solutions@syngr

With more than 1,500,000 copies of our MCSE, MCSD, CompTIA, and Cisco study guides in print, we continue to look for ways we can better serve the information needs of our readers. One way we do that is by listening.

Readers like yourself have been telling us they want an Internet-based service that would extend and enhance the value of our books. Based on reader feedback and our own strategic plan, we have created a Web site that we hope will exceed your expectations.

Solutions@syngress.com is an interactive treasure trove of useful information focusing on our book topics and related technologies. The site offers the following features:

- One-year warranty against content obsolescence due to vendor product upgrades. You can access online updates for any affected chapters.
- "Ask the Author" customer query forms that enable you to post questions to our authors and editors.
- Exclusive monthly mailings in which our experts provide answers to reader queries and clear explanations of complex material.
- Regularly updated links to sites specially selected by our editors for readers desiring additional reliable information on key topics.

Best of all, the book you're now holding is your key to this amazing site. Just go to **www.syngress.com/solutions**, and keep this book handy when you register to verify your purchase.

Thank you for giving us the opportunity to serve your needs. And be sure to let us know if there's anything else we can do to help you get the maximum value from your investment. We're listening.

www.syngress.com/solutions

SYNGRESS®

about itfaqnet.com

Syngress Publishing is a proud sponsor of **itfaqnet.com**, one of the web's most comprehensive FAQ sites for IT professionals. This is a free service that allows users to query over 10,000 FAQs pertaining to Cisco networking, Microsoft networking. Network security tools, .NET development, Wireless technology, IP Telephony, Storage Area Networking, Java development and much more. The content on itfaqnet.com is all derived from our hundreds of market proven books, written and reviewed by content experts.

So bookmark **ITFAQnet.com** as your first stop for mission critical advice from the industry's leading experts.

www.itfaqnet.com

BEST DAMN Cisco Internetworking BOOK PERIOD

Charles Riley Technical Editor

Michael E. Flannagan, CCIE | Ron Fuller, CCIE | Umer Khan, CCIE |
Wayne A. Lawson II, CCIE | Keith O'Brien, CCIE | Martin Walshaw, CCIE |

KEY	SERIAL NUMBER
001	MAXLM3V343
002	G4MBTT6CVF
003	8J9HRQGU3N
004	Z2B4PKURTY
005	U8J3N5R33S
006	X6B7MATTY6
007	G8TR2SH2AK
008	9BKTHQM4S7
009	SW4KP7V6FH
010	5BVF7UM39Z

PUBLISHED BY
Syngress Publishing, Inc.
800 Hingham Street
Rockland, MA 02370

The Best Damn Cisco Internetworking Book Period

Printed in the United States of America

1 2 3 4 5 6 7 8 9 0

ISBN: 1-931836-91-4

Technical Editor: Charles Riley
Technical Reviewer: Jason Campbell
Acquisitions Editor: Catherine B. Nolan
Indexer: J. Edmund Rush

Cover Designer: Michael Kavish
Page Layout and Art by: Patricia Lupien
Copy Editor: Judy Eby, Amy Thomson, Beth Roberts

Distributed by Publishers Group West in the United States and Jaguar Book Group in Canada.

Acknowledgments

We would like to acknowledge the following people for their kindness and support in making this book possible.

Ralph Troupe and the team at Callisma for their invaluable insight into the challenges of designing, deploying and supporting world-class enterprise networks.

Karen Cross, Meaghan Cunningham, Kim Wylie, Harry Kirchner, Kevin Votel, Kent Anderson, Frida Yara, Jon Mayes, John Mesjak, Peg O'Donnell, Sandra Patterson, Betty Redmond, Roy Remer, Ron Shapiro, Patricia Kelly, Andrea Tetrick, Jennifer Pascal, Doug Reil, David Dahl, Janis Carpenter, and Susan Fryer of Publishers Group West for sharing their incredible marketing experience and expertise.

Duncan Enright, AnnHelen Lindeholm, David Burton, Febea Marinetti, and Rosie Moss of Elsevier Science for making certain that our vision remains worldwide in scope.

David Buckland, Wendi Wong, Daniel Loh, Marie Chieng, Lucy Chong, Leslie Lim, Audrey Gan, and Joseph Chan of Transquest Publishers for the enthusiasm with which they receive our books.

Kwon Sung June at Acorn Publishing for his support.

Jackie Gross, Gayle Voycey, Alexia Penny, Anik Robitaille, Craig Siddall, Darlene Morrow, Iolanda Miller, Jane Mackay, and Marie Skelly at Jackie Gross & Associates for all their help and enthusiasm representing our product in Canada.

Lois Fraser, Connie McMenemy, Shannon Russell, and the rest of the great folks at Jaguar Book Group for their help with distribution of Syngress books in Canada.

David Scott, Annette Scott, Delta Sams, Geoff Ebbs, Hedley Partis, and Tricia Herbert of Woodslane for distributing our books throughout Australia, New Zealand, Papua New Guinea, Fiji Tonga, Solomon Islands, and the Cook Islands.

Technical Editor

Charles Riley (CCNP, CSS-1, CISSP, CCSA, MCSE, CNE-3) has a long tenure in information technology, and can remember when the Cisco AGS+ was new. Charles has co-authored several books including *Routing and Configuring Cisco Voice over IP, Second Edition*. Some go bungee jumping, others crochet. Charles writes and tries dangerous network configurations on a non-production rack at home.

The middle son of a tenant farmer and his wife, Charles initially planned to continue the Riley tradition of farming. However, with the collapse of the farm and the kick of an ill-tempered bovine, education became more attractive to the young cowherd. Moving to the metropolis of nearby Remington, he was enticed with the opportunities that urban living offered.

Exhausting the educational offerings of Remington, Charles matriculated at the Model Secondary School for the Deaf in Washington, D.C. before attending Gallaudet University (www.gallaudet.edu). Quick to a decision and even quicker to change his mind, he moved to Florida where he graduated from the University of Central Florida in 1989. Upon graduation, Charles was contacted by and offered a position with the U.S. Army, a relationship that lasted over 10 years.

He started as a U.S. Army telecommunications specialist at Fort Huachuca, Arizona, eventually finishing his Army stretch as the network manager of the 7th Army Training Command in Grafenwoehr, Germany. As a consultant for Sprint, he designed and implemented robust networking solutions for large Fortune 500 and privately held companies. He continues unabated in networking today.

I am blessed to have my wife, René, and daughter, Tess. Your love and support during the countless midnight hours spent crafting this book made it all possible. You lift me when the load is heavy.

Everything has a beginning. My writing started with a wonderful teacher, Barbara Gantley, who saw my potential before I did; your patience and dedication was inexhaustible. You embody all that great teachers are. I hope my antics and inappropriately timed sense of humor never made you reconsider your choice of career.

Special Contributor

Scott Dentler (CISSP, CCSE, CCSA, MCSE, CCNA) is an IT consultant who has served with companies such as Sprint and H&R Block, giving him exposure to large enterprise networks and corporate environments. He is currently providing systems support for a campus network at a Medical Center with national affiliations. Scott's background includes a broad range of Information Technology facets, including Cisco Routers and Switches, Microsoft NT/2000/XP, Check Point firewalls and VPNs, Red Hat Linux, network analysis and enhancement, network design and architecture, and network IP allocation and addressing. Scott Dentler is a contributing author for *Snort 2.0 Intrusion Detection* (Syngress Publishing, ISBN: 1-931836-74-4), and *Cisco Security Professional's Guide to Secure Intrusion Detection Systems* (ISBN: 1-932266-69-0). Additionally, Scott would like to offer his sincere thanks to Alicia Jensen for her unwavering support during the production of this book.

Contributors

Michael E. Flannagan (CCIE #7651, CCDP, CCNA, 3COM-CSA) is Network Consulting Engineer and Team Leader in the Network Supported Accounts (NSA) Group at Cisco Systems. Mike is a member of the global Quality of Service (QoS) Team and has extensive network design experience, with emphasis on Routing Protocol design and Quality of Service mechanisms. Mike's experience, prior to joining Cisco Systems, includes enterprise network architecture, IT management, and consulting. Mike's QoS testing and research was used to recommend the implementation of various QoS mechanisms for one of the world's largest pharmaceutical companies, and he has participated in large-scale QoS designs for several major US companies. In addition to holding various certifications from Cisco, 3Com, and Nortel Networks, Mike has passed both the CCIE Routing/Switching and the CCIE Design written exams and is currently preparing for his CCIE Lab exams. He lives in Morrisville, NC.

Ron Fuller (CCIE #5851, CSS-Level 1, CCNP, CCDP, MCNE) is a Senior Network Engineer with a large financial institution in Columbus, OH. He currently provides design and engineering support for the network infrastructure. His specialties include Cisco routers and LAN switches, strategic network planning, network architecture and design, and network troubleshooting and optimization. Ron's background includes senior systems engineering responsibilities for Cisco and Novell resellers in Central Ohio. Ron has also acted as contributing author to the book *Administering Cisco QoS in IP Networks* (Syngress Publishing, ISBN: 1-928994-21-0). He currently resides in Sunbury, OH with his family, Julie and Max.

Martin Walshaw (CCIE #5629, CCNP, CCDP) is a Systems Engineer working for Cisco Systems in South Africa. His areas of specialty include IP Telephony (including all voice and video applications such as IPCC) and security, both of which keep him busy night and day. During the last 14 years, Martin has dabbled in many aspects of the IT industry, ranging from programming in RPG III and Cobol to PC sales. When Martin is not working, he likes to spend time with his expectant wife Val and his son Joshua. Without their patience, understanding, support, and most importantly love, projects such as this would not be possible.

Wayne A. Lawson II (CCIE # 5244, CCNA, CCDA, NNCSE, CNX, MCSE, CNE, Banyan CBE) is a Systems Engineer with Cisco Systems in Southfield, Michigan. His core area of expertise is in the Routed Wide Area Network (WAN) and Campus Switching. He has provided pre- and post-sales technical support for various dot-com start-ups on redundant ISP access, failsafe security, content networking and verification for local premise, as well as geographical load balancing. His internetworking proficiency includes Layer One and Two, Layer Three, IBM & Voice Technologies, and Network Management and Monitoring Technologies.

Wayne received the "Top Performer" award at Cisco 2000 National Sales Meeting for achieving Cisco's highest level of technical certification. He has also contributed to Syngress Publishing's *Building Cisco Remote Access Networks* (ISBN: 1-928994-13-X). Wayne lives in Holly, MI.

Keith O'Brien (CCIE #2591) is a Consulting Systems Engineer with Cisco Systems specializing in packet voice technologies and multiservice networking. Keith has over 13 years of experience in IT, including large-scale routing, remote access, IP multicast and campus switch designs. Before joining Cisco, Keith worked at MCI Telecommunications, designing international voice and data networks. Keith holds a Bachelors of Science degree in Electrical Engineering from Lafayette College and a Masters of Science degree from Stevens Institute of Technology.

Jason Sinclair (CCIE #9100, CCNP, CCNA) is the Manager of the Network Control Center at PowerTel Ltd., which is Australia's third largest telecommunications carrier. Jason is responsible for all operational aspects of the PowerTel voice, data and IP networks. Jason's technical background is predominantly in large scale IP, Internet, VoIP and DLSW networking. He has also designed and deployed several large-scale networks that have made extensive use of BGP and MPLS technology. Previously Jason worked for a number of ISPs and carriers in the Asia Pacific Region. Jason specializes in IP and IPX routing protocols, with particular focus on BGP, OSPF, and ISIS. He is also an expert in IBM networking, ATM, Frame Relay, ISDN, Token Ring, and Ethernet. Jason has published an article for *Certification Zone*, which is a CCIE level discussion of the theory and configuration of EIGRP. He is also working on articles covering networking case studies, large-scale carrier networks and IBM Networking. Jason lives in Sydney, Australia with his wife, Michelle, and son, Andy.

Edgar Parenti, Jr. (CCNA, CCDA, CCNP, CCDP, CNE-3/4/5, MCNE, PSE, MCSE2000, MCT) has a strong background in network and directory design, network analysis and optimization, system performance tuning, Web application architecture and support, messaging and infrastructure engineering, operating system support, process engineering, and information security. His background also includes working at numerous corporations of all sizes providing senior-level IT consulting services utilizing a wide array of technologies and over six years of designing and managing Cisco internetworks.

Oliver Steudler (CCNP, CCDP, CSE, CNE) is a Senior Systems Engineer at iFusion Networks in Cape Town, South Africa. Oliver specializes in routing, switching, and security and has over 10 years of experience in consulting, designing, implementing and troubleshooting complex networks. He has written articles on TCP/IP, networking, security, and data communications and also co-authored another Syngress title, *Managing Cisco Network Security* (ISBN: 1-928994-17-2).

Sean Thurston (CCDP, CCNP, MCSE, MCP+I) is a Senior Solution Architect with Siemens Business Services. He provides network and data center design solutions for large-scale deployment. His specialties include implementation of multivendor routing and switching equipment and XoIP (Everything over IP installations). Sean's background includes positions as a Technical Analyst for Sprint-Paranet and the director of a brick-and-mortar advertising dot com. Sean is also a contributing author to *Building a Cisco Network for Windows 2000* (Syngress Publishing, ISBN: 1-928994-00-8) and *Cisco AVVID & IP Telephony Design and Implementation* (Syngress Publishing, ISBN: 1-928994-83-0). Sean lives in Renton, WA with his fiancée, Kerry. He is currently pursuing his CCIE.

Tim Blankenship (CCNP, CCDA, CNE-5, CNE-4, CNE-3, MCP, CSEC–Wireless Field Engineer) is a private consultant responsible for leading the design and implementation efforts involving local and wide area networks to clients in the mid-west region of the United States. His specialties include Cisco wireless networking, routers and LAN switches, Novell design and implementation, strategic network planning, network architecture and design, and network troubleshooting and optimization. Tim lives in Grove City, OH with his family, Connie, Morgan, Ben, and Emily.

Umer Khan (SCE, CCIE, MCSE, SCSA, SCNA, CCA, CNX) is the Manager of Networking and Security at Broadcom Corporation (www.broadcom.com). Umer's department is responsible for the design and implementation of global LAN/MAN/WAN solutions that are available with 99.9% up time (planned and unplanned), as well as all aspects of information security at Broadcom. Among other technologies, Broadcom's network consists of Cisco switching gear end-to-end, dark fiber, OC-48 SONET, DWDM, 802.11 wireless, multi-vendor VPNs, and VoIP. The information security group deals with policies, intrusion detection and response, strong authentication, and firewalls. Umer received his bachelor's degree in Computer Engineering at the Illinois Institute of Technology.

Contents

Chapter 1

Cisco Technologies, Routers, and Switches

Best Damn Topics in this Chapter

- The OSI Model
- The TCP/IP Model, DoD Model, or the Internet Model
- Networking Basics
- Wireless Local Area Networks
- Cisco Hardware
- Accessing and Using Routers and Switches
- Connecting to the Router
- SSH
- Cisco Software
- IOS Command Syntax and Basic Configuration
- CATOS Command Syntax and Basic Configurations
- You Are Not Alone—Resources for Cisco Hardware and Software

Introduction

Cisco is almost synonymous with networking. There is almost no area of networking in which Cisco is not a key player, or is not making inroads. You name it Cisco makes it—routers, switches, firewalls, management software, and so on. It can be quite an undertaking to locate and acquire all of the information needed to configure, monitor, and manage these discrete Cisco parts of a network.

Our goal in assembling this book is to create a handy resource for networking (and internetworking) with Cisco. We called on our experiences as networkers to identify and produce information that would be particularly useful consolidated into a single source. The result is what you now hold in your hands.

We know firsthand how rapidly technology changes, and that there are many hidden methods that have not yet been documented. You will discover many of these methods as you configure the topics discussed in this book.

Chapter 1 provides useful information about Cisco networking products, such as its Internet Operating System (IOS), its routers, and its switches. Cisco has standardized management sessions that you will establish to configure Cisco hardware and software.

A fundamental knowledge of networking technologies is essential. This chapter provides a working knowledge of local area network (LAN) technologies while wide area networking (WAN) is covered in Chapter 2. We review network fundamentals in this chapter, as they are a building block to information presented elsewhere in this book. It is important to know and understand the different network technologies, their specific operations, and how they interoperate, if at all.

The Cisco operating systems (OSs) are the heart of all Cisco hardware. Without an OS to tie it all together, the hardware would be just so much silicon and metal. You need to understand how the software and hardware interoperate and their interdependent relationship. The ability to configure and deploy both successfully is your goal, regardless of whether you are doing it to pass an exam, or enhancing your production network.

The OSI Model

All networking can be expressed as a model of operations and functions. Regardless of whether it is Internet Protocol (IP), Internetwork Packet Exchange (IPX), or AppleTalk, all protocols have an established function and a system for the controlled performance of those functions. The ability to correctly identify the functions of a protocol and to know its place in networking is conducive to development, configuration, troubleshooting, and maintenance. Today, when we speak of a network protocol operating at such-and-such a layer, we areusing shorthand provided by the Open System Interconnect (OSI) model.

The OSI model developed by the International Organization for Standardization (ISO), is useful for guiding network development, troubleshooting, and instruction efforts. The OSI model is a seven-layer approach to data networking, with each layer encompassing a specific set of tasks or standards that must be met in order for the network to function.

Knowledge of the OSI model established the language that is used throughout this and other networking books. The concepts and theories of the OSI model apply to all aspects of networking, even when the mapping is not one-to-one mapping (such as the Transmission Control Protocol (TCP)/IP protocol stack to the OSI model). The OSI model is shown in Figure 1.1.

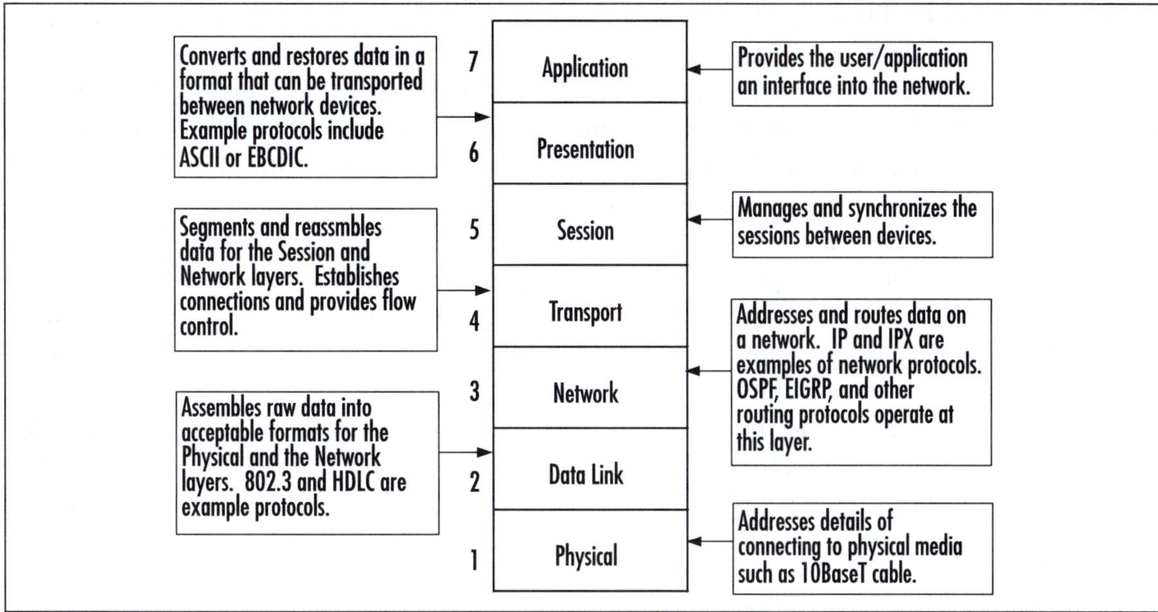

Figure 1.1 The OSI Model

The conventions of the OSI model were developed to provide a framework for simplifying network design and to provide a systematic approach to troubleshooting. As our discussion progresses, the functionality of each layer and how these layers communicate will become clear.

Layer 1: The Physical Layer

The Physical layer is identified as the physical medium that facilitates communication. The Physical layer defines the electrical and mechanical aspects of networking. Issues such as cabling and the methods for placing the 0's and 1's of binary data on the medium are addressed at this layer. Standards such as Category 5, RS-232, and coaxial cable fall within the realm of the Physical layer.

Layer 2: The Data-Link Layer

The Data-link layer defines the protocols that control the Physical layer. Issues such as how the medium is accessed and shared, how devices or stations on the medium are addressed, and how data is framed prior to transmission on the medium are defined here. Common examples of Data-link layer protocols are Ethernet, Token Ring, Fiber Distributed Data Interface (FDDI), and Point-to-Point Protocol (PPP).

Layer 2: Media Access Layer and Logical Link Control.

Within the Data-link layer are two sublayers: Media Access Control (MAC) and Logical Link Control (LLC). Each plays an important role in the operation of a network. The LLC is the liaison between the protocols of the Network layer and the MAC sublayer. The MAC sublayer controls access to the physical medium and uniquely identifies devices on the network.

An example of a protocol that works with MAC is the Carrier Sense Multiple Access/Collision Detect (CSMA/CD). This protocol performs a measure of flow control. Perhaps the best-known services provided by the MAC sublayer are its addresses, such as that for Ethernet.

The destination and source addresses are formally referred to as MAC addresses. The Ethernet MAC (hardware) address is a 48-bit number, which is mostly unique and "burnt into" the device. Data-link frames include a cyclical redundancy checksum (CRC), which provides a metric to allow the receiving device to determine whether the data has been damaged in transit.

When a network interface in a router, switch, PC, server, or any other device that connects to a LAN is created, a globally unique 48-bit address is hard-coded into its Read-Only Memory (ROM). This address must be unique on the network or the network will not operate properly. Each manufacturer of network interfaces has been assigned a range of addresses from the Institute of Electrical and Electronics Engineers (IEEE).

The MAC sublayer is the lower of the two sublayers and determines the access method to the medium, such as token passing (Token Ring or FDDI) or contention (CSMA/CD). Figure 1.2 shows MAC addresses "on the wire" after being passed from the MAC layer to the Physical layer and being converted to 0s and 1s.

Figure 1.2 MAC Layer to Physical Layer

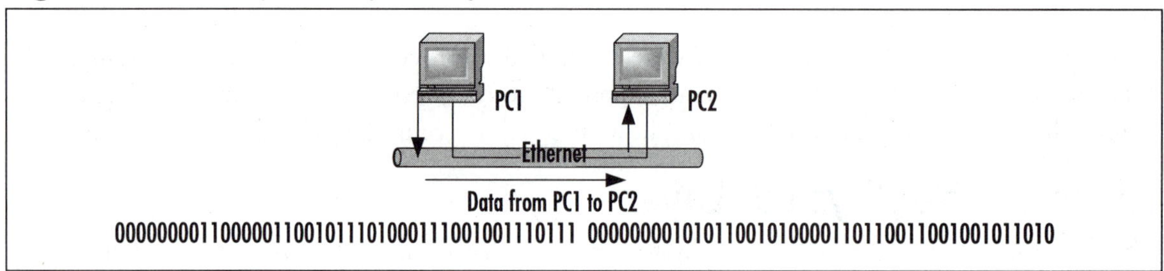

The LLC sublayer handles error control, flow control, framing, and MAC sublayer addressing. The most common LLC protocol is IEEE 802.2, which defines connectionless and connection-oriented variants. IEEE 802.2 defines Service Access Points (SAPs) through a field in the Ethernet, Token Ring, or FDDI frame.

Two SAPs are associated with LLC: the Destination SAP (DSAP) and the Source SAP (SSAP). These SAPs along with the MAC address can uniquely identify the recipient of a frame. Typically, LLC is used for protocols such as Systems Network Architecture (SNA) that do not have a corresponding Network layer.

Layer 3: The Network Layer

The primary function of the Network layer is to determine the best-known path for information to reach its intended destination. The Network layer is responsible for addressing a network above the Data-link layer. It is where protocols such as IP (TCP/IP), IPX and AppleTalk tie into the grand scheme of things. Routing functions are also performed at the Network layer. Routing protocols such as Routing Information Protocol (RIP), Open Shortest Path First (OSPF), and the Border Gateway Protocol (BGP) operate at the Network layer.

Information is formatted, checked for errors, and translated into a message via the Data-link layer. Subsequently, the frame is transmitted into the physical medium. The Network layer deals with packets, which are encapsulated into frames by the Data-link layer. The packets contain information from the layer above the Network layer.

IP addresses, IPX addresses, and other similar logical addresses reside at this layer. They are considered logical because, unlike the MAC address that is permanently "burned" into the network interface, IP addressing provides a method of grouping devices regardless of their physical location. This is an important aspect of network design.

Layer 4: The Transport Layer

The Transport layer provides flow control, orders received data, and acknowledges correctly received data. The Transport layer defines the protocols that control the Network layer, similar to the way the Data-link layer controls the Physical layer. The Transport layer specifies a higher level of flow control, error detection, and correction. Protocols such as TCP, User Datagram Protocol (UDP), Sequenced Packet Exchange (SPX), and Name Binding Protocol (NBP) operate at this layer.

Transport layer protocols may be connection-oriented, such as TCP and SPX, or connectionless, such as UDP. Connection-oriented protocols establish an interaction between two ends on a network. The end devices "shake hands" and agree upon basic conventions for their communications, and then share service information about the ongoing communication. It implies a level of reliability and a guarantee of delivery of services. The processes involved in the protocol function to provide a virtual one-on-one appearance.

Connectionless protocols, such as UDP, do not provide reliability; information is simply placed on the wire and a "best effort" is made to deliver the information to the recipient. What is lost in reliability is gained in efficiency; connectionless protocols are generally chosen when high throughput is necessary and some information loss is acceptable.

Layer 5: The Session Layer

The Session layer establishes the parameters of any upcoming communication. The Session layer establishes, manages, and terminates communication sessions between Presentation layer entities and the Transport layer, where needed. Lightweight Directory Access Protocol (LDAP) and Remote Procedure Call (RPC) are examples of Session layer protocols as are Network File System (NFS), Structured Query Language (SQL), and X Windows. If devices are not using the same protocols, they are essentially speaking different languages.

Session layer protocols determine their communication flow. There are three types: *single mode*, *half-duplex mode*, and *full-duplex mode*. Single-mode communication occurs when only one device at a time transmits information, and it transmits until all the information has been completely sent. Half-duplex mode occurs when the devices take turns transmitting. This is comparable to a conversation between two people using walkie-talkies in which only one person can talk at any given time. (If both people push the Talk button at the same time, neither person will hear anything.) Full-duplex mode occurs when the devices transmit and receive simultaneously. An example of full-duplex communication is when two people talk on a phone—both parties can talk at the same time.

Once the preliminary details have been established, data exchange can proceed. After the exchange is complete, the devices systematically disengage the session. The Session layer can be either connection-oriented or connectionless. A connection-oriented session contains checkpoints or activity management. This system provides a way to efficiently retransmit any data that is lost or is erroneous on receipt. It is efficient because only the data that needs to be transmitted is sent, rather than the entire session. Connectionless sessions, as with IP and UDP, are a best-effort delivery. As with the two other examples, in a connectionless session, the layer above (the Presentation layer) is responsible for providing reliability.

Layer 6: The Presentation Layer

The Presentation layer establishes how information is presented, typically for display or printing. The Presentation layer translates information in a way that the Application layer understands. Likewise, this layer translates information from the Application layer to the Session layer. Data encryption and character set conversion (such as American Standard Code for Information Interchange [ASCII] to Extended Binary Coded Decimal Interchange Code [EBCDIC]) are usually associated with this layer.

The Presentation layer is responsible for ensuring that data sent from the Application layer of one device is comprehensible by the Application layer of another device. IBM's Network Basic Input/Output System (NetBIOS) and Novell's NetWare Core Protocol (NCP) are examples of Presentation layer protocols.

The ISO also developed a Presentation layer protocol named Abstract Syntax Notation One (ASN.1), which describes data types independent of various computer structures and representation techniques. Some other examples of Presentation layer protocols are Secure Sockets Layer (SSL), Hypertext Transfer Protocol (HTTP)/Hypertext Markup Language (HTML) (agent), File Transfer Protocol (FTP) (server), and AppleTalk Filing Protocol.

Layer 7: The Application Layer

The Application layer is where user space programs make requests of network services. The Application layer provides network services to applications such as e-mail, word processing, and file transfer, which are not implicitly defined in the OSI system model. The Application layer relieves software developers from having to write networking routines into their programs. Instead, developers can utilize programming functions on the Application layer and rely upon lower layers to provide the networking services. Some common examples of Application layer protocols include Simple Mail Transfer Protocol (SMTP), HTTP, and Telnet.

The TCP/IP Model, the DoD Model, or the Internet Model

The suite of TCP/IP protocols is known by several names: TCP/IP, the Department of Defense (DOD) model, and the Internet model. Today, it is referred to as TCP/IP. While TCP and IP are the predominant protocols in this stack, there are other protocols that perform important network functions. TCP/IP originally started life in the 1970s as TCP, an all-in-one network solution. As time passed, the value of separating functions into discrete protocols gave rise to TCP/IP.

At around the same time, the Defense Advanced Research Project Agency (DARPA) (ARPA at the time) was using Network Control Protocol (NCP). NCP was not exactly setting the network on fire, and when TCP/IP appeared, it seemed the answer to prayers for structured and controlled networking.

TCP/IP predates the OSI model, so its layers and functions do not map neatly to the OSI model. TCP/IP was one of the first successful attempts to bring structure to networking. If anything, the OSI model owes its existence to the success of TCP/IP.

There is no *official* TCP/IP model. If you adhere to the "ARPANET Reference Model" discussed in RFC871, there are three layers (Network Interface, Host-Host, and Process-Level (Applications). As a *very general* rule of thumb, the TCP/IP model is typically presented as having four layers, and in some cases, five. TCP/IP is adaptable and flexible enough to be modified and created anew by network vendors to suit their needs, or it can be optimized for a new feature. As long as the suite of protocols adhere to the conventions of the TCP and the IP, for example, the customization of TCP/IP does not prevent it from being interoperable with other vendor implementations of TCP/IP. However, if the customization goes too far, such as reducing IP addresses to 24 bits, interoperability will fail, and networking will not be possible.

Our discussion adheres to the four-layer model shown in Figure 1.3. The Network Access layer roughly corresponds to the Data link and Physical layers of the OSI model. However, TCP/IP does not define any Physical layer network standards nor does it care about physical implementation. As long as a vendor builds and provides the ability to bind TCP/IP to some physical standard (Ethernet, Token Ring, and so forth), the layers above the Network Access layer can be used over any physical network types.

Figure 1.3 TCP/IP Model

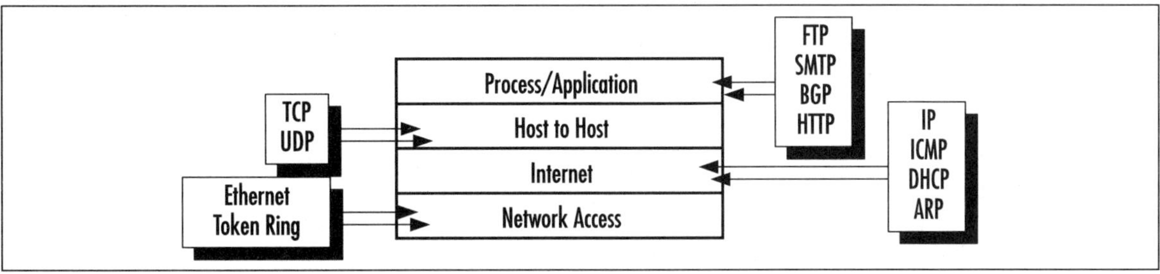

Process/Application Layer (Application, Presentation, and Session)

The Process/Application layer performs functions associated with the Application, Presentation, and Session layers of the OSI model. It addresses interfacing to networks, formats information for network transport, and manages the sessions between two endpoints. HTTP and SMTP are examples of Process/Application layer protocols. Using HTTP as an example, the Application layer is the process and interface used to connect and access the Web, while the Presentation layer could be provided in the form of HTML. The Session layer is evidenced by the flow of request and response commands exchanged between the Web client and the Web server to view a particular Web page.

Host-to-Host Layer (Transport)

The Transport layer provides duplex, end-to-end data transport services between applications. Data sent from the Application layer is divided into segments appropriately sized for the network. TCP and UDP are the chief protocols at this layer.

TCP

TCP provides reliable service by being connection-oriented with error detection and correction. The connection-oriented nature of TCP is used by endpoints to communicate with each other. The connection must be established before a data transfer can occur. Transfers are acknowledged throughout the process. Acknowledgements provide assurance that data is being received properly. The acknowledgement process provides robustness and recovery during periods of network congestion or communication unreliability. TCP also determines when the transfer ends and closes the connection, thus freeing resources for other use. Checksums ensure that the data has not been accidentally modified during transit. Figure 1.4 shows the format of the TCP header.

Figure 1.4 TCP Header

```
⊟ Frame 7 (54 bytes on wire, 54 bytes captured)
    Arrival Time: Oct  5, 2003 10:03:06.190778000
    Time delta from previous packet: 0.000036000 seconds
    Time relative to first packet: 0.116351000 seconds
    Frame Number: 7
    Packet Length: 54 bytes
    Capture Length: 54 bytes
⊟ Ethernet II, Src: 00:e0:18:8a:0f:86, Dst: 00:0b:46:3d:d7:8f
    Destination: 00:0b:46:3d:d7:8f (192.168.1.1)
    Source: 00:e0:18:8a:0f:86 (192.168.1.11)
    Type: IP (0x0800)
⊟ Internet Protocol, Src Addr: 192.168.1.11 (192.168.1.11), Dst Addr:
    Version: 4
    Header length: 20 bytes
  ⊟ Differentiated Services Field: 0x00 (DSCP 0x00: Default; ECN: 0x00)
      0000 00.. = Differentiated Services Codepoint: Default (0x00)
      .... ..0. = ECN-Capable Transport (ECT): 0
      .... ...0 = ECN-CE: 0
    Total Length: 40
    Identification: 0xcbc3 (52163)
  ⊟ Flags: 0x04
      .1.. = Don't fragment: Set
      ..0. = More fragments: Not set
    Fragment offset: 0
    Time to live: 128
    Protocol: TCP (0x06)
    Header checksum: 0xb729 (correct)
    Source: 192.168.1.11 (192.168.1.11)
    Destination:
⊟ Transmission Control Protocol, Src Port: 1804 (1804), Dst Port: http (80), Seq: 2729932844, Ack: 132837570, Len: 0
    Source port: 1804 (1804)
    Destination port: http (80)
    Sequence number: 2729932844
    Acknowledgement number: 132837570
    Header length: 20 bytes
  ⊟ Flags: 0x0010 (ACK)
      0... .... = Congestion Window Reduced (CWR): Not set
      .0.. .... = ECN-Echo: Not set
      ..0. .... = Urgent: Not set
      ...1 .... = Acknowledgment: Set
      .... 0... = Push: Not set
      .... .0.. = Reset: Not set
      .... ..0. = Syn: Not set
      .... ...0 = Fin: Not set
    Window size: 65520
    Checksum: 0x1d14 (correct)
```

TCP ports multiplex TCP to the layer above with multiple applications on the same host. A source port and a destination port are associated with the sending and receiving applications, respectively. The ports from 0 to 1023 are **Well Known Ports**, and are assigned by the Internet Assigned Numbers Authority (IANA). Ports from 1024 to 49151 are **Registered Ports**, while ports from 49152 through 65535 are **Dynamic/Private Ports**. The Well Known and Registered Port numbers are available at www.isi.edu/in-notes/iana/assignments/port-numbers.

Within the TCP header, there are several specialized bits called **flags** that aid in traffic management. They provide information about the importance of the Sequence Number, Acknowledgement Number, and Urgent Pointer fields. They also provide information about how the packet should be treated by the receiving host. These are reflected in Table 1.1.

Table 1.1 TCP Control Bits

Control Bit	Description
URG	Urgent control bit indicates that Urgent Pointer is a valid offset to add to the Sequence Number. The sender of data can indicate to the receiver that there is urgent data pending.
ACK	Acknowledgement control bit indicates that the Acknowledgement Number contains the value of the next sequence number the sender of the segment is expecting to receive. ACK is always set for an established connection.
PSH	Push all data received to this point up to the receiving application. This function expedites the delivery of urgent data to the destination.
RST	Reset the connection. This function flushes all queued segments waiting for transmission or retransmission, and puts the receiver in listen mode.
SYN	Synchronize sequence numbers. The SYN control bit indicates that the Sequence Number contains the initial sequence number.
FIN	Sender has finished sending data. The FIN control bit is set by the application closing its connection.

Sequence numbers allow recovery of data that was lost, damaged, duplicated, or delivered out of order. Each host in the TCP connection selects an Initial Sequence Number (ISN) that is synchronized during connection establishment. The sequence number is incremented for each byte of data transmitted across the TCP connection, including the SYN and FIN flags. Sequence numbers are 32 bits and will wrap to zero when they overflow. The ISN should be unpredictable for a given TCP connection. Some TCP implementations have exhibited vulnerabilities of predictable sequence numbers. Predicting the sequence number can allow an attacker to impersonate a host.

The acknowledgement number has a valid entry when the ACK flag is on. It contains the next sequence number that the receiver is expecting. Since every data segment sent over a TCP connection has a sequence number, it also has an acknowledgement number.

The ACK and RST bits are important in determining whether a connection is established or being established. Cisco uses the **established** keyword in Access Control Lists (ACLs) to check whether the ACK or RST flags are set. If they are, the packet is part of an established TCP session. If neither the ACK nor the RST flags are set, this packet is not part of an existing connection, but an attempt to establish a new connection to the device at the destination TCP address.

HTTP, SMTP, FTP, Telnet, and rlogin are examples of applications that use TCP for transport. Applications that need reliability support from the Transport layer use RPC over TCP. Applications that do not depend on the Transport layer for reliability use RPC over UDP.

TCP Connections

Figure 1.5 shows the establishment of a TCP/IP connection. Establishing a TCP connection requires three segments, known as the "three-way handshake."

1. To initiate the connection, the source host sends a SYN segment (the SYN flag is set), and an ISN in the sequence number field to the destination port and the host address.
2. The destination host responds with a segment containing its ISN. Both the SYN and ACK flags are set. The acknowledgement number will be the source's ISN, incremented by one.
3. The source host acknowledges the SYN from the destination host by replying with an ACK segment and an acknowledgement number that is the destination's ISN incremented by one.

This sequence—SYN, SYN-ACK, ACK—characterizes the handshake.

Figure 1.5 Establishing a TCP Connection (Three-way Handshake)

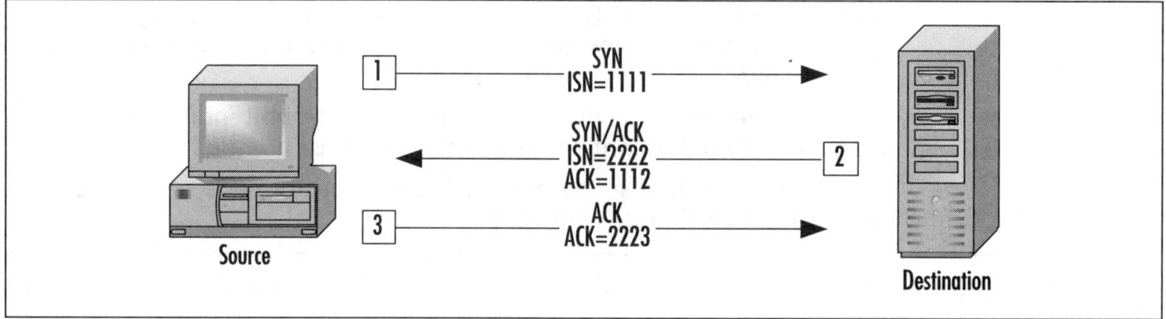

UDP

UDP is a simple, unreliable transport service. It is connectionless, so delivery is not assured. The simple design of the UDP header in Figure 1.6 shows why this is a relatively light and efficient transport protocol. Since connections are not set up and torn down, there is very little overhead. Lost, damaged, or out of order segments will not be retransmitted unless the Application layer requests it. UDP is used for fast, simple messages sent from one host to another. Due to its simplicity, UDP packets are more easily spoofed than TCP packets. If reliable or ordered delivery of data is needed, applications should use TCP.

Figure 1.6 The UDP Header

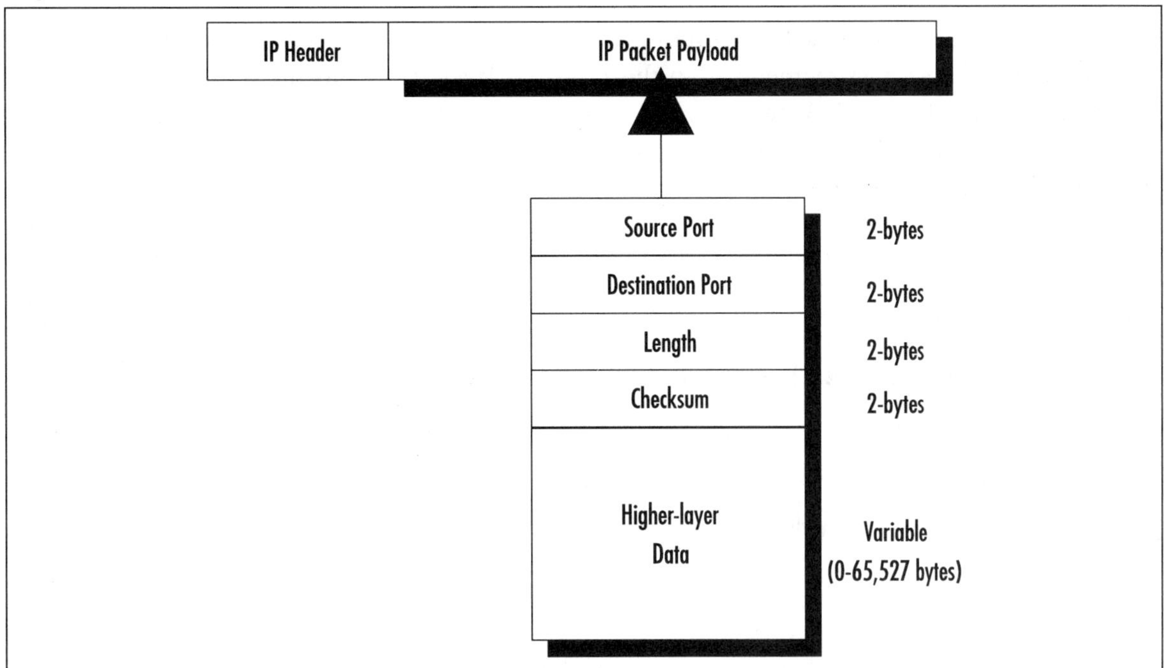

All header fields are 16 bits, meaning that values range from 0 to 65535. The source port is the UDP port on the host that is initiating the session, and to which replies will be returned, while the destination port is the target UDP port (such as UDP port 110 for Post Office Protocol (POP) e-mail). The length field indicates the entire length of the UDP packet, header, and data. The checksum is calculated on the entire UDP packet. The UDP header and its data are encapsulated as payload for an IP packet, as the figure shows.

Simple Network Management Protocol (SNMP), Trivial FTP (TFTP), BOOTstrap Protocol (BOOTP), NFS, and dynamic host control protocol (DHCP) are examples of applications that use UDP for transport. UDP is also suitable for multimedia applications. Unlike the connection-oriented TCP, which can only connect between two hosts, UDP can broadcast or multicast to many systems at once. The small overhead of UDP eases the network load when running time-sensitive data such as audio or video.

The Internet Layer

The Internet layer provides network addressing, routing, error notification, and hop-by-hop fragmentation and reassembly. It manages the delivery of information from host to host. Fragmentation can occur at this layer because different network technologies have different Maximum Transmission Unit (MTU) sizes. IP, Internet Control Message Protocol (ICMP), and Address Resolution Protocol (ARP) are protocols found at this layer.

IP

IP is an unreliable, routable packet delivery protocol. All upper layer protocols use IP to send and receive packets. IP receives segments from the Transport layer, fragments them into packets, and passes them to the Network Access layer.

The IP address is a logical address assigned to each node on a TCP/IP network. IP addressing is designed to allow routing of packets across internetworks. Since IP addresses are easy to change or spoof, they should not be relied upon to provide identification in untrusted environments. As shown in Figure 1.7, the source and destination addresses (DAs) are included in the IP header.

Figure 1.7 IP Header

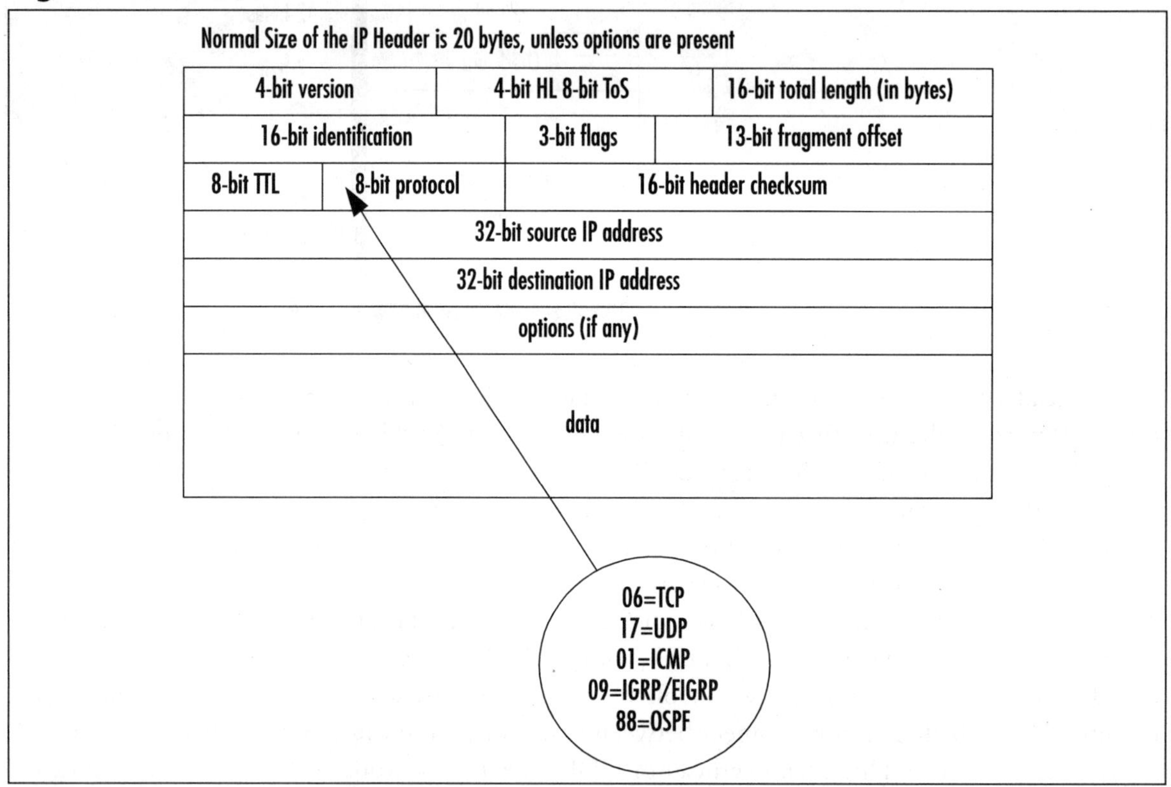

Let's take a look at each of the IP packet fields in Figure 1.7:

- **Ver** IP version number. Version 4 or 6.
- **IHL** Internet Header Length. 32-bits. Indicates the beginning of a data segment. The minimum value is 5, when there are no options.
- **Type of Service** Suggests the desired quality of service. Generally set to zero.
- **Total Length** The length of the datagram. The largest size is 65535 bytes.
- **Identification** A unique identifier prepared by the sender to reassemble packets.

- **Flags** The first bit is reserved, and always set to zero. The second bit is the "Don't Fragment" bit to indicate if routers are not permitted to fragment the packet. The third bit is the "More Fragments" bit that indicates if additional fragments are outstanding.
- **Fragment Offset** Suggests where this packet exists in the datastream, and is measured in units of eight octets. The first fragment has offset zero.
- **Time To Live** Indicates the maximum number of router hops the packet can transit before being discarded. Generated by source, and decremented at each hop.
- **Protocol** Indicates the upper level protocol such as decimal value 6 for TCP and 17 for UDP. A full list of protocol numbers is available at www.isi.edu/in-notes/iana/assignments/protocol-numbers.
- **Checksum** Computed only on the header.
- **SA/DA** The IP address of the respective source and destination.
- **Options** Resembles the TCP options field. Pads with zero to make options plus **padding** a multiple of 32 bits.

ICMP

The ICMP provides diagnostic functions and error reporting for IP. ICMP is protocol type 1. For example, ICMP can provide feedback to a sending host when a destination is unreachable or the time is exceeded (TTL=0). A ping is an ICMP echo request message, and the response is an ICMP echo reply. Utilities such as PING and TRACE use ICMP to gather and provide network diagnostic information such as destination reachability.

ARP

The ARP resolves logical IP addresses to the hardware address. (Note that an ARP packet is not an IP packet as it works below that layer.) If the destination IP address is on the same subnet as the source host, IP will use ARP to determine the hardware address of the destination host. If the destination IP address is on a remote subnet, ARP will be used to determine the hardware address of the default gateway. The ARP cache, a table of translations between IP address and hardware, stores its entries dynamically and flushes them after a short period of time.

NOTE

Some attacks have been based upon gratuitous or forged ARP replies and redirecting IP traffic to a system that sniffs for cleartext passwords or other information. One such attack tool is available at www.monkey.org/~dugsong/dsniff. This attack disables the benefit of a switched Ethernet environment because ARP requests are broadcast to all local network ports. The spoofing machine can respond with its hardware address and become a "man-in-the-middle." Research is being conducted on a new ARP protocol that would be resistant to these types of attacks. It is best to assume that switches do not provide access control, and avoid the use of cleartext passwords or other sensitive information.

The Network Layer

The Network layer includes the network interface card and the device driver. These provide the physical interface to the media of the network. The Network layer controls the network hardware, encapsulates and transmits outgoing packets, and accepts and demultiplexes incoming packets. It accepts IP packets from the higher Internet layer. TCP/IP does not define any specific physical hardware standards, but instead, depends on a variety of data link protocols to handle the formatting and hand off of TCP/IP data to the physical medium. An example of this dependency on other protocols is the use of PPP over dial links.

The following section starts tying the previous concepts together with a discussion of networks.

Networking Basics

A network is a series of points or nodes interconnected by communication paths. The points or nodes may be devices dedicated to a single function, such as a PC used for client applications, or a router used to interconnect networks. The whole purpose of any network is to enable two endpoints, be they networks, servers, routers, and so on, to communicate with each other and pass data. Networks are typically differentiated by the amount of geographical coverage that they provide, as greater coverage and distance requires different technology than smaller coverage and distance networks.

There are three primary types of networks, the LAN, the metropolitan area network (MAN), and the wide area network (WAN). The line between each type is blurring, and is generally used in the context of planning and design for control purposes. Figure 1.8 shows the relationship between the three types.

Figure 1.8 LAN, WAN, and MAN

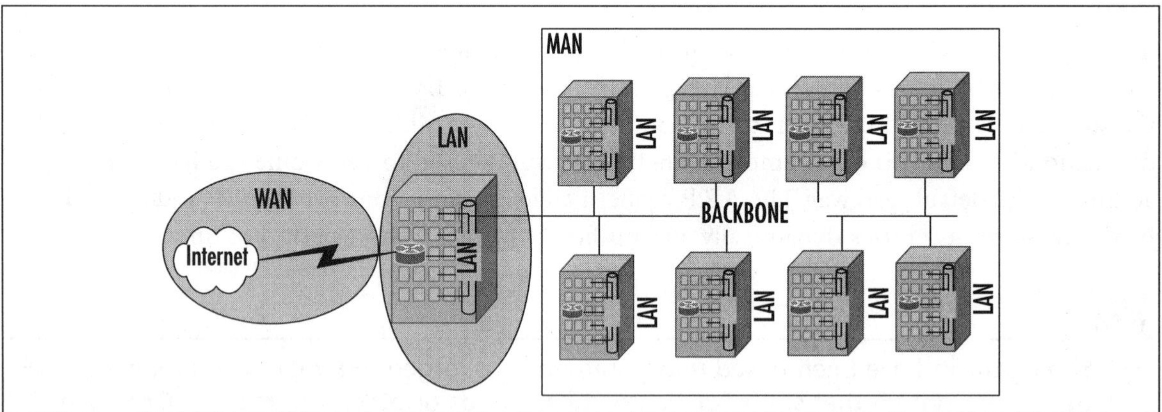

The distinguishing feature of these networks is the spatial distance covered. LANs are typically contained in a single structure or small geographic region such as a campus or building. MANs connect points or nodes in a large geographic region, such as a city-sized grouping of networks sharing a common medium such as a fiber-optic backbone connecting several city blocks worth of networks. Some of the same LAN technologies may be employed in a MAN, such as a Gigabit Ethernet.

WANs are geographically dispersed networks and typically use technologies different from LANs or MANs. WANs are typically comprised of high-speed circuits leased from a telecommunications provider to facilitate connectivity between networks separated by great distances. WANs use certain communications technologies such as point-to-point circuits, Frame Relay, Integrated Services Digital Network (ISDN), X.25, Asynchronous Transfer Mode (ATM), Digital Subscriber Line (DSL) and so on.

LAN technologies such as Ethernet, Fast Ethernet, and Gigabit Ethernet are prevalent, with some Token Ring and FDDI. This chapter focuses on LANs and Chapter 2 covers WAN technology .

Network Topologies

Within the definition of a network, points (or nodes) are connected by communication paths. Networks are structured to take advantage of their features and to optimize their performance. We cover four primary topologies: **bus**, **star**, **ring**, and **mesh**. Each topology has strengths and weaknesses, as well as different associated costs. A good network design will take each topology into consideration to determine the best solution.

NOTE

The word **topology** can refer to either the physical or logical layout of a network. For example, an Ethernet network with a hub would have a physical star topology, but the logical topology would be a bus.

Bus Topology

A bus topology is a linear LAN architecture in which transmissions from network devices or stations propagate the entire length of the medium and are received by all nodes on the medium. The bus topology of Ethernet/IEEE 802.3 networks is illustrated in Figure 1.9.

Figure 1.9 Bus Topology

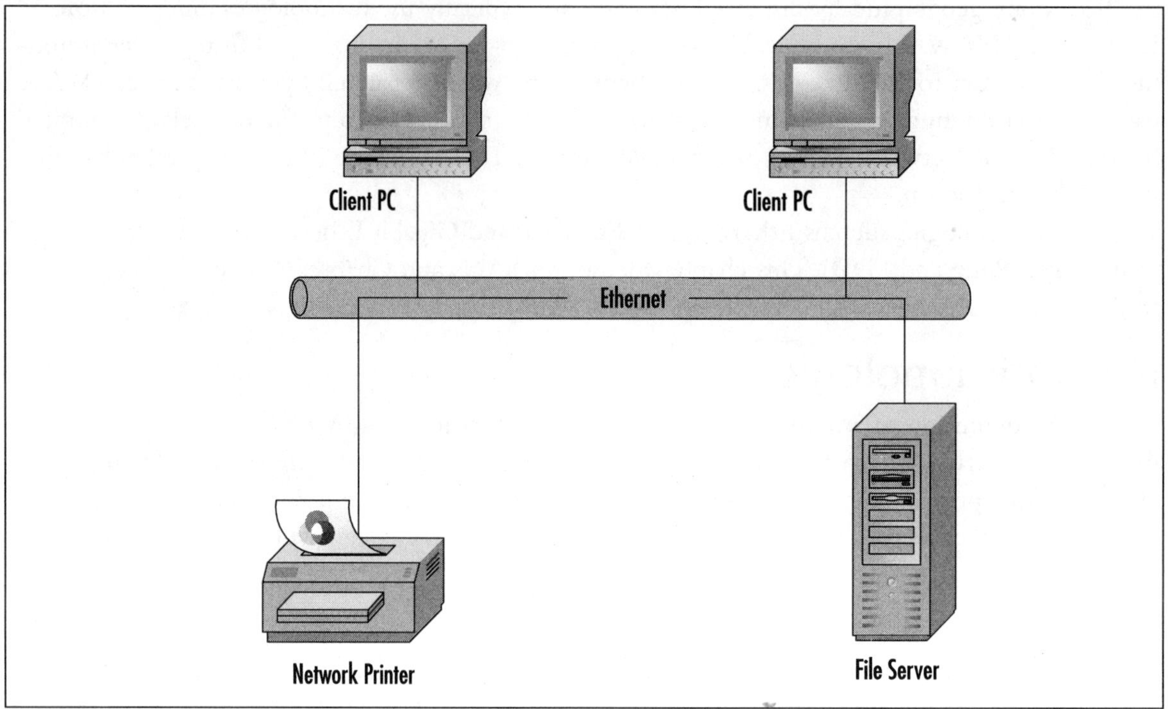

Star Topology

A star topology is a LAN architecture in which the devices or stations on a network are connected to a central communications device, such as a hub or switch. Logical bus and ring topologies are often physically implemented in physical star topologies. Figure 1.10 shows a typical star topology.

Figure 1.10 Star Topology

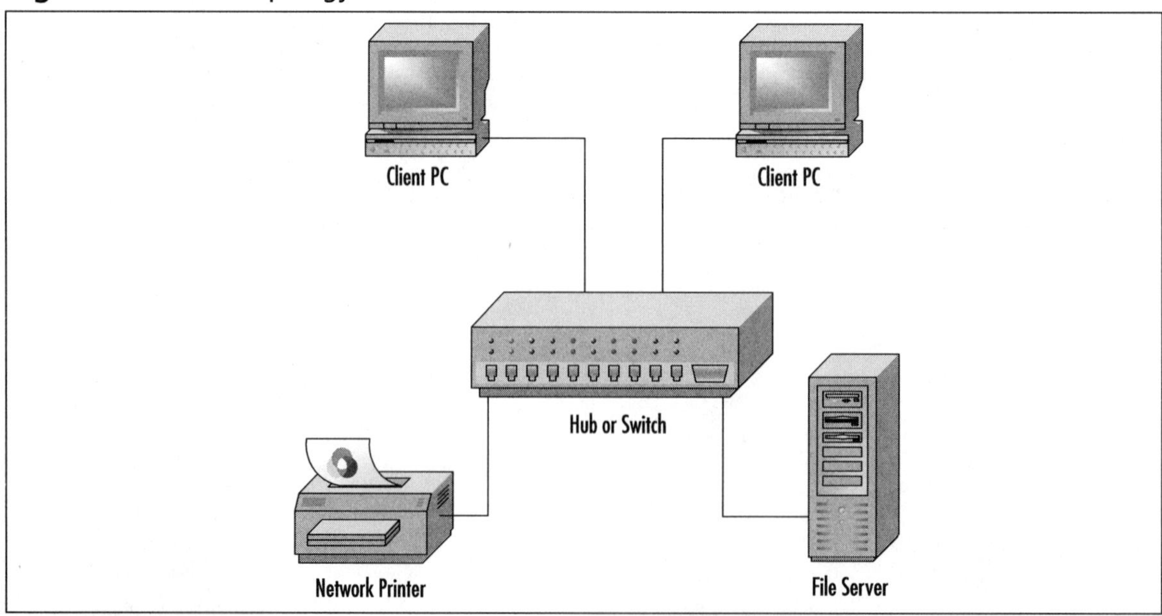

Ring Topology

A ring topology is a LAN architecture in which the devices or stations on a network are connected to each other by unidirectional transmission links to form a single closed loop. Common examples of ring topologies are Token Ring/IEEE 802.5 and FDDI networks, as illustrated in Figure 1.11.

Figure 1.11 Ring Topology

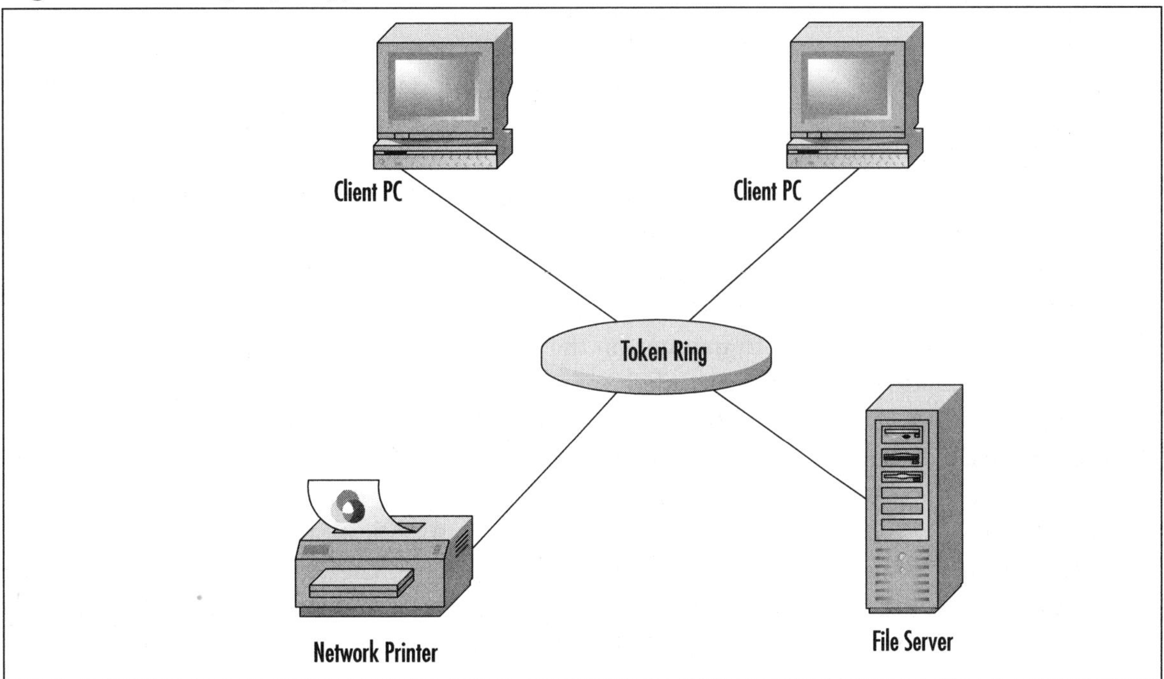

Mesh Topology

A mesh topology is an architecture in which every device or station on a network is connected to every other device or station, typically in certain WAN technologies such as Frame Relay. The degree of "meshiness" will vary, from a full mesh wherein each device is connected to every other device, to simple hub-and-spoke meshes where a few devices are connected to all other devices. In our 20+ years in the IT arena, we have never come across a fully meshed LAN, as it does not make sense in that environment. For example, a server does not need a connection to every other server, nor does a network printer need a physical connection to every client it serves.

A degree of redundancy can be achieved by having more than one network interface on a LAN device, which is sufficient for such needs. Meshed networks make the most sense in a WAN network environment where such redundancy and connectivity is needed. Mesh networking topologies are discussed in Chapter 2.

CSMA/CD versus Deterministic Access

In LANs, there are two predominant methods of controlling access to the physical medium: CSMA/CD and deterministic access. CSMA/CD is the access method for Ethernet. CSMA/CD can be likened to the rules you would follow in a meeting. In a meeting, everyone in the room has the right to speak, but everyone follows the generally accepted rule of "only one person at a time can talk." If you want to speak, you need to listen to see if anyone is else is speaking before you begin. If someone else is speaking, you must wait until they are finished. If nobody is speaking, you can speak, but will continue to listen in case someone else decides to speak at the same time. If they do, both speakers must stop talking, wait a random amount of time, and start the process again. If a speaker fails to observe the protocol of only one speaker at a time, the meeting will quickly lose all effective communication.

In Ethernet, multiple access (MA) describes the connection of many stations to the same cable, each having the right to transmit. No device or station on the cable has priority over any other device or station. All devices or stations on the cable take turns communicating per the access algorithm to ensure that one device on the LAN does not monopolize the media.

The carrier sense (CS) refers to the process of listening before speaking in an Ethernet network. Every device on the network performs the CS operation by looking for energy on the media. If an electrical carrier exists, the cable is in use, and the device must wait to transmit. Many Ethernet devices maintain a deferral or back-off counter defining the maximum number of attempts the device will make to transmit on the cable. If the deferral counter is exceeded (typically 15 attempts), the frame is discarded.

The collision detect (CD) refers to the capability of the devices on the wire to know when a collision occurs. Collisions in Ethernet happen when two devices transmit data at the same time on the cable. Collisions may be caused by the cable distance being exceeded, a defective device, or a poorly written driver that does not adhere to Ethernet specifications. When a collision is detected, the participants generate a collision enforcement signal. The enforcement signal lasts as long as the smallest Ethernet frame size, 64 bytes. This sizing ensures that all stations know about the collision and do not attempt to transmit during a collision event. After the collision enforcement signal has finished, the medium is again open to communications via the CS protocol.

Deterministic access is the protocol used to control access to the physical medium in a Token Ring or FDDI network. Deterministic access means that a control system is in place to ensure that each device on the network has an equal opportunity to transmit.

Ethernet

A LAN by its nature is based on sharing, and this is never truer than with Ethernet. Invented and given form by Robert Metcalfe (founder of 3Com, currently a writer and an inventor), Ethernet was, in the simplest terms, a "cocktail party brought to life." All devices share the medium, but only one can transmit at a time. There are two techniques used to control access. We will discuss the first, which is more prevalent on wired Ethernet networks.

Ethernet refers broadly to a wide variety of data link implementations. Originally, this referred to the DEC, Intel, and Xerox (DIX) implementation of Version 1 or Version 2 Ethernet. When IEEE developed the 802.3 standard, the term was applied to it as well, and characterizes CSMA/CD technology. "Ethernet" refers to several different types of data link protocols, including 802.3u "Fast Ethernet" and 802.3x "Full Duplex." It has evolved from transmission rates of 1/10/100 Mbps to 1 Gbps. Ethernet is even used as a model for 802.11, Carrier Sense Multiple Access/Collision Avoidance (CSMA/CA) within wireless networks.

Ethernet was formalized as a standard by the IEEE 802 committee (its family of standards can be found at http://standards.ieee.org). The IEEE 802.3 standard describes CSMA/CD, which requires that senders first listen to determine if any transmissions are in effect. If so, the sender will delay transmitting. Once the line is clear, transmission may occur. If two or more devices start transmitting simultaneously, the resulting collision is detected by all, and the transmitters back off for an exponential amount of time, which varies by device.

There are numerous types of Ethernet, including wireless, which are discussed more fully in Chapter 3. Table 1.2 shows each current type of Ethernet, including some that are not seen much any more.

Table 1.2 Types of Ethernet

Name (meters)	Speed	Cable	Connector	Distance
10BaseT	10	Twisted Pair	RJ45	100
10BaseFL	10	Multimode Fiber	ST	2000
10Base5	10	Thick Coax	AUI	500
10Base2	10	Thin Coax	BNC Barrel	185
100BaseTX	100	Two-Pair Category 5 UTP	RJ45	100
100BaseT4	100	Four-Pair Category 3-5 UTP	RJ45	100
100BaseFX	100	Multimode Fiber	SC	2000
1000BaseT	1000	Twisted Pair	RJ45	100
1000BaseFX	1000	Fiber Optic	SC or ST	2000

Table 1.2 shows some of the more common types of Ethernet. There are many others that are not as common, or were developed for unique, specific uses. The word "base" means that Ethernet is baseband; that is, it is the only signal present on this wire—it does not share it with any other non-Ethernet signaling.

Knowing Ethernet framing is important to understanding the functions it provides. There are four common types of Ethernet frames found in networks: Version II, 802.3 SNAP, 802.3 raw, and 802.3 LLC. Figure 1.12 examines the Ethernet Version II described on Cisco equipment as Ethernet frame type ARPA, which is probably the most common—it is the default in "pure-play IP" Windows NT and 2000 installations. Figure 1.13 shows the initial format that the 802 committee developed. Notice that it has a Length field rather than a Type field.

Figure 1.12 Ethernet Version II (Original Digital-Intel-Xerox (DIX) Format)

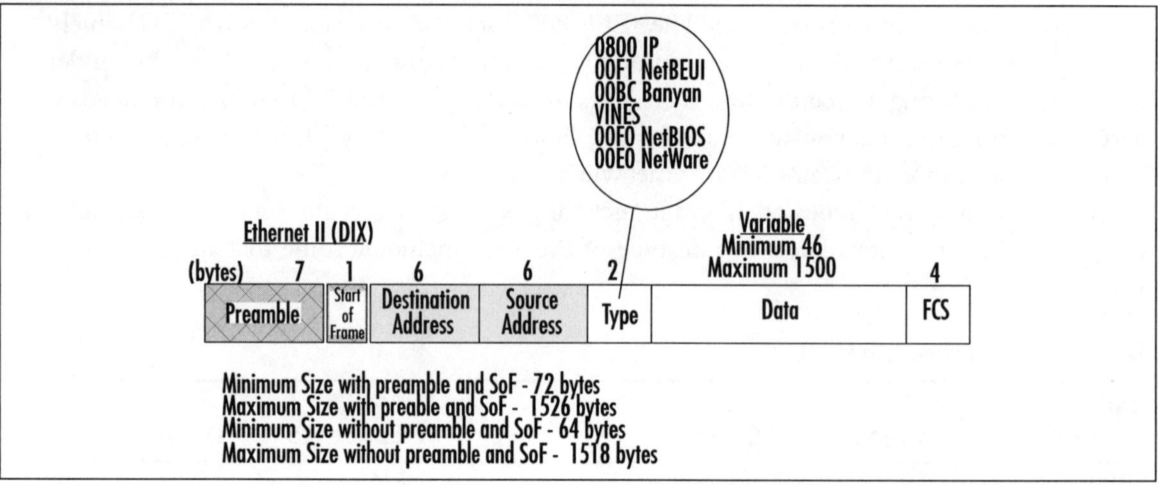

Figure 1.13 Ethernet 802.3 Frame

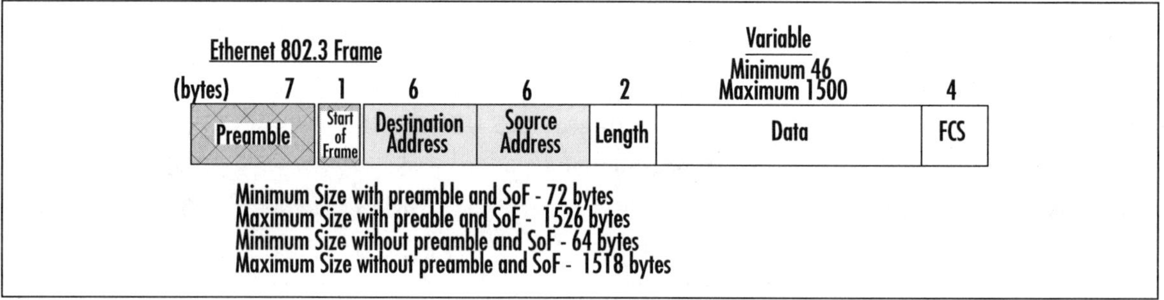

The Ethernet frame fields warrant description of their functions.

- **Preamble** The first field in an Ethernet frame is the preamble. The preamble is a 7-byte long alternating pattern of 0s and 1s that tells receiving devices that a new frame is arriving. 62 bits of alternating 1s and 0s that allow the network interface to synchronize with the beginning of the frame.
- **Start of Frame** A 1-byte field that indicates the start of an Ethernet frame. Its bit pattern (10101011) indicates the start of the frame.
- **DA and SA** A 2- or 6-byte field that contains the MAC address of the source device on the network and the destination. The DA may be a single MAC address in the case of a unicast, a broadcast to all nodes on the network, or a multicast to a group of nodes on the network.
- **Length** A 2-byte field that describes the number of bytes of data following this field.
- **Type** Distinguishes between various types of frames. Values can be found in RFC 1340. For example, IP packets have Ethertype 08 00 while ARP packets have Ethertype 08 03.

- **Data** Contains the user data of the frame and is 46 to 1500 bytes long. Data from the upper layers is encapsulated in the frame; for example the graphic in a Web page requested by your system. This field will vary in length based on the data encapsulated.
- **Frame Check Sequence (FCS)** A 4-byte field. The FCS is a CRC on the frame allowing the receiver to perform basic error control. If a frame fails the CRC check, it is discarded and the upper layer protocol is responsible for retransmission. The FCS is based on the address fields, Ethertype, and data, and is designed to detect errors in transmission.

The destination MAC comes first in the frame. This allows bridges and switches the earliest access to the destination so they can copy the packet to the correct port as quickly as possible.

Figure 1.14 shows the format of the 802.3 format modified to incorporate three 1-byte 802.2 fields. The Destination Service Access Point (DSAP) and the Source Service Access Point (SSAP) identify the network protocol being transported in the Ethernet frame, such as a value of 06 for IP or AA for a SNAP frame (to be discussed next).

Figure 1.14 Ethernet Frame - 802.3 with 802.2 Headers

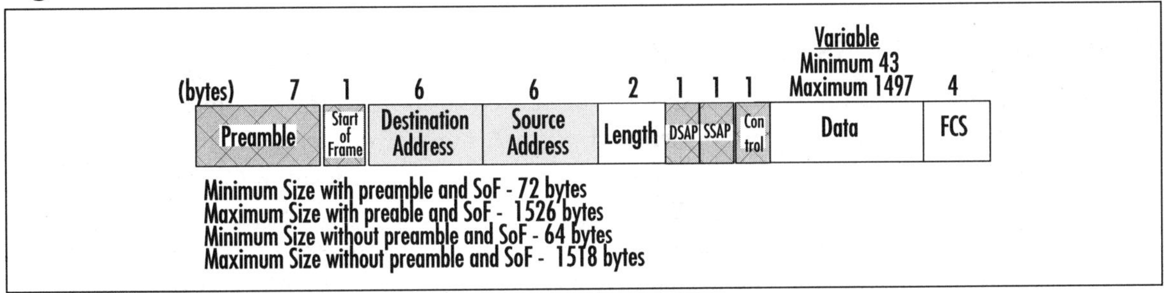

Figure 1.15 examines an 802.3 SNAP Ethernet frame, described on Cisco equipment as Ethernet frame type SNAP. This is an extension of the earlier LLC format, which had only a limited number of Ethertypes.

Figure 1.15 Ethernet Frame: IEEE-Style SNAP

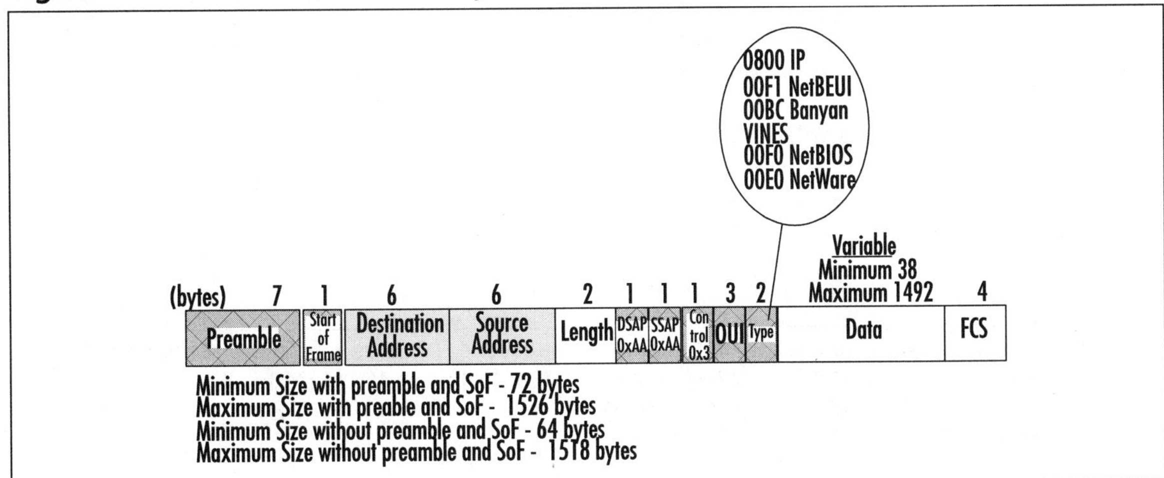

The new fields here are the Destination and Source SAPs, which describe the upper protocol type for the frame; the Control field, generally unused but designed for administrative purposes; and the Organizationally Unique Identifier (OUI), to distinguish protocols from different vendors—the OUI is the same value used in the MAC addresses. A two-byte Type identifier specifies the actual protocol, and maintains compatibility with the earlier Ethernet II frame type.

Wireless LANs

Wireless LANs (WLANs) provide network connectivity almost anywhere, with great cost savings since there is no need to run much network cable, if any. Unfettered access to the network, regardless of physical location, or traditional cable distance limitations is one of the primary drivers for WLANs.

WLANs use radio frequency (RF) signals that enable users to stay connected to the network almost anywhere, as long as they remain within range. Many organizations are merging WLANs into their traditional wired networks. Conference rooms, warehouses, hospitals, and many other organizations are reaping the benefits of WLANs. Wireless networking is briefly introduced here, and discussed more fully in Chapter 3.

OSI and Wireless: Layer 2 and Down

The different technologies used in WLANs can be related to the OSI system model. As the name **wireless LAN** implies, it is networking without wires. A number of various techniques are available for sending data over radio signals. These are covered in greater detail in Chapter 3.

The standards covered by the Cisco WLAN products detailed in this book are based on the IEEE's 802.11 efforts. The 802.11 standards are responsible for defining the Physical and MAC layers of operation in a WLAN. The primary standard we focus on is the 802.11b standard, which is an extension to the original 802.11 standard. 802.11b's primary objective defines the use of the 2.4 GHz band in RF for high-speed data communications. 802.11b supports the original 802.11 data rate of 2 Mbps as well as higher speeds up to 11 Mbps.

The frames generated by a WLAN device differ from the frames generated by an Ethernet device in many ways. WLANs are not physically connected by cables, like an Ethernet LAN, so specialized fields in the frames must be used. While 802.11a, 802.11b, and 802.11g have Ethernet origins, there are differences in the wireless frames to accommodate the underlying technology. An 802.11b frame (illustrated in Figure 1.16) is comprised of nine fields.

Figure 1.16 802.11b Frame

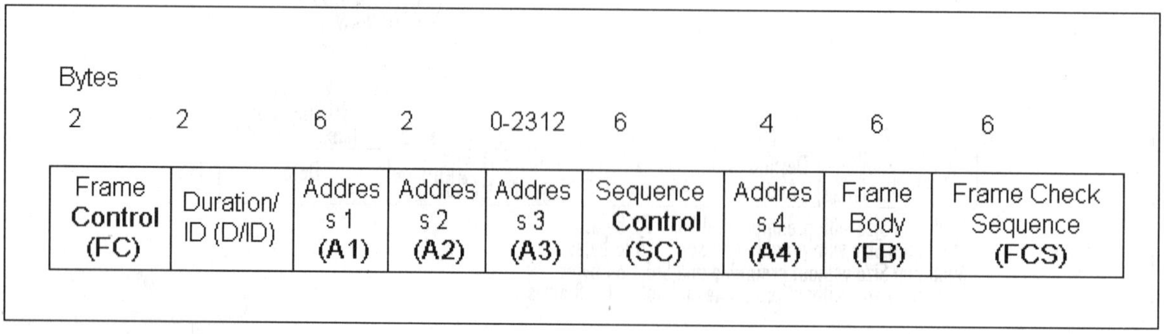

Bytes

2	2	6	2	0-2312	6	4	6	6
Frame **Control** (FC)	Duration/ ID (D/ID)	Addres s 1 **(A1)**	Addres s 2 **(A2)**	Addres s 3 **(A3)**	Sequence **Control** (SC)	Addres s 4 **(A4)**	Frame Body **(FB)**	Frame Check Sequence **(FCS)**

The first field in an 802.11b frame is the 2-byte frame control (FC) field. The FC field contains the ten subfields described next. These fields are some of the prime differentiators in an 802.11b frame.

- **Protocol Version** A 2-bit field within the FC field. The default value is 0 with all other values being reserved at this time.
- **Type** A 2-bit field that works with the 4-bit subtype field to identify the function of the frame. The possible combinations and their descriptions are provided in Table 1.3.
- **To Distribution System** A 1-bit field set to 1 in all frames sent by an associated station with an AP to signify that the frame is destined for the network behind the AP, such as a server connected to the same Ethernet network as the AP. All other frames have this bit set to 0.
- **From Distribution System** A 1-bit field set to 1 on all frames exiting the Distribution System. All other frames have this bit set to 0.
- **More Fragments** A 1-bit field set to 1 in all frames that contain another fragment of the current MAC Service Data Unit (MSDU) or MAC Management Protocol Data Unit (MMPDU). All other frames have the MF bit set to 0
- **Retry** A 1-bit field set to 1 in all frames, data or management, which are retransmissions of earlier frames. Frames that are not retransmissions of a previous frame are set to 0.
- **Power Management** A 1-bit field that indicates the power management mode of a station. Indicates the state the station will be in after the successful completion of the frame exchange sequence. A value of 1 indicates that the station will be in power-save mode, whereas 0 indicates that the station is in active mode.

NOTE

The Power Management field in frames transmitted by an Access Point (AP) will always be set to 0, indicating active mode. It would not be desirable for an AP on your network to go into power-save mode.

- **More Data** A 1-bit field that tells an associated station in power-save mode that one or more frames are buffered for it on the AP. The More Data field is set to 0 for all other directed frames.
- **WEP** A 1-bit field set to 1 if the frame body contains data that has been processed by the WEP algorithm. Frames that have not been processed by WEP have a WEP field value of 0.
- **Order** A 1-bit field set to 1 in any data frame that contains data using the **StrictlyOrdered** service class. All other frames have a value of 0 in the Order field.

NOTE

The Strictly Ordered service class is a mechanism built into the 802.11 standard that provides additional protection against out-of-order frames. This is accomplished by holding any multicast or broadcast traffic that matches addresses for frames that are already queued. Without this mechanism, it would be possible for broadcast or multicast traffic to reach a recipient out of order and create communications problems.

Table 1.3 802.11 Type and Subtype Combinations in the FC Field

Type Value	Type Description	Subtype Value	Subtype Description
00	Management	0000	Association Request
00	Management	0001	Association Response
00	Management	0010	Reassociation Request
00	Management	0011	Reassociation Response
00	Management	0100	Probe Request
00	Management	0101	Probe Response
00	Management	0110-0111	Reserved
00	Management	1000	Beacon
00	Management	1001	Announcement traffic indication message (ATIM)
00	Management	1010	Disassociation
00	Management	1011	Authentication
00	Management	1100	Deauthentication
00	Management	1101-1111	Reserved
01	Control	0000-1001	Reserved
01	Control	1010	Power Save (PS) Poll
01	Control	1011	Request To Send (RTS)
01	Control	1100	Clear To Send (CTS)
01	Control	1101	Acknowledgement (ACK)
01	Control	1110	Contention-Free (CF) End
01	Control	1111	CF-End + CF-ACK
10	Data	0000	Data
10	Data	0001	Data + CF-ACK
10	Data	0010	Data + CF-Poll
10	Data	0011	Data + CF-ACK + CF-Poll
10	Data	0100	Null function (no data)
10	Data	0101	CF-ACK (no data)
10	Data	0110	CF-Poll (no data)
10	Data	0111	CF-ACK + CF-Poll (no data)

Continued

Table 1.3 802.11 Type and Subtype Combinations in the FC Field

Type Value	Type Description	Subtype Value	Subtype Description
10	Data	1000-1111	Reserved
11	Reserved	0000-1111	Reserved

- **Duration/ID** A 16-bit field that carries the association ID of a station with an AP.
- **Address Fields** Destination and source MAC addresses. In 802.11b frames, there may be up to five:
- **Basic Service Set Identifier (BSSID)** The MAC address of the AP.
- **DA** The MAC address of the final recipient.
- **SA** The MAC address of the sending station on the WLAN.
- **Receiver Address (RA)** The MAC address of the intended immediate recipient stations on the WLAN.
- **Transmitter Address (TA)** MAC address of the sending station on the WLAN.
- **Frame Body** A 0 to 2312-byte field that contains the payload (data). This is where the data being transported by the frame is located, for example the graphic in a Web page requested by your system. This field will vary in length based on the data encapsulated.
- **FCS** The FCS has the same function and purpose as it performs for a wired Ethernet frame.

As you can see, there are a number of differences between Ethernet and 802.11b frames. These differences are required to enable high-speed communications on a medium of radio waves rather than copper or fiber media.

OSI and Wireless: Layer 3 and Up

The OSI system model applies to the configuration, management, and troubleshooting of Cisco WLANs far beyond Layers 1 and 2. Certainly Layers 1 and 2 are key to WLANs, but the other layers play key roles as well.

For example, configuration of wireless APs and bridges may be done through Telnet and HTTP, two Application-layer protocols. This is a key topic to understand because if there is a problem accessing the Web interface, you need to be able to use your knowledge of the OSI system model to troubleshoot the problem.

Problems at higher layers that affect wireless operations are varied. The problem could be caused by an ACL on a router between your system and the AP. It could be a problem with general network connectivity (can you ping the AP's IP address?). These all come into play in determining the cause of the failure.

Bridges and APs also use other protocols in the OSI system model. Examples include the following:

- DHCP at Layer 7 to automatically obtain an IP address from a DHCP server.
- Remote Authentication Dial In User Service (RADIUS) at Layer 7 in conjunction with EAP to authenticate WLAN users.
- WEP at Layer 2 to encrypt/decrypt data on the WLAN.

What does all these networking theories and models mean to Cisco? Good question! In the next section, we bring it all together by discussing how Cisco ties it all together in a well-functioning mix of hardware and software. A good working knowledge of Cisco hardware and software is imperative to mastering and taming your networks.

Cisco Hardware

Cisco offers a number of hardware products that run the gamut from routers and switches, to specialized security products such as firewalls. This section covers routers and switches, what they do, and what Cisco offers. It is our goal in this section to help your research and decision-making efforts by organizing otherwise scattered information into a single resource.

Advances in technology have blurred the line between routing and switching, which can make it difficult to understand what device performs what function. Routers can perform certain Layer 2 functions such as bridging, while certain models of switches can route with the right mix of hardware. Instead of worrying and artificially making such distinctions, we have simply chosen to adopt the traditional viewpoint that "routers route and switches switch." That is, regardless of what devices do it or how it is accomplished, we will focus on routers and switches as pure functionaries, rather than a conglomeration of router and switch technologies. We will identify the routers and switches available to you from Cisco, and what functions they perform that may be of use to you.

Our discussion starts with the lowest layer in this equation—Layer 2, the Data Link layer. In this case, that means network switches.

Switches

A working definition of a switch is a hardware device that connects two or more network devices, and supports the delivery of traffic using Layer 2 MAC addresses. A switch is unaware and does not care about upper protocol information; as far as it is concerned, Layer 2 information is simply data payload.

Figure 1.17 shows A and B connected to Switch1. A has a MAC address of 00-02-2D-3A-14-F6 and B has a MAC address of 00-08-02-00-5E-D3. A is using IP address 10.1.1.1 while B has 10.1.1.2; such Layer 3 information is immaterial to the switch as it uses Layer 2 MAC addresses to perform its functions.

Figure 1.17 Basic Switch Operations

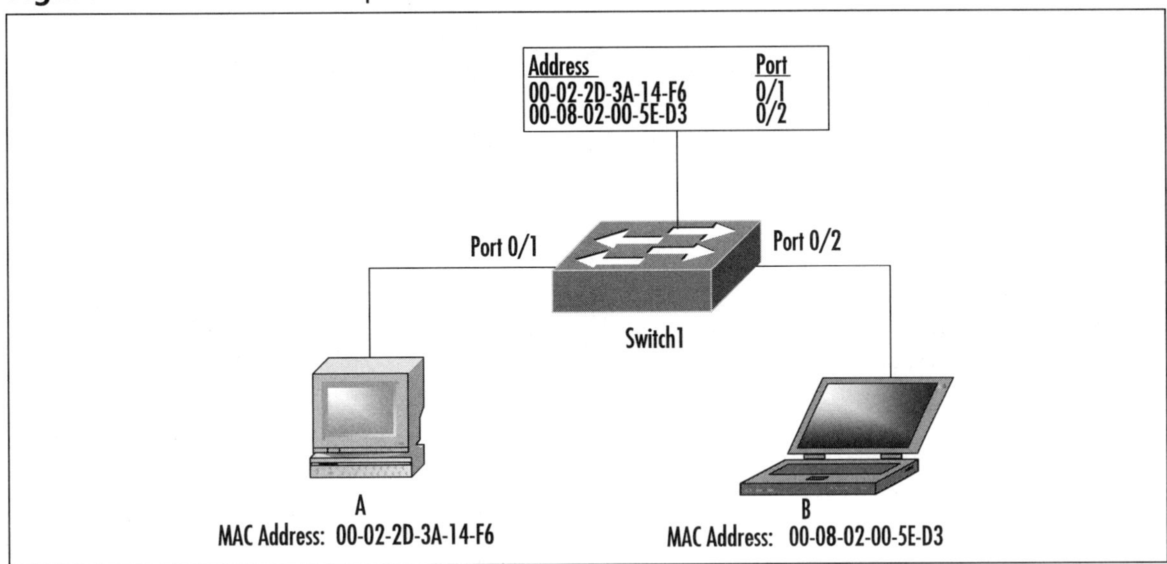

If A needs to communicate with B (in this case, via IP addresses), it must first determine the MAC address of B. It will make this determination using ARP, which will map the MAC address of B to its IP address. Once A has the MAC address of B, it will create the necessary Layer 2 frames (in this case, Ethernet) with its MAC address as the source, and B's MAC address as the destination. Encapsulated within this Ethernet frame is all the higher layer data, including the IP source and the DAs.

When the frame arrives at the switch, the switch reads the destination MAC, checks its MAC address table, and forwards it to the port to which B is connected. When B responds to A, the process is reversed, where B becomes the source, and A the destination. This is a fairly simplistic example, but it serves to illustrate that all LAN switches operate along these same lines. There are several key switch operations and concepts that you need to know at Layer 2. One of the most important as far as switches are concerned is the Spanning Tree Protocol (STP).

Spanning Tree Protocol

No discussion of LANs is complete without covering the STP, officially known as 802.1D for the standard that defines it. The STP provides the necessary mechanisms and processes that allow a network to achieve redundancy, yet suppress network-killing loops. For purposes of discussing STP, ignore the implications of the poor network design evidenced by Figure 1.18, which shows Switch1 and Switch2 providing two paths to B. Switch1 can and will send traffic for B out both its ports, as will Switch2. Host B may find itself the recipient of several copies of the same LAN packets. While that is bad enough, it gets worse with broadcast traffic: both switches will send it out all their ports by default, over and over until the network collapses from saturation.

Figure 1.18 STP

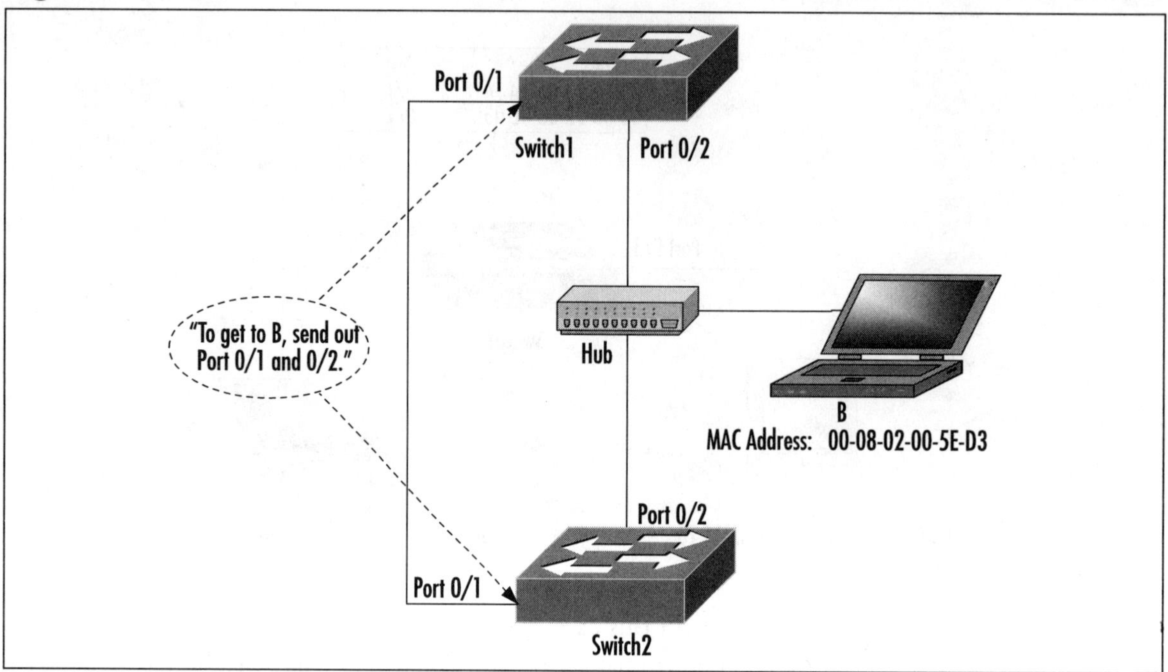

While it is beneficial that there are two paths to B, especially to compensate for any link failures, obviously there is a problem with having both active at the same time. STP solves this problem by forcing one of the switches to be active and the other to be in stand-by, ready to assume duties should the primary link on the other switch fail. To achieve this, STP will hold an election wherein one of the switches will become root, and thus be in a position to make adjustments that eliminate the loop. The loser of the STP elections will put its port to non-forwarding (blocking), and use the other switch to reach B.

There are several states (listed in order in the next section) that a port goes through when STP is activated. STP uses the spanning tree algorithm (STA) to elect the root bridge in a tree, and to determine which ports will block and which will forward. Ports are chosen on the basis of cost, with higher speed ports having a lower cost.

Spanning Tree Port States

Ports participating in STP (which is enabled by default) transition through several states, as shown in Figure 1.19. Notice that if a port is blocked by STP, it will not learn or forward, but is ready to assume duties should the active port link fail.

Figure 1.19 STP States

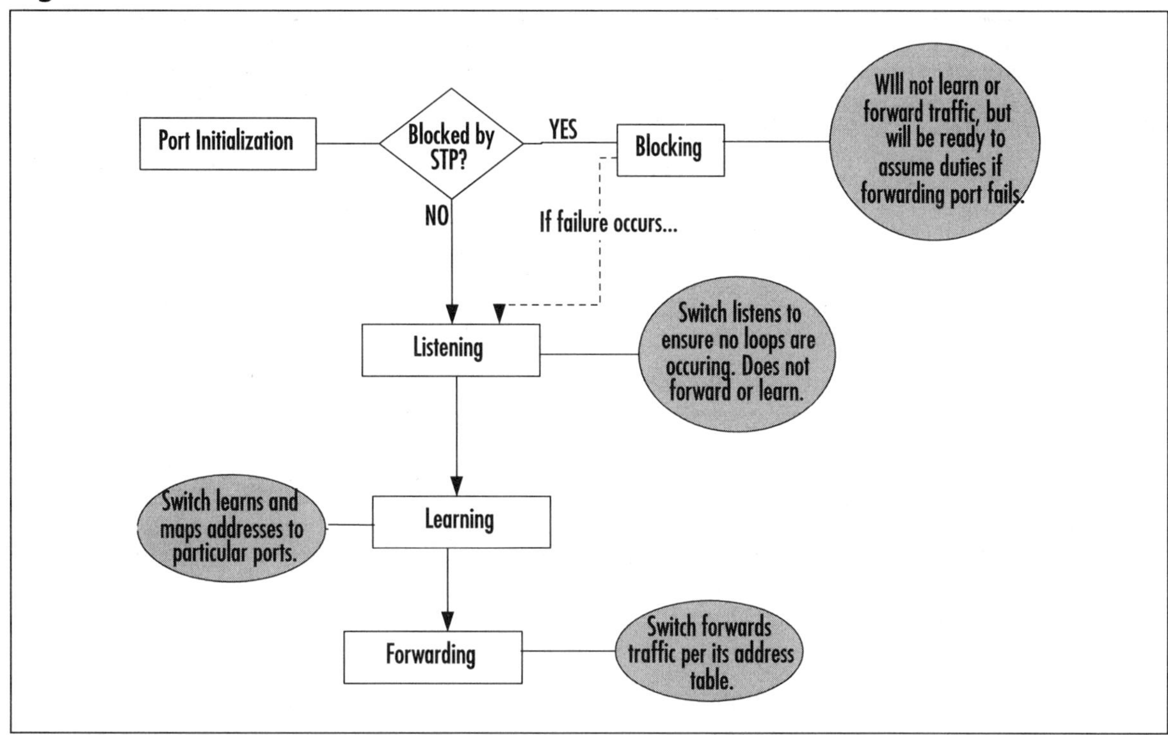

Cisco Catalyst switches support several versions of STP:

- **Common Spanning Tree** One spanning tree for the entire Layer 2 network. All virtual LANs (VLANs) share the same instance of spanning tree. Less computationally intensive but could result in sub-optimal spanning tree.
- **Per VLAN Spanning Tree** Cisco proprietary solution that provides one spanning tree per VLAN for over same or different ISL trunks.
- **Per VLAN Spanning Tree+** Same as the previous bullet, except for 802.1Q trunks.

All LAN switches, regardless of what make and model they are, operate in this same fashion. The speed and efficiency levels may vary, as will the set of features, but when stripped to its essentials, all a LAN switch does is simply forward frames based on MAC addresses. The Cisco Catalyst series contains the switches manufactured and supported by Cisco. They differ by backplane, features, and port density, as well as what types of ports they will support.

Cisco Catalyst Series Models

Tables 1.4 through Table 1.7 list current models of the Catalyst switches and corresponding values. These tables provide a handy summary of the features and capacities of currently available models. More information can be obtained at: www.cisco.com/en/US/products/hw/switches/index.html.

Table 1.4 Catalyst Switches Support Specifications

Catalyst Switch	End Of Sale (EOS)	End Of Life (EOL)
2900	2948G-L3 October 31, 2003	2948G-L3 October 31, 2008
2900XL	June 30, 2003	June 30, 2008
2950	No Plans for EOS	X
3500XL	3512/24/48 July 27, 2002	3512/24/48 July 27, 2007
3550	No Plans for EOS	X
4500	No Plans for EOS	X
6000	No Plans for EOS	X
8500	No Plans for EOS	X

Table 1.5 Catalyst Switch Throughput Values

Catalyst Switch	Maximum throughput speed (Packets per second)
2900	18Mpps
2900XL	2.1Mpps
2950	10.1Mpps
3500XL	8Mpps
3550	9Mpps
4500	48Mpps
6000	210Mpps
8500	24Mpps

Table 1.6 Catalyst Switch Port Availability

Catalyst Switch	Fixed	Modular	Fixed and Modular
2900	X		
2900XL			X
2950			X
3500XL			X
3550			X
4500			X
6000		X	
8500		X	

Table 1.7 Catalyst Switch LAN Interfaces

	2900	2900XL	2950	3500XL	3550	4500	6000	8500
10BaseT	X	X	X	X	X	X	X	
100BaseT	X	X	X	X	X	X	X	
1000BaseTX							X	
10BaseFL							X	
100BaseF		X	X		X	X	X	X
10/100 Autosensing	X	X	X	X	X	X	X	X
10/100/1000							X	
10GBaseLR							X	
Gigabit Ethernet	X	X	X	X	X	X	X	X
ATM							X	X
Integrated Inline Power				X		X	X	
Integrated Server Load Balancing							X	

Switch Architecture

While each model of Catalyst switch differs by hardware architectures, expandability options, and features, they share some common characteristics. Switches can be fixed configuration, where the number and types of ports and features are static or modular, where the density and types of ports and features are dynamic and can be adjusted to fit your networking needs.

All switches need the right mix of hardware and software to process traffic. These components typically include processors (both general and specialized), memory (of which they are several types), and an interconnection mesh that enables ports to pass traffic between each other. These aspects of switches are discussed, and any significant differences between what is available for fixed versus modular switches are noted.

Supervisor Engine

The Supervisor Engine (SE) is the traffic cop of the Cisco Catalyst switch for certain models. It establishes and controls the flow of Layer 2 traffic, and on certain newer models, Layer 3 and 4. The SE controls all aspects of the switch, and provides the user interface for switch management and configuration. On fixed configuration switches, the SE function is part of the integrated circuitry and is typically not upgradeable, while modular switches enable you to upgrade or replace your SE entirely.

What features are available to you depend on the model of SE you have. Table 1.8 contains information about the SEs available and their capacities. As a general rule, capacities and features increase with each new generation of SE.

Table 1.8 Catalyst Switch SEs

Model	Catalyst Series	Capacity	Operating System	MAC Address Table Size	CPU	NVRAM	Flash	Memory
Supervisor II	4xxxx	24Gbps Gbps switching, 18Gbps Gbps forwarding	CATOS	16,384	150	1MB	16MB	64MB
Supervisor III	4xxx	64Gbps Gbps switching, 48Gbps Gbps forwarding	IOS	32,768	300	512K	192MB	256MB
Supervisor IV	4xxxx	64Gbps Gbps switching, 48Gbps Gbps forwarding	IOS	32768	333	512K	192MB	512MB
Supervisor IIG	50xx 1.2 Gbps 55xx 3.6Gbps Gbps	GBIC (mulitlayer) 1.2 Gbps Switching	CATOS/IOS	16,384	37.5MHz MCF5102	256K	8MB	32MB
Supervisor IIIF	50xx 1.2 Gbps 55xx 3.6Gbps Gbps	Fixed GBIC 3.6Gbps Gbps switching	CATOS/IOS	16,384	IDT RISC	512K	8MB	64MB
Supervisor IIIG	50xx 1.2 Gbps 55xx 3.6Gbps Gbps	GBIC (Uplink) 3.6Gbps Gbps switching	CATOS/IOS	16,384	37.5MHz MCF5102	512K	8MB	32MB
Supervisor III	50xx 1.2 Gbps 55xx 3.6Gbps Gbps	GBIC (multiplayer) 3.6Gbps Gbps switching	CATOS/IOS	16,384	150MHz R4700 RISC	512K	8MB	64MB
Supervisor 1-A PFC MSFC2	65xx	32Gbps Gbps switching CEF – NO	CATOS, IOS, Hybrid	128K		N/A	16MB	128MB
Supervisor 2 PFC MSFC2	65xx	256Gbps Gbps switching CEF – YES	CATOS, IOS, Hybrid	128K		N/A	32MB	512MB

Continued

Table 1.8 Catalyst Switch SEs

Model	Catalyst Series	Capacity	Operating System	MAC Address Table Size	CPU	NVRAM	Flash	Memory
Supervisor 1-A PFC	65xx	32Gbps Gbps switching CEF – NO	CATOS, IOS, Hybrid	128K		N/A	16MB	128MB
Supervisor 2 PFC2	65xx	256Gbps Gbps switching CEF – YES	CATOS, IOS, Hybrid	128K		N/A	32MB	512MB
Supervisor 1-A 2GE	65xx	32Gbps Gbps switching CEF – NO	CATOS, IOS, Hybrid	128K		N/A	16MB	128MB
Supervisor 720	65xx	720Gbps Gbps switching CEF - YES	CATOS, IOS, Hybrid	64K		N/A	192MB	1GB

Switch Fabric

The switch fabric is essentially the backplane for all ports and modules on the switch module. When a connection is made from a port on one module to a port on another module, it is made across the switch fabric. Physically, it is the combination of silicon, plastic, and metal that enables ports to connect and pass traffic between themselves.

The switch fabric resides on the SE. When a port has to communicate with another port, it has the supervisor check its tables (Content Addressable Memory [CAM] for Layer 2 addresses and Ternary CAM [TCAM] for Layer 3 addresses) to determine what slot and port it needs. The supervisor then establishes the connection between the ports. The switch fabric can also reside on its own module (such as the Switch Fabric Module 2 (WS-X6500-SFM2) and the Switch Fabric Module (WS-C6500-SFM for the Catalyst 6500 Series), which enables the available capacity to be expanded without replacing the SE, or to expand beyond the capacity of the SE.

The switch fabric can be blocking or non-blocking. Non-blocking fabric ensures that the total bandwidth of all ports that use the switch fabric do not exceed its capacity. What this means is that the density of the ports on the switch are such that their total capacity will never be greater than that of the switch fabric. Switches operating in non-blocking mode ensure that congestion will never occur on the switch, nor will ports ever want for bandwidth between each other.

A blocking switch has a port density capacity that exceeds the total capacity of the switch fabric. Control is possible by blocking traffic flow when the switch fabric capacity is exceeded or otherwise not available.

Backplane

Each Catalyst chassis has a series of interconnected slots into which modules such as the SE or port modules are inserted. The pathway that interconnects these slots is called the backplane, and can be a key determinant of performance. Table 1.9 summarizes the backplanes capacity of current Cisco Catalyst switches.

Table 1.9 Catalyst Switch Backplane Capacities

Catalyst Model	Backplane	Configuration
1912	1Gbps Gbps	Fixed – 12 ports
1924	1Gbps Gbps	Fixed – 24 ports
2980G	24Gbps Gbps	Fixed – 80 ports
2948G	24Gbps Gbps	Fixed – 48 ports
2912MF XL	3.2Gbps Gbps	Fixed – 12 100BaseFX ports
2924MF XL	3.2Gbps Gbps	Fixed – 24 ports
2950G-48EI	13.6Gbps Gbps	Fixed – 48 ports
2950G-24EI	13.6Gbps Gbps	Fixed – 24 ports
2950T-24	8.8Gbps Gbps	Fixed – 26 ports
2950C-24	8.8Gbps Gbps	Fixed – 26 ports
2950-24	8.8Gbps Gbps	Fixed – 24 ports
2950-12	8.8Gbps Gbps	Fixed – 12 ports

Continued

Table 1.9 Catalyst Switch Backplane Capacities

Catalyst Model	Backplane	Configuration
3512XL	10Gbps Gbps	Fixed – 12 ports
3524	10Gbps Gbps	Fixed – 24 ports
3548XL	10Gbps Gbps	Fixed – 48 ports
3508XL	10Gbps Gbps	Fixed – 8 GE ports
3550-48	13.6Gbps Gbps	Fixed – 48 ports
3550-24	8.8Gbps Gbps	Fixed – 24 ports
3550-12G	24Gbps Gbps	Fixed – 12 GE ports
3550-12T	24Gbps Gbps	Fixed – 12GE ports
4003	24Gbps Gbps	Modular – 3 slots (1 for Supervisor)
4006	64Gbps Gbps	Modular – 6 slots (1 for Supervisor)
4912G	24 Gbps Gbps	Fixed – 12GE ports
5500	3.6 Gbps Gbps	Modular – 13 slots (1 for Supervisor)
5505	3.6Gbps Gbps	Modular – 5 slots (1 for Supervisor)
5509	3.6Gbps Gbps	Modular – 6 slots (1 for Supervisor)
6006	32Gbps Gbps	Modular – 9 slots (1 for Supervisor)
6009	32Gbps Gbps	Modular – 9 slots (1 for Supervisor)
6506	256Gbps Gbps	Modular – 6 slots (1 for Supervisor)
6509	256Gbps Gbps	Modular – 9 slots (1 for Supervisor)
6513	256Gbps Gbps	Modular – 13 slots (1 for Supervisor)
8510	10Gbps Gbps	Modular – 5 slots (multiservice switch router)
8540	40Gbps Gbps	Modular – 13 slots (multiservice switch router)

Memory

There are several types of memory used by Cisco Catalyst switches. Memory is typically distributed on a per module, per port, and per supervisor basis. Memory (known as dynamic random access memory [DRAM]) is used to store packets awaiting service, to load and hold images, and to buffer traffic until it can be in processed or transmitted.

Memory is typically allocated to ports in set-sized buffers. This is usually automatically tuned by the switch, with little or no option for the engineer to directly affect buffer allocation. When the switch receives traffic destined to a port that currently is unable to process it immediately, the switch fabric will buffer the traffic until the port is ready.

The size of buffers can impact the efficiency of a switch. Too small and large packets will be segmented too frequently. Too large, and memory will be wasted when large numbers of small packets are received.

How memory is allocated and in what quantities will depend on the model of switch. Some switches such as the 6x00 series allocate 128K per four 10/100 ports, and 512K per four gigabit Ethernet ports. Generally, this is not something that is field-upgradeable, nor that you can directly increase. For the most part, you can deploy Catalyst switches knowing at least this much: Cisco has already mathematically derived the ideal buffer memory based on the capabilities of its switches, and their potential port densities.

Flash

Flash memory is re-writeable memory used to store OS images as well as the configuration files for each switch in some cases. Flash can be an internal Single In-Line Memory Module (SIMM) chip on the supervisor card, or an external Personal Computer Memory Card International Association (PCMCIA) flash card. Flash does not have a significant impact on operations other than when the switch is booting; the image gets loaded into DRAM after booting is complete, and is run from there.

Non-Volatile Random Access Memory (NVRAM)

Most Catalyst models use NVRAM to store their configuration file. In many cases, this is preferable to storing it in flash, as it decreases the likelihood that the configuration will be lost during OS upgrades.

Modules

Unless it is a fixed configuration switch such as the 29*xx*, the 35*xx*, or the 19*xx*, the Cisco Catalyst typically has available slots for expanding the number and type of network interfaces that it can support. Typically, these modules are inserted into the switch directly into its backplane, which places them under the control of the installed SE.

One potential issue with modules, especially new gigabit rate modules, is that older SEs, or SEs with older firmware may not support them. In that case, your only resource is to upgrade the firmware to a new version, or upgrade to the correct SE.

Module types include densely concentrated switched LAN ports (from 8 to 48 Ethernet ports, for example), switch fabric modules that expand capacity, or even router modules that route at wire speed (called Layer 3 switching). A procedure for installing such modules is to power down the switch and insert them, as some modules are hot swappable, and some are not; it is better to err on the side of caution.

Almost all Catalyst switches have slots for various types of uplink interfaces used to connect the switch to other switches, and to trunk traffic. These are usually relatively high-speed interfaces measured in the 100/1000 Mbps range.

Cisco offers switch fabric modules to increase capacity on several of its modules, such as the WS-C6500-SFM= for the 65*xx* line. Such a module is appropriate if the installed switch fabric is not sufficient to handle the load.

Application Specific Integrated Circuits (ASIC)

ASICs are specialized processors that handle the reception and transmission of packets that transit a port. They are optimized to process traffic, rather than being a general processing chip. Their job is to get packets onto the backplane (if necessary) or out the port if that is the destination. Typically, they work with port buffers, which are small amounts of memory used to store packets waiting processing by the ASIC. The Cisco Catalyst switches use ASICs on their ports, SEs, and Layer 3 switching modules.

Switch Commands

Later in this section, we illustrate how to configure a Catalyst switch. Entire books have been written about the Cisco Catalyst line of switches; however, we will provide the basics of configuring these switches. For now, know that these switches primarily concern themselves with switching Layer 2 traffic, though several models blur the line between the switching and routing functions, which brings us to our next topic...Cisco routers.

Routers

The purpose of a router is to route, which is forwarding traffic to its destination based on its Layer 3 network address. While this is an IP-centric book, other network protocols such as AppleTalk and IPX can also be routed. Routers learn the route to a destination using dynamic and static means (discussed in Chapter 5 "IP Routing"). Routers either have the final destination or a next hop (usually another router) that claims to know how to reach the final destination.

Cisco routers can be flexible and adaptable devices that can adjust to support almost any type of network interface, from T-1 circuits, to Ethernet, to Token Ring, to FDDI, to ATM, and so forth. In its way, the router endlessly translates from one network format (like ATM) to another (Ethernet, for example), and vice versa. It is able to do this because Layer 2 details are of little importance to its primary function, which is Layer 3 traffic. As with the switch section, we discuss the hardware and software composition common to most Cisco routers, be they low-end access routers such as the 17xx series, or the more monstrous 12000 carrier class routers. Regardless of their features and port densities, all routers are concerned with sending Layer 3 traffic to its final destination.

Router Architecture

Cisco router hardware architecture shares some similar characteristics with Cisco Catalyst switches. This is especially true for components such as memory and NVRAM. In some cases, cards can be used interchangeably between certain models of routers and switches, such as the 36*xx* series of routes and the 65*xx* series of switches.

Backplane

The backplane is the interconnecting bus into which all modules are plugged, and across which data flows to reach other ports, or to access the central processing unit (CPU) or memory. Router backplanes tend to be of less magnitude than those of switches. This is because routers were not designed to handle the same amount of traffic as switches.

There is also a Layer 2 and Layer 3 reason for this; it takes more processing and time to read through three layers than it does two. While seemingly insignificant to humans (the difference is milliseconds or nanoseconds, in some cases), it does have a processing impact that can be notable. With the advances that Cisco is making in its routers and switches (such as Layer 3 switching, which routes at wire speed), the adaptation of switch technology to router tasks, or the router modules available for installation in Catalyst switches, the difference is rapidly becoming moot.

Memory

DRAM AKA main memory and AKA working memory is used by the router for almost all its functions. At boot time, the IOS image is copied to and run from memory. The configuration is copied from NVRAM and run from memory. What is left is allocated and shared amongst the various components and processes active on the router.

Certain modules use buffer memory to hold input or output awaiting processing or transmissions. Still other modules must take what they can get from available shared memory. The absence of memory for whatever reason can result in total router shutdown. As a rule, if Cisco recommends a set amount of memory to run a particular version of IOS, ensure you have at least that, if not more. Otherwise, while you can install the image and run it with a limited amount of memory, as you enable more features, your router will be running on borrowed time.

Flash

Flash memory exists primarily to hold the IOS image, and to be available to boot the image of your choice. On certain routers, flash memory can also be used to hold the configuration file, though this author prefers that it be store in NVRAM for peace of mind. Flash memory can be a SIMM or an external PCMCIA card.

NVRAM

NVRAM is a small amount of writeable memory, usually no more than 128K, that is used to store the configuration of the router. It retains the configuration, even when the router is turned off, hence the non-volatile in its name.

Cards

Like switches, routers are either fixed or modular. Fixed routers have a set amount of interfaces and features that cannot be expanded. Examples of fixed router configurations are the 25*xx* series (now end of sale). Other router models, such as the 37*xx* and 7*x*00 series, are modular with an adaptable backplane that can accommodate a wide range of network interfaces. While certain models are hot swappable (that is, cards can be inserted while the router is turned on), it might be a good idea to get into the habit of backing up and powering down the router prior to such an insertion or removal.

There are several types of adapter cards for Cisco routers. There are the oversize cards for the high-end routers (7*x*00 and up), and there are carrier adapter modules or port adapter modules, which accept smaller interface cards, allowing for unique mixing and matching.

Cisco Models

Cisco routers range from small office/home office (SOHO) models, to carrier class devices such as the 12000 services. Table 1.10 through 1.17 summarizes the key features of each, which can be useful information to have nearby.

Table 1.10 Cisco Routers: Support Specifications

	End of Sale	End of Life
SOHO	SOHO 71/76/77/77H – April 30, 2004	SOHO 71/76/77/77H – April 30, 2009
800	802/04 – October 8, 2002 806/26/27/27H – April 30, 2004	802/04 – October 8, 2007 806/26/27/27H – April 30, 2009
1700	1720 – August 1, 2003	1720 – August 1, 2004
2600	2610/11, 20/21, 50/51, 91 – April 26, 2003	2610/11, 20/21, 50/51, 91 – April 26, 2008
3600	3620 – December 31, 2003	3620 – December 31, 2008
3700		
7100	November 30, 2003	November 30, 2008
7200	7204 – April 30, 2002 7206 – January 1, 2002	7204 – April 30, 2007 7206 January 27, 2007
7300		
7400		
7500	7507 January 31, 2004 7509 – September 5, 2001	7507 – January 31, 2009 7509 – September 5, 2006
7600	7609 – January 31, 2004	7609 – January 31, 2009
10000	10005 – February 22, 2003	10005 – February 22, 2008
10720		
12000		

Table 1.11 Cisco Routers: Maximum Throughput in Packets Per Second

	Throughput Speed
SOHO	340pps
800	340pps
1700	115.2Kpps
2600	70Kpps
3600	120Kpps
3700	1.55 or 6.22Mpps (depends on version of software used)
7100	93Mpps
7200	800Kpps
7300	1 Mpps
7400	800Kpps

Continued

Table 1.11 Cisco Routers: Maximum Throughput in Packets Per Second

	Throughput Speed
7500	1.4Mpps
7600	170Mpps
10000	34Mpps
10720	34Mpps
12000	480Mpps

Table 1.12 Cisco Routers: Port Availability

	Fixed	Modular	Fixed & Modular
SOHO	X		
800	X		
1700			X
2600			X
3600		3620 and 3640 Only	3660
3700			X
7100			X
7200		X	
7300			X
7400		X	
7500		X	
7600			X
10000		X	
10720		X	
12000		X	

Table 1.13 Cisco Routers: LAN Interfaces

	10MB Ethernet	100MB Ethernet	10/100MB Ethernet	Gigabit Ethernet	Fiber 10MB Ethernet	Fiber 100MB Ethernet	Token Ring	FDDI/CDDI	ATM
SOHO	X		X						X
800	X		X						X
1700	X	X	X						
2600	X	X	X				X		X
3600	X	X	X		X	X	X		X
3700	X	X	X	X			X		X
7100	X	X	X	X	X	X	X		
7200	X	X	X	X	X	X			X
7300				X					
7400	X	X		X	X	X			X
7500	X	X		X	X	X	X	X	X
7600	X	X		X	X	X			X
10000				X		X			X
10720	X	X	X	X		X			
12000		X		X		X			

Table 1.14 Cisco Routers: WAN Interfaces

	Async	Serial	Serial with integrated CSU	ISDN BRI (S/T)	ISDN BRI (U)	ISDN PRI/Ch T1	ISDN PRI w/ CSU	Analog/ POTS	Integrated Modems	Integrated Modem WICs	HSSI	DS3
SOHO												
800		X		X	X			X				
1700	X	X	X	X	X					X		
2600	X	X	X	X	X	X	X	X	X	X	2691	X
3600	X	X	X	X	X	X	X	X	X	X	X	X
3700	X	X	X	X	X	X	X	X	X	X	X	X
7100				X	X	X					X	X
7200		X		X	X	X	X				X	X
7300												
7400		X		X	X	X	X				X	X
7500		X		X	X	X	X				X	X
7600		X				X	X				X	X
10000			X									X
10720												
12000												X

Table 1.14 Cisco Routers: WAN Interfaces (continued)

	ATM	ATM T1/E1	ATM OC3	ATM OC12	POS OCx/STMx	DPT/RPR OC12/ STM4	DPT/RPR OC48/ STM16	DPT/RPR OC192/ STM64	ADSL	ADSL over ISDN	G.SHDSL	IDSL	DPT
SOHO									X	X	X		
800									X	X	X	X	
1700									X		X	X	
2600	X	X	Requires external power source						X		X	X	
3600	X	X	X						X				
3700	X	X	X						X		X	X	
7100	X	X	X		X								
7200	X	X	X	X	X	X							X
7300					X								
7400	X	X	X	X	X								
7500	X	X	X	X	X	X							X
7600	X	X	X	X	X		X						
10000	X		X	X	X		X						X
10720							X						X
12000	X		X	X	X	X	X	X					X

Table 1.15 Cisco Routers: Voice Interfaces

	Analog	Digital
SOHO		
800	X	
1700	X	X
2600	X	X
3600	X	X
3700	X	X
7100		
7200		X
7300		
7400		X
7500		X
7600		X
10000		
10720		
12000		

Table 1.16 Cisco Routers: Integrated Port Switching

	Integrated 16port Switching	Integrated 36port Switching	Inline Power
SOHO			
800			
1700			
2600	X		Requires external power source
3600	X	3660 Only	Requires external power source
3700	X	X	X
7100			
7200			
7300			
7400			
7500			
7600			
10000			
10720			
12000			

Table 1.17 Cisco Routers: Security & VPN Capabilities

	Encryption AIM	Encryption NM
SOHO		
800		
1700		
2600	X	
3600	3660	3620 and 3640
3700	X	X
7100		
7200		
7300		
7400		
7500		
7600		
10000		
10720		
12000		

Recall that we mentioned several models of switches that are blurring the line between switch and router with their ability (or rather, the ability of an optional router module) to route (Layer 3 switching). The following "routers" are Catalysts with these modules installed. They are treated and configured the same as any Cisco router; the key difference is the tightly integrated support for VLANs and the ability to route at wire speeds.

- The 3550 (routing integrated into switch and IOS image [standard or enhanced])
- The 4x00 series with Layer 3 module (WS-X4232-L3=)
- The 5x00 series with Route Switch Module (RSM) (WS-X5302)
- The 6x00 series (routing integrated; this is a multilayer switch (layers 2-4).
- The 8x00 series varies by model (any module with "route processor" in its description).

The process of using any Cisco router or switch starts with its initial configuration, which we cover in the next section.

Accessing and Using Routers and Switches

Cisco routers and switches are accessed initially using a special cable to its console or auxiliary port. Until an IP address is assigned, this is your only way to configure. After the initial configuration, you can use telnet, SSH, or HTTP.

Access Cisco Console and AUX Port Cabling

Although router configurations differ considerably from platform to platform, all routers generally share two common ports: an **auxiliary port** and a **console port**. These two ports have different cabling, pin, and speed requirements. Auxiliary ports are typically attached to a modem or other device for remote management in case of network failure or some other catastrophic event.

We will start with the console port. Most of us have used the console port on a Cisco router to connect to the router for initial setup, configuration, and troubleshooting. The console port on most Cisco routers only supports speeds up to 9600 bps—not a very desirable speed if you want to use Xmodem or similar serial transfer protocol to upload a large image to the router.

However, this speed is more than enough to configure the router, given the simple, textual command line interface (CLI). You will need a special console cable (called a *rolled cable*) to make this connection. A rolled RJ-45 cable is simply a cable in which the cables have been swapped at opposite ends to make the send receive and the receive send. Figure 1.20 illustrates the pin-out diagram for a console cable.

Figure 1.20 Rolled (Console) Cable Pin-out Diagram

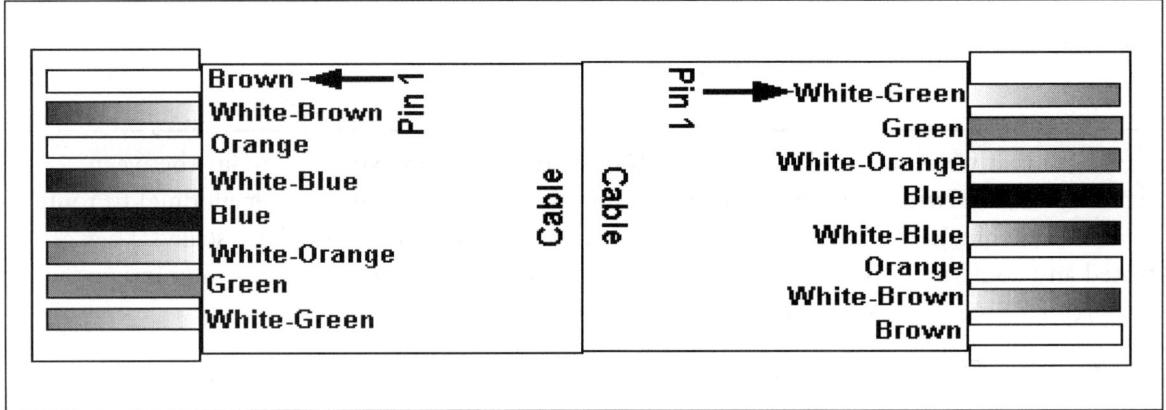

The AUX port, in contrast to the Console port, can have a modem connected to it to enable you to obtain a console session by dialing in. The AUX port on most routers can support speeds up to 38,400 bps, and the newer series of routers, 2600 and 3600 specifically, support speeds up to 115,200 bps. A rolled cable with a modem adapter (typically RJ-45 to DB-25) will suffice. Although the auxiliary port is useful in many cases, we focus our discussion on the console port.

Connecting to the Router

As logic would dictate, to configure a router, you must first be able to connect to it. Out of the box, the IOS is loaded; however, it has no working configuration, and only certain default parameters are enabled. As such, it has no Layer 3 addressing on the interfaces or SNMP strings loaded into the router. This makes it impossible to connect remotely. To configure the router, a physical connection must be made to the router through the use of the *router console port*.

Console Port Connections

The console port provides a console connection to the router for configuration purposes. To access this port you need to use a rolled-RJ45 cable with a 9-pin or 25-pin adapter connected to a PC that is running terminal emulation software, connected to the console port of the router. On older routers, the console port is a 25-pin serial port; a 25-pin to RJ-45 connector with a rolled RJ-45 cable is incorporated to connect to the console ports of these routers.

Figure 1.21 demonstrates the connection between a PC running terminal software and the router's console port. A new router usually comes with a console connection kit with a 9-pin and 25-pin connector as well as an RJ-45 rolled cable.

Figure 1.21 PC Connecting to a Router Console Port

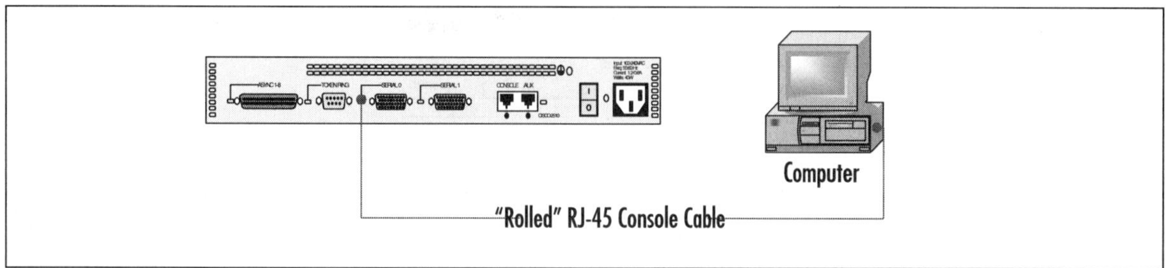

Now that you have an understanding of how the physical connection is made to the router, we can turn our attention to how the logical connection to the router is made. To make a connection to the router, you must run a terminal-emulation software program on your computer. For purposes of this discussion, we use the HyperTerminal software program, which is included in the accessories software package of most Windows-based computers. This configuration is as follows:

1. Go to **Start Menu** | **Programs** | **Accessories** | **Communications**, and launch **HyperTerminal**.
2. In the Connection Description screen, enter a name for your new connection and press **OK** (see Figure 1.22).

Figure 1.22 HyperTerminal Name Settings

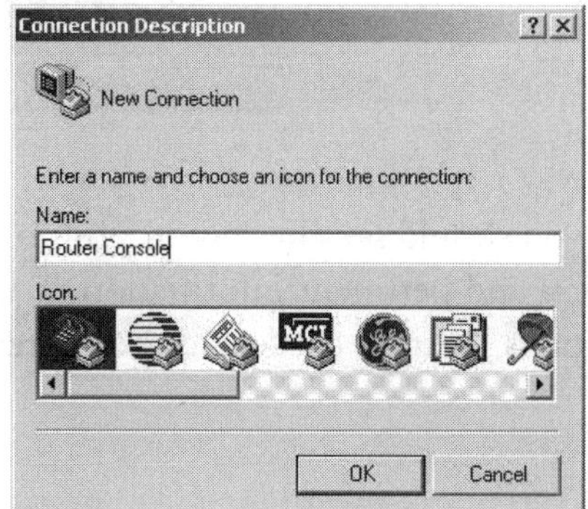

3. In the Connect To screen, choose a COM port from the list (2 to 4 ports are usually available). For the purposes of this example we use **COM 2**, as shown in Figure 1.23.

Figure 1.23 HyperTerminal Connection Settings

4. Make the following changes to the connection: Choose **9600** bps and **None** for the option for flow control. Figure 1.24 demonstrates what the appropriate connection settings should look like.

Figure 1.24 Com Port Settings

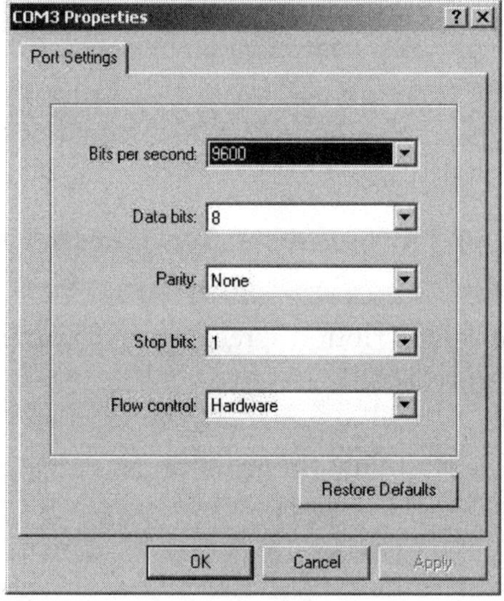

Turn the router on and you should see the system post information. This information includes the boot information and pertinent information to the current configuration. After the router has finished booting, press **Return** twice and the router is ready to accept commands.

Telnet Connection

After you have configured addressing on interfaces and network paths are available to these addresses, you can access the router through the virtual terminal (VTY) interfaces of the router. VTY ports are a set of completely logical interfaces that accept incoming TCP port 23 requests to the router. Unless you are accessing it from a secure network, Telnet should be avoided as it transmits **ALL** its information in the clear; anyone with the time and sniffer can quickly capture your username and password. A new and better solution for VTY access is Secure Shell (SSH).

To access a router via Telnet connection, use a Telnet client to connect to a configured IP address on the router. In the following example, we use the Telnet function built into the Windows OS to access our router. At the command prompt, enter the **telnet <ip address>** command. An example of this command is shown in Figure 1.25.

Figure 1.25 Connecting to the Router with Telnet

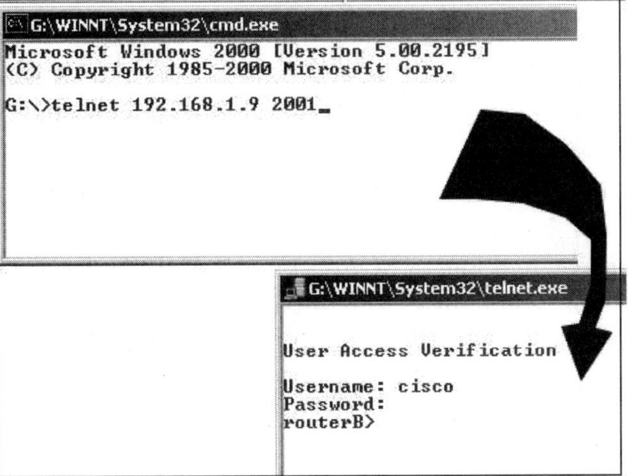

You can see from our example in Figure 1.25 that we issued the **telnet** command for the IP address 192.168.1.9; we are actually accessing this router via terminal server, hence the 2001 at the end of the Telnet command to redirect the TCP port 23. Once the Telnet session is established, we are presented with a login prompt. RouterB prompts for a username and password,.

SSH

SSH performs a similar function to Telnet, with the significant difference that it encrypts its session. Initially, Cisco will support only SSH version 1 on the bulk of its devices; however, it may provide widespread support for version 2 at a later date. SSHv2 has stronger security than SSHv1. Currently, SSHv2 is supported only on a small set of Cisco devices for select versions of the IOS.

Cisco supports SSH in certain versions of 12.2 and later of its IOS. SSH is available on Catalyst switches as well (see Table 1.18). Cisco continually updates its feature support in its software, so check the Software Advisor utility located at: www.cisco.com/kobayashi/support/tac/tools.shtml.

SSHv1 support was introduced in version 12.2(2) T, and is prevalent in later IOS versions. Check the Software Advisor tool for confirmation of whether a particular version supports SSH. For those switches that run Catalyst Operating System (CATOS) (such as the Catalyst 5000 or Catalyst 4000), version 6.1(1) is the minimum version required to obtain SSH, while Cisco recommends 6.4(2). SSH is *not* supported on the following Catalyst switches.

- Cat 1900
- Cat 2800
- Cat 2948G-L3
- Cat 2900XL
- Cat 3500XL
- Cat 4840G-L3
- Cat 4908G-L3

SSH forces the use of username and password for authentication; with SSH enabled, you cannot just establish a session to a Cisco device without providing both a username and password; contrast that with Telnet which will authenticate with either a password, or a password and username combination. This goes a long way towards doubling the protection of a device. The username and password combination can be stored locally or accomplished via a Terminal Access Controller Access Control System Plus (TACACS+) or RADIUS server. SSH is not enabled automatically; at a minimum, you must execute the following commands. The following assumes that any other parameters such as IP addresses have been configured.

```
Router_SSH(config)# username joesmith password cisco
Router_SSH(config)# crypto key generate rsa
```

Also, you need to enable SSH on the virtual lines (0 to 4, by default).

```
lines vty 0 4
transport input ssh
```

Remember that SSH requires a username and password; here, we have chosen to create a local account on the router. We could have configured TACACS+ or RADIUS and authenticated that way. Regardless, the important thing is that SSH be able to authenticate by a username and password. The **crypto key generate rsa** command creates a key that is used in the encryption process.

On those switches that support it and are running CATOS (set commands), the following will enable SSH. In this case, we are specifying a key length of 1024 bits, and are enabling SSH access from addresses on the 10.10.10.0/24 network.

```
CATALYST> (enable) set crypto key rsa 1024
CATALYST> (enable) set ip permit 10.10.10.0 255.255.255.0
CATALYST> (enable) set ip permit enable ssh
```

If you have the correct version, your IOS router can act as a SSH client. You can establish a SSH session from an IOS router using the following command:

```
ssh [-l userid] [-c {des | 3des}] [-o numberofpasswdprompts n] [-p portnum] {ipaddr |
hostname} [command]
```

The following will attempt to SSH with username joesmith to 10.10.10.10.

```
ssh -l joesmith -c 3des 10.10.10.10
```

There is no CATOS equivalent of this command, at least not in current versions, though this may change at a later date. In our focus on hardware so far, we have managed to keep our command examples to a minimum. However, without software (and its assemblage of commands), there is not much that the hardware will do. The next section discusses Cisco software in greater detail.

Cisco Software

All Cisco hardware depends on an OS of some kind to perform its mission. For routers and certain Catalyst switches, this is the IOS. The IOS is a scalable feature-rich OS with a seemingly endless list of configurable parameters. Obviously, like any OS, it has its own syntax and commands for enabling and configuring these parameters.

Several models of switches, especially those models that are a little long in the tooth, use the CATOS. CATOS is rapidly being supplanted by IOS on many of these switches, but you will still encounter it on many networks. One distinguishing feature of the CATOS is its large library of **set** commands to accomplish virtually all its functions. Certain models of Catalyst switches run the CATOS on their SEs, and an appropriate version of the IOS on their Layer 3 or multilayer module; this is referred to as *hybrid software* or a *hybrid OS*. We will confine our attention to IOS and CATOS for ease of discussion.

A working familiarity with IOS is critical. It is also important to be able to distinguish between different versions, and to know what each can do for you. To that end, we cover the Cisco IOS as well as the fundamentals of the Cisco CATOS.

Cisco Software - IOS

Cisco IOS software does not develop in a vacuum. It is continually tested, validated, and released to add new features, fix bugs, or to adapt to changing network conditions. IOS versions are assigned a major release number, such as 12.3, where 12 is the release number, and 3 is the iteration of that release (in this case, the third one). Cisco identifies its images with names such as c2500-i-l.123-1a.bin. The Cisco image identification scheme is dissected in Figure 1.26.

Figure 1.26 Image Identification

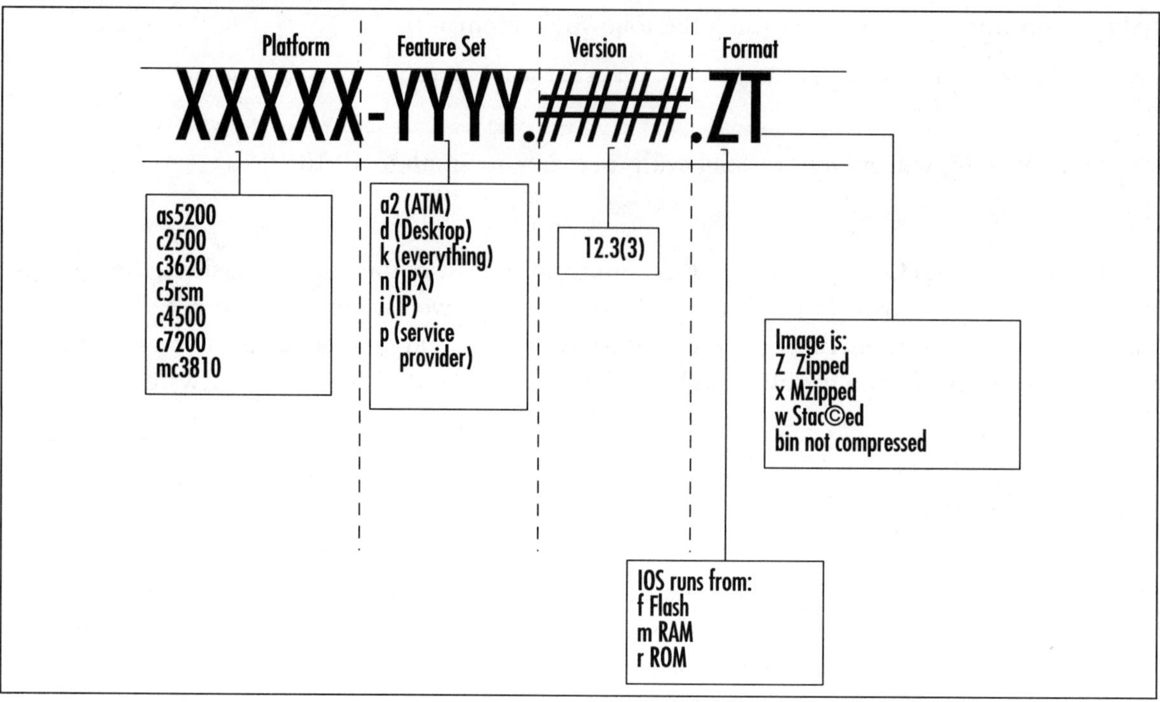

Cisco provides an image identification white paper at: www.cisco.com/warp/public/620/4.html#image. Being able to decode this information can help you determine what feature is active, and whether it is provides all the features you need.

To make things easier, Cisco bundles features into sets to enable its customers to select the IOS version best suiting their needs. The feature set descriptions are provided here, and more feature sets can be found at the Feature Navigator (shown in Figure 1.27) at: http://tools.cisco.com/ITDIT/CFN/jsp/index.jsp.

Figure 1.27 Feature Navigator

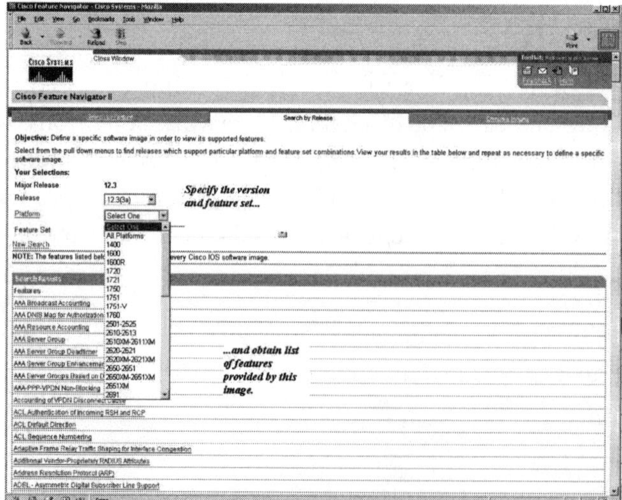

Figure 1.28 shows a partial listing of the features supported by the IP feature set for release 12.3(2)T. This type of information can be used to determine if the IOS release and version we are contemplating has all the features and commands needed. There are other features sets we could have used this tool to investigate, as shown in Figure 1.28.

Figure 1.28 Feature Navigator - Feature Sets

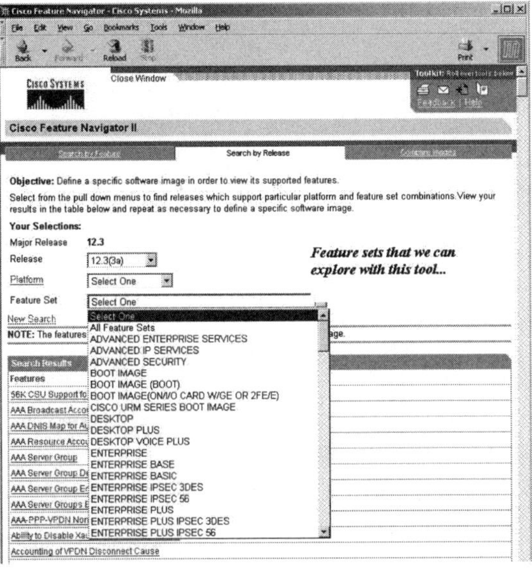

Software Image Lifecycle

Cisco labels its software releases such that its customers can determine where a version is in its lifecycle. Knowing that a particular release is End of Engineering (EOE) or General Deployment (GD) enables you to decide whether you want to acquire it, let alone install it on critical production network infrastructure equipment.

You can check the status of a release via the Software Center page at: www.cisco.com/kobayashi/library/12.2/index.shtml, as shown in Figure 1.29. Cisco has a system for tracking and controlling the lifespan of a release, starting with Early Deployment to End of Life (EOL)

Figure 1.29 Software Advisor

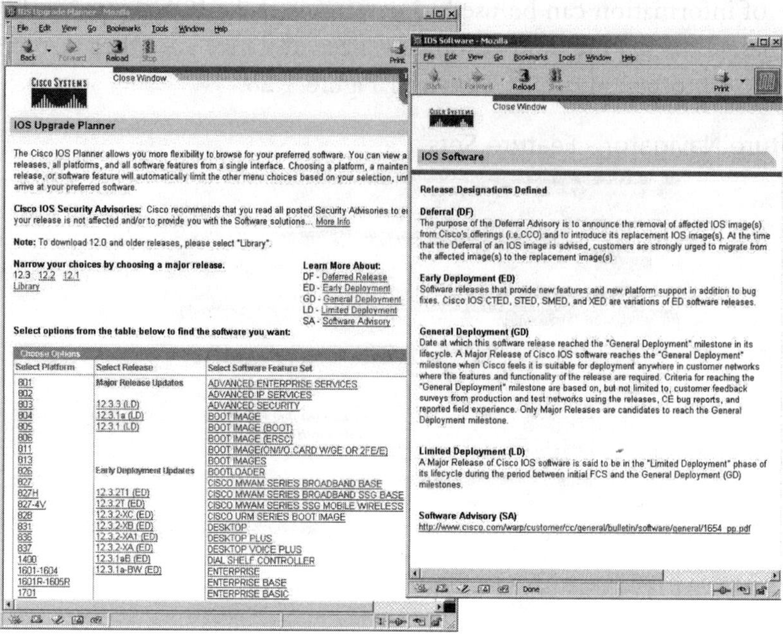

Early Deployment (ED)

IOS images start life as ED releases, which are simply the addition of new features, removal of old features, or new ways of doing things. Since these modifications are new and generally unproven, ED releases should be used only if you have a specific problem that it addresses. Perhaps the best know examples of ED releases are those IOS images marked as "T" (for technology) to show the incorporation of new technologies into the IOS. There are four forms of ED.

- **Consolidated Technology Release (CTED)** Introduces new technologies into the IOS, and are identified by "T", as in 12.3T. Generally contains more bugs and potential to crash than a main release. After the sixth maintenance release, the CTED will increment in version number, such as from 12.2T to 12.3, though Cisco may opt not to do this, depending on stability issues.
- **Specific Technology (STED)** The same concept as the CTED release, except for a narrow focus on a limited set of technologies for a fixed subset of Cisco hardware. STED images are identified by a two-letter combination appended to end of the IOS release number, such as 12.2.12-DA.
- **Specific Market (SMED)** Similar to STED, except targeted towards specific market segments such as service providers. A single letter appended to the end of the version number is used to identify a SMED release such as 12.3S.
- **Short-Lived (X) (XED)** Used as a competitive release tool to allow Cisco business units to rapidly develop and release an IOS image to fulfill some market need. Only exists until these features are incorporated into a maintenance release, which will render

them more stable. XED is identified by an X and another letter appended to the end of the version number, such as 12.3(1)XA. The letter following the X is used to distinguish one XED release from another.

First Customer Ship (FCS)

First Customer Ship (FCS) occurs when the first version (usually coinciding with the first maintenance) is made available to Cisco customers, via direct sales and the CCO Software Center. FCS is considered the start of the Limited Deployment (LD) phase for the IOS.

LD

The LD phase starts from the FCS to the time that the IOS achieves GD status. LD releases have been determined to be largely stable, but not all features have been validated in all possible scenarios. As new features crop up, bugs gets fixed, and changes are made, the LD release will either achieve GD status as a result, or be dropped in favor of a new release that supersedes it with all the necessary fixes. The LD phases generally lasts for about 9 to 14 months.

GD

The GD phase identifies a version that has been declared to be stable and with a mature set of features that have been validated. Customers can install GD versions with confidence that almost all bugs have been fixed. The GD phase for a release generally lasts 10 to 18 months, after which it will enter a mature maintenance phase in which incremental updates are periodically applied to make minor revisions or fixes. Mature maintenance on such GD revisions will address those conditions rated 1 and 2 on Cisco's severity scale.

End Cycles

Eventually, all versions reach the end of their lifecycle, and a process to transition them to obsolescence begins with the declaration of a End of Sale (EOS) period.

EOS means that the image cannot be ordered, and may only be available via special arrangement with Cisco if a particular version is needed to fix a particular problem or to maintain compatibility with a mix of equipment. It will also continue to be available for download from CCO. EOS can last 24 to 36 months before the next phase, EOE.

The EOE phase marks the cessation of active engineering work to fix any future defects; the last released version will stand as is, defects and all. EOE images will continue to be available from CCO. The EOE phase may last 24 to 36 months, depending on Cisco decisions about a release. Support is available via the TAC, but Cisco will not expend any active effort otherwise to support, unless it is by agreement with the customer to do so.

Finally, the end is near when an image reaches the EOL phase. All support (including TAC) stops, and the image is removed from CCO. In other words, no more support and no more downloading from Cisco.

Cisco takes this structured approach rather than outright stopping a product immediately to allow its customers time to adjust. It also provides this opportunity to plan for a transition to any replacement versions. The next section discusses the details of the IOS, and how to configure it.

IOS Command Syntax and Basic Configuration

A common management and configuration framework should be the goal of any network equipment provider. Cisco Systems has achieved this goal in commendable fashion. The Cisco IOS provides a breadth of features, which facilitates a uniform configuration and management platform across nearly its entire line of routing and switching products. One of Cisco's goals has been to unify the core services provided by its IOS to create a standard "look and feel" for its product lines. The CLI, which is used to enter configuration and management commands, has been standardized in recent years and has been emulated by other networking vendors due to its effective structure.

The purpose of the IOS is is to transform the collection of electronics within a particular piece of network equipment into a useable, intelligent device. OSs such as MS-DOS, UNIX, VMS, NT, and Windows 2000 perform a similar function for mid-range and personal computers. At first glance, configuring a Cisco networking product through the IOS CLI seems intimidating. There are complex sets of commands that require intricate syntax to perform even the simplest tasks. The daunting nature of the large command set and complex syntax is offset by its consistency and help facility. Entering commands become routine activities after you have performed them a few times, due to the short learning curve necessary for mastering the CLI.

This section focuses on the necessary procedures to enter commands using the CLI. It covers the steps necessary to connect and describes how to enter commands, work with commands and use the help facility. IOS configuration tasks are demonstrated on a Cisco router. This chapter gives you all the information necessary to help you configure a Cisco router.

SNMP Configurations

The SNMP is an industry open standard used by administrators and network management systems (NMS) to remotely manage systems. SNMP incorporates a system known as management information bases (MIBs) to accomplish this. MIBs are sets of device characteristics that let the NMS know how the device operates. When a certain criterion is met, an event known as a trap is set off. A trap lets the NMS know that a specific event has occurred and whether or not an action should be taken.

Cisco routers are fully compliant with the SNMP standard. Although initial configuration cannot take place through the use of SNMP (due to a lack of an IP address), ongoing management and monitoring is more than possible through it. Cisco routers, through use of SNMP, can interoperate with almost all the major NMS platforms including CiscoWorks, HP OpenView, IBM Tivoli, Micromuse, and SMARTS. SNMP is enabled on a router through the configuration of community strings and privileges.

Web

HTTP can be enabled to allow the configuration and control of routers and switches via a Web browser. This is not exactly the most feature rich or flexible method for configuring your Cisco device, as seen in Figure 1.30.

Figure 1.30 Router Management via Web Browser

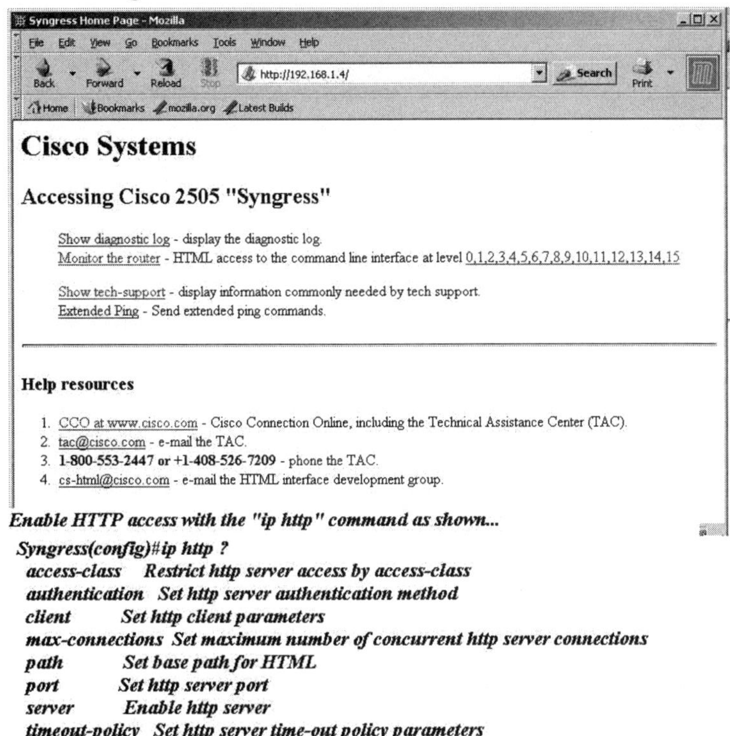

Despite its obvious limitations, HTTP access to your device can be useful if you have personnel monitoring your routers or performing low-level tasks who do not have the necessary knowledge or understanding of IOS commands. In that case, a friendly Web user interface can enable them to perform basic tasks.

Config Maker

For small to medium sized networks, and organizations with limited staff, ConfigMaker (CM) represents an easy solution. CM allows novice engineers or those without the time or means to master the commands required, to configure and maintain their Cisco device at the CLI.

This is a GUI to the CLI that can be used with a limited set of Cisco routers. CM is appropriate for short, simple configurations, but generally does not offer the flexibility needed for complex customization. Figure 1.31 shows the main screen of CM. Notice the routers, hubs, and switches that it supports listed in the left pane of the figure.

Figure 1.31 CM

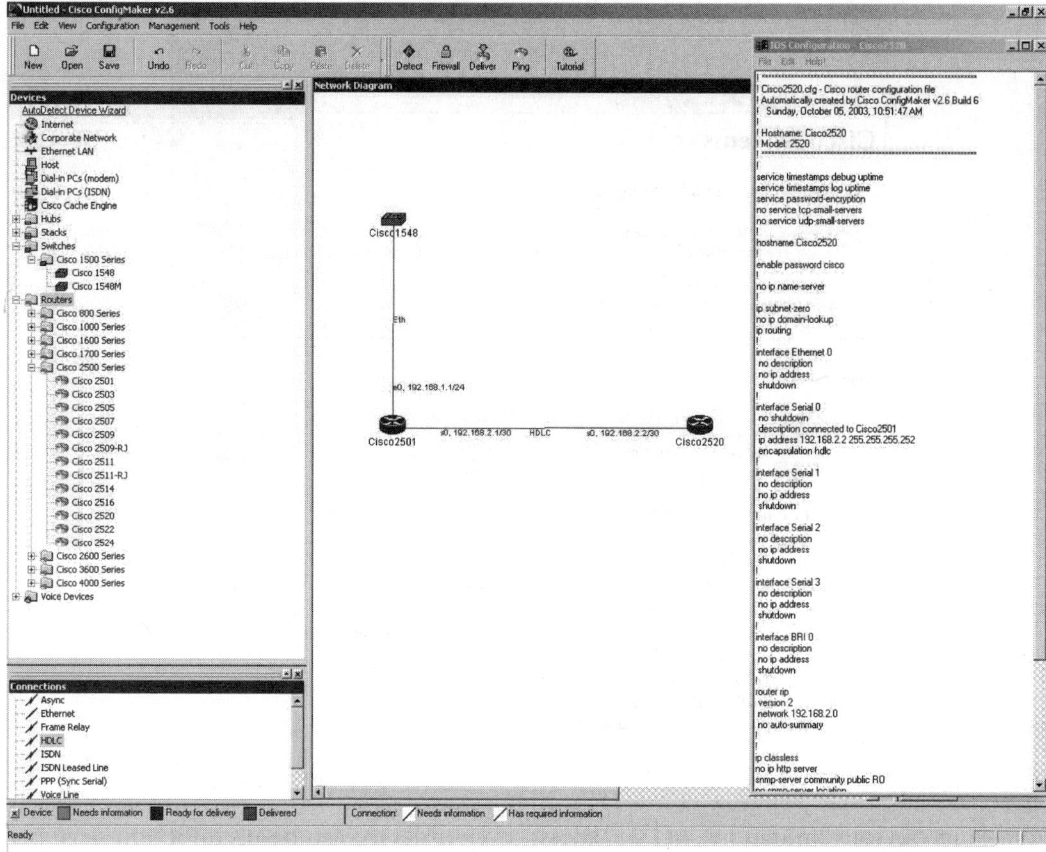

CM is not practical for a network of meaningful size and complexity. However, it can be useful for helping non-Cisco engineers put together a working configuration for a simple network.

Entering Commands to Configure a Cisco Router

Router configuration, as a process, is a relatively simple task, with a basic command structure; however, it has a reputation for being difficult because of the logic that must be incorporated. This section discusses the structure and process for entering commands into a Cisco router.

There are two basic levels of router configuration, *user mode* and *privileged mode*. User mode is for basic administration and verification—no configuration can be done on this level. You are limited to basic functions such as **ping**, low-level **show** commands, and trace routes at this level.

Privileged mode is the configuration level that enables an administrator to make actual configuration changes and high-level **show** commands. This section centers on entering commands at a privileged level. When in doubt as to what you can do at a particular prompt, you can enter a question mark (**?**) to see the commands available to you. When you enter the question mark after a particular command, it will show you all the different parameters available for that command. The following example shows all the commands available in user mode, and then all the particular parameters available for the **ping** command:

```
Router-1> ?
Exec commands:
  <1-99>           Session number to resume
  access-enable    Create a temporary Access-List entry
  access-profile   Apply user-profile to interface
  clear            Reset functions
  connect          Open a terminal connection
  disable          Turn off privileged commands
  disconnect       Disconnect an existing network connection
  enable           Turn on privileged commands
  exit             Exit from the EXEC
  help             Description of the interactive help system
  lock             Lock the terminal
  login            Log in as a particular user
  logout           Exit from the EXEC
  mrinfo           Request neighbor and version information from a
                   multicast router
  mstat            Show statistics after multiple multicast traceroutes
  mtrace           Trace reverse multicast path from destination to
                   source
  name-connection  Name an existing network connection
  pad              Open an X.29 PAD connection
  ping             Send echo messages
  ppp              Start IETF Point-to-Point Protocol (PPP)
  resume           Resume an active network connection
  rlogin           Open an rlogin connection
  show             Show running system information
  slip             Start Serial-line IP (SLIP)
  systat           Display information about terminal lines
  telnet           Open a telnet connection
  terminal         Set terminal line parameters
  traceroute       Trace route to destination
  tunnel           Open a tunnel connection
  udptn            Open an udptn connection
  where            List active connections
  x28              Become an X.28 PAD
  x3               Set X.3 parameters on PAD
```

```
6Router-1>
6Router-1> ping ?
  WORD  Ping destination address or hostname
  ip    IP echo
  ipv6  IPv6 echo
  srb   srb echo
  tag   Tag encapsulated IP echo
6Router-1> ping
```

As mentioned earlier, when you first enter into a router, you enter into basic user mode. You can always tell which level you are in by looking at the router prompt at the far left. When you are in user mode, you will see the router name followed by a greater-than angle bracket (>). To enter into privileged mode, enter the **enable** command. This changes the angle bracket to a pound sign (#). In most cases, and as recommended by Cisco, an enable password governs the capability to enter into privileged mode. You are prompted for the enable password after entering the **enabl***e* command. To return to user mode from privileged mode, enter the **disable** command. The following code example demonstrates this process:

```
6Router-1> enable
Password:
6Router-1# disable
6Router-1>
```

Using Configuration Commands

After you have entered into privileged mode on your router, there are two basic types of commands that you can enter: **configuration** or **show**. Configuration commands change the way the router operates. Some of these changes include interface addressing, routing protocol configuration, password changes, and system-level configuration changes. All of these configuration changes must be made through configuration mode.

To enter configuration mode, use the **configure** command at privilege level. When you enter the **configure** command, it prompts you as to how you wish to configure the router, either by **terminal**, **memory**, or **network**. In this particular instance, select **terminal** to configure it from your terminal connection. Memory and network configuration changes are made if you wish to use the configuration stored either in the router's non-volatile RAM (NVRAM) or if you wish to configure from a network server.

To exit the configuration level of the router, enter **end** or **Ctrl+Z** to exit completely or **exit** to exit the current layer (when at the top layer, the **exit** command takes you out of configuration mode). The following example demonstrates the **configure** command:

```
6Router-1# configure
Configuring from terminal, memory, or network [terminal]? terminal
Enter configuration commands, one per line.  End with CTRL/Z.
6Router-1(config)# ^Z
6Router-1#
```

Notice in the preceding example that when entering into configuration mode the **(config)** prompt is present next to the router name. This will change as you move into the different layers of configuration, such as interface configuration. In configuration mode, you can see all the possible configuration commands by entering a question mark. For reasons of brevity, we shorten this list considerably (more than 100 possible commands exist for the following output):

```
6Router-1(config)# ?
Configure commands:
  aaa                        Authentication, Authorization, and Accounting.
  boot                       Modify system boot parameters
  clock                      Configure time-of-day clock
  config-register            Define the configuration register
  default                    Set a command to its defaults
  do                         To run exec commands in config mode
  downward-compatible-config Generate a configuration compatible with
                             older software
  enable                     Modify enable password parameters
  hostname                   Set system's network name
  ip                         Global IP configuration subcommands
  logging                    Modify message-logging facilities
  multilink                  PPP multilink global configuration
  netbios                    NETBIOS access control filtering
  no                         Negate a command or set its defaults
  parser                     Configure parser
  regexp                     regexp commands
  rif                        Source-route RIF cache
  service                    Modify use of network-based services
  username                   Establish User Name Authentication
  virtual-profile
  access-list                Add an access list entry
  alias                      Create command alias
  alps                       Configure Airline Protocol Support
  arp                        Set a static ARP entry

. . .

6Router-1(config)#
```

You can see the specific parameters for a configuration command by entering it followed by a question mark. In this case, see what possible configuration parameters you can make with the **ipv6** command:

```
6Router-1(config)# ipv6 ?
  access-list       Configure access lists
  hop-limit         Configure hop count limit
  host              Configure static hostnames
  icmp              Configure ICMP parameters
  neighbor          Neighbor
  prefix-list       Build a prefix list
  route             Configure static routes
  router            Enable an IPV6 routing process
  unicast-routing   Enable unicast routing

6Router-1(config)# ipv6
```

It would be nearly impossible to discuss in any degree of detail these entire configuration commands. The next sections discuss some of the more general configuration commands and situations.

Using Passwords to Control Router Access

Passwords are used on a Cisco router just like they are used on any device: to control access. Cisco routers use five different passwords to control access to the router: **console, auxiliary, VTY, enable, and enable secret**.

*The **console** Password*

Use the **console** password to control physical access to the console port of a router. When utilizing a console password, a user is automatically prompted for the console password to access the router even before entering user mode. This secures the console port in case an unauthorized party is able to physically connect to the router console port. To assign or change the console password, you must first specify that interface when working in configuration mode. This is accomplished by entering the **line console 0** command in configuration mode. After entering into the line configuration mode, you will see that the prompt changed from just *(**config**)* to *(**config-line**)*. To change this password, you simply enter the **password** command followed by the password that you wish to use:

```
6Router-1(config)# line console 0
6Router-1(config-line)# password cisco
6Router-1(config-line)# exit
6Router-1(config)
```

*The **auxiliary (aux)** Password*

The auxiliary port is a secondary port commonly used to attach a modem for remote access to the router. It can also be used for dial backup in the case of primary network link failure. This port presents a security problem if not secured. It should also be protected with a password. The configuration for this password is nearly identical to that of the configuration for a console password, except here you specify the **aux 0** port:

```
6Router-1(config)# line aux 0
6Router-1(config-line)# password cisco
6Router-1(config-line)# exit
6Router-1(config)
```

The VTY Password

VTY ports are virtual interfaces into the router for Telnet access. By default, routers have five virtual terminal interfaces (0 through 4). Since there are multiple interfaces, they can be grouped when making configuration changes. Because it is impossible to know which VTY port will answer the Telnet session and because VTY ports allow for remote access to the router, all need to be secured. It is highly recommended that appropriate password protection be implemented on these ports. Configuration for a password on these ports is also very similar to that of the **console** and **aux** passwords:

```
 6Router-1(config)# line vty ?
  <0-4>   First Line number

6Router-1(config)# line vty 0?
<0-4>

6Router-1(config)# line vty 0 ?
  <1-4>   Last Line number
  <cr>

6Router-1(config)# line vty 0 4
6Router-1(config-line)# password cisco
6Router-1(config-line)# exit
```

*Using the **enable** and **enable secret** Passwords*

Use the **enable** and **enable secret** passwords to gain access to the privileged mode of the router—the configuration mode that you can make all your changes in. Out of the box, privileged mode can be entered by using the **enable** command. Unsecured, this is a very large security risk.

To change this, use the **enable** password command in configuration mode. The **enable secret** password is an extension of the **enable** password. The **enable secret** command overrides the **enable** password, making itself the **enable** password. Also, the **enable** password, unless manually encrypted, is a cleartext password, whereas the **enable secret** password is an encrypted password. The following code examples demonstrate configuration of both the **enable** and **enable secret** passwords:

```
6Router-1(config)# enable password cisco
6Router-1(config)# enable secret cisco
```

For good security, use **enable secret** only. The **enable** password has been retained to ensure backwards compatibility with older versions of the IOS that cannot support the use of **enable secret**, but otherwise, it has no useful value and is not worth the risk.

Performing Interface Configuration Tasks

Interface configuration is one of the more fundamental tasks of router configuration. Interface configuration concerns itself with the actual physical, Ethernet, serial, and ATM, as well as logical interfaces such as loopback interfaces. Interface configuration is important because it involves the direct configuration of networks. Configuration tasks that take place on this level include logical addressing, line speed, duplex settings, framing, and so on. To enter into interface configuration, enter the **interface** command from configuration mode, followed by the interface type and number of the particular interface. You can follow the command with a question mark to see the available options:

```
6Router-1(config)# interface ?
  Async               Async interface
  BVI                 Bridge-Group Virtual Interface
  CTunnel             CTunnel interface
  Dialer              Dialer interface
  Ethernet            IEEE 802.3
  Group-Async         Async Group interface
  Lex                 Lex interface
  Loopback            Loopback interface
  MFR                 Multilink Frame Relay bundle interface
  Multilink           Multilink-group interface
  Null                Null interface
  Serial              Serial
  Tunnel              Tunnel interface
  Vif                 PGM Multicast Host interface
  Virtual-Template    Virtual Template interface
  Virtual-TokenRing   Virtual TokenRing
  range               interface range command
6Router-1(config)# interface
```

For purposes of this discussion, select the Ethernet 0 interface by selecting **Ethernet** from the preceding list and selecting the **0** port. Remember, many routers have more than one type of specific port, so it is important to specify the port that you intend to work with:

```
6Router-1(config)# interface ethernet ?
  <0-0>  Ethernet interface number
6Router-1(config)# interface ethernet 0
6Router-1(config-if)#
```

When you enter interface configuration mode, your prompt changes from **(config)** to **(config-if)** for interface configuration. Again, you can enter a question mark to find out the configuration options for this interface:

```
6Router-1(config-if)# ?
Interface configuration commands:
  access-expression       Build a bridge boolean access expression
  arp                     Set arp type (arpa, probe, snap) or timeout
  backup                  Modify backup parameters
  bandwidth               Set bandwidth informational parameter
  bridge-group            Transparent bridging interface parameters
  carrier-delay           Specify delay for interface transitions
  cdp                     CDP interface subcommands
  cmns                    OSI CMNS
  custom-queue-list       Assign a custom queue list to an interface
  default                 Set a command to its defaults
  delay                   Specify interface throughput delay
  description             Interface specific description
  dlsw                    DLSw interface subcommands
  dspu                    Down Stream PU
  duplex                  Configure duplex operation
  exit                    Exit from interface configuration mode
  fair-queue              Enable Fair Queuing on an Interface
  fras                    DLC Switch Interface Command
  help                    Description of the interactive help system
  hold-queue              Set hold queue depth
  ip                      Interface Internet Protocol config commands
  ipv6                    IPv6 interface subcommands
  keepalive               Enable keepalive
  lan-name                LAN Name command
  llc2                    LLC2 Interface Subcommands
  load-interval           Specify interval for load calculation for an
                          interface
  locaddr-priority        Assign a priority group
  logging                 Configure logging for interface
  loopback                Configure internal loopback on an interface
  mac-address             Manually set interface MAC address
  max-reserved-bandwidth  Maximum Reservable Bandwidth on an Interface
  media-type              Interface media type
  mtu                     Set the interface Maximum Transmission Unit (MTU)
  multilink-group         Put interface in a multilink bundle
```

```
  netbios               Use a defined NETBIOS access list or enable
                          name-caching
  no                    Negate a command or set its defaults
  ntp                   Configure NTP
  pppoe                 pppoe interface subcommands
  pppoe-client          pppoe client
  priority-group        Assign a priority group to an interface
  random-detect         Enable Weighted Random Early Detection (WRED) on
                          an Interface
  rate-limit            Rate Limit
  rmon                  Configure Remote Monitoring on an interface
  sap-priority          Assign a priority group
  service-policy        Configure QoS Service Policy
  shutdown              Shutdown the selected interface
  sna                   SNA pu configuration
  snapshot              Configure snapshot support on the interface
  snmp                  Modify SNMP interface parameters
  standby               HSRP interface configuration commands
  timeout               Define timeout values for this interface
  traffic-shape         Enable Traffic Shaping on an Interface or
                          Sub-Interface
  transmit-interface    Assign a transmit interface to a receive-only
                          interface
  tx-ring-limit         Configure PA level transmit ring limit

6Router-1(config-if)#
```

Configuration commands are at the very heart of working with routers. We provide liberal examples of configurations using these commands and more in this book. We will leave our discussion of configuration options with this piece of advice: **Remember the question mark!**

Using **show** Commands

show commands are invaluable tools for diagnosing router and network conditions. As with configuration commands, literally hundreds of potential **show** commands exist, ranging from the very general, such as showing the overall configuration on a router, to the very specific, such as showing the collisions on an Ethernet interface, and everything in between. The following listing is the command output of a **show ?** command. As before, the output was shortened for purposes of brevity. More than 100 possible **show** commands exist.

```
6Router-1# show ?

  aaa                   Show AAA values
  access-expression   List access expression
```

```
access-lists       List access lists
accounting         Accounting data for active sessions
adjacency          Adjacent nodes
aliases            Display alias commands
alps               Alps information
arp                ARP table
async              Information on terminal lines used as router interfaces
backup             Backup status
bgp                BGP information
bridge             Bridge Forwarding/Filtering Database [verbose]
bsc                BSC interface information
bstun              BSTUN interface information
buffers            Buffer pool statistics
caller             Display information about dialup connections
cca                CCA information
cdapi              CDAPI information
cdp                CDP information
cef                Cisco Express Forwarding
class-map          Show QoS Class Map
clock              Display the system clock
cls                DLC user information
cns                CNS subsystem
compress           Show compression statistics
configuration      Contents of Non-Volatile memory
connection         Show Connection
controllers        Interface controller status
cops               COPS information
debugging          State of each debugging option
derived-config     Derived operating configuration
dhcp               Dynamic Host Configuration Protocol status
dialer             Dialer parameters and statistics
dlsw               Data Link Switching information
dnsix              Shows Dnsix/DMDP information
drip               DRiP DB
dspu               Display DSPU information
dxi                atm-dxi information
entry              Queued terminal entries
exception          exception informations
file               Show filesystem information
flash:             display information about flash: file system
```

```
  flh-log              Flash Load Helper log buffer
  frame-relay          Frame-Relay information
  fras                 FRAS Information
  fras-host            FRAS Host Information
  funi                 FUNI information
  history              Display the session command history
  hosts                IP domain-name, lookup style, nameservers, and host
. . .
6Router-1# show
```

As you can see, quite a few potential **show** commands are available to you. Remember that each one of these commands has specific parameters that you can specify, which you can view by issuing the command followed by a question mark. Take a look at the parameters available for **show interface**:

```
6Router-1# show interface ?
  Async                Async interface
  BVI                  Bridge-Group Virtual Interface
  CTunnel              CTunnel interface
  Dialer               Dialer interface
  Ethernet             IEEE 802.3
  Loopback             Loopback interface
  MFR                  Multilink Frame Relay bundle interface
  Multilink            Multilink-group interface
  Null                 Null interface
  Serial               Serial
  Tunnel               Tunnel interface
  Vif                  PGM Multicast Host interface
  Virtual-Template     Virtual Template interface
  Virtual-TokenRing    Virtual TokenRing
  accounting           Show interface accounting
  crb                  Show interface routing/bridging info
  irb                  Show interface routing/bridging info
  mac-accounting       Show interface MAC accounting info
  precedence           Show interface precedence accounting info
  rate-limit           Show interface rate-limit info
  summary              Show interface summary
  |                    Output modifiers
  <cr>
  Lex                  Lex interface

6Router-1# show interface
```

Although hundreds of potential **show** commands are available on a router, you will find a few universally useful in understanding and diagnosing your system configuration and operation, including **show version**, **show running-configuration**, and **show interface**, which we will discuss further.

Using the show version Command

The **show version** command is a very useful command that enables you to discern the following system conditions and parameters:

- System Platform
- System IOS version
- System Boot Rom Version
- System Uptime
- Reason for the last reboot
- System Image File
- Processor and Memory available
- Physical Interfaces
- Configuration Register

This is a truly useful command in fully understanding the general information about your system. This information is also useful in understanding malfunctioning system states such as reboots and gives a good overall picture as to the operation of your router. The following code example demonstrates this command for a Cisco 2500 router running IOS version 12.2(8)T:

```
6Router-1# show version
Cisco Internetwork Operating System Software
IOS (tm) 2500 Software (C2500-IS-L), Version 12.2(8)T,  RELEASE SOFTWARE (fc2)
TAC Support: http://www.cisco.com/tac
Copyright (c) 1986-2002 by cisco Systems, Inc.
Compiled Wed 13-Feb-02 21:11 by ccai
Image text-base: 0x0306DA78, data-base: 0x00001000

ROM: System Bootstrap, Version 5.2(8a), RELEASE SOFTWARE
BOOTLDR: 3000 Bootstrap Software (IGS-RXBOOT), Version 10.2(8a), RELEASE SOFTWA)

6Router-1 uptime is 1 week, 5 days, 21 hours, 39 minutes
System returned to ROM by reload
System image file is "flash:c2500-is-l.122-8.T.bin"

cisco 2500 (68030) processor (revision N) with 14336K/2048K bytes of memory.
```

```
Processor board ID 05606049, with hardware revision 00000000
Bridging software.
X.25 software, Version 3.0.0.
1 Ethernet/IEEE 802.3 interface(s)
2 Serial network interface(s)
32K bytes of non-volatile configuration memory.
16384K bytes of processor board System flash (Read ONLY)

Configuration register is 0x2102

6Router-1#
```

Using the show running-configuration Command

The **show running-configuration** command is a useful tool for obtaining an overall picture of your router. Whereas the **show version** command displays system parameters, the **show running-configuration** command shows the actual system configuration that has been installed on the router to process traffic. You will obtain the following information from issuing this command:

- IOS version
- Service Information
- Hostname
- Enable password (if not encrypted)
- IP and IPV6 static routes
- Access List information
- Host file entries
- Interface addressing information
- Dynamic Routing Processes
- Console, Aux, and VTY parameters

The following is an example of this command output. Keep in mind that this will vary greatly from system to system depending on the configuration. As with a few of the previous command outputs, we have significantly abbreviated this; it can literally be four to five pages and even more in certain instances.

```
6Router-1# show running-configuration
Building configuration...

Current configuration : 2718 bytes
!
```

```
version 12.2
service timestamps debug uptime
service timestamps log uptime
service password-encryption
service tcp-small-servers
!
hostname 6Router-1
!
enable secret 5 $1$kW9A$aKyzOAaklR/ReD6YKiyQa/
!
clock timezone EST -5
clock summer-time EST recurring
ip subnet-zero
ip tcp synwait-time 5
no ip domain-lookup
ip host 6ROUTER-2 2001 192.168.123.50
ip host 2501-2 2001 192.168.123.50
!
ipv6 unicast-routing

interface Ethernet0
 ip address 192.168.123.50 255.255.255.0
 no ip route-cache
 no ip mroute-cache
 ipv6 address 3FFE:4200:1:1::1/64
 ipv6 address 2000:1:2::1/64
 ipv6 rip cisco enable
!
interface Serial0
 ip address 172.16.4.1 255.255.255.0
 no ip route-cache
 no ip mroute-cache
 ipv6 address 2000:1:1::1/64
 ipv6 rip cisco enable
!
router rip
 redistribute ospf 1 metric 3
 passive-interface Serial0
 network 172.16.0.0
!
```

```
 address-family ipv6
 neighbor cisco activate
 neighbor 2000:1:1::2 peer-group cisco
 network 2000:1:1::/64
 network 2000:1:2::/64
 no synchronization
 exit-address-family
!
line con 0
line aux 0
 exec-timeout 0 0
 transport input all
line vty 0 4
 exec-timeout 90 0
 password 7 060A1A2255
 login local
!
end
```

Using the show Interface Command

The **show interface** command gives the physical and logical information for each physical and logical interface. You can use this command to look at a particular interface by specifying it, such as **show interface Ethernet 0**. Information gathered from this **show** command includes the following:

- Physical up/down status
- Line protocol up/down status
- IP or logical addressing information
- MTU information
- Encapsulation
- Queuing
- Collisions
- CRC errors
- Dropped packets

This can be used to diagnose problems with specific interfaces and to check overall health. The following is an example of the **show Ethernet 0** command output:

```
6Router-1# show interface ethernet 0
Ethernet0 is up, line protocol is up
```

```
  Hardware is Lance, address is 00e0.b05a.d998 (bia 00e0.b05a.d998)
  Internet address is 192.168.123.50/24
  MTU 1500 bytes, BW 10000 Kbit, DLY 1000 usec,
     reliability 255/255, txload 1/255, rxload 1/255
  Encapsulation ARPA, loopback not set
  Keepalive set (10 sec)
  ARP type: ARPA, ARP Timeout 04:00:00
  Last input 00:00:00, output 00:00:00, output hang never
  Last clearing of "show interface" counters never
  Input queue: 0/75/0/0 (size/max/drops/flushes); Total output drops: 0
  Queueing strategy: fifo
  Output queue :0/40 (size/max)
  5 minute input rate 0 bits/sec, 0 packets/sec
  5 minute output rate 0 bits/sec, 0 packets/sec
     93866 packets input, 13802455 bytes, 0 no buffer
     Received 47471 broadcasts, 0 runts, 0 giants, 0 throttles
     0 input errors, 0 CRC, 0 frame, 0 overrun, 0 ignored
     0 input packets with dribble condition detected
     234089 packets output, 24304032 bytes, 0 underruns
     0 output errors, 2 collisions, 31 interface resets
     0 babbles, 0 late collision, 19 deferred
     0 lost carrier, 0 no carrier
     0 output buffer failures, 0 output buffers swapped out
```

Increasing Efficiency by Using Shortcuts

Until now, we have purposefully and completely written out the entire string when entering commands. Cisco software does support a shorthand version of its command syntax. You can enter only a partial portion of the command as long as you provide enough for the IOS to recognize it. For example, you can enter **copy run star**, which the router will recognize to mean **copy running-configuration startup-configuration**.

The following example uses shortcuts rather than spelling out the full command. In this example, we are entering privileged mode and configuring an IP address for the Ethernet 0 interface. Our final task is copying the running configuration to NVRAM:

```
6Router-1>en
6Router-1# conf t
Enter configuration commands, one per line.  End with CNTL/Z.
6Router-1(config)# int e0
6Router-1(config-if)# ip add 10.1.1.1
6Router-1(config-if)# ex
6Router-1(config)# ^Z
6Router-1(config)# copy run star
```

In the preceding example, we entered privileged mode by entering **en** instead of typing **enable**, then entered configuration mode by entering **config t**, which the router recognized as **configure terminal**. We next entered interface configuration mode by typing **int e0**, which the router recognized as **interface Ethernet 0**. We then configured an IP address by using the **IP add** command. After existing with **ex** for **exit**, we copied running configuration NVRAM with **copy run star** for the command **copy running-config startup-config**.

The rule for shortcuts is that you can reduce a command as long as it is unique from other commands. For example, you could not reduce disable to DI, because disconnect also starts with DI, so you would need to use DISA, and conversely, disconnect would need to be DISC. If you do not enter enough information to make the command unique, you will be met with an error stating **% Ambiguous command:**. This indicates that you need to type more of the command.

The **auto-complete** feature automatically completes a command when you simply press the **Tab** key. You must enter enough information for the command to be unique or it will not work. The following code example demonstrates this feature. In this example you are trying to enter the **configure terminal** command. You start by trying to enter **con**, but this does not work because both the **configure** and **connect** commands start with ""con," so you have to enter enough information to make it unique by entering **conf**. You follow this by **t** and hit the **Tab** key to get the terminal word to appear:

```
6Router-1# con
6Router-1# conf
6Router-1# configure t
6Router-1# configure terminal
```

A set of shortcuts is also available with specific keystrokes to move the cursor and perform other actions.

- **CTRL + A** Move to the beginning of a line
- **CTRL + E** Move to the end of a line
- **CTRL + R** Redisplay a line
- **CTRL + K** Erase all from cursor to end of line
- **CTRL + X** Erase all from cursor to beginning of line
- **CTRL + W** Erase a Word
- **CTRL + X** Exit Configuration Mode

The autocommand Feature

Cisco routers can automate tasks that are associated with terminal lines using the **autocommand** option. **autocommand** allows the execution of any EXEC mode command when a connection is established to a terminal line. This is convenient when you want to control the operating characteristics of a dial-in modem.

For example, if you want to have users dial in to an access server and connect to a UNIX host, this can be done automatically as soon as the session is established. In the following example, the **autocommand** feature establishes a session to a UNIX host with an IP address of 192.168.1.1.

```
line vty 129
autocommand connect 192.168.1.1
```

The **autocommand** feature can issue any EXEC command, not just Telnet sessions. You can configure the **autocommand** feature for remote support by technical staff; if you want them to be able to dial in and view the TCP/IP routing table, you can use the **autocommand** feature to automate this process, as illustrated in the following example:

```
line vty 129
autocommand show ip route
```

Menus

Menus can be configured within Cisco IOS to provide users connecting to a router with an easy-to-use interface. Users do not need to learn the underlying command syntax to accomplish basic tasks. The following is an example of a basic menu that users can utilize to access network services.

```
Welcome to the Corporate Network
Type a number to select an option;
Type 9 to exit the menu.
1 Connect to VMS (LAT)
2 Connect to the IBM Mainframe (TN3270)
3 Read E-Mail
4 Start PPP
Exit the Menu
```

When users connect to this router, this is the menu they see. The following is the command structure for the menu shown previously:

```
menu Basic title ^C
Welcome to the Corporate Network
Type a number to select an option;
Type 9 to exit the menu.^C
menu Basic text 1 Connect to VMS (LAT)
menu Basic command 1 LAT CENTRAL
menu Basic text 2 Connect to the IBM Mainframe (TN3270)
menu Basic command 2 tn3270 mainframe
menu Basic text 3 Read E-Mail
menu Basic command 3 telnet mail.corp.com
menu Basic text 4 Start PPP
```

```
menu Basic command 4 ppp
menu Basic text 9 Exit the Menu
menu Basic command 9 exit
menu Basic clear-screen
menu Basic default 3
```

Menus can have a title that is displayed when the menu starts, which is created with the **menu *name* title *delimiter*** command. The delimiter is the ASCII character the router will use to signify the end of the character string used for the title. Typically, you would not want to use a standard letter, because that letter may appear in the text you enter. A rarely used character such as a tilde (~) can save you quite a bit of frustration.

To create the entries the users will see when the menu is executed, you use the **menu *name* text *item text*** command.

- **Item** The number that you want to appear next to the text.
- **Number** The number that the users will use to invoke that particular selection.

It is important to note that menus can only have 18 entries, but Cisco has built in the ability to create submenus. When all entries have been created, configure the commands that will be executed when a user picks a menu option. To do this, you use the **menu *name command item text*** format. The item is the number of the command you want to use, while the text is the actual command executed. It is important to note that the value placed in the text portion corresponds exactly to the command a user would enter if they were connected to the router with no menu system.

You also have some additional controls over the way a menu is displayed and operates. Commands such as **menu *title* clear-screen** make the router insert 24 new lines, which effectively clears the screen. It is important to note that the menu system default is a standard "dumb" terminal that only displays text in a 24-line-by-80-column format. With the use of submenus, a very complex and feature-rich menu system can be created. It is important to note that **all** menus should have an exit menu option, otherwise, you can get stuck in a menu loop with no way to exit.

CATOS Command Syntax and Basic Configuration

There are several ways to configure a Cisco Catalyst switch. We do not cover configuration via menu selection or via Web interface, as they provide enough structure and information to guide you through the process of configuration. Instead, we focus on CLI configuration, which is more complex and has more parameters with which to contend.

Our discussion is complicated by the fact that the OS for the Catalyst line has and is still evolving into the more familiar Cisco IOS syntax (variously known as integrated or native mode). However, there is still a large base of switches that have the "original" Catalyst OS on them, known by its legion of trusty set commands. Further compounding the confusion of what commands to use are semi-evolved versions of the Catalyst OS that contain commands that appear to be a mix of IOS and CATOS commands. We discuss and provide examples of using both types of commands to accomplish the same task.

You console or Telnet (if networking is configured) to switch, and execute the necessary commands at the prompt. The CATOS automatically saves the changes as you make; the CAT IOS does not.

Configuring Network Parameters

If you want to manage your switch remotely (Telnet, SNMP, and other means that require an IP address), you need to configure the network parameters of that switch, including an address, mask, and default gateway at a minimum. There are currently three types of management interfaces used by the CATOS for management:

- **SL0** SLIP-based connection to the console port on the SE module for out-of-band management. This can be used for remote dial-in sessions to the switch via a modem.
- **SC0** A logical in-band management interface assigned to VLAN1 by default, but can be assigned to any VLAN. Doing so will make it reachable provided that you have a route to and from its assigned VLAN.
- **ME1** A reserved, dedicated Ethernet port for out-of-band management of the switch. It is not assigned to any VLAN, but exists as a "stand alone" network port.

The following shows how to configure these management interfaces. Notice that since we are using addresses from the same subnet for SC0 and ME1, we downed one interface in favor of the other in order to operate. We also, for fun, put SC0 in VLAN999 before we downed it, just to show that we are the boss of this switch and can put the SC0 interface in any VLAN we want. We also identified the default gateway.

```
set interface sc0 1 10.11.20.111/255.255.254.0 10.11.21.255
set int sc0 999
interface sc0 vlan set.
set interface sc0 down
set interface me1 10.11.20.110 255.255.254.0 10.11.21.255

set ip route default 10.11.20.1
```

On a switch with IOS, the above interfaces do not exist. Instead, you specify and address a VLAN on the switch as follows. While this example shows the management interface in VLAN1, it can actually be in any VLAN.

```
interface vlan 1
ip address 10.11.20.110 255.255.254.0
ip default-gateway 10.11.20.1
```

Once you have configured networking on the Catalyst, you can then Telnet in or perform other network tasks on the switch.

Securing the Switch

To protect the Catalyst, you can use local authentication, or authenticate via a TACACS, RADIUS, or Kerberos. In our example, we show both methods. To use local authentication with CATOS, specify:

```
set password cisco
set enablepass cisco
```

To use TACACS+:

```
set authentication enable tacacs all primary
set authentication login  tacacs all primary
set tacacs server 10.11.20.20 primary
```

With Catalyst IOS, the same thing is accomplished with the following series of commands.

```
enable password cisco
enable secret cisco

vity 0 4
password cisco

aaa new-model
aaa authentication login default
tacacs-server host 10.11.20.20
```

Creating VLANs

VLANs define and contain the broadcasts for a network. The first step in VLAN creation (regardless of which OS is being used) must be to define the Virtual Trunking Protocol (VTP) domain. VTP is used between switches to exchange information about the VLANs that each services. Each switch can belong to only one VTP domain at a time; information is only exchanged by switches in the same VTP domain. Without VTP, switches would not be able to share information about their VLANs. A switch can serve in one of the following VTP domains.

- **Server** Can create and modify VLANs, which are advertised throughout the VTP domain. This is the default mode.
- **Client** Does not originate or modify any VLANs; receives information from the server.
- **Transparent** Does not uses or depend on VTP, nor are VLANs created on it sent to other switches in the VTP domain. Essentially turns off VTP on the switch.

In VTP transparent mode, VLAN configurations are saved in nonvolatile memory, but they are not advertised to other switches. To define VLANs, execute the following series of commands. The **set vlan** command is used to add ports to a VLAN.

```
# vtp
set vtp domain BEST_CISCO_BOOK
set vlan 999 name BEST_CISCO_BOOK

set vlan 999 4/3
```

The native mode equivalent is:

```
vlan database
vtp domain BEST_CISCO_BOOK

vlan database
vlan 999 mtu 1500

interface fa4/3
switchport mode access
switchport access vlan 999
```

Port Configuration

You can change the parameters of a port such as its speed, duplex settings, and other parameters as shown. Port security allows you to restrict what MAC addresses may be connected to a particular port: you can simply enable it with no parameters and the first detected MAC address will be the only one allowed on this port or you can specify MAC addresses (up to 1024) manually. The other port commands used in this section are self explanatory by their names. When port security is enabled, the port cannot be a trunk or have SPAN enabled,

```
set port security 4/3 enable aa-bb-cc-dd-ee-ff-11
set port speed 4/3 100
set port name 4/3 Best_Cisco_Port
set port duplex 4/3 auto
```

The CAT IOS version of the same commands are:

```
interface fastethernet4/3
description Best_Cisco_Port
speed 100
duplex auto
port security
```

The **port security** command is slightly different in the IOS for the Catalyst in that you cannot specify a MAC address.

Enabling Trunking

Trunking is the use of switch ports to transport multiples VLANs, often with several ports grouped together with Etherchannel to provide redundancy and the increased bandwidth necessary to transport multiple networks. The process of configuring a port as trunk is simply a matter of identifying it as such.

Cisco supports two types of trunking. Cisco developed the InterSwitch Link (ISL) trunking protocol for its switches. The IEEE developed 802.1q as a vendor-independent standard for trunking. ISL can only be used on Cisco products, while 802.1q can enable interoperation with non-Cisco switches. Auto-negotiation of a trunking protocol is possible (for example, **set trunk 4/11 desirable negotiate**). Since we are firm believers in vendor-independent standards, we configure for 802.1.q in our examples.

We clarify the parameters and options associated with the various trunk commands.

```
set trunk mod_num/port_num [on | desirable | auto | nonegotiate] dot1q isl negotiate
```

- **On** Converts ports to a trunk.
- **Off** Converts trunk to a regular port.
- **Desirable** Converts port to trunk if neighbor is configured for trunking.
- **Auto** Port is converted to trunk if neighbor trunking state is on or desirable.
- **Nonnegotiate** Neighbor trunk has to be manually configured.
- **ISL** Specifies ISL as the trunking protocol.
- **Dot1q** Specifies 802.1q as the preferred trunking protocol.
- **Negotiate** Will negotiate which trunking protocol to use with a neighbor.

By default, when you define a trunk, all VLANs will be transported over it. If this is not desirable, you can remove all VLANs from the trunk with the **clear trunk** command, and then add only those VLANs you want to trunk with the **set trunk x/x ####** where **x/x** is the port being trunked and **####** is the number of the VLAN to be transported.

The following example shows how to configure a trunk on a switch using CATOS commands.

```
set trunk 4/1-2 on dot1q
```

Complete this command on the neighboring switch, and you will have an 802.1q trunk transporting all VLANs. You can confirm the status of your trunking efforts with:

```
Syngress_4006 (enable) show trunk
* - indicates vtp domain mismatch
Port      Mode         Encapsulation   Status        Native vlan
--------  -----------  -------------  ------------  -----------
 4/1      nonegotiate  dot1q           trunking      1
 4/2      nonegotiate  dot1q           trunking      1
```

```
Port      Vlans allowed on trunk
--------  ---------------------------------------------------------------------
 4/1      1-1005
 4/2      1-1005

Port      Vlans allowed and active in management domain
--------  ---------------------------------------------------------------------
 4/1      1,998-999
 4/2      1,998-999

Port      Vlans in spanning tree forwarding state and not pruned
--------  ---------------------------------------------------------------------
 4/1      1,999
 4/2      1,999
```

Trunking on a Catalyst IOS switch is configured through the process shown. The ports to be used for trunking are configured as pure Layer 2 interfaces. The **switchport** command configures the port to be a trunk, as well as specifying parameters such as 802.1q.

```
interface FastEthernet4/1
no ip address
switchport
switchport trunk encapsulation dot1q
switchport mode trunk

interface FastEthernet4/2
no ip address
switchport
switchport trunk encapsulation dot1q
switchport mode trunk
```

View your trunk port details with **show interface fastethernet 4/1 trunk**, for example.

Networking Monitoring and Packet Capture

All Cisco Catalyst switches have the ability to copy traffic inbound and outbound on any port to another port for monitoring and analysis. This feature is known as Switch Port Analyzer (SPAN) is useful for determining what traffic in what amounts and types is transiting a particular switch port.

On a CATOS switch, span is enabled and disabled with the following commands. If you are going to use SPAN regularly, ensure that the first SPAN command you learn is **set span disable all** to turn off all SPAN operations.

```
set span disable [dest_mod/dest_port | all]
```

```
set span {_mod/src_ports... | src_vlan...} {dest_mod/dest_port} [rx | tx | both]
[filter {vlan}][inpkts {enable | disable}] [learning {enable | disable}]
[multicast {enable | disable}] [create]
```

For example, to monitor all traffic from port 3/1 to monitoring port 4/1, you would execute the following command. By default, traffic transmitted and received on the port is captured.

```
set span 3/1 4/1
```

The CAT IOS equivalent is provided here.

```
{ no } port monitor [interface | vlan vlan-id]
```

Notice that you execute this command on the monitoring interface by identifying the source interface or VLAN, as shown.

```
interface Fastethernet4/1
port monitor fa3/1
```

You are Not Alone—Resources for Cisco Hardware and Software

The configuration of Cisco products can become quite complex as your network grows, or the demand for new services increases. It can be a very delicate balancing act to get the mix of hardware and software working exactly as needed. Complications can arise as you add new hardware, turn on new features, or bugs are discovered at the last minute. When that happens, knowing where to go for assistance can be immeasurably invaluable, especially when it is just you at 2:00 AM in the morning needing a solution by 6AM and it is something that you have never seen before. The following are resources that can be of great assistance for whatever problems you may encounter, or if you need to master new hardware, software, or features in general.

Cisco Technical Support—General

Your starting point for obtaining assistance from Cisco is the Technical Support page at www.cisco.com/en/US/partner/support/index.html is shown in Figure 1.32.

Figure 1.32 Cisco Technical Support

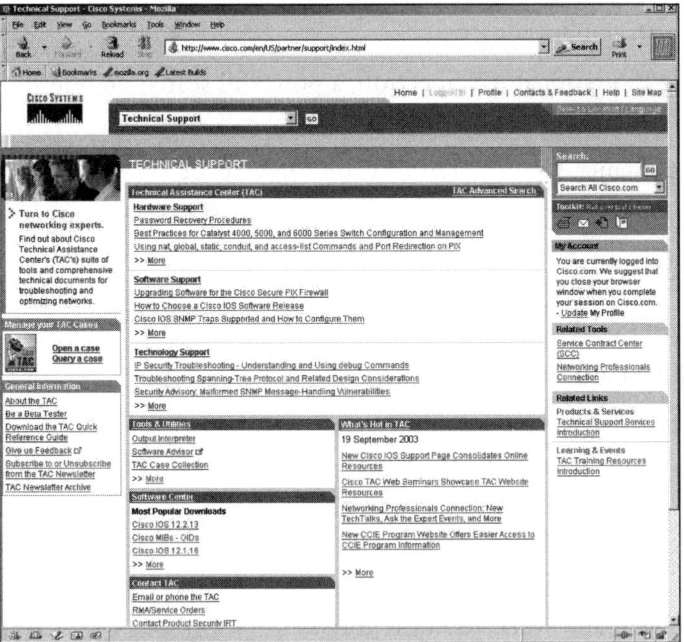

You will need a Cisco Connection Online (CCO) account to access this page which provides links to a variety of support tools, several of which we discuss next.

CCO

Obtaining a CCO account provides you with your portal to many aspects of the Cisco support systems. In fact, it is your first step. There are two levels of CCO access: **guest** and **registered user**. You can find the CCO datasheet at: www.cisco.com/warp/public/cc/serv/mkt/sup/tsssv/opmsup/ctspco/cco02_ds.htm.

Registering as a guest provides you with the following benefits (this information is taken from the CCO data sheet provided at the URL previously provided.

- Cisco worldwide contacts and events calendar
- Press releases
- *Packet*, Cisco's user's magazine
- Product catalogue, brochures, and announcements
- Training and seminar schedules
- General service and support information
- Cisco MarketPlace and electronic Commerce Agents

Notice that guest access does not give you any special assistance access. For that, you need to become a registered user. This requires the purchase of a support contract, such as SmartNet or Comphrensive, or sponsorship by a Cisco partner. Becoming a registered user provides the following benefits (as taken from the Cisco CCO datasheet).

- All Guest-level information
- Interactive user applications
- Networking Professionals Connection, a powerful search engine for Cisco's Q&A database
- Technical Assistance Center (TAC) (Case Open, Case Query, Case Update)
- Bug Toolkit
- Bug Navigator, finds known bugs
- Bug Alert, proactively alerts customers of possible bugs and fixes
- Software Upgrade Planner
- Software updates and upgrades
- Product bulletins
- Software release notes
- Technical tips and references
- Known problem and workaround reports
- Installation notes and case studies
- Partner sales information
- Order status checking
- Pricing and configuration of Cisco products

Several of these support options bear special mention, such as the TAC and the Network Professionals Connection.

TAC

The TAC provides 24 x 7 x 365 support for all manner of questions and problems. Access to the TAC is limited to registered users. Engineers who work for Cisco are responsible for fielding the issues sent to the TAC. Cases can be opened or queried via the Web (www.cisco.com/tac), e-mail (tac@cisco.com), or telephone (Asia-Pacific: +61 2 8446 7411; Australia: 1 800 805 227; EMEA: +32 2 704 55 55 or USA: 1 800 553-2447).

The general process is that you open a case by providing the details of your problem. Cisco will then assign a case number and priority, and maintain a record of efforts (including suggested solutions and any information/feedback you provide.)

To ensure the timeliness of responses by severity and in some cases, by the weight of your contract, Cisco assigns each case the following proprieties.

- **Priority 1 (P1)** Critical and merits round the clock effort until resolved.
- **Priority 2 (P2)** Severe degradation of operations. Normal business hours commitment until resolved.

- **Priority 3 (P3)** Operations are impaired, but your core business is unimpeded. Normal business hours commitment.
- **Priority 4 (P4)** Assistance needed with Cisco hardware and software, but there is little or no impact on your core business. Catch as catch can commitment.

In addition to the TAC, you can also post informally to the Network Professional Connection (NPC) (which replaced the Open Forum that served the same function).

NPC

The NPC consists of engineers and technicians (Cisco and non-Cisco) who voluntarily provide answers and information to posted questions. It is essentially a free-for-all newsgroup where anyone with questions and answers can post. There are a variety of subject areas as shown in Figure 1.33.

Figure 1.33 NPC

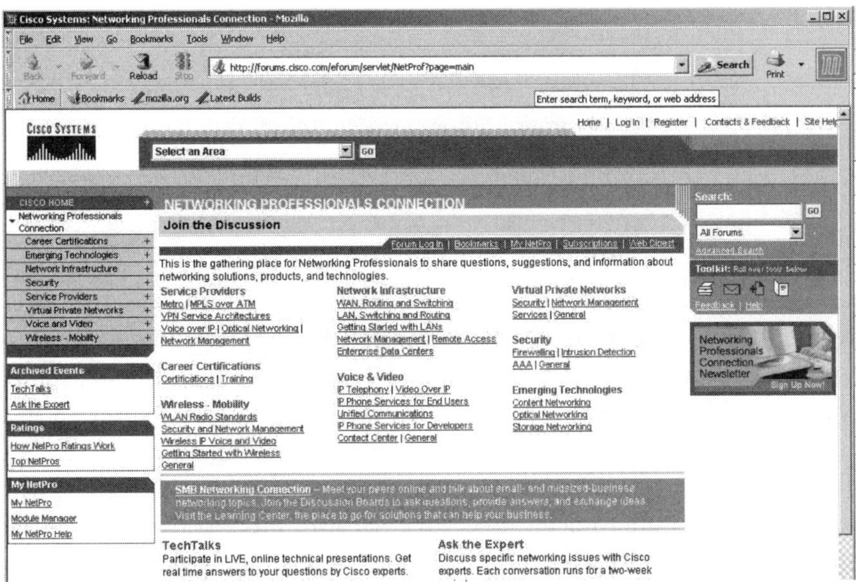

The only requirement for using NPC is that you need a registered user CCO account. In addition to posting questions, you can also avail yourself of the TechTalks, which are online seminars conducted by experts on a variety of topics. NPC is useful for obtaining answers to non-critical questions concerning Cisco products, or particular features. Since this is a voluntary effort, answers to your questions are not subject to a timed schedule, though in this author's opinion, the responses have been fairly rapid for a voluntary effort. NPC is meant to be more of a discussion forum, rather than a technical support tool.

Software Advisor

Cisco provides the Software Advisor (SA) tool to help you select the correct software version and feature set that will satisfy your requirements. Figure 1.34 shows the opening screen for SA.

Figure 1.34 SA

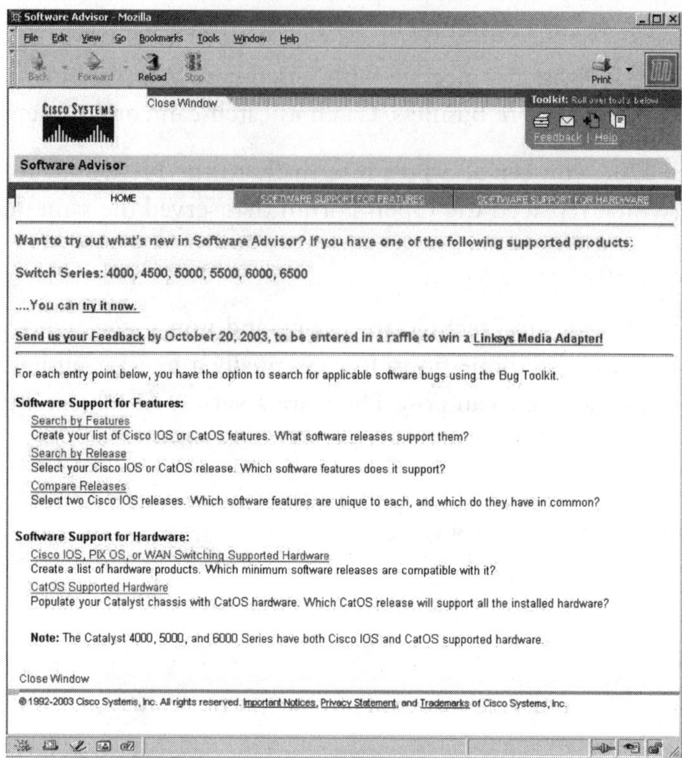

With SA, you can search by features to find the image versions that contain the features that you need. Alternately, you can determine what features are supported by a particular version. As shown in the figure, you can compare two images to determine which is most appropriate. The SA can help you select an image that is comparative with your target hardware platform, with just the right amount of features. Prior to ordering or downloading an image, use SA to ensure you are selecting the correct one. A complement to SA is the Feature Navigator, which allows you to browse feature by feature to determine what versions support particular commands and parameters. Once you have determined what version you need using either method, you are ready to download it from the Software Center.

Software Center

Cisco believes in making life easy for its customers. To that end, it makes almost all software images for all products downloadable to registered CCO account holders. This is a very customer-friendly and convenient feature that allows customers who have the appropriate contract and legal right (via purchase, contracts, and so on) to download image software. The full value of the Software Center becomes apparent when an upgrade to a new version becomes necessary: rather than ordering and waiting for media with the image to arrive via traditional shipping methods where it can be mangled by an indifferent and uncaring delivery person, it can be downloaded in a matter of minutes, which significantly reduces downtime.

You must hold a contract that entitles you to the software you want to download, or have purchased the software you want to download. If you do not satisfy the conditions in the license, you are not entitled legally to download this software.

Selecting and downloading the software is a simple matter of pointing and clicking your way through a series of Web pages until you have selected the appropriate version, feature, and platform, as shown in Figure 1.35.

Figure 1.35 IOS Upgrade Planner

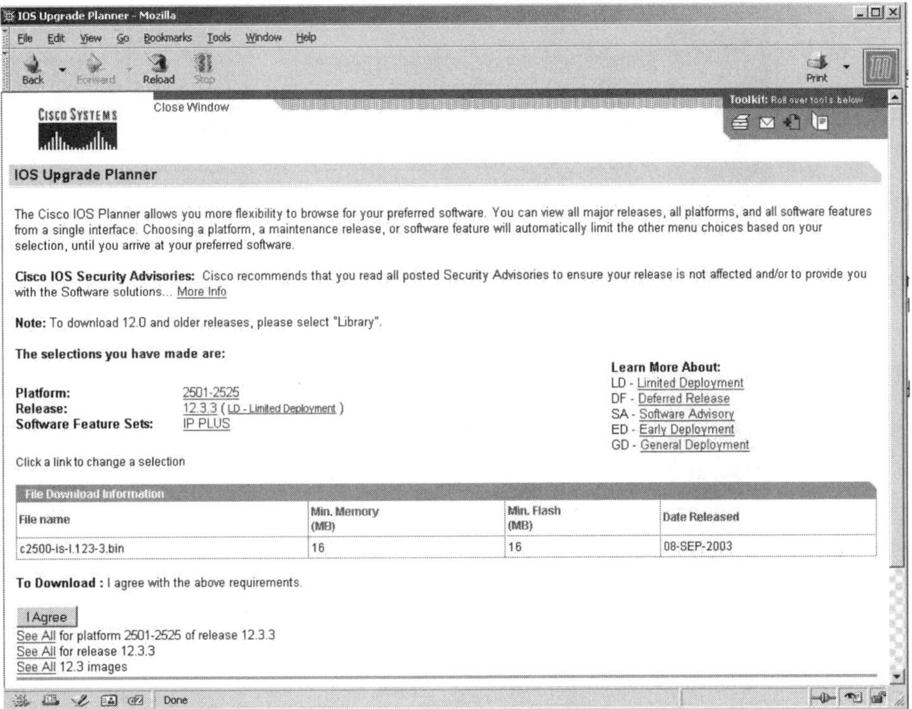

Here we have arrived at the page to download IOS version 12.3.1a with the IP Plus feature for the Cisco 2500 series of routers. This is a LD release that has not achieved GD status. Clicking the "I Agree" button will force you to first agree to the legal restrictions for this image, and then you can download and install.

So far, we have discussed Cisco tools that you have at your disposal. There is one non-Cisco resource that we need to highlight that has helped many an engineer stuck in a tight spot.

Groupstudy.com

Groupstudy.com is a premier collection of newsgroups devoted to networking topics, especially the study of Cisco topics launched in 1998 by Paul Borghese after he achieved his CCIE. GroupStudy is devoted to helping engineers achieve various Cisco certifications such as CCNA, CCNP, CCIE, and others. It has evolved into an important force in the Information Technology (IT) community. It is an excellent resource for posting questions, sharing information, and learning from the most experienced and intelligent people in the business. Contributors and users include newly minted CCNAs, CCIEs, respected authors, and professionals from all walks of life. Figure 1.36 shows the Groupstudy homepage (www.groupstudy.com).

Figure 1.36 Groupstudy

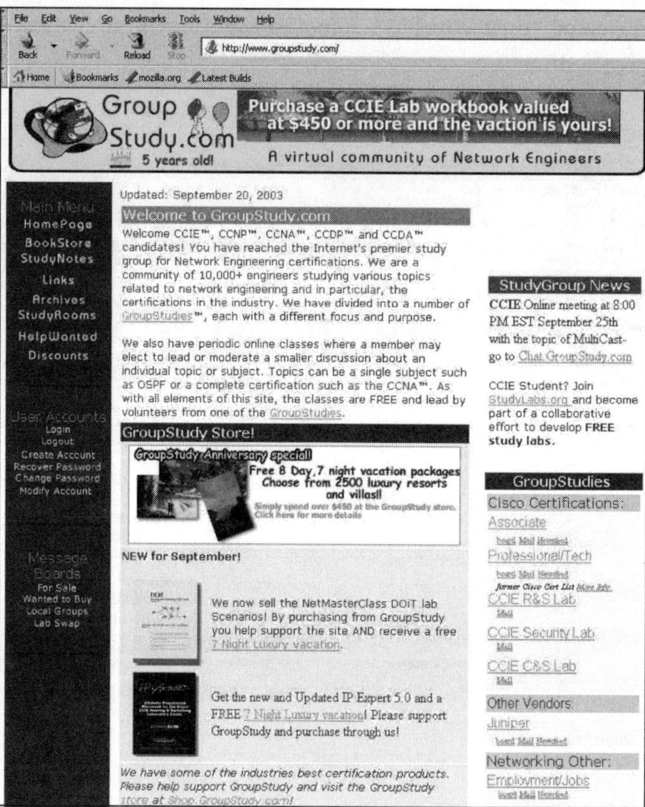

Over time, specialized topic groupstudies have resulted from the specialization of various certifications such as CCIE R&S, Security, and C&S labs. There is also an employment Groupstudy devoted to job information, such as available positions, to discussing any employment-related topic such as salary negotiations, career changes, and so on. Any newsreader or e-mail client can be used to browse and post to Groupstudy.com. You can also elect to subscribe, which will result in Groupstudy postings being sent your e-mail address.

Summary

Networking has grown from its academic and military origins to become a pervasive factor in the lives of organizations and individuals. We discussed networking stripped to its barest essentials to provide you with the information you need to deploy and maintain robust networks. The OSI model is a guidepost for networking, from development to troubleshooting; using its layers to structure your efforts can increase your effectiveness.

Networks can be distinguished by the spatial area that they service. LANs tend to cover a small area, such as a building or small campus. WANs provide the technology necessary to interconnect islands of isolated networks.

Cisco provides many solutions that have become integral to networking. LAN switches provide connectivity to end devices such as workstations and servers. Routers are more concerned delivering traffic to its final destination via the use of network addresses such as that provided by IP.

All Cisco devices can be configured in a number of ways. The simplest and cleanest is the CLI, though it requires knowledge of the command syntax and parameters. On many Cisco products, you can use other means such as SNMP and HTTP to complete your configuration. There are also products such as ConfigMaker that will guide you through the process of creating your configuration.

When all of your devices are working as they should, all is well in the world. However, when problems occur (and they will), you may need to avail yourself of various resources available to you. This can include Cisco aids such as the TAC or NPC. There are non-Cisco options such as the www.groupstudy.com where you can post and receive answers to a variety of Cisco networking questions.

Chapter 2

Wide Area Networking (WAN)

Best Damn Topics in this Chapter:

- Wide Area Network Topologies
- High-Level Data Link Control
- Point-to-Point Protocol
- Circuit Types and Terminology
- Frame Relay
- Asynchronous Transfer Mode
- Integrated Services Digital Networks
- Backing Up Permanent Connections
- Redundant Hardware and Links – Design and Performance Issues

☑ Summary

☑ Solutions Fast Track

☑ Frequently Asked Questions

Introduction

Chapter 2 is concerned with wide area network (WAN) technologies and topologies. A WAN connects other networks, or groups of networks separated geographically or by organizational design. Unlike a local area network (LAN), a WAN does not concern itself with providing direct connectivity to end devices such as workstations, servers, and printers. It provides the means for the networks on which those devices reside to reach remote destinations.

When it comes to networking, hard and fast rules tend to be broken. A WAN can be configured to provide connectivity to any of the end devices previously described; a single server at a distant location can be connected via a WAN to the rest of the organizational network.

This chapter gives an overview of WAN technologies provided by Cisco, including their features and salient points. It also provides configuration details for deployment and support of WANs, especially on routers.

When analyzing the traffic requirements between remote offices and your central site, you may find it is not cost-effective to use ad hoc "dial connection" connection. Under these circumstances, you need to implement a permanent connection. This chapter explores several ways of providing permanent connections: point-to-point links of all types such as High-Level Data Link Control (HDLC), Point-to-Point Protocol (PPP), and the various varieties of T1. Frame Relay and Asynchronous Transfer Mode (ATM) also figure predominantly in this chapter.

Frame Relay is a common method used to connect a WAN; ATM is also commonly used for WAN connections. This chapter covers these technologies and how they can be used to connect remote sites to a central site. As organizations become more reliant on their network infrastructure, network engineers are required to provide a higher level of service. The final section of this chapter looks at ways of backing up these connections to provide different levels of resilience.

You will gain a good understanding of the details of some of the most common WAN technologies. This information will enable you to better understand and support WAN circuits of any type. Of all the WAN protocols that can be used, HDLC is probably the simplest to understand, as well as being one of the oldest.

Point-to-point networks remain a common method for connecting a remote site to another site. When implementing point-to-point connections there are many options to choose from. A point-to-point link can be a simple dial-up connection, a dedicated serial link, or an Integrated Services Digital Network (ISDN) connection. Regardless of the type of link, you will need a protocol to allow communication over that link. Let's look at two protocols that can be implemented over point-to-point links: PPP and HDLC.

Wide Area Network Topologies

There are several types of topologies that can be used to describe networks, including the following:

- Point-to-point topology
- Fully meshed topology
- Hub-and-spoke topology

These topologies are described in additional detail in the following sections.

Point-to-Point Topology

If there are only two sites involved in the design, point-to-point topology should be used. For point-to-point topology to work, each site is connected to the other site, and has mutual end points. A point-to-point design works with almost any network technology from Ethernet to ATM. Point to point networks can be grouped to use multiple links to give additional bandwidth. Figure 2.1 shows a point-to-point topology.

Figure 2.1 Point-to-Point Topology

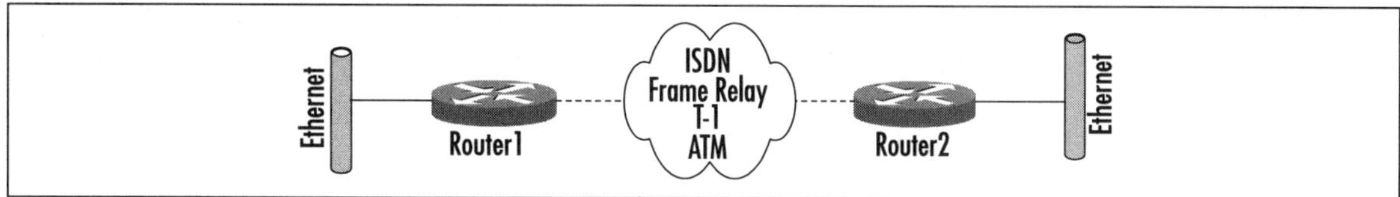

Fully Meshed Topology

A fully meshed network topology is only recommended for a very small network. In the fully meshed design, as shown in Figure 2.2, each router is connected to every other router in the network. An advantage of this design is that it allows each site to communicate directly with each other instead of going through a central site. However, scalability is severely limited. The number of available ports and circuits must also be taken into consideration. Just like any fully meshed topology, the amount of resources required to maintain a full mesh grows exponentially with the number of devices.

Figure 2.2 Fully Meshed Topology

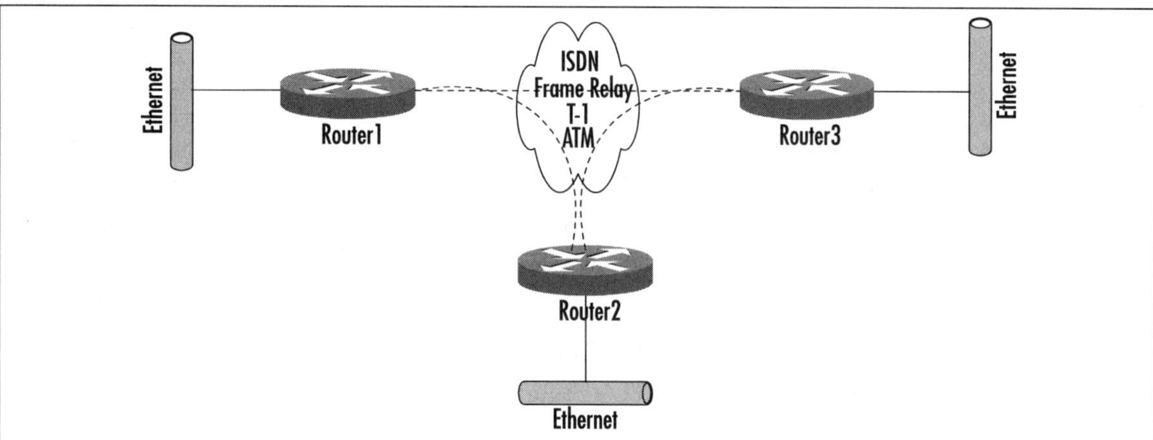

Hub-and-Spoke Topology

A hub-and-spoke network topology is different from the fully meshed design, in that all traffic is sent to a central site (or two) and then re-routed to the final destination. For example, in Figure 2.3, if a computer on Router1's Ethernet network wanted to communicate with a computer on the Ethernet network for Router3, it must pass to the hub, Router2, which has a connection to Router3. This type of design is more suitable for large-scale networks.

In order for this type of design to scale properly, the only site that needs to have significant available resources is the hub. Contrary to the exponential growth in resources (circuits and ports) required in a fully meshed design, the hub-and-spoke design only needs resources equal to the number of sites. Another advantage of the hub-and-spoke design is that it is easy to configure and troubleshoot. The complexity of the design is constrained to the hub router, as the spoke routers will have relatively simple configurations. One key disadvantage to this design (but not to the fully meshed topology) is that there is now a single point of failure in the network. If the hub router goes down, none of the spoke sites are able to communicate with the rest of the network.

Figure 2.3 Hub-and-Spoke Topology

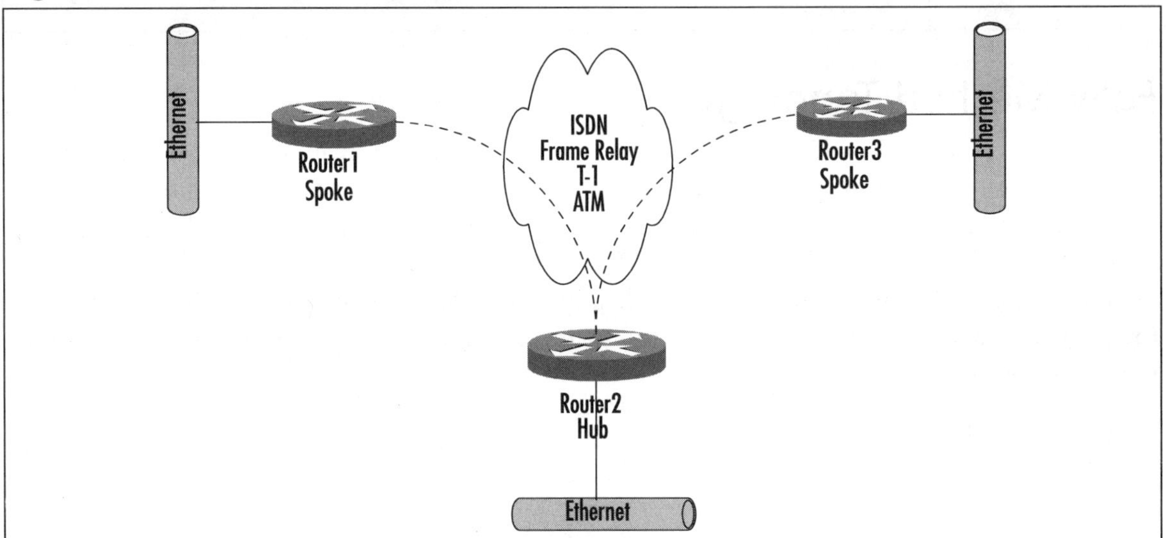

One popular solution to overcoming this potential failure issue is to design a dual-hub-and-spoke network. This works well on large networks, retains the advantages of the hub-and-spoke design, and overcomes the issue of a single point of failure by adding additional hubs to the configuration. Should one hub fail, communications will continue through another hub.

High-Level Data Link Control

HDLC is Layer 2 data link protocol for encapsulation techniques on point-to- point dedicated links. HDLC is derived from IBM's Synchronous Data Link Control (SDLC) protocol suite. HDLC specifies the encapsulation method in point-to-point synchronous links. It is the default encapsulation for Cisco serial interfaces. Figure 2.4 provides a configuration for a simple point-to-point network.

Figure 2.4 Point-to-Point HDLC Configuration

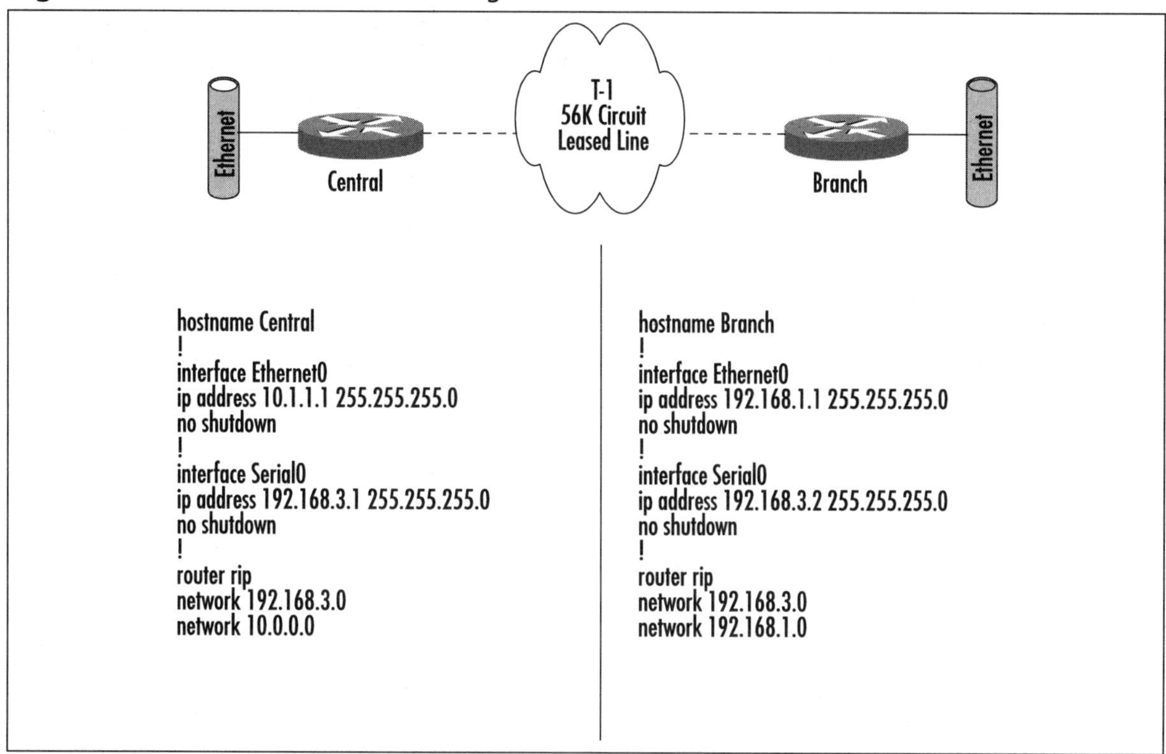
T-1
56K Circuit
Leased Line
Ethernet
Central
Branch
Ethernet
hostname Central
!
interface Ethernet0
ip address 10.1.1.1 255.255.255.0
no shutdown
!
interface Serial0
ip address 192.168.3.1 255.255.255.0
no shutdown
!
router rip
network 192.168.3.0
network 10.0.0.0
hostname Branch
!
interface Ethernet0
ip address 192.168.1.1 255.255.255.0
no shutdown
!
interface Serial0
ip address 192.168.3.2 255.255.255.0
no shutdown
!
router rip
network 192.168.3.0
network 192.168.1.0

Data to be transmitted across a point-to-point link is encapsulated into HDLC frames. Cisco HDLC, while it has an address field, typically does not use it since it is usually deployed in a point-to-point configuration. Since HDLC is the default for Cisco serial interfaces, there is no **encapsulation hdlc** command anywhere in the configuration in Figure 2.4.

HDLC simply concerns itself with transporting data from one router to another. It does not offer much in the way of "extra" services such as authentication or compression. It is used for synchronous communications, and with its low overhead (due to a limited set of capabilities), is amongst the most efficient Layer 2 protocol that you can deploy for point-to-point networks. PPP has its roots in HDLC.

Point to Point Protocol

PPP is designed for links that transport packets between two peers. PPP can operate across asynchronous, synchronous; ISDN, and dial-up point-to- point implementations. PPP is an Open Systems Interconnect (OSI) Layer 2 protocol standard that allows two devices to communicate with each other using point-to-point connections such as an analog phone line, an ISDN line, or a serial link. These point-to-point connections can be client-to-network or router-to-router.

PPP links provide a simultaneous, full-duplex, bi-directional operation, and are assumed to deliver packets in order. PPP encapsulates higher layer protocol packets such as Internet Protocol (IP), Internetwork Packet Exchange (IPX), and AppleTalk into PPP packets for transmission across the link on a first-come, first-served basis. This encapsulation is accomplished by placing the OSI Layer 3 network packet inside the PPP OSI Layer 2 frame and transmitting to the distant end where the PPP encapsulation frame is stripped away. The Layer 3 network packet is then passed up to the next layer of the protocol stack. PPP is a standard international protocol, which can be used in multi-vendor environments

PPP encapsulates network layer protocol information (including, but not limited to IP over point-to-point links. This chapter looks at how this protocol works, and it also looks at the Link Control Protocol (LCP) mechanisms for establishing, configuring, and testing the data-link connection. PPP supports several authentication methods: the Password Authentication Protocol (PAP), and the Challenge Handshake Authentication Protocol (CHAP).

To use PPP instead of HDLC, you would enter the following command in interface configuration mode for each of the connected serial interfaces: **central(config-if)# encapsulation ppp**. Keep in mind that the encapsulation must be the same on both sides of the link, or no communication will be possible over that link.

There are four ways PPP can be used as a data link layer protocol on a Cisco router to provide access to computing resources:

- Provides dial-in access to remote users.
- Provides backup services over an asynchronous or synchronous connection in case a circuit fails between two routers.
- Provides encapsulation between two routers over a leased line.
- Provides dial-on-demand routing (DDR) services between two routers.

PPP Features

PPP offers several features that add the benefits of efficiency, security, and reliability to communications links.

- **Multiple Protocols per Communication Line** PPP allows multiple network protocols (such as IP, IPX, DECnet, Vines, or AppleTalk) to use the same communications link. Each network protocol is transported by use of an additional associated Network Control Protocol (NCP). For example, IP uses the IP Control Protocol (IPCP) and IPX uses the Internet Packet Exchange Control Protocol (IPXCP) as their respective NCPs.
- **Authentication** Security can be implemented over the link by the use of an authentication protocol such as PAP, Challenge-Handshake Authentication Protocol (CHAP), or Microsoft's MS-CHAP. These protocols are explained later in this chapter.
- **Link Configuration and Negotiation** LCP manages link layer parameters (such as the use of special escape characters and a maximum frame size) to add flexibility and reliability to the communications link.
- **Error Detection** Transmission errors can be detected through the use of Frame Check Sequence (FCS) fields in the PPP frame.
- **Header Compression** PPP allows for the compression of packet headers to more efficiently utilize link bandwidth by reducing transmission overhead.

Bonding of Communications Links

PPP allows multiple communications links and/or remote access servers to be "bonded," to increase the amount of bandwidth between end devices. This bonding action allows two physical communications lines to appear as a single virtual link for remote access services. The PPP frame consists of the following six fields, as illustrated in Figure 2.5:

Figure 2.5 PPP Frame Format

	FLAG	ADDRESS	CONTROL	PROTOCOL	DATA	FCS
	0111110	1111111	00000011	00000011	00000011	00000011
SIZE IN BYTES	8	8	8	8-16	VARIABLE	8-16

- **Flag** (8 bits) start of frame consisting of the value 01111110
- **Address** (8 bits) broadcast address consisting of the value 11111111
- **Control** (8 bits) transmission control field consisting of the value 00000011
- **Protocol** (8–16 bits) identifies network protocol encapsulated within frame
- **Data** (Variable length) frame payload (maximum size is 1500 bytes)
- **FCS** (8–16 bits) FCS for error detection. By prior agreement, consenting PPP applications can use 4 bytes for greater error detection

There are several components that make up the PPP. Each of these component sublayers executes specific tasks that enable PPP to exhibit its many capabilities while remaining a stable and robust Link layer protocol.

Link Control Protocol

LCP establishes and negotiates the data-link connection. The two most commonly set options are the Maximum Receive Unit (MRU) and the setting that maps the character escape sequences—the Asynchronous Control Character Map (ACCM).

Escape sequences are used to replace special control characters that may appear naturally in the data stream, causing interruption of communication. An example is the XOFF character. Such control characters are replaced with a two-character representation that is unlikely to appear within the data stream. The use of escape sequences prevents the user data being sent from inadvertently interrupting the data flow by appearing as control signals to the computing devices or the protocol in use.

LCP authenticates point-to-point peers by using either PAP or CHAP. Which authentication protocol that LCP uses is configurable by the user. MS-CHAP is an authentication protocol proprietary to Microsoft that is also supported by Cisco. These three authentication protocols are discussed later in this chapter.

LCP sits on top of the Physical layer and establishes, authenticates, and tests the functionality of the data-link connection through a four phase process:

- **Phase 1** LCP sets up a data-link connection and negotiates configuration parameters.
- **Phase 2** LCP determines sufficiency of link quality (this phase is optional).
- **Phase 3** LCP sets up a network layer connection and configuration.
- **Phase 4** LCP tears down the connection and notifies network layer of the status.

There are three types of LCP frames that correspond with each mandatory phase of the LCP process:

- **Link Configuration** Sets up a data-link connection.
- **Link Management** Maintains and debugs a connection.
- **Link Termination** Tears down a connection.

When two LCP peers initiate the negotiation process, they use their unique LCP parameters to either accept or reject each other's unique LCP option values. LCP peers do this by sending any of the following responses to an initial configuration request:

- **Configure-NACK** Due to unacceptable values.
- **Configure-Reject** Because some or all values are unknown.
- **Configure-ACK** Because all of the values are within accepted parameters.

The default value is used when LCP configuration options are not included in the configuration request packet. When a Configure-NACK or Configure-Reject is received as a configuration response, the values are modified until they are within acceptable limits. At that time, a Configure-ACK is returned to the requestor. Two of the most important parts of the LCP process are the negotiation of the MRU parameter and the authentication of peers (see Figure 2.6).

The MRU instructs the PPP peer as to how many frames to send across the wire (for example. a peer interface must be able to receive frames of up to 1,500 bytes in length). Setting the MRU to lower values may aid the performance of interactive applications over the WAN links. Lower MRU values allow for a "quicker send" of smaller packets that are common to interactive applications.

The MRU parameter limits the size of packets and determines the overall bandwidth of the communications link. The MRU can be different sizes in either direction, or the same size in both directions. This process is completed by the configuration request responses mentioned in the previous list of LCP acknowledgements.

Figure 2.6 LCP Negotiation of MRU and Authentication Values

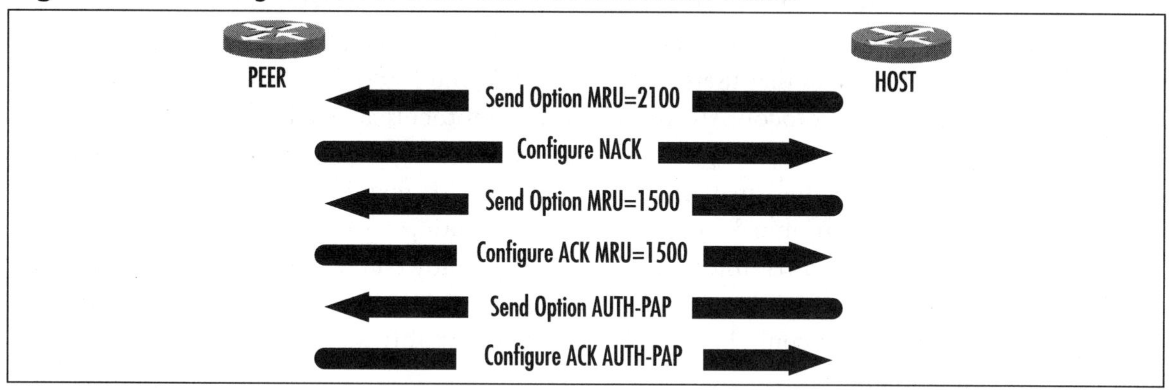

Once LCP has established the Data Link layer for the connection, the responsibility for setting up the network layer is passed up to the NCP. Figure 2.7 shows PPP as a Layer 2 protocol and the placement of LCP and NCP within its suite.

Figure 2.7 Layers of PPP

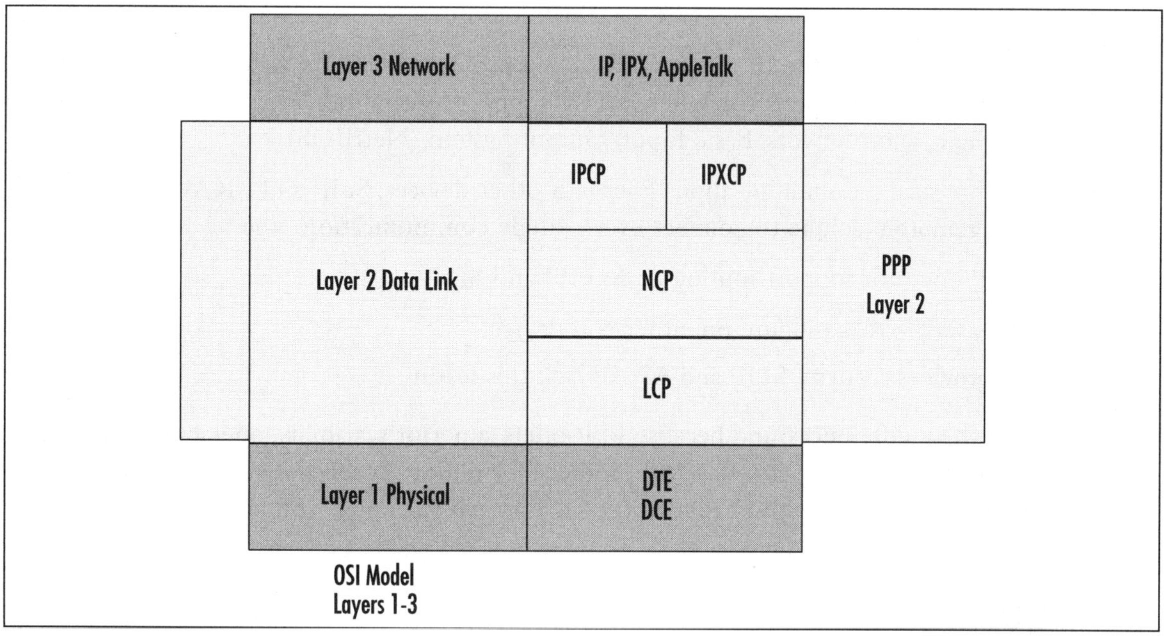

Layer 3 Network
IP, IPX, AppleTalk
IPCP
IPXCP
Layer 2 Data Link
NCP
PPP
Layer 2
LCP
Layer 1 Physical
DTE
DCE
OSI Model
Layers 1-3

Network Control Protocol

NCP resides at a higher layer than LCP, and is responsible for establishing and configuring network layer protocols such as IP, IPX, and AppleTalk (refer back to Figure 2.7). NCP can also signal LCP to terminate the communications link when necessary.

NCP uses the IPCP to manage the use of IP over the communications link. IPCP allows the Dynamic Host Configuration Protocol (DHCP) to be used for IP address assignment to the remote peer (RFC1332). NCP uses IPXCP for IPX protocol support. This permits negotiation of the routing protocol and compressed IPX (RFC1552, RFC1553).

PPP Alternatives…Not Really: PPP vs. SLIP and ARAP

When connecting to the Internet with personal computers running Windows became an option for the masses, the two choices that users had were Serial Line Internet Protocol (SLIP) and AppleTalk Remote Access Protocol (ARAP). These two protocols allowed users to exchange IP packets of data with remote computing systems, and represented an alternative to the straight American Standard Code for Information Interchange (ASCII) text characters that were exchanged between remote terminals and mainframe computing systems.

The ability to send IP packets instead of character text allowed remote users to run a number of applications concurrently, or to have several "virtual" connections due to the various Transport layer (OSI Layer 4) ports that could be used. Believe it or not, this was considered a very big advancement at the time.

While SLIP and ARAP advanced remote connectivity, they had many shortcomings that needed to be addressed in order to support robust applications between distant endpoints. To the great distress of SLIP and ARAP, the solution was PPP. PPP provides the ability to sustain several virtual connections over a single line, and provides a number of other benefits lacking in SLIP and/or ARAP:

- PPP provides error checking, whereas SLIP does not.
- SLIP supports only the IP protocol (it lacks a protocol identifier field); ARAP supports only the AppleTalk protocol, whereas PPP supports several others including IP, IPX, AppleTalk, and Network Basic Input/Output System (NetBIOS).
- PPP can share a communications line with other devices; SLIP and ARAP allow only a single remote machine to connect over a single communications line.
- ARAP does not support routing as do PPP and SLIP.
- PPP is simple to configure on either end device.
- PPP provides security. SLIP and ARAP lack this feature.

Because of these differences, and because PPP offers superior scalability, operability, and reliability, PPP has become the de facto standard protocol for remote access networks. Other than bragging rights, there is no earthly reason to use SLIP or ARAP, unless you are working with very old software and hardware.

Configuring PPP

Configuring PPP on a Cisco router involves the following steps:

1. Configuring Cisco parameters necessary to communicate with a third-party device such as an ISDN switch.
2. Entering global configuration commands to identify the Cisco device and to implement routing over the established link.
3. Entering interface configuration commands to define the router's interface, determine the encapsulation type, and select the kind of authentication performed over the line.

4. Saving the configuration changes to nonvolatile RAM (NVRAM).

To configure IP over PPP on an ISDN interface on a Cisco router, follow these steps:

1. Enter the enable mode using the **enable** command so that the configuration of the router can be changed.
2. Enter the global configuration mode by using the **config terminal** command.
3. Using the **isdn switch-type *switch-type*** command, select the ISDN switch type of your ISDN provider.
4. Enter the remote router host name and password with the **username *remote* password *pwd*** command.
5. Next, use the **dialer-list *number* protocol *ip* permit** command to configure a dialer list of interesting traffic.
6. Then, enter a static route to host end router with the command **ip *route subnet mask next-hop-address***.
7. Enter the interface configuration mode using the **interface bri *number*** command.
8. Next, assign an IP address by using the **ip address *address mask*** command.
9. Then, use **encapsulation ppp** to enable PPP.
10. The next step is to assign a dialer list to the interface by using the **dialer-group *number*** command.
11. Use **ppp authentication *type*** to enable CHAP or PAP.
12. Next, use **dialer map *protocol next hop address* name *hostname* class *classname dial-string*** to map the next hop address.
13. Return to global configuration mode by typing **exit**.
14. Finally, save changes by using the **copy running-config startup-config** command.

More specific examples are provided later in this chapter. Cisco makes it easy for dial-in users to establish their session.

Autoselect

Cisco access routers can automatically allow PPP, ARAP, and SLIP sessions to start when they are requested. This allows the user to be prompted for his username without having to press the "return" key. This can help alleviate any confusion as to the status of the PPP connection to the user during initialization and logon.

To configure a Cisco access server to automatically start PPP sessions when requested, follow these steps:

1. Enter the enable mode by using the **enable** command.
2. Use **configure terminal** to enter the global configuration mode.
3. Use **line *line-number*** to enter the line configuration mode.
4. Finally, enable autoselect with **autoselect *ppp* during-login**.

PPP Addressing Methods

The local interface of the Cisco access router can be assigned a network address for the IP protocol in one of two ways:

- The first method is to use manual assignment by entering an IP address on the router interface with the command **ip address *address mask***.
- The other method is to use an address from the Ethernet interface to conserve an IP address. This is accomplished with the command **ip unnumbered *interface-type number***.

The local interface can also assign a network address for the IPX protocol in one of two ways:

- Similar to IP, a manual assignment can be used by entering an IPX network number on the router interface with the command **ipx network *network-number***.
- The second method is to associate an asynchronous interface with a loopback address (this also involves using IP unnumbered on the interface) with the **ipx ppp-client loopback *number*** command.

This latter task conserves IP address space as the asynchronous interface uses the IP address of the loopback interface. Using unnumbered interfaces is a convenient way to simplify router configuration while saving valuable IP address space for other uses. When **ip unnumbered** is used, the IP address of the loopback interface *does not* have to be on the same subnet as the remote host router being called.

Cisco supports a couple of methods for the assignment of network addresses to remote end-user client computers that dial into Cisco routers and Access Servers:

- **Asynchronous Dynamic Address** Allows clients to enter in their network address after they enter the PPP EXEC command. To select this option, use the **async dynamic address** command in interface configuration mode.
- **DHCP** Allows a third-party DHCP server to assign IP addresses to remote clients. To select this option, use the **ip dhcp-server *address*** command in global configuration mode.

The DHCP option seamlessly integrates the user into the IP addressing scheme of the dial-in network and requires no intervention by the user. The **async** option may be necessary when applications are hard-coded to work only with certain IP addresses, or when static addressing is necessary for administrative or security purposes.

The following is an example configuration for a local IP address pool and Domain Name System (DNS) service to be assigned to dial-in clients.

1. To assign the address pool consisting of 253 IP addresses in the range of 10.10.11.2-10.10.11.254, enter the following configuration command:

```
ip local pool pool_name 10.10.11.2 10.10.11.254
```

2. To assign a primary DNS service with IP address 10.10.13.254 and a secondary DNS service with IP address 10.10.13.253, enter the following command:

```
async-bootp dns-server 10.10.13.254 10.10.13.253
```

PPP provides security with its authentication mechanisms.

PPP Authentication

A common method hackers use to attack computing systems is using software called *war dialers*. A war dialer is a software program that continuously dials telephone numbers until a modem picks up at the other end. Once it detects a modem at the other end, it launches one of a number of attacks attempting to gain access to the computer system. To protect remote access networks from these types of attacks, some means of security needs to be provided that can perform authentication before access is given to the network.

PPP provides several types of authentication methods to enhance the security of providing remote access over publicly accessible communication lines. These authentication protocols need to work at a layer lower than the network layer, to avoid the passing out of IP addresses to unknown systems that may attempt a connection to the network. PAP and CHAP work at the LCP layer of PPP. CHAP is the more secure of the two-link layer authentication protocols. By forcing authentication before a network address is assigned, PPP ensures that only those with a valid account and password are permitted access.

The authentication process and concepts discussed here apply to all PPP authentications. While router-to-router PPP authentication are used in the examples, a similar process is executed for a dial-up user.

Password Authentication Protocol (PAP)

Both the peer (the client requesting access) and the authenticator (the access server) must be configured for PAP authentication, and a matching set of ID/passwords must be entered in both the peer and the authenticator's configuration. First, the link establishment phase is completed. The peer and authenticator send LCP packets to each other until framing is agreed upon and the link is established.

Once the PPP link has been established, the authentication phase begins, in which the peer repeatedly sends its ID/password in cleartext to the authenticator until the authentication is validated or the connection is terminated. The authenticator validates the ID/password by checking for a match of the ID/password in its authentication list. See Figure 2.8 for an illustration of the authentication process. Because PAP sends the password across the link in plain text and is vulnerable to "playback" and repeated heuristic hacking attempts, it is considered a low measure of security. Figure 2.9 illustrates relevant PAP configuration commands of two routers that are configured for PAP authentication using PPP.

Figure 2.8 Client to Access Server PAP Authentication

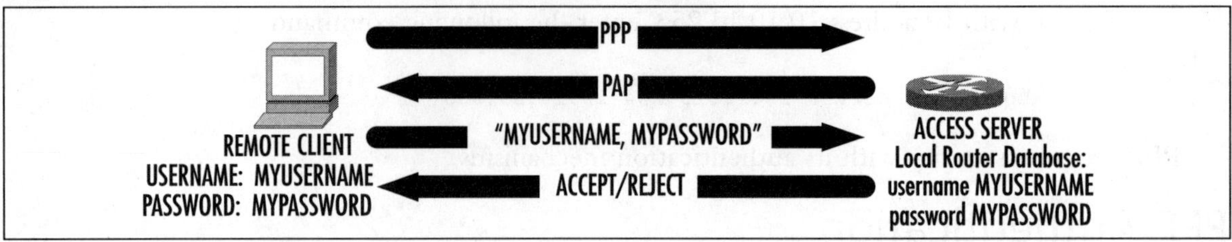
PPP
PAP
REMOTE CLIENT
USERNAME: MYUSERNAME
PASSWORD: MYPASSWORD
"MYUSERNAME, MYPASSWORD"
ACCEPT/REJECT
ACCESS SERVER
Local Router Database:
username MYUSERNAME
password MYPASSWORD

Figure 2.9 Example PAP Configuration

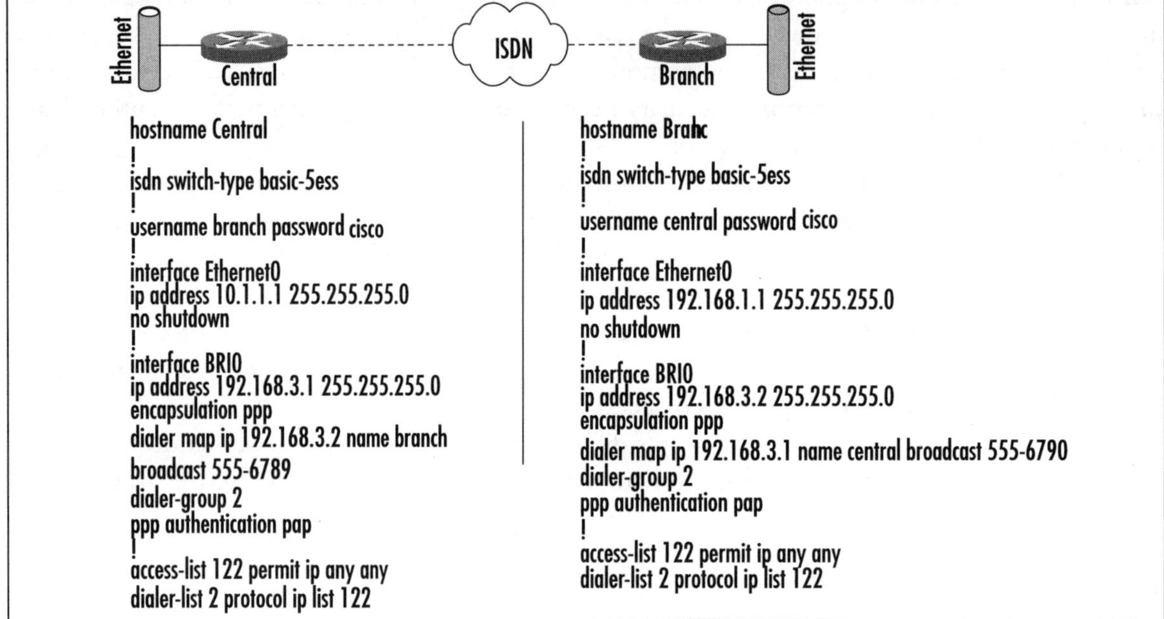
Ethernet
Central
ISDN
Branch
Ethernet
hostname Central
!
isdn switch-type basic-5ess
!
username branch password cisco
!
interface Ethernet0
ip address 10.1.1.1 255.255.255.0
no shutdown
!
interface BRI0
ip address 192.168.3.1 255.255.255.0
encapsulation ppp
dialer map ip 192.168.3.2 name branch
broadcast 555-6789
dialer-group 2
ppp authentication pap
!
access-list 122 permit ip any any
dialer-list 2 protocol ip list 122
hostname Brahc
!
isdn switch-type basic-5ess
!
username central password cisco
!
interface Ethernet0
ip address 192.168.1.1 255.255.255.0
no shutdown
!
interface BRI0
ip address 192.168.3.2 255.255.255.0
encapsulation ppp
dialer map ip 192.168.3.1 name central broadcast 555-6790
dialer-group 2
ppp authentication pap
!
access-list 122 permit ip any any
dialer-list 2 protocol ip list 122

The PAP configuration shown here is not optimal: any IP traffic between Central and Branch will keep the link up, resulting in large ISDN call charges. When it comes to PAP, eschew it in favor of its cousin—the more secure CHAP.

Challenge Handshake Authentication Protocol

CHAP works without having to send the authentication password over the communications link. As with PAP, the link establishment phase is completed before the authentication phase begins.

The authenticator instructs the other end to use CHAP for authentication. The calling peer then requests a challenge. The authenticator issues the CHAP verification "challenge" to the peer in the form of a random selection (like a number) that is encrypted using its ID/password. The peer in turn uses its password to encrypt the challenge using a **one-way hash**, and sends the encrypted result back to the authenticator.

The authenticator authenticates the received response and establishes the authenticated connection if the challenge was validated. If the challenge fails, the connection is rejected. Because a failed challenge has its connection terminated, CHAP is not vulnerable to **brute force** attacks like PAP is.

What's in a Name? Usernames and Passwords

PPP can work with Remote Authentication Dial-In User Server/Service (RADIUS) and Terminal Access Controller Access Control System+ (TACACS+) servers to authenticate against accounts in their databases. However, for brevity and to keep the focus on PPP, local accounts are used (usernames and passwords are defined on the router). When using PPP to perform router-to-router authentication, especially to activate backup links, username and passwords must be configured in a special way.

When configuring the username command-line in each router, the host name of the opposite router as the username must be used. This is a common mistake made by even the most seasoned Cisco professionals. The passwords must be identical. The format should be as follows:

```
username other-router-host password same4both
```

Both the calling peer and the called peer must be configured to use either CHAP or PAP, or the connection will be rejected. There must be agreement on the authentication method. A peer configured to use PAP cannot authenticate to an authenticator that is configured only to use CHAP, and vice versa. Figure 2.10 shows two routers configured to use CHAP authentication.

Figure 2.10 Example CHAP Configuration

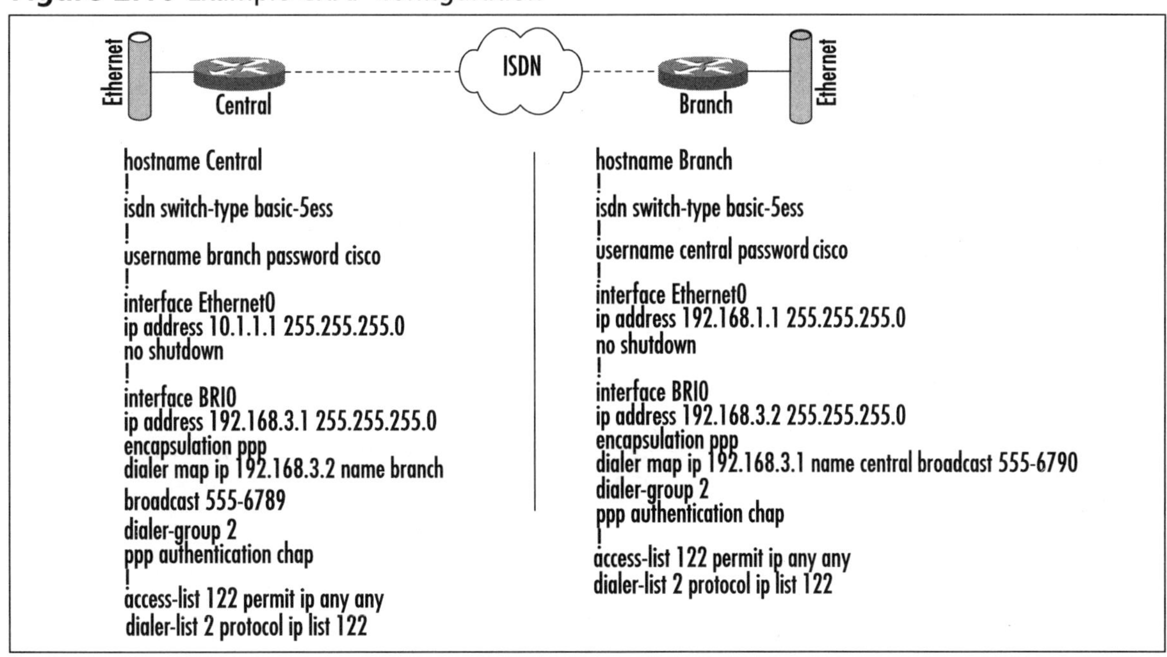
Ethernet
Central
ISDN
Branch
Ethernet
hostname Central
!
isdn switch-type basic-5ess
!
username branch password cisco
!
interface Ethernet0
ip address 10.1.1.1 255.255.255.0
no shutdown
!
interface BRI0
ip address 192.168.3.1 255.255.255.0
encapsulation ppp
dialer map ip 192.168.3.2 name branch
broadcast 555-6789
dialer-group 2
ppp authentication chap
!
access-list 122 permit ip any any
dialer-list 2 protocol ip list 122
hostname Branch
!
isdn switch-type basic-5ess
!
username central password cisco
!
interface Ethernet0
ip address 192.168.1.1 255.255.255.0
no shutdown
!
interface BRI0
ip address 192.168.3.2 255.255.255.0
encapsulation ppp
dialer map ip 192.168.3.1 name central broadcast 555-6790
dialer-group 2
ppp authentication chap
!
access-list 122 permit ip any any
dialer-list 2 protocol ip list 122

Figure 2.11 tries PAP authentication first; if that fails, it next tries CHAP.

Figure 2.11 Using Both PAP and CHAP

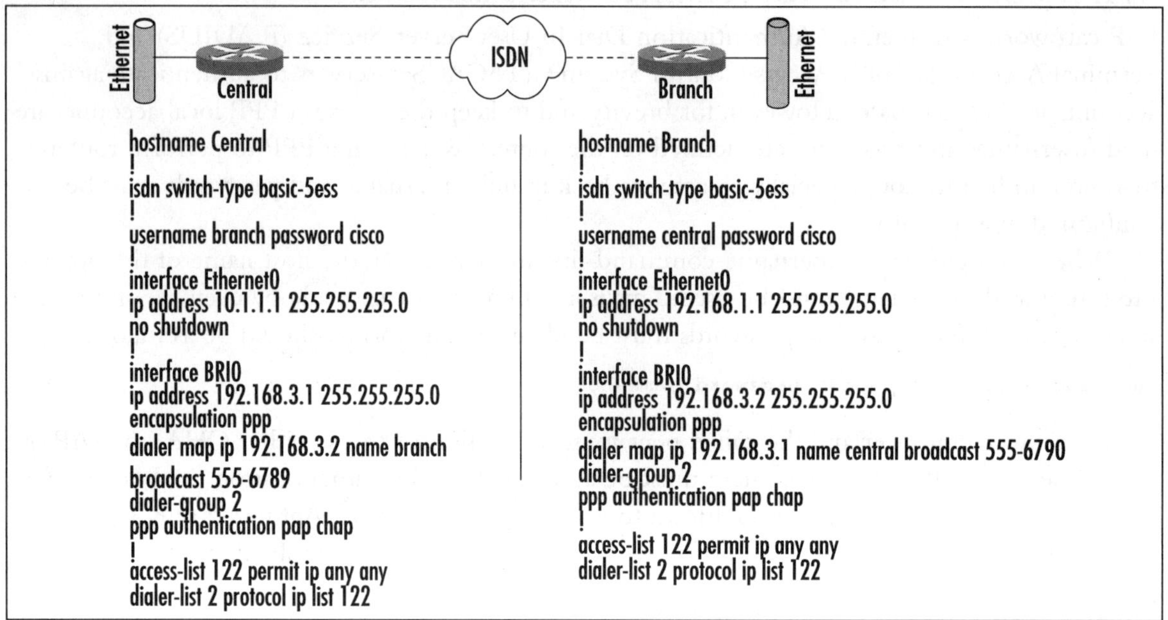
Ethernet
Central
ISDN
Branch
Ethernet
hostname Central
!
isdn switch-type basic-5ess
!
username branch password cisco
!
interface Ethernet0
ip address 10.1.1.1 255.255.255.0
no shutdown
!
interface BRI0
ip address 192.168.3.1 255.255.255.0
encapsulation ppp
dialer map ip 192.168.3.2 name branch
broadcast 555-6789
dialer-group 2
ppp authentication pap chap
!
access-list 122 permit ip any any
dialer-list 2 protocol ip list 122
hostname Branch
!
isdn switch-type basic-5ess
!
username central password cisco
!
interface Ethernet0
ip address 192.168.1.1 255.255.255.0
no shutdown
!
interface BRI0
ip address 192.168.3.2 255.255.255.0
encapsulation ppp
dialer map ip 192.168.3.1 name central broadcast 555-6790
dialer-group 2
ppp authentication pap chap
!
access-list 122 permit ip any any
dialer-list 2 protocol ip list 122

Authentication Failures

Most PAP and CHAP authentication failures using Cisco equipment are due to either the appropriate authentication protocol not being configured on both ends of the PPP link, or the wrong ID/password being configured on the "username" line.

The Cisco username configuration line has the format: **username** *other_end_hostname* **password** *same_password_4both*. When troubleshooting PPP authentication failures, use either the **debug ppp pap** or **debug ppp chap** command to aid in determining the configuration error. These commands are covered later in this chapter.

PPP Callback

PPP callback enhances the security of remote access by verifying the phone number of the initiating client through returning the phone call. It can also be used to reverse phone charges so that billing can be managed from a single hub site. With PPP callback, the initiating client dials into the access server (such as an AS5300) and passes authentication information to it (such as the host name and dialer string). The host router returns the call if the information is authenticated (Figure 2.12). The client could be another router or a dial-up PC.

PPP callback must be configured on both the initiating client and the host router, with the client being configured to make PPP callback requests and the host router being configured to accept and return authenticated callback requests. If a participating router is not configured for callback, the connection will not be successful.

Figure 2.12 PPP Callback Process

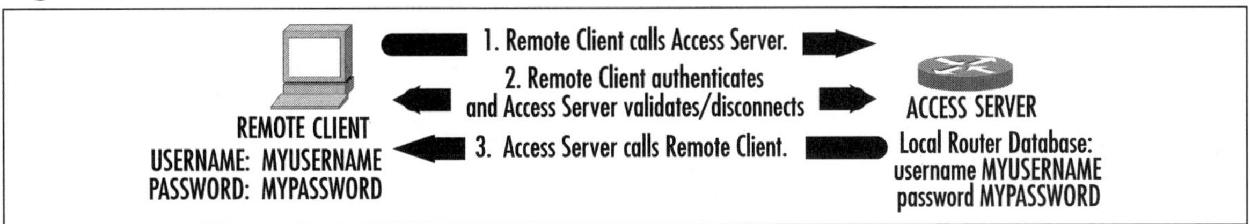

Configuring PPP between two Cisco routers is straightforward. To configure the host router as the call back server, do the following:

1. First enter enable mode using the **enable** command.
2. Next, use **configure terminal** to enter the global configuration mode.
3. Use **interface *type number*** to enter interface configuration mode.
4. Then enable DDR using the **dialer in-band** command.
5. Enable PPP with the **encapsulation ppp** command.
6. Enable CHAP or PAP with the **ppp authentication *type*** command.
7. Next, map the next hop address using the **dialer map *protocol next-hop-address* name *hostname* class *classname dialstring*** command.
8. Then, use the **ppp callback accept** command to set the interface to accept callback.
9. Use the **exit command** to return to the global configuration mode.
10. From here, configure the PPP dialer map class with the **map-class dialer *classname*** command.
11. Next, use the **dialer callback-server *username*** command to configure dialer map class as callback.
12. Finally, save the changes to memory with the command **copy runnin-config startup-**config command.

To configure a remote router as the callback client, do the following:

1. Use **enable** to enter enable mode.
2. Use **configure terminal** to enter global configuration mode.
3. Use **interface *type number*** to enter interface configuration mode.
4. Next, enable DDR with the **dialer in-band** command.
5. Then, enable PPP as the link layer encapsulation with the **encapsulation ppp** command.
6. Then, enable CHAP or PAP authentication with the **ppp authentication *type*** command.
7. Next, map the next hop address with the **dialer map** *protocol next-hop-address* **name** *hostname* **class** *classname dialstring* command.

8. Use the command **ppp callback request** to set the interface to request callback.
9. Finally, save the changes to memory with the **copy running-config startupconfig** command.

PPP Compression

PPP provides an option to conserve bandwidth or to get more across limited bandwidth. PPP Compression minimizes the utilized bandwidth across the link. Payload data within a PPP packet can be compressed by two methods supported by Cisco:

- **Stacker** Compresses each data type once and then determines where each occurs.
- **Predictor** Examines the data to see if it has previously been compressed, to avoid attempting to compress data that is already compressed.

It is important to check the effects of enabling compression on your equipment, as compression can be central processing unit (CPU) and memory intensive. Typically, compression will result in about a 2:1 reduction in payload size.

Multilink PPP

Multilink PPP (MP) allows multiple communications lines to be bound together in a "bundle" between one to two remote peers (Figure 2.13). For example: two 56 Kbps links can be bound together to form a single logical link with a bandwidth of 112 Kbps. Packets are fragmented at the origination end and sent over the multiple links at the same time to the remote end. When they arrive at the remote end, the packets are re-assembled, re-sequenced, and sent on to their destination. (See RFC1717 for more information.)

Figure 2.13 MP: Multiple Physical Links = One Logical Connection

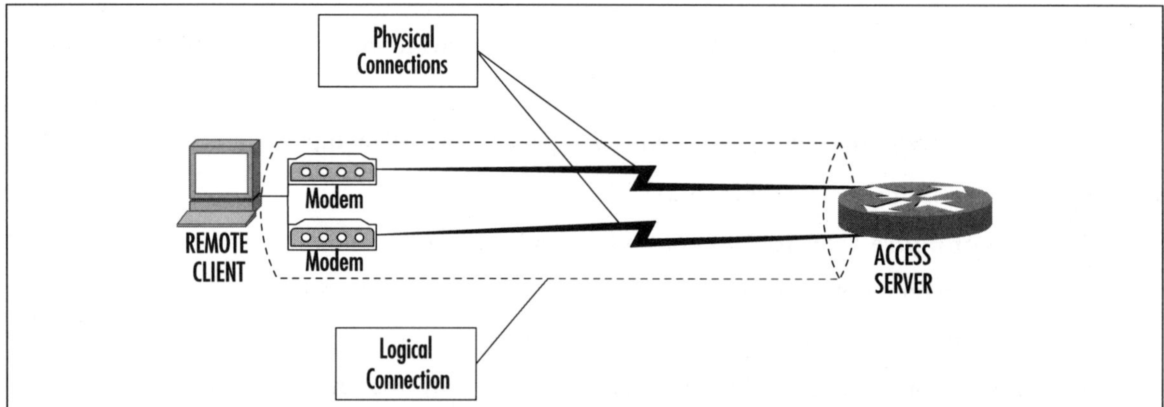

The bandwidth of the logical link has an upper bound of the aggregate bandwidth of each individual physical connection (though the actual aggregation will not be realized as pure data throughput due to link negotiation and protocol overhead).

The individual communication channels do not have to be the same type in order to be bundled. Asynchronous and synchronous lines can be mixed together. For example, four channels can be bound together, with two channels consisting of 56Kbps modem lines and two channels consisting of two B channels of a Basic Rate Interface (BRI) ISDN line. In order to implement this feature, both end devices must support MP and have the necessary facilities to build out the bundle.

For example, a remote user using analog phone lines must have at least two available phone lines and two modems connected to a computer that is configured to support MP (such as Microsoft Windows XP or Windows 2000). The other end must also have at least two lines and two ports available and be configured to support MP. Microsoft refers to MP as *bonding* or MLPPP.

MP uses the Bandwidth Allocation Control Protocol (BACP) to bind several physical connections into a single logical link. It is initiated when a system sends the Maximum Received Reconstruction Unit (MRRU) option during the first stages of LCP option negotiation. The MRRU LCP option defines the bandwidth of the connection.

MP works by splitting the Layer 2 datagrams on one end, ordering them in a sequence, and sending the datagrams across the several different physical connections of the bundle. When received on the other end, the datagrams are re-combined and re-sequenced before being passed up to the Layer 3 network protocol.

To configure MP on an ISDN BRI using the IP protocol, perform the following configuration tasks in **enable** mode:

1. Select the BRI interface with the **interface bri *interface_number*** command.
2. Next, assign an IP address with the **ip address *ip_address mask*** command.
3. Use **encapsulation ppp** to enable PPP.
4. Use **dialer load-threshold *load*** to specify the dialer load threshold.
5. Then, set up an interface to make outbound calls with the **dialer map ip *next_hop_address* name *hostname* broadcast** command.
6. Next, select an access list to control access to the interface with the **dialer-group *group_number*** command.
7. Then select an authentication type with the **ppp authentication *type*** command.
8. Finally, use **ppp multilink** to enable MP.

Multichassis MP (MMP)

Multichassis MP (MMP) is an extension of MP, in that it allows for a bundle to be split and reconstructed across several different communications lines spanning several different Cisco access servers (Figure 2.14). These access servers are combined into a single rotary group that can be accessed via a single phone number. The fact that the different access servers are grouped together is completely transparent to the end user. This allows corporations and Internet Service Providers (ISPs) to publish a single dial-in phone number to automatically distribute user access across all of their bound access servers. Otherwise, users might have to dial a sequence of dial-in numbers until they find an available port—a process that can be time consuming and frustrating.

Figure 2.14 MMP Configuration Using Routers

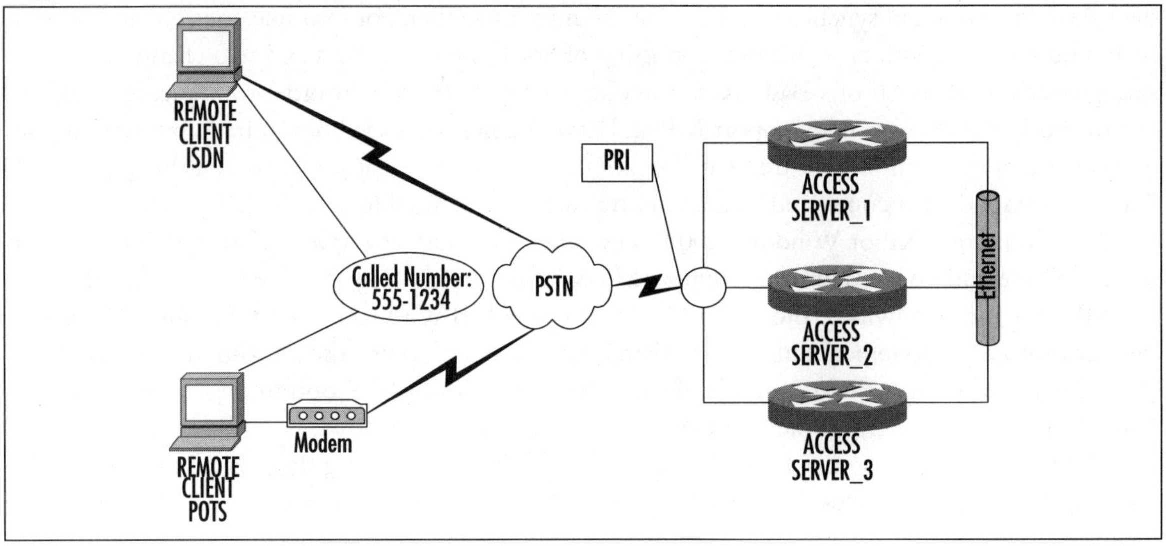

When multiple Cisco access servers are configured for MMP, the grouping is referred to as a "stack group." Supported interfaces for MPP are Primary Rate Interface (PRI), BRI, serial, and asynchronous.

MMP requires that each associated router be configured with the following parameters:

- PPP
- **Stack Group Bidding Protocol (SGBP)** A protocol for arbitrating the location of bundles within a stack group to the "highest bidder" (normally the stack group member that locates the initial bundle for the first link in a multilink connection)
- MP
- Virtual template for interface cloning

Simple stack groups are composed of member peer routers and do not need to have a permanent "lead" router. Any stack group member who answers an incoming call becomes the "owner" of the call if it is the first call in a new session with the particular remote-end device. When a second call comes in from this same remote-end device to the stack group, the answering router forwards the call to the stack group where the member routers "bid" for the call. Since the first router "owns" the session by answering the first call, it wins the bid and the answering router forwards the call to it.

The second router accomplishes this by establishing a tunnel to the "owner" router and forwarding all packets to the owner. The owner router is responsible for re-assembling and re-sequencing the packets. The owner router then forwards these packets to the local network.

There are two basic steps to configuring MMP on Cisco routers and access servers:

1. Configure the stack group and make member assignments.

- Create the stack group on the first router to be configured, where "name" is the hostname of that router.

```
sgbp group group_name
```

- Add additional stack group members.

```
sgbp member router2_hostname router2_ip_address
sgbp member router3_hostname router3_ip_address
<add additional sgbp member lines for each additional member router>
```

2. Configure a virtual template and Virtual Template Interface.
   - Create a virtual template for the stack group.

```
multilink virtual-template template_number
```

- Create an IP address pool (a local pool is used in this example).

```
ip local pool default ip_address
```

- Create a Virtual Template Interface (not required for ISDN interfaces or if physical interfaces are using dialers).

```
interface virtual-template template_number
```

- Use unnumbered IP addressing.

```
ip unnumbered ethernet 0
```

- Configure PPP.

```
encapsulation ppp
```

- Enable MP.

```
ppp multilink
```

- Enable PPP authentication.

```
ppp authentication type
```

Verifying and Troubleshooting PPP

Sometimes problems arise when configuring PPP. Cisco provides a very powerful and robust set of commands to aid in isolating problems and solving communication problems. These commands exist in two different command sets: **show** commands and **debug** commands. **show** commands are used to determine the current status of an interface or protocol, whereas **debug** commands are used to show the processes an interface or protocol executes in order to establish continuity or communication.

Basic troubleshooting involves ensuring that the hardware is functioning correctly, then checking to see that configurations are correct and communication processes are proceeding normally over the wire. The network administrator should start at the physical layer and work their way up the OSI model to determine where the problem(s) are in establishing the connection.

PPP and Cisco Access Servers

Below are some basic steps that can be used to troubleshoot remote connections to a Cisco access server.

1. Does the user's modem connect? If the answer is no, use these commands to determine the status of the modem: **show modem log**, **debug modem**.
2. Does the LCP negotiation succeed? If the answer is no, use these commands to determine the point of failure: **debug PPP negotiation**, **debug PPP error**.
3. Does the authentication succeed? If the answer is no, use this command to determine the cause of failure: **debug PPP authentication**.
4. Does the network layer succeed? If the answer is no, use this command to determine the point of failure: **debug PPP negotiation**.
5. If all of the above is successful, use this command to inspect the user's session: **show caller {line, user, ip, interface}**.

Many communication problems with remote access systems are due to an authentication failure. The following is an example of debugging CHAP. Use the **debug ppp chap** command (make sure the router is in terminal monitor mode and then point the IP address of the BRI0 interface). The output should look similar to the following:

```
12:53:11: %LINK-3-UPDOWN: Interface BRI0: B-Channel 1, changed state to up
12:53:11: PPP BRI0: B-Channel 1: CHAP challenge from ciscortr2
12:53:11: PPP BRI0: B-Channel 1: CHAP response received from ciscortr2
12:53:11: PPP BRI0: B-Channel 1: remote passed CHAP authentication.
12:53:11: PPP BRI0: B-Channel 1: Passed CHAP authentication with remote
```

If the output from the command states, "PPP BRI0: B Channel 1: failed CHAP authentication with remote," check your username and password for correctness—passwords and usernames are case sensitive.

The following is a list of other useful Cisco debug commands:

- **debug ppp ?**
- **debug ppp chap**
- **debug ppp pap**
- **debug ppp multilink**
- **debug isdn events**
- **debug ppp negotiation**
- **debug dialer**

Monitoring PPP Multilink

PPP Multilink allows for multiple circuits to be bonded together providing greater bandwidth than would be possible if the circuits were used singularly. The **show ppp multilink** command can be used to verify PPP multilink operation.

```
Router1# show ppp multilink
Bundle Router2, 2 members, Master link is Virtual-Access2
Dialer Interface is BRI0
0 lost fragments, 0 reordered, 0 unassigned, sequence 0xC/0xE rcvd/sent
0 discarded, 0 lost received, 1/255 load
Member Links: 2 (max not set, min not set)
BRI0:2
BRI0:1
```

The **show ppp multilink** command gives information on the status of the multilink session. It identifies the remote router and the interface connecting to it.

The command **show interface bri 0 1 2** not only gives information about a BRI interface, it also gives information on PPP multilink. The fifth line of the output identifies that multilink is open, which means the PPP multilink session has been established.

```
Router1# show interface bri 0 1 2
BRI0:1 is up, line protocol is up
Hardware is BRI
MTU 1500 bytes, BW 64 Kbit, DLY 20000 usec, rely 255/255, load 1/255
Encapsulation PPP, loopback not set, keepalive set (10 sec)
LCP Open, multilink Open
Last input 00:00:02, output 00:00:02, output hang never
Last clearing of "show interface" counters never
Queueing strategy: fifo
Output queue 0/40, 0 drops; input queue 2/75, 0 drops
5 minute input rate 0 bits/sec, 0 packets/sec
5 minute output rate 0 bits/sec, 0 packets/sec
6825 packets input, 276786 bytes, 0 no buffer
Received 6825 broadcasts, 0 runts, 0 giants, 0 throttles
0 input errors, 0 CRC, 0 frame, 0 overrun, 0 ignored, 0 abort
6888 packets output, 287236 bytes, 0 underruns
0 output errors, 0 collisions, 7 interface resets
0 output buffer failures, 0 output buffers swapped out
234 carrier transitions
BRI0:2 is up, line protocol is up
Hardware is BRI
MTU 1500 bytes, BW 64 Kbit, DLY 20000 usec, rely 255/255, load 1/255
```

```
Encapsulation PPP, loopback not set, keepalive set (10 sec)
LCP Open, multilink Open
Last input 00:00:07, output 00:00:07, output hang never
Last clearing of "show interface" counters never
Queueing strategy: fifo
Output queue 0/40, 0 drops; input queue 0/75, 0 drops
5 minute input rate 0 bits/sec, 0 packets/sec
5 minute output rate 0 bits/sec, 0 packets/sec
87 packets input, 3084 bytes, 0 no buffer
Received 87 broadcasts, 0 runts, 0 giants, 0 throttles
0 input errors, 0 CRC, 0 frame, 0 overrun, 0 ignored, 0 abort
90 packets output, 3240 bytes, 0 underruns
0 output errors, 0 collisions, 7 interface resets
0 output buffer failures, 0 output buffers swapped out
3 carrier transitions
```

Circuit Types and Terminology

Before starting the discussion of the types of WAN circuits that can be used to interconnect networks, a working definition and description of each type is needed. As a rule of thumb, WAN circuits can range in speeds from 64 Kbps up to almost 10 Gbps and reaching higher all the time. The telecommunications industry has its own shorthand for describing these circuits. Each standard described has its own frame formats and techniques for delivering data to its destination.

The lowest common denominator of circuit descriptions is the DS0, which is simply 64 Kbps of bandwidth. Grouping 24 DS0s together composes a DS1, which gives the administrator 1.536 Mbps; basically, a T1. A DS3 has 672 DS0s, for a total capacity of 44.736 Mbps.

North America telecommunications providers use the T carrier standards to describe and package the circuits they sell. A T carrier uses time division multiplexing (TDM) to interleave voice and data in time slices over a digital circuit. For example, a T1 circuit is one such item. Another T carrier circuit is the T3, which weighs in at 44.736 Mbps. The European equivalent is the E carrier, which is essentially the same thing. However, an E1 is faster than a T1 at 2.048 Mbps, while an E3 has less capacity than a T3 at 34 Mbps. E carrier standards are developed and maintained by the European Conference of Postal and Telecommunications Administrations (CEPT). Europe, South America, and Mexico use these standards for their digital circuits. T1 carrier circuits will probably be around for sometime to come; however, Optical Carrier (OC) circuits are fast making inroads, even over fiber optics.

OC standards were birthed as part of the Synchronous Optical Network (SONET) standards (also known as Synchronous Transport Signal (STS), which are standards for digital circuits with capacities far outstripping the T carrier and E carrier systems). Since the large capacities of STS circuits require and demand fiber-optic cable, they are referred to by their OC moniker.

OC circuits range from 155 Mbps (OC3) to 9.6 Gbps (OC192), with OC12 and rounding out the family with 622 Mbps and 2.5 Gbps, respectively. Forty Gbps (OC768) is currently being worked on and products are being offered, though it is not readily available.

T1 and Fractional T1

T1 circuits are almost synonymous with wide area networking, having been around a relatively long time with a large installed base. T1 circuits were developed by AT&T in the 1960s, and were the "high speed" technology (at 1.544 Mbps per second) until the advent of ATM and DS3 circuits. T1s are still fairly prevalent today, and therefore merit some discussion.

A T1 is a digital circuit comprised of 24 DS0 channels each capable of carrying 64 Kbps of data providing a total capacity of 1.536Mbps, plus 8Kbps for framing overhead therefore providing a total of 1.544 Mbps. A T1 is also be referred to a DS1 circuit. A T1 can either be non-channelized or channelized. When non-channelized, all 24 DS0's are grouped to make one single circuit with a total data payload capacity of 1.536Mbps. Figure 2.15 shows both applications of a T1.

Figure 2.15 Channelized versus Non-channelized

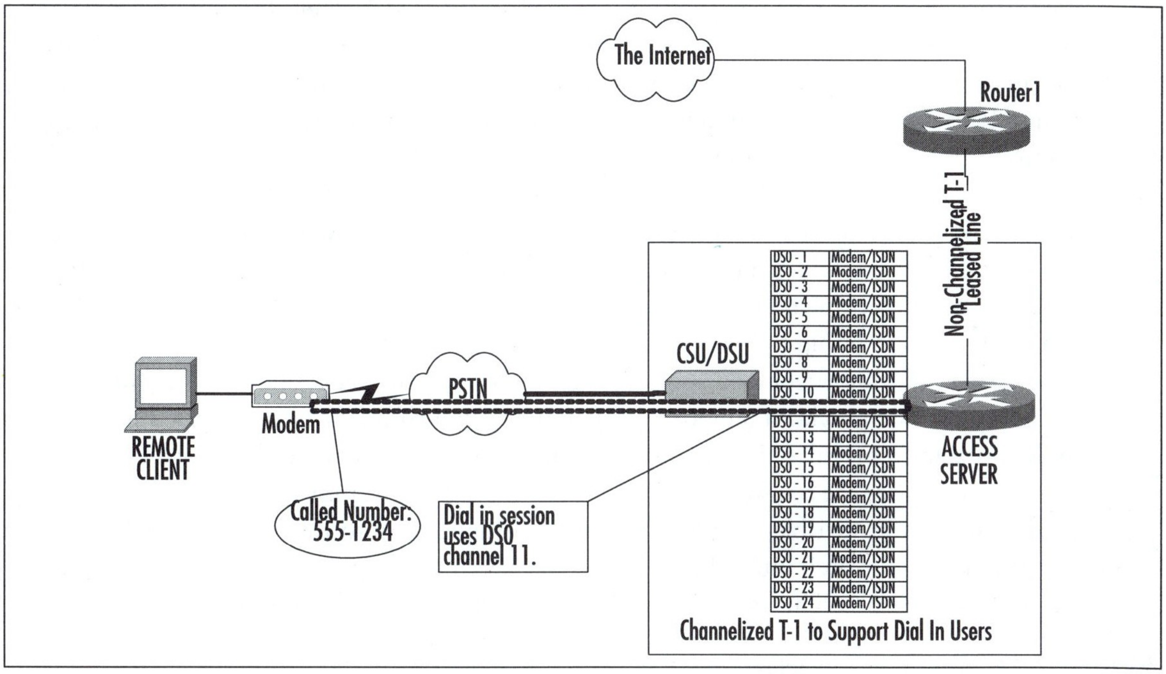

In Figure 2.15, the access server has a full T1 connection to Router1, which is its path to the outside world. The access server also has a channelized T1 that is providing 24 64 Kbps Plain Old Telephone System (POTS) or ISDN lines to dial-in users. The remote client has dialed and established a session over DS0 channel 11. This is a very common application found at ISPs that provide such dial-in services as it is better than installing 24 individual POTS lines to provide the same service. The access server is responsible for multiplexing/de-multiplexing T1 into individual channels for service to the individual modems.

Fractional T1 is simply the installation and use of less than a full T1. For example, , a T1 is ordered in allotments of 128Kbps. A network administrator can order a 384 Kbps fractional T1 if that is all they require. The advantage of fractional T1 is that they can shrink and grow bandwidth as needed, without any physical connection changes; the Telco can simply make adjustments to the number of channels received over the T1 interface to give the bandwidth required.

Frame Relay

Frame Relay is packet-switching technology at the data-link level. It provides an efficient, low-cost communication technology. The Frame Relay protocol was originally part of the ISDN suite of protocols. In the late 80s and early 90s, Frame Relay became a separate protocol. Error checking and re-transmissions are handled by upper layer protocols, which enhances the efficiency and speed of Frame Relay.

Frame Relay offers a high-speed version of packet switching, with many of the same techniques being employed to provide a complete network service. Frame Relay has the potential of operating effectively at much higher speeds (up to 45 Mbps). It is well suited to high-speed data applications, such as LAN connectivity, but is not well suited to delay-sensitive applications (voice, video), because of the variable length of the frames within the network. Cisco has added new features such as traffic shaping that have improved its support for such applications.

A Frame Relay frame is transmitted to its destination by way of virtual circuits, which are logical paths from the origin network to the destination network. Virtual circuits may be one of two types: permanent virtual circuits (PVCs) or switched virtual circuits (SVCs). A PVC is a permanently established connection between two endpoints on a Frame Relay network. PVC's can be used in a case where data transfers occur frequently and require fairly constant connectivity. PVC's do not require the call set-up and tear-down procedures utilized by SVCs. Configuring a PVC requires only a one-time set up by the network administrator, and the connection is permanently available, whereas SVCs are established and terminated on a call-by-call basis. An SVC differs from a PVC in that SVC's only provide a temporary data transmission path. SVC's can be used in situations where only sporadic connectivity is required. Each time data needs to be transmitted; a new SVC must be established. After the transmission is complete, the SVC is terminated.

Data is forwarded in variable-length frames and multiplexed onto the transmission links. Upper lay data is encapsulated into a Frame Relay packet and transported through the Frame Relay network. Figure 2.16 illustrates the fields contained in a Frame Relay packet.

Figure 2.16 Frame Relay Packet

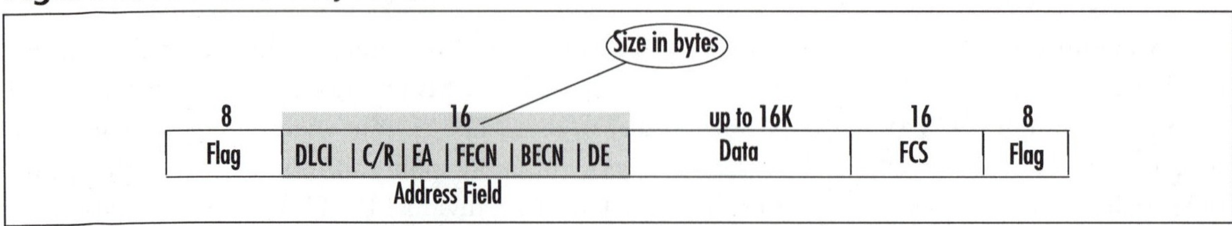

The Frame Relay packet format is designed based on low bit-error rates (1 in 10**10), with upper layers requesting re-transmission of dropped packets or lost packets. The main functionality provided by the Frame Relay switch is threefold:

1. **Error Checking** FCS uses 32-bit polynomial to check cyclic redundancy , and drops the packet if the checksum does not match.
2. **Addressing** The Frame Relay switch checks the routing information in the packet and forwards it through the appropriate output port/PVC.
3. **Congestion Notification** If the switch buffers are full, it sends the congestion notification (forward or backward) depending on how the output/input buffers are filling up.

Refer to Figure 2.16 and take a closer look at the fields contained in the Frame Relay packet.

- **Flag** An 8-bit sequence with bit stuffing, to identify the "start, end, start" sequence to delimit each packet.
- **Link Layer/Frame Relay Header** Contains addressing and error-checking functionality for Frame Relay.

The 16-bit bits of the Address field are divided and assigned specific functions as follows:

- **DLCI** Addressing in Frame Relay is called Data Link Connection Identifier (DLCI) . A DLCI is a 10-bit, Layer 2 address (up to 1,024) that identifies a virtual circuit. Frame Relay networks assign each end of a connection with a DLCI from a pool of locally unused numbers. The service provider's Frame Relay network then maps one DLCI to the other, using a look-up table. Locally significant DLCIs have become the primary method of addressing because the same address can be used in several different locations while still referring to different connections. Thus, local addressing prevents a customer from running out of DLCIs as the network grows.
- **C/R** The command/response (CR) bit, which is not used in most Frame Relay networks.
- **EA** The Extended Address (EA) field signifies up to two additional bytes in the Frame Relay header, thus greatly expanding the number of possible addresses.
- **FECN** The Forward Explicit Congestion Notification (FECN) bit lets the receiving router know that congestion exists in the path that the frame came from.
- **BECN** The Backward Explicit Congestion Notification (BECN) bit lets the receiving router know that congestion exists in the reverse of the path that the frame came from.
- **DE** If the Discard Eligibility (DE) bit is set on a frame, it means that this frame is eligible to be discarded if the Frame Relay network becomes congested.

FECN, BECN, and DE warrant further discussion. When the network becomes congested to the point that it cannot process new data transmissions, it begins to discard frames (frames with the DE bit set to 1). These discarded frames are retransmitted, thus causing more congestion. In an effort to prevent this situation, several mechanisms have been developed to notify user devices at the onset of congestion, so that the offered load may be reduced.

Two bits in the Frame Relay header are used to notify the user device that congestion is occurring on the line. They are the FECN bit and the BECN bit. The FECN is changed to 1 as a frame is sent downstream toward the destination location when congestion occurs during data transmission. In this way, all downstream nodes and the attached user device learn about congestion on the line. The BECN is changed to 1 in a frame traveling back toward the source of data transmission on a path where congestion is occurring. Thus, the source node is notified to slow down transmission until the congestion subsides.

The last two fields in a Frame Relay packet are also important:

- **User Data** Contains the upper layer data encapsulated in the Frame Relay packet. This field can vary in length up to a maximum of 16K bytes.
- **FCS** Used upon receipt of the packet to check the data for any errors that may have occurred during transmission. The transmitting station computes the value before transmission. The receiving station then does the same computation and verifies the value.

Committed Information Rate (CIR)

Committed Information Rate (CIR) is the minimum bandwidth consumed by the user at all times. CIR is usually less than the physical interface speed. The user could have a T1 port, with a CIR of 256K. The user can have data traffic bursting up to T1, but is guaranteed only 256K all the time. A Frame Relay network keeps track of the number of packets for a delta time. When the data rate exceeds CIR in the delta period, the Frame Relay network sets the rest of the packets with the DE bit until the delta expires. If the network is congested, it starts dropping the packets with DE bits, otherwise they will pass through the network. CIR is needed to guarantee certain bandwidth for normal data transmission needs. Certain applications such as file services, application services at a central location, or workstations at a branch location, need to communicate continuously to maintain network drive mappings and application database connections. These applications need certain guaranteed bandwidth.

The provisioning of a Frame Relay circuit with CIR guarantees bandwidth needed for standard applications. Provisioning different PVC's with a different CIR is possible and recommended. For example, the Central Office (CO) connects to two branch offices. Branch1 has 100 users, and Branch2 has 10 users. CO can connect to Frame Relay T1, with PVC1 to Branch1 at 512K CIR, and PVC2 to Branch2 with 64K CIR.

CIR rates can be set to minimize the cost of a Frame Relay circuit. The lower the CIR, the lower the cost. CIR is negotiated when purchasing the circuit from the provider.

Local Management Interface (LMI)

Local Management Interface (LMI) is a signaling (polling) protocol between a service provider network and an end-user device. Poll and acknowledgment (status) messages are exchanged between the user and the network at regular intervals (similar to keepalives on an Ethernet network.). In addition to the polling mechanism, which verifies connectivity, LMI is responsible for providing the end station with its local DLCI address, and keeping an eye on the status of the assigned DLCIs.

LMI Type

When configuring a router supporting Frame Relay, it is very important that the LMI type is correct—if it is incorrect, the Frame Relay circuit will not function properly. LMI signaling comes in three options:

- **ANSI** Annex D defined by American National Standards Institute (ANSI) standard T1.617. ANSI uses DLCI 0 to pass status information between the service provider's Frame Relay switch and the connected router.
- **Cisco** An LMI type developed jointly by StrataCom, Northern Telecom, DEC, and Cisco. This LMI type uses DLCI 1023 to pass status information between the service provider's Frame Relay switch and the connected router.
- **Q933a** ITU-T Q.933 Annex A. This LMI type also uses DLCI 0 to pass status information between the service provider's switch and the connected router. In addition, Q933a provides CIR information for each configured PVC.

All three LMI types accomplish the same thing—they each just do it a little differently. The network administrator must know what their LMI should be set to on their router. If the LMI type between communicating devices is different, the virtual circuit will not establish, DLCIs will not be assigned, and communication over the link will not be possible.

While Internetworking Operating System (IOS) software can autosense the LMI type from the provider network, there may be situations where the administrator needs to configure the type manually, which can be done by executing the following command on the appropriate interface.

```
frame-relay lmi-type {ansi | cisco | q933a}
```

Frame Relay Topologies

Frame Relay provides various mechanisms to connect many remote sites efficiently and economically. When every remote site has a direct connection to every other site, it is called a *fully meshed* network. This type of topology provides connectivity to every site, but it is rarely cost-justified and tends to be a lot harder to support. Figure 2.17 illustrates four remote sites connected together in a fully meshed network. Six network connections are needed to make it fully meshed. As the number of remote sites increase, the number of Frame Relay circuits increases exponentially; and so will the recurring charges for Frame Relay.

Figure 2.17 Fully Meshed Frame Relay

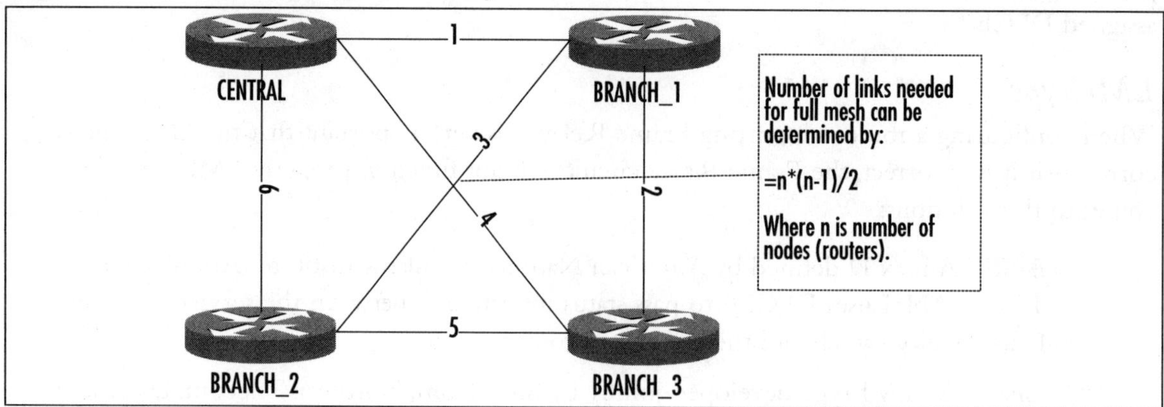

Every branch is guaranteed CIR, with a burst of up to physical port speed. If remote site connectivity (or redundancy) is an issue, a more cost effective method (instead of a fully meshed infrastructure) is to implement ISDN dial backup.

An alternative approach to a full meshed network is to implement a *partially meshed* network. A partially meshed network is also called a *hub-and-spoke network*. This kind of topology can be connected with n-1 connections. All the traffic comes to one central location and then is re-routed back to the appropriate branch location.

Hub-and-spoke designs are more efficient because the full connectivity can be achieved through a minimum number of connections. Hubs can be headquarters and spokes can be branch offices. Figure 2.18 shows Central as a hub, with Branch_1, Branch_2, and Branch_3 as spokes.

Figure 2.18 Hub-and-Spoke Frame Relay Network

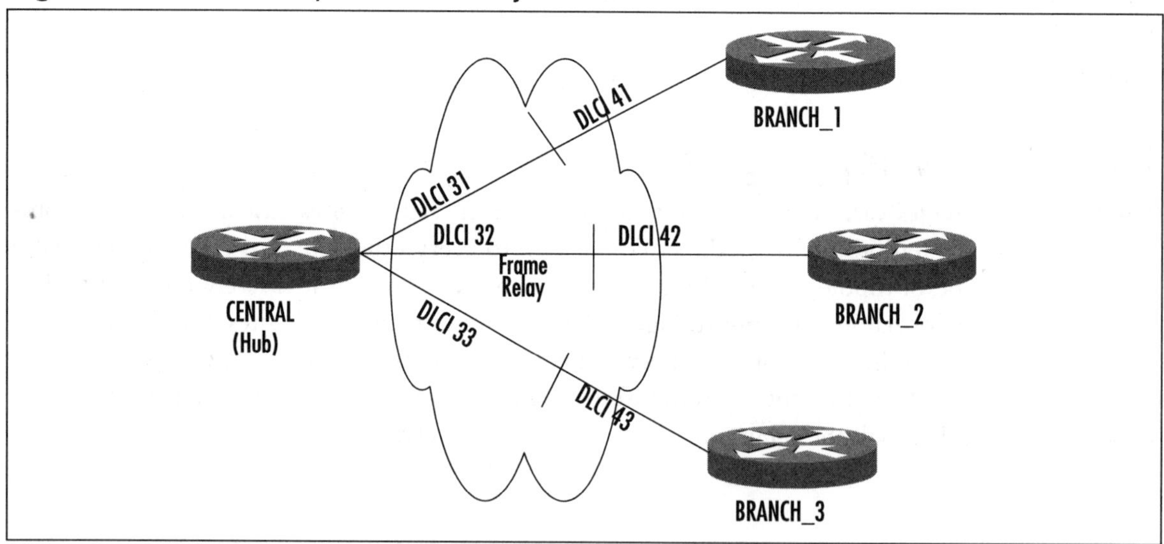

Be aware that split horizon issues may arise from any networks with degrees of meshing in them. Recall that routing processes will not advertise a route back out the interface on which it learned, which is a particular problem for hub-and-spoke topologies. For more information see Chapter 4, "IP Routing." Frame Relay is amenable to many types of interfaces and can be adjusted to fit certain requirements. Certain interfaces such as subinterfaces can be used to overcome limitations.

Subinterfaces

A single, physical interface can be logically divided into multiple, virtual subinterfaces. Subinterfaces are logical interfaces within a physical interface. Subinterfaces are ideal for mapping PVCs in Frame Relay, and VCs in ATM. With their help, nonbroadcast multiaccess (NBMA) networks like Frame Relay can be converted into point-to-point networks. With subinterfaces, split horizon is no longer an issue in Frame Relay.

The subinterface may be defined as either a *point-to-point* or *multipoint* connection. A point-to-point subinterface provides all the advantages of direct point-to-point links. Point-to-point links provide complete control over the traffic, like filtering through access lists and broadcast control.

Frame relay multipoint subinterfaces provide nonbroadcast multiaccess (NBMA), as shown in the following output. In multipoint situations all interfaces are part of a single subnet. Pinging your own IP address on a multipoint Frame Relay interface does not work, because Frame Relay multipoint subinterfaces are non-broadcast (unlike Frame Relay point-to-point subinterfaces).

```
Central Router Configuration
Central#
!
interface Serial0
ip address 192.168.101.1 255.255.255.0
encapsulation frame-relay
frame-relay lmi-type cisco
frame-relay map 192.168.101.2 31 !Maps PVC to Branch_1
frame-relay map 192.168.101.3 32 !Maps PVC to Branch_2
frame-relay map 192.168.101.4 33 !Maps PVC to Branch_3

Branch_1 Router Configuration
Branch_1#

interface Serial0
no ip address ! the ip address is supplied on the subinterface
encapsulation frame-relay
frame-relay lmi-type cisco
!
interface Serial0.41 multipoint
ip address 192.168.101.2 255.255.255.0
frame-relay map 192.168.101.1 41 ! Remote ip address maps to local DLCI
```

Branch_2 Router Configuration

```
Branch_2#
!
interface Serial0
no ip address
encapsulation frame-relay
frame-relay lmi-type cisco
!
interface Serial0.42 multipoint
ip address 192.168.101.3 255.255.255.0
frame-relay map 192.168.101.2 42
end
```

The number of subinterfaces on a given router is limited to 230. The number of DLCI's is limited to a maximum of 796. The Cisco 2500 series router can have 60 DLCIs and Cisco 7500 series provides a maximum of up to 720 DLCIs.

Configuring Frame Relay

Cisco routers can be configured as a Frame Relay switch (carrier side) or Frame Relay Customer Premise Equipment (CPE). Usually the only reason a Cisco router is configured as a Frame Relay switch is for lab and/or testing purposes. In carrier networks, Frame Relay switches like Cisco (Stratacom) or Lucent (Ascend) switches are used. A router as Data Terminal Equipment (DTE) connecting to the Frame Relay cloud is a more popular scenario.

The following is an example of Frame Relay hub-and-spoke configuration. (These configurations are based on Figure 2.18.)

```
Central>
interface Serial0
description Hub site Frame Relay T-1 circuit# 123456
no ip address
encapsulation frame-relay
frame-relay lmi-type ansi
!
interface Serial0.31 point-to-point
description 128k PVC BRANCH_1
ip address 192.168.30.1 255.255.255.0
frame-relay interface-dlci 31
!
interface Serial0.32 point-to-point
description 128k PVC to BRANCH_2 - circuit 31
ip address 192.168.31.1 255.255.255.0
frame-relay interface-dlci 32
```

```
!
interface Serial0.33 point-to-point
description 256k PVC to BRANCH_3 - circuit 32
ip address 192.168.32.1 255.255.255.0
frame-relay interface-dlci 33
!
```

<u>***Remote Sites Configuration*****</u>**

BRANCH_1

```
!
interface Serial0
no ip address
encapsulation frame-relay
frame-relay lmi-type ansi
!

interface Serial0.40 point-to-point
description 128k PVC to CENTRAL to BRANCH_1 - circuit 40
ip address 192.168.30.2 255.255.255.0
frame-relay interface-dlci 41
!
```

BRANCH_2>

```
!
interface Serial0
no ip address
encapsulation frame-relay
frame-relay lmi-type ansi
!
interface Serial0.41 point-to-point
description 128k PVC to CENTRAL to BRANCH_2- circuit 41
ip address 192.168.31.2 255.255.255.0
frame-relay interface-dlci 42
!
```

BRANCH_3>

```
interface Serial0
no ip address
encapsulation frame-relay
frame-relay lmi-type ansi
!
interface Serial0.42 point-to-point
description 256k PVC to CENTRAL to BRANCH_2- circuit 42
```

```
ip address 192.168.32.2 255.255.255.0
frame-relay interface-dlci 43
!
```

Verifying and Troubleshooting Frame Relay

Troubleshooting begins at the physical layer and then moves up to the network layer.

- Layer 1 (Physical layer)
- Layer 2 (Data Link layer, circuit level)
- Layer 3 (Network layer)

Physical Layer Troubleshooting

If you see "serial protocol up, line protocol up" during a **show interface** command, then the interface is physically up and operational. You may not have any physical level problems.

If you see "serial protocol up, line protocol down," then the interface is up from a software configuration point of view, but no physical signal connectivity is established. At this point, look at the leads like Clear to Send (CTS) and Ready to Send (RTS) to see if they are up. Check your cabling, and ensure that your provider has activated your circuit.

Use the **show interface serial 0** command to see the interface statistics for serial 0. The first line in the command output will indicate whether the interface and protocol are up or down. (In the following output example, both serial 0 and line protocol are up. This indicates that there are no problems with the circuit.)

```
Show interface serial 0
Serial0 is up, line protocol is up
Hardware is PowerQUICC Serial
Description: Frame Relay circuit 12345
MTU 1500 bytes, BW 1544 Kbit, DLY 20000 usec,
reliability 255/255, txload 1/255, rxload 1/255

! Makesure the encapsulation is frame relay.
Encapsulation FRAME-RELAY, loopback not set
Keepalive set (10 sec)
LMI enq sent 328460, LMI stat recvd 328460, LMI upd recvd 0, DTE
LMI up - LMI should be up
LMI enq recvd 0, LMI stat sent 0, LMI upd sent 0
LMI DLCI 0 LMI type is ANSI Annex D frame relay DTE ! Compare with
remote LMI type , both ! should be same
Broadcast queue 0/64, broadcasts sent/dropped 87/0, interface broadcasts 373
Last input 00:00:03, output 00:00:08, output hang never
Last clearing of "show interface" counters 5w3d
```

```
Queueing strategy: fifo
Output queue 0/40, 0 drops; input queue 0/75, 0 drops
5 minute input rate 0 bits/sec, 0 packets/sec
5 minute output rate 0 bits/sec, 0 packets/sec
392750 packets input, 24814146 bytes, 0 no buffer
Received 0 broadcasts, 0 runts, 0 giants, 0 throttles
10 input errors, 3 CRC, 3 frame, 0 overrun, 0 ignored, 4 abort
429748 packets output, 29450130 bytes, 0 underruns
0 output errors, 0 collisions, 1 interface resets !crc errors and
interface resets indicate there is !an issue with phyical line.
0 output buffer failures, 0 output buffers swapped out
0 carrier transitions
DCD=up DSR=up DTR=up RTS=up CTS=up
```

Verify that the cable is physically secure and connected. If this is a new installation, you may want to verify that this is the correct cable (**show controllers serial** can help, as shown).

```
Central# show control serial 0
Interface Serial0
Hardware is PowerQUICC MPC860
DTE V.35 TX and RX clocks detected.
idb at 0x8087CD18, driver data structure at 0x80882C28
SCC Registers:
```

If you do not see DTE V.35 or other cable type listed, then there is no cable connected between the router to the Channel Service Unit/Data Service Unit (DSU/CSU), or to the Smart Jack. The Smart Jack is an RJ48 jack provided by Telco and installed at the customer site. If you do not see the clock, you may have to provide the clock from an external source like the CSU/DSU. The clock is usually provided by the network (carrier); it maintains the transmit and receive signal. When you have verified all of the following and the problem still exists, verify the CRC counters, input errors, output errors, and carrier transitions.

```
!
10 input errors, 3 CRC, 3 frame, 0 overrun, 0 ignored, 4 abort
429748 packets output, 29450130 bytes, 0 underruns
0 output errors, 0 collisions, 1 interface resets !crc errors and
interface resets indicate there is !an issue with phyical line.
```

You may have a faulty line if these counters are consistently incrementing. This type of situation will need to be corrected by the carrier.

The **show frame pvc** command provides PVC status, network congestion details, and so forth. The following output is an example of the **show frame pvc** command in action.

```
Central# show frame pvc
PVC Statistics for interface Serial0 (Frame Relay DTE)
```

```
DLCI = 30, DLCI USAGE = LOCAL, PVC STATUS = ACTIVE, INTERFACE = Serial0
input pkts 20 output pkts 12376 in bytes 28400
out bytes 17462536 dropped pkts 0 in FECN pkts 0
in BECN pkts 0 out FECN pkts 0 out BECN pkts 0
in DE pkts 0 out DE pkts 0
pvc create time 5:22:21 last time pvc status changed 5:20:20
DLCI = 31, DLCI USAGE = LOCAL, PVC STATUS = ACTIVE, INTERFACE = Serial0
input pkts 30 output pkts 250 in bytes 42600
out bytes 355000 dropped pkts 0 in FECN pkts 0
in BECN pkts 0 out FECN pkts 0 out BECN pkts 0
in DE pkts 0 out DE pkts 0
pvc create time 10:22:21 last time pvc status changed 10:20:20
```

Loopback Tests

Loopback tests can be performed to verify Frame Relay connectivity at the physical layer. These tests help to isolate a problem with the Frame Relay circuit. Two types of loopback tests are typically run: local loopback and remote loopback.

Local Loopback

Local loopback tests check the connection between the local CSU/DSU and the local router. Set up the near-end CSU/DSU in local loopback, and check to see if the line comes up. If it does not come up, the potential areas to look at are:

- Faulty cable from router to CSU/DSU
- Faulty CSU/DSU
- Faulty router

Remote Loopback

Remote loopback tests check the connection between the local CSU/DSU and the remote router (the router on the other end of the Frame Relay circuit). Configure the local CSU/DSU to provide remote loopback. Monitor the far-end router. If the line comes up, local router, CSU/DSU, and serial circuit up to the remote CSU/DSU are functioning normally. In this situation one of these three could be faulty:

- Remote CSU/DSU
- Remote cable
- Remote router

Frame Relay Problems

Once you have verified that the physical line is not causing the problem, the next step is to begin looking into the data link layer (Layer 2) statistics.

The first item to verify in troubleshooting Frame Relay Layer 2 is whether the Frame Relay LMI type matches the Frame Relay service provider settings. Remember, if the LMI type differs between the two devices, communication will not take place. Using the **show frame-relay lmi** command, you should see what your LMI is set to and that status messages are being sent and received.

```
Central-1# show frame-relay lmi
LMI Statistics for interface Serial0 (Frame Relay DTE) LMI TYPE = ANSI
Invalid Unnumbered info 0 Invalid Prot Disc 0
Invalid dummy Call Ref 0 Invalid Msg Type 0
Invalid Status Message 0 Invalid Lock Shift 0
Invalid Information ID 0 Invalid Report IE Len 0
Invalid Report Request 0 Invalid Keep IE Len 0
Num Status Enq. Sent 328601 Num Status msgs Rcvd 328601
Num Update Status Rcvd 0 Num Status Timeouts 0
```

The debug frame-relay lmi Command

The debug command **debug frame-relay lmi** provides a variety of information, such as: Is the PVC active? Does the DLCI configured on the router match the DLCI broadcast by the carrier? Is the LMI type the same in the Frame Relay local switch and router?

Monitor the keepalives on the debug output.

```
!
*Jun 9 18:18:18.819: KA IE 3, length 2, yourseq 121, myseq 123
*Jun 9 18:18:18.819: PVC IE 0x7 , length 0x3 , dlci 31, status 0x2
   (indicates pvc status is active)
*Jun 9 18:18:18.819: KA IE 3, length 2, yourseq 122, myseq 124
```

Check to see if the PVC is active.

```
Central-1# show frame pvc
PVC Statistics for interface Serial0 (Frame Relay DTE)
Active Inactive Deleted Static
Local 1 1 0 0
Switched 0 0 0 0
Unused 1 2 0 0
DLCI = 30, DLCI USAGE = LOCAL, PVC STATUS = INACTIVE,
INTERFACE = Serial0.30
input pkts 0 output pkts 0 in bytes 0
out bytes 0 dropped pkts 0 in FECN pkts 0
```

```
in BECN pkts 0 out FECN pkts 0 out BECN pkts 0
in DE pkts 0 out DE pkts 0
out bcast pkts 0 out bcast bytes 0
pvc create time 5w0d, last time pvc status changed 5w0d
DLCI = 31, DLCI USAGE = LOCAL, PVC STATUS = ACTIVE, INTERFACE =
Serial0.31
input pkts 64061 output pkts 101345 in bytes 18983910
out bytes 24863788 dropped pkts 0 in FECN pkts 0
in BECN pkts 0 out FECN pkts 0 out BECN pkts 0
in DE pkts 64061 out DE pkts 0
out bcast pkts 87814 out bcast bytes 19797798
pvc create time 5w0d, last time pvc status changed 03:24:11
```

The following URL at Cisco Online provides Frame Relay troubleshooting links: www.cisco.com/univercd/cc/td/doc/cisintwk/itg_v1/tr1918.htm

The following commands can be used to further identify problems related to specific protocols like IP, Novell, AppleTalk, and DECNET:

- **debug frame-relay** Shows the packets coming into the router
- **debug frame-relay packet** Shows the packets going out of the router
- **debug frame-relay events** Provides information about Frame Relay Address Resolution Protocol (ARP) replies

The debug frame-relay Command

The following debugging scenario shows Frame Relay packets *received by* the Frame Relay interface. The data shows what type of protocol packet was received, on what DLCI, and the length of the packet.

```
Router1# debug frame-relay
Router1#
Router1# debug frame
Frame Relay debugging is on
Router1#
Serial2(i): dlci 102(0x1861), pkt type 0x800, datagramsize 96 !traffic coming in on
dlci 102, packet type is ip
Serial2(i): dlci 100(0x1841), pkt type 0x800, datagramsize 116
Serial2.30: Broadcast on DLCI 100 link 65(CDP) !Cisco discovery protocol packet
recieved
Serial2.30(o): dlci 100(0x1841), pkt type 0x2000(CDP), datagramsize 282
Serial2.32: Broadcast on DLCI 102 link 65(CDP)
Serial2.32(o): dlci 102(0x1861), pkt type 0x2000(CDP), datagramsize 282
broadcast dequeue
```

```
Serial2.30(o):Pkt sent on dlci 100(0x1841), pkt type 0x2000(CDP), datagramsize 282
```

The debug frame-relay packet Command

The **debug frame-relay packet** displays the packets being *transmitted through* the interface. The router is queuing Cisco Discovery Protocol (CDP) packets for broadcasting on the serial link. The output also shows IP packets (0x800) being transmitted.

```
Router1# debug frame-relay packet
Serial2.30(o):Pkt sent on dlci 100(0x1841), pkt type 0x2000(CDP), datagramsize 282
broadcast dequeue
Serial2.32(o):Pkt sent on dlci 102(0x1861), pkt type 0x2000(CDP), datagramsize 282
Serial2.30: broadcast search
Serial2.30(o): dlci 100(0x1841), pkt type 0x800(IP), datagramsize 96 broadcast dequeue
Serial2.30(o):Pkt sent on dlci 100(0x1841), pkt type 0x800(IP), datagramsize 96
Serial2.32: broadcast search
Serial2.32(o): dlci 102(0x1861), pkt type 0x800(IP), datagramsize 96 broadcast dequeue
```

Asynchronous Transfer Mode (ATM)

ATM is the building block of Broadband ISDN (B-ISDN) services. ATM is a technology developed to address the needs of both voice and data technologies. Voice traffic requires guaranteed bandwidth on a per-call basis for a call to be reliable. Data traffic is bursty and unpredictable. Voice packets are usually small compared to data packets. To address the requirements of both, ATM Forum and other standards organizations agreed to a 53-byte cell, with a 5-byte header and a 48-byte payload.

ATM technologies scale well at high speeds like OC3, OC12, and so on. Some of the features of ATM are:

- The edge devices provide error and flow control.
- There is no error control on data fields within the network, due to low transmission error rates on fiber.
- There is no flow control on links within the network.
- It is connection-oriented at the lowest level.
- All information is transferred in a virtual circuit assigned for the duration of the connection.
- A fixed cell (packet) size permits high-speed switching nodes.
- There is no constraint on data services (segmentation).
- It has an efficient cell structure for bandwidth allocation, and quality of service.

ATM Cell Format

Data is transported in fixed-length 53-byte cells. The efficiency and speed of ATM is due to its cell being a constant size and small size. Of the 53-bytes, 5 are reserved for the header, and 48 for data. Figure 2.19 depicts the UNI ATM cell format.

Figure 2.19 ATM Cell Format

Size in Bits	4	8	16	3	1	8	
	GFC	VPI	VCI	PTI	CLP	HEC	Data
			Header 5-bytes				48-byte Payload

- **Generic Flow Control (GFC)** Not used, but can support flow control and identify multiple devices connected to same interface.
- **Virtual Path Identifier (VPI)** VPI is 8 bits, which allows 256 virtual paths.
- **Virtual Circuit Identifier (VCI)** VCI is 16 bits, which allows 65K virtual circuits.
- **Payload Type Indicator (PTI)**
- **Cell Loss (CLP)** CLP is the cell loss priority bit, which if set, can discard the packet. This is similar to the DE bit in Frame Relay.
- **Header Error Control (HEC)** Checksum error control on the header itself. HEC is also used as a synchronizing delimiter; after three HEC matches the transmission is synchronized.
- **Payload** 48-bytes of data.

ATM Adaptation Layer (AAL)

The ATM Adaptation Layer (AAL) provides mapping of higher layer application data to and from the ATM cell. AAL provides a Segmentation Assembly and Re-assembly (SAR) layer. It detects lost cells and errors in cells through a 4-bit sequence number protection. Several AAL types are defined, with each type consisting of a separate SAR sublayer:

- **AAL Type 1** Used for connection-oriented, constant-bit-rate services and for circuit emulation.
- **AAL Type 2** Used for connection-oriented, variable-bit-rate services, and for video applications.
- **AAL Type 3/4** AAL Types 3 and 4 are combined; they are designed for data applications and support both connectionless and connection-oriented applications.
- **AAL Type 5** A more commonly used protocol, applied to Variable Bit Rate (VBR) type traffic. AAL Type 5 is used for signaling and Frame Relay over ATM.

The AAL provides the benefits of error detection, circuit emulation, and connectionless or connection-oriented services, depending on the type of AAL used.

ATM Virtual Circuits

ATM virtual circuits are built on top of a VPI/VCI combination. A VC bundle inside of a VP is used to differentiate traffic (like voice, video, and data). The VPI/VCI combination is significant on a physical link between a pair of ATM switches. These circuits are unidirectional, and need mapping in reverse directions to complete conversation between two end-node devices. Circuits can be established as PVCs or SVCs. More popularly used circuits are PVCs, which need mapping and configuration at each ATM switch along the path. SVCs are more dynamic; hence they build and tear the sessions automatically.

Figure 2.20 illustrates that on a given physical ATM network, the VP are the virtual paths that are uniquely identified through VPI. In every virtual path, multiple virtual channels can be defined. VPI is 8 bits long (256 virtual paths), and VCI is 16 bits long (64K circuits), thus providing 256* 64k circuits. The number of channels available gives the granularity needed to provide quality of service (QoS). Each circuit is a VPI/VCI combination. VPI zero (VPI=0) is reserved.

Figure 2.20 VPI/VCI Path and Physical Circuit Relationship

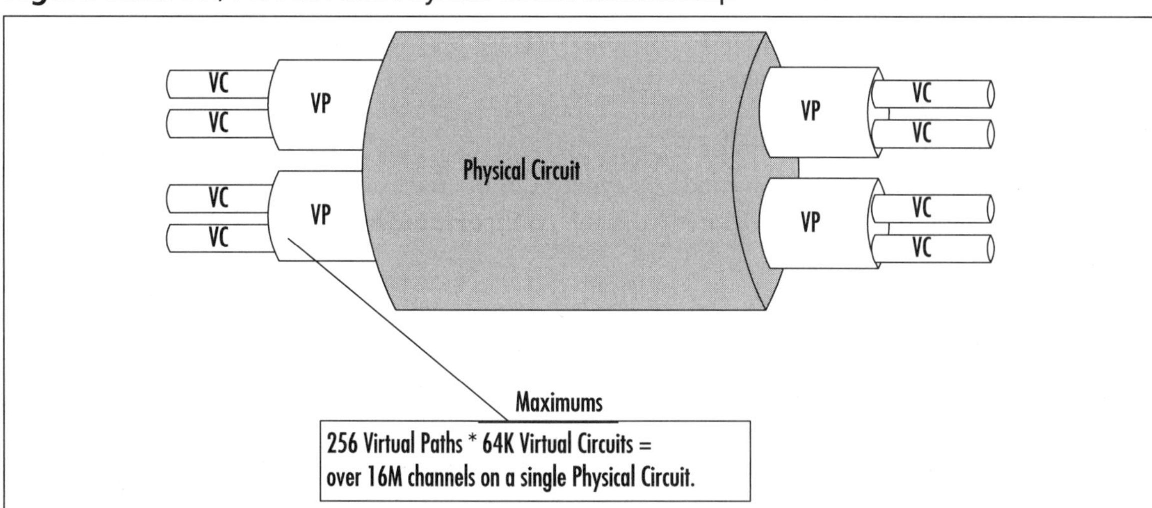

PVC Mapping and Circuit Buildup

Table 2.1 and Figure 2.21 demonstrate PVC mapping and circuit buildup. Notice how the ports, VCI, and VPI in the table relate and map to the switch diagram. Remember, PVC's need to be manually configured on each switch.

Table 2.1 PVC Mapping

Input Port	VPI	VCI	Output	VPI	VCI
1	10	20	2	20	10
2	20	10	1	10	20
3	30	15	4	31	16
4	40	16	3	30	15

Figure 2.21 PVC Mapping and Circuit Creation

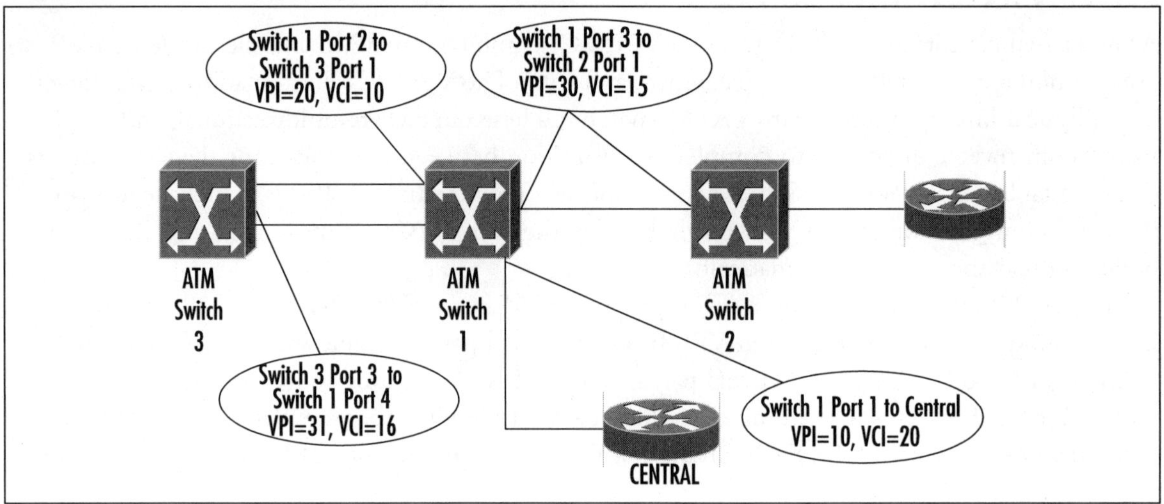

In the case of Cisco routers with an ATM Interface Processor (AIP), the PVC's are mapped point-to-point, or point-to-multipoint.

Configuring ATM

Configuring routers for ATM is similar to any other interface on Cisco routers. Set up the interface subsystem in the configuration mode by typing the interface-related detailed syntax. Figure 2.22 illustrates how to build an ATM network; the configurations are provided as well, using PVC's.

Figure 2.22 ATM PVC Configuration.

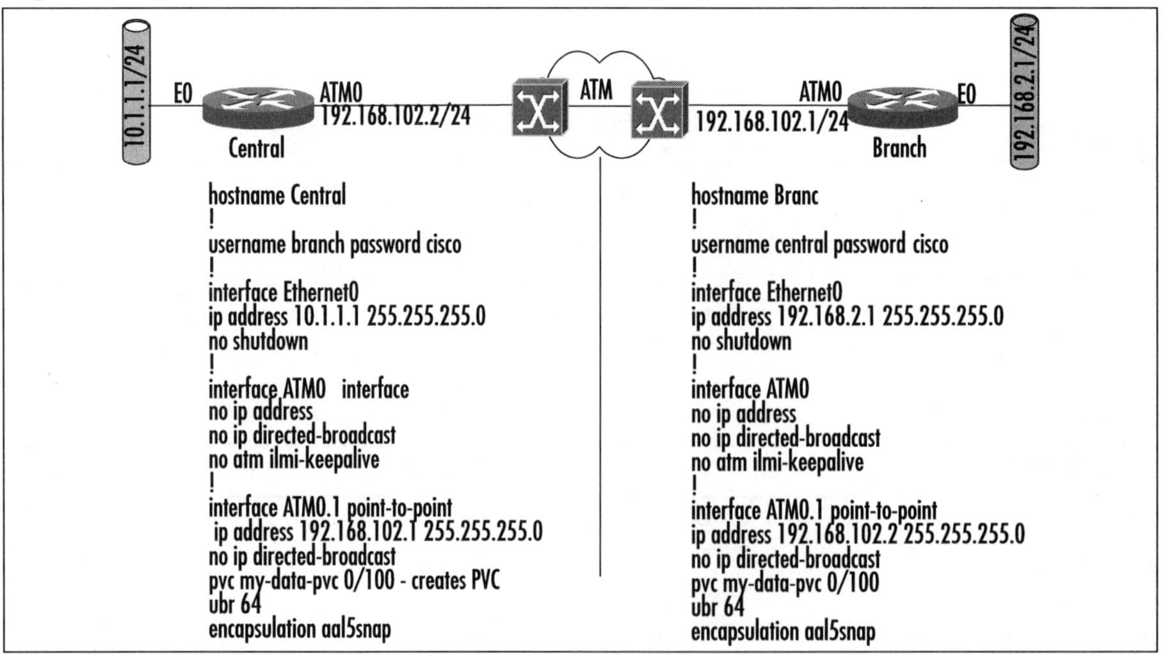

Verifying and Troubleshooting ATM

The methodology applied in troubleshooting ATM networks uses show and debug commands relevant to ATM. Various commands that can be used to monitor an ATM network include the following:

```
Router1# show atm ?
arp-server          ATM ARP Server Table
class-links         ATM vc-class links
ilmi-configuration  Display Top level ILMI
ilmi-status         Display ATM Interface ILMI information
interface           Interfaces and ATM information
map                 ATM static mapping
pvc                 ATM PVC information
signalling          ATM Signaling commands
svc                 ATM SVC information
traffic             ATM statistics
vc                  ATM VC information
vp                  ATM VP information

Router1# show interface atm 0
ATM0 is up, line protocol is up
Hardware is PQUICC Atom1
MTU 1500 bytes, sub MTU 1500, BW 1536 Kbit, DLY 20000 usec,
reliability 255/255, txload 1/255, rxload 1/255
Encapsulation ATM, loopback not set -  shows the encapsulation mode
on the interface
Keepalive not supported
Encapsulation(s):, PVC mode
   1024 maximum active VCs, 2 current VCCs shows Virtual channels supported
VC idle disconnect time: 300 seconds
Last input 00:00:00, output never, output hang never
Last clearing of "show interface" counters never
Input queue: 0/75/0 (size/max/drops); Total output drops: 0
Queueing strategy: weighted fair
 Output queue: 0/1000/64/0 (size/max total/threshold/drops)
Conversations 0/0/256 (active/max active/max total)
Reserved Conversations 0/0 (allocated/max allocated)
5 minute input rate 0 bits/sec, 0 packets/sec
5 minute output rate 0 bits/sec, 0 packets/sec
13 packets input, 1008 bytes, 0 no buffer
Received 0 broadcasts, 0 runts, 0 giants, 0 throttles
```

```
0 input errors, 0 CRC, 0 frame, 0 overrun, 0 ignored, 0 abort
15 packets output, 1166 bytes, 0 underruns
0 output errors, 0 collisions, 2 interface resets
0 output buffer failures, 0 output buffers swapped out
```

The following command shows the details of the subinterface ATM 0.1.

```
Router1# show interface atm 0.1
ATM0.1 is up, line protocol is up
Hardware is PQUICC Atom1
Internet address is 10.0.23.2/24
MTU 1500 bytes, BW 1536 Kbit, DLY 20000 usec,
reliability 255/255, txload 1/255, rxload 1/255
    Encapsulation ATM
12 packets input, 874 bytes
15 packets output, 1106 bytes
0 OAM cells input, 0 OAM cells output
```

The following command shows traffic across the ATM link.

```
Router1# show atm traffic
13 Input packets
14 Output packets
0 Broadcast packets
0 Packets received on non-existent VC
0 Packets attempted to send on non-existent VC
0 OAM cells received
F5 InEndloop: 0, F5 InSegloop: 0, F5 InAIS: 0, F5 InRDI: 0
F4 InEndloop: 0, F4 InSegloop: 0, F4 InAIS: 0, F4 InRDI: 0
0 OAM cells sent
F5 OutEndloop: 0, F5 OutSegloop: 0, F5 OutRDI: 0
F4 OutEndloop: 0, F4 OutSegloop: 0, F4 OutRDI: 0
0 OAM cell drops
```

The following command shows the PVC status.

```
Router1# show atm pvc
On ATM 0.1 interface , my-data-pvc has VPI=0, VCI =100, encapsulation
is SNAP.
Router1# show atm pvc
VCD / Peak Avg/Min Burst
Interface Name VPI VCI Type Encaps SC Kbps Kbps
Cells Sts
0.1 my-data-pv 0 100 PVC SNAP UBR 64 UP
```

```
0.2 my-voice-p 0 200 PVC VOICE VBR 384 192
48 UP (192)
```

The following command shows the mapping between IP addresses and PVCs.

```
Router1# show atm pvc map
Map list ATM0.1_ATM_INARP : DYNAMIC
ip 10.0.23.3 maps to VC 1, VPI 0, VCI 100, ATM0.1
```

ATM Debug Commands

In addition to the show commands, there are also numerous debug commands that can be used to capture information on ATM events as they occur.

```
Router1# debug atm ?

aal-crc      Display CRC error packets
arp Show     ATM ARP events
compress     ATM Compression
errors       ATM errors
events       ATM or FUNI Events
ilmi         Show ILMI events
oam Dump     OAM Cells
packet       ATM or FUNI packets
pvcd         Show PVCD events
sig-all      ATM Signalling all
sig-api      ATM Signalling api
sig-error    ATM Signalling errors
sig-events   ATM Signalling events
sig-ie       ATM Signalling information elements
sig-packets ATM Signalling packets
smap-all     ATM Signalling Static Map all
smap-error   ATM Signalling Static Map errors
smap-events ATM Signalling Static Map events
state        ATM or FUNI VC States
```

Following are several **ATM debug** commands that further aid in troubleshooting ATM implementations.

The debug atm packet Command

The **debug atm packet** command displays all ATM packets.

```
Router1# debug atm packet
ATM packets debugging is on
Displaying all ATM packets
```

```
Router1# conf terminal
Enter configuration commands, one per line. End with CNTL/Z.
Router1(config)# int atm 0
Router1(config-if)# shut
Router1(config-if)# no shut
Router1(config-if)# exit
Router1(config)# exit
Router1# show logging
Syslog logging: enabled (0 messages dropped, 0 flushes, 0 overruns)
Console logging: disabled
Monitor logging: level debugging, 0 messages logged
Buffer logging: level debugging, 351 messages logged
Trap logging: level informational, 47 message lines logged Log Buffer (4096 bytes):
04:45:47: %SYS-5-CONFIG_I: Configured from console by console
04:46:06: %LINK-5-CHANGED: Interface ATM0, changed state to administratively down
04:46:07: %LINEPROTO-5-UPDOWN: Line protocol on Interface ATM0, changed state to down
04:46:21: ATM0.1(O): VCD:0x1 VPI:0x0 VCI:0x64 DM:0x100 SAP:AAAA CTL:03 OUI:000000
TYPE:0800 Length:0x56
   !Shows the 1/100 (64hex) pvc sending an ip packet type0800.
04:46:21: 45C0 004A 0000 0000 0209 96EA 0A00 1702 FFFF FFFF 1105 0001 0003 0000 0000
04:46:21: 53C9 0002 0000 0064 0003 E805 DCFF 0100 0003 00FF FFFF 0100 0501 1043 6973
04:46:21: 0017 0000 07D0 0019 6E05 DCFF 0100
04:46:21:
04:46:22: ATM0.1(O): --o -Outgoing packet VCD:0x1 VPI:0x0 VCI:0x64 DM:0x100 SAP:AAAA
CTL:03 OUI:000000 TYPE:0806 Length:0x20 Arp packet type 0806
04:46:22: 0013 0800 0000 0008 0400 0004 0A00 1702 0000 0000
04:46:22:
04:46:22: ATM0.1(I):
VCD:0x1 VPI:0x0 VCI:0x64 Type:0x0 SAP:AAAA CTL:03 OUI:000000 TYPE:0806 Length:0x20
04:46:22: 0013 0800 0000 0009 0400 0004 0A00 1703 0A00 1702
04:46:23: %LINK-3-UPDOWN: Interface ATM0, changed state to up
04:46:24: %LINEPROTO-5-UPDOWN: Line protocol on Interface ATM0, changed state to up
04:46:25: %SYS-5-CONFIG_I: Configured from console by console
04:46:34: ATM0.1(I): VCD:0x1 VPI:0x0 VCI:0x64 Type:0x0 SAP:AAAA CTL:03 OUI:000000
TYPE:0800 Length:0x56
04:46:34: 45C0 004A 0000 0000 0109 97E9 0A00 1703 FFFF FFFF 1101 0001 0003 0000 0000
04:46:34: 8030 0002 0000 0834 0019 6E05 DCFF 0101 0003 0000 0064 0003 E805 DCFF 0100
04:46:34: 0017 0000 07D0 0019 6E05 DCFF 0100
```

The debug atm state Command

Use the **debug atm state** command to see changes in the state of the ATM VCs.

```
Router1# debug atm state
ATM VC States debugging is on
Router1# conf terminal
Enter configuration commands, one per line. End with CNTL/Z.
Router1(config)# int atm 0
Router1(config-if)# shut
Router1(config-if)# no shut
Router1(config-if)# exit
Router1(config)# exit
Router1# show logging
Log Buffer (4096 bytes):
04:48:02: %SYS-5-CONFIG_I: Configured from console by console
04:48:18: %SYS-5-CONFIG_I: Configured from console by console
04:48:40: %LINK-5-CHANGED: Interface ATM0, changed state to administratively down
04:48:41: %LINEPROTO-5-UPDOWN: Line protocol on Interface ATM0, changed state to down
04:49:12: %LINK-3-UPDOWN: Interface ATM0, changed state to up
04:49:13: %LINEPROTO-5-UPDOWN: Line protocol on Interface ATM0, changed state to up
04:49:18: %SYS-5-CONFIG_I: Configured from console by console
```

The following conversation provides ATM VC status.

```
04:51:08: Changing vc 0/100vc-state to ATM_VC_SHUTTING_DOWN
04:51:08: Changing vc 0/100vc-state to ATM_VC_NOT_IN_SERVICE
04:51:08: Changing vc 0/100vc-state to ATM_VC_NOT_IN_SERVICE
04:51:08: Changing vc 0/200vc-state to ATM_VC_SHUTTING_DOWN
04:51:08: Changing vc 0/200vc-state to ATM_VC_NOT_IN_SERVICE
04:51:08: Changing vc 0/200vc-state to ATM_VC_NOT_IN_SERVICE
04:51:10: %LINK-5-CHANGED: Interface ATM0, changed state to administratively down
04:51:11: %LINEPROTO-5-UPDOWN: Line protocol on Interface ATM0, changed state to down
04:51:41: Changing vc 0/100 vc-state to ATM_VC_NOT_VERIFIED
04:51:41: Changing vc 0/100 vc-state to ATM_VC_ESTABLISHING_VC
04:51:41: Changing vc 0/100 vc-state to ATM_VC_NOT_VERIFIED
04:51:41: Changing vc 0/100 vc-state to ATM_VC_UP
04:51:41: Changing vc 0/200 vc-state to ATM_VC_NOT_VERIFIED
04:51:41: Changing vc 0/200 vc-state to ATM_VC_ESTABLISHING_VC
04:51:41: Changing vc 0/200 vc-state to ATM_VC_NOT_VERIFIED
04:51:41: Changing vc 0/200 vc-state to ATM_VC_UP
04:51:43: %LINK-3-UPDOWN: Interface ATM0, changed state to up
04:51:44: %LINEPROTO-5-UPDOWN: Line protocol on Interface ATM0, changed state to up
```

The debug atm ilmi Command

The **debug atm ilmi** command provides detailed Integrated Local Management Interface(ILMI) conversations. ILMI is used for a variety of ATM functions, from interface type identification (UNI versus NNI) to address registration functions. A failure of ILMI operations can curtail the ATM interfaces.

```
Router1# debug atm ilmi
Setting ILMI debug for all interfaces.
Router1# configure terminal
Enter configuration commands, one per line. End with CNTL/Z.
 Router1(config)# int atm 0
Router1(config-if)# shut
Router1(config-if)# no shut
Router1(config-if)# exit
Router1(config)# exit
Router1# show log
Syslog logging: enabled (0 messages dropped, 0 flushes, 0 overruns)
Console logging: disabled
Monitor logging: level debugging, 0 messages logged
Buffer logging: level debugging, 529 messages logged
Trap logging: level informational, 67 message lines logged
Log Buffer (4096 bytes):
   ILMI conversation starts here
tion error on o/g ILMI Pdu <ilmi_send_pkt> (ATM0)
04:57:33: ILMI: Unable to Send Pdu out <ilmi_send_trap> sends an SNMP
   trap
04:57:35: ILMI(ATM0): Sending ilmiColdStart trap
04:57:35: ILMI(ATM0): No ILMI VC found
04:57:35: ILMI: Encapsulation error on o/g ILMI Pdu <ilmi_send_pkt> (ATM0)
04:57:35: ILMI: Unable to Send Pdu out <ilmi_send_trap>
04:57:37: ILMI(ATM0): Sending ilmiColdStart trap
04:57:37: ILMI(ATM0): No ILMI VC found
04:57:37: ILMI: Encapsulation error on o/g ILMI Pdu <ilmi_send_pkt> (ATM0)
04:57:37: ILMI: Unable to Send Pdu out <ilmi_send_trap>
04:57:38: ILMI(ATM0): Received Interface Down. Shutting down ILMI
04:57:40: %LINK-5-CHANGED: Interface ATM0, changed state to administratively down
04:57:41: %LINEPROTO-5-UPDOWN: Line protocol on Interface ATM0, changed state to down
04:58:01: ILMI(ATM0): Received Interface Up
04:58:01: ILMI(ATM0): Sending ilmiColdStart trap
04:58:01: ILMI(ATM0): No ILMI VC found
 04:58:01: ILMI: Encapsulation error on o/g ILMI Pdu <ilmi_send_pkt> (ATM0)
```

```
04:58:01: ILMI: Unable to Send Pdu out <ilmi_send_trap>
04:58:03: %LINK-3-UPDOWN: Interface ATM0, changed state to up
Router1#no debug all
```

Integrated Services Digital Network

ISDN is an International Telecommunication Union Telecommunication Standardization (ITU-T) standard and technology for digital technology that supplements traditional analog telephony. ISDN differs from traditional analog telephone service (public switched telephone network [PSTN]) in that it is completely digital. To transmit data across the PSTN requires that computers convert digital data into an analog stream, and then reconvert back into digital data at the receiving end. The analog PSTN was developed purely for transmission of voice communications, which limits its data bandwidth and transmission quality. The maximum speed for analog data transfer across PSTN networks is 56 Kbps (assuming that a lot of prerequisites are met such as similar equipment, clean connection, and so forth). Analog data connections require a significant amount of time to establish.

ISDN was developed to fix the problems encountered in the PSTN. In order to make ISDN a public network, standards had to be developed for all companies to follow. The International Consultative Committee for Telegraph and Telephone (CCITT) developed the ISDN standards and specifications. The CCITT became the ITU-T. ISDN is a group of digital services allowing high-speed transmissions of data, voice, and video. It is an end-to-end digital services network. The ITU-T developed groups of standard protocols separated by content.

- **E Series** The E series protocols deal with telephone network standards for ISDN.
- **I Series** The I series protocols deal with various aspects of the ISDN standard.
- **Q Series** The Q series standards deal with call setup and switching processes.

For a complete list of each of these standards, as well as all other ITU-T standards, go to www.itu.int/itu-t/rec.

The ISDN standards focus on how the end-user communicates with the network. In addition to the ITU-T, there are several other organizations involved in setting the standards for ISDN. These organizations work together and, through the ANSI, develop and assure the standards for ISDN.

The actual ISDN circuits consist of channels distinguished by function and bit rate. There are three different channels in the ISDN service model: B channel, D channel, and H channel. ISDN lines can be ordered in several different configurations of grouping of these channels. BRI and PRI are two of the most common groupings. Below are details of the three channel types.

- **B Channel** Used for user services including data, audio, and video, and operates at 64 Kbps (56 Kbps in older equipment) in full-duplex mode.
- **D Channel** Used for signaling between the user and the network, and can carry user packet mode data. The D channel operates at either 16 Kbps or 64 Kbps in full duplex, depending on the interface in use. Both the B and D channels are fully digitized.

- **H Channel** Used in applications that require bit rates higher than the 64 Kbps offered in the B channel. There are four H channels: H0, H10, H11, and H12.
  - H0 is equivalent to six B channels for a total capacity of 384 Kbps.
  - H10 is equivalent to 23 B channels for a total capacity of 1.472 Mbps.
  - The H11 channel is used when the circuit is a T1 line. This is equivalent to 24 B channels for a total capacity of 1.536 Mbps.
  - The H12 channel is used when the circuit is an E1 line. This is equivalent to 30 B channels for a total capacity of 1.92 Mbps.

Basic Rate Interface (BRI)

Small businesses and home users typically use the BRI for remote connectivity and the Internet. Another use for BRI lines is as a backup connection should a primary WAN link fail. The BRI is comprised of two B channels and one D channel, commonly referred to as 2B+D. The available bandwidth of the BRI is:

$$(2 \cdot 64\text{Kbps}) + 16\text{Kbps} = 144\text{Kbps}$$

There are an additional 48 Kbps of bandwidth required to allow the physical connection to operate, giving a total bit rate of 192 Kbps. However, in most cases, the usable bandwidth for data across a BRI line is 128Kbps.

BRI Call Setup

Only the D channel is involved in setting up and breaking down an ISDN call. The following describes what happens at each numbered step in the call setup process, as shown in Figure 2.23.

1. The call is initiated over the D channel. The called number is sent to the CO ISDN switch.
2. The CO ISDN switch sets up a path to the destination switch using the SS7 protocol.
3. The remote switch sends a signal over the remote D channel activating the remote end.
4. The remote end answers the call and establishes a data session through the B channel.

Figure 2.23 ISDN BRI Call Setup Process

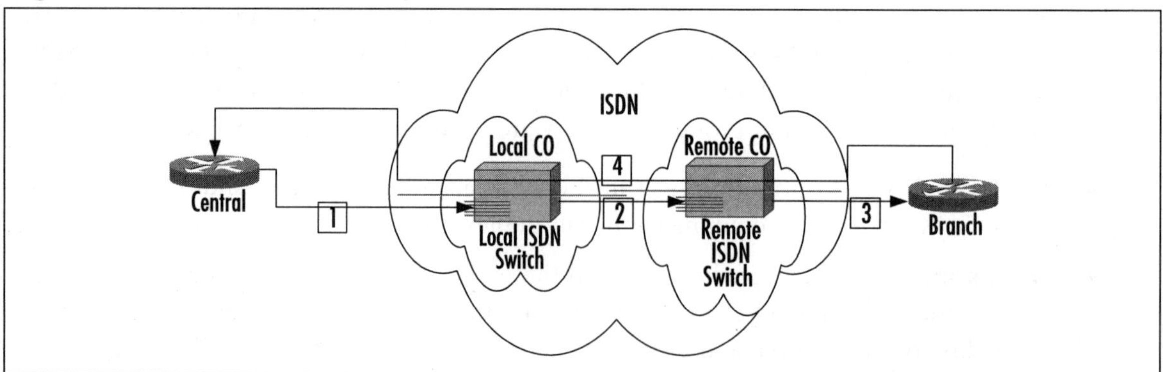

BRI Reference Points and Functional Groups

ISDN reference points identify architectural separations at the customer's site. The functional groups identify the equipment involved in ISDN BRI circuits. Figure 2.24 shows the reference points in relation to the functional groups.

Figure 2.24 ISDN BRI Reference Points and Functional Groups

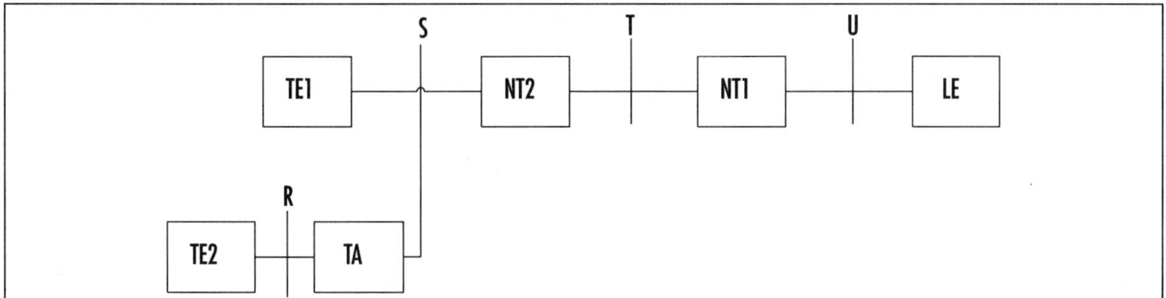

The functional groups from Figure 2.24 are:

- **TE2 (Terminal Equipment 2)** A device that is not compatible with ISDN, such as an analog telephone or a router without an ISDN interface.
- **TA (Terminal Adapter)** Converts standard electrical signals from non-ISDN devices into a form compatible with ISDN. The TA is the link between non-ISDN equipment and the ISDN network.
- **TE1 (Terminal Equipment 1)** A device that is compatible with ISDN, such as a digital telephone or a router with an ISDN interface. It interoperates with ISDN natively, with no additional equipment needed.
- **NT2 (Network Termination 2)** A device that directs traffic to and from the user devices and the NT1, such as a private branch exchange (PBX).
- **NT1 (Network Termination 1)** The device that connects the ISDN wiring (four-wire ISDN wiring) to the conventional local loop (two-wire standard wiring).
- **LE (Local Exchange)** The ISDN switch residing in the CO.

The reference points from Figure 2.24 are:

- **R (Rate)** Reference point between TA and non-ISDN (TE2) device.
- **S (System)** Reference point between NT2 and TE1 or TA that connects the terminals to the ISDN network. The System reference point is the most important point for users.
- **T (Terminal)** Reference point between NT2 and NT1. Both the T and S reference points use the same characteristics and are often represented as S/T.
- **U (User)** Reference point between NT1 and LE, which is only specified by ANSI (not by CCITT) and is only used in North America.

Primary Rate Interface (PRI)

PRI lines are used where more bandwidth is required. They are also used as a dial-up access line giving an organization up to 30 (23 in North America and Japan) 64 Kbps lines. There are several different configurations for the PRI. In North America and Japan, the configuration is noted as 23B+D, or 23 B channels and one D channel operating at 64 Kbps. The bit rate of this type of PRI is (24 · 64 Kpbs) =1.544 Mbps, which is equivalent to a T1. Another configuration of the PRI is noted as 30B+D, which provides a total capacity of 2.048 Mbps, which is equivalent to an E1. 30B+D PRI is commonly offered in Europe and Australia.

PRI Reference Points and Functional Groups

The reference points for PRI lines are simpler than for BRI lines. The functions of the reference points are the same as in the BRI line. The major difference is that PRI does not support multiple ISDN devices on the same line, whereas a BRI network supports connecting multiple devices to the same line. As shown in Figure 2.25, in PRI lines the TE connects directly to the DSU/CSU, which then connects to the LE. The DSU/CSU is similar to a modem but does not convert digital signals into analog signals. Since no support for non-ISDN multiple devices exist, the reference points and functional groups for the PRI line can be kept simple.

Figure 2.25 ISDN PRI Reference Points and Functional Groups

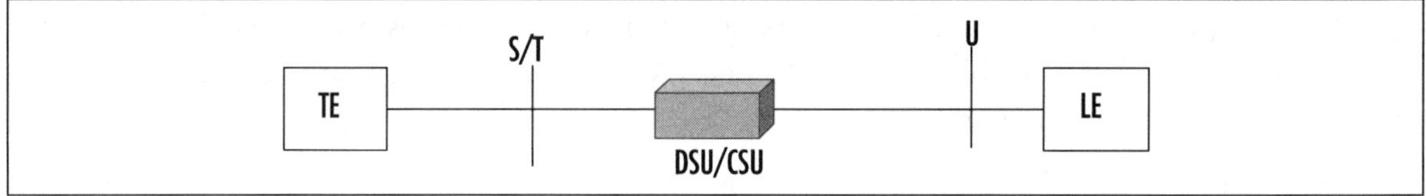

ISDN Protocol Layers

ISDN uses different protocols for control signaling and user data. The protocols can be correlated to the OSI reference model. The OSI reference model regulates all communication between systems to ensure interoperability between vendors.

Since signaling protocols and user data protocols are different yet still operate in the same OSI layers, it further divides the OSI model into protocol planes. The user plane (U-plane) contains the protocols required for sending user data such as voice, video and data. The control plane (C-plane) contains the protocols necessary for exchanging control signaling. Finally, the management plane (M-plane) controls the flow of traffic between the U-plane and the C-plane. All of these planes can operate on the same layers of the OSI model simultaneously.

ISDN services or bearer services operate at the first three layers of the OSI model (see Figure 2.26). These services allow for user-to-user communication and for transmitting all processed information. The actual processing of information takes place at Layers 4 through 7 of the OSI model, which are the responsibility of the computer, not the network.

The B channel carries user data that directly correlates to the U-plane, and the D channel carries signaling information that directly correlates to the C-plane.

Figure 2.26 OSI Reference Model and ISDN Protocols

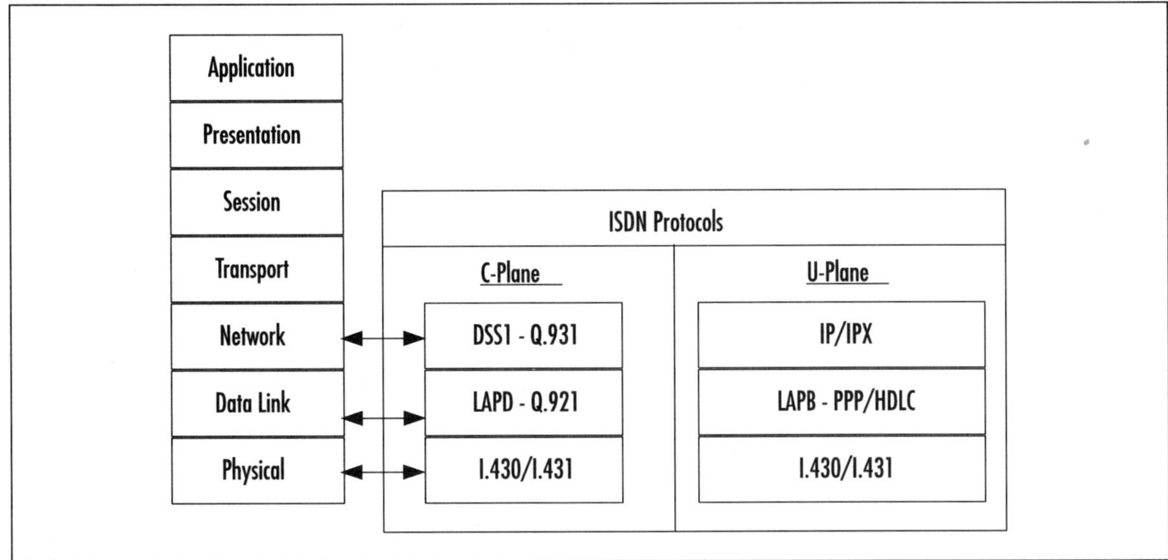

U-plane

At Layer 1, or the physical layer, the B channel is specified by both I.430 for BRI functionality and I.431 for PRI functionality. At this layer, the B channel performs circuit switching, packet switching, and leased circuitry. For both circuit-switched and leased circuits, control signals set up the circuit and the ISDN network does not need to use any Layer 2 or 3 protocols.

When a packet-switched circuit is set up, the X.25 protocols run at Layers 2 and 3 allowing the exchange of data. The Layer 2 protocol for packet-switched circuits is known as Link Access Procedure for the B channel (LAPB). Once LAPB establishes the Layer 2 connection, the Layer 3 connection can be established. Layer 3 protocols on the B channel can be any OSI Layer 3 protocol such as IP or IPX.

C-plane

The D channel operates at the same physical medium as the B channel. Because of this, its physical layer protocols are the same as B channel on both the BRI and PRI. For the D channel, the Layer 2 protocol for packet-switched circuits is known as Link Access Procedure for the D channel (LAPD). LAPD is specified under ITU-T Q.920 and Q.921 standards. The CCITT did not make LAPD a requirement, only a recommendation (I.440 and I.441). The D channel has several Layer 3 protocols to choose from. The most commonly used Layer 3 protocol is Q.931.

ISDN Call Setup and Teardown

Figure 2.27 shows how the call setup process takes place using the Q.931 protocol. Not every ISDN switch uses the same procedures for both call setup and teardown. Figures 2.27 and 2.28 show the setup and teardown of a call through a typical ISDN switch. In addition to the steps shown, an optional progress message can also pass through the system. Not all of these messages are required to take place when placing an ISDN call.

Figure 2.27 ISDN D Channel Call Setup

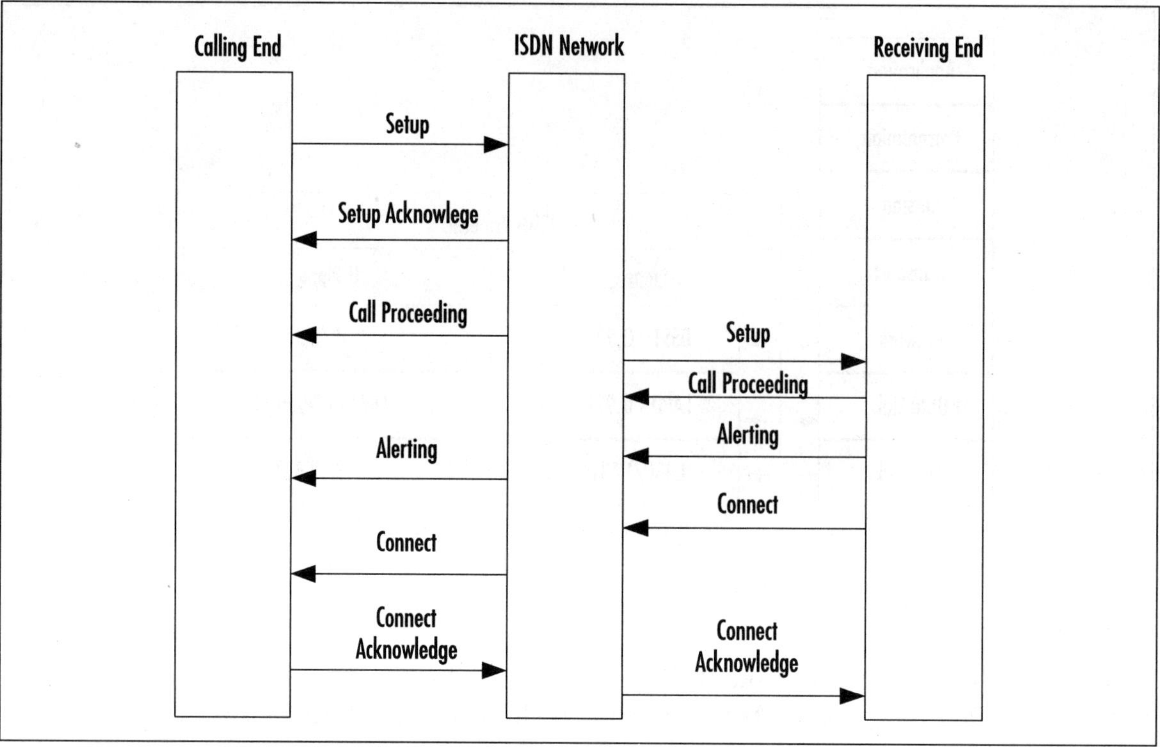

Figure 2.28 ISDN D Channel Call Teardown

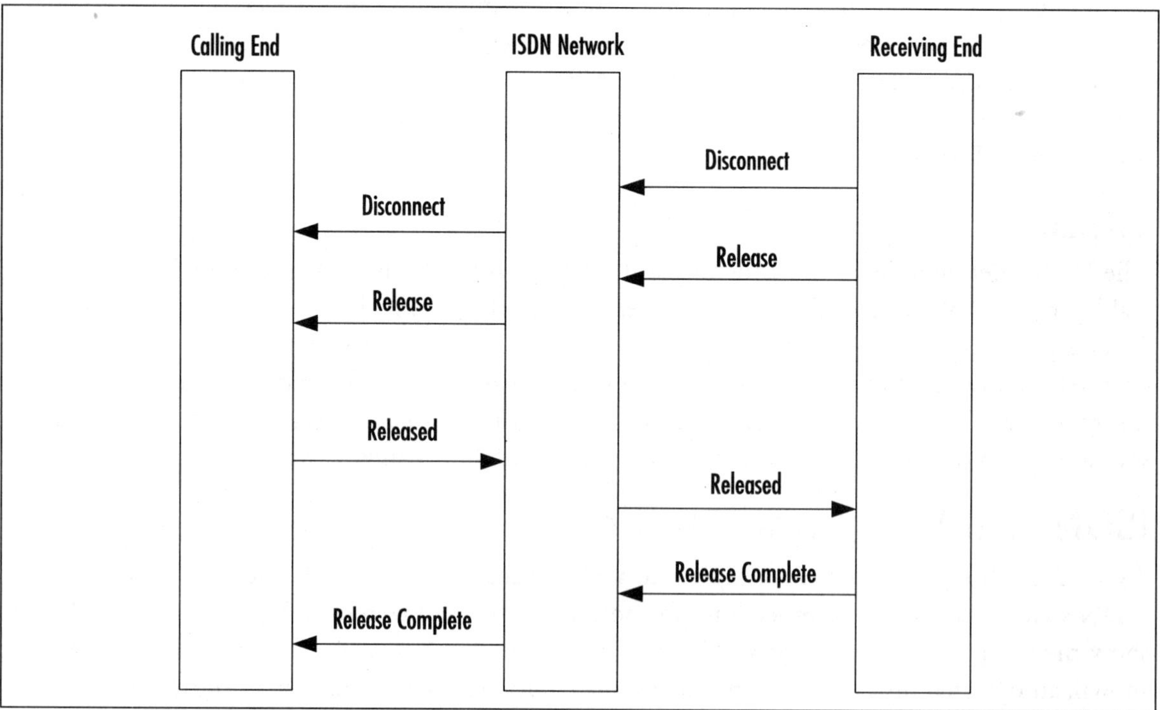

So far, this chapter has focused on what ISDN is. But, what can ISDN do for a network? It can be used to support dial lines as well as backup WAN circuits. ISDN can also help the routing.

Dial-on-Demand Routing (DDR)

DDR is a technology that routers use to dynamically initiate and close a circuit-switched session to remote routers on demand. Once these sessions have been connected, data as well as routing updates can be exchanged between routers. In order for the router to initiate this session, it must first know when to dial. This is accomplished by defining *interesting traffic* that will initiate the session.

Once the call has been established, data can pass to the other end. The DDR session is typically not broken until there is a period of inactivity determined by the *idle-time* value. Multiple locations can be configured to dial based on routing destination. There are several features built into DDR that enhance its operation.

DDR typically runs on an as-needed basis, meaning the session is not established until necessary. By activating DDR only when required, companies can save significant WAN usage costs and ISDN toll charges. DDR operates over circuit-switched networks like ISDN and PSTN. Some of the methods using DDR are legacy DDR, dialer profiles, dial backup, and snapshot routing. All of these methods are covered later in this chapter.

Interesting Traffic

The mechanism that allows DDR to function is the definition of interesting traffic. Interesting traffic is defined as "traffic the router deems important" (based on access lists); all other traffic is deemed *uninteresting*. When interesting traffic enters the router destined for a remote network, the router establishes a call to the remote network and sends the data (see Figure 2.29).

Once the circuit is connected, all traffic (including uninteresting traffic) can flow through the circuit. In the event of uninteresting traffic coming into the router destined for a remote network, the router will not establish a new call and the uninteresting traffic will be dropped.

Interesting traffic is configured on the router with the **dialer-list** command. The dialer-list command is then associated with a protocol and then permitted, denied, or matched to an access list. An example of an interesting traffic definition is **dialer-list 1 protocol ip permit**. This would allow all IP traffic entering the router and destined for the remote network or networks to trigger a DDR session. Another example is:

```
dialer-list 2 protocol ip list 101
dialer-list 2 protocol ipx list 901
dialer-list 2 protocol appletalk deny
```

Figure 2.29 Dial-on-Demand Logic

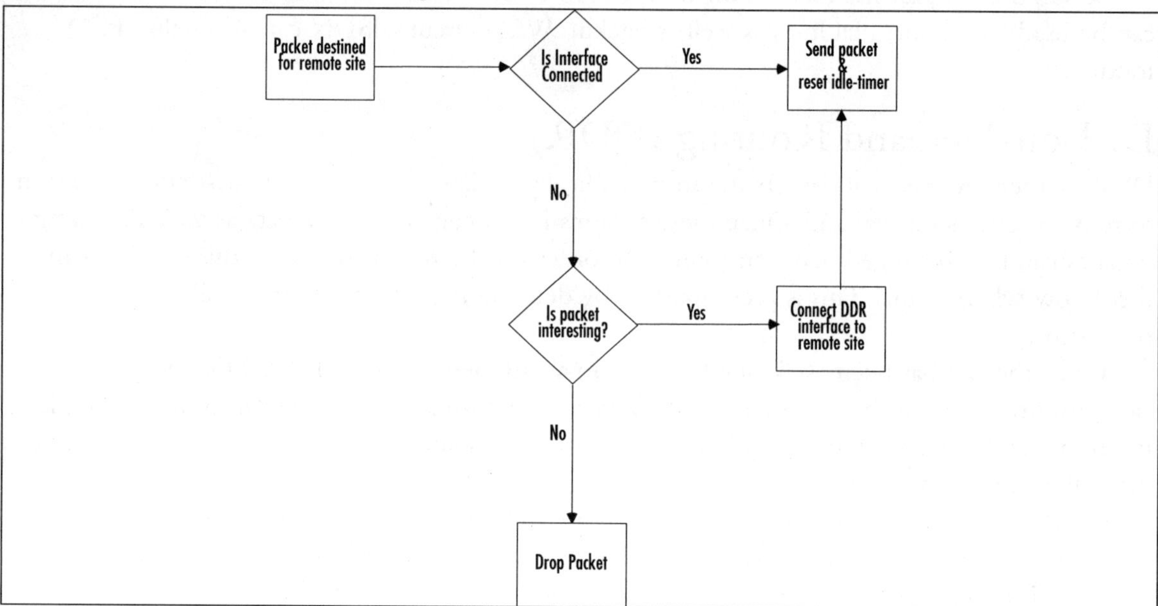

The previous dialer-list would prevent any AppleTalk traffic from initiating a DDR session, and would look at access list 101 to determine what IP traffic should trigger a dial session, as well as performing the same check for IPX using access list 901. If an IP or IPX match were found, the DDR interface would dial.

For example, one reason a network administrator would want to configure an access list permitting only specific traffic to initiate a DDR call would be for "enable only" e-mail and Web traffic. In that instance, other traffic such as routing updates and broadcasts would not initiate a DDR session. If dynamic routing protocols were allowed to trigger the DDR interface, the link would stay connected all the time.

The limit on the number of dialer-lists in a router is 10, but each list can have multiple entries. It is important to use an access list when using DDR and dynamic routing to prevent routing updates or hello packets from initiating and keeping the link active. Once a DDR connection has been made, any traffic passing through the interface (including uninteresting traffic) will keep the session open, but only interesting traffic will reset the idle timer, which keeps the circuit up.

Dialer Interfaces

There are a few different interfaces that Cisco routers can use as a dialer interface: ISDN BRI, synchronous serial, and asynchronous. In order to have an understanding of dialer interfaces, it is important to have an understanding of dialer profiles, dialer rotary groups, dialer addressing, dialer mapping, encapsulation, and supported interfaces. The following list defines these concepts.

- **Dialer Profiles** Dialer profiles were introduced to offer design flexibility in DDR networks. Dialer profiles bound separate logical interfaces to physical interfaces. They involve configuring a profile, which is kept separate from the physical interface. Once the profile has been configured, it is then bound to the physical interface. Multiple profiles can then be linked to one interface, allowing multiple sites to be called from the same interface. A single profile can be linked to multiple interfaces, allowing greater bandwidth per call.

- **Dialer Rotary Groups** Dialer rotary groups are used when there are multiple physical interfaces placing a call. In the event one interface is busy, the rotary group uses the next available interface to make the call. A dialer rotary group does not need to be configured for either BRI or PRI interfaces; the multiple B channels in either interface are automatically placed into a dialer rotary group.
- **Dialer Addressing** There are two different ways to assign dialer interface addresses: using unnumbered interfaces and shared subnetting. Unnumbered interfaces are similar to assigning a point-to-point line an unnumbered address; the address of another interface on the router is used on the dialer interface. Using unnumbered dialer interfaces works because the links are always point-to-point. Shared subnetting is similar to assigning a subnet to a LAN or multipoint WAN to share. Each site in the dialer configuration gets a unique address from a subnetted pool. Using shared subnetting is much simpler than using unnumbered addresses; however, it consumes extra addresses.
- **Dialer Mapping** Dialer maps translate telephone numbers into next-hop addresses. DDR cannot function without statically configured dialer maps. Dialer maps control whether an interface allows broadcasts. Dialer maps can also control call bandwidth, and can link names for PPP authentication. If a site is only going to receive calls and not make any outgoing calls, the phone number can be left off the dialer map statement.
- **Encapsulation** Once a connection is established between two DDR devices, datagrams must be encapsulated and framed before being sent across the media. There are several methods of encapsulation available on Cisco routers, and depending on the interface being used, not all methods are available. Cisco routers support PPP, SLIP, X.25 data link, and HDLC. PPP is the recommended encapsulation method.

Supported Interfaces

There are three types of interfaces on Cisco hardware that support ISDN:

- ISDN interfaces
- Synchronous serial interfaces
- Asynchronous modem connections

These are described in the following sections.

ISDN Interfaces

There are two types of ISDN BRI interfaces used on Cisco hardware. One has the NT1 device built in (labeled with "U") and the other does not (labeled with "S/T"). The NT1 device terminates a four-wire ISDN bus and connects it to the two-wire local loop. Cisco offers ISDN interfaces with or without an NT1 device mainly because a Telco may or may not provide the NT1 device (most in the United States do not).

MP is commonly used in conjunction with ISDN BRI lines. MP bonds multiple B channels together, providing greater bandwidth. Both ISDN BRI and PRI interfaces are automatically configured as dialer in-band interfaces. An in-band interface is simply an interface that sends dialing information over the same connection that carries the data. ISDN interfaces support PPP, HDLC, X.25, and V.120 encapsulation.

Synchronous Serial Interfaces

There are two ways that synchronous serial interfaces can initiate dialing. V.25bis dialing is the ITU standard for in-band dialing and is used with devices such as synchronous modems, ISDN TAs, and switched 56 Kbps DSU/CSUs.

Data Terminal Ready (DTR) dialing is the other method for synchronous serial interface dialing, and does not support incoming calls. DTR does, however, allow for lower cost devices to be used when there is only one number that interface calls. Synchronous serial interfaces support PPP, HDLC, and X.25 encapsulation. To convert a synchronous serial interface into a dialer interface, use the Cisco command **dialer in-band or dialer dtr**.

Asynchronous Modem Connections

Asynchronous connections are made through the auxiliary (aux) port on a router or through the asynchronous ports on a communications server, such as a Cisco 2511 router. Just as with synchronous serial interfaces, you must use the **dialer in-band or dialer dtr** command on the interface for DDR operation. Asynchronous DDR connections can support multiple protocols and encapsulations. Some disadvantages of asynchronous DDR designs are they require more time to establish connections than ISDN, and have much lower bandwidth capability than ISDN or synchronous serial connections. If bandwidth and call establishment time are not important, asynchronous DDR can be a cost-effective solution.

In order to use asynchronous DDR, chat scripts must be configured so that dialing and login commands get sent to the remote end. The chat script sends the modem the proper dialing and login commands. Multiple chat scripts can be assigned to dialer maps to allow for additional flexibility. In addition to chat scripts, modem scripts for configuring outbound modems and logon scripts for remote system logon information can be used. There are two examples in the "Configuring ISDN and DDR" section that show how to configure an asynchronous serial interface.

Configuring ISDN and DDR

This section illustrates how to configure ISDN and DDR. In Example A (Figure 2.30), Router1 will be dialing into Router2 through asynchronous interface line 1. As mentioned earlier, the configuration for a synchronous serial interface would be the same as an asynchronous serial interface. The configuration of Router1 is provided with an explanation of each command in Table 2.2. Only the commands required to set up and initiate the call are shown. This example introduces how to configure an interface for DDR operation.

Examples B through D expand on DDR operation and introduce ISDN configuration. Each of the examples shows only partial router configurations.

Figure 2.30 (Example A) Asynchronous One-To-One

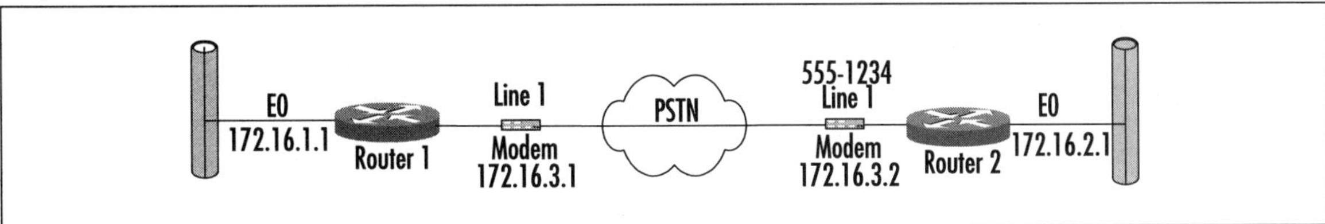

The router configuration used in Figure 2.30 Example A is as follows.

```
Router1(config)# ip route 172.16.2.0 255.255.255.0 172.16.3.2
Router1(config)# dialer-list 1 protocol ip permit
Router1(config)# interface async 1
Router1(config-if)# dialer in-band
Router1(config-if)# ip address 172.16.3.1 255.255.255.0
Router1(config-if)# dialer string 5551234
Router1(config-if)# dialer-group 1
Router1(config-if)# encapsulation ppp
```

Table 2.2 Command Descriptions for Example A

Command	Description
ip route 172.62.2.0 255.255.0 172.16.3.2	This command tells the router to send all traffic destined for the 172.16.20 to the 172.16.3.2 interface. Static routes (for a dynamic routing protocol) must be defined in order for the router to know where to send non-local traffic. Additionally the other end must have a route back to the network or networks. Dynamic routing is covered later in this chapter.
dialer-list 1 protocol ip permit	This command specifies the interesting traffic that can initiate dialing. In this example, the interesting traffic has been identified as all IP traffic. The next example shows how to limit the interesting traffic to a set of protocols.

Continued

Table 2.2 Command Descriptions for Example A

Command	Description
interface async 1	This command enters the subinterface configuration mode for the asynchronous interface.
dialer in-band	This command enables DDR on the asynchronous interface. By default, only ISDN interfaces have this command automatically enabled.
ip address 172.16.31. 255.255.2550	This command configures the asynchronous interface with IP address 172.16.31.1.
dialer string 5551234	This dialer string command tells the router what phone number to dial. In this example the remote site phone number is 555-1234.
dialer-group 1	The dialer-group command identifies what dialer list to use for interesting traffic on that interface. It is possible to have several dialer lists configured on the router and each interface can point to different dialer-lists.
encapsulation ppp	This command tells the router to use PPP encapsulation on the interface.

Examples B through D expand on DDR operation and provide the necessary configuration information to achieve each. Each of the examples shows a partial router configuration to keep the focus on ISDN and DDR.

Example B (Figure 2.31) shows how to configure a router to dial into several different locations using the same dial line. The configuration commands are explained in Table 2.3. In this example, if the line was connected to Router2 and traffic arrived at Router1 destined for Router4, the traffic would be dropped. It would be important to control the amount of time the line was used to prevent this situation. One command that can help control this is **dialer idle-timeout**, which is covered in Example D.

Figure 2.31 (Example B) Asynchronous One-to-Many

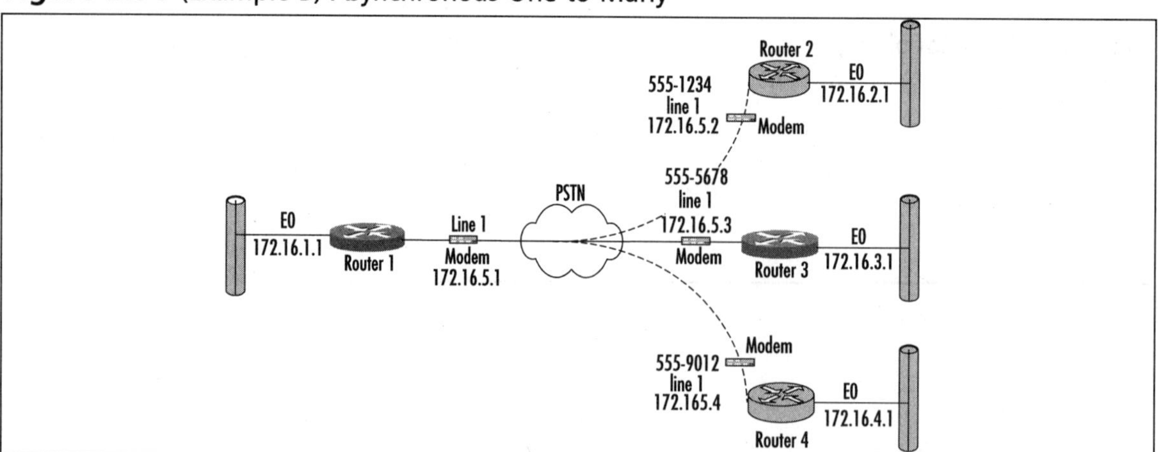

The router configuration used in Figure 2.31 Example B is as follows:

```
Router1(config)# ip route 172.16.2.0 255.255.255.0 172.16.5.2
Router1(config)# ip route 172.16.3.0 255.255.255.0 172.16.5.3
Router1(config)# ip route 172.16.4.0 255.255.255.0 172.16.5.4
Router1(config)# dialer-list 1 protocol ip list 101
Router1(config)# username Router2 password cisco
Router1(config)# username Router3 password cisco
Router1(config)# username Router4 password cisco
Router1(config)# interface async 1
Router1(config-if)# dialer in-band
Router1(config-if)# ip address 172.16.3.1 255.255.255.0
Router1(config-if)# dialer map ip 172.16.5.2 name Router2 5551234
Router1(config-if)# dialer map ip 172.16.5.3 name Router3 5555678
Router1(config-if)# dialer map ip 172.16.5.4 name Router4 5559012
Router1(config-if)# dialer-group 1
Router1(config-if)# encapsulation ppp
Router1(config-if)# ppp authentication chap
Router1(config)# access-list 101 permit tcp any any eq www
Router1(config)# access-list 101 permit tcp any any eq smtp
Router1(config)# access-list 101 permit tcp any any eq pop3
Router1(config)# access-list 101 permit icmp any any
```

Table 2.3 Command Descriptions for Example B

Command	Description
dialer-list 1 protocol ip list 101	As in Example A, this command identifies what traffic will be considered interesting. This example identifies IP traffic, which passes the access list 101 as interesting traffic.
username router 2 password cisco	The username command is required for authentication. This command identifies the shared secret password required when challenged by the remote router.
dialer map ip 172.16.5.2 name router2 5551234 **dialer map ip 172.16.5.3 name router3 5555678** **dialer map ip 172.16.5.4 name router4 5559012**	The dialer map command maps an IP address to the remote router name to the phone number to be dialed. Along with IP route commands, all traffic destined for the 172.16.2.0 network goes through this dialer map. For the authentication to function, the name option must also be used.
ppp authentication chap	This command tells the router to use CHAP authentication on this interface. For CHAP authentication to pass, the remote routers must have this router in their username list and have CHAP authentication configured.

Continued

Table 2.3 Command Descriptions for Example B

Command	Description
access-list 101 permit tcp any any eq WWW access-list 101 permit tcp any any eq smtp access-list 101 permit tcp any any eq pop3 access-list 101 permit icmp any any	Access-list 101 permits all World Wide Web (WWW), Simple Mail Transfer Protocol (SMTP), Post Office Protocol 3 (POP3), and Internet Control Message Protocol (ICMP) traffic. The explicit "deny all" will deny all other types of IP traffic. With this access-list and dialer map command only WWW, SMTP, POP3, and ICMP traffic can initiate the DDR session.

Example C (Figure 2.32) introduces ISDN connectivity. This example is similar to Example A, with several new commands explained in Table 2.4. With ISDN, the network administrator can configure their Cisco router to dial both of the B channels and bond them together, giving them 128 Kbps of bandwidth, which is shown by the Example C configuration. If the ISDN switch type on a Cisco router needs to be changed, the change will not take place until the administrator reboots the router.

Figure 2.32 (Example C) ISDN BRI One-to-One

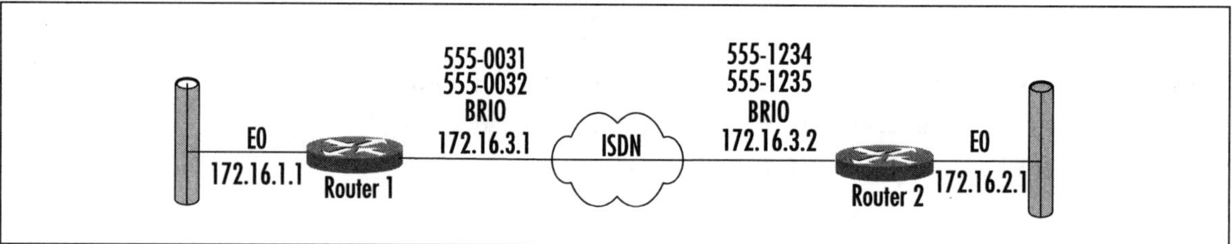

The router configuration for the ISDN BRI one-to-one example C is as follows.

```
Router1(config)# isdn switch-type basic-ni1
Router1(config)# ip route 172.16.2.0 255.255.255.0 172.16.3.2
Router1(config)# dialer-list 1 protocol ip permit
Router1(config)# interface bri 0
Router1(config-if)# ip address 172.16.3.1 255.255.255.0
Router1(config-if)# isdn spid1 0913555000101
Router1(config-if)# isdn spid2 0913555000201
Router1(config-if)# dialer map ip 172.16.3.2 5551234
Router1(config-if)# bandwidth 128
Router1(config-if)# dialer load-threshold 127 either
Router1(config-if)# dialer-group 1
Router1(config-if)# encapsulation ppp
Router1(config-if)# ppp multilink
```

Table 2.4 Command Descriptions for Example C

Command	Description
isdn switch-type basic-ni1	This command configures the ISDN switch type into the router. The telephone company should provide this information when installing an ISDN line.
isdn spid1 0913555000101 **isdn spid2 091355000201**	This command configures the Service Profile Identifiers (SPIDs) into the router. The SPID is not required on all ISDN switch types. The telephone company should provide SPIDs when installing an ISDN line.
bandwidth 128	This command tells the router how much bandwidth is available on the interface. The bandwidth command is used in calculating the load threshold.
dialer load-threshold 127 either	This command configures the router to initiate a second call once the threshold has been met. The value is a number between 1 and 255 and is a percent of the total bandwidth of the line. 127 is equivalent to approximately 50 percent of 64 Kbps of data. Once traffic reaches this data rate the second number is dialed (through the D channel), connecting both B channels. In this example, only one dialer map statement had to be issued for the threshold to operate correctly. Certain ISDN switches automatically recognize when a second call is incoming and re-route the call to the second B channel. If the switch in this example did not support this, there would have been a second dialer map statement pointing the same IP address to the second B channel number.
ppp multilink	This command bonds both B channels together to provide for double the bandwidth of a B channel.

Example D (Figure 2.33) shows how to configure ISDN to dial multiple sites. Example B identified the dialer idle-timeout command to allow for faster disconnection of DDR lines. Example D explains that command. Table 2.5 explains the benefit of the **dialer idle-timeout 5 either** command.

Figure 2.33 (Example D) ISDN BRI One-to-Many

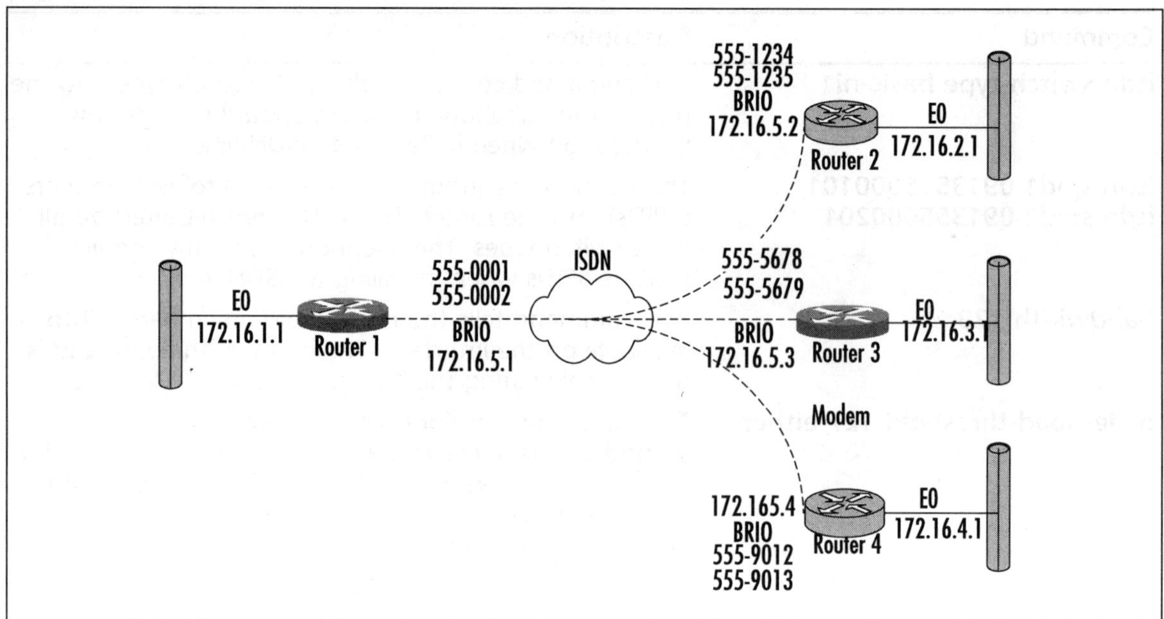

The following is the router configuration for Example D:

```
Router1(config)# isdn switch-type basic-ni1
Router1(config)# ip route 172.16.2.0 255.255.255.0 172.16.5.2
Router1(config)# ip route 172.16.3.0 255.255.255.0 172.16.5.3
Router1(config)# ip route 172.16.4.0 255.255.255.0 172.16.5.4
Router1(config)# dialer-list 1 protocol ip permit
Router1(config)# username Router2 password cisco
Router1(config)# username Router3 password cisco
Router1(config)# username Router4 password cisco
Router1(config)# interface bri 0
Router1(config-if)# ip address 172.16.5.1 255.255.255.0
Router1(config-if)# isdn spid1 0913555000101
Router1(config-if)# isdn spid2 0913555000201
Router1(config-if)# dialer map ip 172.16.5.2 name Router2 5551234
Router1(config-if)# dialer map ip 172.16.5.3 name Router3 5555678
Router1(config-if)# dialer map ip 172.16.5.4 name Router4 5559012
Router1(config-if)# bandwidth 128
Router1(config-if)# dialer load-threshold 127 either
Router1(config-if)# dialer-group 1
Router1(config-if)# encapsulation ppp
Router1(config-if)# ppp multilink
Router1(config-if)# dialer idle-timeout 5 either
```

Table 2.5 Command Descriptions for Example D

Command	Description
idle-timeout 5 either	This command configures the router to disconnect the ISDN interface after five seconds of inactivity in either direction. Configuring this command can improve online usage.

Previous examples showed the basics of connecting a BRI to a BRI. The following examples show how to configure some of the more advanced DDR features. Example E (Figure 2.34) shows a BRI-to-BRI configuration using snapshot routing and route redistribution. In this example, both router configurations are displayed. Example F (Figures 2.35) shows how to configure a BRI to a PRI using Open Shortest Path First (OSPF) on-demand routing, caller ID callback, and caller ID screening. Routing protocols such as Enhanced Interior Gateway Routing Protocol (EIGRP) and OSPF are discussed more fully in Chapter 4.

Figure 2.34 (Example E) Snapshot Routing with Route Redistribution

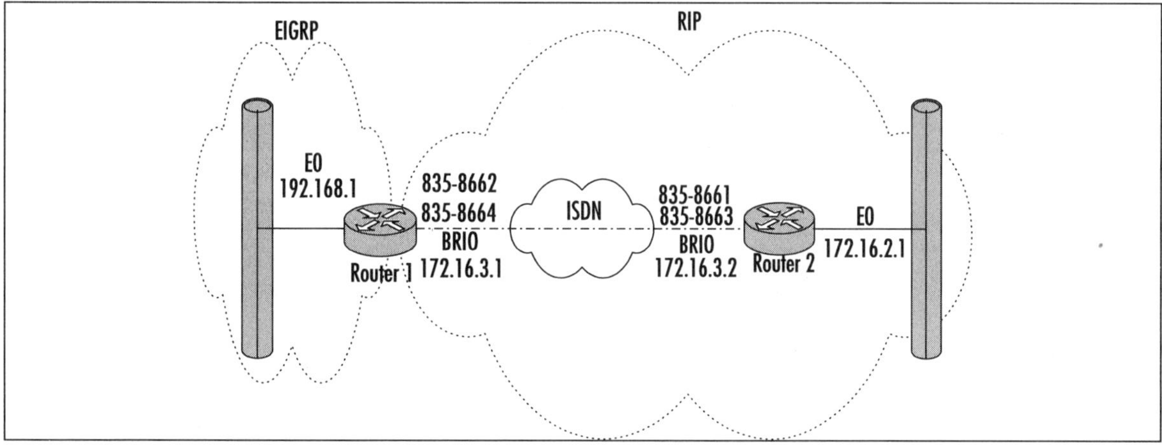

The following is the Router1 configuration for Example E:

```
hostname Router1
isdn switch-type basic-ni1
dialer-list 1 protocol ip permit
!
interface Ethernet0
ip address 192.168.1.1 255.255.255.0
!
interface BRI0
ip address 172.16.3.1 255.255.255.252
encapsulation ppp
bandwidth 128
```

```
dialer map ip 172.16.3.2 name Router2 broadcast 8358661
dialer map snapshot 1 name Router2 broadcast 8358661
dialer load-threshold 127 either
dialer-group 1
isdn spid1 0835866201
isdn spid2 0835866401
snapshot client 10 13 dialer
ppp multilink
!
router eigrp 6243
redistribute rip metric 64 10 255 127 1500
network 192.168.1.0
!
router rip
version 2
redistribute eigrp 6243 metric 2
network 172.16.0.0
neighbor 172.16.3.2
```

The following is the Router2 configuration for Example E:

```
hostname Router2
isdn switch-type basic-ni1
dialer-list 1 protocol ip permit
!
interface Ethernet0
ip address 172.16.2.1 255.255.255.0
!
interface BRI0
ip address 172.16.3.2 255.255.255.252
encapsulation ppp
bandwidth 128
dialer map ip 172.16.3.1 name Router1 broadcast 8358662
dialer map snapshot 1 name Router1 broadcast 8358662
dialer load-threshold 127 either
dialer-group 1
isdn spid1 0835866101
isdn spid2 0835866301
snapshot server 10 dialer
ppp multilink
!
router rip
```

```
version 2
network 172.16.0.0
neighbor 172.16.3.1
no auto-summary
```

Example E shows how to configure snapshot routing as well as route redistribution. To configure snapshot routing, the administrator needs to configure one router as the client and the other as the server. The snapshot client is the end that controls the active and quiet timers. You will notice in the Router1 configuration that the dialer parameter has also been used. In the event the dialer parameter is used, a dialer map must be made between the snapshot process and the phone number. This allows the snapshot update to initiate a DDR session if there is no interesting traffic to bring up the link.

Looking at the Router1 configuration, EIGRP is redistributing routes learned from RIP, and RIP is redistributing routes learned from EIGRP.

This is commonly referred to as *mutual redistribution*. The following output is from the **show ip route** command executed before and after the DDR connection is established. Notice that before the connection is established, the only routes in the routing table are the ones directly connected to the router (192.168.1.0, 172.16.3.2, and 172.16.3.0). After the connection is established, the routing table also shows the 172.16.2.0 network and that it was learned via RIP.

Once the ISDN connection to Router2 is disconnected, the route to 172.16.2.0 stays in the routing table for the quiet period configured in the snapshot command. The following is the Router1 routing table before the DDR connection:

```
Router1# show ip route
Codes: C - connected, S - static, I - IGRP, R - RIP, M - mobile, B - BGP D - EIGRP,
EX - EIGRP external, O - OSPF, IA - OSPF inter area N1 - OSPF NSSA external type 1,
N2 - OSPF NSSA external type 2 E1 - OSPF external type 1, E2 - OSPF external type 2,
E - EGP i - IS-IS, L1 - IS-IS level-1, L2 - IS-IS level-2, * -
candidate default
U - per-user static route, o - ODR
Gateway of last resort is not set
172.16.0.0/16 is variably subnetted, 2 subnets, 2 masks
C 172.16.3.2/32 is directly connected, BRI0
C 172.16.3.0/30 is directly connected, BRI0
C 192.168.1.0/24 is directly connected, Ethernet0
```

The following is the Router1 routing table after DDR connection.

```
Router1# show ip route
Codes: C - connected, S - static, I - IGRP, R - RIP, M - mobile, B -
BGP
D - EIGRP, EX - EIGRP external, O - OSPF, IA - OSPF inter area
N1 - OSPF NSSA external type 1, N2 - OSPF NSSA external type 2
E1 - OSPF external type 1, E2 - OSPF external type 2, E - EGP
```

```
i - IS-IS, L1 - IS-IS level-1, L2 - IS-IS level-2, * -
candidate default
U - per-user static route, o - ODR
Gateway of last resort is not set
172.16.0.0/16 is variably subnetted, 2 subnets, 2 masks
R 172.16.2.0/24 [120/1] via 172.16.3.2, 00:00:13, BRI0
C 172.16.3.0/30 is directly connected, BRI0
C 192.168.1.0/24 is directly connected, Ethernet0
```

Example F (Figure 2.35) and its associated configurations show a BRI-to-PRI connection. In this example, the PRI is also performing caller ID authentication. Both routers are running OSPF on-demand routing across the ISDN link. Following the configurations for Router1 and Router2 is an output of Router1's routing table before and after the ISDN connection is established.

Figure 2.35 (Example F) PRI OSPF On-demand with Caller ID Screening

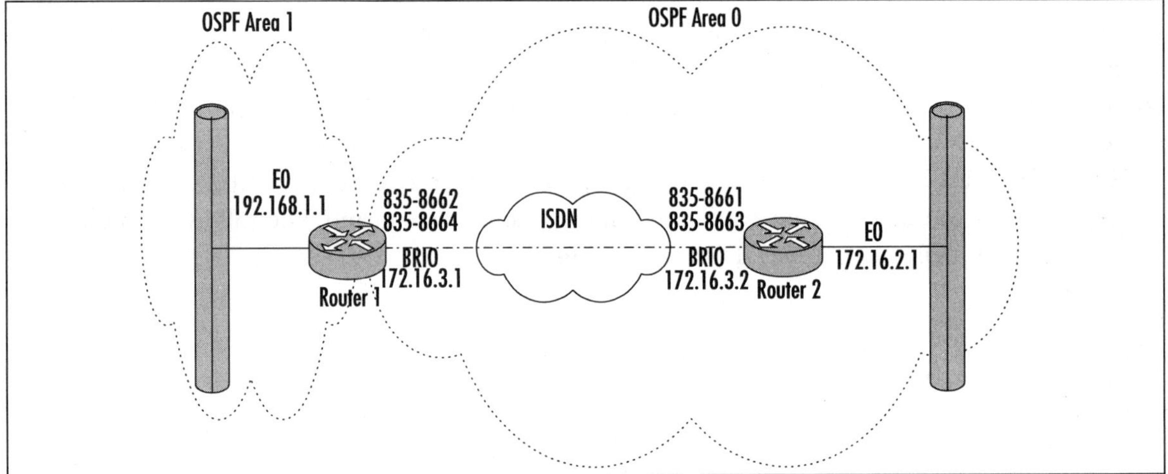

The following is the Router1 configuration for Example F:

```
hostname Router1
isdn switch-type basic-ni1
dialer-list 1 protocol ip permit
!
interface Ethernet0
ip address 192.168.1.1 255.255.255.0
!
interface BRI0
ip address 172.16.3.1 255.255.255.252
encapsulation ppp
bandwidth 128
```

```
ip ospf demand-circuit
dialer map ip 172.16.3.2 name Router1 broadcast 8358661
dialer load-threshold 127 either
dialer-group 1
isdn spid1 0835866201
isdn spid2 0835866401
ppp multilink
!
router ospf 2177
network 172.16.3.0 0.0.0.255 area 0
network 192.168.1.0 0.0.0.255 area 1
```

The following is the Router2 configuration for Example F:

```
hostname Router2
isdn switch-type primary-5ess
dialer-list 1 protocol ip permit
ip local pool dialup 172.16.3.129 172.16.3.152
!
controller T1 0
framing esf
clock source line primary

linecode b8zs
pri-group timeslots 1-24
!
interface Ethernet0
ip address 172.16.2.1 255.255.255.0
!
interface Serial0:23
no ip address
encapsulation ppp
dialer rotary-group 1
dialer-group 1
isdn switch-type primary-5ess
isdn incoming-voice modem
no fair-queue
!
interface Dialer1
ip address 172.16.3.2 255.255.255.0
encapsulation ppp
dialer in-band
```

```
ip ospf demand-circuit
dialer map ip 172.16.3.1 name Router1 broadcast 8358662
dialer-group 1
peer default ip address pool dialup
isdn caller 8358662 callback
isdn caller 8358664 callback
ppp multilink
!
router ospf 2177
network 172.16.2.0 0.0.0.255 area 0
network 172.16.3.0 0.0.0.255 area 0
```

As shown in the Router2 configuration, caller ID authentication requires only two commands: **isdn caller 8358662 callback**, and **isdn caller 8358664 callback**. These commands only allow an incoming call to be connected if its number is 835-8662 or 835-8664. The callback parameter instructs Router2 to hang up and call Router1 back. You can replace any number or numbers with an *x* to mean "I do not care." If, in this example, the **isdn caller 835866*x*** command were used, the following incoming numbers would be allowed:

- 8358660
- 8358661
- 8358662
- 8358663
- 8358664
- 8358665
- 8358666
- 8358667
- 8358668
- 8358669

Both Router1 and Router2 are running OSPF and have configured their ISDN interfaces for OSPF on-demand operation. It only takes one **ip ospf demand-circuit** command (in addition to the normal OSPF configuration) to configure the routers for OSPF on demand. Additionally, since Router2 has a PRI interface, the controller and the serial0:23 interface must be configured. To configure the controller, you need to know the type of controller (T1 or E1), framing, linecode, and number of channels to be used, as well as where the clock source is. The serial0:23 interface is the D channel on a T1 PRI. Notice that the Dialer1 interface is being used for this example. Example E provides the **show ip route** output before and after the ISDN connection is established.

The following is the Router1 routing table before DDR connection for Example E:

```
Router1# show ip route
```

```
Codes: C - connected, S - static, I - IGRP, R - RIP, M - mobile, B - BGP D - EIGRP,
EX - EIGRP external, O - OSPF, IA - OSPF inter area N1 - OSPF NSSA external type 1,
N2 - OSPF NSSA external type 2 E1 - OSPF external type 1, E2 - OSPF external type 2,
E - EGP i - IS-IS, L1 - IS-IS level-1, L2 - IS-IS level-2, * - candidate default
U - per-user static route, o - ODR
Gateway of last resort is not set
172.16.0.0/16 is variably subnetted, 2 subnets, 2 masks
C 172.16.3.2/32 is directly connected, BRI0
C 172.16.3.0/30 is directly connected, BRI0
C 192.168.1.0/24 is directly connected, Ethernet0
```

The following is the Router1 routing table after DDR connection for Example E:

```
Router1# show ip route
Codes: C - connected, S - static, I - IGRP, R - RIP, M - mobile, B - BGP D - EIGRP,
EX - EIGRP external, O - OSPF, IA - OSPF inter area N1 - OSPF NSSA external type 1,
N2 - OSPF NSSA external type 2 E1 - OSPF external type 1, E2 - OSPF external type 2,
E - EGP i - IS-IS, L1 - IS-IS level-1, L2 - IS-IS level-2, * - candidate default
U - per-user static route, o - ODR
Gateway of last resort is not set
172.16.0.0/16 is variably subnetted, 2 subnets, 2 masks
O 172.16.2.0/24 [110/791] via 172.16.3.2, 00:00:18, BRI0
C 172.16.3.0/30 is directly connected, BRI0
C 192.168.1.0/24 is directly connected, Ethernet0
```

Before the connection is first brought up, Router1 has no route to Router2's Ethernet network (172.16.2.0). Notice that after the connection is made, there is an OSPF route to network 172.16.2.0 through the BRI 0 interface. Even after the ISDN line is disconnected, the route to 172.16.2.0 remains in the routing table for Router1.

ISDN and DDR commands

The following section covers the various ISDN and DDR commands covered in the previous examples. This is a list of some of the commands and their associated optional parameters.

- **dialer-list-number protocol operator** The dialer-list command defines interesting traffic.
  - **dialer-list-number** A number between 1 and 10.
  - **protocol** Can be any of the following (depending on IOS): AppleTalk, bridge, clns, decnet, ip, ipx, llc2, netbios, vines, xns.
  - **operator** Can be either **permit**, **deny**, or **list** with list number.
- **dialer map *protocol next-hop-address* [name *hostname*] [speed *speed*] [modem-script *script_name*] [system-script *script_name*] [spc] [class *map_class*] [broadcast] *dial-string*** The dialer map command maps a protocol and next hop address to a phone number. This command is useful when dialing to more than one location.

- **protocol next-hop-address** Specifies the protocol and next hop router address.
- **name *hostname*** Specifies the destination router's host name.
- **speed *speed*** Specifies either 56K or 64K bits per second.
- **modem-script *script_name*** Script to be used for making the connection.
- **system-script *script_name*** Script to be used for system login to the destination host.
- **spc** Specifies whether the connection is semi-permanent.
- **class *map_class*** Specifies a map class for the map.
- **broadcast** Broadcast packets for the given protocol will be sent to the next hop address.
- ***dial-string*** Specifies the telephone number to be called when a packet for the next hop address arrives.

- **dialer in-band** This command enables the interface for DDR operation and sets the interface for V.25bis dialing.
- **dialer string *phone_number*** This command specifies the telephone number to be dialed.
- **dialer-group dialer-list-number** This command assigns the interface to the specified dialer list.
  - **dialer-list-number** Value from 1 to 10.
- **encapsulation *type*** This command sets the encapsulation type for the interface. See the "Encapsulation" section earlier in this chapter for an explanation of types.
- **dialer idle-timeout *time* [either]** This command specifies the allowed inactivity time on the interface before disconnecting it.
  - **time** A value between 1 and 2,147,483 seconds. The default is 120 seconds.
  - **either** Tells the interface to monitor inbound and outbound traffic inactivity. Default is outbound.
- **dialer hold-queue *size* [timeout *seconds*]** This command specifies the output hold queue on the DDR interface. This command tells the router to hold a specified number of packets while the interface is being connected and transmitted once the session is established.
  - **size** Number of packets from 0 to 100 to be held before dropping.
  - **timeout seconds** The length of time the packets will be held before being dropped.
- **dialer load-threshold *percent-load* [direction]** This command identifies when to place an additional call based on the percent of bandwidth used on the interface. When

an ISDN call is initiated, only one B channel is dialed. When configuring this command, the administrator can tell the router how soon to dial the second B channel.

- **percent-load** A value from 1 to 255. A value of 127 would be 49.8 percent of the line, or 63.75 Kbps.
- **direction** Determines what direction of traffic flow is monitored before activating the additional line. This optional parameter can be set to inbound, outbound, or either. Outbound is monitored by default.

- **isdn switch-type *type*** This command sets the type of ISDN switch connected to your router. Several different types of ISDN switches are supported including:
  - **basic-1tr6** 1TR6 switch type for Germany
  - **basic-5ess** AT&T 5ESS switch type for the U.S.
  - **basic-dms100** Northern DMS-100 switch type
  - **basic-net3** NET3 switch type for UK and Europe
  - **basic-ni1** National ISDN-1 switch type
  - **basic-nwnet3** NET3 switch type for Norway
  - **basic-nznet3** NET3 switch type for New Zealand
  - **basic-ts013** TS013 switch type for Australia
  - **ntt** NTT switch type for Japan
  - **vn2** VN2 switch type for France
  - **vn3** VN3 and VN4 switch types for France
- **isdn spid1 spid phone_number** This command sets the SPID for the BRI interface. The phone company provides the SPID, which is usually the phone number with a few numbers added to the front or back or both. 0913555123401 is an example of a SPID. The SPID identifies any services that are part of this ISDN line.

ISDN Troubleshooting

Cisco provides a large toolset of commands that can be used to troubleshoot problems and errors with the ISDN configurations. These tools and troubleshooting methods are described in more detail in the sections that follow.

ISDN Connections between Cisco Routers

The following is a typical scenario to determine the problem(s) that occur when a BRI interface fails to establish a remote connection using PPP over an ISDN line. First, we need to check the status of the physical layer:

```
Cisco command: show isdn stat
The current ISDN Switchtype = basic-nil
```

```
ISDN BRIO interface
Layer 1 Status:
DEACTIVATED
Layer 2 Status:
Layer 2 NOT Activated
Layer 3 Status:
No Active Layer 3 Call(s)
Activated dsl 0 CCBs = 0
Total Allocated ISDN CCBs = 0
```

The output above indicates that there is a problem with the Physical layer. The Layer 1 status being "DEACTIVATED" indicates this. This could be caused by a bad cable, a bad NT1 device (or no power to an external NT1 device), or a bad demarc.

In this instance, there was a bad cable between the NT1 device and the BRI interface of the Cisco router. We replaced our cable and executed the command again:

```
The current ISDN Switchtype = basic-nil
ISDN BRIO interface
Layer 1 Status:
ACTIVE
Layer 2 Status:
Layer 2 NOT Activated
Layer 3 Status:
No Active Layer 3 Call(s)
Activated dsl 0 CCBs = 0
Total Allocated ISDN CCBs = 0
```

The output indicates that the physical layer is functioning properly as evidenced by the Layer 1 status being "ACTIVE." Now we turn our attention to Layer 2 to determine where the problem is within that layer. If Layer 2 were functioning correctly, the router would receive Terminal Endpoint Identifiers (TEIs) from the ISDN switch. To determine whether there are any Layer 2 problems, turn on terminal monitoring (**term mon**), execute the following command, and then ping the IP address of the BRI0 interface. The command **debug isdn q921** (shown next) displays all information that passes between the local router and the ISDN switch.

```
Router# debug isdn q921
ISDN Q921 packets is on
```

(after ping):

```
Type escape sequence to abort.
Sending 5, 100 byte ICMP Echos to 10.1.20.2, timeout is 2 seconds:
12:20:01: TX -> IDREQ ri = 18543 ai = 127 dsl = 0
12:20:03: TX -> IDREQ ri = 1546 ai = 127 dsl = 0
12:20:05: TX -> IDREQ ri = 1834 ai = 127 ds1 = 0
12:20:07: TX -> IDREQ ri = 17456 ai = 127 dsl = 0
```

```
…..
12:21:03: TX -> IDREQ ri = 1654 ai = 127 ds1 = 0
```

The output above indicates a malfunctioning NT1 device, an incorrectly provisioned circuit, or an incorrect IDSN switch type configured on the router. After speaking with the LE carrier (LEC), it was determined that the circuit was not correctly provisioned.

Here is what a good Layer 2 output looks like for this **debug** command:

```
Type escape sequence to abort
Sending 5, 1000 byte ICMP Echos to 10.1.20.2, timeout is 2 seconds:
12:45:17: BRI0: TX -> RRp sapi = 0 tei = 102 nr = 1
12:45:17: BRI0: RX <- RRF sapi = 0 tei = 102 nr = 1
12:45:19: BRI0: TX -> RRp sapi = 0 tei = 101 nr = 3
12:45:19: BRI0: TX <- RRf sapi = 0 tei = 101 nr = 3
12:45:19: BRI0: TX -> INFOc sapi = 0 tei = 101 ns = 1 nr = 2
I = 0x04E120406283703C14033348C4001233
12:45:21: BRI0: TX <- RRr sapi = 0 tei = 101 nr = 2
….
12:45:25: %LINEPROTO-5-UPDOWN: Line protocol on Interface BRI0: BChannel 1, changed
state to up. !!!
Success rate is 60 percent (3/5), round-trip min/avg/max = 100/110/120 ms
```

Q.921 information is a Layer 2 protocol. Please note the reception of TEIs from the ISDN switch. Each time you shut down the BRI0 interface and bring it back up, you should receive new TEIs from the ISDN switch. A fuller listing of information provided by the **debug isdn q921** command is provided here. This example shows a complete log of the activity that occurs at layer to bring up the ISDN line.

```
Router1# debug isdn q921
ISDN Q921 packets debugging is on
02:47:01: %LINK-3-UPDOWN: Interface BRI0:1, changed state to down
02:47:01: %LINK-3-UPDOWN: Interface BRI0:2, changed state to down
02:47:02: %LINK-3-UPDOWN: Interface BRI0, changed state to up
02:47:02: ISDN BR0: TX -> SABMEp sapi = 0 tei = 79
02:47:02: ISDN BR0: RX <- IDREM ri = 0 ai = 127
02:47:02: ISDN BR0: RX <- IDCKRQ ri = 0 ai = 79
02:47:02: %ISDN-6-LAYER2DOWN: Layer 2 for Interface BRI0, TEI 80 changed to down
02:47:02: %ISDN-6-LAYER2DOWN: Layer 2 for Interface BRI0, TEI 79 changed to down
02:47:02: %ISDN-6-LAYER2DOWN: Layer 2 for Interface BR0, TEI 79 changed to down
02:47:02: %SYS-5-CONFIG_I: Configured from console by console
02:47:02: ISDN BR0: TX -> IDREQ ri = 44940 ai = 127
02:47:03: ISDN BR0: RX <- IDCKRQ ri = 0 ai = 79
02:47:04: ISDN BR0: RX <- IDREM ri = 0 ai = 79
02:47:04: ISDN BR0: TX -> IDREQ ri = 43085 ai = 127
```

```
02:47:05: ISDN BR0: RX <- IDASSN ri = 43085 ai = 81
02:47:05: ISDN BR0: TX -> SABMEp sapi = 0 tei = 81
02:47:05: ISDN BR0: RX <- UAf sapi = 0 tei = 81
02:47:05: %ISDN-6-LAYER2UP: Layer 2 for Interface BR0, TEI 81 changed to up
02:47:05: ISDN BR0: TX -> INFOc sapi = 0 tei = 81 ns = 0 nr = 0 i = 0x08007B3A0A303
02:47:05: ISDN BR0: RX <- INFOc sapi = 0 tei = 81 ns = 0 nr = 1 i = 0x08007B3B02828
02:47:05: ISDN BR0: TX -> INFOc sapi = 0 tei = 81 ns = 1 nr = 1 i = 0x08012705040288
02:47:05: ISDN BR0: TX -> IDREQ ri = 11550 ai = 127
02:47:05: ISDN BR0: RX <- INFOc sapi = 0 tei = 81 ns = 1 nr = 2 i = 0x0801A702180189
02:47:05: ISDN BR0: RX <- IDASSN ri = 11550 ai = 82
02:47:05: ISDN BR0: TX -> RRr sapi = 0 tei = 81 nr = 2
02:47:05: ISDN BR0: TX -> SABMEp sapi = 0 tei = 82
02:47:05: ISDN BR0: RX <- UAf sapi = 0 tei = 82
02:47:05: %ISDN-6-LAYER2UP: Layer 2 for Interface BR0, TEI 82 changed to up
02:47:05: ISDN BR0: TX -> INFOc sapi = 0 tei = 82 ns = 0 nr = 0 i = 0x08007B3A0A3038
02:47:05: ISDN BR0: RX <- INFOc sapi = 0 tei = 81 ns = 2 nr = 2 i = 0x0801A707
02:47:05: ISDN BR0: TX -> RRr sapi = 0 tei = 81 nr = 3
02:47:05: %LINK-3-UPDOWN: Interface BRI0:1, changed state to up
02:47:05: ISDN BR0: TX -> INFOc sapi = 0 tei = 81 ns = 2 nr = 3 i = 0x0801270F
02:47:05: ISDN BR0: RX <- INFOc sapi = 0 tei = 82 ns = 0 nr = 1 i = 0x08007B3B028481
02:47:05: ISDN BR0: TX -> RRr sapi = 0 tei = 82 nr = 1
02:47:05: ISDN BR0: RX <- RRr sapi = 0 tei = 81 nr = 3
02:47:05: %LINK-3-UPDOWN: Interface Virtual-Access1, changed state to up
02:47:06: %LINEPROTO-5-UPDOWN: Line protocol on Interface BRI0:1, changed state to up
02:47:06: %LINEPROTO-5-UPDOWN: Line protocol on Interface Virtual- Access1, changed
state to up
```

Now, if you execute the **show isdn status** command, you will receive the following:

```
Cisco command: show isdn status
The current ISDN Switchtype = basic-nil
ISDN BRI0 interface
Layer 1 Status:
ACTIVE
Layer 2 Status:
TEI = 102, State = MULTIPLE_FRAME_ESTABLISHED
TEI = 101, State = MULTIPLE_FRAME_ESTABLISHED
Layer 3 Status:
1 Active Layer 3 Call(s)
Activated ds1 0 CCBs = 1
CCB:called=800C, sapi=0, ces=1, B-chan=1
```

If Layer 3 does not activate, use the **debug isdn q931** command to troubleshoot the Layer 3 problems. The following is an example of output from a router whose Layer 3 is functioning properly (be sure to turn on terminal monitoring, execute the command, then ping the IP address of the router's BRI0 interface):

```
Cisco command: debug isdn q931
Type escape sequence to abort.
Sending 5, 100-byte ICMP Echos to 10.1.20.2, timeout is 2 seconds:
12:51:11: %SEC-6-IPACCESSLOGDP: list 100 permitted icmp 10.1.20.2 ->
10.1.20.2 (0/0), 1 packet
12:51:11: BRI0: TX -> SETUP pd = 8 callref =0x08
12:51:11: BRI0: Bearer Capability I = 0x8890
12:51:11: BRI0: Channel ID I = 0x62
12:51:13: BRI0: Called Party Number I = 0x70, '4097004509'
12:51:13: BRI0: RX <- CALL_PROC pd = 8 callref = 0x82
12:51:13: BRI0: Channel ID I = 0x89
12:51:15: BRI0: ISDN Event: incoming ces value = 1
.....
12:51:17: %LINK-3-UPDOWN: Interface BRI0: B-Channel 1, changed state to
up
   12:51:17: BRI0: TX -> CONNECT_ACK pd = 8 callref = 0x08
 12:51:17: %LINEPROTO-5-UPDOWN: Line protocol on Interface BRI0: BChannel
1, changed state to up!!
Success rate is 60 percent (3/5), round-trip min/avg/max = 110/130/150
Ms
```

(If the line in bold contains "HOST_TERM_REGISTER_NACK – invalid EID/SPID, or TEI not assigned Cause I = 0x8082 – No route to specified network," check to see that your SPIDs are valid and that your ISDN switch-type is correct.) The most common Layer 3 problems are incorrect IP addressing, incorrect SPIDs, or erroneous access lists assigned to the interface.

To verify Layer 3 connectivity, use the **debug isdn q931** command. This command, as shown in the following output, displays all call setup and teardown information across the D channel. Both Q.921 and Q.931 display information on the D channel. To obtain information on the B channel you should use either the **debug dialer** or **debug ip packet** command.

```
Router1# debug isdn q931
ISDN Q931 packets debugging is on
02:50:03: ISDN BR0: TX -> INFORMATION pd = 8 callref = (null) SPID Information i =
'0835866201'
02:50:03: ISDN BR0: RX <- INFORMATION pd = 8 callref = (null) ENDPOINT IDent i =
0x8281
02:50:03: ISDN BR0: TX -> SETUP pd = 8 callref = 0x28
02:50:03: Bearer Capability i = 0x8890
```

```
02:50:03: Channel ID i = 0x83
02:50:03: Keypad Facility i = '8358661'
02:50:03: ISDN BR0: RX <- CALL_PROC pd = 8 callref = 0xA8
02:50:03: Channel ID i = 0x89
02:50:03: Locking Shift to Codeset 5
02:50:03: Codeset 5 IE 0x2A i = 0x809402, ''=', 0x8307, '8358661', 0x8E0B, ' Teltone 1
'
02:50:03: %ISDN-6-LAYER2UP: Layer 2 for Interface BR0, TEI 84 changed to up
02:50:03: ISDN BR0: TX -> INFORMATION pd = 8 callref = (null) SPID Information i =
'0835866401'
02:50:03: ISDN BR0: RX <- CONNECT pd = 8 callref = 0xA8
02:50:03: %LINK-3-UPDOWN: Interface BRI0:1, changed state to up
02:50:03: ISDN BR0: TX -> CONNECT_ACK pd = 8 callref = 0x28
02:50:03: ISDN BR0: RX <- INFORMATION pd = 8 callref = (null) ENDPOINT IDent i =
0x8481
02:50:03: %LINK-3-UPDOWN: Interface Virtual-Access1, changed state to up
02:50:03: %LINEPROTO-5-UPDOWN: Line protocol on Interface BRI0:1, changed state to up
02:50:03: %LINEPROTO-5-UPDOWN: Line protocol on Interface Virtual- Access1, changed
state to up
```

Monitoring the ISDN Interface

The command **show interface bri 0** displays information about the BRI interface. It gives information about the D channel of the interface.

```
Router1# show interface bri 0
BRI0 is up, line protocol is up (spoofing)
Hardware is BRI
Internet address is 172.16.3.1/30
MTU 1500 bytes, BW 128 Kbit, DLY 20000 usec, rely 255/255, load 1/255
Encapsulation PPP, loopback not set
Last input 00:00:01, output 00:00:01, output hang never
Last clearing of "show interface" counters never
Input queue: 0/75/0 (size/max/drops); Total output drops: 0
Queueing strategy: weighted fair
Output queue: 0/1000/64/0 (size/max total/threshold/drops)
Conversations 0/1/256 (active/max active/max total)
Reserved Conversations 0/0 (allocated/max allocated)
5 minute input rate 0 bits/sec, 0 packets/sec
5 minute output rate 0 bits/sec, 0 packets/sec
4723 packets input, 25063 bytes, 0 no buffer
Received 4 broadcasts, 0 runts, 0 giants, 0 throttles
```

```
0 input errors, 0 CRC, 0 frame, 0 overrun, 0 ignored, 0 abort
4957 packets output, 23463 bytes, 0 underruns
0 output errors, 0 collisions, 7 interface resets
0 output buffer failures, 0 output buffers swapped out
5 carrier transitions
```

This command is only valid on routers with internal BRI interfaces. If you are not using an internal BRI interface, you would issue the command **show interface serial** to obtain similar information.

In this example, the second line shows that the interface is up and the protocol is up (spoofing). Spoofing is used to trick the router into believing the interface is permanently connected. This is done so that features such as DDR will function properly. When an interface is down, any entries in the routing table pointing to that interface will be removed.

DDR requires that routing table entries be intact in order to initiate dialing. DDR forces the BRI interface to remain in a spoofing state to maintain routing entries for that interface or network. This command is primarily used to verify that the interface is responding and that the IP address has been configured correctly. Also, when identifying problems, the input and output rates and errors are useful.

As you can see, the command **show interface bri 0 1 2** provides details of both B channels of the BRI interface. You can quickly identify whether either or both of the B channels are up or down, as well as determine the encapsulation protocol. Other useful data is the various input and output information.

```
Router1# show interface bri 0 1 2
BRI0:1 is down, line protocol is down
Hardware is BRI
MTU 1500 bytes, BW 64 Kbit, DLY 20000 usec, rely 255/255, load 1/255
Encapsulation PPP, loopback not set, keepalive set (10 sec)
LCP Closed, multilink Closed
Closed: IPCP, CDPCP
Last input 00:00:17, output 00:00:17, output hang never
Last clearing of "show interface" counters never
Queueing strategy: fifo
Output queue 0/40, 0 drops; input queue 2/75, 0 drops
5 minute input rate 0 bits/sec, 0 packets/sec
5 minute output rate 0 bits/sec, 0 packets/sec
6764 packets input, 273534 bytes, 0 no buffer
Received 6764 broadcasts, 0 runts, 0 giants, 0 throttles
0 input errors, 0 CRC, 0 frame, 0 overrun, 0 ignored, 0 abort
6826 packets output, 283850 bytes, 0 underruns
0 output errors, 0 collisions, 7 interface resets
0 output buffer failures, 0 output buffers swapped out
231 carrier transitions
```

```
BRI0:2 is down, line protocol is down
Hardware is BRI
MTU 1500 bytes, BW 64 Kbit, DLY 20000 usec, rely 255/255, load 1/255
Encapsulation PPP, loopback not set, keepalive set (10 sec)
LCP Closed, multilink Closed
Closed: IPCP, CDPCP
Last input 07:12:56, output 07:12:56, output hang never
Last clearing of "show interface" counters never
Queueing strategy: fifo
Output queue 0/40, 0 drops; input queue 0/75, 0 drops
5 minute input rate 0 bits/sec, 0 packets/sec
5 minute output rate 0 bits/sec, 0 packets/sec
72 packets input, 2468 bytes, 0 no buffer
Received 72 broadcasts, 0 runts, 0 giants, 0 throttles
0 input errors, 0 CRC, 0 frame, 0 overrun, 0 ignored, 0 abort
74 packets output, 2480 bytes, 0 underruns
0 output errors, 0 collisions, 7 interface resets
0 output buffer failures, 0 output buffers swapped out
2 carrier transitions
```

A quick way to identify whether the BRI and B channels are up is to use the **show ip interface brief** command. This command shows whether the interface is up, whether the protocol is up, and also shows the IP address of the interface. Notice in the following output that the BRI0 interface is the only BRI interface that has an IP address assigned to it.

```
Router2# show ip interface brief
Interface          IP-Address      OK?     Method     Status     Protocol
BRI0               172.16.3.2      YES     NVRAM      up         up
BRI0:1             unassigned      YES     unset      up         up
BRI0:2             unassigned      YES     unset      up         up
Ethernet0          172.16.2.1      YES     NVRAM      up         up
Virtual-Access1    unassigned      YES     unset      up         up
Virtual-Access2    unassigned      YES     unset      down       down
```

The **show isdn status** command gives information on all three layers of the ISDN interface. It identifies the ISDN switch type configured, and gives information on SPIDs and active calls. You can see information on all three ISDN layers in the following output.

```
Router1# show isdn status
The current ISDN Switchtype = basic-ni1
ISDN BRI0 interface
Layer 1 Status:
ACTIVE
```

```
Layer 2 Status:
TEI = 118, Ces = 1, SAPI = 0, State =
MULTIPLE_FRAME_ESTABLISHED
TEI = 119, Ces = 2, SAPI = 0, State =
MULTIPLE_FRAME_ESTABLISHED
Spid Status:
TEI 118, ces = 1, state = 5(init)
spid1 configured, no LDN, spid1 sent, spid1 valid
Endpoint ID Info: epsf = 0, usid = 2, tid = 1
TEI 119, ces = 2, state = 5(init)
spid2 configured, no LDN, spid2 sent, spid2 valid
Endpoint ID Info: epsf = 0, usid = 4, tid = 1
Layer 3 Status:
1 Active Layer 3 Call(s)
Activated dsl 0 CCBs = 1
CCB:callid=0x8076, sapi=0x0, ces=0x1, B-chan=1
Total Allocated ISDN CCBs = 1
```

Monitoring the Dialer

The dialer is responsible for making and maintaining DDR connections. The **show dialer** command can be used to verify proper dialing and connectivity.

```
Router1# show dialer
BRI0 - dialer type = ISDN
Dial String Successes Failures Last called Last status
 8358661 235 1 00:01:53 successful
0 incoming call(s) have been screened.
0 incoming call(s) rejected for callback.
BRI0:1 - dialer type = ISDN
Idle timer (120 secs), Fast idle timer (20 secs)
Wait for carrier (30 secs), Re-enable (15 secs)
Dialer state is multilink member
Dial reason: snapshot
Connected to 8358661 (Router2)
BRI0:2 - dialer type = ISDN
Idle timer (120 secs), Fast idle timer (20 secs)
Wait for carrier (30 secs), Re-enable (15 secs)
Dialer state is idle
```

The **show dialer** command gives information on the phone number being dialed and the number of successful and failed calls to that number. It also provides specific information on the interface performing the dialing such as the values for "Idle timer," "Fast idle timer," "Wait for carrier," and "Re-enable." The Idle timer shows how long the router waits to disconnect after not receiving traffic. The Fast idle timer is triggered if there is traffic destined for a different number. This timer disconnects the circuit, allowing the data destined for the different network to be passed.

The command **show dialer maps** displays all static dialer maps configured on that router and the interface where they are configured. Here, there are two dialer maps configured on the BRI0 interface.

```
Router1# show dialer maps
Static dialer map ip 172.16.3.2 name Router1 broadcast (8358661) on BRI0
Static dialer map snapshot 1 name Router2 broadcast (8358661) on BRI0
```

The **debug dialer** command can also be used, which is useful for identifying DDR events such as the dialing cause and phone number being dialed.

```
Router1# debug dialer
Dial on demand events debugging is on
02:55:27: BRI0: Dialing cause ip (s=172.16.3.1, d=172.16.3.2)
02:55:27: BRI0: Attempting to dial 8358661
02:55:27: %ISDN-6-LAYER2UP: Layer 2 for Interface BR0, TEI 87 changed to up
02:55:27: %ISDN-6-LAYER2UP: Layer 2 for Interface BR0, TEI 88 changed to up
02:55:27: %LINK-3-UPDOWN: Interface BRI0:1, changed state to up
02:55:27: %LINK-3-UPDOWN: Interface Virtual-Access1, changed state to up
02:55:27: dialer Protocol up for Vi1
02:55:28: %LINEPROTO-5-UPDOWN: Line protocol on Interface BRI0:1, changed state to up
```

Backing up Permanent Connections

Permanent connections provide connectivity between local and remote sites. Although called *permanent connections*, we all know that nothing is ever really permanent. Like any other physical entity, these permanent connections are susceptible to failure. The problem with these connections is that if and when they fail, all connectivity is lost, resulting in costly downtime for the remote users.

To provide fault tolerance to the remote site, there must be a backup connection in place in case the permanent connection fails. In the event of a permanent connection failure, the backup connection should be able to kick in (transparent to the end-users) without any administrative intervention, and pick up right where the failed link left off. Let's take a look at some of the ways in which this type of backup connection can be provided.

Backup Interface

The backup interface is one of the mechanisms that provide redundancy in a WAN. The backup interface is configured in the primary interface configuration; when the primary goes down, it recognizes the loss of signal on the primary and raises DTR on the secondary interface. Figure 2.36 illustrates how to configure the backup interface on a point-to-point link.

Figure 2.36 Point-To-Point Permanent Connection with an ISDN Backup Connection

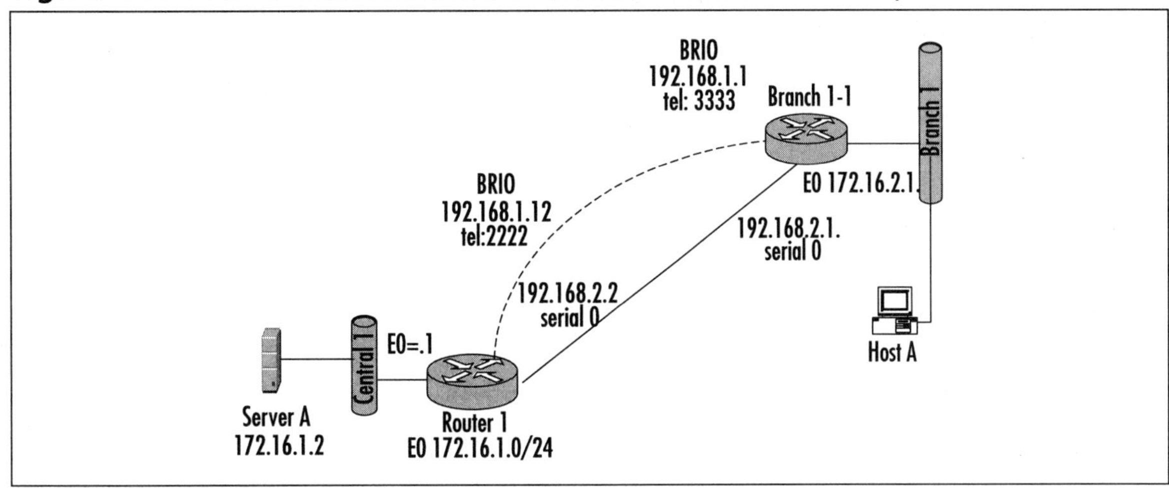


```
! central site
hostname Central-1

isdn switch-type basic-dms100
!
interface Ethernet0
ip address 172.16.1.1 255.255.255.0
no ip route-cache
no ip mroute-cache
!
interface Serial0
backup delay 30 never
backup interface BRI0
backup load 70 40
ip address 192.168.2.2 255.255.255.0
no ip route-cache
no ip mroute-cache
bandwidth 64
no shutdown
!
interface BRI0
ip address 192.168.1.2 255.255.255.0
encapsulation ppp
no ip route-cache
```

```
no ip mroute-cache
bandwidth 64
dialer idle-timeout 1
dialer map ip 192.168.1.1 name Branch1 3333
dialer load-threshold 180 outbound
dialer-group 10
isdn switch-type basic-dms100

 ppp authentication chap
no shutdown
!
ip classless
!
access-list 120 permit ip 172.16.2.0 0.0.0.255 host 192.168.1.1
dialer-list 10 protocol ip permit
!
end

! Branch-1
!
hostname Branch1
!
isdn switch-type basic-dms100
!
interface Ethernet0
ip address 172.16.2.1 255.255.255.0
no ip route-cache
no ip mroute-cache
!
interface Serial0
backup delay 60 20
!When primary fails, it waits for 60 sec,
! When primary comes back, the backup link waits
! for 20 sec before shutting down
backup interface BRI0   BRI 0 will be activated in case of s0 failure
backup load 80 30
ip address 192.168.2.1 255.255.255.0
no ip route-cache
no ip mroute-cache
bandwidth 64
```

```
no shutdown
!
interface BRI0
ip address 192.168.1.1 255.255.255.0
encapsulation ppp
no ip route-cache
no ip mroute-cache
bandwidth 64
dialer idle-timeout 180
dialer map ip 192.168.1.2 name CENTRAL-1 1111 ! Dialer string points
to remote
! side of the link
dialer load-threshold 1 either
dialer-group 10
isdn switch-type basic-dms100 ! ISDN switch type provided by TELCO
ppp authentication chap
no shutdown
!
ip classless
ip route 17.16.1.0 255.255.255.0 192.168.1.2
!
access-list 120 permit ip 172.16.1.0 0.0.0.255 host 192.168.1.2
access-list 120 permit tcp any any established
dialer-list 10 protocol ip list 120
!
end
```

The backup load Command

The **backup load** command allows the network administrator to use a secondary link when a set utilization has been reached. This command will enable or *bring up* a second interface, while the primary is still up and running, giving additional bandwidth as needed. This is desirable when there is heavy traffic on the primary link. For example:

```
interface serial 1
!
backup interface bri 0
!
backup load 85 10
```

If the primary link is 85 percent utilized, the backup line comes up. If the primary line's available bandwidth is less than 10 percent of the utilization of the backup link, the backup comes down.

Floating Static Routes and Default Routes

Static routes are usually preferred to dynamic routes because their default administrative distance is very low. For a dynamic route to be preferred over a static route, higher administrative distance value must be assigned to the static route. Floating static routes are another method of providing redundancy in a network. Similar to the **backup interface** command, it is a more dynamic method that provides a higher level of guarantee.

To understand the way a floating static route works, you must first understand routing metrics. Metrics in a routing environment provide a mechanism for the routing table manager (RTM) to decide which route to prefer. Each routing protocol has a default metric such as 20 for EBGP and 110 for OSPF. If a route can be reached via both EBGP and OSPF, the preferred route will be through EBGP, because it has a low-cost route. Static routes by default have a metric of 1, and directly connected networks have a metric of zero.

When the primary interface fails, the dynamic route is aged out. At this point, the static route becomes the preferred route to the destination. A floating static route provides a mechanism to increase the cost to reach a specific route; therefore, the dynamic routing protocol route is preferred.

A floating static route is more efficient than a backup interface, because a floating static route is already installed in the routing table. There is no convergence time required for a floating static route to be active. In case of the need for a backup interface, the router IOS has to activate the backup interface and make a connection via a dial-up to an ISDN or similar physical line.

The router has to start sending interesting packets, sending routing updates on the new route. The new route injection into the network will take time depending upon the convergence times, the diameter of the network, and so on. To configure a floating static route on the BRI interface, execute the following commands. Assume that all parameters have been configured.

```
router rip
network 10.0.0.0
network 192.168.0.0

! The administrative distance of 240 here is greater than RIP
! This means RIP routes will always be preferred.
! When RIP loses the route, this static route
!will become active.
ip route 192.168.0.0  255.255.0.0 10.10.10.10 240

int bri0
ip address 10.10.10.9 255.255.255.0
```

In Figure 2.37, a Frame Relay WAN is backed up via ISDN. Floating static routes have been configured such that when the Frame Relay circuit fails, it activates the static route, and interesting traffic will trigger the ISDN connection. The complete configuration is provided.

Figure 2.37 Frame Relay Network with ISDN Backup

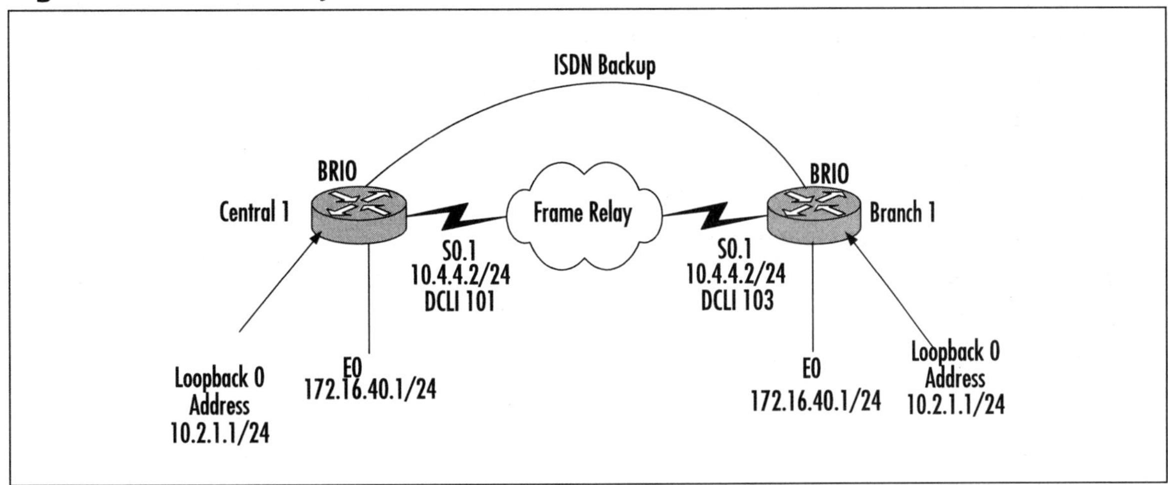


```
CENTRAL-1
!
hostname Central-1
!
isdn switch-type basic-5ess
!
interface Loopback0
ip address 10.2.1.1 255.255.255.0
!
interface Ethernet0
ip address 10.2.2.1 255.255.255.0
no shutdown
!
interface Serial0
no ip address
encapsulation frame-relay
no shutdown
!
interface Serial0.1 point-to-point
ip address 10.4.4.1 255.255.255.0
frame-relay interface-dlci 101
no shutdown
!
```

```
interface BRI0
ip unnumbered Ethernet0
encapsulation ppp
no ip route-cache
no ip mroute-cache
dialer map ip 10.1.1.1 name branch1 3333
dialer-group 1
isdn switch-type basic-5ess
ppp authentication chap callin
ppp chap hostname Central-1
ppp chap password 7 070C285F4D06
hold-queue 75 in
no shutdown
!
router eigrp 100
network 10.0.0.0
!
ip classless
ip route 10.1.1.1 255.255.255.255 BRI0 180 !floating static
! metric 180 will be active when primary fails
ip route 10.3.3.0 255.255.255.0 10.1.1.1 180! Floating static
!
access-list 101 deny ip any host 255.255.255.255
access-list 101 deny eigrp any any
access-list 101 permit ip any any
dialer-list 1 protocol ip list 101
!
end

****Branch1****
!
hostname Branch1
isdn switch-type basic-5ess
!
interface Loopback0
ip address 10.1.1.1 255.255.255.0
!
interface Ethernet0
ip address 10.3.3.1 255.255.255.0
no ip route-cache
```

```
no ip mroute-cache
no shutdown
!
interface Serial0
no ip address
encapsulation frame-relay
no ip route-cache
no ip mroute-cache
no shutdown
!
interface Serial0.1 point-to-point
ip address 10.4.4.2 255.255.255.0
no ip route-cache
no ip mroute-cache
frame-relay interface-dlci 103
no shutdown
!
interface BRI0
ip unnumbered Ethernet0
encapsulation ppp
no ip route-cache
no ip mroute-cache
dialer map ip 10.2.1.1 name Central-1 2222
dialer-group 1
isdn switch-type basic-5ess
ppp authentication chap callin
ppp chap hostname Branch1
hold-queue 75 in
no shutdown
!
router eigrp 100
network 10.0.0.0
!
ip classless
ip route 10.2.1.1 255.255.255.255 BRI0 180
ip route 10.2.2.0 255.255.255.0 10.2.1.1 180
!
access-list 101 deny ip any host 255.255.255.255
access-list 101 deny eigrp any any
access-list 101 permit ip any any
```

```
dialer-list 1 protocol ip list 101
!
```

The route table for routers with floating static routes contains all of the learned and connected routes as well as the floating static. In Figure 2.38, MainRouter1 has a floating static route configured to reach the 172.16.20.0/24 network in the event that the Frame Relay link fails. The following is an example of what you would see in the route table of MainRouter1 (with floating static route configured) *prior* to the primary link failure.

Figure 2.38 ISDN Backup and Floating Static Route

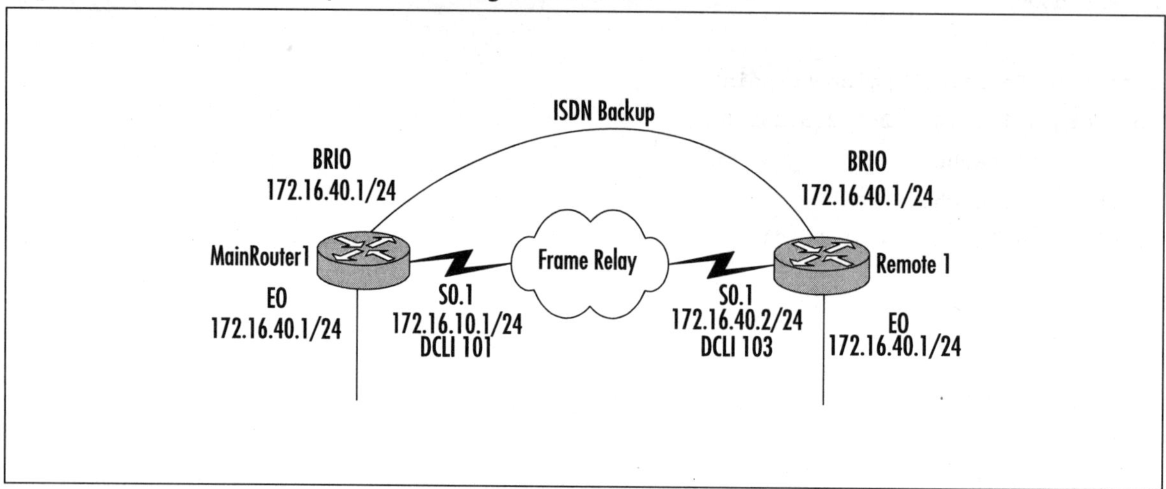


```
MainRouter# show ip route
Codes: C - connected, S - static, I - IGRP, R - RIP, M - mobile, B - BGP D - EIGRP,
EX - EIGRP external, O - OSPF, IA - OSPF inter area N1 - OSPF NSSA external type 1,
N2 - OSPF NSSA external type 2 E1 - OSPF external type 1, E2 - OSPF external type 2,
E - EGP i - IS-IS, L1 - ISIS level-1, L2 - ISIS level-2, * - candidate default
U - per-user static route, o - ODR
Gateway of last resort is not set
172.16.0.0/16 is variably subnetted, 4 subnets, 1 mask
D 172.16.20.0/24 [90/2195456] via 172.16.10.2, 00:07:28, Serial0
C 172.16.30.0/24 is directly connected, Ethernet0
C 172.16.10.0/24 is directly connected, Serial0
C 172.16.40.0/24 is directly connected, BRI0
S* 172.16.20.0/24 [180/0] via 172.16.40.1
```

Notice that MainRouter1 has learned about the 172.16.20.0/24 network via EIGRP. The floating static route has an asterisk specifying that it is candidate default (standby mode). It has an administrative distance of 180 (EIGRP administrative distance is 90), which means that currently the EIGRP route is preferred. If the EIGRP route is removed for any reason, the floating static route becomes the preferred route. Now let's see what happens to the route table after the EIGRP route to the 172.16.20 network disappears due to a Frame Relay link failure.

```
MainRouter# show ip route
Codes: C - connected, S - static, I - IGRP, R - RIP, M - mobile, B - BGP D - EIGRP,
EX - EIGRP external, O - OSPF, IA - OSPF inter area N1 - OSPF NSSA external type 1,
N2 - OSPF NSSA external type 2 E1 - OSPF external type 1, E2 - OSPF external type 2,
E - EGP i - IS-IS, L1 - ISIS level-1, L2 - ISIS level-2, * - candidate default
U - per-user static route, o - ODR
Gateway of last resort is not set
172.16.0.0/16 is variably subnetted, 4 subnets, 1 mask
C 172.16.30.0/24 is directly connected, Ethernet0
C 172.16.10.0/24 is directly connected, Serial0
C 172.16.40.0/24 is directly connected, BRI0
S 172.16.20.0/24 [180/0] via 172.16.40.1
```

Notice that the EIGRP route has disappeared and that the static route is no longer in standby mode (it has no asterisk next to it). It has taken over and is providing a route to the 172.16.20.0 network through the BRI0 interface. It will be the primary route to that network until such a time when the router learns a new route via a routing protocol with a lower administrative distance. The static route would then return to standby mode (candidate default).

Dialer Watch

Dialer watch is used to monitor a specific route in the routing table, which is not to be confused with dialer backup, which monitors a specific interface. The example here monitors 192.168.0.0 255.255.0.0, and will activate a dial session if this route disappears from the routing table.

```
dialer watch-list 99 ip 192.168.0.0 255.255.0.0
interface bri0
dialer watch-group 999
```

Dialer Watch or Dial Backup is used in a DDR environment to monitor an active interface. An ISDN BRI interface can be configured to monitor a Frame Relay interface or a Frame Relay DLCI. The monitoring interface becomes activated when the monitored interface or the DLCI reaches a down status. This method keeps the monitoring interface (ISDN) in a perpetual state of down and cannot be used to send/receive any traffic until the monitored interface goes down or the configured load threshold has been exceeded. To configure a BRI0 interface to back up a serial0 interface, type:

```
Int s0
Backup interface bri0
Backup delay time1 time2
```

Time1 is the time in seconds that the backup interface waits before going into activation after the primary line went down, and *time2* is the time in seconds the backup interface waits before going into standby mode after the primary line is up.

Configuring a Dialer Profile

Another method is to configure a dialer profile. As discussed previously, dialer profiles are logical interfaces that can be configured with most of the parameters of a physical interface. The logical interface now monitors the primary or active interface, and activates the physical ISDN interface only when the active interface fails. This means that the ISDN line could be used to send/receive traffic. The dialer profile configuration follows a similar ISDN configuration except that it is a logical interface.

```
Int dialer n ! where n is an integer
Ip address and other configuration parameters.
Dialer pool x where x is an integer
Dialer string where string is the remote phone number
```

On the BRI0 interface, configure:

```
!
Int bri0
Encapsulation ppp
Ppp authentication chap
Dialer pool-member x
```

On the serial interface, configure:

```
Int s0
Ip address and other parameters
Backup interface dialern
Backup delay time1 time2
```

With the dialer profile configuration, the ISDN interface is only used when needed and released after use.

Verifying and Troubleshooting Backup Connections

Let's look at some of the commands that can be used to troubleshoot and verify your ISDN backup connections. The first command we examine is **show controller** that provides the physical level information on the line.

```
Central1# show controller
BRI unit 0
!On BRI , ISDN the channels are divided into 2B+D. Here in the output below these
channels !show layer1 is activated. The message activated ensures, that the BRI
interface is !successfully communicated with carrier ISDN switch.
D Chan Info:
Layer 1 is ACTIVATED
idb 0x148D68, ds 0x15BE88, reset_mask 0x8 buffer size 1524
RX ring with 2 entries at 0x2101600 : Rxhead 1
```

```
00 pak=0x15C41C ds=0x614FEC status=D000 pak_size=0
01 pak=0x15C614 ds=0x6156AC status=F000 pak_size=0 TX ring with 2 entries at
0x2101640: tx_count = 0, tx_head = 0, tx_tail = 0
00 pak=0x000000 ds=0x000000 status=00 pak_size=0
01 pak=0x000000 ds=0x000000 status=00 pak_size=0
0 missed datagrams, 0 overruns, 0 bad frame addresses
0 bad datagram encapsulations, 0 memory errors
0 transmitter underruns
0 d channel collisions
B1 Chan Info:
Layer 1 is ACTIVATED
idb 0x14E8CC, ds 0x15BF60, reset_mask 0x0
buffer size 1524
RX ring with 8 entries at 0x2101400 : Rxhead 0
00 pak=0x15E108 ds=0x61AE6C status=D000 pak_size=0
01 pak=0x15DF10 ds=0x61A7AC status=D000 pak_size=0
02 pak=0x15DD18 ds=0x61A0EC status=D000 pak_size=0
03 pak=0x15DB20 ds=0x619A2C status=D000 pak_size=0
04 pak=0x15D928 ds=0x61936C status=D000 pak_size=0
05 pak=0x15D730 ds=0x618CAC status=D000 pak_size=0
06 pak=0x15D538 ds=0x6185EC status=D000 pak_size=0
07 pak=0x15D340 ds=0x617F2C status=F000 pak_size=0
TX ring with 2 entries at 0x2101440: tx_count = 0, tx_head = 0, tx_tail = 0
00 pak=0x000000 ds=0x000000 status=5C00 pak_size=0
01 pak=0x000000 ds=0x000000 status=7C00 pak_size=0
0 missed datagrams, 0 overruns, 0 bad frame addresses
0 bad datagram encapsulations, 0 memory errors
0 transmitter underruns
0 d channel collisions
B2 Chan Info:
Layer 1 is ACTIVATED
idb 0x154430, ds 0x15C038, reset_mask 0x2
buffer size 1524
RX ring with 8 entries at 0x2101500 : Rxhead 0
00 pak=0x1601E4 ds=0x621A6C status=D000 pak_size=0
01 pak=0x15FFEC ds=0x6213AC status=D000 pak_size=0
02 pak=0x15FDF4 ds=0x620CEC status=D000 pak_size=0
03 pak=0x15FBFC ds=0x62062C status=D000 pak_size=0
04 pak=0x15FA04 ds=0x61FF6C status=D000 pak_size=0
05 pak=0x15F80C ds=0x61F8AC status=D000 pak_size=0
```

```
06 pak=0x15F614 ds=0x61F1EC status=D000 pak_size=0
07 pak=0x15F41C ds=0x61EB2C status=F000 pak_size=0
TX ring with 2 entries at 0x2101540: tx_count = 0, tx_head = 0, tx_tail = 0
00 pak=0x000000 ds=0x000000 status=5C00 pak_size=0
01 pak=0x000000 ds=0x000000 status=7C00 pak_size=0
0 missed datagrams, 0 overruns, 0 bad frame addresses
0 bad datagram encapsulations, 0 memory errors
0 transmitter underruns
0 d channel collisions
```

Use **show interface BRI 0** to find most of the details about the ISDN interface.

```
Central1# show interface bri 0
BRI0 is up, line protocol is up (spoofing) ! Spoofing indicates that BRI interface is
acting as backup interface
Hardware is BRI
Internet address is 10.2.2.1/24
MTU 1500 bytes, BW 64 Kbit, DLY 20000 usec, rely 255/255, load 1/255
Encapsulation PPP, loopback not set
Last input 00:00:00, output 00:00:00, output hang never
Last clearing of "show interface" counters never
Input queue: 0/75/0 (size/max/drops); Total output drops: 0
Queueing strategy: weighted fair
Output queue: 0/1000/64/0 (size/max total/threshold/drops)
Conversations 0/1/256 (active/max active/max total)
Reserved Conversations 0/0 (allocated/max allocated)
5 minute input rate 0 bits/sec, 0 packets/sec
5 minute output rate 0 bits/sec, 0 packets/sec
108 packets input, 524 bytes, 0 no buffer
Received 20 broadcasts, 0 runts, 0 giants, 0 throttles
0 input errors, 0 CRC, 0 frame, 0 overrun, 0 ignored, 0 abort
106 packets output, 508 bytes, 0 underruns
0 output errors, 0 collisions, 12 interface resets
! Interface resets and carrier transitions do occur, as backup interface comes up when
activated, and reverts back to the spoofing state after the primary link is restored.
0 output buffer failures, 0 output buffers swapped out
3 carrier transitions
```

The **shown isdn status** command allows you to confirm the health and parameters of the ISDN connections as shown.

```
Router1# show isdn status
Central1# show isdn status
```

```
Global ISDN Switchtype = basic-5ess !Identifies the switch type used
ISDN BRI0 interface
dsl 0, interface ISDN Switchtype = basic-5ess
Layer 1 Status:
ACTIVE
Layer 2 Status: !show that layer 2 is active and bonding at 64k on the B1 channel
TEI = 64, Ces = 1, SAPI = 0, State =
MULTIPLE_FRAME_ESTABLISHED
Layer 3 Status:
0 Active Layer 3 Call(s)
Activated dsl 0 CCBs = 0
Total Allocated ISDN CCBs = 0
```

Usually the initial setup problems are a switch type mismatch (like 5ESS or DMS100), or a wrong SPID number. SPID numbers might need a leading or trailing zero, depending what the Telco has programmed.

```
Debug ISDN Event
BRI0: ISDN Event: incoming ces value = 1
BRI0: received HOST_TERM_REGISTER_NACK - invalid EID/SPID or TEI not assigned
Cause i = 0x8082 - No route to specified network
```

To verify that TEI is assigned, show ISDN status. Also look at the ISDN CSU/DSU (ISDSU) to see if it has a TEI link up. On ADTRAN ISU128 models, the ISDN configuration is provided through the keypad. Using the keypad, check the status of the line, which provides the TEI line linkup details.

Routing Issues

Confirm that the configuration for the backup interface, or the floating static, is properly functioning, by disconnecting the primary cable and verifying the routing tables. As the ISDN comes up, see if it is getting activated on the correct interesting traffic.

Redundant Hardware and Links/ Design and Performance Issues

A network could be designed with built-in redundancy such as two T1s (instead of just one) between two sites. In this type of scenario you may see two routers at each physical location (site), with a total of four. Another scenario may be one router with two serial links (with a total of two). See Figure 2.39 for an illustration of the two scenarios.

Figure 2.39 Redundant Hardware and Link Designs For Backups

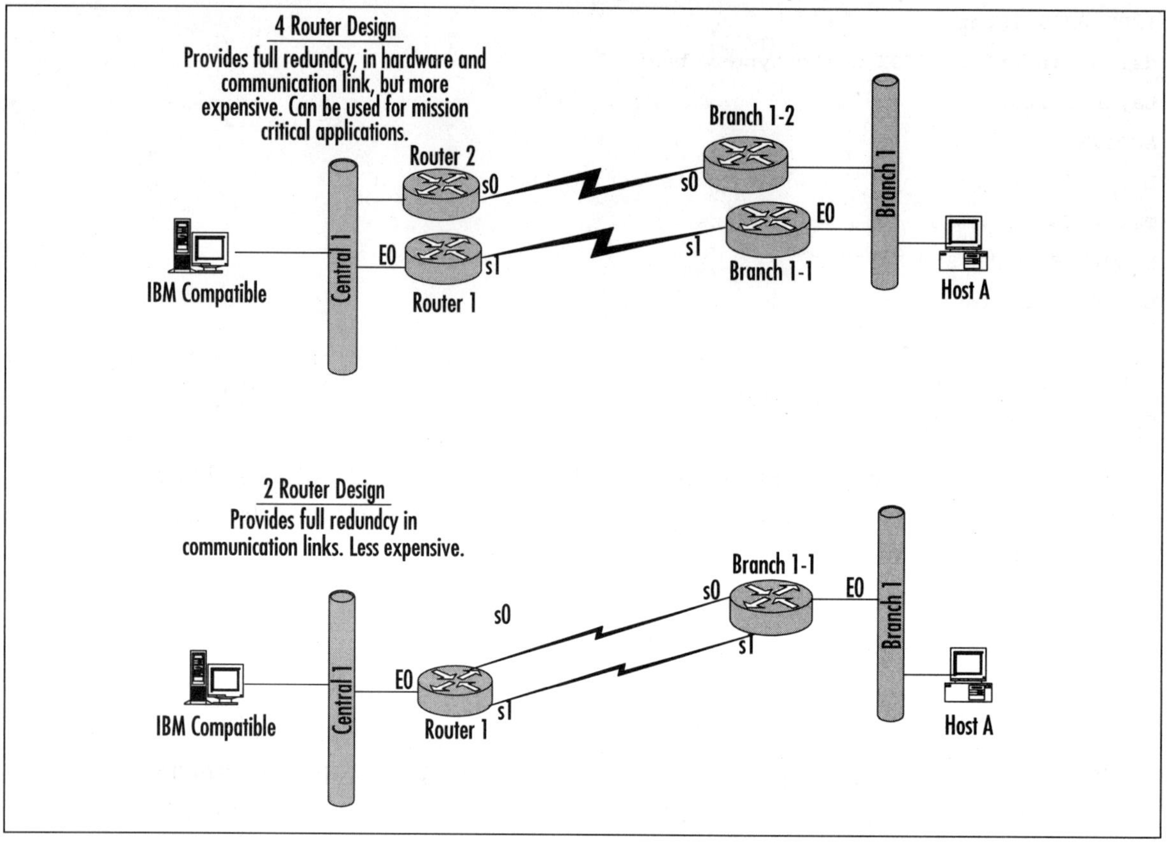

The usual practice entails one router on each end with two serial links, because of the cost of the hardware (two routers instead of four), and a better throughput due to the load balancing. However, using a single router at a site means that it will be a single point of failure. The decision you are faced with is whether the cost of the extra router and circuit are outweighing the costs of an outage. One additional plus of having additional circuits and routers is that you will have a better opportunity to load balance.

Load Balancing

Load balancing is a function that spreads the traffic over multiple devices and circuits, rather than sending it all through a single device and circuit. Cisco routers can support two types of load balancing (sometimes referred to as *load sharing*): per-destination load balancing and per-packet load balancing. Let's look at each of these in detail.

Per-Destination Load Balancing

By default, Cisco routers are in a *fast switching mode*. This means that the first time a router receives a packet addressed to a particular destination, it performs a route-table lookup and selects the route. That information is then stored in the fast switching cache so that any subsequent packets bound for the same destination can be immediately switched and sent over the predetermined route without having to perform another lookup. This means that all packets destined for a particular host will take the same route. All packets destined for another host on the same destination network can and will take a different route. The balance is decided on a per destination basis, as shown in Figure 2.40. Notice that there are two packets destined for each of the two hosts (Host 2 and Host 3). The path that each packet takes is dependent on which destination it is bound for.

Figure 2.40 Per-Destination Load Balancing

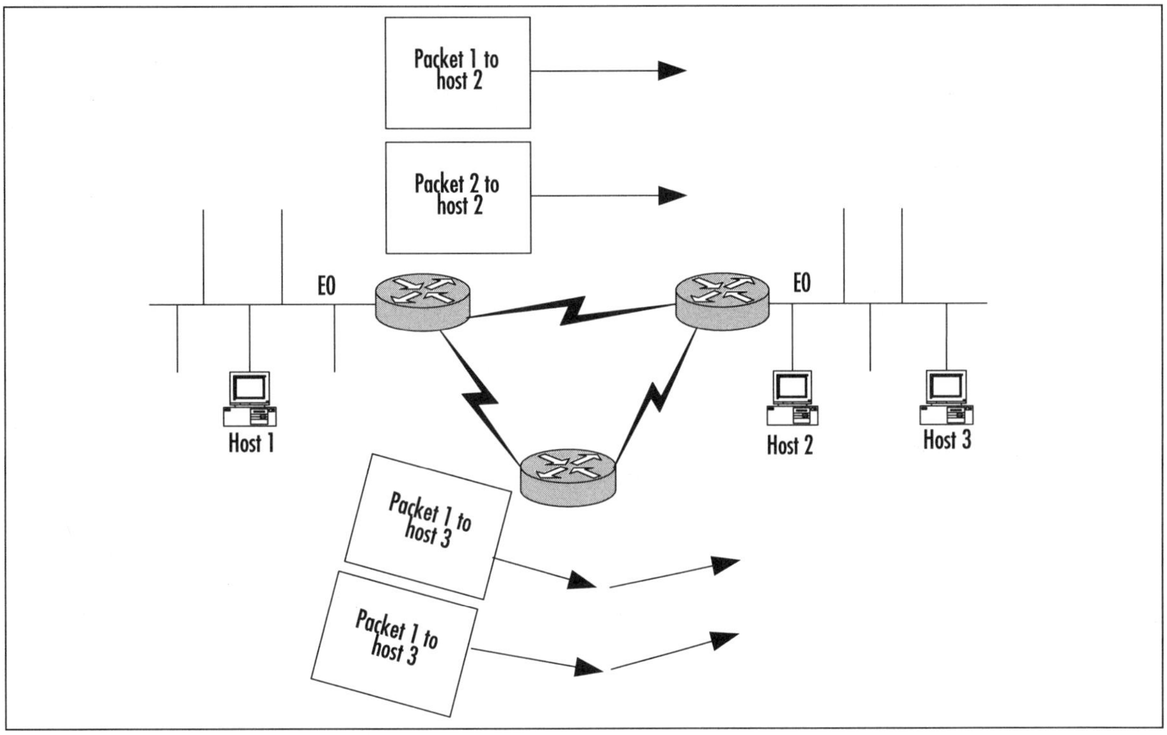

Per-packet Load Balancing

By implementing the command **no ip route-cache** on a Cisco router, two things on the router change. First, the router load-balances traffic across two equal cost paths on a packet-by-packet basis. Second, the router switches from the default setting of fast switching to process switching. Process switching simply means that the router will do a route table lookup for each packet it must process. Because each route decision is independent, packets will be distributed evenly across the two equal cost paths (See Figure 2.41.) Per-packet load balancing results in more evenly balanced traffic over the equal cost links—however, there are a couple of drawbacks to this method. The switching process is not as fast as fast switching (hence the name) and there is added overhead on the CPU. This must be considered when selecting the load-balancing method for a particular network. Notice that, regardless of the destination, the packets are evenly distributed over the two links.

Figure 2.41 Per Packet Load Balancing

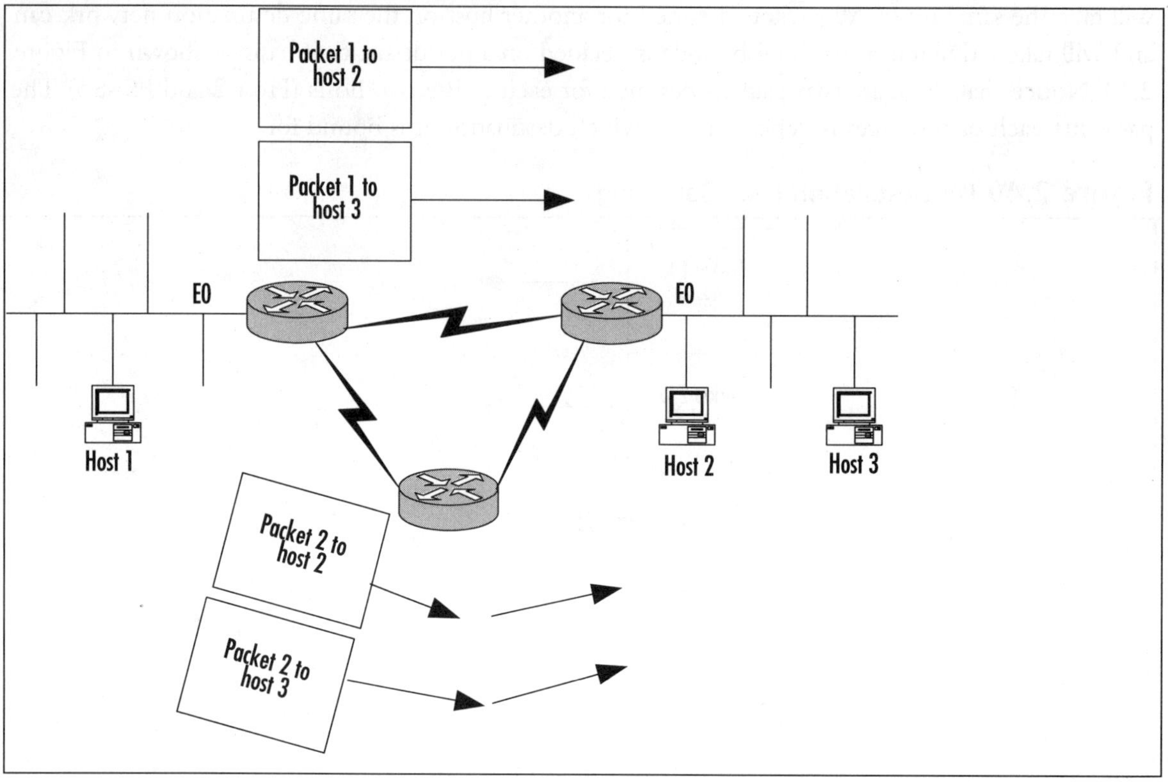

Summary

We covered a lot of material in this chapter! It examined point-to-point connections and their benefit, the related protocols, and a simple point-to point configuration. It covered Frame Relay packets and the fields they contain. It explained LMI, CIR, Frame-Relay Traffic Shaping (FRTS), and subinterfaces as well as Frame Relay topologies and configurations. It described troubleshooting in a Frame Relay environment, the related troubleshooting commands, and some common problems.

ATM connections and the fixed cell length of 53 bytes were described next. We talked about the fact that the fixed cell length cuts down on latency and is much more efficient for transmitting voice or video data. The discussion covered ATM packets and virtual circuits. We looked at some ATM configurations and talked about troubleshooting ATM networks.

The chapter concluded by describing what it takes to provide some level of fault tolerance to your connections. We looked at backup interfaces, backup ISDN circuits, floating static routes, redundant hardware, and load balancing. All of these elements can provide more dependable network connectivity in the event of a link failure.

Chapter 3

Wireless Networking

Best Damn Topics in this Chapter:

- Understanding the Fundamentals of Radio Frequencies
- Communicating with Wireless LAN Technologies
- Wireless Networking Standards
- Wireless Design Considerations
- Implementing a Wireless LAN Architecture
- Security Fundamentals for Wireless Networks
- Wireless Equivalency Privacy
- Cisco Wireless Systems
- Cisco's Aironet 3X0 Series APs and Bridges
- Cisco's Aironet Wireless NICs
- Installing the Cisco Aironet 3X0 APs
- Initial Configuration of the Cisco 3X0 Series APs
- Web-Based Configuration of the Cisco 340 and 350 Series APs
- Web-Based Configuration of the Cisco 340 BSE/BSM Series AP
- Cisco Aironet Wireless Bridges
- Installation of the Cisco Aironet Bridge Unit
- Initial Configuration of the Wireless Bridge Using the Command-Line Interface
- Operational Configuration of the Cisco Aironet Wireless Bridge
- Event Logging
- Viewing Statistics
- Cisco Aironet Wireless Bridge Troubleshooting
- Cisco Aironet Antennas
- Bridge and AP Accessories
- Cabling, Connectors and Bulkhead Extenders

Introduction

Wireless networks have become integral to many organizations over the past few years, and no wonder. The ability to remain connected and mobile without wires provides a wealth of benefits. Entire buildings and campuses can establish a network presence with a minimum of wires. No longer is it necessary to install a wired network drop in every location, which can be an expensive and time consuming undertaking. Wireless networking allows users to be mobile, yet still be able perform tasks such as checking their e-mails, accessing servers, and use the resources of the Internet.

Integrating both wired network and wireless LAN (WLAN) technologies into a single device allows the administrator to have the best of both worlds. In addition to the radio technologies that enable WLANs, other technologies are employed to provide security, efficiency, and stability to the wireless local area network.

Because WLAN radio devices use various aspects of radio technology, this chapter first reviews radio frequency (RF) fundamentals such as the practical information necessary to understand the functionality of any WLAN radio device, including Cisco Aironet products. Because this subject matter represents such a broad range of topics and technologies, discussing them all in one chapter is difficult at best. Instead, this chapter focuses on the fundamentals and standards as they directly relate to WLANs. It discusses current wireless technologies and the advantages and disadvantages of various wireless technology implementations, with greater attention given to the technology used by Cisco Aironet devices.

Understanding the Fundamentals of Radio Frequencies

RF in wireless communications describes devices or equipment that use radio waves to transmit images and sounds from one transmission point to one or more reception points. In networking, RF is used to describe network devices (access points [APs], bridges, and so on) that use radio waves to transmit or receive data instead of using traditional wired data cabling or telephone lines. Wireless systems utilize components of radio technology to prepare, transmit, and receive the digital data.

In 1886, Heinrich Hertz developed a device called a *spark gap coil*, for generating and detecting electromagnetic waves. This spark gap coil would not have been possible if it were not for the mathematical theory of electromagnetic waves formulated by Scottish physicist James Clerk Maxwell in 1865. In 1895, Guglielmo Marconi, recognizing the possibility of using these electromagnetic waves for a wireless communication system, gave a demonstration of the first wireless telegraph, using Hertz's spark coil as a transmitter and a radio detector called a *coherer*, which was developed by a scientist by the name of Edouard Branly, as the first radio receiver. The effective operating distance of this system increased as the equipment was improved, and in 1901, Marconi succeeded in sending the letter "S" across the Atlantic Ocean using Samuel Morse's dot-dash communication coding technique (now known as Morse code). The first vacuum electron tube capable of detecting radio waves electronically was invented (by Sir John Fleming) in 1904.

Two years later, Lee de Forest invented a type of triode (a three-element vacuum tube) called an *audion*, which not only detected radio waves but also amplified them.

To understand wireless, consider AM/FM radio. The radio station impresses (encodes) information, like voice or speech, on a radio wave via a process known as *modulation*. The radio station broadcasts this radio wave with the encoded data (music) on a set frequency. A car radio antenna picks up the broadcast based on the frequency to which the radio dial is tuned. A car radio then decodes the music from the radio wave and plays that information through the speakers as music, as shown in Figure 3.1.

Figure 3.1 Car Radio Transmission and Reception Process

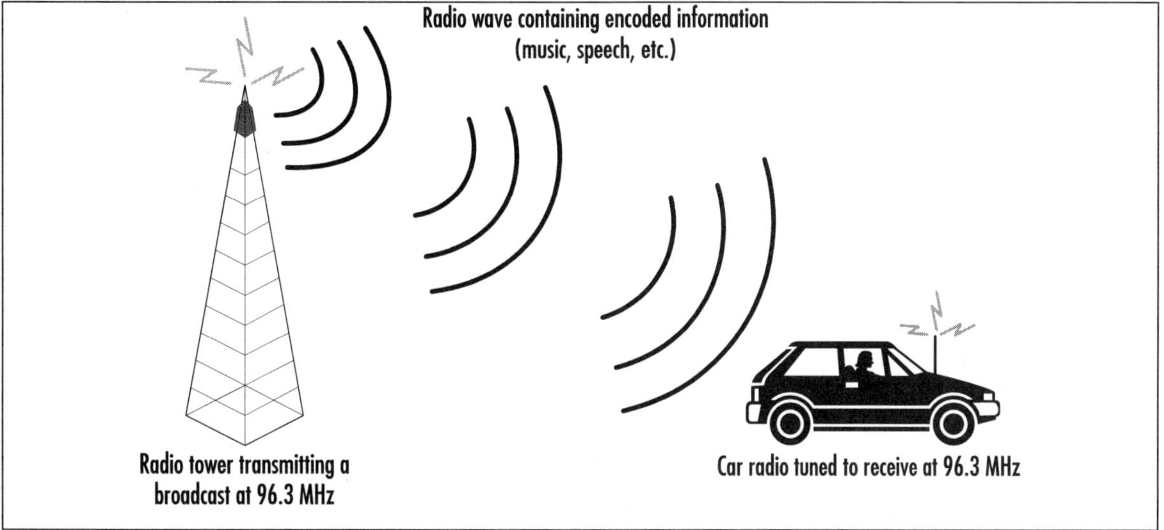

Understanding Wireless Radio Signal Transmission and Reception

RF is a specific type of electric current known as alternating current (AC) that generates an electromagnetic field (RF field) when applied to an antenna. The subsequent electromagnetic radiation of the RF field is used for wireless broadcasting and/or communications. When an electric current flows through a wire, a magnetic field is generated around the wire. When AC flows through a wire, the magnetic field alternately expands and collapses. This expansion and collapse is a result of the electrical current reversing its direction. In the United States, AC reverses direction or alternates at a frequency of 60 Hertz (Hz), or 60 cycles per second. In South America and Europe, AC typically alternates at a frequency of 50 Hz or 50 cycles per second.

As seen in the car radio analogy, a radio wave is broadcast from the radio station tower. To broadcast the radio wave, AC is applied, giving rise to an electromagnetic field that moves and spreads through space, like the ripples caused by dropping a pebble into a pond.

The radio transmitter and antenna generate a moving electric charge. Nonmoving or static electric charges produce electric fields around them. Moving electric charges produce both electric and magnetic fields, or an electromagnetic field. An electromagnetic field is generated when charged particles, such as electrons, are accelerated. Electric fields surround all electrically charged particles. When these charged particles are in motion, they produce magnetic fields. When the speed of the charged particle changes, an electromagnetic field is produced. In the nineteenth century, scientists discovered that arcs or sparks of electrical energy (in the form of an electromagnetic field) could travel between two perpendicular conductive rods without the aid of wires between them. They learned to reproduce this effect over varying distances and led them to believe that it was possible to communicate wirelessly over long distances. These electric arcs were used in the first radio transmitters.

Electrically charged particles in motion produce electromagnetic fields. When the motion of these charged particles regularly repeats or changes, they produce what is called *electromagnetic radiation*. Electromagnetic radiation moves energy from one point to another. This is somewhat like a small ball moving the same way over and over against the inside of a larger ball, causing the larger ball to move in a certain direction. The larger ball represents the electromagnetic radiation and the smaller ball inside the larger ball represents an electrically charged particle in motion. Radio waves are not the only form of electromagnetic radiation.

Light is also electromagnetic radiation, and shares similarities with radio waves such as the speed at which both travel. Both are moving through space in approximately straight lines at a speed of about 299,792 km per second or 186,000 miles per second. In other words, a radio wave as electromagnetic radiation travels at the speed of light.

As the distance from the energy source of electromagnetic radiation increases, the area over which the electromagnetic radiation is spread is increased, so that the available energy from the electromagnetic radiation in a given area is decreased. Radio signal intensity (amplitude), like light intensity, decreases as the distance from the source increases. The signal gets weaker as you move farther away from the source of the transmission. A transmitting antenna is a device that projects electromagnetic radiation as RF energy, into space by a transmitter (the electromagnetic radiation energy source). The antenna can be designed to concentrate the RF energy into a beam and increase its effectiveness in a given direction.

Radio is commonly used for the transmission of voice, music, and pictures, as in broadcast radio and television. The sounds and images used in radio and television are converted into electrical signals by an input device such as a microphone or video camera. They are then amplified and used to encode (modulate) a carrier wave that has been generated by an oscillator circuit (a circuit used to produce AC) in a transmitter.

A carrier wave is the form of the radio wave prior to modulation or transmission. The modulated carrier wave is also amplified and then applied to an antenna that converts the electrical signals to electromagnetic waves for radiation into space. Electromagnetic waves are transmitted by line-of-sight and by deflection from a specific layer of the upper atmosphere, called the ionosphere, 30 to 250 miles above the earth's surface. Ionization of nitrogen and oxygen molecules from ultraviolet radiation and X-rays from the sun produces a layer of charged particles, which allows radio waves to be reflected around the world.

Receiving antennas do not actively search for a radio wave from any source. The electromagnetic radiation from the originating antenna passes across the passive, receiving antenna. Receiving antennas intercept part of this electromagnetic radiation and change it back to the form of an electrical signal. The receiving antennas then feed this signal to a receiver, which in turn takes the incoming signals mixed with a signal from a local oscillator in the receiver, to produce intermediate frequencies that are equal to the mathematical sum and difference of the incoming and local frequencies. In other words, the oscillator acts as a type of filter to weed out all frequencies other than the intended frequency. The oscillator then sends this intended frequency through an amplifier. Because the amplifier operates at the previously determined intermediate frequency (a single frequency), it is designed for optimum selectivity and gain. The tuning control on a radio receiver adjusts the local oscillator frequency. In order for the receiver to amplify the signal and feed it to circuits that demodulate it to separate the signal wave from the carrier wave, the incoming signals must be above the threshold of sensitivity of the receiver and tuned to the frequency of the signal.

Radio transceivers act as both transmitter and receiver for radio signals. When a responding signal is sent back to the originating radio, the radio transceiver changes modes from reception to transmission and back again. Cisco Aironet APs and bridges are transceivers. Transceivers change modes from transmission to reception over and over again. They will do this many thousands of times per second. Though transceivers allow you to transmit and receive with the same device, thus reducing the size and cost of radios, in wireless networking, this capability introduces *latency*, a delay in communications. It is idiosyncratic to radio communications and negatively affects data throughput, albeit minimally.

Radio Frequencies

AC is electric current used to produce electromagnetic fields. AC alternates, or cycles over a period of time known as *amplitude*. The amplitude oscillates from zero to some maximum and back again. The number of times the cycle is repeated in one second is called the frequency, which can range from a single cycle in thousands of years to quadrillions of cycles per second.

Heinrich Hertz invented the spark coil for generating and detecting radio waves. The unit of measurement for frequency (a Hertz) is named after him. A Hertz is usually defined as one cycle per second, or one wave per second. The frequency unit or Hertz is normally abbreviated to Hz. Because frequencies can be very large, the standard units of quantities used in science and commonly seen in the data world are used to annotate them. For example, 1,000 Hz equals 1 KHz (kilohertz), 1,000 KHz equals 1 megahertz (MHz), 1,000 MHz equals 1 GHz (gigahertz), and so on.

At any given instance, a radio wave will have an amplitude variation similar to that of its time variation. Picture the waves produced by a pebble dropped into a still pond. One of the waves traveling on the pond represents a radio wave, the height of that wave represents the amplitude, and the speed at which that wave travels represents the time variation. The distance from the top of one wave to the next is known as the wavelength. The RF of an RF field is directly related to its wavelength. By specifying the frequency of a radio wave (f) in megahertz and the wavelength (w) in meters, the two are interrelated mathematically, according to the following formula:

$$w = 300/f$$

In the car radio example, the radio is tuned to 96.3 MHz. This is the signal frequency of the radio station transmitter we want to "listen to." At 96.3 MHz, the signal has a wavelength of about 3 meters, or about 10 feet. This same formula applies if the wavelength is specified in millimeters (mm) and the frequency is given in gigahertz. Therefore a Cisco Aironet AP that transmits a signal at 2.4 GHz would have an approximate wavelength of 120 mm, or a little less than 5 inches. Remember, all radio waves travel at the speed of light, so a radio wave with a shorter wavelength will cross a specific point in space (such as an antenna) more times than a radio wave with a long wavelength.

As the frequency of a radio gets higher, the corresponding wavelength of the electromagnetic field gets shorter. At 9 KHz, the free space wavelength is approximately 33km or 21 miles. At the highest radio frequencies, the electromagnetic wavelengths measure approximately 1 mm. As the frequency is increased beyond that of the RF spectrum, electromagnetic energy takes the form of various types of light and energy such as infrared light (IR), visible light, ultraviolet light (UV), X-rays, and gamma rays.

Electromagnetic radiation, as radio waves, can be generated and used at frequencies higher than 10 KHz. A considerable segment of the electromagnetic radiation spectrum is available for use, extending from about 9 KHz, the lowest allocated wireless communications frequency, to thousands of GHzs, with the upper ends of the frequency spectrum consisting of gamma and cosmic rays. Many types of wireless devices make use of radio waves. Radio and television broadcast stations, cordless and cellular telephone, two-way radio systems, and satellite communications are but a few. Other wireless devices make use of the visible light and infrared portions of the frequency spectrum. These areas of the spectrum have electromagnetic wavelengths that are shorter than those in RF fields. Examples include most television remote controls, some cordless computer keyboards and mice, and many laptop computers. Table 3.1 depicts the eight bands of the frequency spectrum used in the United States Frequency Allocation, displaying frequency and bandwidth ranges. These frequency allocations vary slightly from country to country.

Table 3.1 The United States Frequency Allocation Chart

Designation	Abbreviation	Frequencies	Free-Space Wavelengths
Very Low Frequency	VLF	9 KHz–30 KHz	33km–10km
Low Frequency	LF	30 KHz–300 KHz	10km–1km
Medium Frequency	MF	300 KHz–3 MHz	1km–100m
High Frequency	HF	3 MHz–30 MHz	100m–10m
Very High Frequency	VHF	30 MHz–300 MHz	10m–1m
Ultra High Frequency	UHF	300 MHz–3 GHz	1 mm–100 mm
Super High Frequency	SHF	3 GHz–30 GHz	100 mm–10 mm
Extremely High Frequency	EHF	30 GHz–300 GHz	10 mm–1 mm

The RF spectrum is divided into several ranges, or bands. Most bands represent an increase of frequency corresponding to an order of magnitude of a power of 10. The exception to this is the extreme low end of the frequency spectrum. Table 3.2 shows examples of the classes of devices assigned to each frequency.

Table 3.2 Example Device Classes by Frequency Allocation

Designation	Abbreviation	Examples
Very Low Frequency	VLF	Radio navigation devices for marine vessels, military communication with nuclear submarines (maritime mobile)
Low Frequency	LF	Marine and aeronautical radio navigation and location devices
Medium Frequency	MF	Marine and aeronautical radio beacons, distress beacons, AM radio broadcasting, and maritime radio voice communications
High Frequency	HF	Amateur radio and satellite communications, radio astronomy, and space research
Very High Frequency	VHF	Amateur radio and satellite, FM radio broadcasting, TV broadcasting (Channels 2 to 13), radio astronomy, mobile satellite communications
Ultra High Frequency	UHF	Fixed satellite communications, meteorological satellite communications, amateur radio, TV broadcasting (Channels 14 to 36 and 38 to 69), WLANs, land mobile communications (cell phones, cordless phones, and so on), radio astronomy, and aeronautical radio navigation
Super High Frequency	SHF	Inter-satellite communications, WLANs, weather radars, land mobile communications
Extremely High Frequency	EHF	Space research, earth exploration satellites, amateur radio and satellite communications, radio astronomy, fixed and mobile satellite communications

Radio Country Options

Allowed RF frequencies differ by country. Many Cisco wireless products encryption is greater than 64-bit and require that special export regulations be followed, or it cannot be exported to particular countries. Cisco groups countries into areas that all have similar requirements. After analyzing the different products that each country allows, it was determined that the countries fell into three different groups, the Americas, Europe, and Japan, as shown in Table 3.3. Cisco created part numbers to reflect these groupings and to indicate which products had greater than 64-bit encryption. Part number AIR-BR350-E-K9 still refers to a 350 Bridge (part #AIR-BR350), however the "-E" means that it used the "European" frequencies and power and the "-K9" means that the encryption is greater than 64 bits.

Table 3.3 Radio Country Groupings and Number of Channels

Group	Abbreviation	# of RF Channels
Americas	A	11
Europe	E	13
Japan	J	14

To ensure that products are not shipped to countries where they are prohibited, Cisco created a product/country matrix showing which products are approved for shipment to which country as well as the group that each country belongs to. For a more detailed list of products as well as countries, please see the Cisco Web site at www.cisco.com/warp/public/779/smbiz/wireless/approvals.html.

What is Bandwidth?

Traditionally, bandwidth is the amount of information that can be carried through a phone line, cable line, satellite feed, or any communications medium. The greater the bandwidth, the higher the speed of the connection, meaning that more data can be transported.

Bandwidth is the capacity (measured in bits per second) for sending and receiving data over a connection. A full page of English text is about 16,000 (16 Kbps) bits; the time it would take to transmit this page depends on the bandwidth available plus any overhead associated with the connection. Full-motion full-screen video requires roughly 10,000,000 bits per second, depending on compression.

In the radio world, bandwidth is defined in a more complicated manner. Bandwidth is the difference between limiting frequencies within which performance of a radio device, in respect to some characteristic, falls within specified limits or the difference between the limiting frequencies of a continuous frequency band. In the 2.4 GHz unlicensed frequency band, which is used in Cisco Aironet products (described fully later in the chapter), the band begins at 2.4 GHz and ends at 2.4835 GHz. The difference between the beginning point and the end point is the bandwidth. Therefore, the total available bandwidth available for use by wireless devices in this band is .0835 GHz or 83.5 MHz.

WLAN Frequency Bands

To prevent interference from radio signals in the United States, the Federal Communications Commission (FCC) is charged with assigning small sections of the RF spectrum for specific uses called *licensed frequencies*. To broadcast radio signals at these frequencies, the administrator must obtain a license from the FCC.

The FCC allocated separate bands of radio frequencies as public bands, allowing use of some of the radio spectrum for devices that would not require a license. No license is required to use equipment transmitting at these frequencies. These are called the Industrial Scientific and Medical (ISM) bands, short for ISM bands.

There are three unlicensed bands within the ISM frequency range. They are the 900 MHz, 2.4 GHz, and 5.8 GHz frequencies (see Figure 3.2). Cisco Aironet products currently use the 2.4 GHz frequency range, which adheres to the Institute of Electrical and Electronic Engineers

(IEEE) 802.11b standard. Recently, the FCC also opened up the 5.2 GHz band, known as the Unlicensed National Information Infrastructure (UNII) bands, for unlicensed use by high-speed data communications devices. 5.2 GHz is the same band that is used for the European Telecommunications Standards Institute (ETSI) HiperLAN specification in Europe.

Figure 3.2 ISM Unlicensed Frequency Bands

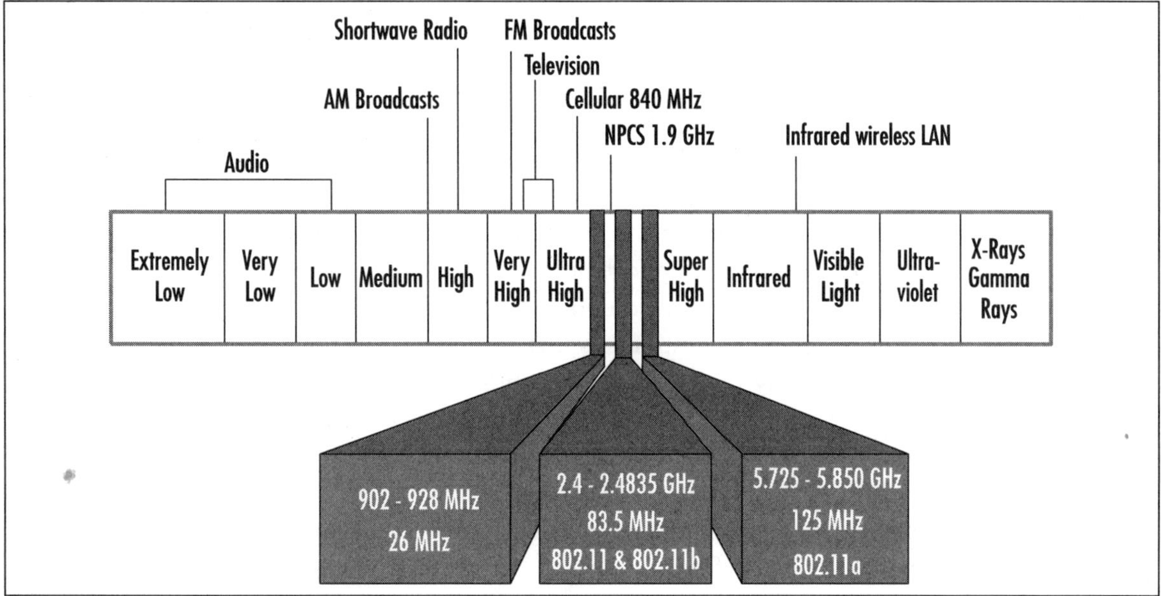

Table 3.4 lists additional 802.11b RF bands by geographic area.

Table 3.4 802.11b RF Bands by Geography

Channel Number	Frequency				
GHz	North America	Europe	Spain	France	Japan
1	2.412	X	X		
2	2.417	X	X		
3	2.422	X	X		
4	2.427	X	X		
5	2.432	X	X		
6	2.437	X	X		
7	2.442	X	X		
8	2.447	X	X		
9	2.452	X	X		
10	2.457	X	X	X	X
11	2.462	X	X	X	X
12	2.467		X		X
13	2.472		X		X
14	2.483				X

Of significant importance is the total number of channels allocated in a given geographical area. The same IEEE 802.11 standard can be more versatile in areas where additional channels (bandwidth) are allocated. The advantage is due to the greater number of channels that can be potentially deployed. By allowing more channels to be deployed in a given area, the possibility of interference from other wireless devices is reduced or eliminated.

Radio Wave Modulation

For the propagation and interception of radio waves, a transmitter and receiver are employed. A radio wave "carries" information-bearing signals through space. This carrier wave may have information encoded directly on it by periodically interrupting its transmission, as in Morse code telegraphy, or encoded on it by what is known as a *modulation technique*.

The actual information in a modulated signal is contained in its sidebands, or frequency components added to the carrier wave. It is important to note that the information is not contained in the carrier wave itself. Those frequency components that are higher than the carrier frequency are called *upper sidebands*. Frequency components that are lower than the carrier frequency are called *lower sidebands*. Usually only one of these sidebands needs to be transmitted because they typically contain equivalent information. The most common types of modulation techniques are analog, such as frequency and amplitude modulation (FM and AM).

All WLAN radio devices including Cisco Aironet bridges and APs must have the capability to encode digital information on an analog signal to prepare it for transmission, and a reverse of the process for reception, much like the functionality of a modem. The conversion process requires modulation techniques that can efficiently convey digital information in analog form. Cisco Aironet devices use a family of modulation techniques, called *phase modulation*, to perform this efficient encoding.

Digital Signal Modulation: Phase Modulation

Phase modulation is the current modulation technique of choice for efficiently converting digital signals in a WLAN. Signal strength is used in AM to modify the carrier wave to send information. FM converts the originating signal into cycles to bear information. Phase modulation takes advantage of a signal wave's shape. It is ideal for sending digital information. Cisco Aironet radios uses several forms of phase shifting for transmitting digital signals.

A digital signal means an ongoing stream of bits. These bits are usually used to communicate information in the form of data for devices capable of receiving and decoding them. These "data bits" are mathematically represented as 0s and 1s and correspond to off and on pulses of electrical energy typically in the form of AC. Because a radio wave is an analog waveform, the off-on-off-on beat of digital electrical signals must be modulated in order to transmit them on a carrier wave.

A digital signal can be sent without a carrier wave, like the earliest wireless telegraphs, but the results would be less than spectacular. Digital signals without a carrier wave are wideband, extremely inefficient, and would have extremely limited data rate capacity.

A radio wave, represented as a *sine wave*, is a continuous wave produced to transmit analog or digital information. The many phases or angles of the sine wave give rise to different ways of sending information. Simple phase modulation schemes begin by encoding a digital stream of bits onto an unchanging analog waveform. There is now a rising and falling pattern, in tune with the 0s and 1s. This pattern is sometimes referred to as on-and-off amplitudes. A digital bit 0 might be marked by anything above the baseline value on the analog waveform, and a digital bit 1 might be marked by anything below the same baseline value. Simple enough, but it gives just two states to send information. Binary Phase Shift Keying (BSPK) is an example of this type of modulation.

Phase modulation techniques have become more complex, to accommodate the need to carry greater amounts of information in the waveform. The following modulation techniques are used in Cisco Aironet radios (described in the following sections):

- BPSK
- Quadrature Phase Shift Keying (QPSK)
- Complimentary Code Keying (CCK)

BSPK

In BPSK modulation, digital on and off states (1 and 0, respectively) are represented by the various phases of an AC waveform or sine wave. BPSK uses one phase to represent a binary 1 and another phase to represent a binary 0 for a total of two bits of binary data (see Figure 3.3). This is utilized to transmit data at 1Mbps.

Figure 3.3 Binary Phase Shift Keying

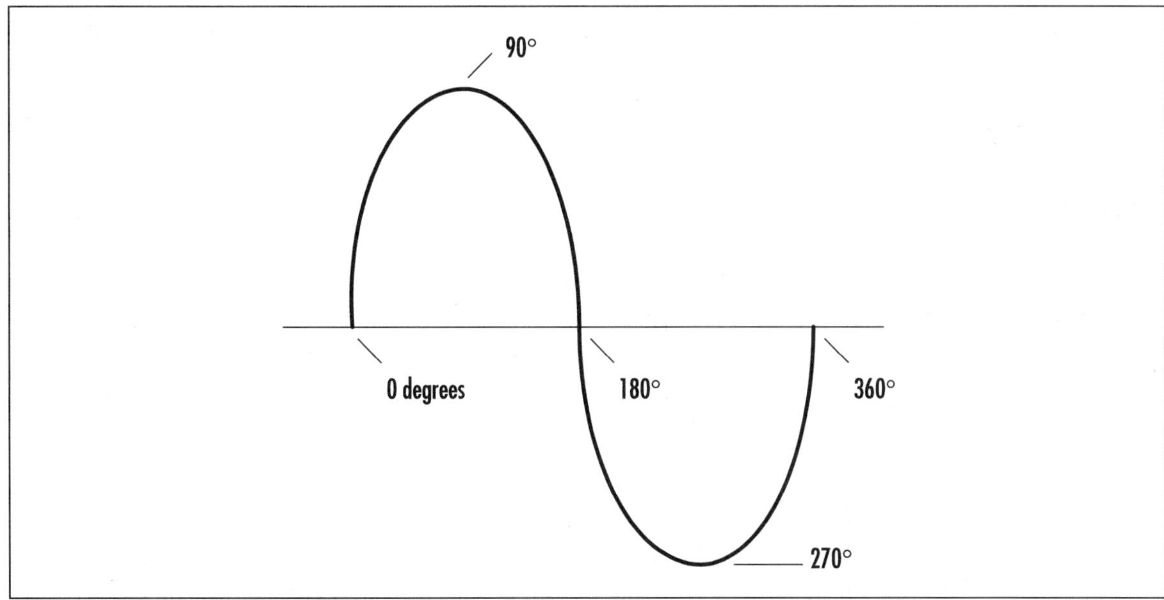

QPSK

With QPSK, the carrier undergoes four changes in phase and can therefore represent four binary bits of data. This scheme, used by most high-speed modems, increases the speed and amount of data transferred by doubling the two states BPSK offers to at least four states to send information. QPSK manipulates or changes a sine wave's normal pattern by shifting its alternation and forcing the wave to fall to its baseline resting point. This fall to the wave's baseline is represented in the example by a premature drop to zero degrees (the baseline) before the wave would naturally drop on its own (see Figure 3.4). By forcing this abrupt drop, we can increase the amount of information conveyed in the wave.

Figure 3.4 Quadrature Phase Shift Keying

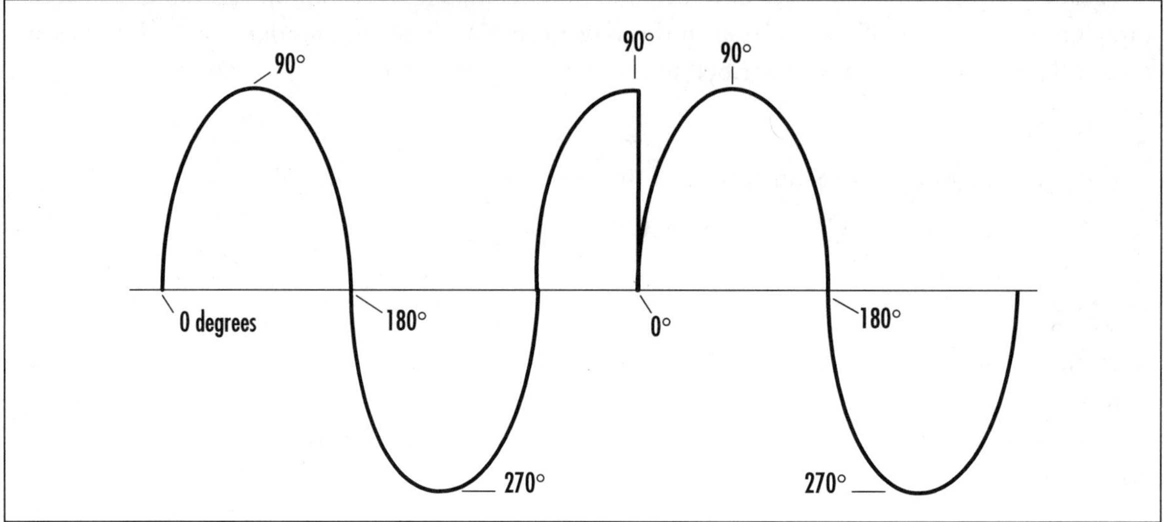

As with BPSK, digital bits must be represented using various phases of the analog waveform. In QPSK, the portion of the phase from 0 degrees to 90 degrees might represent binary digit 0, 90 degrees to 180 degrees could represent binary digit 1, and 180 to 270 degrees and 270 back to 0 degrees might be represented by binary digits 10 and 11, respectively. The wireless radio configured for QPSK arranges a forced shift in the sine wave at each point that a bit or set of bits is transmitted. The receiving wireless radio expects these shifts and decodes them in the proper sequence. QPSK is utilized to transmit data at 2 Mbps.

Complementary Code Keying

Complementary Code Keying (CCK) is a newer modulation standard originally based on another modulation technique called Mary Orthogonal Keying (MOK). It was not a defined modulation technique in the original IEEE 802.11 standard for WLANs, unlike BPSK and QPSK. CCK was designed as a new, modified modulation technique by industry leaders to overcome the limitations of the rate barrier of 2 Mbps within the original standard. It was adopted in the IEEE 802.11b standard currently employed by many vendors.

CCK is a coded QPSK modulation, where the original data bits are mapped to a corresponding modified data symbol, 8 bits for one 8-bit symbol. The data symbol is then applied to the various phases of the analog waveform as in phase shift keying modulations. The resulting waveform is the same as the original 2 Mbps QPSK modulations; however, the resulting data rate is 11 Mbps. CCK uses a complex set of functions known as *complementary codes* to send additional data in the waveform. CCK provides an additional bit to each I (In-phase) and Q (Quadrature) channel by inverting or rotating the waveform 90 degrees and utilizing unmodified versions of the spreading function.

There is a code set as well as a cover sequence defining the waveform. This new symbol type carries 6 bits and can be QPSK-modulated to carry 2 more bits. The result is that 8 bits are transmitted with each symbol, resulting in a waveform that contains 16 bits of complexity. This is why the data rate for a Direct Sequence Spread Spectrum (DSSS) system employing CCK modulation is capable of 11 Mbps throughput rather than 2 Mbps. CCK supports both 5.5 Mbps and 11 Mbps modulation, and is backward compatible with the 1 to 2 Mbps scheme. The data bit structure per codeword for BPSK, QPSK, and CCK is outlined in Figure 3.5. One of the advantages of CCK over similar modulation techniques is that it suffers less from multipath interference than systems based only on QPSK and BPSK.

Figure 3.5 Modulation Techniques

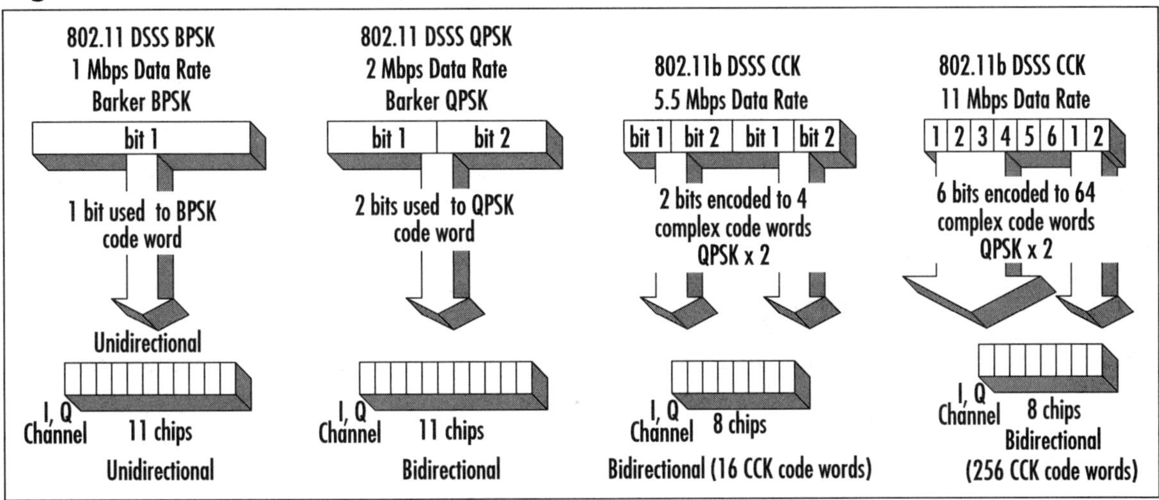

A digital signal produced using any of these techniques modulates the current carrying the signal within the radio. In other words, modulation gets wireless digital information ready for transmission. Once completed, the digital signal can then be actually transmitted over the air with another modulation technique, like direct sequence or frequency hopping spread spectrum.

Communicating with WLAN Technologies

The most effective forms of wireless communications today are produced using radio and microwave technologies. Because of licensing and cost issues, we are focusing on the wireless technology used in Cisco Aironet wireless products; however, brief descriptions of other wireless technologies are presented. The following sections discuss the core aspects of various WLAN technologies and the advantages and disadvantages of each.

The technologies available for use in WLANs include infrared, microwave, and spread spectrum radios. Two spread spectrum techniques are currently prevalent: frequency hopping and direct sequence.

Microwave Technology

Microwave technology is not really a local area network (LAN) technology. Its main use in WLAN capacity is to interconnect LANs between buildings requiring microwave dishes on both ends of the link. The dishes must be in line-of-sight to transmit and collect the microwave signals. Microwave is used to bypass the telephone company when connecting LANs between buildings or as a backup path in the event of a telecommunications infrastructure outage. Microwave is used to replace traditional wired technologies, such as dedicated circuits offered by the telephone company, with a network of microwave dishes to accomplish connectivity between businesses, cities, and states. Microwave communication satisfied the wide area network (WAN) requirements in the geographical area due to the limited availability of dedicated circuits for data transmission and environmental constraints in the state.

Although it is a viable alternative even in private communications, it has two drawbacks. First, microwave communication requires FCC licensing. Once a license is granted for a particular location, that frequency band cannot be licensed to anyone else, for any purpose, within a 17.5-mile radius. Second, the cost of implementing microwave technology (tower/dish infrastructure) is higher than other options. On the other hand, microwave communication is extremely resistant to interference.

Infrared Technology

The infrared spectrum has long been used for such items as television and VCR remote controls. Over the past 10 years, infrared devices for home computers have become extremely popular. Input devices such as wireless keyboards and mice have introduced us to the freedom of working and playing without being tethered to the computer. Typically, an infrared receiver is attached to the keyboard or mouse connector on a computer. The wireless keyboard or mouse has an infrared transmitter built in. Because each wireless component manufacturer designs their own transmitters, the keyboard or mouse operates at a proprietary frequency. Keystroke or mouse movement signals are translated into an infrared signal and are sent to the receiver. Many laptop computers now come with an infrared port, which allows information from another laptop or infrared device to be transferred to each other via infrared transmission.

Just like the infrared connection between the laptops, infrared LANs use infrared signals to transmit data. These LANs can be set up using either a point-to-point configuration (line-of-sight) or a diffused configuration where the signals are reflected off some type of surface. The line-of-sight configuration generally offers the faster data rate of the two.

The advantages and disadvantages of infrared are few, however, the severity of the disadvantages are high in a WLAN scenario. Infrared's best advantage is its capability to carry a high bandwidth. The major disadvantage is its capability to be blocked. Because infrared energy is a form of light, it can easily be obstructed as it cannot pass through solid objects. Because infrared provides high-speed connectivity it is sometimes used for point-to-point connectivity, but infrared communication solutions are very expensive to implement. Because of infrared distance and coverage limitations, many more infrared devices are necessary to provide the same coverage area as radio wireless APs.

Spread Spectrum Technology

Most of the familiar communication technologies—radio, television, two-way radios—use what is called *narrowband communications*. Each station or channel operates over a very thin slice of the radio spectrum. Because the station is assigned a particular band, and the FCC ensures that no other broadcasters in the local area use that same band through licensing, there is no interference. The range of each station is limited, so the same frequency can be reused a great distance away without interference.

Because many devices might use the ISM bands in a local area, additional technology is required to keep the various signals from interfering with each other. Spread spectrum enables bandwidth "sharing" by spreading the radio signal over a wide "spectrum" of radio frequencies. This minimizes the impact of narrowband interference. In most cases, only small parts of the transmission are corrupted by any interference, and coding techniques allow that data to be recaptured.

Spread spectrum is a coding technique for digital transmission. It was developed for the military in the 1950s by engineers from the Sylvania Electronics System Division under a veil of secrecy to avoid jamming and eavesdropping of signals. Though developed and implemented by the U.S. military, the technique was first conceived by Hedy Lamarr and George Antheil. Lamarr, a famous actress of Austrian descent in the 1930s and 1940s, and Antheil, a music composer, patented the idea in 1940. The patent license expired before government and commercial implementation of the concepts occurred. In the mid-1980s, the U.S. military declassified spread-spectrum technology, and the commercial sector began to develop it for consumer electronics.

The military purpose of spread spectrum coding was to transform an information signal so that it looked more like noise. Noise has a flat uniform spectrum with no coherent peaks and can be reduced or eliminated by filtering. This made interception of radio signals extremely difficult.

The spread spectrum transmission technique modifies the signal spectrum to spread it out over a range of frequencies and increase its bandwidth. In other words, instead of transmitting a signal continuously over one narrow frequency band, the several parts are transmitted separately over a wide spectrum of radio frequencies.

The frequencies used consist of the industrial, scientific, and medical (ISM) bands of the electromagnetic spectrum. The ISM bands include the frequency ranges at 902 MHz to 928 MHz and at 2.4 GHz to 2.484 GHz, which do not require a FCC license. Spread spectrum is currently the most widely used transmission technique for WLANs.

Two different spreading techniques are currently used, both using a coded pattern of communication. A receiving unit is synchronized to use the same pattern and successfully receive the transmission. Any other radio unit hears the signal as noise because it is not programmed with the appropriate coding. The two techniques are called frequency hopping spread spectrum (FHSS) and DSSS. All Cisco Aironet products use DSSS. An extremely important and difficult part of designing a spread spectrum radio is to ensure fast and reliable synchronization in the receiver. Acquisition time is the period taken to lock up the receiver from a cold start and is an important measure of the receiver's performance.

Frequency Hopping Spread Spectrum (FHSS)

The first type of spread spectrum developed is known as FHSS. Simply put, frequency hopping is the process of jumping quickly from one frequency to another. A communications signal (voice or data) is split into separate parts. This technique broadcasts the signal over a seemingly random series of radio frequencies. A receiver, hopping between frequencies in synchronization with the transmitter, receives the message.

Frequency hopping has two benefits. Electrical noises as random electromagnetic signals, which are not part of any communications signal, affect only a small part of the signal. Also, the effects of any other forms of radio communications operating in narrow bands of the spectrum are minimized. Any such interference that occurs results in only a slightly reduced quality of transmission, or a small loss of data. Because data networks acknowledge successful receipt of data, any missing pieces will trigger a request to transmit the lost data.

The FCC has made some rules for FHSS technologies. The FCC dictates that the transmitters must not spend more than 0.4 seconds on any one channel every 20 seconds in the 902 MHz band and every 30 seconds in the 2.4 GHz band. Also, the transmitters must hop through at least 50 channels in the 902 MHz band and 75 channels in the 2.4 GHz band. A channel consists of a frequency width, which is determined by the FCC. The IEEE 802.11 committee has drafted a standard that limits FHSS transmitters to the 2.4 GHz band.

Direct Sequence Spread Spectrum (DSSS)

The other type of spread spectrum communication is DSSS. A direct sequence transmitter spreads its transmissions by adding redundant data bits called chips to them. The digital data signal is inserted in a higher data rate *chipping code* according to a predetermined spreading ratio. The chipping code is a bit sequence generally consisting of a redundant bit pattern that incorporates the original bit pattern.

Figure 3.6 is a simplification of how a statistical technique is used to create the chipping code abstraction from the original bit sequence. DSSS adds at least 10 chips to each data bit to protect the receiver from data loss. DSSS does not split a data signal into pieces. Instead, it encodes each data bit into these chips. This technique reduces interference because if the original data pattern is compromised, the data can be recovered based on the remainder of the chipping code. The longer the chipping code, the more likely it is that the original data can be recovered. Long chipping codes have the drawback of requiring more bandwidth. This is currently the most common method used in WLANs.

Figure 3.6 DSSS

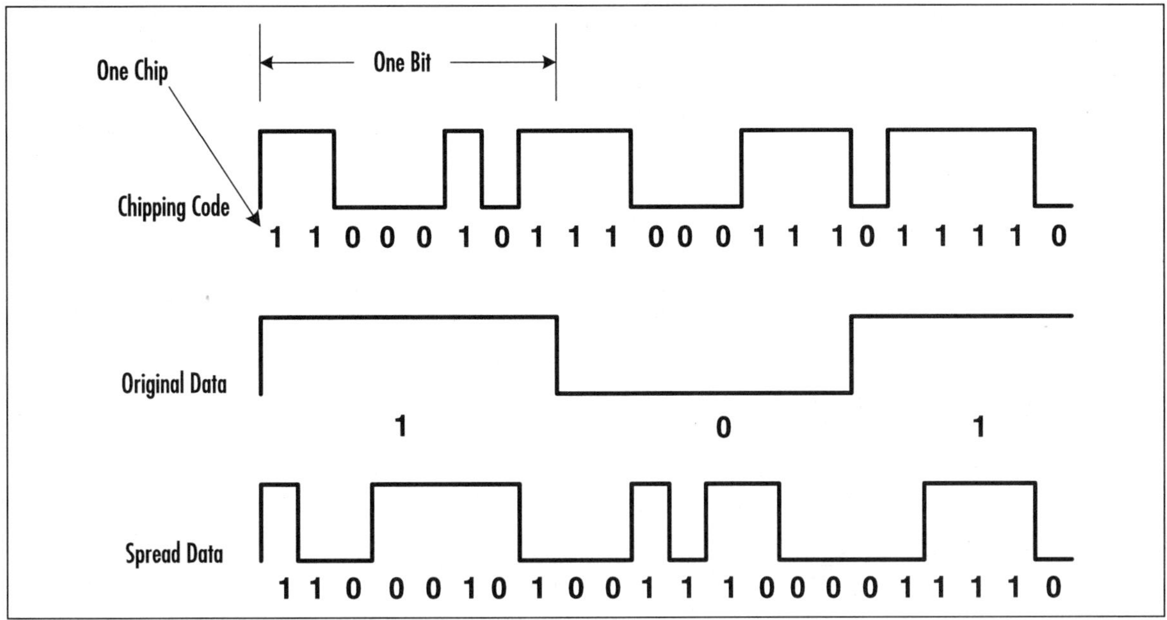

The transmitter sends the same piece of data attached to several chips to provide redundancy. Usually, 11 to 20 bits are used for the chip, depending on the application. An 11-bit chip is illustrated here:

0=10010010110

1=01101101001

After a fixed number of chips are sent, they repeat themselves precisely. This fixed number of chips is also referred to as the *chipping sequence*, or *Barker sequence*.

Similar to a frequency-hopping receiver, a direct sequence receiver must know a transmitter's spreading code in order to properly decode the data stream. This spreading code is what allows multiple direct sequence transmitters to operate in the same area without interference. Once the receiver has received a transmission, it removes all the extraneous chips to produce the original length of the signal and completes the demodulation process.

The number of chips and the frequency used is directly related to a signal's capability to avoid interference. The raw data throughput of direct sequence transmitters in the 2.4 GHz band is 11 Mbps. In addition to other factors, areas of high interference can significantly slow throughput when using DSSS.

DSSS Channel Setup

For direct sequence WLANs, 11 total channels can be used for RF transmission (see Figure 3.10). Each channel is 22 MHz wide, and all channels combined equal the entire spectrum that can be used for 802.11 WLANs—in this case, the 2.4 GHz range of the ISM bands. When designing WLANs, multiple channels become an issue only when overlapping coverage is required. This will be the case in most designs. When two APs have overlapping coverage, each AP must be using a different channel so that the client can distinguish the difference between the RF for each AP. Figure 3.7 illustrates that only three channels do not overlap concurrently: channels 1, 6, and 11.

Figure 3.7 DSSS Channels

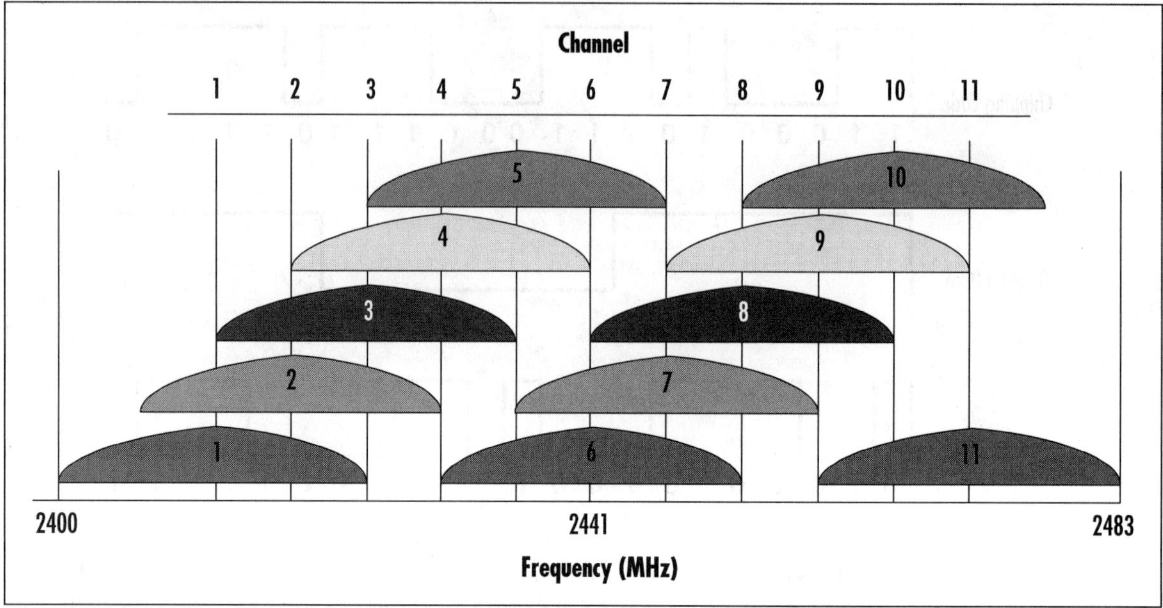

Just as important as the underlying RF technologies that make wireless networking a reality are standards for ensuring that the mix of hardware, software, and infrastructure can all interoperate. Without standards, networking would be awash in competing and incompatible proprietary products that could not communicate with each other. The expense would be tremendous. Thankfully, there are standards for wireless.

Wireless Networking Standards

Standards organizations are groups interested in promoting and coordinating rules for the measure of quantity, weight, extent, value, or quality of a given technology or idea, giving rise to a model or example of the idea or technology. This, in turn, allows others to build on the model or example and improve the existing idea or technology, or in some cases, foster new ideas or technologies. In the wireless networking world, standards organizations have had the welcome impact of allowing new wireless technologies to get from conception to consumer with unprecedented speed. Because the standards are used as a base for the wireless technology most vendors employ, consumers reap the benefits of interoperability, reliability, and efficient technology.

Wireless standards have been developed both in the U.S. and abroad, and the advances made using these standards are shaping the wireless industry constantly. To fully understand wireless fundamentals, architecture, and design considerations, you must understand what the current standards are for WLANs and who created those standards.

IEEE

IEEE is an association that develops standards for almost anything electronic and/or electric. Far from being limited to computer-related topics, IEEE societies cover just about any technical practice, from automobiles to maritime, from neural networks to superconductors. Thirty-six technical societies cover broad interest areas; therefore, more specific topics are handled by special committees that focus on a particular technology or technologies to develop standards that will be used to promote technological advancement. The IEEE 802 LAN/MAN Standards Committee develops LAN standards and MAN standards. The most widely used standards are for the Ethernet family, token ring, WLAN, Bridging, and Virtual Bridged LANs. All standards created by this committee are designated 802.

Standards listed 802.11 designate the WLAN Working Group within the LAN/MAN Standards Committee. Letters after the designations represent revisions or changes to the original standards for the working group. These groups meet several times a year to discuss new trends within their industry or to continue the process of refining a current standard. Prior to the adoption of the 802.11 standard, wireless data-networking vendors made equipment that was based on proprietary technology.

Many of the members of the 802.11 Working Group were employees of vendors making wireless technologies. Therefore, there were many pushes to include certain functions in the final specification. Although this slowed down the progress of finalizing 802.11, it also provided momentum for delivery of a feature-rich standard left open for future expansion.

On June 26, 1997, the IEEE announced the ratification of the 802.11 standard for WLANs. At that time, costs associated with deploying an 802.11-based network had dropped, and WLANs rapidly were being deployed in schools, businesses, and homes.

The primary reason WLANs were initially not widely accepted was the lack of standardization. It is logical to question whether vendors would accept a nonproprietary operating standard, because vendors compete to make unique and distinguishing products. Although 802.11 standardized the physical (PHY) media access control (MAC) layers, the frequencies to send/receive on, transmission rates, and more, it did not absolutely guarantee that differing vendors' products would be 100 percent compatible. In fact, some vendors built in backward-compatibility features into their 802.11 products to support their legacy customers. Other vendors have introduced proprietary extensions (for example, bit-rate adaptation and stronger encryption) to their 802.11 offerings.

802.11

As in all 802.*x* standards, the 802.11 specification covers the operation of the MAC and PHY layers. As seen in Figure 3.8, 802.11 defines a MAC sublayer, MAC services and protocols, and three physical layers.

Figure 3.8 802.11 Frame Format

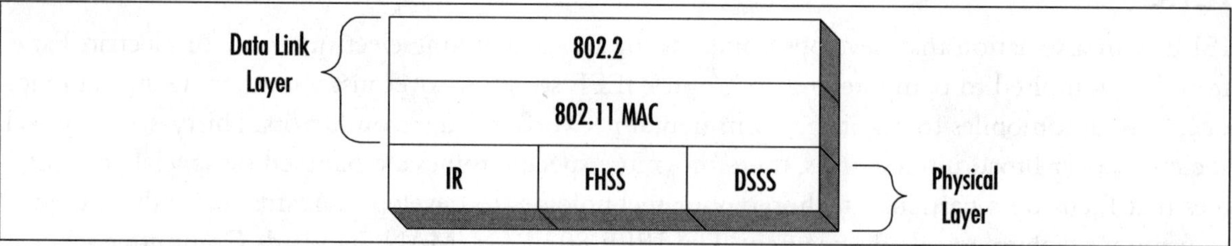

The three physical layer options for 802.11 are infrared (IR) baseband PHY and two RF PHYs (FHSS and DSSS). Due to line-of-sight limitations, very little development has occurred with the IR PHY. The RF physical layer is composed of FHSS and DSSS in the 2.4 GHz band. All three physical layers operate at either 1 or 2 Mbps. The majority of 802.11 implementations utilize the DSSS method.

802.11 Topologies

The topology of a wireless network is dynamic; therefore, the destination address does not always correspond to the destination's location. This raises a problem when forwarding frames through the network to the intended destination.

The IEEE 802.11 topology consists of components, called "sets," to provide a WLAN that allows transparent station mobility. The 802.11 standard supports the following three topology sets:

- **Basic Service Set (BSS) Networks** The basic topology set of 802.11 systems. The BSS consists of at least one AP connected to the wired network infrastructure and a set of wireless end stations (see Figure 3.9). BSS configurations rely on an AP that acts as the logical server for a single WLAN cell or channel. Communications between two end stations actually flows from one station to the AP and from the AP to the other station.

Figure 3.9 BSS Network

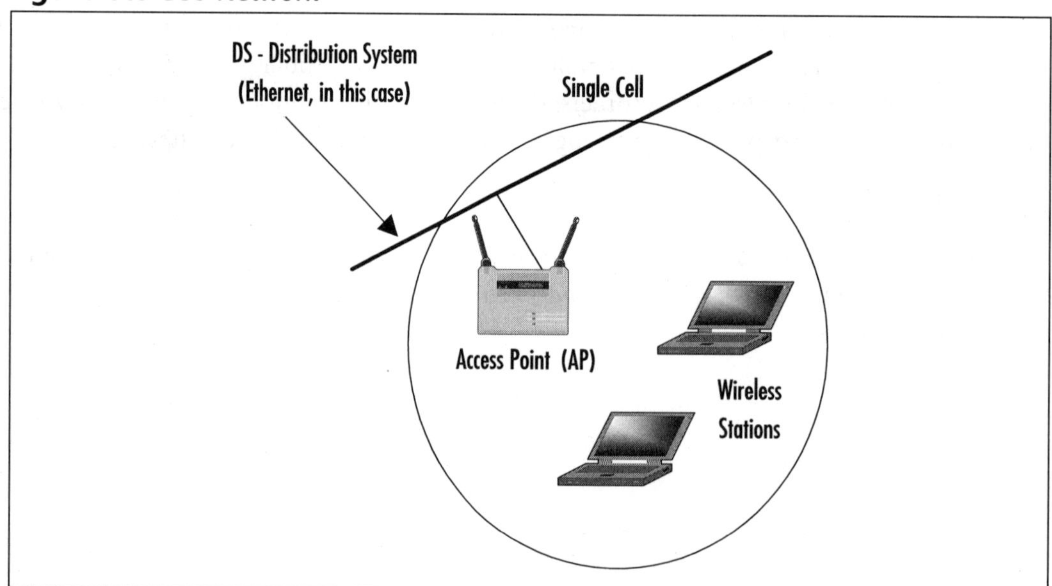

- **Independent Basic Service Set (IBSS) Networks** IBSS networks are also referred to as an *independent configuration* or *ad-hoc network*. Logically, an IBSS configuration is very similar to a peer-to-peer home or office network in which no single node is required to function as a server (see Figure 3.10). IBSS topology sets include a number of wireless end stations that communicate directly with one another, with no intervening AP or any connection to a wired network. It is useful for quickly and easily setting up a wireless network anyplace where a wireless infrastructure does not exist or is not required for services, such as meeting rooms in hotels, airports, or trade shows, or where access to the wired network is barred (such as for consultants at a client site). Generally, ad-hoc implementations cover a small (limited) area and are not connected to any network.

Figure 3.10 IBSS Network

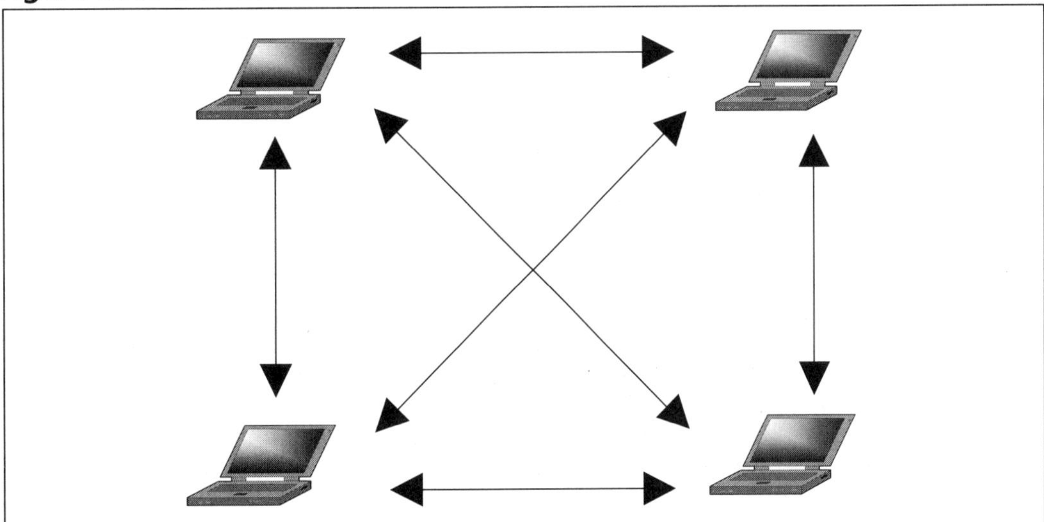

- **Extended Service Set (ESS) Networks** ESS topologies consist of a series of overlapping BSS sets (each containing an AP), commonly referred to as *cells*. These cells are usually connected together by some wired medium typically referred to as a distribution system (DS) (see Figure 3.11). Although the DS could be any type of network, it is almost invariably an Ethernet LAN. Mobile end stations can roam between the APs, making seamless ESS-wide coverage possible. Because most corporate WLANs require access to the wired LAN for services (file servers, printers, Internet links) they operate in a BSS/ESS topology.

Figure 3.11 ESS Network

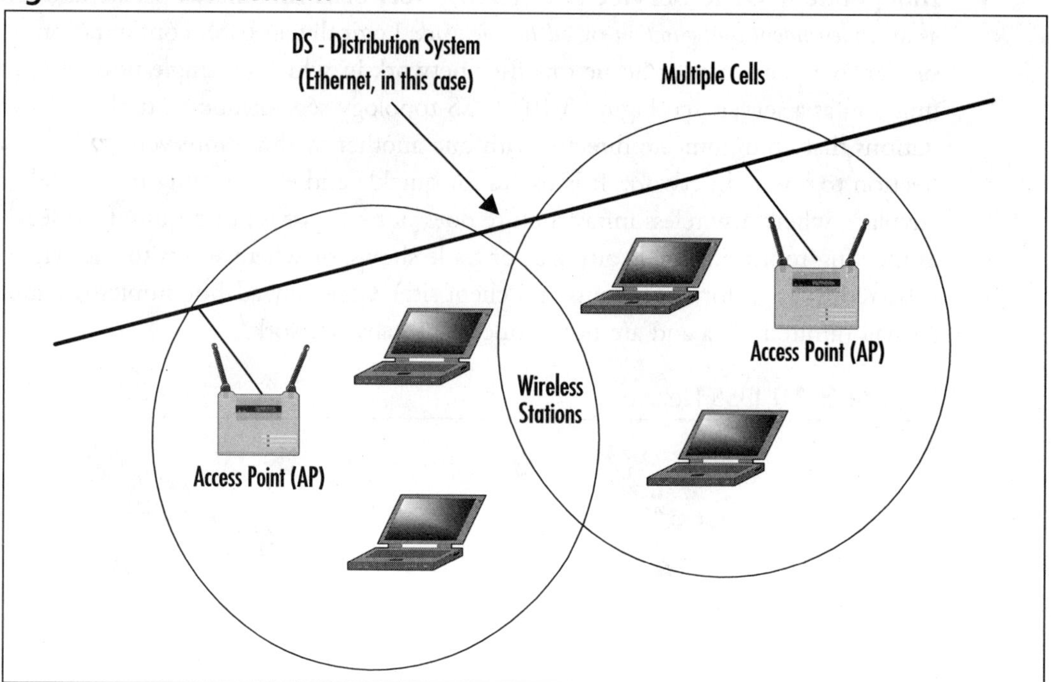

These networks utilize a basic building block: the 802.11 standard referred to as a BSS, providing a coverage area whereby stations of the BSS (or ESS) remain fully connected. A station is free to move within the BSS, but it can no longer communicate directly with other stations if it leaves the BSS/ESS.

The compelling force behind WLAN deployment is that with 802.11, users are free to move about without having to worry about switching network connections manually. If you were operating with a single infrastructure BSS, this moving about would be limited to the signal range of the one AP. Through the ESS, the IEEE 802.11 architecture allows users to move between multiple infrastructure BSSs. In an ESS, the APs communicate about forwarding traffic from one BSS to another, as well as switch the roaming devices from one BSS to another.

802.11 Services

Nine different services provide behind-the-scenes support to the 802.11 architecture. Of these nine, four belong to the *station services* group and the remaining five to the *distribution services* group.

The four station services (*authentication*, *de-authentication*, *data delivery*, and *privacy*) provide functionality equal to what standard 802.3 wired networks would have.

The authentication service defines the identity of the wireless device. Without a distinct identity, the device is not allowed access to the WLAN. Authentication can also be made against a list of MAC addresses allowed to use the network. This list of allowable MAC addresses may be on the AP or on a database somewhere on the wired network. A wireless device can authenticate itself to more than one AP at a time. This "pre-authentication" allows the device to prepare other APs for its entry into their coverage area.

The de-authentication service is used to tear down a previously known station identity. Once the de-authentication service has been started, the wireless device can no longer access the WLAN. This service is invoked when a wireless device shuts down, or when it is roaming out of the range of the AP. De-authentication frees up resources on the AP for other devices.

The privacy service is used to protect the data as it crosses the WLAN. Even though the service utilizes an RC4-based encryption scheme, it is not intended for end-to-end encryption or as a sole method of securing data. Its design was to provide a level of protection equivalent to that provided on a wired network—hence its moniker Wireless Equivalency Privacy (WEP).

Between the Logical Link Control (LLC) sublayer and the MAC, five distribution services make the decisions as to where the 802.11 data frames should be sent. These distribution services make the roaming handoffs when the wireless device is in motion. The five services are *association*, *re-association*, *disassociation*, *integration*, and *distribution*.

The wireless device uses the association service as soon as it connects to an AP. This service establishes a logical connection between the devices, and determines the path the DS needs to take to reach the wireless device. If the wireless device does not have an association made with an AP, the DS will not know where that device is or how to get data frames to it. As seen in Figure 3.12, the wireless device can be authenticated to more than one AP at a time, but it will never be associated with more than one AP.

Figure 3.12 802.11 Authentication, Association, and Re-Association

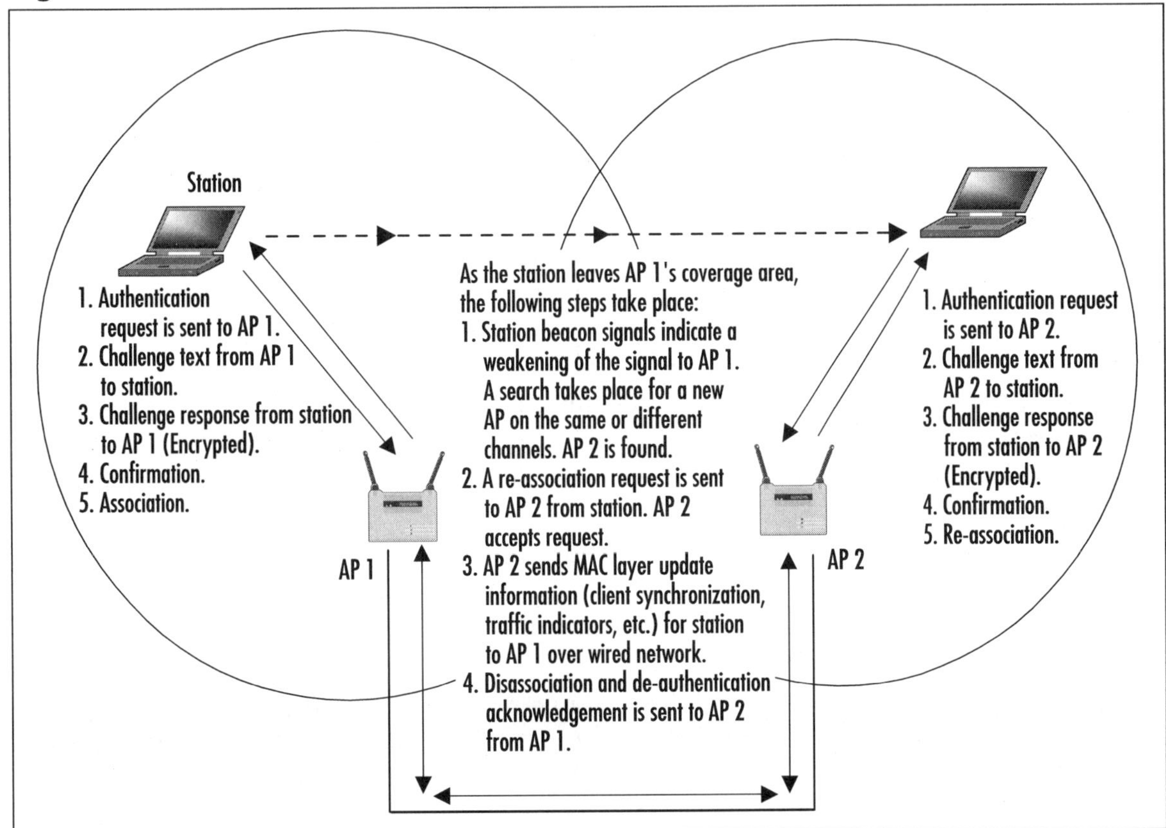

To keep from losing whatever network session information the wireless device has, the re-association service is used. This service is similar to the association service, but includes current information about the wireless device. In the case of roaming, this information identifies the previous AP that the wireless client was associated with to the current AP. This allows the current AP to contact the previous AP to pick up any data frames waiting for the wireless device and forward them to their destination.

The disassociation service is used to tear down the association between the AP and the wireless device. This could be because the device is roaming out of the AP's area, the AP is shutting down, or other causes of disassociation. To keep communicating to the network, the wireless device has to use the association service to find a new AP.

The distribution service is used by APs to determine whether to send the data frame to another AP and possibly another wireless device, or if the frame is destined to head out of the WLAN into the wired network.

The integration service resides on the APs as well. This service does the data translation from the 802.11 frame format into the framing format of the wired network. It also does the reverse, taking data destined for the WLAN, and framing it within the 802.11 frame format.

CSMA-CA Mechanism

The basic access mechanism for 802.11 is Carrier Sense Multiple Access/Collision Avoidance (CSMA/CA) with binary exponential back off. This is very similar to the Carrier Sense Multiple Access Collision Detection (CSMA-CD) of standard 802.3 (Ethernet), but with several differences.

Unlike Ethernet, which sends out a signal until a collision is detected, CSMA/CA network nodes do not transmit unless they have the attention of their intended receivers and no other node is using the network. This is a listening before talking (LBT) approach to networking.

Before a packet is transmitted, the wireless device listens to hear if any other device is transmitting. If a transmission is occurring, the device waits for a random period of time, and then listens again. Only when no other transmissions are active does the device begins transmitting. Otherwise, it waits again for a random time before listening once more.

802.11 DCF/PCF and RTC/CTS Mechanisms

To minimize the risk of a wireless device transmitting at the same time as another wireless device (and thus causing a collision), the 802.11 working group designed two functions known as Distributed Coordination Function (DCF) and Point Coordination Function (PCF), employing a mechanism called Request To Send/Clear To Send (RTS/CTS).

DCF is used by any of the component topologies to determine when a station can transmit during periods of contention on the network and is a best-effort delivery system. If the channel being used is determined to be in an idle state, a specified "wait" period is initiated before transmission actually occurs.

In PCF, a single point in the network (usually a network AP) acts as a centralized "traffic cop," telling individual stations when they may place a packet on the network. In other words, the AP periodically "beacons" each of its associated end stations, polling them to see if they have anything to transmit. Time-sensitive applications, such as voice and video, use this to permit fixed, dependable rate transmissions.

In both DCF and PCF, RTS/CTS is used as the mechanism to perform these functions. For example, if data arrived at the AP destined for a wireless node, the AP would send an RTS frame to the wireless node requesting a certain amount of time to deliver data to it. The wireless node would respond with a CTS frame saying that it would hold off any other communications until the AP had completed sending the data. Other wireless nodes would hear the transaction taking place, and delay their transmissions for that period of time as well. In this manner, data is passed between nodes with a minimal possibility of a device causing a collision on the medium.

This also eliminates a well-documented WLAN issue called *the hidden node*. In a network with multiple devices, the possibility exists that one wireless node might not know all the other nodes that are out on the WLAN. Thanks to RTS/CTS, each node hears the requests to transmit data to the other nodes, and thus learns what other devices are operating in that BSS.

802.11 Data Acknowledgment

When transmitting data using radio signals with an inherent risk of interference, the odds of a packet getting lost between the transmitting radio and the destination unit is much greater than in a wired network model. To counter this risk, an acknowledgment (ACK) mechanism is used in CSMA/CA such that when a destination host receives a packet, it sends an ACK (notification) to the sending unit. If the sender does not receive an ACK, it will know that this packet was not received and transmit it again.

802.11 Fragmentation

In an environment prone to interference, the possibility exists that one or more bits in a packet will get corrupted during transmission. No matter the number of corrupted bits, the packet will need to be re-sent.

When operating in an area where interference is not a possibility, but a reality, it makes sense to transmit smaller packets than those traditionally found in wired networks. This allows for a faster retransmission of the packet to be accomplished.

The disadvantage to doing this is that in the case of no corrupted packets, the cost of sending many short packets is greater than the cost of sending the same information in a couple of large packets. The 802.11 standard has made this a configurable feature, allowing the specification of short packets in some areas and longer packets in more open, non-interfering areas.

802.11 Power Management

Sufficient battery power in the mobile device such as a laptop or Personal Digital Assistant (PDA) to power the communications channel is of prime concern and can affect mobility. The IEEE recognized this and included a power management service, which saves power without losing connectivity to the wireless infrastructure. Utilizing a 20-byte Power Save Poll (PS-Poll) frame, the wireless device sends a message to its AP letting it know that it is going into power-save mode, and the AP needs to buffer all packets destined for the device until it comes back online. Periodically, the wireless device will wake up and see if there are any packets waiting for it on the AP. If there are not, another PS-Poll frame is sent, and the unit goes into a sleep mode again.

802.11 Multicell Roaming

Roaming between APs in the ESS is a very important service of the 802.11 standard. Roaming is based on the capability of the wireless device to determine the quality of the wireless signal to any AP within reach, and decide to switch communications to a different AP if it has a stronger or cleaner signal. This is based primarily upon an entity called the signal-to-noise (S/N) ratio. In order for wireless devices to determine the S/N ratio for each AP in the network, AP's send out *beacon* messages that contain information about the AP as well as link measurement data.

The wireless device listens to these beacons and determines which AP has the clearest and cleanest signal. The wireless device re-associates with the new AP, telling it which AP the device just came from. The new AP continues in progress transactions, and notifies the old AP that it no longer needs to support that wireless device. The 802.11 standard does not define the communications process for re-association, so many vendors have developed their own. An 802.11 Working Group (802.11f) is developing an Inter-Access Point Protocol. This protocol will be of great help in the future as companies who have invested in one vendor's products can integrate APs and devices from other vendors into their ESSs.

802.11b

Ratified on September 16, 1999, by IEEE, 802.11 High Rate (HR/DSSS), better known as 802.11b, operates at 11 Mbps. The architecture, features, and services are defined by the original 802.11 standard, as the revised specification affects only the physical layer, adding higher data rates and more robust connectivity.

The key contribution of the 802.11b addition to the WLAN standard was to standardize the physical layer support of two new speeds, 5.5 Mbps and 11 Mbps. DSSS is the sole physical layer technique for the standard because frequency hopping cannot support the higher speeds without violating current FCC regulations. The implication is that 802.11b systems will interoperate with 1 Mbps and 2 Mbps 802.11 DSSS systems, but will not work with 1 Mbps and 2 Mbps 802.11 FHSS systems. The 802.11b standard has no provision for FHSS, and most vendors have chosen to implement DSSS as the ratified 802.11b (11 Mbps) standard. This makes migration from a 2 Mbps 802.11 DSSS system to an 11 Mbps 802.11b system very easy, as the underlying modulation scheme is very similar. 2 Mbps 802.11 DSSS systems will be able to coexist with 11 Mbps 802.11b systems, enabling a smooth transition to the higher data rate technology. To migrate from FHSS systems to DSSS will require wholesale replacement of radios in areas where the currently used FHSS is either no longer functional or productivity requirements outweigh conversion costs.

802.11b WLANs use dynamic rate shifting, allowing data rates to be automatically adjusted to compensate for interference or range issues on the radio channel. When devices move beyond the optimal range for 11 Mbps operation, or if substantial interference is present, 802.11b devices will transmit at lower speeds, falling back to 5.5, 2, and 1 Mbps. Likewise, if the device moves back within the range of a higher-speed transmission, the connection will automatically speed up again. Rate shifting is a physical-layer mechanism transparent to the user and the upper layers of the protocol stack.

There are many different devices competing for airspace in the 2.4 GHz radio spectrum. Most of the devices that cause interference are especially common in the home environment, such as microwaves and cordless phones. The frequency hopping nature of Bluetooth may also interfere with 802.11b operations.

802.11a

802.11a is one of the physical layer extensions to the 802.11 standard. Abandoning spread spectrum completely, 802.11a uses an encoding technique called Orthogonal Frequency Division Multiplexing (OFDM). This is a major reason why 802.11a cannot interoperate with 802.11b devices.

802.11a equipment operates at 5 GHz and supports up to a 54 Mbps data rate. The FCC has allocated 300 MHz of RF spectrum for unlicensed operation in the 5 GHz block, 200 MHz of which is at 5.15 MHz to 5.35 MHz (UNII), with the other 100 MHz at 5.725 MHz to 5.825 MHz (ISM). In addition to the frequency and bandwidth allocation, one key parameter that is regulated by the various authorities is the allowable transmit output power. The transmit output power is directly related with the range of coverage that a particular radio can achieve. The 5 GHz spectrum is split into three working "domains." The first 100 MHz in the lower section is restricted to a maximum power output of 50 millawatts (mW). The second 100 MHz has a more generous 250 mW power budget, while the top 100 MHz is delegated for outdoor applications, with a maximum of 1 watt power output.

In contrast, 802.11b client cards can radiate as much as 1 watt in the United States. However, most modern cards radiate only a fraction (30 mW) of the maximum available power. This is due mainly for reasons of battery conservation and heat dissipation. Although segmented, the total bandwidth available for IEEE 802.11a applications is almost four times that of the ISM band's 83 MHz of spectrum in the 2.4 GHz range, while the UNII and 5 GHz ISM bands offer 300 MHz.

A drawback to using the 802.11a MAC is that 802.11a has the same inefficiencies resident in 802.11b wireless implementations. The 802.11b MAC is only about 70 percent efficient. Currently, the maximum throughput on an 11 Mbps 802.11b wireless implementation is about 5.5 to 6 Mbps. So even at 802.11a's 54 Mbps, maximum throughput is closer to 30 to 35 Mbps when factoring in driver inefficiencies and some additional overhead at the physical layer, with most real-world performance averaging around 20 Mbps. Unlike 802.11b, 802.11a does not have to transmit its headers at 1 Mbps.

Because 802.11a and 802.11b operate in different frequencies, interoperability is impossible. There is a clear migration path when more bandwidth is needed, but extensive redesign is necessary to move from 802.11b to 802.11a. Coexistence of the two standards in a single environment is possible because there is no signal overlap. 802.11g, which was ratified on June 12, 2003, by the IEEE, has more promise.

802.11g

802.11g offers a theoretical maximum bandwidth of 54 Mbps using the 2.4 GHz spectrum; in other words, the speed of 802.11a and the spectrum of 802.11b. 802.11g is backwards-compatible with 802.11b devices, which protects the investment. Of course, the degree of compatibility varies from vendor to vendor, as product differentiation efforts may add features unique to a particular vendor only. Nonetheless, the IEEE planned for the two standards to be interoperable. The Cisco Aironet 1100 and 1200 series are upgradeable from 802.11b to 802.11g. Be assured that Cisco will offer more 802.11g products as the standard gains acceptance and achieves maturity. Currently, the Cisco 1100 and 1200 series of Aironet products can be upgraded (software) to support 802.11g. No other Cisco Aironet products support 802.11g at this time.

Wireless Design Considerations

The network administrator should consider common WLAN transmission and reception impairments, such as attenuation, RF interference, and application and structural constraints in their design. Point-to-point and point-to-multipoint wireless implementations are the focus of design.

Attenuation

Attenuation is the decrease in strength of a radio wave as distance from the antenna increases. Natural conductivity or resistance of physical matter can cause attenuation. Radiated energy from the earth and interference from trees and buildings, water, and dust particles will cause attenuation. Low-frequency radio wave propagation utilizes propagation of both ground and sky wave transmissions and can be used at varying distances; high-frequency wave propagation (3,000 KHz to 30 MHz) rely more upon sky waves for transmission and may be used at long distances (such as 12,000 miles); and very high frequency wave propagation (above 30 MHz) is reliant upon line-of-sight direct wave transmission.

Antenna cabling can cause 6.7 dBi of loss per 100 feet of cabling. The radiated energy traveling through the cabling from the radio device to the antenna induces a voltage in the cabling, decreasing the strength of the wave as the distance from the radio device to the antenna becomes greater.

Natural elements such as the earth and weather can cause attenuation. Earth bulge comes into play only if the administrator is implementing a point-to-point or point-to-multipoint WLAN, whereas weather is a consideration for any outdoor implementation. Researching any unusual weather conditions that are common to the site location is important. Attenuation due to rain does not require serious consideration for frequencies up to the range of 6 or 8 GHz. When microwave frequencies are at 11 or 12 GHz or above, attenuation due to rain becomes much more of a concern, especially in areas where rainfall is of high density and long duration.

The attenuation rate for snow, rain, and fog is generally higher in comparison to the wavelength of the signal. For example, a 2.4 GHz signal has a wavelength of approximately 125 mms, or 4.9 inches. A 23 GHz signal has a wavelength of approximately 0.5 inches. A raindrop approaches 0.25 of an inch. At 2.4 GHz, rain or snow should not have much of an impact on a wireless system, however in a 23 GHz system, the wavelength is reduced to half by this rain and snow. At this size, the rain or snow becomes a reflective surface and disperses the 23 GHz signal. Fog merits the same consideration as rain, with additional factors such as inversion or still air.

Multipath Distortion

Multipath distortion is caused by the transmitted signal traveling to the receiver via more than one path. A common cause of this is reflection of the signal from bodies of water, hills, or tall buildings. Figure 3.13 shows an example of multipath distortion caused by reflection. The antennas are the same height.

The reflected signal may arrive at the receiving antenna at the same time as the intended signal, but out of phase with the intended signal, causing both signals to cancel each other out or cause distortion. Examples of reflective surfaces include water, asphalt, fields, metal roofs, or any smooth, relatively flat surface. Dispersing extraneous radio waves is better than reflecting them. Examples of dispersal surfaces include rough rocky surfaces, shrubbery, trees, and so on.

Figure 3.13 Multipath Distortion Diagram

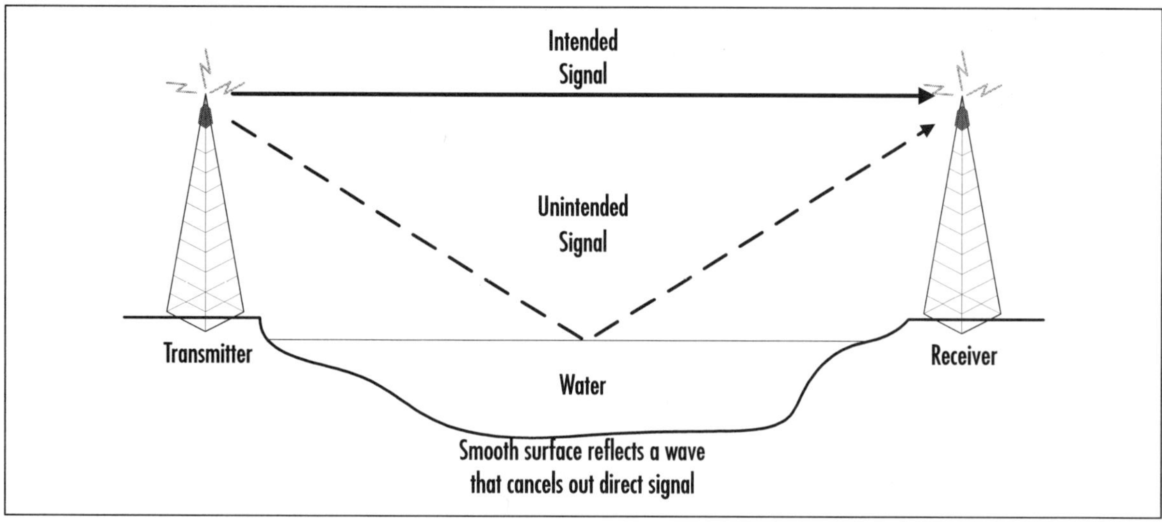

The best way to reduce multipath distortion is to use a directional rooftop antenna (for example, a directional antenna that only picks up signals coming from the direction of the transmitter, and rejects reflections that arrive at its sides or its back. A Yagi antenna is one example of a directional antenna that helps reduce or eliminate multipath distortion (see Figure 3.14).

Figure 3.14 Directional Antenna to Reduce or Eliminate Multipath Distortion (Birds-eye View)

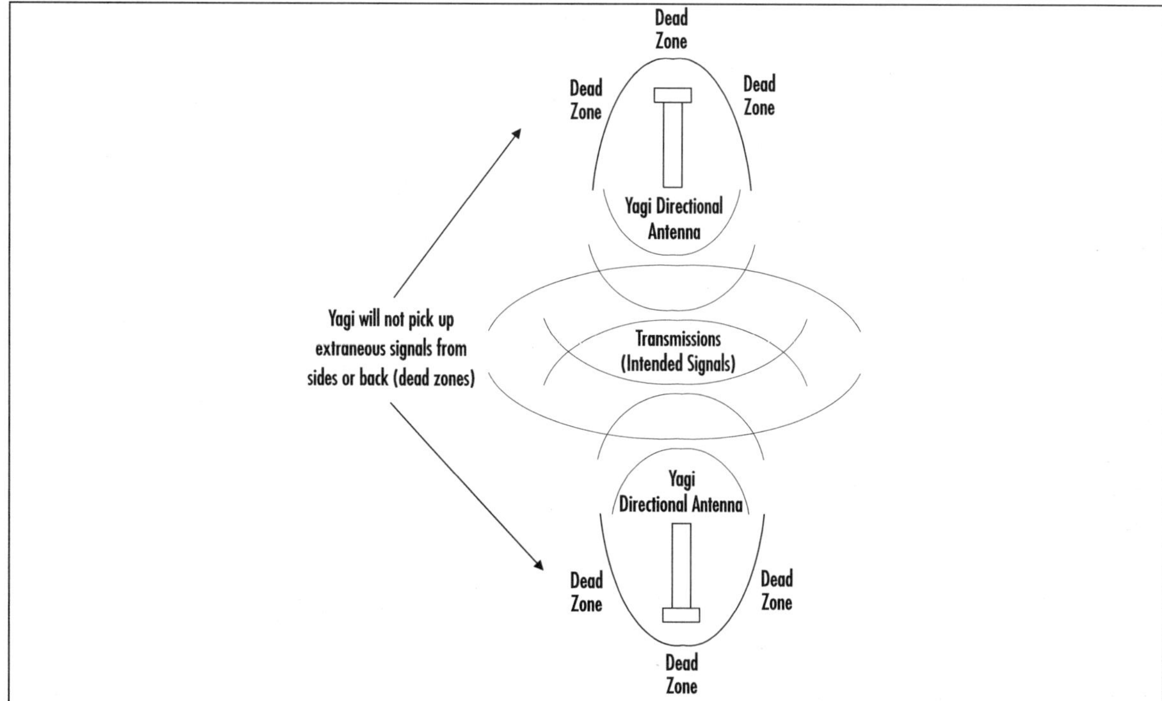

It is also sometimes possible to mount the antenna so that the mounting structure screens it from the reflections but not from the wanted signal. Changing the antenna height can effectively reduce or eliminate the multipath signals by dispersing the signals away from the receiving antenna (see Figure 3.15).

Figure 3.15 Dispersing Multipath Reflections

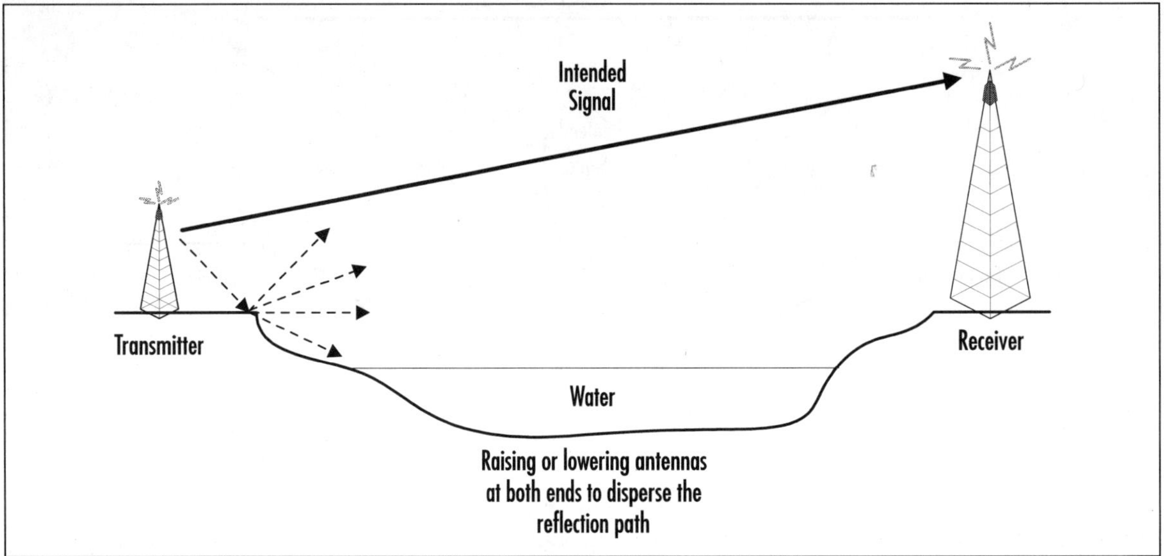

Refraction

When a radio wave travels between two substances of different densities, it bends (refracts) because electromagnetic signals move slower through denser substances. This phenomenon impacts a radio wave as it travels through the atmosphere. The density of the earth's atmosphere decreases as altitude increases. Therefore, the bottom of the radio wave travels through a denser atmosphere than the top of the wave. This means the bottom of the wave moves slower than the top of the wave, causing the signal to bend towards the earth's surface and follow the curvature of the earth, but at an arc radius approximately 1.33 times greater than the earth's arc radius (see Figure 3.16).

Figure 3.16 Refraction

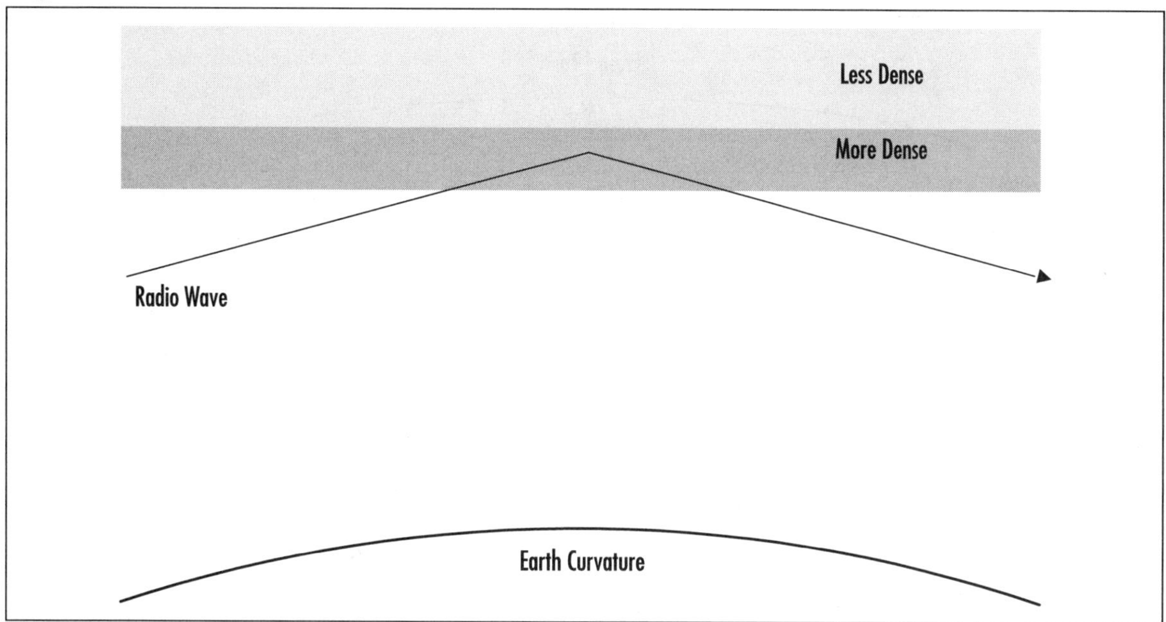

At night, the air cools, and much of the moisture in the air moves closer to the earth's surface. The cool, wet air near the earth is denser than the air higher in the atmosphere, so radio signals can bend farther than they do in the daylight hours. This is known as *super refraction*. *Ducting* happens when radio waves are trapped in a high-density duct between two areas of lower density. *Bending* is similar to super refraction, but is caused by differences in air density in a horizontal plane, like when cooler air over a lake or field and warmer air over a shore or highway cause the radio waves to bend in the direction of the cooler, denser air over the lake or field. Refraction is one reason why radio line-of-sight is not necessarily the same as optical line-of-sight. Refraction is minimal for paths under 10 miles, with the exception of hot, humid areas like the Southeastern U.S.

Accounting for the Fresnel Zone and Earth Bulge

A main consideration of any point-to-point design is the Fresnel zone, as shown in Figure 3.17. An electromagnetic signal traveling between two antennas does not travel in a straight line. The wave spreads out as it propagates. The individual waves that make up the signal do not travel at a constant velocity. A pair of antennas defines a three-dimensional elliptical path for the radio waves that propagate between them. This elliptical path is divided into several Fresnel zones based on the phase and speed of the propagating waves.

Each Fresnel zone differs in phase by up to half a wavelength, or 180 degrees. Radio line-of-sight is not the same as visual line-of-sight. Radio line-of-sight is not a straight line between the antennas, but more of an ellipse. This ellipse should be calculated to determine its optimal size and unobstructed path.

Figure 3.17 Fresnel Zone (Radio Line-of-sight)

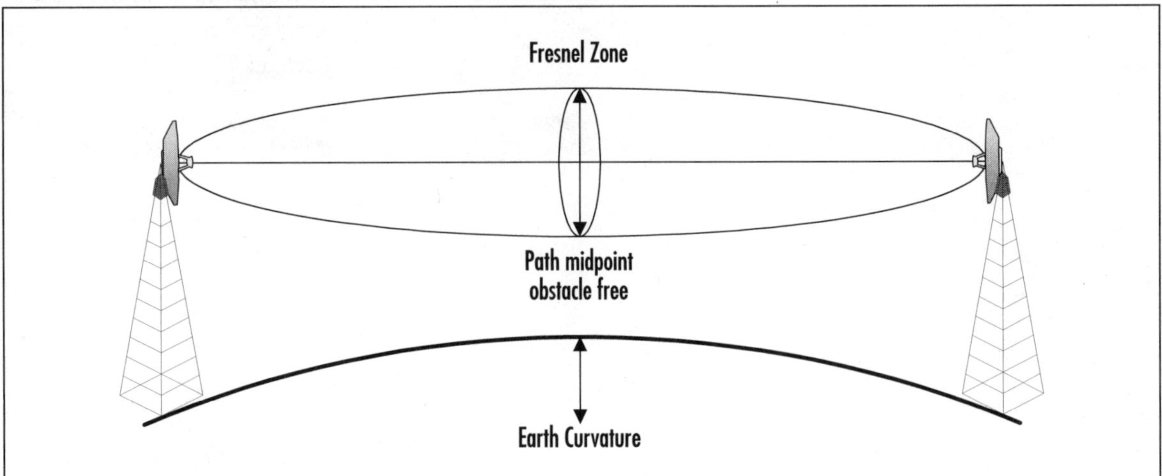

The antennas used in a point-to-point design must be tall enough to provide clearance of the Fresnel zone's radius at the midpoint. As the distance increases, the curvature of the earth makes the line-of-sight more difficult at 6 miles (for a 6-foot tall person) and disappears altogether at 16 miles (for two structures at 10 feet) because the clearance from the earth at the horizon point has minimum clearance (see Figure 3.18). Paths over 20 miles are extremely difficult to align and install.

Figure 3.18 Minimum Clearance for Long Distances

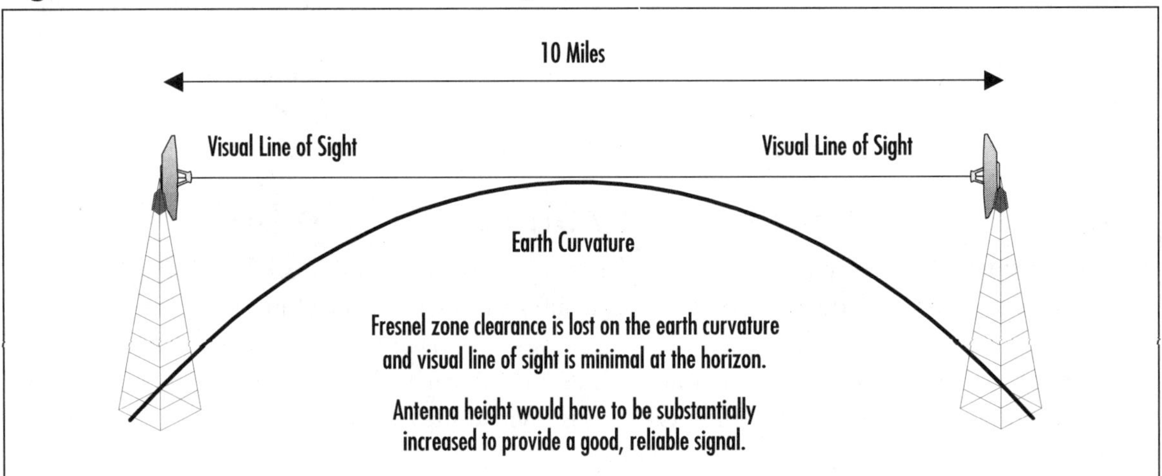

RF Interference

RF interference is extraneous energy that impedes the reception of signals and can be caused by radio emissions from another transmitter at approximately the same frequency.

Both the transmitter and receiver operate within a band of frequencies that is several MHz wide. AP transmitters transmit strongest at frequencies very close to its center frequency, with a decrease in signal strength as you move away from the center frequency. The receiver is most sensitive to frequencies very close to its center frequency. The receiver center frequency can differ slightly from the transmitter center frequency, yet communications will still work.

The width of the center frequency is a major factor in determining the effects of radio interference. If a receiver encounters a second signal that is too close to its center frequency, and overlaps too much, interference results. The closer the interfering signal is to the receiver's center frequency, the less power is needed to cause interference. In the extreme case, if somebody turns on their microwave oven and its emanations are on exactly the same frequency as yours, you may drop down in speed even if the signal is very weak. Conversely, if something is operating on a frequency that is quite far away from the center frequency of your AP's receiver, it can still interfere if its signal is strong enough.

Interference from Radio Transmitters

Interference can occur from other radio transmitters and electronic equipment operating closely. Sources of such interference include:

- Incorrectly installed radio transmitting equipment
- An intense radio signal from a nearby transmitter
- Unwanted signals generated by the transmitting equipment and not enough shielding or filtering in the electronic equipment to prevent it from picking up those unwanted signals

Any signal other than the desired signal is called an unwanted signal, or *spurious radiation*. Spurious radiation includes harmonic radiation, usually in the form of standing or traveling waves. Such problems can be detected using a spectrum analyzer, a calibrated field intensity meter, or a frequency-selective voltmeter.

Harmonics

Harmonics occur when signals are produced at two or three times the station's operating frequency in addition to the desired signals, as shown in Figure 3.19. If the harmonics fall on another locally used frequency, such as an AP channel, they are likely to cause interference. Figure 3.77 shows how a signal from some radio device may interfere with an AP set to channel 1.

These undesired transmissions occur at multiples of the original frequency. In the example, harmonics of Device A, which is transmitting at 804 MHz, may occur at 1.608 MHz (frequency × 2) or 2.412 MHz (frequency × 3). Device A's second harmonic is reduced in power by roughly half of the originating signal's power. The third harmonic's power is roughly half of the second harmonic and so on.

Figure 3.19 Harmonics

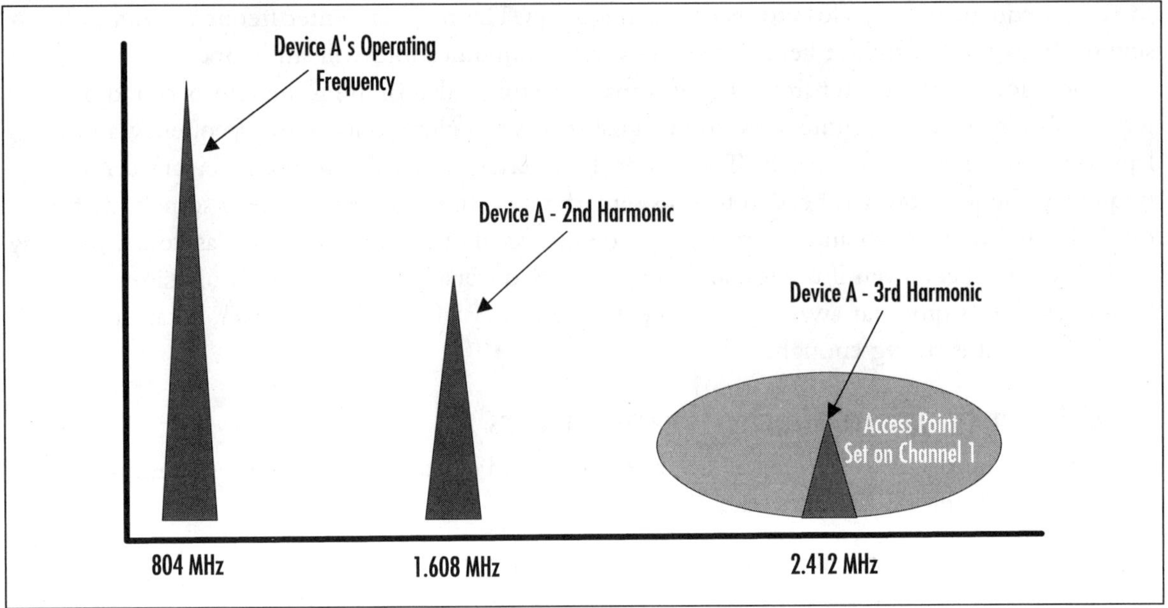

Application Considerations

Applications can drive the details of a wireless implementation with their bandwidth requirements. If the high bandwidth and/or high traffic application is not necessary on the wireless network, filter or remove it from the equation. Network-intensive applications that require the transfer of large amount of data by a significant number of users can place a heavy burden on a network.

Structural Considerations

Physical considerations affecting wireless operations include path fading and propagation loss. Each has its specific causes. Radio waves travel at the speed of light, and attain this speed assuming that there are no obstructions to pass through. The densities of substances through which the waves travel affect the speed. The greater the density of the substance, the slower the wave propagates through it. Under normal circumstances, as the signal radiates out from an antenna and encounters objects within the environment, it will exhibit one or more of the following reactions: it may penetrate the object, reflect off the object, or be absorbed by the object.

All of these reactions will occur to varying degrees, depending on the density and type of object encountered. The strength of the signal decreases as it propagates. Penetration, reflection, and absorption all factor into the signal's journey, each consuming some of its strength, and affecting its direction.

As the radio wave propagates through the earth's atmosphere and encounters objects within the environment, the strength of the signal will decrease. Any distortion of a wave's amplitude, phase, or direction can affect the strength of the received signal, causing *path fading*. The strength of the received signal is equal to the strength of the transmitted signal minus path fading.

Differing environments can have substantial structural considerations to work around or overcome to successfully implement a WLAN solution. Hospitals must be constructed to meet stringent regulations, and contain radiating medical equipment—all factors in signal degradation. Warehouses with their rows and varying stock densities also play havoc with wireless. Buildings constructed of metal can constrain wireless signals and interfere with normal operations. Other potential interfering devices can be arc welding and telemetry equipment, 2.4 GHz lighting systems, and Spectralink phone systems. Spectralink phone systems are used to provide cellular phone coverage within a company and are based on the IEEE 802.11b standard—the same standard used for WLANs.

Implementing a WLAN Architecture

A complete WLAN architecture consists of several key devices and structures, not completely defined by the IEEE 802.11 standards. Figure 3.20 depicts a wireless system and the additional components that may be needed to complete it. Some of the components may already be in place for a particular implementation. In general, most sites already have DS, which may be Ethernet, token-ring, and so on, and may include WAN connectivity as well as LAN.

Figure 3.20 WLAN System

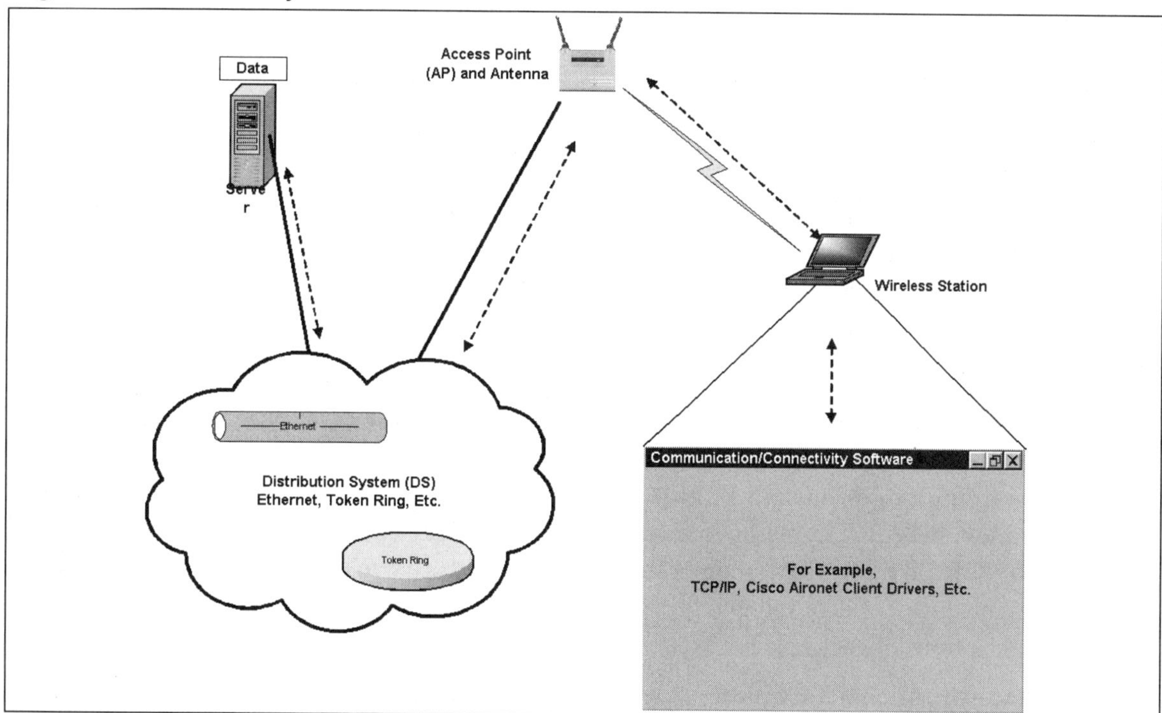

A good way to depict these functions is to specify the network's architecture. This architecture describes the protocols, major hardware, and software elements that constitute the network. Network architecture, whether wireless or wired, may be viewed in two ways, physically and logically.

As seen in the graphic, wireless systems contain both logical and physical components, many of which are not specified in the IEEE 802.11 standards. Some of the components not addressed by the 802.11 standard are DS', connectivity software, such as wireless client drivers and utilities, and communications protocols (for example, Transfer Control Protocol (TCP)/Internet Protocol (IP), Internetwork Packet Exchange (IPX), and so on).

The OSI Reference Model

The physical and logical components of a wireless system implement the physical, data link, and network layer functions of the OSI reference model to satisfy the functionality needed within LANs, WANs, and MANs.

Recall from Chapter 1 that the OSI reference model provides a schematic overview of networking by dividing its functions into seven layers. Each layer performs a different function required to exchange data between two systems. Each individual layer supports the operations of the layers above it.

The data link layer of the OSI model is divided into two parts: the MAC sublayer and the LLC sublayer. The IEEE 802.2 LLC standard defines LLC activity for most networking products. The LLC provides link control between devices and is independent of the transmission medium or MAC technique implemented by a particular network. Wireless systems utilize the first two layers of the OSI reference model: the physical and data link layers.

Logical Wireless System Components

Logical wireless system components are the functions and subsystems required to perform networking in a wireless system. Not to be confused with the actual hardware used in such environments, typical logical components are software-based. In general, many of the logical functions required of wired networks, such as Ethernet and token ring are also needed in a wireless system. Much of this has to do with the standards upon which wired networks are built. The wireless systems must comply with these standards in order to integrate with the wired networks.

- **DS** The DS refers to the topology of the wired network that wireless networks access to use services and applications. Obviously, if all the network services and applications required reside on directly accessible wireless systems, there is no need for a DS.

  In most cases, a wired LAN backbone can be specified to act as the DS. Typically, vendors sell APs capable of connecting to either IEEE-compliant Ethernet or token ring LANs. In addition, WAN components may be necessary to connect LANs separated by longer distances. The following are the logical components of a wireless system and brief descriptions of each.
- **Medium Access Technique** Medium access techniques facilitate the sharing of a common medium. This component is specified in the IEEE 802.11 standard.
- **Synchronization and Error Control** Synchronization and error control mechanisms ensure that each link transfers the data intact. The data link layer of the OSI reference model is used to handle this function of the logical wireless system. IEEE 802.11 specifies the MAC to be used for WLANs.
- **Routing Mechanisms** Routing mechanisms move the data from the originating source to the intended destination. These mechanisms work at the network layer of the OSI reference model.

- **Application Interface** The application interface connects a device, such as a laptop computer or bar-code scanner, to application software hosted on a server. An e-mail program on a wireless laptop is an example of an application interface. These interfaces also include the communication and connectivity software, such as TCP/IP and wireless client drivers.

Physical Wireless System Components

To further understand wireless architecture, it is important to be able to identify the physical wireless system components used in various wireless implementations. This section identifies the general terms for the physical components in the WLAN architecture and gives a brief description of each. In addition, this section gives an overview of each component's place in the overall wireless scheme.

- **Medium** The physical component of the WLAN backbone. This is part of the wireless system's DS. For example, twisted-pair cabling, coax cabling, and fiber-optic cabling are all physical components of logical topologies defined as the DS.
- **AP** An AP is a wireless radio. They are the center points in an all-wireless network, or a connection point between a wired and wireless network. Multiple APs can be placed throughout a facility to provide users equipped with WLAN adapters the ability to move freely throughout an extended area while maintaining uninterrupted access to all network resources.
- **Antenna** The antenna, along with air, can be thought of as the medium for wireless networking outside the DS. It is the physical component that radiates the modulated signal through the air so that the destination can receive it. Types of antennas are differentiated by their propagation patterns, gain, and transmission power.
- **Wireless Station (Client)** This is any appliance that interfaces with wireless medium and operates as an end user device. The wireless station is the user's interface to the wireless system. Examples of wireless stations are laptop computers, desktop computers, and PDAs with wireless network interface cards (radio cards) installed, radio bar code readers, and wireless hubs (like Cisco's Workgroup Bridge product). The wireless hub allows the addition of wired network devices such as print servers or computers with traditional wired network cards to attach to the wireless hub from which the devices gain access to the wireless network.
- **Server** Though not necessarily directly attached to a wireless network, servers are nonetheless a typical component in a wireless system. In many cases, wireless stations need to access servers for such things as print and e-mail services, file sharing, and application access.

Security Fundamentals for Wireless Networks

WLAN security needs to be a prime directive due to the inherent (default) insecure nature of wireless networking. Data passes through the air, and can be vulnerable to anyone within range. In a WLAN scenario, it is impossible for the AP to know if the wireless client is sitting inside your building, passing time in your lobby, or if they are seated in a parked car just outside your office. Acknowledging that passing data across an unreliable radio link could lead to possible snooping, the IEEE 802.11 standard provides three ways to provide a greater amount of security for the data that travels over the WLAN. Adopting any (or all three) of these mechanisms decreases the likelihood of an accidental security exposure.

- **Service Set Identifier (SSID)** The SSID can be associated with one or more APs to create multiple WLAN segments within the infrastructure BSS. The SSID is presented during the authentication process and acts as a crude password. These SSIDs could be shared among users, thus limiting their effectiveness. Changing the SSID for any reason requires that all wireless devices and APs be updated.
- **MAC Address** The AP can authenticate a wireless device against a list of MAC addresses either on the AP itself or on the wired network. This typically provides a good level of security, and is best used with small WLAN networks. With larger WLAN networks, administering the list of allowable MAC addresses requires some back-end services to reduce the amount of time needed to make an addition or subtraction from the list.
- **Encryption** The privacy service, WEP, uses a RC-4 based encryption scheme to encapsulate the payload of the 802.11 data frames. WEP specifies a 40-bit (advertised as 64 bits) encryption key, although some vendors have implemented a 104-bit (advertised as 128 bits) key. WEP is not meant to be an end-to-end encryption solution. WEP keys on the APs and wireless devices can be rotated. The 802.11 standard does not specify a key-management protocol, so all key rotation must be done manually. This rotation affects all APs and wireless users and requires significant effort to accomplish.
- **Virtual Private Network (VPN)** VPNs are a form of encryption. A highly advocated approach is placing the WLAN architecture behind a firewall or VPN device, treating it as an outside network. This would make the wireless client authenticate to the VPN or firewall using third-party software (on top of WEP). The benefit here is that the bulk of the authenticating would be up to a non-WLAN device and would not require additional AP maintenance.

Security protection starts with the preservation of the confidentiality, integrity, and availability (CIA) of data and computing resources. These three tenets of information security, often referred to as "the big three," are sometimes represented by the CIA triad, as shown in Figure 3.21.

Figure 3.21 The CIA Triad

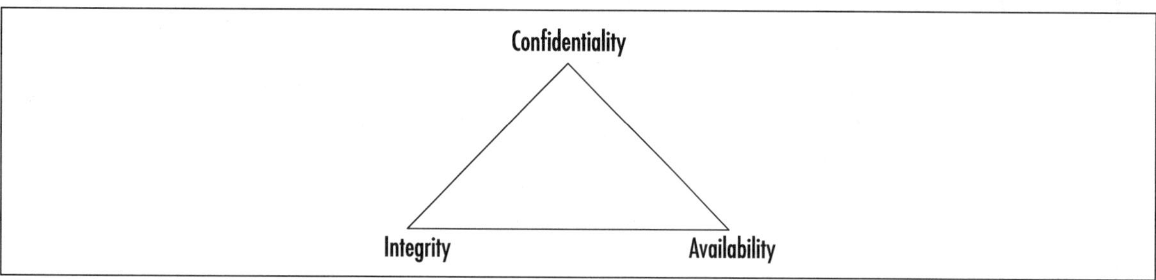

Ensuring Confidentiality

Confidentiality attempts to prevent the intentional or unintentional unauthorized disclosure of communications between a sender and recipient. With the advent of wireless communications, the need for physically connecting to a communication channel to listen in or capture confidential communications was removed. An attacker can join a wireless network by merely being in signal range. Having knowledge that communications channels are possibly compromised allows us to properly implement policies and procedures to mitigate the wireless risk. To ensure confidentiality, *encryption* is used.

The current implementation of encryption in today's wireless networks use the RC4 stream cipher to encrypt the transmitted network packets, and the WEP to protect authentication into wireless networks by network devices connecting to them (that is, the network adapter authentication, not the user utilizing the network resources). Both of which, due mainly to improper implementations, have introduced sufficient problems that have made it possible to determine keys used and then either falsely authenticate to the network or decrypt the traffic traveling across through the wireless network. With these apparent problems, those in charge of wireless network security should utilize other proven and properly implemented encryption solutions, such as Secure Shell (SSH), Secure Sockets Layer (SSL), or Secure Internet Protocol (IPsec).

Ensuring Integrity

Integrity ensures the accuracy and completeness of information throughout its process methods. It is concerned with ensuring that the message was not modified en route by validating with checksums or other techniques. A *checksum* is a value based on the hash of a message, which is appended to the message. When the receiver gets the complete message, they then run the message through the same function and compare the value they generate with the value that was included at the end of the message. These functions can sometimes have their own issues, such as the function not being detailed enough to allow for distinctly separate data that could possibly have identical checksums.

Cyclic redundancy checks (CRCs) were developed to ensure data integrity. CRC algorithms treat a message as an enormous binary number, whereupon another large fixed binary number then divides this binary number. The remainder from this division is the checksum. Using the remainder of a long division as the checksum as opposed to the original data summation, adds a significant chaos to the checksum created, increasing the likelihood that the checksum will not be repeatable with any other separate data stream.

Ensuring Availability

Availability ensures that access data or computing resources needed by appropriate personnel is both reliable and available in a timely manner. The initial design of packet-switched networks did not take into consideration the possibility of an actual attack on the network from one of its own nodes. Wireless networks are experiencing similar design issues, and are finding themselves in conflict with other wireless resources.

Ensuring Authentication

Authentication allows the sender and receiver to confirm their identities with each other. If authentication cannot be accomplished, there is no trust. It is only through authentication that we know exactly with whom we are communicating.

The simplest form of authentication is the transmission of a shared password between the entities. This can be as simple as a password. As with all simple forms of protection, once knowledge of the key used in authentication is disclosed to untrusted parties, all authentications via that key become suspect.

Many methods can be used to acquire a simple secret key, including social engineering, sniffing, or weak keys. However the key is acquired, once obtained, it can be used to falsely authenticate and identify an attacker as a valid party, forging false communications or utilizing the user's access to gain permissions to the available resources.

Public-key cryptography introduced the concept of having keys work in pairs, with an encryption key (public) and a decryption (private) key. Obtaining one key from the other is infeasible, as they are independent of each other. Possession of the public key does not enable an attacker to decrypt a message. In fact, the public key is generally made available to anyone who wants to use it to encrypt a message to a particular user or device. The holder of the private key can decrypt the message encrypted with their public key. A good example of a public-key cryptography is the Pretty Good Privacy (PGP) program that can be downloaded from http://web.mit.edu/network/pgp.html. While PGP can be used to secure wireless networking, it is still a good tool for anyone desiring to learn the fundamentals of public-key cryptography. The longer the key, the harder it is for an attacker to brute-force their way to decryption.

Initial 802.11 network authentication centered on the authentication of the wireless device, not the user. Public-key encryption was not used in the wireless encryption process. Although a few wireless vendors have dynamic keys that are changed with every connection, most wireless products utilize shared-key authentication with static keys.

Shared key authentication is utilized by WEP functions with the following steps:

1. When a station requests service, it sends an authentication frame to the AP it wishes to communicate with.
2. The receiving AP replies to the authentication frame with its own, which contains 128 octets of challenge text.
3. The station requesting access encrypts the challenge text with the shared encryption key and returns to the AP.

4. The access decrypts the encrypted challenge using the shared key and compares it with the original challenge text. If they match, an authentication acknowledgement is sent to the station requesting access, otherwise a negative authentication notice is sent.

This approach does not authenticate the user. It is only a verification that the client has knowledge of the shared secret key installed on the wireless AP. Once authenticated, a client has full access to the wireless network. Effort has been put into improving the lot of wireless security, starting with several authentication protocols such as Extensible Authentication Protocol (EAP) and Light Extensible Authentication Protocol (LEAP).

Extensible Authentication Protocol (EAP)

The EAP provides authentication within Point-to-Point-Protocol (PPP). EAP integrates third-party authentication packages that use PPP. It can be configured to support a number of methods for authentication schemes, such as token cards, public key, certificates, personal identification numbers (PINs), and so on.

When using PPP/EAP, EAP will select a specific authentication method during the authentication phase. This allows the authenticator to request more information to select the authentication method. An AP does not need to understand each request, as it is a conduit for the host. It only needs to know if there is a success or failure code in order to terminate the authentication phase.

EAP can define one or more requests for peer-to-peer authentication. This can happen because the request packet includes a type field, such as Generic Token, one-time password (OTP), or an Message Digest 5 (MD5) challenge. The MD5 challenge is very similar to the Challenge Handshake Authentication Protocol (CHAP).

EAP provides a flexible, link-layer security framework (see Figure 3.22), with the following features:

- EAP mechanisms are Internet Engineering Task Force (IETF) standards-based and allow for the growth of new authentication types when system security needs to be changed:
  - Transport Layer Security (TLS)
  - Internet Key Exchange (IKE)
  - GSS_API (Kerberos)
  - Other authentication schemes (LEAP)
- There is no dependency on IP, because this is a Layer 2 data link protocol.
- There is no windowing as this is a simple ACK/negative acknowledgment (NAK) protocol.
- There is no support for fragmentation.
- Can run over any link layer (PPP, 802.3, 802.5, 802.11, and so on).
- Does not consider a physically secure link as an authentication method to provide security.
- Assumes that there is no reordering of packets.
- Retransmission of packets is the responsibility of authenticator.

Figure 3.22 The EAP Architecture

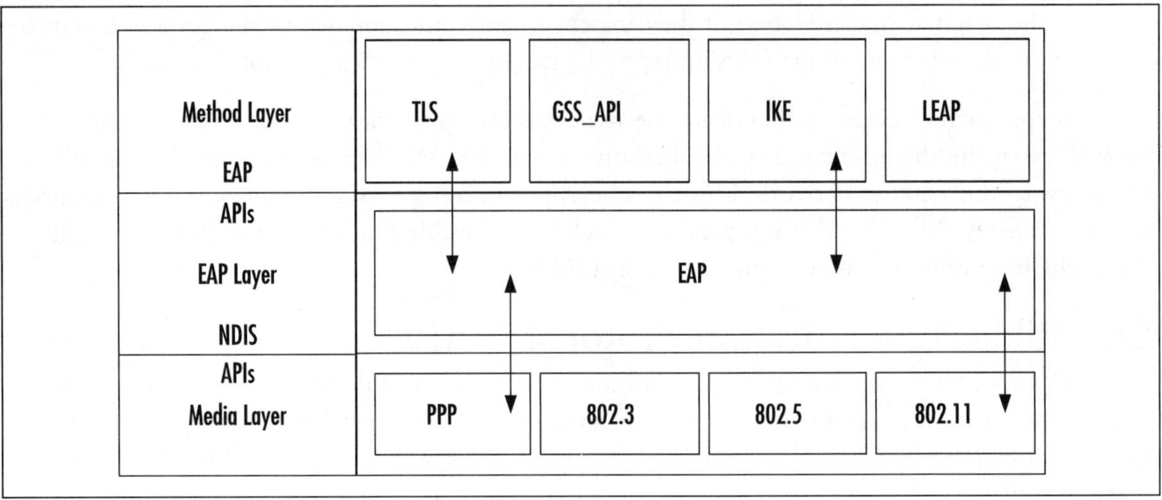

Per-packet Authentication

EAP can support per-packet authentication and integrity protection, but this is not extended to all types of EAP messages. NAK and notification messages are not able to use per-packet authentication and integrity. Per-packet authentication and integrity protection works for the following (packet is encrypted unless otherwise noted):

- TLS and IKE derive session key
- TLS ciphersuite negotiations (not encrypted)
- IKE ciphersuite negotiations
- Kerberos tickets
- Success and failure messages that use derived session key (through WEP)

Possible Implementation of EAP on the WLAN

EAP-MD5 and Public Key Infrastructure (PKI) with EAP-TLS are two main authentication methods for EAP on a WLAN. EAP-MD5 does not support mutual authentication between access servers and wireless clients. PKI is very computation-intensive on client systems, requires much planning and design to ensure the network can support PKI, and is relatively expensive.

Cisco LEAP

LEAP is an enhancement to the EAP protocol. EAP provides a scalable method for a PPP-based server to authenticate its clients and allow for mutual authentication. An extensible packet exchange should allow for the passing of authentication information between the client devices and the PPP servers. PPP usually rely on a centralized authentication server such as Remote Authentication Dial-In User Server/Service (RADIUS) or Terminal Access Controller Access Control System Plus (TACACS+) system to validate the clients for them. The PPP server is a pass through or a relay agent as authentication occurs between the client and the RADIUS server. The RADIUS server shares the authentication results with the PPP server.

LEAP may be a better option because it offers mutual authentication, requires minimal CPU cycles, supports embedded systems, and supports clients that do not natively support EAP or PKI authentication. With LEAP, the client and the AP must authenticate. LEAP can prevent a rogue AP from being used. LEAP authentication works through three phases: the *start phase*, the *authenticate phase*, and the *finish phase*. The following sections show the process that the client and AP go through so that the client can also talk to the RADIUS server. TACACS or RADIUS can be used for the authentication.

Start Phase for LEAP Authentication

In the start phase, information (in packet form) is transferred between the client and APs:

1. **EAPOW-Start** (AKA EAPOL-Start in 802.1x for wired networks). Starts the authentication process. This packet is sent from the client to the AP.
2. **EAP-Request/Identity** Sent from the AP to the client with a request for the clients identity.
3. **EAP-Response/Identity** Sent from the client to the AP with the required information.

Authentication Phase for LEAP Authentication

This sequence changes based on the mutual authentication method between the client and the authentication server. If using TLS for the transfer of certificates in a PKI deployment, EAP-TLS messages are used. For LEAP, the process looks like this:

1. The client sends an EAP-Response/Identity message to the RADIUS server through the AP as a RADIUS-Access-Request with EAP extensions.
2. The RADIUS server then returns access-request with a RADIUS-challenge, to which the client must respond.

Cisco LEAP authentication is a mutual authentication method, and the AP is only a pass through. The AP, in the authenticate phase, forwards the contents of the packets from EAP to RADIUS and from RADIUS to EAP.

The Finish Phase of LEAP Authentication

The steps for the finish phase are as follows:

1. If the client is considered invalid, the RADIUS server sends a RADIUS deny packet with an EAP fail packet embedded within it. If the client is considered to be valid, the server sends a RADIUS request packet with an EAP success attribute.
2. The RADIUS-Access-Accept packet contains the MS-MPPE-Send-Key attribute to the AP, where it obtains the session key that will be used by client.

The RADIUS server and client both create a session key from the user's password when using LEAP. The encryption for the IEEE 802.11 standard can be based on a 40/64-bit or 104/128-bit key. The key derivation process creates a longer key than required. This is so that when the AP receives the key from the RADIUS server (using MS-MPPE-Send-Key attribute), it will send an EAPOL-KEY message to the client. This key tells the client the key length and what key index should be used.

The key value is not sent because the client has already created it on its own WEP key. The data packet is then encrypted using the full-length key. The AP will also send an EAPOL-KEY message that gives information about the length, key index, and value of the multicast key. This message is encrypted using the full-length session unicast key from the AP.

Configuration and Deployment of LEAP

Installation for a LEAP solution consists of a client, an AP, and a RADIUS (or TACACS) server for key distribution in a network.

Client Support for LEAP

A client can be configured to use LEAP mode in one of two modes:

- **Logon Mode** Single sign-on for both the wireless network as well as for networks or servers (Microsoft Networking, NetWare, etc.). This provides users with a transparent security experience.
- **Device Mode** WLAN stores the username/password identification so that the administrator can get non-interactive authentication into the WLAN. Used on wireless devices that can authenticate themselves through these pre-configured credentials.

AP Support for LEAP

APs support 802.1x for 802.11 Authenticator if the following is accomplished:

- The AP is configured to use 40/64-bit or 104/128-bit WEP mode.
- Give the LEAP RADIUS server address and configure the shared secret key that the AP and RADIUS server use, so that they can communicate securely.

Configuring a RADIUS Server for LEAP

To configure the RADIUS server for authentication and key distribution users:

- Create the user databases.
- Configure the APs as Network Access Servers (NASs). This enables users that are configured with Cisco-Aironet RADIUS extensions on the NAS to use RADIUS. RADIUS requests from the AP with EAP extensions are passed as described earlier.

An Introduction to the 802.1x Standard

The current IEEE 802.11a, b, and g standards are limited because they are available only for the current open and shared key authentication non-extensible schemes.

Some of these requirements for future security include the following:

- The creation of new 802.11 authentication methods.
- These authentication methods must be independent of the underlying 802.11 hardware.
- Authentication methods should be dynamic because hard coding makes it difficult to fix security holes when they are found.
- It must have the ability to support PKI and certificate schemes.

The Objectives of the 802.1x Standard

The IEEE 802.1x Working Group was created to develop a security framework for port-based access control that resides in the upper layers. Clients are identified by usernames, not the MAC address of the devices. 802.1x was designed so that it could support extended forms of authentication, using password methods (such as OTPs, or GSS_API mechanisms like Kerberos) and non-password methods (such as biometrics, IKE, and smart cards). The most common method for port-based access control is to enable new authentication and key management methods without changing current network devices. The benefits are:

- Significant decrease in hardware cost and complexity.
- More options, which allows the network administrator to pick and choose their security solution.
- Latest and greatest security technology that should still work with an existing infrastructure.
- Responds to security issues as quickly as they arise.

802.1x in a Nutshell

When a client device connects to a port on an 802.1x switch and AP, the switch port can determine the authenticity of the device. The services offered by the switch can be made available on that port. Only Extensible Authentication Protocol Over LAN (EAPOL) frames can be sent and received on that port until the authentication is complete. When the device is properly authenticated, the port switches traffic as though it were a regular port.

802.1x standard terminology:

- **Port** Single point of connection to the network.
- **Port Access Entity (PAE)** Controls the algorithms and protocols associated with the authentication mechanisms for a port.
- **Authenticator PAE** Enforces authentication before it will allow access to resources on that port.

- **Supplicant PAE** Accesses the services that are allowed by the authenticator.
- **Authentication Server** Verifies the supplicant PAE. It decides whether the supplicant is authorized to access the authenticator or not.
- **EAPOL** Encapsulates EAP messages so that they can be handled directly by a LAN MAC service. 802.1x uses EAP to receive authentication information.
- **Extensible Authentication Protocol Over Wireless (EAPOW)** EAPOL messages encapsulated in 802.11 wireless frames.

Key Derivation Can Be Dynamic

802.1x supports per-user/per-session keys, removing the requirement to configure WEP keys on the client or AP. These WEP keys will be dynamically created at the client for every session, thus making it more secure. The Global key, like a broadcast WEP key, can be encrypted using a unicast session key and then sent from the AP to the client in a secure manner.

Mutual Authentication

When using 802.1x and EAP, some form of mutual authentication should be used. This will make the client and the authentication servers mutually authenticate and prevent man-in-the-middle attacks. To enable mutual authentication, any of the following EAP methods can be used:

- **TLS** Server supplies a certificate and establishes that it has possession of the private key.
- **IKE** Server shows possession of pre-shared key or private key (this can be considered certificate authentication).
- **GSS_API (Kerberos)** Server demonstrates knowledge of the session key.

802.1x and EAP

IEEE 802.1x, EAP, and the Cisco LEAP provide an end-to-end solution. EAP/LEAP allow wireless clients to authenticate to RADIUS and TACACS+ servers. IEEE 802.1x provides network access control that is port-based for MAC filtering. When deployed together, wireless clients associated with APs are not able to gain access to the network unless the user authenticates with a username and password to a RADIUS or TACACS+ server. The RADIUS server and client device then receives a client-specific WEP key by the client for that specific logon session. The user's password and session key is never transmitted in the open, over the wireless connection.

Here is how authentication works and the WEP key is passed:

1. The wireless client associates with an AP.
2. The AP prevents all other attempts made by that client to gain access until the client logs on.
3. The client supplies a username and password.
4. Using 802.1x standard and EAP/LEAP, the wireless client and a RADIUS/TACACS+ server perform authentication through the AP. If using LEAP, the RADIUS server sends an authentication challenge to the client.

After authentication completes successfully, the following steps take place:

5. The RADIUS server and client determine a WEP key unique for the client and session.
6. The RADIUS server transmits this WEP key (session key) across the wired LAN to the AP.
7. The AP encrypts the broadcast key and the session key so that it can then send the new encrypted key to the client. The client then uses the session key to decrypt it.
8. The client and the AP activate the WEP. The APs and clients then use the session and broadcast WEP keys for all communications that occur during the session.
9. The Session key and broadcast key are changed at regular periods that are configured in the RADIUS server.

This process is illustrated in Figure 3.23.

Figure 3.23 Cisco Security Solution Using Session-Based Encryption Keys

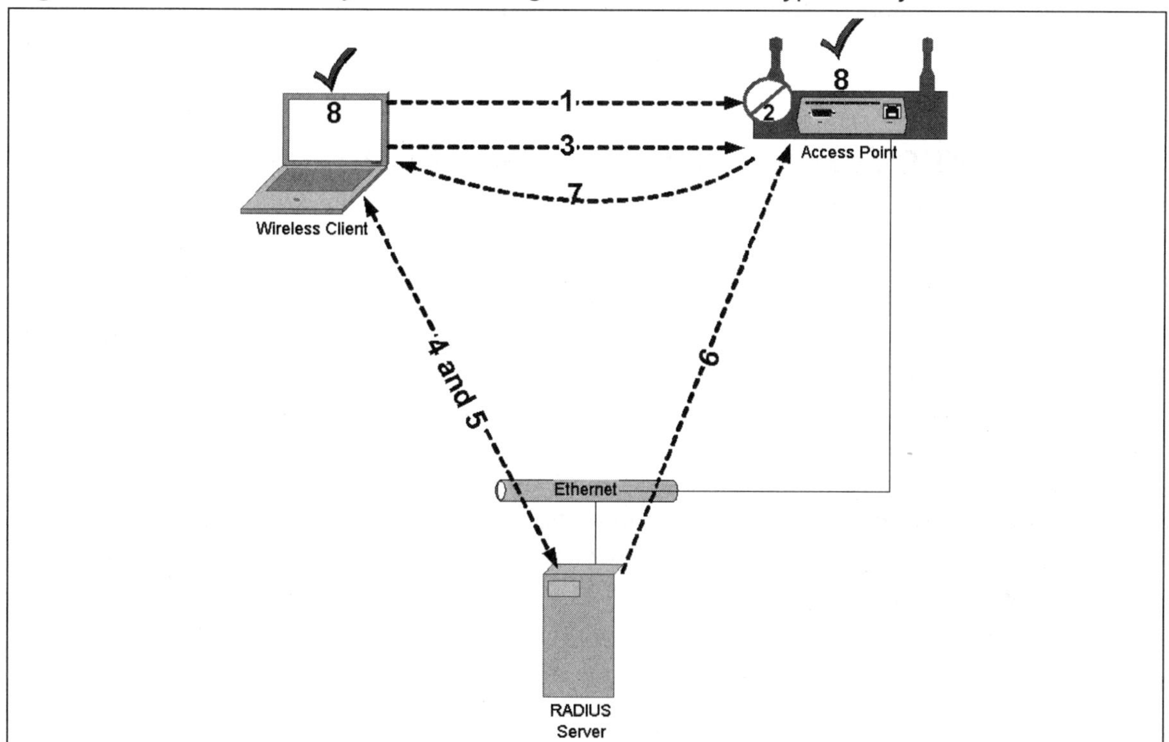

Ensuring Authorization

While authentication is concerned with validating identity, authorization concerns itself with ensuring that a user or device is granted access for which they are cleared. Authorization levels determine the extent of system rights of a particular user or device. Authorization is possible through mechanisms such as RADIUS and TACACS+.

Unfortunately, many wireless devices do not currently support external authorization validation. Most deployments do not control access to or from specific network segments. To fully restrict authorized users to the network devices they are authorized to utilize, the network administrator still needs to deploy an adaptive firewall between the AP and the network. Nonetheless, there are other ways to ensure the proper authorization of a client.

Deploy a firewall to segment wireless and wired networks, and harden the wireless interfaces by utilizing the strongest encryption available to them, disabling SID broadcast and allowing only authorized MAC addresses on the wireless network.

- Disable dynamic host control protocol (DHCP) on the AP, and permit DHCP servers to lease only certain MAC addresses.
- Turn off all routing and forwarding between wireless and wired interfaces.
- Require clients to authenticate via an SSL-protected Web page to gain access to internal resources.

Once a user is properly authenticated, the firewall changes the firewall rules for the IP address that user is supposed to be assigned to, allowing full access to only the network resources they are authorized to access.

Where in the Authentication/Association Process Does MAC Filtering Occur?

When a wireless device wants to connect to a WLAN, it goes though a two-part process called authentication and authorization. After both have been completed, the device is allowed access to the WLAN. When a wireless device attempts to connect to a WLAN, it sends an authentication request to the AP (see Figure 3.24). This request contains the SSID of the target network, or a null value if connecting to an open system. The AP grants or denies authentication based on this string.

Following a successful authentication, authorization of a sort occurs. The requesting device attempts to associate with the AP. It is at this point that MAC filtering plays its role. Depending on the AP vendor and administrative setup of the AP, MAC filtering either allows only the specified MAC addresses, blocking the rest, or it allows all MAC addresses, blocking specifically noted MAC addresses. If the MAC address is allowed, the requesting device is allowed to associate with the AP.

Figure 3.24 MAC Filtering

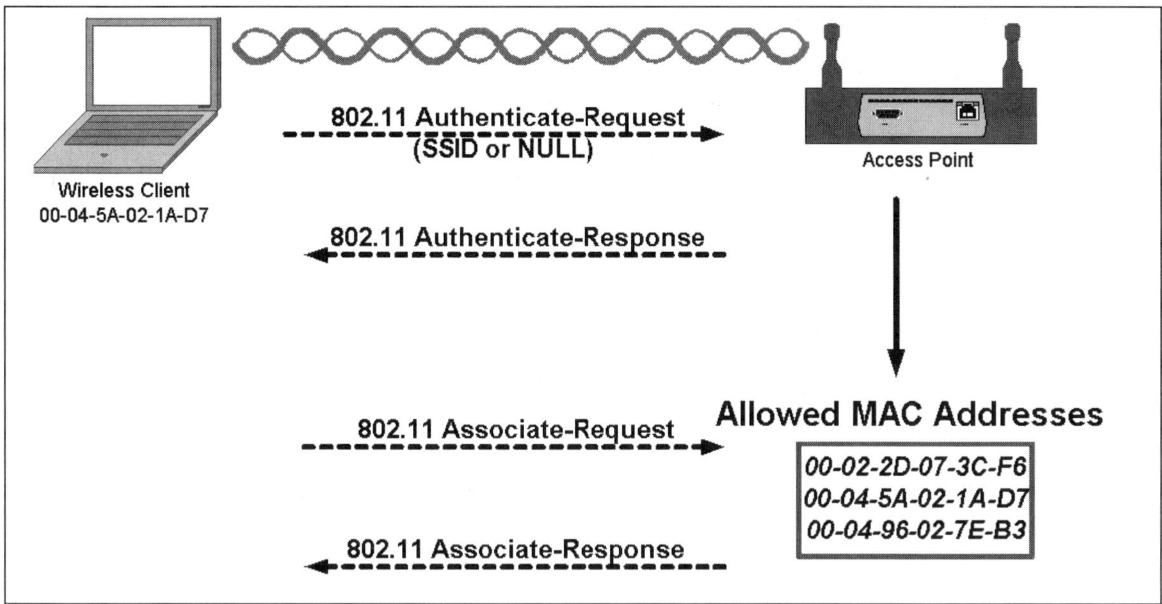

Accounting and Audit Trails

Auditing tracks and logs activities on networks and systems, and can map them to specific users or devices. Audit trails can be useful in restoring data integrity. Auditing can ensure that the activity of authorized individuals can be traced to their specific actions, and that those actions comply with defined policy. Information collected as part of the auditing process can help investigate and curb improper or illegal activities.

The logging features provided on most networks and systems involve the logging of known or partially known resource event activities. Although these logs are sometimes used for analyzing system problems, they are also useful for those whose duty it is to process the log files and check for both valid and invalid system activities.

Most of the current Cisco wireless products do not offer the amount of detail necessary for true auditing. They do provide statistical information, such as how much traffic has transited the AP, or information about the clients that have associated with it. As Cisco wireless products mature and more features are added, auditing will probably top the list.

Wireless Equivalency Privacy (WEP)

Encryption has always played a key role in information security, and has been the center of controversy in the design of the WEP wireless standard. Encryption continues to play a major role in wireless security, especially with the adoption of new and better encryption algorithms and key management systems.

Cryptography offers the obvious advantage that the material it protects cannot be used without the keys needed to unlock it. As long as those keys are protected, the material remains protected. There are a few potential disadvantages to encryption as well. For instance, if the key is lost, the data becomes unavailable, and if the key is stolen, the data becomes accessible to the thief.

The process of encryption also introduces possible performance degradation. When a message is to be sent encrypted, time must be spent to first encrypt the information, then store and transmit the encrypted data, and then later decode it. In theory, this can slow a system by as much as a factor of three.

WEP is a mechanism that strives to give wireless networks as much privacy as their wired counterparts. Because WEP utilizes a cryptographic security countermeasure for the fulfillment of its stated goal of privacy, it has the added benefit of becoming an authentication mechanism. This benefit is realized through a shared key authentication that allows the encryption and decryption of the wireless transmissions. Many keys can be defined on an AP or a client, and can be rotated to add complexity for a higher security standard for a WLAN policy. This is a must! WEP was never intended to be the absolute authority in security.

Most APs advertise that they support at least 64 bits, but often the 128-bit option is also supported. For corporate networks, 128-bit encryption–capable devices should be considered as a minimum. With data security enabled in a closed network, the settings on the client for the SSID and the encryption keys have to match the AP when attempting to associate with the network, or it will fail.

Addressing the Issues with Policy

Wireless users have unique needs that policy must address. The administrator must take diligent care in creating effective policies to protect users, their data, and corporate assets. Wireless networks should be treated as outside networks, and only allow secured and authenticated access. APs should be configured to not broadcast SSID information. All default passwords and insecure configurations should be changed and strong authentication and encryption should be used.

Creating Privacy with WEP

The WEP options are no encryption, 40-bit, or 128-bit encryption. No encryption means transmissions are sent in the clear, and can be viewed by any wireless sniffing application. The 40- and 128-bit varieties offer stronger encryption. This shared key can be in the form of either alphanumeric or hexadecimal strings, and is matched on the client.

WEP uses the RC4 encryption algorithm, a stream cipher. Both the sender and receiver use the stream cipher to create identical pseudorandom strings from a known shared key. The process requires the sender to logically XOR the plaintext transmission with the stream cipher to produce the ciphertext. The receiver takes the shared key and identical stream and reverses the process to gain the plaintext transmission.

A 24-bit initialization vector (IV) is used to create identical cipher streams. The IV is produced by the sender, and is included in the transmission of each frame. A new IV is used for each frame to prevent the reuse of the key, thus weakening the encryption. This means that for each string generated, a different value for the RC4 key is used. Although a secure policy, consideration of the components of WEP bear out one of the flaws in WEP. Because the 24-bit space is so small with respect to the potential set of IVs, in a short period of time, all keys are eventually reused. Unfortunately, this weakness is the same for both the 40- and 128-bit encryption levels, which both use a 24-bit IV. To protect against some rudimentary attacks that insert known text into the stream to attempt to reveal the key stream, WEP incorporates a checksum in each frame.

WEP Benefits and Advantages

WEP provides some security and privacy in transmissions to prevent curious or casual browsers from viewing the contents of the transmissions held between the AP and the clients. WEP benefits include:

- All messages are encrypted using a checksum to provide some degree of tamper resistance.
- Privacy is maintained via the encryption. No key, no decryption.
- WEP is easy to implement. Set the encryption key on the AP, and repeat the process on each client.
- WEP provides a very basic level of security for WLAN applications.
- WEP keys are user definable and unlimited.

WEP Disadvantages

The following are some of the disadvantages of WEP:

- RC4 encryption algorithm takes a finite key and attempts to make an infinite pseudo-random key stream in order to generate the encryption.
- Once the key is altered, the network administrator must tell all users to adjust their settings. The more people told, the more public the information becomes.
- Used on its own, WEP does not provide adequate WLAN security.
- WEP has to be implemented on every client as well as every AP, to be effective.

The WEP Authentication Process

Shared key authentication is a four-step process as shown:

1. The requestor (the client) sends a request for association.
2. The authenticator (the AP) receives the request, and produces a random challenge text and transmits it back to the requestor.
3. The requestor receives the transmission, ciphers the challenge with the shared key stream, and returns it.
4. The authenticator decrypts the challenge text and compares the values against the original. If they match, the requestor is authenticated.

Implementing WEP on the Cisco Aironet AP 340

As seen in Figure 3.25, the Cisco AP340 supports 128-bit encryption. It is configured with either a Hypertext Transfer Protocol (HTTP) connection, or a serial connection. Select **Full Encryption** and then **128 bit** for the key size. Select the **WEP Key** radio button for the transmission key and type the string.

Figure 3.25 WEP Configuration on the Aironet

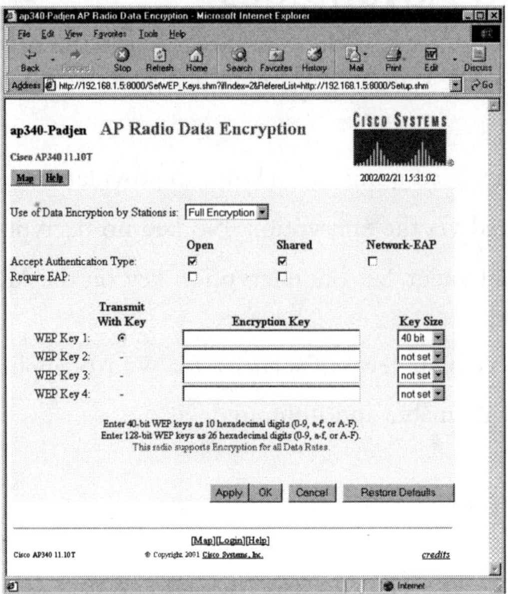

Security of 64-Bit versus 128-Bit Keys

It might seem that something protected with a 128-bit encryption scheme would be more secure than something protected with a 64-bit encryption scheme. This, however, is not the case with WEP. Because the same vulnerability exists with both encryption levels, they can be equally broken within similar time frames.

With 64-bit WEP, the network administrator specifies a 40-bit key—typically ten hexadecimal digits (0 to 9, a to f, or A to F). A 24-bit IV is appended to this 40-bit key, and the RC4 key scheme is built from these 64-bits of data. This same process is followed in the 128-bit scheme. The Administrator specifies a 104-bit key—this time 26 hexadecimal digits (0 to 9, a to f, or A to F). The 24-bit IV is added to the beginning of the key, and the RC4 key schedule is built.

The vulnerability comes from capturing predictably weak IVs, so the size of the original key does not make a significant security difference. This is due to the relatively small number of total IVs possible under the current WEP specification. Currently, there are a total of 2^{24} possible IV keys. It is easy to see that if the WEP key was not changed within a strictly defined period of time, all possible IV combinations could be heard off of a 802.11b connection, captured, and made available for cracking within a short period of time. This is a flaw in the design of WEP, and bears no correlation to whether the wireless client is using 64-bit WEP or 128-bit WEP. WEP used in conjunction with security mechanisms offered by 802.11x provides a more secure solution.

Knowledge of Cisco offerings can help the administrator with their wireless security efforts. The following sections provide useful information about the Aironet line of wireless products, as well as related accessories.

Cisco Wireless Systems

In November 1999, Cisco purchased one of the leading companies in the field of wireless technology (Aironet Wireless Communications, Inc.) in an effort to catch up to other vendors who already had a head start in the field. Aironet was a leading developer of high-speed WLAN products and played an important role on the IEEE 802.11 working group. Since then, Cisco has been aggressively expanding its wireless offerings, including the features on each product. This section discusses several of the wireless products that Cisco offers, including APs and wireless bridges. For ease of understanding, each product is introduced, followed by information about the configuration and management of each.

In most cases, the initial configuration of the wireless bridge or AP is accomplished via a direct console session. The command-line interface (CLI) provides a means to execute commands without navigating through the command menus. The CLI commands use the syntax of the command menus. The CLI can also be used to navigate submenus by entering the command tree structure syntax that is directed to the desired command menu. However, the administrator may be presented with a hierarchical series of menus instead of a CLI.

Cisco's WLAN Product Line

Cisco has a diverse selection of wireless products. Table 3.5 summarizes their offerings. There is a slight distinction that needs to be made between an AP and a bridge. Generally, an AP handles end clients such as laptops with wireless cards, while wireless bridges connect networks (wireless or wired) over greater distances than that handled by an AP. Note that the 340 series is end-of-sale, and can no longer be purchased. Also, Cisco has largely ceased the availability of 40-bit WEP support on its products. Refer to this table throughout the chapter, as the concepts for each of the fields are fully described.

Table 3.5 Cisco Wireless AP and Bridges

	340 AP	350 AP	350 Wireless Bridge	350 Workgroup Bridge	1100 AP	1200 AP (Dual Band) A/B	1400 Wireless Bridge
End of Sale (EOS)	July 31, 2002						
End of Life (EOL)	July 31, 2007						
Maximum throughput speed, packets-per-second	11 Mbps	11 Mbps	11 Mbps	11 Mbps	11 Mbps	54 Mbps	54 Mbps
PORTS							
Wired uplink 10/00	Yes	Yes	Yes	10BastT (8 clients max)	Yes	Yes	Yes
Range - Indoor - No Antenna		130ft		130ft	150ft	60ft/130ft	
Range - Indoor - Antenna		350ft		350ft	400ft	200ft/350ft	
Range - Outdoor - No Antenna		800ft		800ft	800ft	100ft/800ft	2 miles
Range - Outdoor - Antenna		2000ft	12-25 miles	2000ft	2000ft	1200ft/2000ft	23 miles
PROTOCOLS							
802.11a						Yes	Yes
802.11b	Yes	Yes	Yes	Yes	Yes	Yes	
802.11g					Upgradeable	Upgradeable	
SECURITY							
WEP 64-bit	Yes	Yes	Yes	Yes	Yes	Yes	Yes
WEP 128-bit	Yes	Yes	Yes	Yes	Yes	Yes	Yes
EAP/LEAP/PEAP		Yes	Yes	Yes	Yes	Yes	Yes
802.11x		Yes	Yes	Yes	Yes	Yes	Yes
ACCESSORIES							
Antenna	Yes	Yes	Yes	Yes	Yes	Yes	Yes
Integrated In-Line Power	Yes	Yes	Yes	Yes	Yes	Yes	Yes

Cisco devices (APs and clients) can be managed and monitored remotely with Web browsers, Telnet sessions, and Simple Network Management Protocol (SNMP). The APs also allow the administrator to control the throughput of traffic through the WLAN using MAC and protocol-based filters. If there are multiple APs deployed in a network, the administrator can also configure these devices at a central location and manage them through the network. Most of the operating systems are proprietary, and are not the Cisco standard IOS. Cisco efforts are being expended to change this, at least on the high-end models of the Aironet line.

One of Cisco's driving objectives is to create a seamless environment where users can utilize their network regardless of location. Cisco wanted to create a solution for connecting a campus environment or even a metropolitan area together in a reliable and relatively inexpensive manner. The result of this evolution is two different solution sets: one for individuals and one for site-to-site connectivity.

There are two main types of devices on a WLAN: the AP and the bridge. The AP connects the wired LAN to the WLAN to pass data from one to the other. A wireless bridge connects two or more remote networks into a single LAN. The Aironet wireless Ethernet bridge is designed to support three connection types: 10Base2 (Thinnet), 10Base5 (Thicknet), or 10BaseT (twisted pair). The Aironet 340 series bridges have 10Base-T, AUI, and coaxial connection, while the Aironet 350 series devices use 10/100BaseT connections. Most of the 1*x*00 series of the Aironet line are also 10/100BaseT, with a few models sporting coax ports.

Cisco wanted to establish its presence in the small office/home office (SOHO) market. Typically, this market consisted of very small networks, with users who have no need or desire for advanced features such as QoS. Rather than began from scratch, Cisco completed its acquisition of Linksys in June 2003, which gave it an instant toehold in the SOHO market. However, there are no plans to integrate Linksys wireless devices with the Aironet line. In fact, the Linksys brand will continue under its own banner, with insight and direction coming from Cisco.

Cisco's Aironet 3X0 Series APs and Bridges

Three main pieces of hardware go into a successful wireless installation: a base unit (AP or bridge), NIC cards (if using an AP), and an antenna. The base units that Cisco offers are detailed in this section, and the NIC cards and antennas are detailed in later sections. Cisco Aironet 3X0 series APs and bridges consist of the Cisco Aironet 350 and Cisco Aironet 340 series

The 350 series provides a more powerful radio transmitter than the 340 series. The 350 transmitter can operate at power signal strengths up to 100 mW. The 340 transmitters are limited to power strengths up to 30 mW. Depending on the deployment requirements, lower-powered 340 series wireless bridges may suit the networking needs of most bridges located within short proximity to other wireless components. For longer transmission distances or in areas where radio signals are impacted by environmental factors, the more powerful 350 series wireless bridge may be better suited. Selecting the right bridge for each specific environment can be facilitated by testing the throughput of the wireless media using the radio link test menu options.

The Cisco Aironet 350 Series

Cisco has designed the Aironet 350 series to meet the needs of mobile users and satellite offices. The 350 is designed to support a wide array of wireless devices, such as PCs, PDAs, handheld PCs, printers, point-of-sale devices, management and monitoring equipment, and so on. Some of the items that make the 350 so popular are that it has the highest transmit power (100 mW) in its class, it is highly sensitive for receiving transmissions from other units, it can be powered inline, and it allows for centralized security.

The Cisco Aironet 350 is IEEE 802.11b–compliant and interoperates with other vendor devices. The 350 platforms come bundled with client software monitoring the strength of the wireless signal.

The 350 can support a variety of features depending on the version of bridge firmware that is installed, such as the following:

- **Accounting** Collects activity and event data from wireless devices by using RADIUS servers. Available in firmware version 11.10T and above.
- **Protection for WEP Keys** Uses and protects WEP keys for greater security. WEP key hashing, Broadcast WEP key rotation, and Message Integrity Check (MIC). This feature is available in firmware version 11.10T and above.
- **LEAP** Used to authenticate non-root bridges Allows the non-root bridges to authenticate to the network so that they can receive and use dynamic WEP keys. This feature is available in firmware version 11.10T and above.
- **Software Image Management (SWIM) Tool** With CiscoWorks 2000, manages AP and bridge firmware from a centralized location. This feature is available in firmware version 11.08 and above.
- **Publicly Secure Packet Forwarding (PSPF) to Block Inter-client Communication** Prevents wireless devices from unintentionally sharing data. Prevents peer-to-peer sharing, and often sees this feature enabled in campus environments, such as college campuses, airport terminals, and coffee houses. This feature is available in firmware version 11.08 and above.

Cisco wireless software also allows the administrator to have the following:

- **Observation of the Activity on the Radio Transmitter by Frequency that is Used by the Bridge.** Using this tool allows the administrator to configure the bridge to use the most efficient frequency available.
- **Antenna Alignment Tool** Aligns the antenna to optimize signal quality between wireless devices.
- **Port Assignment** Reserves ports for specific use to maintain consistency on the WLAN.
- **Bridge Location Detection** Locates specific wireless devices within the wireless network.

- **Bridge Association Limits** Limits the number of devices that the bridge will accept.
- **Integrated Network Management** Utilizes Cisco Discovery Protocol (CDP) to improve the efficiency of network monitoring. This is a potential security risk, so it must be used carefully.
- **Security** Configures the wireless bridge to restrict access to a group of users. Data could be encrypted the WEP, or EAP/LEAP could be used with MAC-based authentication to a RADIUS server to control access to the network.
- **Filtering** Allows or prevents specific protocols. Controls the forwarding of traffic from the bridge with unicast and multicast filtering.
- **Hot standby** Backs up the AP or the bridge.
- **World Mode** Location-independent WLAN. User connects and works similarly regardless of location.
- **Automatic Load Balancing** Directs client devices to an AP that will allow them the best connection using transmission rate, signal strength, and the number of currently connected users as determinants.

The Cisco Aironet 350 APs are powered *inline*. This means that they receive their power through Ethernet cables. This Ethernet cable can be up to 300 feet in length.

- Powered patch panel
- Switch that is capable of inline power (the Cisco Catalyst 3524, 4000, and the 6500)
- Cisco Aironet power injector (designed for the Aironet 350 line only)

The 350 series product line has three base models: APs, wireless bridges, and workgroup bridges. The AP is used with existing wired infrastructure. The wireless bridges are used to connect disparate parts of the network. Whether that is to connect two different office spaces in the same building or to connect two buildings together, the concept is the same. Workgroup bridges connect smaller remote locations to a central location. The workgroup bridge can connect up to eight wired Ethernet devices to the WLAN. The workgroup bridge only has one 10BaseT port so a switch is used to connect the eight devices.

Aironet 350 AP

The 350 AP connects individual clients who have wireless cards. The AP formats this traffic to transmit to the wired LAN or another wireless segment. Using multiple APs together, users are able to seamlessly travel between coverage areas.

The 350 series APs come in a normal plastic case model and a sturdier metal case or "rugged" model. The rugged model is for environmental airspaces or areas that require plenum-rated equipment. It has a wider range of operating temperatures, –4 to 131 degrees Fahrenheit (–20 to 55 degrees Celsius), compared to the plastic case models, 32 to 122 degrees Fahrenheit (0 to 50 degrees Celsius). If an inline power injector is used, it loses its plenum rating and gains a smaller operating range of 32 to 104 degrees Fahrenheit (0 to 40 degrees Celsius).

Cisco also makes APs with two non-detachable 2.2 dBi diversity dipole antennas or two external, removable 2.2 dBi dipole antennas with RP-TNC connectors.

The 350 series APs are equipped with an auto-sensing 10/100BaseT Ethernet uplink port. The AP and clients communicate at either 1, 2, 5.5, or 11 Mbps depending on signal strength and quality. Speed determines modulation, as shown in Table 3.6. Differential Binary Phase Shift Keying (DBPSK) and Differential Quadrature Phase Shift Keying (DQPSK) modulation techniques are similar in structure. Both are quite different from the CCK technique that is used for the 5.5 and 11 Mbps transmission.

Table 3.6 350 Series AP Features

Description	Specifications
Supported data rates	1, 2, 5.5, 11 Mbps
Supported standard	IEEE 802.11b
Indoor range	11 Mbps at 150 ft; 1 Mbps at 350 ft
Outdoor range	11 Mbps at 800 ft; 1 Mbps at 2,000 ft
Encryption support	128-bit
Authentication?	Yes
Wireless medium	DSSS
MAC	CSMA/CA
Modulation	DBPSK @ 1 Mbps; DQPSK @ 2 Mbps; CCK @5.5 and 11 Mbps
Frequency band	2.4 to 2.497 GHz
Operating systems supported	Windows 95/98/2000/NT/CE, LINUX Netware 4.*x*
Remote configuration support	Telnet; HTTP; FTP; TFTP; and SNMP
AP acts as DHCP client?	Yes
Antenna options	Two external removable 2.2 dBi Dipole with RP-TNC connectors; integrated (non-removable) diversity dipoles
Uplink	Auto-sensing 10/100BaseT Ethernet
Operating temperature range	Plastic case AP: 32 to 122° F (0 to 50° C) Rugged AP: –4 to 131° F (–20 to 55° C) Power injector: 32 to 104° F (0 to 40° C)

No matter which modulation technique is used for the wireless transmission with the APs, the methodology used for the transmission is DSSS. DSSS uses the entire frequency band for transmission of the data, thus allowing for higher throughput than if just one of the frequencies was used. The AP acts as a hub and handles collisions using Carrier Sense Multiple Access with Collision Avoidance (CSMA/CA).

Aironet 350 Wireless Bridge

The 350 series bridge is available only in the rugged, metal case, version. These bridges are plenum-rated and can be installed in environmental air space. Their operating temperature range is –4 to 131 degrees Fahrenheit (–20 to 55 degrees Celsius), which allows them to be installed in

National Electrical Manufacturers Association (NEMA) enclosures outdoors. The 350 series bridges are powered by inline power through the Ethernet cable; the power supply used in most cases will not be plenum-rated nor have the same operating temperature range. The power supply can be up to 300 feet away, rendering this a non-issue.

The bridges are typically used in point-to-point configurations, and can support point-to-multipoint topologies as well. No antennas are supplied with the bridge, though it has RP-TNC connectors that can be attached to an existing antenna. The only uplink port on the 350 series bridge is an auto-sensing 10/100BaseT Ethernet port. The bridge uses DSSS and can transmit at 1, 2, 5.5, or 11 Mbps depending on signal strength and quality. CSMA/CA is used for the MAC protocol. The maximum range (depending on antenna and environmental conditions) is up to 25 miles at 2 Mbps, or 18 miles at 11 Mbps. See Table 3.7 for more information about the 350 series bridge.

Table 3.7 350 Series Bridge Features

Description	Specifications
Supported data rates	1, 2, 5.5, 11 Mbps
Supported standard	IEEE 802.11b
Range	25 miles at 2 Mbps; 18 miles at 11 Mbps
Encryption support	128-bit
Bridging protocol	Spanning tree
Wireless medium	DSSS
MAC	CSMA/CA
Modulation	DBPSK @ 1 Mbps; DQPSK @ 2 Mbps; CCK @5.5 and 11 Mbps
Frequency band	2.4 to 2.497 GHz
Remote configuration support	Telnet; HTTP; FTP; TFTP; and SNMP
Antenna options	2 RP-TNC connectors (no antenna ships with bridge)
Uplink	Auto-sensing 10/100BaseT Ethernet
Operating temperature range	Bridge: –4 to 131° F (–20 to 55° C); Power injector: 32 to 104° F (0 to 40° C)

Aironet 350 Workgroup Bridge

The 350 workgroup bridge connects a small number (up to eight) of wired-attached Ethernet stations to an AP. The 350 workgroup bridge has only one uplink port, and a switch will need to be used if an administrator wishes to connect more than one device. Though the wireless connection usually takes place within a building, it can also be done between buildings. Figure 3.26 shows a typical workgroup bridge configuration.

Figure 3.26 350 Workgroup Bridge

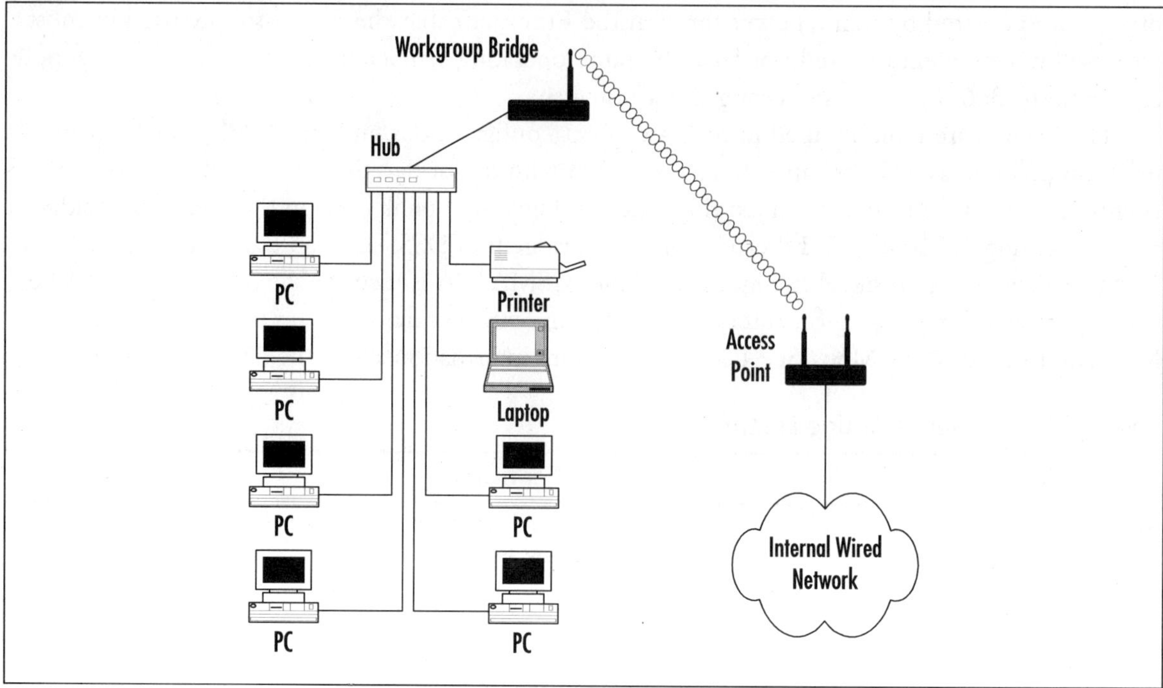

The workgroup bridge is very similar to the other members of the 350 series family. It uses DSSS, CSMA/CA as the MAC protocol, and can communicate at 1, 2, 5.5, or 11 Mbps. The 350 series workgroup bridge does not use inline power. Its only uplink port is a 10BaseT uplink, which deliberately limits the number of devices it can support. Available in a plastic case model only, this bridge is not plenum-rated and is designed for indoor use only. Its operating temperature matches that of the plastic case AP, 32 to 122 degrees Fahrenheit (0 to 50 degrees Celsius). Two antenna options are available: a single non-removable 2.2 dBi dipole antenna, or two RP-TNC connectors with no supplied antennas. For more information on the 350 series workgroup bridge, see Table 3.8.

Table 3.8 350 Series Workgroup Bridge Features

Description	Specifications
Supported data rates	1, 2, 5.5, 11 Mbps
Supported standard	IEEE 802.11b
Range	Indoor: 130 ft @ 11 Mbps; 350 ft @ 1 Mbps Outdoor: 800 ft @ 11 Mbps; 2,000 ft @ 1 Mbps
Encryption support	128-bit
Maximum number of users supported	8
Inline power?	No
Wireless medium	DSSS
MAC	CSMA/CA

Continued

Table 3.8 350 Series Workgroup Bridge Features

Description	Specifications
Modulation	DBPSK @ 1 Mbps; DQPSK @ 2 Mbps; CCK @5.5 and 11 Mbps
Frequency band	2.4 to 2.4897 GHz
Remote configuration support	Telnet; HTTP; FTP; TFTP; and SNMP
Antenna options	One non-removable 2.2 dBi dipole antenna or 2 RP-TNC connectors (no antenna ships with bridge)
Uplink	10BaseT Ethernet
Operating temperature range	Bridge: 32 to 122° F (0 to 50° C)

Features of the Cisco Aironet 340 Series—End-of-Sale

The 340 series of wireless devices closely resemble those of the 350 series. Its feature set is essentially a twin of the 350. One difference between the two product lines is that the 340 series has a base station, something the 350 line does not. Another difference is the 340 series does not have inline power. All 340 series APs, wireless bridges, workgroup bridges, and base stations are detailed in the following sections.

The Cisco Aironet 340 Series AP

The 340 series AP allows individual users to connect to the WLAN, and formats their traffic to transit the wired LAN or other WLANs. Using multiple APs allows users to seamlessly travel between coverage areas.

The 340 series AP uses CSMA/CA as the MAC protocol and DSSS. Transmission speeds range from 1, 2, 5.5, or 11 Mbps using DBPSK, DQPSK, and CCK modulation. There is an auto-sensing 10/100BaseT Ethernet port for connecting to the wired network.

There is no rugged or plenum version of the 340 series AP. The operating temperature range is 32 to 122 degrees Fahrenheit (0 to 50 degrees Celsius). Most models use a 110-volt power source, with a few models using 220 volts. The 340 series supports Telnet, HTTP, File Transfer Protocol (FTP), and SNMP, but not Trivial File Transfer Protocol (TFTP). Three antenna choices are available for the 340 series AP: a single non-removable 2.2 dBi diversity dipole antenna, two redundant non-removable 2.2 dBi diversity dipole antennas, and two RP-TNC connectors with no antenna supplied. Most 340 APs support 128-bit, but a few models support only 40-bit encryption. For more information on the 340 series APs, see Table 3.9.

NOTE

The 340 series is end-of-sale as of July 2003, and will achieve end-of-support on July 2007; Cisco advocates the 350 series as a replacement.

Table 3.9 340 Series AP Features

Description	Specifications
Supported data rates	1, 2, 5.5, 11 Mbps
Supported standard	IEEE 802.11b
Indoor range	11 Mbps at 80 ft; 1 Mbps at 250 ft
Outdoor range	11 Mbps at 300 ft; 1 Mbps at 1,300 ft
Encryption support	40-bit or 128-bit
Authentication?	Yes
Wireless medium	DSSS
MAC	CSMA/CA
Modulation	DBPSK @ 1 Mbps; DQPSK @ 2 Mbps; CCK @5.5 and 11 Mbps
Frequency band	2.4 to 2.4834 GHz
Operating systems supported	Windows 95/98/2000/NT/CE, Linux
Remote configuration support	Telnet; HTTP; FTP; and SNMP
AP acts as DHCP client?	Yes
Antenna options	2 RP-TNC connectors (no antenna ships with AP); Single Integrated (non-removable) diversity dipoles; 2 Integrated (non-removable) diversity dipoles
Uplink	Auto-sensing 10/100BaseT Ethernet
Operating temperature range	32 to 122° F (0 to 50° C)

The Cisco Aironet 340 Series Wireless Bridge

The 340 series bridge is designed to connect multiple buildings in a campus or metropolitan area, or to connect two LANs in the same building. An external antenna can be used to boost the signal.

Data rates, wireless medium, MAC protocol, modulation, and power are shown in Table 3.10. The 340 series bridge has support for 10Base2, 10Base5, and 10BaseT wired connections. The operating temperature range of the 340 series bridge, –4 to 122 degrees Fahrenheit (–20 to 50 degrees Celsius) is rugged enough to handle locations with great temperature variations.

Table 3.10 340 Series Bridge Features

Description	Specifications
Supported data rates	1, 2, 5.5, 11 Mbps
Supported standard	IEEE 802.11b
Range	18 miles at 11 Mbps
Encryption support	128-bit
Bridging protocol	Spanning tree
Wireless medium	DSSS

Continued

Table 3.10 340 Series Bridge Features

Description	Specifications
MAC	CSMA/CA
Modulation	DBPSK @1 Mbps; DQPSK @2 Mbps; CCK @5.5 and 11 Mbps
Frequency band	2.4 to 2.4835 GHz
Remote configuration support	Telnet; HTTP; FTP; and SNMP
Antenna options	2 RP-TNC connectors (no antenna ships with bridge)
Uplink	10Base2, 10Base5, and 10BaseT
Operating temperature range	–4 to 122° F (–20 to 50° C)

The Cisco Aironet 340 Series Workgroup Bridge

The 340 Series workgroup bridge can connect a small (up to eight devices) network to a central wired LAN. It has a single 10BaseT RJ-45 connector, so a switch is used to handle more than one device. The remaining details about the setup of the 340 series workgroup bridge are detailed in Table 3.11.

Table 3.11 340 Series Workgroup Bridge Features

Description	Specifications
Supported data rates	1, 2, 5.5, 11 Mbps
Supported standard	IEEE 802.11b
Range	Indoor: 100 ft@11 Mbps; 300ft @1 Mbps Outdoor: 400 ft@11 Mbps; 1,500 ft@1 Mbps Outdoor with antenna: 10 Miles
Encryption support	40-bit or 128-bit
Wireless medium	DSSS
MAC	CSMA/CA
Modulation	DBPSK @ 1 Mbps; DQPSK@ 2 Mbps; CCK@5.5 and 11 Mbps
Frequency band	2.4 to 2.497 GHz
Remote configuration support	Telnet; HTTP; FTP; and SNMP
Antenna options	One non-removable 2.2 dBi dipole antenna or 2 RP-TNC connectors (no antenna ships with bridge)
Uplink	10BaseT Ethernet
Operating temperature range	32 to 122° F (0 to 50° C)

The Cisco Aironet 340 Series Base Station

The Cisco Aironet 340 Series Base Station provides wireless connectivity to the Internet home and small office users. The base station can be connected to a cable modem or Digital Subscriber Line (DSL) connection via Ethernet RJ-45 port (see Figure 3.27). It can support up to 10 simultaneous devices, and connect multiple users by sharing the Internet connection amongst them. There is also a base station that has a 56K v.90 dialup modem integrated within it.

Figure 3.27 340 Series Base Station

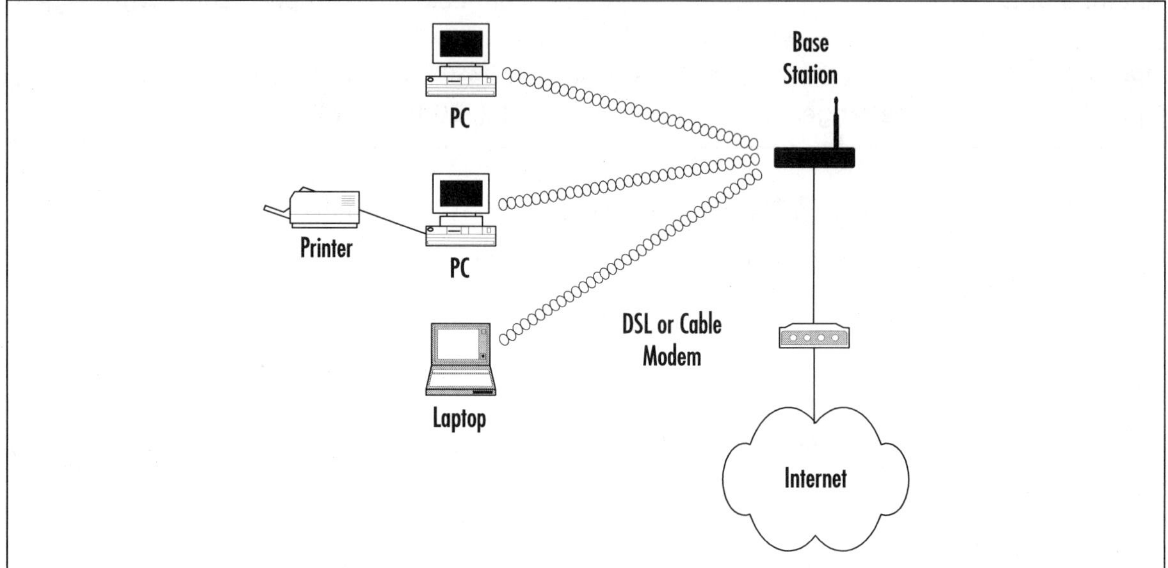

The base station includes Network Access Translation (NAT) and Dynamic Host Configuration Protocol (DHCP) to automatically configure multiple internal devices. The roaming feature that is available with APs is not available in the base station. Complete details are shown in Table 3.12.

Table 3.12 340 Series Base Station Features

Description	Specifications
Supported data rates	1, 2, 5.5, 11 Mbps
Supported standard	IEEE 802.11b
Range	Indoor: 100 ft @ 11 Mbps; 300 ft @ 1 Mbps Outdoor: 400 ft @ 11 Mbps; 1,500 ft @ 1 Mbps
Encryption support	128-bit
Wireless medium	DSSS
MAC	CSMA/CA
Modulation	DBPSK @ 1 Mbps; DQPSK @ 2 Mbps; CCK @5.5 and 11 Mbps
Frequency band	2.4 to 2.497 GHz

Continued

Table 3.12 340 Series Base Station Features

Description	Specifications
Remote configuration support	Telnet; HTTP
Antenna options	One non-removable 2.2 dBi antenna
Uplink	10BaseT Ethernet or RJ-11 line connector for versions with built-in modems
Operating temperature range	32 to 122° F (0 to 50° C)

Cisco's Aironet Wireless NICs

Cisco wireless network cards offer the same functionality as a traditional wired NIC, preparing data for transmissions from a PC to the network.

There are three major types of network cards:

- Industry-Standard Architecture (ISA)
- Peripheral Component Interconnect (PCI)
- Personal Computer Memory Card International Association (PCMCIA) (also called PC Cards) for laptops and notebooks

These cards have dual internal antennas that automatically select the strongest signal so that it can maintain the most efficient connection. The external antenna is designed for transmission from a fixed system, and is also designed to take up a small amount of space. The Cisco Aironet Client Adapter is a fixed solution that works in conjunction with 11 Mbps Cisco Aironet Series APs and bridges. These adapters are designed for DSSS technology and operate at 2.4 GHz. All Cisco wireless client adapters comply with the IEEE 802.11b standard and interoperate with other vendor WLAN products using this standard.

Many Cisco adaptors support a feature called *world mode*. When an adapter is configured for this mode, it automatically inherits channel configuration properties directly from the Cisco Aironet AP to which they associate. This allows a user's client adapter to work around the world while still meeting local or regional standards without the need for any reconfiguration.

Key features of the Cisco wireless network cards include the following:

- IEEE 802.11b standard compliance
- Supports the highest range and throughput performance
- Transmits at up to 100 mW
- Supports 128-bit WEP RC4 encryption for data security
- Offers 802.1x security support via EAP and LEAP
- Offers World mode (roaming) for international mobility
- Dual antenna connectors allow for the support of multi-path compensation
- Support for popular operating systems

- Automatically inherits channel configuration settings directly from Cisco Aironet APs
- Full-featured utilities for easy configuration and management

Installing the Cisco Aironet 3X0 APs

The installation and configuration of the Cisco Aironet 3X0 (340 and 350) APs is relatively simple. There are some complexities that may arise as the installation becomes more complex or involves more APs. In addition, the configuration of the wireless "connections" between the APs and the clients is a little more difficult than following a simple 100-meter rule in wired Ethernet. Interference from cordless phones, walls, partitions, microwaves and other hindrances can quickly complicate the wireless installation.

Many end-users may be concerned regarding the look of the antennas for wireless networks, in addition to the potential health risks that may be associated with them. For this reason, some companies may implement guidelines to increase the distance between the closest user and the antenna, and antenna selection may include directional systems that radiate power in a single direction instead of in all directions.

The installation steps for the Cisco Aironet 3X0 systems are fairly straightforward and include the following:

- Determine the AP placement and appropriate antenna.
- Inline power or plenum installation? 350 series can do both.
- Virtual LAN (VLAN) architecture for wireless networks.
- IP addresses for wireless networks (via DHCP if desired or appropriate).
- SSID values for networks.
- WEP use and key management via RADIUS or static configuration.
- LEAP/EAP for WEP with installation and configuration of RADIUS server.
- AP channels; in the U.S., there are only three non-overlapping channels.
- Wireless management including SNMP and SYSLOG.
- Secure wireless networks using VPNs and IPsec.
- Access control using access control lists (ACLs) and VACLS, as well as using SSL.
- Use PSPF to limit wireless device connectivity.

If the hardware is not yet selected, many administrators will likely choose the Cisco 350 APs and adapters. The Cisco 350 series APs has a few advantages over the 340 series. The fact that the Cisco 350 series can operate at 100 mW translates to greater coverage compared to the Cisco 340's 30 mW configuration. The Cisco 350 can accept inline power or powered Ethernet, which negates the need for a separate power cord. The 350 is also available in a rugged chassis making it suitable for airspace and plenum installation. In all other regards, the configuration of the 340 and 350 series' is virtually identical.

Power Requirements

There are three methods for powering the Cisco 350 Series APs; the 340 platform cannot accept inline power. The simplest installations take advantage of the inline power options, which are available on specific modules of the Catalyst series switches, including the Catalyst 6000 (WS-X6248 with the WS-F6K-VPWR daughter card), the 4006 (with the WS-X4148-RJ45V), and the 3524-PWR-XL. These products can supply power to the Cisco 350 series AP via the standard Ethernet pins 1, 2, 3, and 6. The physical configuration of this installation is shown in Figure 3.28. Cisco has and will continue to increase the number of switches and modules that supply inline power.

Figure 3.28 Inline Power

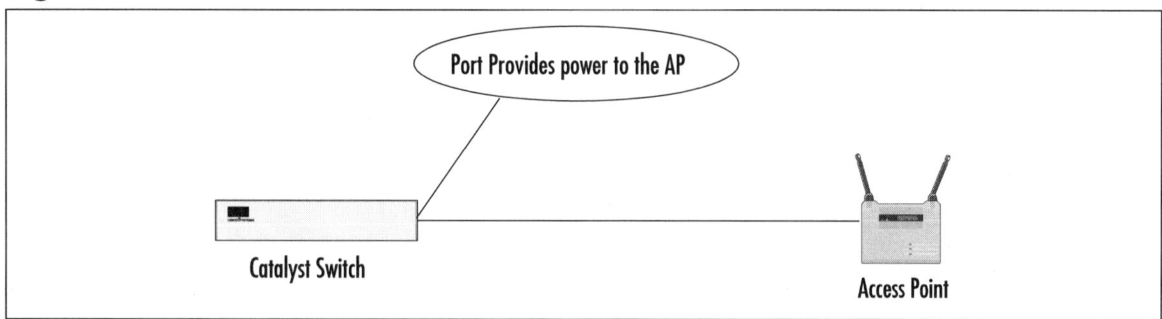

For installations where only Ethernet cable is available to the AP, no electrical wiring is present, and the existing hub or switch infrastructure does not support inline power, users may select the WS-PWR-PANEL patch panel. This panel connects in between the switch or hub and the AP, and is better suited to installations that require a large number of powered Ethernet lines, such as IP telephony.

When a single link solution is required, administrators may opt for the Cisco Aironet Power Injector. This is often used for in-the-ceiling installations. The physical characteristics of the powered patch panel installation are shown in Figure 3.29. Please note that all Ethernet-powered solutions are limited to 300 feet, which should not present a problem for most installations within the 100-meter rule for Ethernet. Administrators should check with their local building codes to ensure their planned configuration will be in compliance.

Figure 3.29 Using the Powered Patch Panel

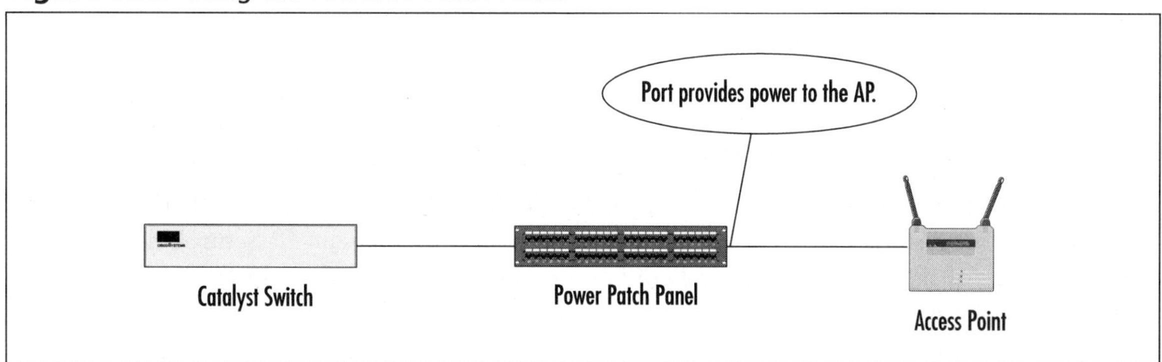

The AP may also be connected to a standard wall outlet for power. These installations use an AC adapter and isolate the power channel from the data path. Figure 3.30 illustrates the connections for this option; note that the Cisco 340 series is powered by this method only.

Figure 3.30 Using Standard Power

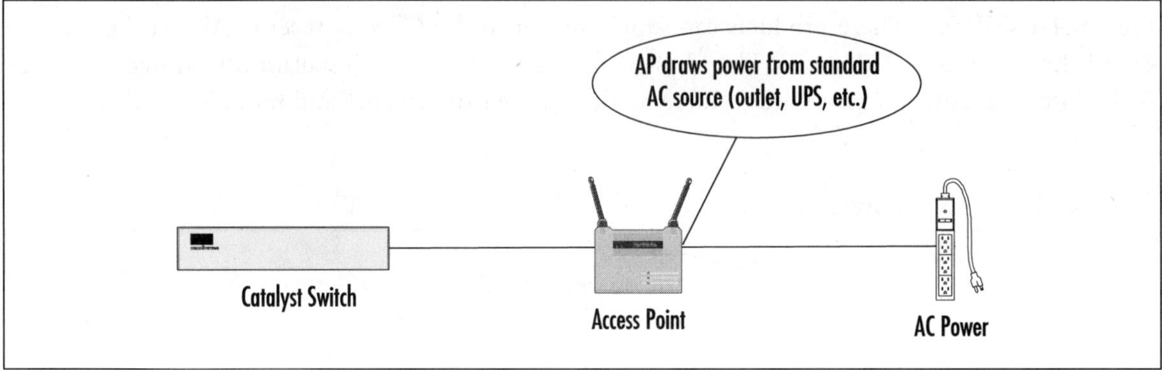

Network Connectivity

The Cisco Aironet 3X0 APs support both 10 Mbps and 100 Mbps Ethernet connections. Network addressing and VLAN designs choices are:

- **Place the AP on the Current Wired Subnet** Simple and quick, this solution nonetheless causes issues. Wireless connectivity problems are not isolated from wired problems. Roaming may require IP address changes.
- **Create a Second Collision Domain with a Second Aubnet per AP** Good for single AP installations, but does not scale well. Roaming will necessitate IP address changes.
- **Place an Overlay Network or VLAN into the Campus or Building that Allows all APs to Reside in One Subnet** Roaming does not require IP address changes. Scalability problems will increase as network grows.

Administrators may wish to address the historical limitations with spanning tree by using 802.1w, MST, Port Fast, Uplink Fast, or other enhancements, ensuring that they address future growth. There is little to differentiate wireless networks from their wired brethren and the same rules of broadcast and collision domains, in addition to support models and administrative controls, remain valid.

Initial Configuration of the Cisco 3X0 Series AP

There are several options for configuring the AP, including initially configuring via the console port, then finishing it via a Web or Telnet session. Cisco also provides an IP Setup Utility (IPSU), which operates at the data link layer and configures a preliminary SSID and IP address. This utility can be skipped altogether and DHCP can assign an IP address to the AP. Remember that

SNMP and LEAP require an IP address to function. There is no IOS command structure to the AP. Configurations are prepared via a menu and navigation-based interface.

IP Setup Utility

The IPSU allows the network administrator to assign an IP address to the AP dynamically via DHCP or statically by entering it. IPSU is usable if the configuring workstation and AP are on the same network. If the obtained address is 10.0.0.1, it signifies that the AP has reverted to a default setting and the DHCP request has failed.

The IPSU program is shown in Figure 3.31. To obtain an IP address with DHCP, select the **Get IP addr** option, then enter the MAC address of the AP, and complete with the **Get IP Address** button. To manually assign an IP address or SSID, choose the **Set Parameters** button and then enter the values.

Figure 3.31 The IPSU

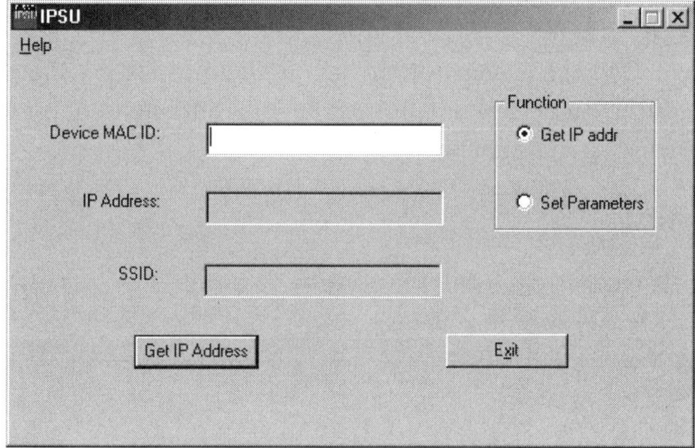

IPSU works only with a default AP configuration— any changes made to the AP will preclude use of IPSU. To set the SSID, the administrator must assign an IP address, even if that address is the same as the one already configured on the AP. Setting the IP address does not require an SSID.

Terminal Emulator Setup

The AP can be configured via its console port, similar to the process for configuring Cisco routers and switches. The console port is a standard DB-9 with a configuration of VT-100, 9600, N, 8, 1, using a straight-through cable is required. The following series of text menus will be presented.

```
ap340-Padjen              Express Setup            Uptime: 6 days, 02:30:03
  System [Name                  ][ap340-Padjen                        ]
 [Terminal Type                 ][teletype]
  MAC Address                   : 00:40:96:32:dd:d1
  Config. Server [Protocol    ][None ]
```

```
  IP [Address                 ][192.168.1.5      ]
  IP [Subnet Mask             ][255.255.255.0   ]
  Default [Gateway            ][192.168.1.1      ]
 [Radio Service Set ID (SSID)][padjen                          ]
 [Role in Radio Network      ][Root Access Point          ]
 [Optimize Radio Network For ][Throughput]  [Hw Radio]
  Ensure Compatibility With:  [2Mb/sec Clients][_]   [non-Aironet802.11][_]
 [SNMP Admin. Community      ][rpadjen                          ]
 [Apply] [OK]   [Cancel] [Restore Defaults]
------------------------------------------------------------
[Home] - [Network] - [Associations] - [Setup] - [Logs] - [Help]
```

The AP also provides a limited help screen function, as shown in the following output.

```
ap340-Padjen   Brief Help For the Console Browser   Uptime: 6 days, 02:29:52
Follow a link:
```

When typing the first few characters for an anchor, the browser goes to the page as soon as it finds a unique match. If the numerical notation for links is on, one can also go to that page by typing in the number for that link directly.

```
Quick Keys:
    =               Go to the home page
    ^R              Force the screen to refresh
    ENTER           Scroll down one page
    Hitting 3 ENTER's in a row will force the screen to refresh.
Use command Line:
    Enter the command line mode by typing in ':' followed by a command
and the ENTER key. Commands are case insensitive.
Supported Commands:
    :AUTO           Turn on/off switch for the Auto-Apply feature
    :BACK           Return to the previous page
    :BOTTOM         Scroll to the bottom of the current page
    :CLEAR          Clear history list
    :CLOSE          Close the telnet session if the connection is open
    :CMD            Enter SNMP Command Line mode
    :DOWN           Scroll down one page
    :FORWARD        Return to next page
    :GOTO           Go to the page specified by the URL following the goto
    :HOME           Go to the home page
    :NUMBERS_ON     Turn on the numerical notation for links
    :NUMBERS_OFF    Turn off the numerical notation for links
    :PING ipAddr    Send 5 IP Echo requests to "ipAddr".
    :REFRESH        Force the screen to refresh
```

```
:RESETALL      Reset ENTIRE configuration to Factory Defaults,
                including security controls.  Only available from
                serial console for the first 2 minutes after a
                reboot.
:TOP           Scroll to the top of the current page
:UP            Scroll up one page
:REFRESH       Refresh the screen
:=             Go to the home page
```

Note that the automatic completion feature may be toggled on and off with the **auto** command. The **resetall** command is quite powerful and is used to restore the entire AP to its default configuration, but is available only within the first two minutes of powering the device. There is also a recessed reset button on the back of the AP.

Web-Based Configuration of the Cisco 340 BSE/BSM Series AP

The Cisco 340 BSM (Base Station AIR-BSM128) is a variant of the standard Cisco 340 AP, and is ideal for up to ten users. It features an integrated modem and fixed antenna. The non-modem version, AIR-BSE128, is suited to cable modem and DSL installations only. The base station supports WEP, incorporates a DHCP server, and terminates cable modems, DSL, or analog modem connections. PPP over Ethernet (PPPoE) is supported and may be required for certain DSL installations.

The configuration of the BSE and BSM models is somewhat different from the other Aironet models as it may be accomplished via the wireless interface. While this was designed to prevent unauthorized access from the Internet connection, it can lead to a more compromised system. The installation of any connection to the Internet should include firewall protection. Many users do not change the default SSID, which is "tsunami."

It cannot be stressed enough that the SSID is not a valid security measure (it can be quickly discovered), and should be changed. With the BSE and BSM APs, the SSID is the only default protection to restrict access. This is unlike the other Cisco APs, which may also be configured with user accounts and passwords.

Many administrators will choose to use the Base Station Client Utility to configure the BSE/BSM. To modify the settings with the client software, select the **Base Station | Set Up Base Station** option, as shown in Figure 3.48. The bottom portion of the screen shows that the AP is associated with the workstation—both the IP address (192.168.200.1) and the MAC address are displayed. This requires that the wireless client be configured with the default SSID of "tsunami." (In Windows, this can be configured without the client utility by using the Control Panel, Network option.)

Figure 3.48 Configuring the Base Station

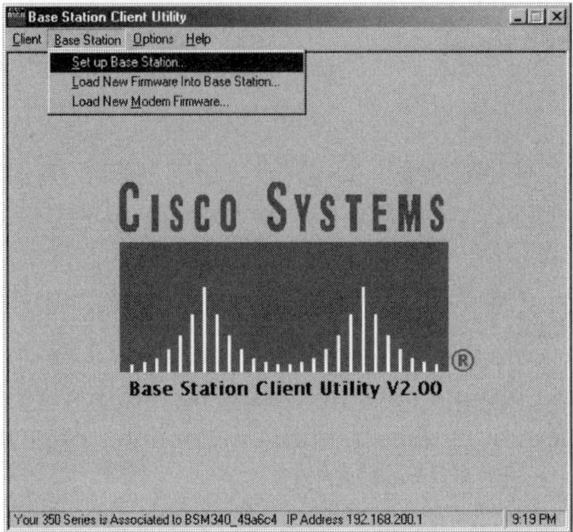

This takes you to the Settings screen, as shown in Figure 3.49. Many of the settings are already provided from the workstation configuration, including Computer Name and Network Name. Selecting **Edit Base Station Settings** will allow modification of the configuration, including selection of the dial-out modem. Note that the BSE/BSM always uses 192.168.200.0/24 and network address translation for the wireless interface. The BSE/BSM is addressed as 192.168.200.1.

Figure 3.49 The Settings Screen

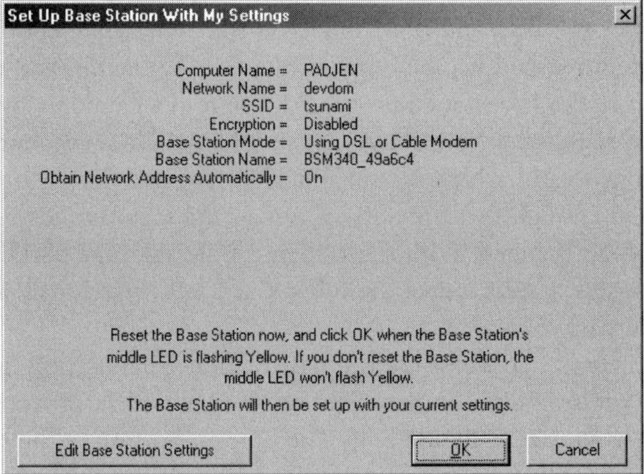

The BSE/BSM AP can be configured via a Web interface and a series of menus via Telnet. No passwords exist to protect the configuration parameters, which makes the BSE/BSM ill-suited for corporate installations. The product is designed for home and small offices where security may not be as important. The Web and Telnet screens are shown in Figures 3.50 and 3.51, respectively.

Figure 3.50 The Web Interface of the BSE/BSM

Item	Value
SSID - Service set identification	a string of at least 1 characters tsunami
WEP encryption key in ASCII	off or a key
WEP encryption key in hex	off or a key
Use new SSID and key	
Operating mode	cable_DSL_modem, accesspoint, PPP over ethernet or dialup
Base station name	a string
Obtain network address automatically	off or on
Log and alarm history	
Load new firmware via browser	Browse... Send

Connection status : Failed, Idle - Ethernet cable problem

Figure 3.51 Menus of the BSE/BSM

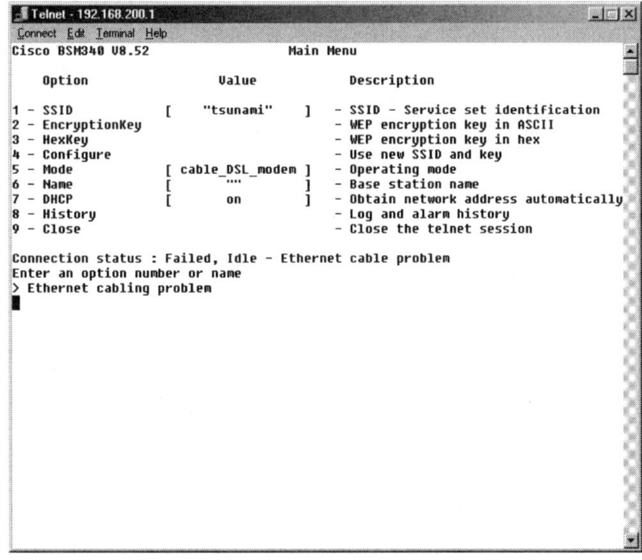

Troubleshooting the Cisco 340 BSE/BSM Series AP

Troubleshooting the BSE and BSM models of the Cisco Aironet APs is comparable to troubleshooting other AP models. Certain features are simpler to eliminate—for example, the BSE/BSM does not support roaming or antenna selection. Base station installations tend to be much smaller in diameter, making the configuration much easier to review and isolate as it relates to problems.

Cisco Aironet Wireless Bridges

Cisco Aironet wireless bridges are similar to traditional wired network bridges in that they are standalone devices providing an interface between two types of network segments: wired and wireless. The wireless bridge is akin to a translating bridge, providing an interface that allows wired networks to communicate to wireless networks, and vice versa.

The wireless bridge is protocol-independent and does not verify, analyze, or modify packets to be forwarded. When the wireless bridge receives multicast packets, it processes the packet based on the packet header. When the wireless bridge receives packets addressed to it directly, the packet is examined and the protocol header is assessed. If the protocol is recognized, the packet is processed. The wireless bridge supports TCP/IP and SNMP conforming to the MIB-I and MIB-II standards.

The Cisco Aironet 340 and 350 wireless bridges use the DSSS radio transmission and modulation technique within the 2.4 GHz ISM band. It supports transmission rates of up to 11 Mbps over a half-duplex radio channel, meaning it can send or receive transmissions but not do both at the same time. The Cisco 1400 wireless bridge is an 802.11a bridge that can bridge at 54 Mbps under optimal conditions over distances of up to 23 miles (with the right antenna and positioning). It is worth mentioning that as a general rule, the greater the distance between bridges, the lower the transmission rate.

Cisco Aironet 3X0 and 1400 wireless bridges can communicate with Cisco Aironet APs and other Cisco Aironet wireless devices, but not with wireless networking devices manufactured by other vendors.

Cisco Aironet 3X0 and 1400 wireless bridges can be used in one of three modes:

- As a wireless bridge between two wired network segments (point-to-point)
- As a wireless bridge between three or more wired network segments (point-to-multipoint)
- As a wireless bridge used as a repeater (repeater)

Cisco Aironet Wireless Bridge—Point-to-Point

Cisco Aironet wireless bridges can interconnect two wired network segments to form a larger contiguous network segment (point-to-point). In this mode, two wireless bridges connected to wired networks communicate with each other to bridge the two wired networks together wirelessly. Both units are configured with the same SSID. One is configured as the Root Node while the other is configured as the Remote Node.

Network resources located on one wired network segment can access network resources located on the other wired network segment via the wireless network bridge connection (see Figure 3.52).

Figure 3.52 Point-to-Point Wireless Bridging

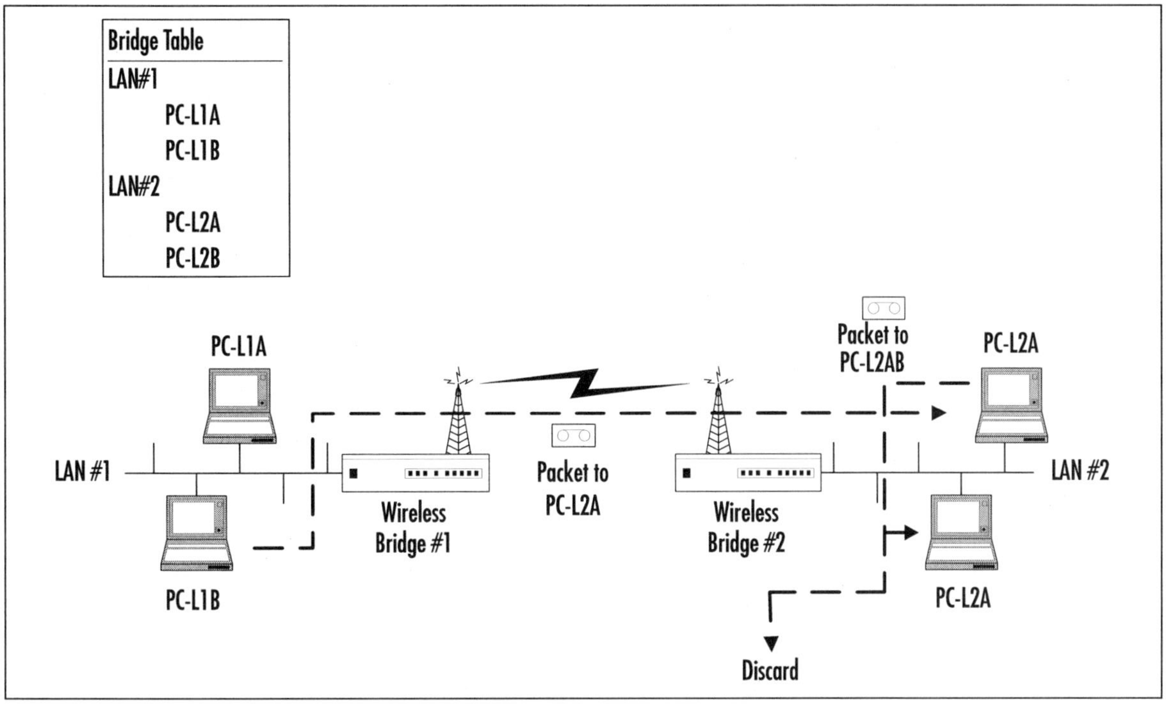

This configuration is useful for interlinking two wired LAN segments located on different floors of a building or between different nearby buildings where traditional cabling solutions may not be feasible or are cost prohibitive. In Figure 3.52, Bridge #1 is used to forward a packet from PC-L1B to PC-L2A and Bridge #2 is used to filter a packet that is sent from PC-L2A to PC-L2B.

Cisco Aironet Wireless Bridge—Point-to-Multipoint

The wireless bridge can connect three or more network segments (point-to-multipoint). In this mode, all of the wireless bridges share the same SSID. One is configured as the Root Node while all other wireless bridges are configured as Remote Nodes (see Figure 3.53).

Figure 3.53 Point-to-Multipoint Wireless Bridging

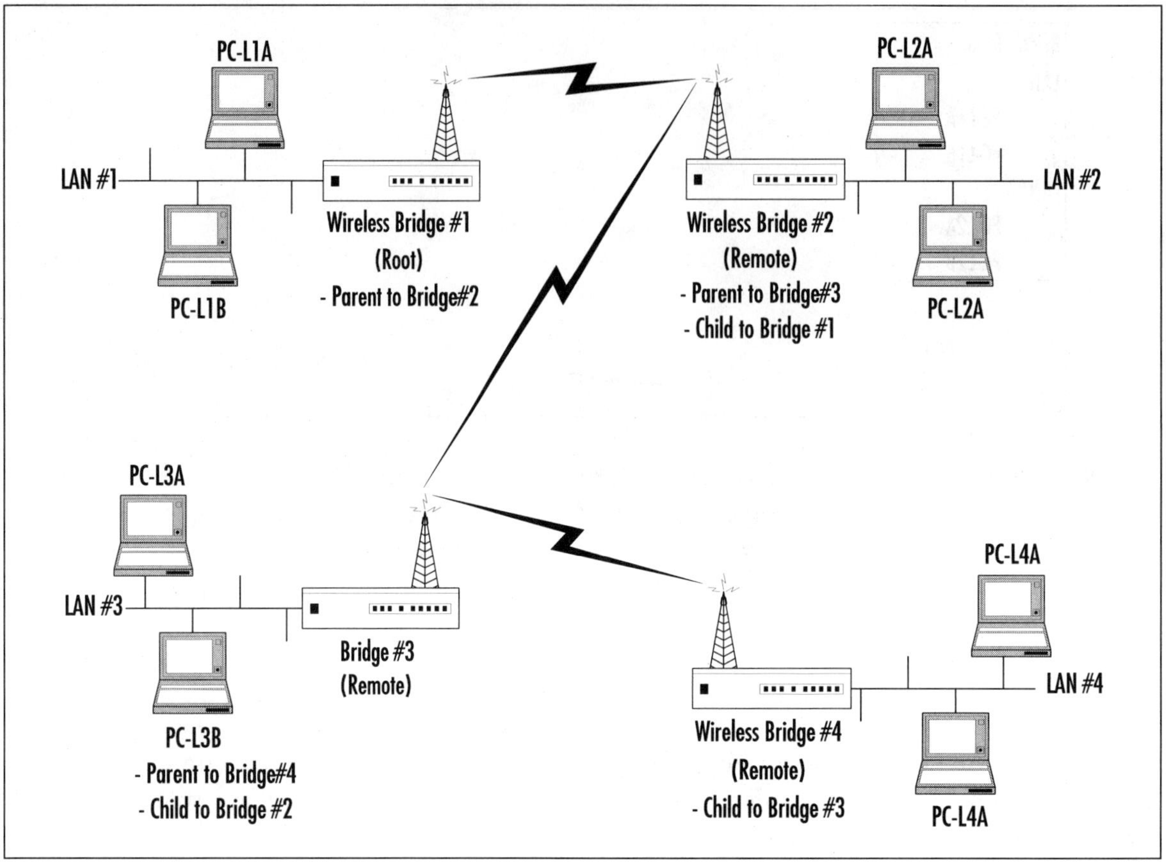

The wireless signals transmitted by one of the Remote Nodes is acknowledged and acted upon only by the Root Node. Signals received by Remote Nodes from the Root Node are acknowledged and acted upon. All other communications are discarded (remote node to remote node).

Cisco Wireless Bridge—Repeater

Remote Nodes are automatically *repeaters*. Repeaters will rebroadcast any and all communications from the Root Node or from Remote Nodes (parent to it) to bridges that are its children. This is effective in increasing the range of the radio signals broadcast by the Root Node and for extending the radio hop count of transmissions.

Wireless bridge repeaters can act as standard Remote Nodes with a connected local wired LAN, or as standalone repeaters with no local wired LAN connections.

Installation of the Cisco Aironet Bridge Unit

The Cisco Aironet 3X0 wireless bridges consist of an antenna connector, a 10Base2 network connector, a 10Base5 network connector, a 10BaseT network connector, a DB-9 female console port connector, and status LEDs. The Cisco Aironet 1400 wireless bridges come with a power injector, mounting hardware, RG-6 coaxial cables, and a rugged power supply and cord. An optional dish antenna for increased distances can be used to increase the 1400's effective distance. Before powering up the wireless bridge, the antenna, network and console/serial port connections should be made.

Installing the Antenna

The Cisco Aironet wireless bridge provides a connector port for an external antenna. A low-loss antenna cable can be used to extend the distance between the wireless bridge and the antenna. Administrators should perform a wireless site survey to assess environmental impacts on transmission and reception. This includes power lines, obstructions, and types of materials through which the radio signals may have to propagate. Radio signals can also be hampered by interference from other devices operating within the 2.4 GHz frequency range, such as microwave ovens and electrical motors. The wireless site survey provides guidance for the type and placement of antennas and helps establish baseline metrics for the expected sensitivity, range, and data communication rates.

A clear line-of-sight should be maintained between communicating antennas (see Figure 3.54). Obstructions can attenuate signals thus limiting the range of the wireless bridge. Directional antennas can also be used to focus the radio signal strength in one direction. This is especially relevant to the Cisco Aironet 3*x*0 wireless bridge transmitting in the 2.4 GHz frequency. Although signals emitted at 2.4 GHz will pass through most solid objects, they do not pass through objects with a high water content very well as they are absorbed by water molecules, which causes these molecules to become excited, otherwise known as heated. This is the same principle that makes microwave ovens work so well with "wet" food and not very well with "dry" food.

Figure 3.54 Line of Sight

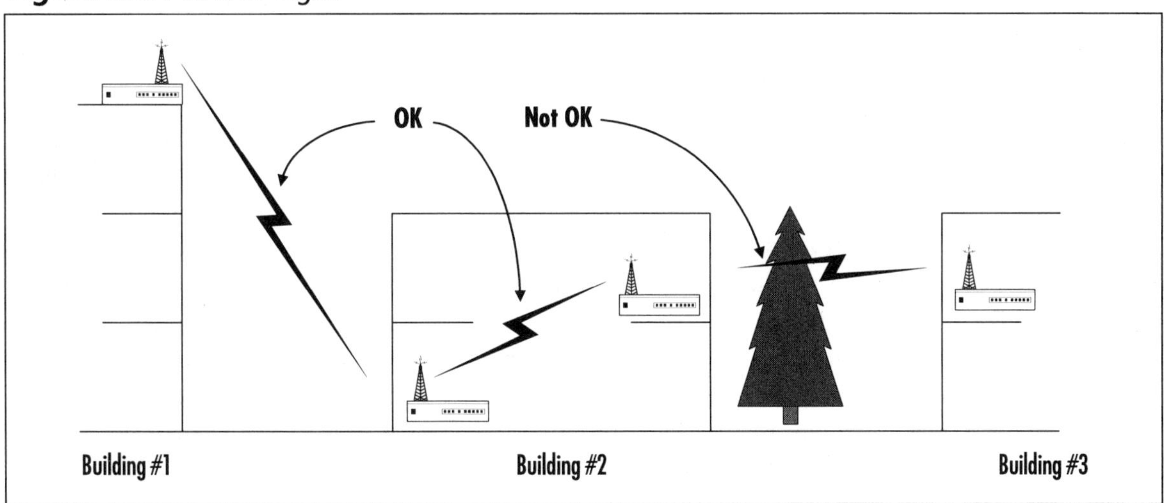

In addition to line-of-sight considerations, network administrators need to consider the Fresnel zone when planning long-distance radio transmissions or transmissions that will be outside of a building. The Fresnel zone refers to an elliptical area that wraps the direct line-of-sight path above, below, and to either side.

Administrators should install a lightning arrestor to the antenna connector on the wireless bridge when using antennas located outside a building. The lightening arrestor will provide protection from voltage surges resulting from a lightning discharge striking the antenna.

Configuring the Network Port

A Cisco Aironet wireless bridge can be connected to 10Base2, 10Base5, or 10BaseT Ethernet LAN segments. The wireless bridge network connection can be used only by one type of network segment at any given time. Segments that are connected to the wireless bridge must conform to the IEEE 802.3 Ethernet specification. If connecting the wireless bridge to a network other than an Ethernet segment, the network administrator can use a third-party network bridge to interface the non-Ethernet network with one of the Ethernet ports on the wireless bridge.

The wireless bridge's 10BaseT network port can be connected to a switch, allowing it to support up to eight devices. A cross over cable or a straight through cable with an uplink port on the switch should be used for this connection. LED indicators are provided on the back of the wireless bridge next to the network interfaces indicating which is the active network interface along with the data transmission activity in terms of when packets are being received or transmitted.

Applying Power

After installing and configuring the antenna, network, and console port connections, the administrator can supply power to the wireless bridge with an external AC/DC power supply. Cisco 350 and 1400 wireless bridges can also get power from Catalyst inline power patch panels, or from Cisco power injectors.

Working with Root and Non-Root Modes on a Wireless Bridge

Administrators should first define the overall wireless topology and determine how wired networks will connect to wireless networks via wireless bridges. At least one wireless bridge should be designated as a Root Node. This Root bridge will be considered the starting point, top, or parent of the network tree. The Root bridge acts as the focal point for all wireless traffic generated by each wireless bridge associated with the SSID of the Root bridge. From a network perspective, the Root Node and all its Remote Nodes appear as a single multiport bridge.

The Root bridge is usually connected to wired network backbone, or it can connect to the wired network that will generate or receive the most wireless traffic. Only one Root bridge can exist. All other wireless network bridges and end nodes are considered subordinates or children of the Root (see Figure 3.55).

Figure 3.55 Wireless Network Tree Diagram

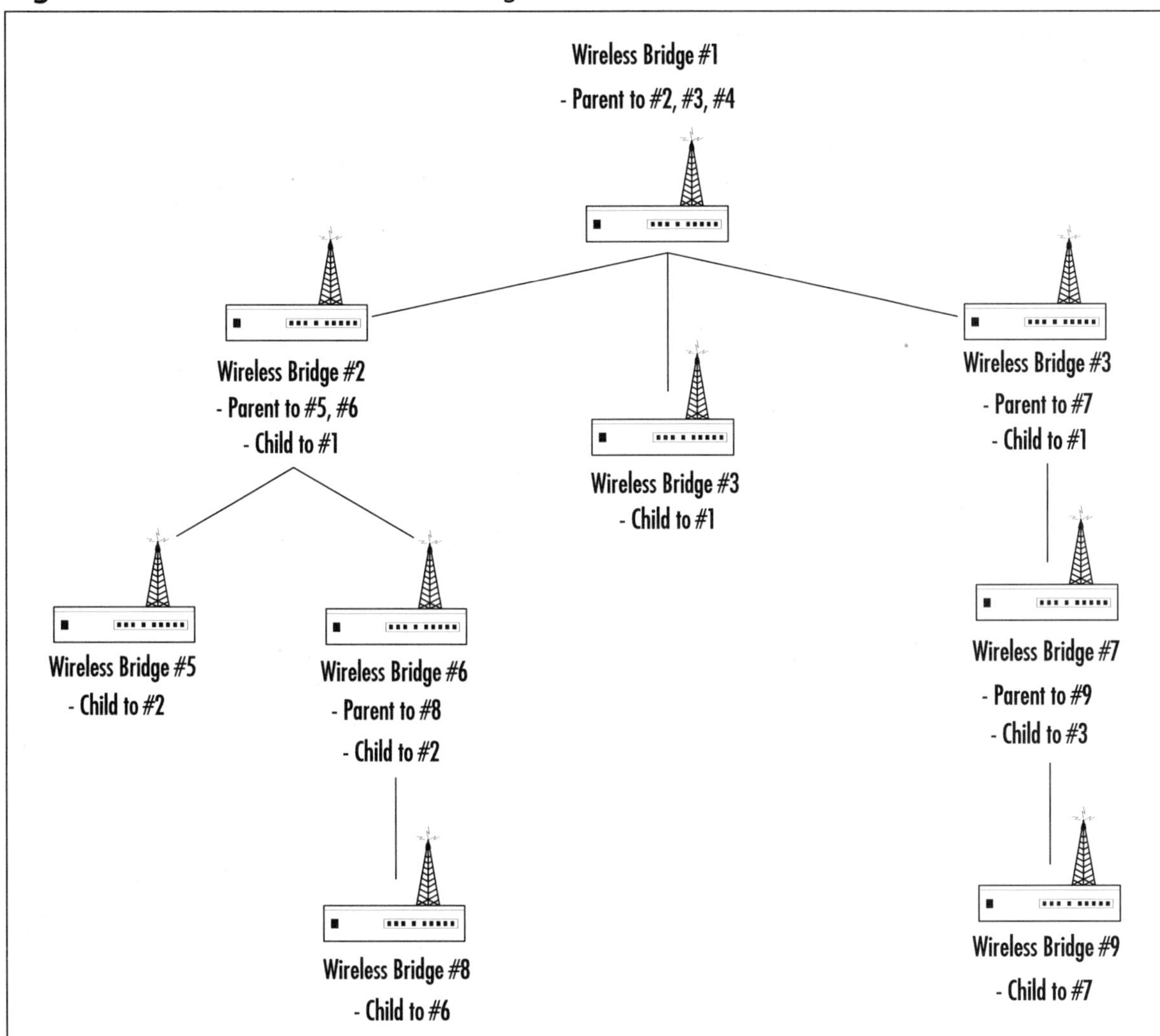

The default configuration for wireless bridges is to have Root mode set to active or "on." On networks containing multiple wireless bridges, only one bridge can be the root; all other bridges must be configured as Remote Nodes (also called repeaters). Remote Nodes communicate with the Root Bridge or other Remote Nodes as if they are its children. Root bridges can only communicate with Remote bridges and not with other Root bridges. To prevent loops, wireless bridges use the Spanning Tree protocol.

Initial Configuration of Wireless Bridge Using the CLI

While this section focuses on the configuration of 3X0 wireless bridges; the concepts and processes are similar on other wireless bridges. Commands are organized to configure the wireless bridge, display settings information, display operational statistics, or test the system. The administrator can navigate the menu by entering the menu option number for the command or by typing the command at the prompt at the bottom of the screen. To return to the previous menu, pressing **Esc** and "=" returns to the main menu. The menus have a consistent look and feel. At a minimum, the following are available:

- A Title Line indicates which menu is being accessed.
- An Option Number lists each command available in that particular menu.
- A Value indicates either the setting for that option's actual value or that the command will drill down to another submenu.
- A Description entry provides basic information on the command.
- A command prompt at the bottom of the screen, where operational and menu navigational commands are entered.

All commands (command-line or menu) are acted upon and saved in flash memory immediately after use. Although administrators do not need to perform further actions or enter other commands in order to save a configuration, they can remotely store wireless bridge configurations for backup purposes and build version control. Whenever the unit is powered up, the main menu is displayed, and is also presented when opening a new Telnet or Web session.

For troubleshooting and ease of configuration, wireless bridges should be configured while in proximity to other wireless devices sharing the same SSID. This facilitates the configuration of network parameters while ensuring that strong radio signals are present. After configuration, the wireless bridge should be relocated to its intended installation point.

When a Telnet session is active, access to the main menu via the console port will be temporarily disabled. If a console connection is made while a Telnet session is active, a message is displayed on the console indicating that a Telnet operation is in progress and from which IP address. A Telnet session can be disconnected from the console by pressing the **Break** key. When performing a Telnet session break, the configuration menu is returned to the console control. All active Telnet sessions should be verified before forcing a disconnection. Breaking a session can cause configuration commands to be cut off midstream or in a state of partial configurations, rendering the wireless bridge inoperable or improperly configured.

This section focuses on the two most critical components to be configured during initial power up. Using the console port of the wireless bridge the administrator should:

- Assign the Radio parameters
  - Set the root parameters
  - Set the SSID
  - Set the data rate
  - Set the distance
- Assign an IP address

A schematic of the menu system on the 3X0 series is provided in Figure 3.56. While this exact menu may not be found on all Aironet devices due to differences in hardware and software, it is a suitable representative of menus currently used.

Figure 3.56 Aironet Menus

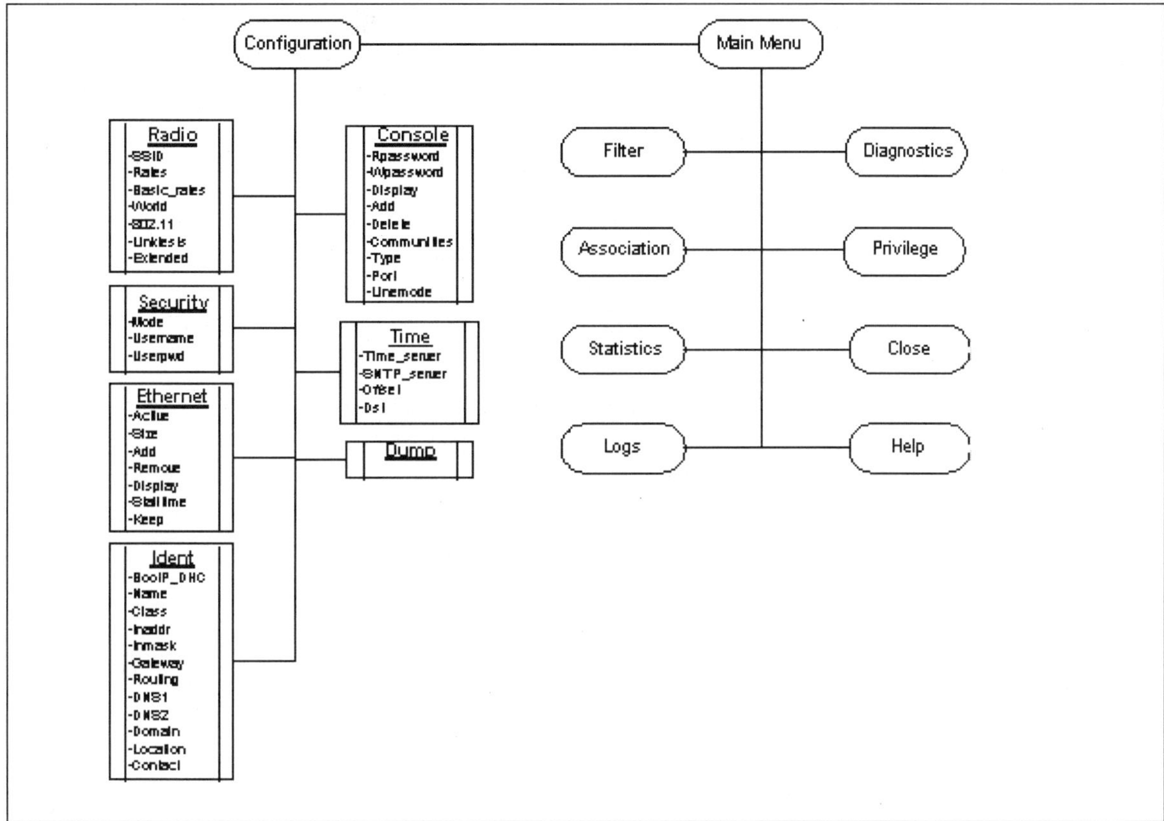

Assigning the Radio Parameters

The network administrator must configure the Radio parameters of the wireless bridge before it can communicate with the other wireless devices. Resetting any of the radio parameters while the wireless bridge is in operation will disconnect all wireless sessions and reinitialize the wireless bridge.

Setting the Root Parameters

If two or more wireless bridges are used to create a wireless network, one must be Root and all others must Remote Nodes. Cisco Aironet 3X0 wireless bridges are configured as Root when shipped from the factory.

After selecting **Configuration** from the main menu, then **Radio**, and then **Root** the administrator is prompted to verify this change. When using the terminal emulator connected to the console port, pressing **Y** toggles the setting from on to off and off to on.

Setting the SSID

The SSID is a unique, case-sensitive, up to 32-characters-long identifier appended to network packets. It defines the name of the wireless network and is used to authenticate and establish communications with other wireless devices sharing the same SSID. The wireless bridge discards all transmissions received from wireless devices not sharing the same SSID.

After selecting **Configuration** from the main menu, then **Radio**, and then **SSID**, the administrator enters the SSID to be associated with this wireless bridge. It must be the same for all wireless devices that are to be included within this wireless network.

Setting the Data Rate

The Data Rate configuration defines the minimum transmission rate with other wireless devices. Wireless devices can transmit data to the wireless bridge at the minimum rate or at any other higher available rates. When a wireless bridge communicates with a Root bridge, the rate used to communicate is the highest rate supported by both units and supported by the media/environment at that time.

After selecting **Configuration** from the main menu, then **Radio**, and then **Rates**, the administrator enters the value for the rate,. being sure to select more than one rate to adapt to media/environment changes due to weather, construction, or other potential interference. If only one rate is selected and it cannot be maintained, wireless communications will be terminated.

Setting the Distance

The travel distance of wireless signals between wireless bridges can be short (3 to 4 meters) or long (40 kilometers). Propagation delay can cause a transmitting bridge to assume that communication never reached its intended recipient. To counter this scenario, the Root Node wireless bridge is configured to adjust system timers responsible for network and transmission control on all of the Remote Nodes under its control.

To configure the distance parameter on the wireless bridge, the administrator should select **Configuration** from the main menu, then **Radio**, and then **Distance**. They should enter the longest expected radio link in terms of kilometers—not miles.

Assigning IP Information

IP addresses are used to remotely communicate with the wireless bridge using Telnet, HTTP, and SNMP. Other IP information can be configured to specifically tailor wireless bridge operations.

To configure the IP address and other related settings; the administrator should select **Configuration** from the main menu, then **Ident**. The **Inaddr** command is used to assign an IP address And the **Inimask** command is used to configure the subnet mask. The **Gateway** command is used to configure the gateway address.

Establishing Communications Using Remote Telnet Access

The menu style and options presented during a Telnet session are similar to that of console sessions. Command menu navigation is similar to console-based command menu navigation.

To access the configuration menu from the command prompt of a PC or workstation, enter the following:

```
telnet <IP address of the bridge>
```

Establishing Communications Using Remote Web Browser Access

Menus are converted to Web pages for access via a Web browser. Each of the menu pages contains links to command options. The mouse is used to point and click various options. **Allow Config Changes** must be clicked first before changes are allowed. Configuration changes take effect immediately. As a precaution, **Disallow Config Changes** should be selected once configuration changes have been completed to prevent accidental reconfigurations.

Configuration commands with fixed options display the options as a list. The active choice is listed in bold. To select another option, click on the option. Configuration commands requiring text input display text boxes. You can type information into the text box and then press **Enter**. A HOME link is provided at the top left of each page as a convenience, to return to the main menu from any submenu.

Operational Configuration of the Cisco Aironet Wireless Bridge

After the initial configuration is defined, the wireless bridge will have the capability to establish elementary wireless communications with other Cisco bridges and APs. In order to support additional networking and security requirements, advanced bridge configuration options may need to be defined. Using only the network capabilities that were configured on the bridge during the initial setup, administrators can now access the bridge via one of three types of connections: via the console, Telnet, or the Web.

The Configuration menu provides the submenus indicated in the following output.

```
Configuration Menu
Option              Value         Description
1 - Radio          [ menu ]       Radio network parameters
2 - Ethernet       [ menu ]       Ethernet configuration
3 - Ident          [ menu ]       Identification information
4 - Console        [ menu ]       Control console access
5 - Stp            [ menu ]       Spanning Tree Protocol
6 - Mobile IP      [ menu ]       Mobile IP protocol configuration
7 - Time           [ menu ]       Network Time Setup
8 - Dump                          Dump configuration to console
Enter an option number or name, "=" main menu, <ESC> previous menu
```

Using the Cisco Aironet Wireless Bridge Radio Main Menu

The Radio menu configures the options supporting the radio (signals), as shown in the following output.

```
Configuration Radio Menu
Option                Value            Description
1 - Ssid              [ "test" ]       Service set identification
2 - Root              [ on ]           Enable root mode
3 - Rates             [ 1_11 ]         Allowed bit rates in megabits/second
4 - Basic_rates       [ 1 ]            Basic bit rates in megabits/second
5 - Frequency         [ "auto" ]       Center frequency in MHz
6 - Distance          [ 0 ]            Maximum separation in kilometers
7 - I80211            [ menu ]         802.11 parameters
8 - Linktests         [ menu ]         Test the radio link
9 - Extended          [ menu ]         Extended parameters
Enter an option number or name, "=" main menu, <ESC> previous menu
```

Configuring the Basic Rates Option

From the **Configure Menu | Radio | Radio Menu**, choose **Basic_rates** (Option four). **Basic_rates** is configured only on the Root Node to establish supported rates within the wireless network. Data traffic is transmitted at the highest sustainable rate available; network control packets, broadcast packets, and multicast packets are transmitted at the lowest transmission rate.

Configuring the Frequency Option

From the **Configure Menu | Radio | Radio Menu**, choose **Frequency**. **Frequency** is configured only on the Root Node and is subject to radio regulations. By default, it is configured for "auto," which supports all frequencies available within the local market radio jurisdiction. When initialized, the Root Node determines and selects an appropriate and available frequency. This option usually remains at its default value, but the administrator may change it to address environmental interference within a specific frequency.

Configuring the IEEE 802.11 Options

From the **Configure Menu | Radio Menu | Radio Menu**, choose **IEEE80211**. **IEEE80211** configures radio protocols, power save, and other node management functions, as shown in the following output. The Default settings are acceptable for most environments.

```
Configuration Radio I80211 Menu
Option                Value            Description
1 - Beacon            [ 100 ]          Beacon period in Kusec
2 - Dtim              [ 5 ]            DTIM interval
```

```
3 - Extend              [ on ]         Allow proprietary extensions
4 - Bcst_ssid           [ on ]         Allow broadcast SSID
5 - Rts                 [ 2048 ]       RTS/CTS packet size threshold
6 - Privacy             [ menu ]       Privacy configuration
7 - Encapsulation       [ menu ]       Configure packet encapsulation
Enter an option number or name, "=" main menu, <ESC> previous menu
```

Configuring the Beacon Period Option

Beacon configures the interval between the broadcast of beacon packets. Beacon packets are pulses used to synchronize the wireless network and nodes. While the default is appropriate for most environments, shorter beacon intervals can improve response times.

Configuring the DTIM Interval

Dtim configures the Delivery Traffic Indicator Map (DTIM) settings. The 802.11 general MAC layer provides power-saving features via the Traffic Indicator Map (TIM) and DTIM "beacons." Power management can conserve laptop battery life, which extends network functionality when operating without A/C power.

TIMs are sent periodically by a wireless AP or bridge, and identify wireless nodes with pending traffic. Wireless network cards are configured to wake upon receiving a TIM.

DTIMs are similar to TIMs, but with broad/multicast traffic indications. DTIMs are sent at lower frequencies, such as 1 DTIM every 5 TIMs. The recommended wake setting for network cards is at every DTIM. The Cisco Aironet 340 wireless bridge provides a facility to configure the interval using the Dtim menu option.

Configuring the Network Management Extension Option

Network Management Extension communicates specific node and network management data in management packets. These include enhanced bridge affiliations and communications path management. Although most non-Cisco products generally ignore these packets, some may attempt to interpret them, causing errors. In these cases, this option should be disabled by setting it to "off."

Configuring Allow Broadcast SSID Option

Broadcast SSID (no-SSID or empty SSID) is a default means (or last resort) for establishing communications. It allows bridges to support or disallow communications using the broadcast SSID. For security reasons, administrators should define an SSID for the wireless network, and require all clients to use it. For most networks, this option should be disabled by setting it to off.

Configuring the RTS/CTS Option

RTS/CTS establishes a formal communications channel between nodes for transmitting packets meeting a size threshold. It prevents collisions and ensures that the broadcast medium is effectively used. When a node is ready to send (RTS) a packet satisfying the threshold, the wireless bridge sends a small RTS packet over the network in order to obtain a clear channel. The receiving node sends out a small CTS packet over the network, thereby declaring a quiet period for all other nodes. The transmitting node sends the packet and the network becomes available again.

This is effective in larger dispersed networks where wireless bridges may be several radio hops away from a transmitting bridge or where a bridge may not be within immediate radio range of another transmitting bridge.

The option can be configured for packets ranging from 100 to 2,048 bytes. The lower the packet size threshold setting, the more RTS/CTS packets sent. This results in lowered network availability for the transmission of actual data packets.

Configuring the Privacy Option

The Privacy option establishes an encrypted communications channel between the wireless devices that make up the network, as shown in the following output.

```
Privacy Options MenuConfiguration Radio I80211 Privacy Menu
Option              Value            Description
1 - Encryption      [ off ]          Encrypt radio packets
2 - Auth            [ open ]         Authentication mode
3 - Client          [ open ]         Client authentication modes allowed
4 - Key                              Set the keys
5 - Transmit                         Key number for transmit
Enter an option number or name, "=" main menu, <ESC> previous menu
```

- **Encryption** Default is off (communications are not encrypted between wireless bridges). When enabled, communications are encrypted with RSA RC4 symmetric encryption algorithm with the same key used to encrypt and decrypt. Key is installed on all wireless nodes wishing to communicate securely. Key updates must be performed on all nodes simultaneously in order for encrypted communications to remain available. When enabled, unencrypted packets will be discarded. The mixed setting supports both encrypted and unencrypted communications, and is not recommended as it allows for capture of both types of traffic.
- **Authentication Mode** Open or shared key authentication used by Remote Nodes to authenticate to the Root Node. Open mode allows any Remote Node to authenticate. Shared key mode uses a challenge-response token to verify the Remote Node is allowed into the network. The Root Node requests that the Remote Node encrypt a token it sent, and the Remote Node is permitted access only if the Root Node can decrypt the result.
- **Client** Authentication using open, shared key, and both options for wireless bridges operating as APs. Specifies the authentication to be used by clients wishing to associate with a wireless bridge.
- **Key** Cisco Aironet 340 wireless bridge supports up to four programmed keys. One key is used at any given time to set up the encrypted session. Each key must be known to all

devices on the network to ensure that data can be encrypted and decrypted by all nodes. The keys must be entered in the same order on each wireless devices.

When the **Key** option is selected, a prompt is displayed requesting the input of the key string. Key strings are made up of 10 hexadecimal characters for 40-bit keys and 26 hexadecimal characters for 128-bit keys. Key entry is repeated twice for each inputted key to guard against mistyped characters.

- **Transmit** Sends keys after they are defined. The receive option does not need to be configured, as only knowledge of the key is required from the receiving station to decrypt messages.

Configuring the Packet Encapsulation Option

By default, Cisco Aironet wireless bridges do not interoperate with equipment from other vendors. However, the signaling and packet assembly can be modified to support basic transmissions for interoperability. This can be accomplished by using packet encapsulation.

The administrator must know the encapsulation method used by non-Cisco equipment to enable communications with Cisco equipment. The encapsulation table is used to configure the specific packet settings. This is an advanced function and must be understood thoroughly before it can be used. When configuring a Cisco Aironet 340-only network, these options can be ignored and left at their default value of 802.1H.

Configuring the Extended Options

The Extended options configure radio parameters that may be modified under certain circumstances (as shown in the following output). These options should be left at their default settings unless environmental conditions or other network factors are causing problems. The default options listed reflect the type of application the wireless unit is called to serve.

```
Configuration Radio Extended Menu
Option              Value               Description
1 - Bridge_mode     [ bridge_only]     Bridging mode
2 - Parentid        [ any ]             Parent node Id
3 - Parent_timeout [ off ]             Time to look for specified parent
4 - Time_retry      [ 8 ]               Number of seconds to retry transmit
5 - Count_retry     [ 0 ]               Maximum number transmit retries
6 - Refresh         [ 100 ]             Refresh rate in 1/10 of seconds
7 - Roaming         [ directed ]       Type of roaming control packets
8 - Balance         [ off ]             Load balancing
9 - Diversity       [ off ]             Enable the diversity antennas
01 - Power          [ 20 ]              Transmit power level
02 - Fragment       [ 2048 ]            Maximum fragment size
03 - Options                            Enable radio options
Enter an option number or name, "=" main menu, <ESC> previous menu
```

- **Bridge Mode** This option establishes which types of communications will be supported by the wireless node.
  - **Bridge_only** Wireless bridges will be the only types allowed to communicate with this node.
  - **Access_point** Any and all wireless devices will be allowed to communicate with this node.
  - **Client** Standalone repeater that will not have any communications with other units.
- **Parentid** When wireless nodes are activated, they listen to determine their parent(s). This is an automatic process, but wireless bridges configured as client, should be assigned a specific parent, which is the purpose of this option.
- **Parent Timeout** Configures timeout period when communications with a parent are not available to find another parent. When off, this unit communicates only with its associated parent and no other parent.
- **Time Retry** Defines parameters affecting transmitter retry timers. It is used with the Count Retry option. If a packet cannot be transmitted to the intended recipient bridge, parent, or child within the specified time, a new association may be established. If the timer expires before then, a new parent bridge is determined. In the case of the time retry counter exceeding the allowed retry time for a child bridge, the parent/child bridge relationship is dissolved. The Time Retry counter can be configured from 1 second to 30 seconds.
- **Count Retry** Affects transmitter retry counters, and used with Time Retry. The number of retries the bridge will make to reestablish the association with the parent. The Count Retry varies from 0 tries to 64 tries. A setting of 0 disables the Count Retry option, making only the Time Retry active.
- **Refresh** Repeaters only. Keep-alive that ensures long periods of inactive communications with a parent are not the result of a loss in communication. Defined in tenths of a second.
- **Roaming** Used where an associated wireless node has the capability to roam within an environment and re-associate to a new parent node. When this re-association occurs, the parent forwards a notification to the other wireless bridges informing them of the new relationship.
  - **Directed** Interrogates the new child and determines the roaming node's previous parent.
  - **Broadcast** Broadcasts new affiliation throughout the network.
- **Balance** Load balancing is used by Root Node bridges in conjunction with the i80211 Extend options to communicate load-balancing configurations. Balances the parent/child associations between different Remote Nodes based on traffic loads, number of existing associations, and other parameters. This option can be configured to off, slow (every 30 seconds), or fast (every 4 seconds).

- **Diversity** Informs the wireless bridge that it has two antennas instead of one. When off, bridge operates as if a single antenna is present. On tells the bridge it has two antennas.
- **Power** Reduces the broadcast power of radio transmitter from full power down to 100 mW or 50 mW. Default setting is appropriate for most operations but can be reduced if interference is caused to other devices.
- **Fragment** Fragment size determines the largest packet size allowed to be transmitted. Packets exceeding this size are segmented into smaller packets meeting the size restrictions. The maximum fragment size can be configured for values ranging from 256 bytes to 2,048 bytes.
- **Options** Activates additional wireless bridge peripheral accessories.

Configuring the Ethernet Port

To configure the Ethernet port, select **Configure | Ethernet**. The Cisco Aironet wireless bridge provides an Ethernet port that can connect an Ethernet LAN. This port is configured using the following menu options shown in the next series of output.

```
Configuration Ethernet Menu
Option          Value           Description
1 - Active     [ on ]          Connection active
2 - Size       [ 1518 ]        Maximum frame size
3 - Port       [ auto ]        Port selection
Enter an option number or name, "=" main menu, <ESC> previous menu
```

- **Active** Enables or disables the Ethernet port. The default setting is **on, or**set to **off** if the unit is a repeater.
- **Size** The maximum frame size allowed, from 1,518 to 4,096 bytes. Requires reboot to effect.
- **Port** Which Ethernet port to be used. Auto scans to determine the active port. Manual is used if port is connected to an Ethernet card already scanning.

Configuring the Network Identifiers

Network identifiers define network address parameters, network service, and other related configurations (see the following Configuring Identifier Menu). These include the following:

- Domain Name Service (DNS)
- Unit Naming
- DHCP

```
Configuration Ident Menu
Option              Value                  Description
1 - Inaddr          [ 10.053.147.031 ]     Internet address
2 - Inmask          [ 255.255.255.000 ]    Internet subnet mask
3 - Gateway         [ 10.053.147.050 ]     Internet default gateway
4 - Routing         [ menu ]               IP routing table configuration
5 - Dns1            [ 10.053.147.254 ]     DNS server 1
6 - Dns2            [ 000.000.000.000 ]    DNS server 2
7 - Domain          [ "Wireless" ]         Domain name
8 - Name            [ "CAWB_3f_SE_P3 ]     Node name
9 - Location        [ "" ]                 System location
01 - Contact        [ "" ]                 System contact name
02 - Bootp_DHCP     [ on ]                 Use BOOTP/DHCP on startup
03 - Class          [ "" ]                 DHCP class id
```

Most of these parameters are self-explanatory so they are not discussed in detail. **Routing** defines how IP packets are routed and forwarded. **Name** provides a 20-character name for the wireless bridge. This name appears on all console port menus and is used to identify the wireless bridge to all of the members of the wireless network.

Console Management Access

Console and remote management features are controlled through tables of user privileges and credentials. Authorized users can access the wireless bridge configurations options and services for which they are cleared, including Telnet, HTTP, FTP, SNMP, and TFTP, among others. Non-authorized users are denied access.

Users can be defined and managed through an IP address or a MAC address listing. Listings can be created and maintained using the **Add**, **Remove**, and **Display** menu options. To prevent any form of remote access, the Remote menu option must be set to **off**. When the Remote menu option is set to **on**, and no entries are made within the right management tables, privileges are deemed to be universally available, that is any user at any location can access the console.

Configuring Passwords

To configure a password for a selected privilege, select **Configuration** from the Main Menu, and then **Console**. The two defined privileges are:

```
Configuration Menu
Option              Value        Description
1 - Radio           [ menu ]     Radio network parameters
2 - Ethernet        [ menu ]     Ethernet configuration
3 - Ident           [ menu ]     Identification information
4 - Console         [ menu ]     Control console access
5 - Stp             [ menu ]     Spanning Tree Protocol
```

```
6 - Mobile IP          [ menu ]        Mobile IP protocol configuration
7 - Time               [ menu ]        Network Time Setup
8 - Dump                               Dump configuration to console
Enter an option number or name, "=" main menu, <ESC> previous menu>
```

Several options are presented as described next.

- **RPassword**
- **WPassword**

The administrator selects the privilege for which a password is to be applied. If they do not want to use a password, type **none**. To configure a password, the administrator enters a character string of at least 5 characters but less than 10 characters. Passwords are case-sensitive. After the password is set, the system monitors for incorrect logins. Failing to enter the correct password at the prompt three consecutive times causes the wireless bridge to drop the connection. A log entry records the failed login attempts. Forgotten passwords can only be recovered by Cisco.

Configuring Privileges

Privileges are configured by selecting the **Privilege** option. Users navigating from a high privilege level to a lower privilege level are not required to re-authenticate. Users navigating from a low privilege level to a higher privilege level must re-authenticate using valid credentials for that level.

Three privilege levels are available:

- **Off** User does not have to be logged on to view the **privilege** and **help** entries of the main menu. You cannot password protect this privilege level.
- **Read-Only** Password controlled read-only access to display configuration, statistics, and other operational commands.
- **Write** Password controlled read-write access.
- **SNMP Support** Defines community strings that are used to view or modify the configurations, as well as monitoring operational characteristics.

Configuring the Time Service

The Network Time Protocol (NTP) synchronizes the bridge by specifying a timeserver and related parameters, as shown in the following Configuration Time Menu. **Offset** calibrates the time with GMT in minutes.

```
Configuration Time Menu
Option                 Value                   Description
1 - Time_server       [ 10.053.147.080 ]     Time protocol server
2 - Sntp_server       [ 000.000.000.000 ]    Network time server
3 - Offset             [ -300 ]                GMT offset in minutes
4 - Dst                [ on ]                  Use daylight savings time
Enter an option number or name, "=" main menu, <ESC> previous menu
```

Setting Up Association Tables

Association tables define and manage the parent-child relationship between Cisco Aironet wireless bridges and end nodes for address information to perform traffic routing, load balancing, and other management functions. Parent wireless bridges can manage up to 2,048 subordinate entries. Entry information provides details on the child node and client name, address, device, and association type. Table entries can be manually edited to create a predetermined wireless network tree.

When a wireless bridge receives a packet originating from its wired or wireless interfaces, it determines the destination. If the destination is on one of its interfaces, it forwards the packet directly; otherwise, it forwards the packet directly to a Root Bridge, child bridge, or an associated dedicated repeater. If not known, the wireless bridge forwards the packet to the Root Bridge.

To configure the association tables, the administrator should select the **Association** option (main menu option 3) from the Association main menu, as shown in the following output.

```
Association Menu

Option                   Value            Description
1 - Display                               Display the table
2 - Summary                               Display the table summary
3 - Maximum              [ 1024 ]         Maximum allowable child nodes
4 - Autoassoc            [ on ]           Allow automatic table additions
5 - Add                                   Control node association
6 - Remove                                Remove association control
7 - Staletime            [ 350 ]          Backbone LAN node stale out time
8 - Niddisp              [ numeric ]      Node Ids display mode
Enter an option number or name, "=" main menu, <ESC> previous menu
```

The **Display** option on the Associations menu lists existing associations. A prompt appears requesting the type of associations to be displayed. These include the following associations:

- **All** Displays all of the entries contained within the table
- **Connected** Displays all of the entries currently connected to the wireless bridge
- **Hierarchy** Displays the association tree with parent and children associations
- **Static** Displays entries that were entered manually
- **Multicast filters** Displays multicast entries for which filters have been defined
- **Node filters** Displays node entries for which filters have been defined

Using Filters

Filters manage and limit traffic by predefined traffic types. They can be applied to traffic originating on a wired LAN (**to_radio** option) or to traffic originating from wired and wireless networks (**both** option). Filters can block certain types of packets and reduce unnecessary wireless transmissions.

Filtering can extend the life of battery-operated wireless nodes by ensuring all wireless communications supported are necessary and allowed. All wireless bridges in the same network should have the same filter sets to ensure a uniform management.

Select **Filter** from the main menu as shown in the following output.

```
Filter Menu
Option              Value         Description
1 - Multicast       [ menu ]      Multicast address filtering
2 - Node            [ menu ]      Node address filtering
3 - Protocols       [ menu ]      Protocol filters
4 - Direction       [ both ]      Packet direction affected by filters
Enter an option number or name, "=" main menu, <ESC> previous menu
```

The following discusses the Filter Menu options.

Configuring the Multicast Option

Multicast defines and manages multicast filters for each multicast address:

- **Default** Applied to multicast traffic not originating from a defined multicast address.
  - **Discard** Discards all multicast traffic not originating from a known address.
  - **Forward** Forwards multicast traffic from unknown multicast addresses.
  - **Accesspt** Forward multicast traffic from unknown multicast addresses to APs and wireless bridges only.
  - **Nonsps** Forwards multicast traffic from unknown multicast addresses to wireless devices that do not operate in power saving mode.

Configuring the Node Option

Node filters packets based on source node addresses. Default actions can be defined for addresses not contained within the table. The node address filters can be populated by using the IP address of the node in question, as shown in the following Filter Node Menu.

```
Filter Node Menu
Option            Value          Description
1 - Ethdst        [ forward ]    Destination address from Ethernet
2 - Raddst        [ forward ]    Destination address from radio
3 - Source        [ off ]        Source addresses
4 - Display                      Display the node address filters
5 - Ipdisplay                    Display the IP address filters
6 - Add                          Add a node address filter
7 - Remove                       Remove a node address filter
Enter an option number or name, "=" main menu, <ESC> previous menu
```

Configuring the Protocols Option

Protocols filters packets based on the encapsulation protocol. Default actions can be defined for protocols not defined within the table. This option can minimize transmissions of protocol traffic not used on remote wireless networks. Options are similar to multicast and source address filters.

Event Logging

Cisco wireless bridges can log information, which can be especially useful for troubleshooting. Event logging documents actions and events that occurred during operation. The wireless bridge provides several types of logs, including the ones shown in Table 3.13.

Table 3.13 Wireless Bridge Logging

Type	Description
Information Log	Records changes in the operation of the wireless bridge
Error Log	Records self-recoverable errors such as transmission errors
Severe Error Log	Records critical errors requiring intervention from an administrator

To view and manage logs, the administrator should select **Log** from the main menu to access the Logs menu shown in the following output. Log levels are severe errors, all errors, and logging off.

```
Logs Menu
Option              Value                 Description
1 - History                               Log and alarm history
2 - Clear                                 Clear the history buffer
3 - Printlevel      [ all ]               Type of logs to print
4 - Loglevel        [ all ]               Type of logs to save
5 - Ledlevel        [ error/severe ]      Type of logs to light status led
6 - Statistics                            Set alarms on statistics
7 - Network         [ off ]               Log network roaming
8 - Bnodelog        [ off ]               Log backbone node changes
9 - Snmp            [ menu ]              Set-up SNMP traps
01 - Syslog         [10.053.147.131]      Unix syslogd address
02 - Syslevel       [ error/severe ]      Type of logs to send to syslog
03 - Facility       [ 16 ]                Syslog facility number to send
04 - Rcvsyslog      [ on ]                Enable reception of syslog messages
Enter an option number or name, "=" main menu, <ESC> previous menu
```

Following is specific information about the Logs Menu options provided.

- **Printlevel** Defines which logs to display on the console screen.
- **Loglevel** Type of logs to save into memory for review on the display log history menu.

- **Ledlevel** Type of error to trigger the indicator LED to amber.
- **Statistics** Defines how and when alarm conditions are to be triggered based on the wireless bridge statistics.
- **Network** Registers the movement of wireless nodes between other bridges.
- **BnodeLog** Logs changes to the backbone.
- **SNMP** Triggers and forwards SNMP traps.
- **Syslog, SysLevel, Facility, and Rcvsyslog** Forward logs of certain levels to a SYSLOG server, including to a bridge where **Rcvsyslog** is turned on.

Viewing Statistics

The Cisco Aironet 3X0 wireless bridges allow viewing of statistical information on several parameters such as general status, throughput, error, routing, and related wireless bridge information. To use the wireless bridge logs, the administrator selects **Statistics** from the main menu (shown in the following output). To refresh on-screen information, the administrator presses the **Spacebar**. To clear the display and the statistics, the administrator presses **Shift + C**, and to exit the display, the administrator presses **q**.

```
Statistics Menu
Option                 Value              Description
1 - Throughput                            Throughput statistics
2 - Radio                                 Radio error statistics
3 - Ethernet                              Ethernet error statistics
4 - Status                                Display general status
5 - Map                                   Show network map
6 - Watch                                 Record history of a statistic
7 - History                               Display statistic history
8 - Nodes                                 Node statistics
9 - ARP                                   ARP table
01 - Display_time     [ 10 ]             Time to re-display screens
02 - IpAdr             [ off ]            Determine client IP addresses
Enter an option number or name, "=" main menu, <ESC> previous menu
```

- The **Throughput statistics** option provides a summary of wireless transmitter statistical throughput information, including the following:
  - **Recent Rate/s** Displays throughput information per second back up to 10 seconds
  - **Total** Displays the throughput totals since the last reset
  - **Average Rate** Displays the throughput total averages since the last reset
  - **Highest Rate** Displays peak throughput since the last reset

- **Packets** Displays the total number of packets sent or received
- **Filtered** Displays the total number of filtered (discarded) packets

- **Radio Error Statistics** Displays an error summary of wireless transmitter and receiver including the following options:
- **Buffer Full Frame Lost** Displays the number of packets discarded due to a buffer overrun
- **Duplicate Frames** Displays the number of packets received more than once
- **CRC Errors** Displays the number of packets received with CRC errors
- **Retries** Displays the cumulative count of packet retransmits attempts
- **Max Retries/Frame** Displays the highest count of a retransmit for a packet
- **Queue Full Discards** Displays the number of discarded packets due to transmissions to a wireless bridge not being successful

Duplicate frame errors are generally indicative of packet receive acknowledgements being lost over the network. CRC errors, retries, and queue full discards are usually caused by interference and noise over the radio path.

- The **Ethernet error statistics** displays an error summary occurring over the Ethernet port, including the following:
  - **Buffer Full Frames Lost** Number of packets discarded due to a buffer overrun
  - **CRC Errors** Number of packets received with CRC errors
  - **Collision**s Number of collisions that have occurred
  - **Frame Alignment Errors** Number of misaligned (not a multiple of eight) packets received
  - **Over-length Frames** Number of packets received which exceeded the maximum packet size
  - **Overruns** Number of first-in-first-out (FIFO) overflow errors
  - **Misses** Number of packets lost due to lack of buffer space
  - **Excessive Collisions** Number of transmission failures due to collisions
  - **Deferrals** Number of times a packet transmission was delayed due to network collisions
  - **Excessive Deferrals** Number of times frames were discarded due to excessive deferrals
  - **No Carrier Sense Present** Number of times the Ethernet carrier was not present during a packet transmission

- **Carrier Sense Lost** Number of times the Ethernet carrier was lost during a packet transmission
- **Out of Window Collision** Number of times a collision indication occurred after the 64th byte of a frame was transmitted
- **Underruns** Number of times the transmit FIFO was empty during transmission
- **Bad Length** Number of times a packet larger than the maximum allowed was attempted to be transmitted

- **Status** The **Display Overall Ethernet Status** menu option (Statistics menu option 4) displays critical operational configurations and runtime statistics for the wireless transmitter (radio), Ethernet LAN port connections, and filtering.
- **Map** The **Display Network Map** menu option (Statistics menu option 5) provides a means for the local wireless bridge to query the other wireless network components on their parent/child relationships and display a network tree.
- **Watch** The **Watch** option (Statistics menu option 6) provides a means to record selected Ethernet statistical information based on a timer. The last 20 saved events are kept.
- **History** The **Static History Display** menu option (Statistics menu option 7) displays the saved events generated from the Watch menu option configuration.
- **Node** The **Node Information Display** menu option (Statistics menu option 8) provides the Ethernet details of a client, including address, signal strength, total number of transmitted and received packets, total number of bytes transmitted and received, and the total number of packets that were retransmitted due to acknowledgements not received.
- **ARP** The **ARP Information Display** menu option (Statistics menu option 9) lists the ARP table of the IP to MAC address and provides details regarding support for Ethernet Type II or IEEE 802.2 framing support.
- **Display Time** The **Screen Display Time** option (Statistics menu option 01) sets the automatic refresh rate for constantly updated screens. The default refresh rate is configured at 10 seconds.
- **Ipadr** The **Client IP Address Determination** option (Statistics menu option 02) configures the wireless bridge to determine the IP address of client notes that are associated.

Cisco Aironet Wireless Bridge Troubleshooting

The troubleshooting functions such as Telnet, link tests, restart, reset, and ping, among others, are available from the Diagnostics menu (shown next). To use the wireless bridge diagnostics functions, the administrator should select **Diagnostics** from the main menu.

```
Diagnostics Menu
Option              Value              Description
1 - Network        [ menu ]            Network connection commands
2 - Linktest       [ menu ]            Run a link test
3 - Restart                            Equivalent to power-up
4 - Defaults                           Return to default configuration
5 - Reset                              Default parts of the configuration
6 - Load           [ menu ]            Load new version of firmware
Enter an option number or name, "=" main menu, <ESC> previous menu
```

There are several key pieces of diagnostic information that can be gathered from the Diagnostic menu, as discussed in the following sections.

Network Menu Option

The Network options submenu provides network-based troubleshooting and support tools. Tools include a facility to establish a Telnet session, ping, and find a wireless bridge.

Connect Option

Starts a Telnet session with another remote wireless bridge, which accesses its console menu to troubleshoot and configure. Administrator's can connect via IP address or the MAC address. When a Telnet session is active, console access is disabled until the Telnet session is terminated (naturally or with Break key at the console). Telnet must be enabled on the remote bridge. The escape sequence is configured for **Ctrl+Z**, but can be changed using the Escape menu. This is required only if the default escape character has an alternate meaning on the host. To enter non-printable characters, the administrator uses the following:

- Enters an escape sequence using the **Ctrl** key, enters the caret (^) character. Example: Enter **Ctrl+Z** as **^z.**
- Enters an escape character using a three-digit octal character number, precedes the entry with a back slash. Example: **\021**.
- Enters an escape character using a two-digit hexadecimal number, precedes the entry with a string. Example: **$4F**.

Find Option

Trigger the blinking of the amber LED indicators on the remote bridge to visually locate it. Telnet to the desired remote wireless bridge and select the **Find** option. Disengage the find setting by pressing **Ctrl+C**.

Ping Option

Send standard ICMP echo request packet to the remote node every three seconds until a reply is received or until 5 ICMP echo request packets have been sent. To stop the ping command, press **Ctrl+C**.

Linktest Menu Options

Administrators must verify the operational quality of the wireless network. Select **Linktest** from the **Diagnostics** menu for the following menu.

```
Configuration Radio Linktests Menu
Option              Value          Description
1 - Strength                       Run a signal strength test
2 - Carrier                        Carrier busy statistics
3 - Multicast                      Run a multicast echo test
4 - Unicast                        Run a unicast echo test
5 - Remote                         Run a remote echo test
6 - Destination    [ any ]         Target address
7 - Size            [ 512 ]        Packet size
8 - Count           [ 100 ]        Number of packets to send
9 - Rate            [ auto ]       Data rate
01 - Errors                        Radio error statistics
02 - Autotest      [ once ]        Auto echo test
03 - Continuous    [ 0 ]           Repeat echo test once started
Enter an option number or name, "=" main menu, <ESC> previous menu
```

The signal strength test can be used to verify the carrier signal strength between nodes. The **carrier busy test** option is used to determine the overall level of activity present and overall availability for each available frequency. This can be used to help determine which frequency is most appropriate for the intended wireless network, and can also be used to investigate the presence of radio signaling and jamming equipment. When a wireless bridge is performing a carrier busy test, it does not perform any of the normal wireless bridge operations, and as a result, all associations and communications are dropped.

The **Multicast**, **Unicast**, and **Remote echo test** options are used to test the reception of packets on a remote wireless bridge from a local wireless bridge. During this test, packets are sent using a Cisco proprietary protocol triggering the remote node to send a reply regarding signal strength and other related parameters. The Multicast option can be used to verify and obtain metrics on the wireless transmissions over a local wireless network. The Unicast option can be used to verify the path between the wireless bridge and other nodes on the wireless and Ethernet segment. The same error recovery considerations are applied to this packet, as would normal user packets. The **Remote** option provides a means of controlling a multicast link test triggered on a remote bridge, from the local bridge console. The test is the same as the standard multicast test.

The **Autotest** option controls the automatic operation of a link test when a repeater associates with its parent. The test uses the existing configured test parameters to define the test options. The acceptable values include **off** (to configure that a test is never triggered), **once** (to configure that a test is to be triggered only the first time a unit associates with its parent), and **always** (where a test is triggered every time a node associates with a parent).

When in **autotest** mode, the wireless bridge LED indicators turn green in a cyclic pattern. Once the test is completed, the LEDs are a solid pattern to indicate the results of the test. The patterns shown in Table 3.14 can be displayed.

Table 3.14 Linktest LED Patterns

LED Pattern	Meaning
Green, green, green	Excellent
Green, green, amber	Very good
Green, green, off	Good
Green, amber, off	Satisfactory
Amber, off, off	Fair
Red, off, off	Poor

Restart Option

The **restart unit** menu option (Diagnostics menu option 3) reboots the Cisco Aironet 340 wireless bridge. The wireless bridge operates as it would if it had just been powered up and all currently existing associations are lost.

Default and Reset Options

The **return unit to default configuration** menu options (Diagnostics menu options 4 and 5) reset the wireless bridge to full factory default using the "default" option, or reset specific configuration selections, such as radio and filter, among others, back to factory default.

Loading Firmware and Configurations

The **load** option (Diagnostics menu option 6) updates firmware and configuration files from a remote host into the local main memory of the wireless bridge (as shown in the following output). Newly downloaded files must be stored into local flash memory before becoming active. Files stored in the flash memory of the bridge are retained during power down. Configuration text files can be edited to act as command line input. These files start with the string **! CONFIGURATION**. Commands that are to be executed are listed line-by-line using the standard command-line syntax and option settings.

```
Diagnostics Load Menu
Option            Value          Description
1 - Xmodem                       Xmodel load from serial port
2 - Crc-xmodem                   Xmodem-crc load from serial port
```

```
3 - FTP            [ menu ]        Load using FTP
4 - Distribute     [ menu ]        Distribute the firmware
5 - Bootp/DHCP     [  on  ]        Use Bootp/DHCP on startup
6 - Class          [<value>]       DHCP class ID
Enter an option number or name, "=" main menu, <ESC> previous menu
```

FTP

FTP is used to upload and download firmware on the wireless bridge. IP addresses must be configured on all of the hosts and wireless bridges actively participating in the file transfer as a host or client. The wireless bridge supports four modes of FTP transfers, as listed in Table 3.15. See the following output from the diagnostics load FTP menu for a listing of the available options.

Table 3.15 FTP Transfer Options

Connection Origin	Connection Destination	Action
Local wireless bridge	Remote PC or host	Retrieve a copy of the new firmware (get)
Local wireless bridge	Remote PC or host	Send a copy of the active firmware
Local wireless bridge	Remote wireless bridge	Send or receive a copy of the active firmware
PC or host	Local wireless bridge	Send a copy of the new firmware

```
Diagnostics Load Ftp Menu
Option           Value                   Description
1 - Get                                  Load a firmware/config file
2 - Put                                  Send a firmware file
3 - Config                               Send a configuration file
4 - Dest         [ 000.000.000.000 ]     Host IP address
5 - Username     [ "" ]                  Host username
6 - Password                             Host password
7 - Filename     [ "" ]                  Host filename
Enter an option number or name, "=" main menu, <ESC> previous menu>
```

Distribute

The **firmware distribution** option (Diagnostics Load menu option 4) distributes firmware and configuration files to one or all of the wireless bridges making up the wireless infrastructure. The **distribute** option provides an efficient means of updating remote wireless bridges. See the following output for menu options.

```
Diagnostics Load Distribution Menu
Option           Value         Description
1 - Go                         Start the distribution
```

```
2 - Type          [firmware]        What to distribute
3 - Control       [ "newer"]        How to control distributions
4 - Add                             Change distributable configuration
5 - Remove                          Remove change
6 - Show                            Show changes
7 - Dump                            Show Configuration
Enter an option number or name, "=" main menu, <ESC> previous menu>
```

BOOTP and DHCP

The BOOTP and DHCP options (Diagnostics Load menu option 5) are used for downloading firmware from a BOOTP or DHCP server. This option is enabled by default.

Backing Up Wireless Bridge Configurations

Whenever custom configurations are entered on the wireless bridge, a copy of the configuration should be saved on a centralized server. The dump operation involves configuring the console terminal emulator program to save or capture the screen information. Once this is configured, the Dump option is selected from the main menu.

Cisco Aironet Antennas

The previous sections provided an overview of Cisco APs and wireless bridges and their configuration. Most of these devices can have their effective networking range extended with optional antennas. Many of the Cisco wireless products have the capability to use an external antenna to maximize network coverage and to compensate for environmental variables. Before going through the available antenna choices, we need to examine a few terms to better explain the terminology used:

- **Decibel (dB)** Unit of measure for ratios describing loss or gain, normally expressed in watts. A decibel is the measurement of power gained or lost between two communicating devices. These units are normally given in terms of the logarithm to Base 10 of a ratio.
- **dBi Value** Ratio of the gain of an antenna as compared to an isotropic antenna. The greater the dBi value, the higher the gain. If the gain is high, the angle of coverage is more acute.
- **Isotropic Antenna** Theoretical construct that an antenna will radiate its signal 360 degrees to cover the area in a perfect sphere. Used as a basis to describe the gain of a real antenna.
- **Line-of-sight Sight** Unobstructed straight line between two transmitting devices. Administrators will most often see the need for a line-of-sight path for long-range directional radio transmissions. Due to the curvature of the earth, the line-of-sight for devices not mounted on towers is limited to 6 miles (9.65 km).

- **Signal Attenuation (Multipath Fading)** Reduction of signal strength based on one of several factors: absorption, diffraction, reflection, and refraction.
    - **Absorption** Obstructions (such as trees) soak up the signal so that it is unable to reach the receiver that it is trying to communicate with.
    - **Diffraction** When a signal bends around an obstruction that has a reflective quality (such as glass).
    - **Reflection** When a signal bounces off a surface (such as a body of water) causing distortion, and sometimes cancellation, of the signal.
    - **Refraction** Bending of the signal based on atmospheric variations (such as fog).

A number of the different antennas described were designed to fit specific needs. Cabling and connectors that attach the antenna to the AP or bridge are equally important. Each antenna is discussed in the following sections, with a summary provided in Table 3.15.

Horizontal coverage (Figure 3.57) and vertical coverage (Figure 3.58) refers to the transmission area of the antenna on the horizontal and vertical axis.

Figure 3.57 Horizontal Coverage Area

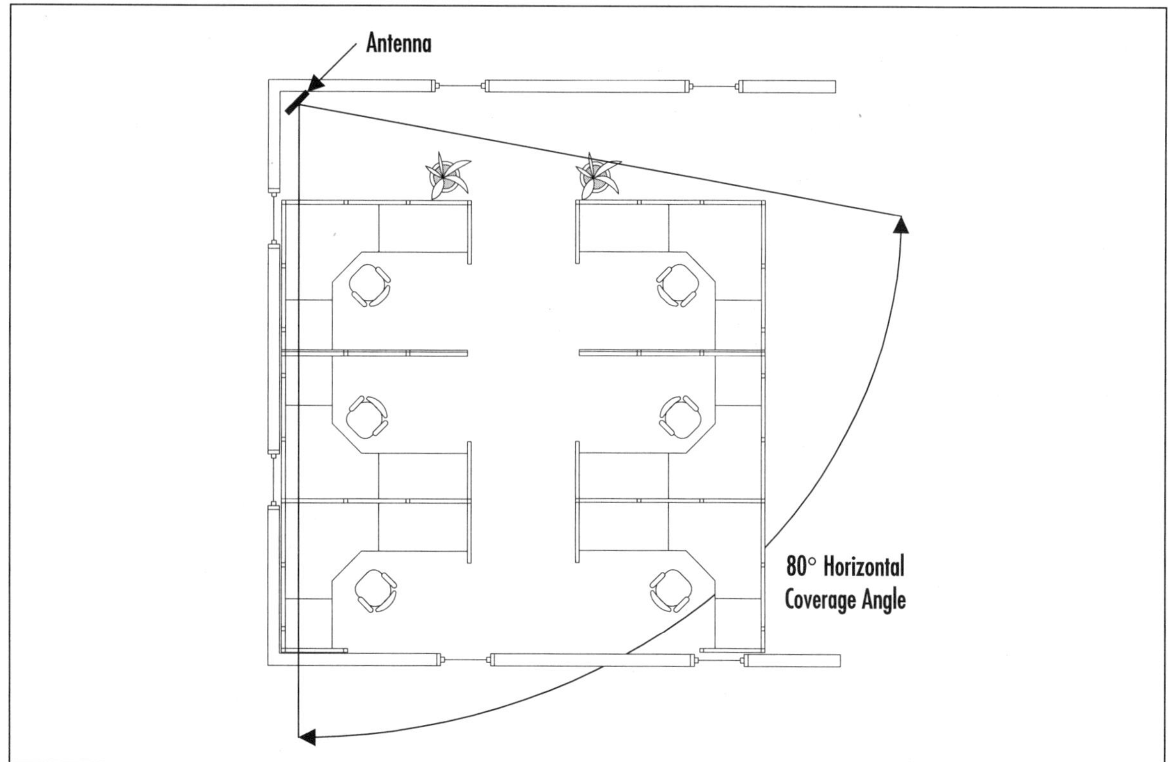

Figure 3.58 Vertical Coverage Area

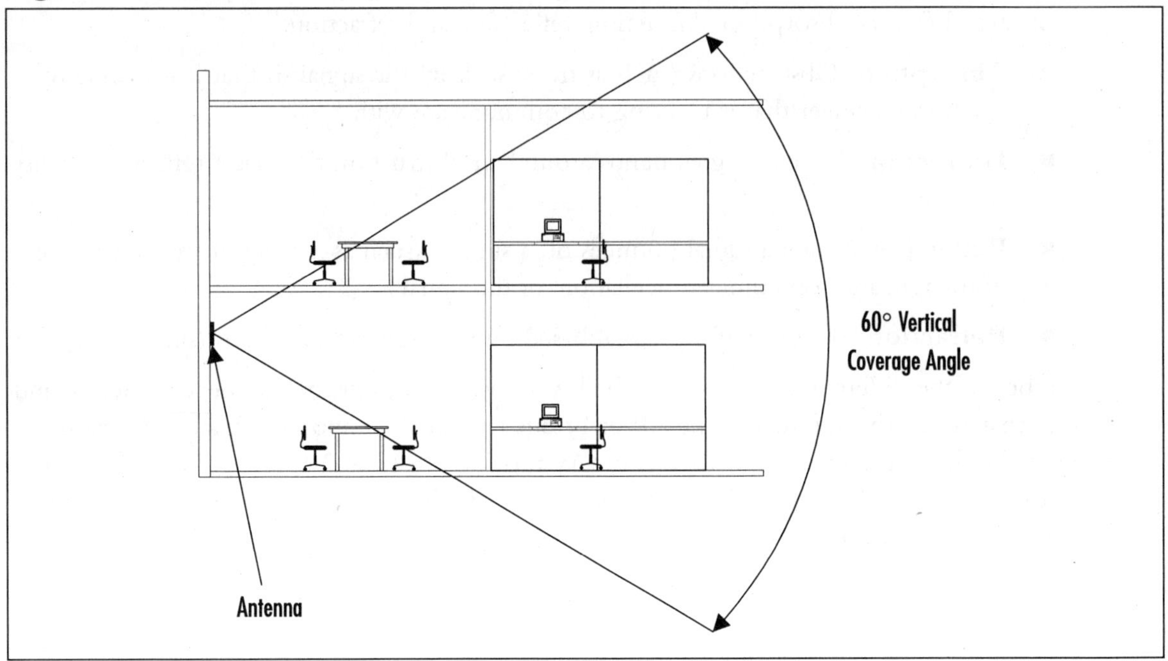

Ceiling Mount Omni-Directional Antenna

This indoor medium-range antenna provides 360-degree coverage in an office environment. It has a 360-degree horizontal coverage and a 38-degree vertical coverage. It is cylindrically shaped and is 9 in. long with a 1-inch diameter. It is light enough, 4.6oz. (131 g), to be hung from a drop ceiling. It has a 3-foot pigtail of coaxial cable at one end that terminates in a RP-TNC connector. Its approximate range is 500 feet at 1 Mbps and 145 feet at 11 Mbps.

Mast Mount Omni-Directional Antenna

The short-range outdoor mast mount omni-directional antenna has a 360-degree horizontal coverage and a 38-degree vertical coverage for point-to-multipoint connections. It can also be used indoors. The mast mount antenna is cylindrical in design, 11.5 in. long and 1.125 in. in diameter. It has a 3-foot pigtail of coaxial cable at the end that terminates in a RP-TNC connector. The approximate range is 5,000 feet at 2 Mbps and 1,580 feet at 11 Mbps.

High-Gain Mast Mount Omni-Directional Antenna

The high-gain mast mounted omni-directional antenna is a medium-range outdoor antenna that has a 360-degree horizontal coverage point-to-multipoint applications. The high-gain antenna has a vertical coverage of only 7 degrees compared to a 38-degree vertical coverage for the normal mast mount antenna. Transmitting at a smaller angle concentrates the signal energy and gives it a range of 4.6 miles at 2 Mbps and 1.4 miles at 11 Mbps. This mast mount antenna is cylindrical and is 40 in. in length, with a diameter of 1.3 inches. The cable used is a 1-foot RG-8 cable with an RP-TNC connector on the end.

Pillar Mount Diversity Omni-Directional Antenna

This indoor, medium-range antenna provides omni-directional service while being unobtrusive. It has two RP-TNC connectors on the end of a 3-foot Siamese coaxial cable. The two inputs allow for the transmission of diverse signals in the event that there is a failure of one of the transmissions. Covered with a tan cloth and mounted, it will sit approximately 6 in. from the wall. It has a rectangular shape and is 1 foot tall by 5 in. wide and 1 inch thick. The antenna has a 360-degree horizontal coverage and a 30-degree vertical coverage with a range of 500 feet at 1 Mbps and 145 feet at 11 Mbps.

POS Diversity Dipole Omni-Directional Antenna

The POS diversity dipole omni-directional antenna is for workstations that LMC adapters with dual MMCX connectors. It has 360-degree horizontal coverage, a 75-degree vertical coverage, and a range of 350 feet at 1 Mbps and 100 feet at 11 Mbps.

Diversity Ceiling Mount Omni-Directional Patch Antenna

This small (5.5 in. by 3 in. by 1 in.) rectangular antenna mounts to a drop ceiling for maximum coverage in a cubicle environment. Its range is 350 feet at 1 Mbps and 130 feet at 11 Mbps. It has two diverse transmitting elements accessed via two 3-foot pigtails each with their own RP-TNC connector.

Directional Wall Mount Patch Antenna

The horizontal and vertical coverage area for this antenna is 60 degrees. It is installed at the edge of its environment. The wall mount patch antenna is a long-range (700/200 feet at 1/11 Mbps) indoor antenna for use with the AP products, or can also be installed as a medium-range (2 miles/3,390 feet at 1/11 Mbps) outdoor bridge antenna. Small (5 in. by 5 in.) and light colored, it requires four screws to attach it to a wall. It has a 3-foot pigtail that terminates in an RP-TNC connector for connecting the antenna to an AP or bridge. Another version of this antenna has a larger vertical and horizontal angle (75-degree horizontal and 60-degree vertical) appropriate for indoor or outdoor applications. Its effective range is 540 feet at 1 Mbps and 150 feet at 11 Mbps if used with an AP, or 1.1 miles at 1 Mbps and 1,900 feet at 11 Mbps if used with a bridge.

Diversity Directional Wall Mount Patch Antenna

This compact directional antenna is designed primarily for indoors with a medium range (550/170 feet at 1/11 Mbps). It has two radiating elements with their own 3-foot pigtail attached to them for connecting dual RP-TNC connectors on many Cisco.

Yagi Antenna

The compact (18 in. long by 3 in. diameter), cylindrical Yagi antenna is designed for outdoor use in a point-to-point configuration. The signal comes out the end of the cylinder, and signal gains are due to limiting the horizontal and vertical radiation pattern. With a 30-degree horizontal and 25-degree vertical pattern, the maximum range is 6.5 miles at 2 Mbps and 2.0 miles at 11 Mbps. The Yagi antenna comes with a 3-foot pigtail with an RP-TNC connector on the end.

Dish Antenna

The small (2-foot diameter) dish antenna provides the longest range of any Cisco antennas with a maximum range of 25 miles at 2 Mbps and 11.5 miles at 11 Mbps. Both the vertical and horizontal radiation angles are the same at 12.4 degrees. This small area can make aligning two dish antennas over a large distance a difficult task if not done with care. The dish antenna is specifically designed for point-to-point applications. The dish antenna connects to a bridge via the attached 2-foot pigtail with RP-TNC connector.

The features and capabilities of the various antennas are summarized in Table 3.16.

Table 3.16 Summary of Antenna Features

Antenna	Indoor/Outdoor	Gain (dBi)	Radiation Pattern	Range (Adapter/AP/Bridge)
Ceiling Mount Omni	Indoor	5.2	360° H 38° V	AP: 500 ft @ 1 Mbps AP: 145 ft @ 11 Mbps
Mast Mount Omni	Indoor/Outdoor	5.2	360° H 38° V	Bridge: 5,000 ft @ 2 Mbps Bridge: 1,580 ft @ 11 Mbps
High-Gain Mast Mount Omni	Outdoor	12.0	360° H 7° V	Bridge: 4.6 miles @ 2 Mbps Bridge: 1.4 miles @ 11 Mbps
Pillar Mount Diversity Omni	Indoor	5.2	360° H 30° V	AP: 500 ft @ 1 Mbps AP: 145 ft @ 11 Mbps
POS Diversity Dipole (for use with LMC cards)	Indoor	2.2	360° H 75° V	Adapter: 350 ft @ 1 Mbps Adapter: 100 ft @ 11 Mbps
Ceiling Patch Omni	Indoor	2.0	360° H 80° V	AP: 350 ft @ 1 Mbps AP: 130 ft @ 11 Mbps
Directional Wall Patch	Indoor/Outdoor	9.0	60° H 60° V	AP: 700 ft @ 1 Mbps AP: 200 ft @ 11 Mbps Bridge: 2 miles @ 1 Mbps Bridge: 3,390 ft @ 11 Mbps

Continued

Table 3.16 Summary of Antenna Features

Antenna	Indoor/Outdoor	Gain (dBi)	Radiation Pattern	Range (Adapter/AP/Bridge)
Directional Wall Patch (lower gain)	Indoor/Outdoor	6.0	75° H 65° V	AP: 540 ft @ 1 Mbps AP: 150 ft @ 11 Mbps Bridge: 1.1 miles @ 1 Mbps Bridge: 1,900 ft @ 11 Mbps
Diversity Directional Wall Patch	Indoor	6.5	80° H 55° V	AP: 550 ft @ 1 Mbps AP: 170 ft @ 11 Mbps
Yagi	Outdoor	13.5	30° H 25° V	Bridge: 6.5 miles @ 2 Mbps Bridge: 2.0 miles @ 11 Mbps
Dish	Outdoor	21	12.4° H 12.4° V	Bridge: 25 miles @ 2 Mbps Bridge: 11.5 miles @11 Mbps

Antenna Accessories

Antennas can greatly increase the range and usability of a wireless system. Once an antenna has been chosen for a given application, the correct accessories for it such as lightning suppression and mounting kits must be chosen. The specific mounting kits that looked at are the Yagi articulating mount and the magnetic mount.

Yagi Articulating Mount

This mounting kit is for the Yagi antenna, a directional antenna that needs to be properly aligned in order to function optimally. The Yagi articulating mount, as shown in Figure 3.59, mounts a Yagi antenna on either a flat surface or a mast. This mount then allows for both horizontal and vertical adjustment of the antenna to assist in the alignment process. Proper use of this mount also allows the Yagi antenna to retain its wind rating of 110 miles per hour.

Figure 3.59 Yagi Articulating Mount

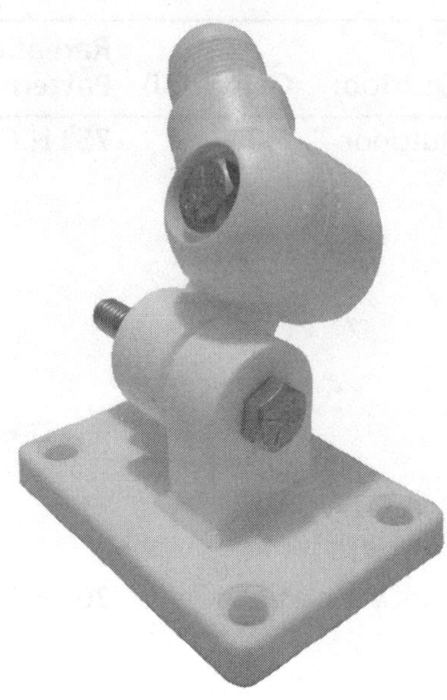

Magnetic Mount

The magnetic mount adapter, as shown in Figure 3.60, is used for dipole antennas and a 1-foot coaxial RG-58 pigtail cable for easy connection to in-house wiring. The mount base is cylindrical and approximately 5.25 in. in diameter and approximately 2 in. tall. Its magnet firmly attaches to a flat metallic surface. The magnet is strong enough to hold the antenna on a wall or even upside-down. The base has a thin rubber coating to protect the surface on which the mount is installed.

Figure 3.60 Magnetic Mount

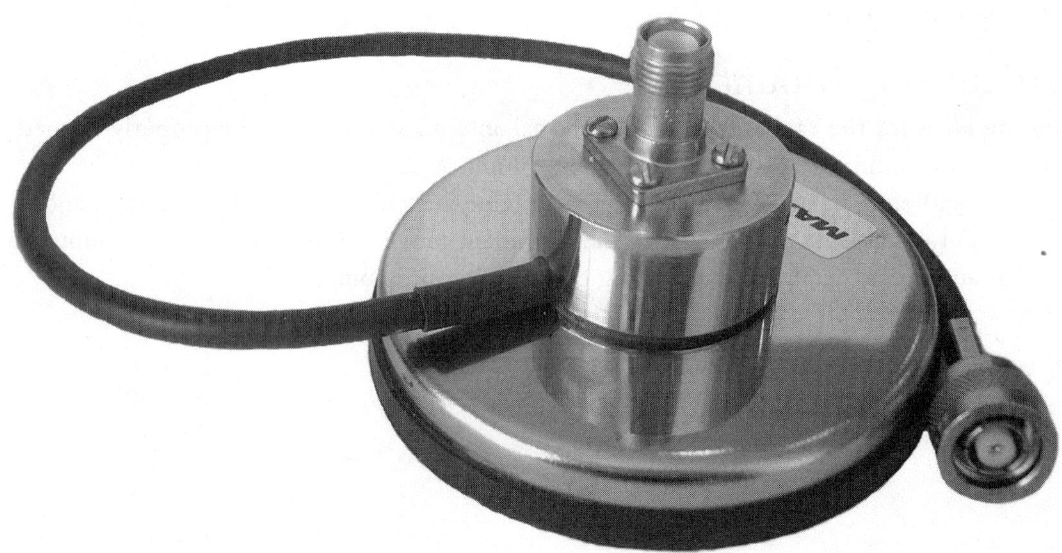

Lightning Arrestor with Grounding Ring

Lightning protection should cover exterior equipment and interior equipment. Costs involved include not only the equipment or protection itself but also the indirect legal and business costs incurred for not having the protection. Exterior antennas are protected by installing them in areas less likely to be hit by lightning or in areas that have lighting rods. Additional protection such as the Cisco lightning arrestor with grounding ring, as shown in Figure 3.61, protects interior equipment from nearby (not direct) lightning strikes.

The lightning arrestor is an inline device that connects to the coaxial cable between the antenna and the Cisco wireless device. It has a 50 ohm transmission line and a gas discharge tube that grounds in approximately 100 nanoseconds when experiencing an electrical surge. It protects against transient spikes of up to 5,000 amps, ensuring that the surge to the equipment connected to the line is limited to a maximum of 50 volts.

To install, first disconnect or power off any powered components connected to the coaxial cable. Install it indoors, as close to the bulkhead as possible or in a protected area outside. Connect the lightning arrestor to an earth ground (usually an 8-foot copper or steel rod, placed 6 or 7 feet into the ground). Administrators should make this connection with the ground lug attached to the lightning arrestor and with at least a #6 copper wire. Verify the connections are sound, then power on or connect the equipment.

Figure 3.61 Lightning Arrestor with Grounding Ring

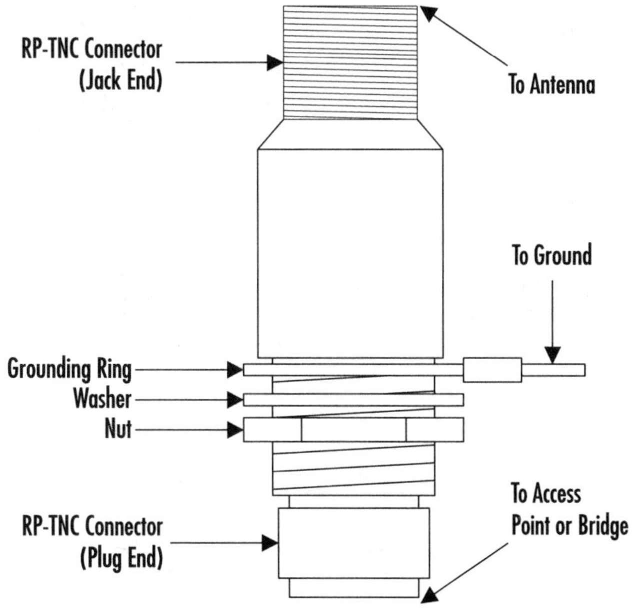

Bridge and AP Accessories

Cisco provides several types of accessories that can enhance the ability of its APs and wireless bridges to operate in a variety of environments. These include mounting kits, power supplies, and serial configuration cables. Location is important and can affect the performance of the Cisco wireless device. When installing the AP or bridge, be sure to choose a location that is free from large metal structures (such as filing cabinets or shelving), microwave ovens, and 2.4 GHz cordless phones that could interfere with the performance of the AP or bridge. Spare power supplies can help minimize the downtime of a wireless system. The AP or bridge serial cable allows for the configuration of the AP even when the network to it is unavailable.

Bridge Mounting Kit

An AP or bridge can be mounted several different ways. The easiest method is to simply put a couple of screws into either a plywood backboard or drywall and attaching the AP or bridge to them. The necessary mounting hardware can be obtained from Cisco, as well as print out templates to mark where the screw holes need to be made. For more information, see: www.cisco.com/en/US/products/hw/wireless/ps469/prod_installation_guide09186a008007f8fe.html.

AP/Bridge Spare Power Supplies

One of the easiest and most inexpensive spare components to keep in inventory is a spare power supply for an AP or bridge. Having such a spare can mean the difference between a minor short-term outage and a long-term outage that has a major impact on a business.

The 350 series bridge and AP have another option: the inline power injector, as shown in Figure 3.62. The power injector is connected to both the AP or bridge via a standard Category 5 UTP cable which carries the power needed to run the AP or bridge. The power injector supplies this power by utilizing the unused pairs in the Cat5 cable. Specifically, the negative current is sent on the cables on pins 4 and 5, and the positive is sent on the cables on pins 7 and 8.

The 350 series products can also obtain their power from a Catalyst 3524-PWR-XL switch or an inline power patch panel. These solutions send the power via the Cat5 UTP cable.

Figure 3.62 In-Line Power Injector

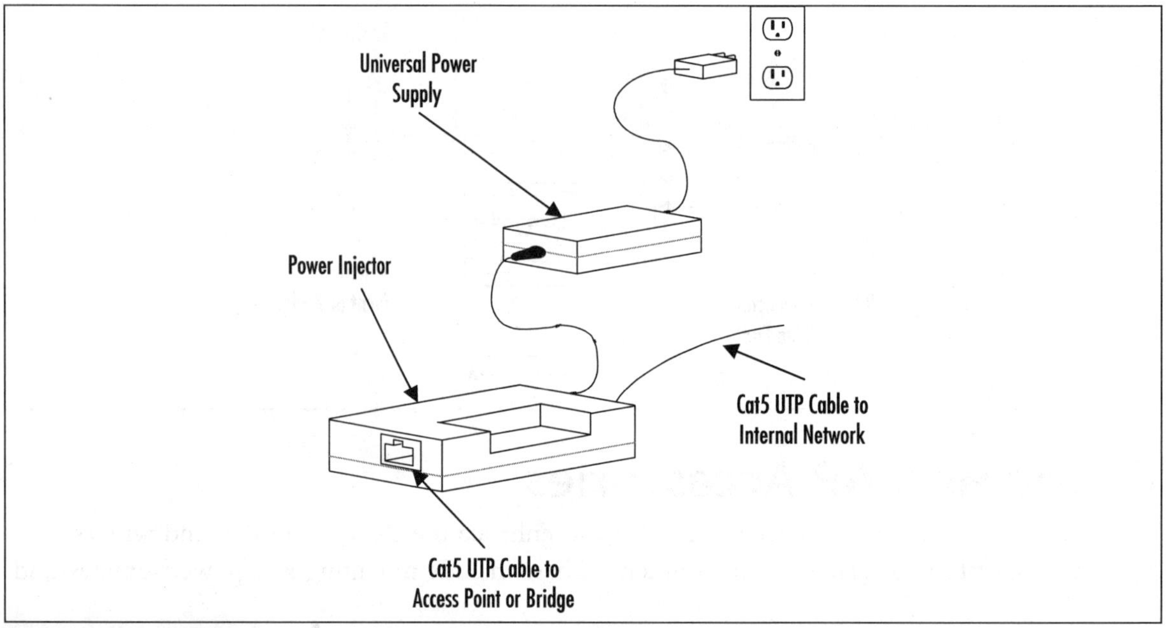

AP/Bridge Serial Cable

This cable is a straight-through cable that has a male DB-9 connector on one end and a female DB-9 connector on the other. The male end of the cable is connected to the AP or bridge and the female end is connected to a serial port on a PC. The communication settings are 9,600 bits per second, 8 data bits, no parity, 1 stop bit, and Xon/Xoff. Table 3.17 shows the standard pinout and function of a PC serial port.

Table 3.17 DB-9 Pinouts and Signal Description from PC's (DTE) Perspective

Pin Number	Use Description	Signal Direction	
1	DCD	Carrier detect	AP/bridge to PC
2	RXD	Receive data	AP/bridge to PC
3	TXD	Transmit data	PC to AP/bridge
4	DTR	Data terminal ready	PC to AP/bridge
5	GND	Ground	NA
6	DSR	Data set ready	AP/bridge to PC
7	RTS	Request to send	PC to AP/bridge
8	CTS	Clear to send	AP/bridge to PC
9	RI	Ring indicator	AP/bridge to PC

NEMA Enclosures

If a Cisco wireless device will be exposed to wide ranges of temperatures or inclement weather, a *NEMA enclosure* may be needed. NEMA enclosures are typically watertight boxes used to mount equipment outside to protect it from the elements. NEMA enclosures are available that are heated and/or cooled, and conform to NEMA guidelines. Specification 250-1997 describes the applications and features available specifically for enclosures (with a power rating under 1,000 volts) available at www.nema.org. This document divides enclosures into different types according to the type of protection they are designed to provide, as shown in Table 3.18. Cisco does not make NEMA enclosures; they must be obtained from a third party supplier such as Anixter (www.anixter.com).

Table 3.18 NEMA Enclosure Classifications

Enclosure Type	Location	Indoor/Outdoor	General Use/Comments
1	Non-hazardous	Indoor	Provides a degree of protection against contact with enclosed equipment.
2	Non-hazardous	Indoor	Provides some protection from small amounts of falling water and dirt.
3	Non-hazardous	Outdoor	Provides protection against windblown dust, rain, sleet, and external ice formation.

Continued

Table 3.18 NEMA Enclosure Classifications

Enclosure Type	Location	Indoor/Outdoor	General Use/Comments
3R	Non-hazardous	Outdoor	Provides protection against falling rain, sleet, and external ice formation.
3S	Non-hazardous	Outdoor	Provides protection against windblown dust, rain, sleet, and operation of the external components of the enclosure when ice-laden.
4	Non-hazardous	Either	Provides protection against windblown dust rain, and splashing or hose-directed water.
4X	Non-hazardous	Either	Provides protection against windblown dust, rain, and splashing or hose-directed water; corrosion-resistant.
5	Non-hazardous	Indoor	Provides protection from settling dust, falling dirt, and dripping (noncorrosive) liquids.
6	Non-hazardous	Either	Provides protection against the entry of water during temporary submersion in water at a limited depth.
6P	Non-hazardous	Either	Provides protection against the entry of water during prolonged submersion in water at a limited depth.
7	Hazardous	Indoor	For use in locations classified as a Class I (Groups A, B, C, D) as defined in the National Electrical Code. Will contain internal explosion without causing an external hazard.
8	Hazardous	Either	For use in locations classified as a Class I (Groups A, B, C, D) as defined in the National Electrical Code. Will prevent combustion through the use of oil-immersed equipment.
9	Hazardous	Indoor	For use in locations classified as a Class II (Groups E, F, G) as defined in the National Electrical Code. Will prevent the ignition of combustible dust.
10	Hazardous	Either	Meet applicable requirements of the Mine Safety and Health Administration. Will contain internal explosion without causing an external hazard.
11	Non-hazardous	Indoor	Provides protection, by oil immersion, from the corrosive effects of liquids and gases
12	Non-hazardous	Indoor	Provides some protection from settling dust, falling dirt, and dripping (noncorrosive) liquids.

Continued

Table 3.18 NEMA Enclosure Classifications

Enclosure Type	Location	Indoor/Outdoor	General Use/Comments
12K	Non-hazardous	Indoor	Provides protection from settling dust, falling dirt, and dripping (noncorrosive) liquids. 12K enclosures contain knockouts. This protection does not apply to the knockout area.)
13	Non-hazardous	Indoor	Provides protection from dust, and spraying water, oil, and noncorrosive coolant.

Cabling, Connectors, and Bulkhead Extenders

This section discusses items involved in getting the signal to and from the antenna. This communication occurs over cabling and through connectors and bulkheads.

Cabling

Choosing the wrong cabling between the AP and the antenna can mean the difference between the success or failure of a wireless system. This cabling carries both the signals from the AP or bridge to the antenna and from the antenna to the AP or bridge. The cable choices are RG58, RG8, or Belden 9913 (including 9913F). Distance is the prime determinant of what cable to use.

Connectors

Along with the cabling, one of the items that can have the largest impact on the quality of the signal that the bridge or AP receives is the connector that is used. Connectors are used to interface the cabling with the AP or bridge as well as the antenna or bulkhead. As previously discussed, the primary type of cabling used to connect the AP or bridge to the antenna is coaxial. Some of the more popular types of coaxial conductors are BNC, F, N, and TNC.

RP-TNC Connectors

Cisco APs, bridges, and accessories primarily use the RP-TNC connector, as shown in Figure 3.63. The design of the RP-TNC connector looks exactly like a TNC connector because it was based on the TNC design. The TNC connector was first made in the 1950s as an improvement upon the Bayonet-Neill-Concelman (BNC) connector. The threaded TNC connector allows for a consistent fit that will not be easily compromised by movement or vibration. The RP-TNC connector can handle frequencies up 11 GHz, well within the range used by Cisco wireless devices. In a RP-TNC connector, the female contact is in the plug connector and the male connector is in the jack.

Figure 3.63 RP-TNC Connectors (Jack on the Left, Plug on the Right)

Bulkhead Extenders

Bulkhead extenders are cables that have a standard connector, such as an RP-TNC on one end and a bulkhead connector on the other. A bulkhead is nothing more than a mounting style of connector inserted through a pre-made panel or precut hole and secured by a nut screwed onto the end of the connector. Bulkhead extenders can be used to easily move a bulkhead connector to another location. This methodology allows for a watertight seal around the cable that can easily be relocated if necessary. The main bulkhead extender that Cisco sells for use with its APs and bridges is a 60-inch extender, as shown in Figure 3.64. This bulkhead extender is made from RG-58 cable with RP-TNC connectors. The jack side of the RP-TNC connector has the bulkhead connector on it.

Figure 3.64 60-Inch Bulkhead Extender

There is an excellent resource maintained by Cisco at www.cisco.com/en/US/partner/products/hw/wireless/ps469/index.html, which provides more information on the various accessories available for supplementing core wireless components.

Summary

This chapter provided a comprehensive overview of wireless networking. Radio technologies that made wireless networking a reality were the beginning. Were it not for the efforts of a certain Austrian actress and other radio pioneers, wireless networking would not have come about. Standards developed by the 802.11 committee have made great strides in ensuring that diverse devices can interoperate.

Cisco provides a number of wireless networking products, from wireless APs that enable clients to function, to wireless bridges that connect networks over great distances. Cisco strives to provide a standard method of networking wireless via consistent interfaces for configuration and monitoring. Menus, commands, and Web interfaces can be used to configure any Cisco wireless network device.

Cisco wireless AP and bridges have fairly large coverage areas. Coverage can be expanded with the use optional antennas, which can also compensate for obstructions and distance that would otherwise degrade wireless rates. This chapter provided an overview of the various antenna types, and their appropriate use.

Security in initial wireless network deployments was limited at best, and nonexistent at worst. Advances such as EAP and 802.11x have done much to improve the security lot of wireless networks. Almost all Cisco wireless products support these new security mechanisms, as were illustrated in this chapter.

While this chapter provided a wealth of information about wireless networking in general, and Cisco wireless products specifically, the technology is advancing at a rapid clip. It is a good idea to keep up on the technology to ensure that your wireless networks have the latest in security, features, and other options that enable you to maximize your return on investment.

Chapter 4

IP Addressing, Multicasting, and IPv6

Best Damn Topics in this Chapter:

- IPv4 Addressing and Header Formats
- Strategies to Conserve Addresses
- RFC1918 – Private Network Addresses
- The Fundamentals of Subnetting
- Multicast Addresses and Protocols
- Participating in Multicasting
- Distribution Trees
- Multicast Routing
- Network Address Translation
- NAT Architectures
- TCP Load Distribution
- NAT Monitoring and Troubleshooting Commands
- Considerations about NAT and PAT
- IP Version 6
- IPv6 Addresses
- IPv6 Headers
- IPv6 Security
- Upper Layer Protocol Issues
- Understanding ICMPv6
- Configuring IPv6 Addressing

Introduction

In the 1970s, Internet Protocol (IP) was developed as part of the Transmission Control Protocol (TCP)/IP effort to provide logically addressed and structured networking. Since then, IP has matured greatly, and can convey a wide array of information and services. The primary role of IP is to provide logical addresses, and to support the routing of traffic to its destination. Recent efforts to expand the capacity of IP addresses (which are nearly exhausted) have resulted in the next generation of the protocol, IP version 6 (IPv6). IP supports the ability to send to a group via multicasting. These topics are covered in this chapter, starting with IP version 4 (IPv4).

IP provides the network layer addressing and functions for the TCP/IP protocol stack, as shown in Figure 4.1. The TCP/IP protocol stack does not map neatly to the Open Systems Interconnect (OSI) model, as the OSI model was developed after TCP/IP.

Figure 4.1 TCP/IP Protocol Stack

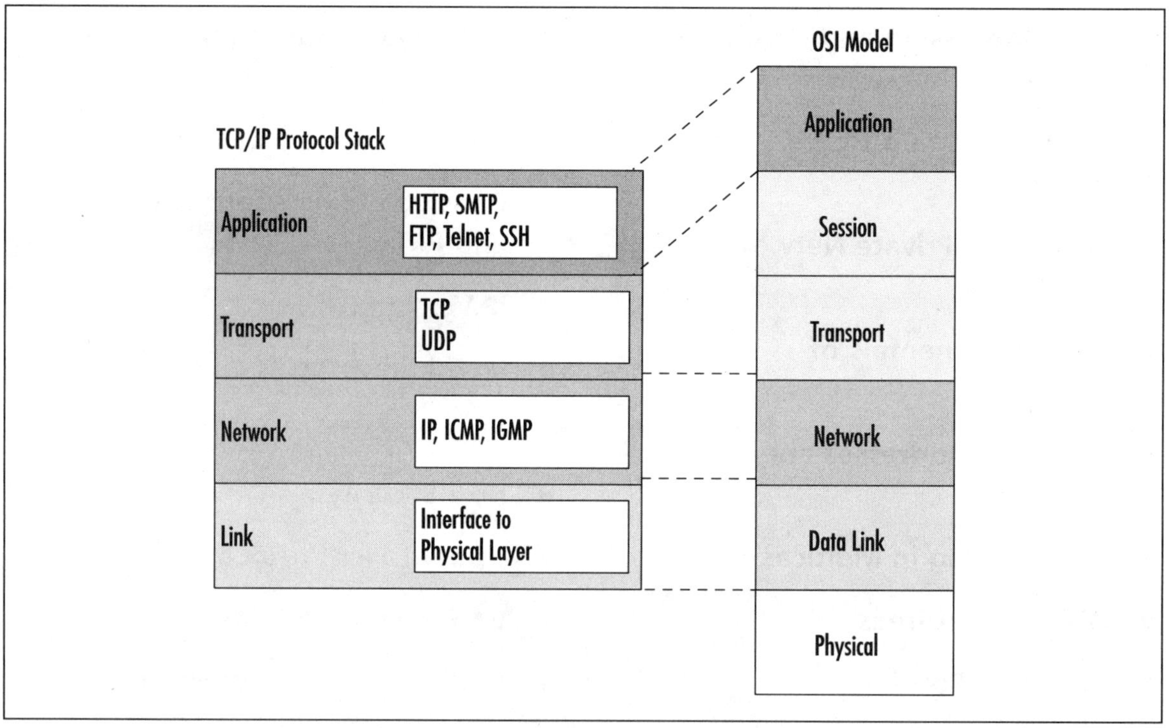

IPv4 has structure and processes developed around its address space. Information is transported in IP packets, of which the header remains consistent in terms of size and fields.

IPv4 Address and Header Format

IP is responsible for addressing and delivery by providing a logical address scheme. "Original" IP (referred to as IPv4) consists of 32 bits spread over four 8-bit octets, expressed in "dotted decimal" format. For example, a 32-bit address may look like this in binary:

```
00001010000001011000011000001101
```

To improve readability, the 32-bit IP address splits into four blocks of 8 bits like this:

```
00001010    00001011    00001100    00001101
```

Finally, each 8-bit block is converted to decimal and the decimal values are separated with periods or "dots." The converted IPv4 address, expressed as a dotted decimal address, is:

```
10.11.12.13
```

It is much easier to remember an IP address of 10.11.12.13 than to remember a string of bits such as 00001010000010110000110000001101. IP addresses and their values and uses are discussed in detail later in this chapter.

All information transported over IP is carried in IP packets with the format shown in Figure 4.2. The header length can vary somewhat depending on whether the options field is present and the number of bits that are used to specify these options. This variation in length adds to the processing burden, as predictability and consistency are not achieved.

Figure 4.2 The IPv4 Header

bits	
4	Version
4	Header Length
8	Type of Service
16	Total Length
16	Identification
3	Flags
13	Fragment Offset
8	Time to Live
8	Protocol
16	Header Checksum
32	Source Address
32	Destination Address
0 - 40	Options
variable	Data

- **Version** 4-bit field. Identifies the version of the IP (4 or 6). Makes IPv6 backward-compatible with IPv4.
- **Header Length** 4-bit field. Indicates the length of the header, as the IPv4 header is a variable between 20 and 64 bytes.
- **Type of Service (ToS)** Identifies the priority of packet.

- **Total Length** The entire length of the IP portion of the packet. Called payload length in IPv6.
- **Identification, Flags, Fragment Offset** Handles the fragmentation and reassembly of packets. Not necessary in the IPv6 header as they are handled by the source.
- **Time To Live (TTL)** Limits the number of hops the packet is allowed to transit. At each hop, a router decrements this field, and when it reaches zero, the packet is removed from the network.
- **Protocol** Indicates the next protocol (header) following the IPv4 header, such as TCP or User Datagram Protocol (UDP).
- **Header Checksum** Maintains the integrity of the IPv4 header.
- **Source and Destination Address** 32-bit addresses that identify the source and destination for this packet.
- **Options** If enabled, each intermediate node in the path needs to examine it, which can cause inefficient router performance.

Familiarity with the IP address classes, masks, and structure are essential to mastering and using IP. The most fundamental aspect of IP is its addresses.

Classful Addressing - Structure and Size of Each Type

IPv4 addressing assigns a logical address to a physical device. While physical addresses are sufficient for communicating while on the same network, more is necessary for communicating with devices on other networks. The role of a network address such as IP is to address and route traffic between networks.

A 32-bit address is large enough to provide 4,294,967,296 individual addresses. Since all networks are not the same size, the addresses are grouped together for administrative purposes into address classes to ease allocation and control.

IP Address Classes

There are five classes of IP addresses. Only three classes are used to assign unicast addresses to end devices such as routers, workstations, servers, and so on. Table 4.1 shows IP address classes and their starting and ending addresses. The "n's" represent the network number bits in the address, and the "h's" are the locally administered portions of the address.

Table 4.1 IP Address Classes

Class	Format	Starting Address	Ending Address
A	0nnnnnnn hhhhhhhh hhhhhhhh hhhhhhhh	1.0.0.0	127.255.255 255
B	10nnnnnn nnnnnnnn hhhhhhhh hhhhhhhh	128.0.0.0	191.255.255.255
C	110nnnnn nnnnnnnn nnnnnnnn hhhhhhhh	192.0.0.0	233.255.255.255

Continued

Table 4.1 IP Address Classes

Class	Format	Starting Address	Ending Address
D	1110mmmm mmmmmmmm mmmmmmmm mmmmmmmm	224.0.0.0	239.255.255.255
E	1111rrrr rrrrrrr rrrrrrrr rrrrrrrr	240.0.0.0	255.255.255.255

Class A

Class A is the largest grouping of addresses. The first 8 bits indicate the network number. The remaining 24 bits can be modified to represent addresses assigned to "local" devices.

The first bit of a Class A network address is always a zero, which means network numbers begin at 1 and end at 127. Class A IP addresses range from 1.0.0.0 to 127.255.255.255. With a 24-bit locally administered address space, the total number of addresses in a Class A network is 16,777,216. The default mask for Class A addresses is 255.0.0.0.

Class B

The first bits are always 10 in a Class B address. The first 16 bits of a Class B address indicate the network number. The remaining 16 bits represent addresses assigned to "local" hosts. Class B network numbers begin at 128 and end at 191, which is an effective address range of 128.0.0.0 to 191.255.255.255.

The first two dotted decimal numbers are included in the network number because the network number in a Class B address is 16 bits long. The 16-bit locally administered address space allows each Class B network to contain 65,536 addresses. The number of Class B networks available for administration is 16,384. The default mask for Class B addresses is 255.255.0.0.

Class C

The first 24 bits of a Class C address are the network number, leaving 8 host bits. A Class C address is identified by the "110" in the first 3 bits. Class C network numbers begin at 192 and end at 223, creating IP addresses from 192.0.0.0 and 223.255.255.255. The 8-bit locally administered address space allows each Class C network to contain 256 addresses. The number of Class C networks available for administration is 2,097,152. The default mask associated with Class C addresses is 255.255.255.0.

Class D

Class D addresses, ranging from 224.0.0.0 to 239.255.255.255, are used for multicast applications. Unlike broadcasts which are directed to all devices on a network or a unicast address which is destined for a single device, multicast addresses are targeted to a group of devices that run some type of service (such as Open Shortest Path First [OSPF]) or group application (such as video), where the same data needs to go to multiple devices, but not all devices, on a particular network.

Class E

Class E addresses (240.0.0.0 to 255.255.255.255) are "reserved" for special experimental purposes. The only use of Class E addresses to date is the all hosts broadcast, 255.255.255.255.

Class A, B, and C addresses include default masks. It is advantageous to use only the amount of addresses necessary to cover a particular network. For example, it would be wasteful to allocate 500 IP addresses to a network that will never contain more than 12 addressable devices. Various strategies have been developed to more effectively handle IP addresses, including subnetting.

Strategies to Conserve Addresses

Several strategies have been developed and implemented to help the Internet community cope with the exhaustion of IP addresses. These strategies help reduce the load on Internet routers and also help administrators use globally unique IP addresses more efficiently. The following three strategies were mentioned in previous sections, and are discussed in more detail in the following paragraphs:

- Classless Inter-Domain Routing (CIDR)
- Variable-Length Subnet Mask (VLSM)
- Private Addressing

CIDR

CIDR (RFCs 1517, 1518, and 1519) reduces route table sizes as well as IP address waste. Instead of full Class A, B, or C addresses, organizations can be allocated subnet blocks. For example, if a network needed 3,000 addresses, a single Class C network (256 addresses) would be insufficient. However, if a Class B network were assigned (65,536 addresses), 62,000 addresses would be wasted. With CIDR, a block of 4,096 addresses can be allocated—the equivalence of 16 Class C networks. This block of addresses covers the immediate addressing needs, allows room for growth, and uses global addresses efficiently.

VLSM

VLSM conserves IP addresses by tailoring the mask to each subnet. Subnet masks are appropriated to meet the amount of addresses required. The idea is to assign "just the right amount" of addresses to each subnet. Many organizations have point-to-point wide area network (WAN) links. Normally, these links comprise a subnet with only the 2 addresses required. By using a routing protocol that supports VLSM, administrator's can use a block of addresses much more efficiently.

Private Addresses

The most effective strategy for conserving globally unique (public) IP addresses is not using any. If an enterprise network is using TCP/IP protocols but is not communicating with hosts in the global Internet, public IP addresses are not needed. If the internetwork is limited to one organization, the IP addresses need only be unique within that organization. Only networks that interface with public networks such as the Internet need public addresses. Using public addresses on the outside and private addresses for inside networks is very effective. Network Address Translation (NAT) is used to convert those private (inside) addresses to public (outside) addresses.

Public versus Private Address Spaces

The IP requires that each interface on a network have a unique address. If the scope of a network is global, the addresses must be globally unique. Since global uniqueness must be assured, a centralized authority must be responsible for making sure IP address assignments are made correctly and fairly.

To meet the demands of a growing Internet community, the Internet Assigned Numbers Authority (IANA) was replaced by the Internet Corporation for Assigned Names and Numbers (ICANN). If an organization wants to use IP protocols and applications in its network, but is not connecting its network to the global Internet, the IP addresses it uses do not need to be globally unique. A network of this type is called a "private network," and the addresses used are called "private addresses."

RFC 1918 - Private Network Addresses

RFC1918 conserves globally unique IP addresses by providing three blocks of addresses that are never officially allocated to any organization. These blocks can then be used in private networks without fear of duplicating any officially assigned IP addresses in other organizations.

The Three Address Blocks

RFC1918 designates three ranges of IP addresses as private:

- 10.0.0.0 through 10.255.255.255
- 172.16.0.0 through .31.255.255
- 192.168.0.0 through 192.168.255.255

Table 4.2 summarizes the private address blocks defined by RFC1918. Notice the CIDR shorthand for the mask.

Table 4.2 Private IP Address Blocks

Address Block	Classful Equivalent	Prefix Length	Number of Addresses
10.0.0.0–10.255.255.255	1 Class A 256 Class B 65,536 Class C	/8	16,777,216
172.16.0.0–172.31.255.255	16 Class B 4,096 Class C	/12	1,048,576
192.168.0.0–192.168.255.255	1 Class B 256 Class C	/16	65,536

Considerations

The address blocks in Table 4.2 can be used in any network at any time. However, devices using these addresses will not be able to communicate with other hosts on the Internet without some kind of address translation. Some benefits of using private addresses are:

- **Number of Addresses** There are plenty of addresses for most internal networking needs.
- **Security** Private addresses are not routable on the Internet. The translation from private to public addresses further obscures internal network information.
- **Renumbering** If using NAT, no readdressing of privately addressed networks is necessary in order to access public networks.
- **Networks** Treating private addresses as public addresses when allocating ensures that efficiency and design are maximized.

The Fundamentals of Subnetting

Subnetting allows administrators to apportion IP addresses for more efficient use. For example, if an administrator has a Class B address and they assign it "as is" to a network of 10 devices, the waste of address space is incredible. However, if that address is divided so that only 10 addresses are used from it, an administrator can address a small network and retain the remaining addresses for their other networks. The process of using a subnet mask is described in RFC950.

What the Mask Does

Masks (which are 32 bits) indicate the range of addresses in use on a particular network. Masks identify the network, subnet, and host bits in an address. The subnet mask is used to interpret addresses to determine how they are subnetted.

Assume that 172.31.0.0 is a Class B network address, which means that the first 16 bits of the address are the network number. Using the mask assigned to this network, it can be determined that a certain device is on the 172.31.240.0 subnet. Each class has a "default" or natural mask associated with it.

```
Class A 255.0.0.0
Class B 255.255.0.0
Class C 255.255.255.0
```

The default or "natural mask" for the Class A address is 255.0.0.0. In this case, the mask indicates that the first 8 bits represent the network number and must be used when evaluating a Class A address for subnetting. If a device has a Class A address assigned with the natural mask 255.0.0.0, there is no subnetting in that network. If a device has a Class A address and a mask that is not 255.0.0.0, the network has been subnetted and the device is in a subnet of the Class A network.

Subnet Mask Components

A mask is a 32-bit binary number that is expressed in dotted decimal notation. By default, a mask contains two fields, the network field and the host field. These correspond to the network number and the locally administered part of the network address. When an administrator subnets, they are adjusting the way they view the IP address.

In the following example, the network is indicated by the first two 255 entries (16 bits) and the host field is indicated by the ending 0.0 (last 16 bits).

```
172.31.88.250 255.255.0.0
```

The network number is 172.31 and the host number is 88.250. In other words, the first 16 bits are the network number and the remaining 16 bits are the host number.

Subnetting converts the address hierarchy from the network and the host to the network, subnet and host. Subnetting the 172.31.0.0 network with a mask of 255.255.255.0 adds more information: the subnet bits. As with the previous example, the 172.31 is still the network number. With a mask of 255.255.255.0, the third octet is used to indicate where the subnet number is located. The subnet number is .88 and, finally, the host number is 250.

```
255.255.255.0 for a Class B network

255          255        255        0

11111111     11111111   11111111   00000000

Network      Network    Subnet     Host
```

The locally administered portion of the network address can be subdivided into subnetworks using the mask to identify the subnet bits. A certain number of bits are allocated to the subnet field and the remainder becomes the new host field.

Binary Determination of Mask Values

The first task in subnetting is determining how many networks containing how many hosts per network are needed. This information helps administrators divide and assign addresses efficiently. Addressing should be settled in the design phase; however, it can be done on any network that needs address optimization. Once this is complete, the next task is determining the right address and mask combinations that will achieve the addressing goals.

Decimal Equivalent Mask Values

Tables 4.3, 4.4, and 4.5 show the possible subnet masks that can be used in Class A, Class B, and Class C networks. These tables are useful for quickly determining the amount of hosts per subnet that would be achieved with a particular mask.

Table 4.3 Class A Subnet Table

Subnets	Hosts	Mask	Subnet Bits	Host Bits
2	8,388,606	255.128.0.0	1	23
4	4,194,302	255.192.0.0	2	22
8	2,097,150	255.224.0.0	3	21
16	1,048,574	255.240.0.0	4	20
32	524,286	255.248.0.0	5	19
64	262,142	255.252.0.0	6	18
128	131,070	255.254.0.0	7	17
256	65,534	255.255.0.0	8	16
512	32,766	255.255.128.0	9	15
1,024	16,382	255.255.192.0	10	14
2,048	8,190	255.255.224.0	11	13
4,096	4,094	255.255.240.0	12	12
8,192	2,046	255.255.248.0	13	11
16,384	1,022	255.255.252.0	14	10
32,768	510	255.255.254.0	15	9
65,536	254	255.255.255.0	16	8
131,072	126	255.255.255.128	17	7
262,144	62	255.255.255.192	18	6
524,288	30	255.255.255.224	19	5
1,048,576	14	255.255.255.240	20	4
2,097,152	6	255.255.255.248	21	3
4,194,304	2	255.255.255.252	22	2

Table 4.4 Class B Subnet Table

Subnets	Hosts	Mask	Subnet Bits	Host Bits
2	32,766	255.255.128.0	1	15
4	16,382	255.255.192.0	2	14
8	8,190	255.255.224.0	3	13
16	4,094	255.255.240.0	4	12
32	2,046	255.255.248.0	5	11
64	1,022	255.255.252.0	6	10
128	510	255.255.254.0	7	9
256	254	255.255.255.0	8	8
512	126	255.255.255.128	9	7
1,024	62	255.255.255.192	10	6

Continued

Table 4.4 Class B Subnet Table

Subnets	Hosts	Mask	Subnet Bits	Host Bits
2,048	30	255.255.255.224	11	5
4,096	14	255.255.255.240	12	4
8,192	6	255.255.255.248	13	3
16,384	2	255.255.255.252	14	2

Table 4.5 Class C Subnet Table

Subnets	Hosts	Mask	Subnet Bits	Host Bits
2	126	255.255.255.128	1	7
4	62	255.255.255.192	2	6
8	30	255.255.255.224	3	5
16	14	255.255.255.240	4	4
32	6	255.255.255.248	5	3
64	2	255.255.255.252	6	2

These subnet mask tables make it easier to determine which subnet mask to use for any given situation. As the table shows, the number of subnets increases and the number of hosts in each subnet decreases. As the number of subnet bits increases, the number of host bits decreases. Since there are a fixed number of bits to work with in each class of network address, each bit can be used in only one way as specified by the mask. Each bit must be either a subnet bit or a host bit. An increase in the number of subnet bits causes a reduction in the number of host bits, and vice versa.

These tables assume that an administrator has been allocated their initial addresses with respect to the natural masks for the class of the address. For example, 192.168.1.0 would be allocated with a mask of 255.255.255.0 because it is a Class C address. However, it is possible to be allocated a range of addresses that exceed the boundaries of the class. For example, 192.160.0.0 with a mask of 255.255.0.0 provides an administrator with a Class C address with a Class B amount of addresses. In that case, the administrator would have 16 host bits to subnet that they would not normally have. This concept is called "classless addressing," and is revisited later in this chapter.

Addresses and Mask Interaction

An IP address identifies a device on a network. IP addresses are assigned from classes that contain different groups of addresses. Each IP network has a network number. Each IP subnet has the network number of its parent network and a subnet number. The subnet number can be found by locating the subnet field in the subnet mask.

If an administrator has an IP address of 172.31.8.0 with a mask of 255.255.255.0, they know that they have an address in the 172.31.8.0 network. The mask of 255.255.255.0 for this Class B address states that the first two octets (172.31) are network numbers; the third octet (8) is the subnet number, and the fourth octet is for host addresses.

The address and mask combination can be expressed as 172.31.8.0 255.255.255.0 or as 172.31.8.0/24. The latter is classless addressing shorthand, called "prefix-length," which identifies the total number of network and subnet bits used with this address. In our example, the first three octets are used for this purpose, which gives a total of 24 bits so used. When working with subnet masks in a professional environment, the prefix-length format is more common and easier to use. The network 172.31.8.0/24 would read 172 dot 31 dot 8 dot 0 slash 24. For consistency and learning purposes, we will continue to use the longhand format of expressing masks.

In a Class B network, the first 16 bits are the network number. If devices have identical first 16 bits, they are in the same network with a Class B address. When the source network (172.31.8.0) shown here wants to communicate with the destination network (172.31.9.0), the first thing that needs to be determined is if they are on the same network.

```
Source        172.31.8.0    10101010    00011111    00001000    00000000
Destination   172.31.9.0    10101010    00011111    00001001    00000000
```

This determination is made by what mask is associated with these networks. If the natural mask for Class B is used (255.255.0.0), they are on the same network—the first 16 bits match, putting them on the 172.31.0.0 network. However, if they were subnetted and are using a mask such as 255.255.255.0, then these would be two separate networks, in which case, a router is needed in order for the two networks to communicate.

The following example shows how the masks make this distinction. This is a logical mathematical process using a logical AND process. This AND process states that a 1 and 1 equal 1, and any other combinations (0 and 0 and 1 and 0) equal 0. This enables us to determine the true network/subnet numbers.

If using the natural mask for Class B (255.255.0.0), then both of these addresses are on the same network range.

```
Source        172.31.8.0    10101010    00011111    00001000    00000000
      AND     255.255.0.0   11111111    11111111    00000000    00000000
              -------------------------------------------------------------
RESULT        172.31.0.0    10101010    00011111    00000000    00000000

Destination   172.31.9.0    10101010    00011111    00001001    00000000
        AND   255.255.0.0   11111111    11111111    00000000    00000000
              -------------------------------------------------------------
RESULT        172.31.0.0    10101010    00011111    00000000    00000000
```

NOTE

The previous operation shows that 172.31.8.0 and 172.31.9.0 are both on the 172.31.0.0 network.

If a different subnet mask is applied for Class B (255.255.255.0), then both of these addresses are on different networks.

```
Source         172.31.8.0       10101010    00011111    00001000    00000000
    AND        255.255.255.0    11111111    11111111    11111111    00000000
               --------------------------------------------------------------
RESULT         172.31.8.0       10101010    00011111    00001000    00000000

Destination    172.31.9.0       10101010    00011111    00001001    00000000
       AND     255.255.255.0    11111111    11111111    11111111    00000000
               --------------------------------------------------------------
RESULT         172.31.9.0       10101010    00011111    00001001    00000000
```

NOTE

The previous example shows that 172.31.8.0 and 172.31.9.0 are separate networks, and will need routing to communicate.

Reserved and Restricted Addresses

In any subnet, there are certain addresses that cannot be assigned to an individual device because they have a special purpose. The subnet address is the first address in a range and identifies the subnet. The broadcast address is the last address in the range, and all hosts on the subnet receive traffic if anything is sent to it. Assume that a subnet address is 172.31.9.0 with a mask of 255.255.255.0. The subnet address is 172.31.9.0, and the broadcast address is 172.31.9.255. It is important to understand that the mask determines the subnet address and the broadcast address for a particular range. For example, if 255.255.255.128 is used with 172.31.9.0, the subnet address is still 172.31.9.0, but the broadcast address is now 172.31.9.127.

Determining the Range of Addresses within Subnets

Once an administrator determines what mask to use and understands the special subnet address and subnet broadcast address, they can begin the process of determining what assignable addresses are available. They will need to "calculate" which addresses are in each subnet. The following is a structured approach for accomplishing this.

```
IP Address:  172.31.9.0
Mask:         255.255.255.248
Bit Values in a Octet:      128   64   32   16   8   4   2   1
```

Only the fourth octet in the mask (248) is important to our calculations. Convert 248 to binary 11111000. The value of the last bit, 8, is the lowest incrementing value that is used to derive the addresses in this range. Start with 0, add 8 to derive the next IP network, add 8 to that, and so on until you reach 256, which is invalid, meaning the one before it is the true last subnet in the span of addresses. This calculation derives all possible subnets possible with this particular mask.

```
SUBNET
172.31.9.0
172.31.9.8
172.31.9.16
.
.
.
172.31.9.248
172.31.9.256 <- INVALID!
```

To derive the broadcast address, subtract one from the subsequent subnet, as shown.

```
SUBNET                  BROADCAST
172.31.9.0              172.31.9.7   (subtract 1 from 172.31.9.8)
172.31.9.8              172.31.9.15  (subtract 1 from 172.31.9.16)
172.31.9.16             172.31.9.23
.
.
.
172.31.9.248            172.31.9.255
172.31.9.256 <- INVALID!
```

Assignable addresses are between the subnet and broadcast addresses as shown.

```
SUBNET        FIRST ASSIGNABLE  LAST ASSIGNABLE    BROADCAST
172.31.9.0    172.31.9.1        172.31.9.6         172.31.9.7   (subtract 1 from
                                                     172.31.9.8)
172.31.9.8    172.31.9.9        172.31.9.14        172.31.9.15 (subtract 1 from
                                                    172.31.9.16)
172.31.9.16   172.31.9.17       172.31.9.22        172.31.9.23
.
.
.
172.31.9.248 172.31.9.249       172.31.9.254       172.31.9.255
172.31.9.256 <- INVALID!
```

Not only do the subnets increment by the incrementing value (8), but so do the first and last assignable IP addresses and the broadcast addresses. Knowing this can make subnet calculations much easier. Assignable addresses are addresses that can actually be assigned to a network device. The approach shown here is but one of many other ways that can be used to derive the same information.

Determining Subnet Addresses Given a Single Address and Mask

If an administrator has an IP address and a subnet mask, they can determine the subnet where the device is located. Everything between these two numbers represents IP addresses that may be assigned to devices. The following process shows how to derive the subnet number and broadcast address. The address of the device is 172.31.9.2 and the subnet mask is 255.255.255.224.

1. Convert the locally administered portion of the address to binary (in this case, the fourth octet [2]).

   ```
   00000010
   ```

2. Convert the locally administered portion of the mask to binary (in this case, the fourth octet [224] in the mask).

   ```
   11100000
   ```

3. Logically AND binary the numbers created in Steps 1 and 2 to derive the subnet octet.

   ```
   00000010
   11100000
   --------
   00000000  (or 0 in decimal)
   ```

Thus, the subnet of the host with the address 172.31.9.2 and a mask of 255.255.255.224 is 172.31.9.0.

To find the broadcast for this range, subtract 1 from the incrementing value (32) (as discussed previously) and the result is 172.31.9.31.

Strategies for Subnetting

A subnetting strategy should seek to achieve the following goals.

- **Simplicity** Address assignment should be simple and understandable, allowing the administrator to identify the location and function by the address alone.
- **Ease of Administration** Should allow for growth and reduced administrative burdens.
- **Router Efficiency** The routing tables should be kept as small as possible.
- **Documentation** The documentation should be consistent, clear, and with as few exceptions as possible.

Creating and Managing Variable Length Subnets

The process of creating a VLSM subnetting structure requires careful and thoughtful planning. Administrators should perform a network survey that includes the number of required subnets, the number of planned but not deployed subnets, the number of devices currently in each subnet, and the number of planned but not deployed devices in each subnet. A plan should be developed that covers what they currently have and what they will probably have in the future.

Creating a variable length subnet mask addressing design requires the completion of four separate phases. Each phase must be completed before moving to the next phase.

1. **Analyze Subnet Needs** You must know exactly what you have today and what you will need in the future for each subnet. A simple spreadsheet or matrix detailing each subnet will help you determine your needs. Remember to locate and list all networks.
2. **Enumerate Each Subnet and Number of Required Nodes** When the detailed needs survey is completed, the matrix you develop will contain all of the local area networks (LANs) and WANs with the number of hosts in each subnet. The purpose of sorting the matrix is to group subnets together based on the number of hosts in the subnets. Subnets with similar numbers of host addresses will have the same subnet mask.
3. **Determine Mask Size to Use in Each Subnet** Review the previous subnetting exercise to determine which mask and address combinations you need for each of your networks. Ensure that you leave enough room for growth in each subnet specified. If you need 150 devices in a subnet, leave room for 200. If you need 40 devices, leave room for 60. Select a mask that gives you the allocation you need today and may need in the future.
4. **Allocate Addresses Based on Need for Each Subnet** Now it is time to determine which range of addresses will be assigned in each subnet. With fixed-length subnetting, the ranges of addresses are uniform and easily determined; with variable-length mask subnetting, the address ranges are just as important but more difficult to assign. Intimate familiarity with the subnetting process is important.

Determine Addressing Requirements

When you need to develop an IP addressing plan, whether for fixed- or variably subnetted networks, you must start by determining exactly what your needs are. You must be able to determine the proper range of addresses for each network or subnet, and how to derive the correct mask and address combination to support the number of devices you have. Assume that we have been assigned 172.31.0.0 255.255.0.0; in the following sections, we will determine how to derive masks that give us a set number of subnets and a certain number of addresses per subnet.

Review Your Internetwork Design

If this is a newly designed IP network, you will need the design specifications. If the network has been in operation for some time, you can use the "as built" documentation. These specifications should include information such as:

- The number and type of devices on each LAN segment
- An indication of which of those devices need an IP address
- The devices connecting the segments (for example: routers, bridges, and switches)

How Many Subnets do You Need?

As you review your design, identify and list each subnet, noting the number of IP addresses needed in each. Figure 4.3 depicts a sample network layout.

Figure 4.3 Sample Network Layout

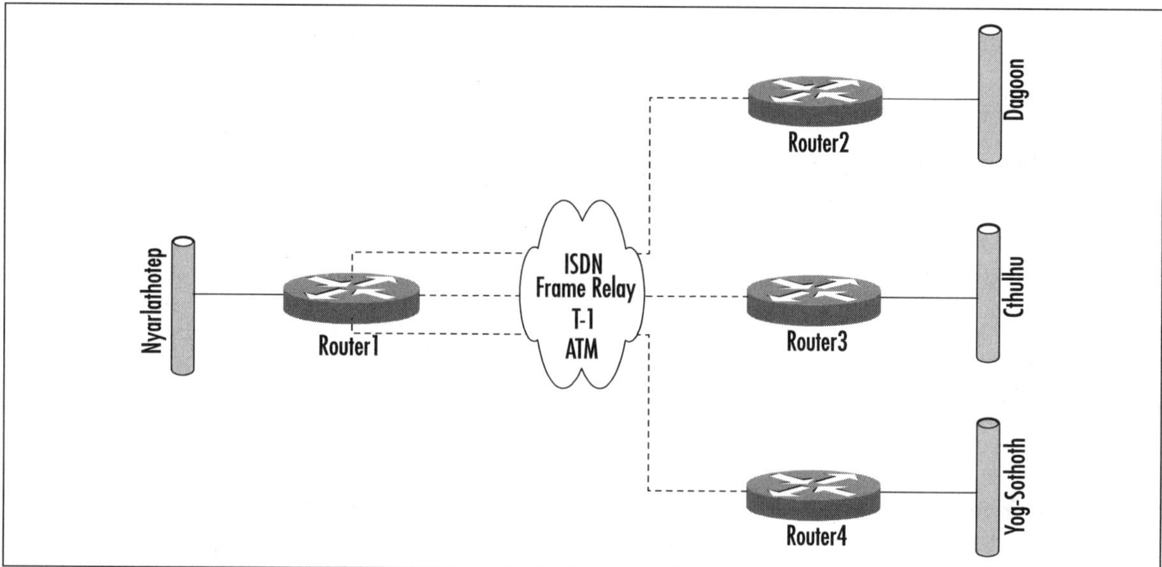

Router1 has four interfaces—one LAN interface and three WAN interfaces, which means it needs 4 IP addresses for four different networks. Router2 has two interfaces—a LAN interface and a WAN interface, and needs two addresses. The same holds for the other two branch office routers. All told, seven subnets are needed.

How Many IP Addresses are Needed in Each Subnet?

We must determine how many addressable hosts will be on each network. Table 4.6 summarizes our addressing needs.

Table 4.6 Devices in the Sample Network

LAN	Devices
Nyarlathotep	60
Dagoon	30
Cthulhu	30
Yog-Sothoth	4
WAN: Router1 to Router2	2
WAN: Router1 to Router3	2
WAN: Router1 to Router4	2

Determining a Mask to Get a Certain Number of Subnets

First we must determine what subnet mask will produce the seven subnets needed in Figure 4.3.

Recall the address 172.31.0.0 255.255.0.0; the first two octets cannot be subnetted; they are fixed and assigned. That leaves the last octets to subnet and modify as needed. We need a minimum of seven subnets.

1. The subnet bit values (from right to left) for the last two octets are:

   ```
   32768  16384  8192  4096  2048  1024  512  256 .128  64  32  16  8  4  2  1
   ```

2. Turn on the bits that will give you seven subnets.

   ```
   0  0  0  0  0  0  0.0  0  0  0  0  1  1  1 = 7
   ```

3. Flip the bits:

   ```
   1  1  1  0  0  0  0  0.  0  0  0  0  0  0  0  0
   ```

4. Flipping turns the last two octets into:

   ```
   224.0
   ```

5. This results in a mask of:

   ```
   255.255.224.0
   ```

   The incrementing value is the last turned-on lowest bit value in the third octet (224), which is 32. We will use that to derive the seven subnets, starting with 0.

   ```
   172.31.0.0
   172.31.32.0
   172.31.64.0
   172.31.96.0
   172.31.128.0
   172.31.160.0
   172.31.192.0
   172.31.224.0
   172.31.256.0 ▪ INVALID!
   ```

Notice that we end up with eight subnets, and that each subnet has 8,190 assignable addresses, which is far more than we need. This also means that we can use a portion of one subnet for our needs, as illustrated in the following. We will use 172.31.0.0 255.255.224.0, as its 8, 190 available addresses more than satisfies our needs.

Determining a Mask to Get a Certain Number of Addresses per Subnet

Recall that we need two subnets with 30 hosts, one subnet with 60 hosts, and one subnet with four hosts. Additionally, we have three point-to-point WAN links interconnecting the routers that need two addresses for each router interface on the link. The process is somewhat similar to what was used previously.

Recall the address 172.31.0.0 255.255.244.0; the first two octets plus the first 3 bits of the third octet cannot be subnetted; they are fixed and assigned as per our previous calculations. It is important to understand that this is an imaginary fixation: we could actually use 172.31.0.0 255.255.0.0 as our starting point. However, for the sake of consistency and education, we will respect the results of our previous efforts. The best rule of thumb is to take care of the largest address needs first, then work down to the smallest; in this case, we need to take care of the 60 address subnets first, and work downwards to the two address WAN subnets.

1. The available subnet bit values (from right to left) for the last 5 bits of the third octet and the entire fourth octet are:

```
4096    2048    1024    512    256 .128    64    32    16    8    4    2    1
```

2. Turn on the bits that would give us 60 addresses (the following gives us 63 addresses total, subtract 1 for the broadcast, which leaves 62):

```
0  0  0  0  0  0  0  0.0  0  1  1  1  1  1  1 = 63
```

3. Invert the bits (do not flip as we previously did):

```
1  1  1  1  1  1  1  1.  1  1  0  0  0  0  0  0
```

4. Inverting turns the last two octets into:

```
255.192
```

5. This results in a mask of:

```
255.255.255.192
```

The incrementing value is the last turned-on lowest bit value in the fourth octet (192), which is 64. This gives us a total of four subnets each containing 62 assignable addresses. We will use the first (172.31.0.0 255.255.255.192) to satisfy our 60-host subnet requirement.

```
172.31.0.0
172.31.0.64
172.31.0.128
172.31.0.192
172.31.0.256 <- INVALID!
```

We will next subnet 172.31.0.64 255.255.255.192 to satisfy our requirement for two 30-host subnets.

1. Your available subnet bits in the last five bits of the fourth octet are:

```
32    16    8    4    2    1
```

2. Turn on the bits that would give us 60 addresses (the following gives us 31 addresses total, subtract 1 for the broadcast, which leaves us with 30, which is what we want):

```
0  0  0  1  1  1  1  1 = 31
```

3. Invert the bits:

```
1 1 1 0 0 0 0 0
```

4. Inverting turns the last octet into:

```
224
```

5. This results in a mask of:

```
255.255.255.224
```

The incrementing value is the last turned-on lowest bit value in the fourth octet (192), which is 32. This gives us a total of two subnets each containing 30 assignable addresses. Apply this to 172.31.0.64 255.255.255.192) to satisfy our 30-host subnet requirement. You must use the mask of 255.255.255.224 for these two subnets.

```
172.31.0.64 <- First 30-host subnet.
172.31.0.96 <- Second 30-host subnet.
172.31.0.128 <- STOP! Overlaps and exceeds boundaries we set earlier.
```

We will next subnet 172.31.0.128 255.255.255.192 to satisfy our requirement for a 4-host network.

1. The available subnet bit are the last 5 bits of the fourth octet are:

```
32    16    8    4    2    1
```

2. Turn on the bits that would give us 4 addresses (the following gives us 7 addresses total; subtract 1 for the broadcast, which leaves us with 6):

```
0 0 0 0 0 1 1 1 = 7
```

3. Invert the bits:

```
1 1 1 1 1 0 0 0
```

4. Inverting turns the last octet into:

```
248
```

5. This results in a mask of:

```
255.255.255.248
```

The incrementing value is the last turned-on lowest bit value in the fourth octet (248), which is 8. This gives us a total of eight subnets each containing 6 assignable addresses. Apply this to 172.31.0.128 255.255.255.192) to satisfy our 30-host subnet requirement. You must use the mask of 255.255.255.248 for these two subnets.

```
172.31.0.128 <- First 6-host subnet.
172.31.0.136
```

```
172.31.0.144
172.31.0.152
172.31.0.160
172.31.0.168
172.31.0.176
172.31.0.184
172.31.0.192 <- STOP! Overlaps and exceeds boundaries we set earlier.
```

Finally, we need to determine what mask will support the three 2-address WAN links. In the interest of consistency and address allocation control, we will use 172.31.0.136 255.255.255.248, and if that is not enough, we will also use 172.31.0.144 and 172.31.0.152, both with a mask of 255.255.255.248.

1. The available subnet bits are the last 3 bits of the fourth octet:

   ```
   4  2  1
   ```

2. Turn on the bits that would give us 2 addresses (the following gives us 3 addresses total, subtract 1 for the broadcast, which leaves us with 2):

   ```
   0  0  0  0  0  0  1  1 = 7
   ```

3. Invert the bits:

   ```
   1  1  1  1  1  1  0  0
   ```

4. Inverting turns the last octet into:

   ```
   252
   ```

5. This results in a mask of:

   ```
   255.255.255.252
   ```

   The incrementing value is the last turned-on lowest bit value in the fourth octet (252), which is 4. This gives us a total of three subnets, each containing 2 assignable addresses. Apply this to 172.31.0.136 255.255.255.248) to satisfy our 30-host subnet requirement. You must use the mask of 255.255.255.252 for these two subnets.

   ```
   172.31.0.136 <- First 2-host subnet address for WAN.
   172.31.0.140 <- Second 2-host subnet address for WAN.
   172.31.0.144 <- Third 2-host subnet address for WAN.
   172.31.0.148
   172.31.0.152 <- STOP! Overlaps and exceeds boundaries we set earlier.
   ```

Table 4.7 shows the results of our calculation efforts and the subnet addresses and masks to be used on each network and WAN link.

Table 4.7 Subnet Addresses and Masks

LAN	Devices	Subnet Address and Mask
Nyarlathotep	60 devices	172.31.0.0 255.255.255.192
Dagoon	30	172.31.0.64 255.255.255.224
Cthulhu	30	172.31.0.96 255.255.255.224
Yog-Sothoth	4	172.31.0.128 255.255.255.248
WAN: Router1 to Router2	2	172.31.0.136 255.255.255.252
WAN: Router1 to Router3	2	172.31.0.140 255.255.255.252
WAN: Router1 to Router4	2	172.31.0.144 255.255.255.252

Notice how our careful calculations and methodical approach have left us plenty of room for growth, as well as minimized IP address waste. We still have 172.31.0.148 through 172.31.255.255 at our disposal for future address allocation.

You can use a few techniques to save addresses or increase the number available to you as described next.

- **Use Unnumbered Interfaces** Configure an interface to use the IP address of another interface.
- **Ask for a Bigger Block of Addresses** This is difficult with the limited amount of available public IP addresses.
- **Private Addresses** Use private addresses for all internal networks, and reserve your public addresses for interfaces that connect to the outside world.
- **Use Subnet Zero** Subnet zero permits you to use IP addresses which contain an 0 value octet such as 172.31.0.1.

Document Your Addresses

Quite a bit of time so far has been spent working out the details of this project. A small additional investment of time can yield big dividends down the road. Document your addresses and how you have allocated them within your network. Spreadsheets, databases, and visual diagrams can be used to accomplish this. Whatever method you use should allow you to track and control how your addresses are deployed throughout your network.

Multicast Addresses and Protocols

With the continuously expanding use of networks, more and more people are deciding that one-to-one networking is not enough anymore. The need to have one to many networks has become more important. This is true for large corporations who benefit from e-mail, file sharing, and mirrored servers in two different cities (or countries). New technologies are developed every day.

Multicasting can reduce travel expenses while maximizing benefits. Imagine the cost of sending several employees half-way around the world for a conference that lasts less than a day. Not only would you incur the cost of travel, but also the cost of the employees' time as they travel.

A better solution in this case would be to videoconference, which allows viewing a presentation in one window while watching the speaker in another. Questions can be typed while the presentation is in progress, and prioritized for answering at the end of the conference. These are just a few of the features that can be provided by multicasting. Other benefits can include interactive distance learning and corporate announcement transmissions.

Multicasting benefits are not limited to video/audio needs. Multicast can be used to push updates to multiple hosts simultaneously, thus reducing the effort and time involved in doing one update at a time. Multicasting can push computer operating system images to their hosts.

The possibilities seem endless and are rapidly growing. The following sections cover the basics of multicasting and its communication methods. We also discuss the use of bandwidth and how Cisco has developed strategies to prevent bandwidth-intensive applications from curtailing network operations.

- Understanding the Basics of Multicasting
- Multicast IP Addressing
- Participating in Multicasting
- Distribution Trees
- Multicast Routing

Understanding the Basics of Multicasting

Bandwidth utilization is the first thing on our minds when discussing streaming video and other live information feeds to an individual's PC. It is important to understand the differences between unicast, broadcast, and multicast traffic.

Multicasting is UDP-based. While UDP is not a great example of reliability, it makes more sense for multicasting than TCP. For starters, having a multitude of hosts acknowledge receipt of a multicast would be counterproductive. Additionally, UDP has lower overhead, which provides the speed necessary to support the traffic needs of multicasting.

Multicast addresses cannot be used as source addresses for any traffic. While multicast addresses can be associated with particular interfaces on particular devices (such as 224.0.0.5 for OSPF-enabled interfaces on a router), traffic cannot be sourced from a multicast address because it does not identify a specific host; rather, a multicast address identifies a group of hosts sharing the same address.

Multicast addresses are not "assigned" to a device. Rather, a device proceeds to listen for and receive traffic destined to a multicast group that it has joined by some process. For example, routers can join the OSPF multicast group on their network by having OSPF configured, and having interfaces configured to participate in OSPF routing. In this case, it means that the router will receive traffic destined to multicast IP addresses reserved for OSPF routing. Hosts can opt to join a multicast group by having certain applications (such as videoconferencing software) installed and configured.

Unicast Traffic

Unicast is the transmission of data from one host to another, one host at a time. This is a one-to-one session between one host and another, such as a client and server arrangement. Unicasts can be used to support multiple sessions (i.e., multicast) by establishing multiple one-to-one communications to transport the same datastream to multiple hosts. An example of this is seen in Figure 4.4.

Figure 4.4 Unicast Network Video Feed Example

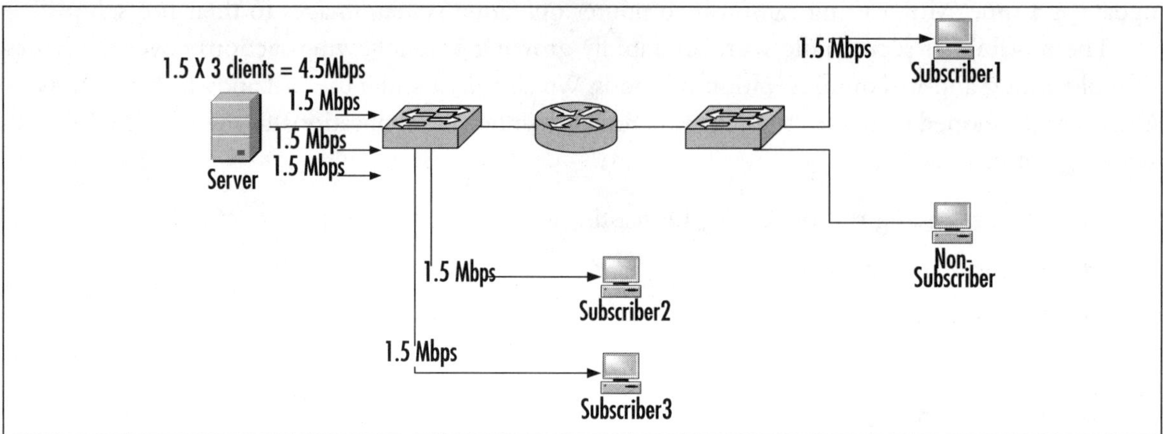

If the session is required by multiple hosts, a one-to-one connection is established, with the same data transmitted repeatedly to each host. This form of transmission will not transmit to every computer on a network; however, multiple requests for the same conference or data would cause that data to be pushed across the network media at the same time. Thus, as seen in Figure 4-4, a video feed of 1.5 Mbps unicasted to 10 computers on a network requires 15 Mbps of bandwidth. While this might not seem significant, it can degrade network performance as the feed size and quantity increase.

The toll of network usage is realized on the network equipment traversed from source to destination for the video feed. All of the routers and switches will have a considerable amount of data traffic to process.

Broadcast Traffic

Broadcast is another option that can be used for transmitting data to a large number of host systems simultaneously. Broadcasts can consume a significant amount of bandwidth; connections are based on a one-to-all method transmission. This can be seen when using the Network Basic Input/Output System (NetBIOS) protocol and Address Resolution Protocol (ARP), as well as many others. Any hosts on a network where a broadcast is generated will process that broadcast (at least far enough to know it is not intended for that system). An example of a broadcast can be seen in Figure 4.5.

Figure 4.5 Broadcast Network Video Feed Example

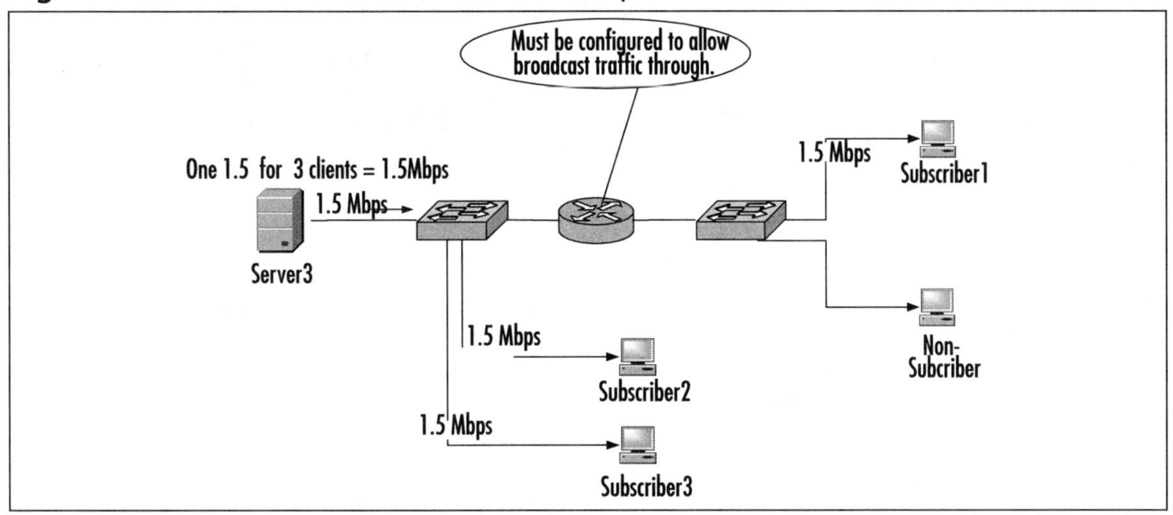

As seen in Figure 4.5, the broadcast traffic is sent to all computer systems that can be reached on the network. This process launches the 1.5 Mbps video stream to all the interfaces possible, thus not creating the intense bandwidth consumption of a unicast.

The problem is that each host receiving the broadcast has to process the 1.5 Mbps datastream continuously until it is finished. If the receiving host does not want the broadcast traffic, valuable resources of the host still accept the datagram and then distinguish what to do with it—accept it or reject it. Because this is also a video feed, this large bit of data needs to be processed, which can take a considerable toll on the host system.

Another disadvantage of using the broadcast transmission for video feeds is the network architecture. On a small network, with no routers, this may be a desirable option. On larger networks, or if there are any routers in the path to a host, the default action is to filter (block) the broadcast, meaning that broadcasts must be explicitly allowed to traverse the path to the host.

Multicast Traffic

Obviously, neither unicast nor broadcast is optimized to handle traffic destined to multiple hosts. Multicasting more than addresses this need. Multicast traffic establishes a one-to-many type of transmission. This allows the data traffic to only be sent to those who specifically requested the information, and only sends one stream of traffic to each requesting broadcast domain. A multicast example is shown in Figure 4.6.

Figure 4.6 Multicasting in Action

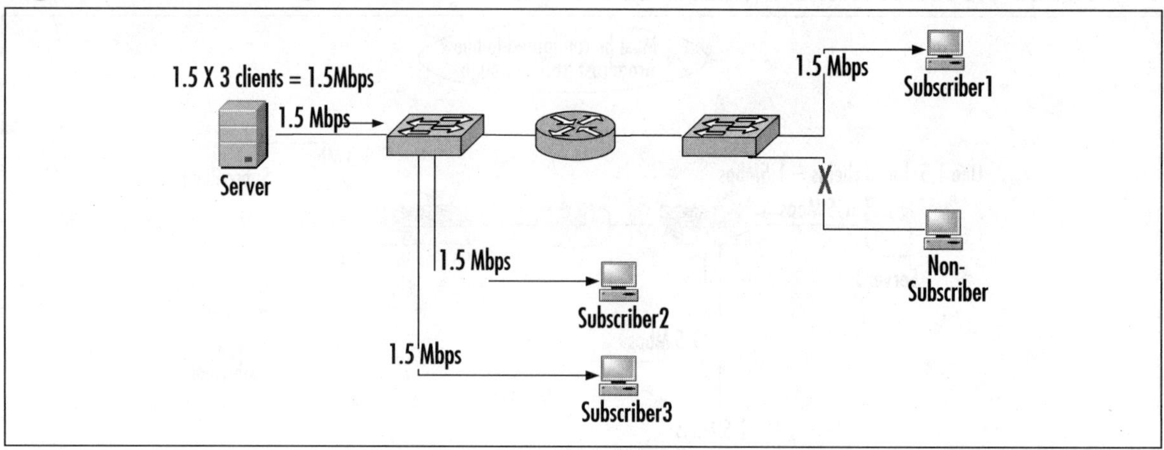

Multicast (RFC1112) is a technology used to address multiple hosts as a group. A source multicasts to a group of hosts by sending an IP packet to a special IP address associated with that group. The IP address that defines a multicast group is a Class D address (224.0.0.0 to 239.255.255.255), with unique groups allocated their own IP address in that range. This allows multiple multicast groups to be defined at the same time with different IP addresses. Multicasting sends the datastream only to the group of hosts that specifically want it. All other hosts ignore and do not process the multicast traffic.

Multicast differs from broadcast because it sends traffic to a group of hosts, not to all hosts on a network. Hosts that are not part of the group will not process the multicast packet because it is not addressed to them.

A typical multicast application is videoconferencing. Not all network users want or need to participate in a videoconference; only those users that need to will join the multicast group to receive the video feed.

The advantage of multicast becomes apparent when you consider that using unicast addresses would result in an individual video feedback to each receiver. More users means more bandwidth used. By using multicast, only one channel is used, independently of the number of users: 1,000 users only require one channel. Multicast traffic is bi-directional: a host can receive or send multicast packets.

Multicast IP Addressing

If only one datastream is being transmitted, how can all of the requesting systems receive the data? Multicasting uses IP addresses to establish multicast groups, which host systems' can join to receive multicast data. The multicast data is sent to the group IP address and all listed group members receive the traffic.

IP Address Designations

Class D IP addresses comprise the whole of multicast addresses, with a range of 224.0.0.0 through 239.255.255.255. Multicast IP addresses are easily recognized by their binary numeration, as their high-end bits are always 1110. For instance 11100000 is equal to 224 and 11101111 is equal to 239. These first 4 bits account for a portion of the IP address; the remaining 28 bits are used for multicast group identification. Two types of multicast IP addresses are used: *dynamic* and *static*.

Transient (dynamic) addresses are used for the duration of the session, and relinquished when no longer needed. Dynamic multicast IP addressing allows applications to acquire an IP address for the length of the multicast transmission. This IP address allocation has a certain expiration time and must be considered by the application requesting the address in order to retain functionality. For example, a transient address is used to multicast a videoconference of an event. After the event is finished, the transient address can be reused. Transient addresses must be coordinated to ensure that two people or organizations do not use the same transient address for different needs.

Static multicast IP addresses are a group of IP addresses, ranging from 224.0.0.0 to 224.255.255.255, that have been specifically assigned by the IANA. The permanent addresses are defined in the protocol itself, such as the all-hosts (224.0.0.1), all-routers (224.0.0.2), or RIPv2 group address (224.0.0.9) addresses. Permanent addresses can also be assigned by the IANA for other protocols or uses. These addresses are reserved for particular purposes and referred to as "well-known" addresses. Table 4.8 shows some of these assigned static IP addresses. For a complete listing of statically assigned Class D IP address, see www.iana.org/assignments/multicast-addresses site.

Table 4. 8 Permanent (Static) Multicast Addresses

Static IP Address	Assigned Use
224.0.0.0	Base IP address for multicasting
224.0.0.1	All host systems on a subnet
224.0.0.2	All routers on a subnet
224.0.0.3	Unassigned
224.0.0.4	All Distance Vector Multicast Routing Protocol (DVMRP) routers, (covered later)
224.0.0.5	All OSPF routers
224.0.0.6	All OSPF designated routers
224.0.0.7	ST routers
224.0.0.8	ST hosts
224.0.0.9	All RIPv2 routers
224.0.0.10	All Interior Gateway Routing Protocol (IGRP) routers
224.0.0.11	Mobile agents
224.0.0.12	Dynamic host control protocol (DHCP) server or relay agent
224.0.0.13	All Protocol Independent Multicast (PIM) routers, (covered later)

All reserved static Class D addresses that are used for multicast management and multicast data are never forwarded to these addresses. Static addresses such as 224.0.0.2 include all multicast-enabled router interfaces. Multicast-enabled routers automatically join this "all routers" group upon initialization. In turn, all multicast-enabled hosts must join the all-host systems group 224.0.0.1. Others become active upon activation or configuration of some feature such as OPSF on a router.

Scope of Multicast Addresses Using the Time-to-Live Field

Multicasting network diameters must be controlled to reach only as far as necessary. This is accomplished using *scoping*, where the diameter (span) of a multicast session is controlled by manipulating the Time-to-live (TTL) field. Using TTL = 1 tells the IP router not to forward this packet to another network, since each router must decrement the TTL field by 1; if the TTL = 0, the packet is not forwarded.

The scoping of multicast addresses is based on the TTL value of the IP packet and controlled by the source. Scoping using the TTL has some limitations because it is based on the number of routers in the network topology, not on the administrative boundaries. It also conflicts with routing functions such as pruning.

TTL Thresholds

TTL thresholds can be implemented for managing the location of multicast traffic, preventing loops, or keeping traffic from being broadcast to other networks outside the intended area. These TTL thresholds restrict the transmission of datagrams by adjusting the TTL field within the IP packet itself.

TTL thresholds are implemented on all multicast-enabled interfaces and all data is compared to these thresholds. If a TTL on a datagram is equal to or less than the interface's TTL threshold, the datagram is dropped and not forwarded. If the TTL of a datagram is greater than a TTL threshold on an interface, the packet is decremented by one and forwarded out the interface.

NOTE

Because the TTL value is within the IP packet, it should be noted that this method might be misleading when used on a switched network. Layer 2 switches will not check a packet at Layer 3. This may seem obvious; however, simple items like this are the type of thing that are easily overlooked.

Administrative Scopes

A better scoping approach, as defined in RFC2365, is based on special multicast addresses in the range of 239.0.0.0 to 239.255.255.255. *Administrative scoping* allows an administrator to develop boundaries, or *scope zones*, by disallowing certain multicast address to be forwarded from one point to another, essentially boundary A to boundary B or vice versa. It is based on an administrative scope instead of a network topology scope. These addresses are used to restrict all multicast traffic from leaving a specific zone, hence keeping excessive network traffic to a minimum.

The following scopes are defined:

- **IPv4 Local Scope (239.255.0.0/16)** Local multicast channels. The locality is site dependent, but a local scope can be defined to have one site in a city by configuring its site boundary routers not to forward local scope multicast packets.
- **IPv4 Organization Local Scope (239.192.0.0/14)** An organization scope that can include many sites.
- **Link-Local Scope (224.0.0.0/24)**
- **Global Scope (224.0.1.0-238.255.255.255)** Full Internet.

More information about administrative scoping through RFC2365 can be found at ftp://ftp.rfc-editor.org/in-notes/rfc2365.txt.

Mapping Multicast IP Addresses to MAC Addresses

Multicast has been defined for the link layers of Ethernet, Token Ring, and others such as Fiber Distributed Data Interface (FDDI). On Ethernet, the low-order 23 bits of the IP multicast address are placed in the lower part of the Ethernet multicast address 01-00-5E-00-00-00. All Ethernet multicast MAC addresses begin with 01-00-5E.

When sending data to a particular multicast IP address groups, a method to eliminate the need for Layer 2 to Layer 3 address mapping (ARP) was adopted, wherein the lower 23 bits of the multicast IP address are incorporated as the lower 23 bits of the Media Access Control (MAC) address.

There are several requisites for the mapping process:

1. The first 4 high-order bits of the multicast IP address are reserved for Class D addressing and not mapped.
2. The next 5 bits are not mapped and ignored.
3. Only the 23 low order bits of the multicast IP address are actually mapped.

A standard multicast address would be mapped to the last 23 bits of a MAC address as shown:

```
nnnn nnnn.nxxx xxxx.xxxx xxxx.xxxx xxxx
```

The **n** indicates those bits that will not be mapped, and the **x** indicates the bits that will be mapped. These 23 bits of the multicast IP address are converted and expressed as hexadecimal. We will review the conversion process using 224.2.99.254 as our example.

1. Convert the IP address to binary:

   ```
   224.2.99.254 becomes 1110 0000.0000 0010.0110 0011.1111 1110
   ```

2. Recall that only the last 23 bits of the multicast IP address are mapped, so we are concerned with only the bits that are bolded here.

   ```
   1110 0000.0000 0010.0110 0011.1111 1110
   ```

We want to convert these bits to hexadecimal; use the hexadecimal table to guide your efforts.

```
0 0000
1 0001
2 0010
3 0011
4 0100
5 0101
6 0110
7 0111
8 1000
9 1001
A 1010 (10)
B 1011 (11)
C 1100 (12)
D 1101 (13)
E 1110  (14)
F 1111  (15)
```

3. For ease of conversion, view the 23 bits of the IP multicast address as blocks of four.

```
000     0010     .0110     0011.     1111     1110
```

4. Convert each 4 bits to their hexadecimal equivalent. Use the hexadecimal table if necessary.

```
000     0010     .0110     0011.     1111     1110 becomes
          02              .          63            .          FE
```

5. Prepend the Ethernet multicast address prefix (01:00:5E) to the result obtained in Step 4; use the MAC address format for consistency and clarity. This is the Ethernet multicast address for 224.2.99.254.

```
01:00:5E:02:63:FE
```

One indirect lesson that can be gleaned during this process is that because the first 9 bits of the IP multicast address are ignored, the resulting Ethernet multicast address is not unique to 225.2.99.254. 226.2.99.254, 227.2.99.254, and 224.2.99.254 would all be mapped to 01:00:5E:02:63:FE. As a result, hosts that are members of any of these multicast groups would receive packets destined for all the other groups. There is generally a 32 to 1 ratio that says regardless of what Ethernet multicast address is derived, it is associated with 32 multicast IP addresses. This should be kept in mind as plan your multicast design.

To review, multicast prefixes are indicated by the first 8 high-order bits, which results in 224 through 239, and always start with 1110 (in binary). The IANA has provided a similar type of address designation for Ethernet addressing, which is 01:00:5E that was mentioned during the decimal to hex conversion discussion. Figure 4.7 shows an example of an Ethernet address in binary.

Figure 4.7 Multicast Ethernet Address Structure for 01:00:5E:00:00:00

01	00	5E	Not Used	00	00	00
0000 0001	0000 0000	1101 1110	0	000 0000	0000 0000	0000 0000
8 bits	8 bits	8 bits	1 bit	7 bits	8 bits	8 bits

The IANA-designated Ethernet addresses used for multicasting commence with 01:00:5E. This accounts for 24 bits of the 48-bit address. The 25th bit is always a "0" and is not used. With this extra bit not being used for mapping, the Ethernet address range for multicast can be 01:00:5E:00:00:00 through 01:00:5E:7f:ff:ff. With the 25th bit always set to 0, the second octet in the IP address can reach a maximum of 127, which is notated as 7f in the MAC address when the mapping is accomplished. This leaves 23 bits for mapping to the multicast group IP address to the MAC address. A multicast group IP address prior to mapping is shown in Figure 4.8.

Figure 4.8 Multicast Group IP Address Structure for 224.136.168.8

224	128 - Not Used	8	168	8
1110 0000	1	000 1000	1010 1000	0000 1000
8 bits	1 bit	7 bits	8 bits	8 bits

This first 9 bits of the multicast address are not mapped to the Ethernet address. Mapping the remaining 23 bits of 224.8.168.8 is illustrated in Figure 4.9.

Figure 4.9 Ethernet to IP Addressing for 224.136.168.8

Octet	First			Second		Third	Fourth
IP Address	224			(128 + 8) 136		168	8
Binary	0000 0001	0000 0000	1101 1110	1	000 0001	1010 1000	0000 1000
Ethernet Address	01	00	5E	Not Used	08	A8	08

Since we are not using the 9th bit in the IP address (or 25th bit in the MAC address), the value of 136 becomes 8 as we lose 128 from our calculations as a result. The last 23 bits of the address are indicative of the *Multicast Group ID*, 8.168.8. Thus, using the conversion process discussed earlier, our multicast IP address is mapped to the MAC address as follows:

```
224.136.168.8 mapped to IEEE-802 MAC-layer address 01:00:5E:08:A8:08
```

Participating in Multicasting

To join a multicast group is a matter of configuring the host to listen and accept traffic destined for a particular multicast address associated with the group, or using an application (such as a videoconference client) to activate the necessary multicast address on the host. If the multicast channel originates on a remote network, by default, this channel is likely not currently multicast on the local network of the host.

The joining host must inform its neighbor router that it wants to receive traffic to this multicast address. The router will try to get that channel from its source and send the multicast packets of that channel to the local network. This entire process involves routing multicast over the larger network. There are several protocols used to enable and support multicast communications. These protocols are involved in the establishment and routing of multicast traffic. Each multicast protocol has its own set of rules and procedures to handle multicast traffic, as well as accessory tasks such as joining and leaving a group.

Internet Group Management Protocol Versions

Internet Group Management Protocol (IGMP) is the protocol used by the hosts to join (or leave) multicast groups to receive (or cease) the data of the groups. The host system sends an IGMP message to its respective multicast router (at the all-routers address 224.0.0.2). The router, which is also running IGMP, builds a list of active multicast groups. It becomes the querier for the LAN; that is, it will regularly send out queries to which hosts respond with a report message.

The multicast router manages the various multicast groups and handles the membership queries and reports and any other IGMP messages. When a host joins a multicast group, the router interface to the network of that host will receive the multicast traffic. The host simply lets the router know to which broadcast domain to allow the traffic. The important thing to know about IGMP is that it is concerned with the membership control for multicast purposes. There are currently three versions of IGMP available.

IGMPv1

IGMP version 1 (IGMPv1) is currently being phased out. With IGMPv1, when a host joins a multicast group, it sends a report to the all-hosts group (224.0.0.1) on its local network. The membership query works at adding multicast hosts from the routers perspective as well as manages the subnets need of a multicast transmission. A query is sent to the all-hosts group multicast address, 224.0.0.1. This query asks for any host on an interfaces subnet if they are members of a multicast group.

The membership query has a TTL of one, which constrains traffic to the local subnet. Hosts respond with the multicast address. If no host replies to the membership query, two more queries are sent at the default, 60-second query-interval time, (unless otherwise configured with the **query-interval** command). If the query-interval expires after the third attempt, the routers interfaced to that subnet will be removed from the multicast group membership and no longer receive the multicast data. Thus, the multicast router will only need to monitor a particular interface, as opposed to individual hosts

Routers can then learn who is joining which group via the membership reports sent to it at the all-routers multicast address, 224.0.0.2. It receives that message and marks the appropriate interface to receive the requested multicast.

When a host departs a multicast group, it does so quietly and without sending a report to the report for its network. It can take up to 3 minutes before the departed host is removed from the group, as the router will send three membership queries to the group before removing any non-respondents. That means that the router can continue streaming multicast traffic for up to 3 minutes to a group that no longer exists. This behavior is one of the reasons that IGMPv1 is being phased out.

Only one host in the group and on the same subnet replies to a membership query. This is possible because all intended hosts reside on the same subnet and all receive the multicast data. This bandwidth saving process is called *response suppression*. Response suppression works by using a countdown timer, which is a randomly chosen number within the default of 10 seconds for ICMPv1, (between 0 and 10 seconds). Once the timer reaches 0, the host sends a membership report for the correlating multicast group. If the host receives a membership report from another host on the subnet, it cancels its countdown timer and does not reply.

The packet structure for an IGMPv1 multicast frame is shown in Figure 4.10

Figure 4.10 IGMPv1 Packet Structure

Bits	4	4	8	16	32
	Version	Type	Unused	Checksum	Multicast (Group) Address

- **Version** The version number of IGMP being used
- **Type** Indicates if the type is:
  - Host Membership Query (1)
  - Host Membership Report (2)
- **Unused** This field is disregarded by a receiving system and zeroed out when a message is sent
- **Checksum** This area is zeroed when sent
- **Group Address** This field can have two different meanings:
  - **Membership Query** Zeroed when sent and disregarded when received
  - **Membership Report** Contains the IP address of the multicast group being conveyed

To activate IGMPv1 on an interface, simply join the multicast group, using the commands shown. Notice that prior to executing the join command, the IGMP status can be checked on the interface with **show ip igmp interface Ethernet 0** as shown.

```
IGMPv1# show ip igmp interface ethernet 0
Ethernet0 is up, line protocol is up
  Internet address is 192.168.1.4/24

  IGMP is disabled on interface
  Multicast routing is disabled on interface
  Multicast TTL threshold is 0
  No multicast groups joined by this system
```

Executing the following commands puts interface Ethernet 0 in the multicast group served by address 225.0.0.1. Version 1 must be specifically chosen in order to get IGMPv1.

```
IGMPv1(config)#interface ethernet 0
IGMPv1(config-if)#ip igmp join-group 225.0.0.1
IGMPv1(config-if)#ip igmp version 1
```

Rerun the **show ip igmp interface ethernet 0** command to confirm that IGMPv1 is enabled.

```
IGMPv1# show ip igmp interface ethernet 0
```

```
Ethernet0 is up, line protocol is up
  Internet address is 192.168.1.4/24
  IGMP is enabled on interface
  Current IGMP host version is 1
  Current IGMP router version is 1
  IGMP query interval is 60 seconds
  Inbound IGMP access group is not set
  IGMP activity: 1 joins, 0 leaves
  Multicast routing is disabled on interface
  Multicast TTL threshold is 0
  Multicast groups joined by this system (number of users):
      225.0.0.1(1)
```

IGMP version 2

IGMP version 2 (IGMPv2) is based on the first version, and uses membership queries and membership reports, the message formats of IGMPv1. IGMPv2 is currently the default enabled on Cisco routers. IGMPv2 maintains backward functionality with IGMPv1. IGMPv2 adds an option to actively leave a group, which in turn provides the ability to reduce multicast traffic on a particular subnet.

IGMPv2 takes a more active approach to announcing departures. When a host departs a multicast group, it sends a report to the all-routers group (224.0.0.2) on its local network. This enables the router to remove the host from its table immediately, rather than 3 minutes later as IGMPv1 did. Routers also send queries periodically to the all-hosts address (224.0.0.1) to request reports of group membership from all hosts on each multicast network to which it connects. In this way, a multicast router knows the membership of all groups for all multicast hosts.

When establishing a multicast session, the process works as it did under IGMPv1 with hosts sending membership reports to the all-routers group (224.0.0.2) or the router sending a query to the all-hosts group (224.0.0.1). The receiving multicast router will receive a join message initially, or in response to its query, and check its current addresses within its IGMP table. If the address is not in the table, the router will add it and activate the interface the message was received on for the multicast group.

A *multicast querier* maintains the IGMP group membership table, both joining and departing. Upon initialization, all multicast routers treat their interfaces as queriers and transmit query messages. All multicast routers check these queries and determine the IP address of the source interface.

The multicast router interface with the lowest IP address on the subnet is elected the multicast querier. If another router's interface is currently the multicast querier and receives a query from another with a lower IP-addressed interface, the current multicast querier will succeed and relinquish the position to the new router interface. To view which interface, (or router), is acting as a multicast querier, use the following **show** command.

```
Router1# show ip igmp interface s0
Serial0 is up, line protocol is up
```

```
Internet address is 10.30.30.10/24
IGMP is enabled on interface
Current IGMP host version is 2
Current IGMP router version is 2
IGMP query interval is 60 seconds
IGMP querier timeout is 120 seconds
IGMP max query response time is 10 seconds
Last member query count is 2
Last member query response interval is 1000 ms
Inbound IGMP access group is not set
IGMP activity: 1 joins, 0 leaves
Multicast routing is enabled on interface
Multicast TTL threshold is 0
IGMP querying router is 10.30.30.10 (this system)
Multicast groups joined by this system (number of users):  224.0.1.40(1)
```

The method that IGMPv2 uses allows hosts to leave multicast groups, which reduces excess multicast traffic sent to a particular subnet. The host sends a leave message to the all-routers multicast address of 224.0.0.2. The multicast querier in turn sends a query to determine if any other hosts on the network want to remain in the multicast group and thus leave the interface in a multicast group table. If no other host system responds, the router will *prune* the interface in question from the multicast group table.

Figure 4.11 shows an example of the packet structure for an IGMPv2 packet.

Figure 4.11 IGMPv2 Packet Structure

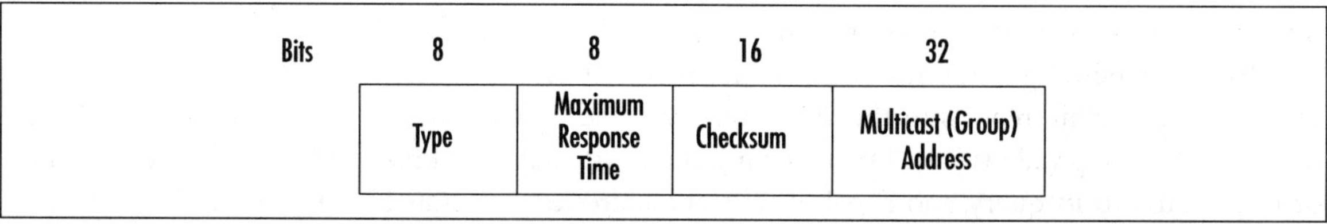

The frame in Figure 4.11 contains the following:

- **Type** Indicates if the type is:
  - A Host Membership Query represented by a 0x11
  - A Host Membership Report represented by a 0x12 (Version 1)
  - A Host Membership Report represented by a 0x16 (Version 2)
  - A Leave Report represented by a 0x17
- **Maximum Response Time** Only used in membership queries to indicate the time to wait before sending a responding report. Default is 10 seconds
- **Checksum** This area is zeroed when sent

- **Group Address** This field can have two different meanings:
  - **Membership Query** Zeroed when sent and disregarded when received
  - **Membership Report** Contains the IP address of the multicast group being conveyed
- **Group-Specific Query** Contains the IP address of the multicast group being conveyed

The process of configuring IGMPv2 is similar to IGMPv1, only you do not need to specify a version, as Cisco Internetworking Operating System (IOS) routers default to IGMPv2 by default.

```
IGMPv2(config)# interface loopback 0
IGMPv2(config-if)# ip igmp join-group 225.0.0.1
```

To confirm the successful acvtivation of IGMPv2, use the **show ip igmp interface** command.

```
IGMPv2# show ip igmp interface loopback 0
Loopback0 is up, line protocol is up
  Internet address is 192.168.0.1/32
  IGMP is enabled on interface
  Current IGMP host version is 2
  Current IGMP router version is 2
  IGMP query interval is 60 seconds
  IGMP querier timeout is 120 seconds
  IGMP max query response time is 10 seconds
  Last member query count is 2
  Last member query response interval is 1000 ms
  Inbound IGMP access group is not set
  IGMP activity: 1 joins, 0 leaves
  Multicast routing is disabled on interface
  Multicast TTL threshold is 0
  Multicast groups joined by this system (number of users):
      225.0.0.1(1)
```

Notice that no multicast routing is enabled on any of the interfaces. This is because IGMP is designed to handle joins and departures of hosts from multicast groups. It is not designed to route multicast traffic. The lesson here is that IGMP is not a routing protocol. Several multicast routing protocols are discussed later in this section.

IGMP version 3

IGMP version 3 (IGMPv3) is supported in Cisco IOS 12.1(5)T and later. IGMPv3 adds a process called *source filtering* that allows a host system to contact its corresponding multicast router and request the groups from which it wishes to receive multicast traffic. The multicast router then only forwards traffic from the multicast groups and hosts that were requested.

The joining process is the same as for versions 1 and 2 with some slight differences. Only a host can specify what groups and from what sources it wants to receive multicasts. It sends this join message to IGMPv3 routers (224.0.0.22). The multicast router for a subnet maintains its tables by sending queries to all hosts, and all hosts respond (to 224.0.0.22). Contrast this with version 1 and 2 where only one host in the group responds to such queries.

The packet structure for IGMPv3 is much more complex than its two predecessor's and can be seen in Figures 4.12 and 4.13. By viewing these structures, we can get a better understanding of the newest IGMP version.

Figure 4.12 IGMPv3 Query Packet Structure

8	Type (0x11)
8	Maximum Response Code
16	Checksum
32	Multicast (Group) Address
4	Reserved
1	S
3	QRV
8	QQIC
16	Number of Sources
32	Source Address (1)
32	Source Address (2)
32	...
32	...
32	Source Address (N)

Figure 4.13 IGMPv3 Membership Report Packet

8	Type (0x22)
8	Reserved
16	Checksum
16	Reserved
16	Number of Group Records (X)
32	Group Record (1)
32	...
32	...
32	Group Record (X)

There are some similarities and some progressive differences in these structures. The Type and Checksum are essentially the same, so we will cover the newer features.

- **S** Indicates that router processing is suppressed
- **Query Robustness Value (QRV)** Indicates certain timers and retry attempts
- **Querier's Query Interval Code (QQIC)** Specifies the elected querier query intervals in seconds
- **Number of Sources (N)** Number of sources in a query; N represents the total number
- **Source Address** Represents the source address
- **Number of Records (X)** Number of records in a report
- **Group Record** Contains information pertaining to the host systems' membership within one multicast group. The Group Record includes the fields shown in Figure 4.14.

Configuring IGMPv3 is similar to what we did for the previous versions: select an interface and enable as shown. For IGMPv3, we have enabled Protocol Independent Multicast (PIM), (discussed later) instead of enabling IGMP, by having the router join a multicast group as done in the previous examples. Notice that since **ip multicast-routing** is not enabled, this router will not forward any multicast traffic. In other words, any multicast traffic on this router will stay on its own network.

```
IGMPv3(config)# interface loopback 0
IGMPv3(config-if)# ip pim sparse-mode
    WARNING: "ip multicast-routing" is not configured, IP Multicast packets
    will not be forwarded
IGMPv3(config-if)# ip igmp version 3
```

Execute the **show ip igmp interface** command to confirm that IGMPv3 is enabled.

```
IGMPv3# show ip igmp interface loopback 0
oopback0 is up, line protocol is up
 Internet address is 192.168.0.1/24
 IGMP is enabled on interface
 Current IGMP host version is 2
 Current IGMP router version is 3
 IGMP query interval is 60 seconds
 IGMP querier timeout is 120 seconds
 IGMP max query response time is 10 seconds
 Last member query count is 2
 Last member query response interval is 1000 ms
 Inbound IGMP access group is not set
 IGMP activity: 1 joins, 0 leaves
```

```
Multicast routing is enabled on interface
Multicast TTL threshold is 0
Multicast designated router (DR) is 192.168.0.1 (this system)
IGMP querying router is 192.168.0.1 (this system)
Multicast groups joined by this system (number of users):
    224.0.1.40(1)
```

Multicasting via Switches

Earlier, we showed how multicast IP addresses are mapped to Ethernet MAC addresses, which are Layer 2 addresses. Layer 2 switches are involved in support multicasting. With the right configuration, switches can selectively transmit multicast traffic to their ports that contain members of the multicast group. Several protocols have been developed to enable switches to intelligently process multicast traffic. These include Cisco Group Management Protocol, (CGMP), IGMP Snooping, and Router-Port Group Management Protocol (RGMP).

CGMP

CGMP is a Cisco proprietary protocol that controls multicasting from the switch to the hosts. Catalyst switches can learn about multicast clients on the network from routers, and intelligently forward multicast traffic out the correct ports.

CGMP must be enabled on the interface connected to the upstream, multicast router. This router receives a join message from a switch on behalf of a client, which triggers the router to create and return a CGMP join message to the switch, which passes it to the requesting client. The CGMP message includes the type of message, (join or leave), the multicast group IP address, and the client's MAC address. Using this information, the switch updates its Content-Addressable Memory (CAM) table to map the host MAC address to the appropriate switch port.

From this point on, the switch listens to CGMP join and leave messages from the router, and switches multicast traffic per its CAM table entries. This method is very efficient and fast, and reduces the load on the switch process and fabric.

Before CGMP can be implemented, IGMP snooping must be disabled, which causes the multicast router to act as a server and the switch to act as the client. The router monitors the multicast groups and sessions and uses access switches as traffic management tools.

The process of configuring CGMP involves enabling it with a single command:

```
CGMP> (enable) set cgmp enable     [CATOS]  OR
CGMP(config)# ip cgmp              [IOS]
```

The switch will then monitor traffic and build its tables. CGMP is not efficient or effective, and has largely been bypassed by IGMP snooping, which offers the flexibility needed by modern applications.

IGMP Snooping

IGMP Snooping allows a Layer 2 switch to examine IGMP packet information at Layer 3 to determine the type of multicast packet currently being switched to a host system or multicast router. Once the switch has determined the packet type (join or a leave), the port of the requesting host(s) are dynamically added to (or removed from) the switch's IGMP Snooping Forwarding table.

The IGMP Snooping Forwarding Table will configure two primary mappings to manage the flow of IGMP and multicast traffic. Figure 4.14 shows an example of an IGMP Snooping Forwarding table.

Figure 4.14 IGMP Snooping Forwarding Table

Destination Address	Packet Type	Ports
01.00.5e.NN.NN.NN	IGMP	0
01.00.5e.NN.NN.NN	!IGMP	0, 1, 2 ...

- The first entry IGMP Snooping creates will be to direct all multicast IGMP packets (indicated by the multicast MAC address and IGMP packet type) directly to the central processing unit (CPU) for processing (indicated by port 0).
- The second entry contains the requested multicast MAC address, all *non-IGMP* packets, (indicated by !IGMP), and the appropriate switch port to reach the requesting host. This entry allows all non-IGMP multicast traffic to traverse the switch at Layer-2 and only to the appropriate ports.

Analyzing the IGMP packets above Layer 2 improves switch performance.

If an IGMPv2 leave message is detected, IGMP Snooping allows the switch to dynamically remove the switch port interface that the message was received on from the forwarding table. This is made possible through an IGMPv2 feature called *Fast-Leave Processing*.

While IGMP Snooping works dynamically, static mappings may be used as well. These static mappings take priority and will replace any existing dynamic IGMP snooping parameters that conflict. Static mappings and dynamic mappings can work in conjunction with one another to create a multicast membership list. The **ip igmp snooping static** command is used for statically configuring multicast groups on a switch.

NOTE

If there is more than one host system residing on a switch port (for instance connected to a hub), IGMP Snooping may cause multicast sessions on that port to have intermittent problems.

IGMP Snooping can become resource-intensive due to its examination of Layer 3 information. IGMP Snooping should only be used on the beefier models of the Cisco Catalyst line such as the Catalyst 6500 series. If processor utilization on the switch is a concern, consider the use of CGMP to manage the multicast traffic on the switch.

NOTE

IGMPv3, using source-based address filtering, supports the IGMP Snooping process.

To configure IGMP Snooping, use the following commands. Note that this is available on only IOS-based switches.

```
IGMP_Snooping (config)# ip igmp snooping [vlan ####]
```

This command is sufficient for configuring IGMP Snooping and enabling the switch to monitor and process multicast traffic that transits its ports. Notice in the example how you could have enabled IGMP Snooping on a particular virtual LAN (VLAN), which may better suit your requirements.

Distribution Trees

To ensure all intended recipients receive multicast traffic, multicast routers create *distribution trees*. A distribution tree provides a path from the source to the destination for multicast traffic flow and delivery. This provides a loop-free path to all multicast routers and the routers only replicate data when the tree branches to different networks.

Distribution trees come in different flavors, though all work on the same basic principles and seek to set up a path for efficiently sending multicast traffic. Distribution trees are also dynamically updated, which creates new branches in the tree, or prunes existing branches when the multicast is not requested any more. There are two types of distribution trees, *shared* and *source*.

Shared

The Shared Distribution Tree (SDT) uses distribution centers to build one shared tree. All multicast recipients will receive their data via this path. SDT most closely resembles a tree as it has a thick trunk (the main path), and branches out to the leaves (individuals systems). All of the data follows the same path until it is necessary to branch out. This is the case even if a clearly shorter path exists.

A rendezvous point is created as a common point (root) for all members of a particular tree. This method creates a shared path for each individual multicast group. A host system must request to join a particular multicast group with a join message to be added and will be pruned when the system no longer requests the data. An advantage of SDT is that it requires few system resources from the routers involved. On the downside, it does not consider or select the best path to a client, which may cause latency.

Source

The SDT process (sometimes referred to as the Shortest Path Tree [SPT]), locates the shortest possible path for all multicast recipients. This method creates many different paths for distribution from the source to the requesting subnets. It uses Reverse Path Forwarding (RPF) to create these paths.

RPF sends a multicast packet from the source to the next hop router. If the router receives this packet on an interface, which is also the best return interface (or the RPF interface), the router forwards the multicast packet out all other interfaces. This process occurs on all routers in the network until the destination has been reached for each multicast recipient.

Multicast forwarding is the ability of a router to use RPF to discover which interfaces are facing upstream to the multicast source and which interfaces are downstream to the receiving client systems. With this direction established, the multicast traffic could be forwarded toward the receivers. Interfaces receiving inbound multicast traffic are considered *parent links*. Interfaces that are used to send outbound multicast traffic are considered *child links*. Generally speaking, the parent link accepts the multicast traffic and forwards it to the child link.

Multicast Routing

So far, we have discussed multicasting between hosts, with routers as support devices charged with tracking what hosts should receive what multicasts. As a network expands and the distance between multicast sources and destinations increase, there needs to be a way to route multicast traffic to the appropriate receivers. This section highlights several multicast routing protocols and provides configuration information about each. Multicast routing protocols can be classified as either *sparse* ("pull") or *dense* ("push") mode.

Sparse mode protocols send multicast traffic only when it is specifically requested. Hosts must join a multicast group and signal their desire to receive particular multicast traffic. Dense mode protocols, on the other hand, push traffic out regardless of whether it is requested or noted. Hosts that are on the receiving end that do not want the traffic they received must let the sender know. Dense mode protocols then prune the tree by removing hosts from the group that do not want the traffic. The pattern of flood and prune is repeated every few minutes, and, if not managed properly, can degrade network operations. While dense mode is easier to set up, the cost in bandwidth may outweigh this advantage. Sparse mode takes a more conservative approach to bandwidth use.

Sparse Mode Routing Protocols

Sparse Mode (SM) routing protocols assume that there is limited bandwidth and that only a few routers will participate within multicast session maintenance. This is a good choice for WAN environments in that SM does not use bandwidth-wasting flooding. It caters to situations in which the receiving multicast clients are broadly distributed. To avoid flooding the network while discovering multicast members, SM routing protocols assume all clients are not group members unless they specifically request to join. Perhaps the best-known example of a sparse protocol is Protocol Independent Multicast Sparse Mode (PIM-SM)—RFC2362.

To construct a distribution tree, PIM-SM uses something similar to a "core" router (used with CBT) called a rendezvous point (RP). This RP accepts requests from clients (and sources), and registers the client for a particular multicast group. Once registered, the multicast traffic is forwarded to the appropriate network segment. The routers in the path will automatically optimize the path between the multicast source and the group.

This protocol is a good choice for multicast sessions with a few receivers and sporadic traffic. It is also a good choice where bandwidth available and constraints are a concern. To configure PIM-SM, execute the following series of commands on all routers that will participate in multicast routing.

```
PIM-SM(config)# ip multicast-routing
PIM-SM(config)# ip pim rp-address 192.168.0.1   ! Defines a RP at 192.168.0.1
PIM-SM(config)# interface loopback 0
PIM-SM(config-if)# ip pim sparse-mode
```

Dense Mode Routing Protocols

While SM routing protocols factor available bandwidth and widely distributed clients systems, Dense Mode (DM) does just the opposite. DM routing protocols assume that all multicast clients are located together and that there is plenty of bandwidth to spare. DM also assumes that each router on the network will be participating in the multicast distribution tree. Flooding the network with multicast information is imperative for dense mode routing protocols to establish and maintain distribution trees, and therefore a network running this protocol must be able to handle the load. Several DM routing protocols are discussed, including:

- DVMRP—RFC1075
- PIM-DM—Protocol Specification (Revised)
- Multicast Open Shortest Path First (MOSPF)—RFC1584

Each dense mode routing protocol provides different advantages, or disadvantages, for setting up distribution trees and are covered next.

NOTE

Dense mode and SM configurations can work on the same network, for different multicast groups, simultaneously. This is known as *Sparse-Dense Mode.*

DVMRP

Popular with Internet multicast backbones, or MBONE, configurations, DVMRP uses reverse path flooding (RPF) to reach its targets and construct distribution trees. RPF floods are sent out periodically to discover any new hosts wishing to join a particular multicast group. This flooding will reach every network. When a LAN is found to not have any multicast group members, routers will send prune messages to indicate LAN segments that do not need to receive multicast packets. These messages are sent back through the distribution tree and prevent further multicast packets from being sent to these segments.

DVMRP uses its own variation of a unicast routing protocol (similar to RIP). DVMRP is used to reach the multicast data source. *Cisco IOS does not support full DVMRP.* Instead, its support of DVMRP works in conjunction with other routing protocols such as PIM to obtain forward and receive multicast traffic. A separate DVMRP table is maintained for those multicast neighbors that can only use DVMRP. You can configure a DVMRP tunnel with the commands shown:

```
DVMRP(config)# interface tunnel99
DVMRP(config-if)# ip address 192.168.99.99 255.255.255.0
DVMRP(config-if)# tunnel source 192.168.99.100
DVMRP(config-if)# tunnel destination 192.168.99.101
DVMRP(config-if)# tunnel mode dvmrp
DVMRP(config-if)# ip pim sparse-mode
```

This will be enough for the router to tunnel DVMRP traffic between itself and the DVMRP speaker, including obtaining neighbor and route information.

Other DVMRP interface commands you can use to adjust parameters are summarized:

```
DVMRP(config-if)# ip dvmrp ?
  accept-filter        DVMRP incoming Report filters
  auto-summary         Enable DVMRP auto summarization
  default-information  DVMRP advertise default route
  metric               DVMRP Report metric
  metric-offset        DVMRP metric offset for Reports
  output-report-delay  Delay sending DVMRP Reports
  reject-non-pruners   Do not peer with non pruning/grafting DVMRP neighbors
  summary-address      Do DVMRP route summarization
  unicast-routing      Enable DVMRP unicast routing
```

PIM Dense Mode (PIM-DM)

PIM Dense Mode (PIM-DM) works similar to DVMRP. PIM-DM sends multicast packet floods out all but incoming interfaces to construct its distribution tree. It allows routers to prune interfaces that do not want certain multicast group data.

PIM-DM can be used with all unicast IP routing protocols and is best suited for networks in which there is a short distance between the sending system and the receiving system. PIM-DM is also best suited for environments in which there are only a few source systems and many receiving clients systems, and when there is a high amount of continuous traffic. Enabling PIM-DM is much simpler than PIM-SM, only the following command is necessary.

```
PIM-DM(config-if)# ip pim dense-mode
```

The activation of PIM-DM on an interface adds that interface to the multicast table, as opposed to PIM-SM where the interface gets added only when a host on that interface generates a join request.

MOSPF

MOSPF works in conjunction with OSPF, which MOSPF uses as its unicast routing protocol. In other words, OSPF is a unicast routing protocol that helps MOSPF to get from point A to Point B, just like any other routed network protocol. However, Multicast OSPF on Cisco IOS routers is not supported.

In MOSPF, as with OSPF, each router contains a topology map of the entire network and uses link-state advertisements to propagate this information. MOSPF information is included within link-state advertisements and are distributed when a link-state change occurs or a distribution tree cache times out. This link-state information is used to create a distribution tree for each "source-to-group" pair.

MOSPF is best used in a self-contained network such as an organizational Intranet. To minimize excess traffic, network links also need to be reliable. MOSPF is best used for networks with only a few multicast group sessions; however, Cisco routers do not support MOSPF.

Cisco OSPF routers ignore LSA Type 6 (MOSPF) packets, but will generate a SYSLOG message by default. If you do not want these messages to be generated, suppress them using the following command:

```
MOSPF(config-router)# ignore lsa mospf
```

NAT

NAT is designed for IP address simplification and conservation. NAT is a feature of the Cisco IOS that permits an organization's IP address structure to appear differently to outside networks than the actual address space it is using. This allows organizations to connect to the Internet without having to use globally unique addressing schemes internally. It enables private IP networks that use non-registered RFC1918 IP addresses to connect to the Internet.

Generally, NAT is used when a company's internal addresses are not globally unique and thus cannot be routed on the Internet (for instance, using RFC1918 private addresses), or because two separate networks that need to communicate are using an overlapping IP address space.

NAT allows (in most cases) hosts on a private network (inside network) to transparently communicate with destination hosts (outside network) in a global or public network. This is achieved by modifying the source address portion of an IP packet as it traverses the NAT device. The NAT device tracks each translation (conversation) between the source host (inside network) and the destination host (outside network), and vice versa.

NAT converts IP addresses from the private address space to the public address space. When a device performing NAT receives a packet from the Intranet, it changes the source IP address, recalculates the appropriate checksums, and sends it to the Internet. This obscures the true source address.

NAT is a method by which IP addresses are mapped from one address realm to another. This type of translation provides transparent routing from host to host. There are many variations of address translation that assist in translating different applications.

NAT Terminology and Concepts

Cisco uses specific NAT terminology for referring to hosts in the Intranet and the Internet, both before translation and after translation. Figure 4.15 illustrates those terms. **Azathoth** is on the inside network and the router (**Arkham**) is running NAT and connects to the Internet. Azathoth is communicating with **Cthulhu** on the Internet.

Figure 4.15 NAT Terminology

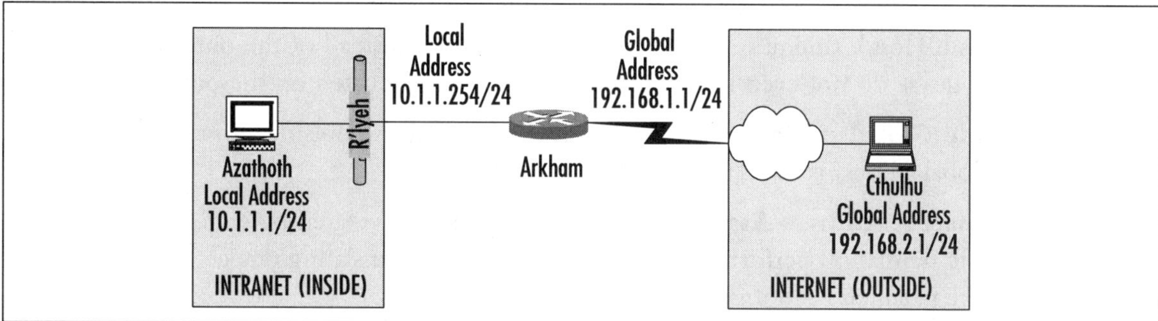

- **Address Realm** An address realm is a network in which the network addresses (IP addresses) are uniquely assigned to hosts so traffic can be routed to them. Often referred to as "inside" and "outside" networks, address realms define zones that are separate but need to intercommunicate. In Figure 4.15, the 10.1.1.0/24 addresses are one realm (inside) while the 192.168.2.0/24 addresses are another realm (outside).
- **Inside** An administrative domain controlled by an organization (Intranet). This includes all hosts, servers, and networks that are internal to a company, such as Azathoth.
- **Outside** An administrative domain not controlled by an organization (the Internet).
- **Local Address** An IP address used internally that will be translated. Host Azathoth's local address is 10.1.1.1, and the router's local address is 10.1.1.254. These addresses will not traverse the Internet (outside) and therefore are considered local to (or inside).
- **Global Address** A registered and legitimate IP address that can traverse the Internet. In Figure 4.15, there are two global addresses: the router's global address is 192.168.1.1 and Host Cthulhu's global address is 192.168.2.1.

NOTE

Global addresses are RFC1918 addresses and are only used to illustrate this topic. These addresses should never be used on Internet-facing devices.

- **Inside Local Address** An IP address assigned to a host residing on the inside. This address can be either a public or private IP address. Host Azathoth has an inside local address. Note that the inside local address is the same as the local address.

- **Inside Global Address** A public IP address assigned to an inside local address after a NAT translation. This is the IP address of the inside host or hosts as it appears on the outside network. When Host Azathoth communicates with Host Cthulhu, the router assigns Host Azathoth a registered global address to use over the Internet.
- **Outside Local Address** An IP address of a host on the outside as it appears on the inside after a NAT translation. Host Cthulhu's IP address (192.168.2.1) can be NAT-translated to a different IP address prior to traversing the inside network. This IP address can be in the same address pool as the company's internal IP addresses. This makes it seem as if Host Cthulhu is on the inside of a network instead of the outside. The hosts on the inside do not even realize that Host Cthulhu is located on the outside.
- **Outside Global Address** An IP address of a host on the outside. Host Cthulhu's outside global address is 192.168.2.1.
- **Transparent Address Assignment** A static (manually created by engineer) or dynamic translation performed by the router or other translating device in accordance with the parameters configured for translation.
- **Transparent Routing through Address Translation** Routes traffic between separate address realms (from an "inside" network to an "outside" one), by modifying address contents in the IP header to be valid in the address realm to which the traffic is routed.
- **Public, Global, and External Networks** An address realm with a unique network address assigned by the IANA or an equivalent address registry.
- **Private and Local Networks** An address realm independent of external network addresses. A private or local network uses IP addresses specified in RFC 1918.

In Figure 4.15, Arkham will translate between Azathoth and Cthulhu as these two devices communicate; neither will know the other's true address.

NAT Operation

Figure 4.16 illustrates a router performing NAT translation on a packet sent from the inside to the outside. The inside local address of the packet is depicted as SA, and the inside global address after the NAT translation is shown as SA*. The router translates all inside addresses to outside addresses and outside addresses to inside addresses. Note in the diagram that SA* can either be the IP address of the router's physical interface or any other IP address that the engineer has configured.

Figure 4.16 Packet Conversion through a NAT Router

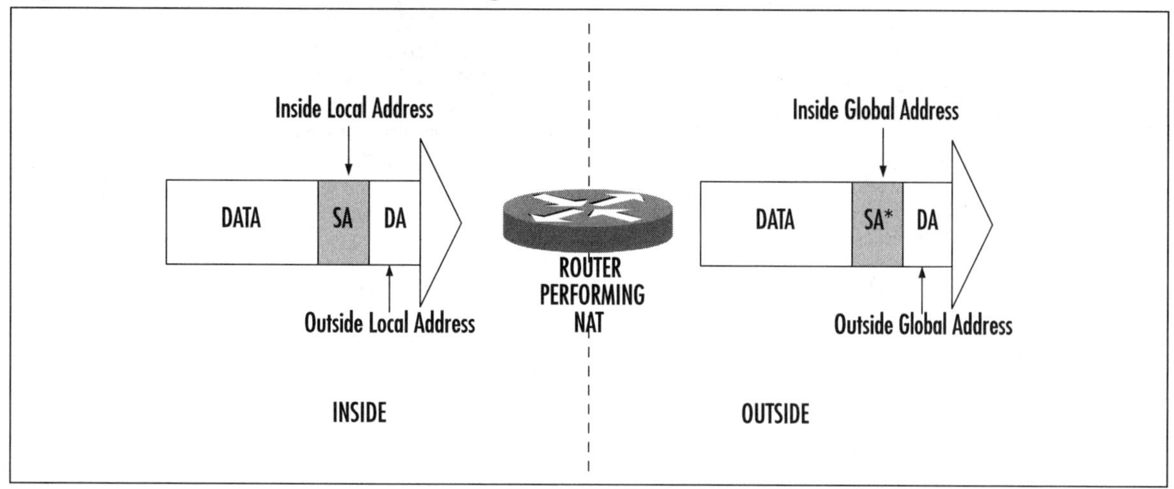

The router maintains a NAT translation table, which is continually updated as new connections are made and old connections are deleted after a set period of inactivity. This deletion ensures that the router can reallocate these addresses to other hosts. If there were no timeouts, the router resources would be quickly depleted.

Figure 4.17 shows an example of transparent routing when a company's "inside" network uses the subnet 10.1.1.0/24, and the "outside" network uses the subnet 192.168.221.0/24. Transparent routing would occur on the device that separates the two subnets. Instead of using a router to route packets based on destination address, NAT alters the source address of an IP packet originating from the "inside" network and changes it to a valid IP address in the "outside" network. The NAT device then builds a table to keep track of the translations that have occurred, to maintain communications between a host on the "inside" network and a host on the "outside" network.

Figure 4.17 NAT Translation

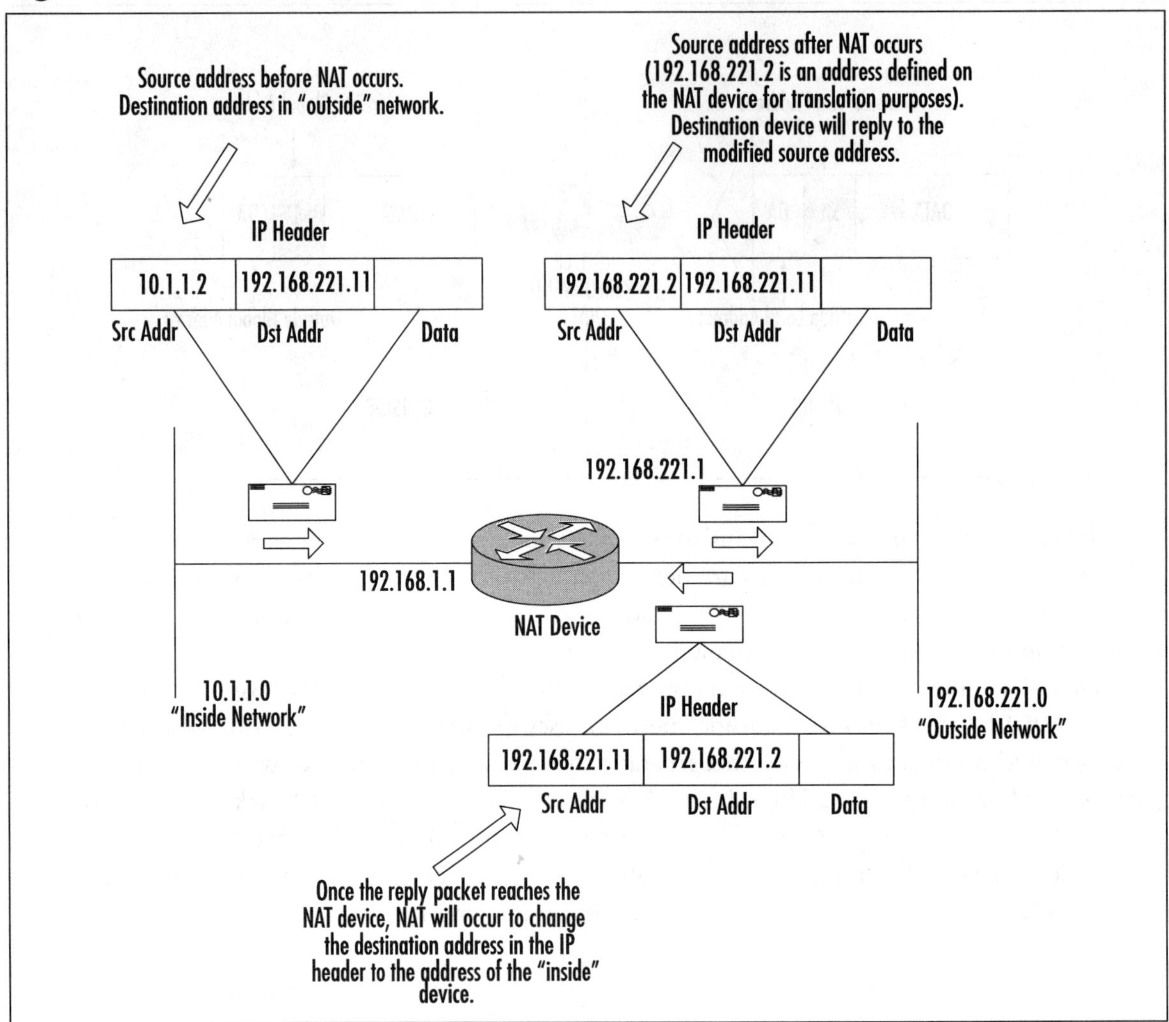

Configuring NAT on Cisco IOS

The NAT session limit on a router depends on the amount of Dynamic Random Access Memory (DRAM) available on the router, and its load. Each NAT translation consumes approximately 160 bytes of DRAM. As a result, 10,000 translations would consume about 1.6MB. Port Address Translation (PAT) is handled differently as its translations occur with 1 global IP address. Since TCP and UDP port numbers are encoded in 16 bits, there are theoretically 65,536 possible values, resulting in 65,536 simultaneous sessions for each protocol.

Configuration Commands

This section covers the commands necessary to implement NAT on a Cisco IOS router. The configuration commands necessary to implement NAT on a Cisco Secure PIX firewall are covered in Chapter 8.

1. Before NAT can be implemented, the inside and outside networks must be defined. To define the inside (the network to be translated) and outside networks, use the **ip nat** command.

   ```
   ip nat inside | outside
   ```

2. Mark the interface as being on the inside or outside realms with the following:

   ```
   interface ethernet0
   ip nat inside

   interface serial1
   ip nat outside
   ```

3. Once the inside and outside network interfaces have been defined, an access control list (ACL) must be created to define the traffic that will be translated. This will only define the traffic to be translated and will not control any NAT functions by itself. To create an ACL, use the **access-list** command:

   ```
   access-list access-list-number permit source [source-wildcard]
   access-list 10 permit ip 192.168.1.0 0.0.0.255 any
   ```

   This specifies that traffic originating from the 192.168.1.0 subnet destined for any other network should be translated. By itself, the ACL will not translate the specified traffic.

4. A pool of IP addresses must be defined for dynamic NAT translations. To do this, use the **ip nat** command:

   ```
   ip nat pool name start-ip end-ip {netmask netmask | prefix-length prefix-length}
   [type rotary]
   ```

   - **Name** The name of the pool.
   - **Start-ip** The starting IP address for a range of addresses in address pool.
   - **End-ip** The ending IP address for a range of addresses in address pool.
   - **Netmask *netmask*** Specifies the netmask of the network to which the pool addresses belong.
   - **Prefix-length *prefix-length*** Indicates how many bits of the netmask are ones.
   - **Type-rotary (optional)** Indicates that the range of addresses in the address pool identify real, inside hosts where TCP load distribution will occur.

5. Define a pool of global addresses to be allocated as needed.

   ```
   ip nat pool net-207 207.139.221.10 207.139.221.128 netmask 255.255.255.0
   ```

The previous example specifies a pool of global IP addresses with the name net-192 that will contain the range of IP addresses 192.168.221.10 thru 192.168.221.128.

1. To enable NAT for the inside destination address, the **ip nat inside destination** command is used:

   ```
   ip nat inside destination list {access-list-number | name} pool name
   ```

   - **list *access-list-number*** Standard IP ACL number. Packets with destination addresses that match ACL entries are translated using global addresses from the named pool.
   - **list *name*** Standard IP ACL.
   - **pool *name*** Pool from which global IP addresses are allocated during dynamic translation.

2. Define a pool of global IP addresses called **net-207** with the IP addresses 192.168.221.10 thru 192.168.221.128.

   ```
   ip nat pool net-192 192.168.221.10 192.168.221.128 netmask 255.255.255.0
   ```

3. Specify that traffic destined for the network address 10.1.1.0 will be translated to global addresses defined in the pool net-192.

   ```
   access-list 10 permit any 10.1.1.0 0.0.0.255
   ```

4. Enable NAT for traffic defined in ACL 10 to be translated to addresses from the net-192 pool. This will translate the destination address, not the source.

   ```
   ip nat inside destinationn list 10 pool net-192
   ```

5. To enable NAT for the inside source address; use the **ip nat inside source** command.

   ```
   ip nat inside source {list {access-list-number | name} pool name  [overload] |
   static local-ip global-ip
   ```

- **List *access-list number*** Standard IP ACL number. Packets with source addresses that match ACL entries are dynamically translated using global addresses from the named pool.
- **List *name*** Name of the standard IP ACL.
- **Pool Name** Name of the pool from which global IP addresses are allocated dynamically.
- **Overload (optional)** Enables the router to use 1 global address for many local addresses (PAT).
- **Static local-ip** Sets up a single static translation.
- **Global-ip** Sets up a single static translation. This argument establishes the globally unique IP address which an inside host will be translated to.

Establish dynamic source translation using an ACL to define the traffic to be translated based on the source address.

1. Define a pool of IP addresses with the name **net-207** and a range of IP addresses from **192.168.221.10 thru 192.168.221.128**.

```
ip nat pool net-192 192.168.221.10  192.168.221.128  netmask 255.255.255.0
```

Specify that traffic originating from the 10.1.1.0 network will be translated.

```
access-list 10 permit ip 10.1.1.0 0.0.0.255 any
```

2. Enable dynamic NAT for traffic defined in ACL 10 to be translated to addresses from the net-207 pool. This will translate the source address and not the destination address.

```
ip nat inside source list 10 pool net-192
```

3. To enable static NAT translation for the "inside" host 10.1.1.10 to the global IP address 192.168.221.10, use the following command:

```
ip nat inside source static 10.1.1.10 192.168.221.10
```

4. To enable PAT in conjunction with, or instead of, NAT:

```
ip nat pool net-192 192.168.221.10  netmask 255.255.255.0
```

Define a single global IP address with the name **net-192** and an IP address of **192.168.221.10**.

1. Specify that traffic originating from the 192.168.1.0 network will be translated.

```
access-list 10 permit ip 10.1.1.0 0.0.0.255
```

2. Enable PAT for traffic defined in ACL 10 to be translated to the address defined in the net-192 pool. This will translate the source address.

```
ip nat inside source list 10 pool net-192 overload
```

3. To enable NAT of the outside source address, use the **ip nat outside source** command:

```
ip nat outside source {list {access-list-number | name} pool name | static
global-ip local-ip}
```

- **List *access-list-number*** Packets with source addresses that pass the ACL are translated using the local addresses from the named pool.
- **List *name*** Name of a standard IP ACL.
- **Pool *name*** Name of the pool from which local IP addresses are allocated.
- **Static *global-ip*** Sets up a single static translation. This argument establishes the globally unique IP address assigned to an outside host.
- **Local-ip** Sets up a single static translation. Establishes the local IP address of an outside host as it appears to the inside world.

Dynamic NAT translations have several timers associated with them to remove stale (inactive) NAT entries from the table. For most deployments, the default values are usually acceptable. However, if necessary, the following command can be used to adjust these timers:

```
ip nat translation {timeout | udp-timeout | dns-timeout | tcp-timeout | finrst-timeout}
seconds
```

- **Timeout** Dynamic translations except for overload translations. The default is 86400 seconds (24 hours).
- **UDP-timeout** The UDP port. The default is 300 seconds (5 minutes).
- **DNS-timeout** The connections to the Domain Naming System (DNS). The default is 60 seconds.
- **TCP-timeout** The TCP port. The default is 86400 seconds (24 hours).
- **Finrst-timeout** Finish and reset TCP packets, which terminate a connection. The default is 60 seconds.
- **Seconds** The number of seconds the specified port translation times out.

1. This example specifies that translations will timeout after 300 seconds (5 minutes) of inactivity.

   ```
   ip nat translation timeout 300
   ```

2. This example specifies that NAT translations will timeout after 600 seconds (10 minutes) of inactivity.

   ```
   ip nat translation timeout 600
   ```

NAT Architectures

In the previous sections, we discussed the fundamentals of NAT, and provided the examples and commands necessary for a basic configuration. However, there are several variations of NAT that can be used for different situations. In our examples, we use RFC1918 addresses.

- Traditional/Outbound NAT
- Dynamic Translation
- Static Translation
- Dual Address Translation (Overlapping Networks)

Traditional NAT or Outbound NAT

Traditional NAT is a dynamic translation that allows hosts within the "inside" network to transparently access hosts in the "outside" network. In traditional NAT, the initial outbound session is unidirectional (one-way)—outbound from the private network. Once a session has been established with a device on the "outside" network, bi-directional communication occurs for the duration of that session.

IP addresses of hosts in the "outside" network are unique; while IP addresses of hosts on the "inside" network use RFC1918 private IP addresses. Since the IP addresses of the "inside" network are private and cannot be used globally, they must be translated into global addresses.

A traditional NAT router, as shown in Figure 4.18, would allow Host A to initiate a session to Host Z, but not the other way around. Also, the address space from the global address pool used on the "outside" is routable, whereas the "inside" address space cannot be routed globally.

Figure 4.18 Traditional NAT

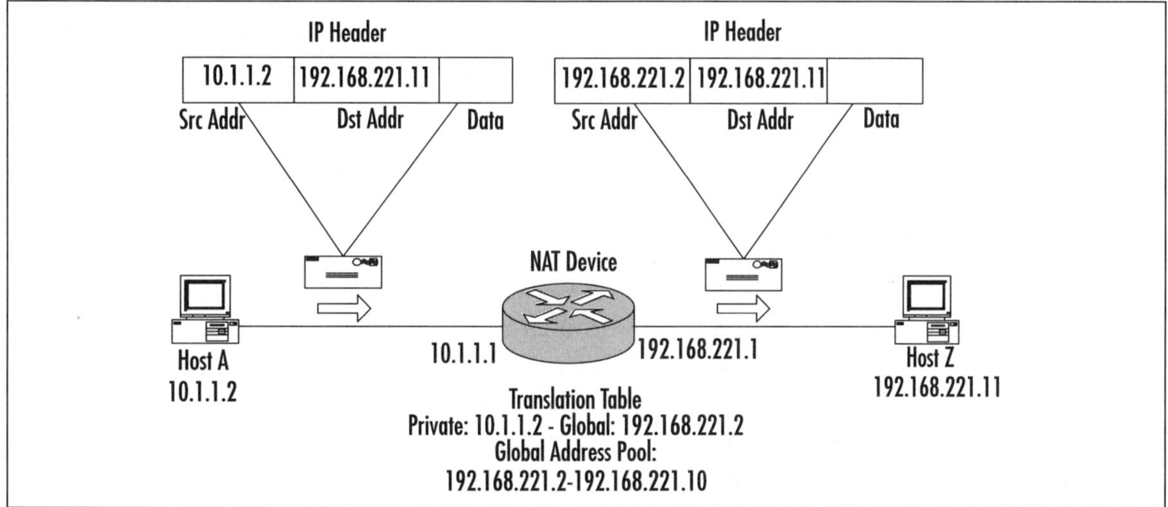

Figure 4.19 shows the reply packets sent by Host Z to Host A. Since Host A originated a session from inside, any packets originating from Host Z in response to Host A will be permitted provided that the security rules on the NAT device permit it. If Host Z attempted to initiate a session with Host A, traditional NAT will not permit this because Host A has a private IP address.

From the perspective of Host Z, Host A's IP address is 192.168.221.2 (the translated address). If Host Z attempts to initiate a session with this IP address, the NAT device will not be able to associate 192.168.221.2 with an "inside" IP address with traditional NAT. To allow Host Z to initiate a session with Host A, Static NAT must be configured.

Figure 4.19 Traditional NAT Reply

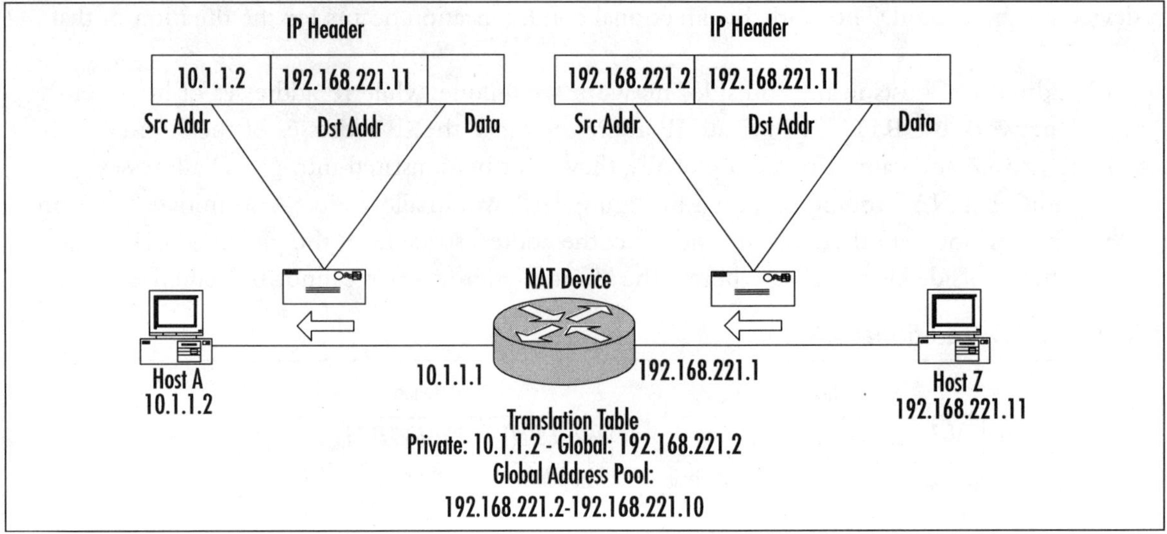

Dynamic Translation

Typically, traditional outbound NAT (inside addresses to outside networks) is dynamic. Static NAT is typically reserved for inbound sessions to map a public address to a private address, and especially for inside hosts that are providing a service such as Hypertext Transfer Protocol (HTTP). Figure 4.20 illustrates dynamic NAT. The router is performing dynamic NAT translations from the inside to the outside. It is configured with a pool of addresses from the 192.168.1.0/24 network. The hosts on the inside are using IP addresses from the 10.0.0.0 network and the outside Host D is on the Internet. Following Figure 4.20 is an example that walks through how Host A on the inside would communicate with Host D on the outside.

Figure 4.20 Dynamic NAT Translation

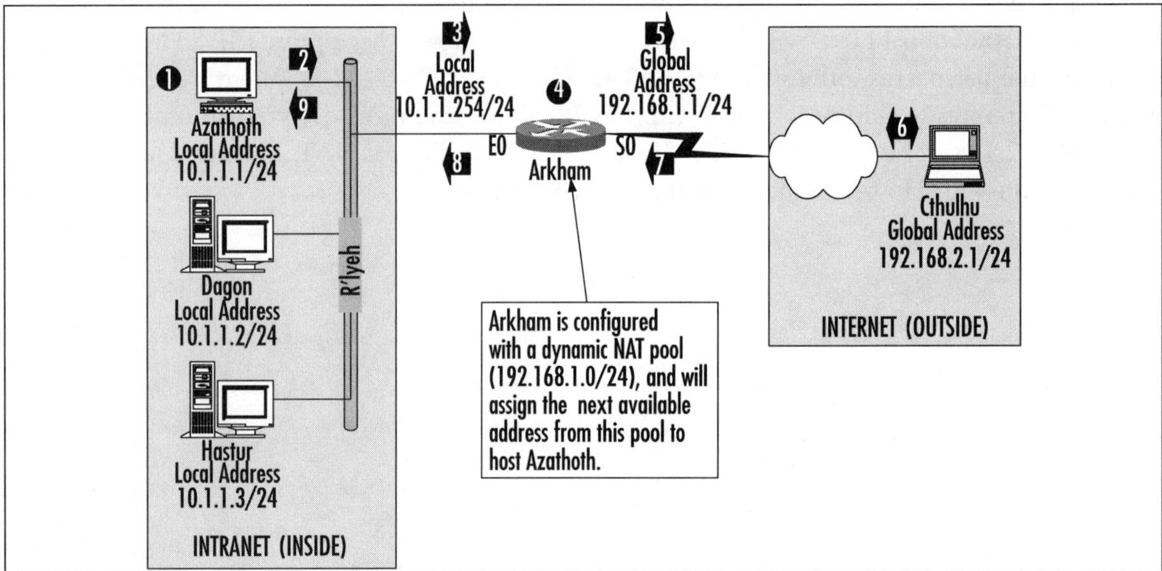

1. Upon receiving the packet, the router, Arkham, consults its NAT table and determines that IP address 10.1.1.1 (Azathoth's inside local address) has not been mapped to an inside global address.
2. Arkham was configured with a global NAT pool consisting of an IP address from the 192.168.1.0/24 subnet. It chooses an available inside global address (192.168.1.1) from its NAT pool and dynamically maps it to Host Azathoth's inside local IP address (10.1.1.1). If the router does not have an address available to assign to Host Azathoth, it will refuse the connection to the outside.
3. The router changes the source IP address in the packet to 192.168.1.1 and leaves the destination IP address as 192.168.2.1.
4. Cthulhu receives the packet and replies to Azathoth using its source address (192.168.2.1) and Azathoth's destination (192.168.1.1).
5. Upon receiving the packet, the router consults its NAT table and determines that 192.168.1.1 is dynamically mapped to 10.1.1.1.
6. The router changes the destination IP address to 10.1.1.1 and leaves the source IP address as 192.168.2.1.
7. Azathoth receives the packet and continues the conversation.
8. When Azathoth and Cthulhu complete their conversation, the NAT software within the router detects this and, after some time (user configurable), releases IP address 192.168.1.1 and returns it to the NAT pool.

Configuring Dynamic NAT

Dynamic NAT translations use standard Cisco ACLs to specify which addresses on the inside should be translated. This list comprises inside local IP addresses and only those addresses for which translations are permitted. The steps that are involved in configuring a dynamic NAT translation follow.

1. Create an ACL containing the inside local IP addresses to be translated. The source below is the IP address on the inside that is permitted to access the outside.

```
arkham(config)# access-list access-list-number permit source [sourcewildcard]
```

2. Define NAT pools by name. Create as many pools as necessary to accommodate all inside local hosts requiring simultaneous access.

- **Name** The name given to the pool of addresses on the router.
- **Start-ip and end-ip** The beginning and ending IP addresses of the NAT pools
- **netmask and the prefix-length** Indicates the subnet mask of the IP addresses within the pool.

```
arkham(config)# ip nat pool name start-ip end-ip {netmask netmask| prefixlength
prefix-length}
```

3. Bind the NAT pools to the ACL. Use the name of the pool and the ACL configured in Step 1 above.

   arkham(config)# **ip nat inside source list** *access-list-number* **pool** *name*

4. Identify the interface from which the inside local addresses in the ACL are being sourced; this will be referred to as the "inside" interface. The **interface-number** should be in the form of **Ethernet0**, **Serial0**, and so on.

   arkham(config)# **interface** *interface-number*

5. The following command will denote the interface above as the inside interface:

   arkham(config-if)# **ip nat inside**

6. Repeat the steps above for the outside interface.

   arkham(config-if)# **interface** *interface-number*

   arkham(config-if)# **ip nat outside**

The completed configuration is provided.

```
access-list 1 permit 10.1.1.0 0.0.0.255
!
ip nat pool employees 192.168.1.1 192.168.1.254 netmask 255.255.255.0
ip nat inside source list 1 pool employees
!
interface ethernet0
ip address 10.1.1.254 255.255.255.0
ip nat inside
!
interface serial0
ip address 192.168.1.254 255.255.255.0
ip nat outside
```

Dynamic NAT Translation Commands

The configuration file above was used to configure the NAT router in Figure 4.4. The following illustrates the output from executing the **show** and **debug** commands on the router.

The output of the **show ip nat translation** command is shown. Hosts Azathoth, Dagon, and Hastur were used to send pings to Cthulhu on the outside to set up the translations. Note how the router has assigned each host its own inside global address.

```
arkham# show ip nat translations
Pro Inside global Inside local Outside local Outside global
--- 192.168.1.1 10.1.1.1 --- ---
--- 192.168.1.2 10.1.1.2 --- ---
--- 192.168.1.3 10.1.1.3 --- ---
```

The following shows the output from the **show ip nat translation verbose** command. The **create** field specifies how long ago the translation was created. The **use** field specifies how long ago the translation was last used. The **left** field shows how much time is remaining before the entry is deleted.

```
arkham# show ip nat translations verbose
Pro Inside global Inside local Outside local Outside global
--- 192.168.1.1 10.1.1.1 --- ---
create 00:07:54, use 00:02:04, left 23:57:55, flags: none
--- 192.168.1.2 10.1.1.2 --- ---
create 00:04:57, use 00:04:57, left 23:55:02, flags: none
--- 192.168.1.3 10.1.1.3 --- ---
create 00:04:32, use 00:04:31, left 23:55:28, flags: none
```

The output below shows the result of typing the **show ip nat statistics** command:

```
arkham# show ip nat statistics
Total active translations: 3 (0 static, 3 dynamic; 0 extended)
Outside interfaces:
Serial1
Inside interfaces:
Serial0
Hits: 47 Misses: 3
Expired translations: 0
Dynamic mappings:
-- Inside Source
access-list 1 pool employees refcount 3
pool employees: netmask 255.255.255.0
start 192.168.1.1 end 192.168.1.254
type generic, total addresses 254, allocated 3 (1%), misses 0
```

Cisco also provides several debug commands to check the NAT operations. Azathoth (10.1.1.1) was used to send five pings to Cthulhu (192.168.2.1). The debug output shows that an ICMP packet is being translated from either the inside or the outside. If the packet is sourced from the inside, it is shown as an **i** and if it is from the outside it is shown as an **o**. Note that when outside Host D (192.168.2.1) responds to the inside host it uses IP address 192.168.1.1, which is the address that the NAT router has assigned to inside Cthulhu.

```
arkham# debug ip nat detailed
IP NAT detailed debugging is on
01:51:38: NAT: i: icmp (10.1.1.1, 8328) -> (192.168.2.1, 8328) [60]
01:51:38: NAT: o: icmp (192.168.2.1, 8328) -> (192.168.1.1, 8328) [60]
01:51:38: NAT: i: icmp (10.1.1.1, 8329) -> (192.168.2.1, 8329) [61]
01:51:38: NAT: o: icmp (192.168.2.1, 8329) -> (192.168.1.1, 8329) [61]
```

```
01:51:38: NAT: i: icmp (10.1.1.1, 8330) -> (192.168.2.1, 8330) [62]
01:51:38: NAT: o: icmp (192.168.2.1, 8330) -> (192.168.1.1, 8330) [62]
01:51:38: NAT: i: icmp (10.1.1.1, 8331) -> (192.168.2.1, 8331) [63]
01:51:38: NAT: o: icmp (192.168.2.1, 8331) -> (192.168.1.1, 8331) [63]
01:51:38: NAT: i: icmp (10.1.1.1, 8332) -> (192.168.2.1, 8332) [64]
01:51:39: NAT: o: icmp (192.168.2.1, 8332) -> (192.168.1.1, 8332) [64]
```

NAT translations can be cleared as shown. Note that the inside global IP address has to be specified first and then the inside local address. After clearing the entry for 10.1.1.1, the **show ip nat translation verbose** command is typed to verify that the translation no longer exists.

```
arkham# clear ip nat translation inside 192.168.1.1 10.1.1.1
01:58:34: NAT: deleting alias for 192.168.1.1
arkham# show ip nat translation verbose
Pro Inside global Inside local Outside local Outside
global
--- 192.168.1.2 10.1.1.2 --- ---
create 00:13:01, use 00:13:01, left 23:46:58, flags: none
--- 192.168.1.3 10.1.1.3 --- ---
create 00:12:36, use 00:12:35, left 23:47:24, flags: none
```

The output below shows how to clear all NAT translations.

```
arkham# clear ip nat translation *
01:58:57: NAT: deleting alias for 192.168.1.2
01:58:57: NAT: deleting alias for 192.168.1.3


arkham# show ip nat translation verbose
```

Static NAT

Static NAT works just like dynamic NAT except that the translations are statically created, typically by a network engineer. Static NAT is appropriate for handling inbound sessions initiated from outside sources (such as an HTTP session to an inside server), or when the outbound session of an inside host must use the same global address each time. A translation that occurs from the "inside" network to the "outside" network will be translated with the statically configured address. When a session must be established from an "outside" network to an "inside" network, the static translation must already be manually set up on the router. By creating a static translation, you are translating an "inside" IP address to a fixed "outside" global IP address. This translation will never change and will always remain in the translation table. With a static NAT, the translation is always active; the global IP address will never be allocated dynamically to another host on the "inside" network for translation purposes.

Figure 4.21 illustrates a static NAT translation. A session is initiated from Host Z on the "outside" network. Since the NAT device has a static translation for Host A's IP address to a global IP address, the NAT device can forward the packet from Host Z to Host A's static NAT public IP address. An outbound static is configured such that Host A will establish a session to Host Z's inside address (192.168.1.3), which gets translated by the router to Host Z's global address (192.168.221.11).

Figure 4.21 Static NAT

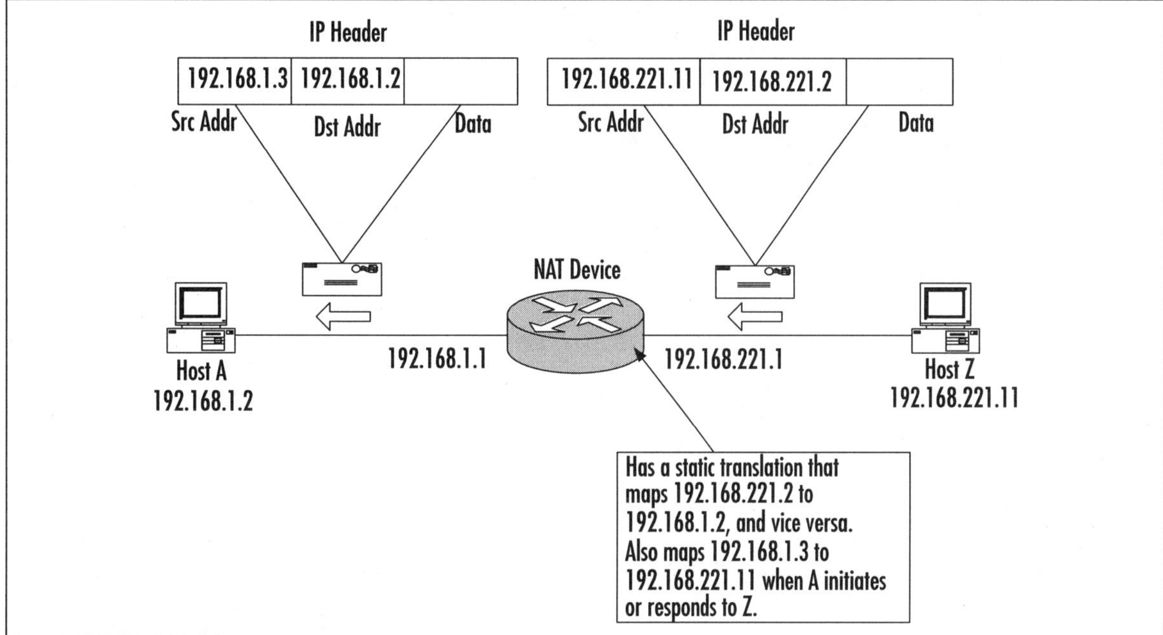

Static Translation Process

Static NAT translation is not configured with a pool of addresses to assign to inside hosts, but rather with one-to-one IP address mappings between inside local addresses and inside global addresses. Figure 4.22 illustrates a router performing static translation. Cthulhu from the outside (Internet) is accessing the Web server Azathoth on the inside. The NAT translation table on the router is configured to assign an inside global address of 192.168.1.1 to the server. This will guarantee that this IP address is not assigned to other inside hosts.

Figure 4.22 Static NAT Translation

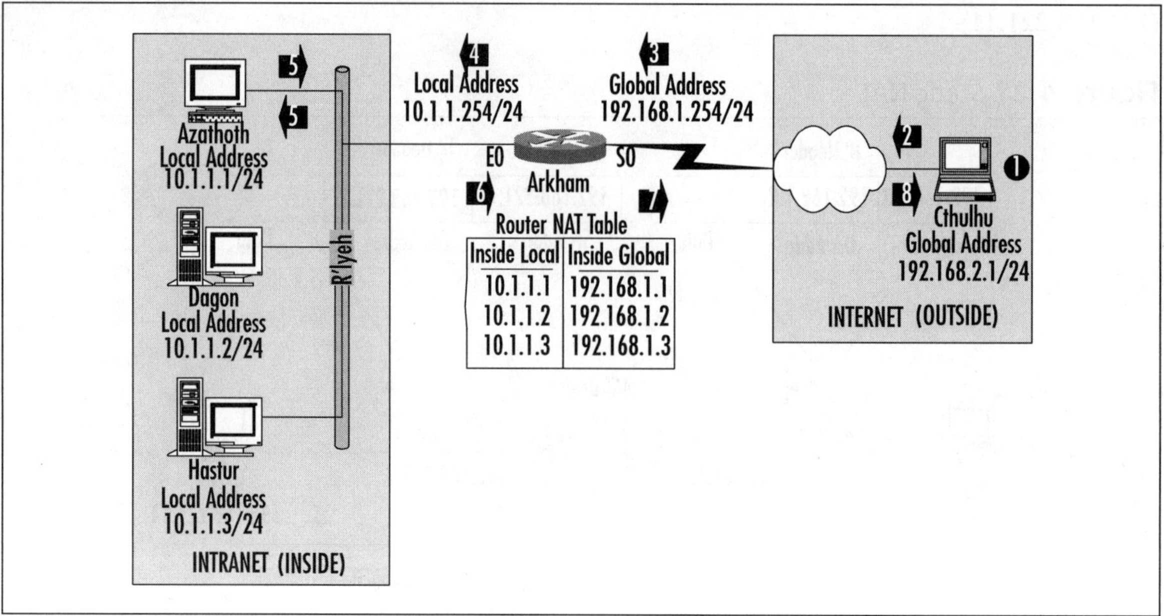

1. Outside host Cthulhu wishes to communicate with Web server Azathoth on the inside network.
2. Host Cthulhu sends all traffic to Web server Azathoth with the source IP address 192.168.2.1 and the destination IP address 192.168.1.1.
3. Upon receiving the packet, the router consults its NAT table and determines that IP address 192.168.1.1 is statically mapped to 10.1.1.1 (the Web server's inside local address).
4. The router changes the destination IP address in the packet to 10.1.1.1 and leaves the source IP address as 192.168.2.1, which converts the server's IP address from an inside global address to an inside local address.
5. Web server Azathoth receives the packet and replies to Host Cthulhu using Cthulhu's destination address 192.168.2.1 and Azathoth's source 10.1.1.1.
6. Upon receiving the packet, the router consults its NAT table and determines that 10.1.1.1 is statically mapped to 192.168.1.1.
7. The router changes the source IP address to 192.168.1.1 and leaves the destination IP address as 192.168.2.1.
8. Host Cthulhu receives the packet and continues the conversation.

Configuring Static NAT Translations

Define static NAT translations by entering all addresses for which static mappings are required, and mark which interfaces are outside and inside. Here are the steps that are involved in configuring static NAT translation:

1. Specify that this is a static translation by identifying the inside local address and the inside global address that the local address will map to:

```
arkham(config)#  ip nat inside source static inside-local-ip-address inside-global-ip-address
```

2. Identify the interface from which the inside local address is being sourced; this will be the "inside" interface. The **interface-number** below should be of the form **Ethernet0**, **Serial0**, and so on.

```
arkham(config)# interface interface-number
```

3. Designate the interface above as the inside interface.

```
arkham(config-if)#ip nat inside
```

4. Designate the outside interface (the interface from which traffic will exit after the NAT translation).

```
arkham(config-if)# interface interface-number
arkham(config-if)# ip nat outside
```

For Figure 4.23, the config file would look like:

```
ip nat inside source static 10.1.1.1 192.168.1.1
ip nat inside source static 10.1.1.2 192.168.1.2
ip nat inside source static 10.1.1.3 192.168.1.3
!
interface ethernet0
ip address 10.1.1.254 255.255.255.0
ip nat inside
!
interface serial0
ip address 192.168.1.254 255.255.255.0
ip nat outside
```

The status of the static translations can be checked as shown.

```
arkham#sh ip nat  translations verbose
Pro Inside global        Inside local        Outside local        Outside global
--- 192.168.1.1          10.1.1.1            ---                  ---
    create 00:00:26, use 00:00:26,
    flags:
static, use_count: 0
--- 192.168.1.2          10.1.1.2            ---                  ---
    create 00:00:26, use 00:00:26,
    flags:
```

```
static, use_count: 0
--- 192.168.1.3          10.1.1.3          ---          ---
    create 00:00:26, use 00:00:26,
    flags:
static, use_count: 0
```

Dual Address Translation (Overlapping Networks)

Overlapping networks are two or more autonomous networks that share the same IP address space. Two different autonomous systems (ASs) can share the same address space if both of them use the same non-registered addresses from RFC 1918, or if one of the ASs selects an address space that is registered to the other AS. When both of these networks are connected together, a routing problem exists because the routers within each AS will not be able to determine if a particular network is reachable from within its AS, or from the other AS.

With dual-address translation, the router interconnecting both companies performs NAT translations and a DNS server is used to resolve host names to IP addresses. Hosts must be registered in their organization's DNS. When a host receives a response to its DNS query, the NAT device intercepts it and translates the address in the DNS response to a pre-configured outside local address and passes it to the requesting host.

Figure 4.23 illustrates Company A communicating with Company B. Both companies are using subnets from the 10.0.0.0 network. Azathoth, from Company A, and Cthulhu, from Company B, are both on the 10.1.1.0/24 subnet. The DNS server (192.168.2.1) is located somewhere on the Internet and includes all host name-to-IP address mappings for Company B. We will concentrate on the operation of Router Arkham, which is performing dual address translation.

Figure 4.23 Dual Address Translation (Overlapping Networks)

Inside Local	Inside Global	Outside Global	Outside Local
10.1.1.1 (Azathoth)	192.168.1.254 (Azathoth outside address)	10.1.1.2 (Cthulhu)	10.1.2.1 (Cthulhu inside address)

(after translation)

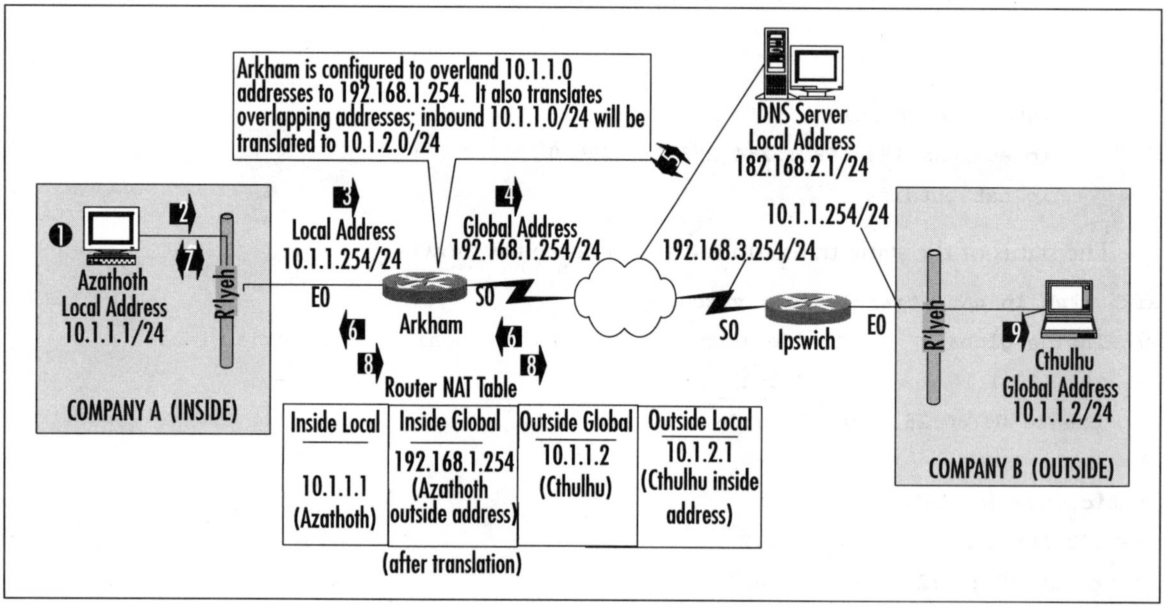

1. Azathoth wishes to communicate with Cthulhu. The only information that Azathoth has is Cthulhu's hostname *Cthulhu*. Azathoth and Cthulhu are on the same IP subnet.
2. Azathoth sends a DNS query to DNS server 192.168.2.1 to resolve Cthulhu's name to an IP address.
3. The router is configured for address overloading and will use 192.168.1.254 for all outbound traffic. It translates 10.1.1.1 (Host Azathoth's inside local address) to 192.168.1.254 (the inside global address).
4. The router changes the source IP address of the packet to 192.168.1.254 and leaves the destination IP address as 192.168.2.1 (the DNS server).
5. The DNS server sends a reply to 192.168.1.254. The information in the DNS reply packet specifies that Cthulhu's IP address is 10.1.1.2, which is in the same IP subnet space as Azathoth.
6. Arkham receives the DNS reply and interprets the data within the packet. It translates the data portion of the DNS reply packet by changing the IP address of Cthulhu to 10.1.2.1 from 10.1.1.2. The router does not change the source and destination IP addresses of the packet, only the data within the packet. The source address remains that of the DNS server (192.168.2.1) and the destination address that of Azathoth (10.1.1.1).
7. Azathoth receives the DNS reply and notes that Cthulhu's IP address is 10.1.2.1. Azathoth opens a session to Cthulhu using a source address of 10.1.1.1 and a destination address of 10.1.2.1.
8. The router translates source address 10.1.1.1 to 192.168.1.254 because it is performing address overloading. The router will also translate the destination address 10.1.2.1 to 10.1.1.2 because it is performing dual-address translation. Arkham will forward the translated packet to Cthulhu using a source address of 192.168.1.254 and a destination address of 10.1.1.2.
9. Cthulhu receives the packet and continues the conversation using source address 10.1.1.2 and destination address 192.168.1.254.

Configuring Overlapping Networks

To configure dual-address translation, first configure the PAT for the inside local addresses, and then configure the dual-address translation for the outside global addresses.

Here are the steps that are involved:

1. Create an ACL containing the inside local IP addresses to be translated. These include all addresses from Company A that are permitted to access services on the outside (in this case, Company B).

```
arkham(config)# access-list access-list-number permit source [sourcewildcard]
```

2. Define as many NAT pools as necessary.

```
arkham(config)# ip nat pool name start-ip end-ip {netmask netmask|prefixlength
prefix-length}
```

3. Bind the NAT pools to the ACL. Note the word **overload,** which specifies to use address overloading.

   ```
   arkham(config)# ip nat inside source list access-list-number pool name
   overload
   ```

4. Designate the "inside" interface from which the inside local addresses in the ACL are being sourced. The **interface-number** should be of the form **Ethernet0**, **Serial0**, and so on.

   ```
   arkham(config)# interface interface-number
   arkham(config-if)# ip nat inside
   ```

5. Designate the outside interface (the interface from which traffic will exit after the NAT translation).

   ```
   arkham(config)# interface interface-number
   arkham(config-if)# ip nat outside
   ```

The following steps configure dual-address translation for outside global addresses. Global addresses can be NAT-translated using either static or dynamic translations. In our example, we use dynamic translations.

1. Create an ACL containing the outside global IP addresses that will be translated. These include addresses from the IP address space that contains Cthulhu.

   ```
   arkham(config)# access-list access-list-number permit source [sourcewildcard]
   ```

2. Define a NAT pool by name to translate the outside global addresses.

   ```
   arkham(config)# ip nat pool name start-ip end-ip {netmask netmask|prefixlength
   prefix-length}
   ```

3. Link the NAT pools to the ACLs by specifying which pool should use which ACL.

   ```
   arkham(config)#  ip nat outside source list access-list-number pool name
   ```

The resulting configuration is shown.

```
access-list 1 permit 10.1.1.0 0.255.255.255
access-list 2 permit 10.1.1.0 0.255.255.255
!
ip nat pool CompanyA 192.168.1.254 192.168.1.254 netmask 255.255.255.0
ip nat inside source list 1 pool CompanyA overload
 !
ip nat pool CompanyB 10.1.2.1 10.1.2.254 netmask 255.255.255.0
ip nat outside source list 2 pool CompanyB
!
interface ethernet0
```

```
ip address 10.1.1.254 255.255.255.0
ip nat inside
!
interface serial0
ip address 192.168.1.254 255.255.255.0
ip nat outside
```

One variations of NAT is PAT, which translates many addresses to a single address, such as many private addresses to a single public address. This solution only works if the application does not rely on an IP address in the data portion of the packet for functionality.

Port Address Translation

PAT extends the concept of translation one step further by also translating transport identifiers like TCP and UDP port numbers, and Internet Control Message Protocol (ICMP) query identifiers. This allows the transport identifiers of a number of private hosts to be multiplexed into the transport identifiers of a single global IP address. PAT allows numerous hosts from the "inside" network to share a single "outside" network IP address. The advantage of this type of translation is that only one global IP address is needed, whereas with NAT, each "inside" host must translate to a unique "outside" IP address. PAT can be particularly useful for locations or users connected via cable modem, Digital Subscriber Line (DSL), or other similar arrangement wherein they are provided a single global, public IP address. In such scenarios, all inside addresses are translated to this single address.

Figure 4.24 illustrates PAT. Host A on the "inside" network needs to communicate with Host Z on the "outside" network. Because these two hosts are on different networks and the "inside" network uses IP addresses from a private address space, NAT/PAT is needed to allow the two hosts to communicate. Unfortunately, the administrator only has a limited number of global IP addresses, many of which have already been assigned to various devices. Therefore, NAT cannot be used for translations. As an alternative, PAT can be used instead.

Figure 4.24 Port Address Translation (PAT)

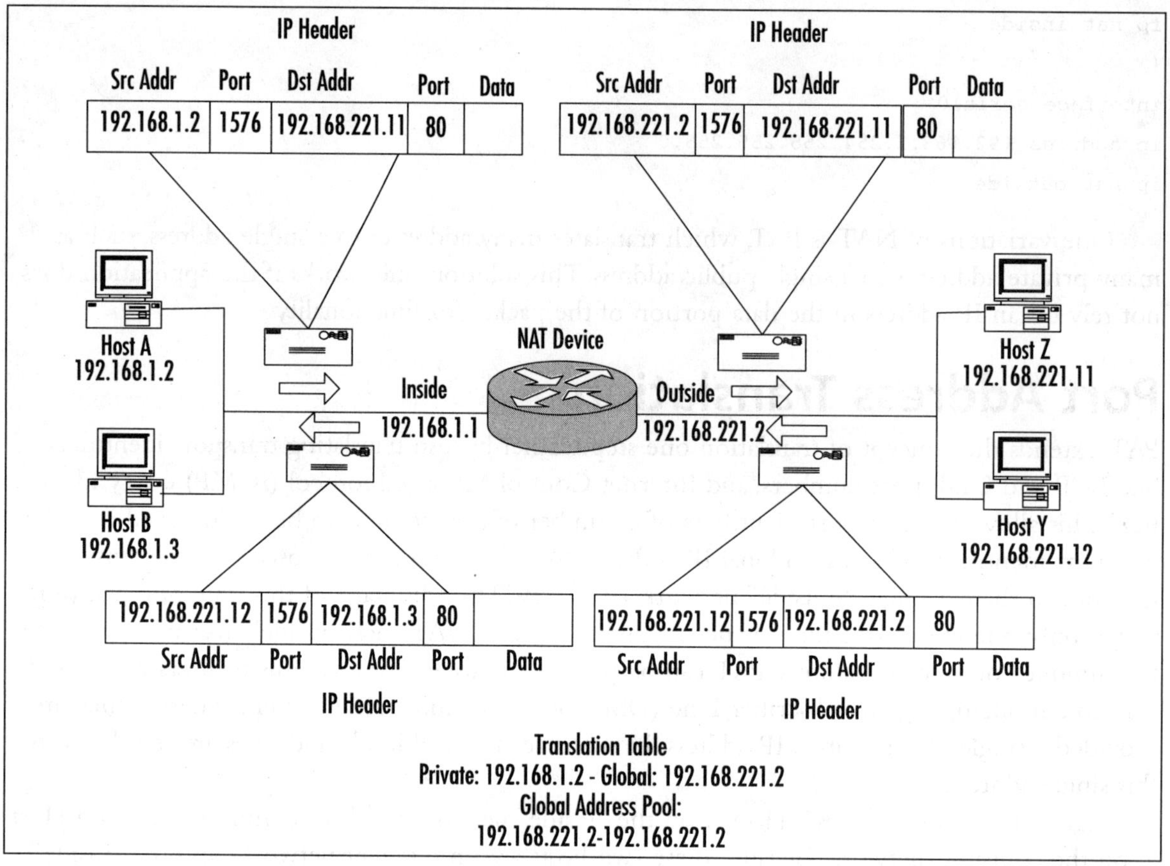

IP Header
Src Addr | Port | Dst Addr | Port | Data
192.168.1.2 | 1576 | 192.168.221.11 | 80 |

IP Header
Src Addr | Port | Dst Addr | Port | Data
192.168.221.2 | 1576 | 192.168.221.11 | 80 |

Host A 192.168.1.2
Host B 192.168.1.3
NAT Device
Inside 192.168.1.1
Outside 192.168.221.2
Host Z 192.168.221.11
Host Y 192.168.221.12

192.168.221.12 | 1576 | 192.168.1.3 | 80 |
Src Addr | Port | Dst Addr | Port | Data
IP Header

192.168.221.12 | 1576 | 192.168.221.2 | 80 |
Src Addr | Port | Dst Addr | Port | Data
IP Header

Translation Table
Private: 192.168.1.2 - Global: 192.168.221.2
Global Address Pool:
192.168.221.2-192.168.221.2

When Hosts A or B establish a session with Hosts Z or Y, their inside addresses are translated to 192.168.221.2 using PAT, which maintains a table of port to address mappings. Responses from Hosts Z and Y are sent to 192.168.221.2 to the correct source TCP or UDP port. The router translates the destination addresses back to the appropriate 192.168.1.2 and 192.168.1.3 addresses for Hosts A and B, respectively.

PAT is simply the process of using one inside global address to translate all inside hosts that require access to the outside. With PAT, multiple inside local addresses can all be translated to the same inside global address. All conversations are differentiated using source TCP or UDP port numbers. Therefore, all hosts permitted to access the outside will be able to do so, without the NAT router running out of IP addresses.

The most significant advantage PAT has over NAT is that no host will be denied access due to a depleted address pool. PAT also helps conserve scarce public addresses. Figure 4.25 illustrates a router performing address overloading using an inside global address of 192.168.1.1. It can be seen from the router's NAT translation table, that all conversations are unique. Each inside host is mapped to the same global address, and the router uses TCP or UDP port numbers to distinguish each conversation.

Figure 4.25 Address Overloading

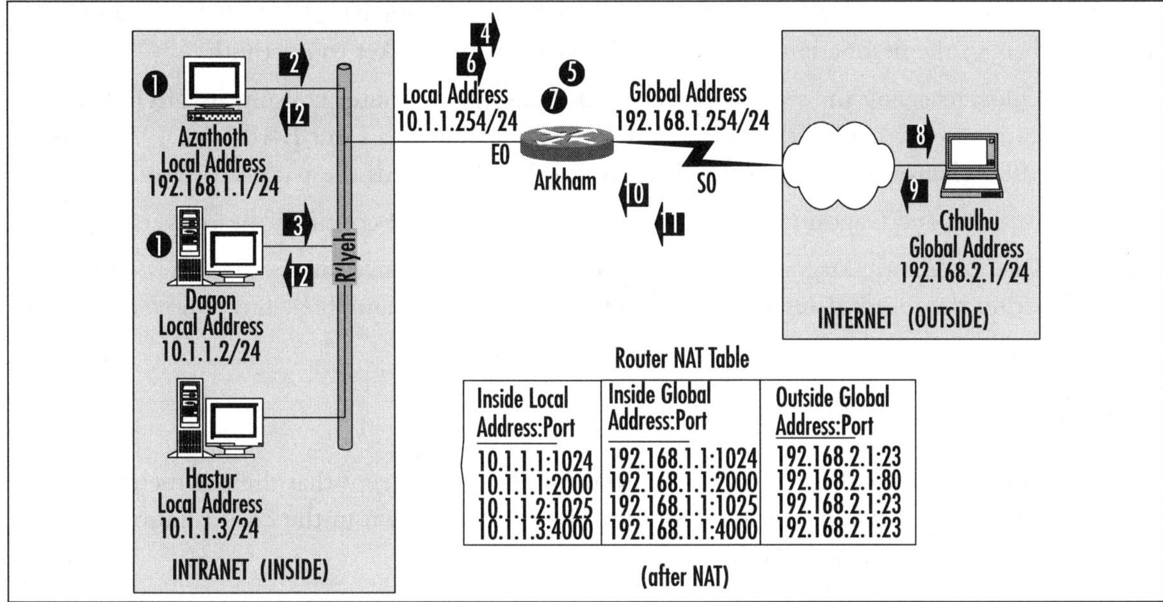

1. Inside Azathoth and Dagon on the Intranet wish to Telnet to outside Cthulhu on the Internet.
2. Azathoth sends all traffic to Cthulhu with source IP 10.1.1.1, source port number 1024, destination IP address 192.168.2.1, and destination port number 23.
3. Dagon sends all traffic to Cthulhu with source IP 10.1.1.2, source port number 1025, destination IP address 192.168.2.1, and destination port number 23.
4. Upon receiving the packet from Azathoth, the router consults its NAT table and determines that IP address 10.1.1.1 (Host Azathoth's inside local address) has not been mapped to a global address.
5. The router changes the source IP address of Azathoth to 192.168.1.1 (the inside global address) and updates its NAT table. Note that the router does not alter the source port number and the destination IP address of Cthulhu.
6. The router also receives the packet from Dagon and performs the same tasks. It consults its NAT table and determines that IP address 10.1.1.2 (Dagon's inside local address) has not been mapped to a global address.
7. The router changes the source IP address of Dagon to 192.168.1.1 also (the inside global address), and updates its NAT table. Note that both Azathoth and Dagon have been mapped to the inside global address of 192.168.1.1.
8. Cthulhu receives both packets and assumes that they were sent from the same host, since the source IP addresses are the same.
9. Cthulhu replies to both packets using Cthulhu's source address 192.168.2.1 and a destination of 192.168.1.1. Cthulhu does not alter any port numbers.

10. Upon receiving the first packet from Cthulhu, the router consults its NAT table and determines that 192.168.1.1:1024 is mapped to Azathoth 10.1.1.1:1024. The router changes the destination IP to 10.1.1.1 and sends the packet to Azathoth.
11. Upon receiving the second packet from Cthulhu, the router consults its NAT table again and determines that 192.168.1.1:1025 is mapped to Host B 10.1.1.2:1025. The router changes the destination IP to 10.1.1.2 and forwards the packet to Dagon.
12. Azathoth and Dagon receive their respective packets and continue the conversation.
13. When Azathoth, Dagon, and Cthulhu complete their conversation, the NAT software within the router detects this after some time (user configurable), and removes the mapping.

Configuring PAT

The configuration process for PAT is similar to dynamic NAT except that the parameter **overload** is specified when linking the NAT pool to the ACL, as shown in the configuration here.

```
access-list 1 permit 10.1.1.0 0.0.0.255
!
ip nat pool employees 192.168.1.1 192.168.1.1 netmask 255.255.255.0
ip nat inside source list 1 pool employees overload
!
interface ethernet0
ip address 10.1.1.254 255.255.255.0
ip nat inside
!
interface serial0
ip address 192.168.1.254 255.255.255.0
ip nat outside
```

NAT can also be used in conjunction with other features on Cisco IOS routers. For example, it can help with load balancing, as described in the next section.

TCP Load Distribution

TCP load distribution can be used to load-balance TCP (and only TCP) traffic across multiple servers using a virtual IP address and NAT translation. This is used for network services such as File Transfer Protocol (FTP) or HTTP that use TCP as their transport protocol. The collection of multiple servers can be assigned one virtual IP address and a single host name. When outside hosts need access to the servers, they can use the single IP address and hostname to connect. The cluster of servers are front-ended by a router running NAT services and configured for TCP load distribution.

The router is configured with the virtual IP address assigned to the cluster of servers, and a pool of addresses that include the real IP addresses of the servers. When outside hosts need to communicate with the servers, they direct their traffic to the virtual IP address; the router will recognize this and send the data to the servers. The router directs traffic to each server using a *round-robin* mechanism. Each time a new connection is received by the NAT router, it forwards the packet to the next server in line.

The advantage to TCP load distribution is that traffic from one over-utilized server is load-distributed across several servers serving similar content. The router does not consider the respective utilizations of each server. It simply uses a round-robin mechanism to forward data. Each time a new connection is requested, it notes this and sends the connection to the next server in line.

Figure 4.26 illustrates a router implementing the TCP load distribution function. The organization has configured Web servers A, B, and C to serve similar Web content. The router is configured to use a virtual IP address of 192.168.1.1. There are four hosts (Hosts D, E, F, and G) on the Internet that wish to connect to the company's Web site. These hosts are not aware that the company has multiple Web servers serving the same purpose, as the server has been registered in the DNS using the virtual IP address. When the hosts connect to the Web site, they send all traffic to the virtual IP address, and the router passes the data to the respective Web server.

Figure 4.26 TCP Load Distribution

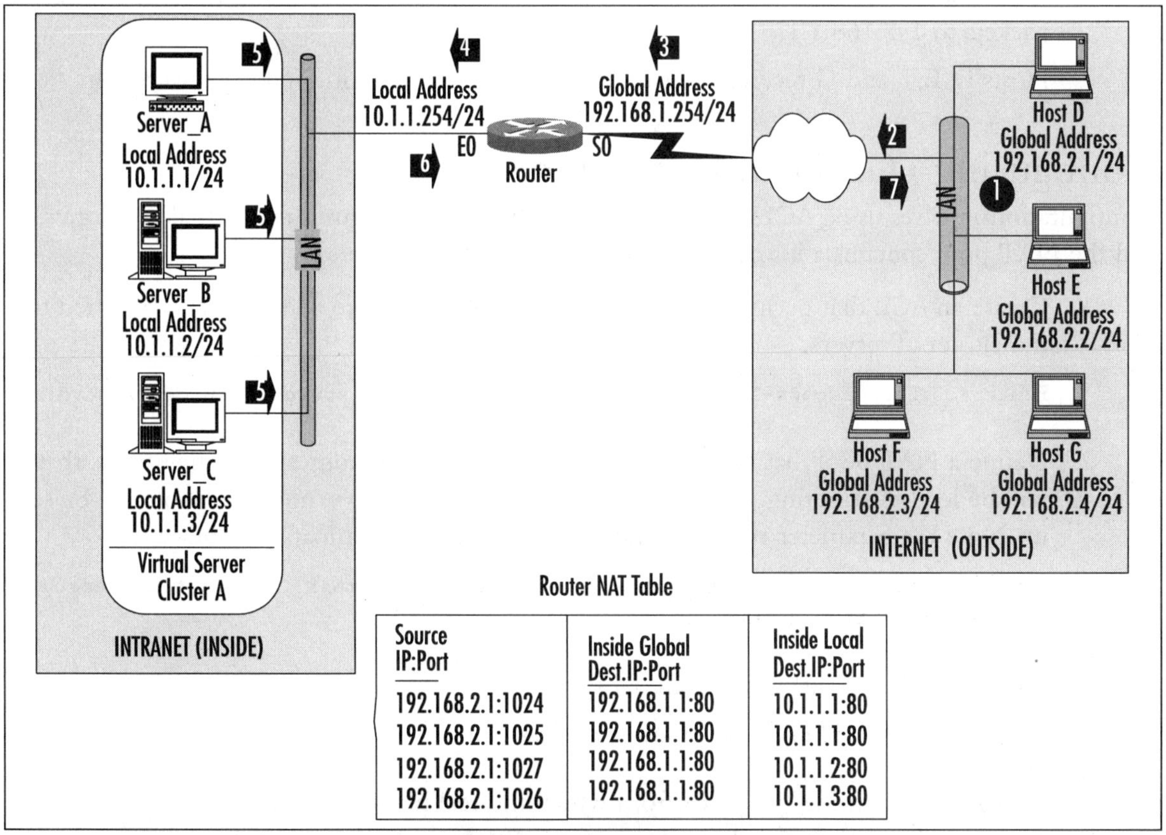

Source IP:Port	Inside Global Dest.IP:Port	Inside Local Dest.IP:Port
192.168.2.1:1024	192.168.1.1:80	10.1.1.1:80
192.168.2.1:1025	192.168.1.1:80	10.1.1.1:80
192.168.2.1:1027	192.168.1.1:80	10.1.1.2:80
192.168.2.1:1026	192.168.1.1:80	10.1.1.3:80

1. Hosts D, E, F, and G on the Internet want to connect to the company's Web site (comprised of servers A, B, and C). The hosts are considered to be on the outside, and the servers are on the inside.

2. Each host sends traffic to the virtual server IP address 192.168.1.1 with a destination port of 80 (HTTP). The DNS will resolve the company's Web site address to the virtual IP address.
3. Upon receiving the packets, the router consults its NAT table and determines that 192.168.1.1 (the inside global address) is set up as a virtual IP address that is mapped to servers A, B, and C.
4. The router changes the destination IP address to 10.1.1.1 for the packet received from Host D, and forwards it to server A. It translates Host E's destination IP address to 10.1.1.2 and forwards it to server B, and Host F's destination to server C and son for the remaining hosts. The router is implementing a round-robin mechanism to distribute the load across the servers.
5. Each of the servers uses its real IP address as the source address to respond. Server A will respond to Hosts D and G using a destination IP address of 192.168.2.1 for Host D and 192.168.2.4 for Host G, and a source IP address of 10.1.1.1, and so on for the other servers.
6. The router consults its NAT table and translates the source addresses for all four of these packets to 192.168.1.1.
7. Hosts D, E, F, and G receive their respective packets and continue the conversation.

Configuring TCP Load Distribution

Configuration involves using ACLs and NAT pools. The ACL configures the virtual IP address, and the NAT pool contains a list of the real IP addresses of the servers.

1. Create an ACL that permits the virtual IP address. This is the address that is assigned to the cluster of servers.

```
router(config)# access-list access-list-number permit source [sourcewildcard]
```

2. Define a NAT pool that contains all of the inside local IP addresses of the servers that will be load-distributing. If the list of hosts is not consecutive, multiple pools can be set up. Note the parameter **rotary**, which specifies that this is a load distribution.

```
router(config)# ip nat pool name start-ip end-ip {netmask netmask|prefixlength
prefix-length} type rotary
```

3. Link the NAT pool(s) to the ACL by specifying which pool should use which ACL.

```
router(config)# ip nat inside destination list access-list-number pool name
```

4. Designate the "inside" interface from which the real hosts can be accessed. The **interface-number** below should be of the form **Ethernet0**, **Serial0**, and so on.

```
router(config)# interface interface-number

router(config-if)# ip nat inside
```

5. Designate the outside interface (the interface from which traffic will be received from the outside):

```
router(config)# interface interface-number
router(config-if)# ip nat outside
```

The completed configuration is provided.

```
access-list 1 permit 192.168.1.1 255.255.255.255
!
ip nat pool webservers 10.1.1.1 10.1.1.3 netmask 255.255.255.0 type rotary

 ip nat inside destination list 1 pool webservers
!
interface ethernet0
ip address 10.1.1.254 255.255.255.0
ip nat inside
!
interface serial0
ip address 192.168.1.254 255.255.255.0
ip nat outside
```

Verifying TCP Load Distribution

The TCP load distribution operations can be checked using a variety of **show** and **debug** commands. The following output is for the **show ip nat translation** command.

```
NATRouter# show ip nat translation
Pro Inside global Inside local Outside local Outside global
tcp 192.168.1.1:23 10.1.1.1:23 192.168.2.1:11018 192.168.2.1:11018
tcp 192.168.1.1:23 10.1.1.3:23 192.168.2.2:11017 192.168.2.2:11017
tcp 192.168.1.1:23 10.1.1.2:23 192.168.2.3:11016 192.168.2.3:11016
tcp 192.168.1.1:23 10.1.1.1:23 192.168.2.4:11015 192.168.2.4:11015
```

The following output is from the **show ip nat translation verbose** command. The **extended** parameter specifies that the NAT router is using one global IP address (192.168.1.1) to mask several inside local addresses (10.1.1.1 through 10.1.1.3). The **dest** parameter indicates that the entry is being used for a TCP load distribution. And the **timing-out** parameter means that the entry will no longer be used because a TCP RST or FIN bit was received.

```
NATRouter# show ip nat translation verbose
Pro Inside global Inside local Outside local Outside global
tcp 192.168.1.1:23 10.1.1.1:23 192.168.2.1:11018 192.168.2.1:11018
create 00:00:09, use 00:00:07, left 00:00:52, flags: extended, dest, timing-out
tcp 192.168.1.1:23 10.1.1.2:23 192.168.2.2:11017 192.168.2.2:11017
```

```
create 00:00:13, use 00:00:10, left 00:00:49, flags: extended, dest, timing-out
tcp 192.168.1.1:23 10.1.1.3:23 192.168.2.3:11016 192.168.2.3:11016
create 00:00:17, use 00:00:14, left 00:00:44, flags: extended, dest, timing-out
tcp 192.168.1.1:23 10.1.1.1:23 192.168.2.4:11015 192.168.2.4:11015
create 00:00:22, use 00:00:20, left 00:00:39, flags: extended, dest, timing-out
```

The output from the **show ip nat statistics** command is shown below.

```
NATRouter# show ip nat statistics
Total active translations: 4 (0 static, 4 dynamic; 4 extended)
Outside interfaces:
Serial1
Inside interfaces:
Serial0
Hits: 799 Misses: 22
Expired translations: 9
Dynamic mappings:
-- Inside Destination
access-list 1 pool webservers refcount 4
pool webservers: netmask 255.255.255.0
start 10.1.1.1 end 10.1.1.3
type rotary, total addresses 3, allocated 4 (133%), misses 0
```

The debug output is shown below. Host D (192.168.2.1) was used to Telnet to the Web servers using virtual IP address 192.168.1.1. Note that when Host D opens the session to the virtual IP address, Web server 10.1.1.2 responds. This is because this particular conversation was passed to Web server 10.1.1.2 by the NAT router.

```
NATRouter# debug ip nat detailed
IP NAT detailed debugging is on
12:51:13: NAT: o: tcp (192.168.2.1, 11019) -> (192.168.1.1, 23) [0]
12:51:13: NAT: i: tcp (10.1.1.2, 23) -> (192.168.2.1, 11019) [0]
12:51:13: NAT: o: tcp (192.168.2.1, 11019) -> (192.168.1.1, 23) [1]
12:51:13: NAT: o: tcp (192.168.2.1, 11019) -> (192.168.1.1, 23) [2]
12:51:13: NAT: o: tcp (192.168.2.1, 11019) -> (192.168.1.1, 23) [3]
12:51:13: NAT: i: tcp (10.1.1.2, 23) -> (192.168.2.1, 11019) [1]
12:51:13: NAT: o: tcp (192.168.2.1, 11019) -> (192.168.1.1, 23) [4]
12:51:13: NAT: o: tcp (192.168.2.1, 11019) -> (192.168.1.1, 23) [5]
12:51:13: NAT: o: tcp (192.168.2.1, 11019) -> (192.168.1.1, 23) [6]
. . .
. . .
. . .
```

Cisco provides a command to clear a rotary NAT translation. Observe how the specific port numbers have to be specified. All NAT translations can also be cleared using the **clear ip nat translation** command.

```
NATRouter# show ip nat translation
Pro Inside global Inside local Outside local Outside
global
tcp 192.168.1.1:23 10.1.1.3:23 192.168.1.253:11269
192.168.1.253:11269
NATRouter# clear ip nat translation tcp inside 192.168.1.1 23 10.1.1.3
23 outside 192.168.1.253 11269 192.168.1.253 11269
```

NAT Monitoring and Troubleshooting Commands

Several commands are available to monitor, maintain, and troubleshoot NAT. There are different commands to show NAT translations and statistics, clear NAT translations, and perform extensive troubleshooting using the debug commands.

1. Clear all dynamic NAT translations from the NAT table before they timeout.

   ```
   router# clear ip nat translation *
   ```

2. Clear a dynamic translation that contains an inside translation.

   ```
   router#  clear ip nat translation inside global-ip local-ip
   ```

3. Clear a dynamic translation entry containing an outside translation.

   ```
   router#  clear ip nat translation outside local-ip global-ip
   ```

4. Clear a PAT translation.

   ```
   router#  clear ip nat translation protocol inside global-ip global-port local-
   ip local-port [outside local-ip local-port global-ip global-port]
   ```

5. Display all active NAT translations. The verbose option displays how long ago the translation was created and used.

   ```
   router# show ip nat translations [verbose]
   ```

6. Display all NAT translation statistics, such as what is configured as the outside and inside interfaces, the total number of translations, the IP address pools, and so on.

   ```
   router#  show ip nat statistics
   ```

7. Debug IP NAT translations. This command can be used to display information about every packet that is NAT-translated. The **ACL** option is the number of a standard ACL that defines a set of IP addresses to be included in the debug. The **detailed** option provides a description of each packet considered for NAT translation, error information, and failure conditions.

```
router#  debug ip nat
```

8. Display PAT statistics and the active sessions on a 700 series router.

```
router#  show ip pat
```

The following are the commands used to verify the operation of NAT on a Cisco router.

- **show ip nat statistics** Displays NAT statistics.
- **show ip nat translations [verbose]** Displays NAT translations, where **Verbose** optionally displays additional information for each translation table entry.

The following is sample output from the **show ip nat statistics** command. Table 4.9 outlines the significant fields in the sample output.

```
Router# show ip nat statistics
Total translations: 2 (0 static, 2 dynamic; 0 extended)
Outside interfaces: Serial0
Inside interfaces: Ethernet1
Hits: 135  Misses: 5
Expired translations: 2
Dynamic mappings:
-- Inside Source
access-list 1 pool net-208 refcount 2
 pool net-208: netmask 255.255.255.240
        start 171.69.233.208 end 171.69.233.221
        type generic, total addresses 14, allocated 2 (14%), misses 0
```

Table 4.9 Explanation of the Significant Fields from the **show ip nat statistics** command Sample Output

Field	Description
Total translations	Number of translations active in the system. This number is incremented each time a translation is created, and is decremented each time a translation is cleared or times out.
Outside interfaces	List of interfaces marked as outside with the **ip nat outside** command.
Inside interfaces	List of interfaces marked as inside with the **ip nat inside** command.
Hits	Number of times the software does a translation table lookup and finds an entry.

Continued

Table 4.9 Explanation of the Significant Fields from the **show ip nat statistics** command Sample Output

Field	Description
Misses	Number of times the software does a translation table lookup, fails to find an entry, and must try to create one.
Expired translations	Cumulative count of translations that have expired since the router was booted

Considerations about NAT and PAT

Even though NAT helps get around the problem of scarce globally routable IP addresses, it does have an impact on the functionality of certain protocols, therefore complicating their deployment. This section outlines some of the problems associated with NAT.

IP Address Information in Data

Numerous applications fail when packets traverse a NAT device. These packets carry IP address or port information in the data portion of the packet. Since NAT only alters the IP header to perform the translation, the data portion is left untouched. With the aid of an application gateway, a workaround may be provided in some cases. But if the packet data is IPSec-secured (or secured by another transport or application level mechanism), the application will fail.

Bundled Session Applications

Bundled session applications such as FTP, H.323, Serial Interface Protocol (SIP), and Real Time Streaming Protocol (RTSP), which use a control connection to establish data flow, are also usually broken up by NAT devices. This occurs because the applications exchange address and port information within the control session to establish data sessions and session orientations. NAT cannot know the interdependency of the bundled sessions and would therefore treat each session as if they were unrelated to one another.

Peer-to-Peer Applications

Peer-to-peer applications are more prone to failure than client-server-based applications, and can be originated by any of the peers, even if those peers are located in different realms. NAT translations, however, may not be established because the hosts on the "inside" network are not visible to the host on the "outside" network. This is problematic with traditional NAT (dynamic NAT and PAT) where connections are client to server.

IP Fragmentation with PAT en Route

IP fragmentation with PAT can occur when two hosts send fragmented TCP/UDP packets to the same destination host, and they happen to use the same fragmentation identifier. When the target host receives the two unrelated packets (which carry the same fragmentation ID from the same assigned host address), the target host is unable to distinguish which of the two sessions the packets belong to (due to the translation of the local source address when compared to the global PAT address), causing both sessions to be corrupted.

IPSec and IKE

NAT operates by modifying source addresses within the IP header while it passes through the NAT device. Due to the nature of IPSec, the AH protocol is designed to detect alterations to IP packet headers. So, when NAT alters the source address information, the destination host receiving the altered packet discards the packet since the IP headers have been altered. The IPSec AH-secure packet traversing NAT will simply not reach the target application.

IPSec Encrypted Security Payload (ESP) encrypted packets may be altered by NAT devices in only a limited number of cases. In the case of TCP/UDP packets, NAT would need to update the checksum in the TCP/UDP headers whenever the IP header is changed. However, as the TCP/UDP header is encrypted by the ESP, NAT would not be able to make this checksum update because it is now encrypted. TCP/UDP packets that are encrypted and traverse a NAT device will fail because the TCP/UDP checksum validation on the receiving end will not reach the target application.

Internet Key Exchange (IKE) Protocol can potentially pass IP addresses as node identifiers during the Main, Aggressive, and Quick modes. In order for an IKE negotiation to correctly pass through NAT, these data portions should be modified. However, these payloads are often protected by encryption. For all practical purposes, end-to-end IPSec is almost impossible to accomplish with NAT translation en route.

One of the reasons that NAT and PAT were developed was to conserve IP address space. Another solution to the address exhaustion problem was the development of IPv6, which provides more addresses.

IPv6

Issues such as address exhaustion that made version 4 of the IP (IPv4) inadequate, require robust solutions. While 32 bits of address space were originally thought to be "more than enough," time and growth have proven this to not be the case. Additionally, IPv4 suffers from a lack of hierarchical structure; while addresses may be sequentially allocated and summarized, they are not optimized by routing or allocation.

Designers of IPv6 worked diligently to ensure that the same issues would not be encountered. Members of the Internet community who were responsible for developing the protocol carefully scrutinized each new RFC penned for IP. This section covers IPv6, which was developed to overcome the exhaustion of IPv4 addresses, and to improve on it in general.

Benefits of IPv6

The following sections look at the two main problems solved by IPv6—address depletion and routing scalability—in more detail. Some added benefits that IPv6 gives to network designers and administrators include:

- Increased IP address size
- Increased addressing hierarchy support

- Simplified host addressing (unified addressing: global, site, local)
- Simplified autoconfiguration of addresses (easier readdressing, DHCPv6, Neighbor Discovery instead of ARP broadcasts)
- Improved scalability of multicast routing
- The **anycast** address
- A streamlined header
- Improved security (security extension headers, integrated data integrity)
- Better performance (aggregation, neighbor discovery instead of ARP broadcasts, no fragmentation, no header checksum, flow, priority, integrated quality of service [QoS])

How does IPv6 compare with its predecessor, IPv4?

IPv4 versus IPv6

IPv6 eases the network administrator's burden, in that Aggregatable Global Unicast (to be discussed later) addresses do not require address translation when used to access external networks such as the Internet. In IPv4, private address spaces are used when global addresses are unavailable. These private addresses must be translated to a limited set of global addresses when accessing external networks. IPv4 address translation schemes include NAT and PAT. IPv6 virtually eliminates the need for address translation as a means of accessing external networks.

Table 4.10 illustrates the reduced address administration burden placed upon IPv6 network administrators.

Table 4.10 Address Administration Comparison

Address Administration Issues	IPv4 Private Class A Block	IPv6 Aggregatable Global Unicast
Address Length	32 bits	128 bits
Length of Pre-assigned Upstream Fields	8 bits	48 bits
Length of Delegated Addressing Fields	24 bits	80 bits
Host Identifier Length	24 subnet bits	64 bits
Subnet Identifier Length	24 host bits	16 bits (SLA ID)
Allocate host addresses for subnet identifiers	Yes	No
Determine subnet identifiers	Yes	Yes
Determine host identifiers	Yes	No
Address Translation Required (NAT/PAT)	Yes	No

Header Comparison

Five fields are eliminated, including the variable-length IPv4 **options** field. Removal of the variable-length field and other fields permits the IPv6 header to have a fixed header of 40 bytes in length. A comparison of the two types of headers is summarized in Table 4.11.

Table 4.11 Header Comparison

Header	IPv4	IPv6
Header Format	Variable	Fixed
Header Fields	13	8
Header Length	20 to 60 bytes	40 bytes
Address Length	32 bits	128 bits
Header Checksum	Yes	No
Fragmentation Fields	Yes	No
Extension Headers	No	Yes

To provide for additional options, IPv6 defines the following extension headers, which are used to provide specific information needed for particular operations.

- Hop-by-Hop Options header
- Destination Options header
- Routing header
- Fragment header
- Authentication header (AH)
- Encapsulating Security Payload header

These headers are discussed in the following sections.

Feature Comparison

The IPv6 architecture contains integrated features that are not contained in IPv4. Table 4.12 contrasts the features of IPv4 and IPv6.

Table 4.12 Feature Chart

Feature	IPv4	IPv6
Anycast Address	No	Yes
Multicast Scoping	No	Yes
Security Support	No	Yes
Mobility Support	No	Yes
Autoconfiguration	No	Yes
Router Discovery	No	Neighbor Discovery
Multicast Membership	IGMP	Multicast Listener Discovery
Router Fragmentation	Yes	Source only

IPv6 Addresses

IPv6 splits its addresses into a set of definite scopes, or boundaries, by which IPv6 delegates addresses. The format prefix (FP) is used to show that an address is Globally Routable Unicast (GRU), or another type of address, and is always set to the same value. This allows a router to quickly discern what type of IPv6 packet it has received. By obtaining this information quickly, the routing device can more efficiently send the packet to its next hop or final destination. The Top-Level Aggregation Identifier (TLA ID) field and the Next-Level Aggregation Identifier(NLA ID) field are key to understanding IPv6's support for an aggregatable addressing hierarchy

The TLA ID designates a large block of addresses from which smaller blocks of addresses are allocated to downstream networks. This makes address assignment more structured and eases routing burdens. IPv6 global addresses are assigned to service provider's or Top-Level Aggregation (TLA) organizations. The TLA organizations in turn allocate addressing space to the Next-Level Aggregation (NLA) organizations. This hierarchical method of allocating address space encourages address aggregation to reduce the size of core routing tables.

The (NLA ID address block is a block of addresses that are assigned downstream out of a TLA block. These addresses are aggregated as much as possible into bigger TLA blocks when they are exchanged between providers in the Internet core. This stabilizes routing through the network.

The Site-Level Aggregation Identifier (SLA ID) enjoys most of the benefits that an NLA does, except for its size: the SLA is usually a network or network provider with a much smaller network. Unlike the TLA ID and the NLA ID, the SLA ID is not usually delegated to a downstream organization with a pre-assigned value. Per RFC 3587, the SLA ID allows an organization to define its own local subnets and addressing hierarchy. Because of this, a smaller delegation of address space is needed.

SLA ID retains the value of aggregation in that its routing tables are kept smaller, even when receiving a full Internet routing table from its upstream provider. It also enjoys the benefits of global route stability, in that its upstream provider, whether an NLA or a TLA, aggregates according to the principles of the IPv6 aggregations model. The 16 bits provided by the SLA ID for subnet identifiers can support 65,535 subnets, enough for all but the largest organizations. To support even larger networks, a downstream organization may request that a lower-order portion of the NLA ID be delegated.

The IPv6 architecture provides advantages in network performance and scalability. These advantages include:

- **Reduced Address Translation Overhead** Address translation to overcome address space limitations is unnecessary.
- **Reduced Routing Overhead** IPv6 addresses are allocated via service providers to encourage an addressing hierarchy that reduces routing overhead.
- **Increased Route Stability** A single provider can aggregate the routes of many networks and allow route flapping to be isolated to that provider's network. Routing changes need only be advertised between peer routers in a provider's network.

- **Reduced Broadcasts** IPv6 uses Neighbor Discovery to perform a similar function during the autoconfiguration process, without the use of ARP broadcasts.
- **Scoped Multicasts** In IPv6, a multicast address contains a **scope** field that can restrict multicast packets to the node, the link, or the organization.
- **Streamlined Header** The IPv6 header has only eight fixed-length fields. To implement extended functions, extension headers can be used that need not be checked by intermediate routers. This streamlined header architecture lowers network overhead.
- **No Intermediate Node Fragmentation** Only the source node will perform packet fragmentation. To assist the source node, IPv6 provides a **Path MTU Discovery** function to determine the Maximum Transmission Unit (MTU) size for the path from source to destination.
- **No Header Checksum** IPv6 eliminates the **header checksum** field. While this may cause erroneous packets to be forwarded, the reliability of current links reduces that probability. Checksum verification is already performed at the source and destination by upper-layer processes such as TCP and UDP. In IPv6, checksum processing is solely the responsibility of the source and destination. This greatly reduces network overhead.

IPv6 Address Space

The 128 bits that IPv6 has available for addressing (2^{128} addresses) are used differently depending on the address format and type. For example, GRUaddresses set the first 3 bits (FP) to 001. This leaves 125 bits for addresses (2^{125} addresses) before GRU address space is depleted.

The IPv6 Aggregatable Global Unicast Address is 128 bits long and is comprised of a subnet prefix and an interface identifier (Interface ID). The first 64 bits are used for network numbering, and the last 64 bits are used for host numbering. The 48 bits of the last 64 bits of the host ID are derived from the MAC address, with 16 bits of padding. The format is shown in Figure 4.27.

Figure 4.27 IPv6 Address Structure

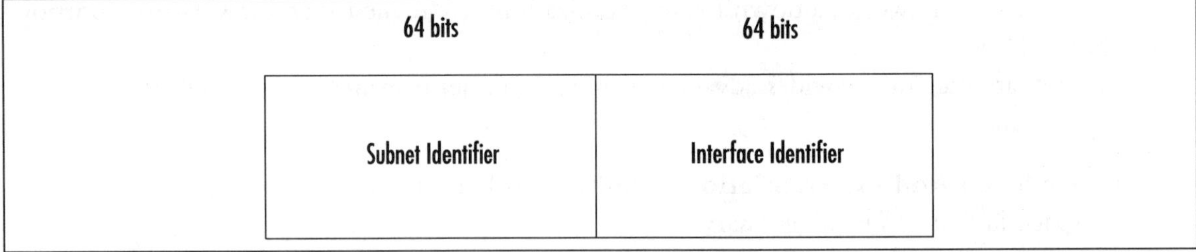

The subnet prefix is the network number assigned to the link. The interface identifier is derived from the node's MAC address. IPv6 uses the last 64 bits of the address to distinguish hosts from one another on the same subnet. Regardless of the address format, the last 64 bits on a device will remain the same. During IPv6 address autoconfiguration, the host node supplies its own interface ID from MAC components such as network cards, and queries the local router or DHCPv6 server for a subnet prefix. Today's MAC addresses are only 48-bits long, so each one is padded with a 16-bit prefix. The Institute of Electrical and Electronic Engineers (IEEE) has proposed a MAC address that is 64 bits long, known as EUI-64.

This amount of host addresses is more than adequate as there will rarely be 2^{64} addresses in use on a typical LAN. Table 4.13 compares the address sizes of IPv4 and IPv6.

Table 4.13 Address Space Comparison

Specification	IPv4	IPv6
Address Length	32 bits	128 bits
Host Identifier Length	2 to 24 bits	64 bits
Network Identifier Length	2^2 to 2^{24} bits	2^{64}
Maximum Number of Hosts per Subnet	2^2 to 2^{24}	2^{64}
Maximum Number of Hosts	3.7 E+09	4.25 E+037
Number of Hosts	3.7 E+09	4.25 E+037

IPv6 addresses are classified as unicast, multicast, or anycast addresses. The following information discusses IPv6 addresses and their structure, as well as the different types. The IPv6 address space utilizes a 128-bit format that consists of an eight-part hex address separated by colons (:). Each part of the IPv6 address space represents 16 bits, which provides a theoretical address space of 340,282,366,920,938,463,463,374,607,431,768,211,456 addresses. Due to the fact that IPv6 has reserved addresses, the total assignable address space is smaller than this.

The size and scope of the IPv6 address space enables allocations of addresses in a more hierarchal fashion than IPv4, which in turn enables independent customers of service providers to obtain and deploy globally routable addresses within their environments. The IPv6 address space provides more than enough space to reassign public IPv6 addresses to all entities that require global routing over the Internet.

The Fundamentals of IPv6 Addresses

IPv6 utilizes hex notation. This is a fundamental change from the dotted decimal notation used in the IPv4 addressing. Utilization of dotted decimal notation to express and address space equivalent to the size of the IPv6 scope would be complex and cumbersome. To express the same address space as IPv6 in decimal notation, the current IPv4 string would have to be expanded four times. If dotted decimal notation were used, addresses would appear as 15.25.35.45.55.65.75.85.95.105.115.125.135.145.155.165, which would make it very difficult to remember IP addresses. Using hexadecimal notation allows for the expression of these numbers using two hexadecimal numbers. Conversion from decimal to hexadecimal and vice versa is a necessary evil for anyone considering IPv6, especially if IPv4 addresses are incorporated into the IPv6 address. Table 4.14 depicts decimal to hexadecimal equivalents. This table is useful when converting smaller numbers.

Table 4.14 Decimal to Hexadecimal Equivalents

Decimal Notation	Hex Notation
0	0
1	1
2	2
3	3
4	4
5	5
6	6
7	7
8	8
9	9
10	a
11	b
12	c
13	d
14	e
15	f

How are hexadecimal numbers used within the IPv6 addressing architecture? RFC3513 provides an addressing structure for IPv6 addressing architectures. Cisco requires that all addressing comply with RFC3513. Although the hexadecimal notation shortens the number of digits required to express a decimal value, the address structure is much longer than IPv4 due to the amount of address space.

As previously discussed, IPv6 addresses utilize a 128-bit format that consists of an eight-part hex address separated by colons (:). Expressed another way, there are eight 16-bit hexadecimal values separated by colons as shown generically, where **X** is 16 bits of two hexadecimal values.

```
X:X:X:X:X:X:X:X
```

Therefore, an IPv6 address is expressed as follows:

```
ADBF:0:FEEA:0:0:00EA:00AC:DEED (or ADBF:0000:FEEA:0000:0000:00EA:00AC:DEED)
```

IPv6 provides two methods for compressing the syntax of the address space. The first is the omission of leading zeroes and the second is the replacement of multiple groups of zeroes by double colons (::). Using these methods, the preceding address can be shortened considerably.

For example, using the first method, omitting the leading zeroes provides an address of ADBF:0:FEEA:0:0:EA:AC:DEED. If the second method is applied, the address is represented as ADBF:0:FEEA::EA:AC:DEED. However, the double colon can appear only once in the address. In addition to replacing multiple groups of zeroes within the address, the double colon can be used to represent the leading or trailing zeroes in an address.

IPv4 Addresses as IPv6 Addresses

RFC3513 outlines a structure for representing IPv4 addresses with IPv6 address space and format. IPv4 addresses can be embedded or mapped.

Embedded IPv4 addresses are where IPv4 unicast addresses are transported over IPv6 networks. The format (from RFC3513) is shown in Figure 4.28. This is an odd format because the first 96 bits are expressed as hexadecimal, while the last 32 bits are decimal notation for the IPv4 address.

Figure 4.28 Embedded IPv4 Address

80 bits	16	32 bits
0000 0000	0000	IPv4 Address

The six high-order hexadecimal values (16 bits each) of the IPv6 address space are represented as leading zeroes. The last two 16-bit spaces are broken into four 8-bit spaces for the IPv4 address. This provides an address in the form of 0:0:0:0:0:0.A.B.C.D, where ABCD is expressed in standard IPv4 syntax. For example, the IPv4 address of 192.168.100.10 can be represented as 0:0:0:0:0:0.192.168.100.10. Notice that within the IPv6 address the IPv4 address space is delimited by dots (.), not colons. The IPv6 address can be further truncated by omitting the leading zeroes. The result is an IPv6 address in the form of ::192.168.100.10. Embedding is appropriate for allowing IPv4 traffic to be transported over IPv6 networks.

IPv4 addresses can be mapped to IPv6 addresses, making them a form of IPv6 address. This is a conversion process in that IPv4 addresses are transformed into IPv6 addresses. The format is shown in Figure 4.29

Figure 4.29 Mapped IPv4 Address

80 bits	16	32 bits
0000.. 0000	FFFF	IPv4 Address

The 16 bits preceding the IPv4 portion are turned on (all ones). The Internet community adopted CIDR notation to extend the life of the IPv4 address space, which is also used by IPv6. CIDR does not solve the problem of multiple entries in the Internet routing tables, but rather presents a method for aggregating address space only outside the normal Class A, B, and C network boundaries.

As with IPv4 addresses, specific types of reserved address divisions are within the IPv6 addressing architecture. The leading bits within the address identify reserve addresses. Table 4.15 shows the reserved addresses.

Table 4.15 IPv6 Address First-Bits Standards

Allocation	Prefix (Binary)	Fraction of Address Space
Reserved	0000 0000	1/256
Unassigned	0000 0001	1/256
Reserved for NSAP Allocation	0000 001	1/128
Reserved for IPX Allocation	0000 010	1/128
Unassigned	0000 011	1/128
Unassigned	0000 1	1/32
Unassigned	0001	1/16
Aggregatable Global		
Unicast Addresses	001	1/8
Unassigned	010	1/8
Unassigned	011	1/8
Unassigned	100	1/8
Unassigned	101	1/8
Unassigned	110	1/8
Unassigned	1110	1/16
Unassigned	1111 0	1/32
Unassigned	1111 10	1/64
Unassigned	1111 110	1/128
Unassigned	1111 1110 0	1/512
Link-Local Unicast Addresses	1111 1110 10	1/1024
Site-Local Unicast Addresses	1111 1110 11	1/1024
Multicast Addresses	1111 1111	1/256

Each of these reserved address spaces defines a specific type of address. The addresses defined have scope. A node or router may have multiple addresses configured that define the scope as local to the link, local to the site, or globally significant. In addition, there are loopback and local use, multicast, and anycast addresses. The types of addresses are as follows:

- Unicast Address
- Multicast Address
- Anycast Address
- Nodes-Required Address

IPv6 Unicast Addresses

A unicast address represents an end node or host. Unicast addresses are aggregatable and use contiguous bits to represent the subnet mask. By incorporating clear and concise definitions, IPv6 provides a structured addressing architecture for allocating addresses. IPv6 unicast addresses are segmented into the following formats:

- Aggregatable Global Unicast Addresses
- Loopback Addresses
- Unspecified Addresses
- Interface Identifiers
- Local-use Unicast Addresses
- NSAP Addresses
- IPX Addresses

Aggregatable Global Unicast Address

The Aggregatable Global Unicast Address format is used to define a tiered structure for the assignment and allocation of the IPv6 address space. The new structure calls for the address space to be broken into six separate components. These components are the FP), the TLA ID, Reserved (RES), NLA ID, SLA ID, and the Interface ID. Figure 4.30 depicts the Global Unicast Address format.

Figure 4.30 Global Unicast Address Format

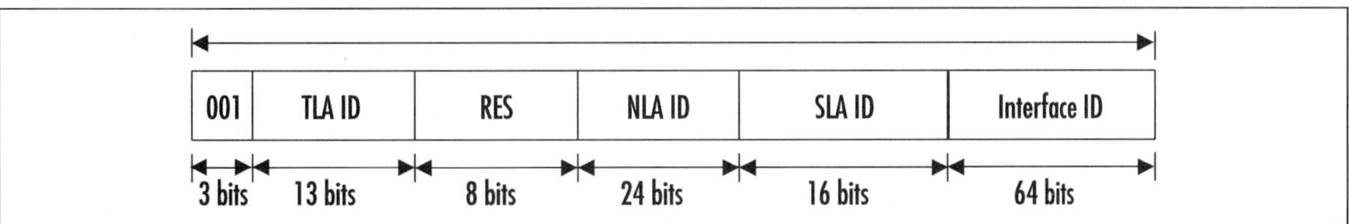

The public routing topology prefix (from FP to the RES field) consists of the first 48 bits of unicast address space. This includes the FP bits plus the TLA, RES, and NLA bits. The next 16 bits define the site topology and the final 64 bits are the Interface ID. The public topology is address space assigned to exchanges and Internet Service Providers (ISPs) that provide transit Internet services. The site topology can be defined as the customers of the providers and exchanges and the Interface ID is an end host or node Interface ID.

- **FP** The first three bits are always set to 001 for GRU addresses.
- **TLA ID** 13 bits. TLAs reside at the highest point of the routing hierarchy, and are assigned one of the 8,192 TLA IDs. Allocates addresses to downstream customers.
- **RES** Reserved.
- **NLA ID** 24 bits. From an upstream TLA, which is broken into chunks, which will be delegated to the customers of the NLA.
- **SLA ID** A SLA ID describes an entity that has no downstream customers who are network service providers. An example of an SLA is a cable modem service provider.
- **Interface ID** The final 64 bits of the Global Unicast address is reserved for the Interface ID. This is typically comprised of a MAC address and any padding necessary to make 64 bits.

The policies governing the assignment of IPv6 unicast address space must be done in a manner that ensures that each unicast address is efficiently allocated, globally routable, unique, and supports aggregation. RFC 3587 organizes the IPv6 address space into a topological hierarchy. The topologies are public topology, site topology, and interface topology. An IPv6 address can be expressed in the same manner as IPv4 addresses. An IPv4 address contains network and host bits. The network and host portions of an IPv6 address are shown in Figure 4.31.

Figure 4.31 Unicast Address Network and Host Bits

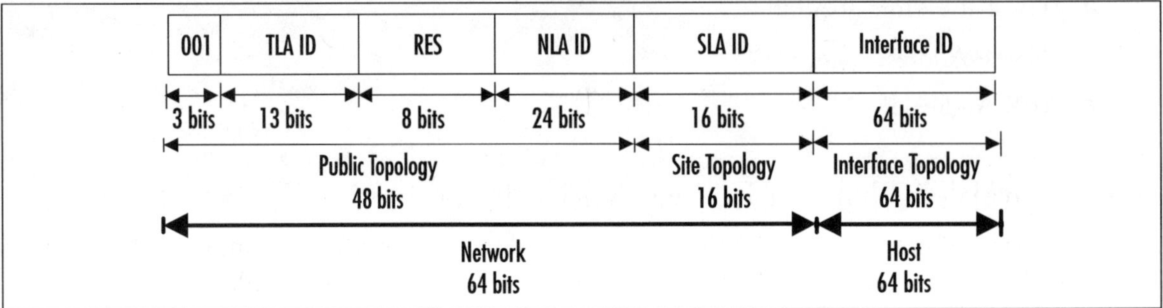

The network portion of an IPv6 address is 64 bits and the host portion is 64 bits. The expression of IPv6 addresses uses CIDR notation to divide the address into network and host portions. An address with a /48 mask represents an aggregatable network prefix assigned out of the public topology allocation.

The regional Internet Registry (IR) agencies use a modified version of the TLA field to allocate the initial address space. This requires dividing the TLA space into a sub-TLA, which allows for allocating less of the address space to the original TLAs as previously planned. The IR reserves the additional 6 bits for the TLA so that if the need arises, it can allocate the address space to the TLA. The reservation preserves the aggregation policies but allows for efficient allocation on an as-needed basis. This policy creates a modified format to the IPv6 address space. The modified version is shown in Figure 4.32.

Figure 4.32 Modified Sub-TLA Format

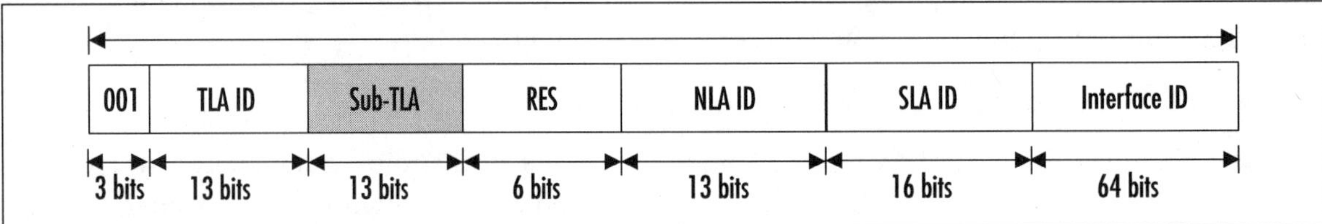

The address allocation policy for IPv6 is as follows:

1. Regional IRs assign addresses to qualified sub-TLAs (TLA ISPs).
2. TLA ISPs assign NLA addresses to NLA ISPs (TLA customers).
3. NLA ISPs assign SLA addresses to their customers.

TLA providers have to be able to allocate SLA addresses to customers. TLA ISPs provide direct Internet connectivity to end users as well as NLAs. Subnetting the address space within the TLA and NLA providers' networks is left up to the discretion of the individual providers. Regardless of how providers subnet the address space within their networks, aggregation of the address space falls on the prefix boundaries shown in Table 4.16.

Table 4.16 Aggregation Prefix Boundaries

ID	Longest Prefix	Length in Bits
TLA	/16	13
Sub-TLA	/29	13
RES		
NLA	/48	13
SLA	/64	16

The Loopback Address

The loopback interface is not a physical interface and has no hardware associated with it. It is a software interface that is always reachable regardless of the physical interface status. RFC3513 defines the loopback interface address as 0:0:0:0:0:0:0:1, or ::1 in condensed form. An IPv6 node uses the loopback interface to send packets to itself. The standard prohibits a node from forwarding a packet with a destination address of a loopback.

The Unspecified Address

The unspecified address (0:0:0:0:0:0:0:0 or ::) is never assigned to any node, and may not be used as a destination address in an IP packet, nor can it be used in routing headers. Unspecified addresses are used during the auto configuration process.

Interface IDs

Interface IDs, derived substantially from MAC addresses, are used to uniquely identify interfaces on a link. IPv6 utilizes a modified EUI-64 format to construct Interface IDs. EUI-64 addresses are a derivation of the 24-bit company ID value assigned by the IEEE registration authority.

Conversion to the EUI-64 format is accomplished by modifying the 48-bit MAC address assigned to the hardware interface. Cisco routers contain pools of MAC addresses that are used for internal identifiers. The exceptions to these rules are tunnels that are used with IPv6 overlay tunnels. For these types of interfaces the Interface ID is the IPv4 address with zeroes in the high-order 32 bits.

To create EUI-64 addresses from vendor MAC addresses, perform the following steps:

1. Insert **ff-ee** between the third and fourth bytes of the MAC address.
2. Complement the Universal/Local (U/L) bit by inverting the bit from the original value and set it to either a 0 or a 1. Setting the bit to 0 means that the Interface ID is locally administered; setting it to 1 indicates a globally unique Interface ID.)

Local-Use Unicast Addresses

Two types of local-use addresses exist within the IPv6 address space:

- **Link-local Addresses (Used on a Single Link)** Significant only on the physical medium connected to the router (that is, Ethernet, Token Ring, or WAN segment
- **Site-local Addresses (Used within a Site)**

Only the hosts and router interface connected to the same segment are aware of the link-local addresses for that segment. The router does not advertise link-local addresses, which considerably simplifies renumbering. After the addresses have been assigned (either manually or via auto configuration), the Global Unicast Address space can change without having to reconfigure the link-local addresses. In addition, link-local addressing is used in neighbor discovery and internal routing. Figure 4.33 shows the format for the link-local address.

Figure 4.33 Link-Local Unicast Address Format

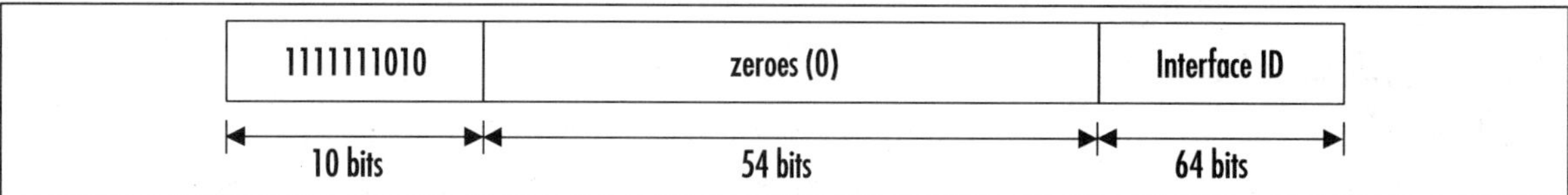

The leftmost 10 bits shown in Figure 4.6 translate into the prefix FE80::/64. Appending the Interface ID to the FE80::/64 prefix derives link-local addresses. Figure 4.34 depicts a segment utilizing link-local addressing.

Figure 4.34 Link-Local Address Space

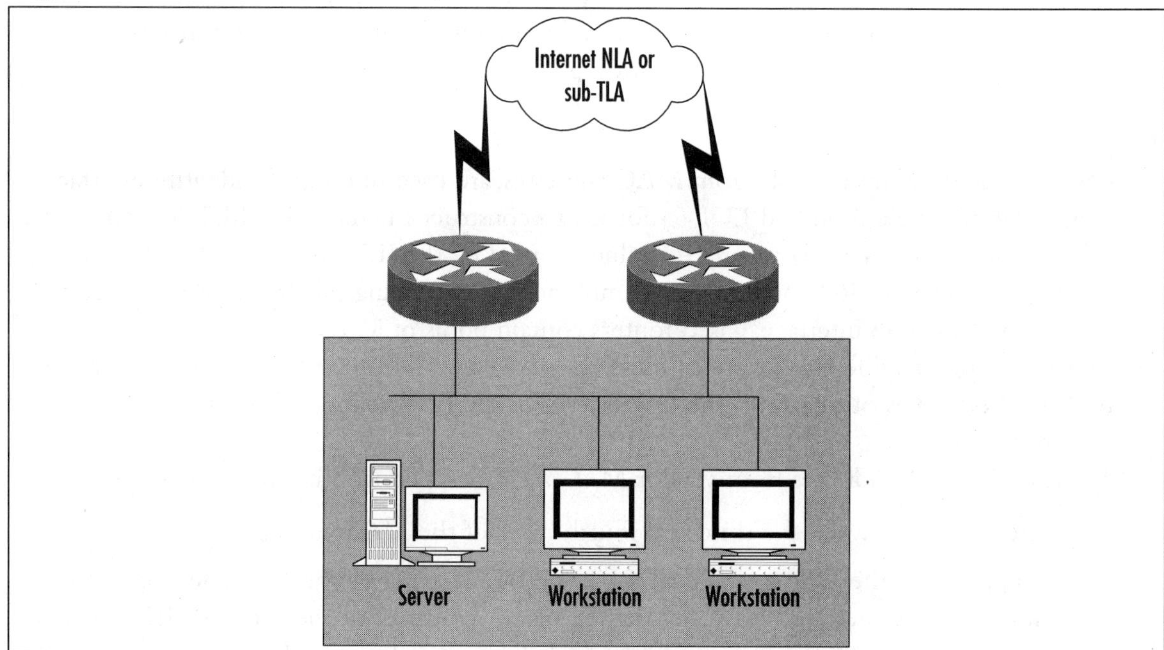

Link-local devices are configured using a MAC address or the EUI-64 format prepended by FE80. Figure 4.35 depicts the address assignments for the devices in link format.

Figure 4.35 Link-Local Assigned Addresses

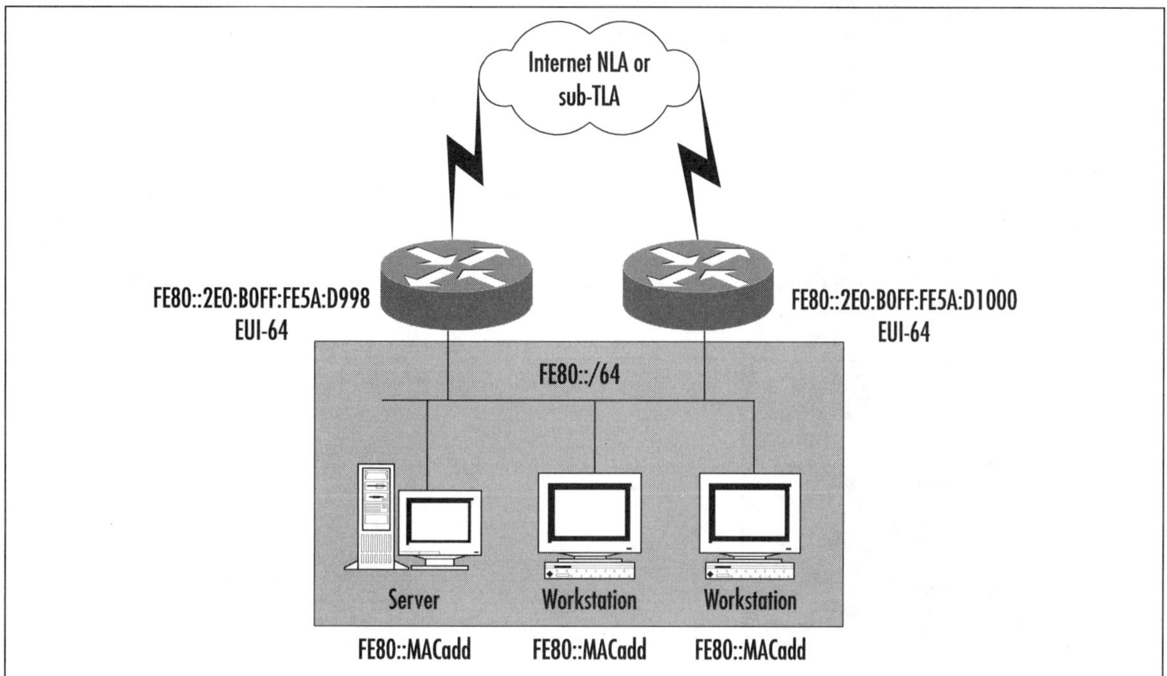

In this example, the routers are utilizing EUI-64 format for the Interface ID; the server and workstations are using MAC addresses. These addresses are never visible outside the local segment on which they are configured. If the devices need to be reached from hosts outside the local segment, site-local unicast addresses are assigned.

A site-local address is an address that is routable within a site only. This means that hosts that are configured with a site-local address can communicate with other hosts within the same environment but are not globally routable. These addresses are assigned without a global unicast prefix. Site-local addresses are used in the same fashion as RFC 1918 addresses are in the IPv4 world. Site-local addresses are considered private and form the addressing structure for an internal domain. Figure 4.36 shows the format for the site-local address.

Figure 4.36 Site-Local Address Format

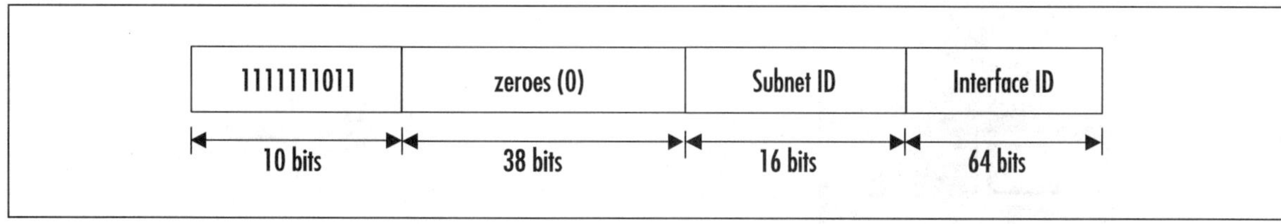

The leftmost 10 bits shown in Figure 4.9 translate into the prefix FEC0::/10. Concatenating the 16-bit SLA field (subnet ID) with the interface ID derives the site-local address. Figure 4.37 shows a topology that utilizes site-local addresses.

Figure 4.37 Site-Local Address Space

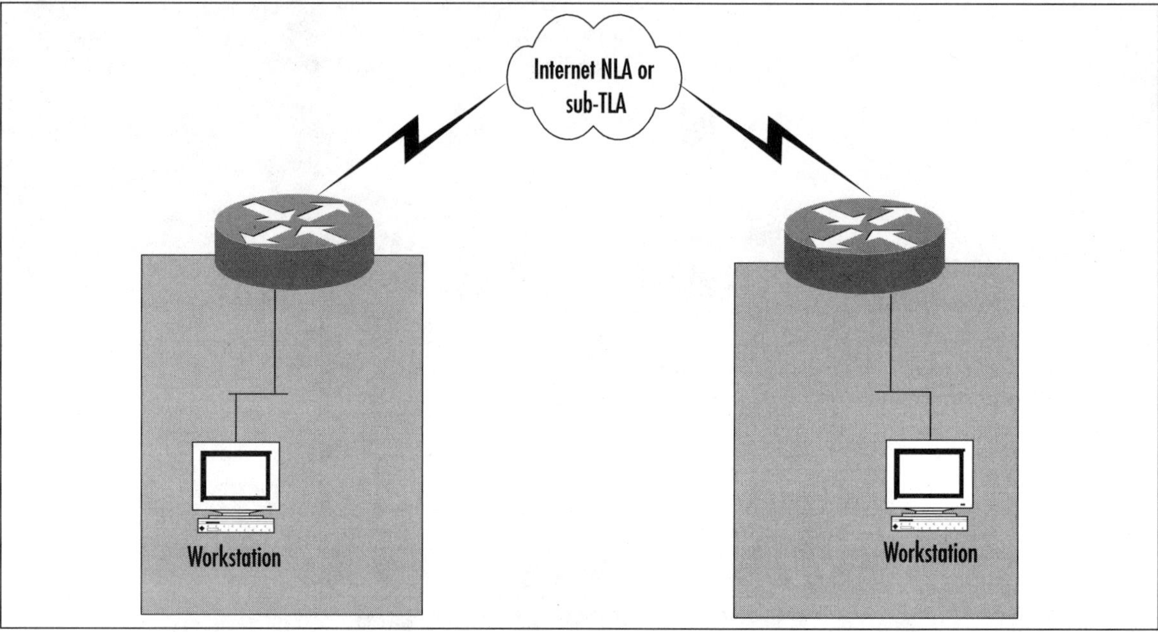

Site-local devices are configured using a MAC address or the EUI-64 format prepended by FEC0. Figure 4.38 depicts the address assignments for the devices in site-local format.

Figure 4.38 Site-Local Assigned Addresses

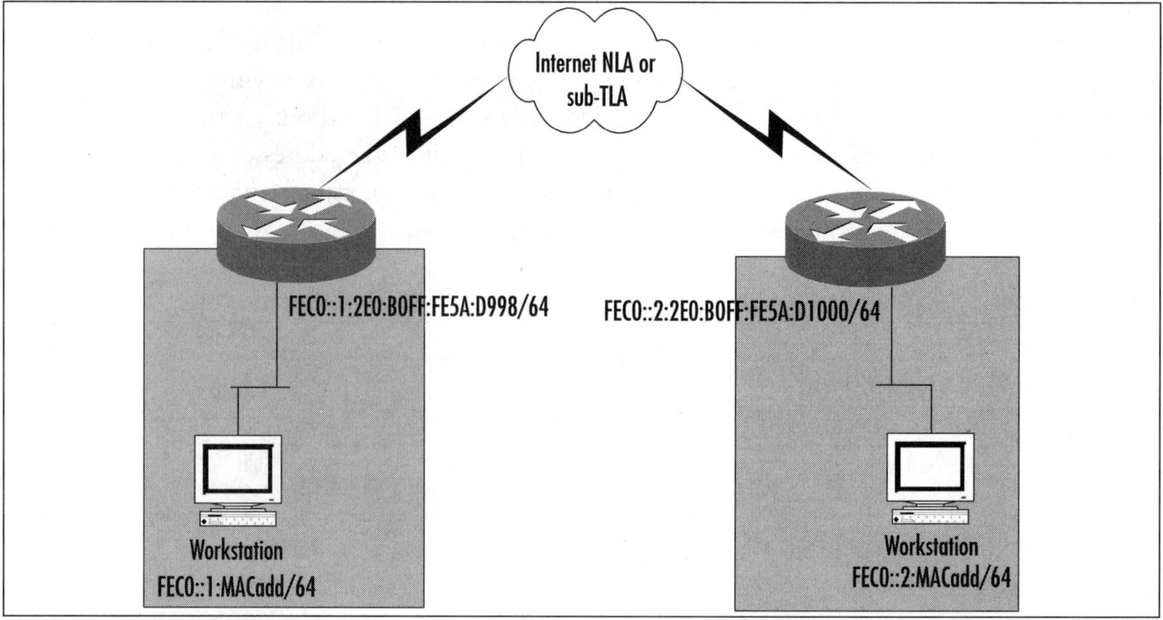

In this example, the routers utilize site-local addresses and interface IDs in the EUI-64 format. The workstations are using the MAC address as the interface ID. The numbers 1 and 2 before the interface ID represent the subnet ID. Workstations on subnet 1 can communicate with workstations on subnet 2 and vice versa. These addresses are never advertised outside the internal domain to the global Internet. If future Internet connectivity is required, it makes sense to initially configure the host with a GRU address. Again, this introduces the issue of renumbering in the event that the customer changes providers.

Subnetting and Prefixes for IPv6 Aggregation

IPv6 was developed with a structure and format that is conducive to high levels of aggregation. In the previous section, you learned that IPv6 addresses are broken up into prefixes of TLA, sub-TLA, NLA, and SLA allocations. Providers allocate addresses in a hierarchical fashion that provides aggregation from the lower-level prefixes to the higher-level TLAs. RFC3513 provides a clear method for the allocation of the IPv6 address space.

ARIN, RIPE, and APNIC allocate sub-TLA address space to the TLA providers. These providers in turn allocate NLA address space to downstream providers who in turn allocate to SLAs. Remember that TLAs can also allocate SLAs. Figure 4.39 depicts the hierarchy of Global Unicast Address allocation.

Figure 4.39 Global Unicast Address Allocation

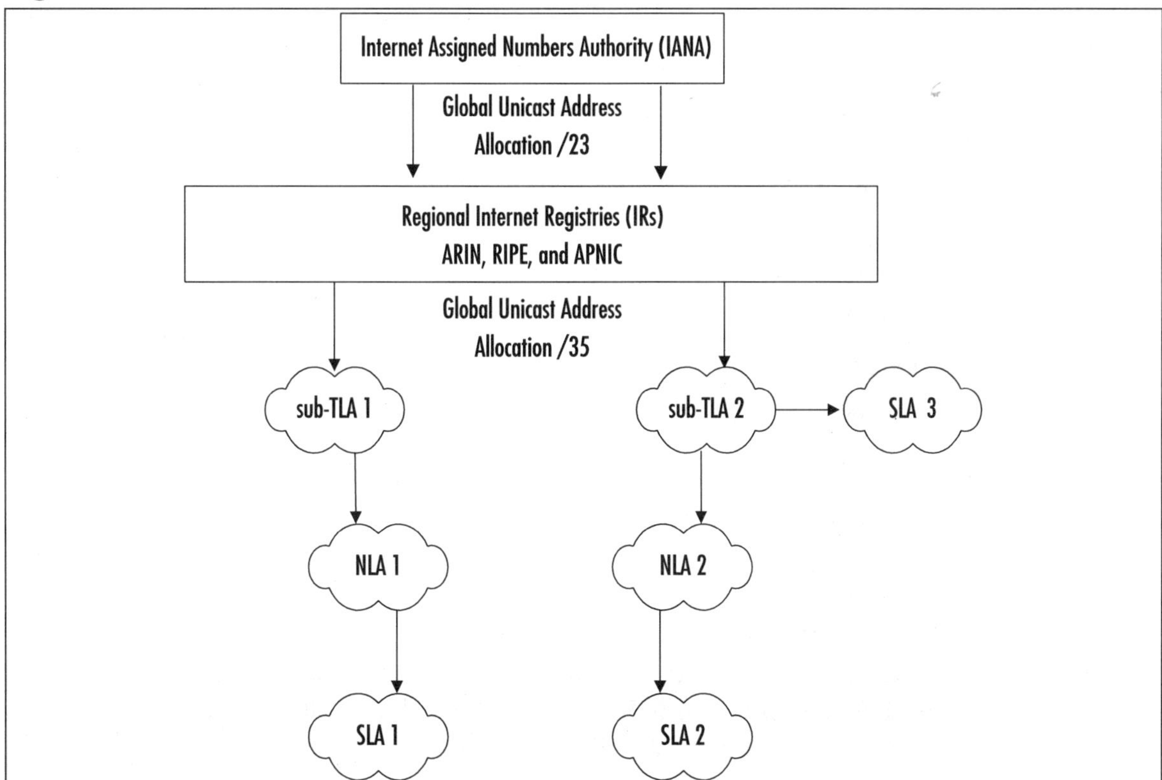

The following IPv6 address assignments have been allocated to the three IRs:

- 2001:0400::/23 - ARIN
- 2001:0200::/23 - APNIC
- 2001:0600::/23 - RIPE

ARIN is used as an example to demonstrate the aggregation capabilities of IPv6. ARIN has adopted assignment guidelines for IPv6 address allocation from RFC 3177. These guidelines provide the following recommendations for IPv6 address space allocation:

- Allocate /35 addresses to TLAs—this is a sub-TLA address space.
- TLAs allocating address space to NLAs are responsible for prefix/network length determination.
- As a general rule, allocate a /48 to all SLAs (except for very large SLAs).
- Allocate a /64 to SLAs that have only one subnet.
- Allocate a /128 to SLAs with only one subscriber.

These policies relate more to SLA end customers, but they provide efficient guidelines that facilitate aggregation. ARIN is responsible for assigning the slow-start sub-TLA addresses out of the 2001:0400::/23 block to providers. Say that ARIN allocates the following addresses:

- 2001:0420::/35 - sub-TLA1
- 2001:0428::/35 - sub-TLA2

This allocation gives each of these sub-TLA providers the capability to subnet this space and allocate it to the NLAs. These rules govern the subnetting of the NLA address space. This subnetting should be done at the NLA provider's discretion. The TLAs can allocate the following address space to the downstream NLAs:

- Sub-TLA1 provides the following prefixes to its NLA customers:
  - 2001:0420:0001::/48
  - 2001:0420:0002::/48
  - 2001:0420:0003::/48 etc
- Sub-TLA2 provides the following prefixes to its NLA customers
  - 2001:0428:0001::/48
  - 2001:0428:0002::/48
  - 2001:0428:0003::/48 etc

Each NLA provider can subnet and allocate the address space delegated to them by the sub-TLAs. Using the guidelines established in RFC3177, the NLAs should allocate /48s to their downstream SLA customers. For example, an NLA provider with the address space of 2001:0420:0001::/48 can allocate the following address space:

- 2001:0420:0001:1:/48

- 2001:0420:0001:2:/48
- 2001:0420:0001:3:/48, and so on

The allocation policies described previously provide the aggregation desired for a hierarchical IPv6 infrastructure. Figure 4.40 shows the distribution of the ARIN-allocated IPv6 addresses to the NLA providers and SLA customers.

Figure 4.40 ARIN

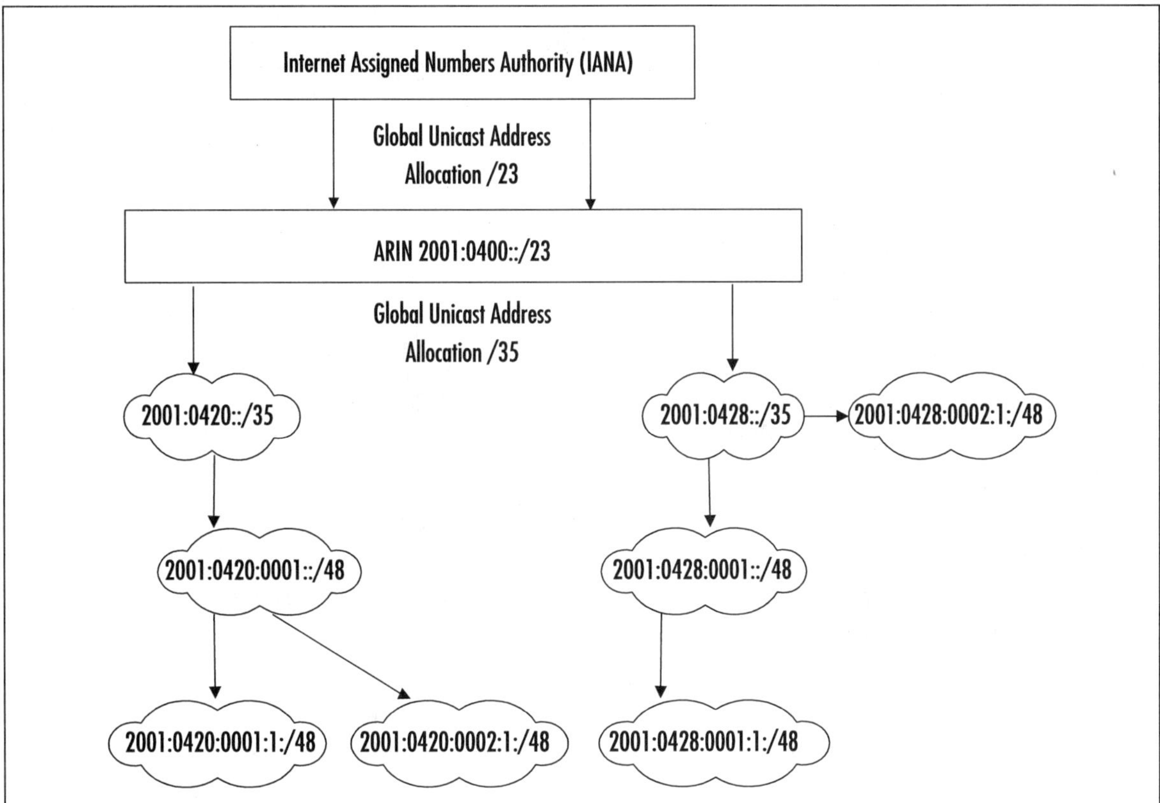

Internet providers use BGPv4 to propagate addresses throughout the Internet. Addresses are aggregated and advertised to the upstream provider when possible. The inefficiencies of IPv4 allocation and advertisement policies have created an abundance of routes with small prefixes. With the IPv6 aggregation capabilities, the SLA can advertise the entire prefix assigned to them to the NLA. All SLA space is a subset of the NLA to which the customer is connected. This enables the NLA to generate one prefix announcement to the sub-TLA for all SLA customers. The same holds true for the NLA space. The NLA allocates all addresses out of the sub-TLA assignment, enabling the sub-TLA to generate one prefix advertisement to its peers. Figure 4.41 depicts the aggregate announcements.

Figure 4.41 Aggregate Route Announcements

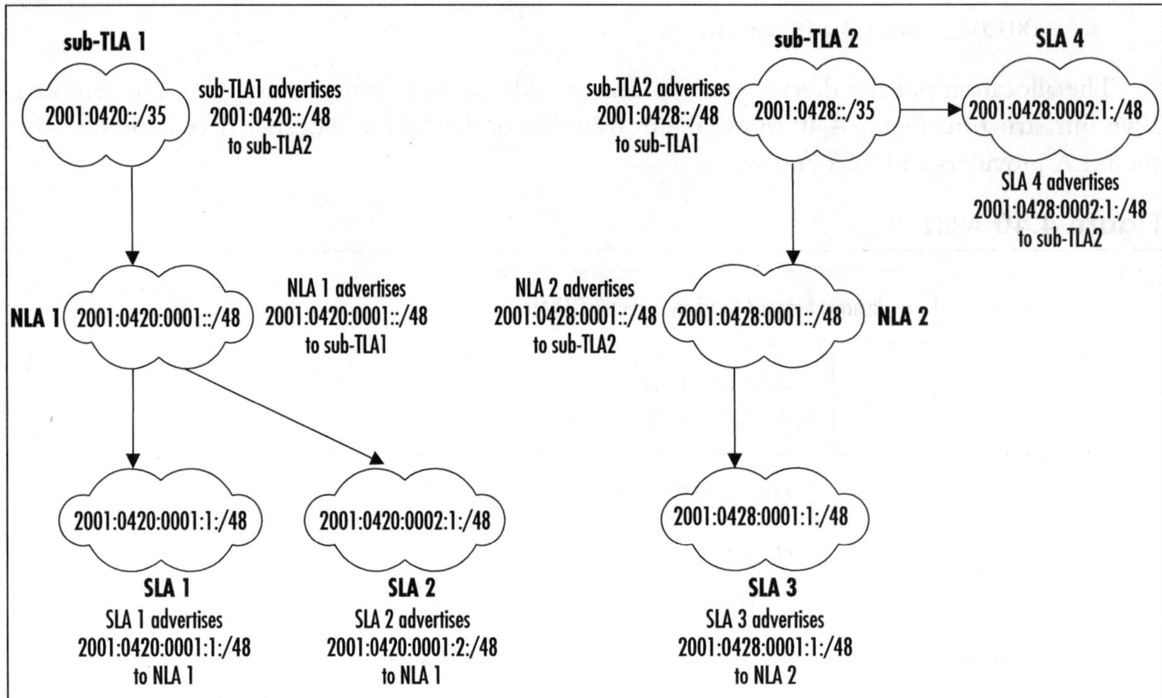

Using this hierarchical aggregation model substantially reduces the size of the Internet routing table. The routing table for sub-TLA1 comprises only NLA prefixes and prefixes learned from other sub-TLAs (or TLAs). Address space assigned to TLAs is not portable. This means that the addresses have to be advertised to the TLA that allocated the address space, which reduces the de-aggregation of addresses demonstrated in current IPv4 allocations. Non-portability does have its drawbacks. If a customer is unsatisfied with the level of service provided by their upstream provider and switches providers, the entire network has to be renumbered out of the new provider's address space.

Switching providers creates issues not only with addressing, but also with the subject of dual homing. IPv6 address space is not intended to be portable; in other words, a secondary provider does not accept prefix advertisements from other providers, which prevents customers from dual homing to multiple providers.

IPv6 Multicast Addressing

A multicast address is identified by the presence of eight 1 bits at the start of the IPv6 address, as shown in Figure 4.43. IPv6 uses the concept of multicast scoping where certain multicast streams are routed only within a certain area, and never leave that area. This scoping is well known and understood by all routing entities to constrain multicast data and multicast routes so that they do not get outside the routing domain for which they are meant to exist. Figure 4.42 presents the multicast addressing format in a little more detail.

Figure 4.42 IPv6 Multicast Address Format

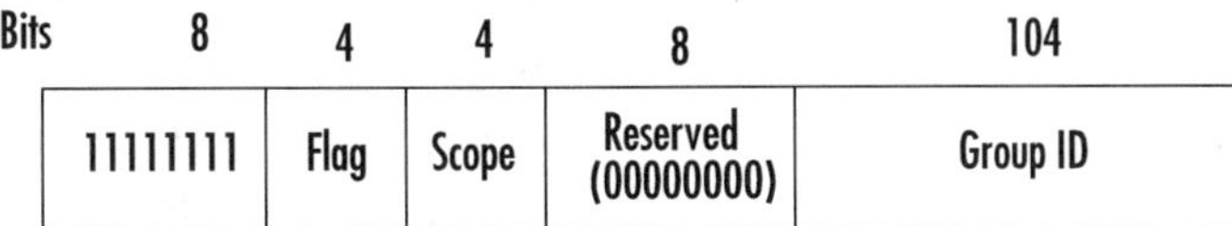

As can be seen, the multicast addressing architecture is a little different than that of the GRU addressing format. The first 8 bits are set to one, which will allow a routing device to know immediately that the packet is multicast in nature, and subject to the special handling associated with this packet type.

The next 4 bits are used for flags. Currently, the first 3 bits in the **flags** field are reserved and undefined, so they should always be set to zero. The fourth bit is known as the **T bit** (see RFC2460), and is used to decide whether the multicast address is a permanently assigned address (well-known) or a temporary assignment (transient). This field identifies if the multicast address is standard (perhaps a group address used to contact all nodes within a given routing domain, for example) or a temporarily assigned address (perhaps the Monday night football game broadcast over the Internet).

The **scope** field determines how far the multicast packet can go, in what areas of a routing domain the packet can travel, and the group address that can be advertised. The **scope** field takes the values shown in Table 4.17. It uses 4 bits to specify the scope of the multicast group.

Table 4.17 Multicast Scope Field

Scope Value	Scope
0	RES
1	Node-local scope
2	Link-local scope
3	Unassigned
4	Unassigned
5	Site-local scope
6	Unassigned
7	Unassigned
8	Organization-local scope
9	Unassigned
A	Unassigned
B	Unassigned
C	Unassigned
D	Unassigned
E	Global scope
F	RES

Depending on how we assign our multicast address, we can control how far the multicast packets travel, and how widely the routing announcements associated with that multicast group are advertised. A scope of E (1110 in binary) would broadcast all networks, while a scope of 5 would be limited to the local networks, or even 2, which would limit the scope to the LAN.

The RES field has all 8 of its bits set to 0. The remaining 104 bits provide the Group ID; that is, the address for the multicast group to which this packet is destined.

The **Flag** field is a set of 4 bits with the first 3 reserved and the fourth used to flag whether the multicast address is permanently or non-permanently assigned. A 0 indicates permanent and a 1 indicates non-permanent. The global Internet numbering authority assigns permanent multicast addresses.

The **Group ID** field identifies multicast addresses as permanent or non-permanent within a scope. It is important to distinguish between permanent addresses within a scope and permanent addresses across a scope.

Permanent addresses within a scope are those addresses that are reserved for multicast functions for that particular scope. For example, FF01 indicates a node-local scope. Addresses FF01:0:0:0:0:0:0:1 and FF01:0:0:0:0:0:0:2 are reserved within the FF01 scope.

Permanent addresses across a scope are those addresses that have a reserved group ID value for any scope range. For example, the group ID of 100 is reserved for the Versatile Message Transaction Protocol (VMTP) Managers Group (RFC1045). This address is a permanent address across any of the scope values shown in Table 4.18. Table 4.18 defines addresses reserved for multicast groups of both fixed-scope and variable-scope allocations.

Table 4.18 Reserved Multicast Addresses

Node-Local Scope Reserved For	Multicast-Address
All Nodes Address	FF01:0:0:0:0:0:0:1
All Routers Address	FF01:0:0:0:0:0:0:2
Link-Local Scope Reserved For	**Multicast-Address**
All Nodes Address	FF02:0:0:0:0:0:0:1
All Routers Address	FF02:0:0:0:0:0:0:2
Unassigned	FF02:0:0:0:0:0:0:3
DVMRP Routers	FF02:0:0:0:0:0:0:4
OSPFIGP	FF02:0:0:0:0:0:0:5
OSPFIGP Designated Routers	FF02:0:0:0:0:0:0:6
ST Routers	FF02:0:0:0:0:0:0:7
ST Hosts	FF02:0:0:0:0:0:0:8
RIP Routers	FF02:0:0:0:0:0:0:9
EIGRP Routers	FF02:0:0:0:0:0:0:A

RFC3513 also provides a method for mapping multicast addresses into MAC addresses. The low-order 32 bits of the multicast address generate the MAC address. This is only feasible for group IDs that have 32 bits or fewer. IPv6 multicast address assignment should be done so that the group ID is always in the low-order 32 bits.

IPv6 Anycast Addresses

An anycast address is an IPv6 address that is assigned to a group of one or more hosts, all of which serve a common purpose or function. Any address assigned to more than one interface is considered an IPv6 anycast address. When packets are sent to the IPv6 anycast address, routing dictates which member of the group receives the packet via the machine *closest to the source*, as determined by the routing protocol. Packets sent to an anycast address are routed dynamically to the nearest interface configured with the anycast address.

Routing protocols determine the "nearness" of the closest (in terms of routing distance) anycast interface. *Anycast addresses are indistinguishable from a unicast address.* Anycast addresses are beneficial because they can be used to augment dynamic routing protocols when choosing the shortest path to a destination.

Although both the anycast and the multicast addresses are assigned to more than one host, the anycast address serves for data transmissions that are 1-to-1, whereas multicast addressing is used when a data transmission to multiple destinations is required. While multicast addresses operate on a one-to-many principle, anycast addresses operate on a one-to-nearest. That is, many geographically dispersed devices share the same anycast address, but only the device nearest will respond to anycast traffic to the address.

One application that benefits from anycast addresses is DNS. It is efficient for deploying multiple DNS servers and spreading them out geographically. This allows for failover if one DNS server becomes unreachable due to network failures, and it also allows the administrator to distribute the load of their DNS service between these servers. An illustration of anycast in use is provided in Figure 4.43.

Figure 4.43 Anycast Message

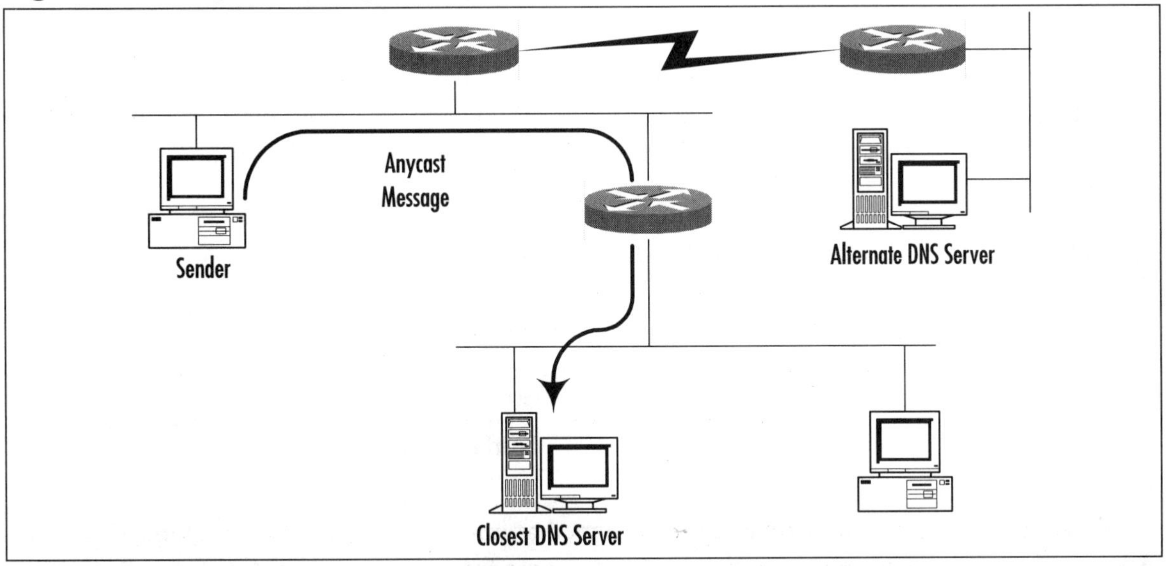

Anycast addressing enables load sharing among multiple hosts. For example, a user can initiate a connection to the anycast address, which results in the packet being routed to the nearest server based on the dynamic route. The user does not have to specify a server to which to connect. However, each server must be configured with the anycast address. For example, routers are associated with the **subnet-router** anycast address. All routers are required to support this address for the interfaces that are configured as subnets. Figure 4.44 depicts the format of the subnet-router anycast address.

Figure 4.44 Anycast Address

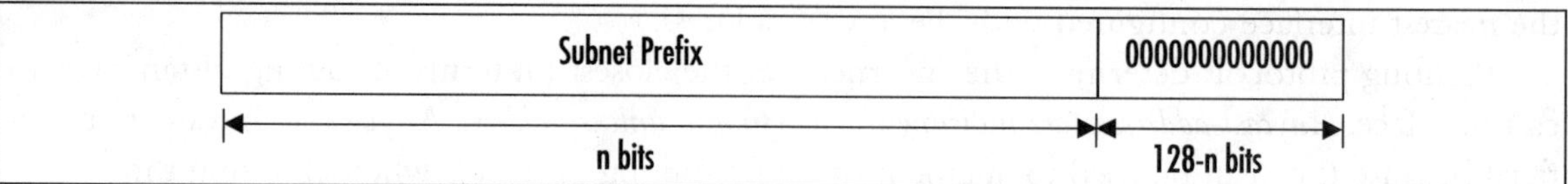

There are two other reserved anycast addresses. The format of these addresses is dependent on the type of IPv6 address configured. A simple rule to remember is: if the leading bits of an address equals 000, the interface ID can have any width; if the leading bits of an address are not equal to 000, then the interface ID is 64 bits wide. The only exception is the multicast address discussed earlier. Figure 4.45 depicts the anycast address structure for the types of addresses that require the 64-bit interface ID.

Figure 4.45 Anycast Addresses - EUI-64 Format

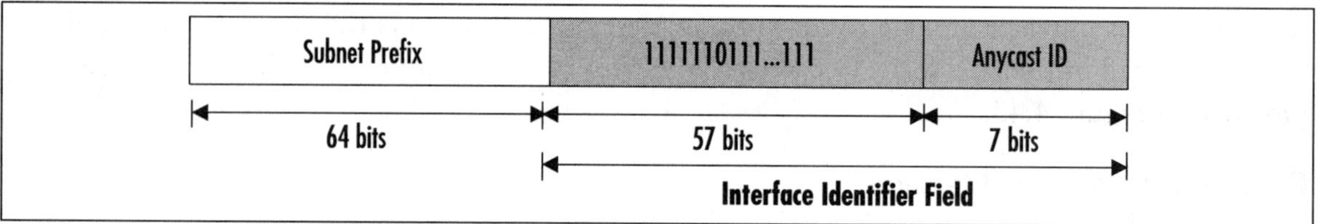

The universal/local bit must be set to 0 for this type of anycast address. The second reserved anycast address covers all addresses whose FP equals 000. These are addresses whose interface ID is not in EUI-64 format, as shown in Figure 4.46. The Interface ID length is dependent upon the subnet prefix.

Figure 4.46 Anycast Address - Non–EUI-64 Format

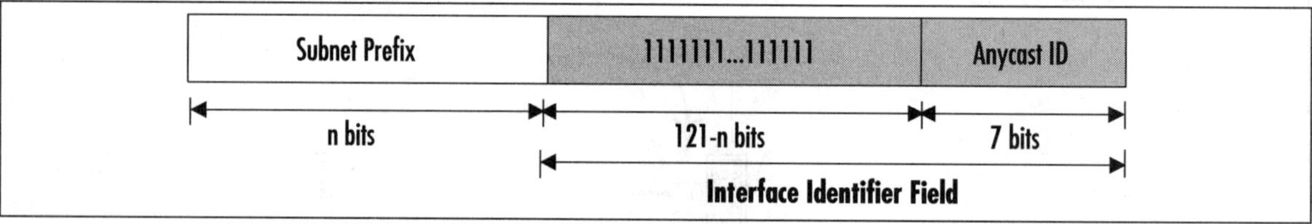

Anycast addresses in this format are not assigned as unicast addresses on any interface. Additional anycast identifiers are anticipated in the near future. Currently three reserved subnet anycast identifiers exist:

- 7E = 126 Decimal (used for Mobile IPv6 Home-Agents anycast)
- 7F = 127 Decimal

- 00 = 0 Decimal

If written, the mobile IPv6 home agents IPv6 EUI-64 interface ID address would be represented as follows:

```
1111110111111111    1111111111111111    1111111111111111    1111111111111110
```

The 0 in the first 16 bits is the universal local bit and means this address is local. The last 8 bits of the address represent 7E. 11111110 = 7E in hex.

IPv6 Address Autoconfiguration

One of IPv6's best perks is that not only is the Host ID determined prior to configuring an IPv6 device, but the network on which it resides can be deduced as well, making it possible for autoconfiguration to take place. Autoconfiguration assigns a unique IPv6 address and additional parameters such as the default gateway. Autoconfiguration is similar to DHCP or Bootstrap Protocol (BOOTP), without the need to track and manage address assignments.

When an IPv6 device initializes on a network, it sends a well-known multicast packet onto the network to which it is attached. This packet is destined to the Solicited Node Multicast address prefaced with **FF02::1:FF00:0**. The router replies with the network address that the device should assign itself.

The device receives the packet and, in turn, reads the network number that the router has sent. It then creates an IPv6 address by appending its Host ID (its MAC address on the interface connected to that subnet) to that network number. See Figure 4.47 for a graphical representation of autoconfiguration. Once the host has a routable address, it can learn the default route to reach non-local networks.

Figure 4.47 Autoconfiguration Mechanism

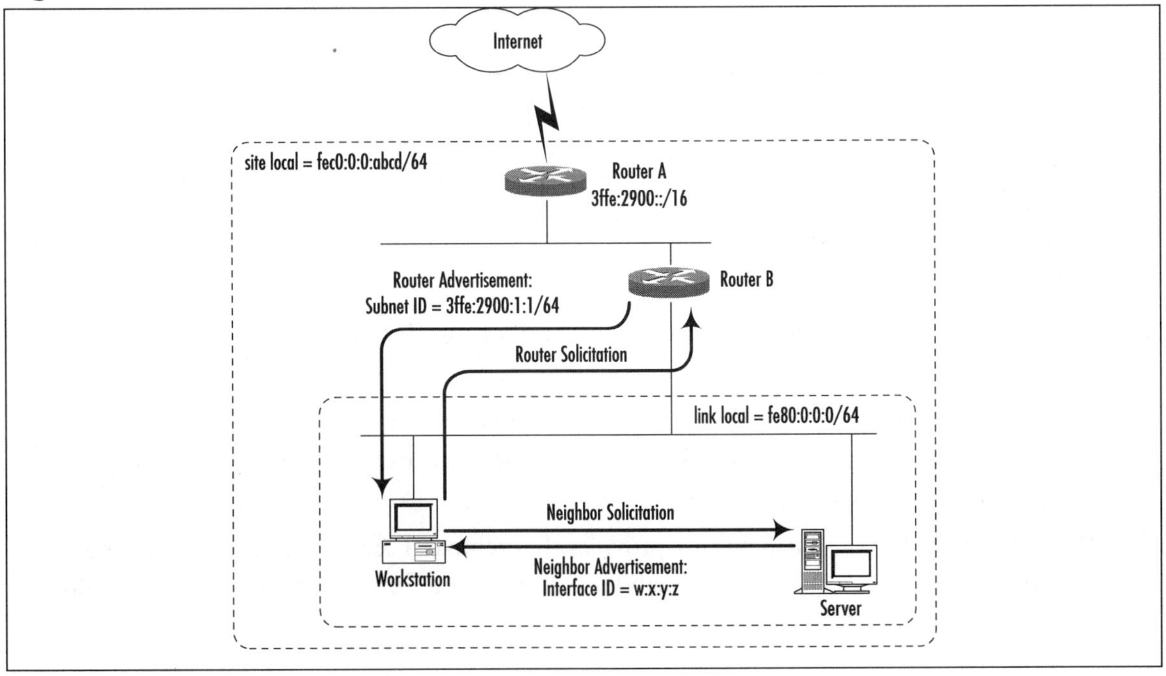

IPv6 Headers

The IPv6 header is fixed in length and aligned at an 8-octet boundary, unlike the IPv4 header, which is of variable length and aligned at a 4-octet boundary. The IPv6 header is simpler and more streamlined than the IPv4 header. The new header has only six fields and 2 addresses, while an IPv4 header contains 10 fixed fields, 2 addresses, and a variable-length **options** field. The length of the IPv6 header (or extension headers) is designed to be a multiple of 8 octets for 8-octet alignment. With a fixed IPv6 header, a router can efficiently process a packet. Several characteristics of the header are:

- **Simplified Format** A fixed format with fewer fields and no variable-length **options** field. Other IPv4 fields have been eliminated or changed to optional extension headers. Reduces the protocol overhead of IPv6.
- **No Header Checksum** Only hosts need to compute the checksum, not routers.
- **No Hop-by-Hop Fragmentation Procedure** The source determines the MTU size prior to transmission.

The IPv6 header is 40 bytes long and contains fields pertaining to version, traffic class, flow label, payload length, next header, hop limit, source address, and destination address, all of which are discussed later. Figure 4.48 shows the format of an IPv6 header.

Figure 4.48 The IPv6 Header

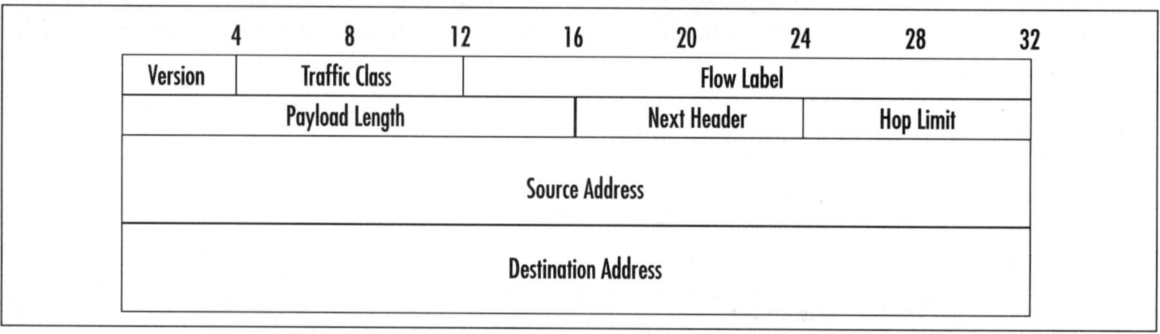

The IPv6 header stores the information necessary to route and deliver packets to their destination. IPv6 header fields are as follows.

- **Version** The 4-bit field indicates the version of the IP being used, and its value is 6 (0110 in binary).
- **Traffic Class** A 8-bit field used to provide differentiated services based on the nature of the data being transmitted. Similar to the intended use of the **type of service** field in the IPv4 header.
- **Flow Label** A 20-bit field that provides differentiated services and supports applications requiring special per-flow handling. Identifies a flow that requires special handling by intermediate routers.

- **Payload Length** A 16-bit field indicates the length of the packet, not including the length of the IPv6 header.
- **Next Header** An 8-bit field indicates the next header following the IPv6 header.
- **Hop Limit** Limits the number of intermediate hops a packet is allowed to visit, which can prevent packets from being circularly routed in a network.
- **Source and Destination Address** 128-bit IPv6 addresses for source and destination.

Figure 4.49 illustrates a transmission frame of a TCP segment (or UDP datagram) using IPv6. Notice there are optional extension headers, which are discussed next.

Figure 4.49 Transmission Frame with IPv6

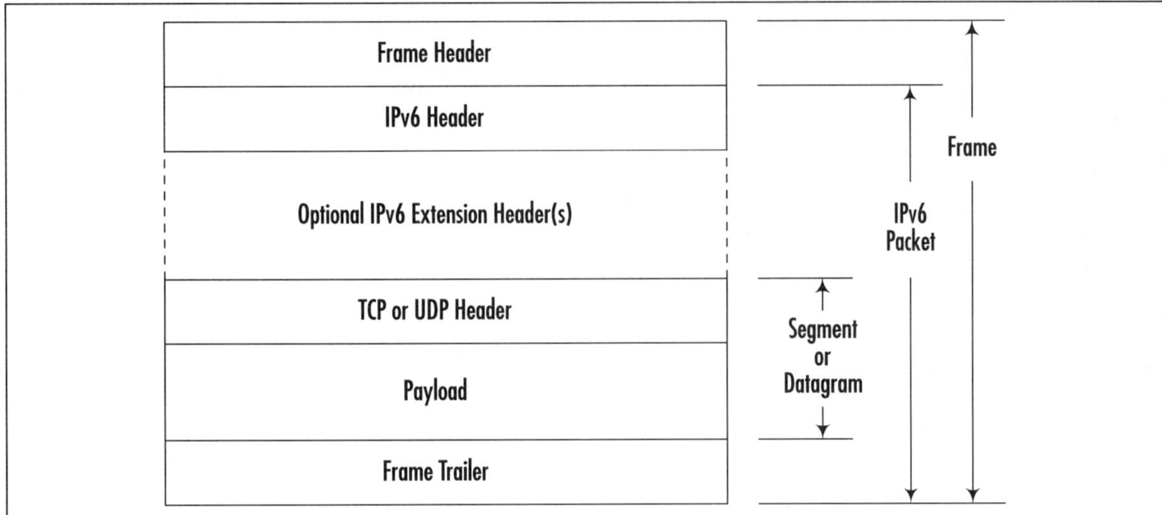

The IPv6 Extension Headers

Extension headers, placed between the IPv6 header and the upper-layer protocol header (see Figure 4.50), carry optional Internet-layer information in a packet. An IPv6 packet may carry zero or more extension headers. The **Next Header** field in the IPv6 header and extension headers is used to indicate which extension header or upper-layer protocol header follows the current header. Some values for these fields are shown in Table 4.19.

Table 4.19 Next Value Headers

Next Header Value	Next Header
0	Hop-by-Hop Options header
4	IP
6	TCP
17	UDP
43	Routing header
44	Fragment header

Continued

Table 4.19 Next Value Headers

Next Header Value	Next Header
45	Inter Domain Routing Protocol
46	Resource Reservation Protocol
50	Encapsulating Security Payload
51	AH
58	ICMP
59	No next header
60	Destination Options header

A full implementation of IPv6 includes the following extension headers: Hop-by-Hop Options, Routing (Type 0), Fragment, Destination Options, Authentication, and Encapsulating Security Payload. The recommended ordering of extension headers when multiple extension headers are present in a packet is as follows:

- IPv6 header
- Hop-by-Hop Options header
- Destination Options header (processed by all destination nodes appearing in the routing header)
- Routing header
- Fragment header
- AH
- Encapsulating Security Payload header
- Destination Options header (to be processed only by the final destination of the packet)
- Upper-layer header

Except for the Destination Options header, which can appear twice, each extension header should appear no more than once in a packet.

Except for the Hop-by-Hop Options header, extension headers are examined or processed only by the destination node (or nodes, in the case of multicast) of the packet. Thus, an IPv6 packet may carry optional information applicable only to its destination node without impacting the performance of the intermediate nodes. The Hop-by-Hop Options header can be used to carry optional information that needs to be examined or processed at all intermediate nodes.

The value of the **Next Header** field in the current header determines the next action to be taken, and the semantics of the current extension header determine whether to continue processing the next header. Thus extension headers must be examined in the order they appear in a packet. When a node receives an unrecognized Next Header value in a packet, it discards the packet and sends an ICMP Parameter Problem message to the source of the packet, with an ICMP Code value of 1—**unrecognized Next Header type encountered**. Because the Hop-by-Hop Options header must immediately follow the IPv6 header, a Next Header value of zero in any header other than IPv6 header will be treated as a packet with an unrecognized Next Header value.

Currently, the Hop-by-Hop Options header and the Destination Options header carry a variable number of options encoded in Type-Length-Value (TLV) format, as seen in Figure 4.50.

Figure 4.50 TLV-Encoded Option Format for Hop-By-Hop Options Header and Destination Options Header.

Option Type 8 bits	Opt Data Len 8 bits	Option Data variable length

Option Type	8-bit identifier of the type of option
Opt Data Len	8-bit unsigned integer. Length of the Option Data field of this option, in octets.
Option Data	Variable-length field. Option-Type-Specific data.

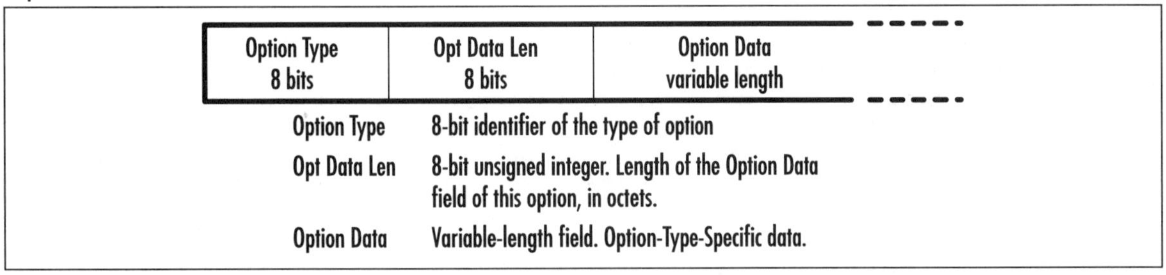

The Option Type identifiers are encoded so that the highest-order 2 bits specify the action to be taken when the processing node does not recognize the Option Type, and the third highest bit specifies whether or not the Option Data of that option can change en route to the packet's final destination. For instance, when a node encounters an unknown Option Type value of 130 (1000 0010), the highest-order 2 bits indicate that the node must discard the packet and send an ICMP Parameter Problem, Code 2, message to the source of the packet. Table 4.20 describes the encoding of Option Type.

Table 4.20 Option Type Encoding

Highest-order two bits	Action to be taken
00	Skip over this option and continue processing the header.
01	Discard the packet.
10	Discard the packet and, regardless of whether or not the packet's Destination Address was a multicast address, send an ICMP Parameter Problem, Code 2, message to the packet's Source Address, pointing to the unrecognized Option Type.
11	Discard the packet and, only if the packet's Destination Address was *not* a multicast address, send an ICMP Parameter Problem, Code 2, message to the packet's Source Address, pointing to the unrecognized Option Type.

Extension headers are designed to be multiples of 8 octets in length. To ensure that the end of the **option data** field is aligned with the 8-octet boundary, specific Option Types may be associated with alignment requirements in the form **xn+y**, indicating that the Option Type must appear at an integer multiple (**n**) of **x** octets from the start of the header, plus **y** octets. For instance, a 4n+2 alignment requirement indicates that the Option Type must start at any 4-octet offset from the start of the header, plus 2 octets, such as 2, 6, 10, 14, and so on.

Two padding options, the Pad1 option and the PadN option, may be used to force headers containing options to be multiples of 8 octets in length. The Pad1 option is used to insert 1 zero-valued octet of padding, and the PadN option is used to insert more than one octet of padding. The format of the PadN option is shown in Figure 4.51. To insert 2 octets of padding (Pad2), 1 octet with the value of one and one octet (**option data length** field) with the value of zero can be used. The Pad2 option is a special case in that there is no Option Data, or Option Data of zero length is used.

Figure 4.51 PadN Option Format

1 8 bits	Opt Data Len 8 bits	Option Data variable length

Opt Data Len — For N octets of padding, a value of N-2.
Option Data — For N octets of padding, N-2 zero-valued octets.

Hop-by-Hop Options Header

The Hop-by-Hop Options header, identified by a Next Header value of zero in the IPv6 header, carries optional information that must be processed by every node along a packet's delivery path. The use of the Hop-by-Hop Options header allows routers to selectively examine packets for special handling, if necessary. The format of the Hop-by-Hop Options header is shown in Figure 4.52. Note that the **header extension length** field is the length of the Hop-by-Hop Options header in 8-octet units, not including the first 8 octets. In other words, when the length of the TLV-encoded option(s) is less than or equal to 6 octets, the header extension length field is zero. Examples of Hop-by-Hop Options include the Router Alert Option and Jumbo Payload Option.

Figure 4.52 Hop-by-Hop Options Header

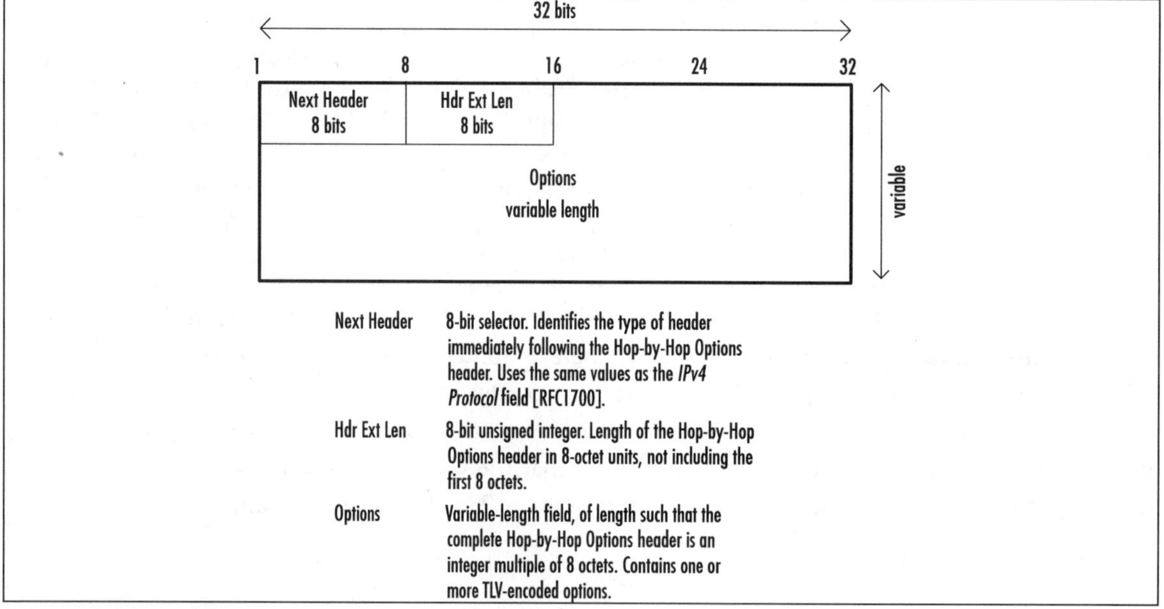
32 bits
1
8
16
24
32
Next Header
8 bits
Hdr Ext Len
8 bits
Options
variable length
variable
Next Header
8-bit selector. Identifies the type of header immediately following the Hop-by-Hop Options header. Uses the same values as the IPv4 Protocol field [RFC1700].
Hdr Ext Len
8-bit unsigned integer. Length of the Hop-by-Hop Options header in 8-octet units, not including the first 8 octets.
Options
Variable-length field, of length such that the complete Hop-by-Hop Options header is an integer multiple of 8 octets. Contains one or more TLV-encoded options.

A call set-up control message that uses the RSVP protocol will need special provisioning at each router along the path of the connection. Using the Router Alert Hop-by-Hop option, routers can provide special handling. Processing a Hop-by-Hop option may result in processing an upper-layer protocol such as RSVP. RSVP is a protocol used for end-to-end flow control and is detailed in numerous RFCs.

Figure 4.53 (a) illustrates a packet containing a Router Alert Hop-by-Hop Option. The value of the **next header** field in the IPv6 header is zero, indicating that a Hop-by-Hop Options header follows. All nodes in the path of this packet examine and process this packet. The **next header** field of the Hop-by-Hop Options header indicates the next header following this Hop-by-Hop header—a TCP header in this sample packet. The **extension header length** field is zero since there is only one option (the Router Alter option), and the total length of the TLV encoding of this option is 4 octets. Since there is no alignment requirement associated with this option, its TLV-encoded option is placed first, and the Pad2 Option is used to make the length of this Hop-by-Hop Options header exactly 8 octets.

The IPv6 header uses the 16-bit **payload length** field, which limits the maximum length of a packet to 65536. However, advances in hardware have enabled the transmission of a jumbogram, a packet with payload larger than 65536 octets. This option supports jumbograms up to 4,294,967,296 octets. When a path MTU can support payloads larger than 65535, this option may be used to transmit jumbograms.

The Option Type of the Jumbo Payload Option is 192 (1100 0010), indicating that nodes not recognizing this option type must discard this packet and send an ICMP, Parameter Problem, Code 2, message to its sender (only if the destination is not a multicast), and the Option Data must not change en route. The **option length** field of this option is 4 octets, and the Option Data is the length of the IPv6 jumbogram, not including the IPv6 header. When this option is used, the **payload length** field in IPv6 is set to zero. This option has an alignment requirement of 4n+2.

Figure 4.53 (b) illustrates a packet that includes the Jumbo Payload Hop-by-Hop option. The **next header** field in the IPv6 header indicates that the Hop-by-Hop Options header follows. Note that the **payload length** field in the IPv6 header is set to zero. The **next header** field in this Hop-by-Hop options header indicates that the next header is a TCP header. The **extension header** field has a value of zero because the total length of the TLV-encoded Jumbo Payload option is 6 octets. The value of the Option Data of this packet indicates that the payload is 2,818,048 octets (0x002A FFFF). Since the end of the Option Data is aligned with an 8-octet boundary, no padding option is necessary.

The processing of a Jumbo Payload option must detect several possible format errors and send an appropriate ICMP Parameter Problem message if one is present. These format errors include the absence of the Jumbo Payload option when the IPv6 Payload and the IPv6 Next Header are both zero, the use of the Jumbo Payload option when the IPv6 Payload is not zero, the use of the Jumbo Payload option when the actual payload is less than 65,535, and the use of the Jumbo Payload option when the Fragment Header is present.

Figure 4.53 Packets with the Hop-by-Hop Options Header

(a) Router Alert Option (32 bits; bit positions 1, 8, 16, 24, 32)

6 (ver)	(traffic cl.)	(flow label)	
(payload length)		0 (next hdr)	(hop limit)
(source address)			
(destination address)			
6 (next hdr)	0 (hdr len)	5 (op. type)	2 (op. len.)
(option data)		1 (Pad2)	0 (Pad2)
upper-layer protocol header (TCP header, for example)			
data			

(b) Jumbo Payload Option (32 bits; bit positions 1, 8, 16, 24, 32)

6 (ver)	(traffic cl.)	(flow label)	
0 (payload length)		0 (next hdr)	(hop limit)
(source address)			
(destination address)			
6 (next hdr)	0 (hdr len)	192 (op. type)	4 (op. len.)
0x002A FFFF (option data)			
upper-layer protocol header (TCP header, for example)			
data			

Routing Header

The Routing Header, identified by a Next Header value of 43 in the header immediately preceding it, allows an IPv6 source to determine routes to reach its destination by listing one or more intermediate nodes to be visited. (This is similar to the Loose Source and Record Route options in IPv4.) The format of the Routing Header is shown in Figure 4.54.

Figure 4.54 Routing Header

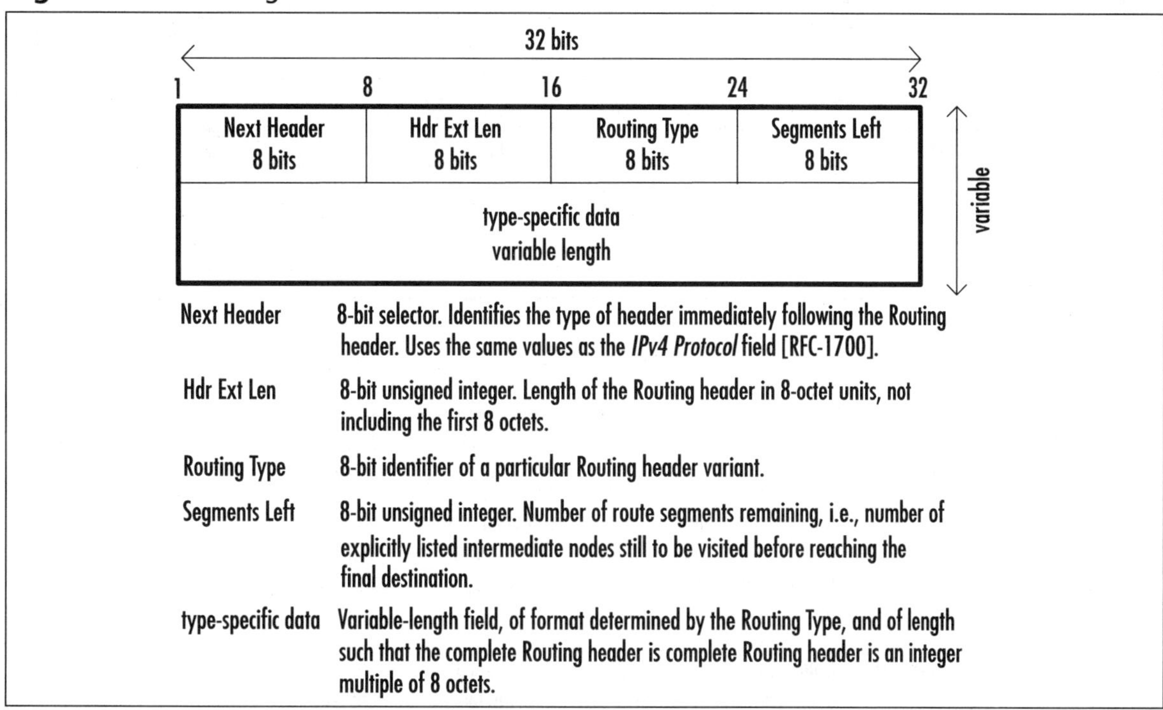
32 bits
1
8
16
24
32
Next Header
8 bits
Hdr Ext Len
8 bits
Routing Type
8 bits
Segments Left
8 bits
type-specific data
variable length
variable
Next Header 8-bit selector. Identifies the type of header immediately following the Routing header. Uses the same values as the IPv4 Protocol field [RFC-1700].
Hdr Ext Len 8-bit unsigned integer. Length of the Routing header in 8-octet units, not including the first 8 octets.
Routing Type 8-bit identifier of a particular Routing header variant.
Segments Left 8-bit unsigned integer. Number of route segments remaining, i.e., number of explicitly listed intermediate nodes still to be visited before reaching the final destination.
type-specific data Variable-length field, of format determined by the Routing Type, and of length such that the complete Routing header is complete Routing header is an integer multiple of 8 octets.

When a node encounters an unrecognized Routing Type, and the value of **segments left** is zero, it ignores the Routing header and continues to process the next header. However, if segments left is not zero, a node discards the packet and sends an ICMP Parameter Problem, Code 0 message to the packet's source address. Currently, only Type 0 has been defined; Figure 4.55 shows the format of a Type 0 Routing header.

Figure 4.55 Type 0 Routing Header

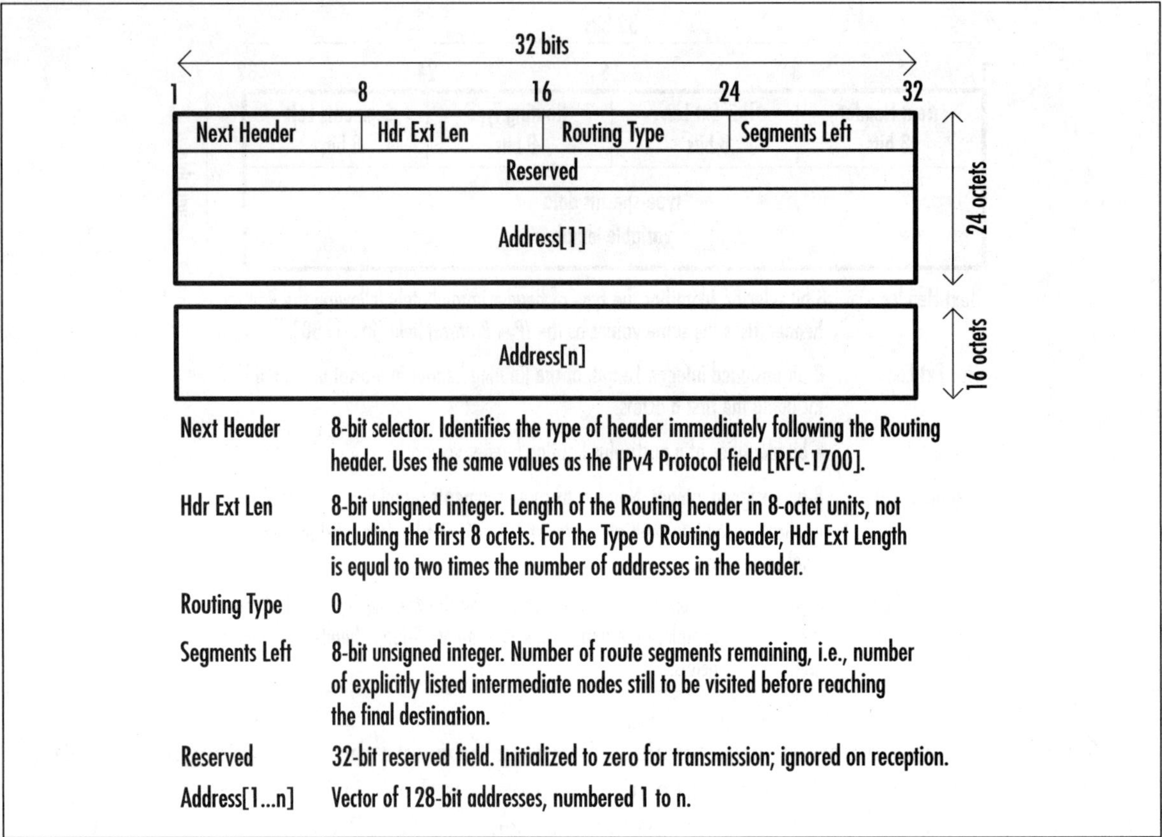
32 bits
1
8
16
24
32
Next Header
Hdr Ext Len
Routing Type
Segments Left
Reserved
Address[1]
24 octets
Address[n]
16 octets
Next Header
8-bit selector. Identifies the type of header immediately following the Routing header. Uses the same values as the IPv4 Protocol field [RFC-1700].
Hdr Ext Len
8-bit unsigned integer. Length of the Routing header in 8-octet units, not including the first 8 octets. For the Type 0 Routing header, Hdr Ext Length is equal to two times the number of addresses in the header.
Routing Type
0
Segments Left
8-bit unsigned integer. Number of route segments remaining, i.e., number of explicitly listed intermediate nodes still to be visited before reaching the final destination.
Reserved
32-bit reserved field. Initialized to zero for transmission; ignored on reception.
Address[1...n]
Vector of 128-bit addresses, numbered 1 to n.

One application of the Type 0 Routing header is in supporting new protocols, such as RSVP. In RSVP, a connection path may be established whereby all packets belonging to that connection follow the same path to reach the destination. The source of this connection may then use a Type 0 Routing header to specify the path to its destination.

Another use of a Routing header is to communicate with a mobile node away from its home network. Without route optimization, which may or may not be supported, packets may have to be sent to the mobile node's home network and be forwarded by the home agent (creating triangle routing) when a mobile node is away from its home network. The source of such a connection can specify the path using a Type 0 Routing header in order to allow the source of a connection to specify its path and avoid triangle routing.

Fragment Header

In IPv6, only source nodes perform fragmentation. A source node first finds the path MTU and then segments the fragmentable part of the original packet so that the length of each fragmented packet does not exceed the path MTU. Before fragmentation, the original packet consists of two parts: the unfragmentable part and fragmentable part. The IPv6 header and any extension headers that need to be processed at each hop on the way to the destination are unfragmentable, and extension headers processed only by the final destination node (or nodes in the case of multicast) are considered to be fragmentable.

The Hop-by-Hop Options header is always unfragmentable, since it must be processed by each hop in the path. Thus, when the Hop-by-Hop Options header is present, the unfragmentable part of the original packet includes the IPv6 header and the Hop-by-Hop Options header. Whether the Destination Options header is fragmentable depends on whether there is a Routing Options header. If there is no Routing Options header, the Destination Options header is fragmentable, since it only needs to be processed by the final destination. If there is a Routing Options header, the Destination Options header is unfragmentable, since it will need to be processed by every node appearing in the Routing header.

The Fragmentation header is identified by a Next Header value of 44 in the immediately preceding header. Figure 4.56 shows the format of the Fragmentation header. The source node generates a unique 32-bit identifier for every fragmented packet sent to the same destination. Except for the last fragmented packet, the fragmentable part of the original packet is divided so that each fragmented part is of a length that is an integer multiple of 8 octets. The **fragment offset** field is used to indicate the offset of the data following this Fragmentation header relative to the start of the Fragmentable part of the original packet.

Figure 4.56 The Fragmentation Header

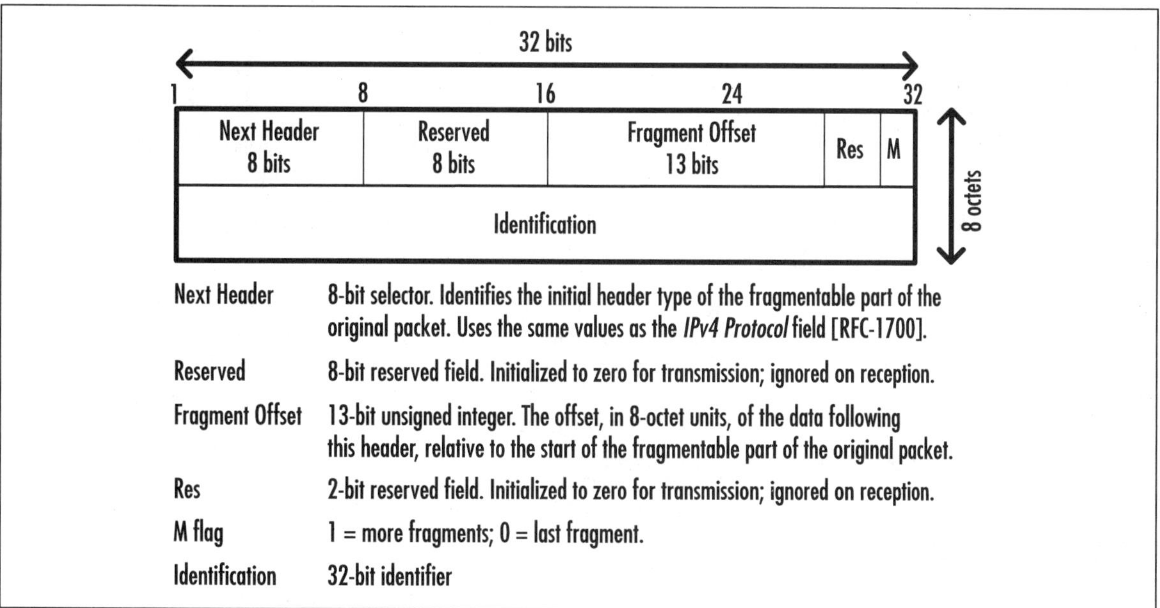

Destination Options Header

A source node may need to convey optional information that needs to be processed by a destination node. In an IPv6 network, such optional messages can be handled efficiently using either an extension header dedicated for handling specific optional information or using the Destination Options header. Packet fragmentation or authentication information is handled as an extension header, as shown previously. The IPv6 Mobility Support Internet-Draft proposes four Destination Options to support Mobile IPv6.

The optional information may be encoded either in a separate extension header or in the Destination Options header, based on the desired action to be taken at the destination node when the node does not recognize the option. Optional information that requires a few octets to send an ICMP Unrecognized Type message to the sender only if the destination node is not a multicast address, may be encoded in a separate extension header.

The Destination Options header, identified by a Next Header value of 60 in the immediately preceding header, carries optional information that needs to be examined and processed only by a packet's destination node (or nodes, in multicast). The format is shown in Figure 4.57.

Figure 4.57 The Destinations Options Header

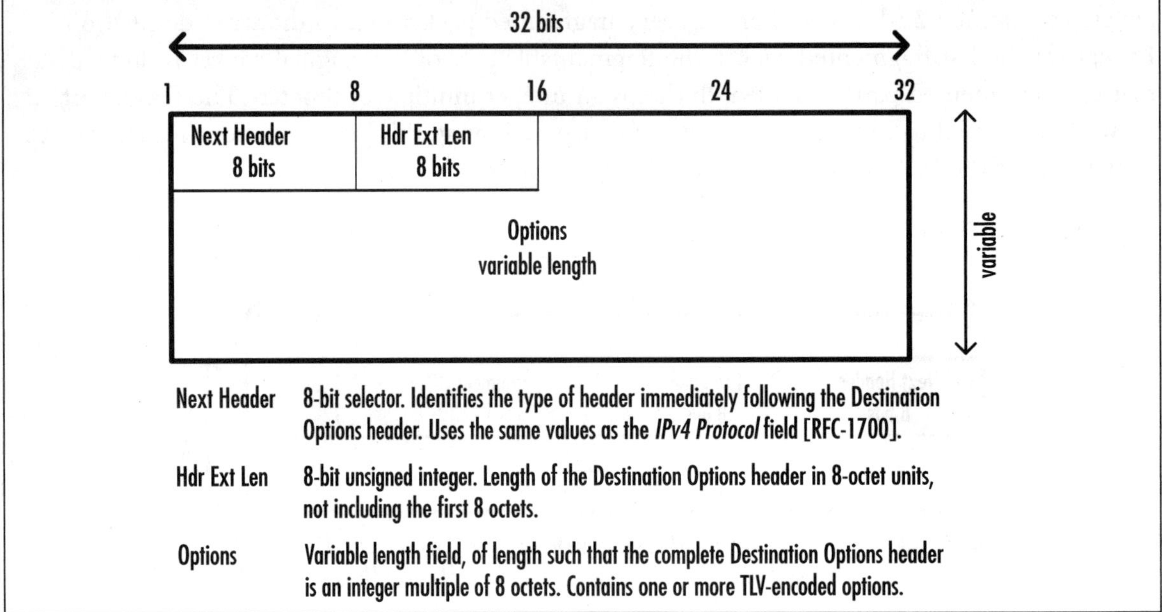

Next Header 8-bit selector. Identifies the type of header immediately following the Destination Options header. Uses the same values as the *IPv4 Protocol* field [RFC-1700].

Hdr Ext Len 8-bit unsigned integer. Length of the Destination Options header in 8-octet units, not including the first 8 octets.

Options Variable length field, of length such that the complete Destination Options header is an integer multiple of 8 octets. Contains one or more TLV-encoded options.

By now, you should have a good understanding of IPv6 fundamentals. Such knowledge will enable you to configure IPv6 on Cisco routers.

IPv6 Security

One goal of IPv6 designers was to support interoperable encryption-based security. IPv6 seeks to ensure confidentiality and integrity with its security features. IPv6 integrates security into its architecture by introducing the AH and the ESP headers.

AH

The AH provides authentication for the IPv6 header, upper-layer protocol headers, user data, and IPv6 extension header fields that may not change en route. For instance, the **destination address** field in the IPv6 header changes at every hop when the Type 0 Routing header is used, so in this case the AH cannot provide the authentication of the **destination address** field. Figure 4.58 shows the format of the AH.

Figure 4.58 The AH

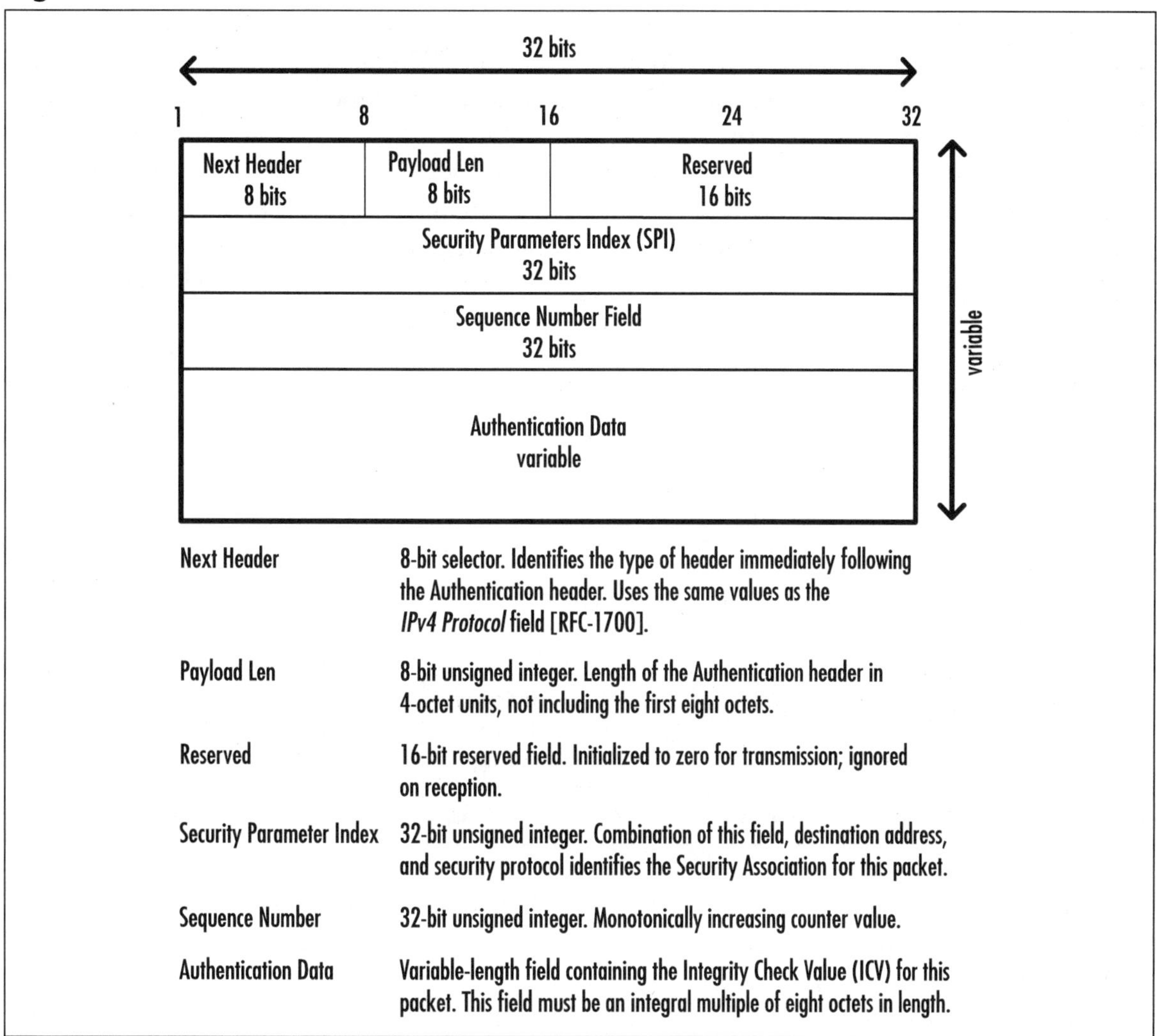
32 bits
1
8
16
24
32
Next Header
8 bits
Payload Len
8 bits
Reserved
16 bits
Security Parameters Index (SPI)
32 bits
Sequence Number Field
32 bits
Authentication Data
variable
variable
Next Header
8-bit selector. Identifies the type of header immediately following the Authentication header. Uses the same values as the *IPv4 Protocol* field [RFC-1700].
Payload Len
8-bit unsigned integer. Length of the Authentication header in 4-octet units, not including the first eight octets.
Reserved
16-bit reserved field. Initialized to zero for transmission; ignored on reception.
Security Parameter Index
32-bit unsigned integer. Combination of this field, destination address, and security protocol identifies the Security Association for this packet.
Sequence Number
32-bit unsigned integer. Monotonically increasing counter value.
Authentication Data
Variable-length field containing the Integrity Check Value (ICV) for this packet. This field must be an integral multiple of eight octets in length.

The **sequence number** field detects packet replay attacks, which consume receiving system resources. By examining the sequence numbers, we can spot the arrival of duplicate IP packets. When a Security Association (SA) is established between source and destination nodes, counters at the sending and receiving ends are initialized to zero. It is mandatory for the sender to increment this field for every transmission; however, the receiver may elect not to process the transmission. This service is effective only if the receiver processes this field.

The **authentication data** field contains the Integrity Check Value (ICV) for the packet, which is computed by the source and computed again by the destination for verification. The authentication algorithm, selected when the Security Association is established between the sender and the receiver, specifies the length of the ICV, the comparison rules, and the necessary processing steps. This value is computed over the packet by the source node and verified by the destination node, which compares the value to its own recomputed value. This procedure provides both connectionless integrity and data origin authentication.

The AH may be applied in transport or tunnel mode. The transport mode AH, implemented in hosts, provides protection for the upper-layer protocol header and any fields in the IPv6 header, as well as extension headers that do not change in transit. The tunnel mode AH is applied to the original IPv6 packet, encapsulating the original packet by constructing a new IPv6 packet that uses a distinct IPv6 addresses, such as a security gateway.

In transport mode, the AH is viewed as an end-to-end payload and is placed after the IPv6 header and Hop-by-Hop, Routing, and Fragmentation extension headers. The Destination Options header may appear once before the Routing header, as the options in the Destination Options header are applicable to intermediate nodes specified in the Routing header. In this case, the AH comes after the Destination Options header, as shown in Figure 4.59.

Figure 4.59 Header Order with AH in Transport Mode

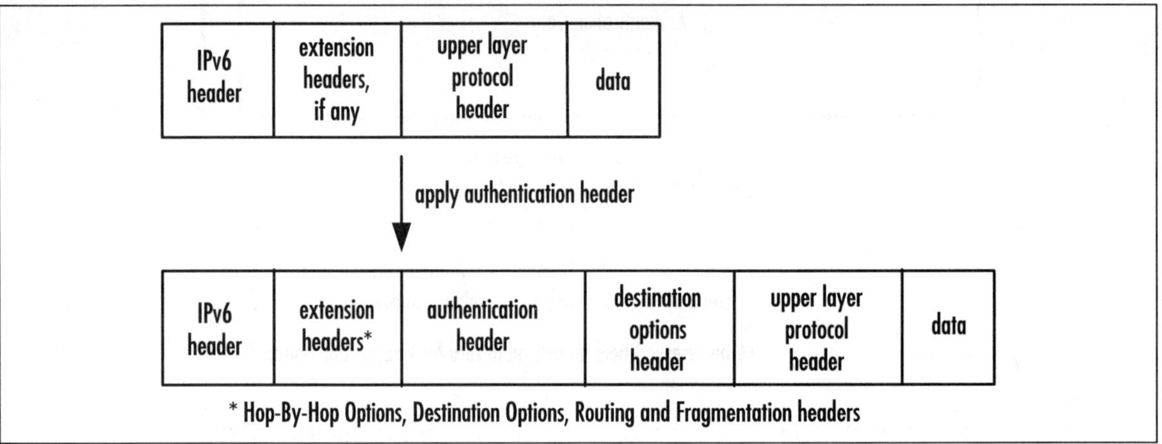

In tunnel mode, the AH is applied to the original IPv6 packet using distinct IPv6 addresses as communication end points, and a new IPv6 header is constructed using addresses of security gateways for source and destination addresses. Fragmentation processing may be necessary after applying the AH; thus, a newly constructed IPv6 packet may undergo further processing. Figure 4.60 shows the order of headers after applying the AH in tunnel mode.

Figure 4.60 Header Order with AH in Tunnel Mode

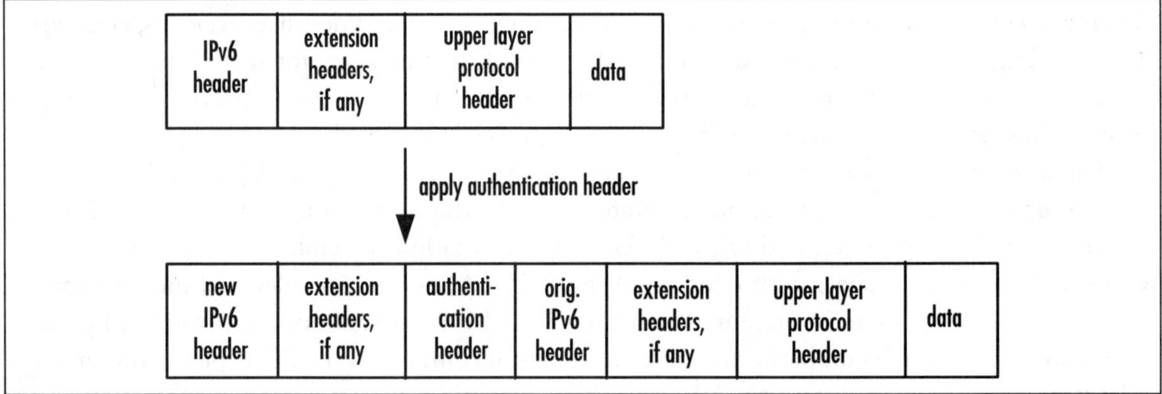

ESP

The ESP header used in transport mode or in tunnel mode also provides security services in both IPv4 and IPv6 networks. The security services provided through the ESP include confidentiality, authentication (data origin authentication and connectionless integrity), an anti-replay service, and limited traffic flow confidentiality. The implementation and options chosen at the time the Security Association is established determine the security services provided. ESP provides confidentiality by encrypting the payload.

The IPV6 ESP header contains a security parameter index (SPI) field that refers to a security association telling the destination how the payload is encrypted. ESP headers may be used for end-to-end or for tunneling. When tunneling, the original IPv6 header and payload are both encrypted and jacketed by outer IPv6 and ESP headers.

As in the case of the anti-replay service provided by the AH, the source increments the sequence number; however, the destination node must check this field to enable the anti-replay service. To provide traffic flow confidentiality service, true source and destination information should be hidden. Thus, this service requires that the ESP header be used in a tunnel mode.

Figure 4.61 shows the format of the ESP header. The Next Header value of 50 in the immediately preceding header indicates that the ESP header processing is necessary.

Figure 4.61 The ESP Header

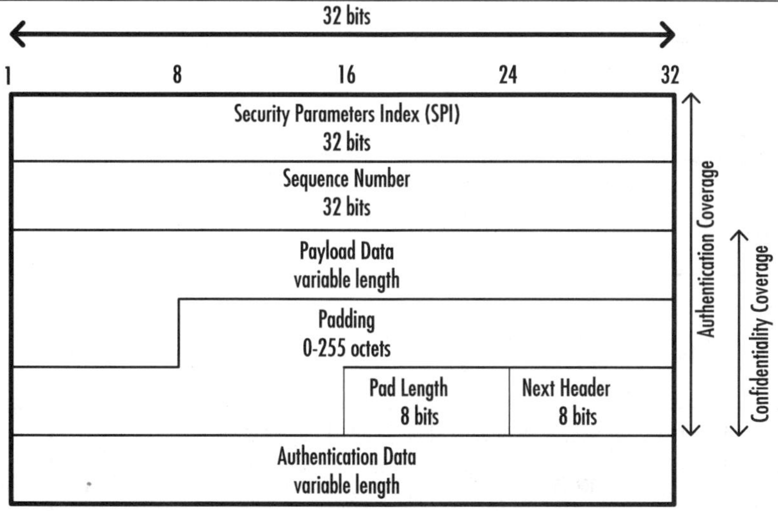

Security Parameter Index	32-bit unsigned integer. Combination of this field, destination address, and Security Protocol (ESP) identifies the Security Association for this packet.
Sequence Number	32-bit unsigned integer. Monotonically increasing counter value.
Payload Data	Variable-length field containing data described by the *Next Header* field.
Padding	Variable-length field containing 0 to 255 octets of 8-bit padding.
Pad Length	8-bit unsigned integer. Indicates the number of pad octets immediately preceding it.
Next Header	8-bit selector. Identifies the type of data contained in the Payload Data.
Authentication Data	Variable-length field containing the Integrity Check Value (ICV) computed over the ESP packet minus the Authentication Data.

The mandatory **payload data** field contains encrypted data described by the **next header** field. The encryption algorithm used specifies the length and the location of the structure of the data within the **payload data** field. Padding may be necessary to fulfill the encryption algorithm requirement of the length of the plain text or the 4-octet boundary alignment of the **payload data** field.

Figures 4.62 and 4.63 illustrate the sequence of an IPv6 packet with its encrypted portion when ESP headers are used in transport mode and tunnel mode, respectively.

Figure 4.62 Header Order with ESP in Transport Mode

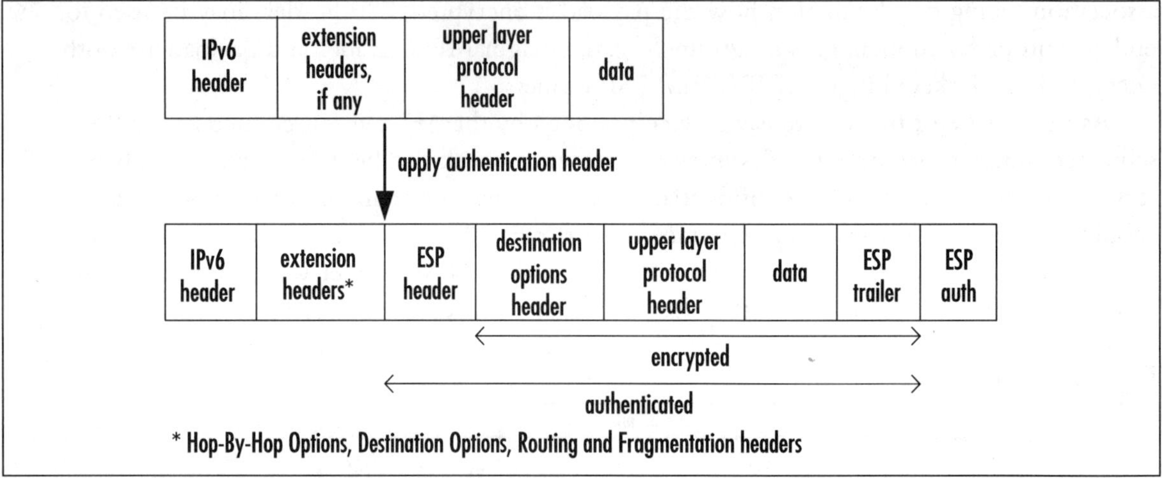

Figure 4.63 Header Order with ESP in Tunnel Mode

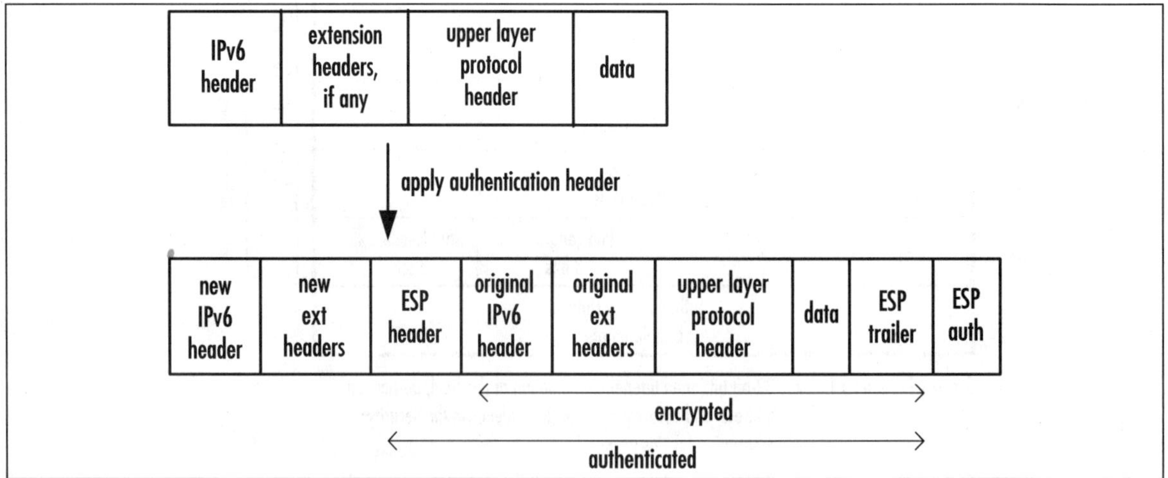

Upper-Layer Protocol Issues

Upper layer protocols that compute checksums over packets must account for changes in IPv6, including the use of 128-bit addresses, having a final destination instead of intermediate ones when the Routing header is used, and so on.

The **TTL** field has been renamed the **hop limit**. Any upper-layer protocol that relies on the original meaning of the TTL may have to make necessary adjustments. The maximum upper-layer payload size also needs to be adjusted to reflect the length of the IPv6 header (40 bytes).

- **Upper-Layer Checksums** TCP and UDP pseudo headers must be expanded to include the larger addresses, the upper-layer packet length, and the **next header** field. The checksum is computed over the IPv6 pseudo header, the TCP or UDP header, and the TCP or UDP payload. Figure 4.64 illustrates the checksum being calculated over an IPv6 pseudo header.
- **Maximum Packet Lifetimes** IPv6 has the **Hop Limit** field, which replaces the TTL.
- **Maximum Upper-Layer Payload Size** The nominal IPv6 header is 40 bytes long, which will result in larger packet sizes, which may have upper-layer consequences.
- **Routing Headers and Security** The IPv6 routing header extension contains the intermediate nodes that the packet must traverse on the way to its destination. When a packet with a routing header is received by the destination, it should not assume that the reverse path to the source is appropriate. In fact, responding along the reverse path may facilitate certain types of security breaches.
- **DNS** IPv6 enhancements to DNS include new record types with the 128-bit IPv6 address and a new service that can return a hostname when given its IPv6 address.
- **Application Programming Interface (API)** Application programs written for IPv4 must be converted to use APIs written for IPv6.

Figure 4.64 TCP/UDP Checksum Calculation

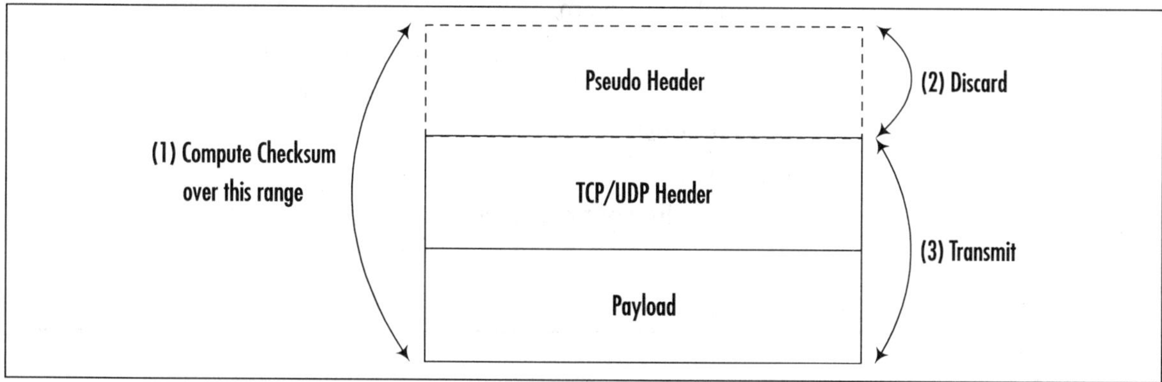

Like IPv4, IPv6 has several useful information utilities for checking network conditions. There are also changes to other protocol behavior. For example, ICMP in IPv6 does more than it did in IPv4.

Understanding ICMPv6

The ICMP version 6 (ICMPv6) is a key part of the IPv6 architecture. ICMPv6 performs the feedback functions necessary to ensure the smooth operation of IPv6 processes. These functions include:

- Packet Processing Error Reporting
- Diagnostics
- Neighbor Discovery
- Multicast Membership Reporting

ICMPv6 combines the functions of three separate IPv4 protocols: ICMPv4, IGMP, and ARP. ICMPv6 messages can be divided into **error messages** and **information messages**, which are summarized in Table 4.21.

Table 4.21 ICMP Error Message Types

Message Type	Message Cause	Included Sub-Messages
Error Message	Destination Unreachable	No route
		Administratively prohibited
		Address unreachable
		Port unreachable
	Packet too big	N/A
	Time exceeded	N/A
	Parameter problem	Erroneous header field
		Unrecognized next header type
		Unrecognized option
Informational Message	Echo request	N/A
	Echo reply	N/A
	Multicast listener discovery	Query
		Report
		Done

Error Messages

ICMPv6 error messages pertain to packet processing and include:

- **Destination Unreachable** A packet cannot be delivered for any reason other than congestion.
- **Packet Too Big** A packet cannot be forwarded because it is larger than the MTU of the next hop link. The MTU of the next link is returned in the message. This message is used by the Path MTU Discovery function.

- **Time Exceeded** The IPv6 header contains a Hop Limit that is decremented by each router that forwards the packet. When this hop limit reaches zero, the router discards the packet and returns a Time Exceeded message to the source node.
- **Parameter Problem** Generated when a problem with some part of an IPv6 header keeps a router from successfully processing the packet.

Each ICMPv6 error message includes three fixed-length fields plus a variable-length message body. Figure 4.65 illustrates the format of the error message.

Figure 4.65 ICMPv6 Error Message

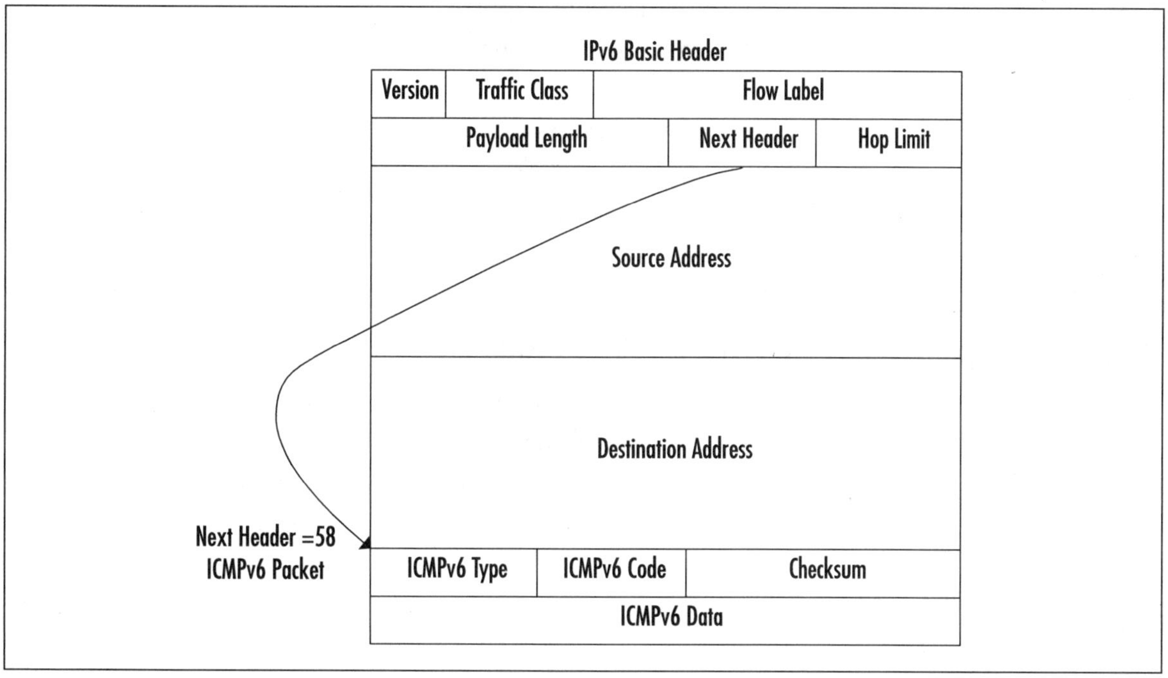

IPv6 Basic Header
Version
Traffic Class
Flow Label
Payload Length
Next Header
Hop Limit
Source Address
Destination Address
Next Header =58
ICMPv6 Packet
ICMPv6 Type
ICMPv6 Code
Checksum
ICMPv6 Data

Informational Messages

ICMPv6 can also report informational messages. These include:

- **Diagnostic Messages** Diagnostic messages include the echo request and reply.
- **Multicast Listener Discovery (MLD) Messages** Enable a router to discover neighboring nodes that wish to receive multicast packets, and what multicast addresses are of interest to them.
- **Neighbor Discovery Messages** Router solicitation and advertisement, neighbor solicitation and advertisement, and redirect. These messages include information options such as the source link-layer address, the target link-layer address; prefix information, the redirected header, and the MTU size.

ICMPv6 informational messages have the same format as the ICMPv6 error messages. The **type** field values for informational messages range from 128 to 255. Table 4.22 shows some of the common **type** fields for ICMPv6 informational messages.

Table 4.22 ICMPv6 Informational Messages

Type Field Value	ICMPv6 Informational Message
128	Echo Request
129	Echo Reply
130	Multicast Listener Query
131	Multicast Listener Report
132	Multicast Listener Done
133	Router Solicitation
134	Router Advertisement
135	Neighbor Solicitation
136	Neighbor Advertisement
137	Redirect

Understanding Neighbor Discovery

IPv6's Neighbor Discovery protocol is used to obtain information that facilitates the packet-forwarding process. The information gathered by the Neighbor Discovery protocol can be used for:

- Next Hop Determination
- Address Resolution
- Prefix Discovery
- Parameter Discovery
- Redirection

Several ICMPv6 messages are used in the Neighbor Discovery protocol., which are discussed later.

Router Solicitation and Advertisement

During the autoconfiguration process, after the workstation generates a unique link-local address, it queries for a router. The workstation sends a Router Solicitation message and listens for a Router Advertisement message.

The presence of a router indicates that there may be other subnets connected to the router. Each subnet must have its own subnet identifier because routing is dependent on unique subnet numbers. Host identifiers are not used to make routing decisions. The workstation address must now have a unique subnet identifier. The link-local address, with its zero subnet ID, is not sufficient for inter-subnet communications.

The Router Advertisement contains a network number or prefix. The prefix may contain an aggregatable global unicast prefix or simply a subnet identifier. Router Advertisements for each router interface contain different prefixes. This prefix will be concatenated with the Interface ID to form the workstation's IPv6 address.

The workstation uses information from the Router Advertisement to update its caches. The subnet ID is added to the workstation's Prefix List cache. This cache is used to determine if an address is on the workstation's subnet (on-link) or not (off-net). The router's information is added to the Neighbor cache and the Destination cache. If the router can be used as a default router, an entry is added to the Default Router List cache.

Neighbor Solicitation and Advertisement

To communicate with a destination host on the same subnet, the workstation must discover the destination's Interface ID. To do so, the workstation uses the functions provided by the IPv6 Neighbor Discovery protocol. The workstation sends a Neighbor Solicitation message to the destination, and the Interface ID is returned in a Neighbor Advertisement message. This interface ID is placed in a header before the IPv6 header and transmitted on the subnet. The workstation then adds an entry to its Neighbor Cache containing the destination IPv6 address and Interface ID, a pointer to packets pending transmission, and a flag indicating whether the destination is a router. This cache will be used for future transmissions (instead of sending duplicate solicitation messages).

Figure 4.66 illustrates how Neighbor Solicitation and Advertisement messages play a key role in the Neighbor Discovery process. The workstation solicits the local router and receives the subnet identifier it needs to complete its host IPv6 address.

Figure 4.66 Router and Neighbor Discovery

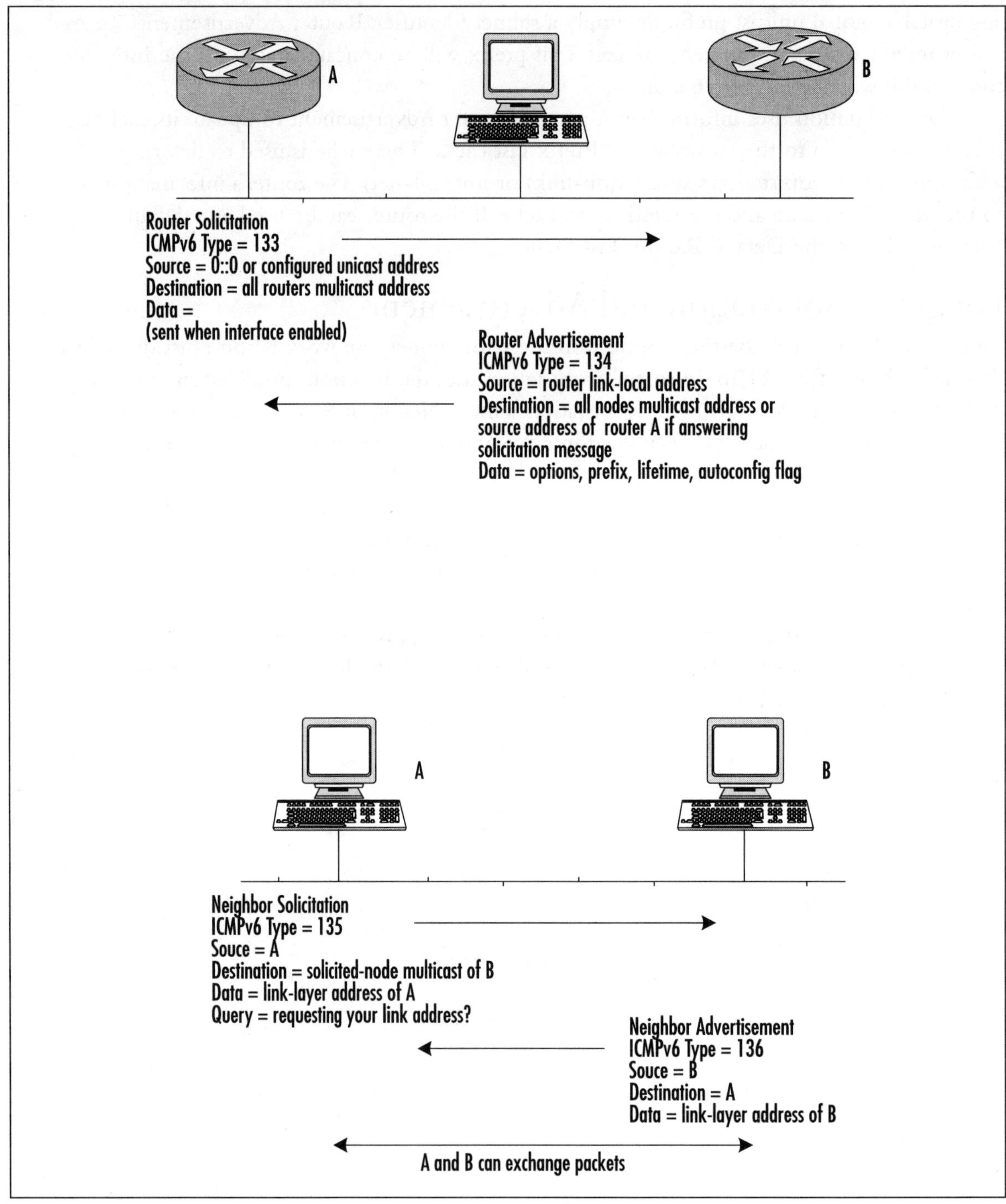

The router solicitation packet contains a value of 133 in the ICMP packet header and is sent to an all-routers multicast address when an IPv6 interface is enabled to request an immediate router advertisement from the neighboring routers, rather than wait for their next periodic router advertisement. The router solicitation message causes neighboring IPv6 routers to respond with a router advertisement message, which enables the host to immediately auto-configure its interface.

The router advertisement packet contains a value of 134 in the ICMP packet header and is periodically sent to an all-nodes multicast address to announce their presence, or is sent in response to a router solicitation packet and is sent in response to the router solicitation message. The advertisement typically contains prefixes that local-link nodes can use to auto-configure their IPv6 addresses, the lifetime information for each advertised prefix, the flags indicating a stateless or stateful auto-configuration, whether the router sending the advertisement should be used as a default router, and host information such as hop limit and MTU.

Neighbor solicitation packets contain a value of 135 in the ICMP packet header and are sent to solicited-node multicast addresses to determine the link-layer address of a neighbor on the same local link. The neighbor solicitation can also be sent to a neighbor's unicast address to verify neighbor reachablity and is used for duplicate address detection. Neighbor reachablity identifies the failure of a neighbor or the failure of the forwarding path to the neighbor. The neighbor solicitation message causes a neighbor advertisement to be sent from the neighboring routers.

The neighbor advertisement packet contains a value of 136 in the ICMP packet header and is sent in response to a neighbor solicitation message. A neighbor advertisement message is sent with the source address of the IPv6 interface sending the neighbor advertisement. After the sender of the neighbor solicitation receives the neighbor advertisement, the two nodes can communicate. A node may also send unsolicited neighbor advertisements to announce a link-layer address change. This concept is illustrated in Figure 4.67.

Figure 4.67 Neighbor Discovery: Neighbor Solicitation/Advertisement Messages

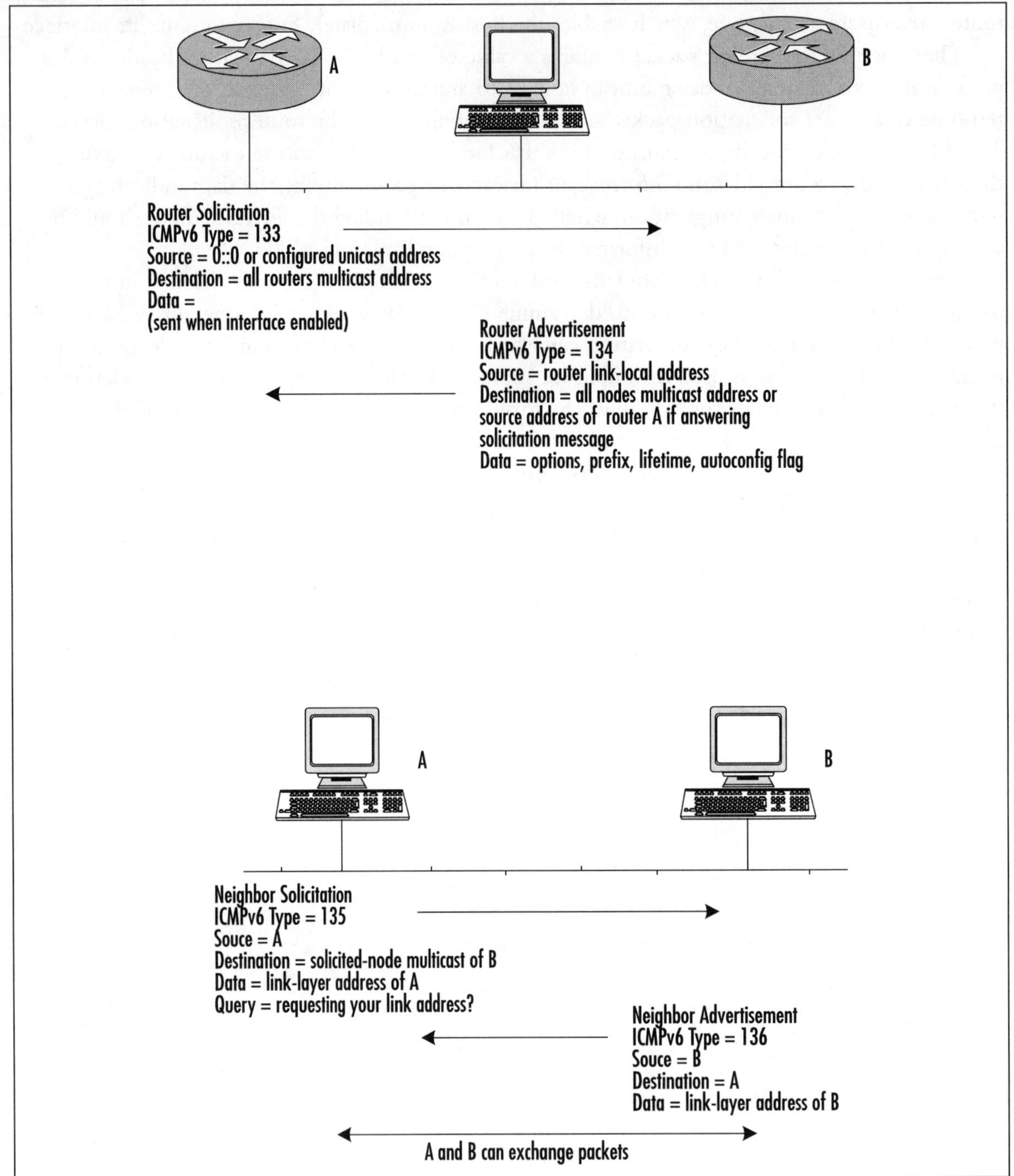

A redirect packet contains a value of 137 in the ICMP packet header. Routers use a redirect packet to inform hosts of a better first hop for a destination. Routers also use the redirect packet when the destination address of the packet is not a multicast address, when the packet is not addressed to the router, when the packet is about to be sent out the interface it was received on, or when the source address of the packet is a global IPv6 address of a neighbor on the same link or a link-local address.

Redirect Message

Routers issue the Redirect message to inform other nodes of a better first hop to the destination. A node can be redirected to another router on the same link.

When the workstation is ready to send a packet to a destination host, it queries the Prefix List to determine whether the destination's IPv6 address is on-link or off-link. If the destination host is off-link, the packet is transmitted the next hop, which is the router in the Default Router List. The workstation then updates its Destination cache with an entry for the destination host and its next hop address. If the default router selected is not the optimal next hop to the destination, the router sends a Redirect message to the source workstation with the new recommended next hop router for the destination. The workstation then updates its Destination Cache with the new next hop for the destination.

Message Options

Neighbor Discovery messages may contain additional information options. These options include:

- **Source Link-Layer Address Option** The ink-layer address of the **source** of the message that is used in Router Solicitation, Router Advertisement, and Neighbor Solicitation messages.
- **Target Link-Layer Address Option** The link-layer address of the **target** of the message that is used in Neighbor Advertisement and Redirect messages.
- **Prefix Information Option** Prefixes for address autoconfiguration and used in Router Advertisements.
- **Redirected Header Option** All or part of the packet that is being redirected.
- **MTU Option** The MTU size of the link. It is used in Router Advertisements.

Configuring IPv6 Addressing

The first step in configuring IPv6 on a router is making sure that at least IOS version 12.2(1)T Technology release is installed, which is the earliest version that supports IPv6

Some of the commands from the router are listed below to give a quick overview of the various commands that can be configured just for IPv6. The first mode shown is the global configuration mode. The second list shown is one from an interface; in this case an Ethernet interface.

```
6Router-1(config)# ipv6 ?
  access-list       Configure access lists
```

```
  cef                Cisco Express Forwarding for IPv6
  hop-limit          Configure hop count limit
  host               Configure static hostnames
  icmp               Configure ICMP parameters
  local              Specify local options
  neighbor           Neighbor
  prefix-list        Build a prefix list
  route              Configure static routes
  router             Enable an IPV6 routing process
  source-route       Process packets with source routing header options
  unicast-routing    Enable unicast routing

6Router-1(config-if)# ipv6 ?
IPv6 interface subcommands:
  address            Configure IPv6 address on interface
  cef                Cisco Express Forwarding for IPv6
  enable             Enable IPv6 on interface
  mtu                Set IPv6 Maximum Transmission Unit
  nd                 IPv6 interface Neighbor Discovery subcommands
  redirects          Enable sending of ICMP Redirect messages
  rip                Configure RIP routing protocol
  traffic-filter     Access control list for packets
  unnumbered         Preferred interface for source address selection
  verify             Enable per packet validation
```

Once you have verified that the Cisco IOS version you are using supports IPv6, the next step is to enable IPv6 globally on the router. This is done while in the **configuration** mode with the command **ipv6 unicast-routing**. If this command is not enabled globally, the rest of the commands on the interfaces will not operate.

```
6Router-1# configure terminal
Enter configuration commands, one per line.  End with CNTL/Z.
6Router-1(config)# ipv6 unicast-routing
6Router-1(config)#
```

Enabling IPv6 globally does not do much good until IPv6 is configured on individual interfaces, so the next step is to enable IPv6 on LAN and WAN interfaces.

Configuring LAN Addresses

There are a few steps involved in configuring the LAN address. Assuming that the IPv6 global routing has already been configured, the first step is to configure the actual interface. In most cases this will be an Ethernet interface, although it is possible to configure IPv6 on other types of LAN interfaces such as Token Ring.

The three types are **link-local**, **site-local**, and the **global** addresses. The global and site-local addresses are assigned at the same time. If a global address is already assigned by the architecture of your network, then the full address will be typed in during configuration. If only the first 64 bits are specified, then the Extended Unique Identifier (EUI) command at the end of the global address will have an Interface ID assigned for the global address. Configure IPv6 addresses on each interface. Each of the commands can be seen below, the first with the full address and the second using the EUI parameter at the end of the command to have the router assign the last 64 bits of the address.

If the EUI is used, only the first 64 bits of the address need to be specified; the rest of the address will be filled in automatically using the MAC address of the router. If there are multiple interfaces using the EUI parameter, you will notice that all of the interfaces will have addresses with the same last 64 bits.

Router configuration for predetermined global address

```
6Router-1(config)# int e0
6Router-1(config-if)# ipv6 address 2000:1:1::1/64
6Router-1(config-if)#
```

Router configuration for global address to be assigned Interface ID

```
6Router-1(config)# int e0
6Router-1(config-if)# ipv6 address 2000:1:1:1::/64 eui-64
6Router-1(config-if)#
```

When the EUI parameter is used, the remaining 64 bits of the address are automatically completed by the router. The address produced by the command above can be seen below. Notice that only the first 64 bits were defined above. Also notice that the link-local address has the same last 64 bits as the global address.

```
6Router-1# show ipv6 interface ethernet 0
Ethernet0 is up, line protocol is up
  IPv6 is enabled, link-local address is FE80::200:CFF:FE47:58E1
  Global unicast address(es):
    2000:1:1::1, subnet is 2000:1:1::/64
  Joined group address(es):
    FF02::1
    FF02::2
    FF02::1:FF00:1
    FF02::1:FF47:58E1
```

When the IPv6 address has been assigned to the interface, a link-local address gets assigned as well. The router automatically assigns a link-local address, and will typically use the EUI identification of the router for the last 64 bits of the address. If the architecture of your network requires that the local links have specific addresses, you can assign an address as link-local by simply typing

link-local after the IPv6 address in the configuration. For link-local to be enabled, the address must be a valid one between FE80 and FEBF.

```
6Router-1(config)# int e0
6Router-1(config-if)# ipv6 address fe80::1:1:1:1 link-local


6Router-1(config-if)# ipv6 addr 2001::1 link-local
Invalid link-local address
```

Sometimes an interface may not require an IPv6 interface, as is the case when subinterfaces are used for tunneling. The configuration of an unnumbered interface is similar to the equivalent IPv4 configuration. Simply type the command **IPv6 unnumbered** and the interface will have no IPv6 address assigned to it, although it will be associated with the interface specified at the end of the command. The command for enabling IPv6 on an interface while maintaining an unnumbered interface is shown here:

```
6Router-1(config)# int s1
6Router-1(config-if)# ipv6 unnumbered loopback0
6Router-1(config-if)# ipv6 enable
```

Secondary addresses can be assigned by entering another IPv6 address on the desired interface. When an IPv6 address is assigned to an interface, it will join several multicast groups including the all-nodes, the all-routers, and the solicited-node multicast groups. Figure 4.68 is a quick diagram of the network as configured above.

Figure 4.68 LAN Diagram

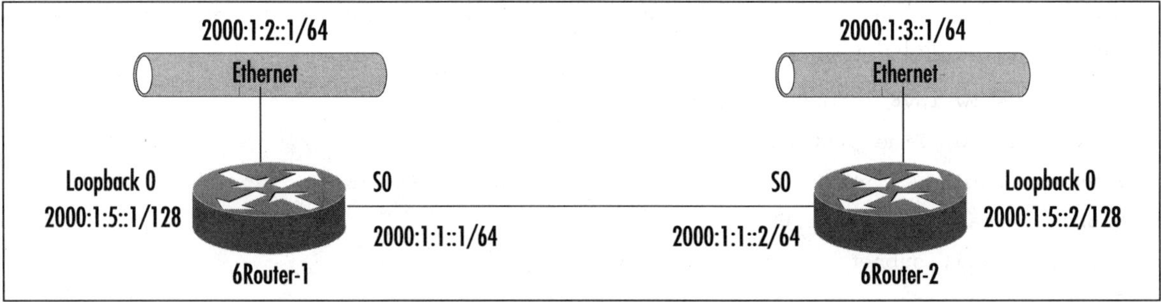

Configuring Duplicate Address Detection

Duplicate address detection (DAD) verifies that a new IPv6 address is unique to the router. The router will check using neighbor solicitation messages, and if the address is not unique, an error message identifying the offending interface is returned. This is a default feature with no configurable parameters, though the number of solicitation messages sent out an interface can be adjusted. It must fall in the range from 0 to 600.

```
6Router-1(config-if)# ipv6 nd dad attempts 2
```

The DAD can be turned off by setting the value of **attempts** to zero. The command, **no ipv6 nd dad attempts,** resets the number of attempts to the default of one.

Configuring DNS

Configuring DNS for IPv6 contains almost the same steps you would use to configure it for IPv4.

```
6Router-1(config)# ip domain-lookup
```

Identify the DNS server you want to use by its IPv6 address:

```
6Router-1(config)# ip name-server 1000:1000:2ad::2000:2000:2
```

You can also perform static hostname to IPv6 address mappings:

```
6Router-1(config)# ipv6 host 6Router-2 2000:1:1::2
6Router-1(config)# ipv6 host backup  2001 2000:1:5::1
```

Configuring WAN Addresses

The basic concepts of addressing WAN interfaces still apply with IPv6, with slight variations to allow for its unique characteristics. The mapping of data link addresses to IPv6 addresses needs to be address thoroughly.

Configuring ATM

The configuration of ATM using IPv6 is not very different from the configuration for IPv4. The **ipv6 address** command assigns an IPv6 address to the ATM interface. For a point-to-point interface, only an IPv6 address would be required to configure the ATM interface.

If the interface is multipoint, then **protocol ipv6** must be entered on the interface for the particular PVC. Examples of some configurations are shown here.

Point-to-Point

```
6Router-1(config-if-atm-vc)# ipv6 address 2000:1:20::1/64


6Router-2(config-if-atm-vc)# ipv6 address 2000:1:20::2/64
```

Point-to-Multipoint

```
6Router-1(config-if-atm-vc) protocol ipv6 2000:1:20::2
6Router-1(config-if-atm-vc) protocol ipv6 fe80::1:1:20:2
6Router-1(config-if-atm-vc) ipv6 address 2000:1:20::1

6Router-2(config-if-atm-vc) protocol ipv6 2000:1:20::1
6Router-2(config-if-atm-vc) protocol ipv6 fe80::1:1:20:1
6Router-2(config-if-atm-vc) ipv6 address 2000:1:20::2
```

Configuring Frame-Relay

IPv6 is configured similarly to IPv4, with the same steps and issues that you would use and find with IPv4. Figure 4.69 and 4.70 provide two frame-relay scenarios.

Figure 4.69 Frame-Relay Point-to-Point

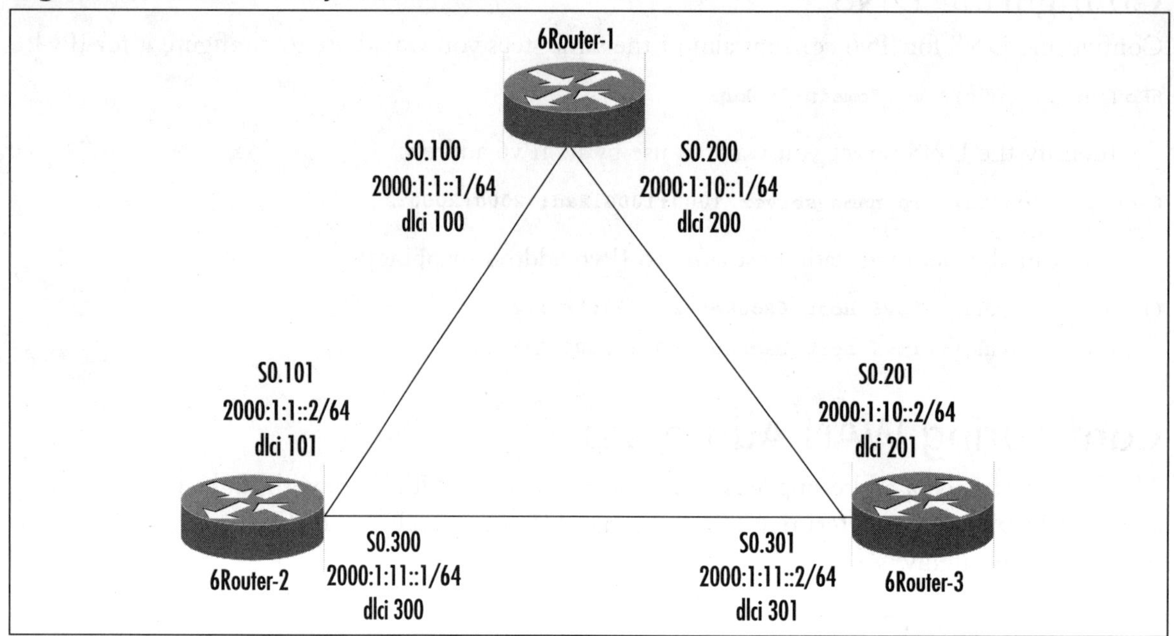


```
Point-to-Point
6Router-1(config)# int s0
6Router-1(config-if)# encapsulation frame-relay
6Router-1(config)# int s0.100 point-to-point
6Router-1(config-subif)# ipv6 address 2000:1:1::1/64
6Router-1(config-subif)# frame-relay interface-dlci 101
6Router-1(config)# int s0.200 point-to-point
6Router-1(config-subif)# ipv6 address 2000:1:10::1/64
6Router-1(config-subif)# frame-relay interface-dlci 201

6Router-2(config)# int s0
6Router-2(config-if)# encapsulation frame-relay
6Router-2(config)# int s0.101 point-to-point
6Router-2(config-subif)# ipv6 address 2000:1:1::2/64
6Router-2(config-subif)# frame-relay interface-dlci 100
6Router-2(config)# int s0.300 point-to-point
6Router-2(config-subif)# ipv6 address 2000:1:11::1/64
6Router-2(config-subif)# frame-relay interface-dlci 301

6Router-3(config)# int s0
6Router-3(config-if)# encapsulation frame-relay
6Router-3(config)# int s0.201 point-to-point
```

```
6Router-3(config-subif)# ipv6 address 2000:1:10::2/64
6Router-3(config-subif)# frame-relay interface-dlci 200
6Router-3(config)# int s0.301 point-to-point
6Router-3(config-subif)# ipv6 address 2000:1:11::2/64
6Router-3(config-subif)# frame-relay interface-dlci 300
```

Notice that the commands are almost identical to what is used to configure IPv4 in a similar scenario.

Figure 4.70 Frame-Relay Point-to-Multipoint

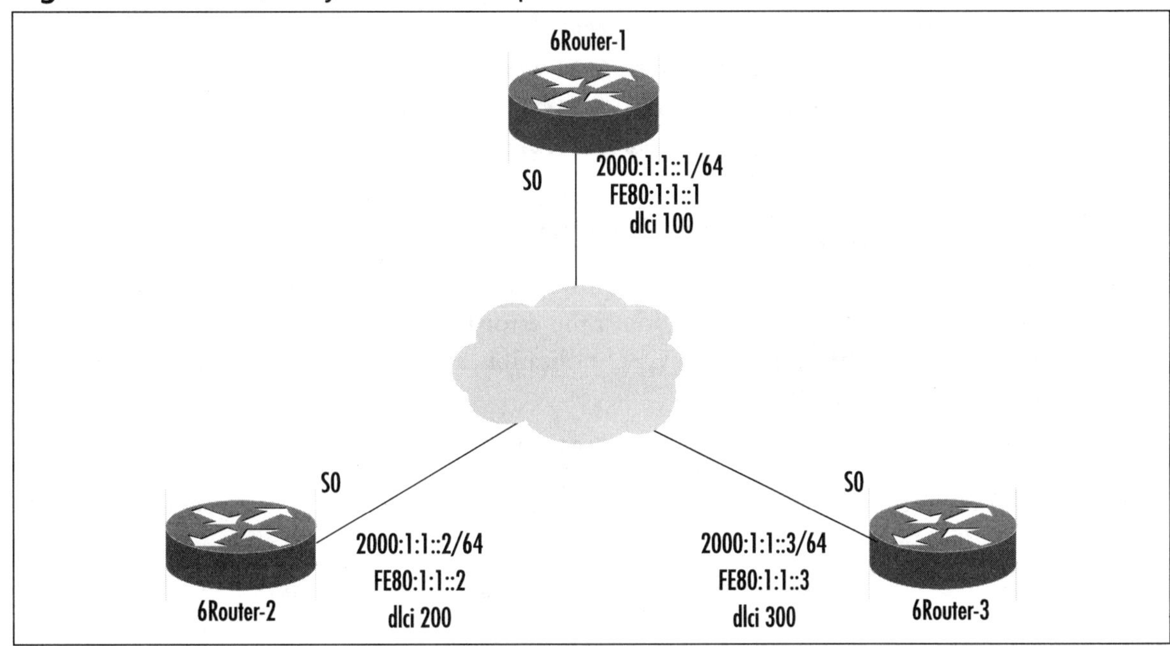


```
Point-to-Multipoint
6Router-1(config)# int s0
6Router-1(config-if)# encapsulation frame-relay
6Router-1(config-if)# ipv6 address 2000:1:1::1/64
6Router-1(config-if)# ipv6 address fe80:1:1::1 link-local
6Router-1(config-if)# frame-relay map ipv6 2000:1:1::2 200
6Router-1(config-if)# frame-relay map ipv6 2000:1:1::3 300
6Router-1(config-if)# frame-relay map ipv6 fe80:1:1::2 200
6Router-1(config-if)# frame-relay map ipv6 fe80:1:1::3 300

6Router-2(config)# int s0
6Router-2(config-if)# encapsulation frame-relay
6Router-2(config-if)# ipv6 address 2000:1:1::2/64
6Router-2(config-if)# ipv6 address fe80:1:1::2 link-local
```

```
6Router-2(config-if)# frame-relay map ipv6 2000:1:1::1 100
6Router-2(config-if)# frame-relay map ipv6 2000:1:1::3 300
6Router-2(config-if)# frame-relay map ipv6 fe80:1:1::1 100
6Router-2(config-if)# frame-relay map ipv6 fe80:1:1::3 300

6Router-3(config)# int s0
6Router-3(config-if)# encapsulation frame-relay
6Router-3(config-if)# ipv6 address 2000:1:1::3/64
6Router-1(config-if)# ipv6 address fe80:1:1::3 link-local
6Router-3(config-if)# frame-relay map ipv6 2000:1:1::1 100
6Router-3(config-if)# frame-relay map ipv6 2000:1:1::2 200
6Router-3(config-if)# frame-relay map ipv6 fe80:1:1::1 100
6Router-3(config-if)# frame-relay map ipv6 fe80:1:1::1 100
```

Configuring ICMPv6 and Neighbor Discovery

You can adjust your ICMPv6 parameters to improve CPU utilization rates, and to certain traceroute features. In the command shown, we adjust the error interval and the bucket size (number of tokens in the bucket). The latter affects CPU utilization, and pertains to the number of outstanding messages the router has.

```
6Router-1(config)# ipv6 icmp error-interval 100 10
```

Neighbor discovery in IPv6 is equivalent to IP ARP in IPv4. You can create static entries as shown.

```
6Router-1(config)# ipv6 neighbor 2000:1:2::10 ethernet0 0000.1234.5678
```

Notice the error message received when attempting to configure neighbor cache on a serial interface:

```
6Router-1(config)# ipv6 neighbor 2000:1:1::10 serial0 0000.1111.2222
% Static Neighbor Cache entries not supported on this interface type
```

Monitoring and Troubleshooting IPv6

Cisco provides a wealth of tools to support IPv6 networks. These consist primarily of **show** and **debug** commands used to examine IPv6 past and present activity on the router.

Using Basic show Commands

Cisco provides several show commands that can be used to check many aspects of the IPv6 configuration, as shown.

```
6Router-1# show ipv6 ?
  access-list   Summary of access lists
  cef           Cisco Express Forwarding for IPv6
```

```
interface     IPv6 interface status and configuration
local         IPv6 local options
mtu           MTU per destination cache
neighbors     Show IPv6 neighbor cache entries
prefix-list   List IPv6 prefix lists
protocols     IPv6 Routing Protocols
rip           RIP routing protocol status
route         Show IPv6 route table entries
routers       Show local IPv6 routers
traffic       IPv6 traffic statistics
tunnel        Summary of IPv6 tunnels
```

We will discuss several of these commands and provide sample output. The **show ipv6 interface** command displays the status and operational information about interfaces. The full command syntax is as follows:

```
show ipv6 interface [brief] [interface-type interface-number]
```

```
6Router-1# show ipv6 interface serial0
Serial0 is up, line protocol is up
     ! denotes the status of the interface
  IPv6 is enabled, link-local address is FE80::2E0:B0FF:FE5A:D998
     ! displays the status of the IPv6 on the interface and the
     ! link--local address assigned
  Global unicast address(es):
    2001::1000:1000:1, subnet is 2001::/64  Joined group address(es):
     ! shows the multicast groups this interface belongs to
    FF02::1
    FF02::2
    FF02::1:FF00:1
    FF02::1:FF5A:D998
  MTU is 1500 bytes
  ICMP error messages limited to one every 500 milliseconds
     ! frequency of ICMP messages
  ICMP redirects are enabled
  ND DAD is enabled, number of DAD attempts: 1
     ! neighbor discovery status
  ND reachable time is 30000 milliseconds
  Hosts use stateless autoconfig for addresses.
```

The IPv6 interface status is derived through the use of DAD. If DAD has identified the link-local address of the interface as being a duplicate address, the processing of IPv6 packets is disabled on the interface and the interface is marked **stalled**. If IPv6 is not enabled, the interface is marked **disabled**. During the DAD process, the interface may also display DUPLICATE, TENTATIVE, or OK. The TENTATIVE status informs you that the DAD process is in progress.

The joined group addresses list the multicast groups to which this interface belongs. The ICMP error messages line indicates ICMP messages are periodically sent every 500 milliseconds (default) and the rate can be modified using the **ipv6 icmp error-interval** command, which can ultimately reduce link-layer congestion.

ND DAD indicates that the Neighbor Discovery Duplicate Address Detection is enabled. The number of DAD attempts indicates the number of Neighbor Solicitation messages that were sent while the DAD process was being performed.

You can use the **show ipv6 interface brief** command to obtain a summary listing of all IPv6 interfaces.

The **show ipv6 route** command displays the routing table and the next hop to a remote network. The full command syntax for **show ipv6 route** command is as follows:

```
show ipv6 route [ipv6-address | ipv6-prefix/prefix-length | protocol].
6Router-1
    # show ipv6 route
IPv6 Routing Table - 9 entries
Codes: C - Connected, L - Local, S - Static, R - RIP, B - BGP
       I1 - ISIS L1, I2 - ISIS L2, IA - ISIS interarea
    ! legend of possible protocol types that may be displayed below
Timers: Uptime/Expires


L   2000:1:1::1/128 [0/0]
     via ::, Serial0, 20:45:43/never
     ! neighboring network information
C   2000:1:1::/64 [0/0]
     via ::, Serial0, 20:45:46/never
L   2000:1:2::1/128 [0/0]
     via ::, Ethernet0, 20:46:12/never
C   2000:1:2::/64 [0/0]
     via ::, Ethernet0, 20:46:13/never
B   2000:1:3::/64 [20/1]
     via 2000:1:1::2, Serial0, 20:45:37/never
L   3FFE:4200:1:1::1/128 [0/0]
     via ::, Ethernet0, 1d19h/never
C   3FFE:4200:1:1::/64 [0/0]
     via ::, Ethernet0, 1d19h/never
L   FE80::/10 [0/0]
     via ::, Null0, 1w5d/never
L   FF00::/8 [0/0]
     via ::, Null0, 1w5d/never
```

The command displays the routing protocol used to learn the route it is using. It also shows the prefix of the remote network (2000:1:1::1/128), the administrative distance and metric for the link (0/0), and the interface to forward packets through (Serial0). The output also indicates the last time the route was updated and when the route expires [20:45:43/never] (local and connected routes never expire).

The **show ipv6 route** command enables you to specify the IPv6 address/network and prefix and/or the protocol type to enable more granularity in the output. The full command syntax is listed here:

```
show ipv6 route [ipv6-address | ipv6-prefix/prefix-length | protocol]
```

The **show ipv6 route summary** command is used to display the number of routes per route source and each prefix length. This command lists the total number of entries in the IPv6 routing table and provides a quick look at the total number of locally connected, directly connected, statically mapped, and dynamically derived networks as well as a summary of the total number of routing table entries per given prefix length.

```
6Router-1# show ipv6 route summary
IPv6 Routing Table Summary - 9 entries
     ! total routing table entries
  5 local, 3 connected, 0 static, 0 RIP, 1 BGP 0 IS-IS
     ! route source
  Number of prefixes:
    /8: 1, /10: 1, /64: 4, /128: 3
     # number of accessible networks by prefix
```

The **show ipv6 neighbors** command displays the contents of the neighbor discovery cache constructed through the exchange of Router Solicitation/Advertisement, Neighbor Solicitation/Advertisement, and Redirect ICMP messages. This command helps determine which neighbors are inaccessible or the last time the neighbor was contacted.

```
show ipv6 neighbors [interface-type interface-number | ipv6-address]


6Router-1# show ipv6 neighbors
IPv6 Address                              Age Link-layer Addr State Interface
2000:1:2::10                                - 0000.1234.5678  REACH Ethernet0
     ! list of each IPv6 neighbor
```

The above shows the neighbor's IPv6 address (2000:1:2::10), the last time it was confirmed to be reachable (a hyphen (-) indicates a static entry), its link-layer (MAC) address, and so on. Table 4.23 lists the various neighbor communication states. The listed states apply only to non-static neighbor cache entries.

Table 4.23 Neighbor Cache Entry States

Neighbor Cache Entry	Definition
INCMP - Incomplete	Neighbor resolution has not been completed. The Neighbor Solicitation ICMP message has been sent but the Neighbor Advertisement message has not yet been received.
REACH - Reachable	The neighbor has been confirmed as reachable within the last Reachable Time (default 30000 ms). The Reachable Time is displayed in the show IPv6 interface output.
STALE	The neighbor has not been successfully contacted within the Reachable Time setting. No action is taken until a packet is sent.
DELAY	The DELAY state follows the STALE state and indicates a packet was sent within the last DELAY_FIRST_PROBE_TIME. If a confirmation is not received, the state changes to the PROBE state and sends a Neighbor Solicitation message.
PROBE	Neighbor Solicitation messages will continue to be sent at an interval specified by the neighbor discovery-related variable RetransTimer (RFC 2461, Neighbor Discovery for IPv6), until reachability is confirmed. The RetransTimer interval is specified in milliseconds
????	The neighbor is in an unknown state.

Use the **show ipv6 protocols** command to display the IPv6 routing protocols configured on the router.

```
6Router-1# B
IPv6 Routing Protocol is "connected"
IPv6 Routing Protocol is "static"
IPv6 Routing Protocol is "bgp 64999"
     ! the BGP network configured on this router
  IGP synchronization is disabled
  Redistribution:
    None
  Neighbor(s):
    Address                  FiltIn FiltOut Weight RoutemapIn RoutemapOut
    2000:1:1::2
IPv6 Routing Protocol is "rip cisco"
     ! RIP is configured on the Serial0 and Ehternet0 interfaces
  Interfaces:
    Serial0
    Ethernet0
  Redistribution:
    Redistributing protocol rip cisco
     ! RIP is being redistributed
```

The **show ipv6 protocols** command also displays if neighbor route maps or AS filter lists have been applied to each of the interfaces. You can also add the **summary** keyword at the end of the command to display each configured protocol, as shown here:

```
6Router-1# B
Index Process Name
0      connected
1      static
5      bgp 64999
6     rip cisco
```

The **show ipv6 traffic** command provides statistics for IPv6, ICMP, and UDP packets that have been received by or originated from the IPv6-configured router.

```
6Router-1# show ipv6 traffic
IPv6 statistics:
  Rcvd:  17489 total, 14367 local destination
     ! total number of IPv6 packets received by this router
         0 format errors, 0 hop count exceeded
         0 bad header, 0 unknown option, 0 bad source
         0 unknown protocol, 0 not a router
         0 fragments, 0 total reassembled
         0 reassembly timeouts, 0 reassembly failures
  Sent:  67630 generated, 0 forwarded
     ! total number od IPv6 packets sent from this router
         0 fragmented into 0 fragments
         1 encapsulation failed, 3122 no route, 0 too big
  Mcast: 0 received, 0 sent

ICMP statistics:
  Rcvd: 61 input, 0 checksum errors, 0 too short
     ! total number of IPv6 ICMP packets reeived by this router
        0 unknown info type, 0 unknown error type
        unreach: 0 routing, 0 admin, 0 neighbor, 0 address, 0 port
        parameter: 0 error, 0 header, 0 option
        0 hopcount expired, 0 reassembly timeout, 0 too big
        25 echo request, 25 echo reply
     ! total number of ping request/replies to this router
        0 group query, 0 group report, 0 group reduce
        0 router solicit, 0 router advert, 0 redirects
        2 neighbor solicit, 9 neighbor advert
     ! neigbor discovery statistics
```

```
  Sent: 6000 output, 0 rate-limited
     ! total number of ICMP packets sent by this router
        unreach: 0 routing, 0 admin, 0 neighbor, 0 address, 0 port
        parameter: 0 error, 0 header, 0 option
        0 hopcount expired, 0 reassembly timeout,0 too big
        30 echo request, 25 echo reply
     ! total number of ping request/replies from this router
        0 group query, 0 group report, 0 group reduce
        0 router solicit, 5880 router advert, 0 redirects
     ! number of router advertisements sent by this router
        32 neighbor solicit, 33 neighbor advert
     ! ICMP neighbor advertisements and solicitations
     ! used in neighbor discovery sent by this router

UDP statistics:
  Rcvd: 9089 input, 0 checksum errors, 0 length errors
        0 no port, 0 dropped
  Sent: 56804 output
```

Using the show bgp Commands

The **show bgp ipv6** command displays the Border Gateway Protocol (BGP) table version, the next hop address to reach the listed network along with the metric, a local preference (if configured), weight, and AS path.

```
show bgp ipv6 [ipv6-prefix/prefix-length] [longer-prefixes]
6Router-1# B
BGP table version is 13, local router ID is 172.16.0.1
     ! the BGP table version number and IP address used as the router ID
Status codes: s suppressed, d damped, h history, * valid, > best, i - internal,r RIB-
failure
Origin codes: i - IGP, e - EGP, ? - incomplete
     ! indicates the origin of the entry

   Network          Next Hop              Metric LocPrf Weight Path
*  2000:1:1::/64    2000:1:1::2                              0 65000 i
     ! the accessible BGP networks and the next hop address to reach them
*>                    ::                                 32768 I
     ! the :: indicates the router has non-BGP routes to this network
*> 2000:1:2::/64    ::                                   32768 i
*> 2000:1:3::/64    2000:1:1::2                              0 65000 i
```

The **show bgp ipv6** command output contains similar information as the **show ipv6 route** command but displays only BGP routing information.

The **show bgp ipv6 summary** command provides an overview of the BGP configuration on the router.

```
6Router-1# B
BGP router identifier 172.16.0.1, local AS number 64999
     ! the BGP router ID and AS assigned to this router
BGP table version is 13, main routing table version 13
3 network entries and 4 paths using 659 bytes of memory
     ! memory used by the BGP routing protocol
2 BGP path attribute entries using 120 bytes of memory
1 BGP AS-PATH entries using 24 bytes of memory
0 BGP route-map cache entries using 0 bytes of memory
0 BGP filter-list cache entries using 0 bytes of memory
BGP activity 10/41 prefixes, 14/10 paths, scan interval 60 secs

Neighbor         V     AS MsgRcvd MsgSent    TblVer  InQ OutQ Up/Down  State/PfxRcd
2000:1:1::2      4 65000    4293    4300        13     0    0 1d22h            2
```

The **show bgp ipv6 neighbors** command is useful for determining the status of the BGP neighbor communications.

```
show bgp ipv6 neighbors [ipv6-address] [received-routes | routes | flap-statistics |
advertised-routes | paths regular-expression | dampened-routes]
```

Pay particular attention to the current BGP state and length of time the the peer connection has been established.

```
6Router-1# show bgp ipv6 neighbors
BGP neighbor is 2000:1:1::2,  remote AS 65000, external link
     ! the BGP neighbors address and AS number
 Member of peer-group cisco for session parameters
     ! update policy peer group this router belongs to
  BGP version 4, remote router ID 172.16.8.33
  BGP state = Established, up for 00:51:16
     ! current state of the BGP session and how long the
     ! underlying TCP connection has been established
  Last read 00:00:16, hold time is 180, keepalive interval is 60 seconds
     ! BGP configuration settings
  Neighbor capabilities:
     ! the BGP capabilities advertised and received from this neighbor
    Route refresh: advertised and received(old & new)
    Address family IPv6 Unicast: advertised and received
```

```
  Received 1528 messages, 0 notifications, 0 in queue
     ! IPv6 unicast-specific properties of this neighbor

  Sent 1535 messages, 1 notifications, 0 in queue
  Default minimum time between advertisement runs is 30 seconds

 For address family: IPv6 Unicast   BGP table version 13, neighbor version 13
     ! confirms router and neighbor are using the same BGP routing table
  Index 1, Offset 0, Mask 0x2
  cisco peer-group member
  Route refresh request: received 0, sent 0
  2 accepted prefixes consume 136 bytes
  Prefix advertised 11, suppressed 0, withdrawn 1

  Connections established 4; dropped 2
     ! number of times the peers have agreed to speak BGP
     ! and the how often a good connection has failed or been taken down
  Last reset 22:53:50, due to BGP Notification sent, hold time expired
Connection state is ESTAB, I/O status: 1, unread input bytes: 0
Local host: 2000:1:1::1, Local port: 179
     ! peering address of the local router
Foreign host: 2000:1:1::2, Foreign port: 11631    # peering address of the neighbor

Enqueued packets for retransmit: 0, input: 0  mis-ordered: 0 (0 bytes)

Event Timers (current time is 0x3D6B4AF8):
Timer          Starts    Wakeups            Next
Retrans            58          2             0x0
TimeWait            0          0             0x0
AckHold            55         26             0x0
SendWnd             0          0             0x0
KeepAlive           0          0             0x0
GiveUp              0          0             0x0
PmtuAger            0          0             0x0
DeadWait            0          0             0x0

iss: 2268213783  snduna: 2268215016  sndnxt: 2268215016     sndwnd:  15152
irs:  840903895  rcvnxt:  840905059  rcvwnd:       15221  delrcvwnd:   1163

SRTT: 302 ms, RTTO: 323 ms, RTV: 21 ms, KRTT: 0 ms
```

```
minRTT: 4 ms, maxRTT: 424 ms, ACK hold: 200 ms
Flags: passive open, nagle, gen tcbs

Datagrams (max data segment is 1440 bytes):
Rcvd: 84 (out of order: 0), with data: 55, total data bytes: 1163
Sent: 82 (retransmit: 2, fastretransmit: 0), with data: 82, total data bytes: 45
20
```

Cisco provides several **clear ipv6** commands as shown.

```
6Router-1# clear ipv6 ?
  neighbors     Clear IPv6 ND Entry Cache
  prefix-list  Prefix-list
  route         Clear IPv6 route table entries
  traffic       Clear traffic counters
```

Finally, you have a choice of IPv6 specific debug commands.

```
6Router-1# debug ipv6 ?
  icmp      ICMPv6 debugging
  nd        IPv6 Neighbor Discovery debugging
  packet   IPv6 packet debugging
  rip       RIP Routing Protocol debugging
  routing  IPv6 routing table debugging
```

…and of course, you can always view your configuration.

```
6Router-1# show running-config

(omitted)
!
hostname 6Router-1
!
ipv6 unicast-routing
!
interface Loopback0
 no ip address
 no ip route-cache
 no ip mroute-cache
```

The command, **ipv6 unicast-routing,** enables IPv6 globally, and is mandatory.

Verifying WAN Addressing

Cisco provides commands for checking the mapping of data link addresses to IPv6 addresses.

```
6Router-1# show atm map
```

```
Map list ATM0pvc1:  PERMANENT
Ipv6 FE80::1:1 maps to VC 1,  VPI 1, VCI 32, ATM0,
Broadcast
Ipv6 2000:1:1::1 maps to VC 1, VPI 1, VCI 32, ATM0

Frame-Relay

6Router-1# show frame-relay map
Serial1 (up): ip 10.10.10.2 dlci 200(0xC8,0x3080), static,
              CISCO, status defined, active
Serial1 (up): ipv6 2000:1:1::2 dlci 200(0xC8,0x3080), static,
              CISCO, status defined, active
Serial1 (up): ipv6 2000:1:1::3 dlci 300(0x12C,0x48C0), static,
              CISCO, status defined, active
```

Verifying ICMPv6 and Neighbor Discovery Configuration

To view a router's neighbor discovery cache, use the **show ipv6 neighbors Ethernet0** command. This command lists discovered neighbors that the router has in its cache. Both discovered and statically configured entries are shown. A hyphen (-) in the age field indicates that the entry is static.

```
6Router-1# show ipv6 neighbors ethernet0
IPv6 Address                         Age Link-layer Addr State Interface
2000:1:2::10                           - 0000.1234.5678  REACH Ethernet0
2000:1:2::15                           0 0000.2345.5678  REACH Ethernet0
2000:1:2::17                           1 0000.2222.5678  REACH Ethernet0
```

To view ICPMv6 traffic and other general traffic on the router, issue the command **show ipv6 traffic**. This will give the IPv6 statistics as shown here.

```
6Router-1# show ipv6 traffic
IPv6 statistics:
  Rcvd:  4903 total, 4892 local destination
         0 format errors, 0 hop count exceeded
         0 bad header, 0 unknown option, 0 bad source
         0 unknown protocol, 0 not a router
         0 fragments, 0 total reassembled
         0 reassembly timeouts, 0 reassembly failures
  Sent:  27330 generated, 0 forwarded
         0 fragmented into 0 fragments
         1 encapsulation failed, 11 no route, 0 too big
  Mcast: 0 received, 0 sent
```

```
ICMP statistics:
  Rcvd: 36 input, 0 checksum errors, 0 too short
        0 unknown info type, 0 unknown error type
        unreach: 0 routing, 0 admin, 0 neighbor, 0 address, 0 port
        parameter: 0 error, 0 header, 0 option
        0 hopcount expired, 0 reassembly timeout, 0 too big
        15 echo request, 10 echo reply
        0 group query, 0 group report, 0 group reduce
        0 router solicit, 0 router advert, 0 redirects
        2 neighbor solicit, 9 neighbor advert
  Sent: 2561 output, 0 rate-limited
        unreach: 0 routing, 0 admin, 0 neighbor, 0 address, 0 port
        parameter: 0 error, 0 header, 0 option
        0 hopcount expired, 0 reassembly timeout,0 too big
        15 echo request, 15 echo reply
        0 group query, 0 group report, 0 group reduce
        0 router solicit, 2480 router advert, 0 redirects
        25 neighbor solicit, 26 neighbor advert
UDP statistics:
  Rcvd: 4797 input, 0 checksum errors, 0 length errors
        0 no port, 0 dropped
  Sent: 24701 output
```

Using debug Commands

Debug commands are useful for gathering real-time information on IPv6 events as they occur. The Cisco IOS provides several IPv6 debug commands, as shown.

```
6Router-1# debug ipv6 ?
  access-list  IPv6 access list debugging
  cef           IPv6 CEF information
  icmp          ICMPv6 debugging
  interface    IPv6 interface debugging
  nd            IPv6 Neighbor Discovery debugging
  packet        IPv6 packet debugging
  pool          IPv6 prefix pool debugging
  rip           RIP Routing Protocol debugging
  routing       IPv6 routing table debugging
```

The **debug ipv6 packet** command displays information on the IPv6 packets received, generated, and forwarded on this router. Fast-switched packets do not generate messages. The **debug**

ipv6 packet command creates substantial overhead on the router and should only be used when traffic levels are very low.

```
6Router-1# debug ipv6 packet
IPv6 unicast packet debugging is on
6Router-1#
1w6d: IPV6: source 2000:1:1::2 (Serial0)
      ! the source address in the IPv6 header
1w6d:        dest 2000:1:1::1
      ! the destination address in the IPv6 header
1w6d:        traffic class 192, flow 0x0, len 79+4, prot 6, hops 64, forward to ulp
      !the contents of the traffic class, flow, length, protocol, and hops fields
1w6d: IPV6: source 2000:1:1::1 (local)
1w6d:        dest 2000:1:1::2 (Serial0)
1w6d:        traffic class 192, flow 0x0, len 60+0, prot 6, hops 64, originating
      !indicates this packet originated from this router
…
1w6d: IPV6: source FE80::2E0:B0FF:FE5A:D998 (local)
1w6d:        dest FF02::9 (Serial0)
1w6d:        traffic class 224, flow 0x0, len 112+1388, prot 17, hops 255, originating
1w6d: IPv6: Sending on Serial0
1w6d: IPV6: source FE80::2E0:B0FF:FE5A:D998 (local)
1w6d:        dest FF02::9 (Ethernet0)
1w6d:        traffic class 224, flow 0x0, len 112+1388, prot 17, hops 255, originating
1w6d: IPv6: Sending on Ethernet0
1w6d: IPV6: source FE80::2E0:B0FF:FE5A:D998 (local)
1w6d:        dest FF02::9 (Serial0)
1w6d:        traffic class 224, flow 0x0, len 112+1388, prot 17, hops 255, originating
1w6d: IPv6: Sending on Serial0
1w6d: IPV6: source FE80::2E0:B0FF:FE5A:D998 (local)
1w6d:        dest FF02::9 (Ethernet0)
1w6d:        traffic class 224, flow 0x0, len 112+1388, prot 17, hops 255, originating
1w6d: IPv6: Sending on Ethernet0
1w6d: IPV6: source 2000:1:1::2 (Serial0)
1w6d:        dest 2000:1:1::1
1w6d:        traffic class 192, flow 0x0, len 79+4, prot 6, hops 64, forward to ulp
      ! indicates this was received by the router and forwarded
      ! to an upper-layer protocol
1w6d: IPV6: source 2000:1:1::1 (local)
1w6d:        dest 2000:1:1::2 (Serial0)
1w6d:        traffic class 192, flow 0x0, len 60+12, prot 6, hops 64, originating
```

The **debug ipv6 icmp** command is useful for troubleshooting ICMP communication on the router. The neighbor discovery process, MTU determination, and MLD all use ICMP, although a separate **debug** command exists for troubleshooting the neighbor discovery process.

```
6Router-1# debug ipv6 icmp
ICMP packet debugging is on
6Router-1# ping ipv6 2000:1:1::2

Type escape sequence to abort.
Sending 5, 100-byte ICMP Echos to 2000:1:1::2, timeout is 2 seconds:
!!!!!
Success rate is 100 percent (5/5), round-trip min/avg/max = 8/10/12 ms
6Router-1#
1w6d: ICMPv6: Sending echo request to 2000:1:1::2
     ! indictaes ICMPv6 packet has been sent
1w6d: ICMPv6: Received ICMPv6 packet from 2000:1:1::2, type 129
      ! ICMPv6 packet received, type 129 = echo reply
1w6d: ICMPv6: Received echo reply from 2000:1:1::2
```

The **debug ipv6 nd** command is useful for troubleshooting the neighbor discovery process where adjacencies are attained by passing ICMPv6 packets between routers to establish neighbor adjacencies.

```
6Router-1# debug ipv6 nd
ICMP Neighbor Discovery events debugging is on
6Router-1#
2w0d: ICMPv6-ND: Sending RA to FF02::1 on Ethernet0
     ! indicates a router advertisement is being sent to
     ! all-nodes multicast group
2w0d: ICMPv6-ND:      prefix = 3FFE:4200:1:1::1/64 onlink autoconfig
2w0d: ICMPv6-ND:      prefix = 2000:1:2::1/64 onlink autoconfig
     ! indicates the type of autoconfiguration
```

The following **debug** output shows a more complete communication flow. Reviewing the flow shows that the Neighbor Solicitation (NS) and Neighbor Advertisement (NA) are being passed between the FastEthernet0/0 interface and a neighbor at 2000:0:0:3::2.

```
13:22:40:ICMPv6-ND:STALE -> DELAY:2000:0:0:3::2
     ! indicates ND cache entry used to be reachable but is now stale,
     ! reachability needs to be confirmed
13:22:45:ICMPv6-ND:DELAY -> PROBE:2000:0:0:3::2
     ! indicates reachability being confirmed
13:22:45:ICMPv6-ND:Sending NS for 2000:0:0:3::2 on FastEthernet0/0
     ! sending neighbor solicitation
```

```
13:22:45:ICMPv6-ND:Received NA for 2000:0:0:3::2 on FastEthernet0/0 from 2000:0:0:3::2
      ! receiving neighbor advertisement confirming reachability
13:22:45:ICMPv6-ND:PROBE -> REACH:2000:0:0:3::2
      ! entry flagged as reachable
13:22:45:ICMPv6-ND:Received NS for 2000:0:0:3::1 on FastEthernet0/0 from
FE80::203:A0FF:FED6:1400
      ! received neighbor solicitation to determine link-local address
13:22:45:ICMPv6-ND:Sending NA for 2000:0:0:3::1 on FastEthernet0/0
      ! sending neighbor advertisement in response to previous NS
13:23:15: ICMPv6-ND: Sending NS for FE80::1 on Ethernet0/1
13:23:16: ICMPv6-ND: DAD: FE80::1 is unique.
      ! duplicate address detection was performed and address is unique
13:23:16: ICMPv6-ND: Sending NS for 2000::2 on Ethernet0/1
13:23:16: ICMPv6-ND: Sending NS for 3000::3 on Ethernet0/1
13:23:16: ICMPv6-ND: Sending NA for FE80::1 on Ethernet0/1
13:23:17: ICMPv6-ND: DAD: 2000::2 is unique.
13:23:53: ICMPv6-ND: Sending NA for 2000::2 on Ethernet0/1
13:23:53: ICMPv6-ND: DAD: 3000::3 is unique.
13:23:53: ICMPv6-ND: Sending NA for 3000::3 on Ethernet0/1
```

The **debug ipv6 routing** command displays **debug** messages for IPv6 routing table updates and route cache updates. The following output displays routes being added to the routing table:

```
13:18:43:IPv6RT0:Add 2000:0:0:1:1::/80 to table
      ! specifies addition of the network to the routing table
13:18:43:IPv6RT0:Better next-hop for 2000:0:0:1:1::/80, [120/2]
      ! indicates the entry was in the routing table but a lower
      ! cost path was added
13:19:09:IPv6RT0:Add 2000:0:0:2::/64 to table
13:19:09:IPv6RT0:Better next-hop for 2000:0:0:2::/64, [20/1]
13:19:09:IPv6RT0:Add 2000:0:0:2:1::/80 to table
13:19:09:IPv6RT0:Better next-hop for 2000:0:0:2:1::/80, [20/1]
13:19:09:IPv6RT0:Add 2000:0:0:4::/64 to table
13:19:09:IPv6RT0:Better next-hop for 2000:0:0:4::/64, [20/1]
13:19:37:IPv6RT0:Add 2000:0:0:6::/64 to table
13:19:37:IPv6RT0:Better next-hop for 2000:0:0:6::/64, [20/2]
```

The **debug bgp ipv6** command enables the debugging of IPv6 BGP information. The full command syntax is as follows:

```
debug bgp ipv6 {dampening [neighbor-acl] | updates [neighbor-address |
 neighbor-acl | in | out]}
```

The following output displays BGP keepalive messages.

```
6Router-1# debug bgp ipv6
BGP debugging is on
6Router-1#
2w0d: BGP: 2000:1:1::2 rcv message type 4, length (excl. header) 0
2w0d: BGP: 2000:1:1::2 send message type 4, length (incl. header) 19
```

Summary

This chapter introduced you to IPv4 and IPv6. Regardless of the version used, IP is used to provide logical addressing, and to get traffic to its destination. IPv4 and IPv6 handle their responsibilities differently, starting with differences in address formats and lengths.

Both have special addresses such as multicast that are used in specific situations. For example, multicast addresses enable groups of network devices to receive the same datastream, rather than requiring multiple unicast streams. Multicast can be efficient and conserve network bandwidth.

We are just starting to see more development and support for IPv6, starting with its incorporation into Cisco software, as well as on end-user devices such as workstations and servers. Ultimately, IPv6 will ensure that address exhaustion will not plague the legions of networks that depend on IP.

Chapter 5

IP Routing

Best Damn Topics in this Chapter:

- Routing Terminology
- CIDR
- Cisco Routing in General
- Routing Information Protocol
- IGRP
- RIP versus IGRP
- EIGRP
- Intermediate System to Intermediate System
- Border Gateway Protocol
- Dial-on-Demand Routing
- OSPF Demand Circuits
- IPv6 Routing
- Configuring IS-IS for IPv6
- Configuring BGP Extensions for IPv6

Introduction

This chapter discusses routing, which is simply the processes that get traffic to its destination using network addresses such as IP. Specialized intermediaries called routers make this movement of traffic from its origin to its destination possible. Routing protocols enable routers to gather and exchange the information needed to build the necessary tables containing path information to reachable destinations.

Routing protocols for IP are the main focus of this chapter. We will cover the routing protocol concepts and terminology. We will also cover the various routing mechanisms used, including static and dynamic techniques.

- Classless Interdomain Routing (CIDR)
- Router Information Protocol (RIP)
- Interior Gateway Routing Protocol (IGRP)
- Enhanced Interior Gateway Routing Protocol (EIGRP)
- Open Shortest Path First (OSPF)
- Intermediate System to Intermediate System (IS-IS)
- Border Gateway Protocol (BGP)
- Dial-on-Demand Routing (DDR)

Routing Terminology

Before we get into the specifics of routing, we need to describe routing concepts and define terminology that will aid our discussion. It is important to distinguish between distance vector and link state routing protocols, for example. Understanding the terminology used to describe and classify routing aids the configuration of routing protocols such as RIP or BGP.

- **Administrative domain (AD)** Routing involves logical boundaries that encompass the AD. An AD is a collection of networks and network devices (including and especially routers) that adhere to a common policy for routing, addressing, and interconnection. An AD is controlled by a single entity.
- **Interior Gateway Protocol (IGP)** Responsible for the routing within a single AD. It handles the passage of traffic from source to destination within the same AD. OSPF, RIP, EIGRP, and IGRP are examples of IGPs.
- **Exterior Gateway Protocol (EGP)** Handles routing between separate ADs. Typically, EGPs will summarize the multitude of routing information within an AD and share the summarized view with another foreign AD whom their home AD needs to be able to reach. The best-known example of an EGP is BGP.
- **Distance vector protocols** Based primarily on the Bellman-Ford algorithm. This algorithm bases its metric calculation on a single-path tree concept, using the parameter

of weight. It enables the protocol to select from several paths to a destination network, using a Boolean expression to determine the weight of a particular path and to select the path with the best metric. The term *distance vector* comes from the function of the protocols. Protocols use a vector, or list, of distances or hop counts to determine the optimal routes to a given destination network. IGRP, RIP, and EIGRP are examples of distance vector routing protocols. EIGRP is a special instance of a distance vector protocol since it routes by hops, but builds its tables using techniques similar to that of a link-state routing protocol.

- **Link state** Link state routing protocols use the Dijkstra algorithm to determine the shortest path to a destination. Link-state routers place themselves at the center of the network, and build the complete routing picture of all reachable networks. Each network or interface is considered a link, and all routers running the same link-state protocol are aware of all advertised networks, the distance and cost associated with each path to any network, and the shortest (best) path to each. OSPF and IS-IS are examples of link-state protocols.

  Link-state protocols are immune to the problems that plague distance vector protocols such as routing loops or convergence issues. Link-state protocols also only update upon a change, as opposed to sending updates because a schedule mandates it.

  Link state routing protocols offer much more scalability and many more features than their distance vector predecessors did. Link state protocols also offer a system of hierarchy that affords greater control and scalability. It is for these reasons, along with several others, that link state protocols are the protocols of choice within large enterprise organizations as well as within the networks of major service providers.

  Link state protocols derive their name from the manner in which they view the network. They take the state, or conditions, of the path into account when making a routing determination. Routers examine not only the state of the specific link, but also the link and its relation to the neighboring router. Information such as bandwidth of the links and delay are taken into consideration, as is information pertaining to interface types, IP addresses, and subnet mask. This provides better path selection.

  Link state protocols are typically more difficult to configure than distance vector protocols. Central processing unit (CPU) and memory utilization are typically greater than for distance vector routing protocols.

- **Link state advertisements (LSAs)** The primary means of communication for link state protocols. Flooding the network with LSAs enables other routers to discover the network topology, build neighbor relationships, and form adjacencies.

  The initial flooding of LSAs ensures that all routers in a link state environment learn all routes, for an accurate picture of the network. LSAs inform routers of network topology changes as a change triggers a LSA. If the receiving router does not know the updated information already (from another source, perhaps), it requests a link state update (LSU) containing the new information. LSAs are coded with sequence numbers; if a router receives an LSA older than the last one it received, it will discard it. LSAs also have an aging mechanism (the default is 30 minutes), which renders a LSA invalid and requires a new one to be sent.

- **Neighbors** Routers have reached agreement and formed the necessary relationships to exchange routing information. Typically, neighbors are in the same autonomous system (AS), in the same area, or on the same network.
- **Link state database** A collection of all the information a router has obtained through the reception of LSAs. Every time a new LSA is received, its information is compared to the router's link state database. If the sequence number is newer, the information is added to the database. A router maintains a link state database for every area of which it is a member.
- **Areas** Link state routing protocols use *areas* to establish hierarchy within a routed network. Areas are logical, not physical, groupings of routers to control route propagation. Every router within an area has the same link state database. Routers belonging to more than one area will maintain a link state database for each area to which they belong.
- **Triggered updates** A mechanism used by routing protocols to deal with sudden network changes such as link failure. Upon detection of a network change, the affected router(s) will send updates informing its neighbors of the new conditions. The neighbors will in turn forward this information to their neighbors, thus helping to prevent conditions such as routing loops and decreasing convergence time. Triggered updates augment periodic updates to ensure that routers will not have to wait until the next periodic update to know about a network change.

  When sending a periodic update, routers transmit their entire routing table. Triggered updates send only information regarding the change. Triggered updates are more efficient than periodic updates, and help speed convergence.
- **Routing loops** A problem for distance vector protocols, but not for link state protocols. Routing loops are a state in which, due to incorrect information being propagated through a network, packets will continually encircle a network unable to reach their destination.

  In a routing loop, a network has become unreachable due to a link failure or some other unforeseen circumstance. The directly affected router will transmit this change to its directly connected neighbors, informing them of the inability to reach this network; however, this update might not make it to every router within the network, and another router might transmit its ability to reach the network in the meantime, using the link through the first router that saw the link was down. As a result, all routers will update their tables to use the new router as the next hop, which in turn will forward them back to the original router, which will forward them to the transmitting router, so it can reach the network, with the end result: an endless loop.
- **Split horizon** Loops in a production environment can be a major service effacing, if not service halting, problem. Split horizon is a mechanism employed by distance vector routing protocols used to control or eliminate routing loops. A network will not be advertised out of the same interface through which it was learned. Routers will omit these routes from their advertisements sent out the interface through which the route was initially learned. Split horizon cannot prevent routing loops in every situation.

Many people dealing with split horizon encounter a problem with nonbroadcast multi-access mediums such as Frame Relay or asynchronous transfer method (ATM). Many implementations of NBMA functionality work in a basic hub and spoke topology, a central router, or hub router, with several spoke routers hanging off it. The problem arises when all of these spoke routers terminate into one single interface on the hub router (for example, a multipoint Frame Relay interface). According split horizon, the hub router cannot send the update to the other routers also attached to that interface.

This has been recognized as a problem by Cisco, and split horizon is disabled by default on all Frame Relay physical interfaces. However, split horizon is enabled on all point-to-point subinterfaces and all point-to-multipoint sub-interfaces. When using point-to-point subinterfaces, each link is treated like a separate point-to-point link (so there is no conflict with the rule of split horizon). With point-to-multipoint subinterfaces, all subinterfaces are treated as a shared medium and must be in the same subnet to communicate. Obviously, this creates a problem with the rule of split horizon. Disabling split horizon leaves the possibility of routing loops, so you must be very careful in this type of environment. Figure 5.1 demonstrates split horizon in that A and B are not advertised out the interface through which they were initially learned.

Figure 5.1 Split Horizon

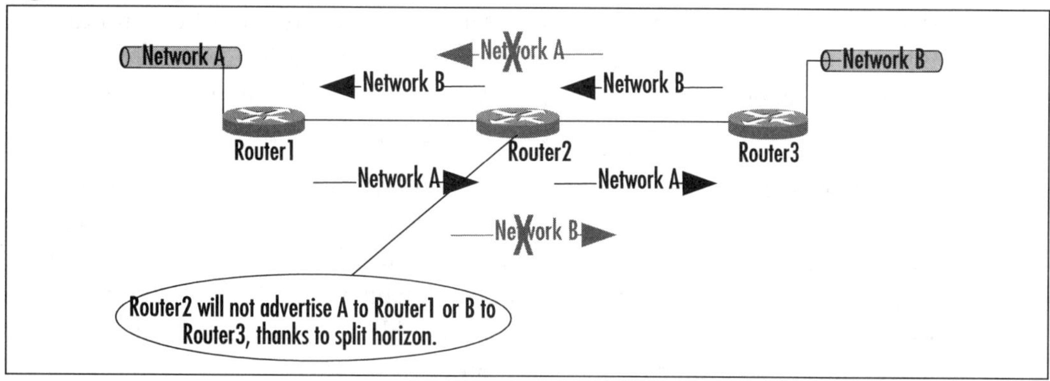

- **Counting to infinity** Some distance vector protocols derive their metric from the number of hops or routers that must be traversed to reach a given destination. The maximum number of hops, or infinity, is a number set specifying the maximum distance or diameter of a network that a packet can cross to reach a given destination network before it is considered unreachable. RIP has an infinity number set at 16 hops. If a destination network is 16 or more hops away, it will be considered unreachable and will not be considered for packet forwarding by the router.

  Counting to infinity is incorporated into distance vector routing protocols as a means of eliminating the possibility of packets traversing the network aimlessly for an eternity due to a downed link and the routing loop that could ensue thereafter. Counting to infinity is not by itself a loop-prevention mechanism.

- **Poison reverse** A solution to the problem of counting to infinity, or packets circling the network until they have reached the maximum number of hops—16, in the case of RIP.

In a standard application of split horizon, a rule states that a network cannot be advertised out of the interface through which the network was learned. Using this as a basis, poison reverse takes this a step further. When using poison reverse and split horizon, networks learned via a certain interface are advertised back out the same interface, with one major difference: the route is given a metric of unreachable, or infinity, so that the receiving router will not the use it, and will not add it to the routing tables.

- **Hold-down timers** In distance vector protocols, hold-downs prevent regular routing update messages from reinstating a route that is down due to link failure or other cause. When a router or link to a network fails, the neighboring routers recalculate their routing metrics to select a new path to reach the downed network. However, during this time, a nondirectly connected router could possibly retransmit a routing update specifying that the link is up, before triggered updates can reach it to inform it otherwise. This router could potentially update all the devices that had just been notified that the link was down, and cause them to reinstate the route.

  Hold-down timers specify the time that a router should wait before accepting any changes to the status of the route. These timers should be greater than the period needed to update every router in the network of the failed link.
- **Redistribution** Enables multiple routing protocols and processes to work in harmony, sharing their information. In simplest terms, the information of one routing protocol is injected into another routing protocol. It enables you to run multiple instances of a routing protocol on a select few routers, which in turn share the information they obtain with their brethren who are running a single routing protocol.
- **Administrative distance** Cisco routers incorporate this concept when making routing decisions. Administrative distance is a scale from 0 to 255 that specifies the reliability of a given route; 0 is the most reliable and 255 is the least reliable (unreachable). Each routing protocol is given a specified default administrative distance; however, these values can be manipulated when necessary. Table 5.1 provides the administrative distances of routing protocols on Cisco routers.

Table 5.1 Administrative Distances

Routing Protocol	Administrative Distance
Connected Interface	0
Static Route	1
EIGRP Summary Route	5
External BGP	20
Internal EIGRP	90
IGRP	100
OSPF	110
IS-IS	115
RIP v1, v2, IPv6 RIP	120

Continued

Table 5.1 Administrative Distances

Routing Protocol	Administrative Distance
EGP	140
External EIGRP	170
Internal BGP	200
Unknown (Unreachable)	255

We will be discussing the routing protocols used by IP to get traffic to its destination. You will see that each routing protocol differs in its ability to support CIDR, which was conceived to improve address allocation, and to reduce routing table sizes.

CIDR

CIDR was developed to stave off the exhaustion of IP address space. CIDR allows for a more efficient allocation of IP addresses than the original Class A, B, and C address and mask scheme, as discussed in Chapter 4. This original scheme is often referred to as *classful* addressing, whereas CIDR is referred to as *classless* addressing.

Another term for CIDR supernetting is *prefix-based addressing.* As you can see in Figure 5.2, the boundary between the network ID and host ID is not fixed. CIDR helps reduce the routing load by shrinking routing tables and ensuring that the most important routes are carried by the most routers.

Figure 5.2 Prefix Length of a Classless Address

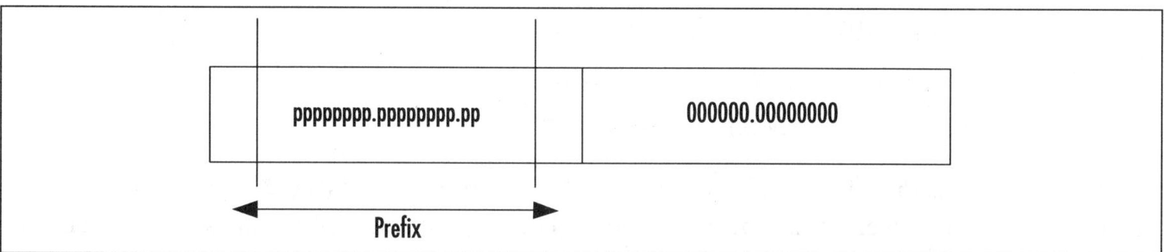

CIDR combines networks into *supernets,* whereas subnetting divides networks into smaller, more manageable *subnets* through the use of the subnet mask. CIDR eliminates the concept of Class A, B, and C networks, and replaces them with a generalized IP prefix consisting of an IP address and the mask length. For example, a single class C address would appear as 192.168.1.0/24, in which /24 refers to the number of bits of the network portion of the IP address.

With the traditional Class A, B, and C addressing scheme, the addresses were identified by converting the first eight bits of the address to their decimal equivalent. Table 5.2 shows the breakdown of the three address classes, and how many bits appear in the host ID and the network ID.

Table 5.2 The Familiar Delineations of the IP Address Classes

Address Class	# Network Bits	# Hosts Bits	Decimal Address Range
Class A	8 bits	24 bits	1–126
Class B	16 bits	16 bits	128–191
Class C	24 bits	8 bits	192–223

Using the classful Class A, B, and C addressing scheme, the Internet could support the following:

- 126 Class A networks that could include up to 16,777,214 hosts each
- 65,000 Class B networks that could include up to 65,534 hosts each
- Over 2 million Class C networks that could include up to 254 hosts each

A CIDR supernet consists of numerous contiguous IP addresses. Each supernet has a unique supernet address that consists of the upper bits that are shared between all IP addresses in the supernet. For example, the address is contiguous (192.168.0.0 through 192.168.7.0 in decimal notation).

```
11000000 10101000 00000  000 00000000
11000000 10101000 00000  001 00000000
11000000 10101000 00000  010 00000000
11000000 10101000 00000  011 00000000
11000000 10101000 00000  100 00000000
11000000 10101000 00000  101 00000000
11000000 10101000 00000  111 00000000
```

The supernet address for the block is 11000000 10101000 00000 (the 21 upper bits) because every address in the supernet has this in common. The complete supernet address consists of the address and the mask.

- The address is the first 32-bit address in the contiguous address block. In our case, this would be 11000000 10101000 00000000 00000000 (192.168.0.0 in decimal notation).
- The mask is a 32-bit string, similar to the subnet mask, which contains a set bit in the supernet portion of the address. In our case, this would be 11111111 11111111 11111000 00000000 (255.255.248.0 in decimal notation). The masked portion, however, contains the number of bits that are in the on position; in our case, this would be 21.

The complete supernet address would be 192.168.0.0/21. The /21 indicates that the first 21 bits are used to identify the unique network, leaving the remaining bits to identify the specific host.

CIDR can then be used to employ a supernet address to represent multiple IP destinations. Rather than advertise a separate route for each of the members of the contiguous address space, the router can now advertise the supernet address as a single route, called an *aggregate* route. This aggregate route will represent all the destinations within the supernet address, thereby reducing the amount of information that needs to be contained in the routing tables of the routers.

Table 5.3 shows how the CIDR block prefix is used to increase the number of groups of addresses that can be used, thereby offering a more efficient use of addressing than the Class A, B, or C method.

Table 5.3 Characteristics of Each CIDR Block Prefix

CIDR Block Prefix	Subnet Mask	# Equivalent Class C	# of Host Addresses
/27	255.255.255.224	1/8th of a Class C	32 hosts
/26	255.255.255.192	1/4th of a Class C	64 hosts
/25	255.255.255.128	1/2 of a Class C	128 hosts
/24	255.255.255.0	1 Class C	256 hosts
/23	255.255.254.0	2 Class C	512 hosts
/22	255.255.252.0	4 Class C	1,024 hosts
/21	255.255.248.0	8 Class C	2,048 hosts
/20	255.255.240.0	16 Class C	4,096 hosts
/19	255.255.224.0	32 Class C	8,192 hosts
/18	255.255.192	64 Class C	16,384 hosts
/17	255.255.128.0	128 Class C	32,768 hosts
/16	255.255.0.0	256 Class C (= 1 Class B)	65,536 hosts
/15	255.254.0.0	512 Class C	131,072 hosts
/14	255.252.0.0	1,024 Class C	262,144 hosts
/13	255.248.0.0	2,048 Class C	524,288 hosts

Contiguous Subnets

The most important rule to remember with CIDR classless addressing is that subnets must be contiguous. A router cannot process subnet routes for networks to which it is not directly connected. The example in Figure 5.3 illustrates this rule more clearly.

Figure 5.3 Illegal Subnetting = Routing Confusion

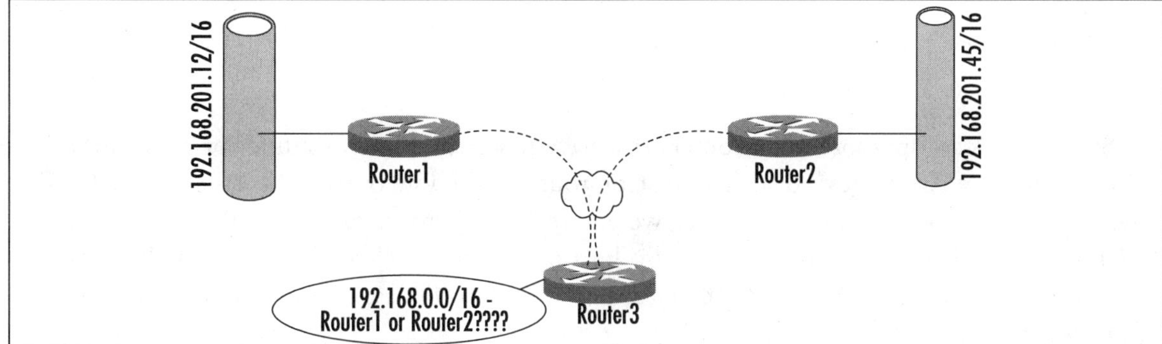

If a router is to take part in the same classful network in order to interpret the prefix length, it must be connected directly to the network.

In Figure 5.3, the router is not a part of the contiguous network, so it has no way of knowing the prefix length that is being used. More specifically, Router1 and Router2 cannot advertise their routes to Router3 because Router3 is not a part of the 192.168.201.0 network. The only route that can be advertised to Router3 is 192.168.201.0. This poses a problem because Router3 has no indication of which direction to send a packet with the prefix of 192.168.201.0; it will undoubtedly send packets to the wrong network.

The problem with the network configuration shown in Figure 5.3 is that the 192.168.201 networks are not contiguous. If we configured a direction connection between Router1 and Router2, we would have a contiguous network, and could benefit from CIDR addressing. The addition of Router3 injects another classful network between the 192.168.201 networks, thus making it discontiguous.

Cisco Routing in General

It is important that you at least be familiar with what CIDR is, given its implications for routing. Some routing protocols, such as RIP, do a very poor job of supporting CIDR, while others such as OSPF and EIGRP do much better. In this section, we will discuss routing in general; that is, routing that is not specific to any one routing protocol.

Cisco routers need to know where to send traffic, and learn this information via a variety of techniques. Dynamic routing protocols such as RIP or OSPF gather the necessary information for the Cisco router to build its routing table, which it uses to determine where to send traffic. There are also alternatives to dynamic methods such as static routes or default routes.

Static Routes

A routing table can be built via static routes such as the **ip route** command shown here. This command is manually entered and does not adapt to any changing network conditions.

```
Router_Static(config)# ip route 0.0.0.0 0.0.0.0 ?
  A.B.C.D    Forwarding router's address
  Ethernet   IEEE 802.3
  Null       Null interface
  Serial     Serial


ip route 10.0.0.0 255.0.0.0 192.168.1.1
ip route 192.168.1.1 255.255.255.255 Ethernet0
ip route 0.0.0.0 0.0.0.0 ethernet 0 254
```

Static routes are appropriate on routers that have few networks and still fewer paths from which to choose. The biggest advantage of static routes is the low overhead costs associated with them. In our previous command example, we entered a static route with a next hop IP address 192.168.1.1. Notice that an interface can also be a next hop as well; traffic for the address will be sent out that interface. Finally, a default route was created in the last example, and assigned an administrative distance of 254. You also send certain destinations to a routing black hole by pointing to the null (nonexistent) interface as the next hop.

You can create a floating static route that will not appear in the routing table to be used until the same route learned via a routing protocol disappears. You accomplish this by setting the administrative distance of the static route higher than that of the competing routing protocol. Floating static routes are useful in dial backup of situations where such an interface as the next hop is activated only the primary permanent link fails (and thus loses the route as learned via the dynamic routing protocol).

Default Routes and Networks

Default routes are known by many names, including default gateway, gateway of last resort, and others of that ilk. Default routes are special routes to which traffic having no particular route is sent. The presumption is that the next hop for this default route will know where to send such traffic. There are several commands and options available to create a default route.

If the router is not running any dynamic routing protocols (that is, **no ip routing** has been executed on this router), you would use the **ip default-gateway** command as shown. This command is to be used when the router is nothing more than a host (not doing any routing):

```
Router_Default(config)# ip default-gateway 10.10.10.10
```

Assuming that you have a routing table built either via dynamic or static means, you can identify a network in that table as the default network that all traffic with no associated route will be sent:

```
interface Loopback0
 ip address 10.10.10.11 255.255.255.255
 no ip directed-broadcast
!
interface Loopback1
 ip address 10.10.10.12 255.255.255.255
 no ip directed-broadcast


Router_Default(config)# ip default-network 10.0.0.0
```

Run the **show ip route** command and you will see that one of the networks in the 10.0.0.0/8 range has been flagged as the preferred default route; two other networks are waiting the wings to take over as the default should the selected default route fail or be removed.

```
Router_Default# show ip route
Codes: C - connected, S - static, I - IGRP, R - RIP, M - mobile, B - BGP
       D - EIGRP, EX - EIGRP external, O - OSPF, IA - OSPF inter area
       N1 - OSPF NSSA external type 1, N2 - OSPF NSSA external type 2
       E1 - OSPF external type 1, E2 - OSPF external type 2, E - EGP
       i - IS-IS, L1 - IS-IS level-1, L2 - IS-IS level-2, * - candidate default
       U - per-user static route, o - ODR
```

```
Gateway of last resort is 10.10.10.11 to network 10.0.0.0
 *    10.0.0.0/8 is variably subnetted, 4 subnets, 2 masks
C        10.10.10.11/32 is directly connected, Loopback0
C        10.10.10.12/32 is directly connected, Loopback1
C        10.10.10.13/32 is directly connected, Loopback3
S*       10.0.0.0/8 [1/0] via 10.10.10.11
```

We previously mentioned that you could create a special instance of a static route that will serve as the default route. This approach is more manual, but also more flexible and gives you better control over your default, including its metric and the next hop as shown.

```
ip route 0.0.0.0 0.0.0.0 10.10.10.10 120
```

This command creates a default route (indicated by the *0.0.0.0 0.0.0.0*) with an administrative distance of *120* (same as RIP) and a next hop of *10.10.10.10*. If you do not specify a metric, it will be assigned an administrative distance of 1, which is lower than any dynamic routing protocol.

Many Are Learned, Few Are Chosen

So, how does the Cisco router determine which route makes it into its routing table, and which are understudies for the chosen route? The router has a strict criterion that it uses to make such decisions. It judges each route and deems it worthy of the routing table as follows.

Specific beats general anytime. The most specific routes will always make it into the table, and will always be used to route traffic. For example, traffic to 10.10.10.10 will be sent to the next hop associated with the route of 10.10.10.10/32 rather than the static route of 10.0.0.0/8 because the former is the more specific and matches the most bits in the destination address.

What if two techniques have the same specificity? In that case, the administrative distance is the next tiebreaker. The routing technique with the lowest administrative distance will win the routing battle and have its routes inserted into the table.

What if the administrative distances are the same (such as two instances of the same protocols)? In that case, the router looks at the costs (metrics) associated with the routes, and chooses the one with the best metrics.

Dynamic routing protocols such as RIP automate the drudgery associated with obtaining routes to particular destinations. Perhaps the oldest and still active routing protocol is RIP, which we will use to kick off our discussion.

Routing Information Protocol (RIP)

RIP is a distance vector routing protocol limited to a maximum of 15 hops (anything 16 or more hops is considered unreachable). RIP sends its entire routing update to all directly connected neighbors through the use of periodic updates, *every 30 seconds* in this case, using UDP port 520 for this broadcast. This update occurs regardless of any network change and or link failure.

NOTE

When discussing RIP, unless we specify a version, the information provided applies to both versions 1 and 2.

These metric counts of hops to the destination determine the most efficient route; that is, the quickest path to the destination network. In other words, a route with five hops is more efficient than a route with eight hops. However, the route with the least number of hops might not be the fastest route to a destination. The hops do not take into account the speed of the route. For example, a route with five hops might cross slower serial links to reach a destination, rather than another route with seven hops that crosses an Ethernet network. For this reason, a router can advertise a higher hop count for a slow link to compensate for the slower link. This will deter the use of the slower link.

RIP classifies routers as *active* and *passive*. An active router will advertise its routes to other routers. Passive routers will receive these routes, but they do not advertise their own routes. The update will consist of an IP network address and the integer distance to that network.

Routing Update Impact

One of the disadvantages of RIP routing is the extensive use of broadcasts. A router updates its own routing table with information received from neighboring routers. Response packets contain destination network information and metrics (hops). When the host or router receives this routing information it will rebuild its database by adding new routes and modifying existing routes.

To modify an existing route, the host or router will determine if the new route has a better path to the destination, which is a lower hop count. RIP will also delete a route that contains more than 15 hops to the destination. Routes will also be removed from the router's database if no updates are received within a certain period of time. This is a dynamic means of purging routes in the database that have not been used recently. Routes are usually broadcast every 30 seconds, and routes are deleted from the route database if they are not updated within 180 seconds.

RIP Timers

A set of three timers is incorporated into RIP: the *update interval*, the *hold-down interval*, and the *flush timer*. The update interval is the amount of time that a router will wait before sending its entire routing table to all its neighbors. The default value for this is 30 seconds. The update interval should be uniform across your RIP network to avoid your routers being out of sync.

When a route is placed in the hold-down state, no routing updates are accepted for that route, and it will not be advertised. The hold-down timer is the amount of time that the router will wait without receiving updates before putting a route into hold-down state. The default value for this is 180 seconds; this value is also configurable.

The flush timer specifies the amount of time in seconds that the router will wait before completely removing a route, after which a new route to the destination network is sought. The default value for this is six times the update interval, or 240 seconds. This value is also configurable.

RIPv1

RIP uses the update to verify neighbor connectivity and activity. Figure 5.4 shows the format of the RIPv1 packet used to transport routing information. A single RIP packet can contain as many as 25 networks, making the size of a single RIP packet as large as 512 bytes. Add that to the corresponding 20 to 24 bytes of the IPv4 header attached and you have a large amount of traffic traversing your network!

Figure 5.4 RIPv1 Packet

bits	RIPv1 Packet
8	Command
8	Version
16	Unused (zeros)
16	Address Family Identifier (1)
16	Unused (zeros)
32	IP Address
32	Unused (zeros)
32	Unused (zeros)
32	Metric
	...
	...
	...
16	Address Family Identifier (25)
16	Unused (zeros)
32	IP Address
32	Unused (zeros)
32	Unused (zeros)
32	Metric

- **Command** Indicates if this is a response or request.
- **Version** Indicates the version of RIP (in this case, 1 for RIPv1).
- **Address Family Identifier** Indicates the network protocol advertised by RIP (in this case, IP).

- **IP Address** The IP address being advertised on classful boundary, as appropriate for its class.
- **Metric** Number of hops from the advertising router to this IP address.

RIPv1 has several limitations that can make it unsuitable.

- RIP cannot support an internal network with more than 15 hops within the same network.
- RIPv1 cannot support variable-length subnet masking.
- RIP will broadcast updates about every 30 seconds.
- RIP has limited security. It is possible to obtain an unauthorized list of routes from other neighboring routers, and it might be possible for a hacker to inject false routes on the network.
- Routing problems are difficult to diagnose in RIP.
- RIP has a slower convergence time due to its period of hold-down, garbage collection, and will slowly time-out information during the convergence process.
- RIP has no concept of slow links or network delays. Routing decisions are only made by metrics hop counts.
- RIP networks are not hierarchical, and have no concept of areas, domains, and ASs.
- RIP does not support classless routing, which has become increasingly necessary.
- Routers using the RIP protocol exchange their entire routing table, which can be inefficient.

Not everything about the RIP protocol is negative. Since it is one of the most widespread interior routing protocols, RIP can be supported almost anywhere. RIP is very easy to configure, which makes it very attractive because of the minimal amount of configuration required. Many the weaknesses of RIPv1 were addressed in RIPv2.

RIPv2

RIPv2 increases the amount of information in the packet itself, and increases security. The following is a list of features added in RIPv2:

- **Optional authentication** Simple password authentication (plaintext and MD5) between neighbors.
- **Routing Domain field** Enables you to ignore logical domains on the same physical network. The default routing domain is assigned the value 0.
- **Route Tag field** Separates internal RIP routes from external ones.
- **Subnet Mask field** Contains a subnet mask that is applied to the IP address to determine the host network on which the destination is located. Supports CIDR and VLSM.

- **Next Hop** Forwards packets to the immediate next hop.
- **Multicasting** Sends multicast packets out on the network. The RIPv2 multicast address is 224.0.0.9.

RIPv2 is completely backward compatible with RIPv1, and can run in RIPv1 emulation mode or RIPv1 compatible mode. Other than the features detailed above, RIPv2 is similar to RIPv1 in every other way.

As you can see in Figure 5.5, the size and number of packet fields do not change between the two versions; however, RIPv2 has added the Route Tag, subnet mask, and next hop field. These additional fields enable RIP v2 to support VLSM as well as authentication. Each RIPv2 router assumes that addresses are subnetted consistently according to the masks configured on their interfaces. A workaround would be to summarize on a classful boundary and advertise that to the neighbors, fooling them into thinking the mask is the same throughout the AS.

Figure 5.5 RIPv2 Packet

bits	RIPv2 Packet (with Authentication)
8	Command
8	Version
16	Unused (all zeros)
16	Address Family Identifier (1) OxFFFF
16	Authentication Type (Plaintext or MD5)
128	Password
32	Address Family Identifier (2)
32	Route Tag (Internal or External)
32	IP Address
32	Subnet Mask
32	Next Hop
32	Metric
	...
	...
	...
32	Address Family Identifier (25)
32	Route Tag (Internal or External)
32	IP Address
32	Subnet Mask
32	Next Hop
32	Metric

Configuring RIP

We will briefly discuss the commands you use to configure RIP. Of all the routing protocols to choose from, RIP is probably the simplest, with the smallest set of parameters of any routing protocol. As you study the RIP configuration examples provided here, pay attention to the router prompt information on each command line: some commands are global, others are interface commands.

First, enable RIP on the router.

```
Router1(config)# router rip
```

Specify the networks that you want RIP to advertise:

```
Router1(config-router)# network 10.0.0.0
Router1(config-router)# network 172.16.0.0
Router1(config-router)# network 192.168.1.0
```

The previous commands are the bare minimum that you must execute to enable RIP. There are more commands to tune and customize RIP, as shown next.

If you do not want RIP to broadcast (or multicast if using RIPv2), manually identify the neighbor; RIP updates will then be unicast to the IP address specified. This can be a useful command if you have configured a broadcast interface (such as Ethernet) as passive, but want to advertise to a specific RIP router on that network.

```
Router1(config-router)# neighbor ip-address
Router1(config-router)# neighbor 10.10.10.10
```

You can specify the RIP version globally, in which case that is the version to be used with all neighbors, or on a per-interface basis to ensure that the router uses the correct version with each neighbor. The interface setting overrides the global setting. *By default, RIP on Cisco routers will receive both versions 1 and 2, but send only version 1.* The global **version** command is:

```
Router1(config-router)# version {1 | 2}
```

On each interface, you can specify what version is used to send and receive updates. Here we are using both versions.

```
Router1(config-if)# ip rip send version 1 2
Router1(config-if)# ip rip receive version 1 2
```

You can adjust the RIP timers previously discussed using the following command.

```
Router1(config-router)# timers basic update invalid holddown flush [sleeptime]
```

- Update Interval (in seconds) between updates <0–4294967295>
- Invalid Time (in seconds) to wait before invalidating a route <1–4294967295>
- Holddown Time (in seconds) before advertising a newly learned route. <0–4294967295>
- Flush Time (in seconds) time to wait before deleting invalid routes <1–4294967295>
- Sleeptime Time (in milliseconds) to hold off on posting updates. <1–4294967295>

The following command adjusts the metric (hop count) of an incoming or outbound route. This is the only direct command that you have in RIP to make such an adjustment. Our example increases the hop count of all networks specified by ACL 99 by two hops.

```
Router1(config-router)# offset-list [access-list-number | name] {in | out} offset [hop count]
Router1(config-router)# offset-list 99 in 2
Router1(config-router)# offset-list 99 out 2
```

The following commands are RIPv2 specific. We enable authentication on per-interface basis. The first command specifies the key, while the second command specifies the authentication mode. Both must match between neighbors.

```
Router(config-if)# ip rip authentication key-chain name-of-chain
Router(config-if)# ip rip authentication mode {text | md5}
```

You can summarize the addresses you advertise using the following command. We will discuss summarization more fully later in this chapter, but suffice to say for now that it is the act of reducing many routes to a few or one. In this case, we are supernetting all 10.x.x.x addresses and advertising them as 10.0.0.0/8.

```
Router(config-if)# ip summary-address rip ip_address ip_network_mask
Router(config-if)# ip summary-address rip 10.0.0.0 255.0.0.0
```

An example of a RIP configuration is provided:

```
interface Ethernet0
 ip address 10.10.10.9 255.255.255.0
 no ip directed-broadcast
 ip rip send version 1
 ip rip receive version 2
 ip rip authentication mode md5
 ip rip authentication key-chain test password
 ip summary-address rip 10.0.0.0 255.0.0.0

router rip
 version 2
 timers basic 1 2 3 4
 offset-list 99 in 2
 offset-list 99 out 4
 network 10.0.0.0
 network 172.16.0.0
 network 192.168.1.0
 neighbor 10.10.10.10
```

Use the **show ip protocols** command to validate your RIP configuration.

```
Routing Protocol is "rip"
 Sending updates every 1 seconds, next due in 0 seconds
 Invalid after 2 seconds, hold down 3, flushed after 4
 Outgoing update filter list for all interfaces is
 Incoming update filter list for all interfaces is
 Outgoing routes will have 4 added to metric if on list 99
 Incoming routes will have 2 added to metric if on list 99
 Redistributing: rip
 Neighbor(s):
   10.10.10.10
 Default version control: send version 2, receive version 2
   Interface             Send  Recv   Key-chain
   Ethernet0             1     2       test password
 Routing for Networks:
   10.0.0.0
   172.16.0.0
   192.168.1.0
 Routing Information Sources:
   Gateway          Distance       Last Update
 Distance: (default is 120)
```

We'll close our discussion of RIP with a mention of how it generates a default route, and its ability to handle discontiguous subnets. It is a limitation of RIP that it will not advertise a default route unless it was learned via RIP, or unless you force it to generate one. In our example, we have created a static default route pointing to *Null0* as the next hop. To force RIP to advertise this route to its neighbors, we do a redistribute static, which makes the route a "RIP route."

```
ip route 0.0.0.0 0.0.0.0 Null0


router rip
 redistribute static
```

We could also force RIP to generate a default route, regardless of whether it has one or not. It will advertise a 0.0.0.0 0.0.0.0 route to its neighbors, which will install it into their routing tables.

```
router rip
  default-information originate
```

RIP has constraints that make it unattractive for larger networks, or for networks with any degree of complexity. To overcome these limitations, Cisco developed IGRP.

IGRP

When the networking community began to realize the limitations of the RIP protocol, they started working on a replacement. The Internet Engineering Task Force (IETF) had not yet formalized the specifications for OSPF, so Cisco implemented their own protocol, which turned out to be IGRP.

IGRP is a distance vector protocol in which routers exchange routing information only with adjacent routers. When the adjacent router receives the update, it will compare the information with its own routing table. Any new paths or destinations will be added. Paths in the adjacent router's update will also be compared with existing paths to determine if the new route is more efficient than the route that currently exists in the routing table. If the new path is better, it will replace the existing one. This is the general procedure used in all distance vector protocols. IGRP can route traffic up to 255 hops; anything more is considered unreachable.

IGRP coordinates routing between a number of routers. There were a number of routing goals with Cisco's IGRP protocol:

- Stable routing, even in a very large or complex network
- No routing loops should occur
- Fast response to changing network topology
- Low overhead, meaning IGRP should not use more bandwidth than it needs for its own use
- Splitting traffic among parallel routes when they are of equal desirability
- Factor in error rates and levels of traffic on different paths
- The ability to handle multiple "types of services" with a single set of information

IGRP maintains a very accurate representation of the internal network topology. Convergence is very important because the paths to networks must be quickly rerouted in the event a link fails. IGRP is concerned with providing the optimal route when packets are being routed.

Working together and exchanging routing information with only their adjacent routers, IGRP routers can determine the best route a packet can take. In other words, no one router needs to maintain the information for the entire network.

IGRP goes beyond RIP when it comes to metrics. IGRP performs a more complex mathematical comparison of routes to select the best one for its table, instead of using a simple hop count. IGRP metrics include:

- **Topological delay time** The amount of time for a packet to reach its destination if the network was not busy. You can incur additional delays if there is network traffic on the network.
- **Bandwidth** Narrowest bandwidth segment of the path. The bandwidth is in bits per second.
- **Channel occupancy** Indicates how much of the bandwidth in the path is currently in use. This number will change often as the network traffic increases and decreases.

- **Reliability** of the path. Indicates the reliability of the path based on the number of packets that actually arrive at the destination, based on the number of packets that were originally sent.

IGRP calculates these factors and determines the best route, as indicated by the smallest metric value. IGRP also has substantial stability features, such as h*old-down timers*, *split horizon*, and *poison-reverse*. IGRP uses timers and variables that contain time intervals. The timers include an update timer, an invalid timer, a hold-time period, a flush timer, and a sleep timer.

- **Update timer** Specifies how frequently update messages will be sent. Default is every 90 seconds.
- **Invalid timer** Specifies how long a router will wait if it is not receiving update messages before a route is declared invalid. Default is three times the update timer (180 seconds).
- **Hold timer** Specifies the amount of time before new route can be entered into the routing table. Default is three times the update timer plus 10 seconds (190 seconds).
- **Flush timer** Specifies how much time should pass before a route is flushed from a routing table. Default is seven times the update period (630 seconds).
- **Sleep timer** Amount of time that update messages will be postponed. The sleep value should be less than the update timer, as routing tables will never be synchronized if it is higher than the update timer.

Configuring IGRP

IGRP has largely been superseded by EIGRP, so we will not spend a large amount of time discussing its features or configuration. We will provide the commands necessary for a basic IGRP configuration.

Enable IGRP on the router. Notice that we can have multiple IGRP processes running on the same router (unlike RIP, which can only have one). You can assign one IGRP process to each administrative domain.

```
Router_IGRP(config)# router igrp 65535
```

Specify the networks that you want IGRP to advertise:

```
Router_IGRP(config-router)# network 10.0.0.0
Router_IGRP(config-router)# network 172.16.0.0
Router_IGRP(config-router)# network 192.168.1.0
```

The previous commands are the bare minimum that you must execute to enable IGRP. There are more commands to tune and customize IGRP, as shown next.

If you do not want IGRP to broadcast, you can manually identify the neighbor; which will unicast information directly to that neighbor. This command is useful if IGRP is used on an NBMA network such as Frame Relay, which by default does not support broadcasts.

```
Router_IGRP(config-router)# neighbor ?
```

```
  A.B.C.D  Neighbor address
Router_IGRP(config-router)# neighbor 10.10.10.10
```

Other IGRP commands you can use are shown; these are all global commands.

```
Router configuration commands:
  default                  Set a command to its defaults
  default-information      Control distribution of default information
  default-metric           Set metric of redistributed routes
  distance                 Define an administrative distance
  distribute-list          Filter networks in routing updates
  exit                     Exit from routing protocol configuration mode
  help                     Description of the interactive help system
  input-queue              Specify input queue depth
  maximum-paths            Forward packets over multiple paths
  metric                   Modify IGRP routing metrics and parameters
  neighbor                 Specify a neighbor router
  network                  Enable routing on an IP network
  no                       Negate a command or set its defaults
  offset-list              Add or subtract offset from IGRP or RIP metrics
  passive-interface        Suppress routing updates on an interface
  redistribute             Redistribute information from another routing protocol
  timers                   Adjust routing timers
  traffic-share            Algorithm for computing traffic share for alternate routes
  validate-update-source   Perform sanity checks against source address of routing
                           updates
  variance                 Control load balancing variance
```

An example of an IGRP configuration is provided:

```
router igrp 65535
 redistribute rip metric 1 2 3 4 5
 passive-interface Ethernet0
 network 10.0.0.0
 network 172.16.0.0
 network 192.168.1.0
 neighbor 10.10.10.10
 default-information out 1
```

Use the **show ip protocols** command to validate your IGRP configuration.

```
Router_IGRP# show ip protocols
Routing Protocol is "igrp 65535"
  Sending updates every 90 seconds, next due in 36 seconds
```

```
  Invalid after 270 seconds, hold down 280, flushed after 630
  Outgoing update filter list for all interfaces is
  Incoming update filter list for all interfaces is
  Default networks flagged in outgoing updates, if matching access list 1
  Default networks accepted from incoming updates
  IGRP metric weight K1=1, K2=0, K3=1, K4=0, K5=0
  IGRP maximum hopcount 100
  IGRP maximum metric variance 1
  Redistributing: igrp 65535, rip
  Neighbor(s):
    10.10.10.10
  Routing for Networks:
    10.0.0.0
    172.16.0.0
    192.168.1.0
  Passive Interface(s):
    Ethernet0
  Routing Information Sources:
    Gateway         Distance      Last Update
  Distance: (default is 100)
```

IGRP can generate and receive default routes, as follows. To generate a default route, IGRP must already have a default route or network identified in its routing table, either through the commands we mentioned earlier or learned dynamically.

```
Router_IGRP(config-router)# default-information ?
  allowed  Allow default information
  in       Accept default routing information
  out      Output default routing information
```

Not shown is that you specify an access control list (ACL) containing the networks this router will accept (in) as its default routes, or advertise to its neighbors as default routes.

RIP versus IGRP

RIP and IGRP are both distance vector routing protocols. Other than this, there are few other similarities between the two, as shown in Table 5.4.

Table 5.4 RIP versus IGRP—A Comparison

RIP	IGRP
Smaller networks	Large, complex networks
Hop count of 15	Larger metric hop count includes factors such as delay, bandwidth, and reliability

Continued

Table 5.4 RIP versus IGRP—A Comparison

RIP	IGRP
Difficult to load balance over multiple links to same destination	Easy to load balance over multiple links to same destination
No support for AS	Supports AS
Distributes default route like other routes	Flags reachable network as default route

IGRP has fallen into disfavor, and has been largely abandoned in favor of its superior descendant, EIGRP (discussed next), which can exchange routing information with IGRP.

EIGRP

EIGRP is an enhanced version of the IGRP routing protocol. EIGRP uses the same distance vector-based mechanisms of IGRP. However, EIGRP has improved convergence and operating efficiency. The main enhancement with EIGRP is the sophisticated Diffusing Update Algorithm (DUAL). This algorithm is significantly more advanced than the distance vector algorithm used by RIP and previous versions of IGRP. The new algorithm decreases routing loops drastically.

Convergence is improved by implementing a new algorithm that enables all routers involved in a topology change to synchronize their internal routing tables at the same time. EIGRP is network protocol-independent, which means it can support other protocol suites such as IPX or AppleTalk.

EIGRP can be implemented seamlessly within a network of IGRP routers. This makes it possible to benefit from the features of both protocols simultaneously, while providing an upgrade path from IGRP to EIGRP.

Cisco defines the four basic components of EIGRP as follows:

- **Neighbor Discovery/Recovery** Dynamically learn the status of other routers on the directly attached networks. Routers must also continually poll their neighbors by sending Hello packets on a regular basis.
- **Reliable Transport Protocol** Responsible for the guaranteed delivery of packets in the correct order by sending a multicast Hello packet to the neighbors that states the packet does not have to be acknowledged.
- **DUAL Finite State Machine** The decision process for route computations that tracks routes advertised by all neighbors. The metric hop count is the distance information used to create loop-free paths. The routes are selected based on feasible successors.
- **Protocol Dependent Modules** Sends and receives EIGRP packets that are encapsulated in a protocol, such as IP. This module has support for other network protocols.

EIGRP Concepts

This section describes the concepts for Cisco's EIGRP implementation.

- **Neighbor table** Tracks neighboring (adjacent) routers. When a new neighbor is learned, its address and interface are recorded into this database.
- **Topology table** Populated with protocol-dependent modules containing all destinations advertised by the neighbors. Each entry consists of the destination address and list of neighbors that have advertised this particular destination, as well as associated metrics.
- **Feasible successors** Feasible successors are downstream neighbors to the neighboring router; they are the neighbor's neighbors. Neighbors that have an advertised metric route that is less than the current routing table metric are considered feasible successors.
- **Route states** A route is considered passive when the router is not performing a route recomputation. The route is considered active when a router is performing route computation.

EIGRP neighbors multicast to each other at 224.0.0.10 by default, although they can be configured to use unicast addresses via the **neighbor** command. EIGRP can route up to 224 hops; anything more is considered unreachable. Redistribution between IGRP and EIGRP processes with the same AS number is automatic; they will share routing knowledge without any special configuration. EIGRP offers great support for VLSM and CIDR and has none of the issues with subnetting that RIP and IGRP do. It also performs route summarization to reduce the routing table size.

Configuring EIGRP

Configuring EIGRP is similar to configuring IGRP; only EIGRP has more features to configure. We will take you through the process of configuring EIGRP.

Enable EIGRP on the router as shown.

```
Router_EIGRP(config)# router eigrp 65535
```

Specifying networks is the same as on IGRP:

```
Router_EIGRP(config-router)# network 10.10.10.10
Router_EIGRP(config-router)# network 192.168.1.0
Router_EIGRP(config-router)# network 172.31.0.0
```

When you enter the previous commands to specify networks that should be advertised via EIGRP, EIGRP summarizes the networks on their classful boundaries…just like IGRP as shown in the resultant configuration.

```
router eigrp 65535
 network 10.0.0.0
 network 172.31.0.0
 network 192.168.1.0
```

This is all you need to execute to enable EIGRP on the router. The following commands are optional and tune the operation of EIGRP.

EIGRP multicasts its updates to 224.0.0.10, which sends them to any EIGRP neighbors listening on any interface. You convert these multicasts to unicasts with the **neighbor** command as shown.

```
Router_EIGRP(config-router)# neighbor 10.10.10.9
```

Other EIGRP commands you can use are shown; these are all global commands and by their Cisco descriptions, are self-explanatory. However, there are a few commands (highlighted here) that bear further description.

```
Router_EIGRP(config-router)# ?
Router configuration commands:
  auto-summary          Enable automatic network number summarization
  default               Set a command to its defaults
  default-information   Control distribution of default information
  default-metric        Set metric of redistributed routes
  distance              Define an administrative distance
  distribute-list       Filter networks in routing updates
  eigrp                 EIGRP specific commands
  exit                  Exit from routing protocol configuration mode
  help                  Description of the interactive help system
  maximum-paths         Forward packets over multiple paths
  metric                Modify IGRP routing metrics and parameters
  neighbor              Specify a neighbor router
  network               Enable routing on an IP network
  no                    Negate a command or set its defaults
  offset-list           Add or subtract offset from IGRP or RIP metrics
  passive-interface     Suppress routing updates on an interface
  redistribute          Redistribute information from another routing protocol
  timers                Adjust routing timers
  traffic-share         Algorithm for computing traffic share for alternate routes
  variance              Control load balancing variance
```

The command, **auto-summary**, is enabled by default, and will summarize your networks on their classful boundaries. For example, 10.10.10.0 will be advertised as 10.0.0.0/8, as that is the natural mask and address combination. **auto-summary** can have undesirable effects, such as less specific routes being advertised. If the address is not subnetted or used elsewhere in your network, leave this command enabled to reduce your routing table size. Otherwise, use **ip summary-address eigrp** for finer control over how addresses are summarized and advertised to specific neighbors. For example, **ip summary-address eigrp 65535 10.10.10.0 255.255.0.0** will summarize and advertise 10.10.0.0/16.

EIGRP by default permits four paths to a destination; that is, it can inject four routes into the routing table to a particular network. This provides redundancy and load balancing in a round robin fashion, more or less. You can increase or decrease the number of paths with the following command:

```
Router_EIGRP(config-router)# maximum-paths ?
  <1-6>   Number of paths
```

An example of an EIGRP configuration is provided:

```
router eigrp 65535
 passive-interface Ethernet0
 network 10.0.0.0
 network 172.31.0.0
 network 192.168.1.0
 network 192.168.3.0
 neighbor 10.10.10.9
 maximum-paths 6
 default-information out 1
```

Use the **show ip protocols** command to validate your EIGRP configuration.

```
Routing Protocol is "eigrp 65535"
  Outgoing update filter list for all interfaces is
  Incoming update filter list for all interfaces is
  Default networks flagged in outgoing updates, if matching access list 1
  Default networks accepted from incoming updates
  EIGRP metric weight K1=1, K2=0, K3=1, K4=0, K5=0
  EIGRP maximum hopcount 100
  EIGRP maximum metric variance 1
  Redistributing: eigrp 65535, igrp 65535
  Automatic network summarization is in effect
  Routing for Networks:
    10.0.0.0
    172.31.0.0
    192.168.1.0
    192.168.3.0
  Passive Interface(s):
    Ethernet0
  Routing Information Sources:
    Gateway          Distance      Last Update
  Distance: internal 90 external 170
```

EIGRP handles the generation and reception in the same manner as IGRP as evidenced by the command here:

```
Router_EIGRP(config-router)# default-information ?
```

```
  allowed  Allow default information
  in        Accept default routing information
  out       Output default routing information
```

Cisco provides several commands you can use to check EIGRP.

The **show ip eigrp interface** command determines what interfaces are participating in EIGRP:

```
Router_EIGRP# show ip eigrp interface
IP-EIGRP interfaces for process 65535

                      Xmit Queue   Mean   Pacing Time   Multicast    Pending
Interface     Peers  Un/Reliable  SRTT   Un/Reliable  Flow Timer   Routes
AT1/1/0.45      1        0/0        25       0/10         110          0
AT1/1/0.51      1        0/0        30       0/10         130          0
```

You can determine who your EIGRP neighbors are:

```
Router_EIGRP# show ip eigrp neighbors
IP-EIGRP neighbors for process 65535
H   Address                Interface    Hold Uptime    SRTT   RTO  Q  Seq
                                        (sec)          (ms)        Cnt Num
17  10.254.254.30         AT1/1/0.78    10 19:26:35   241   1446  0  735875
12  10.254.254.102        AT1/1/0.74    12 20:16:48    65    390  0  735874
```

The following command identifies your feasible successors and their current state:

```
Router_EIGRP# show ip eigrp topology
IP-EIGRP Topology Table for process 65535

Codes: P - Passive, A - Active, U - Update, Q - Query, R - Reply,
       r - Reply status

P 0.0.0.0/0, 0 successors, FD is Inaccessible
         via 10.254.254.1 (218112/256), ATM1/1/0.51
```

How much EIGRP traffic has been processed?

```
Router_EIGRP# show ip eigrp traffic
IP-EIGRP Traffic Statistics for process 65535
  Hellos sent/received: 31530651/33623388
  Updates sent/received: 7915119/8718500
  Queries sent/received: 6818201/6060031
  Replies sent/received: 5907058/7109303
  Acks sent/received: 21449468/21583924
  Input queue high water mark 70, 0 drops
```

With the following **debug** commands, you can gather information on EIGRP events as they happen. Use them sparingly, as these commands can place quite a burden on the router.

```
Router_EIGRP# debug ip eigrp ?
  <1-65535>       AS number
  neighbor        IP-EIGRP neighbor debugging
  notifications   IP-EIGRP event notifications
  summary         IP-EIGRP summary route processing
  <cr>
```

As mentioned earlier, EIGRP is a distance vector protocol, with link state characteristics. Link state protocols have a unique approach to routing, which we will discuss starting with OSPF.

OSPF

Open Shortest Path First (OSPF) is a thoroughly modern link state routing protocol where all routers have the same database containing information about all links in the network. This renders issues such as split horizon moot. OSPF has the following features that make it attractive as an IGP.

- Plaintext or MD5 Authentication of routing updates
- Well-integrated support for subnetting and VLSM
- Logical separation of network into routing areas for control and efficiency
- Fast response to topology changes with low overhead

OSPF selects and determines the shortest path to a destination via the Dijkstra algorithm. Each OSPF router considers itself the center of the networking universe, and derives the shortest path accordingly to each destination.

OSPF neighbors go through a series of steps to achieve what is known as *adjacency*, a term for when they have both exchanged and agreed on key parameters to become neighbors, and have provided a copy of their databases to their neighbor. Once adjacency is achieved, the OSPF neighbors can then exchange routing information, or refresh their routing tables as needed.

OSPF routers multicast (rather than broadcast) using 224.0.0.5 (all OSPF routers) and 224.0.0.6 (DRs/BDRs) for multi-access broadcast networks. OSPF can also unicast its updates if configured to do so via the **neighbor** command.

OSPF offers a great opportunity to logically organize your routing by enabling you to specify boundaries and to summarize, filter, or otherwise control routing at those boundaries. OSPF is more conducive to planning, and will respond better (more route summarization, and so forth).

Becoming Neighbors

The first task that OSPF routers must accomplish successfully before they can begin exchanging routing information is to become neighbors. To do so, they must agree on the following parameters:

- **Hello and Dead intervals** Must be the same on all routers on a network; otherwise, routers that are mismatched in these parameters will be constantly declared dead, then alive, then dead, and so on.
- **Stub area flag** A small flag in the Hello packet that indicates that the area to which the routers belong is a stub area. Routers must agree if it is on or off for their common area.
- **Authentication** Routers have to have the same password and encryption configured.
- **Area Identification** Routers must be in the same area in order to become neighbors in that area.
- **IP network and mask** Router interfaces in an area must be on the same subnet and have the same mask. The only exceptions to this rule are point-to-point links using IP unnumbered.

OSPF routers cannot progress to exchanging routing information unless the neighbor relationship is successfully formed.

Achieving Adjacency

Only after routers have become neighbors can they take their first steps toward achieving adjacency. Adjacency is the process of OSPF-enabled routers exchanging routing information to build their complete picture of the network, which will enable them to route traffic over the shortest paths. The adjacency process involves the steps that OSPF to fully synchronize their databases by exchanging LSAs to build a complete and correct picture of the network.

Figure 5.6 shows the neighbor states that each router transits through on its way to full adjacency. We will explain each step.

Figure 5.6 Adjacency Process

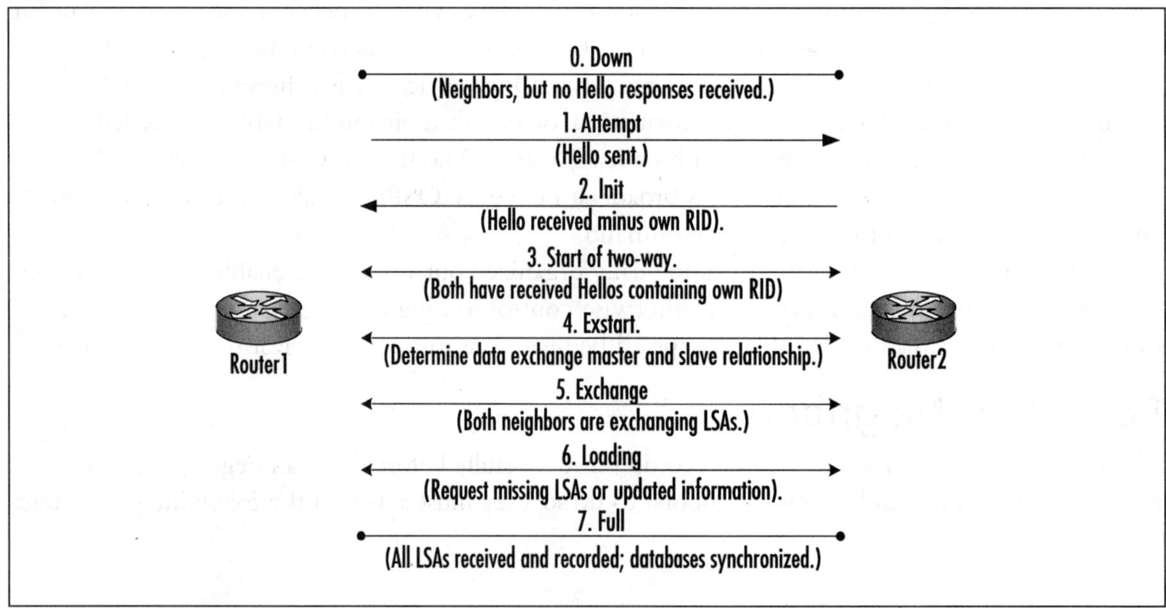

- **Down** A Down state might indicate that no Hello has been received from the neighboring router before the Dead interval has expired.
- **Attempt** This state is only applicable to NBMA networks, and only in those cases where the neighbor relationship is attempted using the **neighbor** command. Hellos have been sent to the neighbor, but responses to that Hello have not yet been received.
- **Init** This indicates that the neighbor has initiated first contact by sending a Hello. This then places the responsibility of responding on the receiving router. While a Hello has been received, it does not contain the router ID of the router receiving it.
- **2-way** The 2-way state means that communications from this point onward will be bidirectional. Each router has received a Hello from its neighbors with its router ID in the header. Routers that have made it to the 2-way state are neighbors and can now proceed to actually start exchanging routing information.

  On broadcast networks such as Ethernet, routers will only go past the 2-way state with their duly elected Designated Router (DR) and Backup Designated Router (BDR). It will remain in the 2-way state with all its other neighbors. Should the DR and BDR fail, and be replaced by a new DR and BDR, the router restarts the process from the down state with the new DR and BDR, instead of starting from the 2-way state.
- **Exstart** The routers start the business of exchanging routing information by determining which of them will be the master and which will be the slave. All this simply means is that one of the routers (the master, typically the router with highest router ID) will initiate and increment the sequence number necessary to track and maintain database description packet synchronization.
- **Exchange** Routers start exchanging the actual LSAs, with the master incrementing the sequence numbers, which must be acknowledged. Each router will send advertisements for all networks that it knows how to reach, including information such as masks, costs, and so forth.
- **Loading** In the loading state, routers will send link state requests (LSRs) to obtain any missing LSAs, or to update an old LSA.
- **Full** When all LSAs have been received from a neighbor, the state transitions to Full, which indicates that the neighbors databases are fully synchronized, that they have the same consistent picture of the network.

Types of OSPF Packets

OSPF uses a number of packet types to conduct its operations. Certain packets are used to convey a specific type of routing information, while others are more general-purpose and maintenance oriented. Regardless, OSPF depends heavily on its Hello packet.

Hello Packets

Hello packets keep the relationships between OSPF routers alive. Hello packets maintain (keep alive) the relationship and are critical to the adjacency process. OSPF routers will broadcast

Hellos periodically at default intervals shown in Table 5.5. Notice that the Dead timer is four times the Hello timer by default, and that the Wait (Hold) timer is equal to the Dead timer.

Table 5.5 Default Timer Values

Network Type	Hello	Dead	Wait
Point to Point	10	40	40
Broadcast	10	40	40
Non-Broadcast Multi-Access (NBMA)	30	120	120
Point to Multipoint	30	120	120

OSPF uses two reserved multicast addresses: 224.0.0.5, which is listened by and received by all OSPF routers, and 224.0.0.6 that is only received by the DRs/BDRs on broadcast networks. During the adjacency process, Hellos are initially sent to the allrouters multicast, 224.0.0.5. All routers running OSPF, and with interfaces participating in OSPF will receive the packet and process it. If you use the **neighbor** command, a unicast with the destination router's IP address will be used.

The format of the Hello packet is shown in Figure 5.7. We will briefly describe each field in the Hello packet.

Figure 5.7 OSPF Hello Packet

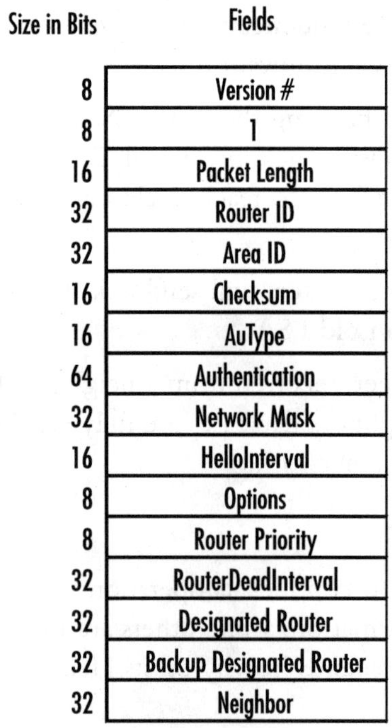

Size in Bits	Fields
8	Version #
8	1
16	Packet Length
32	Router ID
32	Area ID
16	Checksum
16	AuType
64	Authentication
32	Network Mask
16	HelloInterval
8	Options
8	Router Priority
32	RouterDeadInterval
32	Designated Router
32	Backup Designated Router
32	Neighbor

- **Version #** Indicates the version of OSPF used on this router. Cisco's current implementation is 2.

- **Packet Length** Total length of the Hello packet in bytes, from Version # field to last Neighbor field.
- **Router ID** IP address used by this router to uniquely identify itself to its neighbors.
- **Area ID** The area that this router's interface on which it sent this Hello belongs.
- **Checksum** Value calculated based on Hello packet contents for error detection.
- **AuType** Identifies the type of authentication: null (the default), plaintext, or MD5.
- **Authentication** Plaintext: Plaintext password. MD5: MD5 hashed value.
- **Network Mask** The subnet mask that this router knows for this network.
- **HelloInterval** Time in seconds that this router expects Hellos from its neighbors on this interface.
- **Options** Any special type of service levels supported on this interface. Typically not implemented.
- **Router Priority** Used for DR purposes on NBMA or broadcast networks.
- **RouterDeadInterval** Amount of time in seconds that will elapse before a neighbor is declared dead.
- **Designated Router** IP address of which router this router thinks is the DR.
- **Backup Designated Router** IP address of which router this router thinks is the BDR.
- **Neighbor** Known neighbors of this router on this particular network.

Link State Advertisements

OSPF uses Link State Advertisements (LSA) encapsulated in Link State Updates (LSU) encapsulated in IP packets as shown in Figure 5.8 to provide routing information to neighbors. LSUs are encapsulated in IP packets and delivered to the neighbors of the source router.

LSAs are generated upon any link state "changes," which include failures, new links coming on line, and interface changes such as cost. OSPF is a self-secure protocol that minimizes chattiness: it exchanges small Hellos regularly to maintain the neighbor relationships, and only does a refresh of all LSAs every 30 minutes by default. Other than that, updates are only sent upon changes in the network.

Figure 5.8 The OPSF LSA and LSU, and IP Packet Relationship

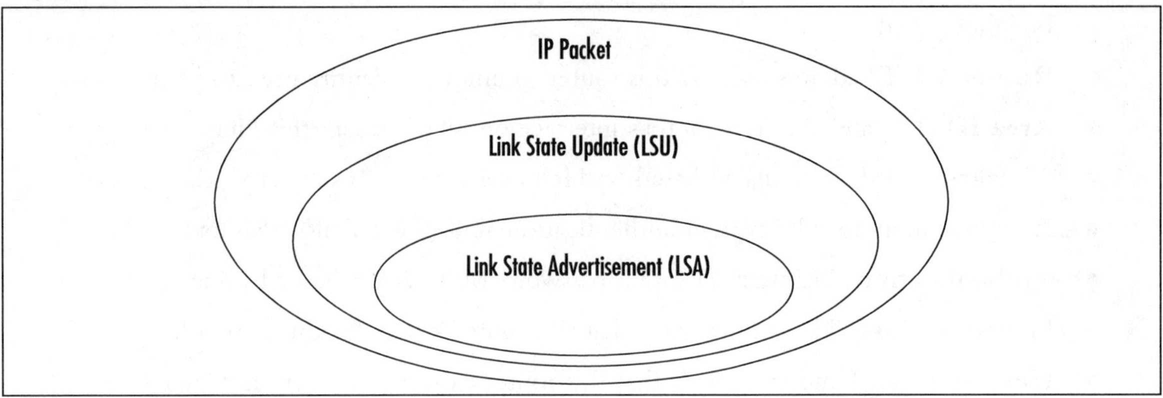

The Function of Link State Advertisements

LSA carry information a router's links (interfaces). Such information includes IP address and mask on a particular interface, the cost associated with that interface, and several other attributes that OPSF uses to build its databases. Some LSAs are applicable within an area, while others are used to advertise information outside the area. Still others carry information from one AS to another.

There are five basic LSA types that OSPF uses to convey link state information. Table 5.6 offers a quick summary of the five basic LSA types we are going to discuss.

Table 5.6 LSA Type Descriptions

LSA Name	Type	Description	Generated By	Flooded
Router Links	1	Links attached to router generating LSA.	Area routers	Intra-area
Network Links	2	Broadcast or NBMA networks attached to router generating LSA	DR	Intra-area
Summary (IP Network)	3	Inter-area networks; Destination is an IP Network	ABR	Inter-area
Summary (ASBR)	4	Inter-area networks; destination is an ASBR	ABR	Inter-area
External Networks	5	Destinations external to this OSPF AS; also default routes	ASBR	All areas except stub areas

Common LSA Header

All of the LSA types have the same 20-byte header shown in Figure 5.9. The header contains various fields that identify the source of the LSA, and the information it contains.

Figure 5.9 OSPF LSA Header

Size in Bits	Fields
8	Version #
8	1
16	Packet Length
32	Router ID
32	Area ID
16	Checksum
16	AuType
64	Authentication
32	Network Mask
16	HelloInterval
8	Options
8	Router Priority
32	RouterDeadInterval
32	Designated Router
32	Backup Designated Router
32	Neighbor

- **Link State Age** Amount of time in seconds since the LSA was originated.
- **Options** Options supported by this router and this LSA.
- **Link State Type** Identifies what LSA type this LSA is; in our case here, it will be 1-5.
- **Link State ID** IP network number being advertised or of the DR for the network.
- **Advertising Router** Router ID of the router that originated this LSA or the router ID of the DR.
- **Link State Sequence Number** Incrementing number that helps detect old or duplicate LSAs.
- **Link State Checksum** Error checking of entire contents of the LSA except for the age.
- **Length** The total length of the LSA, including this 20-byte header.

We will now discuss the various LSA types and describe their function in an OSPF design.

LSA Type 1 Router LSA

LSA Type 1, the router LSA, is flooded only in the area where it originated by each OSPF router for each interface participating in OSPF. It describes the router's interfaces and their associated states. It includes information such as the advertising router ID, the IP address and mask of the interface, costs or metrics associated with the link, and so on. All of this information is passed to the neighbors. Router LSAs are strictly constrained to whatever area they originated: they do not leave the area. All routers in an area will exchange LSAs with each other. Figure 5.10 shows the format of the router LSA.

Figure 5.10 OSPF LSA Type 1 (Router)

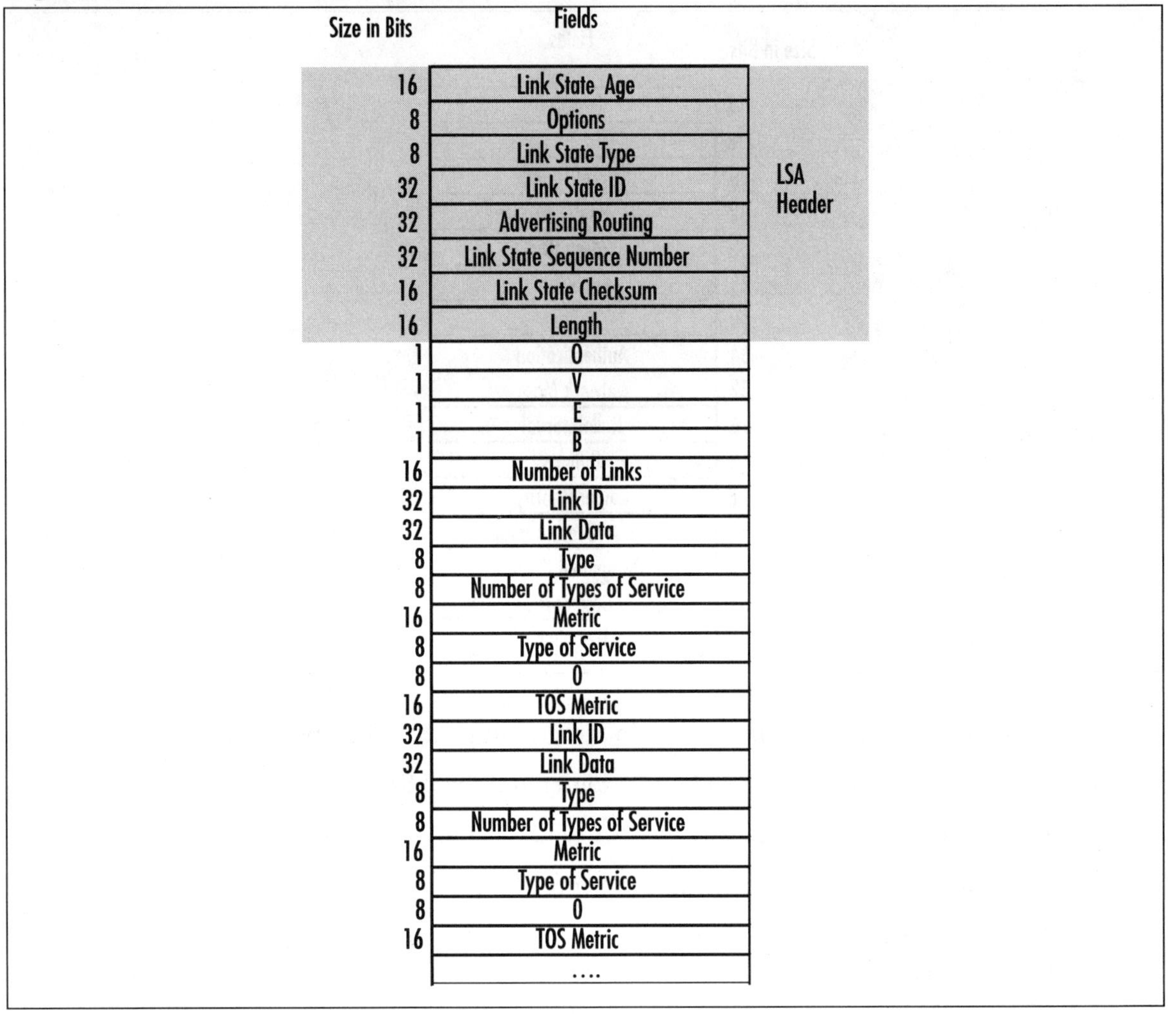

Size in Bits	Fields	
16	Link State Age	LSA Header
8	Options	
8	Link State Type	
32	Link State ID	
32	Advertising Routing	
32	Link State Sequence Number	
16	Link State Checksum	
16	Length	
1	0	
1	V	
1	E	
1	B	
16	Number of Links	
32	Link ID	
32	Link Data	
8	Type	
8	Number of Types of Service	
16	Metric	
8	Type of Service	
8	0	
16	TOS Metric	
32	Link ID	
32	Link Data	
8	Type	
8	Number of Types of Service	
16	Metric	
8	Type of Service	
8	0	
16	TOS Metric	
	....	

- **V** When this bit is turned on, it indicates that the router, which originated this LSA, is an end point of a virtual link.
- **E** When this bit is turned on, it indicates that this router is an ASBR.
- **B** When this bit is turned on, it indicates that this router is an ABR.
- **Number of Links** Total number of links that the router LSA contains information about.
- **Link ID** A network number (IP Address/Mask) that is being advertised by this router.
- **Link Data** This field will vary depending on what the type field is set to.
- **Type** What type of connection this router has to the router advertised in this LSA.
- **Number of Types of Service** Identifies the quantity of ToSs associated with this link.
- **Metric** Only one that OSPF uses: cost of this link.

- **Type of Service** Optional. Identifies any special service to be given to this link.
- **TOS Metric** Cost associated with this level of service.

Depending on how many links are being advertised in this LSA, the fields from Link ID to TOS metric will repeat until there are no more links to be advertised in this LSA.

LSA Type 2 Network LSA

LSA Type 2, the network LSA, is generated by the DR for broadcast and NMBA networks. It contains information about the mask assigned to this network, as the DR sees it, and a list of all OSPF routers attached to this network. These routers are identified by their router IDs.

The structure of LSA type 2 is shown in Figure 5.11. You will see that it is mostly the LSA header, with two additional fields, which will be described.

Figure 5.11 OSPF LSA Type 2 (Network)

Size in Bytes	Field	
2	Link State Age	LSA Header
1	Options	
1	Link State Type	
4	Link State ID	
4	Advertising Routing	
4	Link State Sequence Number	
2	Link State Checksum	
2	Length	
4	Network Mask	
4	Attached Router	

- **Network Mask** The IP network or subnet mask for this network. All routers on the network must agree on this, or they will not become neighbors.
- **Attached Router** Describes the router IDs of all OSPF routers attached to this network that have achieved full adjacency with the DR for this network. The router ID of the DR is also included in this list.

LSA Type 3 Summary LSA (Network) and LSA Type 4 Summary LSA (ASBR)

LSA Type 3 and LSA Type 4 are summary LSAs, and share the same LSA format as shown in Figure 5.12. The difference between the two besides the type is what they advertise. Summary LSAs are used for inter-area routing updates; they are generally a summary of the networks within a particular area.

Both LSAs carry the same information; the difference is their destinations. The destination of a LSA type 3 is an IP network address. The destination of a LSA type 4 is an ASBR. For LSA type 3, the advertising router field contains the router ID of the router that produced this particular LSA. For LSA type 4, the advertising router field will contain the IP address of the ASBR. Summary LSAs can be used to transport default routes.

Figure 5.12 OSPF LSA Type 3 and 3 (Summary)

Size in Bytes	Field	
2	Link State Age	LSA Header
1	Options	
1	Link State Type (3 or 4)	
4	Link State ID	
4	Advertising Routing	
4	Link State Sequence Number	
2	Link State Checksum	
2	Length	
4	Network Mask	
2	Metric	
1	TOS	
2	TOS Metric	

- **Network mask** The IP network or subnet mask for this network. All routers on the network must agree on this, or they will not become neighbors.
- **Metric** Only one that OSPF uses: cost of this link.
- **Type of Service** This is an option field that might or might not be implemented. It identifies any special service to be given to this link.
- **TOS Metric** Cost associated with this level of service.

LSA Type 5 External LSA

LSA Type 5, External LSA (Figure 5.13) is originated *only* by an ASBR. The External LSA describes routes external to the receiving OSPF AS. External LSAs are created by OSPF when you redistribute from one routing protocol into OSPF, or if you redistribute static routes. External LSAs are also created when a router originates a default route; the destination will be 0.0.0.0 with a mask of 0.0.0.0. Basically, LSA 5 carries any routing information not learned via the OSPF process. The External LSA is flooded throughout the entire OSPF routing domain.

Figure 5.13 OSPF LSA Type 5 (External LSA)

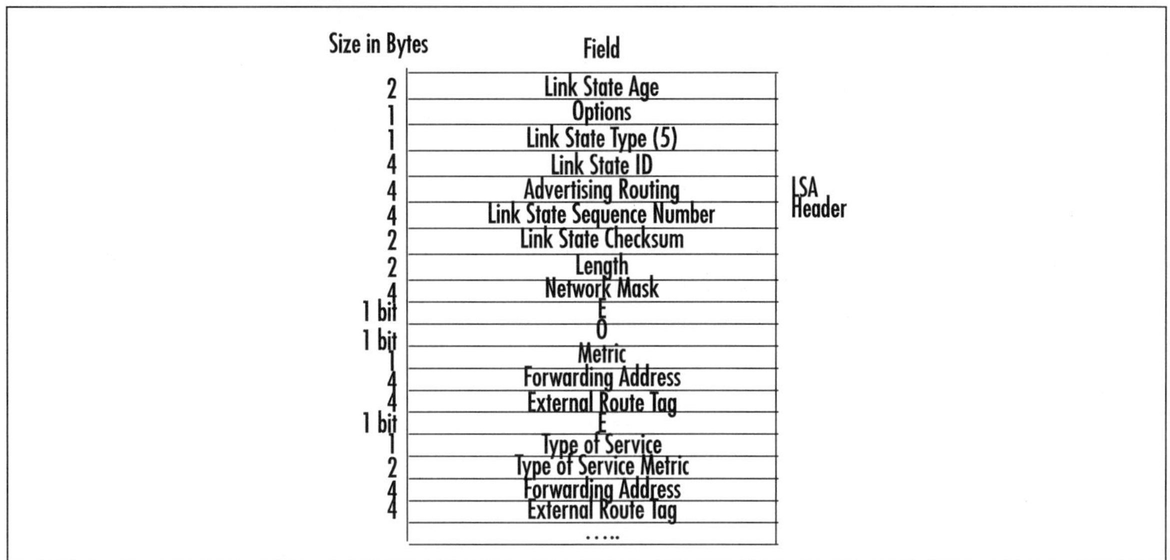

- **Network Mask** Subnet mask for this network.
- **E** E1 is more accurate than E2, and is therefore preferred
  - **On** Type 1 external information (E1—total cost will factor in original external cost plus any internal costs along the way.
  - **Off** Type 2 external (E2) information, meaning that only the original external cost is carried.
- **Metric** Only one that OSPF uses: cost of this link.
- **Forwarding Address** To reach the destination in this LSA, send to this particular IP address.
- **External Route Tag** Special tag used by ASBRs to communicate between themselves.
- **Type of Service** Optional. Identifies any special service to be given to this link.
- **Type of Service Metric** Cost associated with this level of service.

OSPF enables you to logically organize your networks into areas for superior routing and summarization. Mastery of OSPF requires a good understanding of the types of areas it has, and how they are best used.

Types of OSPF Areas

OSPF uses areas to organize network and routers into logical groupings. This enables it to maximize summarization, control routing updates, place contiguous networks together, and group together networks needing to communicate frequently. The design and placement of OSPF areas can also reflect organizational structure.

OSPF basically has a two-level architecture, much like its cousin, IS-IS: a backbone area (top level) and nonbackbone areas (sub level). The most important is the backbone area (also known as area 0), which interconnects all other areas. "Normal" areas do not have any special restrictions on the routing information that can enter it. Stub areas, of which there are several types, are similar to normal areas, except that they restrict what routing information can enter.

The Backbone Area, a.k.a. Area 0

The backbone area connects all other areas to each other. All inter-area traffic must traverse area 0. Figure 5.14 shows several routers configured in area 0.

Figure 5.14 Backbone Area, a.k.a. Area 0

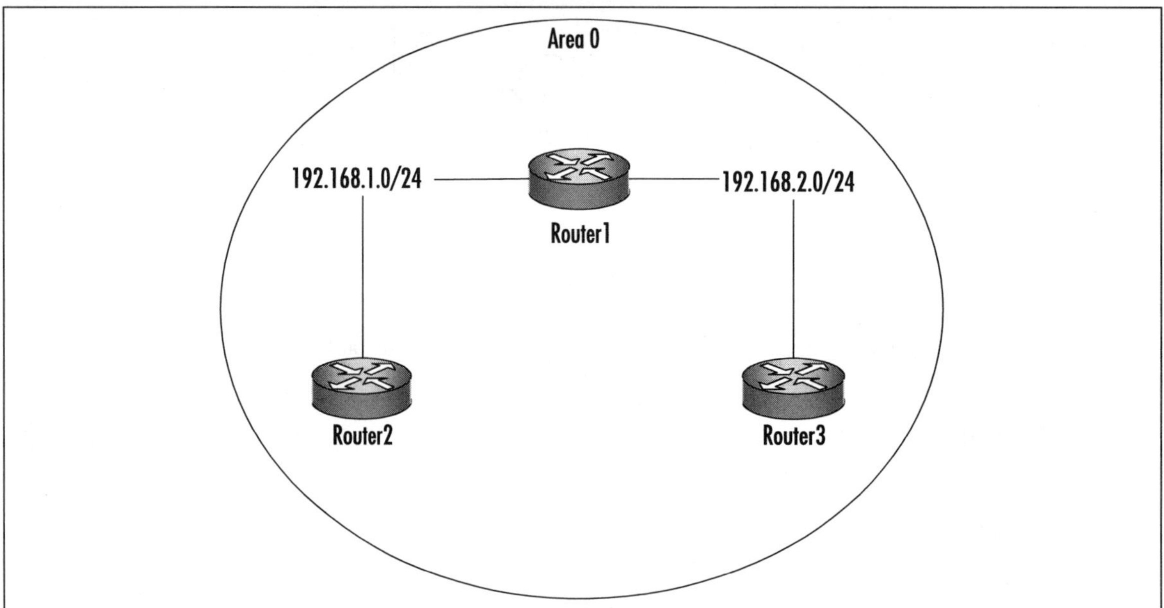

Area 0 supports all LSA types, from its LSAs 1 and 2 generated for area 0 networks, to LSA 3 and 4 from other areas, to passing LSA 3 and 4 from area to area, to passing external network LSAs. Unless your routers are specifically configured to pass traffic between areas, they should not be in area 0.

The design shown in Figure 5.14 should not be implemented unless this is a single area configuration that will never grow. None of these routers are connected to other areas; they will needlessly fill area 0 with LSAs about their links. Assuming there were other areas connected to this area 0, the backbone routers would have to contend with LSAs 1 and 2, which they should not have to do. As a rule of thumb, unless the router is an ABR, or a backbone router connecting ABRs, put it in a nonbackbone area.

We have provided the following configuration for Figure 5.14 to demonstrate how routers can be configured in area 0. Notice that the only command of significance here is the one that identifies the area as area 0. Excepting for that, this would be a configuration for a normal area, which is where these routers really belong.

```
Router1

interface ethernet 0
ip address 192.168.1.1 255.255.255.0

interface ethernet 1
ip address 192.168.2.1 255.255.255.0

router ospf 1
network 192.168.1.1 0.0.0.0 area 0
network 192.168.2.1 0.0.0.0 area 0.0.0.0

Router2
interface ethernet 0
ip address 192.168.1.2 255.255.255.0

router ospf 1
network 192.168.1.2 0.0.0.0 area 0

Router3
interface ethernet 0
ip address 192.168.2.2 255.255.255.0

router ospf 1
network 192.168.2.2 0.0.0.0 area 0.0.0.0
```

Notice that we express area 0 using the decimal notation (0), and "dotted decimal" IP address format (0.0.0.0). Either format is fine, as long as they equal zero.

There are no restrictions on the LSAs that can be transmitted, received, and traversed in area 0. The one exception to LSAs being allowed across the backbone area is LSA type 7, which is restricted to the NSSA where it originated. You cannot configure area 0 as a stub area.

Configuring a "Normal" Area

We now turn our attentions to normal areas. We are using "normal" to describe those areas that are neither backbone, nor stub. In a default configuration, normal areas will originate and receive LSA types 1 to 5. Figure 5.15 shows several normal areas connected to area 0. Notice the direction of the LSA type flow, including external routes, which can come from an ASBR connected to this area, or transit the backbone area to this area.

Figure 5.15 OSPF "Normal" Area LSA Flow

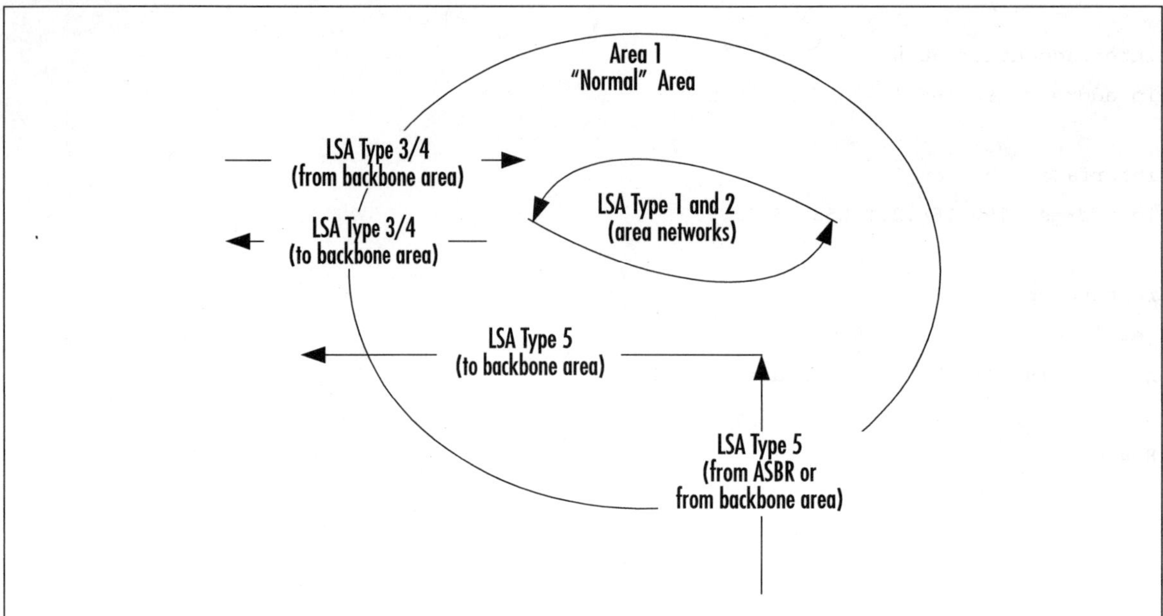

The router and network LSAs (1 and 2) stay in the area they originate in to advertise networks in that area. An ABR for the area will pass area network information into the backbone area as summary LSAs (3 and 4), and will also receive summary LSAs. Should an area have an ASBR, the area ABR will also pass those to the backbone area. The backbone area is responsible for passing the summary and external network LSAs to other areas.

Normal areas have to connect to area 0 to reach other areas. Default routes can be originated in normal areas for the rest of the OSPF routing domain.

Ideally, when planning your normal areas, you should design your IP addressing such that contiguous networks are in the same area; this will enable you to maximize your summarization opportunities. In fact, you can even make the area number the same as the major IP network number in that area. This will enable easier diagnosis and resolution of routing problems.

Stub Areas

Stub areas are configured in a manner similar to "normal" areas. The primary characteristic of stub areas is that they place restrictions on the routing information that they will allow into the area. You would typically define an area as a stub area if it only has one exit and entry point into the area, and if default would be sufficient to reach any external networks. You would also define an area as a stub area if it has multiple routes to other areas. The amount of routing information in a stub area will depend on its stubbiness.

Stub areas will contain intra-area routes; that is, routes that originate within the area. Stub areas will also receive inter-area routes; that is, routes from other areas in the AS. If one is generated for the AS, the stub area will also accept default routes. *The defining characteristic for a stub area is that it has are no external routes (no LSA type 5).* Traffic destined to an external network will be sent to the default network.

Figure 5.16 shows a schematic view of LSA flow in and out of area 1, which is configured as a stub area. The stub area is the least stubby of the stub areas as it only disallows external network LSAs (type 5). A check of any of the stub area routing tables will show router, network, and summary LSAs, plus a default route. There will be no LSA type 5 information in these tables

Figure 5.16 OSPF Stub Area LSA Flow

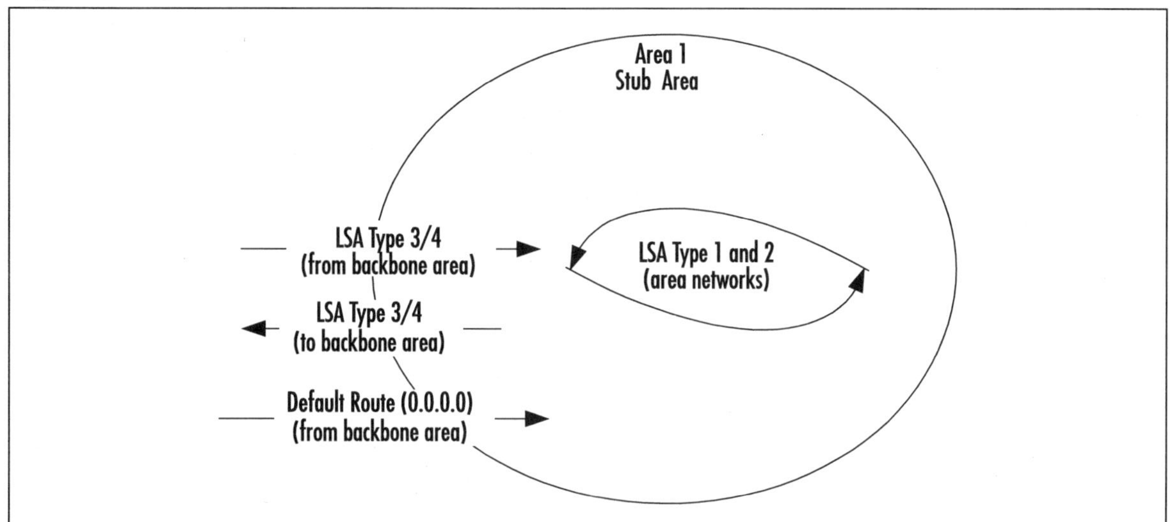

Each router in the stub area must have the **area stub** command configured on it, as shown.

```
RouterA(config-router)# area 1 stub
```

This command turns on the stub area flag bit in the Hello packet.

Any router in the area that does not have this command on it will not become a neighbor with the other routers on its network in the same area. Recall that for routers to become neighbors, they must agree on the stub area flag.

Totally Stubby Areas

The most extreme stub area is the totally stubby area (TSA). TSAs contain intra-area routes and a default route. No inter-area routes (specifically, the summary LSAs) and no external network LSAs (type 5) are permitted into a TSA. You would define an area as totally stubby if it only had one exit and entry point to all other destinations, both other areas, area 0, and external networks. If that is the case, you would be doing the area a disservice if you sent it all the routing information that you had, since it only has one way reach it.

Figure 5.17 shows the LSA flow in a TSA. The **stub** command must be entered on all routers in the TSA, or the routers will not become neighbors. The flow of LSAs into and out of the area is also shown.

Figure 5.17 OSPF Totally Stubby Area LSA Flow

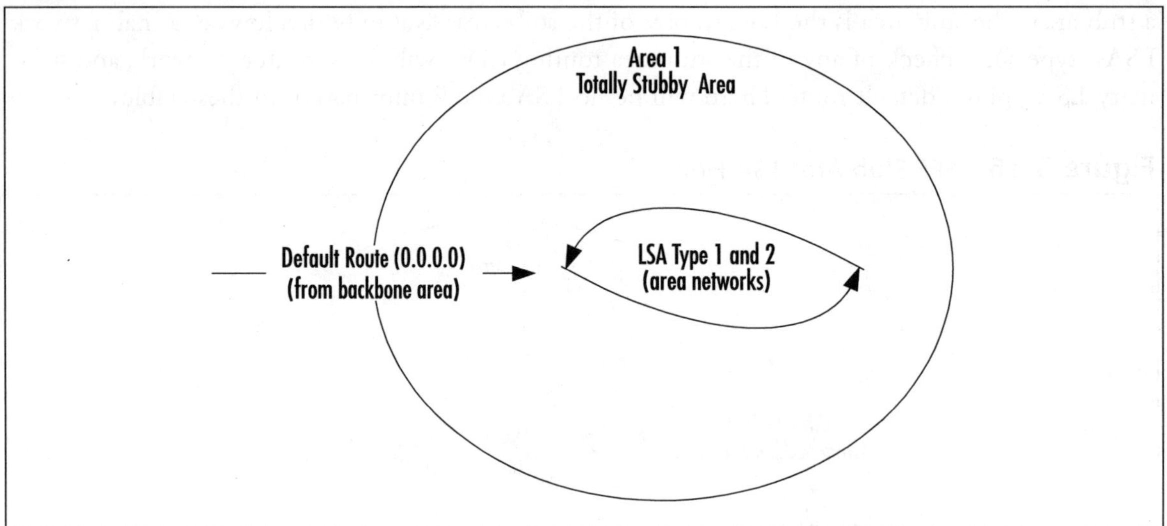

TSAs are the most restrictive when it comes to allowing in routing information. These areas permit a default route to enter the area, but no other routes are allowed into the area. The routing tables of TSA routers are the smallest of any of the area types, potentially containing only router and network LSAs, and a default route.

The command for creating a TSA is shown next. This command must be entered on all routers in the TSA for them to become neighbors and achieve adjacency.

```
RouterA(config-router)# area 1 stub  no-summary
```

The **no-summary** command prevents LSA type 3 and 4 from entering the area.

Not So Stubby Areas

Not So Stubby Areas (NSSA) have some of the characteristics of a normal area, and some of the restrictions of a stub area. The earmark of a NSSA is the injection and transmission of external routes into and from the area. This NSSA concept was introduced to allow external routes to be injected into a stub area. You would configure an area as NSSA if you had a situation where a stub area had a router connected to another AS, or was learning routes via another routing protocol that the rest of the OSPF routing domain needed to know.

Figure 5.18 shows the LSA flow in a NSSA. The area 1 ASBR is redistributing from another routing protocol (such as RIP, IGRP, and so forth) into area 1. These redistributed routes are encapsulated into an LSA type 7, a special case of the external LSA for propagating external routes into a NSSA. In addition to LSAs 1-4, the LSA type 7 is the only other LSA allowed into the NSSA.

Figure 5.18 OSPF NSSA LSA Flow

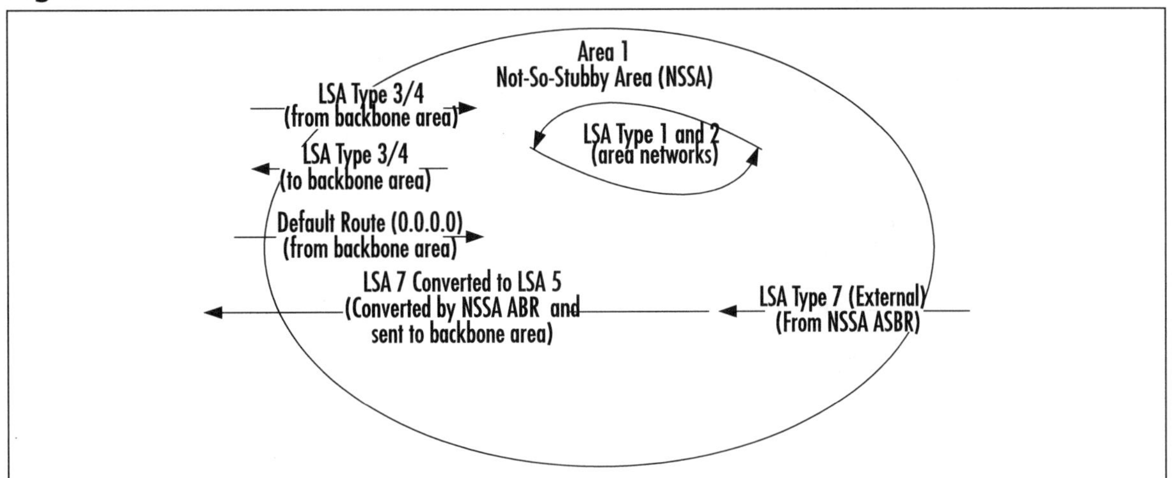

If there is an ABR configured into this area (to area 0), it will convert the LSA type 7 to an LSA type 5.The LSA type 5 that was a LSA type 7 gets passed to the backbone area, where it gets distributed as a normal LSA type 5 to the rest of the OSPF routing domain.This LSA type 5 does not get sent into the NSSA because the NSSA does not allow LSA type 5 into the area…not to mention that the NSSA routers already have this information via the LSA type 7. By default, type 5 LSAs cannot be summarized at an ASBR or ABR, although Type 7 can.This is a major reason to use a NSSA when configuring your OSPF network.

An area is configured as a NSSA with the **area 1 nssa** command in OSPF configuration mode.The **area 1 nssa** command must be entered on all routers in the area for them to become neighbors.

Not So Stubby Totally Stubby Areas

The Not So Stubby Totally Stubby Area (NSSTSA) is a special definition of the NSSA. It is more restrictive regarding what it allows into the area.The NSSTSA is similar to the NSSA, except that it does not allow LSA type 3 and 4 into the area. Otherwise, the NSSTSA is just like a NSSA.

Figure 5.19 shows LSA flow in an NSSTSA.You can see that except for the disallowing of LSA type 3 and 4 into the area, the NSSTSA is just like a NSSA.The NSSTSA ASBR creates LSA type 7 for the routes that it is redistributing from another routing protocol into the NSSTSA.The NSSTSA ABR converts the 7 into a 5 for propagation to the rest of the OSPF domain.A default route, sent as a LSA type 3 summary, is the only exception to NSSTSA rule that no 3 or 4 is allowed into the area.

Figure 5.19 OSPF NSSTSA LSA Flow

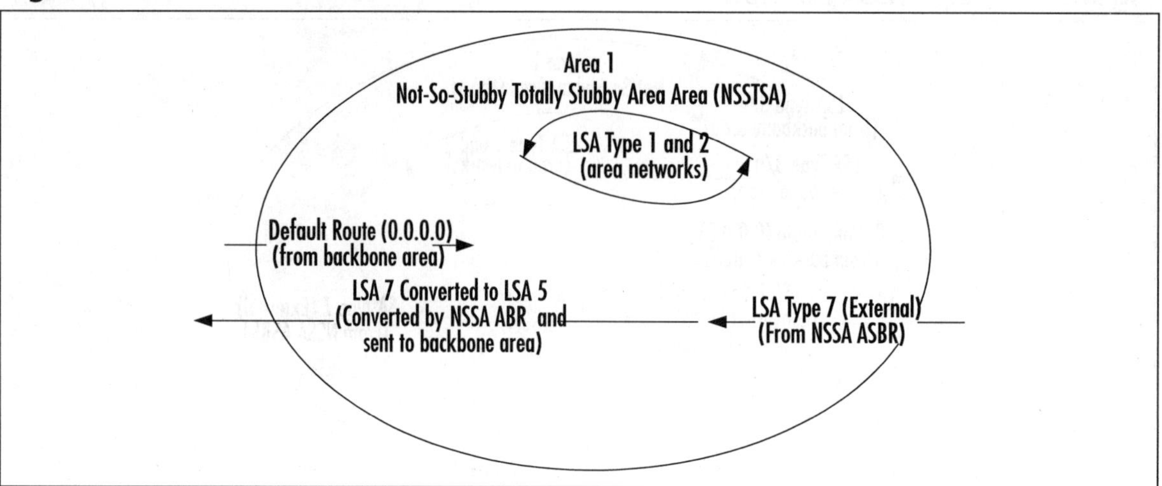

To configure a NSSTSA, enter the following command on the NSSTSA ABR only. This configures the ABR *not* to send LSA type 3 and 4 into the NSSTSA. All routers will be configured with the NSSA command, as previously discussed.

On the NSSTSA ABR only:

```
area 1 nssa no-summary
```

On all other NSSTSA routers:

```
area 1 nssa
```

Multiple OSPF Areas

Multi-area OSPF is OSPF configured with more than one area. The most important thing to remember is that all areas (not routers!) must touch (connect to) area 0! The OSPF novice will sometimes take this statement to mean that all routers in an area must have area 0 configured on them. This is not a requirement of OSPF. As long as one router in the area (which would make it an ABR) connects the area to area 0, OSPF will work.

There will be times when it is not possible for an area to connect to area 0, either because the cost of doing so is prohibitive, or there are other barriers. You can use virtual links to connect such areas. Virtual links should be treated as a temporary solution, and not a part of a permanent design.

All LSAs except 1–2 can be advertised into areas other than the ones in which they originated. The information that is advertised via type 1 and 2 can and will be translated into a 3 or 4, and be advertised outside its originating area. Figure 5.20 shows the LSAs and where they will be flooded in a multi-area design.

Figure 5.20 OSPF Multi-Area LSA Flow

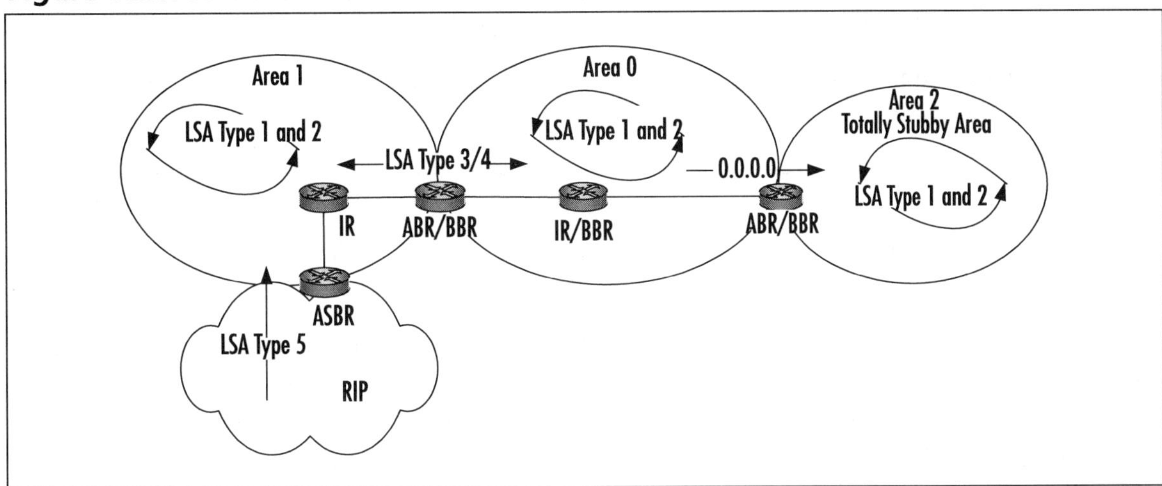

As you see in Figure 5.20, LSA type 1 and 2 are flooded only within the area where they originated. LSA 3 and 4 are flooded between areas. Our ASBR is redistributing RIP routes into OSPF external networks, which are LSA type 5; this will be flooded to all areas except those that do not allow LSA type 5 such as stub areas. Area 2 is configured as a TSA, which means that it will only allow a single default route to be injected into it. TSA routers will have this default route plus any intra-area (LSA 1 and 2) routes. Notice the location of area 0: in the middle, with all areas connected to it.

We have mentioned that OSPF classifies routers according to their place in the OSPF world. In the next section, we will illustrate the various roles that a router can have when running OSPF.

Types of OSPF Routers

There are four types of routers associated with OSPF as illustrated in Figure 5.21.

Figure 5.21 OSPF Router Roles

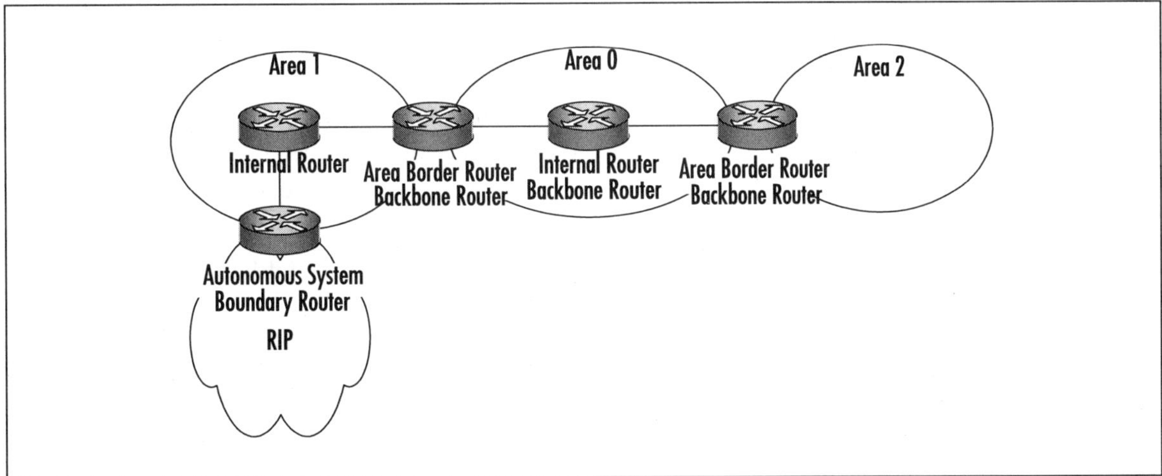

- **Internal routers (IR)** Responsible for routing packets within a single area. Can also be a backbone router if it has no physical interfaces to another area.
- **Area border routers (ABR)** Routes packets between multiple areas on which this router has interfaces.
- **Backbone routers (BB)** Have a physical interface to the backbone. Often called border routers.
- **Autonomous system boundary routers (ASBR)** Exchange information with other ASs using EGP protocols like BGP.

Backbone routers can treat certain areas as stubs. This means that the border routers will not forward any information about external routes to these stub areas. These border routers can also be configured not to forward any internal information about internal OSPF routes. These four types of routers make it possible for OSPF to divide an AS into areas.

Designated Routers

Designated routers (DRs) and backup designated routers (BDRs) are more or less fairly elected, and only on NMBA and broadcast networks. The purpose of a DR is to reduce the number of adjacencies that must be formed by OSPF routers on such networks. The DR and BDR have the responsibility of forming the adjacencies with all routers on its network, and disseminating the routing updates it collects via its adjacencies to all the routers with which it is adjacent. The BDR transparently takes over should the DR fail.

You can see the results of the DR and BDR mechanisms with the **show ip ospf neighbor** command. All routers on the NBMA and broadcast network will attain the Full state only with the DR and BDR; all other neighbor relationships will remain as "2-way/DROTHER." Executing this command on the DR and BDR will show Full states with all neighbors. Executing this command on non-DR routers will show full states with the DR and BDR, and 2-way state with all other routers.

Both the DR and BDR listen for multicasts destined for 224.0.0.6, and will process any traffic destined for that address. The other, non-DR routers on the network, once they know the network is either NBMA or broadcast, will attempt to form their adjacencies with whichever router is listening to this address.

Figure 5.22 shows what things would look like if OSPF did not have the DR mechanism to reduce the adjacencies formed on NBMA and broadcast networks. Figure 5.22 shows a broadcast network without a DR. Notice that among the five routers, each has to form four adjacencies with the other routers on the network. LSAs will be sent out on each of these adjacencies. Imagine the amount of traffic that would have to be generated if you had a flapping link or a faulty router that kept going up and down on the network!

Figure 5.22 Broadcast Network Adjacencies (without DR/BDR)

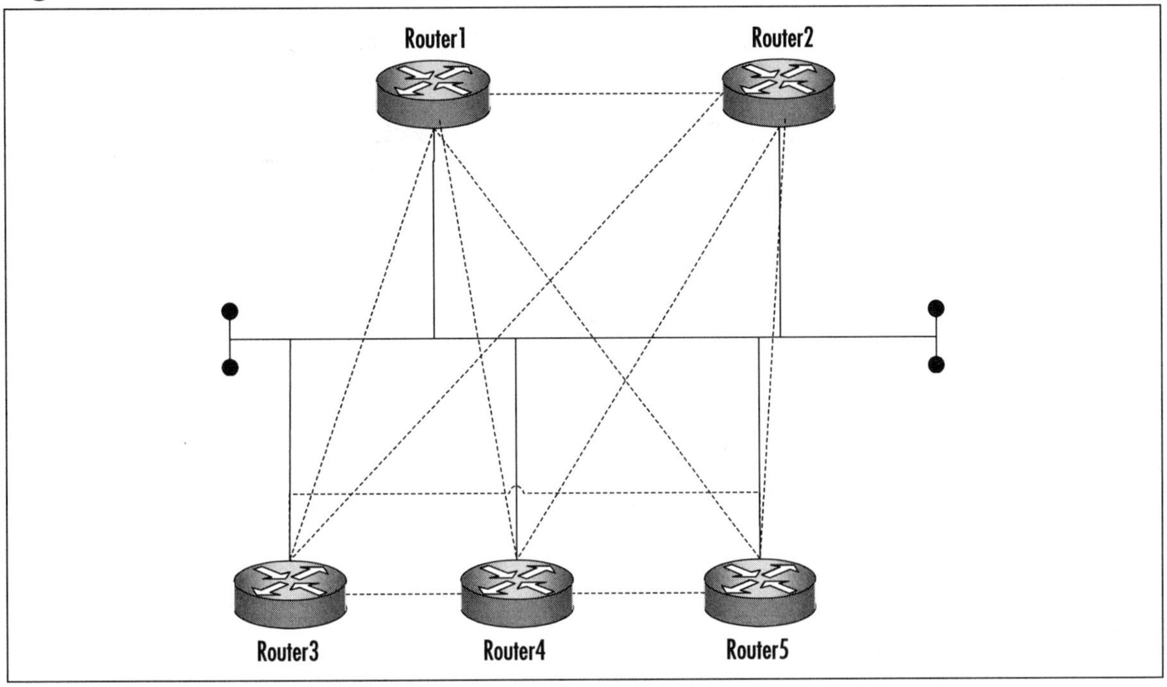

Each of the dashed lines represents the adjacencies that have to be formed by each router. Routing updates will be exchanged over each adjacency. This can create an excessive amount of traffic, especially if you have a database of any meaningful size.

Figure 5.23 shows the same network, only this time using the OSPF DR and BDR mechanism. Notice that the number of adjacencies has been reduced to two adjacencies per non-DR router, and four adjacencies per DR and BDR router. This is huge reduction in adjacencies and in the amount of routing update traffic that will be sent between each router. This will result in bandwidth savings, and improve overall network efficiency.

Figure 5.23 Broadcast Network Adjacencies (with DR and BDR)

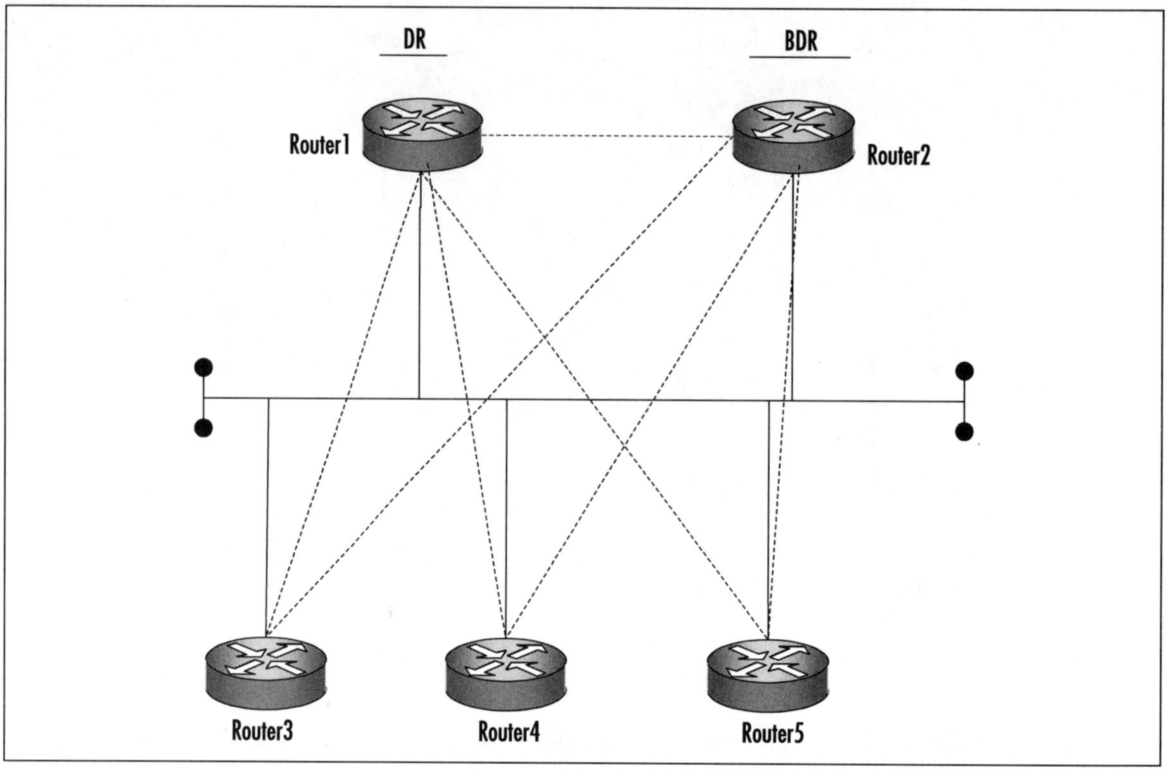

Numerous factors can influence which router gets to be the DR and the BDR. The first decision point is the priority, which can be manually set, but by default is the same for all routers on the network. The router with the highest priority will become the DR, the router with the second highest will become the BDR, and routers with a priority of 0 will never become either. Setting a priority on a particular router that you want to be a DR after a DR has already been elected will have no effect until the router is rebooted.

If all routers have the same priority, the next tiebreaker is the router ID. OSPF naturally prefers loopback interfaces for its source of router RID, so those routers with loopback interfaces will get their router ID from that. If there are multiple loopback interfaces on a router, OSPF chooses the one with the highest IP address for the router ID.

OSPF Router ID and Loopback Interfaces

Before you configure OSPF on a router, it would be a good idea for stability's sake to create a loopback interface first. OSPF prefers to use loopback interfaces as the source of router ID for stability: a loopback interface will never go down, whereas a physical ("real") interface might.

The loss of the router ID can introduce instabilities and add to the burden on the router. The interface that you want to serve as the source for the router ID does not have to participate in OSPF routing. If the router ID is based on a physical interface, and that interface goes down after OSPF is operational, OSPF will select a new router ID from its available pool, and the adjacency process has to restart.

The Cisco IOS allows you to manually select and identify the router ID for a Cisco router using the command **router-id**. The address does not have to be assigned to any of the router's links, but it must unique within the OSPF routing domain. If you use the **router-id** command after OSPF is already up and running, you will either need to restart OSPF (delete and re-create), restart the router (reboot), or use the **clear ip ospf** command to make it take effect.

Types of OSPF Databases

OSPF maintains a large amount of information to support its operations. This includes information on network topology, neighbors, and routes. All this information is stored in several OSPF databases, and one of the most important is the topology database.

What Is the Topology Database?

Each router running OSPF uses Hellos and LSAs to discover the topology of each network to which it is attached. The information that it gathers is stored in the topology database. As we have repeatedly stated throughout this chapter, each router puts itself at the center of the network to gather information. To drive that point home, Figure 5.24 shows Router1 building its picture of the network by viewing itself as being at the center.

Figure 5.24 OSPF Router as the Center of the Network Universe

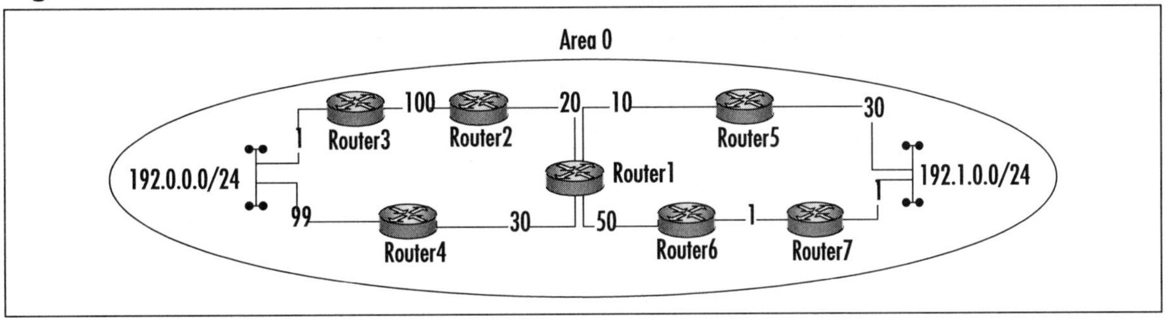

The topology database contains information about the links, costs, other routers, and areas. A router will have one topology database for each area in which it has an interface. Even a small topology database can contain a huge amount of data. For this reason, Cisco recommends that each router belong to no more than two areas at a time, with a maximum of three recommended, and only if the third area is engaged in massive summarization.

By the time it has finished building its picture, Router1 will know all the links between it, and network 192.0.0.0/24 and 192.1.0.0/24. Router1 will know that it has two paths to reach 192.0.0.0/24: the path via Router2 has a total cost of 121, and the path via Router4 has a total cost of 129. It will put the shortest path with the cost 121 into its routing table, and retain information about the path with a cost of 129 in its topology database. Should the 121 path fail, it already has an alternate waiting to be used.

You can view the topology database using the **show ip ospf database** command. Be prepared for reams and reams of information, even if you have a small network. This **show** command has a variety of options. In our sample display, we have wisely opted to look only at summary routes.

The full complement of options available to you is shown here.

```
Router1> show ip ospf data ?
  adv-router          Advertising Router link states
  asbr-summary        ASBR summary link states
  database-summary    Summary of database
  external            External link states
  network             Network link states
  nssa-external       NSSA External link states
  opaque-area         Opaque Area link states
  opaque-as           Opaque AS link states
  opaque-link         Opaque Link-Local link states
  router              Router link states
  self-originate      Self-originated link states
  summary             Network summary link states
  |                   Output modifiers
```

This is the information that Router1 has about the summary links that it has learned about.

```
RouterA> show ip ospf data summary
```

This is this OSPF router's router ID, and the process that it learned about this route.

```
      OSPF Router with ID (192.1.1.1) (Process ID 1)
```

This indicates that this is a summary link with origins in area 0.

```
       Summary Net Link States (Area 0.0.0.0)
```

The following looks familiar if you read the LSA section. It's a summary LSA type 3 for this network number.

```
  Routing Bit Set on this LSA
  LS age: 1007
  Options: (No TOS-capability, DC, Upward)
  LS Type: Summary Links(Network)
  Link State ID: 192.0.0.0 (summary Network Number)
  Advertising Router: 192.0.0.1
  LS Seq Number: 80000B4D
  Checksum: 0x7EE3
  Length: 28
  Network Mask: /24
  TOS: 0  Metric: 1
```

What we did not show in our sample output is that there is a similar entry for every LSA that an OSPF router receives! OSPF does not merely read a LSA to get the information for its routing table; it actually stores every one of them. LSAs will be purged from the database upon failures, age out, and so on, but until then, they are stored.

Processing of Received Updates

When a router receives an LSA containing routes, it stores this information in its topology database. Next, it runs the SPF algorithm to determine those LSAs that have the shortest path to the advertised destination. Once it derives the shortest path, it will insert that into the routing table. We are assuming that a rival protocol with a lower administrative distance and more specific routes is not running on the router to challenge OSPF's chosen routers.

OSPF Cost

The metric that OSPF uses to select a route to put in the routing table is cost. Cost is the only metric that OSPF uses when selecting amongst multiple paths to a destination. The range of OSPF costs is 1–65,535; the lower the cost, the more preferred the route. OSPF relies on the SPF algorithm to arrive at the total cost for the link.

OSPF routers calculate the total costs for a path (the series of links that must be traversed to reach a destination) by adding the costs of the egress interfaces. That is, OSPF does not use the cost of the interface that it used to enter a router; rather, it uses the cost of the interface that it uses to exit the router.

OSPF derives its costs based on the bandwidth value on the interface. The formula that it uses is 10^8 divided by the bandwidth of the interface. In that case, assuming the default values have not changed, a 10BaseT Ethernet interface will have a cost of 10 (100,000,000/10,000,000).

Each OSPF router runs the cost formula on each interface participating in OSPF. The value it derives will be used by other OSPF routers when they run the SPF algorithm to find the shortest path. You can say that the SPF calculations start with the determination of interface (link) costs.

OSPF has a default formula that applies to each interface to derive their costs. OSPF obviously runs this calculation against only those interfaces that are actually participating in OSPF. The formula is very simple…and somewhat limited when dealing with interfaces that have speeds greater than 100Mbps; we will show you how to handle that. This formula is shown here.

10^8/Bandwidth of Interface   or   100Mbps/Bandwidth of Interface

You can influence cost calculations by setting the bandwidth of an interface to a value you want such that it arrives at the cost you want. You can set the bandwidth of the interface such that the formula will calculate the cost you want. For example, if you wanted a cost of 100, you could set the bandwidth to 1,000,000, and OSPF will figure it out for you. In the following example, we have configured the bandwidth on serial 0 to be 1,000,000 (approximately 1Mbps).

```
interface  serial 0
bandwidth 1000000
```

Of course, even though OSPF will calculate the cost for you indirectly, you will still need to figure out the math beforehand. You can directly specify the cost yourself using the command given here.

```
ip ospf cost (1-65535)
```

In our example here, we want the cost of the Ethernet interface to be 1000, yet we will make no changes to its default bandwidth of 10Mbps.

```
interface Ethernet 0
ip ospf cost 1000
```

OSPF will use the cost of 1000 for this Ethernet interface when it does its SPF calculations.

Multiple Paths of Equal Cost

OSPF can load-balance on up to four equal-cost routes to a destination in its routing tables. It will also put the lowest-cost routes into its routing table, up to four routes. It will store information about any other routes in its topology table, as part of its complete picture of the network. Should a selected route fail, it can and will choose an alternate from its topology database.

Cost Calculation with Gigabit Ethernet and Faster Interfaces

OSPF's default formula for calculating costs ceases to provide an accurate cost when bandwidth is greater than 100Mbps, as shown. Here we have a gigabit Ethernet interface, which has a value of 1,000,000,000. Running this through the OSPF formula yields the unusable result shown.

```
100,000,000 / 1,000,000,000 = 0.1
```

It is not even in the range of allowable OSPF costs (1–65,535). You could set the bandwidth gigabit interface to equal that of a megabit interface; however, that would be inaccurate, and might result in OSPF choosing a suboptimal path. A better solution is to use the command that OSPF has to fix this.

The following command will use the default bandwidth that OSPF uses to calculate the cost from 100Mbps to whatever value you want. Negating this command with **no** resets the reference bandwidth back to 100Mbps.

```
ospf  auto-cost reference-bandwidth  Mbps
```

This command is executed under the OSPF process. Its values range from 1 to 4294967 megabits per second, with a default value of 100. Let's change the reference bandwidth to 10000Mbps and see what cost we get with our gigabit interface this time.

```
ospf auto-cost reference-bandwidth 10000
```

We run the gigabit interface through this formula and get a cost of 10.

```
10,000,000,000,000/1,000,000,000,000 = 10
```

OSPF recognizes several types of networks on which it will run. Its behavior is modified to accommodate the uniqueness of a particular network type.

Types of Recognized Networks

OSPF is also capable of supporting four types of physical networks:

- **Point-to-point networks** Consist of two routers in which the point-to-point interfaces can be set up as numbered or unnumbered interfaces.
- **Broadcast networks** For networks with potentially more than two routers, but the OSPF has the ability to send the same broadcast to all of the routers.
- **Nonbroadcast networks** Networks with potentially more than two routers; however, OSPF does not have the ability to send a broadcast to all of the routers.
- **Point-to-multipoint networks** Resemble a bicycle wheel, with the main router as the hub and the other routers branching off in spokes from the central hub.

Point to Point

A point-to-point network is any network having two, and only two, routers directly connected to each other. This is the simplest network topology to configure OSPF on, and is shown in Figure 5.25. There is no DR or BDR elected on a point-to-point network.

Figure 5.25 Point-to-Point Network Topology

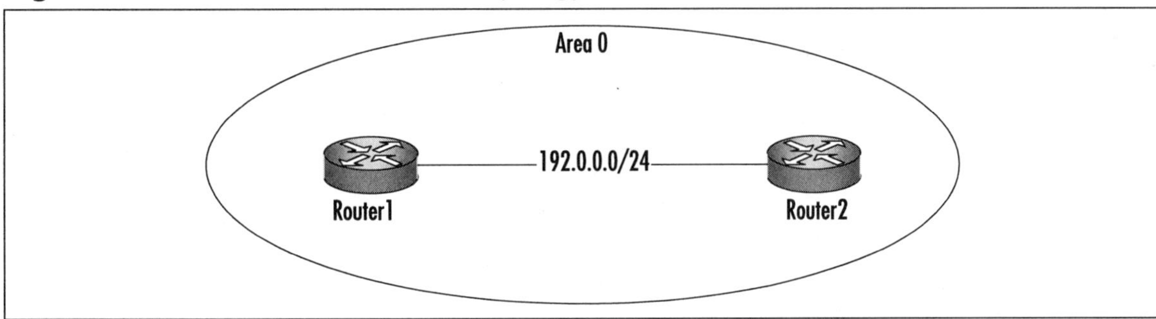

Notice in the configuration for Router1 and Router2, that there is not much to do to get OSPF operating over a point-to-point network.

```
Router1
interface serial 0
ip address 192.0.0.1 255.255.255.0

router ospf 0.0.0.0
network 192.0.0.1 0.0.0.255 area 0

Router2
interface serial 0
ip address 192.0.0.2 255.255.255.0

router ospf 9999
network 192.0.0.2 0.0.0.0 area 0
```

You could adjust the Hello interval using the command shown next. In this example, we are setting the interval to one Hello every 900 seconds. As always, if you make the change on one router on the network, make the same change on all routers on the same network. We are setting the Dead interval to 3,600 seconds, which is unnecessary since this particular value would have been calculated automatically when we changed the Hello interval.

```
ip ospf hello-interval 900
ip ospf dead-interval 3600
```

Point to Multipoint

The point-to-multipoint (PtMP) network is also known as a hub-and-spoke network, and is shown in Figure 5.26. The hub is Router1 that has a connection to all other routers on the network, the spokes. The spokes (Router2 and Router3) have only a connection to the hub, and not to each other. Since the PtMP topology is essentially a collection of point-to-point links, there is no DR or BDR election. In fact, configuring OSPF over a PtMP topology requires the same effort as a point-to-point network.

Figure 5.26 Point-to-Multipoint Network

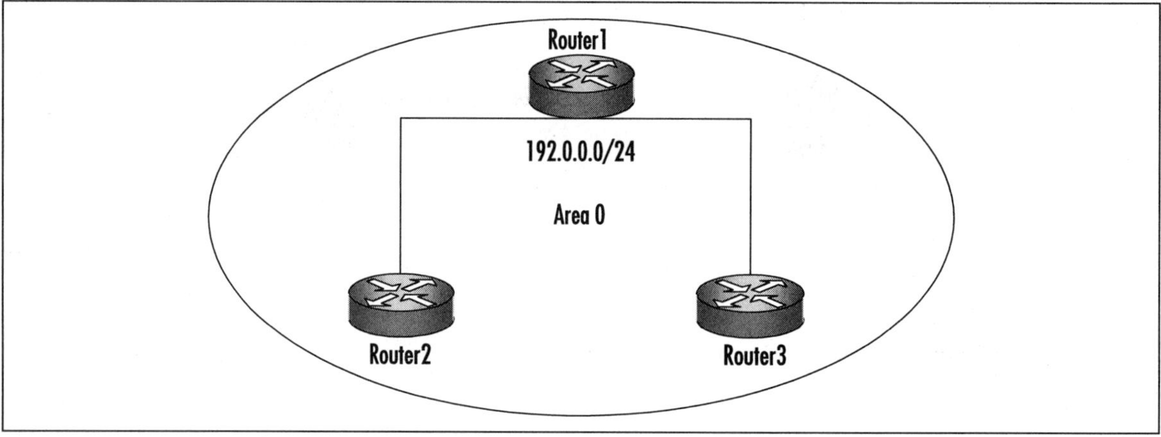

Router1

```
interface serial 0
encapsulation frame-relay
ip ospf network point-to-multipoint
ip address 192.0.0.1 255.255.255.0

router ospf 0.0.0.0
network 192.0.0.1 0.0.0.0 area 0
```

Router2

```
interface serial 0
encapsulation frame-relay
```

```
ip ospf network point-to-multipoint
ip address 192.0.0.2 255.255.255.0

router ospf 9999
network 192.0.0.2 0.0.0.0 area 0
```

Router3

```
interface serial 0
encapsulation frame-relay
ip ospf network point-to-multipoint
ip address 192.0.0.3 255.255.255.0

router ospf 9999
network 192.0.0.3 0.0.0.0 area 0
```

Each router will have what OSPF calls "host routes"; that is, IP routes with a /32 mask, for all routers on the network. This is a routing table entry with a mask of 255.255.255.255 and the IP address of a neighbor on the network. Each spoke will use the hub as the next hop to reach the other spokes; the hub will simply pass this out the interface toward the next hop.

The **ip ospf network** command can treat a physical broadcast or NMBA network as a logical point to point to avoid DR issues. In fact, on NBMA networks configured in a physical hub-and-spoke topology, the PtMP network type is recommended to avoid various DR, reachability, and scalability issues. Prior to this option being available, the only recourse was to manually define neighbors using the **neighbor** command. This was necessary since NBMA networks did not support broadcasts.

In Figure 5.26, for example, Router3 would have an entry of 192.0.0.2 255.255.255.255 for Router2, and similar entries for Router1. Router2 and Router3 would have similar entries for the other routers on the network. If N were the number of neighbors on the network, you would have N-1 entries for all your neighbors.

Broadcast

Broadcast networks are multi-access networks with broadcast capabilities. LANs such as Ethernet or Token Ring are broadcast networks. On broadcast networks, OSPF sends Hellos every 10 seconds, and the dead interval is 40 seconds. A DR and BDR are elected to keep the number of adjacencies reasonable, and to reduce the amount of LSA traffic. Figure 5.27 shows a broadcast network configured in area 0. Notice that if you accept the defaults, the configuration is as simple as a point-to-point network…at least on the surface. Not shown in Figure 5.27 or in the configuration are the DR and BDR elections and the adjacency formation with the DR and BDR.

Figure 5.27 OSPF Broadcast Network

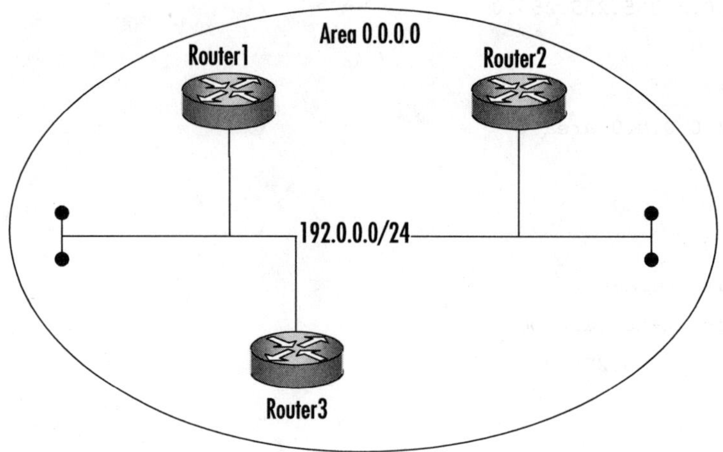


```
Router1
interface ethernet 0
ip address 192.0.0.1 255.255.255.0

router ospf 0.0.0.0
network 192.0.0.1 0.0.0.0 area 0.0.0.0

Router2
interface ethernet 0
ip address 192.0.0.2 255.255.255.0

router ospf 9999
network 192.0.0.2 0.0.0.0 area 0.0.0.0

Router3
interface ethernet 0
ip address 192.0.0.3 255.255.255.0

router ospf 0
network 192.0.0.3 0.0.0.0 area 0
```

Notice that area 0 can be written as 0 or 0.0.0.0. Both will achieve the same result.

Non-Broadcast Multi-Access (NBMA)

X.25, Frame Relay, and ATM are examples of NBMA networks. NBMA network types have OSPF issues that you will not encounter with any of the other network types. In fact, Cisco recommends that you avoid it like the plague, and configure NBMA networks as point-to-multipoint networks instead. Figure 5.28 shows a NBMA network. The Hello timer is 30 seconds, and the Dead timer is 120 seconds by default.

Figure 5.28 Non-Broadcast Multi-Access Network

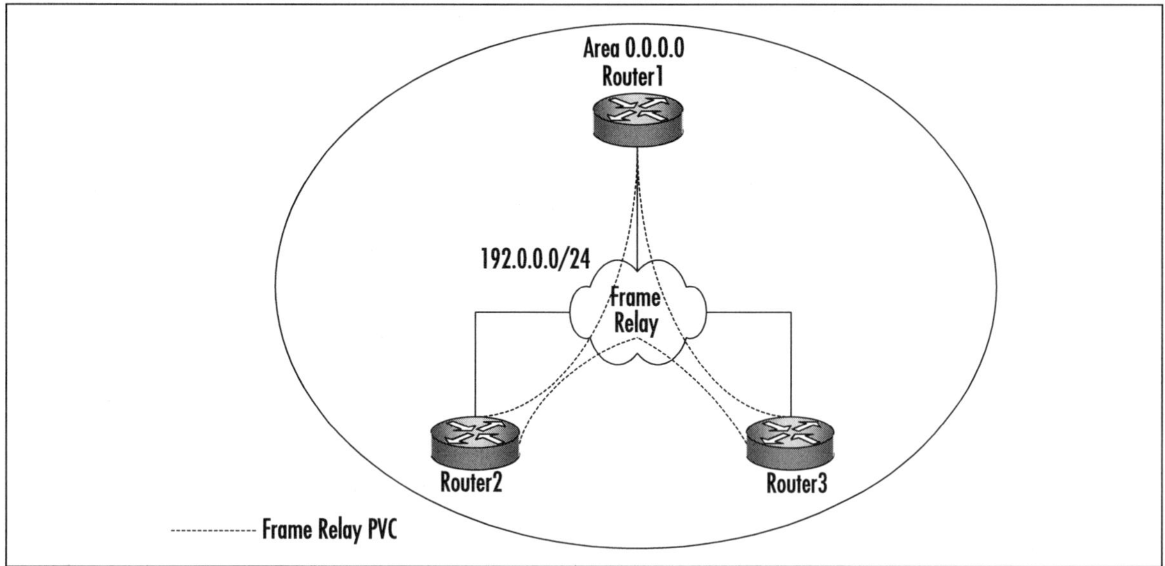

Why is the NBMA network type such a problem child? First, NMBA networks can have multiple routers like a broadcast network, and even elect a DR and BDR. However, NBMA networks cannot support broadcasts, which means that OSPF cannot use multicasts either for its Hellos, adjacency formation process, or to exchange updates. Implied in all this is the fact that you will have to implement a full-mesh NBMA network where all routers have a link to each other. This obviously means many virtual circuits, perhaps too many to be scalable. You could implement a partial mesh, but you must ensure that routers having a connection to all other routers become the DR and BDR.

Despite these issues, OSPF can operate over a NBMA network. You will need to manually form neighbors using the **neighbor** command. In Figure 5.28, the network is fully meshed, so it does not matter which router becomes the DR and BDR. Otherwise, we would have to adjust the priorities so that the routers with connectivity to all other routers would become the DR and BDR. There are no Frame Relay map statements in this configuration, as we are assuming that inverse ARP is operational.

Router1

```
interface serial 0
encapsulation frame-relay
ip address 192.0.0.1 255.255.255.0

router ospf 0.0.0.0
network 192.0.0.1 0.0.0.0 area 0.0.0.0
neighbor 192.0.0.2
```

```
neighbor 192.0.0.3
```

Router2

```
interface serial 0
encapsulation frame-relay
ip address 192.0.0.2 255.255.255.0

router ospf 9999
network 192.0.0.2 0.0.0.0 area 0.0.0.0
neighbor 192.0.0.1
neighbor 192.0.0.3
```

Router3

```
interface serial 0
encapsulation frame-relay
ip address 192.0.0.3 255.255.255.0

router ospf 0
network 192.0.0.3 0.0.0.0 area 0
neighbor 192.0.0.1
neighbor 192.0.0.3
```

Physical Interfaces, Point-to-Point Subinterfaces, and Point-to-Multipoint Subinterfaces

While not specific to OSPF per se, it can be helpful to know the various classifications of router interfaces. We will briefly discuss each type of interface, and explain what they mean to OSPF.

A physical interface is just that: the actual physical interface of the router. They are referred to as serial 0, ATM 0, Ethernet 0, and so forth. By default, OSPF will treat physical serial interfaces as point to point, unless they are using an NBMA encapsulation such as Frame Relay.

Subinterfaces are logical interfaces created under the physical interface; they do not exist, except as logical extensions of the physical interface. You will see them given designators such as serial 0.1, ATM 0.5, and so on. When dealing with subinterfaces, you usually address them, and run OSPF on them, but not the physical interface, which is usually operating at Layer 2.

On NBMA networks, subinterfaces can be classified as point to point or point to multipoint. You will need to execute the **ip ospf network** command to match that of the subinterface to avoid problems. If you do not, OSPF will default to the NBMA network simply because it knows it is on a Frame Relay interface.

It is better to have all the interfaces on the network on all the routers to be the same type. When you start mixing and matching the various types, you will have issues with timers and with OSPF adjacencies being accomplished, and some interfaces attempting to elect a DR, while others do not.

In the next few sections, we will provide configuration examples of OSPF in various types of networking situations.

Basic OSPF Configuration

Figure 5.29 shows a basic OSPF configuration in area 0. All the routers are internal routes and backbone routers by the virtue of having all their interfaces in area 0. Notice that we have defined loopback interfaces on each router to establish a stable source for the router IDs.

Figure 5.29 Basic Single Area OSPF Configuration

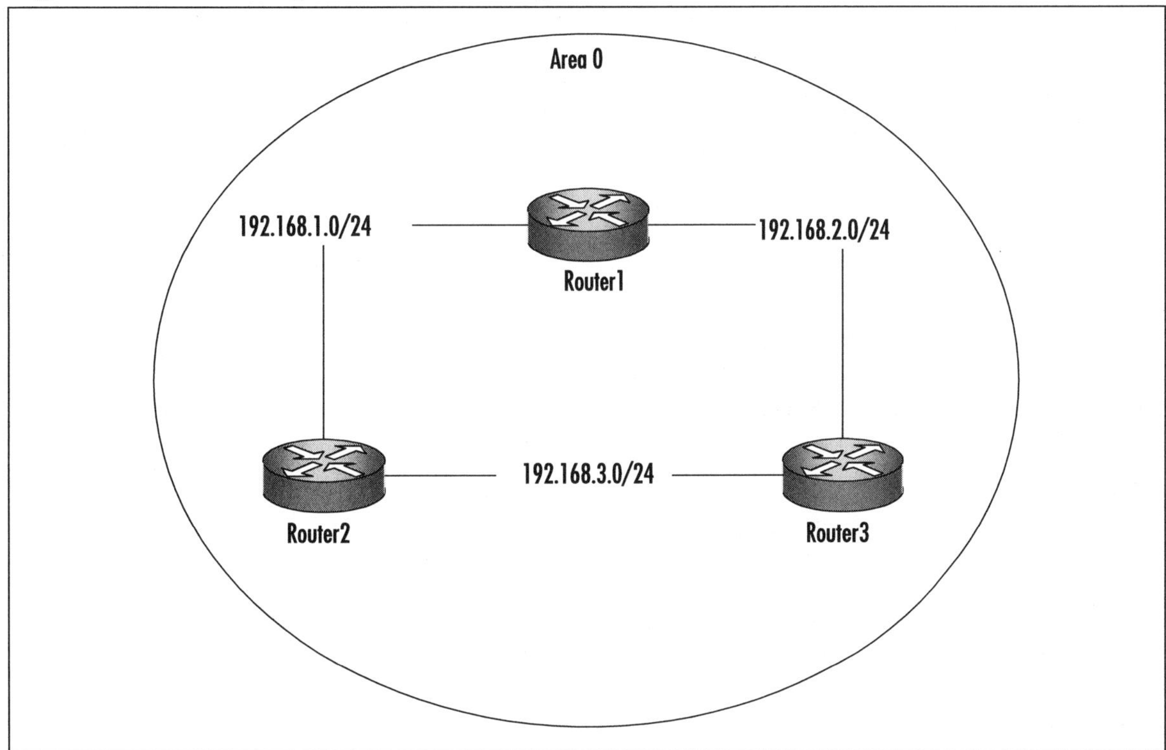

Router1

```
interface loopback 0
ip address 192.0.1.1 255.255.255.255

interface serial 0
ip address 192.1.0.1 255.255.255.0

interface serial 1
ip address 192.2.0.1 255.255.255.0

router ospf 0.0.0.0
network 192.1.0.0 0.0.0.255 area 0
```

```
network 192.1.0.0 0.0.0.255 area 0
```

Router2

```
interface loopback 0
ip address 192.0.2.2 255.255.255.255

interface serial 0
ip address 192.1.0.2 255.255.255.0

interface serial 1
ip address 192.3.0.1 255.255.255.0

router ospf 2
network 192.1.0.0 0.0.0.255 area 0
network 192.3.0.0 0.0.0.255 area 0
```

Router3

```
interface loopback 0
ip address 192.0.3.3 255.255.255.255

interface serial 0
ip address 192.2.0.2 255.255.255.0

interface serial 1
ip address 192.3.0.2 255.255.255.0

router ospf 3
network 192.2.0.0 0.0.0.255 area 0
network 192.3.0.0 0.0.0.255 area 0
```

Notice in our configurations that we do not have the loopback interfaces participating in OSPF. This is to underscore that an interface does not have to be participating in OSPF in order to be the source for the router ID.

OSPF over Frame Relay Point to Point (Subinterfaces)

Figure 5.30 shows OSPF configured over Frame Relay, using point-to-point subinterfaces. In addition to creating the point-to-point subinterfaces with Frame Relay, we have also used the **ip ospf network point-to-point** command to identify this as a point-to-point network to OSPF. All Frame Relay mapping has been handled by inverse ARP.

Figure 5.30 OSPF over Frame Relay: Point-to-Point Subinterfaces

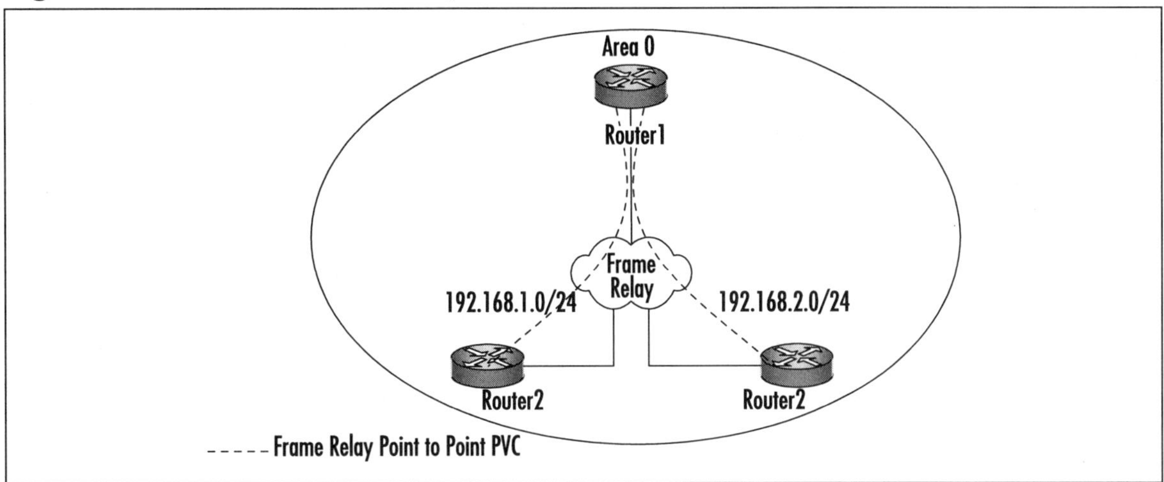

Router1

```
interface loopback 0
ip address 192.0.1.1 255.255.255.255

interface serial 0
encapsulation frame-relay
no ip address

interface serial 0.1 point-to-point
ip address 192.1.0.1 255.255.255.0
ip ospf network-type point-to-point

interface serial 0.2 point-to-point
ip address 192.2.0.1 255.255.255.0
ip ospf network-type point-to-point

router ospf 0.0.0.0
network 192.1.0.1 0.0.0.0 area 0
network 192.2.0.1 0.0.0.0 area 0
network 192.0.1.1 0.0.0.0 area 0
```

Router2

```
interface loopback 0
ip address 192.0.2.2 255.255.255.255

interface serial 0
```

```
encapsulation frame-relay
no ip address

interface serial 0.1 point-to-point
ip address 192.1.0.2 255.255.255.0
ip ospf network-type point-to-point

router ospf 2.2.2.2
network 192.1.0.2 0.0.0.0 area 0
network 192.0.2.2 0.0.0.0 area 0
```

Router3

```
interface loopback 0
ip address 192.0.3.3 255.255.255.255

interface serial 0
encapsulation frame-relay
no ip address

interface serial 0.1 point-to-point
ip address 192.2.0.2 255.255.255.0
ip ospf network-type point-to-point

router ospf 3
network 192.2.0.2 0.0.0.0 area 0
network 192.0.3.3 0.0.0.0 area 0
```

We are advertising all of our interfaces to all routers via OSPF. If we did not use the **opsf network** command, OSPF would default to NBMA mode. This would require use of the **neighbor** command to form neighbors.

OSPF over Frame Relay (NBMA and Physical Interfaces)

Figure 5.31 shows OSPF operating in NMBA mode (by default) over Frame Relay physical interfaces. A DR and BDR are elected. In our configuration, we will set the priority to ensure that Router1 becomes the DR, as it is the only router that has connectivity to all routers. There will be no BDR, so Router2 and Router3 will have their priority set accordingly (0) so that they cannot become a DR or BDR. NBMA do not support broadcasts or multicasts; therefore, the normal neighbor formation process of OSPF will not occur. You will need to use the **neighbor** command to establish neighbors manually.

Figure 5.31 OSPF over Frame Relay Physical Interfaces Configured in NBMA Mode

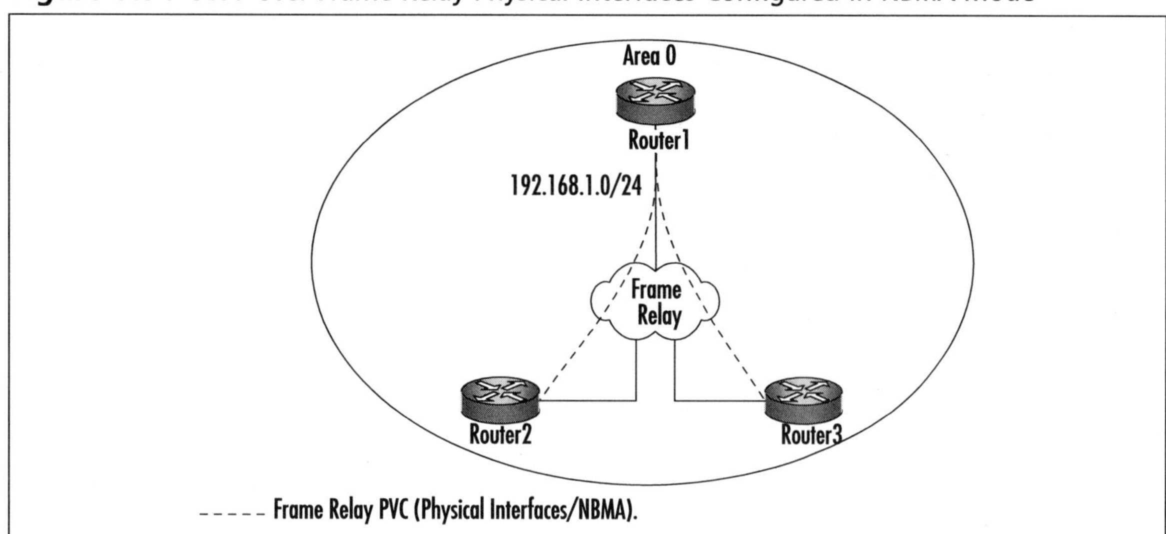

Ideally, the network in Figure 5.31 should be fully meshed. If that were the case, we would not have to set the priorities to ensure that Router1 becomes the DR. We would also have a BDR. However, in our case, it might not be cost effective to pay for a PVC between Router2 and Router3 just to support OSPF. Router2 and Router3 will become adjacent with Router1, but not with each other; they will exchange LSAs only with Router1, but not with each other. Router1 will have to be the next hop for Router2 and Router3 to reach each other's networks. After reviewing this configuration, you will see why Cisco strongly advocates that the point-to-multipoint network type be used for this type of situation.

Router1

```
interface loopback 0
ip address 192.1.1.1 255.255.255.255

interface serial 0
encapsulation frame-relay
ip address 192.168.1.1 255.255.255.0

router ospf 0.0.0.0
network 192.1.1.1 0.0.0.0 area 0
network 192.168.1.1 0.0.0.0 area 0
neighbor 192.168.1.2
neighbor 192.168.1.3
```

Router2

```
interface loopback 0
ip address 192.2.2.2 255.255.255.255
```

```
interface serial 0
encapsulation frame-relay
ip address 192.1.1.2 255.255.255.0
ip ospf priority 0

router ospf 2.2.2.2
network 192.2.2.2 0.0.0.0 area 0
network 192.168.1.2 0.0.0.0 area 0
neighbor 192.168.1.1

Router3
interface loopback 0
ip address 192.3.3.3 255.255.255.255

interface serial 0
encapsulation frame-relay
ip address 192.168.1.3 255.255.255.0
ip ospf priority 0

router ospf 3
network 192.3.3.3 0.0.0.0 area 0
network 192.168.1.3 0.0.0.0 area 0
neighbor 192.168.1.1
```

OSPF over Frame Relay Point-to-Multipoint Subinterfaces

Figure 5.32 shows an OSPF configured over Frame Relay point-to-multipoint network type. This is the same network we used in the previous NMBA example. The PtMP mode treats the links as a collection of point-to-point networks, a fact that we are going to dramatize in our example by configuring Router1's end as PtMP, and Router2 and Router3's end as point to point. The PtMP network type removes the need for neighbor statements.

There is no DR or BDR elected on a PtMP network. Broadcasts are supported, so all routers will become adjacent. In Figure 5.32, we have a true PtMP network: Router2 and Router3 do not have a direct PVC to each other; they will depend on Router1 to pass their LSAs to the other. In other words, as mentioned previously, each router will have host entries to each other; Router2 and Router3 will use Router1 as the next hop to reach each other. However, since we are setting Router2 and Router3 to use the point-to-point network type, they will not have host routes in their tables. We also set the timers on Router1 to match the default values of a point-to-point network so that the neighbor and adjacency formation will be successful.

Figure 5.32 OSPF over Frame Relay Point-to-Multipoint Subinterfaces

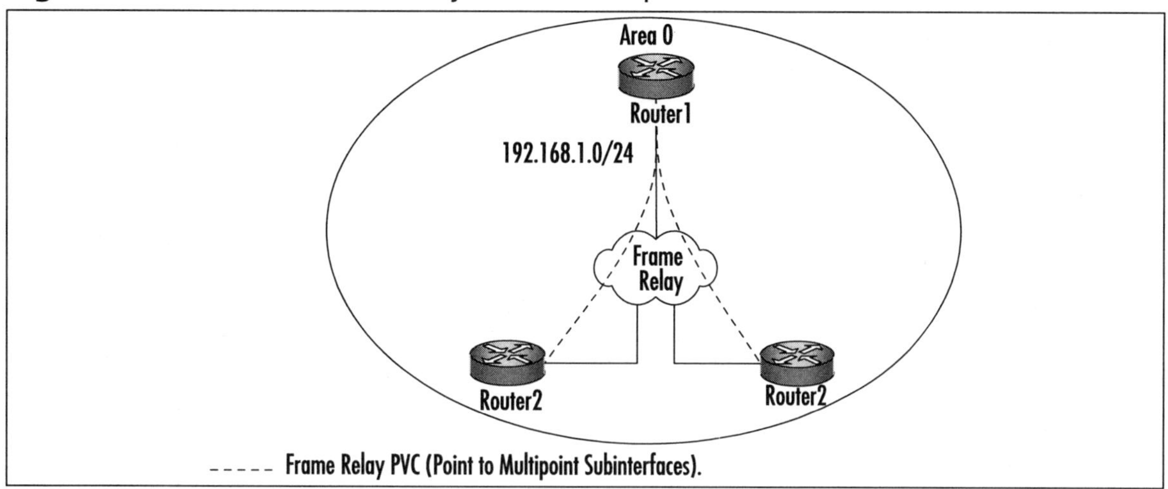

Router1

```
interface loopback 0
ip address 192.1.1.1 255.255.255.255

interface serial 0
encapsulation frame-relay
no ip address

interface serial 0.1 multipoint
ip address 192.168.1.1 255.255.255.0
ip ospf network-type point-to-multipoint
ip ospf hello-interval 10

router ospf 0.0.0.0
network 192.1.1.1 0.0.0.0 area 0
network 192.168.1.1 0.0.0.0 area 0
```

Router2

```
interface loopback 0
ip address 192.2.2.2 255.255.255.255

interface serial 0
encapsulation frame-relay
no ip address

interface serial 0.1 point-to-point
```

```
ip address 192.1.1.2 255.255.255.0

router ospf 2.2.2.2
network 192.2.2.2 0.0.0.0 area 0
network 192.168.1.2 0.0.0.0 area 0
```

Router3

```
interface loopback 0
ip address 192.3.3.3 255.255.255.255

interface serial 0
encapsulation frame-relay
no ip address

interface serial 0.1 point-to-point
ip address 192.168.1.3 255.255.255.0

router ospf 3
network 192.3.3.3 0.0.0.0 area 0
network 192.168.1.3 0.0.0.0 area 0
```

OSPF over Frame Relay Point-to-Multipoint Subinterfaces

Figure 5.32 shows OSPF configured over Frame Relay point-to-multipoint network type. This is the same network we used in the previous NMBA example. The PtMP mode treats the links as a collection of point-to-point networks, a fact that we are going to dramatize in our example by configuring Router1's end as PtMP, and Router2 and Router3's end as point to point. The PtMP network type removes the need for neighbor statements.

There is no DR or BDR elected on a PtMP network. Broadcasts are supported, so all routers will become adjacent. In Figure 5.32, we have a true PtMP network: Router2 and Router3 do not have a direct PVC to each other; they will depend on Router1 to pass their LSAs to the other. In other words, as mentioned previously, each router will have host entries to each other; Router2 and Router3 will use Router1 as the next hop to reach other. However, since we are setting Router2 and Router3 to use the point-to-point network type, they will not have host routes in their tables. We also set the timers on Router1 to match the default values of a point-to-point network so that the neighbor and adjacency formation will be successful.

Figure 5.32 OSPF over Frame Relay Point-to-Multipoint Subinterfaces

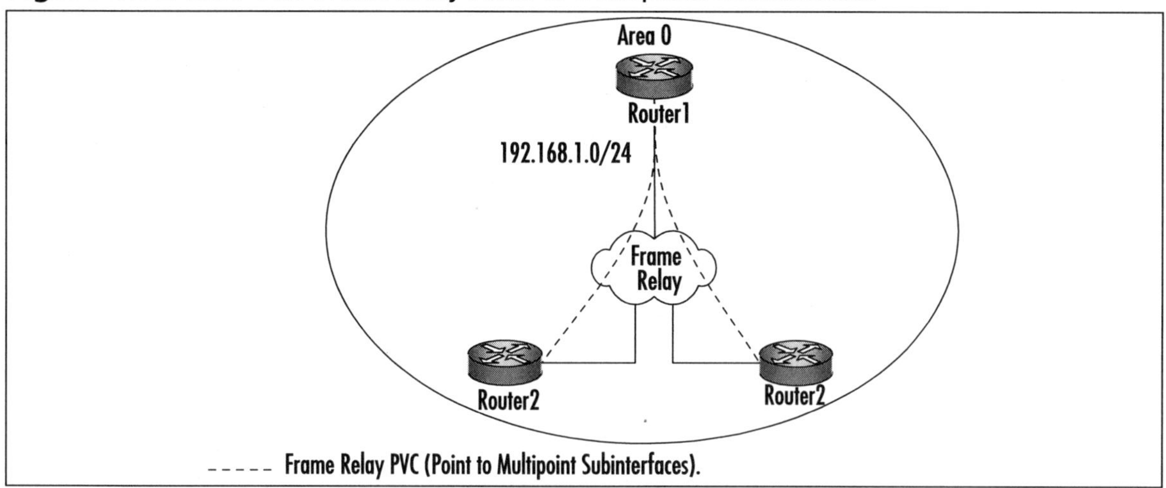

Router1

```
interface loopback 0
ip address 192.1.1.1 255.255.255.255

interface serial 0
encapsulation frame-relay
no ip address

interface serial 0.1 multipoint
ip address 192.168.1.1 255.255.255.0
ip ospf network-type point-to-multipoint
ip ospf hello-interval 10

router ospf 0.0.0.0
network 192.1.1.1 0.0.0.0 area 0
network 192.168.1.1 0.0.0.0 area 0
```

Router2

```
interface loopback 0
ip address 192.2.2.2 255.255.255.255

interface serial 0
encapsulation frame-relay
no ip address

interface serial 0.1 point-to-point
```

```
ip address 192.1.1.2 255.255.255.0

router ospf 2.2.2.2
network 192.2.2.2 0.0.0.0 area 0
network 192.168.1.2 0.0.0.0 area 0
```

Router3

```
interface loopback 0
ip address 192.3.3.3 255.255.255.255

interface serial 0
encapsulation frame-relay
no ip address

interface serial 0.1 point-to-point
ip address 192.168.1.3 255.255.255.0

router ospf 3
network 192.3.3.3 0.0.0.0 area 0
network 192.168.1.3 0.0.0.0 area 0
```

OSPF on Broadcast Networks

Figure 5.33 shows OSPF running on a broadcast network. On broadcast networks, OSPF will elect a DR and BDR to reduce the number of adjacencies formed. In our example configuration, we want Router1 and Router2 to become the DR and BDR, and we do not want Router3 through 5 to ever become the DR and BDR.

Each of the routers in our example has a loopback interface configured, which will by default be the preferred source of loopback addresses. While the way we have assigned IP addresses here ensures that Router1 and Router2 will become the DR and BDR, another router added later with a numerically higher router ID could become the DR. Our configuration will avoid that with the **priority** command.

Figure 5.33 OSPF on a Broadcast Network

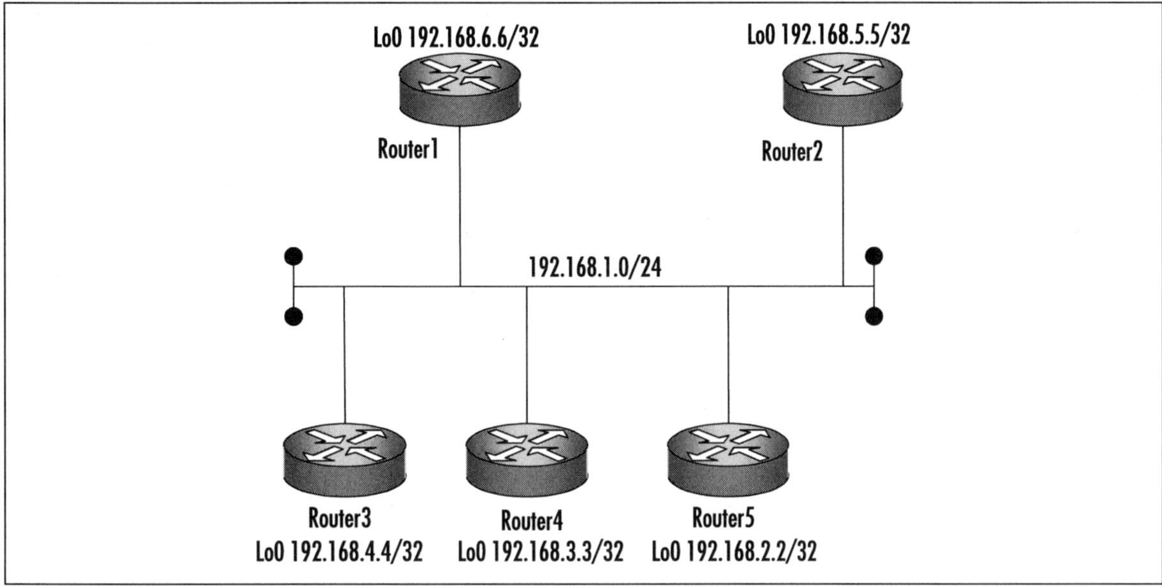

Router1

```
interface loopback 0
ip address 192.168.6.6 255.255.255.255



interface ethernet 0
ip address 192.168.1.1 255.255.255.0
ip ospf priority 127

router ospf 0.0.0.0
network 192.1.1.1 0.0.0.0 area 0
network 192.168.6.6 0.0.0.0 area 0
```

Router2

```
interface loopback 0
ip address 192.168.5.5 255.255.255.255

interface ethernet 0
ip address 192.1.1.2 255.255.255.0
ip ospf priority 126

router ospf 2.2.2.2
network 192.168.5.5 0.0.0.0 area 0
network 192.168.1.2 0.0.0.0 area 0
```

```
Router3
interface loopback 0
ip address 192.168.4.4 255.255.255.255

interface ethernet 0
ip address 192.168.1.3 255.255.255.0
ip ospf priority 0

router ospf 3
network 192.168.1.3 0.0.0.0 area 0
network 192.168.4.4 0.0.0.0 area 0

Router4
interface loopback 0
ip address 192.168.3.3 255.255.255.255

interface ethernet 0
ip address 192.168.1.4 255.255.255.0
ip ospf priority 0

router ospf 5
network 192.168.1.3 0.0.0.0 area 0
network 192.168.3.3 0.0.0.0 area 0

Router5
interface loopback 0
ip address 192.168.2.2 255.255.255.255

interface ethernet 0
ip address 192.168.1.5 255.255.255.0
ip ospf priority 0

router ospf 5
network 192.168.1.5 0.0.0.0 area 0
network 192.168.2.2 0.0.0.0 area 0
```

In our configuration, we set the priority of Router3, Router4, and Router5 to 0, so that they have no chance of ever becoming the DR or BDR on this network. Router1 has the high priority, guaranteeing that it will become the DR on this network, while Router2 has the second highest priority, guaranteeing it as the BDR.

OSPF Summarization

Summarization is the process of aggregating multiple routing updates into a single routing update. Summarization is a manual process; its quality and effectiveness will depend on the person who configures it. OSPF offers no auto-summary capabilities whatsoever. You will have to configure and implement any summarization that you want. When summarizing in OSPF, it is best to summarize at either the ABR for the area containing the networks being summarized, or at the ASBR summarizing any external routes. You can also summarize routes in the backbone area, although as a rule, it is best to summarize at the ABR for the area that sourced the route.

Summarize at the ABR that connects to the backbones so that the ABR will advertise a summarized route into area 0. The area 0 routers will then inject this summarized route into their areas. Another argument for the "summarize at the ABR" technique is that it pinpoints where summarization occurs for each area, rather than having to do router configuration analysis to track it down.

Why Summarize?

The benefits of summarization are most evident when you execute the **show ip route** command before and after summarization. You will see a smaller routing table. This directly translates into saved router CPU cycles (less entries to go through to find a route means less CPU resources consumed). It also means less memory required due to the smaller size of the routing table. There are also benefits to your troubleshooting efforts: you have fewer entries to go through in the routing table. Summarization also indirectly introduces stability, as the loss of a specific link does not modify the routing table that contains the summary.

The summary-address Command

The **summary-address** command is configured on an ASBR to summarize external network advertisements. That is, it is used to summarize those networks being injected into the OSPF domain, which are routes that were learned by means other than OSPF. The LSA type summarized by the **summary-address** command is LSA type 5. Figure 5.34 shows a typical application of the **summary-address** command.

Figure 5.34 summary-address Command in Action

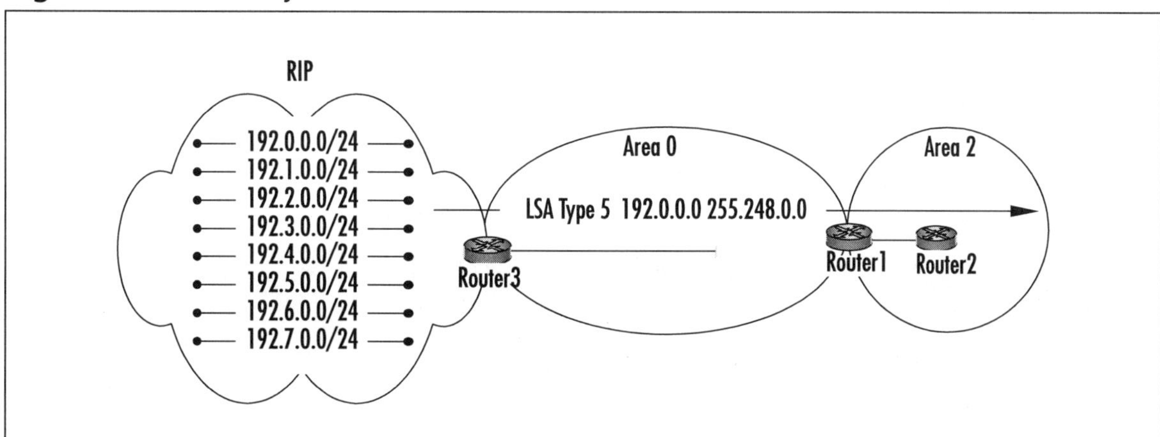

In Figure 5.34, Router3 is the ASBR that is injecting and summarizing the eight networks that it learns from RIP into OSPF. Following is the syntax of the command as culled from the Cisco IOS. You need to work out the appropriate prefix and mask before you execute the command.

```
Router3(config-router)# summary-address ip-address mask prefix mask [not-advertise]
[tag tag]
```

- **ip-address** IP address to be summarized.
- **mask** Mask of the address to be summarized.
- **prefix** Address used as summary of the IP address.
- **mask** Summary address (prefix) mask
- **not-advertise** Specifies that the IP address is not be advertised as part of the summary. Instead, the specified IP address will be advertised in its own LSA (type 5).

We will use Router3 in Figure 5.34 to discuss the different ways you can use this command to summarize. There are about three techniques you can use: summarize all in one statement, summarize all in individual statements, and summarize some in one statement and others in individual statements.

Summarizing All in a Single Statement

The following configuration summarizes all eight networks with a single statement.

```
summary-address 192.0.0.0 255.248.0.0 192.0.0.0 255.248.0.0
```

All addresses that match the IP address and mask will be summarized and advertised in LSA type 5 as shown in the second tuple. This method has the advantage of quickly and easily summarizing large numbers of networks; the disadvantage is that you might summarize more than you want.

Summarizing All Network in Multiple Individual Statements

The following configuration summarizes all eight networks with eight individual statements.

Notice that the same prefix and mask is used for all of them; all of them will be summarized and advertised in a single LSA 5 under this prefix.

```
summary-address 192.0.0.0 255.255.255.0 192.0.0.0 255.248.0.0
summary-address 192.1.0.0 255.255.255.0 192.0.0.0 255.248.0.0
summary-address 192.2.0.0 255.255.255.0 192.0.0.0 255.248.0.0
summary-address 192.3.0.0 255.255.255.0 192.0.0.0 255.248.0.0
summary-address 192.4.0.0 255.255.255.0 192.0.0.0 255.248.0.0
summary-address 192.5.0.0 255.255.255.0 192.0.0.0 255.248.0.0
summary-address 192.6.0.0 255.255.255.0 192.0.0.0 255.248.0.0
summary-address 192.7.0.0 255.255.255.0 192.0.0.0 255.248.0.0
```

All addresses that match the IP address and mask will be summarized and advertised in LSA type 5 as shown in the second tuple. You can also mix and match these techniques to suit your needs.

no-advertise

The following configuration summarizes all eight networks with a single statement. However, this time, we do not want 192.4.0.0 to be summarized. Instead, we want 192.4.0.0 to be advertised in its own individual LSA, and the rest of the networks in this range to be advertised in the summary update.

```
summary-address 192.0.0.0 255.248.0.0 192.0.0.0 255.248.0.0
summary-address 192.4.0.0 255.255.255.0 no-advertise
```

The **no-advertise** command will ensure that 192.4.0.0 gets advertised in its own LSA.

The area range Command

The **area-range** command performs summarization on a per-area basis for routes learned via the OSPF process. Specifically, it summarizes LSA type 1 and 2 LSAs of an area into a single summary LSA type 3 or 4. This is different from the **summary-address** command that summarizes external networks (LSA type 5). This command is executed on the ABR routers for the area.

Figure 5.35 shows a typical situation where the **area-range** command would be useful. Here we have eight networks in area 1 that are being summarized in a single summary LSA. This LSA gets sent to the rest of the OSPF routing domain.

Figure 5.35 OSPF area-range Command

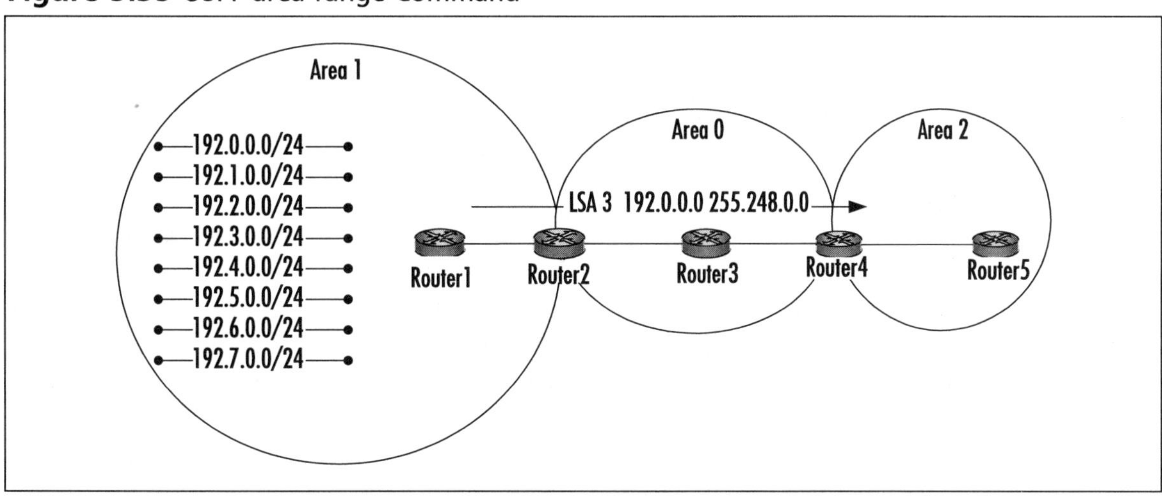

The syntax of the **area-range** command and description of its options are shown here.

```
Router1(config-router)# area area-id range ip-address mask [advertise | not-advertise]
```

- **area-id** The area-id (number) of the area containing the networks to be summarized.

- **range ip-address mask** Specifies the prefix and mask to be used as the summary address and mask. This option serves a double purpose, as it not only defines the summary address and mask to be advertised; it also identifies the range of networks to be summarized. Any thing matching the prefix and mask combination will be summarized.
- **advertise** Can be used to specify networks to be advertised that might have been prohibited from doing so with a **not-advertise** statement. Overrides the **not-advertise** keyword.
- **not-advertise** Specifies the networks not to be advertised. This option allows you to advertise more specific networks in their own LSA. Overrides default summary statement.

In Figure 5.35, Router2 is the ABR for area 1. It is summarizing network 192.0.0.0/24 to 192.7.0.0/24 into a single summary update of 192.0.0.0/24. Not shown in the figure is that we want 192.3.0.0/24 advertised in its own LSA. This means that Router2 will advertise a summary LSA for 192.0.0.0/16, and a individual LSA for 192.3.0.0/24. The configuration to accomplish this is given here.

```
RouterB
router ospf 1
area 1 range 192.3.0.0 255.255.255.0 not-advertise
area 1 range 192.0.0.0 255.248.0.0
```

The first **area-range** command states that 192.3.0.0 will not be part of a summary; the second statement summarizes the networks in range of 192.0.0.0 to 192.7.0.0.

Authentication

OSPF provides authentication measures to prevent undesirables from corrupting your routing. There is an authentication field in the OSPF Hello packet that indicates if authentication is enabled. OSPF authentication can be enabled in a particular area, and then turned on on a per-interface basis.

Plaintext versus Message Digest 5

OSPF provides three methods of authentication: null, plaintext, and Message Digest 5 (MD5). Null authentication is the default, and indicates that authentication is not used in this area, or network. In fact, you can selectively use the **ip ospf authentication null** command to disable authentication in certain areas of your networks.

Plaintext is a simple, unsecured password exchange mechanism that sends the password as unencrypted text…anyone with a packet capture program can easily obtain the password.

MD5 does not transmit the password at all. MD5 hashes the password, and exchanges the result of that hash, which is encrypted garbage unless you have the correct key to decrypt. If the results match, then the authentication is successful, and packets can be exchanged. MD5 is impervious to packet captures: anyone who captures the packets during a MD5 authentication session will end up with a garbled hash that gives no clue to the true password.

Support for authentication is first turned on in the area; however, no authentication takes place until it is enabled on the interfaces. Enabling area authentication is analogous to creating an access list: it doesn't affect anything until you enable it on the interfaces. Just because you enable authentication in an area does not mean that all routers in the area must run authentication. Routers on the same network must agree on a form of authentication: none, plaintext, or MD5. Passwords can be up to 16 bytes long, and key-IDs, where applicable, range from 1 to 255.

Area Authentication

When you enable area authentication, you are specifying that this area will support authentication of a certain type. An area can only support one type of authentication: either plaintext or MD5. If you opt for one over the other, you must remember to use the same authentication method on each interface. Authentication does not have to match between areas since a network can be in one, and only one, area.

The command to accomplish authentication is **area 0 authentication {message}**. If you do not provide the **message** keyword, area authentication will default to plaintext.

Enable authentication and specify the password on each interface with either **the ip ospf message-digest-key 1 md5 <key>** where <key> is the password using MD5, or **ip ospf authentication <key>** to use plaintext. The "1" in the MD5 string is the key-ID; it is specific to each router and does not have to match between neighbors. The password can be different on each network in an area, but all routers on the same network must use a matching password. In Figure 5.36, we have opted to use MD5 authentication for area 0.

Figure 5.36 OSPF Area Authentication

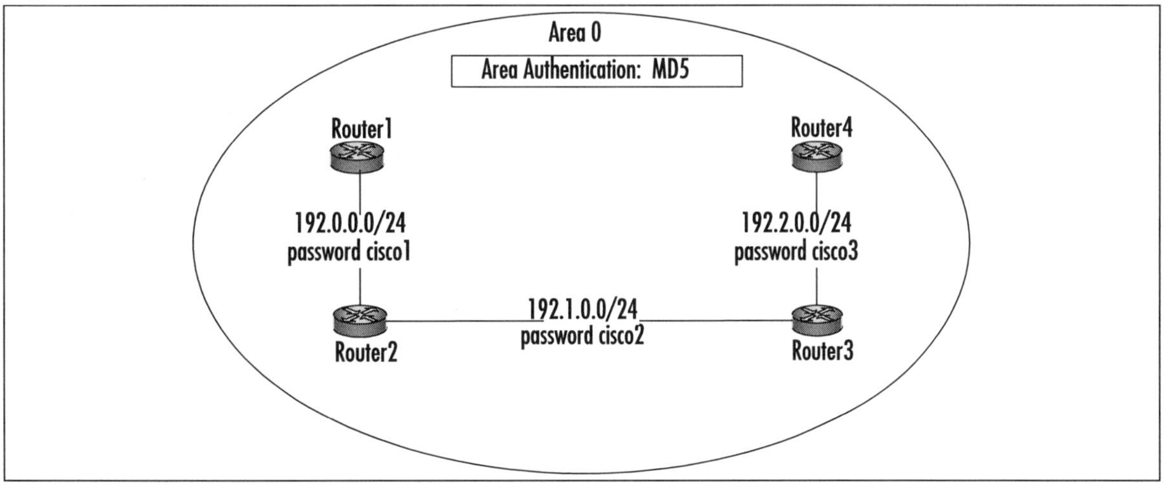

Router1

```
! We enable MD5 authentication on Serial 0.

interface serial 0
ip address 192.0.0.1 255.255.255.0
ip ospf message-digest-key 1 md5 cisco1
```

```
! We have specified MD5 as the standard authentication method for area 0.
router ospf 99
network 192.0.0.1 0.0.0.0 area 0
area 0 authentication message-authentication
```

Router2

```
interface serial 0
ip address 192.0.0.2 255.255.255.0
ip ospf message-digest-key 1 md5 cisco1

interface serial 1
ip address 192.1.0.1 255.255.255.0
ip ospf message-digest-key 1 md5 cisco2

router ospf 99
network 192.0.0.2 0.0.0.0 area 0
network 192.1.0.1 0.0.0.0 area 0
area 0 authentication message-authentication
```

Router3

```
interface serial 0
ip address 192.2.0.1 255.255.255.0
ip ospf message-digest-key 1 md5 cisco3

interface serial 1
ip address 192.1.0.2 255.255.255.0
ip ospf message-digest-key 1 md5 cisco2

router ospf 99
network 192.1.0.2 0.0.0.0 area 0
network 192.2.0.1 0.0.0.0 area 0
area 0 authentication message-authentication
```

Router4

```
interface serial 0
ip address 192.2.0.2 255.255.255.0
ip ospf message-digest-key 1 md5 cisco3

router ospf 99
network 192.1.0.2 0.0.0.0 area 0
```

```
network 192.2.0.1 0.0.0.0 area 0
area 0 authentication message-authentication
```

The important thing that you should get out of this example is that the **area authentication** command specifies the authentication method for all routers in an area. The **interface authentication** command enables authentication in the network, and specifies the password to be used. You can choose not to authenticate over certain links; by default, if you do not configure authentication on an interface, it will not authenticate. If you had enabled authentication, and wanted to disable it, use the **ip ospf authentication null**, or **ip ospf message-digest-key 1 md5 null** command.

OSPF Virtual Links

Virtual links should not be a part of your permanent OSPF design, as they are intended to be temporary solutions. Treat them as indicators of design flaws or network problems. Virtual links are simply a knob for binding disconnected areas or patching together a split backbone area. Situations where areas are not able to connect to area 0, or noncontiguous area 0 occurr during mergers of separate OSPF domains. Area 0 might also become split during link failures.

Figure 5.37 shows a typical virtual link configuration where area 2 does not have a connection to area 0. We will need to use area 1 to build our virtual link from area 2 to area 0. We would like to add that a better solution would be to put the networks of area 2 into area 1, or add another link (physical or tunnel) that would enable area 2 to touch area 0 directly.

Figure 5.37 OSPF Virtual Link

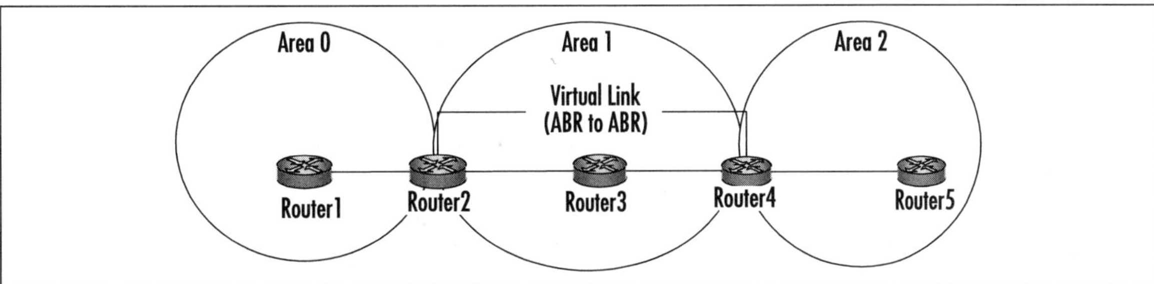

Placement of the **virtual link** commands should be on the ABR connecting the transit area (area 1) to the disconnected area (area 2), and the ABR connecting the transit area (area 2) to the backbone area (area 0). In Figure 5.37, that would be Router4 and Router2, respectively. The following configuration demonstrates how to accomplish this. With virtual links, you must use the router ID to identify the endpoint routers of the virtual link. You should ensure that whatever interfaces are used for the router IDs are advertised via OSPF, or use the router ID command to change the router ID to that of an interface that is advertised via OSPF. In our example, we are choosing the latter option.

```
Router2
router ospf 9999
! Add RouterB to RouterA link to OSPF.
```

```
network 192.0.0.2 0.0.0.0 area 0

!Add RouterB to RouterC link to OSPF.
network 192.1.0.1 0.0.0.0 area 0

! Use the RouterB to RouterC link for router ID since we are advertising that.
router-id 192.1.0.1

! Create virtual link on RouterB to RouterD;  the address here is RouterD's router ID.
area 1 virtual-link 192.2.0.2
```

Router4

```
router ospf 9999
! Add RouterD to RouterC link to OSPF.
network 192.2.0.2 0.0.0.0 area 0

! Use the RouterD to RouterC link for router ID since we are advertising that.
router-id 192.2.0.2

! Create virtual link on RouterD to RouterB;  the address here is RouterB's router ID.
area 1 virtual-link 192.1.0.1
```

Monitoring and Troubleshooting OSPF

The Cisco IOS provides a comprehensive and exhaustive library of commands for monitoring and troubleshooting OSPF. We will discuss some of those commands and provide examples of their output. We will highlight key points of each key command, and how they can be useful for you.

Before we discuss the various **ospf show** and **debug** commands, we need to discuss a command that is neither. The **ospf log-adj-changes** command can be enabled under the OSPF configuration mode to allow the router to record adjacency state changes as they occur. Adjacency state changes will be sent in real time to whatever SYSLOG server you have configured for this router. It provides the same output as **debug ip ospf adjacency**.

The show ip ospf database Command

The **show ip ospf database** command displays the contents of the link state database, and will show every LSA learned and sourced by a particular router. In the following example, Router1 (router ID of 192.168.1.5) has learned about a router link (LSA type 1) from 192.168.1.1. It has also learned about 192.168.0.0 from 192.168.1.6. Both of these links are in area 0. The Age value indicates how old the information is; if it increments, and then resets, it indicates a flapping link.

```
Router1# show ip ospf database
       OSPF Router with ID (192.168.1.5) (Process ID 2)
```

```
                Router Link States (Area 0)
Link ID         ADV Router      Age         Seq#       Checksum Link count
192.168.1.1     192.168.1.1     1008        0x80000795 0xDD6C   26

                Summary Net Link States (Area 0)
Link ID         ADV Router      Age         Seq#       Checksum
192.168.0.0     192.168.1.6     641         0x800000E8 0x785A
```

The show ip ospf database router (LSA 1) Command

Appending the **router** keyword at the end of the **show ip ospf database** command will enable you to narrow your focus to only LSA type 1. In our example, we are looking at a router LSA that Router1 received from 192.168.1.1.

```
Router1# show ip ospf database router
                Router Link States (Area 0)
  Routing Bit Set on this LSA
  LS age: 1177
  Options: (No TOS-capability, DC)
  LS Type: Router Links
  Link State ID: 192.168.1.1
  Advertising Router: 192.168.1.1
  LS Seq Number: 80000795
  Checksum: 0xDD6C
  Length: 336
  AS Boundary Router
   Number of Links: 26
    Link connected to: a Stub Network
     (Link ID) Network/subnet number: 192.168.1.1
     (Link Data) Network Mask: 255.255.255.255
      Number of TOS metrics: 0
       TOS 0 Metrics: 1
    Link connected to: another Router (point-to-point)
     (Link ID) Neighboring Router ID: 192.168.1.14
     (Link Data) Router Interface address: 192.168.1.141
      Number of TOS metrics: 0
       TOS 0 Metrics: 1
```

show ip ospf database network (LSA Type 2)

The **show ip ospf database network** command produces the same output as the previous command, only for broadcast networks attached to a particular router. Another indication that this is a broadcast network is that the link state ID contains the address of the DR. LSA type 2 contains the router IDs of all routers attached to this network.

```
Router2# show ip ospf database network
            OSPF Router with ID (192.168.2.2) (Process ID 1)


                Net Link States (Area 0)
  Routing Bit Set on this LSA
  LS age: 1900
  Options: (No TOS-capability, DC)
  LS Type: Network Links
  Link State ID: 192.168.4.2 (address of Designated Router)
  Advertising Router: 192.168.5.3
  LS Seq Number: 80000DA5
  Checksum: 0x66B8
  Length: 40
  Network Mask: /29
        Attached Router: 192.168.5.3
        Attached Router: 192.168.4.4
        Attached Router: 192.168.4.3
        Attached Router: 192.168.5.2

  Routing Bit Set on this LSA
  LS age: 1220
  Options: (No TOS-capability, No DC)
  LS Type: Network Links
  Link State ID: 192.168.4.11 (address of Designated Router)
  Advertising Router: 192.168.4.18
  LS Seq Number: 80001248
  Checksum: 0xDDC8
  Length: 40
  Network Mask: /29
        Attached Router: 192.168.4.18
        Attached Router: 192.168.4.3
        Attached Router: 192.168.4.17
        Attached Router: 192.168.4.4
```

The show ip ospf database summary (LSA 3) Command

The **show ip ospf database summary** command enables you to view summary LSAs. Recall that LSA type 3 is used to exchange information about links between areas. As you can see in the following example, the link state type is "Summary Links (Networks)." Notice that this LSA includes information about the mask on this link.

```
Router1# show ip ospf database summary
       OSPF Router with ID (192.168.1.5) (Process ID 2)
                Summary Net Link States (Area 0)
  Routing Bit Set on this LSA
  LS age: 696
  Options: (No TOS-capability, DC, Upward)
  LS Type: Summary Links(Network)
  Link State ID: 192.168.0.0 (summary Network Number)
  Advertising Router: 192.168.1.6
  LS Seq Number: 800000E8
  Checksum: 0x785A
  Length: 28
  Network Mask: /16
        TOS: 0  Metric: 1
```

The show ip ospf database asbr-summary (LSA 4) Command

The most important thing you can take away from the **show ip ospf database asbr-summary** command is that it is structurally similar to LSA type 3. The main difference between the two is that LSA type 4 identifies an ASBR, as shown by the "Link State ID: 192.168.116.194 (AS Boundary Router address)" field. The router with router ID 192.168.1.3 is advertising that it can reach this particular ASBR.

```
Router1> show ip ospf database asbr-summary
       OSPF Router with ID (192.168.1.5) (Process ID 2)

                Summary ASB Link States (Area 0)

  Adv Router is not-reachable
  LS age: 808
  Options: (No TOS-capability, DC, Upward)
  LS Type: Summary Links(AS Boundary Router)
  Link State ID: 192.168.1.3 (AS Boundary Router address)
  Advertising Router: 192.168.1.4
  LS Seq Number: 80000016
  Checksum: 0xA5E8
  Length: 28
  Network Mask: /0
        TOS: 0  Metric: 20
  Routing Bit Set on this LSA
  LS age: 262
  Options: (No TOS-capability, DC, Upward)
```

```
  LS Type: Summary Links(AS Boundary Router)
  Link State ID: 192.168.116.194 (AS Boundary Router address)
  Advertising Router: 192.168.1.3
  LS Seq Number: 800006D1
  Checksum: 0xEFBD
  Length: 28
  Network Mask: /0
        TOS: 0  Metric: 1
```

The show ip ospf database external Command

The **show ip ospf database external** command will show any external LSAs in a router's link state database. Router1 has learned the default route (as evidenced by a link state ID of 0.0.0.0) from 192.168.1.1. The particular LSA shown here will make 192.168.1.1 the gateway of last resort for Router1; anything it does not have a route for will be sent to 192.168.1.1.

```
Router1> show ip ospf database external
       OSPF Router with ID (192.168.1.5) (Process ID 2)
                Type-5 AS External Link States
  Routing Bit Set on this LSA
  LS age: 1465
  Options: (No TOS-capability, DC)
  LS Type: AS External Link
  Link State ID: 0.0.0.0 (External Network Number )
  Advertising Router: 192.168.1.1
  LS Seq Number: 80000D54
  Checksum: 0xD7B9
  Length: 36
  Network Mask: /0
        Metric Type: 2 (Larger than any link state path)
        TOS: 0
        Metric: 1
        Forward Address: 0.0.0.0
        External Route Tag: 2
  Routing Bit Set on this LSA
  LS age: 1009
  Options: (No TOS-capability, DC)
  LS Type: AS External Link
  Link State ID: 0.0.0.0 (External Network Number )
  Advertising Router: 192.168.1.2
  LS Seq Number: 80000D55
  Checksum: 0xCFBF
```

```
Length: 36
Network Mask: /0
      Metric Type: 2 (Larger than any link state path)
      TOS: 0
      Metric: 1
      Forward Address: 0.0.0.0
      External Route Tag: 2
```

The show ip ospf database nssa-external (LSA 7) Command

We have come to the end of viewing the LSA database with the **show ip ospf database nssa-external** command. It enables us to view LSA type 7, which you will recall is specific to a NSSA. As shown in the following example, area 1 is configured as a NSSA. The external network 192.168.0.0 was learned by the ASBR with a router ID of 192.168.1.1 and injected into this area as a LSA type 7. Under options, *type 7/5 translation* means that this LSA can be translated from 7 to 5 by the NSSA ABR (into area 0, to be exact).

```
Router1# show ip ospf database nssa-external
 OSPF Router with ID (192.168.1.5) (Process ID 2)
                Type-7 AS External Link States (Area 1)
  Routing Bit Set on this LSA
  LS age: 1913
  Options: (No TOS-capability, Type 7/5 translation, DC)
  LS Type: AS External Link
  Link State ID: 192.168.0.0 (External Network Number )
  Advertising Router: 192.168.1.1
  LS Seq Number: 60000191
  Checksum: 0XA143
  Length: 36
  Network Mask: /16
        Metric Type: 2 (Comparable directly to link state metric)
        TOS: 0
        Metric: 9
        Forward Address: 192.168.1.1
```

show ip ospf neighbor

The **show ip ospf neighbor** command lists the neighbors of a particular router. Router1 in the following example has three neighbors. The *neighbor ID* corresponds to each neighbor's router ID. The *Dead time* decrements until it resets back to some default value upon receiving a Hello. *Address* is the neighbor's address on this particular link.

```
Router1# show ip ospf neighbor
```

```
Neighbor ID     Pri   State           Dead Time   Address         Interface
192.168.1.1       1   FULL/  -        00:00:39    192.168.1.97    Vlan19
192.168.1.2       1   FULL/  -        00:00:39    192.168.1.105   Vlan21
192.168.1.6       1   FULL/  -        00:00:39    192.168.1.114   Vlan23
```

By appending the **detail** keyword, you can obtain more information about your neighbors.

The show ip ospf interface Command

The **show ip ospf interface** command will list all interfaces, and show which ones are participating in OSPF. In the following example, we have the output of this command for a broadcast network. Notice that it identifies the DR on this link, which happens to be Router1! You can also see the timer values for Hello, Dead, and Wait. This command is very useful to determine what links on the router are participating in OSPF.

```
Router1# show ip ospf interface
Vlan6 is up, line protocol is up
  Internet Address 192.168.200.2/23, Area 1.12.16.1
  Process ID 2, Router ID 192.168.1.5, Network Type BROADCAST, Cost: 1
  Transmit Delay is 1 sec, State DR, Priority 1
  Designated Router (ID) 192.168.1.5, Interface address 192.168.200.2
  No backup designated router on this network
  Timer intervals configured, Hello 10, Dead 40, Wait 40, Retransmit 5
    No Hellos (Passive interface)
  Index 1/14, flood queue length 0
  Next 0x0(0)/0x0(0)
  Last flood scan length is 0, maximum is 0
  Last flood scan time is 0 msec, maximum is 0 msec
  Neighbor Count is 0, Adjacent neighbor count is 0
  Suppress hello for 0 neighbor(s)
  Message digest authentication enabled
      No key configured, using default key id 0
```

The show ip ospf Command

The **show ip ospf** command provides a quick overview of the OSPF processes running on this router. It will show how many areas and the number of interfaces for a specific router, and what roles the router plays in each area. In the following example, Router1 is an ABR and ASBR. It has four of its links in area 0, and one link in area 1.12.16.1. The number of times the SPF algorithm has executed can be a good troubleshooting indicator; if this number rapidly increments, it could indicate unstable links.

```
Router1# show ip ospf
 Routing Process "ospf 2" with ID 192.168.1.5
 Supports only single TOS(TOS0) routes
```

```
Supports opaque LSA
It is an area border and autonomous system boundary router
Redistributing External Routes from,
   static
SPF schedule delay 5 secs, Hold time between two SPFs 10 secs
Minimum LSA interval 5 secs. Minimum LSA arrival 1 secs
Number of external LSA 97. Checksum Sum 0x35AADC
Number of opaque AS LSA 0. Checksum Sum 0x0
Number of DCbitless external and opaque AS LSA 0
Number of DoNotAge external and opaque AS LSA 0
Number of areas in this router is 3. 3 normal 0 stub 0 nssa
External flood list length 0
   Area BACKBONE(0)
       Number of interfaces in this area is 4
       Area has message digest authentication
       SPF algorithm executed 17 times
       Area ranges are
       Number of LSA 136. Checksum Sum 0x471A3D
       Number of opaque link LSA 0. Checksum Sum 0x0
       Number of DCbitless LSA 0
       Number of indication LSA 0
       Number of DoNotAge LSA 0
       Flood list length 0
   Area 1.12.16.1
       Number of interfaces in this area is 1
       Area has message digest authentication
       SPF algorithm executed 4 times
       Area ranges are
       Number of LSA 153. Checksum Sum 0x50C401
       Number of opaque link LSA 0. Checksum Sum 0x0
       Number of DCbitless LSA 0
       Number of indication LSA 0
       Number of DoNotAge LSA 0
       Flood list length 0
```

The show ip ospf borders-routers Command

The **show ip ospf borders-routers** command identifies the ABRs and ASBRs by area, and the next hop address to reach them. In the example, Router1 can reach the area 0 ABR/ASBR 192.168.1.3 via the next hop 192.168.1.105. Obviously, this command is very helpful when you need to identify the ABRs and ASBRs in your OSPF routing domain.

```
RouterA# show ip ospf border-routers
OSPF Process 2 internal Routing Table
Codes: i - Intra-area route, I - Inter-area route

i 192.168.1.3 [8] via 192.168.1.105, Vlan21, ABR/ASBR, Area 0, SPF 17
```

The show ip ospf database self-originate Command

show ip ospf database self-originate is a particularly useful command if you want to know what LSAs are being sourced by the router that you are on. In the following example, Router1 is originating the LSAs shown. This command will show all LSAs originated by a router.

```
Router1# show ip os data self-originate
       OSPF Router with ID (192.168.1.5) (Process ID 2)

                Router Link States (Area 0)

Link ID         ADV Router      Age         Seq#       Checksum Link Count
192.168.1.5      192.168.1.5      1534        0x80001258 0xF2FA    7

                Summary Net Link States (Area 0)

Link ID         ADV Router      Age         Seq#       Checksum
192.168.2.0      192.168.1.5      1534        0x80000185 0x2C08
192.168.3.0      192.168.1.5      1534        0x80000185 0x2112
192.168.4.0      192.168.1.5      1534        0x80000185 0x161C
```

The show ip ospf database adv-router Command

The **show ip ospf database adv-router** command enables you to view LSAs by advertising a router. If you do not specify an IP address of an advertising router at the end of the command, it will default to showing LSAs sourced by the current router. In the following example, we are viewing the LSAs learned by Router1 from the router with router ID 192.168.1.5.

```
RouterA# show ip ospf database adv-router  192.168.1.5


       OSPF Router with ID (192.168.1.5) (Process ID 2)

                Router Link States (Area 0)
Link ID         ADV Router      Age         Seq#       Checksum Link count
192.168.1.5      192.168.1.5      1581        0x80001258 0xF2FA    7

                Summary Net Link States (Area 0)
```

```
Link ID         ADV Router      Age         Seq#        Checksum
192.16.2.0      192.168.1.5     1581        0x80000185  0x2C08
192.16.3.0      192.168.1.5     1581        0x80000185  0x2112
```

debug Commands

debug should be used sparingly and specifically. Following are the debug commands that are specific to OSPF monitoring, taken directly from the Cisco IOS. Each command is self-explanatory. We will mention that **debug ip ospf adj** is the best command for isolating and resolving the cause of adjacency failures.

```
Router1# debug ip ospf ?
  adj                OSPF adjacency events
  database-timer     OSPF database timer
  events             OSPF events
  flood              OSPF flooding
  hello              OSPF hello events
  lsa-generation     OSPF lsa generation
  packet             OSPF packets
  retransmission     OSPF retransmission events
  spf                OSPF spf
  tree               OSPF database tree
```

Intermediate System to Intermediate System (IS-IS)

IS-IS is the forgotten, overlooked link state routing protocol. Its better-known cousin, OSPF, has all but eclipsed it. Further compounding the neglect of IS-IS is the fact that there are not as many sources of information about it as there are about OSPF.

IS-IS is a link state routing protocol that is very similar to OSPF. This is no accident, as the developers borrowed and improved on IS-IS when developing OSPF. IS-IS runs the Dijkstra algorithm to build a complete picture of the routing domain (AS). Its backbone area (area 0) is called the L2 area, while all other areas are classified as L1 areas. *IS-IS routes by area within the AS (L2 routing) and by the system ID within an area (L1 routing).* That is, IS-IS uses the area address to determine how to reach the area, and the system ID to reach a particular device once it gets to the destination area. Therefore, it can be said that IS-IS routes on two levels: area and station.

There are two main flavors of IS-IS available: one for CLNS-only routing, and one for routing both CLNS and IP. The latter is officially called Integrated IS-IS by Cisco. While IS-IS was developed by the ISO to route CLNS, it has been modified to route IP. Its modular architecture means that it can be further adapted to route other protocols such as IPX, should anyone need or choose to develop that particular aspect of it.

The "integrated" in Integrated IS-IS simply refers to the support that IS-IS has for non-CLNS protocols such as IP. When you configure Integrated IS-IS, it is subject to the same principles and requirements that other IP routing protocols are (subnetting, masks, and so forth).

With IS-IS, even if you choose to route only IP, you still need to assign a CLNS address (NET), as each IS communicates using CLNS, not IP. You need to enable CLNS, and assign NET, to route IP. While Integrated IS-IS can and does route IP, it does so using its native tongue: CLNS. It speaks CLNS to its peers, encapsulates routing updates in CLNS LSPs, and so on.

The first process that you enable on the IS automatically defaults to L1L2 configuration to support any L2 interarea routing that might be required. This means that the IS will try to determine what the area it is attached to is. Subsequent processes automatically default to L1.

ISO Terminology

It is important to know the ISO terminology associated with IS-IS.

- **Intermediate System (IS)** What the ISO calls a router.
- **End System (ES)** The ISO elected to call hosts ESs. ESs do not route.
- **End System-Intermediate System Protocol (ES-IS)** ES-IS is a discovery and registration protocol used by ESs to identify themselves to an IS, and to discover the IS in their area. ES-IS is also used to register an ES with the IS, which builds a reachability table of ES. ES-IS is *not* a routing protocol.
- **International Standard Organization Interior Gateway Routing Protocol (ISO-IGRP)** ISO-IGRP was Cisco's first and only distance vector protocol for routing CLNS. It does not route IP.
- **Link State Protocol data units (LSP)** LSPs perform the same function for IS-IS and ISO-IGRP that LSAs do for OSPF. Information about the networks in each area is encapsulated within an LSP, and passed to neighboring routers.
- **Connectionless Network Protocol (CLNP)** CLNP is the OSI equivalent of IP. CLNP is a best-effort, unreliable, datagram protocol. It depends on higher layers to provide any needed reliability, including error detection and correction.
- **Connectionless Network Service (CLNS)** CLNS is an amalgam of several OSI protocols, including CLNP for addressing and datagram service, network service access points (NSAP) for access points to higher layer protocols for various services, and so on. It is analogous to TCP/IP, and the various layers in that stack.
- **Protocol Datagram Unit (PDU)** PDU is the OSI term for the units of data that get passed from one layer to the other.
- **Network Service Access Point (NSAP)** NSAP is a logical point in the OSI suite that identifies a particular network service. NSAP provides the addressing for a network device, plus a special byte that identifies the particular service on a network device.
- **Network Entity Title (NET)** This is the NSAP address for a particular network device, ES or IS. The format, fields, and structure of the NET is the same as that of an

NSAP address; the only difference is that the NET SEL value is always 0. Contrast this with a NSAP address with its SEL byte set to a nonzero value to identify a service on a network device.

- **Level 1 (L1)** Defining an area as L1 is the IS-IS equivalent of OSPF defining a "normal" nonbackbone area. Areas that are not backbone areas (that is, do not provide transit support to other areas) are classified as L1 areas.
- **Level 2 (L2)** Backbone area that provides transit services to all other areas.
- **TLV** A tuple in the CLNS PDU that enables a designer to add features, or support for other network protocols. The best-known use of the TLV is to add routing support for IP in IS-IS. The function that it performs is similar to the process of encapsulating one network protocol's traffic inside the packets and datagrams of another network protocol.

ISO Addressing and Topologies

An NSAP address can be likened to the combination of IP address and IP port numbers that identify what protocols are being carried in the IP datagram. NSAP addresses are read from right to left to determine the area, domain, and so forth. You do not assign NSAP addresses to an interface; you assign them to the network device, and each interface is uniquely identified by data link addresses such as the MAC address. On Cisco platforms, assign CLNS addresses to an IS by creating a network entity title (NET) (a NSAP address with its SEL set to 0). NSAP SEL uniquely identifies a particular network service.

Figure 5.38 shows the NSAP address format.

Figure 5.38 NSAP Address Format

Size in Bytes	Field	
1	Authority Format Identifier (AFI)	Initial Domain Part (IDP)
Variable	Initial Domain Identifier (IDI)	
Variable	Address Administration	Domain Specific Part (DSP)
2	Area	
6	Station (System ID)	
1	Selector	

- **Authority Format Identifier (AFI)** One-byte field that defines the structure and format of the rest of the NSAP address, including the length of the IDI field.
- **Initial Domain Identifier (IDI)** Variable length. Identifies the domain that this particular address falls under.
- **Address Administration** Variable length. Allows the NSAP address to be divided into subaddresses, with authority for those addresses delegated. Commonly treated as part of a domain.

- **Area. Logical grouping of IS and ES** L1 (intra-area traffic only), L2 (inter-area traffic), or L1L2 (both types of traffic).
- **System ID** CLNS address for the IS or ES. In many cases, it is a MAC address of a particular interface used to identify a particular network device. It can be set manually.
- **Selector (SEL or NSEL)** Identifies a particular network service, and is analogous to the port number in an IP packet. The SEL value of 00 is reserved, and indicates a network entity title (NET).

NSAP Address Format

Figure 5.39 shows a NSAP address such as that commonly used by ISO-IGRP or IS-IS. If you were simply given an NSAP address such as this, and read it like you would an IP address (left to right), you would have problems. The reason for that is that the domain part of this address is variable: it can be anywhere from one to ten bytes. So, how do you determine what part of a NSAP address is your area, for example? As you can see in Figure 5.39, NSAP addresses are written in hexadecimal format.

Figure 5.39 NSAP Address Illustrated

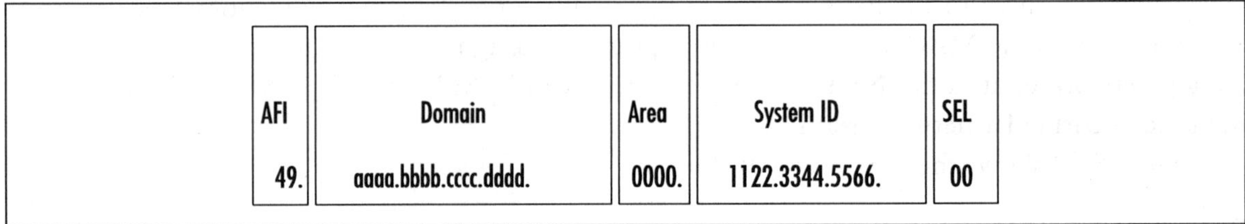

Starting at the right, the SEL field is always one byte. The six bytes to the left of that will always be the system ID. The byte to the left of that is the area number. Anything left of the area will be the domain and AFI.

IS-IS View of NSAP Address

IS-IS has its own interpretation of the NSAP address as shown in Figure 5.40. Notice that there is no domain, and that the two bytes that ISO-IGRP views as the area address are treated as High Order-Domain Specific Part (HO-DSP). Up to the first 12 bytes of the NSAP address are treated as the area address; the next six bytes are the system ID, and we conclude with the SEL byte set to 0 identify a NET.

Figure 5.40 IS-IS Address Format

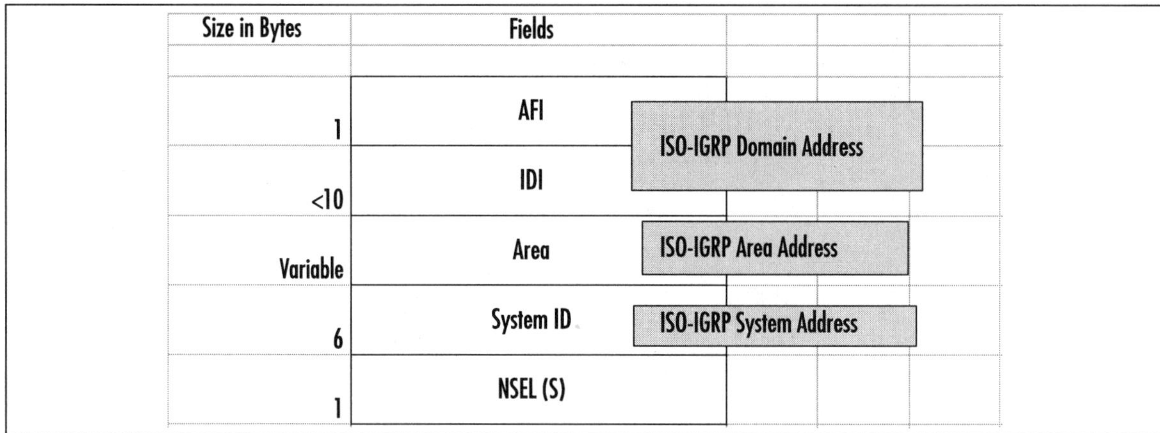

IS-IS routes by the area and the system ID; the lack of a domain indicates that IS-IS, like OSPF, was not designed to route between ASs. Within an AS, IS-IS will use the area address to deliver data to the correct area, and once in that area, use the system ID to deliver to the correct IS.

Using the NSAP address, 49.aaaa.bbbb.cccc.dddd.0000.1111.1111.1111.00, here is how IS-IS interprets NSAP addresses. NSAP addresses are expressed in hexadecimal, with a minimum length of 8 bytes, and a maximum length of 20 bytes.

```
Area: 49.aaaa.bbbb.cccc.dddd.0000
System ID: 1111.1111.1111
SEL: 00
```

Configuring CLNS-Only IS-IS

You create the IS-IS process using the **router isis** command. Next, assign it a NET (essentially creating the areas and system ID) with the **net** command. Finally, put interfaces into the IS-IS routing process using the **clns router isis** command. This command enables routing for CLNS only; we will show you how to enable IP routing with IS-IS. Whenever you create an IS-IS routing process, CLNS routing is automatically enabled.

Configuring Single Area IS-IS

Figure 5.41 shows a single area, CLNS-only IS-IS configuration. The area in this case is 49.dddd.eeee.ffff, and each IS has a unique system ID. Since they are in the same area, all routers are doing L1 routing updates.

Figure 5.41 Single Area CLNS-Only IS-IS

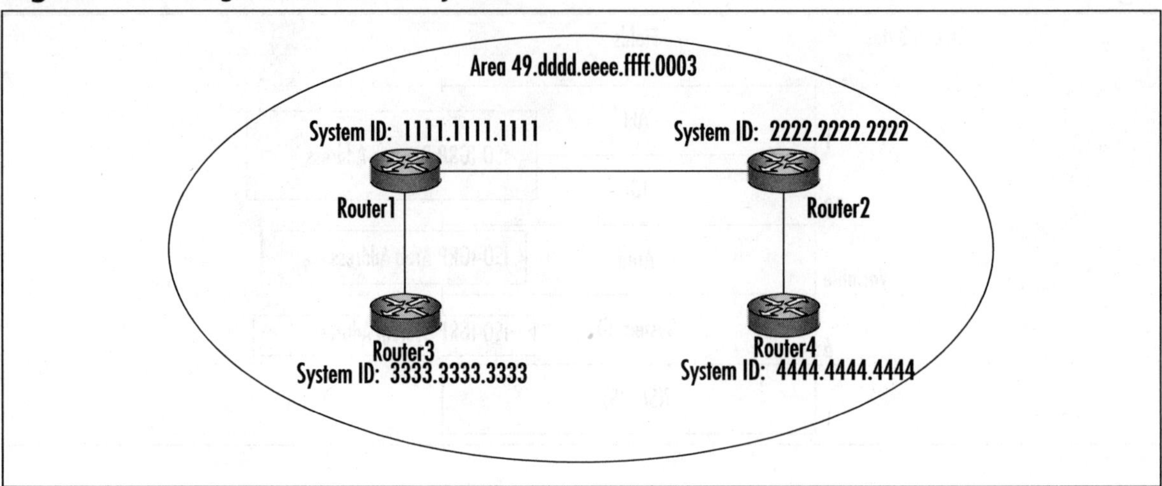

The following configurations are for each router in Figure 5.41. Notice that the routing process is configured, assigned a unique NET, and enabled on the appropriate interfaces.

Router1

```
clns routing
!
interface Serial0
 no ip address
 clns router isis area3
!
interface Serial1
 no ip address
 clns router isis area3
!
router isis area3
 net 49.dddd.eeee.ffff.0003.1111.1111.1111.00
```

Router2

```
clns routing
!
interface Serial0
 no ip address
 clns router isis area3
!
interface Serial1
 no ip address
 clns router isis area3
```

```
!
router isis area3
 net 49.dddd.eeee.ffff.0003.2222.2222.2222.00
```

Router3

```
clns routing
!
interface Serial0
 no ip address
 clns router isis area3
!
router isis area3
 net 49.dddd.eeee.ffff.0003.3333.3333.3333.00
```

Router4

```
clns routing
!
interface Serial0
 no ip address
 clns router isis area3
!
router isis area3
 net 49.dddd.eeee.ffff.0003.4444.4444.4444.00
```

Configuring Multi-area IS-IS.

The following demonstrates the necessary commands to configure multi-area IS-IS in Figure 5.42.

Figure 5.42 CLNS-Only Multi-Area IS-IS

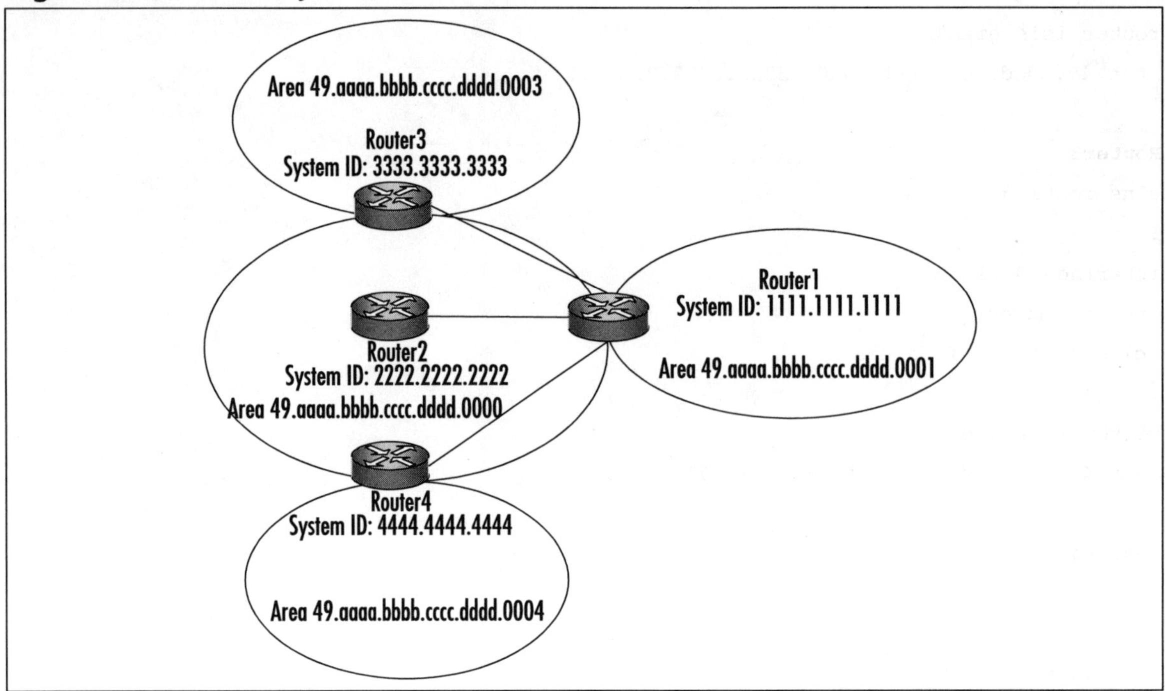

When you are reading through the configurations that follow, notice how area 49.aaaa.bbbb.cccc.dddd.0001 is an L2 area, thanks to Router1, which passes L2 updates through this area to all other routers, with the exception of Router2, which has all its links in the same area, and functions as a L1 router.

Router1

```
clns routing
cns event-service server
!
interface Serial0
 no ip address
 clns router isis area00
!
interface Serial1
 no ip address
 clns router isis area00
!
interface Serial2
 no ip address
 clns router isis area00

!
```

```
router isis area01
 net 49.aaaa.bbbb.cccc.dddd.0001.1111.1111.1111.00
 net 49.aaaa.bbbb.cccc.dddd.0000.1111.1111.1111.00
```

Router2

```
clns routing
!
interface Serial1
 no ip address
 clns router isis area00
!
router isis area00
 net 49.aaaa.bbbb.cccc.dddd.0000.2222.2222.2222.00
 net 49.aaaa.bbbb.cccc.dddd.0001.2222.2222.2222.00
```

Router3

```
clns routing
!
interface Loopback1
 no ip address
 clns router isis area03
!
interface Serial0
 no ip address
 clns router isis area01
!
router isis area00
 net 49.aaaa.bbbb.cccc.dddd.0001.3333.3333.3333.00
!
router isis area03
 net 49.aaaa.bbbb.cccc.dddd.0003.3333.3333.3333.00
 is-type level-1
```

Router4

```
clns routing
!
interface Loopback1
 no ip address
 clns router isis area04
!
```

```
interface Serial0
 no ip address
 clns router isis area04
!
router isis area04
 net 49.aaaa.bbbb.cccc.dddd.0001.4444.4444.4444.00
 net 49.aaaa.bbbb.cccc.dddd.0004.4444.4444.4444.00
```

Configuring Integrated IS-IS

We took you through the previous examples of configuring IS-IS for CLNS-only routing because it is a building block to using Integrated IS-IS to route IP. We now turn our attention to configuring Integrated IS-IS by turning on the IP routing features of IS-IS. The bulk of Integrated IS-IS configuration is the same as CLNS-only IS-IS with the interface command **ip router isis** enabled. This essentially makes IS-IS advertise that particular link (interface) to the rest of the IS-IS speakers.

Assuming that you have already assigned IP addresses to your interfaces, the process of enabling Integrated IS-IS then starts with **router isis**. While in IS-IS configuration mode, assign a NET to the IS. Finally, enable the actual advertisement of IP via the interface command **ip router isis**.

Single-Area Integrated IS-IS

Figure 5.43 shows the same single-area configuration we used in our CLNS-only IS-IS example. Notice that except for the IP addresses on each interface, and the **ip router isis** command, the configuration is almost the same. In our example, we have left the **clns router isis** command on each interface; this command routes CLNS. It is *not* necessary to the routing of IP.

Figure 5.43 Single-Area Integrated IS-IS

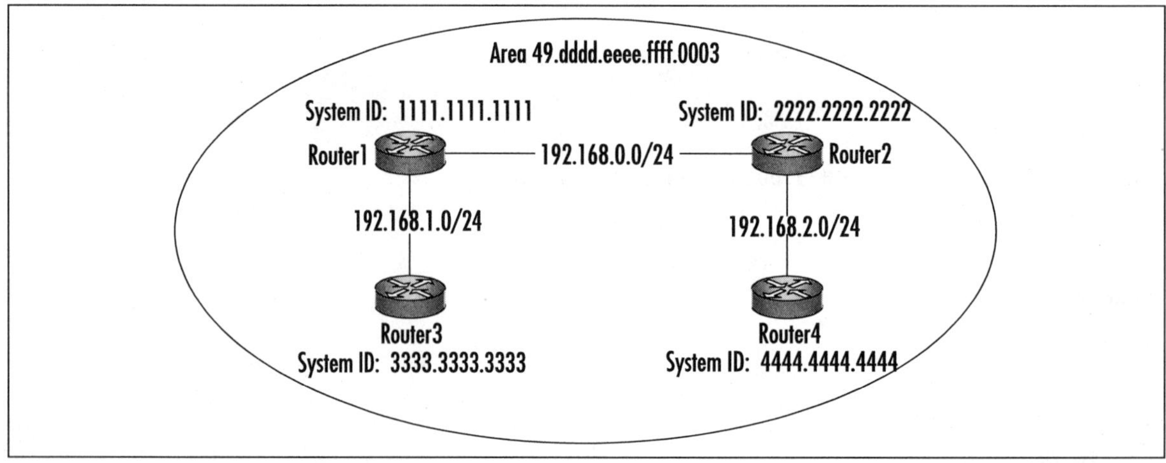


```
Router1
clns routing
```

```
!
interface Serial0
 ip address 192.168.1.1 255.255.255.0
 ip router isis
 clns router isis area3
!
interface Serial1
 ip address 192.168.0.1 255.255.255.0
 ip router isis
 clns router isis area3
!
router isis area3
 net 49.dddd.eeee.ffff.0003.1111.1111.1111.00
```

Router2

```
clns routing
!
interface Serial0
 ip address 192.168.0.2 255.255.255.0
 ip router isis
 clns router isis area3
!
interface Serial1
 ip address 192.168.2.2 255.255.255.0
 ip router isis
 clns router isis area3
!
router isis area3
 net 49.dddd.eeee.ffff.0003.2222.2222.2222.00
```

Router3

```
clns routing
!
interface Serial0
 ip address 192.168.1.2 255.255.255.0
 ip router isis
 clns router isis area3
!
router isis area3
 net 49.dddd.eeee.ffff.0003.3333.3333.3333.00
```

```
Router4
clns routing
!
interface Serial0
 ip address 192.168.2.1 255.255.255.0
 ip router isis
 clns router isis area3
!
router isis area3
 net 49.dddd.eeee.ffff.0003.4444.4444.4444.00
```

Multi-Area Integrated IS-IS

The process of configuring multi-area Integrated IS-IS follows the same steps as configuring multi-area CLNS, only using IS-IS. The biggest differences are the addition of IP addresses and the **ip router isis** command. Figure 5.44 and its configuration demonstrate this.

Figure 5.44 Multi-Area Integrated IS-IS

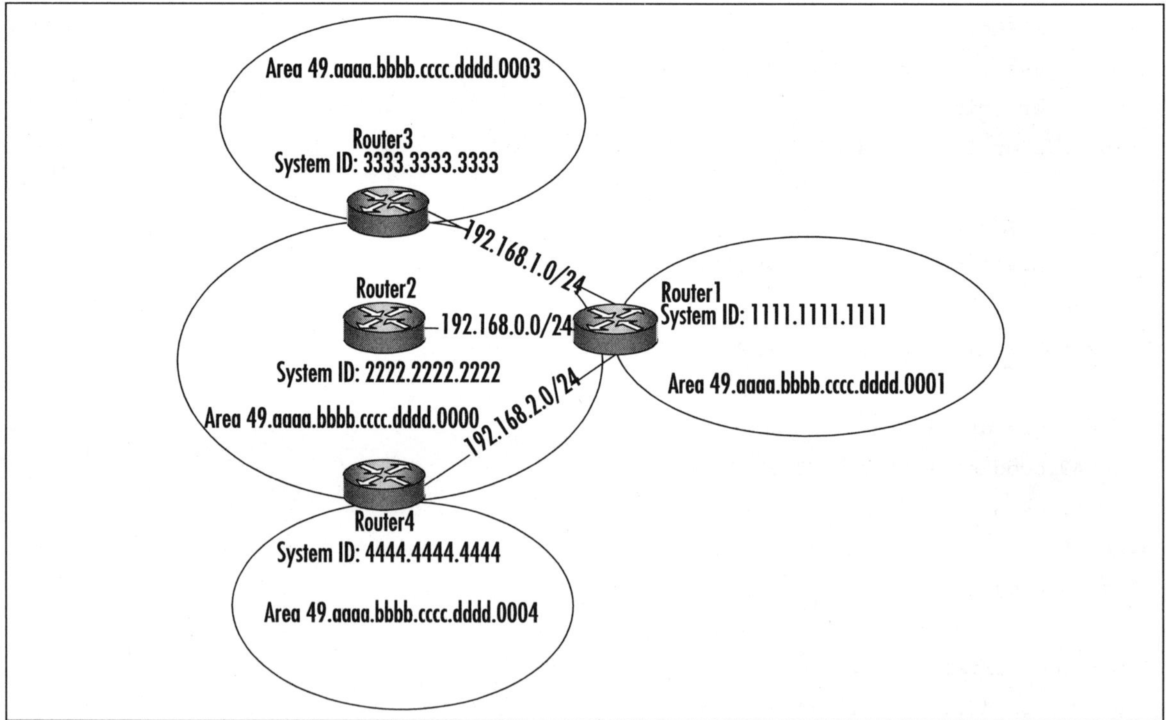


```
Router1
clns routing
!
interface Serial0
```

```
 description Connection to Router3
 ip address 192.168.1.1 255.255.255.0
 ip router isis
 clns router isis area00
!
interface Serial1
 description Connection to Router2
 ip address 192.168.0.1 255.255.255.0
 ip router isis
 clns router isis area00
!
interface Serial2
 description Connection to Router4
 ip address 192.168.2.1 255.255.255.0
 ip router isis
 clns router isis area00
!
router isis area00
 net 01.aaaa.bbbb.cccc.dddd.0001.1111.1111.1111.00
 net 02.aaaa.bbbb.cccc.dddd.0000.1111.1111.1111.00
 net 03.aaaa.bbbb.cccc.dddd.
```

Router2

```
clns routing
cns event-service server
!
interface Serial1
 description Connection to Router1
 ip address 192.168.0.2 255.255.255.0
 ip router isis
 clns router isis area02
!
router isis area02
 net 02.aaaa.bbbb.cccc.dddd.0000.2222.2222.2222.00
```

RouterC

```
clns routing
!
interface Loopback1
 no ip address
```

```
 clns router isis area03
!
interface Serial0
 ip address 192.168.1.2 255.255.255.0
 ip router isis
 clns router isis area00
!
router isis area00
 net 02.aaaa.bbbb.cccc.dddd.0000.3333.3333.3333.00
 net 03.aaaa.bbbb.cccc.dddd.0003.3333.3333.3333.00
!
router isis area03
 net 03.aaaa.bbbb.cccc.dddd.0003.3333.3333.3333.00
 is-type level-1
```

RouterD

```
clns routing
!
interface Loopback1
 no ip address
 clns router isis area04
!
interface Serial0
 ip address 192.168.2.2 255.255.255.0
 ip router isis
 clns router isis area04
!
router isis area04
 net 02.aaaa.bbbb.cccc.dddd.0000.4444.4444.4444.00
 net 03.aaaa.bbbb.cccc.dddd.0004.4444.4444.4444.00
```

Monitoring IS-IS

Cisco provides many commands and facilities for monitoring and troubleshooting IS-IS. Several of these commands and their output are shown in the following example. Some of these commands are not necessarily specific to IS-IS; instead, they provide information about CLNS, but knowing them can help verify and troubleshoot IS-IS.

```
Router3# show isis database ?
  WORD      LSPID in the form of xxxx.xxxx.xxxx.xx-xx or name.xx-xx
  detail    Detailed link state database information
  l1        IS-IS Level-1 routing link state database
```

```
  l2        IS-IS Level-2 routing link state database
  level-1   IS-IS Level-1 routing link state database
  level-2   IS-IS Level-2 routing link state database
  verbose   Verbose database information
  |         Output modifiers
```

You can view the details and contents of the IS-IS database as shown.

```
router3# show isis database
Area area00:
IS-IS Level-1 Link State Database:
LSPID                 LSP Seq Num  LSP Checksum  LSP Holdtime      ATT/P/OL
routerA.00-00         0x00000008   0x0836        1096              1/0/0
2222.2222.2222.00-00  0x00000009   0x6362        557               0/0/0
routerC.00-00       * 0x00000005   0xE1BF        554               1/0/0
IS-IS Level-2 Link State Database:
LSPID                 LSP Seq Num  LSP Checksum  LSP Holdtime      ATT/P/OL
routerA.00-00         0x00000002   0x0AF7        556               0/0/0
2222.2222.2222.00-00  0x00000007   0xCADD        557               0/0/0
routerC.00-00       * 0x00000003   0x31C1        560               0/0/0

Area area03:
IS-IS Level-1 Link State Database:
LSPID                 LSP Seq Num  LSP Checksum  LSP Holdtime      ATT/P/OL
routerC.00-00       * 0x00000004   0x0175        560               1/0/0
```

Details of the IS-IS topology are available as well.

```
Router3# show isis topology
Area area00:
IS-IS paths to level-1 routers
System Id        Metric  Next-Hop          Interface        SNPA
routerA          20      2222.2222.2222    Se0              *HDLC*
2222.2222.2222   10      2222.2222.2222    Se0              *HDLC*
routerC          --

IS-IS paths to level-2 routers
System Id        Metric  Next-Hop          Interface        SNPA
routerA          20      2222.2222.2222    Se0              *HDLC*
2222.2222.2222   10      2222.2222.2222    Se0              *HDLC*
routerC          --

Area area03:
IS-IS paths to level-1 routers
System Id        Metric  Next-Hop          Interface        SNPA
```

All the routing protocols discussed previously were designed to handle intra-AS routing. To route effectively between different ASs requires a routing protocol such as BGP.

Border Gateway Protocol (BGP)

BGP is "the" exterior gateway protocol for routing between ASs, and between an AS and the Internet. BGP is a path vector protocol, meaning that it routes AS by AS, rather than by hop or by link. BGP updates are unicast to TCP port 179, meaning that it depends on TCP to recover from network errors.

The current version is BGPv4, which is the focus of this section. Entire books have been written about BGP, and some network engineers do nothing but BGP in their full-time career. All of this is testament to the importance and complexity of BGP. Our intent in this section is to provide with you an overview of BGP, and enough information that you can configure its fundamental features.

BGP can advertise classless routes that do not fall on a strict classful boundary. This support of CIDR enables BGP to shrink routing tables and to consolidate multiple routes into a single advertisement. Before we discuss the configuration of BGP on Cisco routers, we need to cover several key BGP concepts and terms.

BGP Terminology

The following terms are bandied about when dealing with BGP.

- **Interior BGP (IBGP)** BGP between routers in the same AS. The peering process and exchange of routes are different from EBGP.
- **Exterior BGP (EBGP)** BGP between routers in different ASs.
- **Prefix** Consolidation of multiple routes into a single advertisement.
- **Peers** Two BGP routers that have become neighbors for the purpose of exchanging routing information.

Figure 5.45 illustrates IBGP and EBGP. Router1 and Router4 are in the same AS (65003), and are IGBP peers. Router1, Router2, and Router3 are in different ASs, making them EBGP peers.

Figure 5.45 Interior and Exterior BGP

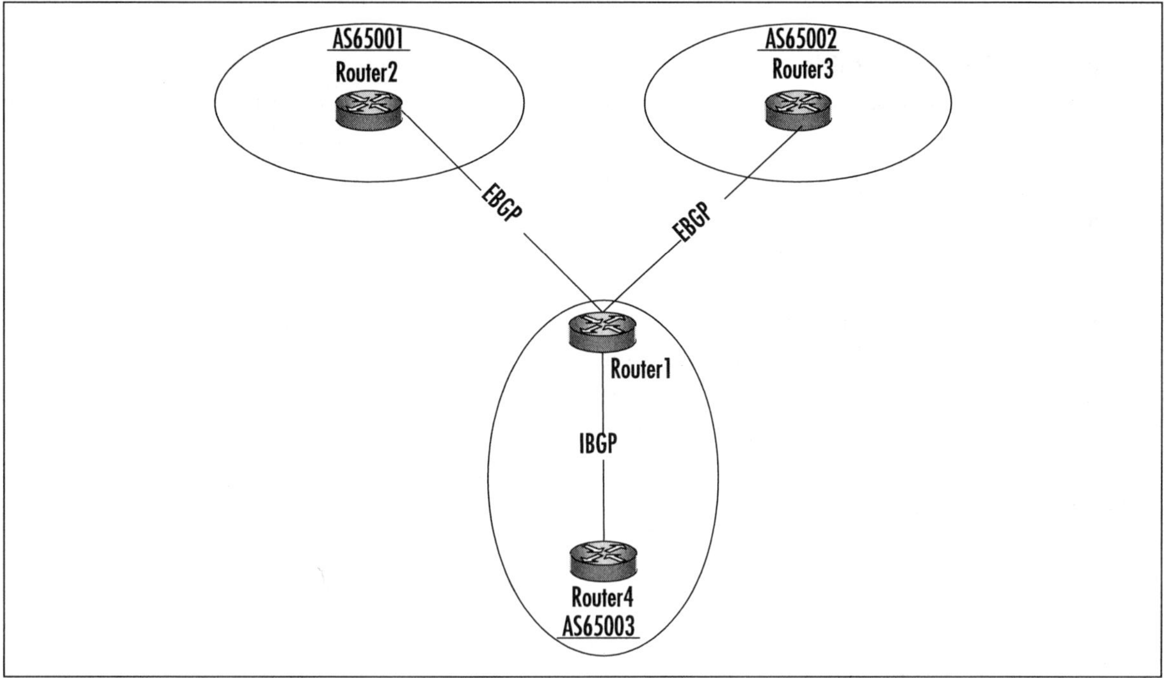

BGP Concepts

BGP operates by routers peering with each other over a TCP connection (port 179). This peering is necessary to enable the routers to exchange BGP routes. The peering can be IBGP (same AS) or EBGP (different AS), as previously discussed. Cisco routers running BGP can be in only one AS, which is identified by its AS number (ASN), both public and private. Private ASN can be used if a public ASN is not needed, or to do internal BGP routing.

EBGP peers must be directly connected. IBGP peers do not have to be directly connected, but the router must have a route to its IBGP peer in its routing table via an IGP or static route. EBGP can forego being directly connected in special circumstances, but must use a special multihop command provided by Cisco for such a configuration.

The propagation of information differs by the peering type. EBGP peers by default share all information they receive from their peers, whereas IBGP peers will not advertise any IBGP information to other IBGP peers, although they will share it with their EBGP peers.

Since BGP typically has a vast amount of routes to support, stability is its number-one goal. Features such as route dampening that penalizes flapping routes are used to minimize updates caused by network problems.

BGP will not advertise any prefix (supernetted or not) unless it has at least one route within the routing table; that prefix can be learned via IBGP or EBGP, IGP, or other means, but it must be present in the table to be advertised via BGP. This requirement is called synchronization, which is enabled by default; Cisco provides a knob (no synchronization) to turn it off, meaning that BGP will advertise regardless of whether it has the prefix in its table or not. BGP uses the following tables to store its information.

- **Neighbor table** Used to host information on each neighbor (view with the **show ip bgp neighbor** command).
- **BGP Routing table** Contains routes learned by BGP, including suppressed routes to the same destination deemed not to be the best. Such routes will replace the "best" route should its next hop become unreachable. View with **show ip bgp**. It also stores routes that were dampened for any reason.
- **IP Routing table** Not a BGP-specific table, but does have the best route to a destination injected into it by BGP and other routing protocols.

BGP uses a very strict process to choose the best route to add to the routing table as illustrated in Figure 5.46. BGP uses attributes (described in the figure) to make decisions at each point between competing routes. One or more alternative routes to a destination will be stored in the BGP routing table, while the best route will be used in the main routing table, as shown.

Figure 5.46 BGP Route Selection Process

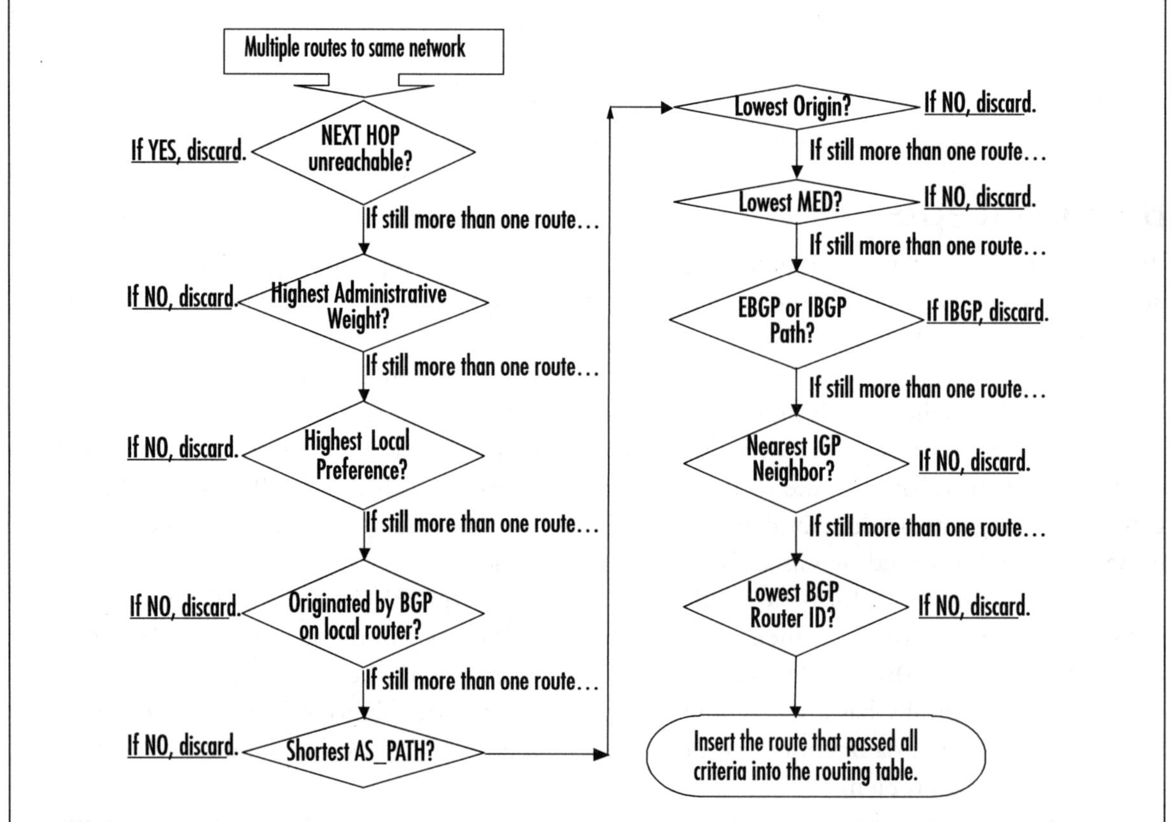

Configuring BGP

To enable BGP, you must identify the BGP process, and remember that the process is tied to your ASN. If you are going to route traffic on the Internet or with other external ASs, you must use an official ASN number assigned to you by ARIN (www.apnic.net/services/asn_guide.html). Recall that BGP uses the ASN to route. If you are only using BGP internally (that is, will not be peering with any AS outside your control), then you can use a private ASN in the range of 64512 through 65535. As with private IP addresses, you can use and assign these as you want. Cisco routers can strip these numbers and use a public ASN should you later need to peer with an external AS.

Bare Minimum BGP—EBGP

The bare minimum you need to enable BGP is to identify the process and at least one neighbor, as shown here. Notice that we are using private ASN in our examples based on the network in Figure 5.47.

NOTE

Only one AS per router translates to one BGP process per router.

Figure 5.47 Minimum BGP

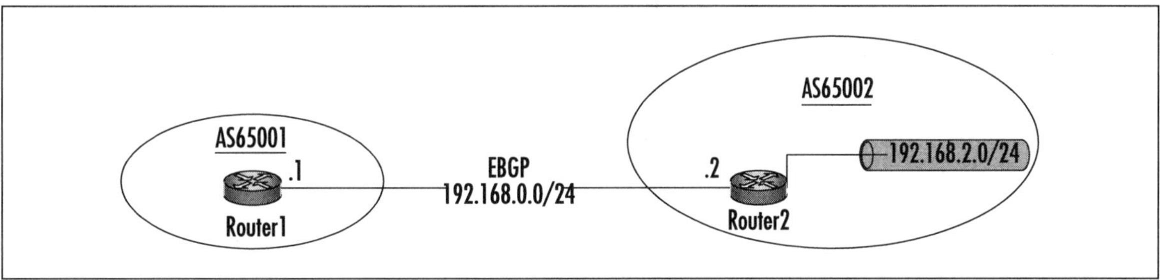

Router1

```
router bgp 65001
neighbor 192.168.0.2 remote-as 64002
```

Router2

```
router bgp 64002
neighbor 192.168.0.1 remote-as 65535
network 192.168.2.0 mask 255.255.255.0
```

This establishes an EBGP peering between Router1 and Router2. Router1 will receive 192.168.2.0/16 from Router2, but will not route via BGP. It is not required that the common network between two peers be advertised or participate in the BGP routing process, unlike most IGPs.

Bare Minimum BGP—IGBP

IBGP, as mentioned earlier, is the establishment of BGP peering relationships between routers in the same AS. Recall that an IBGP peer will not share (advertise) any routes it learns via IBGP with any of its IBGP peers. As a result, all IBGP peers must be fully meshed as shown in Figure 5.48, a requirement that can become unmanageable as the number of peers increases.

Figure 5.48 IBGP Peering

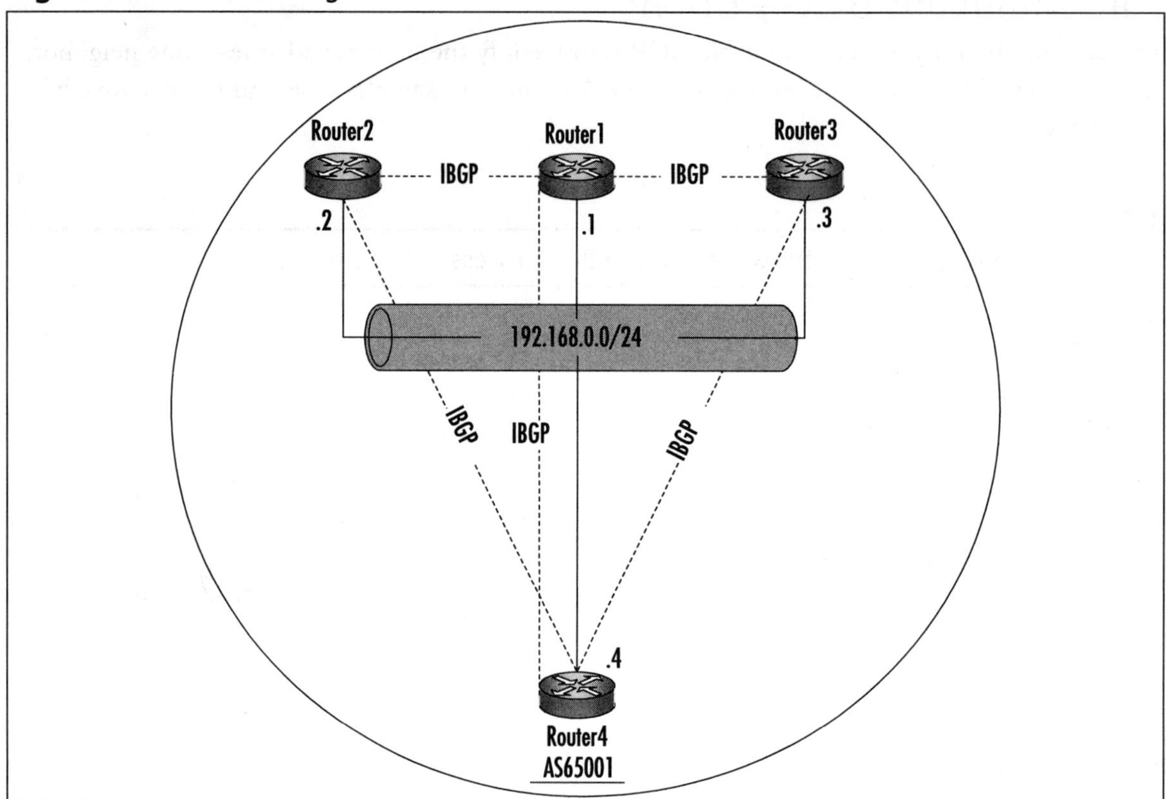

In Figure 5.48, there are four routers, and each has to have an IBGP peering statement to three other routers in order for IBGP to be effective (indicated by the dashed lines), and to ensure that all the routers have all the IBGP routes. The configuration for Figure 5.48 is provided to illustrate the amount of effort required to execute this design. We turned on synchronization here to decrease the time to get the route into the routing table. On Router1, we used the **neighbor** command with its **description** keyword, which enables us to associate a descriptive string of text to the neighbor.

Router1

```
interface Ethernet0
 ip address 192.168.0.1 255.255.255.0
!
router bgp 65001
```

```
 no synchronization
 bgp log-neighbor-changes
 network 192.168.1.0
 neighbor 192.168.0.2 description Router2
 neighbor 192.168.0.2 remote-as 65001
 neighbor 192.168.0.3 description Router3
 neighbor 192.168.0.3 remote-as 65001
 neighbor 192.168.0.4 description Router4
 neighbor 192.168.0.4 remote-as 65001
```

Router2

```
interface Ethernet0
 ip address 192.168.0.2 255.255.255.0
!
router bgp 65001
 no synchronization
 bgp log-neighbor-changes
 network 192.168.1.0
 neighbor 192.168.0.1 remote-as 65001
 neighbor 192.168.0.3 remote-as 65001
 neighbor 192.168.0.4 remote-as 65001
```

Router3

```
interface Ethernet0
 ip address 192.168.0.3 255.255.255.0
!
router bgp 65001
 no synchronization
 bgp log-neighbor-changes
 network 192.168.1.0
 neighbor 192.168.0.1 remote-as 65001
 neighbor 192.168.0.2 remote-as 65001
 neighbor 192.168.0.4 remote-as 65001
```

Router4

```
interface Ethernet0
 ip address 192.168.0.4 255.255.255.0
!
router bgp 65001
 no synchronization
 bgp log-neighbor-changes
 network 192.168.1.0
 neighbor 192.168.0.1 remote-as 65001
```

```
neighbor 192.168.0.2 remote-as 65001
neighbor 192.168.0.3 remote-as 65001
```

This is a fairly sizable configuration for a very small IBGP network. Imagine if this was a network with even more routers…the configuration and management effort would be much greater. Fortunately, Cisco offers several techniques for controlling IBGP peering, such as route reflectors or confederations.

Route Reflectors

Route reflectors are a solution to reducing the number of IBGP peers needed to stabilize and synchronize routing. Recall that IBGP peers do not advertise the routes of other IBGP peers by default, yet all IBGP peers must have each other's prefixes to maintain a consistent routing picture. However, in a network of significant size, the number of IBGP peers can become unmanageable.

Route reflectors will pass the routing information that they receive from an IBGP peer, and pass it (reflect it) to other IBGP peers in the AS. All IBGP peers will peer only with the route reflect, rather than with every IBGP router in the AS. Only the route reflector needs to be configured; all other routers (called router reflector clients, to use the lingo correctly) are configured to peer with the route reflector.

Figure 5.49 shows the design and configuration of the previous example; only this time, Router1 is a route reflector. Notice how much this has lessened our configuration requirements.

Figure 5.49 IBGP—Route Reflector

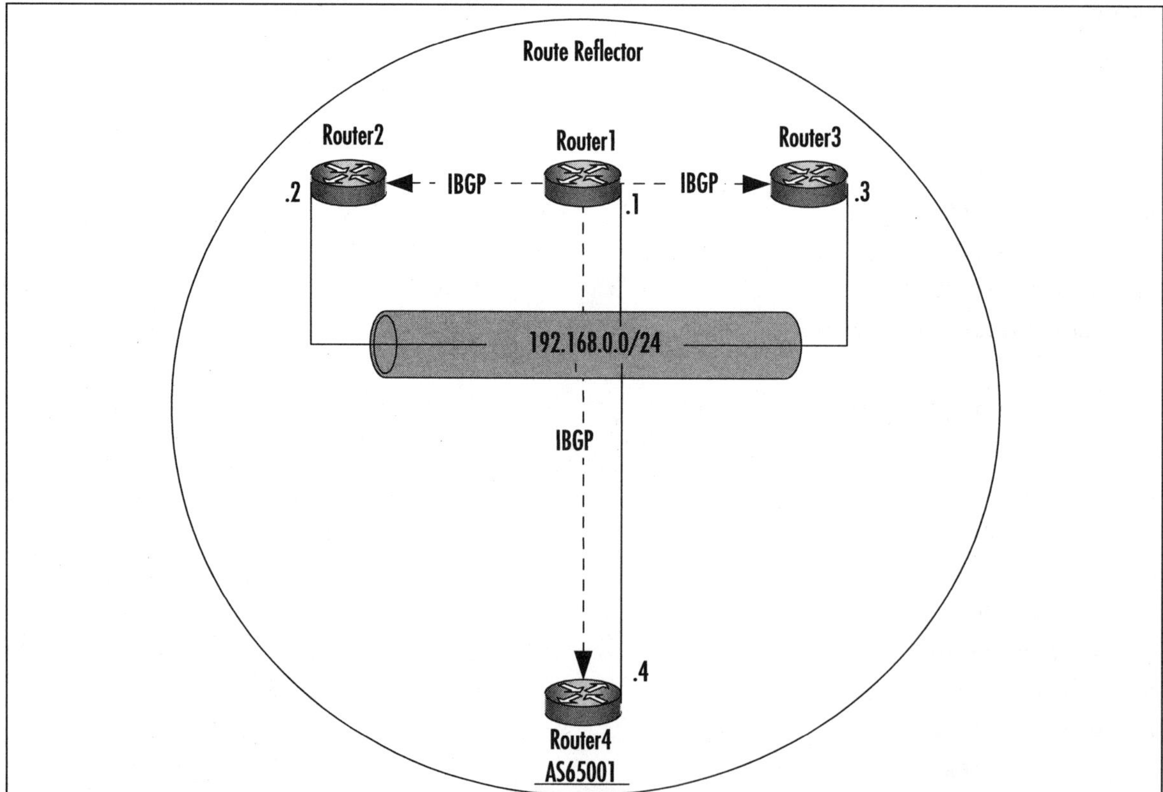

Router1

```
interface Ethernet0
 ip address 192.168.0.1 255.255.255.0
!
router bgp 65001
 no synchronization
 bgp log-neighbor-changes
 network 192.168.1.0
 neighbor 192.168.0.2 description Router2
 neighbor 192.168.0.2 remote-as 65001
 neighbor 192.168.0.2 route-reflector-client
 neighbor 192.168.0.3 description Router3
 neighbor 192.168.0.3 remote-as 65001
 neighbor 192.168.0.3 route-reflector-client
 neighbor 192.168.0.4 description Router4
 neighbor 192.168.0.4 remote-as 65001
 neighbor 192.168.0.4 route-reflector-client
```

Router2

```
interface Ethernet0
 ip address 192.168.0.2 255.255.255.0
!
router bgp 65001
 no synchronization
 bgp log-neighbor-changes
 network 192.168.1.0
 neighbor 192.168.0.1 remote-as 65001
```

Router3

```
interface Ethernet0
 ip address 192.168.0.3 255.255.255.0
!
router bgp 65001
 no synchronization
 bgp log-neighbor-changes
 network 192.168.1.0
 neighbor 192.168.0.1 remote-as 65001
```

Router4

```
interface Ethernet0
 ip address 192.168.0.4 255.255.255.0
!
router bgp 65001
```

```
no synchronization
bgp log-neighbor-changes
network 192.168.1.0
neighbor 192.168.0.1 remote-as 65001
```

As you can see, route reflectors "reflect" prefixes learned from one IBGP peer to another IBGP peer. Notice how the number of IBGP peers has been reduced in this simple scenario. As the configuration shows, route reflectors are enacted with the **neighbor a.b.c.d route-reflector-client** for each client of the route reflector, and only on the route reflector.

BGP Confederations

Confederations are another technique to reduce the amount of IBGP peering by building an AS within an AS. These confederations ASs are used to peer with other confederation ASs. This essentially creates a holding AS used to interface with other ASs on behalf of the AS group. Figure 5.50 shows AS65001 that has grouped Router1 and Router3 into confederation AS65011, and Router2 and Router4 into AS65021.

Router1 (AS65011) and Router2 (AS65021) are EBGP peers on behalf of their confederation. Notice that where we previously had three IBGP peer statements per router, we now have a total of two for the entire network, plus one EBGP peer relationship. The EBGP peers will share whatever routing information they obtain with any IBGP peers they have.

Figure 5.50 BGP Confederation

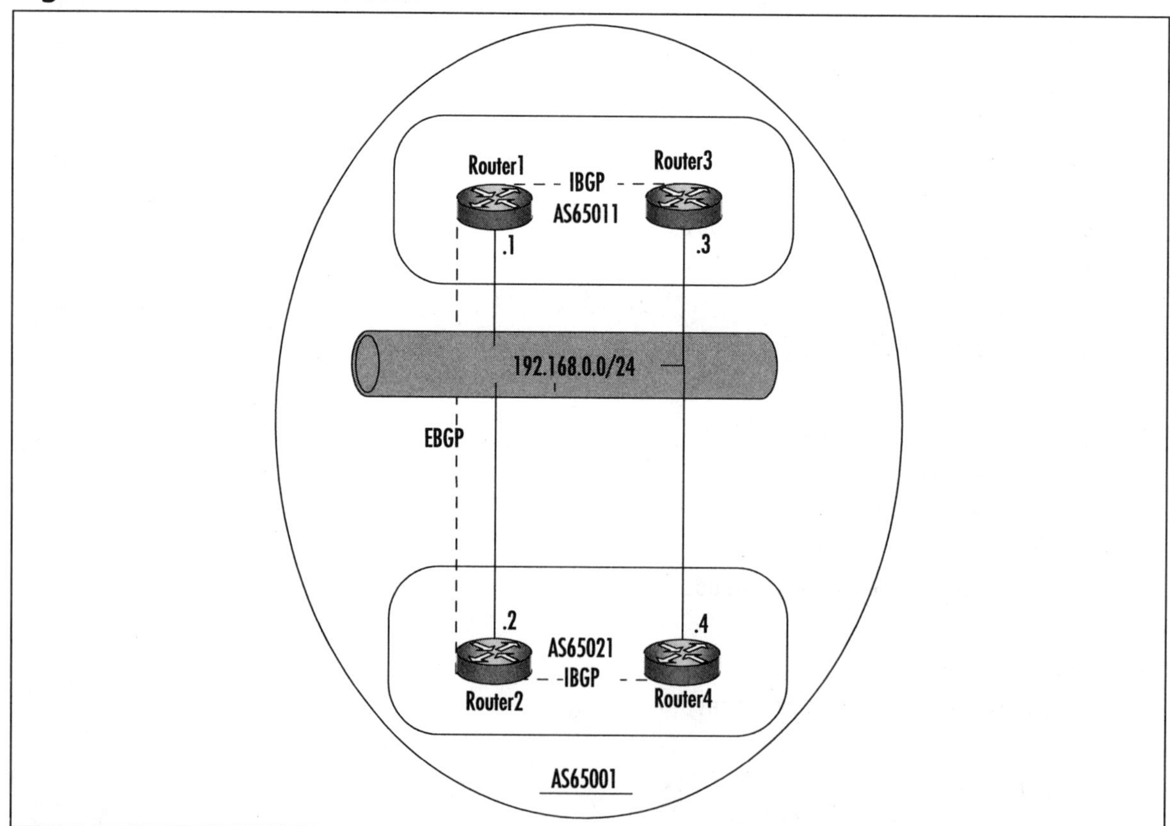

The following creates the necessary configuration to support the BGP design in Figure 5.50.

Router1

```
interface Ethernet0
 ip address 192.168.0.1 255.255.255.0
!
router bgp 65011
 bgp log-neighbor-changes
 bgp confederation identifier 65001
 bgp confederation peers 65021
 neighbor 192.168.0.3 remote-as 65011
 neighbor 192.168.0.2 remote-as 65021
 no auto-summary
```

Router2

```
interface Ethernet0
 ip address 192.168.0.2 255.255.255.0
!
router bgp 65021
 bgp log-neighbor-changes
 bgp confederation identifier 65001
 bgp confederation peers 65011
 neighbor 192.168.0.1 remote-as 65011
 neighbor 192.168.0.4 remote-as 65021
 no auto-summary
```

Router3

```
interface Ethernet0
 ip address 192.168.0.3 255.255.255.0
!
router bgp 65011
 bgp log-neighbor-changes
 bgp confederation identifier 65001
 neighbor 192.168.0.1 remote-as 65011
 no auto-summary
```

Router4

```
interface Ethernet0
 ip address 192.168.0.4 255.255.255.0
!
router bgp 65021
 bgp log-neighbor-changes
 bgp confederation identifier 65001
 neighbor 192.168.0.2 remote-as 65021
 no auto-summary
```

The **bgp confederation peers** command only needs to be entered on routers that have an EBGP relationship within this confederation. The **bgp confederation identifier** needs to be entered on all routers in the confederation.

Filtering

Prefixes in BGP can be filtered using the **distribute-list** command shown here, where the peer in AS65001 is filtering routes in both directions for AS65001 and AS65003. The **distribute-list** points to an ACL composed of deny and permit statements.

The **distribute-list** is configured under BGP. You can reference an ACL, which we will do in our example here.

```
Router1(config-router)# distribute-list ?
  <1-199>        IP access list number
  <1300-2699>   IP expanded access list number
  WORD           Access-list name
  gateway        Filtering incoming updates based on gateway
  prefix        Filter prefixes in routing updates


Router1(config-router)# distribute-list 99 ?
  in    Filter incoming routing updates
  out   Filter outgoing routing updates
EXAMPLE
access-list 99 permit 192.168.0.0 0.0.255.255
access-list 99 deny any
neighbor 192.168.0.2 distribute-list 99 out
neighbor 192.168.0.4 distribute-list 99 in
```

Deny means do not advertise, while permit allows the specified routes to be advertised to (out) or received from (in) a particular neighbor.

You can also implement a global filter by not tying the **distribute-list** to a specific neighbor, something that we did not do in this case; otherwise, the command would have been **distribute-list 99 out**.

There are also other filtering techniques beyond the scope of this chapter, but worth mentioning here. There is **ip as-path** and community filtering, enacted as shown.

```
Router1(config)# ip as-path access-list 99 ?
  deny     Specify packets to reject
  permit   Specify packets to forward
```

At the end of the **ip as-path** statement, you would specify a regular expression to match certain AS paths.

Community filtering is accomplished with route maps that permit or deny matching certain attributes. You can also use route maps to manipulate the attributes of routes. For more information about route filtering and control in BGP, see www.cisco.com/en/US/partner/products/sw/iosswrel/ps1835/products_command_reference_chapter09186a00800ca79d.html.

Summarization

BGP can summarize multiple routing advertisements into a single update using BGPs consolidation effort. This is made possible with the use of the **aggregate address** command.

```
Given:
172.16.0.0
172.17.0.0
172.18.0.0
172.19.0.0

aggregate-address 172.16.0.0 255.252.0.0  summary-only
```

In our example, we are summarizing four networks into one prefix, a reduction of 75 percent, and are advertising the summary only. There many more options with this command as shown here.

```
Router1(config-router)# aggregate-address 172.16.0.0 255.252.0.0 ?
  advertise-map  Set condition to advertise attribute
  as-set          Generate AS set path information
  attribute-map  Set attributes of aggregate
  nlri            Nlri aggregate applies to
  route-map       Set parameters of aggregate
  summary-only   Filter more specific routes from updates
  suppress-map   Conditionally filter more specific routes from updates
  <cr>
```

BGP Security

Cisco BGP supports neighbor authentication, a good way to decrease the likelihood that a rogue or unauthorized router will peer with your router, and inject bad routing information into its tables. This is a simple MD5 password authentication configured as shown with the following command. It must be configured on both authenticating peers, or BGP will fail between the neighbors.

```
router bgp 65001
neighbor 192.168.0.1 password THIS_IS_THE_MD5_PASSWORD
```

Just as important as configuring is being able to monitor and troubleshoot BGP.

Monitoring and Verifying BGP

Cisco provides several commands that you can use to view and monitor all aspects of BGP operations. View the contents of the BGP routing table with **show ip bgp**.

```
Router1# show ip bgp
BGP table version is 10229354, local router ID is 216.117.84.1
Status codes: s suppressed, d damped, h history, * valid, > best, i - internal
Origin codes: i - IGP, e - EGP, ? - incomplete

   Network          Next Hop            Metric LocPrf Weight Path
 h 192.168.0.0      192.168.3.146        1098             0 209 7018 80 i
 h                   192.168.160.254      4363    100      0 (64520) 701 1 3356 7018
80 i
*  192.168.236.0/22 192.168.160.254      1839    100      0 (64520) 701 1 3356 3561 i
*>                   192.168.3.146        1101             0 209 3561 i
*  192.168.0.0      192.168.160.254              100      0 (64520) 701 1 i
*>                   192.168.3.146        1098             0 209 3356 i
*> 192.168.225.0/24 192.168.3.146        1098             0 209 1239 11853 6496 i
*> 192.168.226.0/23 192.168.3.146        1098             0 209 1239 11853 6496 i
*> 192.168.251.0/24 192.168.3.146        1101             0 209 3561 11853 6496 i
*> 192.168.252.0/23 192.168.3.146        1101             0 209 3561 11853 6496 I
```

To check the status of your BGP neighbors:

```
BGP neighbor is 192.168.160.254, remote AS 64520, external link
 Description: router2.fortwayne
 Index 2, Offset 0, Mask 0x4
  NEXT_HOP is always this router
  BGP version 4, remote router ID 192.168.11.193
  Neighbor under common administration
  BGP state = Established, table version = 10229698, up for 12w3d
  Last read 00:00:13, last send 00:00:24
  Hold time 180, keepalive interval 60 seconds
  Neighbor NLRI negotiation:
    Configured for unicast routes only
    Peer negotiated unicast routes only
    Exchanging unicast routes only
  Received route refresh capability from peer
(omitted for brevity)
```

You can get specific and determine what you are advertising to a neighbor, which is useful for determining why a route is not appearing in the neighbor's tables.

```
Router# show ip bgp neighbors 192.168.160.254 advertised-routes
   Network          Next Hop            Metric LocPrf Weight Path
*> 192.168.236.0/22   192.168.3.146        1101             0 209 3561 i
*> 192.168.0.0           192.168.3.146        1098             0 209 3356 i
```

```
*> 192.168.225.0/24    192.168.3.146        1098             0 209 1239 11853 6496
i
*> 192.168.226.0/23    192.168.3.146        1098             0 209 1239 11853 6496
i
*> 192.168.251.0/24    192.168.3.146        1101             0 209 3561 11853 6496
i
*> 192.168.252.0/23    192.168.3.146        1101             0 209 3561 11853 6496
I
```

What prefixes have been summarized? Use the following command:

```
Router1# show ip bgp 192.168.0.0/8 longer-prefixes
BGP table version is 10229889, local router ID is 192.168.84.1
Status codes: s suppressed, d damped, h history, * valid, > best, i - internal
Origin codes: i - IGP, e - EGP, ? - incomplete

   Network          Next Hop            Metric LocPrf Weight Path
*  192.168.0.0      192.168.160.254       1839    100      0 (64520) 701 1 3356 7018
i
*>                  192.168.3.146         1098             0 209 7018 i
*  192.168.19.0/24 192.168.160.254       1839    100      0 (64520) 701 1 3356 7018
27487 i
*>                  192.168.3.146         1101             0 209 3561 27487 i
*  192.168.48.0/20  192.168.160.254       1839    100      0 (64520) 701 1 3356 174
16631 1742 I
```

Other **show** commands associated with BGP are summarized in the following output table:

```
Router1# show ip bgp ?
  A.B.C.D            IP prefix <network>/<length>, e.g., 35.0.0.0/8
  A.B.C.D            Network in the BGP routing table to display
  cidr-only          Display only routes with non-natural netmasks
  community          Display routes matching the communities
  community-list     Display routes matching the community-list
  dampened-paths     Display paths suppressed due to dampening
  filter-list        Display routes conforming to the filter-list
  flap-statistics    Display flap statistics of routes
  inconsistent-as    Display only routes with inconsistent origin ASs
  neighbors          Detailed information on TCP and BGP neighbor connections
  paths              Path information
  peer-group         Display information on peer-groups
  quote-regexp       Display routes matching the AS path "regular expression"
  regexp             Display routes matching the AS path regular expression
  summary            Summary of BGP neighbor status
  |                  Output modifiers
```

Dial-on-Demand Routing

Dial-on-Demand Routing (DDR) is a technology that routers use to dynamically initiate and close a circuit-switched session to remote routers on demand. Once these sessions have been connected, data as well as routing updates can be exchanged between routers. For the router to initiate this session, it must first know when to dial. This is done through what is called *interesting traffic*. Once the call has been established, data can pass to the other end. The DDR session is typically not broken until there is a period of inactivity called *idle-time*. Multiple locations can be configured to dial based on routing destination. Several features built into DDR enhance its operation.

DDR typically runs on an as-needed basis, meaning that the session is not established until necessary. By running DDR on an as-needed basis, companies can save significant toll costs. DDR operates over circuit switched networks like ISDN and public switched telephone network (PSTN). Some of the methods using DDR are legacy DDR, dialer profiles, dial backup, and snapshot routing.

Static and Default Routes

Static routing is the simplest of the DDR routing options. Configuring static routing for DDR is the same as configuring static routing for any other Cisco interface. The command **ip route *destination-address subnetmask next-hop-address*** will configure a static route on the router. For static routing to function, the remote network must also have a route back to you.

Assuming that you have configured ISDN to back up and track your primary interface, you can create a floating static route (which can be specific or default) with the next hop to the dialer interface. The command to accomplish this is provided; notice the high administrative distance for this route, which ensures that it will not be injected into the routing table until the primary route fails.

```
ip route 0.0.0.0 0.0.0.0 Serial0
ip route 0.0.0.0 0.0.0.0 Dialer0 250
```

When serial 0 fails, ISDN will initiate and bring Dialer0 online, which will result in the floating static route becoming active.

Snapshot Routing

Static routing works well on small networks and in areas where a DDR link is the end of a routed network (stub network). If you have a medium-sized network, maintaining the static routing table can be time consuming and tedious. Snapshot routing is one method of overcoming the shortfalls of static routing.

Snapshot routing allows dynamic routing protocols to run across DDR links without requiring the line to remain connected. Snapshot routing works by having an active period when the link is active and routing information passed between neighboring routers, and then having a quiet period when the routing tables are frozen. The active period can be initiated by either user data triggering the DDR link, or by the quiet period timer expiring. Once in the active period, both routers exchange routing information, updating their routing tables. After the active period, the link is terminated, and the routers enter the quiet period and freeze their routing tables. Once the quiet period begins, a timer starts counting down to zero. As soon as the timer hits zero, the routers enter the active state and initiate a DDR connection. Both the active and quiet periods are user-configurable values.

Snapshot routing supports all periodic update routing protocols:

- Internet Protocol–Routing Information Protocol (IP–RIP)
- Interior Gateway Routing Protocol (IGRP)
- Internetwork Packet Exchange–RIP (IPX–RIP)
- Service Advertising Protocol (SAP)
- AppleTalk–Routing Table Maintenance Protocol (RTMP)
- Vines–Routing Table Protocol (RTP)

Snapshot routing does not support link state routing protocols because of the way they exchange routing information. Link state protocols—IS-IS, Open Shortest Path First (OSPF), and NetWare Link Service Protocol (NLSP)—exchange information between neighboring routers every 5 to 10 seconds. This update period would essentially require the link to remain active indefinitely for the routing protocol to function properly. Snapshot routing has been designed to work for hub-and-spoke and point-to-point topologies. For the dialer parameter to function, you need to configure a dialer map for snapshot routing.

To configure snapshot routing, configure the routing protocol and DDR interface as normal. Additionally, use the **snapshot server** ***active-time*** **[dialer]** interface command on the dialed router, and the **snapshot client** ***active-time*** **quiet-time [suppress-statechange-updates] [dialer]** interface command on the dialing router.

- **Active time** 5 to 100 minutes.
- **Quiet time** 8 to 100,000 minutes.
- **Dialer optional** Allows the router to dial if not already connected.
- **Optional parameter suppress-statechange-updates** Prevents the routers from exchanging routing updates during a connection established by interesting traffic.

Route Redistribution

When configuring DDR networks, it is important to remember to redistribute the remote networks into the rest of your network. However after the DDR network is configured, it is recommended that you redistribute the static, OSPF on-demand, or snapshot networks into the rest of your network. To do this, use the redistribute **routing-protocol** command within the primary network routing protocol process.

Configuring Snapshot Routing and Route Redistribution

Snapshot routing requires several tasks to be completed in order to offer proper network support. This includes setting up ISDN, determining what is to be routed, and so on. The configuration (Figure 5.51) for Router1 and Router2 show a BRI-to-BRI configuration using snapshot routing and route redistribution. In this example, both router configurations are shown.

Figure 5.51 Snapshot Routing with Route Redistribution

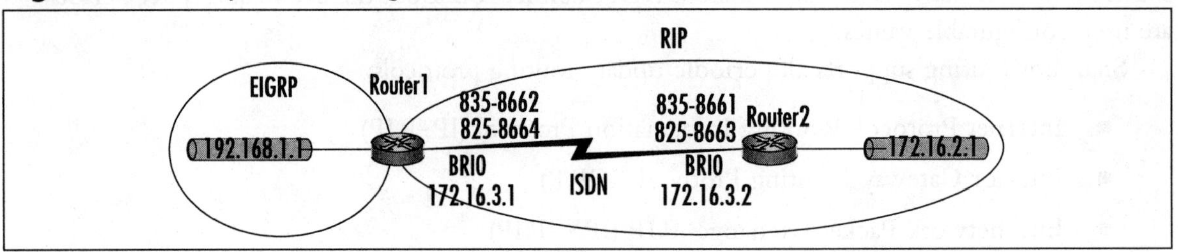


```
Router1 (client)
isdn switch-type basic-ni1
dialer-list 1 protocol ip permit
!
interface Ethernet0
ip address 192.1681.1 255.255.255.0
!
interface BRI0
ip address 172.16.3.1 255.255.255.252
encapsulation ppp
bandwidth 128
dialer map ip 172.16.3.2 name Router2 broadcast 8358661
dialer map snapshot 1 name Router2 broadcast 8358661
dialer load-threshold 127 either
dialer-group 1
isdn spid1 0835866201
isdn spid2 0835866401
snapshot client 10 13 dialer
ppp multilink
!
router eigrp 6243
redistribute rip metric 64 10 255 127 1500
network 192.168.1.0

router rip
version 2
redistribute eigrp 6243 metric 2
network 172.16.0.0
neighbor 172.16.3.2

hostname Router2
isdn switch-type basic-ni1
```

```
dialer-list 1 protocol ip permit
!
interface Ethernet0
ip address 172.16.2.1 255.255.255.0
!
interface BRI0
ip address 172.16.3.2 255.255.255.252
encapsulation ppp
bandwidth 128
dialer map ip 172.16.3.1 name Router1 broadcast 8358662
dialer map snapshot 1 name Router1 broadcast 8358662
dialer load-threshold 127 either
dialer-group 1
isdn spid1 0835866101
isdn spid2 0835866301
snapshot server 10 dialer
ppp multilink
!
router rip
version 2
network 172.16.0.0
neighbor 172.16.3.1
no auto-summary
```

The preceding configuration configures snapshot routing and route redistribution. To configure snapshot routing, you simply need to configure one router as the client and the other as the server. The snapshot client is the end that controls the active and quiet timers. You will notice in the Router1 configuration that the **dialer** parameter has also been used.

In the event the **dialer** parameter is used, a dialer map must be made between the snapshot process and the phone number. This will allow the snapshot update to initiate a DDR session if there is no interesting traffic to bring up the link. Looking at the Router1 configuration, EIGRP is redistributing routes learned from RIP, and RIP is redistributing routes learned from EIGRP. This is commonly referred to as *mutual redistribution*. The following **show ip route** output shows the routing table for Router1 before the DDR connection is established.

```
Router1# show ip route
Codes: C - connected, S - static, I - IGRP, R - RIP, M - mobile, B - BGP
D - EIGRP, EX - EIGRP external, O - OSPF, IA - OSPF inter area N1 - OSPF NSSA
external type 1, N2 - OSPF NSSA external type 2 E1 - OSPF external type 1, E2 - OSPF
external type 2, E - EGP i - IS-IS, L1 - IS-IS level-1, L2 - IS-IS level-2, * -
candidate default U - per-user static route, o - ODR
Gateway of last resort is not set
172.16.0.0/16 is variably subnetted, 2 subnets, 2 masks
```

```
C 172.16.3.2/32 is directly connected, BRI0
C 172.16.3.0/30 is directly connected, BRI0
C 192.168.1.0/24 is directly connected, Ethernet0
```

Compare the previous output to the following output. Notice that before the connection is established, the only routes in the routing table are the ones directly connected to the router (192.168.1.0, 172.16.3.2, and 172.16.3.0). After the connection is established, the routing table also shows the 172.16.2.0 network learned via RIP. Once the ISDN connection to Router2 is disconnected, the route to 172.16.2.0 stays in the routing table for the quiet period configured in the **snapshot** command.

```
Router1# show ip route
Codes: C - connected, S - static, I - IGRP, R - RIP, M - mobile, B - BGP
D - EIGRP, EX - EIGRP external, O - OSPF, IA - OSPF inter area N1 - OSPF NSSA
external type 1, N2 - OSPF NSSA external type 2 E1 - OSPF external type 1, E2 - OSPF
external type 2, E - EGP i - IS-IS, L1 - IS-IS level-1, L2 - IS-IS level-2, * -
candidate default
U - per-user static route, o - ODR Gateway of last resort is not set
172.16.0.0/16 is variably subnetted, 2 subnets, 2 masks
R 172.16.2.0/24 [120/1] via 172.16.3.2, 00:00:13, BRI0
C 172.16.3.0/30 is directly connected, BRI0
C 192.168.1.0/24 is directly connected, Ethernet0
```

Monitoring Snapshot Routing

The following commands can be useful in monitoring snapshot routing. When issued from the server, the **show snapshot** command shows how long the server has been configured for the active period. It also shows the interface being used for the snapshot routing.

```
Router2# show snapshot
BRI0 is up, line protocol is upSnapshot server
Options: dialer support
Length of active period: 10 minutes
```

When issued from the client router, the **show snapshot** command gives more information about the snapshot session, such as the amount of active time and quiet time, and the interfaces being used for the snapshot session. In the following example, the active time has been set to 10 minutes and the quiet time is set to 13 minutes.

```
Router1# show snapshot
BRI0 is up, line protocol is upSnapshot client
Options: dialer support
Length of active period: 10 minutes
Length of quiet period: 13 minutes
Length of retry period: 13 minutes
```

```
For dialer address 1
Current state: active, remaining/exchange time: 9/0 minutes
Connected dialer interfaces:
BRI0:1, BRI0:2
```

You can use **debug snapshot** to capture snapshot routing events as they occur. This can be particularly useful if you encounter problems with your configuration and need to isolate the cause.

```
Router1# debug snapshot
Snapshot support debugging is on
03:20:02: SNAPSHOT: BRI0[1]: Move to active queue (Post active timeout)
03:20:02: SNAPSHOT: BRI0[1]: moving to active queue
03:20:03: %ISDN-6-LAYER2UP: Layer 2 for Interface BR0, TEI 89 changed to up
03:20:03: %ISDN-6-LAYER2UP: Layer 2 for Interface BR0, TEI 90 changed to up
03:20:03: %LINK-3-UPDOWN: Interface BRI0:1, changed state to up
03:20:03: SNAPSHOT: BRI0[1]: Avoiding active: in active queue (Dial connection set)
03:20:03: %LINK-3-UPDOWN: Interface Virtual-Access1, changed state to up
03:20:04: %LINEPROTO-5-UPDOWN: Line protocol on Interface BRI0:1, changed state to up
03:20:04: %LINEPROTO-5-UPDOWN: Line protocol on Interface Virtual-
Access1, changed state to up 03:20:09: %ISDN-6-CONNECT: Interface BRI0:1 is now
connected to 8358661 Router2
```

We mentioned earlier that snapshot routing does not work with a link state protocol such as OSPF. OSPF has a feature called demand circuits to accomplish essentially the same function that snapshot routing provides for distance vector routing protocols.

OSPF Demand Circuits

As mentioned in the previous section, snapshot routing does not support OSPF. Cisco developed support for RFC 1793 "Extending OSPF to Support Demand Circuits" to overcome the lack of link state routing support across DDR networks. OSPF on-demand works by initially bringing up the DDR line when the routers exchange LSA information for the first time, and when a change occurs during normal operation. As long as the network topology is stable, the circuit does not need to be connected. Under normal circumstances, OSPF will age out the LSAs in its topology table. However, when using the on-demand feature, the age will be marked as Do Not Age (DNA). This flag tells the OSPF process not to age out this LSA, which prevents the use of the demand link unnecessarily.

OSPF neighbor relationships are dependent on regular exchanges of Hellos to maintain the relationship. While that is well and good on permanent circuits or broadcast networks such as Ethernet, such behavior over ISDN means that you will have a very expensive bill on a monthly basis. Yet in many cases, it is important for an organization to be able to run OSPF over ISDN, without incurring the expense of keeping an ISDN up and active. How to achieve the balance? The OSPF demand-circuit feature is nothing more than a suppression of OSPF Hellos (every 10 to 20 seconds by default, depending on the link type) and periodic LSA refreshes (every 30 minutes by default).

The demand-circuit feature enables OSPF to run over ISDN, maintain the neighbor relationships, and exchange routing updates to keep its the tables updated, yet not incur a large expense while doing so. Using the demand circuit feature, Hellos and LSAs will only be exchanged either during initial (first) exchange of routing information between neighbors, or upon changes that trigger the circuit up.

When interesting traffic (as defined by a dialer list) activates the link, the OSPF demand-circuit will take advantage of that opportunity to refresh its link state database and routing table. If there are no network changes necessitating the exchange of LSAs, the demand-circuit will remain down, and the entries learned over it previously will not be aged out of the routing table.

If we were implementing a dialer backup scheme, there would be a permanent link between the routers, and the dialer link would monitor that interface, and if it went down, activate. At that activation point, OSPF would exchange routes while the link was up, and refresh its tables. The point is that the OSPF demand-circuit feature does not care if you are using the dialer link as a primary link, or as a backup to a primary: it will behave the same.

Configuring OSPF on-demand circuits is fairly simple. In addition to the normal OSPF and DDR configuration, use the **ip ospf demand-circuit** command in the interface configuration mode. For this feature to work, all routers in the area must have it loaded. Additionally, only one of the routers needs to configure this command. If using a point-to-point topology, either end can be configured with this command. If using a point-to-multipoint topology, the hub (or multipoint end) must be configured with this command. The second example in the "Walkthrough" section shows an example OSPF on-demand configuration. It is recommended that you put OSPF on-demand circuits into stub areas or NSSAs to isolate as many of the topology changes as possible.

Do Not Age (DNA)

When you configure OSPF demand circuits, any updates learned over this circuit are marked DNA by turning on the DNA bit in the LSA. This simply means that they will not be aged out of the routing table due to a lack of refreshing.

Of course, without a mechanism to alert the OSPF router that the updates and Hellos are suppressed due to a demand-circuit configuration, these routing updates would ordinarily be removed from the routing table since the neighbor that sent the update would be perceived as being down. When **demand-circuit** is used, OSPF marks the updates learned over the demand circuit with "DNA," and thus prevents them from being removed from the routing table.

When an update is marked DNA, it is not subject to the refresh requirements that normal updates are. That is, the next hop of the update does not have to be receiving Hellos at regular intervals. You can view entries marked as DNA using **show ip ospf database**, as shown in the following example. 192.168.1.2 was learned over an ISDN link running the **demand circuit** command.

```
RouterA# show ip ospf database


        OSPF Router with ID (192.168.1.1) (Process ID 9)
```

```
        Router Link States (Area 0)

Link ID         ADV Router      Age         Seq#       Checksum Link count
192.168.1.1     192.168.1.1     1059        0x80000011 0xE2EB   2
192.168.1.2     192.168.1.2     1     (DNA) 0x80000009 0x385A   2
```

Configuring an OSPF Demand Circuit

We will not spend much time on the details of configuring dialer features on Cisco products, as we are more interested in OSPF over dialer links. We will keep our dialer configuration here as simple as possible to maintain our focus on the commands necessary to configure demand circuits.

Figure 5.52 shows that Router1 and Router2 are connected via an ISDN link. OSPF adjacencies will be formed between these two routers, and after the initial exchange of routing updates, the link will be deactivated unless interesting traffic defined by a dialer list keeps the link up. Both routers will mark the updates they learn over the ISDN link as DNA entries, as explained in the previous sections.

Figure 5.52 OSPF Demand Circuit

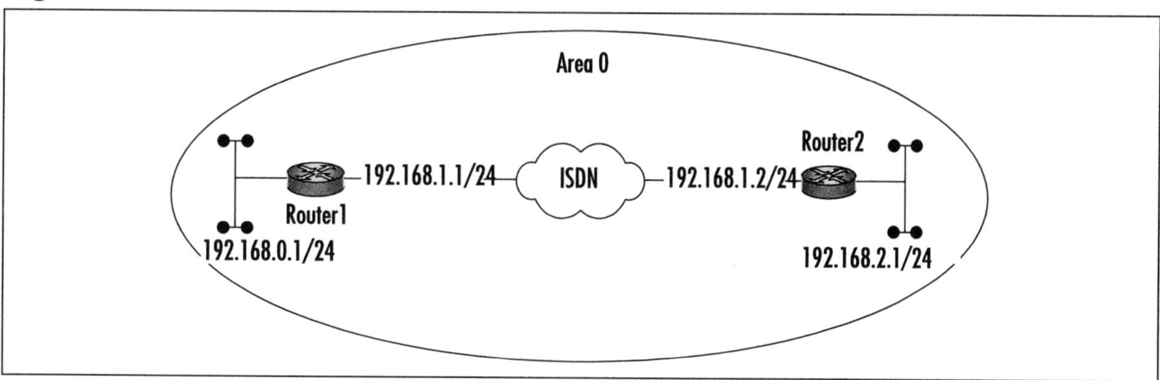

In the following example, we are using dialer interfaces on each router. Notice that the physical ISDN interface does not have an IP address; the dialer interface is the one that actually participates in OSPF.

Router1

```
interface ethernet 0
ip address 192.168.0.1 255.255.255.0

interface BRI0
 no ip address
 no ip directed-broadcast
 encapsulation ppp
 dialer pool-member 1
 isdn switch-type basic-ni
```

```
 isdn spid1 55512340101
 isdn spid2 55512350101
 ppp authentication chap
!
interface Dialer1
 ip address 192.168.1.1 255.255.255.0
 no ip directed-broadcast
 encapsulation ppp
 dialer remote-name routerb
 dialer string 5556789
 dialer string 5556790
 dialer pool 1
 dialer-group 1
 ppp authentication chap
!
router ospf 99
 network 192.168.1.1 0.0.0.0 area 0
 network 192.168.0.1 0.0.0.0 area 0

! Dialer-list 1 defines what traffic may bring the link up.
dialer-list 1 protocol ip permit
```

Router2

```
interface ethernet 0
ip address 192.168.2.1 255.255.255.0

interface BRI0
 no ip address
 no ip directed-broadcast
 encapsulation ppp
 dialer pool-member 1
 isdn switch-type basic-ni
 isdn spid1 55556780101
 isdn spid2 55556900101
 ppp authentication chap
!
interface Dialer1
 ip address 192.168.1.2 255.255.255.0
 no ip directed-broadcast
 encapsulation ppp
```

```
 ip ospf demand-circuit
 dialer remote-name routera
 dialer string 5556789
 dialer string 5556790
 dialer pool 1
 dialer-group 1
 ppp authentication chap
!
router ospf 99
 network 192.168.1.2 0.0.0.0 area 0
 network 192.168.2.1 0.0.0.0 area 0

! Dialer-list 1 defines what traffic may bring the link up.
dialer-list 1 protocol ip permit
```

Notice that the **ip ospf demand-circuit** command was configured on Router2 only. If your version of IOS supports it, this will work. Since it can be difficult to ascertain which versions of IOS support which commands, you might want to consistently execute the command on both routers on a point-to-point link to ensure that the demand-circuit feature will work consistently.

If this were a point-to-multipoint network, then all routers on the point-to-multipoint network that were linked via dialer links would need to have the **ip ospf demand-circuit** command enabled. Cisco makes several design recommendations for using the demand-circuit feature. According to Cisco, you should put your demand circuits within a stub or NSSA. Cisco's reasoning is that stub areas do not experience as many topology change updates since they restrict what information enters the area.

Our efforts so far have focused on routing for IPv4. IPv6, the next generation of IP, is gaining a foothold with its increased address size and other features useful to your network, as discussed in Chapter 4.

IPv6 Routing

The IPv6 routing, while achieving the same goals as IPv4 routing, does have some significant differences, not the least of which is the larger address size. New versions of routing protocols have been developed to support dynamic routing on IPv6 networks, because there have been only a few routing protocols built into the Cisco IOS to this point. RIP, IS-IS, and BGP have been updated and built into the Cisco IOS already. New versions of OSPF and EIGRP supportive of IPv6 will be part of future IOS releases.

Configuring RIP for IPv6

RIPng does offer a few enhancements to the original RIP standard; these include, of course, full support for the IPv6 standard and prefixes as well as support for an all-routers RIP multicast address group for routing update messages to all RIPng routers. This offers an alternative to the broadcast messaging solution used by previous implementations of RIP.

Basic IPv6 RIP Configuration

To enable the RIP routing process for IPv6, the **ipv6 router rip <word>** command is used. The **word** command is actually a process identifier consisting of numbers or letters that identify the specific RIP process. This enables multiple segregated RIP processes to run on the same router. To add specific networks to the RIPng routing domain, the **ipv6 rip <word> enable** command is used. This command places that specific IPv6-enabled interface into the specified IPv6 RIP routing domain. The following listing shows an example of this process on the router:

```
6Router-1# configure terminal
Enter configuration commands, one per line.  End with CNTL/Z.
6Router-1(config)# ipv6 router rip cisco
6Router-1(config-rtr)# exit
6Router-1(config)# interface ethernet 0
6Router-1(config-if)# ipv6 rip cisco enable
6Router-1(config-if)# exit
6Router-1(config)# interface serial 0
6Router-1(config-if)# ipv6 rip cisco enable
6Router-1(config-if)# exit
6Router-1(config)#
```

In the preceding example, we enabled the Ipv6 RIP routing process by using the **ipv6 router rip cisco** command. We then included both the Ethernet 0 and Serial 0 interfaces into the IPv6 RIPng routing process by issuing the **ipv6 rip cisco enable** command on each interface in interface configuration mode.

Figure 5.53 shows an example of a simple IPv6 RIPng network.

Figure 5.53 IPv6 RIPng

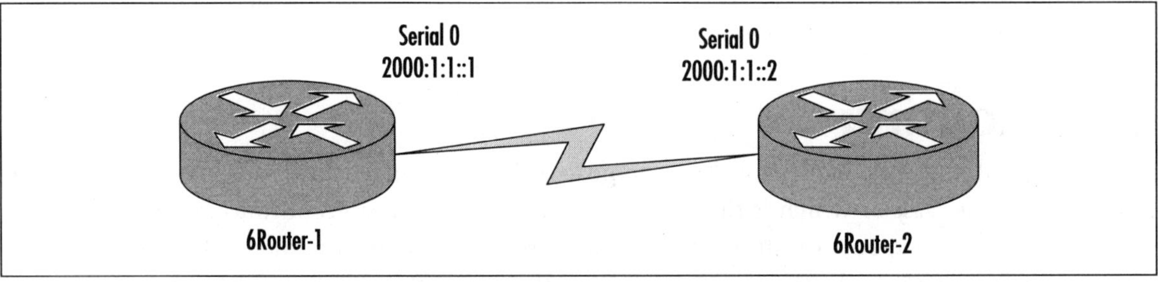

In the example shown in Figure 5.53, we created a RIPng routing domain with three separate subnets, 2000:1:1::/64, which is the network that runs between the two router's serial links, and we have two networks off the Ethernet 0 routers of each of the routers 2000:1:2::/64 and 2000:1:3::/64, respectively. By issuing **show ipv6 protocol**, we can see all the IPv6 routing protocols currently running on the router. In the following listing, we see that we have both connected networks, static routes, and of course RIPng running on our 6Router-1 router.

```
6Router-1# show ipv6 protocol
```

```
IPv6 Routing Protocol is "connected"
IPv6 Routing Protocol is "static"
IPv6 Routing Protocol is "rip cisco"
  Interfaces:
    Serial0
    Ethernet0
  Redistribution:
    Redistributing protocol rip cisco
```

By issuing the **show ipv6 route** command, you can see the routes derived for IPv6. The following **show ipv6 route** output confirms that IPv6 can support seven types of routes (connected, local, static, RIP, BGP, IS-IS levels one and two, as well as interarea IS-IS. Routes derived from a RIP routing process are denoted with an *R*. The following example shows that 6Router-1 has derived one route from the RIP routing process, a connection to 2000:1:3:: /64, which, of course, is the network off the Ethernet 0 interface on 6Router-2. We also see the interface that RIP uses to get to that network; in this case, the Serial 0 interface of 6Router-1.

```
6Router-1# show ipv6 route
IPv6 Routing Table - 7 entries
Codes: C - Connected, L - Local, S - Static, R - RIP, B - BGP
       I1 - ISIS L1, I2 - ISIS L2, IA - ISIS interarea
Timers: Uptime/Expires

L    2000:1:1::1/128 [0/0]
      via ::, Serial0, 1d05h/never
C    2000:1:1::/64 [0/0]
      via ::, Serial0, 1d05h/never
L    2000:1:2::1/128 [0/0]
      via ::, Ethernet0, 1d05h/never
C    2000:1:2::/64 [0/0]
      via ::, Ethernet0, 1d05h/never
R    2000:1:3::/64 [120/2]
      via FE80::2E0:B0FF:FE55:B035, Serial0, 00:00:13/00:02:46
L    FE80::/10 [0/0]
      via ::, Null0, 1d05h/never
L    FF00::/8 [0/0]
      via ::, Null0, 1d05h/never
6Router-1#
```

Default Routes and RIPng

IPv6 RIPng default routes are enabled on an interface level by using the **default-information** command. This command tells the router to inject a ::/0 route into the RIPng routing domain as a default route. Follow the **default-information** command by one of two parameters: **originate** or **only** settings.

The **originate** setting tells the router to inject this ::/0 route into the RIP routing domain and to advertise this route along with all the other routes in its RIP routing advertisements. The **only** parameter instructs the router running IPv6 RIP to advertise only this default route, and to suppress advertisement of any other routes.

The following is an example of default route configuration in an IPv6 RIPng routing process. We have configured the serial 0 interface of our 6Router-1 router to originate a default route and to advertise it to the rest of the IPv6 RIPng routing domain.

```
6Router-1(config)# interface serial0
6Router-1(config-if)# ipv6 rip cisco default-information ?
  only        Advertise only the default route
  originate   Originate the default route

6Router-1(config-if)# ipv6 rip cisco default-information originate
6Router-1(config-if)# exit
```

In the preceding example, we entered interface configuration mode and entered the **ipv6 rip cisco default-information originate** command, thus telling the router to use the network attached to the serial 0 interface as the default route.

Verifying RIPng Operation

You have a few commands to verify that IPv6 RIPng is working correctly. The first of these is **show ipv6 rip**. This command gives you all the specific information relating to the operation of IPv6 RIP, including the following:

- Timer information
- Port information
- Update frequency
- Update types
- Default route information

This command is a very useful tool for verifying that RIPng is functioning correctly. The following listing shows an example of a command output from the **show ipv6 rip** command.

```
6Router-1# show ipv6 rip
RIP process "cisco", port 521, multicast-group FF02::9, pid 71
     Administrative distance is 120.  Routing table is 0
     Updates every 30 seconds, expire after 180
```

```
     Holddown lasts 180 seconds, garbage collect after 120
     Split horizon is on; poison reverse is off
     Default routes are generated
     Periodic updates 24667, trigger updates 2
6Router-1#
```

The **show ipv6 protocols** command is useful for showing all the IPv6 protocols, including RIPng, that are running on a router. Information included from this output includes the following:

- Routing protocols in use
- Interfaces used by routing protocols
- Redistribution information

The following listing shows an example of this command output.

```
6Router-1# show ipv6 protocols
IPv6 Routing Protocol is "connected"
IPv6 Routing Protocol is "static"
IPv6 Routing Protocol is "rip cisco"
  Interfaces:
    Serial0
    Ethernet0
  Redistribution:
    Redistributing protocol static with metric 4
    Redistributing protocol rip cisco
```

Although we have already used this command throughout our discussion of RIP numerous times, the **show ipv6 route** command is also important in verifying RIPng operation. This command shows all IPv6 routes that have been learned, as well as the protocol used to obtain the routes in question. The following listing shows an example of this command output.

```
6Router-1# show ipv6 route
IPv6 Routing Table - 7 entries
Codes: C - Connected, L - Local, S - Static, R - RIP, B - BGP
       I1 - ISIS L1, I2 - ISIS L2, IA - ISIS interarea
Timers: Uptime/Expires

L   2000:1:1::1/128 [0/0]
     via ::, Serial0, 5d17h/never
C   2000:1:1::/64 [0/0]
     via ::, Serial0, 5d17h/never
L   2000:1:2::1/128 [0/0]
     via ::, Ethernet0, 1w2d/never
C   2000:1:2::/64 [0/0]
```

```
      via ::, Ethernet0, 1w2d/never
R    2000:1:3::/64 [120/2]
      via FE80::2E0:B0FF:FE55:B035, Serial0, 02:45:40/00:02:32
L    FE80::/10 [0/0]
      via ::, Null0, 1w2d/never
L    FF00::/8 [0/0]
      via ::, Null0, 1w2d/never
6Router-1#
```

Integrated IS-IS

Support for IP is not inherent in IS-IS, as we discussed before—it was designed for CLNS-only routing. You need to make only a few configuration changes to your CLNS routing configuration to be able to use IS-IS. The first of these is the **ip router isis** command. If IP addresses are not configured, you must configure them on the interface at this time. You must then also assign the interfaces to an area by using the **area** command. This enables the IS-IS process to advertise the IP address to other IS-IS routers. This is a brief introduction to a fairly complex topic, but we will cover more IS-IS configuration in our discussion of IPv6 IS-IS.

Configuring IS-IS for IPv6

A specific version of IS-IS was not written to support IPv6; rather, extensions were written into the protocol to provide this support. This is because of the modular architecture of IS-IS.

You perform initial configuration for IPv6 IS-IS the same as you do for standard IPv4 IS-IS: through the use of the **router isis** command. Follow this command with the **net** command, specifying the network entity address for the router. IPv6 support comes into play at the interface level when assigning an IPv6 address to the router by using the **ipv6 address** command followed by the **ipv6 router isis <area>** command. Figure 5.54 shows an example of a basic IS-IS network.

Figure 5.54 IPv6 IS-IS

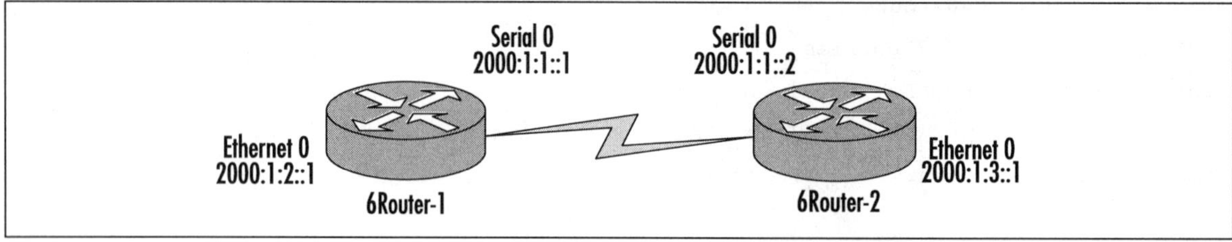

In the following configuration, we are using the two routers shown in Figure 5.54, 6Router-1 and 6Router-2, respectively.

```
6Router-1(config)# clns routing
6Router-1(config)# router isis cisco
6Router-1(config-router)# net 49.aaaa.bbbb.cccc.dddd.0000.2222.2222.2222.00
6Router-1(config-router)# exit
```

```
6Router-1(config)# interface ethernet 0
6Router-1(config-if)# ipv6 address 2000:1:2::1/64
6Router-1(config-if)# ipv6 router isis cisco
6Router-1(config-if)# interface serial 0
6Router-1(config-if)# ipv6 address 2000:1:1::1/64
6Router-1(config-if)# ipv6 router isis cisco
6Router-1(config-if)# exit

6Router-2(config)# clns routing
6Router-2(config)# router isis cisco
6Router-2(config-router)# net 49.aaaa.bbbb.cccc.dddd.0000.2222.2222.2223.01
6Router-2(config-router)# exit
6Router-2(config)# interface ethernet 0
6Router-2(config-if)# ipv6 address 2000:1:3::1/64
6Router-2(config-if)# ipv6 router isis cisco
6Router-2(config-if)# interface serial 0
6Router-2(config-if)# ipv6 address 2000:1:1::2/64
6Router-2(config-if)# ipv6 router isis cisco
6Router-2(config-if)# exit
```

We enabled IS-IS routing by issuing the **clns routing** command on both routers in global configuration mode, after which we enable integrated IS-IS by issuing the **router isis cisco** command. We then assigned the NSAP address of 49.aaaa.bbbb.cccc.dddd.0000.2222.2222.2223.00 and 49.aaaa.bbbb.cccc.dddd.0000.2222.2222.2223.01, respectively, by using the **net** command. Then, we assigned IPv6 addresses to both the Ethernet and serial interfaces of each router by using the **ipv6 address** command on both routers in interface configuration mode. We then assigned the interfaces to the IS-IS routing process by issuing the **ipv6 router isis cisco** command on each interface.

We can verify proper IS-IS operation by performing **show ipv6 route** (note the I1 address, a level-1 IS-IS route running between our two test routers).

```
6Router-1# show ipv6 route
IPv6 Routing Table - 7 entries
Codes: C - Connected, L - Local, S - Static, R - RIP, B - BGP
       I1 - ISIS L1, I2 - ISIS L2, IA - ISIS interarea
Timers: Uptime/Expires

L   2000:1:1::1/128 [0/0]
     via ::, Serial0, 5d20h/never
C   2000:1:1::/64 [0/0]
     via ::, Serial0, 5d20h/never
```

```
L    2000:1:2::1/128 [0/0]
      via ::, Ethernet0, 1w2d/never
C    2000:1:2::/64 [0/0]
      via ::, Ethernet0, 1w2d/never
I1   2000:1:3::/64 [120/2]
      via FE80::2E0:B0FF:FE55:B035, Serial0, 05:57:49/00:02:43
L    FE80::/10 [0/0]
      via ::, Null0, 1w2d/never
L    FF00::/8 [0/0]
      via ::, Null0, 1w2d/never
```

IS-IS Default Routes

IS-IS uses default routes to reach destination networks for which routers do not have routes in their routing tables. However, entering default route information for IS-IS IPv6 is somewhat different from that for RIP. Configuration for a default route for IPv6 in IS-IS is a two-step process.

First, enter the IPv6 address family configuration mode in IS-IS configuration. This is accomplished by using the **address-family ipv6** command in IS-IS configuration mode. Use the **address-family** identifier to specify which group of addresses, either IPv4 or IPv6, is to be configured. Next, execute the **default-information originate** command. Exit by entering the **exit-address-family** command. If a route map is not used, the default route will be advertised to the rest of the routing domain as a Layer 2 route. The following listing is an example of this configuration.

```
6Router-1(config)# router isis cisco
6Router-1(config-router)# address-family ipv6
6Router-1(config-router-af)# default-information originate
6Router-1(config-router-af)# exit-address-family
```

Maximum Paths for IS-IS

IS-IS automatically supports load balancing for up to two paths. However, this value can be increased by up to four by manipulating the **maximum paths** value. You manipulate the **maximum paths** command at the IS-IS configuration level. Specify the appropriate address family that you want to change by using the **address-family ipv6** command. Next, execute the **maximum-paths <number-paths>** command. The *number paths* parameter specifies the number of maximum paths that you want the router to support. The maximum for this number is four. The following listing shows an example of this configuration.

```
6Router-1(config)# router isis cisco
6Router-1(config-router)# address-family ipv6
6Router-1(config-router-af)# maximum-paths 4
6Router-1(config-router-af)# exit-address-family
```

Configuring BGP Extensions for IPv6

As with IS-IS, a new version of BGP was not developed specifically for the purpose of routing IPv6; rather, new multiprotocol extensions were added to the protocol to support IPv6. Enhancements made to the protocol include the support for IPv6, support for IPv6 next-hop addressing information, and support for link-local IPv6 addressing.

IPv6 BGP is configured the same as IPv4 BGP: through the use of the **router bgp** ***<as number>*** command. Upon entering the BGP configuration mode, enter the **no bgp default ipv4-unicast** command. This command turns off IPv4 BGP unicasts. This is a necessary step because, by default, IPv4 address information is advertised for each BGP neighbor configured on the router. IPv6 cannot work if this is taking place.

Configuring an IPv6 Neighbor Relationship

It is slightly more involved to set up IPv6 neighbor relationships than IPv4 neighbors. To set up an IPv6 neighbor in BGP, you must first specify the IPv6 address and remote-as number of the neighbor router by using the neighbor ***<ipv6 address>*** **remote-as** ***<as number>*** command. Next, enter the IPv6 address family configuration and activate the neighbor. You do this with **the ipv6 address-family** command, followed by the **neighbor** ***<ipv6 address>*** **activate** command. The networks to be advertised via IPv6 BGP are also specified here through use of the **network** command.

Figure 5.55 shows a basic IPv6 BGP network, along with configuration details for this network. In Figure 5.55, we have two routers, 6Router-1 and 6Router-2. On 6Router-1 we created a BGP process with the AS of 64999 and a neighbor relationship with the router at the 2000:1:1::2 address with an AS number of 65000. We also instructed the router to advertise the 2000:1:1::0/64 and 2000:1:2::0/64 networks.

```
6Router-1(config)# router bgp 64999 (Enable BGP routing with AS 64999)
6Router-1(config-router)# no bgp default ipv4-unicast (Disable 1Pv4 unicasts)
6Router-1(config-router)# neighbor 2000:1:1::2 remote-as 65000 (Neighbor)
6Router-1(config-router)# address-family ipv6 unicast (Allow Ipv6 unicasts)
6Router-1(config-router-af)# neighbor 2000:1:1::2 activate (Activate neighor
6Router-1(config-router-af)# network ?
6Router-1(config-router-af)# network 2000:1:1::0/64 (Advertise network)
6Router-1(config-router-af)# network 2000:1:2::0/64 (Advertise network)
6Router-1(config-router-af)# exit
6Router-1(config-router)# exit
6Router-1(config)#
```

Figure 5.55 IPv6 BGP

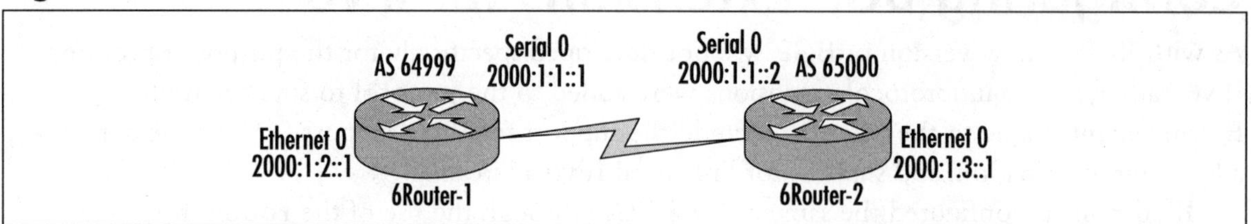

On 6Router-2 we created a BGP process with an AS of 65000 and a neighbor relationship with 2000:1:1::1 with an AS ID of 64999. We also instructed the router to advertise the 2000:1:1::0/64 and 2000:1:3::0/64 networks.

```
6Router-2(config)# router bgp 65000 (Enable BGP routing with AS 65000)
6Router-2(config-router)# no bgp default ipv4-unicast (Disable 1Pv4 unicasts)
6Router-2(config-router)# neighbor 2000:1:1::1 remote-as 64999 (Neighbor)
6Router-2(config-router)# address-family ipv6 unicast (Allow Ipv6 unicasts)
6Router-2(config-router-af)# neighbor 2000:1:1::1 activate (Activate neighor
6Router-2(config-router-af)# network 2000:1:1::0/64 (Advertise Network)
6Router-2(config-router-af)# network 2000:1:3::0/64  (Advertise Network)
6Router-2(config-router-af)# exit
6Router-2(config-router)# exit
6Router-2(config)# exit
```

We can verify the success of our BGP configuration by using the **show BGP neighbors** command on 6Router-1. The following shows that we have established a neighbor relationship with 2000:1:1::2 and that IPv6 unicast traffic is going between the two routers. The more important information to be gained from this output would be the first line of the configuration, verifying that we do in fact have a neighbor relationship between the two routers as well as the information contained in the following bolded lines concerning version, router ID, BGP state, and up time. This is followed by the information concerning the IPv6-specific information about the BGP table and neighbor version as well as connected/dropped connection information.

```
6Router-1# show bgp neighbors
BGP neighbor is 2000:1:1::2,  remote AS 65000, external link
  BGP version 4, remote router ID 172.16.8.33
  BGP state = Established, up for 00:13:43
  Last read 00:00:43, hold time is 180, keepalive interval is 60 seconds
  Neighbor capabilities:
    Route refresh: advertised and received(old & new)
    Address family IPv6 Unicast: advertised and received
  Received 18 messages, 0 notifications, 0 in queue
  Sent 18 messages, 0 notifications, 0 in queue
  Default minimum time between advertisement runs is 30 seconds
```

```
 For address family: IPv6 Unicast
  BGP table version 3, neighbor version 3
  Index 1, Offset 0, Mask 0x2
  Route refresh request: received 0, sent 0
  1 accepted prefixes consume 68 bytes
  Prefix advertised 2, suppressed 0, withdrawn 0

  Connections established 1; dropped 0
  Last reset never
Connection state is ESTAB, I/O status: 1, unread input bytes: 0
Local host: 2000:1:1::1, Local port: 179
Foreign host: 2000:1:1::2, Foreign port: 11000

Enqueued packets for retransmit: 0, input: 0  mis-ordered: 0 (0 bytes)

Event Timers (current time is 0x33538748):
Timer          Starts    Wakeups            Next
Retrans            17          0             0x0
TimeWait            0          0             0x0
AckHold            17         10             0x0
SendWnd             0          0             0x0
KeepAlive           0          0             0x0
GiveUp              0          0             0x0
PmtuAger            0          0             0x0
DeadWait            0          0             0x0

iss: 1756584196  snduna: 1756584638  sndnxt: 1756584638     sndwnd:  15943
irs: 2281490682  rcvnxt: 2281491115  rcvwnd:       15952  delrcvwnd:    432

SRTT: 269 ms, RTTO: 516 ms, RTV: 247 ms, KRTT: 0 ms
minRTT: 4 ms, maxRTT: 300 ms, ACK hold: 200 ms
Flags: passive open, nagle, gen tcbs

Datagrams (max data segment is 1440 bytes):
Rcvd: 25 (out of order: 0), with data: 17, total data bytes: 432
Sent: 27 (retransmit: 0, fastretransmit: 0), with data: 27, total data bytes: 19
6Router-1#
```

You can also verify that IPv6 BGP is functioning by using the **show ipv6 route** command. The following **show ipv6 route** output shows that the 6Router-1 has learned of the 2000:1:3::/64 network by way of the BGP routing process.

```
6Router-1# show ipv6 route
IPv6 Routing Table - 7 entries
Codes: C - Connected, L - Local, S - Static, R - RIP, B - BGP
       I1 - ISIS L1, I2 - ISIS L2, IA - ISIS interarea
Timers: Uptime/Expires

L   2000:1:1::1/128 [0/0]
     via ::, Serial0, 5d23h/never
C   2000:1:1::/64 [0/0]
     via ::, Serial0, 5d23h/never
L   2000:1:2::1/128 [0/0]
     via ::, Ethernet0, 1w2d/never
C   2000:1:2::/64 [0/0]
     via ::, Ethernet0, 1w2d/never
B   2000:1:3::/64 [20/1]
     via 2000:1:1::2, Serial0, 00:00:47/never
L   FE80::/10 [0/0]
     via ::, Null0, 1w2d/never
L   FF00::/8 [0/0]
     via ::, Null0, 1w2d/never
6Router-1#
```

Configuring a BGP Router ID

BGP uses router IDs to identify BGP speaking routers. In IPv4, this address was automatically set to the loopback interface of the router. If this address did not exist, then the address was set as the highest IPv4 address on the router. BGP does not, however, do this for a router running only IPv6 BGP; therefore, you must manually configure this value. *Although you are not running BGP for IPv4 traffic, you will need to configure the Router ID as an IPv4 address.* To do this, you use the **bgp router-id** ***<ip address>*** command in BGP configuration mode. The following listing shows an example of this configuration.

```
6Router-1(config)# router bgp 64999
6Router-1(config-router)# bgp router-id 172.16.0.1
6Router-1(config-router)#
```

Configuring BGP Peer Groups

Peer groups are a management mechanism that Cisco routers can use to make policy changes to multiple routers. This functionality is very advantageous for administrators who have to replicate policy changes to multiple BGP-speaking routers. You define peer groups on routers with a name and a set of routing policies. You configure a peer group for IPv6 BGP by using the ***<name> peer-group*** command. Then, create a neighbor relationship, as we discussed earlier, and then activate the peer group by using the **neighbor** ***<peer group name>*** **activate** command in address family configuration mode. Finally, add the neighbor's IPv6 address to the peer group by using the **neighbor** ***<ipv6 address>*** **peer group** ***<peer group name>*** command. The following listing shows an example of this configuration.

```
6Router-1(config)# router bgp 64999
6Router-1(config-router)# neighbor cisco peer-group (Establish peer group)
6Router-1(config-router)# neighbor 2000:1:1::2 remote-as 65000 (neighbor est)
6Router-1(config-router)# address-family ipv6 unicast (Enable IPV6 unicast)
6Router-1(config-router-af)# neighbor cisco activate (activate neighbor)
6Router-1(config-router-af)# neighbor 2000:1:1::2 peer-group cisco (add to peer group)
6Router-1(config-router-af)# exit
6Router-1(config-router)#
```

Configuring Link-Local Addressing

You use link-local addresses for routers on a single link. They are an inherent part of the IPv6 protocol. Each router assigns each of its active IPv6 interfaces a link-local address. Therefore, a unique address, specific to the link running between the two routers, can be used. BGP has the capability to use this address for neighbor addressing to automatically assign a link-local address to peer routers. You configure link-local addressing in the BGP configuration mode by using the **update-source** ***<interface type>*** command in neighbor configuration mode. This command specifies that the router should use the address configured on the interface specified for the neighbor relationship. After this, you should enter into address-family configuration mode and activate the neighbor relationship. At this point, you also have the option of configuring a route map. The following example shows this configuration:

```
6Router-1(config)# router bgp 64999
6Router-1(config-router)# neighbor 2000:1:1::2 update-source ? (Specify update source)
  Async              Async interface
  BVI                Bridge-Group Virtual Interface
  CTunnel            CTunnel interface
  Dialer             Dialer interface
  Ethernet           IEEE 802.3
  Lex                Lex interface
  Loopback           Loopback interface
  MFR                Multilink Frame Relay bundle interface
  Multilink          Multilink-group interface
  Null               Null interface
  Serial             Serial
  Tunnel             Tunnel interface
  Vif                PGM Multicast Host interface
  Virtual-Template   Virtual Template interface
```

```
  Virtual-TokenRing  Virtual TokenRing

6Router-1(config-router)# neighbor 2000:1:1::2 update-source serial ?
  <0-1>  Serial interface number

6Router-1(config-router)# neighbor 2000:1:1::2 update-source serial 0?
.  :  <0-1>

6Router-1(config-router)# neighbor 2000:1:1::2 update-source serial 0
6Router-1(config-router)# neighbor 2000:1:1::2 update-source serial 0
6Router-1(config-router)# address-family ipv6
6Router-1(config-router-af)# ?
Router Address Family configuration commands:
  aggregate-address     Configure BGP aggregate entries
  bgp                   BGP specific commands
  default               Set a command to its defaults
  default-information   Control distribution of default information
  default-metric        Set metric of redistributed routes
  distribute-list       Filter networks in routing updates
  exit-address-family   Exit from Address Family configuration mode
  help                  Description of the interactive help system
  neighbor              Specify a neighbor router
  network               Specify a network to announce via BGP
  no                    Negate a command or set its defaults
  redistribute          Redistribute IPv6 prefixes from another routing protocol
  synchronization       Perform IGP synchronization
  table-map             Map external entry attributes into routing table

6Router-1(config-router-af)# neighbor 2000:1:1::2 activate (Activate neighbor
6Router-1(config-router-af)# exit-address-family
6Router-1(config-router)#
```

Verifying BGP Operation

Several commands are available to ensure that your IPv6 BGP configuration is running correctly. We will review some of these commands, their applications, and the command syntax in the following sections.

Using the show bgp Command

You can verify your BGP operation by using the **show bgp ipv6** command. This command is very useful in diagnosing the overall health of the IPv6 BGP process, as well as verifying that the protocol is advertising the appropriate networks. This output, shown in the following listing, shows the local router ID, networks being advertised and learned via BGP, BGP table version, as well as path and weights for the networks.

```
6Router-1# show bgp ipv6
BGP table version is 13, local router ID is 172.16.0.1 (Table version and local router ID)
Status codes: s suppressed, d damped, h history, * valid, > best, i - internal,
              r RIB-failure
Origin codes: i - IGP, e - EGP, ? - incomplete

   Network          Next Hop            Metric LocPrf Weight Path
*  2000:1:1::/64    2000:1:1::2                            0 65000 i
*>                  ::                                 32768 i
*> 2000:1:2::/64    ::                                 32768 i
*> 2000:1:3::/64    2000:1:1::2                            0 65000 i
(Advertised Networks)
6Router-1#
```

Using the show bgp ipv6 summary Command

The **show bgp ipv6 summary** command gives an overall picture of the IPv6 BGP routing process; however, it does it in a different way than the **show bgp ipv6** command. As the following illustrates, this command shows the BGP router identifier, local AS number, and BGP table version. Instead of listing the individual network entries, as does the **show bgp ipv6** command, it shows the number of network entries with the available number of paths. Neighbor information is listed at the bottom of this command output. The command output also displays memory utilization as well as route-map and filter-list usage.

```
6Router-1# show bgp ipv6 summary
BGP router identifier 172.16.0.1, local AS number 64999 (Local BGP info)
BGP table version is 13, main routing table version 13 (Table version)
3 network entries and 4 paths using 659 bytes of memory (Network entries)
2 BGP path attribute entries using 120 bytes of memory (Path attribute info)
1 BGP AS-PATH entries using 24 bytes of memory
0 BGP route-map cache entries using 0 bytes of memory
0 BGP filter-list cache entries using 0 bytes of memory
BGP activity 10/23 prefixes, 14/10 paths, scan interval 60 secs

Neighbor        V    AS MsgRcvd MsgSent   TblVer  InQ OutQ Up/Down  State/PfxRcd
2000:1:1::2     4 65000    1482    1489       13    0    0 00:05:04        2
6Router-1#
```

Summary

This chapter covered routing for IP, both version 4 and 6. Routing is simply the processes and mechanisms used to get network traffic to its final destination. Routing protocols are structured methods for collecting the information necessary to build the tables for forwarding traffic.

Static routes are manual entries into the routing table specified by an engineer. A default route is used when there is no specific route for a particular destination. When all else fails, traffic will be sent to the next hop specified by the default route.

Routing protocols can be classified in a number of ways. Interior gateway protocols are concerned with routing within an AS, while exterior gateway protocols handle inter-AS routing. Interior gateway protocols can be either distance vector or link state. Distance vector protocols route by hop count, while link state protocols build and route by the complete network picture.

OSPF and IS-IS are link state protocols. RIP, IGRP, and EIGRP are distance vector protocols. EIGRP builds its tables in link state manner. BGP is an exterior gateway protocol, and is classified as a path vector protocol. BGP routes by AS, not by hop.

One of the most important things you can do for routing is planning. Ensure that you understand your network architecture before deploying any routing protocol. Your chosen routing protocol should reflect and support your architecture.

Chapter 6

Quality of Service (QoS)

Best Damn Topics in this Chapter:

- QoS Overview
- Bandwidth Reservation
- Queuing
- Selecting a Cisco IOS Queuing Method
- First-In, First-Out Queuing
- Low Latency Queuing
- Priority Queuing
- Custom Queuing
- Weighted Fair Queuing
- Class-Based Weighted Fair Queuing
- Why Packet Classification?
- IP Precedence
- Traffic Shaping
- Link Fragmentation and Interleaving
- Weighted Random Early Detection
- Data Compression Overview
- Configuring Packet Classification
- Policy Routing
- Call Admission Control

Introduction

Delay. Limited bandwidth. Sensitive traffic. All of these issues and more have to be addressed on your network. Regardless of how much verbiage is used to describe it, you may find yourself facing a network situation where certain traffic has to be differentiated and given priority over all other traffic. Even more complicated is the deployment and management of multiple priorities. What scheme or mechanism will give you the ability to prioritize in the best way for your situation? There is much available, and you need to understand your options. All of these fall under the umbrella of quality of service (QoS)

QoS ensures that a minimum level of service will be provided to certain classes of traffic. By prioritizing, these techniques enable business-critical or delay-sensitive applications to operate properly in a congested network or in limited bandwidth environments.

There are three levels of QoS:

- **Best effort** Every possible attempt to deliver a packet to its destination is made. This service type carries no guarantees a packet will reach the destination.
- **Integrated services** Provides applications with a guaranteed level of service by negotiating network parameters end to end. Applications request the level of service necessary to operate properly and rely on the QoS mechanism to reserve the necessary network resources before the application begins its transmission.
- **Differentiated services** Differentiated service includes a set of classification tools and queuing mechanisms to provide certain protocols or applications with a certain priority over other network traffic. Differentiated services rely on the edge routers to perform the classification of the various types of packets traversing a network.

QoS can be implemented in any number of ways via one or more of these methods. Many of the options discussed in this chapter can be used either on their own or in conjunction with other QoS techniques. For that reason, the process of deploying QoS on a network can be very complex. The aim of this chapter is to highlight the QoS methods available in order to make the decision process and implementation easier. Because each network is different, it is impossible to provide a single scheme for providing QoS. Each network must be evaluated individually and provided a solution tailored to its specific needs. We will discuss individual techniques, describing the purpose, basics of operation, advantages and disadvantages, and configuration information for each.

Managing congestion over wide area network (WAN) links is important due to the mismatch in speed between local area networks (LANs) and WANs. One way that network devices can handle overflow of arriving traffic is to use a queuing algorithm to sort and prioritize outbound traffic, and then prioritize the traffic on the output link as indicated. It is important to note that queuing/prioritization works most effectively on WAN links that experience bursty traffic. If a WAN link is congested 100 percent of the time, queuing/prioritization may not remedy the issue—look to additional bandwidth instead.

QoS Overview

There are several options for implementing QoS on your networks. These measures include several methods of bandwidth maximization via various queuing techniques as well as packet classification and bandwidth reservation.

The demand for more bandwidth and faster response times is due to ever-increasing traffic and applications that require more bandwidth and faster response times. Cost constraints mean that we are unlikely to have unlimited bandwidth available. It is most likely your job to ensure that networked applications can maintain a satisfactory level of performance and responsiveness as well as make efficient use of the available bandwidth.

Congestion management is a generic term that encompasses various types of queuing strategies used to manage situations in which network applications' bandwidth demands exceed the total bandwidth that the network can provide. Congestion management does not control congestion before it occurs. It controls the injection of traffic into the network so that certain network flows have priority over others. In this chapter, we examine the following congestion management techniques:

- Real-Time Transport Protocol (RTP)
- Compressed Real-Time Transport Protocol (cRTP)
- Queuing
- Priority queuing
- Custom queuing
- Weighted fair queuing (WFQ)
- Class-based WFQ (CB-WFQ)
- Priority queuing with WFQ
- Packet classification
- Internet Protocol (IP) precedence
- Policy routing
- Resource Reservation Protocol (RSVP)
- Call Admission Control (CAC)

Implementing and configuring queuing requires planning and forethought. You must have a good understanding of the traffic flows and how the traffic should be prioritized to engineer an efficient queuing strategy. Poorly planned prioritization can lead to situations worse than the congestive state itself. Certain default mechanisms such as first-in, first-out (FIFO) and weighted fair queuing require little or no configuration. In the Cisco IOS, WFQ is enabled by default on links of E1 speed (2.048Mbps) or slower. Conversely, FIFO is enabled by default on links faster than E1 speeds.

Each queuing algorithm was designed to solve a specific network traffic problem and each will have a different effect on network performance. As described in the following sections, queuing is an effective way to control the order of traffic.

Bandwidth Reservation

You can use bandwidth reservation protocols to ensure available bandwidth for certain traffic such as voice over IP (VoIP). Cisco advocates two such schemes: Real-Time Protocol (RTP) and Resource Reservation Protocol (RSVP). This section covers each and provides troubleshooting guidance.

Real-Time Transport Protocol

Real-Time Transport Protocol priority grants absolute priority to delay-sensitive user datagram protocol (UDP) data transmissions. This is a priority-based queuing algorithm. Via the **ip rtp priority** command, you can specify particular RTP ports that will have priority over other queues on the same interface. RTP, which is described in RFC1889, provides such services as sequencing to identify lost packets and 32-bit values to identify and distinguish between multiple senders in a multicast stream. Once configured, packets that are identified with the RTP port number are given priority over all other packets on the interface.

The RTP priority queue polices based on *total bandwidth*, not the number of individual connections. Therefore, if the queue is configured for 128Kbps, it simply reserves that amount of bandwidth but does not prevent other voice calls from being admitted, for example. The result, in this case, is that if five calls requiring 24Kbps each were in progress, a sixth could be admitted, reducing the actual per-call bandwidth to 21Kbps and jeopardizing call quality. For this reason, it is up to the user to ensure that the reserved bandwidth is not exceeded.

Understanding Real-Time Transport Protocol

IP RTP priority (which is commonly known as *priority queuing with WFQ*) identifies and expedites time- sensitive RTP/UDP traffic. RTP features a priority queue, reserved bandwidth queues, and an unreserved queue. It is optimized for RTP and all other traffic treated with a WFQ algorithm. The strict priority applied here means that if datagrams exit a port in the priority queue, they are dequeued first, ahead of any other traffic. One aspect to particularly note with this method is the lack of bandwidth enforcement for any of the supported queues.

IP RTP priority gives absolute priority to selected traffic, when implemented along with CB-WFQ. This also allows the user to set up additional classes within CB-WFQ for other traffic types requiring something better than best-effort service but not a strict priority. All other traffic will be serviced fairly by WFQ according to its assigned weight.

For example, when configuring RTP for VoIP traffic, ensure that you specify only the range of ports that VoIP uses. Otherwise, it will make reservations for ports not used by VoIP, which can steal bandwidth rightfully needed by VoIP. *RTP marks voice traffic as priority over everything else*, as shown in Figure 6.1. All other traffic not explicitly assigned to a queue is placed in queues are that prioritized and queued by either weighted fair queuing or class-based WFQ; they contend for bandwidth not claimed by RTP.

Figure 6.1 Real-Time Protocol in Action

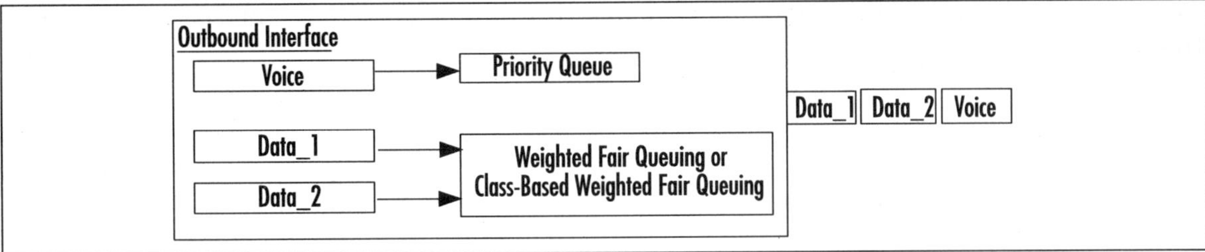

Configuring RTP

RTP is configured in interface configuration mode. Bandwidth is expressed in *kilobits* per second. RTP is enabled with a single command string, as follows:

In this example, we are reserving 64k for any traffic for 16,000 UDP ports starting with UDP port number 14,000. This means that UDP ports from 14,000 to 30,000 receive prioritized service on this interface:

```
ip rtp priority starting-UDP-port number-of-UDP-ports b/w-reserved-for-VOIP
```

Example:

```
ip rtp priority 14000 16000 64
```

Remember that RTP makes a hard reservation: its selected bandwidth is locked and reserved, regardless of whether traffic is flowing over the selected ports or not. As far as our traffic is concerned, our configuration example was bad because it starts with 14,000. This means that our traffic could be dropped due to other protocols that use UDP ports specified in this range. Additionally, if we make a reservation for 16,000 ports and starting with port number 14,000, traffic could overwhelm the 64k reservation we created and steal bandwidth from priority traffic. We could be giving precedence to non-critical ports such as 14000 to 16383. We should adjust our values accordingly to grant priority only to ports in a range that services our ports.

The key to successful RTP use is identifying which and how many UDP ports are used by your traffic and lock in the bandwidth for that range. When specifying the bandwidth, understand that this is the maximum amount of bandwidth that will be reserved for your traffic. Your calculations should factor the amount of bandwidth needed, the number of simultaneous sessions, and a small burst budget. In addition to doing these calculations, you must be sure that you have enough bandwidth available on the circuit to support your requirements.

Configuring Priority Queuing with WFQ (IP RTP Priority)

Configure RTP on an interface by issuing the **ip rtp priority** command while in interface configuration mode. This command specifies a starting port number, port number range (number of ports that qualify), and total queue bandwidth. For instance, if you want to configure RTP on interface Serial 1/0 for ports 16384 through 17000, with a total bandwidth of 128kbps, the commands would be as follows:

```
!
Router1(config)# interface s1/0
Router1(config-if)# ip rtp priority 16384 616 128
```

Note that the second parameter is the range—that is, a number that, when added to the starting number, results in the highest port number that is to be used. In the preceding example, 16384 + 616 = 17000.

Context:

```
ip rtp priority starting-rtp-port-number port-number-range bandwidth
```

When configuring IP RTP priority for voice, use the following guidelines:

- **starting-rtp-port** Lower bound of UDP port. The lowest port number to which the packets are sent. For VoIP, set this value to **16384**.
- **port-number-range** The range of UDP destination ports. A number that, added to the *starting-rtp-port-number*, yields the highest UDP port number. For VoIP, set this value to **16383** because the upper port for VoIP traffic is 32767 (32767 – 16384 = 16383).
- **bandwidth** Maximum allowed bandwidth (kbps) in the priority queue. Set this number according to the number of simultaneous calls you require the system to support.

The following sample configuration enables IP RTP priority to 720Kbps for VoIP on a serial interface:

```
Router1(config)# interface Serial0/0
Router1(config-if)# ip rtp priority 16384 16383 720
```

Note that if the interface configured for IP RTP priority is greater than 2Mbps, you need to enable WFQ with the **fair-queue** interface configuration command.

Header compression is another option to consider. For example, VoIP packets are composed of one or more speech codec samples or frames encapsulated in 40 bytes of IP/UDP/RTP headers. 40 bytes is a large amount of overhead for VoIP payloads, considering that the voice payload is usually about 20 bytes. This is especially true when voice is traveling over low-speed links. For this reason, RTP header compression (detailed in RFC 2508) was created to reduce the RTP header size.

Compressed Real-Time Transport Protocol

cRTP reduces the header overhead for RTP traffic by eliminating redundant information between packets. For instance, imagine a data stream consisting of 100 packets, where the first 99 have identical headers and the last one signals the end of the transmission. Why should the router have to continue to use up valuable bandwidth to send the exact same information 99 times? It shouldn't. Therefore, it simply sends the first packet, then tags each packet after that to let the far end know where to look for the header info—in this case, to packet number 1—thereby greatly reducing overhead.

RTP Header Compression

RFC 2508 specifies two formats of cRTP:

- **Compressed RTP (CR)** Used when the IP, UDP, and RTP headers remain consistent. All three headers are compressed.
- **Compressed UDP (CU)** Used when there is a large change in the RTP timestamp or when the RTP payload type changes. The IP and UDP headers are compressed, but the RTP header is not.

Compressing the IP/UDP/RTP header in an RTP packet can effectively reduce the amount of bandwidth required in a VoIP network. Results from compression can be great, reducing the header size from 40 bytes to approximately 2 bytes where no checksums are being sent and 4 bytes with checksums (see Figure 6.2).

Figure 6.2 RTP/UDP/IP Packet Headers cRTP Reductions

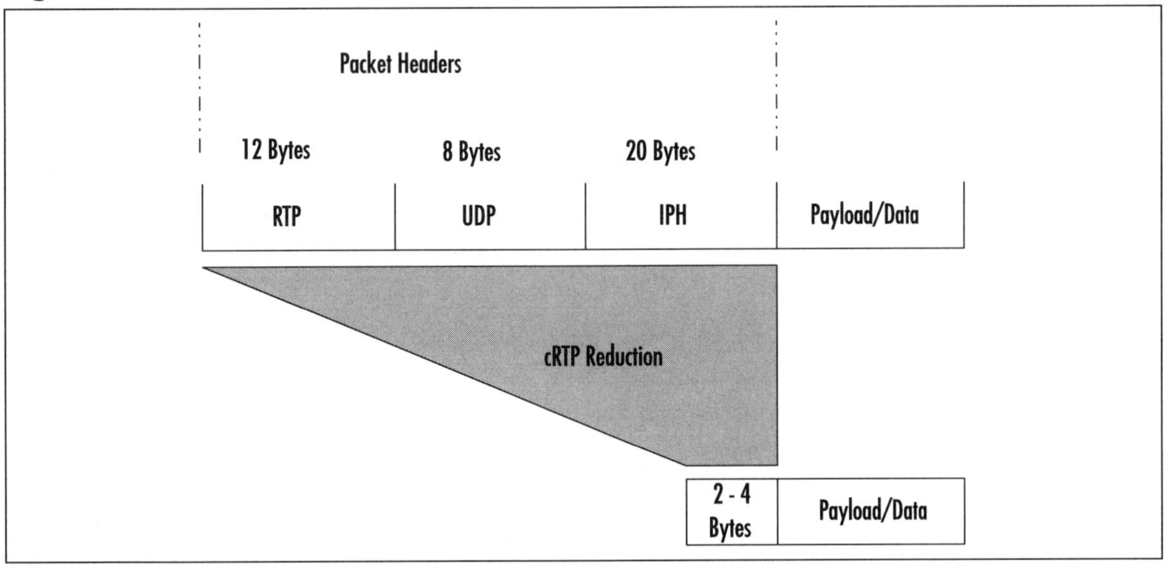

In Figure 6.3 we see the RTP header compression process. Queuing occurs before the compression process. The engine then determines RTP traffic, and only RTP packets are compressed. All packets, non-RTP and cRTP, are then passed on to the interface.

Figure 6.3 RTP Header Compression

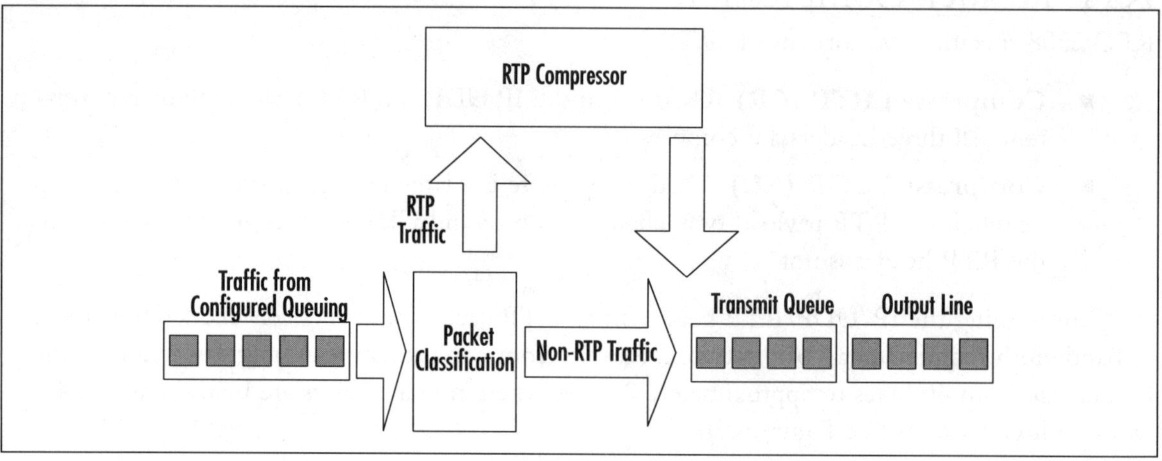

cRTP Implementation

cRTP should not be used on links greater than 2Mbps.You should configure cRTP if the following conditions exist in your network:

- Slow links
- Need to save bandwidth

Enabling compression on both ends of a low bandwidth serial link can greatly reduce the network overhead if there is a relatively large amount of RTP traffic. cRTP is supported on serial lines using Frame Relay, high-level data link control (HDLC), or point-to-point protocol (PPP) encapsulation. It is also supported over integrated services digital network (ISDN) interfaces.

It is important to mention that the available router resources (such as CPU and memory) should be considered when implementing cRTP—or any QoS technique. cRTP depends heavily on the CPU, and could cause utilization to rise, depending on your traffic amounts.

cRTP offers an opportunity to increase bandwidth availability with its header compression. This feature can reduce the IP header from 40 bytes to 2 or 4 bytes, as shown in Figure 6.4. This is a per-packet reduction and is very significant for traffic such as VoIP where a typical call can generate hundreds or thousands of packets per minute. Only a single command, executed on the interface, is needed to enable cRTP:

```
ip rtp header-compression [passive]
```

The **passive** keyword must be entered on only one end. **passive** turns on compression for outgoing packets if incoming packets have already been compressed.

Figure 6.4 cRTP Header Compression

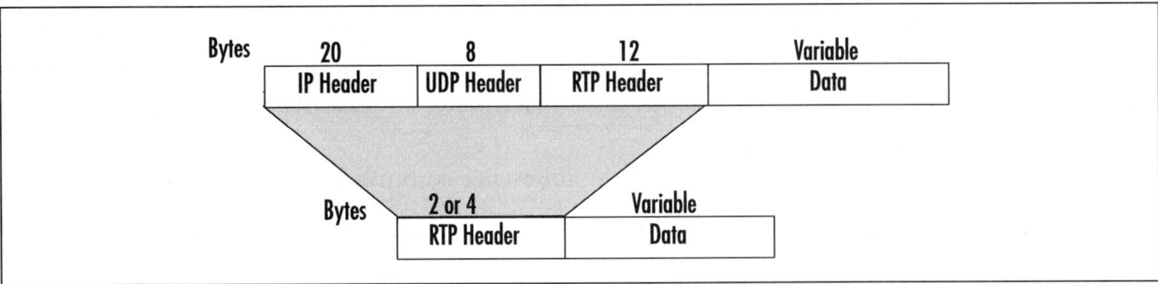

Before you can enable RTP header compression, you must have configured a serial line that uses Frame Relay, HDLC, or PPP encapsulation, or an ISDN interface. The following sections describe how to enable cRTP header compression for these interface types.

Enable cRTP on a HDLC or PPP Serial Interface

To enable cRTP header compression on HDLC or PPP serial interfaces, use the following command while in interface configuration mode (you must enable compression on both ends of a serial connection). The following command enables RTP header compression:

```
ip rtp header-compression [passive]
```

If you include the **passive** keyword, the software compresses outgoing RTP packets only if incoming RTP packets on the same interface are compressed. If you use the command without the **passive** keyword, the software compresses all RTP traffic.

Enable cRTP with Frame Relay Encapsulation

To enable cRTP headers with Frame Relay links, use one of the following commands while in interface configuration mode.

If you would like to enable RTP header compression on the physical interface and all the interface maps will inherit it, you should use the **frame-relay ip rtp header-compression [passive]** command. Subsequently, all maps will perform RTP/IP header compression.

However, if you only would like to enable RTP header compression only on the particular map specified, you should use the **frame-relay map ip *ip-address dlci* [broadcast] rtp header-compression [active | passive]** command.

Finally, to enable both RTP and TCP header compression on the link, use the **frame-relay map ip *ip-address dlci* [broadcast] compress** command.

Change the Number of Header Compression Connections

By default, the Cisco IOS supports a total of 16 RTP header compression connections on an interface. To change that number and specify the total number of RTP header compression connections supported on an interface, use the following command while in interface configuration mode:

```
ip rtp compression connections number
```

Displaying Statistics

You can display specific statistics, such as the contents of IP routing tables, caches, and databases. The information provided can be used to determine resource utilization and solve network problems. You can also display information about node reachability and discover the routing path your packets are taking through the network.

To display compressed RTP statistics, use the following commands while in EXEC mode.

- To display Frame Relay RTP header compression statistics, use the **show frame-relay ip rtp header-compression [interface *type number*]** command.
- To display RTP header compression statistics use the **show ip rtp header-compression [*type number*] [detail]** command.

cRTP Configuration Examples

The following example enables RTP header compression for a serial, ISDN, or asynchronous interface. For ISDN, you also need a broadcast dialer map:

```
interface serial 0 (or interface bri 0)
ip rtp header-compression
encapsulation ppp
ip rtp compression-connections 25
```

The following example for Frame Relay encapsulation enables RTP header compression on the specified map:

```
interface serial 0
ip address 1.0.0.2 255.0.0.0
encapsulation frame-relay
no keepalive
frame-relay map ip 1.0.0.1 17 broadcast rtp header-compression
```

Verifying IP RTP Priority

Verify your IP RTP priority configuration by displaying the interface with the **show** command. Sample output for the serial interface described previously is as follows:

```
!
interface Serial0/1
 bandwidth 64
 ip address 10.10.10.101 255.255.255.252
 no ip directed-broadcast
 ip rtp priority 16384 16383 720
```

Cisco provides several commands to check and monitor RTP. You can view the queuing operations on an interface with **show queue serial 0** to view queuing on interface serial 0, for example:

```
RR1# show queue serial 1/0
  Input queue: 0/128/0/0 (size/max/drops/flushes); Total output drops: 0
  Queueing strategy: weighted fair
  Output queue: 0/1000/128/0 (size/max total/threshold/drops)
     Conversations  0/1/16 (active/max active/max total)
     Reserved Conversations 0/0 (allocated/max allocated)
     Available Bandwidth 112 kilobits/sec
```

Several **debug** commands enable you to monitor RTP operations as they occur. The **debug priority** command is not RTP-specific; rather, it shows the operation and errors of any queuing feature. This allows you to see if any packets are being dropped from your queue, which indicates that the maximum bandwidth you specified is enough or that you need to increase or decrease your range of UDP ports. You can also focus on specific RTP operations with **debug ip rtp header-compression** and **debug ip rtp packets** commands.

Resource Reservation Protocol

RSVP is an IP service that guarantees, or "reserves," bandwidth across a network. RSVP is an ideal QoS method for real-time traffic (audio and video). Real-time traffic is consistent and very sensitive to latency; therefore, it requires a guaranteed network consistency. Without this consistency, there is risk of jitter, delay variations, and information loss due to insufficient bandwidth, which can be devastating to a call.

RSVP supports two types of real-time traffic:

- **Multicast traffic** Primarily a flow in one direction from a single host sending packets to many hosts
- **Unicast traffic** Guaranteed bandwidth between two hosts

There are three RSVP-supported reservation styles: wildcard-filter style, fixed-filter style, and shared-explicit style. A reservation style is a set of control options that specify a number of supported parameters. There are two groups of reservation styles: *distinct* and *shared*. A distinct reservation notes each individual flow, as in a video stream. A shared reservation notes a group of flows, as in an audio environment.

The three types of reservation styles are:

- **Wildcard-filter (WF) style** A shared reservation style. A single reservation is created, into which flows from all upstream senders are mixed. The reservation is extended to new senders.
- **Fixed-filter (FF) style** A distinct reservation request is created for data packets from a particular sender.

- **Shared-explicit (SE) style** A shared reservation style. A single reservation is created, into which flows from all upstream senders are mixed. The scope is explicitly specified by the receiver. The bandwidth reserved by WFQ can be statically defined or dynamically allocated.

A major difference between RSVP and routing protocols is that RSVP works on the entire flow, rather than routing individual datagrams. The reservation is actually made from the sending node to the receiving node, and the connection is a simplex session, so two-way traffic requires two individual RSVP sessions. A session consists of a flow of data to a particular destination and protocol, identified by the destination address, protocol ID (PID), and destination port. There are three types of RSVP traffic:

- **Best-effort** Standard IP connectionless traffic, where upper-level protocols are responsible for error checking and flow control.
- **Rate-sensitive** Sometimes referred to as *guaranteed bit-rate service*, it is a class in which the flow requires a constant rate (such as 128kbs or 384kbps) and is able to withstand queuing delays as a tradeoff for the guaranteed bandwidth.
- **Delay-sensitive** Split into two classifications:
  - *Controlled-delay* traffic is for non-real-time applications.
  - *Predictive service* traffic is used for voice, video, and other real-time applications.

The originating RSVP host requests a path through the network that can support its bandwidth requirements. RSVP then queries each RSVP-enabled router to find the path that can support the bandwidth needed for the call. Once that path is built from source to destination, the call is switched along that path.

RSVP is enabled on an interface basis using a single command, as shown in the following syntax. You can specify that up to 75 percent of the interface bandwidth be reserved for RSVP traffic. In the command syntax, the **bandwidth** keyword specifies how much of the interface bandwidth to reserve for RSVP traffic. RSVP reservations are expressed in *kilobits per second*, so calculate accordingly:

```
ip rsvp bandwidth [interface-kbps] [single-flow-kbps]
```

Example:

```
ip rsvp bandwidth 64 64
```

Our example reserves 64k for our RSVP marked traffic, and of that, a single flow can use all 64k if necessary.

You can request RSVP support for your VoIP traffic when you define the dial peer statements by including the following command. This syntax basically enables VoIP to mark traffic with precedence in the ToS field indicated by RSVP:

```
! Request RSVP (enter this command in the dial peer statement)
 req-qos controlled-load
```

Configuring RSVP

RSVP is enabled on individual interfaces with the **ip rsvp bandwidth** command. The process is shown next.

```
interface interface-type interface-number
bandwidth bandwidth
ip rsvp bandwidth available-bandwidth max-bandwidth
```

While in interface configuration mode, specify the bandwidth of the link. Then enter the **ip rsvp bandwidth** command to specify the total amount of bandwidth reserved for RSVP and the maximum speed of any individual reservation.

For instance:

```
Router1 (config)# interface s1/0
Router1 (config-if)# bandwidth 1536
Router1 (config-if)# ip rsvp bandwidth 1152 128
```

In this example, interface Serial 1/0 is configured for 1536kbps. RSVP is then configured to reserve a maximum of 1152kbps, and no individual connection will be allocated more than 128kbps. Remember that only 75 percent of the total link speed can be used for RSVP:

Verifying RSVP

Cisco provides several commands that you can use to troubleshoot and verify RSVP operation. The **show ip rsvp** command enables you to verify several aspects of RSVP, as described here. The **debug ip rsvp** command allows you to capture detail on RSVP activity as it occurs, either high level or detailed, depending on the amount of information you need:

```
show ip rsvp  { atm-peak-rate-limit |  installed |  interface |  neighbor }
```

- **atm-peak-rate-limit** Maximum rate this ATM interface will handle (peak cell rate).
- **installed** Queues configured on this interface.
- **interface** Detailed RSVP information on this information.
- **neighbor** RSVP neighbors of this router.

You can capture real-time statistics and information on RSVP activity using the **debug ip rsvp { detail | detail sbm }** command. You can confirm that your RSVP configuration is entered properly with the **show run** command, but there are other commands that you will find useful to monitor the status of RSVP. With the **show ip rsvp installed** command, all the current reservations can be displayed for each interface:

```
Router1# show ip rsvp installed
RSVP: Ethernet2/0 has no installed reservations
RSVP: Serial5/0:0
BPS To From Protoc DPort Sport Weight Conversation
128K 10.0.1.2 10.0.6.2 TCP 0 0 6 271
64K 10.0.1.3 10.0.6.3 TCP 0 0 12 272
```

In the previous example, two reservations are made of outbound traffic on Serial5/0:0 from the senders 10.0.1.2 and 10.0.1.3 to the receivers 10.0.6.2 and 10.0.6.3. The first reservation is for 128Kbps, and the second is for 64Kbps. The weight listed is the weighting factor used by WFQ. The conversation is the number assigned to that flow. Since the session flow is toward Client B from Client A, and because weighted fair queuing (WFQ) and weighted random early detection (WRED) works on output interfaces, there is no reservation on the Ethernet 2/0, even though the session is flowing *into* the router through this interface. To see interface-specific information, such as how much total bandwidth has been reserved for RSVP (i/f max) and the amount currently being used (allocated), issue the **show ip rsvp interface** command:

```
Router1# show ip rsvp interface
interface allocated i/f max flow max pct UDP IP UDP_IP UDP M/C
Et2/0 0M 7500K 7500K 0 0 2 0 0
Se5/0:0 192K 1152K 1152K 16 0 1 0 0
```

Sometimes it is helpful to see all neighboring nodes that are participating in RSVP. To do this, use the **show ip rsvp neighbor** command:

```
Router1# show ip rsvp neighbor
Interfac Neighbor Encapsulation
Et2/0 10.0.6.3 RSVP
Et2/0 10.0.6.2 RSVP
Se5/0:0 10.0.101.5 RSVP
```

This tells us that there are two RSVP neighbors on the Ethernet 2/0 interface and another on Serial 5/0:0. These neighbors can be any nodes that are currently using RSVP. They could be end stations (10.0.6.3 and 10.0.6.2) or RSVP-participating router interfaces (10.0.101.5). To display RSVP information such as requests flowing upstream and receiver and sender information currently in the database, use the following commands, respectively:

```
Router1# show ip rsvp request
To From Pro DPort Sport Next Hop I/F Fi Serv BPS Bytes
10.0.1.2 10.0.6.2 TCP 0 0 10.0.6.2 Et2/0 FF LOAD 128K 64K
10.0.1.3 10.0.6.3 TCP 0 0 10.0.6.3 Et2/0 FF RATE 64K 1K
Router1# show ip rsvp reservation
To From Pro DPort Sport Next Hop I/F Fi Serv BPS Bytes
10.0.1.2 10.0.6.2 TCP 0 0 10.0.101.5 Se5/0 FF LOAD 128K 64K
10.0.1.3 10.0.6.3 TCP 0 0 10.0.101.5 Se5/0 FF RATE 64K 1K
Router1# show ip rsvp sender
To From Pro DPort Sport Prev Hop I/F BPS Bytes
10.0.1.2 10.0.6.2 TCP 0 0 10.0.6.2 Et2/0 128K 1K
10.0.1.3 10.0.6.3 TCP 0 0 10.0.6.3 Et2/0 64K 1K
```

The **show ip rsvp request** and **show ip rsvp reservation** commands also indicate the type of service desired, either controlled-load (**LOAD**) or guaranteed-rate (**RATE**).

Queuing

Many applications currently in use are of an interactive, transaction-based or time-sensitive nature. These applications are commonly referred to as *real-time* applications. An example of a real-time application is *Voice over X (VoX)*. VoX can refer to voice over IP, voice over Frame Relay, or voice over Asynchronous Transfer Mode (ATM). Voice traffic does not tolerate excessive delays because it will devastate the content of the call. Therefore, QoS mechanisms must be provisioned to reduce end-to-end delay or jitter.

Cisco routers route IP packets from input ports to output ports based on the most specific route entry in the routing table. During periods when interface traffic volumes are low, packets traverse a given interface in a first-in, first-out manner. As packets arrive faster than they can be forwarded out of an interface, they are placed in a queue. Therefore, queuing happens when network congestion occurs (that is, the queue depth is greater than or equal to 1); otherwise all packets are forwarded out of an interface as they arrive.

Various queuing methods have been developed and implemented on Cisco routers. We will explain how the queuing algorithms work, and how each method improves performance, allowing faster access to the outgoing interface. Queuing algorithms allow different traffic streams to be prioritized on network interfaces. These queuing algorithms can allow real-time traffic to be transmitted before other, less time-sensitive traffic. You can optimize network traffic flow resulting in better traffic management and support of all end-user applications.

It is important to understand the basics of the queuing process. In a router, queues act as a *holding area*. Queues hold packets until enough resources are available to forward the packets out the egress port. The packets will be forwarded immediately, provided there is no congestion in the router. Network queues are used to handle traffic bursts arriving faster than the egress interface can handle. For example, a router connecting a Fast Ethernet LAN interface to a T1 WAN circuit often sees chunks of traffic arriving on the LAN interface faster than it can send it out to the WAN. In this case, the queue holds the traffic so that the T1 circuit can process the packets at its own pace. This is a normal operation necessary to handle traffic transiting an interface and does not necessarily indicate a congestion problem.

Several queuing types are useful and provide traffic benefits. This section discusses the following queuing strategies.

- Custom queuing
- Priority queuing
- Weighted fair queuing
- Class-based weighted fair queuing
- First-in, first-out

Each of these queuing techniques has advantages and disadvantages pertaining to the design and configuration of each individual network. We will examine how each queuing method works, then provide a decision process for selecting the best queuing scheme for your needs.

Selecting a Cisco IOS Queuing Method

Steps 1 through 6 should be followed when determining which queuing option to implement:

1. Is the WAN link congested with network traffic?
   - If there is no congestion on the link, there is no need to sort the traffic into queues.
   - If the link is consistently congested, traffic queuing may not resolve the problem.
   - If the link is only congested for short periods of time, queuing may resolve the flows.
2. What type of traffic is traversing the network and is it congested?
   - Learn traffic flows and study the link during peak usage. This will help determine which traffic is utilizing the link and what can be done with that traffic.
   - Determine whether control over individual streams has to be enforced and/or if generic protocols have to be queued to improve response time. Remember, traffic utilization is dynamic and will have to be analyzed often to determine whether changes are required.
3. After the traffic analysis is completed, can traffic be serviced by WFQ?
   - Determine whether packet trains are utilizing the link during peak times. If so, automatic queuing provided by WFQ may meet current needs. Remember, traffic patterns are dynamic and subject to change. It is recommended that a recurring traffic analysis be performed to determine whether queuing optimization is required.
4. What is your organization's queuing policy?
   - Queuing policies are based on application requirements in conjunction with a detailed traffic study. All interfaces require basic queuing configuration. These configuration values may have to be adjusted based on application requirement or location.
5. Does control over individual streams have to be taken into account?
   - If certain applications are failing, but sufficient bandwidth remains available, custom queuing (CQ), WFQ, or CB-WFQ can be utilized. This will allow the network administrator to prioritize the critical traffic to be serviced while the other network flows will contend for remaining bandwidth.
6. Can network delay be tolerated?
   - If so, develop priority queuing (PQ) schemes. Determine which flows need servicing first and then determine how the other flows can be spread among the remaining queues. If the network cannot handle delays in packet arrival, then CQ can be used. CQ can guarantee that all applications gain some access to the link.

The queuing method selection process is illustrated in Figure 6.5.

Figure 6.5 Queuing Method Selection

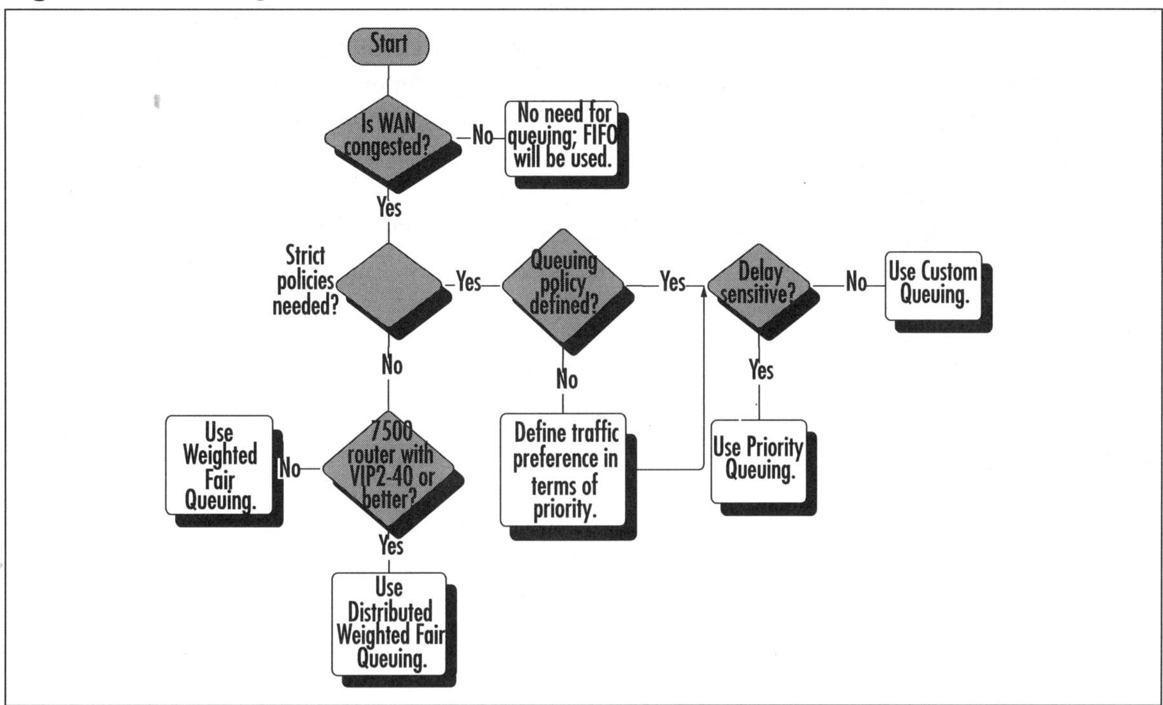

When managing congestion on links that have very low physical bandwidth, consider the amount being used by the routing protocol active on the interface. For locations that are stub sites that have only one link connected to the backbone, consider using a default route or gateway of last resort. This will avoid the overhead associated with dynamic routing protocols. Other things to consider are dynamic routing protocol selection, such as Routing Information Protocol (RIP) versus Open Shortest Path First (OSPF). Distance Vector protocols such as RIP will propagate the entire routing table every 30 seconds, requiring more bandwidth than link state protocols such as OSPF, which propagate changes in a given topology as they occur.

Table 6.1 provides a comparison of queuing techniques.

Table 6.1 Queuing Technique Selection

Weighted Fair Queuing	Priority Queuing	Custom Queuing
No queue lists	4 queues	16 queues
Low volume given priority	High queue serviced first	Round-robin service
Conversation dispatching	Packet dispatching	Threshold dispatching
Interactive traffic gets priority	Critical traffic gets priority	Allocation of available bandwidth
File transfer gets balanced access	Designed for low-bandwidth links	Designed for high-speed low-bandwidth links
Enabled by default	Must configure	Must configure

First-In, First-Out Queuing

FIFO queuing is the default state on most network interfaces: traffic is processed in the order it was received. Packets arrive in sequential order at the network interface. They are then inserted into the output buffer in their received sequence, and processed in the exact order that they arrive at the buffer. The packet buffer or processor on the interface does not give precedence to the type of packets or traffic arriving or when it has to exit the interface. All packets exit the interface sequentially, in the same order in which they arrived. This is the default queuing method for all interfaces, except for serial interfaces operating at a rate of 2.048 Mbps and slower. Figure 6.6 illustrates FIFO queuing.

Figure 6.6 FIFO Queuing

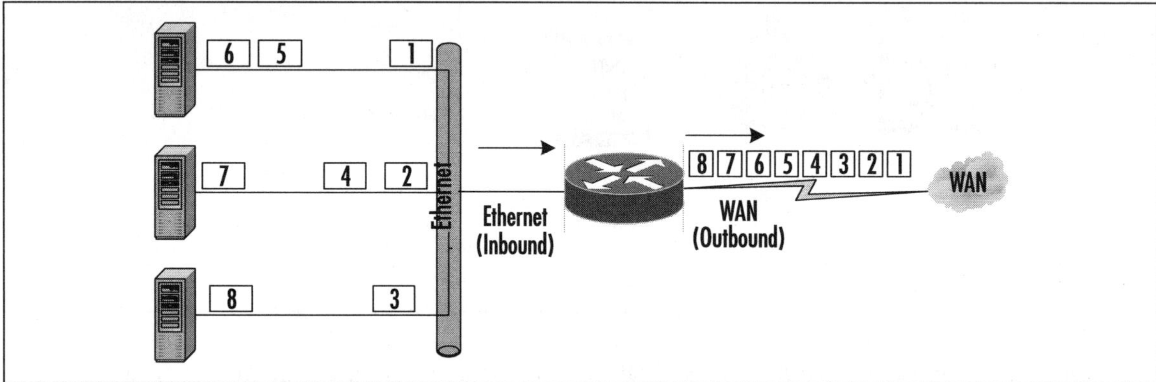

When designing router hardware and software, a methodology had to be derived to provide all packet flows fair access to an outgoing interface. A packet flow is a conversation between two end stations. Problems occur when large continuous packet transfers (packet troops or packet trains, such as a large file transfer), consume the bulk of the available bandwidth and prevent other traffic from using the link. Under sustained heavy utilization, time-sensitive traffic like voice and video may not reach its destination in a timely manner, which may cause unacceptable user results. In theory, such large file transfers could decrease its utilization of the network link and allow time-sensitive traffic fair access to interface bandwidth.

The queuing algorithms described in the next sections were implemented to give network managers the ability to balance interface bandwidth allocation between multiple applications and assign priority to mission-critical applications. Note that, because FIFO is the default queuing method when no other queuing is specified, there are no specific commands to configure FIFO queuing.

Low Latency Queuing (LLQ)

LLQ offers the flexibility to support multiple queues, enabling you to prioritize sensitive traffic such as VoIP. LLQ can ensure that critical traffic gets requisite bandwidth needed for its operation yet still sets aside minimum bandwidth needed for other traffic. Such queuing is on a hop-by-hop basis and is effective only if enabled on each hop that the voice traffic must transit.

LLQ segregates traffic into four classes: a high priority class, two guaranteed bandwidth classes, and a default class. The priority class is guaranteed a priority over all other classes, regardless of how much bandwidth the other classes may need. The two guaranteed bandwidth classes ensure that a certain minimum of bandwidth is available for traffic placed in these queues. The default class is for any traffic not specifically allocated to either the priority or guaranteed classes.

To enable LLQ, define an access list that permits the target traffic. Next, build class and policy maps that specify the bandwidth to be guaranteed. Apply this queuing policy to transit interface. An example configuration using VoIP is provided.

```
! Permit range of UDP ports used by VoIP traffic.
access-list 199 permit udp any any range 16384 37276
! TCP port used H.323 control channels.
access-list 199 permit tcp any any eq 1720
!
class-map voip
match access-group 199
!
policy-map PRIORITY
class voip
priority 32
!
interface Serial1/0
bandwidth 256
service-policy output PRIORITY
```

Cisco provides several commands to verify and troubleshoot LLQ. The **debug priority** command can monitor LLQ activity in real time. The **show queue** command shows priority queuing statistics such as packets passed or dropped through the priority queue. You can use the **show policy interface** command to check your interface to determine the policy that is running on it.

Priority Queuing (PQ)

PQ provides a granular means for the network administrator to determine which traffic must be dequeued and serviced first. With priority queuing techniques, you must know and understand how traffic flows within the network. This type of control is important when specific mission-critical traffic must receive servicing. You can create different interface packet queues that are serviced in a hierarchical order. Each network flow can be categorized by the following:

- Protocol or sub-protocol type
- Incoming interface
- Packet size
- Fragments
- Access lists

NOTE

The priority queues are known as high, medium, normal, and low.

The router services the queues from highest to lowest priority. The service order on the four queues works such that if the high queue has traffic in it, the normal queue cannot forward any packets until all packets in the high priority queue are transmitted, which can become a major issue when developing and deploying the queuing strategy for a network. You may inadvertently starve a certain network stream, preventing use and operation of certain applications and services on the network. However, PQ may be ideal for networks in which critical applications are not able to run because network users are running less important applications. Figure 6.7 illustrates the PQ packet flow. When using PQ, packets are compared with a statically defined priority list. If there is any capacity in the priority queue associated with the incoming traffic, the packet is placed in the designated queue to await its turn to be serviced out of the interface. If there is no room left in the queue, the packet is dropped. Dropped packets do not go into another queue.

Figure 6.7 PQ Selection Process

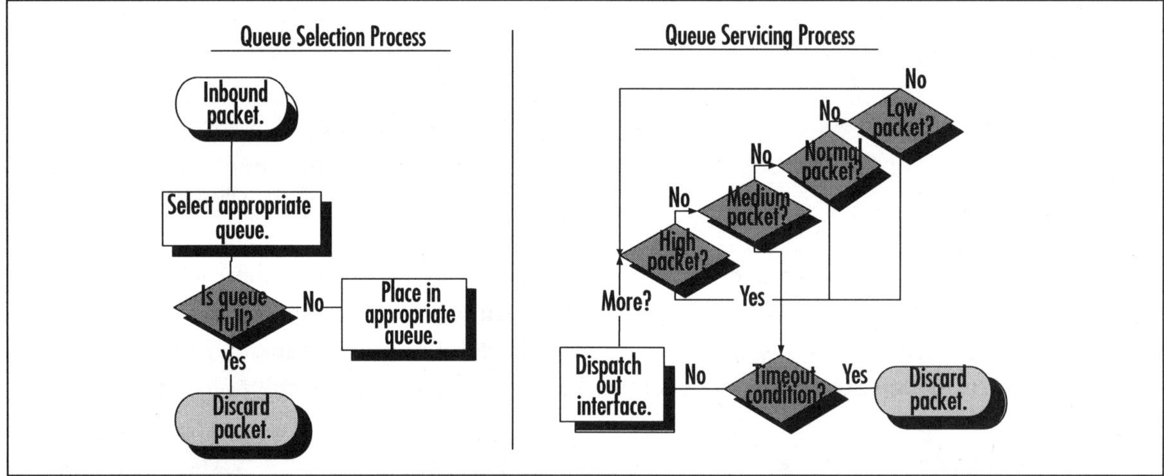

PQ defines how traffic is prioritized in the network. The router places traffic in these queues, based on predefined filters (lists). The queue with the highest priority is serviced first until it is empty, then the lower queues are serviced in sequence. As its name suggests, traffic is processed based on priority. Traffic with the highest priority is given precedence over low priority queues. Four output queues exist, and traffic is placed in these queues based on user-configured criteria. Packets that are not classified by priority fall into the normal queue. Figure 6.8 shows how PQ works.

Figure 6.8 Priority Queuing

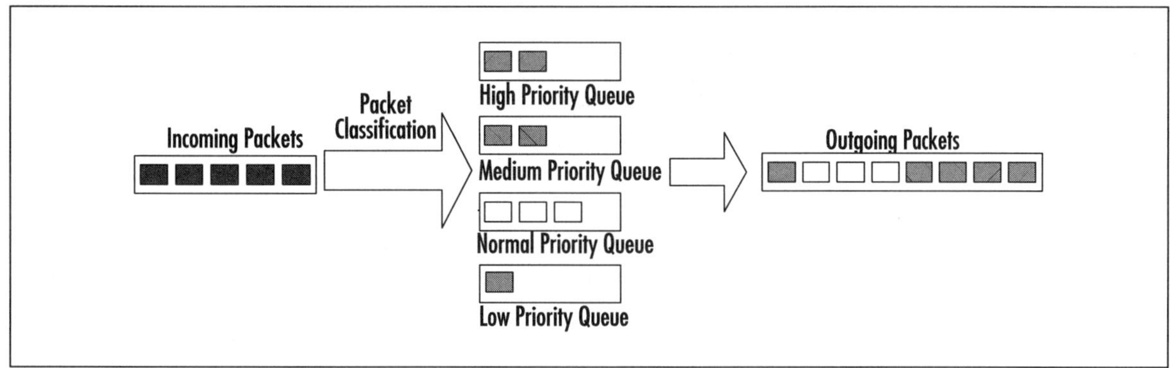

Since the definitions for queues are not open to interpretation, a packet either fits into a queue, or it does not. Even though packets are sent into queues, there is no guarantee they will be processed in time to reach their destination, especially if the high queue remains busy. PQ enables control of the priority of mission-critical traffic.

You should have a good understanding of the effect of PQ on the flow of other traffic. PQ requires recurring reassessment, since traffic pattern and requirements change as well; traffic that was once considered high priority may become a low priority.

PQ can have a notable (some would say degradation) effect on CPU utilization. Cisco routers will process switch packets on interfaces that have priority queuing enabled, which means more work for the CPU. The packet-switching performance will be degraded compared with other interfaces using caching schemes. PQ is not supported on logical, tunnel interfaces.

Priority queues on an interface are scanned for packets in descending order of priority, starting with the high priority queue, then the medium priority queue, and so forth. The packet at the head of the highest queue is then chosen for transmission. This process repeats itself each time a packet is to be sent. It should be noted that priority queuing can lead to situations in which lower priority queues are *starved* (not serviced); this can occur when higher priority queues remain full and active.

Configuring Priority Queuing

The tasks involved in configuring priority queuing are as follows:

1. Define a priority list.
2. Assign the priority list to an interface.

As with custom queuing, the definition of the priority list is vital to the proper operation of priority queuing. The following discussion highlights multiple ways to classify network traffic, which will help you apply priority queuing to your network.

Enabling Priority Queuing

The first step in configuring priority queuing is to define the priority list. The following explicates the **priority-list** command and its parameters:

```
Router1(config)# priority-list ?
      <1-16> Priority list number
Router1(config)# priority-list 1 ?
      default       Set priority queue for unspecified datagrams
      interface     Establish priorities for packets from an interface
      protocol      Priority queuing by protocol
      queue-limit   Set queue limits for priority queues
```

Create a priority list, which can be numbered between 1 and 16.Multiple priority lists can be configured on a single router and applied to different interfaces to deploy differing priority queuing policies. Identify which traffic you want to prioritize; you can prioritize by inbound interface or by protocol type.You can also select the default priority of unclassified traffic and set the queue limits in packets.

Consider the following sample requirements. All packets that enter the router from interface Ethernet 0/0 should be classified as medium priority. The default priority of all unclassified packets should be low. AppleTalk traffic should have priority over all other traffic (assign it to the high priority queue). TCP/IP traffic should be relegated to the normal queue. The following configuration will accomplish our goals using PQ.

```
Router1# configure terminal
Enter configuration commands, one per line. End with CNTL/Z.
Router1(config)# priority-list 1 protocol appletalk high
Router1(config)# priority-list 1 interface ethernet 0/0 medium
Router1(config)# priority-list 1 protocol ip normal
Router1(config)# priority-list 1 default low
Router1(config)# end
```

Configuring the Queue Limits

The default queue size values are 20, 40, 60, and 80 packets for the high, medium, normal, and low priority queues, respectively. To modify these default values, the **queue-limit** parameter is used at the global configuration level. In the following code output, the high, medium, normal, and low priority queues are adjusted to values of 200, 400, 600, and 800 packets, respectively:

```
Router1# configure terminal
Enter configuration commands, one per line. End with CNTL/Z.
Router1(config)# priority-list 4 queue-limit ?
<0-32767> High limit
Router1(config)# priority-list 4 queue-limit 200 ?
<0-32767> Medium limit
Router1(config)# priority-list 4 queue-limit 200 400 ?
<0-32767> Normal limit
Router1(config)# priority-list 4 queue-limit 200 400 600 ?
<0-32767> Lower limit
Router1(config)# priority-list 4 queue-limit 200 400 600 800
```

Be careful when changing these default values. Using larger queue sizes could have a negative impact on router operations due to the amount of memory taken by the queuing process. Large high priority queues servicing large amounts of traffic can cause the queuing process to spend exorbitant amounts of time servicing them. The end result, in this case, will be that the lower priority queues will be denied timely service, and upper-layer protocols may fail. Conversely, reducing the queue sizes to values that are too small will result in unnecessary tail drop, negatively affecting protocols serviced by PQ.

Applying Your Priority List to an Interface

Configuring PQ is similar to defining and applying an access list using the **access-list** and **access-group** commands. First, define the priority list, and apply it to the interface using the interface command **priority-group**. The following example applies priority lists 1 and 2 to interfaces serial 0/0 and 0/1, respectively:

```
Router1# configure terminal
Enter configuration commands, one per line. End with CNTL/Z.
Router1(config)# interface serial 0/0
Router1(config-if)# priority-group 1
Router1(config-if)# exit
Router1(config)# interface serial 0/1
Router1(config-if)# priority-group 2
Router1(config-if)# end
```

Verifying Priority Queuing

As with custom queuing, verify PQ operations by confirming that it is configured and enabled on the appropriate interfaces using the **show interface** command:

```
Router1# show interface serial 0/0
Serial0/0 is up, line protocol is up
Hardware is PowerQUICC Serial
Internet address is 192.168.10.1/24
MTU 1500 bytes, BW 1544 Kbit, DLY 20000 usec,
reliability 255/255, txload 1/255, rxload 1/255
Encapsulation HDLC, loopback not set, keepalive set (10 sec)
Last input 00:00:04, output 00:00:00, output hang never
Last clearing of "show interface" counters never
Input queue: 0/75/0 (size/max/drops); Total output drops: 0
Queuing strategy: priority-list 1
Output queue (queue priority: size/max/drops):
high: 0/20/0, medium: 0/40/0, normal 0/60/0, low 0/80/0
5 minute input rate 0 bits/sec, 0 packets/sec
5 minute output rate 0 bits/sec, 0 packets/sec
```

```
937 packets input, 84028 bytes, 0 no buffer
Received 937 broadcasts, 0 runts, 0 giants, 0 throttles
1 input errors, 0 CRC, 1 frame, 0 overrun, 0 ignored, 0 abor
820 packets output, 51295 bytes, 0 underruns
0 output errors, 0 collisions, 15 interface resets
0 output buffer failures, 0 output buffers swapped out
0 carrier transitions
DCD=up DSR=up DTR=up RTS=up CTS=up
Router1#
```

Check the current state of queuing for details such as the maximum size and tail drops for each queue. You can do this, as well as verifying the configuration of the priority lists with the command **show queuing priority**:

```
Router1# show queuing priority
Current priority queue configuration:
List Queue Args
1 low default
1 medium interface Serial0/0
1 high protocol appletalk
1 normal protocol ip
2 low default
2 normal interface Ethernet0/0
2 high protocol ip tcp port telnet
2 medium protocol ip gt 1000
2 high protocol ip list 101
```

The queuing process is listed alphanumerically, followed by details about the characteristics of the queuing policy alphanumerically; this does not show the order in which queuing is processed.

Priority Queuing Examples

Users "surfing" the Web and downloading non-work related files can cause performance problems with time-sensitive Software Network Architecture (SNA) traffic and other tn3270 (Telnet) traffic on certain networks, to use an example. The following situation grants SNA traffic (Data-Link Switching (DLSw)) and Telnet traffic high priority and designates all other traffic a low priority. There may be some exceptions that can be controlled using an access list to make a normal priority.

```
!
priority-list 1 protocol ip normal list 100
priority-list 1 protocol ip high tcp telnet
priority-list 1 protocol dlsw high
priority-list 1 default low
!
```

The **priority-list 1 protocol ip normal list 100** command references access list 100 to identify which IP traffic will be relegated to the normal priority queue. To configure Telnet traffic as high priority, use **priority-list 1 protocol ip high tcp telnet** . To configure DLSw traffic as high priority, the **priority-list 1 protocol dlsw high** command is used.

For traffic that does not match any of the previous statements, the **priority-list 1 default low** command will place them in the low priority queue. If no default queue is defined the normal queue is used.

```
!
interface Serial0
priority-group 1
!
```

The interface **priority-group 1** command is configured under the whole interface to specify that priority list 1 is used for that interface.

```
c2507# show interface serial 0
Serial0 is up, line protocol is up
Hardware is HD64570
MTU 1500 bytes, BW 1544 Kbit, DLY 20000 usec, rely 255/255, load 1/255
Encapsulation FRAME-RELAY, loopback not set, keepalive set (10 sec)
LMI enq sent 0, LMI stat recvd 0, LMI upd recvd 0, DTE LMI up
LMI enq recvd 0, LMI stat sent 0, LMI upd sent 0
LMI DLCI 1023 LMI type is CISCO frame relay DTE
Broadcast queue 0/64, broadcasts sent/dropped 0/0, interface broadcasts 0
Last input 00:00:03, output 00:00:03, output hang never
Last clearing of "show interface" counters 00:00:03
Input queue: 0/75/0 (size/max/drops); Total output drops: 0
Queueing strategy: priority-list 1
Output queue (queue priority: size/max/drops): high: 0/20/0, medium: 0/40/0, normal:
0/60/0, low: 0/80/0
5 minute input rate 0 bits/sec, 0 packets/sec
5 minute output rate 0 bits/sec, 0 packets/sec
0 packets input, 0 bytes, 0 no buffer
Received 0 broadcasts, 0 runts, 0 giants, 0 throttles
0 input errors, 0 CRC, 0 frame, 0 overrun, 0 ignored, 0 abort
0 packets output, 0 bytes, 0 underruns
0 output errors, 0 collisions, 0 interface resets
0 output buffer failures, 0 output buffers swapped out
0 carrier transitions DCD=up DSR=up DTR=up RTS=up CTS=up
c2507#
```

Using the **show interface serial 0** command, the type of queuing is displayed on the queuing strategy line of the interface output. The syntax for queues is size/max/drops, where size is the current used depth of the queue, max is the maximum depth of the queue before packets are dropped, and drops is the number of packets dropped after the max has been reached. The size and drops reset to 0 when the counters are cleared.

```
!
priority-list 1 queue-limit 30 60 60 90
!
```

The command **priority-list 1 queue-limit <*high*> <*med*> <*norm*> <*low*>** configures the different queues to different depths.

Custom Queuing (CQ)

Custom queuing seems like a logical progression for those who need a queuing solution with more flexibility than PQ. CQ guarantees some level of service to all created queues, unlike PQ where a busy high priority queue could prevent the servicing of lower priority queues. CQ gives consideration to all queues by servicing a set percentage of traffic from all queues in an equitable and balanced fashion. The percentage can be defined by the protocol, source/destination address, or incoming interface. Servicing each queue by set percentages ensures that each will be regularly guaranteed a share of the bandwidth.

CQ allows a specified number of bytes to be forwarded from a queue during servicing. CQ handles traffic by specifying the number (maximum) of packets or bytes to be serviced for each class of traffic. This process cycles through the queues, sending the portion of allocated data for each queue before moving to the next queue. When an empty queue is encountered, it sends packets from the next queue with packets, and so on. While a particular queue is being processed, packets are sent until the number of bytes sent exceeds the queue byte count or the queue is empty. Bandwidth used by a particular queue is specified bytes and queue length. Figure 6.9 shows CQ in action.

Figure 6.9 Custom Queuing

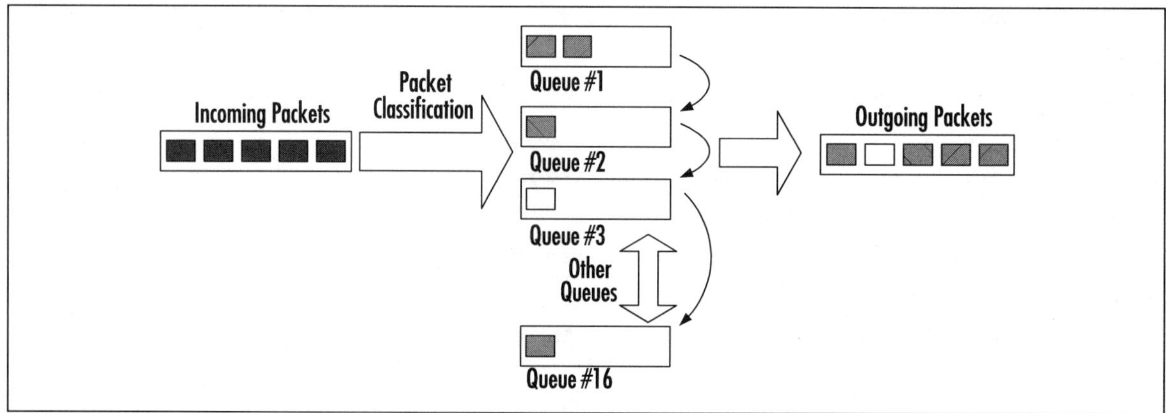

You are more involved in queue sizing and control with CQ, so planning and traffic analysis is more critical. You will need to know the long and short of packet sizes for each application or network service to which you want to apply CQ. With CQ, you can set limits for bandwidth utilization such as ensuring that no application is ever provided more than the capacity allows when the network is congested. The configuration of CQ is not dynamic, so it will not alter existing network conditions.

There are 17 queues defined in CQ. Queue 0 (system queue) is reserved for system messages such as keepalives and signaling. Queues 1 through 16 are available for custom configuration; that is, for you to specify the QoS for your network applications.

The system queue is always serviced first. The algorithm will allow you to specify the number of bytes to be serviced by the queue and/or the number of packets to be forwarded by the queue before moving to the next queue in the sequence. Bandwidth for each queue is configured in terms of bytes and queue length. When using CQ under congestive conditions, no application receives more bandwidth than allowed to the queue to which it is assigned. The CQ process is shown in Figure 6.10.

Figure 6.10 The CQ Servicing Process

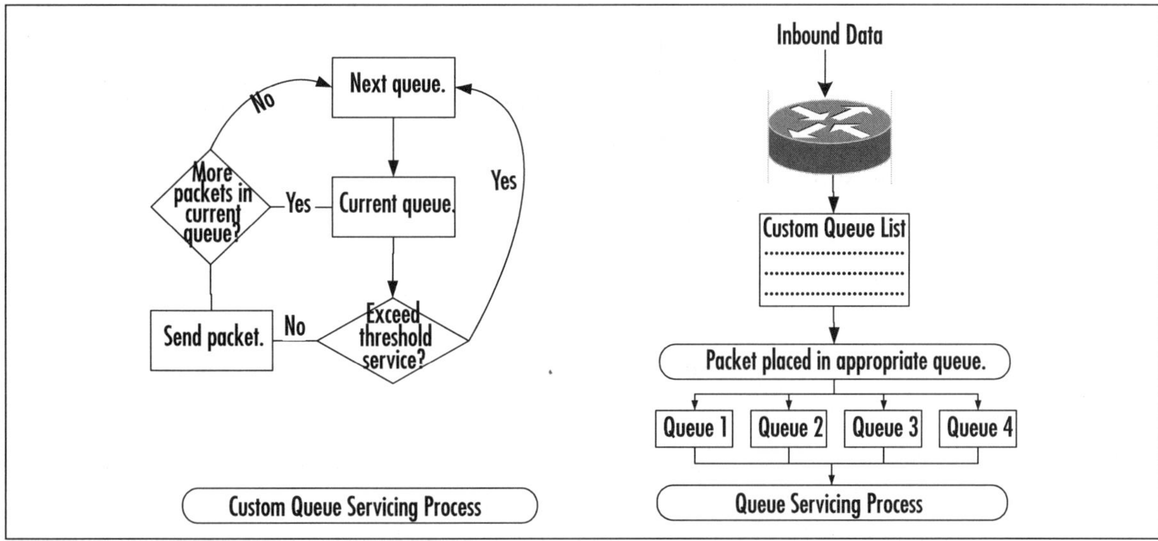

Set the byte count parameters correctly to achieve consistent results, which is best explained using a real-world example. Assume that you want a custom queue that shares 128Kbps bandwidth evenly across four different applications. Assume also that you have not performed any traffic analysis and have configured four CQs with a byte count of 250 under the assumption that all the applications are similar. Now suppose that each application transmits 100-, 300-, 500-, and 700-byte frames consecutively.

The net result is not a 25/25/25/25 ratio. When the router services the first queue, it forwards three 100-byte packets; when it services the second queue, it forwards one 300-byte packet; when it services the third queue, it forwards one 500-byte packet; and when it services the fourth queue, it forwards one 700-byte packet. The result is an uneven distribution of traffic flowing through the queue. You must determine the correct byte count for each queue based on the behavior and requirements of the applications to be serviced by each queue. To determine the bandwidth that a custom queue will receive, use the following formula:

```
(queue byte count / total byte count of all queues) * bandwidth capacity of the
interface.
```

In our example, that would mean:

```
(100/1600) * (128000Kbps/8=16000bytes) = 1000
(300/1600) * (128000Kbps/8=16000bytes) = 3000
(500/1600) * (128000Kbps/8=16000bytes) = 5000
(700/1600) * (128000Kbps/8=16000bytes) = 7000
```

Your custom queue sizes in this case will have byte counts of 1000, 3000, 5000, and 7000.

Configuring Custom Queuing

The tasks involved in configuring custom queuing are:

1. Define a custom queue list.
2. Assign the custom queue list to an interface.

The priority list identifies specific traffic that will be assigned to a queue, and it can refer to an access list containing more entries. One this list is created, it must be applied to an interface in order to be effective. This section examines several examples of custom queuing and explains the potential pitfalls to be avoided when preparing a custom queue list.

Enabling Custom Queuing

The first task in configuring custom queuing is to craft a valid custom queue list. This is accomplished using the global configuration command, **queue-list**. As with priority queuing, custom queue lists are identified using a list number (0-16) for up to 17 queues.

```
Router1(config)# queue-list 1 ?
default         Set custom queue for unspecified datagrams
interface       Establish priority for packets from an interface
lowest-custom Set lowest number of queue to be treated as custom
protocol        Priority queueing by protocol
queue           Configure parameters for a particular queue
stun            Establish priorities for stun packets
```

As you can see, you can group and specify traffic by interface or protocol type. You can also specify a default queue for traffic not matching any entry in the queue list.

In the following example, we have configured a queue list to satisfy the following requirements.

- All default traffic will be assigned to Queue 1.
- All AppleTalk and IPX traffic will be assigned to Queue 2.

- All Telnet traffic will be assigned to Queue 3.
- All traffic from IPX host 3C.ABCD.ABCD.ABCD will be assigned to Queue 4.
- All traffic originating behind interface Ethernet 0/0 will be assigned to Queue 5.
- All remaining IP traffic will be assigned to Queue 6.

Unlike priority queuing, the queue numbers used by custom queuing do not represent assigned priority levels. The following custom queue list configuration meets these requirements:

```
Router1(config)# access-list 801 permit 3c.abcd.abcd.abcd -1
Router1(config)# access-list 801 deny -1
Router1(config)#
Router1(config)# queue-list 1 default ?
<0-16> queue number
Router1(config)# queue-list 1 protocol appletalk 2
Router1(config)# queue-list 1 protocol ipx 2
Router1(config)# queue-list 1 protocol ip 3 tcp telnet
Router1(config)# queue-list 1 protocol ipx 4 list 801
Router1(config)# queue-list 1 interface serial 0/0 5
Router1(config)# queue-list 1 protocol ip 6
Router1(config)# queue-list 1 default 1
Router1(config)# end
```

We have used a single queue list to reference six separate queues. Notice that queue 4 references an IPX access list (801) to grant priority to IPX host 3C.ABCD.ABCD.ABCDst. Custom queuing can classify traffic with a same level of granularity similar to that of priority queuing. Each queue has a default byte count of 1,500 bytes and a default queue length of 20 packets. This means that the custom queuing process should service an equal number of bytes among each queue. However, this does not always remain true when larger packets reach the custom queuing process as we demonstrated earlier.

Adjusting Byte Counts and Queue Sizes

You can modify the byte count and size of each queue using the **queue** keyword of the **queue-list** command. Each queue is individually configured with this command. In the following example, we are changing the byte count of Queues 1, 2, and 3 to 3,000 bytes and the queue depth of Queues 4, 5, and 6 to 60 packets:

```
Router1# configure terminal
Enter configuration commands, one per line. End with CNTL/Z.
Router1(config)# queue-list 1 queue 1 ?
byte-count   Specify size in bytes of a particular queue
limit         Set queue entry limit of a particular queue
Router1(config)# queue-list 1 queue 1 byte-count ?
<0-16777215> size in bytes
```

```
Router1(config)# queue-list 1 queue 1 byte-count 3000
Router1(config)# queue-list 1 queue 2 byte-count 3000
Router1(config)# queue-list 1 queue 3 byte-count 3000
Router1(config)# queue-list 1 queue 3 limit ?
<0-32767> number of queue entries
Router1(config)# queue-list 1 queue 4 limit 60
Router1(config)# queue-list 1 queue 5 limit 60
Router1(config)# queue-list 1 queue 6 limit 60
Router1(config)# end
```

The **queue-list <*list*> queue <*queue#*> limit <*depth*>** command configures the queue depth for each custom queue.

Applying Your Configuration to an Interface

Once you have configured your custom queue list, you must apply it to an interface in order to activate. Otherwise, the CQ you desire will not be implemented. The interface command, **custom-queue-list,** will apply the specified CQ queue list to the interface as shown here with Serial 0/0.

```
Router1# configure terminal
Enter configuration commands, one per line. End with CNTL/Z.
Router1(config)# interface serial 0/0
Router1(config-if)# custom-queue-list 1
Router1(config-if)# end
```

At this point, you have a functional custom queuing configuration. Cisco provides several commands that you can use to validate your efforts.

Verifying Custom Queuing

Has CQ been enacted on the target interface? You can use the **show interface** command to verify by obtaining information similar to that shown here.

```
Router1# show interface serial 0/0
Serial0/0 is up, line protocol is up
Hardware is PowerQUICC Serial
Internet address is 192.168.10.1/24
MTU 1500 bytes, BW 1544 Kbit, DLY 20000 usec,
reliability 255/255, txload 1/255, rxload 1/255
Encapsulation HDLC, loopback not set, keepalive set (10 sec)
Last input 00:00:07, output 00:00:08, output hang never
Last clearing of "show interface" counters never
Input queue: 0/75/0 (size/max/drops); Total output drops: 0
Queueing strategy: custom-list 1
```

```
Output queues: (queue #: size/max/drops)
0: 0/20/0 1: 0/20/0 2: 0/20/0 3: 0/20/0 4: 0/60/0
5: 0/60/0 6: 0/60/0 7: 0/20/0 8: 0/20/0 9: 0/20/0
10: 0/20/0 11: 0/20/0 12: 0/20/0 13: 0/20/0 14: 0/20/0
15: 0/20/0 16: 0/20/0
5 minute input rate 0 bits/sec, 0 packets/sec
5 minute output rate 0 bits/sec, 0 packets/sec
17212 packets input, 1533621 bytes, 0 no buffer
Received 16828 broadcasts, 0 runts, 0 giants, 0 throttles
2 input errors, 0 CRC, 2 frame, 0 overrun, 0 ignored, 0 abor
15098 packets output, 940003 bytes, 0 underruns
0 output errors, 0 collisions, 15 interface resets
0 output buffer failures, 0 output buffers swapped out
0 carrier transitions
DCD=up DSR=up DTR=up RTS=up CTS=up
```

The previous output shows that custom queue list 1 is applied to interface serial 0/0, as well as the state of each queue since the configuration was applied. In our example output here, the queue depths for Queues 4, 5, and 6 were adjusted to 60 packets. Notice that all 16 custom queues are displayed. This means that the IOS allocated memory space for all possible configurable queues, even though we have used only six of them. We can also use the command **show queuing** to show the actual configuration of the custom queues, as shown in the following output:

```
Router1# show queuing ?
custom          custom queuing list configuration
fair            fair queuing configuration
priority        priority queuing list configuration
red             random early detection configuration
Router1# show queuing custom
Current custom queue configuration:
List Queue Args
1 2 protocol appletalk
1 2 protocol ipx
1 3 protocol ip tcp port telnet
1 4 protocol ipx list 801
1 5 interface Ethernet0/0
1 6 protocol ip
1 1 byte-count 3000
1 2 byte-count 3000
1 3 byte-count 3000
1 4 limit 60
1 5 limit 60
1 6 limit 60
```

Custom Queuing Examples

In our next example, we have a low-speed serial connection handling all of the network traffic. To improve operations, we need more control over the different traffic types, which we can accomplish with CQ. In an environment where users are having problems getting Dynamic Host Configuration Protocol (DHCP) information when booting up, you can create a configuration that grants DHCP traffic high priority. The following configuration shows **telnet** and **bootpc** with the highest priority and traffic matching access list 100 with the lowest priority.

```
!
queue-list 1 protocol ip 1 list 100
queue-list 1 protocol ip 2 tcp telnet
queue-list 1 protocol ip 3 udp bootpc
queue-list 1 default 4
!
```

To use an extended access list to make specific IP traffic flow into queue 1, specify **queue-list 1 protocol 1 list 100.**

Telnet traffic is prioritized through queue 2 with **queue-list 1 protocol 2 tcp telnet**.

UDP bootpc (DHCP) traffic will be granted a high priority (queue 3) using **queue-list 1 protocol 3 udp bootpc**.

All other traffic not specifically identified in any of the CQs will be relegated to a default queue configured with the **queue-list 1 default 4** command. If no specific queue is configured as the default queue, queue 1 is assumed to be the default.

```
!
queue-list 1 queue 1 byte-count 1000
queue-list 1 queue 2 byte-count 4000
queue-list 1 queue 3 byte-count 4000
queue-list 1 queue 4 byte-count 2000
!
```

Queue 1 has been configured for 1000 bytes per cycle, queue 2 has been configured for 4,000 bytes per cycle, and queue 3 has been configured for 4,000 bytes per cycle. The default queue 4 has been allocated 2,000 bytes per cycle. Configuring the byte count of the different queues indicates which queue has high priority. The higher the byte count, the more bandwidth is dedicated to that queue.

```
!
interface Serial 0
custom-queue-list 1
!
```

To apply CQ to a specific interface, the **custom-queue-list 1** command is used. Confirm the results of your efforts with the **show interface** command as shown.

```
c2507# show interface serial 0
```

```
Serial0 is up, line protocol is up
Hardware is HD64570
MTU 1500 bytes, BW 1544 Kbit, DLY 20000 usec, rely 255/255, load 1/255
Encapsulation FRAME-RELAY, loopback not set, keepalive set (10 sec)
LMI enq sent 0, LMI stat recvd 0, LMI upd recvd 0, DTE LMI down
LMI enq recvd 0, LMI stat sent 0, LMI upd sent 0
LMI DLCI 1023 LMI type is CISCO frame relay DTE
FR SVC disabled, LAPF state down
Broadcast queue 0/64, broadcasts sent/dropped 0/0, interface broadcasts 0
Last input 00:00:07, output 00:00:07, output hang never
Last clearing of "show interface" counters 00:00:03
Input queue: 0/75/0 (size/max/drops); Total output drops: 0
Queueing strategy: custom-list 1
Output queues: (queue #: size/max/drops)
0: 0/20/0 1: 0/20/0 2: 0/20/0 3: 0/20/0 4: 0/20/0
5: 0/20/0 6: 0/20/0 7: 0/20/0 8: 0/20/0 9: 0/20/0
10: 0/20/0 11: 0/20/0 12: 0/20/0 13: 0/20/0 14: 0/20/0
15: 0/20/0 16: 0/20/0
5 minute input rate 0 bits/sec, 0 packets/sec
5 minute output rate 0 bits/sec, 0 packets/sec
0 packets input, 0 bytes, 0 no buffer
Received 0 broadcasts, 0 runts, 0 giants, 0 throttles
 0 input errors, 0 CRC, 0 frame, 0 overrun, 0 ignored, 0 abort
0 packets output, 0 bytes, 0 underruns
0 output errors, 0 collisions, 1 interface resets
0 output buffer failures, 0 output buffers swapped out
2 carrier transitions DCD=up DSR=up DTR=up RTS=up CTS=uph
c2507#
!
queue-list 1 queue 1 limit 40
```

Weighted Fair Queuing

Weighted fair queuing is a flow-based algorithm that provides fair bandwidth allocation to all network traffic. WFQ interweaves low volume traffic flows with high volume traffic flows, resulting in the breakup of packet trains that restrict lower bandwidth traffic's access to network resources. WFQ automatically places interactive low volume traffic at the front of the queue (to improve response time) and allows high volume traffic to compete for the remaining capacity. WFQ applies priority, or weights, to classify traffic into conversations.

WFQ determines how much bandwidth each conversation is allowed relative to other conversations. In other words, WFQ allows you to give low volume traffic, such as Telnet sessions, priority over high volume traffic, such as File Transfer Protocol (FTP) sessions. WFQ gives concurrent file transfers balanced use of link capacity such that when multiple file transfers occur, they are given an equal share of bandwidth. WFQ can identify and prioritize mixed traffic streams to fairly allocate access to an interface rather than just servicing packets in FIFO fashion. WFQ minimizes configuration efforts and automatically adapts to changing network traffic conditions.

WFQ dynamically sorts traffic into messages that make up a conversation. WFQ segments the train of packets within a conversation to ensure that bandwidth is shared fairly between individual conversations and that low-volume traffic is transferred in a timely fashion. WFQ classifies traffic into different flows based on:

- Source and destination network address
- MAC address
- Protocol
- Destination port and socket numbers of the session
- Frame Relay data link connection identifiers (DLCI)
- Type of service (ToS) value

There are two categories of flow:

- High-bandwidth sessions
- Low-bandwidth sessions

Low-bandwidth traffic has effective priority over high-bandwidth traffic due to the fact that it will not consume all the bandwidth. Low-bandwidth traffic streams, which make up the majority of traffic, receive preferential service, allowing their entire loads to be sent in a timely fashion. High volume traffic streams share the remaining capacity proportionally among themselves according to their assigned weights.

WFQ orders packets of the various conversations in the fair queues before transmission. The order of removal from the fair queues is determined by the virtual time of delivery of the last bit of each arriving packet.

New messages for high-bandwidth flows are discarded after the congestive-messages threshold has been reached. However, low-bandwidth flows, which include control-message conversations, continue to queue data. As a result, the fair queue can occasionally contain more messages than are specified by the threshold number.

NOTE

WFQ is the default queuing mechanism for all serial interfaces operating below 2.048 Mbps that do not use Linked Access Procedure, Balanced (LAPB), X.25, and Synchronous Data Link Control (SDLC) encapsulations.

WFQ can provide consistent response time to heavy and light network users alike without adding additional bandwidth. WFQ automatically adapts to changing network traffic conditions.

WFQ is a queuing method that automatically provides fair allocation of bandwidth to high-bandwidth traffic flows, and prioritizes low-bandwidth connections to each network resource, as shown in Figure 6.11. This algorithm dynamically tracks traffic flows and allocates bandwidth accordingly.

Figure 6.11 Weighted Fair Queuing in Action

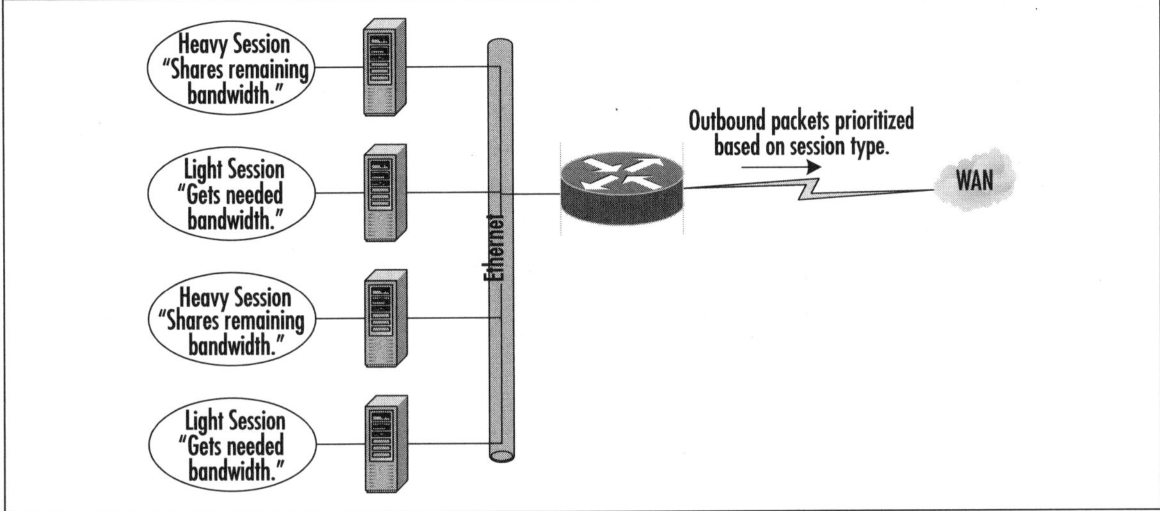

When WFQ is running in conjunction with Frame Relay, the algorithm will adjust the queuing schedule to compensate for link congestion, as identified by the receipt of forward explicit congestion notification (FECN) and backward explicit congestion notification (BECN) frames. This function is enabled by default and requires no manual configuration.

For example, assume we have a mid-sized hub-and-spoke network for a national retail chain. The links between the hub and spokes are T1 circuits. Users primarily use FTP for batch processing and Telnet for access to their order entry system located at the hub site. Remote users have been complaining about intermittent response time problems. Batch processing is degrading performance of the more interactive applications. By enabling WFQ, Telnet is automatically given priority over FTP, resulting in improved response time.

The interface command used to enable and configure WFQ is **fair-queue**. It has several optional parameters such as congestive discard threshold, number of dynamic queues, and number of reservable queues. The congestive discard threshold is set to 64 messages (packets) by default, meaning that once this threshold is reached, new packets belonging to that flow will be discarded.

You can change this parameter to an integer based on a power of 2 resulting in values from 16 to 4,096. Changing this parameter should be considered only after completion of a traffic analysis. If this parameter is changed, the router should be carefully monitored thereafter for memory issues. In most networks, this variable should remain at its default setting. Dynamic queues are used to support best-effort conversations. The default number of dynamic queues allocated is directly proportional to the configured interface bandwidth, as listed in Table 6.2.

Table 6.2 Allocation of Dynamic Queues

Bandwidth Range	Number of Dynamic Queues
Less than or equal to 64Kbps	16
More than 64Kbps and less than or equal to 128Kbps	32
More than 128Kbps and less than or equal to 256Kbps	64
More than 256Kbps and less than or equal to 512Kbps	128
More than 512Kbps	256

The last parameter (reservable queues) specifies the number of flows reserved for features such as Resource Reservation Protocol (RSVP). The default value is determined by dividing the configured interface bandwidth value by 32 Kbps. The value can be statically defined as an integer from 0 to 1000. In practice, this value should not be changed unless a traffic analysis determines that it would solve a specific problem. The following is an example of a serial interface configured for WFQ using all default configuration values:

```
interface Serial0
ip address 10.10.10.1 255.255.255.252
fair-queue
```

The next example illustrates a serial interface configured for a congestive discard of 100 and 128 dynamic queues:

```
interface Serial0
ip unnumbered Ethernet0
bandwidth 384
fair-queue 100
```

WFQ and IP Precedence

WFQ uses the IP precedence field in the IP packet header to allocate bandwidth. The IP precedence bits are located in the type of service (TOS) field of an IP packet and have a value between 0 (default/low) and 7 (high). The precedence values of 6 and 7 are actually reserved. As IP precedence values increase, the algorithm allocates more bandwidth to the flow, causing such marked traffic to be served before lower-precedence traffic. These values will traverse the network intact unless explicitly changed. Packets with higher precedence/priority will be serviced throughout a network (end-to-end) based on their IP precedence.

Planning Considerations

How much bandwidth is needed for your application? How much bandwidth is available? The default for a Cisco router is that 75 percent of available bandwidth is reservable. How much bandwidth is needed for other data traffic? You do not want to squelch traffic simply to serve other traffic.

The higher the value of IP precedence, the more bandwidth allocated to the IP traffic flow by WFQ. Non–real-time traffic flows normally have an IP precedence value of 0. Assigning real-time applications an IP precedence value greater than 0 ensures they will be serviced as high priority by the queuing algorithm.

The method that WFQ uses to calculate flow priority is complex, as shown by the following examples. In WFQ, each IP flow is given a percentage of the total interface bandwidth based on precedence and the number of flows assigned to each precedence level. The following formula simplifies the issue:

```
Percentage of interface bandwidth assigned to a flow =
Precedence level+1
The sum of [(each flow's precedence level+1) *
(the number of flows at that precedence level)]
```

To further clarify, consider the following two examples. In the first example, our object is to determine what percentage of bandwidth is assigned each flow with a precedence value of 0 and 4. We have eight flows using precedence levels 0 through 7 (Table 6.3) with one flow allocated per precedence level.

precedence level+1 (0+1)*1+(1+1)*1+(2+1)*1+(3+1)*1+(4+1)*1+(5+1)*1+(6+1)*1+(7+1)*1

Table 6.3 IP Precedence Values.

Precedence Number	Value Name
0	Routine
1	Priority
2	Immediate
3	Flash
4	Flash-override
5	Critical
6	Internet
8	Network

To determine the bandwidth for precedence 0, we will insert 0 for precedence level and calculate the lower half of the formula:

0+1

1+2+3+4+5+6+7+8=36

To determine the bandwidth for precedence 4, we will insert 4 for precedence level and calculate the lower half of the formula:

4+1

1+2+3+4+5+6+7+8=36

In the previous formulas, precedence 0 traffic will be allocated 1/36 of the interface bandwidth and precedence 4 will receive 5/36 of the interface bandwidth.

In our next example, we have adjusted the formula to represent 12 traffic flows and three individual precedence levels. Our objective is to determine the amount of interface bandwidth assigned to a single flow at each precedence level.

Example criteria:

Five flows with a precedence of 0

Ten flows with a precedence of 2

Two flows with a precedence of 4

precedence level+1

(0+1)*5+(2+1)*10+(4+1)*2

To determine the bandwidth for precedence 0, we will insert 0 for precedence level and calculate the lower half of the formula:

0+1

(1*5)+(3*10)+(5*2)=45

To determine the bandwidth for precedence 2, we will insert 2 for precedence level and calculate the lower half of the formula:

2+1

(1*5)+(3*10)+(5*2)=45

To determine the bandwidth for precedence 4, we will insert 4 for precedence level and calculate the lower half of the formula:

4+1

(1*5)+(3*10)+(5*2)=45

The output of the formula states that precedence 0 flows receive 1/45 of the interface bandwidth, precedence 2 flows receive 3/45 of the interface bandwidth, and precedence 4 flows receive 5/45 of the interface bandwidth. For example, assume we have two locations interconnected via a T1 circuit, as illustrated in Figure 6.12.

By default, WFQ is enabled on each WAN interface. Traffic is distributed between VoIP and Internet traffic, with 10 flows for VoIP traffic and 70 flows for Internet traffic. All voice traffic has been assigned an IP precedence value of 4 and all Internet traffic a precedence value of 0. During periods of congestion, using the formula above, WFQ will allocate 1/120 of the interface bandwidth to each precedence 0 flow and 5/120 or 1/24 of the interface bandwidth to each Internet flow. This equates to about 64 Kbps per VoIP session and 12.8 Kbps per Internet session.

Figure 6.12 IP Precedence Used to Allocate More Bandwidth to Voice Traffic

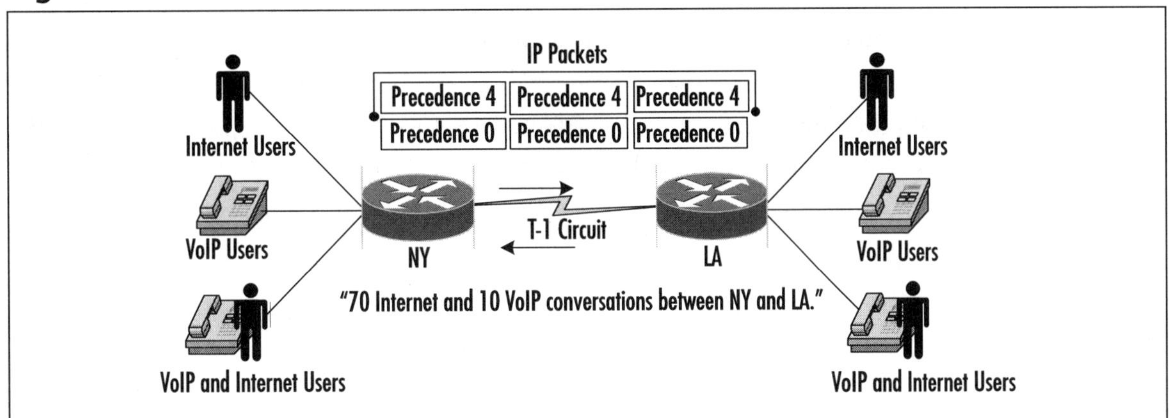

VIP Distributed Weight Fair Queuing (DWFQ)

VIP DWFQ is a high-speed version of WFQ for Cisco 7X00 series routers with VIP2-40s or later modules. Although the VIP2-40 is the minimum required to run DFWQ, VIP2-50s should be used when the aggregate port speed on the VIP exceeds 45 Mbps. In addition, distributed Cisco express forwarding (dCEF) is required to run DWFQ. dCEF provides increased packet routing performance because the entire route forwarding information base (FIB) resides on each VIP card. Routing table lookups happen locally on the VIP card without querying the router CPU. In flow-based DWFQ, all traffic flows are equally weighted and guaranteed equal access to the queue, thus preventing any single flow from monopolizing resources.

To enable DWFQ, activate fair queuing by enabling **ip cef** in global configuration mode and **fair-queue** under the VIP2 interface configuration as shown in the following example.

```
!
ip cef
!
interface FastEthernet0/0
ip address 172.20.10.2 255.255.255.0
full-duplex
!
interface Hssi4/0
ip address 172.20.20.2 255.255.255.0
fair-queue
!
router ospf 100
network 172.20.0.0 0.0.255.255 area 0
!
```

DWFQ has the following requirements and restrictions:

- Can be configured only on main interfaces; per IOS 12.1.0, there is no sub-interface support.
- Can be configured only on an ATM interface with AAL5SNAP encapsulation. Per IOS 12.1.0, there is no support for AAL5MUX or AAL5NLPID encapsulations.
- Is not supported on any virtual, tunnel, or Fast EtherChannel interfaces.
- Cannot be configured in conjunction with RSP-based WFQ, PQ, or CQ.

Configuring Weighted Fair Queuing

Configuring WFQ is fairly simple: apply WFQ to the interface requiring the service. Keep in mind that WFQ is enabled by default on links of E1 speeds (2.048Mbps) or less. These configurations will not show up in the router's configuration when the **show running-config** command is issued, but they are visible through the **show interface** command.

Enabling Weighted Fair Queuing

The interface command **fair-queue** is configures WFQ on an interface. Optional parameters inlcude congestive discard threshold, the maximum number of dynamic conversation queues, and the maximum number of RSVP queues. The number of conversation queues must be a power of 2 (16, 32, 64, 128, 256, 512, 1024); otherwise, the IOS will refuse the command. The following code configures serial interface 0/0 with a congestive discard threshold of 512 bytes, a maximum of 1024 dynamic conversation queues, and 10 reservable queues for RSVP:

```
Router1(config)# interface serial 0/0
Router1(config-if)# fair-queue 512 1048 10
Number of dynamic queues must be a power of 2 (16, 32, 64, 128, 256,512, 1024)
Router1(config-if)# fair-queue 512 1024 10
```

Verifying Weighted Fair Queuing

As with the other queuing processes discussed, use the **show interface** command to verify WFQ configuration by determining if it is enabled on that interface:

```
Router1# show interface serial 0/0
Serial0/0 is up, line protocol is up
Hardware is PowerQUICC Serial
Internet address is 192.168.10.1/24
MTU 1500 bytes, BW 1544 Kbit, DLY 20000 usec,
reliability 255/255, txload 1/255, rxload 1/255
Encapsulation HDLC, loopback not set, keepalive set (10 sec)
Last input 00:00:01, output 00:00:00, output hang never
Last clearing of "show interface" counters never
Input queue: 0/75/0 (size/max/drops); Total output drops: 0
```

```
Queuing strategy: weighted fair
Output queue: 0/1000/512/0 (size/max total/threshold/drops)
Conversations 0/1/1024 (active/max active/max total)
Reserved Conversations 0/0 (allocated/max allocated)
5 minute input rate 0 bits/sec, 0 packets/sec
5 minute output rate 0 bits/sec, 0 packets/sec
341 packets input, 30537 bytes, 0 no buffer
Received 341 broadcasts, 0 runts, 0 giants, 0 throttles
4 input errors, 0 CRC, 4 frame, 0 overrun, 0 ignored, 0 abor
298 packets output, 18667 bytes, 0 underruns
0 output errors, 0 collisions, 16 interface resets
0 output buffer failures, 0 output buffers swapped out
2 carrier transitions
DCD=up DSR=up DTR=up RTS=up CTS=up
```

The output shown previously confirms that WFQ is enabled on this interface, as well as providing the status of WFQ when the command was issued. In this example, 0 packets were in the output queue. The queue itself has a maximum size of 1000 packets, and WFQ starts the congestive discard process as the queue reaches a depth of 512 packets. There have been 0 tail drops so far. We can also see the state of the conversations. Of a total maximum of 1024 conversations, 0 conversations are currently active. In addition, 0 of 10 RSVP reservable queues are in operation. The **show interface** command properly reflects the configuration we applied to the interface.

We can use the command **show queuing fair** to display the configuration of the WFQ process:

```
Router1# show queuing fair
Current fair queue configuration:
Interface Discard Dynamic Reserved
threshold queue count queue count
BRI0/0 64 256 0
BRI0/0:1 64 256 0
BRI0/0:2 64 256 0
Serial0/0 512 1024 10
Serial0/1 64 256 0
Router1#
```

We can see that the router has properly configured the WFQ process on interface serial 0/0 with the non-default values we entered.

Class-Based Weighted Fair Queuing (CB-WFQ)

CB-WFQ is an extension of WFQ, with support for user-defined traffic classes added. CB-WFQ can separate traffic into queues based on criteria such as protocol, access control lists (ACLs), or originating interface. Each packet is analyzed to match a defined traffic class. The packet is then forwarded to the appropriate queue for servicing.

Classes are defined by parameters called *class characteristics*. Examples of class characteristics are bandwidth, weight, and maximum packet limit. The bandwidth assigned is the minimum bandwidth required for that specific class of service during periods of congestion. The weight value is derived from the bandwidth value assigned to each class. The weight value is used to calculate the average queue length and packet limit. The packet limit defines the queue depth in packets. The queue will drop all packets that exceed the configured queue depth or packet limit unless a policy is applied to the class. An example of such a policy is weighted random early detection.

CB-WFQ does not allow more than 75 percent of the interface bandwidth to be assigned to classes. The additional 25 percent is reserved for overhead such as routing updates. While you can override this threshold, you must consider all the bandwidth required for your overhead needs. A good example is an ATM interface where you would need to take into account the overhead required to package data into ATM cells at Layer 2 as well as any control packet flows traversing the link.

CB-WFQ is not bound to packet flows. Up to 64 classes can be defined for a more granular classification than is possible with traditional WFQ. The total number of flows traversing an interface does not affect CB-WFQ, and classes do not compete for bandwidth with other classes. The caveat is that multiple flows can compete for bandwidth within a defined class; therefore, significant thought is required when defining your queuing strategy.

CB-WFQ is not supported in conjunction with traffic shaping or ATM unspecified bit rate (UBR) permanent virtual circuits. Please review Figure 6.12, which illustrates CB-WFQ operation. CB-WFQ allocates bandwidth to a queue by guaranteeing the minimum amount of bandwidth to each class. There are 64 definable queues; WFQ is used to allocate bandwidth within each class or queue, unlike CQ, which services each queue on a FIFO basis.

Figure 6.13 CB-WFQ in Action

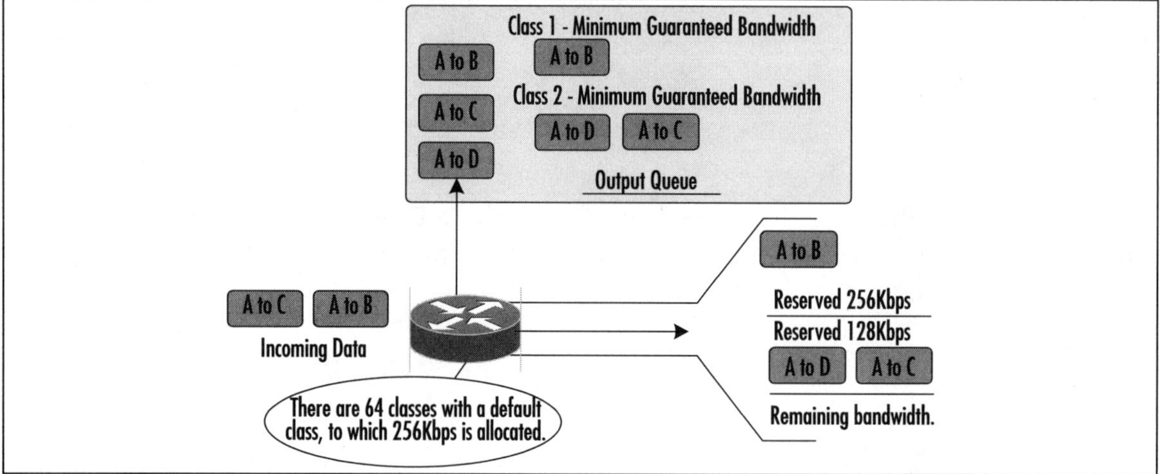

Packets satisfying the criteria for a class constitute the traffic for that class. A queue is reserved for each class, and traffic belonging to a class is directed to its queue. Once a class has been defined with the appropriate criteria, you can assign it characteristics such as bandwidth, weight, and maximum packet limit. The bandwidth assigned to a class is the guaranteed bandwidth delivered to the class during congestion.

You also specify the queue limit for a class, which is the maximum number of packets allowed to accumulate in the queue. Packets belonging to a class are subject to the bandwidth and queue limits set for that class.

After a queue has reached its queue limit, packets over that limit will cause tail drop or packet drop, depending on the class policy. Tail drop is used for CB-WFQ classes unless you explicitly configure the policy to use WRED to drop packets as to avoid congestion. If you use WRED packet drop instead of tail drop for one or more classes in a policy map, you must ensure that WRED is not configured for the interface to which you attach that service policy.

If a default class is configured with the **bandwidth policy-map** class command, all unclassified traffic is placed in a single queue and treated according to the configured bandwidth. If a default class is configured with the **fair-queue** command, all unclassified traffic is flow classified and given best-effort treatment. If no default class is configured, the traffic that does not match any of the configured classes is flow classified and given best-effort treatment. Once a packet is classified, all the standard mechanisms that can be used to differentiate service among the classes apply.

Flow classification is standard WFQ treatment. That is, packets with the same source IP address, destination IP address, source TCP or UDP port, or destination TCP or UDP port are classified as belonging to the same flow. WFQ allocates an equal share of bandwidth to each flow. Flow-based WFQ is also called *fair queuing* because all flows are equally weighted.

CB-WFQ extends the standard WFQ concept of fair queuing by specifying that the weight for a class becomes the weight for each packet that meets the criteria of the class. Packets that arrive at the output interface are classified according to the criteria you define, and assigned the appropriate weight. The weight for a packet belonging to a specific class is derived from the bandwidth you assigned to the class when you configured it; in this sense the weight for a class is user-configurable.

After the weight for a packet is assigned, the packet is placed in the appropriate class queue. CB-WFQ uses the weights assigned to the queued packets to ensure that the class queue is serviced fairly.

Configuring Class-Based Weighted Fair Queuing

Before configuring CB-WFQ, determine how many classes are needed to categorize all your traffic. You also need to know the criteria that will be used to map traffic into those classes and the bandwidth guarantees for each class. If you have already classified your traffic at the edge of the network, IP precedence might be the only criterion you need. If you are configuring a more modest, point-to-point implementation of CB-WFQ, you will probably use extended ACLs to categorize incoming traffic into classes. There are three steps to configure CB-WFQ:

1. Define class maps.
2. Create policy maps.
3. Attach policies to interfaces.

Class maps identify the traffic to be handled by each class and can be used in one or more policy maps. Policy maps determine the way that traffic is handled. No QoS is provided until the policy map is applied to the interfaces.

Defining Class Maps

The **class-map** command allows you to determine how traffic should be classified. The configured class must have a name for reference by subsequent commands. Set your match criteria within the class map as shown.

```
router1(config)# class-map Gold
router1(config-cmap)# match access-group name Gold
```

In this example, we created a class map with the name Gold. This could be a premium service offered to applications that guarantees a certain bandwidth. Furthermore, while in the **class-map (config-cmap)** command mode, we entered a match criterion—namely, the ACL named Gold. All traffic that matches the ACL will be part of the Gold class map. We have used the same name, Gold, for both the class map and the ACL name for consistency. It is necessary to configure the ACLs if you want the class maps to use them. In this case, the ACL might be configured like this:

```
router1(config)# ip access-list extended Gold
router1(config-ext-nacl)# permit ip any any precedence flash-override
```

An extended ACL is used so we can specify a match for any IP packet with a precedence of 4 (the fourth level of precedence is traditionally given the name **flash-override**).

If you have a topology where packets are not marked at the edge of the network with IP precedence, you can use an ACL that classifies traffic based their protocols and port numbers. ACLs can provide granular control over the traffic that ends up in your QoS classes. We can configure more class maps as shown:

```
router1(config)# class-map Silver
router1(config-cmap)# match access-group name Silver
router1(config-cmap)# class-map Bronze
router1(config-cmap)# match access-group name Bronze
```

The extended access lists would be defined as follows:

```
router1(config-ext-nacl)# ip access-list extended Silver
router1(config-ext-nacl)# permit ip any any precedence flash
router1(config)# ip access-list extended Bronze
router1(config-ext-nacl)# permit ip any any precedence immediate
```

This gives us three classes, Gold, Bronze, and Silver, mapped to the IP precedence levels 4, 3, and 2, respectively.

Creating Policies

After defining your class maps for CB-WFQ, your next task is to create the policy maps that specify the QoS for the classes. Let's configure the policy for the Gold class we configured in the previous example:

```
router1(config)# policy-map PPP-T1
router1(config-pmap)# class Gold
router1(config-pmap-c)# bandwidth 216
```

We have given the name PPP-T1 to the policy map. You should use a descriptive name, such as one that describes the kind of circuit bandwidth it was meant to run on. This leads us into the policy map command context (**config-pmap**). We now enter the class that we want to specify parameters for, in this case, Gold. Under this new context (**config-pmap-c**), we specify the bandwidth reserved for this class in Kbps. You can enter the following commands to configure the QoS the class will be given:

- **bandwidth** Bandwidth (in Kbps)
- **queue-limit** Maximum queue threshold for tail drop
- **random-detect** Enable WRED as drop policy

The bandwidth is the rate guaranteed to this class in kilobits per second (Kbps). By default, the sum of all bandwidth rates for a policy cannot exceed 75 percent of the interface's total bandwidth to ensure bandwidth remains available for overhead traffic such as Layer 2 keepalives, routing updates, and so on. Determine the amount of bandwidth required for each class based on the needs of the traffic being classified.

The **queue-limit** and **random-detect** commands specify the drop policy for the class. By default, the drop policy is tail drop with a queue limit of 64 for that class. You may use the **queue-limit** command to change this value as long as it is 1 and 64. A shorter queue drops packets more quickly in times of congestion.

WRED can be configured with the **random-detect** command. The **random-detect exponential-weighting-constant** command can be used to adjust how adaptive WRED is to bursts of traffic. See the discussion on WRED later in this chapter for details.

Unclassified traffic—that is, traffic that is not matched by any of the user-defined classes—is put into a special class called **class-default**. This class does not appear explicitly in the router configuration unless you configure it. By default, unclassified traffic will be flow-classified and queued by WFQ. However, if you configure this class specifically, you can give it a bandwidth guarantee, as shown in the following example.

```
router1(config)# policy-map PPP-T1
router1(config-pmap)# class class-default
router1(config-pmap-c)# bandwidth 31
```

Instead of being fair-queued, the default class will now be guaranteed at least 31Kbps of bandwidth. We can configure the policy map (PPP-T1) with the other classes we defined, resulting in the configuration given here.

```
class-map Gold
match access-group Gold
class-map Bronze
match access-group Bronze
class-map Silver
match access-group Silver
!
policy-map PPP-T1
class Gold
bandwidth 216
class Silver
bandwidth 169
class Bronze
bandwidth 108
class class-default
bandwidth 31
. . .
!
ip access-list extended Gold
permit ip any any precedence flash-override
ip access-list extended Bronze
permit ip any any precedence immediate
ip access-list extended Silver
permit ip any any precedence flash
```

Attaching Policies to Interfaces

Your previous efforts amount to nothing until you have enabled the service policy on an interface:

```
router1(config)# interface serial 0/0
router1(config-if)# service-policy output PPP-T1
```

Once a service policy is defined, it can be enabled on multiple interfaces, assuming that the interface has enough bandwidth to support all the guarantees. Only one policy can be applied to a single interface. After the policy is applied, certain commands relating to queuing and WRED are disabled, since the policy now controls these functions.

The preceding three-step approach to enabling CB-WFQ uses a modular approach that allows you to not only to modify policies without disturbing interfaces and to attach policies to multiple interfaces, but also to copy a policy to like routers, thereby making network-wide configuration of QoS easier.

Verifying CB-WFQ

You can ensure your policies are configured correctly by viewing the configuration with the **show running-config** command. After that, you can view a particular policy with the **show policy-map** command:

```
router1# show policy-map
Policy Map PPP-T1
Weighted Fair Queuing
Class Gold
Bandwidth 216 (kbps) Max Thresh 64 (packets)
Class Silver
Bandwidth 169 (kbps) Max Thresh 64 (packets)
Class Bronze
Bandwidth 108 (kbps) Max Thresh 64 (packets)
Class class-default
Bandwidth 31 (kbps) Max Thresh 64 (packets)
```

This shows the configured bandwidth for each class within the policy and the maximum threshold for the queue before tail drop is enacted. If you have multiple policies configured, you can specify the name of the policy with the command **show policy-map policy-map-name,** and you can even drill down to specific classes within the policy:

```
router1# show policy-map PPP-T1 class Gold
Class Gold
Bandwidth 216 (kbps) Max Thresh 64 (packets)
```

To view the statistics on how the policy has been functioning on the interface, use the **show policy-map interface** command:

```
router1# show policy-map interface serial 0/0
Serial0/0 output : PPP-T1
Weighted Fair Queuing
Class Gold
Output Queue: Conversation 265
Bandwidth 216 (kbps) Packets Matched 248318 Max Threshold 64
(packets)
(discards/tail drops) 95418/84680
Class Silver
Output Queue: Conversation 266
Bandwidth 169 (kbps) Packets Matched 248305 Max Threshold 64
(packets)
(discards/tail drops) 119558/109829
Class Bronze
Output Queue: Conversation 267
```

```
Bandwidth 108 (kbps) Packets Matched 248292 Max Threshold 64
(packets)
(discards/tail drops) 156598/148956
Class class-default
Output Queue: Conversation 268
Bandwidth 31 (kbps) Packets Matched 428362 Max Threshold 64
(packets)
(discards/tail drops) 234720/222514
```

You can use this command to see your class composition with respect to the number of packets matched into the classes and the effect of tail drop (or WRED) on each class. You can always see the overall performance of the interface to which the policy is applied by using the **show interface** or **show queue** command:

```
router1# show queue serial 0/0
Input queue: 0/75/0 (size/max/drops); Total output drops: 778978
Queuing strategy: weighted fair
Output queue: 0/1000/64/778978 (size/max total/threshold/drops)
Conversations 0/4/256 (active/max active/max total)
Reserved Conversations 4/4 (allocated/max allocated)
```

To properly verify queuing operation, use the **show queuing** command.

```
Router1# show queuing
Current fair queue configuration:
Interface Serial 0
Input queue: 0/75/0 (size/max/drops); Total output drops: 0
Output queue: 18/64/30 (size/threshold/drops)
Conversations 2/8 (active/max active)
Reserved Conversations 0/0 (allocated/max allocated) (depth/weight/discards) 3/4096/30
Conversation 117, linktype: ip, length: 556, flags: 0x280
source: 172.16.128.110, destination: 172.16.58.90, id: 0x1069, ttl: 59, TOS: 0 prot:
6, source port 514, destination port 1022
(depth/weight/discards) 14/4096/0
Conversation 150, linktype: ip, length: 1504, flags: 0x280
source: 172.16.128.110, destination: 172.16.58.90, id: 0x104D, ttl:
59, TOS: 0 prot: 6, source port 20, destination port 1554
```

Why Packet Classification?

Reasons for classifying traffic vary from network to network but can range from marking packets with a "flag" (to make them relatively more or less important than other packets on the network) to identifying packets to drop. This section introduces you to several different theories of traffic classification and discusses the mechanics of how these "flags" are set in a packet.

You can set these flags in several ways, and the levels of classification depend on which method is used. Classification can be viewed as infusing data packets with a directive intelligence with regard to network devices. The use of prioritization schemes such as random early detection (RED) and adaptive bit rate (ABR) force the router to analyze data streams and congestion characteristics and then apply congestion controls to those data streams.

These applications can involve the utilization of the TCP sliding window or backoff algorithms, the utilization of leaky or token bucket queuing mechanisms, or a number of other strategies. The use of traffic classification flags within the packet removes decision functionality from the router and establishes the service levels that are required for the packet's particular traffic flow. The router then attempts to provide the packet with the requested QoS.

Each packet must be mapped to a corresponding data flow and the accompanying class of service. The packet classifier then sets each class to be acted upon as an individual data flow subject to the negotiated QoS for that flow.

IP Precedence

IP precedence is a definable parameter used to provide priority values for algorithms such as CB-WFQ. It has other uses as well, such as manually assigning priority to a particular dial peer in a VoIP configuration mode as follows:

```
dial-peer voice 10 VoIP
ip precedence 5
```

This command should be used to prioritize VoIP packets over less sensitive data packets when they share the same available bandwidth. You should also use IP precedence when RSVP is not being used to ensure proper real-time response. In the following sections, you will see how IP precedence settings affect the CB-WFQ algorithms and how they help achieve greater performance for voice traffic.

There are advantages and disadvantages to using either method of QoS for VoIP. One of the most important factors to take into account is the kind of QoS features your network can use. It is important to understand the types of traffic that the network is passing for data as well as voice so that you do not degrade data traffic in favor of voice traffic. Keep in mind the following points when deciding which algorithms to use:

- IP precedence is more controllable. You can choose the level of precedence that is available to the target traffic. It cannot be controlled dynamically, but is set manually. Therefore, QoS will have a higher administration overhead if the network has to be adjusted.
- RSVP is harder to set up initially, since traffic levels have to be analyzed and adjusted on each physical port. RSVP is useful on highly congested links and slow WAN links. It also has the extra benefit of being a dynamically controlled solution. RSVP pipes are built and torn down as needed, so there is no bandwidth wasted.

IP QoS

IP QoS uses IP precedence to provide faster service to select (marked) traffic. Simply enabling QoS is not enough; you also need to configure your queuing methods and bandwidth reservation protocols. QoS by itself merely marks traffic for priority over all other traffic. QoS relies on features and protocols such as RTP and RSVP to accomplish its mission.

QoS ensures that critical traffic is given the bandwidth it needs, that it bypasses congested links, and that it suffers no intolerable delays. Failure to do so means that your transmission quality will suffer, meaning that users will have difficulty communicating. We will use VoIP as an example.

The starting point for QoS is the IP header (Figure 6.14). For purposes of QoS, we are most interested in the Type of Service, or ToS (precedence) field. It is in this field that you manipulate the settings to grant priority to your critical traffic such as VoIP.

Figure 6.14 IP Packet Type of Service and Precedence

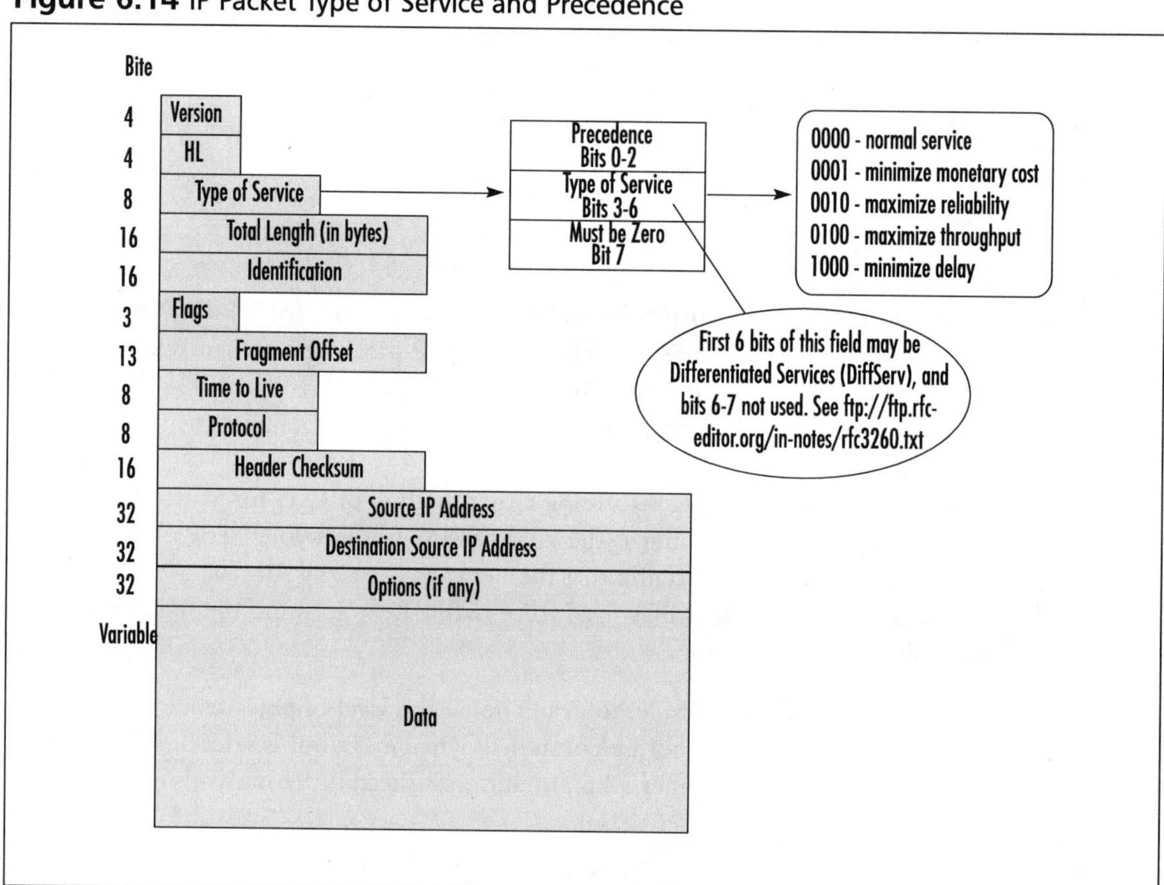

The 8-bit ToS field in the IP header is where the precedence is set. Several values can be set to indicate the QoS desired. The 8-bit ToS field is broken down as shown in Table 6.4.

Table 6.4 Type of Service Bits and Meanings

Bits	Meaning
0–2	Precedence
3	Delay (0-normal, 1-low)
4	Throughput (0-normal, 1-high)
5	Reliability (0-normal, 1-high)
6–7	Reserved

The first three bits are used to set the precedence of an IP packet. They are set per the values shown in Table 6.5. Precedence values for VoIP should at least be priority (001); normal (non-prioritized) IP packets have their ToS set to 000 (routine).

Table 6.5 Precedence Bit Settings and Meanings

Bit Value	Meaning
111	Network Control
110	Internetwork Control
101	CRITIC/ECP
100	Flash Override
011	Flash
010	Immediate
001	Priority
000	Routine

When you want VoIP traffic to have precedence over other traffic, you need to mark it using the commands that follow—specifically, the **ip precedence** command. In our example, we are setting the precedence to 5 (which is written in binary as 101), meaning that VoIP traffic will be marked as critical, giving it a very high priority:

```
dial-peer voice 999 voip
destination-pattern 999
session target ipv4:192.168.99.99
ip precedence 5
```

This setting ensures that VoIP traffic is given priority over many other traffic types.

Traffic Shaping

Traffic shaping smoothes data transmissions by restricting outbound traffic to a particular speed while buffering bursts in the traffic that exceed the set limit. The result is a more consistent data stream, which more easily conforms to downstream requirements. There are two basic traffic-shaping features: Frame Relay traffic shaping (FRTS) and generic traffic shaping (GTS).

FRTS uses a variety of parameters to manage traffic flows in order to avoid or reduce congestion in the network. Parameters include committed information rate (CIR), forward explicit congestion notification, backward explicit congestion notification and excess information rate (EIR). For example, rate enforcement, in which traffic is limited to a particular bit rate, can be configured on a per-VC basis for CIR, EIR, or some other value. Traffic can also be throttled dynamically using BECN tagged packets, on a per-VC basis. During throttling, packets are queued and transmitted at a reduced rate until the congestion has cleared.

GTS is an interface-specific flow control mechanism. Outbound traffic is constrained to a particular bit rate (using a token bucket system), and periodic bursts are queued to limit the flow. Traffic that meets a certain profile can be shaped to eliminate congestion due to downstream rate mismatches. GTS can be used on an interface configured for Frame Relay and to respond to BECN signals, or to simply smooth traffic to a specified rate. GTS can also respond to RSVP signaling on ATM permanent virtual circuits (PVCs).

Configuring Traffic Shaping

FRTS and GTS use similar methods for maintaining traffic rates while buffering bursty traffic. The parameters for each function in the same way, but they use different terminology, as shown in Table 6.6.

Table 6.6 Traffic-Shaping Terminology

FRTS Term	GTS Term	Definition
CIR	Bit rate	Committed information rate; the average rate of traffic to be sent out the interface.
Bc	Burst size	Committed burst; number of bits to be transmitted over a specific time period (Tc).
Be	Excess burst size	Excess burst; number of bits that can be transmitted during the first interval of transmission after a period of no transmission.
Mincir	N/A	Minimum transmission rate during periods of congestion.
Tc	Tc	Time interval that is equal to Bc/CIR.

Traffic shaping is configured in interface configuration mode with the **traffic-shape rate** command for GTS or the **frame-relay traffic-shaping** command for Frame Relay. When traffic shaping is applied to an interface, it reverts to fast switching. All parameters are input in bits per second.

Tc cannot be configured; instead, it is calculated internally and can be no larger than 125ms. Therefore, Bc can be no more than one-eighth of CIR. The smaller the value for Tc, the less tolerant the interface will be of traffic bursts. If Be is not specified, it defaults to the value for Bc. For Frame Relay interfaces, adaptive traffic shaping can also be configured where the interface will respond to BECN by reducing its transmission rate.

The following example shows how to configure GTS on interface Serial 1/0 with a CIR of 128kbps and a committed burst of 16kbps. The transmission rate must never drop below 32kbps:

```
!
Router1 (config)# interface s1/0
Router(config-if)# traffic-shape ?
  group  configure token bucket: group <access-list> CIR (bps) [Bc (bits) [Be
(bits)]]
  rate   configure token bucket: CIR (bps) [Bc (bits) [Be (bits)]]
Router(config-if)# traffic-shape group 1 8000 ?
  <0-100000000>  bits per interval, sustained
Router(config-if)# traffic-shape group 1 8000 0 ?
  <0-100000000>  bits per interval, excess in first interval
Router(config-if)# traffic-shape group 1 8000 0 1 ?
  <1-4096>  Set buffer limit
Router(config-if)# traffic-shape group 1 8000 0 1 1 ?
Router(config-if)# traffic-shape group 1 8000 0 1 1
Router1 (config-if)# traffic-shape rate 128000 16000
```

Context:

```
traffic-shape rate CIR [Bc [Be]]
traffic-shape adaptive mincir
```

Configuring a Frame Relay interface is very similar to the previous example, with a few differences. The same parameters described previously can be used to configure FRTS:

```
 !
Router1 (config)# interface s1/0
Router1 (config -if)# encapsulation frame-relay
Router1 (config -if)# frame-relay traffic-shaping
Router1 (config)# interface s1/0.100 point-to-point
Router1 (config -if)# ip address 10.10.10.101 255.255.255.252
Router1 (config -if)# frame-relay traffic-rate 128000 144000
Router1 (config -if)# frame-relay adaptive-shaping becn
Router1 (config -if)# frame-relay mincir 32000
Router1 (config -if)# frame-relay interface-dlci 100
```

Context:

```
frame-relay traffic-rate CIR [peak]
frame-relay adaptive-shaping {becn | foresight}
frame-relay mincir mincir
```

The optional peak value in the **frame-relay traffic-rate** command is the highest possible rate and is equal to CIR + Bc. For our example, the CIR is 128k, and the Bc is 16k, meaning the **peak** is 128 + 16, or 144k. Adaptive shaping can respond to either BECN or to Foresight, if the interface will be connected to a Cisco StrataCom device using foresight traffic shaping.

Verifying Traffic Shaping

You can use several **show** commands to verify FRTS operation. The following output from the **show running-configuration** command displays the configuration for FRTS on a serial port with a CIR of 128Kbps and a committed burst of 32Kbps:

```
interface Serial1/0
no ip address
no ip directed-broadcast
encapsulation frame-relay
no ip mroute-cache
no fair-queue
service-module t1 timeslots 1-4
frame-relay traffic-shaping
!
interface Serial1/0.100 point-to-point
ip address 10.10.10.100 255.255.255.252
no ip directed-broadcast
frame-relay traffic-rate 128000 144000
frame-relay adaptive-shaping becn
frame-relay mincir 32000
frame-relay interface-dlci 100
!
```

Link Fragmentation and Interleaving

Link fragmentation and interleaving (LFI) reduces serialization delay for time-sensitive applications, such as VoIP. Consider a 1500-byte FTP packet over a 128k serial link, which would take 94ms to be serialized. A VoIP packet that arrived after the FTP packet could be queued for up to 94ms. Given that the overall end-to-end delay for a VoIP packet should not exceed 150ms (G.114), this imposed wait can degrade voice quality. LFI resolves this issue by fragmenting large packets so that smaller time-sensitive packets can be interleaved with these fragments, reducing delay.

The fragmented packets are reassembled at the far end. LFI requires that the interface be configured to use multilink PPP with interleaving enabled. LFI is generally configured on serial interfaces of 768kbps or slower. Figure 6.14 shows traffic flow without LFI, and Figure 6.15 shows the same flow with LFI enabled. The large FTP packet is labeled *FTP*, VoIP packets are labeled *V*, and the fragmented FTP packet is labeled *F*.

Figure 6.15 Serialization Without LFI

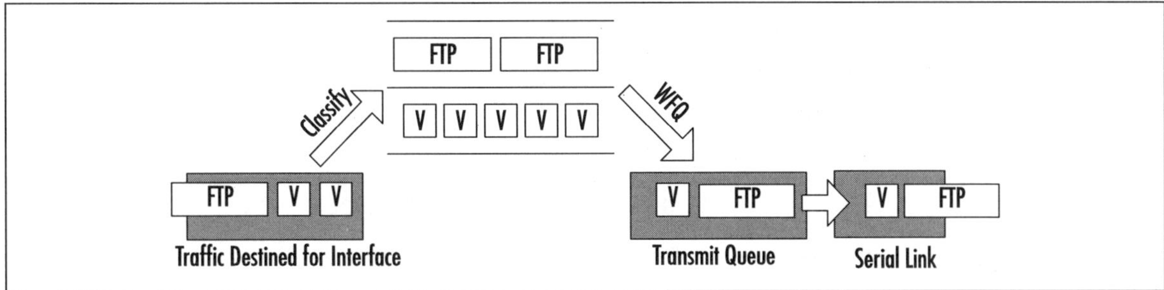

Figure 6.16 Serialization with LFI Enabled

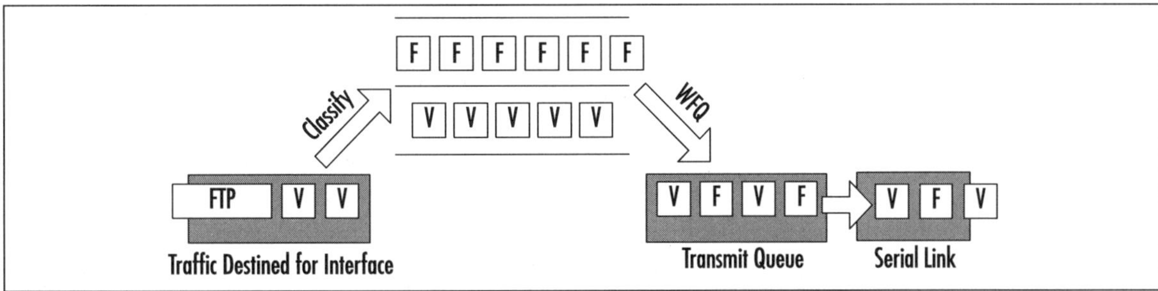

Configuring Link Fragmentation and Interleaving

You must configure multilink PPP on the interface in order to apply LFI to it. Multilink PPP is usually invoked to bundle multiple PPP-encapsulated circuits, but it can also be used on a single link to facilitate LFI. Create a multilink interface, and then associate it with a parent serial interface.

To configure multilink PPP, create a multilink interface while in global configuration mode. Apply an IP address to the new interface, activate interleaving, and turn on WFQ as shown in the example here.

```
router1(config)# interface Multilink 1
router1(config-if)# ip address 10.10.10.101 255.255.255.252
router1(config-if)# ppp multilink interleave
router1(config-if)# fair-queue
```

When the multilink interface is bound to the serial interface, its assigned IP address becomes the address of the serial link. To avoid an addressing conflict, the IP address of the serial link should be removed prior to configuring the multilink interface. Activation of the interleaving feature with the **ppp multilink interleave** and **fair-queue** commands is crucial; otherwise, the fragmented packets would not be interleaved with other packets, and there would be no benefit to the fragmentation process.

Fragmentation delay can be configured to specify a maximum serialization delay (default is 30ms). A delay of 10 to 20ms is desirable for VoIP implementations. The command for this configuration is performed in interface configuration mode:

```
router1(config-if)# ppp multilink fragment-delay 20
```

Your final task is to associate the multilink interface to its parent serial interface:

```
router1(config)# interface s1/0
router1(config-if)# ppp multilink
router1(config-if)# multilink-group 1
```

Verifying Link Fragmentation and Interleaving

After configuring PPP multilink, view the status using the **show ppp multilink** command:

```
router1# show ppp multilink
Multilink1, bundle name is router2
0 lost fragments, 0 reordered, 0 unassigned, sequence 0x2BF/0x524 rcvd/sent
0 discarded, 0 lost received, 1/255 load
Member links: 1 active, 0 inactive (max not set, min not set)
Serial0/0 1920 weight
```

Even though we are using only one serial interface, multilink still shows as a bundle, with the bundle name being the host name of the far router. If there are any problems with multilink encapsulation, you will see it as fragments, or reordered, unassigned, discarded, or lost packets. We can also display interface statistics with the **show interfaces** command just as we would any other interface:

```
router1# show interfaces multilink 1
Multilink1 is up, line protocol is up
Hardware is multilink group interface
Internet address is 10.0.101.10/30
MTU 1500 bytes, BW 1536 Kbit, DLY 100000 usec,
reliability 255/255, txload 43/255, rxload 1/255
Encapsulation PPP, loopback not set
Keepalive set (10 sec)
DTR is pulsed for 2 seconds on reset
LCP Open, multilink Open
Open: IPCP, CDPCP
Last input 00:00:00, output never, output hang never
Last clearing of "show interface" counters 5d21h
Input queue: 2/75/0 (size/max/drops); Total output drops: 0
Queuing strategy: weighted fair
Output queue: 6/1000/64/0 (size/max total/threshold/drops)
Conversations 1/3/256 (active/max active/max total)
Reserved Conversations 0/0 (allocated/max allocated)
5 minute input rate 3000 bits/sec, 10 packets/sec
5 minute output rate 264000 bits/sec, 35 packets/sec
1003558 packets input, 128454537 bytes, 0 no buffer
```

```
Received 0 broadcasts, 0 runts, 0 giants, 0 throttles
0 input errors, 0 CRC, 0 frame, 0 overrun, 0 ignored, 0 abort
35573 packets output, 24346968 bytes, 0 underruns
0 output errors, 0 collisions, 0 interface resets
0 output buffer failures, 0 output buffers swapped out
0 carrier transitions
```

Weighted Random Early Detection

Weighted random early detection is a congestion avoidance technique based on random early detection . WRED is a method by which routers manage their queues, thereby avoiding congestion before it occurs. WRED is Cisco's version of RED. When this service is used, routers will anticipate and subsequently avoid network congestion. This differs from queuing techniques that attempt to control congestion after it has occurred on an interface. WRED builds on the RED algorithm, which monitors traffic throughout the network and drops packets as congestion increases. An understanding of RED will help you understand WRED.

RED makes packet-switched networks aware of congestion before it becomes a problem. RED controls the average queue size by using TCP congestion control mechanisms to inform a sending device that it needs to throttle its transmissions. RED will randomly drop packets during periods of high congestion, which causes the source to decrease its transmission rate. Since TCP restarts quickly once a packet is lost, it can adapt its transmission rate to one the network can support. RED is recommended only for TCP/IP networks. It is not recommended for protocols such as AppleTalk or Internetwork Packet Exchange/ Sequenced Packet Exchange (IPX/SPX), which respond to dropped packets by re-transmitting the packets at the original rate.

WRED overcomes tail dropping problems by randomly discarding packets before the buffers get congested. WRED determines when to start dropping packets based on the average queue length. Once the packet count within the queue exceeds the defined upper queue threshold, WRED begins dropping packets in the upper queue range. When the source detects the dropped packet, it slows transmission. Packet dropping is indiscriminate to the network flow, which causes only a few sessions to restart. This gives the network a chance to drain the queues. Since remaining sessions are still flowing, the buffers can empty and allow other TCP sessions a chance to recover.

WRED, CQ, PQ, and WFQ are mutually exclusive on an interface. The router software produces an error message if you configure WRED and any other queuing strategy simultaneously. WRED is RSVP-aware and adds the use of IP precedence to the RED algorithms, enabling the router to drop lower priority traffic first.

Tail Drop

A queue has limited depth (capacity) to handle packets: once full, it will simply tail drop packets because there is nowhere to send them. Tail dropping is undesirable because it is indiscriminate; the router does not have a chance to identify the priority. Tail dropping occurs when the egress queues become so full that no more packets can enter. These packets are dropped from the tail end of the queue, hence the term, tail drop.

Once packets start to tail drop, the current network session will timeout, cuing each sender to simultaneously retransmit. Since all TCP sessions restart at the same time, more packets get congested in the queue simultaneously, essentially causing a cyclic effect. In other words, traffic can go through a wave of congestion that increases and decreases at regular intervals. WRED addresses this problem by setting thresholds for dropping packets of varying precedence levels. For instance, consider a network with the following thresholds set:

- Minimum threshold for IP precedence of 0 = 20
- Minimum threshold for IP precedence of 1 = 22
- Minimum threshold for IP precedence of 2 = 24

If the queue depth is 21, packets with a precedence of 0 can be dropped, but those with 1 or 2 will not. If the queue depth increases to 22, the packets with a 0 or 1 can be dropped, whereas those with a precedence of 2 will not be.

WRED works best with TCP traffic because when packets are dropped, TCP throttles back, reducing congestion. UDP is not so effective with WRED, and WRED can cause problems in networks with large amounts of UDP traffic. UDP does not respond to drops the same way TCP does, and will not throttle its transmission rate. As congestion occurs, UDP packets will continue to be transmitted and re-transmitted at their original rate.

Flow-Based WRED

Flow-based WRED factors in the types of packets and protocols it attempts to drop and tracks flow states. If it needs to drop any flows, it will look for new flows within the queue rather than sacrificing a currently connected flow.

To allow for irregular bursty traffic, a scaling factor is applied to the common incoming flows. This value allows each active flow to reserve a number of packets in the output queue. The value is used for all currently active flows. When the scaling factor is exceeded, the probability of packets being dropped from the flow is increased.

Flow-based WRED uses a fair method to determine which packets are tail-drops during periods of congestion. WRED automatically tracks flows to ensure that no single flow can monopolize resources. This is accomplished by actively monitoring traffic streams, learning which flows are not slowing down packet transmission, and fairly treating flows that do slow down packet transmission.

Configuring Congestion Avoidance with WRED

Issue the **random-detect** command in interface configuration mode to enable WRED with its default parameters. You can modify WRED defaults if necessary. The WRED algorithm uses the average queue depth to determine the probability of packet drops. The weighting factor of this average can be reconfigured from its default of 9, although Cisco does not recommend doing so. A higher number makes the queue less sensitive to changes in speed, whereas a lower number makes it more sensitive. Note that an excessively high weight can make the algorithm react too slowly to congestion situations, and excessive low value can cause unnecessary packet drops.

You can also adjust the weighting of each IP precedence level. Minimum threshold, maximum threshold, and the mark probability denominator (MPD) for each precedence level can be reconfigured with the **random-detect precedence** command. Table 6.7 shows the default values for each precedence level.

As mentioned previously, packets will be dropped starting at the minimum threshold, and above the maximum threshold. The MPD is the fraction of packets that will be dropped below the maximum threshold (1/MPD).

Table 6.7 Default Values for WRED Parameters

IP Precedence	Minimum Threshold	Maximum Threshold	MPD
0	20	40	10
1	22	40	10
2	24	40	10
3	26	40	10
4	28	40	10
5	31	40	10
6	33	40	10
7	35	40	10
RSVP	37	40	10

All WRED configuration commands are performed in interface configuration mode. Available WRED commands are:

```
random-detect
random-detect precedence precedence min-threshold max-threshold mark-prob-denominator
random-detect exponential-weighting-constant weighting-factor
```

WRED is enabled on a per-interface basis with the following command.

```
Router(config-if)# random-detect
```

You can adjust parameters such as the factor used to derive the queues, and establish thresholds for IP precedence.

```
Router(config-if)# random-detect exponential-weighting-constant exponent
Router(config-if)# random-detect precedence precedence min-threshold max-threshold mark-
prob-denominator
```

Flow-based WRED is enabled on a per-interface basis with the following command *after* you have enabled WRED with random-detect. Notice what WRED commands are available to you before and after WRED is enabled.

```
Router (config-if)# random-detect ?
  dscp-based  Enable dscp based WRED on an inteface
  prec-based  Enable prec based WRED on an interface
Router (config-if)# random-detect ?
```

```
  dscp                            parameters for each dscp value
  dscp-based                      Enable dscp based WRED on an inteface
  exponential-weighting-constant  weight for mean queue depth calculation
  flow                            enable flow based WRED
  prec-based                      Enable prec based WRED on an interface
  precedence                      parameters for each precedence value
Router(config-if)# random-detect flow
```

Verifying WRED

After enabling WRED, check the configured parameters and the number of drops per class (IP precedence) using the **show queuing random-detect** command:

```
router1# show queuing random-detect
Current random-detect configuration:
Serial5/0:0
Queuing strategy: random early detection (WRED)
Exp-weight-constant: 9 (1/512)
Mean queue depth: 0
Class    Random        Tail     Minimum      Maximum       Mark
              drop         drop  threshold  threshold  probability
     0          0          0         20         40       1/10
     1          0          0         22         40       1/10
     2          0          0         24         40       1/10
     3          0          0         26         40       1/10
     4          0          0         28         40       1/10
     5          0          0         31         40       1/10
     6          0          0         33         40       1/10
     7          0          0         35         40       1/10
   rsvp         0          0         37         40       1/10
```

This **show** command provides information on the types of traffic, with respect to IP precedence (or *class*), flowing through the router and what dropping is being used—random drop or tail drop. We can see from this output that each IP precedence level (0 to 7) dropped approximately the same number of packets. For congestion notification responsive flows such as TCP traffic, you should not see a lot of tail drops. Tail drop occurs when the upper threshold has been exceeded. When this occurs, packets are dropped wholesale. In this example, there are a large number of tail drops because the traffic was created with a packet generator that did not throttle.

Data Compression Overview

Traffic optimization is a strategy that reduces cost and improves link utilization and throughput rates. Many techniques are used to optimize traffic flow, which include queues, filters, and access lists. To this list, we will now add data compression.

Data compression can significantly reduce frame size, which in turn helps reduce travel time between endpoints. Data compression techniques differ, with some reducing packet headers and others reducing the payload. These methods ensure the correct reconstruction of the frames at the receiving end. The types of traffic and the network link type and speed must be considered when selecting a data compression method. For example, compression techniques used on voice and video differ from those applied to file transfers. We will review these compression methods and highlight the differences between them.

The Data Compression Mechanism

Data compression provides a coding scheme at both ends of a transmission link. The sending end manipulates the data packets by replacing them with a reduced number of bits, which are restored to the original data stream at the receiving end without loss.

Lossless compression algorithm is required by routers to transport data across the network. Voice and video compression schemes are referred to as *lossy* or *nonreversible compression*. The nature of voice or video data streams is such that retransmission due to packet loss is not required. Lossy compression allows for some degradation in order to gain greater compression and other benefits such as speed. Cisco IOS supports teleconferencing standards such as Joint Photographic Experts Group (JPEG) and Moving Picture Experts Group (MPEG).

Lossless compression schemes use two basic encoding techniques:

- Statistical compression
- Dictionary compression

Statistical compression is a fixed, non-adaptive encoding scheme that suits single applications where data is consistent and predictable. Hardly any current network is consistent or predictable, making this scheme rarely used.

Dictionary compression is based on the Lempel-Ziv (LZ) algorithm, which uses a dynamically encoded dictionary of symbols to replace a continuous bit stream with codes. The symbols represented by the codes are stored in memory in a dictionary format. The code and the original symbol vary as the data patterns change. The dictionary changes to accommodate changes in traffic patterns. Dictionaries can vary in size from 32Kb and much larger to accommodate high compression optimization.

Compression ratios are expressed as ratio x:1, where *x* is the number of input bytes divided by the number of output bytes. Dictionary algorithms require the dictionaries at the sending and receiving ends to remain synchronized. Synchronization is accomplished over a reliable data link such as X.25 or PPP. Synchronization ensures that transmission errors do not cause the dictionaries to diverge.

Dictionary-based algorithms operate in two modes—continuous and packet. Continuous mode constantly monitors the character stream to create and maintain the dictionary. The data stream consists of multiple network protocols (for example, IP and DECnet). Synchronization of end dictionaries is therefore important.

Packet mode also monitors a continuous stream of characters to create and maintain dictionaries, but limits the stream to a single network packet. The synchronization of dictionaries must occur only within the packet boundaries.

Selecting a Cisco IOS Compression Method

Due to ever-increasing bandwidth requirements, capacity planning is key to maintaining good throughput and minimizing congestion. Planners have to consider additional factors when adding compression to the mix:

- **CPU and memory utilization** When utilizing link compression, of the two compression algorithms, Predictor tends to use more memory, but STAC uses more CPU power. Payload compression uses more memory than link compression; however, link compression will be more CPU-intensive.
- **WAN topology** With the addition of more remote sites (more point-to-point connections), more dedicated memory is required due to the increased number of dictionary-based compression algorithms.
- **Latency** Latency is increased when compression is applied to the data stream. It remains a function of the type of algorithm used and the router CPU power available.

Encrypted data cannot be compressed; it will actually expand if run through a compression algorithm since it does not have a repetitive pattern.

Header Compression

TCP/IP header compression adheres to the Van Jacobson algorithm defined in RFC 1144. TCP/IP header compression is most effective with data streams of smaller packets where the header is large in proportion to the payload. While this header compression can reduce the amount of bandwidth required, it is quite CPU-intensive. It is not recommended for WAN links larger than 64 Kbps.

To enable TCP/IP header compression for Frame Relay encapsulation:

```
router(config-if)# frame-relay ip tcp header-compression [passive]
(for interface configuration)
```

Or, on a per dlci basis:

```
router(config-if)# frame-relay map ip ip-address dlci [broadcast] cisco tcp header-
compression {active | passive}
```

Another form of header compression, RTP, transports packets of audio and video traffic over an IP network. RTP provides end-to-end network transport for audio, video, and other network services.

The minimal 12 bytes of the RTP header, combined with 20 bytes of IP header and 8 bytes of UDP header, create a 40- byte IP/UDP/RTP header. The RTP packet has a payload of about 20 to 150 bytes for audio applications that use compressed payloads. This is clearly inefficient since the header could end up being twice the size of the payload.

With RTP header compression, the 40-byte header can be compressed to a more reasonable 2 to 5 bytes. To enable RTP header compression for PPP or high-data-rate digital subscriber line (HDSL) encapsulations:

```
router(config-if)# ip rtp header-compression [passive]
```

If the **passive** keyword is included, the software compresses outgoing RTP packets only if incoming RTP packets on the same interface are compressed. If the command is used without the passive keyword, the software compresses all RTP traffic.

To enable RTP header compression for Frame Relay encapsulation:

```
router(config-if)# frame-relay ip rtp header-compression [passive]
router(config-if)# frame-relay map ip ip-address dlci [broadcast] rtp
header-compression [active | passive]
router(config-if)# frame-relay map ip ip-address dlci [broadcast]
compress (enables both RTP and TCP header compression)
```

Link and Payload Compression

Variations of the LZ algorithm are used in many programs such as STAC (Lempel Ziv STAC, or LZS), ZIP and UNIX compress utilities. Cisco supports the STAC (LZS) and Predictor compression algorithms. LZS is used on Cisco's Link Access Procedure, HDLC, X.25, PPP, and Frame Relay encapsulation types. Predictor and Microsoft Point-to-Point Compression (MPPC) are only supported under PPP.

STAC (LZS) or Stacker was developed by STAC Electronics. This algorithm searches the input for redundant strings of data and replaces them with much shorter tokens. STAC uses the encoded dictionary method to store these string matches and tokens. This dictionary is used to replace the redundant strings found in new data streams. The result is a reduced number of packets transmitted.

The Predictor compression algorithm predicts the incoming sequence of data stream by using an index to locate sequences in the compression dictionary. The next sequence in the data stream is checked for a match. If it matches, that sequence replaces the sequence in the dictionary. If not, the algorithm locates the next character sequence in the index and the process begins anew. The index updates itself by hashing a few of the most recent character sequences from the input stream.

A third and more recent form of compression supported by Cisco IOS is MPPC. MPPC, as described in RFC 2118, is a PPP-optimized compression algorithm. MPPC, while it is an LZ-based algorithm, occurs at Layer 3 of the OSI model. STAC, Predictor, and MPPC are supported on most Cisco routers, from the 1000 series to the 7500 series.

Per-Interface Compression (Link Compression)

Per-interface compression handles larger packets and higher data rates. It is applied to the entire data stream to be transported—that is, it compresses the entire WAN link as if it was one application. Per-interface compression uses STAC or Predictor to compress the traffic, which in turn is encapsulated in a link protocol such as PPP or LAPB. This last step applies error correction and ensures packet sequencing.

Per-Virtual Circuit Compression (Payload Compression)

Per-virtual circuit compression is usually used across virtual network services such as X.25 (Predictor or STAC) and Frame Relay (STAC). The header is unchanged during per-virtual circuit compression; instead, the payload portion is compressed. Payload compression is appropriate for routers with a single interface, but does not scale well in scenarios with multiple virtual circuit destinations.

Continuous-mode compression algorithms cannot be applied realistically due to the multiple dictionary requirements of the multiple virtual circuit destinations. It places a heavy load on the router for CPU and memory.

Packet-mode compression algorithms, which use fewer dictionaries and less memory, are better suited for packet networks. Performing compression before or after WAN encapsulation on the serial interface is a prime goal. Applying compression on an already encapsulated data payload reduces the packet size, but not the number of packets. This suits Frame Relay and Switched Multimegabit Data Service (SMDS). Applying compression before WAN serial encapsulation will benefit the user from a cost perspective when using X.25, where service providers charge by the packet. This method reduces the number of packets transmitted over the WAN.

To configure compression, use the **compress** interface configuration command. To disable compression on the interface, use the **no** form of this command, as illustrated below.

```
router(config-if)# compress {stac | predictor | mppc(ignore-pfc)}
router(config-if)# no compress {stac | predictor | mppc(ignore-pfc)}
```

Another form of payload compression used on Frame Relay networks is FRF.9. FRF.9 is a compression mechanism for both switched virtual circuits (SVC) and permanent virtual circuits. Cisco currently supports FRF.9 mode 1 and is evaluating mode 2, which provides flexibility during the LCP compression negotiation.

To enable FRF.9 compression on a Frame Relay interface you can use either the **frame-relay payload-compress frf9 stac** or **frame-relay map payload-compress frf9 stac** commands.

Per-interface compression adds delay at each hop due to compression and decompression on every link between the endpoints. External compression devices or integrated compression hardware can relieve the router of compression duties. Otherwise, a router must have sufficient CPU and RAM for compression and dictionaries, respectively.

Hardware Compression

Cisco has developed hardware compression modules to relieve the primary CPU of the router. On the 2600 and 3660 routers, there is an Advanced Integration Module (AIM) slot that can be populated with compression modules. For the 7000, 7200, and 7500 series routers, there are Compression Service Adapters (CSAs) that offload the compression from the primary CPU. CSAs require a VIP2-40 or greater. The 7200 VXR series does not support CSA-based compression.

The 2600 can use an AIM-COMP2= to increase its compression capabilities from 256 Kbps to 8 Mbps of compressed data throughput. On the 3660, the AIMCOMPR4= module increases compression throughput from from 1024 Kbps to 16 Mbps.

There are two available modules for the 7X00 routers: the SA-COMP/1 and the SA-COMP/4. Their function is identical, but the SA-COMP/4 has more memory to maintain a larger dictionary. The SA-COPMP/1 and SA-COMP/4, while supporting 16 Mbps of bandwidth, can support up to 64 and 256 compression contexts, respectively. One context is essentially one bi-directional reconstruction dictionary pair. This may be a point-to-point link or a point-to-point Frame Relay sub-interface.

Verifying Compression Operation

To verify and monitor the various compression techniques, use the following **show** and **debug** commands:

For IP header compression:

```
router# show ip tcp header-compression
router# debug ip tcp header-compression
```

For RTP header compression:

```
router# show ip rtp header-compression
router# debug ip rtp header-compression
router# debug ip rtp packets
```

For payload compression:

```
router# show compress {detail-ccp}
router# debug compress
```

Due to the volume and amount of data that these commands generate, use them sparingly.

Configuring Packet Classification

Packet classification can be performed in a variety of manners including IP precedence and policy-based routing (PBR), which support specialized traffic such as VoIP. Each of these methods can be implemented individually, but they can also be mixed such that your policy can set the IP precedence for a packet. We have previously discussed IP precedence and demonstrated its usefulness to queuing; we will simply rehash it in the context of packet classification, a more pure use of IP precedence.

IP Precedence

Valid values for IP precedence are from zero (low priority, first to be dropped) to seven (high priority, last to be dropped). Actual configuration of IP precedence is very simple and can be done either from a dial peer, a Frame Relay port, or as part of a policy map:

```
Router1(config-dial-peer)#ip precedence precedence
```

IP precedence in a VoIP implementation is often configured on individual dial peers. When performing this configuration, you can either set the precedence bits for all dial peers to be high priority—a six or seven—and leave all other traffic at zero or one, or you can choose to specify a different precedence for each dial peer based on the importance of the communications on that port. For instance, to configure a dial peer to assign a precedence of six, enter the following in global configuration mode:

```
Router1(config)# dial-peer voice 1 voip
Router1(config-dial-peer)# ip precedence 6
```

You can also use IP precedence to classify packets for protocols such as RSVP as shown.

```
ip rsvp precedence conform precedence-value exceed precedence-value
```

Verifying IP Precedence

Use **show** commands to verify IP precedence configuration, such as the **show running-configuration** output provided here.

```
!
dial-peer voice 1 voip
  destination pattern 1234
  ip precedence 4
  session target ras
!
dial-peer voice 2 pots
  destination pattern 1001
  ip precedence 3
  port 0/0/0
!
dial-peer voice 3 pots
  destination pattern 1002
  ip precedence 2
  port 0/0/1
```

Policy Routing

Policy-based routing is a method by which a packet can be directed, based on a given set of criteria (policy), to take a path other than that which would have been taken if routed via standard routing protocols. PBR classifies traffic based on configured ACL entries and then applies the configured policy accordingly.

Classification and policy application is performed by a packet filter called a *route map*. Route maps consist of two types of statements: Match and Set. The Match statement compares a packet to either a standard or extended ACL and/or matches packet length. The Set statement determines the action to be performed on matching packets. Set actions can include setting IP precedence, IP next-hop, interface, IP default next-hop, or default interface.

With Cisco IOS release 12.0 and later, PBR can be fast-switched rather than process-switched, which improves performance. With fast switching, the **set IP default next-hop** and **set default interface** commands are not available. The **set interface** command is available only on point-to-point links unless there is a route-cache entry for the specified interface. When fast-switched PBR is used, a matching packet is forwarded blindly, without checking the routing table to ensure that it is a valid route.

Configuring Policy Routing

PBR is fairly simple to configure. Begin by creating an ACL for the traffic that is to be classified. Next, create **route-map** statements that act on the ACLs. A route map that specifies **permit** applies the policy to any packet that matches the ACL; all others will be routed normally. A **deny** route map does just the opposite, routing the packets that match and applying the policy to those that do not.

Each **route-map** statement must also have a sequence number. The router will apply the statements in order to each packet and classify each based on the first statement it matches. Following the **match** statements are **set** statements, which tell the router what policy to apply. **Set** statements can be used with each other, so it is possible to send a matching packet to a particular interface and to adjust the precedence. After the **route-map** statements are complete, apply the route map to an interface with the **ip policy route-map** command. Some PBR applicable commands are:

- **route-map *map-name* [permit | deny] *sequence-number***
- **match length *min max***
- **match ip address [*access-list-number* | *name*]**
- **set ip precedence [*number* | *name*]**
- **set ip next-hop *ip-address***
- **set interface *interface-type interface-number***
- **set ip default next-hop *ip-address***
- **set default interface *interface-type interface-number***

- **interface** ***interface-type interface-number***
- **ip policy route-map** ***map-name***

Verifying Policy Routing

You should use **show** commands to verify your policy routing configuration. Our execution of **show running-configuration** confirms that an IP precedence of 5 is assigned to all H.323 packets, which are sent out interface Serial 0/1:

```
!
interface vlan 1
   ip address 10.10.10.1 255.255.255.0
   ip policy route-map voip
!
route-map voip permit 10
match ip address 101
set ip precedence 5
set interface s0/1
!
access list 101 permit tcp any any eq 1300
!
```

Call Admission Control

Call Admission Control (CAC) describes a method by which a node can prevent over-subscription of network resources, thus preserving the quality of existing transmissions. Often used with voice applications or videoconferencing, CAC rejects a request for network resources if the requesting application requires more bandwidth than is currently available.

For example, if an interface is configured for 128k, and five VoIP calls requiring 24k each are in progress, CAC will prevent a sixth call from being completed, as it would degrade the quality of *all six* calls. This system ensures that all existing connections maintain the bandwidth they need. When a connection is rejected, the originating node will, depending on the network configuration, either look for an alternate path or provide a reorder tone or fast busy signal to the calling party.

In Figures 6.17, 6.18 and 6.19, assume that each call requires 24k of bandwidth. In Figure 6.17, two calls exist between Router1 and Router3 (labeled 1 and 2).

Figure 6.17 Rerouting a Call Due to CAC Rejection: Two Calls Exist

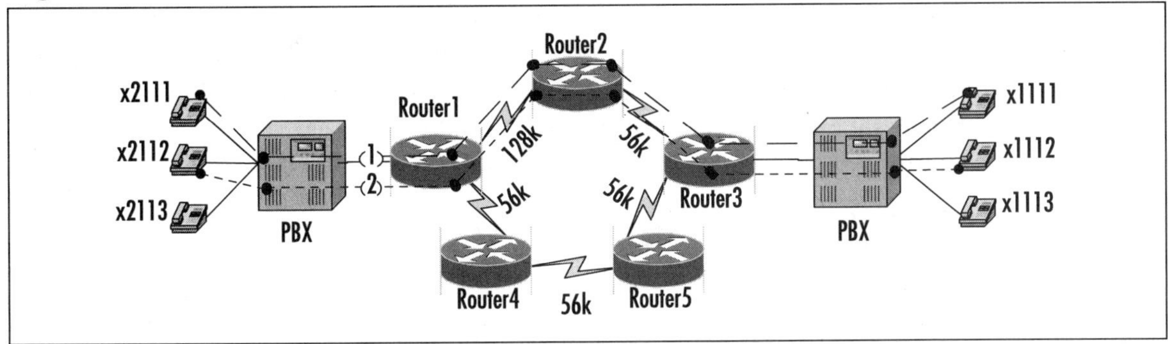

In Figure 6.18, a third call is placed (labeled 3), and Router1 sends the call to the next hop, Router2. However, there is not enough bandwidth to support the new call, so CAC rejects it.

Figure 6.18 Rerouting a Call Due to CAC Rejection: Third Call Is Rejected

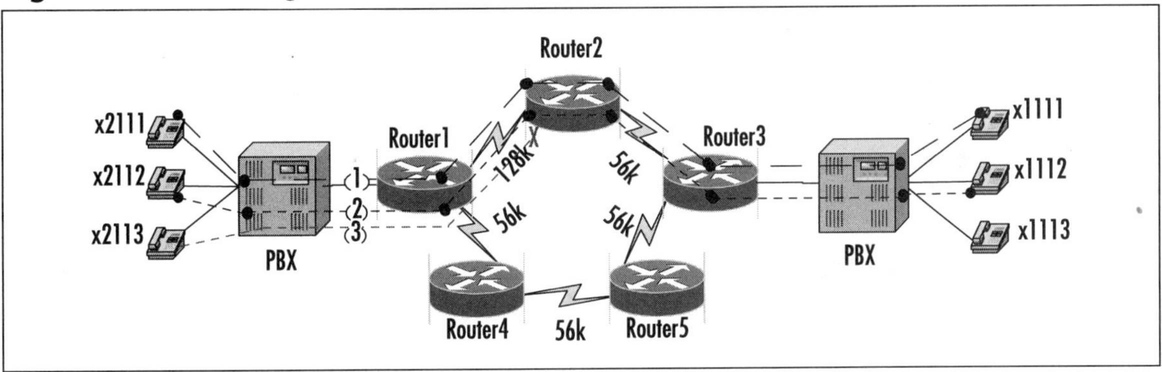

In Figure 6.19, after the rejection, Router1 is able to reroute the call via Router4 to complete the call.

Figure 6.19 Rerouting a Call Due to CAC Rejection: Third Call Is Rerouted

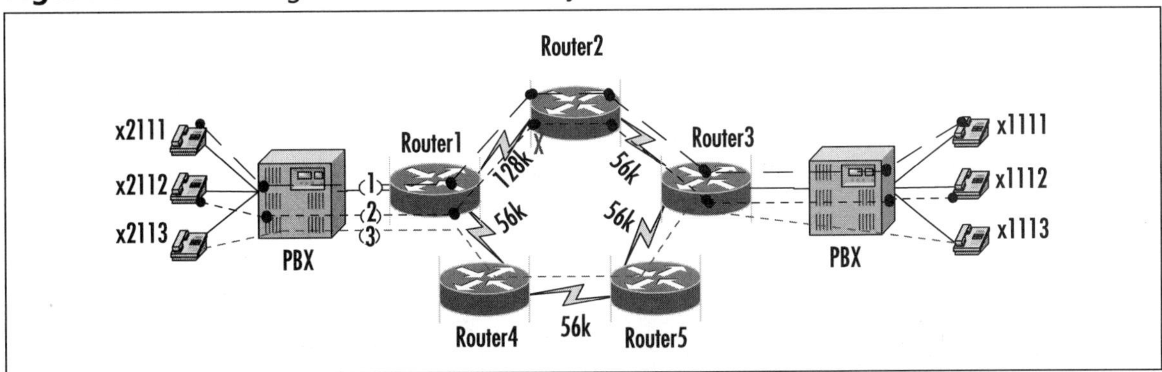

There are several different methods for implementing CAC, but for the purposes of VoIP, the most commonly used are RSVP and H.323 gateway zone bandwidth. The H.323 gatekeeper

monitors the network and makes decisions on call admission based on static calculations to either accept or reject a call, similar to the illustration in Figure 6.18. The gatekeeper does not know how much bandwidth is currently being used and makes no bandwidth reservations. Instead, it relies on configured bandwidth for WAN links and preset values for per-call bandwidth use. The gatekeeper then merely subtracts that rate from the total bandwidth for each active call and rejects a call request that would drop the bandwidth below zero.

Configuring Call Admission Control (CAC)

We will configure an H.323 gateway zone bandwidth for CAC. From Gatekeeper Configuration mode, enter the **bandwidth** command. To configure a specific bandwidth from the current zone to another zone, use the **interzone** parameter. The **total** parameter specifies the total bandwidth available within the current zone, and the **session** parameter specifies a maximum bandwidth for an individual call. Bandwidth is entered in Kbps, and valid values are 1 to 10,000,000Kbps for interzone or total configurations and 1 to 5,000Kbps for session configurations. In Figure 6.20, there are three routers, each with two POTS (plain old telephone service) lines, arranged into two zones, with a gatekeeper.

Figure 6.20 Call Admission Control

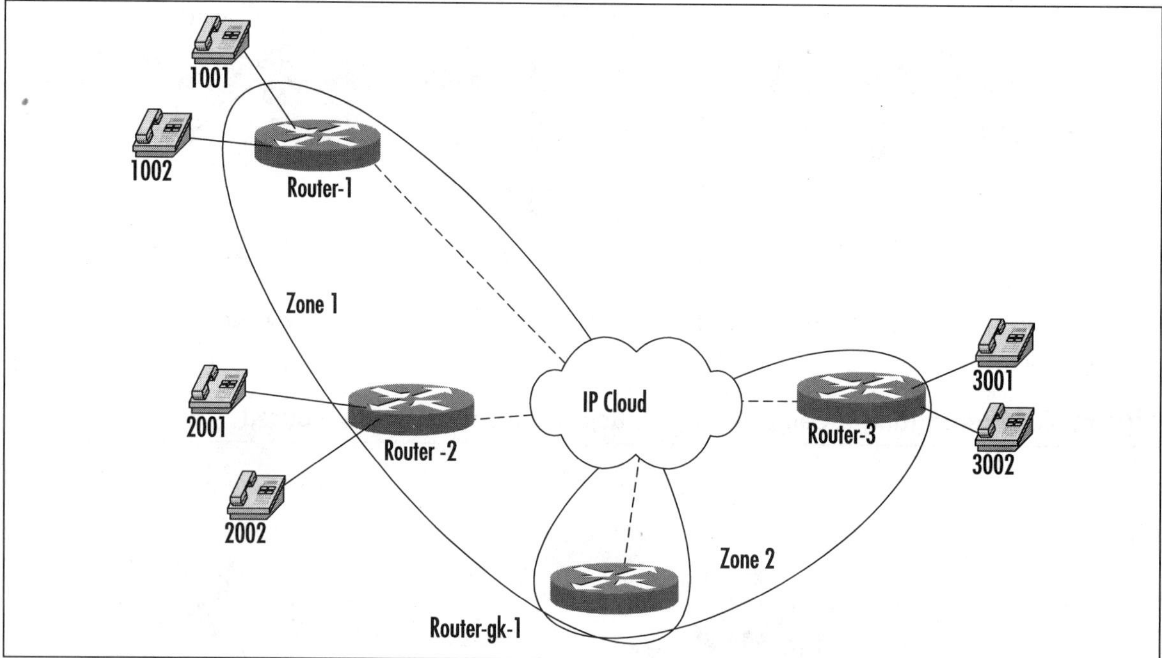

The necessary configuration commands are provided in the following output:

```
hostname Router-1
!
interface ethernet 1/0
  ip address 10.10.10.101 255.25.255.0
```

```
  h323-gateway voip interface
  h323-gateway voip id zone1 ipaddr 10.10.10.104
  h323-gateway voip h323-id gw_1
  h323-gateway voip bind srcarrd 10.10.10.101
!
voice-port 0/0/0
!
voice-port 0/0/1
!
dial-peer voice 1 voip
  destination pattern ….
  session target ras
!
dial-peer voice 2 pots
  destination pattern 1001
  port 0/0/0
!
dial-peer voice 3 pots
  destination pattern 1002
  port 0/0/1
!
gateway
```

Verifying Call Admission Control

Verification of your CAC configuration can be done with simple **show** commands:

```
hostname Router-2
!
interface ethernet 1/0
  ip address 10.10.10.102 255.25.255.0
  h323-gateway voip interface
  h323-gateway voip id zone1 ipaddr 10.10.10.104
  h323-gateway voip h323-id gw_2
  h323-gateway voip bind srcarrd 10.10.10.102
!
voice-port 0/0/0
!
voice-port 0/0/1
!
!
```

```
dial-peer voice 1 voip
  destination pattern ….
  session target ras
!
dial-peer voice 2 pots
  destination pattern 2001
  port 0/0/0
!
dial-peer voice 3 pots
  destination pattern 2002
  port 0/0/1
!
gateway
!
hostname Router-3
!
!
interface ethernet 1/0
  ip address 10.10.10.103 255.25.255.0
  h323-gateway voip interface
  h323-gateway voip id zone2 ipaddr 10.10.10.104
  h323-gateway voip h323-id gw_3
  h323-gateway voip bind srcarrd 10.10.10.103
!
voice-port 0/0/0
!
voice-port 0/0/1
!
dial-peer voice 1 voip
  destination pattern ….
  session target ras
!
dial-peer voice 2 pots
  destination pattern 3001
  port 0/0/0
!
dial-peer voice 3 pots
  destination pattern 3002
  port 0/0/1
!
```

```
gateway
!
hostname Router-gk-1
!
interface Ethernet 1/0
  ip address 10.10.10.104 255.255.255.0
!
gatekeeper
  zone local zone1
  zone local zone2
  zone prefix zone1 1… gw-priority 10 gw_1
  zone prefix zone1 2… gw-priority 10 gw_2
  zone prefix zone2 3… gw-priority 10 gw_3
  bandwidth interzone zone1 64
  bandwidth total zone zone1 128
```

Notice that bandwidth is limited to 64Kbps for Zone 1 for interzone calls, with 128Kbps of total bandwidth. Because the gatekeeper assumes 64Kbps per call, this limits Zone 1 to a maximum of one call from outside the zone and two calls total. Assuming that no calls are currently in progress, if a call is placed from 3001 to 1001, it will be connected. If a call is then attempted from 3002 to 2002, it will be rejected because there is already one interzone call in progress. However, a call from 1002 to 2001 would be allowed because there can be up to two simultaneous calls within Zone 1. For a graphical representation of this scenario, see Figure 6.21.

Figure 6.21 H.323 Gateway Call Flow

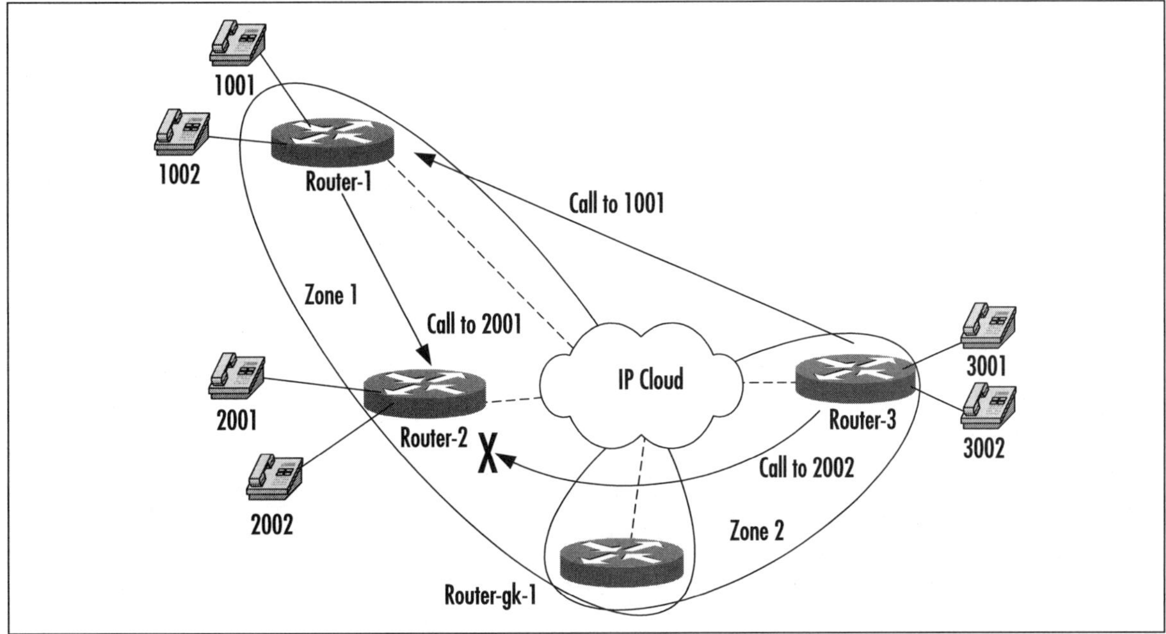

Summary

Democracy is a wonderful thing, but sometimes, in the world of networking, it needs to be suspended to grant preferential treatment to a select few. Certain traffic has requirements that make it more sensitive to delays and time issues than others. With such traffic, you need to grant it priority.

We covered several approaches for prioritizing. Queuing methods such as priority queuing and custom queuing have their own approaches to moving key traffic to the head of the line. IP can enter the fray by enabling its packets marked with higher than normal precedence to get better service. Without explicit configuration, Cisco routers default to either a FIFO basis, or in certain mixes of hardware and software, to weighted fair queuing.

Your bandwidth is limited, and any opportunity to conserve should be considered. Compression can reduce packet sizes, which can translate into faster transmittal as smaller packets take less time. Compression can place a burden on your routers, so you might want to consider hardware options that offload this task.

Routing via protocols such as RIP or OSPF is usually an adequate solution. If not, you can always modify routing behavior using policy based routing and adjusting attributes with route maps. Ultimately, all these tools are designed to give you the control you need over your network.

Chapter 7

Cisco Network Security

Best Damn Topics in this Chapter:

- Attacks and Threats
- Password Attacks
- Malicious Code Attacks
- Attacker Aids
- Detecting Breaches
- AAA Overview
- Configuring AAA
- Security Protocols
- Using RADIUS and TACAS+ for AAA Services
- Monitoring and Verifying AAA Access Control
- Complete AAA Configuration Example
- Authentication Proxy
- Cisco Secure Access Control Server
- Cisco IP Security Hardware and Software
- Access Lists
- Lock-and-Key Access Lists
- Reflexive Access Lists
- Context-Based Access Control
- Configuring Port to Application Mapping
- Applying Perimeter Security in IPv6
- Overview of VPN Technologies
- Layer 2 Transport Protocol
- Understanding Cryptography Concepts
- IPsec Concepts
- Remote Access VPN
- Wireless Security
- Implementing WEP

Introduction

Threats to a network can come from someone intending to do harm, or from a malicious source a user inadvertently activates. Both can arise as a result of security policy violations. Threats can compromise the following three goals of network security:

- **Confidentiality** Protects information from unauthorized disclosure or intelligible interception by permitting it to be seen only by the intended parties in a conversation. Encryption (such as virtual private networks [VPNs]) can ensure confidentiality.
- **Integrity** Ensures that information is not altered (intentionally or accidentally) without authorization or while en route to the authorized receiver. Checksum or hash values from protocols such as Message Digest 5 (MD5) or Secure Hash Algorithm (SHA) (used in Secure Internet Protocol [IPsec]]) can validate the integrity of received information.
- **Availability** Assures that information and services are accessible and functional when needed and authorized. There are a variety of means, including design redundancy (Hot Standby Router Protocol [HSRP], firewall failover), data backups, spare parts, uninterruptible power supplies, and secure architectures.

Threats are many and varied. Some are natural such as weather and climate, while others are human. Threats from humans (hackers, crackers, disgruntled employees, and so forth) are the most difficult to predict and control. As a security engineer, the "why" (the reason for the attack) is not as important as the "how" (how to prevent and stop the attack).

Malicious code includes Trojan horses (where a harmful function is hidden inside an application that appears harmless. Viruses are threats to networks and information. Self-replicating and propagating worms can destroy a network. Smurf attacks use Internet Control Message Protocol (ICMP) to flood and overwhelm a target with responses. Transmission Control Protocol (TCP) is vulnerable to synchronous (SYN) flood attacks that take advantage of its nature. Attacks are becoming increasingly sophisticated at circumventing normal protections; witness the increase and effectiveness of attacks such as W32.Blaster.F.Worm and its similar variants.

While some such threats spring from bored script kiddies, many seek to perpetrate Denial of Service (DOS) attacks. The "why" behind these attacks is not important. What is important is protecting your network and assets. Specifically, there are tools and features of Cisco hardware and software that can be used for protection.

This chapter discusses threats and dangers to networks, and what tools and features Cisco provides to counter them. Security is a continual process of analyzing, testing, and validating your security. You must keep abreast of your networks, a task for which Cisco provides an ample toolbox of commands.

Attacks and Threats

Understanding common threats and attacks is useful when handling them. To that end, this chapter discusses brute force attacks, DOS attacks, and others. Sometimes, you can be your own worst threat if you do not properly manage and configure your security.

Active Attacks

Active attacks can be described as attacks in which the attacker is actively attempting to cause harm to a network or system. The attacker is not just listening on the wire, but is attempting to breach or shut down a service. Active attacks tend to be very visible because the damage caused is very noticeable. Some of the most well-known active attacks are DOS and distributed DOS (DDOS), buffer overflows, SYN attacks, and Internet Protocol (IP) spoofing. These and many more are detailed in the following sections.

DOS/DDOS

A DOS attack reduces the quality of service delivered by some measurable degree, often to the point where the target infrastructure of the DOS attack cannot deliver any services. The fundamental objective of a DOS attack is to degrade service, whether on a single server or an entire network infrastructure (routers, switches, and so on).

A DOS attack attempts to reduce the ability to service clients by either overloading the target or by sending traffic that causes targets to behave unpredictably (usually crashes). DOS attacks can be difficult to detect or deflect.

Although DOS attacks do not by definition generate a risk to confidential or sensitive data, they can act as an effective tool to mask more intrusive activities that could take place simultaneously. While administrators and security officers are attempting to rectify what they perceive to be the main problem, the real penetration can be happening elsewhere.

Most DOS attacks occur over networks, with the perpetrator launching the attack remotely. Other attacks can be launched against the local machine. Local DOS attacks are generally easier to locate and rectify because the parameters of the problem space are well defined (local to the host). A common example of a locally based DOS attack is the fork bomb that repeatedly spawns processes to consume system resources. The two elemental types of DOS attacks are:

- **Resource Consumption Attacks** SYN flood attacks and amplification attacks that deplete the resources of the target.
- **Malformed Packet Attacks** Network packets created with deliberate violations of length and format that will wreak havoc with the target.

As bad as the effects of DOS attacks are, their spin-off, DDOS does even more damage. DDOS attacks advance the DOS conundrum one more step forward. During the first phase of a DDOS attack, the perpetrator compromises computers scattered across the Internet and installs specialized software on these hosts to aid in the attack. In the second phase, these compromised hosts (referred to as *zombies*) are then instructed through intermediaries (called *masters*) to commence the attack. Hundreds, possibly thousands, of zombies can be co-opted into an attack by diligent hackers. Using control software, each of these zombies can then be used to mount its own DOS attack on the target. The cumulative effect of the zombie attack is to either overwhelm the victim with massive amounts of traffic, or to exhaust resources such as connection queues.

Buffer Overflows

A buffer is a temporary area of memory used to store data or instructions. To create a buffer overflow attack, the attacker simply writes too much data to that area of memory, overwriting its contents. This extra data can be garbage characters that would cause the program to fail or, more commonly, new instructions that the victim's computer runs. These instructions can contain information that will install software on the victim's computer to allow the attacker access.

SYN Attacks

A SYN attack exploits a basic weakness found in the TCP/IP protocol, and its concept is fairly simple. A standard TCP session consists of the two communicating hosts exchanging a SYN | SYN/ACK | ACK packet. The expected behavior is that the initiating host sends a SYN packet, to which the responding host issues a SYN/ACK and waits for an ACK reply from the initiator. With a SYN attack, or SYN flood, the attacker sends only the SYN packet, leaving the victim waiting for a reply. The attack occurs when the attacker sends thousands and thousands of SYN packets to the victim, forcing them to wait for replies that never come. While the host is waiting for so many replies, it cannot accept any legitimate requests, so it becomes unavailable, thus achieving the purpose of a DOS attack. For a graphical representation of a SYN attack, refer to Figure 7.1

Figure 7.1 SYN Attack

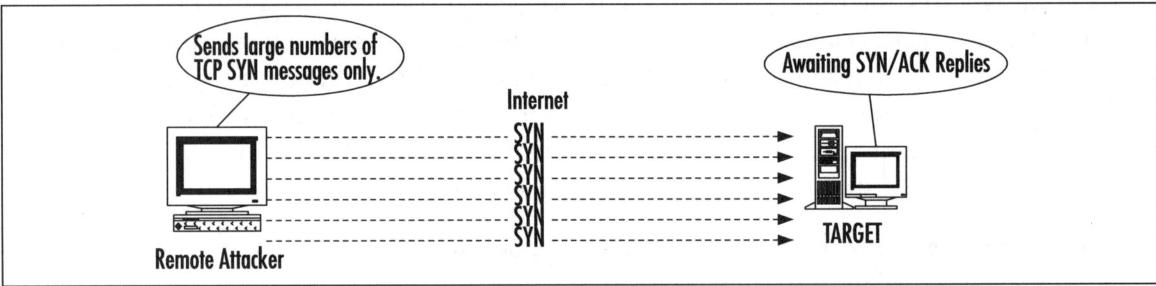

Spoofing

Spoofing means providing false information about your identity in order to gain unauthorized access to systems, or, in even simpler terms, pretending to be someone you are not. The most classic example of spoofing is *IP spoofing,* wherein an attacker fakes its source IP address, perhaps using the IP address of a legitimate host as its own.

There are different types of spoofing attacks, including *blind spoofing attacks* in which the attacker can only send and has to make assumptions or guesses about replies, and *informed attacks* in which the attacker can monitor, and therefore participate in, bi-directional communications. The theft of all of the credentials of a victim (that is, the username and password) is not usually considered spoofing, but does give the attacker much of the same power.

Spoofing is not always malicious. Some network redundancy schemes rely on automated spoofing in order to take over the identity of a downed server. This is because the networking technologies never accounted for the need for one server to take over for another, and so have a hard-coded idea of one address, one host.

Unlike the human characteristics we use to recognize each other, which we find easy to use and hard to mimic, computer information is easy to spoof. It can be perfectly stored, categorized, copied, and replayed.

Technologies and methodologies exist that can help safeguard against spoofing of these capability challenges. These include:

- Using firewalls to guard against unauthorized transmissions.
- Not relying on *security through obscurity*, the expectation that using undocumented protocols will protect you.
- Using various cryptographic algorithms to provide differing levels of authentication.

Spoofing is an easy attack due to inherent flaws in TCP/IP. TCP/IP basically assumes that all computers are telling the truth. There is little or no checking done to verify that a packet really comes from the address indicated in the IP header. When the protocols were being designed in the late 1960s, engineers did not anticipate that anyone would or could use the protocol maliciously. There are ways to combat spoofing, however. One really easy way to defeat harmful spoofing attacks is to disable source routing in your network at your firewall, at your router, or both. Source routing is, in short, a way to tell your packet to take the same path back that it took while going forward. Disabling this will prevent attackers from using it to get responses back from their spoofed packets.

Man-in-the-Middle Attacks

The TCP/IP were not designed with security in mind and contain a number of fundamental flaws. One issue resulting from TCP/IP insecurity is the Man-in-the-Middle (MITM) attack. To fully understand how a MITM attack works, remember that TCP uses a three-way handshake.

As seen in Figure 7.2, a host (Host A) that wants to send data to another host (Host B) initiates communication by sending a SYN packet. The SYN packet contains, among other things, the source and destination IP address and the source and destination port numbers. Host B responds with a SYN/ACK. The SYN from Host B prompts Host A to send another ACK and the connection is established.

Figure 7.2 TCP Handshake Process

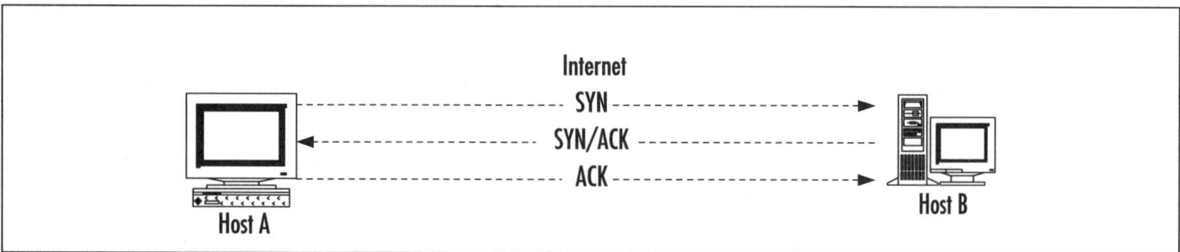

If a malicious individual places himself between Host A and Host B, for example, compromising an upstream router belonging to the Internet Service Provider (ISP) of one of the hosts, they can monitor the packets moving between the two hosts. It is then possible for the malicious individual to analyze and change the packets coming and going to the host. It is easy for a malicious person to perform this type of attack on Telnet sessions, but the attacker must first be able to predict the right TCP sequence number and properly modify the data—all before the session times out waiting for the response. Obviously, doing this manually is hard to pull off; however, tools designed to watch for and modify specific data have been written and work very well.

There are a few ways to prevent MITM attacks from happening. First, use a TCP/IP implementation that generates TCP sequence numbers that are as close to truly random as possible. It is important to note that random TCP sequence numbers do not make a connection secure if that connection is in cleartext.

Replay Attacks

Replay attacks, while possible in theory, are unlikely due to multiple factors such as the level of difficulty of predicting TCP sequence numbers. Performing a replay attack requires first capturing enough sensitive traffic, and then replaying it back to the host in an attempt to replicate the transaction. For example, consider an electronic money transfer. User A transfers a sum of money to Bank B. Malicious User C captures User A's network traffic, then replays the transaction in an attempt to cause the transaction to be repeated multiple times. Obviously, this attack has no benefit to User C, but could result in User A losing money. It has been proven, especially in older versions of Windows NT, that the formula for generating random TCP sequence numbers is not truly random or even that difficult to predict, which makes this attack possible. As with MITM attacks, more random TCP sequence numbers and encryption like SSH or IPsec can help defend against this problem.

TCP/IP Hijacking

TCP/IP hijacking, or *session hijacking*, is a problem that has appeared in most TCP/IP-based applications, ranging from simple Telnet sessions to Web-based e-commerce applications. In order to hijack a TCP/IP connection, a malicious user must first have the ability to intercept a legitimate user's data, and then insert themselves into that session. A tool known as Hunt (http://lin.fsid.cvut.cz/~kra/index.html) is commonly used to monitor and hijack sessions. It works especially well on basic Telnet or File Transfer Protocol (FTP) sessions.

Lately, a more interesting and malicious form of session hijacking has surfaced, involving Web-based applications (especially e-commerce and other applications that rely heavily on cookies to maintain session state). The first scenario involves hijacking a user's cookie, which is normally used to store login credentials and other sensitive information, and using that cookie to then access that user's session. The legitimate user simply receives a "session expired" or "login failed" message and probably is not even aware that anything suspicious has happened. The other issue with Web server applications that can lead to session hijacking is incorrectly configured session timeouts. A Web application is typically configured to timeout a user's session after a set period of inactivity. If this timeout is too large, it leaves a window of opportunity for an attacker to potentially use a hijacked cookie or even predict a session ID number and hijack a user's session.

To prevent these types of attacks, as with other TCP/IP-based attacks, use encryption. In the case of Web applications, unique and pseudo-random session IDs and cookies should be used along with secure sockets layer (SSL) encryption.

WarDialing

WarDialing is the act of dialing large blocks of telephone numbers via modem, searching for a computer with which to connect. The attacker in this case uses a program known as a *WarDialer* to automate the process. These programs are usually quite flexible and dial a given block of numbers at a set interval, logging whatever they find. While this technique was previously heavily used, advances in telecommunications technology make it easier to identify WarDialers, therefore making it slightly more risky.

For someone in charge of securing a large corporate infrastructure, it makes sense to war dial all known company lines to check for modems that may be connected without their knowledge. Though the practice is on a decline, the installation of unauthorized modems by employees still represents a huge threat to enterprise security, as anyone with a modem can set up a backdoor into an otherwise secure network.

Social Engineering

Social engineering is often overlooked in security plans, which is unfortunate because it is one of the most dangerous and easily used methods of infiltrating a victim's network. The concept is nothing more than creative lying. The lies are often backed up by materials found while *dumpster diving*, which involves digging through a victim's trash, looking for important documents, phone lists, and so forth. Knowing a few important names, for example, can make an attacker seem more authentic and can allow them to pose as someone they are not, perhaps asking for classified information over the telephone. This information can be something as trivial as someone's telephone number, or as confidential as someone's server password and login ID.

Unfortunately, you cannot firewall employees, but you can make them aware of policies regarding the disclosure of information, especially over the telephone or via e-mail. The human factor is often the weakest link in network security. However, the positive side is that most employees do not wish to harm their company, and will follow disclosure procedures if they are aware of the problem.

Passive Attacks

During a passive attack (the direct opposite of an active attack), the attacker is not directly affecting the victim's network. Rather, the attacker is passively listening to network traffic or otherwise gathering information. Some passive attacks can be likened to eavesdropping on someone's conversation, or using binoculars to spy on someone. There are quite a few interesting ways that passive attacks can occur, which are described in detail in the following sections.

Vulnerability Scanning

Vulnerability scanning is important both to attackers and those responsible for securing hosts and networks, and refers to the act of probing a host in order to find an exploitable service or process. There are a number of tools that can assist in vulnerability scanning. A basic example is a tool called *NMAP* (www.insecure.org), a port scanner that sends packets to a host in order to generate a list of services that the host is running. NMAP can also identify the operating system

(OS) on the target. With this information, an attacker can get a better idea of what type of attack may be suitable for that particular host.

A more sophisticated vulnerability scanning tool is *Nessus* (www.nessus.org), a freeware tool that scans for vulnerabilities using a list of known attack types. Nessus has several modes of operation, but in its default mode, it generates a readable output detailing which services are currently exploitable, and which may be exploitable. It also offers suggestions on how to improve the security of a host.

Sniffing and Eavesdropping

Sniffing means eavesdropping on a network. A *sniffer* is a tool that enables a machine to see all of the packets that are passing over the wire (or through the air on a wireless network), even those not destined for that particular host. This very powerful technique is used for diagnosing network problems, but it can also be used maliciously to scan for passwords, e-mail, or any other type of data sent in the cleartext. TCPDUMP (www.tcpdump.org) is the most common UNIX sniffing tool, and is included with many Linux distributions. Snoop is the Solaris equivalent. These two programs are command-line-based, and will simply begin dumping all of the packets they see in a readable format. They are fairly basic in their functionality, but can be used to gain information about routing, hosts, and traffic types.

For more detailed command line scanning, *Snort* (www.snort.org), a freeware tool, offers many more functions than TCPDUMP, such as the ability to dump the entire application layer, and to generate alerts based on the types of traffic seen.

Even more advanced, *Ethereal* (www.ethereal.com) is a graphical sniffer program that has many advanced features. One of the more powerful features of Ethereal is the ability to reassemble TCP streams and sessions. After capturing an amount of data, an attacker can easily reassemble Web pages viewed, files downloaded, or e-mail sent, all with a click of the mouse. The threat from sniffing is yet another argument for the use of encryption to protect any kind of sensitive data on a network.

Nowadays, a sniffer used on modern switched networks allows you, by default, to sniff your own traffic. To sniff on a switched network, it be must explicitly configured, an action sure to alert any network engineer that a security breach is occurring.

Password Attacks

Password attacks are extremely common, as they are easy to perform and often result in a successful intrusion. There are two basic types of password guessing that can be performed: *brute force* and *dictionary-based* attacks. Each of these methods is explained in detail in the following sections.

Brute Force Attacks

A brute force attack is the simple act of guessing keys and passwords until the correct one is found. Brute force attacks always work because the key space, no matter how large, is always finite. Making key lengths long enough can render brute force attacks ineffective. For example, the 56-bit Data Encryption Standard (DES) can be cracked by trying every key combination, from 56 zeros to 56 ones. Spreading the load among several attackers, with each trying different combinations, can speed up the cracking process.

Applying brute force techniques to RSA and other public key encryption (PKE) systems is not quite as simple. Because the Rivest, Shamir, Adleman (RSA) algorithm is broken by factoring, if the keys being used are sufficiently small (smaller than any program using RSA would allow), it is conceivable that a person could crack the RSA algorithm using a pencil and paper. However, for larger keys, the time required to perform the factoring becomes excessive. Factoring also does not lend itself to distributed attacks.

Brute force is commonly used to obtain passwords, especially if the encrypted password list is available. While the exact number of characters in a password is usually unknown, most passwords are estimated to be between 4 and 16 characters. Since only about 100 different values can be used for each character of the password, there are only about 100^4 to 100^{16} likely password combinations. Though massively large, the number of possible password combinations is finite and is therefore vulnerable to brute force attack.

Brute force attempts to discover passwords usually involve stealing a copy of the username and hashed password listing and then methodically encrypting possible passwords using the same hashing function. If a match is found, the password is considered cracked. Some variations of brute force techniques involve simply passing possible passwords directly to the system via remote login attempts. However, these variations are rarely seen anymore due to account lockout features and the fact that they can be easily spotted and traced.

Dictionary-based Attacks

Appropriate password selection minimizes, but cannot completely eliminate, a password's ability to be cracked. Simple passwords such as any individual word in a language make the weakest passwords because they can be cracked with an elementary dictionary attack. In this type of attack, long lists of words of a particular language called *dictionary files* are searched to find a match to the encrypted password. More complex passwords that include letters, numbers, and symbols require a different brute force technique that includes all printable characters and generally takes much longer to run.

Malicious Code Attacks

Malicious code attacks are carefully crafted programs written by attackers and designed to do damage. Trojan horses, viruses, and malicious software (*malware*) are all examples of this kind of attack. These programs are written to be independent and do not always require user intervention or for the attacker to be present for their damage to be done. This section discusses these types of attacks.

Malware

There are two common types of malware: *viruses* and *Trojan horses*. Viruses self-replicate and spread without user interaction, and the really advanced ones can modify themselves to avoid detection. A Trojan horse (or *Trojan*) is a program that appears to do one thing but does something else instead of or in addition to its claimed use. Trojan horses typically trick a user into running them by promising that they do something great, such as make the e-mail transfer faster, or offering a money-making opportunity.

Viruses

A computer virus is defined as a self-replicating computer program that interferes with a computer's hardware, OS, or application software. Viruses are designed to replicate and to elude detection. Like any other computer program, a virus must be executed to function (it must be loaded into the computer's memory) and then the computer must follow the virus's instructions. Those instructions constitute the *payload* of the virus. The payload may disrupt or change data files, display a message, or cause the OS to malfunction.

Viruses spread when the instructions (executable code) that run programs are transferred from one computer to another. A virus can replicate by writing itself to floppy disks, hard drives, legitimate computer programs, and across networks. Chances are good that if you download a virus to your computer and do not explicitly execute it, the virus may contain the logic to trick your OS into running the viral program. Other viruses exist that have the ability to attach themselves to otherwise legitimate programs. This can occur when programs are created, opened, or even modified. When the program is run, so is the virus.

Numerous different types of viruses can modify or interfere with code. Unfortunately, developers can do little to prevent these attacks from occurring. Developers cannot write tighter code to protect against a virus. They can, however, detect modifications that have been made, or perform a forensic investigation. Developers can also use encryption and other methods for protecting code from being accessed in the first place. Following are the different categories that a virus can fall under and definitions of each:

- **Parasitic** Parasitic viruses infect executable files or programs in the computer, and leaves the contents of the host file unchanged but appends to the host in such a way that the virus code is executed first.
- **Bootstrap Sector** Bootstrap sector viruses live on the first portion of the disk, known as the boot sector (including both hard and floppy disks). This virus replaces either the programs that store information about the disk's contents or the programs that start the computer. This type of virus is most commonly spread via the physical exchange of floppy disks.
- **Multi-partite** Multi-partite viruses combine the functionality of the parasitic virus and the bootstrap sector viruses by infecting either files or boot sectors.
- **Companion** Instead of modifying an existing program, a companion virus creates a new program with the same name as an already existing legitimate program. It then tricks the OS into running the companion program, which delivers the virus payload.
- **Link** Link viruses function by modifying the way the OS finds a program, tricking it into first running the virus and then the desired program. This virus is especially dangerous because entire directories can be infected. Any executable program accessed within the directory will trigger the virus.
- **Data File** A data file virus can open, manipulate, and close data files. Data file viruses are written in macro languages and automatically execute when the legitimate program is opened. A well-known type of data file virus is the *macro* virus.

Trojan Horses

A Trojan horse closely resembles a virus, but is actually in a category of its own. The Trojan horse is a program in which malicious code is contained inside what appears to be harmless data or programming. It is most often disguised as something fun, such as a game. The malicious program is hidden, and when called to perform its functionality, can ruin a hard disk.

A common way to become the victim of a Trojan horse is for someone to send you an e-mail with an attachment that purports to do something useful. It could be a screensaver, a computer game, or a macro quiz. Regardless, as soon as the file is opened or used, the Trojan is installed, and will commence to get down to business at its convenience or per some trigger event.

Two common Trojan horse remote control programs are Back Orifice and NetBus, which are not used much anymore because of advances in firewalls, antivirus software, and other security mechanisms. However, they serve to illustrate how a Trojan application may function.

Back Orifice consists of two key pieces: a *client application* and a *server application*. The client application runs on one machine and the server application runs on a different machine. The client application connects to the other machine using the server application. However, the only way for the server application of Back Orifice to be installed on a machine is for it to be deliberately installed. Once installed, the attacker can gain remote control of the host. To safely see what this process looks like, experiment with TightVNC (www.tightvnc.com), a legitimate administration tool that can be installed to remotely access your hosts.

Logic Bombs

A logic bomb is a type of malware that can be compared to a time bomb. Logic bombs are designed to do damage after a certain condition is met, such as the passing of a certain date or time, or it can be based on the deletion of a user's account. Often, attackers leave logic bombs behind when they have entered a system to try to destroy any evidence that system administrators might find. One well-known logic bomb was the *Chernobyl virus*. It spread via infected floppy disks or through infected files, and replicated itself by writing to an area on the boot sector of a disk. What made Chernobyl different from other viruses is that it did not activate until a certain date, in this case, April 26, the anniversary of the Chernobyl disaster. On that day, the virus caused havoc by attempting to rewrite the victim's system basic input/output system (BIOS) and by erasing the hard drive. Machines that were the unfortunate victims of this virus required new BIOS chips from the manufacturer to repair the damage. While most logic bombs are not this well publicized, they can easily do similar or greater damage.

Worms

A worm is a self-replicating program that does not alter files, but resides in active memory and duplicates itself by means of computer networks. Worms use the automated functionality found in OSs and are invisible to the user. Often, worms are not noticed on systems until the network resources are completely consumed, or the victim PC's performance is degraded to unusable levels. Some worms are not only self-replicating but also contain a malicious payload. They have become a force to be reckoned with, as they are easily created, and require more logic proficiency than programming skill.

There are many ways worms can be transmitted, but the most common are through e-mail or via Internet chat rooms. Some recent examples of worms are the W32. family that has been replicated in many different variants. For more information, see http://securityresponse.symantec.com/avcenter/venc/auto/index/indexW.html.

Back Door

There are different types of back doors. A back door is essentially any program or deliberate configuration designed to allow for unauthenticated access to a system. Sometimes this is done in stealth and other times not. Types of backdoors include legitimate programs like Virtual Network Computing (VNC) (www.tightvnc.com) and PC Anywhere (www.symantec.com), and malicious programs specifically written to provide back door access like SubSeven and T0rnkit.

A rootkit is a collection of programs that an intruder can use to mask his presence. A typical rootkit, like T0rnkit, replace commonly used programs with versions modified to specifically hide the presence of the attacker while giving the attacker remote access to the system. Because of their stealthy nature, rootkits are more difficult to detect than the average back door.

Most antivirus software will detect specific malicious backdoors, but unfortunately cannot help when a legitimate program is configured to allow back door access (such as TightVNC). You will only detect such a scenario by being aware of what services are running on your system. Personal firewalls that block outgoing and incoming connections based on user configurable rulesets are much more effective in blocking legitimate programs configured as back doors.

Attacker Aids

While almost any encryption standard can be cracked with brute force, it certainly is not the most desirable method to use when "theoretically enough time" is longer than the age of the universe. Thus, any shortcut method that an attacker can use to break encryption will be much more desirable to them than brute force methods. None of the encryption algorithms discussed in this chapter have any serious flaws associated with the algorithms themselves.

Bad Key Exchanges

Diffie-Hellman (DH) handles the exchange of keys to be used during a session. If the DH exchange is not authenticated, it will be vulnerable to MITM attacks. As an example, SSH-1 does not authenticate the client or the server, making it possible to eavesdrop. SSH-2, on the other hand, authenticates both the client and the server, and warns of or prevents any possible MITM attacks; however, SSH-2 is vulnerable to MITM attacks prior to the first key exchange. This vulnerability can enable an attacker to intercept and send their public key in place of the sender and receiver public keys, thus enabling them to decrypt messages.

Clearly, this type of communication is undesirable because an attacker not only has access to confidential information, but can modify it at will. In this type of attack, no encryption is broken because the attacker does not know the private keys, so the DH algorithm is not really at fault. If the key exchange protocol does not authenticate at least one (preferably both sides) of the connection, it may be vulnerable to MITM attacks. Authentication systems generally use some form of digital certificates (usually X.509), such as those available from Thawte or VeriSign.

Hashing Pieces Separately

Older Windows-based clients store passwords in a format known as LanManager (LANMAN) hashes, which is a an insecure authentication scheme. LANMAN passwords are never stored on a system in cleartext format; they are always stored in a hash format. The problem is that the hashed format is implemented in such a way that even though DES is used to encrypt the password, the password can still be broken with relative ease. Each LANMAN password can contain up to 14 characters, and all passwords less than 14 characters are padded to bring the total password length up to 14 characters. During encryption, the password is split into a pair of 7-character passwords, and each of these 7-character passwords is encrypted with DES. The final password hash consists of the two concatenated DES-encrypted password halves.

Using the maximum possible password length of 14 characters, there should be about 100^{14} or 1.0×10^{28} possible password combinations. LANMAN passwords are further simplified because there is no distinction between upper- and lowercase letters—all letters appears as uppercase. Furthermore, if the password is less than 8 characters, then the second half of the password hash is always identical and never even needs to be cracked.

If only letters are used (no numbers or punctuation), then there can only be 26^7 (roughly 8 billion) password combinations. The bottom line here is that dictionary-based attacks on a pair of 7-character passwords (or even just one) are much faster than those on single 14-character passwords. LANMAN hashing can and should be disabled in the registry if possible, though this will make it difficult for Windows clients to authenticate.

Using a Short Password to Generate a Long Key

PKE schemes such as PGP generate public and private keys using passwords or passphrases. The generation process can be vulnerable to brute force attacks. If a password is selected that is not of significant length, that password can be attacked to generate the same keys as the user. Thus, PKE systems such as RSA can be broken by brute force, not because of any deficiency in the algorithm itself, but because of deficiencies in the key generation process. The best way to protect against these types of roundabout attacks is to use strong passwords when generating any sort of encryption key. Strong passwords include the use of uppercase and lowercase letters, numbers, and symbols, preferably throughout the password. Eight characters are generally considered the minimum length for a strong password.

Improperly Stored Private or Secret Keys

Your keys must be safeguarded at all costs. Since keys are simply strings of data, they are usually stored in a file somewhere in your system's hard disk. For example, private keys for SSH-1 are stored in the identity file located in the .ssh directory under a user's home directory. Once others have your private or secret key, reading your encrypted communications becomes trivial.

Detecting Breaches

In any network exposed to an uncontrolled environment like the Internet, there will always be risk of a systems compromise, and over time, that risk approaches a level of certainty. You should be prepared to detect breaches, and take appropriate actions such as recovering from the attack and documenting it for historical and learning purposes, and in some cases, reporting it to the appropriate authorities.

NOTE

We do not have the necessary volume in this book to cover all of the details of breach detection and containment. For more information, see *Scene of the Cybercrime: Computer Forensics Handbook* by Debra Shinder (www.syngress.com/catalog/sg_main.cfm?pid=2250).

What are the Key Steps after a Breach is Detected?

After detecting a breach, several steps should be followed. Precise details will vary depending upon site security policy, the nature of the event, and other constraints, but most should adhere to the following steps:

1. **Identification and Classification** Confirm that a breach has actually occurred and identify its circumstances.
2. **Containment** Take steps to limit the damage and fallout from the breach.
3. **Eradication** Eliminate the cause of the breach and install protective safeguards against its recurrence.
4. **Recovery** Restore operations to normalcy.
5. **Follow-up** Post-breach and post-recovery assessment to garner lessons learned and report to responsible authorities.

While you can never completely eliminate such breaches, you can prevent certain types of attacks and reduce the likelihood of others.

The easiest step is to reduce vulnerabilities that allow threats to take hold. You do not have to be "completely" bulletproof, but you should be aware and in control of your weak spots. Use a security architecture that is easy to diagnose and offers enough visibility into your network that you can detect inappropriate activity. Using access controls to partition your network will help with simple, controlled designs. Develop a culture of security within your company. Documentation allows you to plan your security architecture, and helps you recover after an incident.

Reducing Vulnerabilities

The security of a system is never greater than the security of its weakest element. Improve your security by conducting a thorough assessment regularly and addressing any vulnerabilities. Tools such as Cisco Secure Scanner can be used to build vulnerability reports, identifying any vulnerabilities in your network needing correction. Ensure that your organization is prepared to handle any attacks, and that it has a policy and process for doing so. Keep protection software such as antivirus and Integrated Decision Support (IDS) signatures updated. Ensure that your network devices are patched for security and operating fixes.

Providing a Simple Security Network Architecture

Complex architectures equate to difficult and ineffective security. Keep the network architecture simple and with the minimum of services and devices necessary to function. This will make security manageable and effective. Compartmentalize your network, with distinctions between outside, inside, and demilitarized networks such that there are appropriate levels of security assigned to them. Such designs mean reduced risks.

Developing a Security Policy

Without a security policy, you cannot develop and enforce security, and your network architecture will likely develop in an uncontrolled, ad hoc fashion, which introduces vulnerabilities. Security policies help you understand what you need to do, and the necessary steps you need to take to ensure your goals are achieved. Without such a policy, any control you deploy will be hit or miss, and there is no guarantee you will achieve your purpose. Your security policy should include acceptable usage, requirements for documentation, and processes for handling operations, attacks, and recovery. Above all, it should be simple and clear, and understood by all to whom it applies.

AAA Overview

Authentication, authorization, and accounting (AAA) are the framework that controls and monitors network access. AAA provides a flexible, modular solution for controlling access to your network. The benefits of AAA are:

- **Scalability** Scales to networks of all sizes. Further access control can easily be added when required.
- **Greater Flexibility and Control** Per-user, per-group, or per-service control.
- **Standard Authentication Methods** Remote Authentication Dial-In User Server/Service (RADIUS), Terminal Access Controller Access Control System Plus (TACACS+), and Kerberos.
- **Multiple Backup Systems** Replicated to multiple servers to provide redundancy.

A network access server (NAS) is a device such as a router that is connected to both the backbone and to the Telco (Plain Old Telephone System [POTS] or Integrated Services Digital Network [ISDN]) that receives calls from remote clients who wish to access the backbone via dial-up services. NAS and router are used interchangeably in this section, although other devices can also be a NAS. Clients can be a router, firewall, NAS, or other network devices providing access. A security server is a server running TACACS+, RADIUS, or another service that enforces security.

AAA provides many benefits, such as increased flexibility and control, and the ability to scale as networks grow larger. AAA supports the use of standard protocols such as RADIUS, TACACS+, and Kerberos for authentication and the ability to define backup AAA servers if the primary one fails. You configure the type of AAA you want by creating lists that define the method to perform these functions and applying those lists to specific services or interfaces. Cisco documentation refers to these lists as "method-lists," which is used for clarity throughout this chapter.

Authentication

Authentication validates user identity before allowing access to the network. It parses a predefined list of authentication methods (method-lists). Interfaces with no user-defined method-lists automatically use a default method-list, which is called **default**. Any user-defined method-lists will automatically override the default list. Authentication can rely on up to three factors:

- **Something the User Knows** *Authentication by knowledge*, which verifies identity by something known only by the user such as a username and password.
- **Something the User Possesses** *Authentication by possession*, which verifies identity by something possessed only by the user such as an ATM card or similar token.
- **Something the User Is** *User characteristic* or *biometrics*, which verify identity by something that is unique about the user. This is the strongest authentication as it avoids common problems with the other approaches (for example, the password being guessed or a card being lost or stolen).

Authentication occurs when a client passes the appropriate credentials to an AAA server for validation. The server will respond with either an accept or a deny message.

Authorization

Authorization determines the actions that a user, group, system, or service is allowed to perform. AAA generates attributes that identify allowed actions, and compares them with a security database specific to the user. Attribute-value (AV) pairs that define the user rights are associated with the user to determine the specific user rights. This database can be local or server based (TACACS or RADIUS).

Clients query the AAA server to determine what actions a user is authorized to perform, and the server provides AV pairs that define user authorization. The client is then responsible for enforcing user access control based on those AV pairs. AAA authorization provides authorization for actions attempted while logged into a network device, and for attempts to use network resources.

Accounting

Accounting tracks resource utilization such as the services that users are accessing and the amount of resources they are consuming. This information is used for security auditing, network management, and billing purposes. Account records are made up of accounting AV pairs. Accounting methods must be defined through AAA and applied to an interface. The client sends accounting records with accounting AV pairs to the AAA server for centralized storage.

AAA Servers

A NAS or router must be able to access security information for a specific user to provide AAA services. There are two main options for storing this information—locally, or on a remote AAA server (see Figure 7.3).

Figure 7.3 AAA Servers

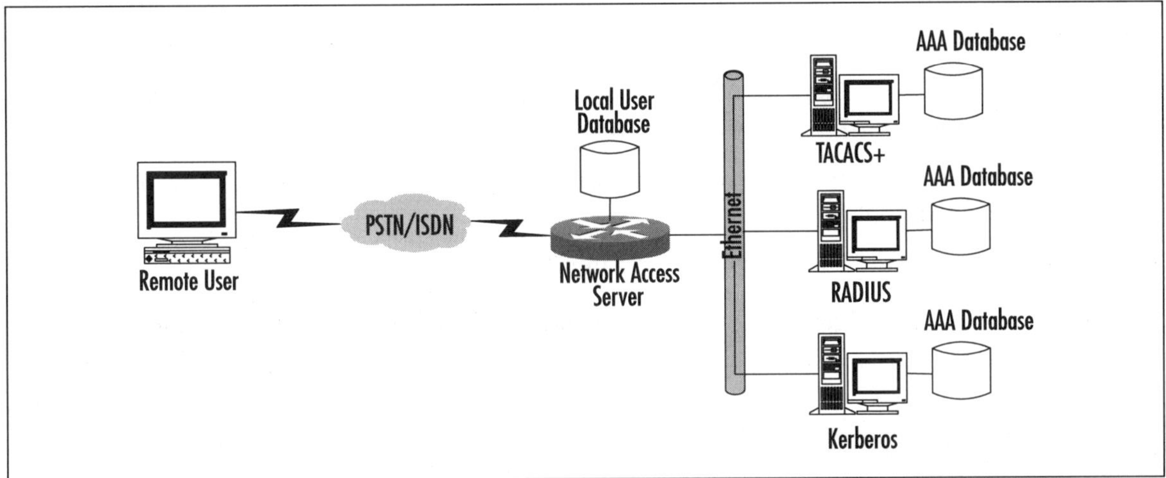

Local AAA information is created and stored on the Cisco device (such as a router), and used to control access. Only a limited number of Cisco-specific security attribute values are supported. Server-based AAA provides more capabilities, and security information is stored on the server, not the network device. Protocols such as TACACS+, RADIUS, or Kerberos are used and support many security attributes. Server-based AAA has superior fault tolerance and redundancy. With multiple security servers, if one becomes inaccessible, the user can be authenticated via another source.

Method-Lists

Method-lists contain sequenced AAA entries. When a user attempts to authenticate, the access server contacts each entry in sequence to validate the user. One or more security servers may be specified to offer fault tolerance and backup of authentication databases. Authentication responses are either a PASS or FAIL message; a lack of response is treated as an ERROR. A PASS or FAIL stops list processing, while an ERROR will move to the next entry. If all entries are processed without obtaining a PASS message, access is denied.

The following is an example method-list configured on a Cisco router:

```
router(config)# aaa authentication login default tacacs+ radius local none
```

An AAA authentication method-list named **default** is used to verify user logins. The method-list consists of three entries, **tacacs+**, **radius**, and **local**. This means that initially the NAS will try to authenticate the login by TACACS+, and if this does not respond, RADIUS is attempted; if RADIUS does not respond, a local database is interrogated. If all of these authentication methods fail, access is denied.

Configuring AAA

The AAA configuration process occurs in several stages. First, AAA must be enabled on the router and then method-lists must be defined for each of the AAA components. Associate these method-lists with interfaces or lines. Access server means any router, switch, firewall, or other network service that avails itself of AAA services from the TACACS+ or RADIUS host.

To configure AAA on a Cisco network device:

1. Enable AAA by using the **aaa new-model** global configuration command.
2. If you are using a separate AAA server, configure the appropriate protocol parameters (for example, RADIUS, TACACS+, or Kerberos).
3. Define the appropriate method-lists for the desired service (authentication, authorization, accounting).
4. Apply the method-lists to the desired interface or service, if required.

We return to the configuration of AAA later in this chapter. First, we need to discuss two key security protocols.

Security Protocols

Security protocols such as TACACS+ or RADIUS provide access control for your network. Each has key features that are appropriate for certain environments. Which one you will use depends on your environment and requirements. In a typical architecture that uses either, accounts are stored in a single database that is queried for authentication requests by a NAS or router.

RADIUS

RADIUS is a connectionless, client-server authentication and authorization protocol. RADIUS uses less central processing unit (CPU) overhead and memory than TACACS+. The RADIUS client is typically a NAS, router, or switch, which requests a service such as authentication or authorization from the RADIUS server. RADIUS uses User Datagram Protocol (UDP), and its software handles any retransmissions. It supports only IP-based networks and requests. The RADIUS authentication specification (RFC2868) is a standard security protocol. RADIUS accounting standard (RFC2867) is informational and for accounting purposes.

A RADIUS server is usually a daemon running on a UNIX machine or a service running on a Windows server. It can also be software, such as Cisco Secure Access Control Server (ACS) or another RADIUS program that services requests from RADIUS clients. The RADIUS server can also act as a proxy to other RADIUS servers or non-RADIUS servers.

RADIUS encrypts not only the password sent between the Cisco access client and RADIUS server, but between the workstation and the Cisco access client. When authorization is needed, the client queries the RADIUS server and passes the user credentials. The server then acts on the configuration information necessary for the client to deliver services to the user. Figure 7.4 illustrates what happens when a user attempts to log in and authenticate to a NAS or router via RADIUS.

Figure 7.4 Authenticating with RADIUS

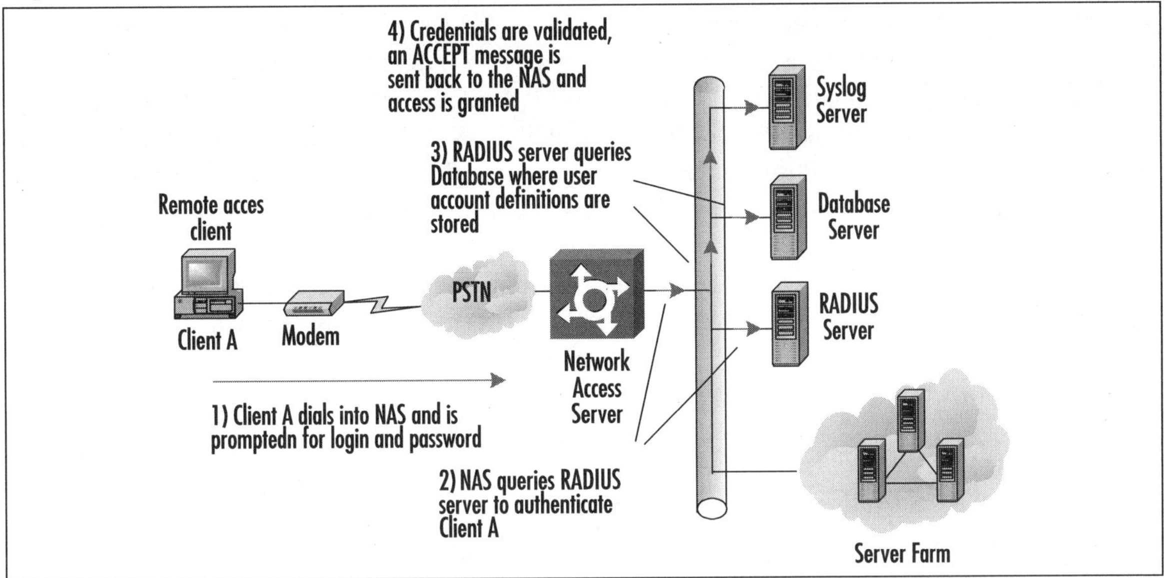

1. The remote user dials into a NAS and provides credentials such as a username and password when promoted.
2. The username and encrypted password are sent from the RADIUS client (NAS) to the RADIUS server via the network.
3. The RADIUS server queries the database where user account definitions are stored.
4. The RADIUS server evaluates the credentials and replies with one of the following responses:
   - **REJECT** Not authenticated. User prompted to re-enter credentials, otherwise access is denied.
   - **ACCEPT** Authenticated.
   - **CHALLENGE** Requests additional information from the user.
   - **CHANGE PASSWORD** User must change their current password.

TACACS+

TACACS provides a method to validate users attempting to gain access to a service through a router or NAS. TACACS, "enhanced" several times by Cisco, provides separate AAA services using the connection-oriented TCP (port 49). By separating authentication from authorization, it is possible to create a dynamic authorization process, which can be integrated with other security negotiations such as Point-to-Point Protocol (PPP). Each of the AAA mechanisms can be tied into separate databases.

TACACS+ encrypts the entire payload of the packet thus protecting the password, username, and other information exchanged between the client and the server. Communication between the end workstation and the Cisco client providing access services is not encrypted.

TACACS+ supports multiple protocols such as IP, AppleTalk Remote Access Protocol (ARAP), Novell Asynchronous Services Interface (NASI), X.25 PAD connection, and NetBIOS. With TACACS+, you can control router management in either non-privileged or privileged mode by authenticating users or groups rather than a shared password. Explicit commands can be allowed or denied.

TACACS+ supports 16 privilege levels, and controls a greater range of service than other security protocols. It can control enable, shell, and standard login. TACACS+ can also block services from certain ports, and control

Cisco supports three versions of the TACACS security protocol:

- **TACACS** Authentication requests only.
- **XTACACS** Authentication and accounting.
- **TACACS+** All elements of AAA using TCP. Can encrypt a body of traffic between the server and the client. Only the TACACS+ header is left unencrypted.

TACACS and XTACACS are now deprecated and are not compatible with the AAA security features in Cisco. This section focuses on the operation and configuration of TACACS+.

Figure 7.5 illustrates the process that occurs when a user attempts to log in by authentication to a NAS using TACACS+:

Figure 7.5 Authenticating with TACACS+

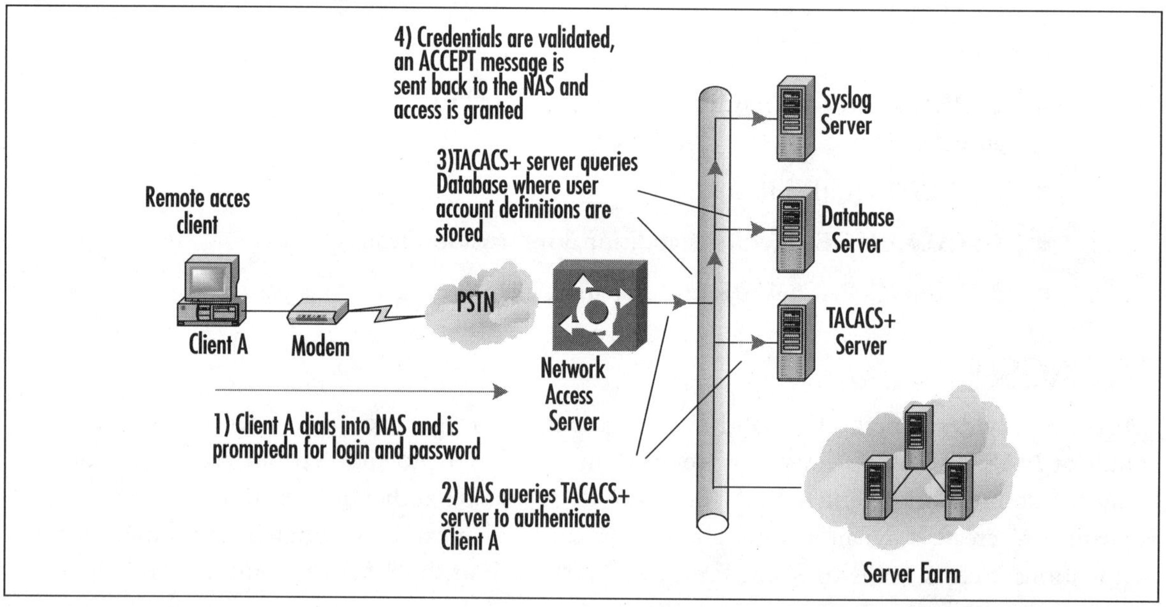

1. When the connection is established, the NAS contacts the TACACS+ server to obtain an authentication prompt (username/password) to which the user provides their credentials.

2. The credentials are then sent to the TACACS+ server.
3. The TACACS+ server queries the user database and validates the user's credentials.
4. The NAS will eventually receive one of the following responses:
   - **ACCEPT** The user is authenticated and the service may begin.
   - **REJECT** The user is not authenticated, and will either be denied access or re-prompted.
   - **ERROR** Error during authentication either at the TACACS+ server or on the network.
   - **CONTINUE** Prompted for additional authentication information.

Comparing TACACS+ and RADIUS

TACACS+ has more Cisco security features than RADIUS. RADIUS has wide industry acceptance and vendor interoperability. Table 7.1 summarizes the key differences between TACACS+ and RADIUS. TACACS+ encrypts the entire body *except* the header.

Table 7.1 TACACS+ and RADIUS Comparison

TACACS	RADIUS
Connection-oriented, uses TCP.	Connectionless. Uses UDP
Encrypts entire body of packet (more secure).	Encrypts only the password in an access-request packet (less secure).
Uses AAA, with separate AAA processes.	Combines authentication and authorization.
Multiprotocol support.	Limited protocol support; does not support NetBIOS, AppleTalk, X.25, or Novell.

Using RADIUS and TACACS+ for AAA Services

AAA functions are independent with TACACS+, but authentication and authorization are combined in RADIUS. AAA information is stored on the RADIUS or TACACS+ server, which is queried by the NAS when a user attempts to authenticate or perform an action. If accounting is configured, information on all defined accounting events is sent to the security server.

The IP addresses or names of security servers and other parameters are configured on the router. For example, all defined TACACS+ servers are attempted for providing authentication services when TACACS+ is specified as an accounting method.

Configuring the RADIUS or TACACS+ Parameters

The configuration of TACACS+ and RADIUS both use a single required command followed by a number of optional commands, depending on your specific requirements.

Configuring TACACS+ Parameters

To configure TACACS+ as your security protocol for AAA, you must specify the host running the TACACS+ server software, and a secret text string that it shares with the TACACS+ client. The **tacacs-server** command sets TACACS+ server parameters such as the IP address of the TACACS+ server, the encryption key used by the server, client-server timeouts, the maximum number of failed attempts at executing commands, and other settings.

Defining a TACACS+ Server Host

The optional **timeout** keyword sets the amount of time an access server waits for a reply before timing out. The optional **key** keyword sets the encryption key used between the access server and the TACACS+ daemon. Any timeout or key settings made here for this specific host will override any global settings for these values.

```
router(config)# tacacs-server host name [single-connection] [port integer] [timeout
integer] [key string]
```

- ***Name*** The host name or IP address of the server to which TACACS+ requests will be directed.
- **Single-connection (Optional)** Specifies that the client should maintain a single open connection when exchanging information with the TACACS+ server.
- **Port Integer (Optional)** Specifies the TCP port on the server to which the client will send TACACS+ requests. This value should match the configuration of the TACACS+ server (default is 49).
- **Timeout Integer (Optional)** Specifies the time (in seconds) that the TACACS+ client will wait for the TACACS+ server to respond. This setting overrides the default timeout value set with the **tacacs-server timeout** command for **this server only**.
- **Key *String* (Optional)** Specifies the shared secret text string used between the TACACS+ client and server. The key must be the same on both devices. The key specified here will override the key specified in the **tacacs-server key** command.

You can specify the shared secret text string used between the TACACS+ client and server with the **tacacs-server key *key*** command. It is also possible to group different TACACS+ servers into distinct lists and distinct methods:

```
aaa group server tacacs+ group-name
```

- ***Group-name*** Specifies the character string name used by the group of servers.
- **Server** A server that belongs in the group server.
- **Server *ip-address*** After using the **aaa group server** command to define a TACACS+ group server, specify the IP address of a TACACS+ server that belongs in the group server.
- ***IP*-address** Specifies the IP address of the TACACS+ server.

Optional TACACS+ Commands

The following details optional configuration commands that might suit your security requirements. There can be limits on the number of times a client searches the list of servers:

```
tacacs-server retransmit retries
```

The number of seconds to wait for reply before timing out is specified with:

```
tacacs-server timeout seconds
```

You can restrict the number of login attempts that can be made on a line:

```
tacacs-server attempts count
```

Encryption will protect the client-server communications, so set the encryption key between the client and the TACACS+ server:

```
tacacs-server key key
```

The following enables AAA and defines multiple TACACS+ servers with different IP addresses, different ports for authentication requests, and timeout or retry settings different from the default.

```
aaa new-model
tacacs-server host 192.168.1.11 port 1149 timeout 10 key tacacsPassword1
tacacs-server host 192.168.2.11 port 2149 timeout 10 key TacacsPassword2
```

Configuring RADIUS Parameters

To use RADIUS, specify the RADIUS server and a secret text string that it shares with the RADIUS client. The global configuration commands and parameters needed to configure a RADIUS on a Cisco router are provided:

Defining a RADIUS Server Host

The following command and its parameters are used to specify the details of your radius host.

```
router(config) radius-server host {hostname | ip-address} [auth-port port-number] [acct-port port-number] [timeout seconds] [retransmit retries] [key string] [alias {hostname | ip-address}]
```

- ***ip-address*** or ***hostname*** The IP address or host name to which RADIUS requests will be directed.
- **auth-port *port-number* (Optional)** The UDP port for authentication requests (default is 1645).
- **acct-port *port-number* (Optional)** The UDP port for accounting requests (default is 1646).

- **timeout seconds** Retransmits the time interval to wait for the RADIUS server reply (1 to 1000). Overrides the global value of the radius-server timeout command.
- **key string (Optional)** The authentication and encryption key used between the router and the RADIUS server. Overrides the global setting of the **radius-server key** command.
- **alias {*hostname* | *ip-address*} (Optional)** A maximum of eight aliases per line for any RADIUS server.

The following command sets the authentication and encryption key for all RADIUS communications between the device and the RADIUS server.

```
radius-server key {0 string | 7 string | string}
```

- **0 *string*** The 0 specifies that an unencrypted (**string**) key will follow.
- **7 *string*** The 7 specifies that a hidden key (**string**) will follow.
- ***string*** The unencrypted (cleartext) shared key.

The **radius-server** command is used to set RADIUS server parameters in global configuration mode.

Optional RADIUS Commands

The following lists optional RADIUS configuration commands. For instance, you can set the shared secret between the client and the RADIUS server with the **radius-server key string** command.

It is possible to specify the number of times the router transmits each RADIUS request to the server before giving up with the **radius-server retransmit *retries*** command (the default retries value is 3). To disable retransmission, use the **no** form of this command.

The **radius-server timeout *seconds*** command configures the number of seconds a router waits for a reply to a RADIUS request before retransmitting the request (the default is 5).

The **radius-server deadtime *minutes*** sets how many minutes a RADIUS server, which is not responding to authentication requests, is passed over by requests for RADIUS authentication.

The **aaa group server radius *group-name*** command groups different RADIUS server hosts into distinct lists and distinct methods. The **group-name** is the character string used to name the group of servers.

One would employ the **server** command to specify a server that belongs in the group server.

```
server ip-address [auth-port port-number] [acct-port port-number]
```

After using the **aaa group server** command to define a RADIUS group server, use this command to specify the IP address of a RADIUS server that belongs in the group server.

- ***ip-address*** Enters the IP address of the RADIUS server
- **auth-port *port-number* (Optional)** The UDP port for authentication requests (the default is 1645).

- **acct-port *port-number*** (Optional) The UDP port for accounting requests (the default is 1646).

The following command enables AAA and defines multiple RADIUS servers with unique IP addresses, different ports for authentication requests, and timeout or retry settings that are different from the default. If RADIUS authentication is specified in a method-list, the defined RADIUS servers will be queried in order of definition.

```
aaa new-model
radius-server host 192.168.1.10 auth-port 4645 timeout 10 retries 5 key
RadiusPassword1 radius-server host 192.168.2.10 auth-port 5645 timeout 10 retries 5
key RadiusPassword2
```

Configuring AAA Authentication

There are many different authentication types defined by AAA, including login, enable, AppleTalk Remote Access Protocol (ARAP), NASI, and PPP. The following are the most commonly used types of authentication. A basic form of authentication is, by default, already provided on Cisco devices. The default authentication on these devices only requires one set of credentials (a password) in order to continue.

To configure authentication, first define a method-list of authentication methods. Apply the list to VTY lines (Telnet), console lines, or groups of asynchronous interfaces (modems) and services such as the ability to use Hypertext Transfer Protocol (HTTP) through a router or Private Internet Exchange (PIX) before it will become active. There is also a default method-list that may be altered. This default list is automatically applied to interfaces or services that require a login unless another method-list is applied to that interface or service. The following sections discuss how to enable AAA authentication and some of its parameters.

Configuring Login Authentication Using AAA

Login authentication controls access to the device itself. The steps you need to follow to enable login authentication using AAA are identified and described next.

1. Enable AAA on the device by issuing the global **aaa new-model** command.
2. Specify parameters such as the IP address of the RADIUS or TACACS+ server and the secret key for client-server communications., as shown in the RADIUS example shown here:

   ```
   radius-server host 192.168.1.10
   radius-server key RadiusPassword1
   ```

3. To specify the same parameters for a TACACS+ server:

   ```
   tacacs-server host 192.168.1.11
   tacacs-server key TacacsPassword1
   ```

4. Define a method-list that specifies one or more authentication mechanisms and their order. The following example creates a named method-list called **login_auth_example**, and specifies that the default group of RADIUS servers be queried first, then the default group of TACACS+ servers, followed by the local database. Creates a login authentication method-list.

   Command Description: `aaa authentication login {default | *list-name*} *method1* [*method2...*]`

   - **default** Applied to all interfaces that do not have a method-list explicitly applied to them.
   - ***list-name*** The name of the method to be referenced when applying the method-list to an interface.
   - ***method1* [*method2...*]** One or more keywords to specify authentication mechanisms.

   Example: `aaa authentication login login_auth_example group radius group tacacs+ local`

5. Apply the method-lists to a particular interface, line, or service, if required. Identify the interface to which you want to apply the authentication list.

   Command Description: `line [aux | console | tty | vty] *line-number* [*end-line-number*]`

   - **aux** Enters configuration mode for the aux port.
   - **console** Enters configuration mode for the console port.
   - **tty** Enters configuration mode for the tty line.
   - **vty** Enters configuration mode for the vty (Telnet) line.
   - **line-number** Enters the starting line number.
   - **end-line-number** Enters the end line number.

   `login authentication [default | *list-name* ]`

   - **login authentication** Applies the authentication list to a line or set of lines.
   - **default** Specifies that the default method-list should be used for authentication.
   - ***list-name*** Specifies the method-list to use for authentication.

   Example:

   ```
   line vty 0 4
   login authentication auth_example
   ```

The **aaa authentication login local** command specifies that the local database on the device will be queried to perform authenticated requests.

The **aaa authentication login krb5** command specifies that a Kerberos 5 server will be queried to perform authentication requests.

A login authentication method-list defined using the **aaa authentication login** command must specify one or more of the **method** keywords identified and described in Table 7.2.

Table 7.2 AAA Authentication Login Methods

Method Keyword	Description
enable	Uses the enable password for authentication.
krb5	Uses Kerberos 5 for authentication.
krb5-telnet	Uses Kerberos 5 Telnet authentication protocol when using Telnet to connect to the device.
line	Uses the line password for authentication.
local	Uses the local username database for authentication.
local-case	Uses case-sensitive local username authentication.
none	Uses no authentication.
group radius	Uses the list of all RADIUS servers for authentication.
group tacacs+	Uses the list of all TACACS+ servers for authentication.
group group-name	Uses a subset of RADIUS or TACACS+ servers for authentication, as defined by the **aaa group server radius** or **aaa group server tacacs+** command.

This specifies that servers at IP addresses 192.168.1.1, 192.168.1.2, and 192.168.1.3 are members of the **radiuslogin** group. Login authentication will use this group of servers to perform authentication requests. If all of the RADIUS servers are unavailable, then no authentication will be required.

```
aaa server group radius radiuslogin
   server 192.168.1.1
   server 192.168.1.2
   server 192.168.1.3
aaa authentication login group radiuslogin none
```

This specifies that the servers at IP addresses 172.16.1.1, 172.16.1.2, and 172.16.1.3 are members of the **logintacacs** group.

```
aaa server group tacacs+ logintacacs
   server 172.16.1.1
   server 172.16.1.2
   server 172.16.1.3
aaa authentication login group logintacacs local
```

Configuring PPP Authentication Using AAA

Using AAA for PPP authentication is very similar to login authentication. When a user configures a workstation to dial their ISP, they must enter their login ID and password. If they are successfully authenticated, they will then be able to access the services for which they are authorized.

The steps you need to follow to enable PPP login authentication using AAA are identified and described next.

1. Enable AAA with the global **aaa new-model** command.
2. Specify parameters such as the IP address of the AAA authentication server and the secret key for client-server communications. To specify the parameters for a RADIUS server, use:

   ```
   radius-server host 192.168.1.10
   radius-server key RadiusPassword1
   ```

   To specify the parameters for a TACACS+ server, use the following commands:

   ```
   tacacs-server host 192.168.1.11
   ```

3. Define a method-list that specifies one or more authentication mechanisms and their order. Use the **aaa authentication ppp** command shown in the following command, which creates a method-list called **ppp_auth_example**.

   ```
   aaa authentication ppp ppp_auth_example group radius group tacacs+ local
   ```

4. Apply the method-lists to a particular interface, line, or service if required.

   ```
   interface async 4
      encapsulation ppp
      ppp authentication chap ppp_auth_example
   ```

A **ppp** authentication method-list defined using the **aaa authentication ppp** command must specify one or more of the method keywords identified and described in Table 7.3.

Table 7.3 AAA Authentication PPP Methods

Method Keyword	Description
if-needed	Does not authenticate if the user has already been authenticated on a TTY line.
krb5	Uses Kerberos 5 for authentication.
Local	Uses the local username database for authentication.
local-case	Uses case-sensitive local username authentication.
none	Uses no authentication.
group radius	Uses the list of all RADIUS servers for authentication.
group tacacs+	Uses the list of all TACACS+ servers for authentication.

Continued

Table 7.3 AAA Authentication PPP Methods

Method Keyword	Description
group *group-name*	Uses a subset of RADIUS or TACACS+ servers for authentication, as defined by the **aaa group server radius** or **aaa group server tacacs+** command.

Enabling Password Protection for Privileged EXEC Mode

When a user successfully authenticates on a device via the console (if configured) or via Telnet, they are in execute (EXEC) mode. To enter privileged EXEC mode, the user must use the **enable** command. The **aaa authentication enable default** command creates a method-list authenticate **enable** mode access. The command to specify a method-list that will be used with the **enable** command is:

```
aaa authentication enable default method1 [method2...]
```

- Enables user ID and password checking for users attempting to enter privileged EXEC mode.
- **method [method2...]** One or more keywords to specify authentication mechanisms. See Table 9.13 for a list of method keywords that can be used in this command.

An enable default authentication method-list defined using the **aaa authentication enable default** command must specify one or more of the method keywords identified and described in Table 7.4.

Table 7.4 AAA Authentication Enable Default Methods

Method Keyword	Description
enable	Uses the enable password for authentication.
line	Uses the line password for authentication.
none	Uses no authentication.
group radius	Uses the list of all RADIUS servers for authentication.
group tacacs+	Uses the list of all TACACS+ servers for authentication.
group *group-name*	Uses a subset of RADIUS or TACACS+ servers for authentication as defined by the **aaa group server radius** or **aaa group server tacacs+** command.

The following example creates a named method-list called **admin-enable**.

```
aaa authentication enable admin-enable group tacacs+ enable
```

The aaa authentication login Command

The **aaa authentication login** command enables AAA authentication. With this command, you define a list of one or more login authentication methods that will be tried when a user logs in, and then apply this list to an interface.

To create a local login authentication list use:

```
router(config)# aaa authentication login {default | list-name} method1 [method2..]
```

The **list-name** is a character string used to identify the method-list. It is this name you use when you apply the list to a line. There can be one or more **methods** that identify which authentication methods are attempted and in which order. If you want to allow a user access even if all authentication methods fail, add the **none** keyword at the end of the method-list.

To apply an authentication login list to a line or set of lines, use:

```
router(config)# line [aux | console | tty | vty ] line number [end-linenumber]
router(config-line)# login authentication {default | list-name}
```

The following configuration is an example of how a router may be configured to use AAA login authentication. The authentication list is first defined and then applied to the appropriate interfaces.

```
router(config)# aaa new-model
router(config)# aaa authentication login default tacacs+ radius
router(config)# aaa authentication login customers tacacs+ radius local none
router(config)# line 0
router(config-line)# login authentication default
router(config-line)# exit
router(config)# line 1-16
router(config-line)# login authentication customers
```

The aaa authentication ppp Command

The **aaa authentication ppp** command is used to specify authentication methods for use on serial interfaces using PPP. To create a ppp authentication list, use:

```
router(config)# aaa authentication ppp {default | list-name} method1 [method2..]
```

The method-list is then applied to an interface using:

```
router(config)# interface interface-type interface-number
ppp authentication {chap | pap | chap pap | pap chap } [if-needed] {default | list-name} [callin]
```

The following configuration is an example of how a router may be configured to use AAA PPP authentication. The authentication list is first defined and then applied to serial interface 0.

```
router(config)# aaa new-model
router(config)# aaa authentication ppp default tacacs+ radius
router(config)# interface serial 0
```

```
router(config-if)# encapsulation ppp
router(config-if)# ppp authentication chap default
```

In the previous example, a default PPP authentication method-list has been created. Initially, TACACS+ is used to try to authenticate the user, and then RADIUS is used. If both authentication methods fail, authentication fails. The default method-list is then applied to interface serial 0.

The aaa authentication enable default Command

The **aaa authentication enable default** command is used to determine whether a user can access the privileged-command level.

```
router(config)# aaa authentication enable default method1 [method2..]
```

The following lists the methods supported by **aaa authentication enable**; if no method is specified, no authentication is used. Therefore, access is always allowed.

- **line** The line password is used for authentication.
- **if-needed** Does not authenticate if the user has already been authenticated on a TTY line.
- **none** No authentication is used.
- **radius** RADIUS is used for authentication purposes.
- **tacas+** TACAS+ is used for authentication purposes.

Configuring AAA Authorization

Authorization is used to restrict access. Authorization is configured by the **aaa authorization** global command. AAA supports four types of authorization:

- **Network** This applies to network connections, including PPP, ARAP, or Serial Line Internet Protocol (SLIP).
- **EXEC** Applies to the user EXEC terminal session.
- **Commands** Applies to EXEC mode commands issued by a user. Authorization is attempted for all EXEC mode commands associated with a particular access level.
- **Reverse Access** Applies to reverse Telnet sessions.

AAA supports six authorization methods used to determine a user's access to each of the authorization types:

- **Local** The access server local database used to provide authorization.
- **Database** Defined by using the **username** command and can only be used to authorize certain functions.
- **None** Authorization is not performed for this function.

- **RADIUS** RADIUS is used to provide authorization functions by associating attributes held in the RADIUS database with a particular user.
- **TACACS+** TACACS+ is used to provide authorization functions by associating a user with AV pairs stored in the TACACS+ security database.
- **Kerberos Instance Map** The instance is defined by the **kerberos instance map** command.

The steps to configure authorization are identified and described next.

1. Enable AAA with the global **aaa new-model** command.
2. Configure AAA authentication as previously described.
3. Specify parameters such as the IP address of the AAA and the secret key used for client-server communications. For RADIUS:

```
radius-server host 192.168.1.10
radius-server key RadiusPassword1
```

For TACACS+:

```
tacacs-server host 192.168.1.11
tacacs-server key TacacsPassword1
```

4. Define a method-list that specifies one or more authorization mechanisms and their order using the **aaa authorization** command, as shown.

```
aaa authorization exec default group tacacs+ local
aaa authorization network default group tacacs+ local
```

The following identifies and describes the commands to specify and apply an AAA authorization method-list. It sets parameters that restrict a user's network access.

```
aaa authorization {network | exec | commands level | reverse-access | configuration}
{default | list-name} method1 [method2...]
```

- **network** Authorization applicable for all network-related service requests.
- **exec** Authorization will run to determine if the user is permitted to run an EXEC shell.
- **commands level** Authorization will run for all commands at the specified privilege level. Valid level entries are 0 through 15.
- **reverse-access** Authorization will run for reverse access connections.
- **configuration** Configuration will be downloaded from the AAA server.
- **default** Modifies the default method-list, which will automatically be applied to all interfaces.

- **list-name** The name of the method-list to be referenced when applying the method-list to an interface.
- ***method1* [*method2...*]** One or more keywords to specify authorization mechanisms. See Table 9.15 for a list of method keywords that can be used in this command.

Configuration commands are authorized by AAA using the **aaa authorization config-commands** command.

In line configuration mode, this enables AAA for a specific line or group of lines. To disable authorization, use the **no** form of this command.

```
authorization {arap | commands level | exec | reverse-access} [default | list-name]
```

- **arap** Enables authorization for lines configured for ARA protocol.
- **commands *level*** Enables authorization on the selected lines for all commands at the specified privilege level. Valid entries are 0 through 15.
- **exec** Enables authorization to determine if the user is allowed to run an EXEC shell on the selected lines.
- **reverse-access** Enables authorization to determine if the user is allowed reverse access privileges.
- **default | *list-name* (Optional)** Enables the default method-list created with the **aaa authorization** command or specifies the name of a list of authorization methods to use.

To effect PPP authorization on an interface, us the **ppp authorization [default | *list-name*]** command. The **default | *list-name*** parameter is optional. This command enters the default method-list created with the **aaa authorization** command or specifies the name of a list of authorization methods to use.

An authorization method-list defined using the **aaa authorization** command must specify one or more of the method keywords identified and described in Table 7.5.

Table 7.5 AAA Authorization Methods

Method Keyword	Description
if-authenticated	Allows the user to access the requested function if the user is authenticated.
krb5-instance	Uses the instance defined by the **kerberos instance map** command.
Local	Uses the local username database for authorization.
None	Uses no authorization.
group radius	Uses the list of all RADIUS servers for authorization.
group tacacs+	Uses the list of all TACACS+ servers for authorization.

Continued

Table 7.5 AAA Authorization Methods

Method Keyword	Description
group *group-name*	Uses a subset of RADIUS or TACACS+ servers for authorization as defined by the **aaa group server radius** or **aaa group server tacacs+** command.

TACACS+ Configuration Example

The following example defines two TACACS+ servers that provide both authentication and authorization as the authorization depends on authentication. The example that follows accomplishes several important tasks:

1. Enables AAA.
2. Defines two TACACS+ servers and the key they will use for communication with clients.
3. Defines the login authentication named method-list called **admins**.
4. Defines the **ppp** authentication named method-list called **remote**.
5. Defines the default authorization method-list for users attempting to enter privileged EXEC mode.
6. Defines the default AAA authorization method-list for users attempting to use network services. Only the TACACS+ group server will be queried.
7. Applies the remote named method for ppp authentication.
8. Applies the admins named method-list to the console.
9. Applies the admins named method-list to the VTY (Telnet) lines 0 through 4.

```
aaa new-model
tacacs-server host 192.168.1.11
tacacs -server host 192.168.2.11
tacacs-server key TacacsPassword
aaa authentication login admins group tacacs+ local
aaa authentication ppp remote group tacacs+ local
aaa authorization exec default group tacacs+ local
aaa authorization network default group tacacs+
interface group-async1
 ppp authentication chap remote
group-range 1 16
line console 0
 login authentication admins
line vty 0 4
login authentication admins
```

When using basic AAA authorization, only a single method is used to attempt to authorize a user. If this method fails, no authorization is granted.

```
router(config)# aaa authorization {network | exec | commands level | reverse-access}
{if-authenticated | local | none | radius | tacacs+ | krb5-instance}
```

For example, the command **aaa authorization exec tacacs+** would cause the access server to use a TACACS+ database to provide authentication for EXEC mode commands. By using an authorization method-list, several authorization methods may be used in sequence to attempt to authorize a user to carry out a particular function.

```
router(config)# aaa authorization {network | exec | commands level | reverse-
access}{default | list-name} [method1 [method2...]]
```

The authorization method-list is assigned to a line as follows:

```
router(config)# line [aux | console | tty | vty ] line-number [endingline- number]
router(config-line)# authorization {arap | commands level | exec | reverse-access}
{default | list-name}
```

The authorization method-list is assigned to an interface as follows:

```
router(config)# interface interface-type interface-number
router(config-if)# ppp authorization {default | list-name}
```

The following sample shows how a router can be configured to use AAA authorization:

```
router(config)# aaa new-model
router(config)# aaa authorization network default tacacs+ local ifauthenticated
router(config)# aaa authorization exec admins tacacs+ local
router(config)# interface serial 0
router(config-if)# ppp authorization default
router(config)# line console 0
router(config-line)# authorization admins
```

In the previous example, two authorization method-lists are defined, network **default** and **admins**. The **default** network list attempts authorization by TACACS+, and then checks the NAS database. If both of these methods fail, the **if-authenticated** keyword will cause the user to be granted authorization only if they have been successfully authenticated. The **admins** exec list attempts to authorize access to an EXEC session first by TACACS+, then by the local user database. If both fail, authorization is denied. The **default** network method-list is applied to interface serial 0. The **admins** method-list is applied to the console line.

Configuring AAA Accounting

Accounting is a very powerful auditing feature that collects and stores user activity information on your security server. The **aaa accounting** global command configures up to five types of AAA accounting.

- **Network** Monitors and reports information on network connections (such as PPP, ARAP, or SLIP). Information includes byte or packet count, protocol used, username, and start and stop times.
- **EXEC** Reports on user EXEC terminal sessions on the access server. Information includes start and stop times, the IP address of the NAS, and the number used for dial-up users.
- **Commands** All EXEC terminal commands executed by a user, recording information such as the command used, privilege level of the command, and username. Only available with TACACS+.
- **System** System level events, such as reboots and when accounting is turned on or off. Only available with TACACS+. Does not support named method-lists (default only).
- **Connection** Reports on outbound connections made from the NAS, such as Telnet, local address table (LAT), PAD, TN3270, and rlogin.

AAA supports only two accounting methods:

- **RADIUS** Only limited types of accounting are supported.
- **TACACS+** Basic AAA accounting is enabled using the following command:

The following are the **aaa accounting** commands that enable accounting of requested services when using RADIUS or TACACS+.

```
aaa accounting {auth-proxy | system | network | exec | connection | commands level}
{default | list-name} {start-stop | stop-only | wait-start | none} [broadcast] group
groupname
```

- **auth-proxy** Provides information about all authenticated-proxy user events.
- **system** Designates keywords to perform accounting for all system-level events.
- **network** Accounts for all network-related service requests such as PPP,. SLIP, and ARAP.
- **exec** Accounts for EXEC sessions (user shells).
- **connection** Provides information about all outbound connections from the router or NAS.
- **commands** Accounts for all commands at the specified privilege level. Valid entries are 0 through 15 in increasing level of privilege.
- **default** Specifies that the listed accounting methods that follow will be used as the default list of methods for accounting services.
- **start-stop** Specifies that accounting notices be sent at both the beginning and the end of a process.

- **wait-start** Specifies that accounting notices be sent at both the beginning and the end of a process.
- **stop-only** Specifies that accounting notices be sent only at the end of a process.
- **none** Specifies that accounting services be disabled on this line or interface.
- **broadcast (Optional)** Sends accounting records to multiple AAA servers. Simultaneously sends accounting records to the first server in each group. If the first server is unavailable, failover occurs using the backup servers defined within that group.
- ***group groupname*** One or more keywords to specify accounting mechanisms. See Table 7.6 for a list of method keywords that can be used in this command.

The **aaa accounting update [newinfo] [periodic *number*]** command enables periodic interim accounting records to be sent to the accounting server. To disable interim accounting updates, use the **no** form of this command.

- **newinfo (Optional)** Specifies that an interim accounting record be sent to the accounting server whenever there is new accounting information to report.
- **periodic *number* (Optional)** Specifies that an interim accounting record be sent to the accounting server periodically, as defined by the argument **number**, which specifies the number of minutes.

In line configuration mode, the **accounting {arap | commands *level* | connection | exec} [default | *list-name*]** command enables AAA accounting services to a specific line or group of lines. To disable AAA accounting services, use the **no** form of this command.

- **arap** Accounting is enabled on lines configured for ARAP.
- **commands *level*** Specifies that accounting be enabled on the selected lines for all commands at the specified privilege **level**. Valid privilege level entries are 0 through 15.
- **connection** Specifies that both challenge-handshake authentication (CHAP) and PAP be enabled, and that PAP authentication be performed before CHAP.
- **exec** Specifies that accounting be enabled for all system-level events not associated with users.
- **default (Optional)** Specifies the default method-list.
- ***list-name* (Optional)** Specifies a named accounting method-list *(list-name)*.

In interface configuration mode, the **ppp accounting [default | *list-name*]** command enables AAA accounting services on the selected interface. To disable AAA accounting services, use the **no** form of this command.

- **default (Optional)** Specifies the default method-list.
- ***list-name* (Optional)** Specifies a named accounting method-list (**list-name**).

An accounting method-list defined using the **aaa accounting** command must specify one or more of the method keywords identified and described in Table 7.6. This command logs keystrokes for high privilege (15) level commands.

Table 7.6 AAA Accounting Methods

Method Keyword	Description
group radius	Uses the list of all RADIUS servers for accounting.
group tacacs+	Uses the list of all TACACS+ servers for accounting.
group *group-name*	Uses a subset of RADIUS or TACACS+ servers for accounting as defined by the **aaa group server radius** or **aaa group server tacacs+** command.

Suppress Generation of Accounting Records for Null Username Sessions

To prevent accounting records from being generated for users whose username string is NULL, and for situations such as console sessions where a login is not required, use the **aaa accounting suppress null-username** command:

RADIUS Configuration Example: AAA Accounting

The following example uses RADIUS to implement AAA accounting, including implementing wait-start accounting for remote users, start-stop accounting for local users, and stop-only accounting for any commands. The example does the following:

- Enables AAA.
- Defines two RADIUS servers and the key used to communicate with clients.
- Defines the login authentication named method-list called **admins**.
- Defines the default **ppp authentication method-list**.
- Defines the exec authorization named method-list called **adminauth** for all exec sessions. The RADIUS group server will be used for authorization.
- Defines the default authorization method-list for network-related service requests. The RADIUS group server will be used for authorization.
- Defines the default accounting method-list for all exec sessions.
- Defines the exec accounting named method-list called **remoteacc**.
- Defines the default accounting method-list for all network-related service requests.
- Applies the admins named method-list to the console.
- Applies the authentication named method-list **admins** to the VTY (Telnet) lines 0 through 4.

- Applies the exec authorization method-list **adminauth** to the VTY (Telnet) lines 0 through 4.
- Applies the exec accounting method-list **remoteacc** to VTY (Telnet) lines 0 through 4.

```
aaa new-model
radius-server host 192.168.1.10
radius -server host 192.168.2.10
radius-server key RadiusPassword
aaa authentication login admins group radius local
aaa authentication ppp default group radius local
aaa authorization exec adminauth group radius if-authenticated
aaa authorization network default group radius if-authenticated
aaa accounting exec default start-stop group radius
aaa accounting exec remoteacc wait-start group radius
aaa accounting network default wait-start group radius
line console 0
     login authentication admins
line vty 0 4
     login authentication admins
     authorization exec adminauth
     accounting exec remoteacc
```

Table 7.7 lists the options used when an accounting record is to be generated.

For example, the **aaa accounting connection stop-only tacacs+** global configuration command would report on outbound connections from the NAS to a TACACS+, only when the event has ended.

By using an accounting method-list, accounting records may be sent to several accounting servers.

```
router(config)# aaa accounting {system | network | connection | exec | commands level }
{default | list-name} {start-stop | wait-start | stoponly} [method1 [method2…]]
```

The following commands apply an accounting method-list to a line:

```
router(config)# line [aux | console | tty | vty ] line-number [endingline- number]
router(config-line)#accounting {arap | commands level | exec | connection} {default |
list-name}
```

The arap keyword reports on network accounting events. The following commands are used to apply an accounting method-list to an interface:

```
router(config)# interface interface-type interface-number
router(config-if)# ppp accounting {default | list-name}
```

The following configuration commands show how accounting can be configured on a router and then applied to a group of lines.

```
router(config)# aaa new-model
router(config)# aaa accounting connection sessions stop-only tacacs+
router(config)# aaa accounting network users wait-start tacacs+
router(config)# aaa accounting commands 10 admins start-stop tacacs+ radius
router(config)# line tty 8 16
router(config-line)# accounting connection sessions
router(config-line)# accounting arap users
router(config-line)# accounting commands 10 admins
```

Table 7.7 AAA Accounting Report Triggers

Keyword	Description
Start-stop	The accounting record is sent when the process starts and stops.
Wait-start	The accounting record is sent when the process starts; it must be acknowledged before the user can continue with process.
Stop-only	The accounting record is sent when the process stops.

In the previous example, three accounting method-lists are defined: sessions, users, and admins. The **Sessions** method-list reports outbound connections from the NAS to a TACACS+ server on their completion. The **users** method-list reports network events to a TACACS+ server; however the TACACS+ server must acknowledge receipt of the accounting record before the user may proceed. The **Admins** method-list reports information on privilege level 10 commands when they begin, and when they end. A TACACS+ server is sent records first, and a RADIUS server is used if TACACS+ fails. The three method-lists are applied to TTY lines 8 through 16.

Typical RAS Configuration Using AAA

The following configuration enables remote analog customers to dial into the NAS and access the Internet. Authentication and accounting are enabled and RADIUS is being used. Login authentication will occur on each asynchronous interface, the VTY lines on the NAS (Telnet), and the console. The AAA configuration shown illustrates this configuration.

```
!
hostname NAS
!
aaa new-model
Enable AAA globally
aaa server group radius loginradius
server 172.16.1.200
server 172.16.1.210
```

```
interface Loopback0
 ip address 172.16.1.254 255.255.255.0
!
interface Ethernet0
 ip address 172.16.1.2 255.255.255.0
!
interface Serial0:23
 no ip address
 encapsulation ppp
 isdn incoming-voice modem
!
interface Serial1:23
 no ip address
 isdn incoming-voice modem
!
interface Group-Async1
 ip unnumbered Loopback0
 encapsulation ppp
 async mode interactive
 peer default ip address pool dialin_pool
 no cdp enable
 ppp authentication chap pap dialin
 group-range 1 48
!
ip local pool dialin_pool 172.16.1.10 172.16.1.250
ip default-gateway 172.16.1.1
ip classless
!
dialer-list 1 protocol ip permit
!
line con 0
 login authentication console
line 1 48
 autoselect ppp
 autoselect during-login
 login authentication dialin
```

Set the authentication method for lines 1 through 48 to that specified in the **dialin** method-list.

```
 modem DialIn
line aux 0
```

```
login authentication console
```

Set the authentication method for the console to that specified in the **console** method-list.

```
line vty 0 4
 login authentication vty
```

Set the authentication method for Telnet to that specified in the **VTY** method-list.

```
transport input telnet rlogin
```

Virtual Profiles and AAA

Virtual profiles allow per-user configurations defined on central security servers to be applied to dialer interfaces. Virtual profiles are a PPP feature used with dialer profiles to provide a unique interface to each user, and are media independent. ISDN and analog dial users can use the same profiles, which can be derived from a virtual interface configuration, per-user configuration stored on an AAA security server, or from a combination of the two. Virtual profiles overcome network scalability limitation issues:

- **AAA Implementation** Allows more Cisco-specific attributes to be used (in addition to AAA AV pairs.
- **Media** Allows a user configuration to be dynamically bound to an interface when it is accessed.
- **Network Protocols** Network numbers are assigned dynamically on dial-in.
- **Dial-on-demand Routing (DDR)** Dynamically adding and removing routes improves scalability.
- **Dialer Profiles** Virtual profiles can scale to many thousands of dial-in users.
- **ISDN** Bind user configurations to individual B-channels. **LIMITATIONS:** Do not support fast-switching, virtual private dial-up network (VPDN), or Layer 2 Forwarding Protocol (L2F) tunneling.

When using virtual profiles, per-user configuration is separated into two logical parts:

- **Generic** Specifies an interface configuration common to all dial-in users. Overrides any physical interface configuration.
- **User-dependent** Stored in a file on the AAA security server, and sent to a NAS when a user is authenticated; can override any previous configuration information.

The two parts can be used independently or combined, allowing for three possible configuration scenarios. The following example shows how virtual profiles and configuration commands are added to a virtual interface when a user dials in.

Example of Virtual Profiles Using Virtual Templates

This code listing shows an example of how virtual profiles might be configured to support virtual templates on a typical router. Table 7.8 describes a few select virtual interface commands.

```
! Enable AAA
aaa new-model
aaa authentication ppp default tacacs
aaa authorization network tacacs
!
! Specify virtual-template 1 to be used for virtual profiles virtual-profile virtual-
template 1
!
! Configure virtual-template 1
interface virtual-template 1
ip unnumbered ethernet 0
encapsulation ppp
ppp authentication chap
!
interface serial 0
encapsulation ppp
no ip route-cache
ppp authentication chap
dialer in-band
dialer rotary-group 0
!
interface bri 0
encapsulation ppp
no ip route-cache
dialer rotary-group 0
ppp authentication chap
!
interface bri 1
encapsulation ppp
no ip route-cache
dialer pool-member 1
ppp authentication chap
!
interface dialer 0
ip address 10.26.1.1 255.255.255.0
encapsulation ppp
dialer in-band
no ip route-cache
dialer map ip 10.26.1.2 bud 1234
dialer map ip 10.26.1.3 simon 5678
```

```
dialer-group 1
ppp authentication chap
```

In the previous example, users dialing in on interface serial 0 or bri 0 would have the virtual template interface applied to their virtual access interface. Any non-interface-specific configuration commands defined on the TACACS+ server for the user would also be applied. Interface bri 1 would not use virtual profiles as a dialer profile defined through the **dialer pool-member** command.

Table 7.8 Virtual Interface Commands

Command	Description
interface virtual-template number	Creates the virtual interface template.
ip unnumbered ethernet 0	Enables IP by using the IP address of Ethernet 0.
encapsulation ppp	Enables PPP on the virtual template.
virtual-profile virtual-template number	Specifies the virtual template to be used for virtual profiles. The number can range from 1 to 30.

Configuring Virtual Profiles Using AAA Configuration

To use virtual profiles with AAA, per-user configurations must be defined on the AAA security server. AAA must be configured on the router and specified as the source of virtual profiles. **virtual-profile aaa** specifies the source of the per-user configuration as AAA.

Example of Virtual Profiles Using AAA Configuration

This following configures the virtual profile to use AAA for per-user configuration.

```
! Enable AAA
aaa new-model
aaa authentication ppp default tacacs
aaa authorization network tacacs
! Specify virtual profile configuration by AAA
virual-profiles aaa
```

Table 7.9 details the commands necessary to configure virtual profiles using a combination of virtual templates and AAA.

Table 7.9 Virtual Profiles Using Virtual Templates and AAA

Command	Description
interface virtual-template number	Creates the virtual interface template.
ip unnumbered ethernet 0	Enables IP by using the IP address of Ethernet 0.
encapsulation ppp	Enables PPP on the virtual template.
virtual-profile virtual-template number	Specifies the virtual template to be used for virtual profiles. The number can range from 1 to 30.

Continued

Table 7.9 Virtual Profiles Using Virtual Templates and AAA

Command	Description
virtual-profile aaa	Specifies the source of per-user configuration as AAA

Example of Virtual Profiles Using Virtual Templates and AAA Configuration

The following router configuration shows how a router might be configured to use both virtual templates and AAA for per-user configuration.

```
! Enable AAA
aaa new-model
aaa authentication ppp default tacacs
aaa authorization network tacacs
!
! Specify virtual-template 1 to be used for virtual profiles virtual-profile virtual-
template 1
! Specify that virtual profiles are to be used virtual-profile aaa
!
! Configure virtual-template 1
interface virtual-template 1
ip unnumbered ethernet 0
encapsulation ppp
ppp authentication chap
!
interface bri0
encapsulation ppp
ppp authentication chap
no ip route-cache
!
```

In the previous example, both virtual templates and AAA configuration are defined. Users dialing into bri 0 will have the virtual interface configuration applied to their virtual access interface. If they have a user entry on the AAA server, their user-specific configuration will also be applied. Any configuration commands defined on the AAA server will override those of the virtual interface.

Per-user Configuration Example

The AAA authorization response holds all per-user configuration information (if any), formatted in AV pairs. The AV pairs available depend on the type of security server you use. The following example shows the application of a user named "remote" dialing into a Cisco router named "central"; the virtual template interface is cloned to produce a unique virtual access interface, then further per-user configuration commands are applied to this interface.

User Remote RADIUS Configuration

The following is the user's configuration entry on a typical RADIUS server.

```
remote Password = "entry"
User-Service-Type = Framed-User,
Framed-Protocol = PPP,
Cisco-avpair = "ip:route=40.0.0.0 255.0.0.0",
Cisco-avpair = "ip:route=50.0.0.0 255.0.0.0",
Cisco-avpair = "ip:inacl#2=10.26.2.1"
```

NAS Configuration (Central)

The Cisco router at the central site is configured as follows.

```
hostname central
!
aaa new-model
aaa authentication ppp default radius
aaa authorization network radius
enable secret 5 $1$IIN8$6BG9B9q8.Qi7mwBKDwF5D1
enable password digest
!
username remote password 0 entry
isdn switch-type basic-net3
!
interface Ethernet0
ip address 10.26.1.1 255.255.255.0
no ip mroute-cache
!
interface Virtual-Template1
ip unnumbered Ethernet0
no cdp enable
!
interface BRI0
ip unnumbered Ethernet0
no ip mroute-cache
encapsulation ppp
no ip route-cache
dialer idle-timeout 300
```

```
dialer map ip 10.26.2.1 name remote broadcast 20842254
dialer-group 1

ppp authentication chap
!
no ip classless
ip route 0.0.0.0 0.0.0.0 10.26.1.254
!
virtual-profile vtemplate 1
dialer-list 1 protocol ip permit
radius-server host 10.26.1.10
radius-server key rabbit
```

Monitoring and Verifying AAA Access Control

There are a wide range of Cisco IOS commands available for monitoring and resolving issues with AAA. Cisco **debug** commands provide detailed information on dynamic security processes, and **show** commands can be used to check current configuration values.

AAA debug and show Commands

The **debug ppp authentication** command details information on authentication transactions between the NAS and dial-in client. This is a good starting point if access is being denied by the NAS. In the following example you can see that the remote client "mark" is successfully authenticating to a NAS named "3260" via BRI0/0.

```
00:07:04: %LINK-3-UPDOWN: Interface BRI0/0:1, changed state to up
00:07:04: %ISDN-6-CONNECT: Interface BRI0/0:1 is now connected to unknown
00:07:04: BR0/0:1 PPP: Treating connection as a callin
00:07:04: BR0/0:1 CHAP: O CHALLENGE id 5 len 25 from "3620"
00:07:05: BR0/0:1 CHAP: I RESPONSE id 5 len 25 from "mark"
00:07:06: BR0/0:1 CHAP: O SUCCESS id 5 len 4
00:07:06: %LINK-3-UPDOWN: Interface Virtual-Access1, changed state to up
00:07:06: Vi1 PPP: Treating connection as a dedicated line
00:07:07: %LINEPROTO-5-UPDOWN: Line protocol on Interface BRI0/0:1, changed state to
up
00:07:07: %LINEPROTO-5-UPDOWN: Line protocol on Interface Virtual- Access1, changed
state to up
00:07:10: %ISDN-6-CONNECT: Interface BRI0/0:1 is now connected to mark
```

The **debug aaa authentication** command shows the authentication process between a NAS and AAA security. The **debug aaa authorization** command details how a NAS provides authorization to a user request, and on what interface the user is connecting, the username, the resource requiring authorization, the method-list being used by the interface, and the actual methods that are used. It will also indicate if authorization is successful or not.

In the following example, the user "mark" dials into BRI0/0 using PPP encapsulation. The interface identifies the "general" method-list as being the network method-list for this interface. A RADIUS server then gives an authorization PASS reply to the requesting user.

```
00:08:55: %LINK-3-UPDOWN: Interface BRI0/0:1, changed state to up
00:08:55: %ISDN-6-CONNECT: Interface BRI0/0:1 is now connected to unknown
00:08:56: BR0/0:1 AAA/AUTHOR/FSM: (0): LCP succeeds trivially
00:08:56: AAA: parse name=BRI0/0:1 idb type=14 tty=-1
00:08:56: AAA: name=BRI0/0:1 flags=0x55 type=2 shelf=0 slot=0 adapter=0 port=0
channel=1
00:08:56: AAA: parse name=<no string> idb type=-1 tty=-1
00:08:56: AAA/MEMORY: create_user (0x61DD835C) user='mark' ruser='' port='BRI0/0
:1' rem_addr='isdn/842633' authen_type=CHAP service=PPP priv=1 00:08:58: BR0/0:1
AAA/AUTHOR/LCP: Authorize LCP
00:08:58: BR0/0:1 AAA/AUTHOR/LCP (3064768274): Port='BRI0/0:1' list='general'
service=NET
00:08:58: AAA/AUTHOR/LCP: BR0/0:1 (3064768274) user='mark'
00:08:58: BR0/0:1 AAA/AUTHOR/LCP (3064768274): send AV service=ppp
00:08:58: BR0/0:1 AAA/AUTHOR/LCP (3064768274): send AV protocol=lcp
00:08:58: BR0/0:1 AAA/AUTHOR/LCP (3064768274): found list "general"
00:08:58: BR0/0:1 AAA/AUTHOR/LCP (3064768274): Method=radius (radius)
00:08:58: BR0/0:1 AAA/AUTHOR (3064768274): Post authorization status = PASS_REPL
00:08:58: BR0/0:1 AAA/AUTHOR/LCP: Processing AV service=ppp
00:08:59: %LINK-3-UPDOWN: Interface Virtual-Access1, changed state to up
00:08:59: %LINEPROTO-5-UPDOWN: Line protocol on Interface BRI0/0:1, changed state to
up
00:09:00: %LINEPROTO-5-UPDOWN: Line protocol on Interface Virtual- Access1, changed
state to up
00:09:01: %ISDN-6-CONNECT: Interface BRI0/0:1 is now connected to mark
```

The **debug aaa accounting** command shows AAA accounting events as they occur. The **debug virtual-template** command gives detailed information on how a virtual template interface is cloned to produce a virtual access interface when a user dials in, and is a good command to use when a virtual access interface is not behaving as expected.

```
00:13:20: %LINK-3-UPDOWN: Interface BRI0/0:1, changed state to up
00:13:20: %ISDN-6-CONNECT: Interface BRI0/0:1 is now connected to unknown
00:13:21: Vi1 VTEMPLATE: Reuse Vi1, recycle queue size 0
00:13:21: Vi1 VTEMPLATE: Hardware address 0010.7b1b.c761
00:13:21: Vi1 VTEMPLATE: Has a new cloneblk vtemplate, now it has vtemplate
00:13:21: Vi1 VTEMPLATE: ************* CLONE VACCESS1 *****************
00:13:21: Vi1 VTEMPLATE: Clone from Virtual-Template1
```

The **debug tacacs** command monitors security transactions with TACACS+ security server, including all TACACS+ packets exchanged, along with PASS or FAIL results. The **debug radius** command provides the same for RADIUS, as shown in the following output.

```
00:14:18: RADIUS: Initial Transmit BRI0/0:1 id 8 10.26.2.1:1645, Access-Request, len
83
00:14:18: Attribute 4 6 0A1A0202
00:14:18: Attribute 5 6 00007531
00:14:18: Attribute 3 19 09F5D352
00:14:18: Attribute 7 6 00000001
00:14:18: RADIUS: Received from id 8 10.26.2.1:1645, Access-Accept, len 126
00:14:18: Attribute 2 8 6A6F7264
00:14:18: Attribute 7 6 00000001
00:14:18: Attribute 26 38 0000000901062269
00:14:18: Attribute 7 6 00000001
00:14:18: Attribute 8 6 FFFFFFFE
00:14:18: Attribute 18 30 0A417574
```

The **show interface virtual-access *number*** command displays the configuration of the virtual-access interface dynamically created when a user dials in. You can see from the following example that the IP address is displayed along with other protocol characteristics.

```
Virtual-Access1 is up, line protocol is up
Hardware is Virtual Access interface
Interface is unnumbered. Using address of Dialer5 (192.168.1.1)
MTU 1500 bytes, BW 100000 Kbit, DLY 100000 usec,
reliability 255/255, txload 1/255, rxload 1/255
Encapsulation PPP, loopback not set
Keepalive set (10 sec)
DTR is pulsed for 5 seconds on reset
LCP Open
Open: IPCP
Last input never, output never, output hang never
Last clearing of "show interface" counters 00:01:08
Queueing strategy: fifo
Output queue 1/40, 0 drops; input queue 0/75, 0 drops
5 minute input rate 0 bits/sec, 0 packets/sec
5 minute output rate 0 bits/sec, 0 packets/sec
14 packets input, 580 bytes, 0 no buffer
Received 0 broadcasts, 0 runts, 0 giants, 0 throttles
0 input errors, 0 CRC, 0 frame, 0 overrun, 0 ignored, 0 abort
27 packets output, 1062 bytes, 0 underruns
0 output errors, 0 collisions, 0 interface resets
```

```
0 output buffer failures, 0 output buffers swapped out
0 carrier transitions
```

Complete AAA Configuration Example

The following configuration uses most of the AAA functions discussed so far to provide secure remote access. Commands relevant to AAA are annotated in the listing.

```
hostname 3620
!
! configure the router for AAA services
aaa new-model
! create a default login authentication method-list using a TACACS+
! server, then a local database.
aaa authentication login default group tacacs+ local
! create an authentication method-list for PPP connections named
! 'general' using only TACACS+ for authentication
aaa authentication ppp general group tacacs+
! create an authorization method-list for network connections named
! 'general' using only TACACS+
aaa authorization network general group tacacs+
! create an accounting method-list for network activity reporting to a
! TACACS+ server. Events are reported when they begin and when they end.
aaa accounting network monitor start-stop group tacacs+
!
username master password 0 letmein
!
! specify that virtual templates are to be used for virtual profiles
virtual-profile virtual-template 1
isdn switch-type basic-net3
isdn voice-call-failure 0
cns event-service server
!
interface Loopback0
ip address 10.1.1.1 255.255.255.255
no ip directed-broadcast
!
interface Ethernet0/0
ip address 10.26.2.2 255.255.255.0
no ip directed-broadcast
!
```

```
interface BRI0/0
no ip address
no ip directed-broadcast
encapsulation ppp

no ip route-cache
no ip mroute-cache
dialer rotary-group 5
isdn switch-type basic-net3
!
! specify the configuration of the virtual template
interface Virtual-Template1
ip unnumbered Dialer5
no ip directed-broadcast
peer default ip address pool lab
!
interface Dialer5
ip address 192.168.1.1 255.255.255.0
no ip directed-broadcast
encapsulation ppp
no ip route-cache
no ip mroute-cache
dialer in-band
dialer-group 1
peer default ip address pool lab
! use the 'general' method-list for PPP authentication
ppp authentication chap general
! use the 'general' method-list for PPP authorization
ppp authorization general
! use the 'monitor' method-list for PPP accounting
ppp accounting monitor
!
ip local pool lab 192.168.1.10 192.168.1.20
dialer-list 1 protocol ip permit
!
! specify the IP address of the TACACS+ server to be used
tacacs-server host 10.26.2.1
! specify the shared secret to used by the TACACS+ server and NAS

tacacs-server key rabbit
```

The previous configuration uses the TACACS+ server (10.26.2.1) for AAA. The general authentication method-list is used to authenticate the users dialing in on BRI0/0, with authorization checked by the general authorization method-list. All networking processes are reported to the TACACS+ server. Successful dials will create a virtual-access interface based on the interface virtual-template 1. Any per-user configuration commands held on the TACACS+ server are sent in the authorization reply packet. In this configuration, only non-interface-specific, per-user commands are applied for the user.

Authentication Proxy

Authentication proxy (IOS 12.0.5.T and later) allows administrators to apply security policies on a per-user basis. The authentication proxy enforces a security policy on a per-user basis. Access profiles are automatically retrieved and applied from a Cisco Secure ACS server or some other RADIUS or TACACS+ authentication server. These profiles are active only while traffic is being passed to and from the specific user.

How the Authentication Proxy Works

The authentication proxy works as follows:

1. The user initiates an HTTP session and triggers the authentication proxy.
2. The authentication proxy checks if the user has already been authenticated. If so, the connection is completed. If not, the user is promoted for a username and password.
3. The authentication profile is downloaded and used to add dynamic access control entries (ACEs), which are added to the inbound access control list (ACL) of an ingress interface, and to the outbound ACL of an egress interface. Profiles determine what services the user can access.
4. Inbound and/or outbound ACLs are altered with the IP address of the authenticated host.
5. Successful authentication starts a timer for each user profile. As long as traffic is being passed through the firewall, the user will not have to re-authenticate.

Benefits of Authentication Proxy

Every policy or networking concept has its advantages and disadvantages. The following are some of the benefits provided by the authentication proxy:

- Dynamic, per-user AAA authentication and authorization via TACACS+ or RADIUS.
- No static IP addresses needed to authenticate and authorize users, which supports DHCP.
- Individualized user profiles that support multilevel authorization.
- Use any HTTP browser. Transparent to the user.

Restrictions of Authentication Proxy

There are some minor restrictions of the authentication proxy as follows:

- Only HTTP connections will trigger the authentication proxy.
- HTTP services must be running on the IOS firewall on the default port 80.
- Does not yet support accounting.
- JavaScript must be enabled in the client browsers.
- Access lists apply to traffic passing through the IOS firewall. Traffic destined to the router is authenticated by the existing authentication methods.
- Does not support concurrent usage.
- Load balancing through multiple AAA servers is currently not supported.

Configuring Authentication Proxy

This section identifies and describes the steps necessary to configure AAA for the authentication proxy on the IOS firewall:

1. Enable AAA functionality on the router by using the **aaa new-model** command.
2. Identify the AAA server and specify its related parameters with the following commands.

```
tacacs-server host hostname
tacacs-server key sting
```

3. Define the AAA authentication login methods with the **aaa authentication login default** command.
4. Use the **aaa authorization auth-proxy default [*method1* [*method2...*]]** command to enable the authentication proxy for AAA methods.
5. Use the **access-list** *access-list-number* **permit tcp host** *source* **eq** *tacacs* **host** *destination* command to create an ACL entry to allow the AAA server return traffic to the firewall.

Configuring the HTTP Server

In order to use the authentication proxy, the HTTP server must be enabled on the IOS firewall, and the authentication method should be set to use AAA. To do this, perform the following steps:

1. Enable the HTTP server as it is used to communicate with the client with the **ip http server** command.
2. Using the **ip http authentication aaa** command, set the HTTP server authentication method to AAA.
3. Specify the access list for the HTTP server with the **ip http access-class *access-list-number*** command.

The following describes HTTP server commands.

1. Enable the HTTP server on the device with the **ip http server** command. To disable the HTTP server, use the **no** form of this command.
2. Next, specify the authentication method for HTTP server users.

```
ip http authentication {aaa | enable | local | tacacs}
```

- **aaa** Specifies that the AAA facility is used for authentication.
- **enable** Specifies that the enable password method is used for authentication (default)..
- **local** Specifies that the local user database is used for authentication
- **tacacs** Specifies that a TACACS or eXtended Terminal Access Controller Access Control System (XTACACS) server is used for authentication.

3. Assign an access list to the HTTP server.

```
ip http access-class {access-list-number | access-list-name}
```

- **access-list-number** Specifies a standard IP access list number in the range 0 to 99.
- **access-list-name** Specifies the name of a standard IP access list.

Configuring the Authentication Proxy

To configure the authentication proxy, use the global commands described next.

1. Set the global authentication proxy idle timeout value in minutes.

```
ip auth-proxy auth-cache-time min
```

2. (Optional) Display the name in the authentication proxy login page.

```
ip auth-proxy auth-proxy-banner
```

3. Create authentication proxy rules.

```
ip auth-proxy name auth-proxy-name http [auth-cache-time min] [list std-
access-list
```

4. Specify the interface type on which to apply the authentication proxy.

```
interface type
```

5. Apply the named authentication proxy rule at the interface.

```
ip auth-proxy auth-proxy-name
```

Authentication proxy commands are described as follows.

- The **ip auth-proxy auth-cache-time *min*** command sets the global authentication proxy idle timeout value in minutes.
- If the timeout expires, user authentication entries are removed, along with any associated dynamic access lists. Enter a value in the range 1 to 2,147,483,647. The default value is 60 minutes.
- (Optional) The **ip auth-proxy auth-proxy-banner** command displays the name of the firewall router in the authentication proxy login page.

Create the authentication proxy rules that define how you apply authentication proxy. This command associates connection initiating HTTP protocol traffic with an authentication proxy name.

```
ip auth-proxy name auth-proxy-name http [auth-cache-time min] [list std-access-list]
```

- **auth-proxy-name** The name of the authentication proxy.
- **auth-cache-time (Optional)** Keyword to override the global authentication proxy cache timer.
- **list (Optional)** Designates a keyword to specify the standard access list to apply to a named authentication proxy rule.
- **std-access-list** Specifies the standard access list for use with the list keyword.
- **interface *type*** Enters interface configuration mode by specifying the interface type on which to apply the proxy. For example, interface *Ethernet0.*

Enable the authentication proxy with that name.

```
ip auth-proxy auth-proxy-name
```

Authentication Proxy Configuration Example

The following examples highlight the specific authentication proxy configuration entries.

AAA Configuration

```
aaa new-model
aaa authentication login default tacacs+ radius
!Set up the aaa new model to use the authentication proxy.
aaa authorization auth-proxy default tacacs+ radius
!Define the AAA servers used by the router
tacacs-server host 172.31.54.143
tacacs-server key cisco
radius-server host 172.31.54.143
radius-server key cisco
```

HTTP Server Configuration

```
! Enable the HTTP server on the router:
ip http server
! Set the HTTP server authentication method to AAA:
ip http authentication aaa
!Define standard access list 61 to deny any host.
access-list 61 deny any
! Use ACL 61 to deny connections from any host to the HTTP server.
ip http access-class 61
```

Authentication Proxy Configuration

```
!set the global authentication proxy timeout value.
ip auth-proxy auth-cache-time 60
!Apply a name to the authentication proxy configuration rule.
ip auth-proxy name HQ_users http
```

Interface Configuration

```
! Apply the authentication proxy rule at an interface.
interface e0
ip address 10.1.1.210 255.255.255.0
ip auth-proxy HQ_users
```

Cisco Secure ACS

Cisco Secure is a suite of access control software that centralizes security policies. The Cisco Secure Access Control Server (ACS) enables full control over all AAA configurations and management. The Cisco Secure ACS provides AAA for users accessing network services. It supports TACACS+ and RADIUS, as well as pass-through Windows authentication. ACS can be a centralized server or a distributed system comprised of multiple ACS systems. Accounting can record user sessions authenticated by the server. It is available on both Windows and Solaris platforms.

Overview of the Cisco Secure ACS

Cisco Secure ACS manages access control and accounting for dial-up access servers, VPNs and firewalls, Voice Over Internet Protocol (VoIP) solutions, broadband access, content networks, and Cisco wireless solutions. Administrators can quickly manage user and group accounts on the entire network through security level changes and network policy alterations. Secure ACS is also designed for interoperability; administrators can leverage existing user database infrastructures such as Lightweight Directory Access Protocol (LDAP) servers or Windows-based domain authentication mechanisms in combination with RADIUS and TACACS+ functionality to manage users.

Benefits of the Cisco Secure ACS

Secure ACS enables the centralized management of AAA for Cisco devices within the enterprise. The easy-to-use Web-based interface simplifies AAA configuration and permits distributed administration of Cisco device security. ACS uses a Web graphical user interface (GUI) and can support large networks. It is interoperable with LDAP, TACACS+, RADIUS, Windows 2000 Active Directory, Windows NT database, and third party security such as RSA SecurID, Passgo, and others.

The Cisco Secure products currently available are Cisco Secure ACS for Windows, Cisco Secure ACS for UNIX, and Cisco Secure Global Roaming Server for UNIX. Features of both are summarized in Table 7.9.

Table 7.9 Cisco Secure ACS for Windows and UNIX

Cisco Secure ACS for Windows	Cisco Secure ACS for UNIX
Workgroups and enterprises that need a standard security policy would benefit from this product:	Larger corporation and ISPs that need increased security and reliability would benefit from this product.
Easy-to-use ACS running on Windows NT	Powerful ACS running on UNIX
Windows NT or flat-file database	Relational database
TACACS+ and RADIUS support	TACACS+ and RADIUS support
Unlimited NAS support	Unlimited NAS support

Authentication

As users require access to network resources, authentication must be used to verify their identity and correlate the necessary user information. Authentication mechanisms range from simple, cleartext methods to more secure techniques such as encrypted passwords or One-Time-Password (OTP) token systems.

With Secure ACS, several methods are available for authentication such as TACACS+ and RADIUS protocols. This authentication connectivity is between the ACS server and the network device only.

Authorization

As users access services on a network device or access server, the Secure ACS sends the users' profiles to the device to determine allowed levels of service. This enables different users and groups to possess different levels of services, access times, or security to specific devices.

Accounting

Secure ACS can track user actions. Secure ACS writes accounting records to Comma Delimited (CSV) log files or to open database connector (ODBC)-compliant data sources.

Placing Cisco Secure ACS in the Network

Secure ACS can control access to many devices and services on a network. Figure 7.6 depicts a typical placement of a Secure ACS server in the network.

Figure 7.6 Secure ACS Server Placement

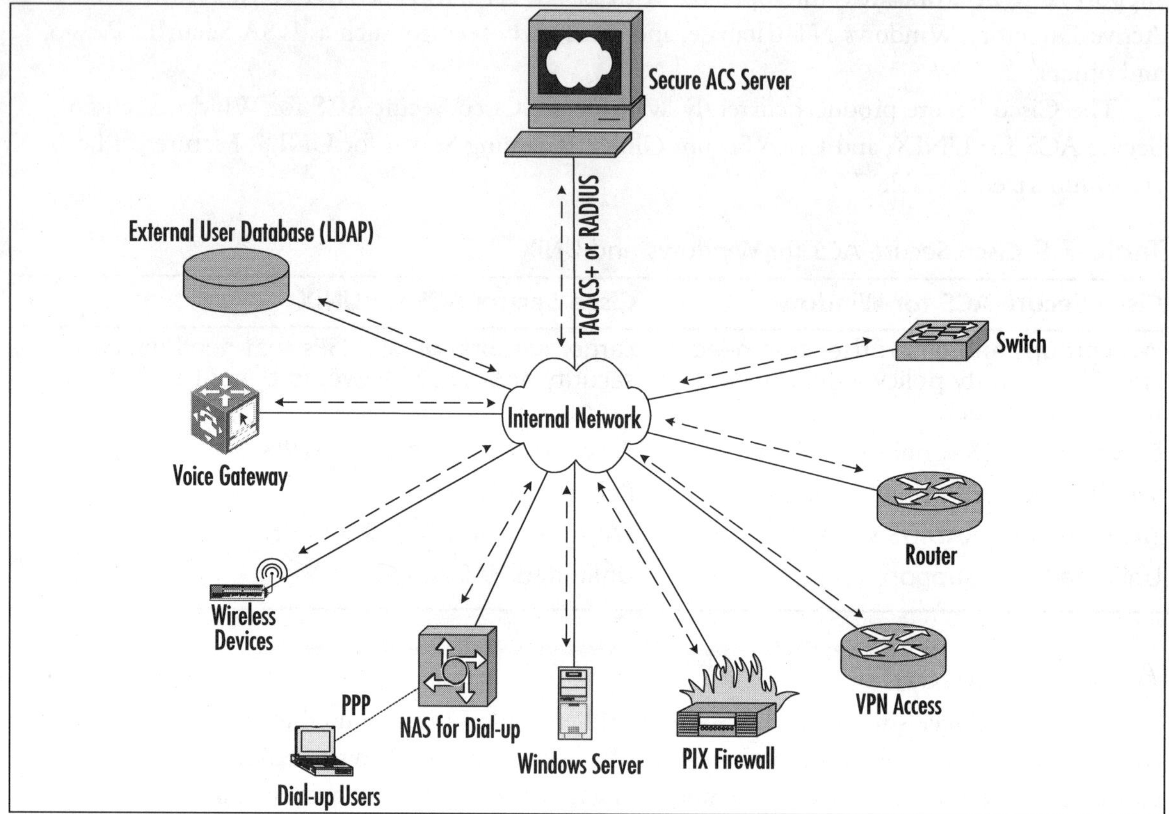

As can be seen, Cisco Secure ACS can be used with dial-up access servers, VPNs and firewalls, VoIP solutions, content networks, and Cisco wireless solutions. Windows servers or external databases/directories, such as LDAP, can be used to manage the username database for access to network devices and dial-up user access.

Between the access devices and Secure ACS, TACACS+ or RADIUS can provide authentication and authorization for network users. The ACS server checks external user databases or local accounts on the ACS server. Dial-up users from remote locations can use PPP or other methodologies to authenticate with the NAS, and the NAS can use TACACS+ or RADIUS to interact with the ACS server.

Configuration Example: Adding and Configuring an AAA Client

After installing and configuring ACS, add AAA clients as necessary. This example provides information regarding the addition of new AAA clients. Begin from the Network Configuration screen shown in Figure 7.7 in order to add a device within the enterprise that requires the ACS server for AAA.

Figure 7.7 Configuring Network Devices Using Cisco Secure ACS

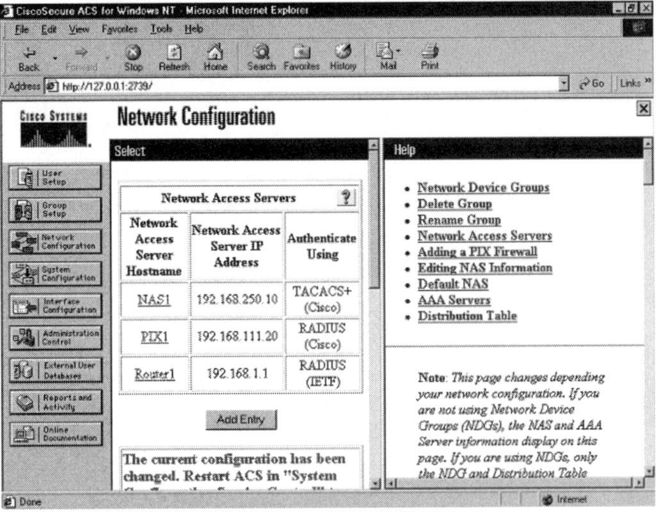

Click **Add Entry** below the AAA Clients table. The Add AAA Client page appears, as shown in Figure 7.8.

Figure 7.8 Device Configuration Changes in Cisco Secure ACS

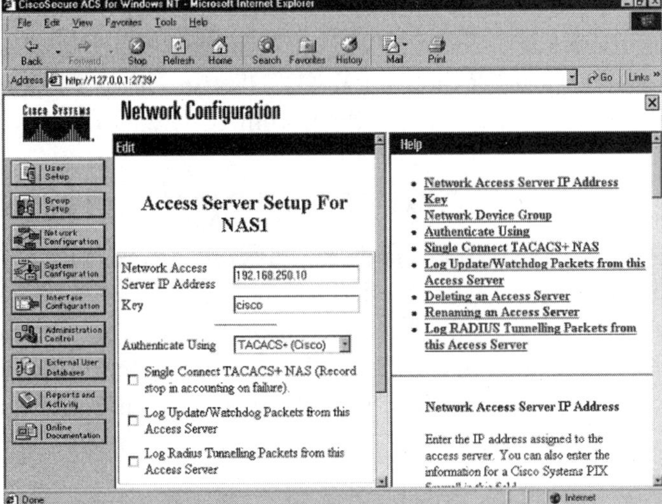

The Network Configuration page allows you to assign the following to the new AAA client:

- The Hostname
- The Client IP address
- The shared secret that the AAA client and Cisco Secure ACS use to encrypt data

If using Network Device Groups, select the name of the Network Device Group to which the AAA client belongs from the Network Device Group list, or select **Not Assigned**. Determine the network security protocol used by the AAA client by configuring one of the following options:

- TACACS+ (Cisco IOS)
- RADIUS (Cisco Aironet)
- RADIUS (Cisco BBMS)
- RADIUS (IETF)
- RADIUS (Cisco IOS/PIX)
- RADIUS (Cisco VPN 3000)
- RADIUS (Cisco VPN 5000)
- RADIUS (Ascend)
- RADIUS (Juniper)
- RADIUS (Nortel)

To enable a static connection for all requests from the AAA client, select the **Single Connect TACACS+ AAA Client** check box. Enable Watchdog packets by selecting the **Log Update/Watchdog Packets** from this AAA Client check box. Watchdog packets are interim packets sent periodically during a session and serve to enable an approximation of session length if the AAA client fails.

To allow RADIUS tunneling accounting packets to be logged in the RADIUS Accounting reports of Reports and Activity, select the **Log RADIUS tunneling Packets** from the AAA Client check box. Save the changes and apply them immediately by clicking **Submit | Restart**.

Cisco IP Security Hardware and Software

Cisco provides a variety of products, both hardware and software, which constitute its security solutions. The breadth and depth of Cisco's offerings are beyond the scope of this chapter for a detailed discussion. Instead, we have identified what those products are, and how and where you can find more information on the Cisco Web site. It is not our intention to act as a sales representative, but rather to point you in the direction where you can find more information.

Cisco PIX Firewall

Cisco provides several hardware and software security solutions, including firewalls. Firewalls are typically placed at borders to create a security perimeter, and to protect an internal network from external access. They can create internal security delineations between departments in an organization. Firewalls are typically deployed at network ingress and egress points to provide sensitive areas. The Cisco PIX Firewall line contains its flagship firewall offerings. PIX firewalls are discussed thoroughly in Chapter 8.

Cisco IOS Firewall Feature Set

The Cisco Firewall Feature Set was introduced in version 11.2(11)P, and new features have been added with each release. It runs on a variety of Cisco hardware platforms and adds firewall features, enhances current IOS security, and improves intrusion detection. With certain caveats, it enables routers to function as firewalls. The Firewall Feature Set is scalable and will run on almost all Cisco routers.

Used with IPsec, Quality of Service (QOS), and Layer 2 Tunneling Protocol (L2TP) tunneling, this feature set can provide VPN solutions. This enables telecommuters, customers, and suppliers to securely connect to your private network using public networks.

The IOS Firewall Feature Set is a comprehensive security solution for networks with existing Cisco devices. Several of its features are discussed in the next few sections. Some features such as access lists are common to all Cisco IOS feature sets, while others are available only with firewall feature sets. For more information, see www.cisco.com/en/US/partner/products/sw/secursw/ps1018/products_data_sheet09186a00800a3be2.html.

Cisco Secure Intrusion Detection System

Cisco Secure Intrusion Detection System (formerly called NetRanger) is a real-time, network intrusion detection system (NIDS) composed of sensors and managers. It can be implemented in multiple locations either singularly or multiply. Cisco sensors passively analyze network traffic for unauthorized activity. Cisco sensors cannot only report events, but also modify access lists to block attacks (known as *shunning*). As of this writing, only Ethernet, Token Ring, and Fiber Distributed Data Interface (FDDI) are supported. The Cisco Secure Policy Manager (CSPM) receives alerts from the sensors. Cisco also has host-based IDS (HIDS) (acquired from Entercept). HIDS detects malicious activity at the target itself and can block such activity. For more information, see www.cisco.com/en/US/products/sw/secursw/ps2113/products_data_sheet09186a008014873f.html.

CSPM

CSPM is a comprehensive security management system for Cisco Secure products. You can define, distribute, enforce, and audit security policies for multiple security devices from a central location. CSPM supports IPsec VPN, user authentication, IDS, and scanning. It requires Cisco Secure Integrated Software be installed on managed routers. It can ensure a consistent application of policies across hundreds of devices, and will save you time by automating portions of the policy creation and distribution. Visit www.cisco.com/en/US/products/sw/secursw/ps2133/index.html for more information.

Cisco routers, switches, and firewalls all have some minimum amount of security. One feature that is very common (especially on routers and Layer 3 switches) is access lists. ACLs, while conceived as a security tool, have evolved to provide a number of services such as dialer lists or routing protocol filters.

ACLs

ACLs can control and filter the flow of data within a network. ACLs can:

- Control access to networks by permitting or denying particular traffic.
- Limit the contents of routing updates advertised by various routing protocols,
- Secure the router itself by limiting access to services such as Simple Network Management Protocol (SNMP) and Telnet.
- Define "interesting traffic" to initiate a dial connection.
- Define queuing features by determining what packets are given priority over others.

An ACL is comprised of a sequential series of filters defined globally on the router. Each filter permits or denies a packet across an interface, based on the information contained inside the packets.

Once an ACL is defined globally, it needs to be applied on the interface. Traffic transits inbound and outbound on the interface, so ensure you apply the ACL accordingly. Clarify the direction by assuming you are inside the router. Simply ask yourself if you want to apply the ACL statements as traffic enters (inbound) or as traffic exists (outbound). You can have one ACL per protocol, per interface, per direction. So, for example, it is possible to have one ACL for outbound IP traffic and one ACL for inbound IP traffic applied to the same interface, as shown in Figure 7.9.

Figure 7.9 Inbound and Outbound Traffic on an Interface

Outbound traffic exits the router interface.
Inbound traffic enters the router interface.
Outbound
Inbound
Inbound
Outbound
Serial 0
Ethernet0

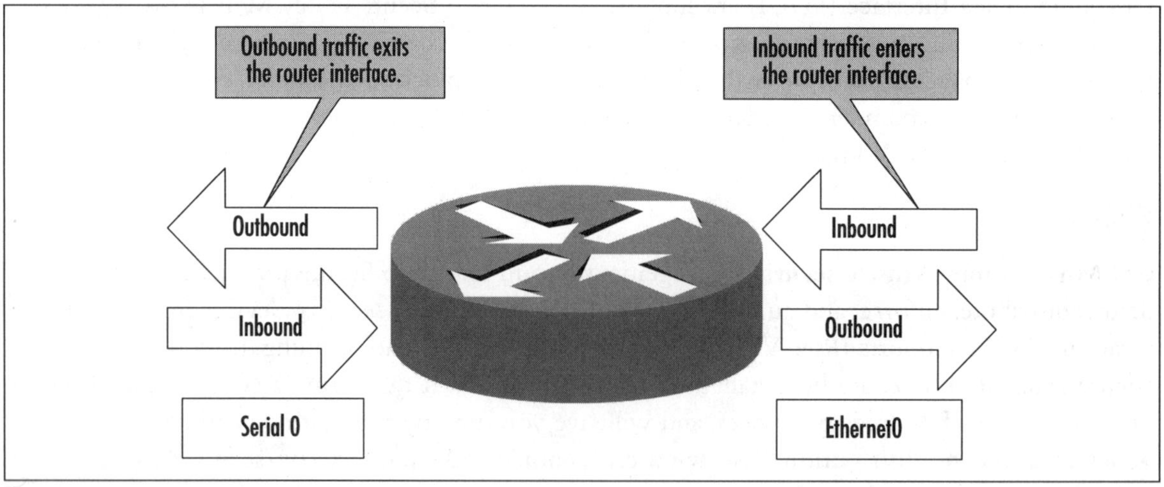

ACL Operation

When a packet enters a router, the destination address in the packet is checked against the routing table to identify the egress interface. The packet is checked against any ACLs assigned to that interface, and will either be permitted or denied accordingly. Think of each line of your ACL as a filter. The following example represents a user-defined ACL with three filters. A complete description on the ACL syntax is given in a later section.

```
access-list 1 permit 192.168.10.15
access-list 1 permit 192.168.10.16
access-list 1 deny 192.168.10.17
```

Assuming this list is applied in the outbound direction, the packet exiting the router will be tested against each condition until a match occurs. If no match occurs on the first line, the packet moves to the second line and the matching process happens again. When a match is established, a permit or deny action, which is specified on each filter statement, will be executed. What happens if the packet ends up at the end of the stack, or last line of our ACL, and a match has never occurred? *There is an implicit deny all command at the end of every ACL.* Any packet that has no match in the ACL is automatically dropped. You will not see this line on any ACL you build. In Figure 7.10, we can see the direction of a packet as it flows through the ACL.

Figure 7.10 ACL Checking

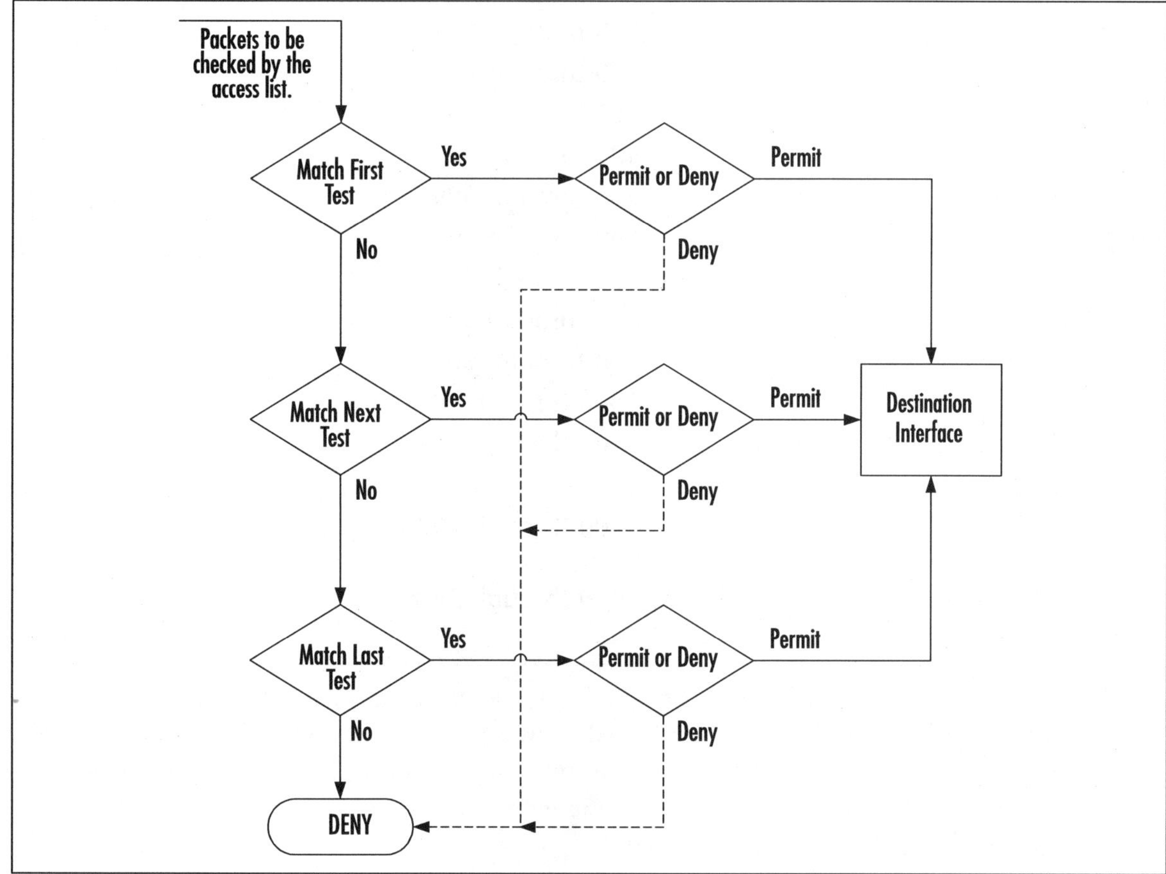

In some cases, you may want to enter the last line of the ACL as a **permit any** statement, as shown next:

```
access-list 1 deny 192.168.10.15
access-list 1 deny 192.168.10.16
access-list 1 permit any
```

With this line in place, all of the packets that do not match the first two lines will be permitted by the third line and will never reach the implicit **deny all** statement.

Types of ACLs

Cisco provides several types of ACLs on its hardware. Numbers, and in some cases, names, uniquely identify ACLs and their types. Standard IP ACLs are numbered 1 through 99, while extended ACLs are numbered 100 through 199. There are format and syntax differences between the two. Table 7.11 shows the various number ranges of ACLs, and what type of traffic they are meant to filter.

Table 7.11 ACL Types and Numbering

ACL Type	ACL Number
Standard IP	1 through 99
Extended IP	100 through 199
Ethernet Type Code	200 through 299
DECnet and Extended DECnet	300 through 399
XNS	400 through 499
Extended XNS	500 through 599
AppleTalk	600 through 699
48-bit Ethernet Address	700 through 799
Standard IPX	800 through 899
Extended IPX	900 through 900
IPX SAP	1000 through 1099
Extended 48-bit Ethernet Address	1100 through 1199
NLSP route summary	1200 through 1299
Standard IP (IOS 12.1 number ranges were extended)	1300 through 1999
Extended IP (IOS 12.1 number ranges were extended)	2000 through 2699

Named ACLs can easily identify the type and purpose of the ACL, as well as the increasing number that can be used. Unlike their numbered counterparts, named ACLs allow you to delete one statement within the ACL, although you are still limited to only adding new entries at the bottom of the list. Although a Cisco router is designed to operate with multiple protocols, we will only cover IP standard and extended ACLs.

Standard IP ACLs

The standard IP ACL only filters on the source address and ignores all other information in the IP header. This allows you to easily permit or deny access to your entire network for a list of addresses and/or subnets.

ACLs are defined in global configuration mode. The syntax of the standard IP ACL is:

```
access-list list-number {permit | deny} source-address [wildcard-mask][log]
```

- **access-list *list number*** Numbers the ACL (standard ACL numbers range from 1-99).
- **permit** Matching traffic will be allowed.
- **deny** Matching traffic will be denied.
- **source-address** Identifies the host or network from which traffic originated, and is either an IP address or the keyword any.
- **wildcard-mask** The default is 0.0.0.0. Defines wildcard bits applied to the source address.
- **log** Logs packets that match the permit or deny statement.

The keywords **permit** or **deny** indicate the action to be performed if a match occurs. For example, the keyword **permit** would allow the packet to be forwarded by the interface. The keyword **deny** will drop the packet if a match is found. If a packet is dropped, an ICMP error message of "destination unreachable" will be sent back to the source.

Source Address and Wildcard Mask

When using a standard IP ACL, the source address must always be specified. The source address can refer to the address of a host, a group of hosts, or an entire subnet. The wildcard mask specifies the scope of the source address.

When using a wildcard mask, a zero is used for each bit that should be matched and a one is used when the bit position does not need to be matched. The easiest way to create a wildcard mask is to first decide what subnet mask applies to the traffic you want to filter, and then use it to create the wildcard mask. To get a wildcard mask for a subnet mask, all you need to do is change all the 1s to 0s, and the 0s to 1s, as seen in the following example. Assume that we want to deny the IP entire subnet 172.16.130.0 with a mask of 255.255.255.0.

```
Subnet Mask       11111111.11111111.11111111.00000000 = 255.255.255.0
Wildcard Mask     00000000.00000000.00000000.11111111 = 0.0.0.255
```

The following ACL line will deny any traffic that has a source address in the range of 172.16.130.0 through 172.16.130.255, because the wildcard mask tells us that the first three octets (24 bits) must match, but the last octet (8 bits) can be anything.

```
Router(config)# access-list 5 deny 172.16.130.0 0.0.0.255
```

For a more complicated example, say we want to only deny the IP address range of 172.16.130.32 through 172.16.130.63. The mask associated with this range is 255.255.255.224, so we would write this in binary and derive the wildcard mask as shown next.

```
Source address - 10101100.00010000.10000010.00100000 = 172.16.130.32
Subnet Mask    - 11111111.11111111.11111111.11100000 = 255.255.255.224
Wildcard Mask  - 00000000.00000000.00000000.00011111 = 0.0.0.31
```

To create an ACL that allows all traffic except those packets that come from the range 172.16.130.32 to 172.16.130.63, enter the following:

```
Router(config)# access-list 8 deny 172.16.130.32 0.0.0.31
Router(config)# access-list 8 permit 0.0.0.0 255.255.255.255
```

The any and host Keywords

The keywords **any** and **host** ease ACL creation. For example, if you want to create a statement that allowed all traffic through:

```
Router(config)# access-list 14 permit 0.0.0.0 255.255.255.255
```

Or use **any**, which accomplishes the same thing.

```
Router(config)# access-list 14 permit any
```

How about a specific host?

```
Router(config)# access-list 15 permit 172.16.134.23 0.0.0.0
```

Or use **host** to accomplish the same thing…

```
Router(config)# access-list 15 permit host 172.16.134.23
```

Using the **any** and **host** keywords in the **ACL** command makes them easier to read and reduces the amount of typing.

ACL Logging

When the keyword **log** is included in an **ACL** statement, a match of that statement is logged. That is, any packet that matches the ACL will cause a message to be sent to the console, memory, or to a syslog server.

The following example shows how this works:

```
Router(config)# access-list 17 deny 172.16.130.88 log
Router(config)# access-list 17 deny 172.16.130.89 log
Router(config)# access-list 17 deny 172.16.130.90 log
Router(config)# access-list 17 permit any
```

Suppose the interface receives 10 packets from host 172.16.130.88, 15 packets from host 172.16.130.89, and 20 packets from host 172.16.130.90 over a five-minute period. The first log would look as follows:

```
list 17 deny 172.16.130.88 1 packet
list 17 deny 172.16.130.89 1 packet
list 17 deny 172.16.130.90 1 packet
```

The **log** keyword is useful for gathering information on network activity, specifically the denial and permission of access to resources.

Applying an ACL

Once you have created your ACL, you need to apply it to the target interface with the **ip access-group** command as shown.

```
Router(config)# interface serial 0 ip access-group {list number} {in|out}
Router(config-if)# ip access-group 25 in
```

in or **out** specifies the direction that the ACL is to be applied.

Extended IP ACLs

An extended ACL enables you to filter on more than just the source address. Both the source and destination address are checked, and if desired, the TCP or UDP ports as well. The format and command syntax for an extended ACL is shown. We will not rehash key concepts that were covered in our standard ACL discussion.

```
access-list access-list-number {permit | deny} protocol source source-wildcard
[operator source-port] destination destination-wildcard [operator destination-port]
[precedence precedence-number] [tos tos] [established] [log | log-input]
```

- **protocol** Defines the IP protocol to be filtered such as TCP or UDP, or a protocol number .
- ***Operator source-port*** The source TCP or UDP port.
- **Destination-address** The host or network to which the packet is being sent.
- **Destination wildcard-mask** The wildcard bits assigned to the destination address.
- **Operator destination-port** The destination TCP or UDP port.
- **precedence precedence-number** Filters by the precedence level name or number (0 through 7).
- **tos tos** Filters by the Type of Service (TOS) level specified by a name or number (0 through 15).
- **established** Allows established TCP sessions through the list.
- **log | log-input** Logs the event when a packet matches the ACL statement. Log-input shows the same information as the log keyword, except it also adds the interface on which the packet was received.

The following ACL illustrates a typical use of extended ACLs. In the first three lines, we are permitting or allowing packets from individual hosts on subnet 172.16.130.0 to any host on network 10.0.0.0. In line 4, we are denying packets with the source address that belongs to subnet 172.16.130.0 to the destination of host 192.168.10.118. Line 5 tells us that we are permitting all IP packets with no concern of a source or destination address. The implicit **deny all** at the end of the list will never be matched against a packet because the previous **permit** statement will match all packets. In Figure 7.11, we would apply this ACL on the serial 0 interface in the outbound direction as follows:

```
Router(config)# interface serial 0
Router(config-if)# ip access-group 141 out
```

An example of an extended ACL is as follows:

```
! Allow host 172.16.130.88 to send ICMP messages to any host on network 10.0.0.0.
access-list 141 permit icmp host 172.16.130.88 10.0.0.0 0.255.255.255
! Allow host 172.16.130.89 to initiate TCP sessions from port 734 to any port between
10000 and 10010 on any host on network 10.0.0.0.
access-list 141 permit tcp host 172.16.130.89 eq 734 10.0.0.0 0.255.255.255 range
10000 10010
! Allow host 172.16.130.90 to send files via TFTP (UDP port 69) to any host on network
10.0.0.0.
access-list 141 permit udp host 172.16.130.90 10.0.0.0 0.255.255.255 eq tftp
! Deny any host on network 172.16.130.0 to host 192.168.10.118.  Since we configured
some permit statements from hosts within these previous two subnets, this entry will
deny everything between these two networks that isn't explicitly permitted in the
earlier listing.
access-list 141 deny ip 172.16.130.0 0.0.0.255 host 192.168.10.118
! Allow all hosts from any network to any network, if it has not matched one of the
preceding lists.  Take a good look at the order of these commands to get a feel for
the importance of the list order.
access-list 141 permit ip any any
```

Figure 7.11 Inbound and Outbound Traffic on an Interface

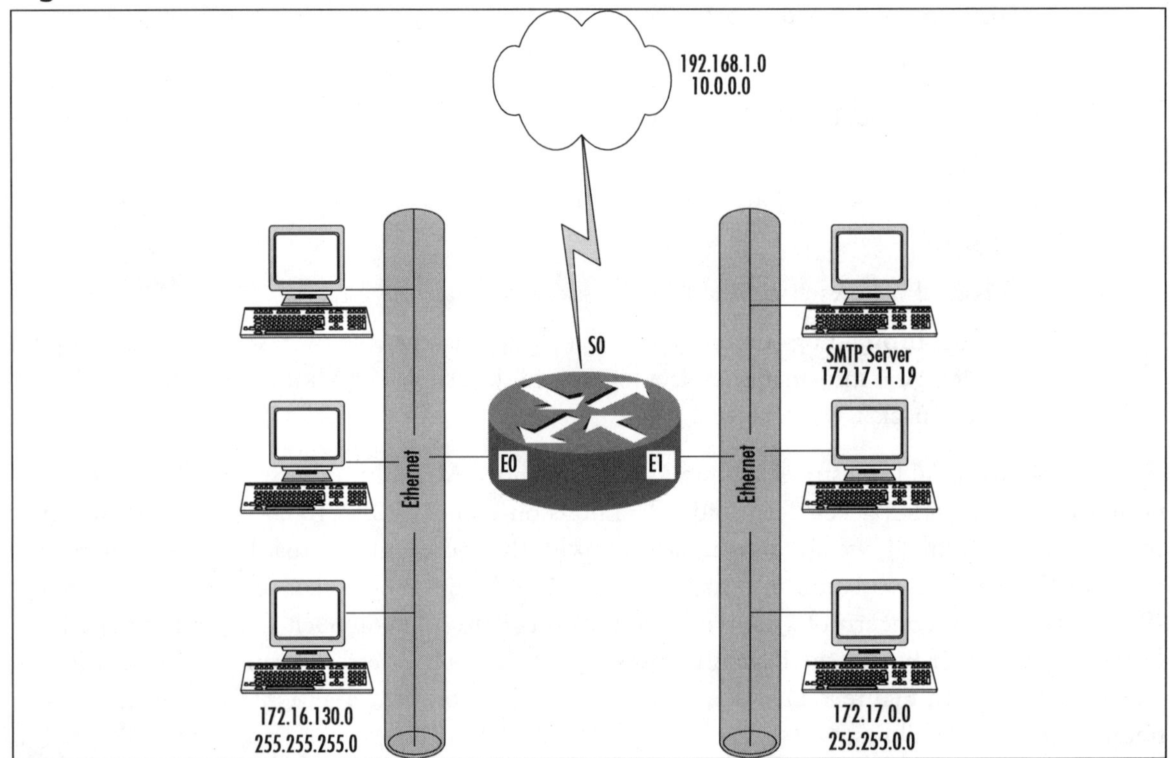

Protocol

Extended ACLs can filter by protocol. The protocol field in the IP header is an 8-bit number that defines what protocol is being serviced by IP. TCP and UDP are only two of the possible protocols that can be filtered. Other protocols, such as ICMP and Enhanced Interior Gateway Routing Protocol (EIGRP), have their own protocol numbers because they are not encapsulated inside TCP or UDP.

```
Router(config)# access-list 191 permit ?
  <0-255>  An IP protocol number
  ahp      Authentication Header Protocol
  eigrp    Cisco's EIGRP routing protocol
  esp      Encapsulation Security Payload
  gre      Cisco's GRE tunneling
  icmp     Internet Control Message Protocol
  igmp     Internet Gateway Message Protocol
  igrp     Cisco's IGRP routing protocol
  ip       Any Internet Protocol
  ipinip   IP in IP tunneling
  nos      KA9Q NOS compatible IP over IP tunneling
  ospf     OSPF routing protocol
  pcp      Payload Compression Protocol
  pim      Protocol Independent Multicast
  tcp      Transmission Control Protocol
  udp      User Datagram Protocol
```

Protocols not on the preceding list may also be filtered with extended ACLs; however, they must be referenced by their protocol number.

Source and Destination Port Number

You can restrict access to and from a particular port, allowing access only to those ports and services you choose. For example, when you deploy a Web server, you can permit access to port 80 (WWW), and deny access to all other ports. Restricting access to this level of detail is a benefit of extended ACLs. We have the option of specifying a source and destination port number in the ACL as shown here.

```
Router(config)# interface Serial 0
! Applies access list inbound on interface.
Router(config-if)# ip access-group 111 in
! Permits SMTP from anywhere to host
Router(config)# access-list 111 permit tcp any host 172.17.11.19 eq 25
! Permits Telnet from anywhere to host
Router(config)# access-list 111 permit tcp any host 172.17.11.19 eq 23
```

Extended ACLs can make liberal use of operators to control the granularity of filtering.

- **eq** Equal to
- **neq** Not equal to
- gt Greater than
- **lt** Less than
- **range** Specifies an inclusive range or ports. (Here, two port numbers are specified.)

The established Keyword

The **established** keyword permits the responses in a TCP session. If the **established** keyword is used on a line of the ACL, it will only allow a packet through if it matches the line of the list, and has either the ACK or RST bit set in the TCP header. The following ACL illustrates the use of this keyword. In this case, we want to allow all workstations access to the Internet, but obviously, we cannot create individual lines in an ACL to permit traffic back from every Web server on the entire Internet.

```
Router(config)# interface Serial 0
Router(config-if)# ip access-group 111 in

access-list 111 permit tcp any host 172.17.0.0 0.0.255.255 established
access-list 111 permit tcp any host 172.17.11.19 eq 25
access-list 111 permit tcp 12.0.0.0 0.255.255.255 172.22.114.0 0.0.0.255 eq 23
```

In the TCP segment there are 6 flag bits, 2 of which are the ACK and RST. If one of these two bits is set, a match on the established keyword will occur. The SYN bit indicates that a connection is being established. A packet with a SYN bit without an ACK bit is the very first packet sent to establish a connection, and will be denied by a line with the established keyword due to the lack of an ACK flag. Figure 7.12 shows the TCP setup handshake.

Figure 7.12 A TCP Session Being Established

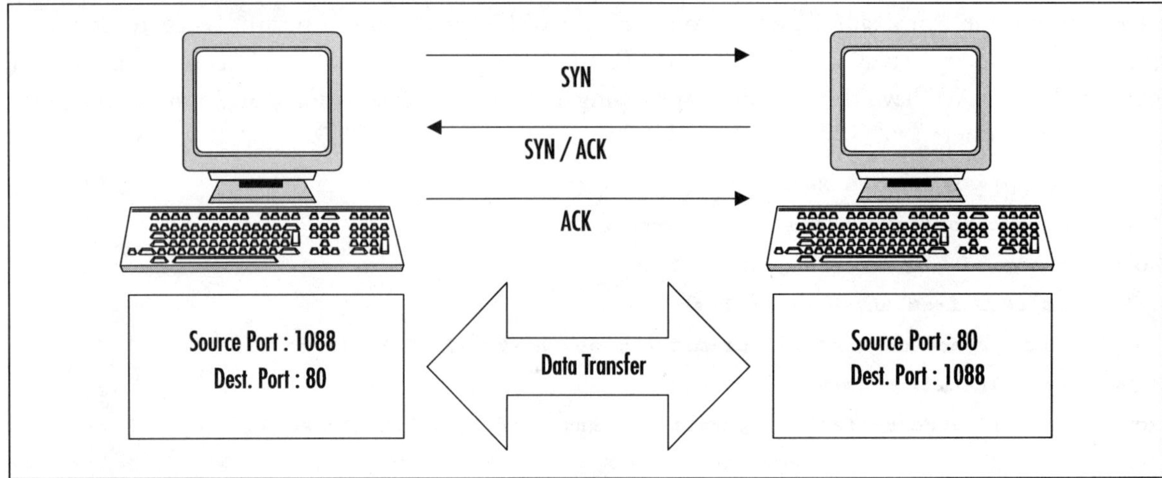

What about the connectionless UDP? To allow Trivial File Transfer Protocol (TFTP) access to host 172.17.11.19, unrestricted DNS access to host 172.17.11.20, and unrestricted SNMP access to the entire network (UDP protocols all) in Figure 7.13, our ACL will now looks like this:

```
access-list 111 permit tcp any host 172.17.0.0 0.0.255.255 established
access-list 111 permit tcp any host 172.17.11.19 eq 25
access-list 111 permit tcp 12.0.0.0 0.255.255.255 172.22.114.0 0.0.0.255 eq 23
access-list 111 permit udp 192.168.10.0 0.0.0.255 host 172.17.11.19 eq 69
access-list 111 permit udp any host 172.17.11.20 eq 53
access-list 111 permit udp any any eq 161
```

There is no **established** keyword for UDP since it is connectionless.

Figure 7.13 Allowing UDP Traffic

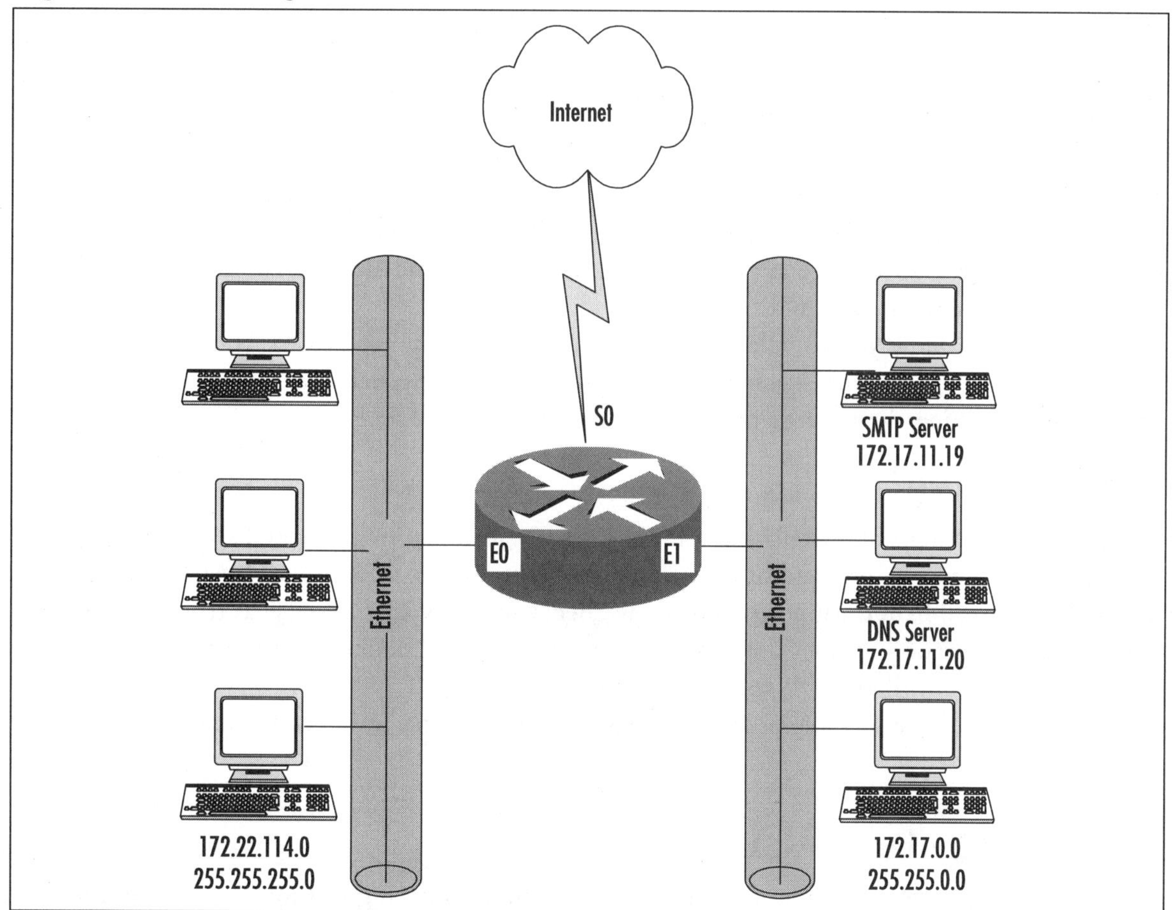

Named ACLs

Named ACLs are referenced by name instead of number, which provides a useful description and allows specific entry deletion. New entries are added to the end.

Named ACLs are case-sensitive. Named ACLs use the same syntax as numbered ACLs, but the creation is slightly different. You must use the keyword **ip** before the main ACL statement, and enter a configuration mode specifically for the named ACLs. In this mode, you start with the **permit** or **deny** keyword, and do not have to type **access-list** at the beginning of every line. Named ACLs are applied with the **ip access-group** command just like numbered ACLs.

```
Router(config)# ip access-list extended filter_tx
Router(config-ext-nacl)# permit tcp any 172.17.0.0 0.0.255.255 established
Router(config-ext-nacl)# permit tcp any host 172.17.11.19 eq smtp
Router(config-ext-nacl)# permit tcp 12.0.0.0 0.255.255.255 172.22.114.0 0.0.0.255 eq 23
Router(config-ext-nacl)# permit udp 192.168.10.0 0.0.0.255 host 172.17.11.19 eq 69
Router(config-ext-nacl)# permit udp any host 172.17.11.20 eq 53
Router(config-ext-nacl)# permit udp any any eq 161
Router(config-ext-nacl)# exit
```

Applying and Editing ACLs

ACLs are evaluated from the top down. The most frequently recurring traffic should be placed at the beginning of the ACL. Once a match is made, processing ceases. Standard ACLs should be placed closest to the destination where traffic needs filtering. Outbound extended ACLs should be placed as close to the source as possible, while inbound extended ACLs fall under the same recommendations as standard ACLs.

Named ACLs allow you to delete a specific entry. With numbered ACLs, you would need to add an entry to a specific line (such as the fifth line), you need to delete and recreate the list, or update the list offline, then merge into the configuration using TFTP.

Problems with ACLs

While ACLs can filter traffic well, they cannot properly secure a network. ACLs will examine each packet individually but cannot determine if a packet is part of an upper layer conversation. The keyword **established** cannot perform any checks to verify that a packet is truly part of an established conversation. It does not protect against forged TCP packets (commonly used to probe networks), nor filter UDP sessions.

To help solve some of these problems, Cisco has added some advanced features to the IOS software, as discussed next.

Lock-and-Key ACLs

Lock-and-key (also referred to as dynamic ACLs) is a traffic-filtering feature that can automatically create an opening in an ACL to allow incoming traffic from an authenticated source. You can add dynamic entries that are only active after the user has been authenticated with the router. After the authentication process, the dynamic entry will disappear after the configured timeout value, or after the maximum lifetime of the temporary entry has been reached. Once the entry is terminated, the interface is restored to its original state.

Figure 7.14 illustrates the lock and key process. After the user Telnets to the router and successfully authenticates, the session is closed. A temporary entry is created in the dynamic ACL to permit traffic from the user's source IP address to some predetermined destination. It will be deleted when a timeout is reached, or can be cleared by the administrator. The authentication process can be done locally or via AAA.

Figure 7.14 Lock-and-Key ACL in Action

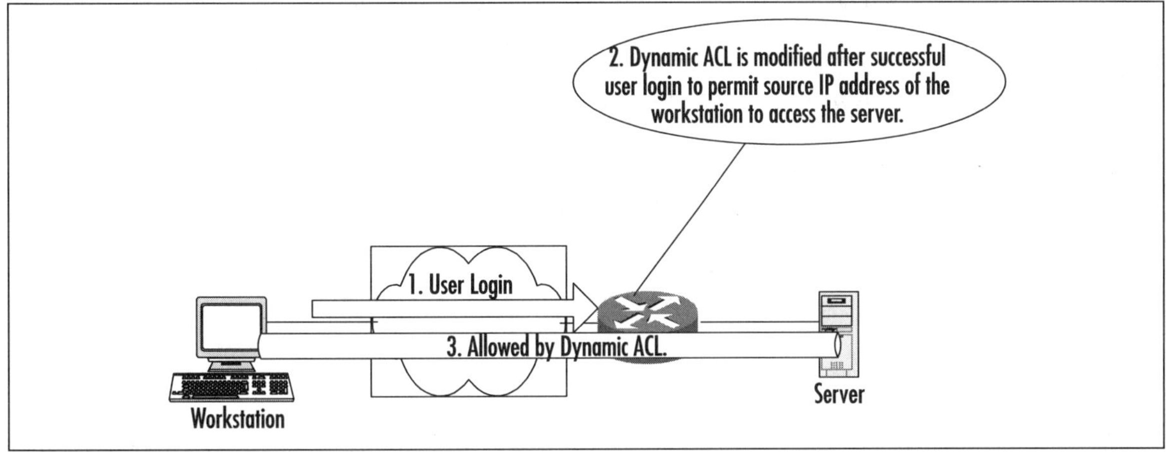

Lock-and-key ACLs can implement a higher level of security without creating large holes in your network. The format of a lock-and-key ACL is identical to an extended ACL, except for two extra fields.

```
access-list access-list-number [dynamic dynamic-name[timeout minutes]]  {deny | permit}
protocol source source-wildcard destination destination-wildcard[precedence precedence]
[tos tos] [established] [log | log-input]
```

- **Access-list List Number** Extended ACL 100-199.
- **Dynamic** Designates this particular entry as part of a dynamic ACL and provides a name assigned to the dynamic entries.
- **Timeout Minutes (Optional)** Designates the absolute timeout for dynamic entries.

Building the ACL and applying it to an interface are required for lock-and-key ACLs, as well as a few extra steps. To open the temporary entries defined in the list, the user must type the **access-enable** command at the prompt, or it can be accomplished with **autocommand** (discussed next). The **access-enable** command is shown here:

```
access-enable [host] [timeout minutes]
```

This **timeout** value is an idle timeout, unlike the one specified in the **access-list** command. If no traffic matches the **dynamic** entry in the number of minutes specified, the temporary entry will be removed from the list.

The **autocommand** feature will automatically run a command upon login.

By default, the router has five VTY ports available for Telnet sessions, numbered 0 through 5. When a user connects to a router, the connection will reserve a VTY port for the duration of that session. First, we will cover the VTY configuration to allow users lock-and-key access:

```
Router(config)# line vty 0 4
Router(config-line)# login
Router(config-line)# password OpenUp
Router(config-line)# autocommand access-enable host timeout 10
```

Using the previous configuration, as soon as someone enters the appropriate password into the Telnet session, the command **access-enable host timeout 10** will be executed and the Telnet session will be disconnected. This also means you will be unable to use the VTY ports for administrative purposes, so this solution is not very appealing. A better way to configure the router for lock-and-key is as follows:

```
Router(config)# username susan password OpenUp
Router(config)# username susan autocommand access-enable host timeout 10
Router(config)# username admin password supersecret
Router(config)# line vty 0 4
Router(config)# login local
```

The previous commands create two users: **susan** and **admin**. If someone logs into the router as Susan, the command **access-enable host timeout 10** will be executed and the session disconnected. If, on the other hand, someone logs in with the admin user, they will have regular access to the router for configuration purposes.

Reflexive ACLs

Reflexive ACLs filter IP packets based on upper-layer session information. Reflexive ACLs create dynamic openings for IP traffic that are part of the allowed session by maintaining information about existing connections. This allows you to permit IP traffic for sessions originating within your network, while denying IP traffic for sessions originating elsewhere. A reflexive ACL is a feature added to an extended ACL and can only be defined using extended named IP ACLs.

A reflexive ACL can be used to permit returning IP upper-layer sessions (such as TCP or UDP). The incoming traffic will only be permitted if it is part of the session and all other traffic will be denied. A temporary ACL will be created inside the reflexive ACL when an outbound TCP packet is forwarded outside of your network. This temporary ACL will permit ingoing traffic corresponding to the outbound connection.

Reflexive ACLs contain entries that define criteria for permitting IP packets, evaluated in a top-down process. Reflexive ACLs contain only temporary entries.

Reflexive ACLs are not applied directly to an interface. They are placed within an extended named IP ACL that is applied to the interface. Reflexive ACLs do not have the implicit **deny all** at the end of the list. Once the reflexive ACL has been processed, the router will continue with the rest of the extended ACL.

A reflexive ACL creates a mirror image of the reflected entry. For example, in Figure 7.15, host0 on network 172.22.114.0 initiates a Telnet session to host1 on network 172.17.0.0. Telnet uses the TCP protocol, therefore host0 will pick a random source port number—let's use port 1028. Also, here we will have a source IP address, destination IP address, and destination TCP port number. Since we are using Telnet, the destination port number will be 23. So far, we have the following information:

Figure 7.15 Example Network Using Reflexive ACLs

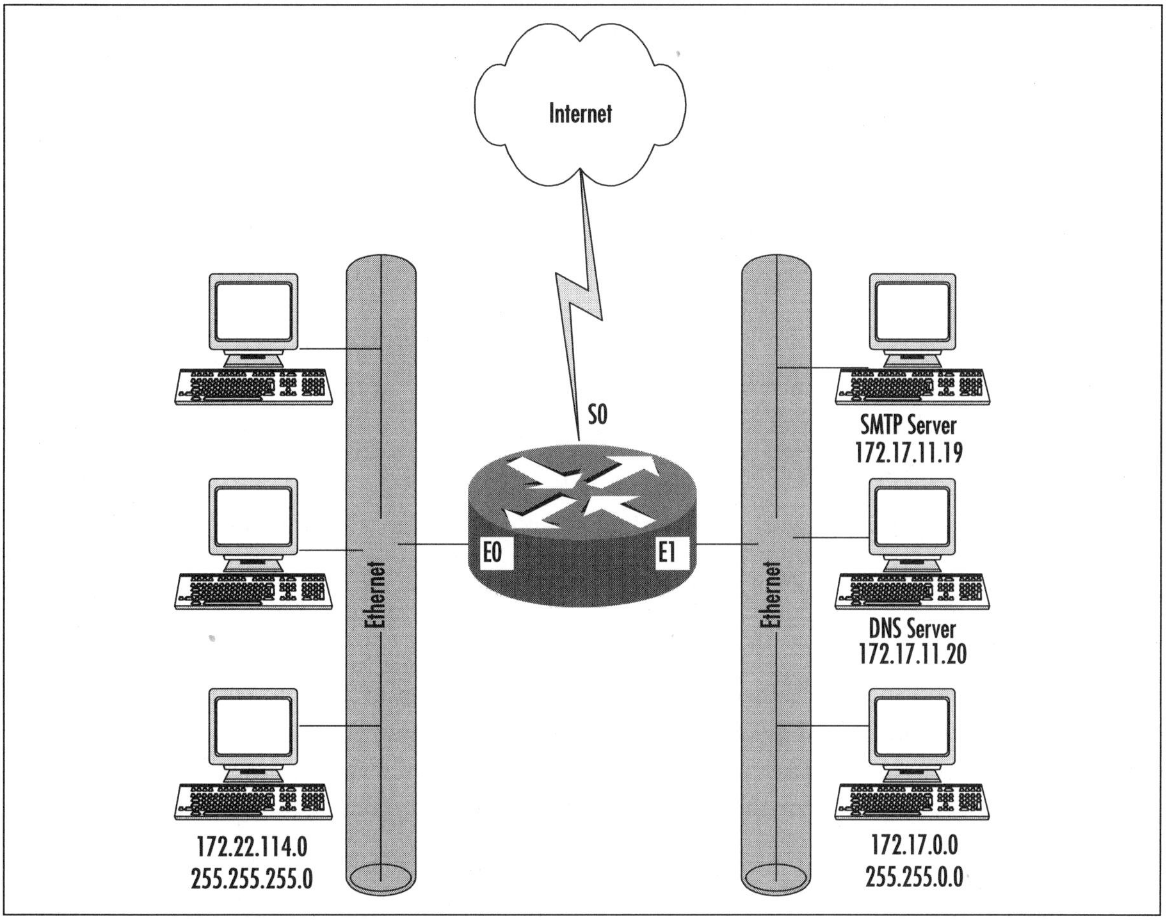

```
Source TCP port-1028
Destination TCP port-23
Source IP address-172.22.114.1
Destination IP address-172.17.0.1
```

In our configuration, we will have a **reflexive access-list** statement that will trigger a reflected ACL entry. This will allow inbound return traffic.

```
Source TCP port-23
Destination TCP port-1028
```

```
Source IP address-172.17.0.1
Destination IP address-172.22.114.1
```

The following shows our information as a reflected ACL entry:

```
permit tcp host 172.17.0.1 eq 23 host 172.22.114.1 eq 1028
```

The source and destination address have been swapped, along with the source and destination port numbers giving the "mirror image."

Building Reflexive ACLs

When building a reflexive ACL, you must first design an extended named ACL. You must use an extended named ACL when defining your reflexive ACL. There is no implicit **deny all** at the end. Here, we enter a **permit** statement to allow all protocols in which you want a reflected entry created. You need to use the keyword **reflect** in each of your **permit** statements, which indicates reflexive openings. The following example shows the format of a reflexive ACL.

```
permit protocol source source-wildcard destination destination-wildcard reflect name
[timeout seconds]
```

- ***name*** The name of the reflexive ACL, which must be specified so that the router can add the reflected entries into this list.
- **timeout (Optional)** The default value is 300 seconds.
- **permit** and **reflect** work hand in hand to create a temporary opening.

To nest a reflexive ACL within an ACL, use the **evaluate** command. By default, an ACL does not evaluate. With **evaluate**, traffic entering your network will be checked against the reflexive ACL.

For example, to support a Telnet session, we will create three ACLs: **Outbound-List**, **Inbound-List**, and **Reflected-List**. The Outbound-List ACL will look at the outbound traffic and decide what should be reflected. The Inbound-List is the ACL that will deny all inbound traffic to the network except for the traffic we will be evaluating. The Reflected-List is the reflexive ACL.

```
Router(config)# ip access-list extended Outbound-List
Router(config-ext-nacl)# permit tcp any any reflect Reflected-List
Router(config-ext-nacl)# exit
Router(config)# ip access-list extended Inbound-List
Router(config-ext-nacl)# evaluate Reflected-List
Router(config-ext-nacl)# exit
```

As traffic leaves the network, it will match the traffic in the Outbound-List ACL. The **reflect** statement will add the mirror image entry to the Reflected-List ACL. When return traffic is checked against the Inbound-List ACL, which runs the **evaluate** command on Reflected-List, it will be allowed back to the original host. If the **evaluate** statement is not in place within the Inbound-List, then no traffic will be allowed back into the network.

While there is not an implicit **deny** at the end of a reflexive ACL, there is an implicit **deny** at the end of the Inbound-List ACL. If the implicit **deny** was at the end of the Reflected-List, then the router would never check any other statements that might be in the Inbound-List after the **evaluate** command.

The timeout can be set on a line-by-line basis in the extended ACL configuration, or you can set a global timeout with the **ip reflexive-list timeout seconds** command.

Reflexive ACLs are only capable of handling single-channel applications such as Telnet, which uses a single static port that stays the same throughout the conversation. Reflexive ACLs do not offer the ability to support applications that change port numbers in a session. This includes protocols such as FTP, Remote Procedure Call (RPC), SQL*Net, Streamworks, and multimedia such as H.232 (Netmeeting, Proshare).

Applying Reflexive ACLs

Reflexive ACLs are applied to an interface in the direction that you specify. As part of your planning, you must determine which interfaces need which ACLs applied to them. In the following example, to reflect sessions, we need to apply both ACLs to the egress interface as shown here:

```
Router(config)# interface ethernet0
Router(config-if)# ip access-group Outbound-List in
Router(config-if)# ip access-group Inbound-List out
```

Do not be confused by the names and directions in the **access-group** commands. Remember that ACLs are applied with respect to the interface. So, any traffic that is heading outbound **from our network** will be considered inbound **to the ethernet0 interface**. The same logic applies to traffic flowing in the opposite direction.

When using a reflexive ACL nested in an extended ACL, the extended ACL entries are tested sequentially up to the **evaluate** command. Then the reflexive ACL entries are tested sequentially, and finally the remaining entries in the extended ACL are tested sequentially. After a packet matches **any** of these entries, no more entries are tested.

Context-based Access Control

Context-based Access Control (CBAC) overcomes the single channel limitation of reflexive ACLs. CBAC inspects outgoing sessions and creates temporary openings to enable the return traffic. CBAC can examine and securely handle various types of application-layer information. This stateful inspection continually monitors each connection state to decide how it should be handled. For example, when the traffic you specify leaves the internal network through an interface, an opening is created that allows returning traffic based on the traffic being part of a data session that was initiated from an internal network. The openings also allow additional data channels to enter your internal network back through the router if it is part of the same session as the originating traffic.

CBAC examines the network layer and transport layer along with application-layer protocol information to learn about the state of the TCP or UDP session. Some protocols create multiple channels above the network and transport layers as a result of negotiations used in the control channel. By examining the information at the application layer, CBAC supports these protocols. Packets are examined when transiting an interface and the information is placed in a packet state information table. The information may be an IP address and port numbers from Layer 4, and is used to create a temporary opening in the ACL for return traffic.

CBAC will automatically determine which ACLs would block the return traffic and add the temporary entry as the very first line in the ACL. CBAC also inspects application-layer information to ensure that the traffic being allowed back through the router is applicable. CBAC observes the outgoing session, and then permits the data connection that will be established from the server to the client by creating an opening in the inbound ACL. The following is a listing of the protocols where CBAC performs the equivalent function:

- Single-channel TCP
- Single-channel UDP
- CU-SeeME
- FTP
- H.323
- Java applets transported via HTTP
- Microsoft Netshow
- UNIX r commands
- RealAudio
- RPC
- SMTP
- SQL*Net
- StreamWorks
- TFTP
- VDOLive

Just as with everything, there are a few limitations when using CBAC.

- Packets with the router as the source or destination will not be inspected.
- Only TCP and UDP packets are inspected.
- CBAC cannot inspect IPsec traffic, unless the router is configured as the IPsec tunnel endpoint.

CBAC cannot track stateless protocols such as UDP and ICMP. UDP replies are allowed through temporary openings that timeout after a specified period of time. ICMP must be permitted or denied by extended ACLs and will not be tracked by CBAC.

The CBAC Process

The following describes the CBAC process.

1. The outgoing packet reaches the router and is evaluated against the outbound ACL. If permitted, it will be inspected by CBAC. Otherwise, it will be dropped and no CBAC inspection will occur.
2. The CBAC records source and destination IP addresses and port numbers in a state table entry created for the new connection.
3. A temporary ACL entry is created based on the previous state information. It is placed at the beginning of the extended ACL configured to filter inbound traffic.
4. This temporary opening permits inbound packets that are part of the same connection as the outbound packets inspected previously. The outbound packet now leaves the interface.
5. Return packets are tested against the inbound ACL and permitted because of the temporary entry created by CBAC. Here, CBAC will modify the state table and inbound ACL, if necessary.
6. All future inbound and outbound traffic will be tested; therefore, the state table ACL will be modified as required.
7. When the connection is closed, the state table entry is deleted along with the temporary ACL.

Configuring CBAC

Configuring CBAC requires specifying protocols for inspection, and applicable interfaces and direction. CBAC will only inspect the protocols we specify. We must configure an outbound ACL (standard or extended) so that CBAC will know what traffic to inspect. The inbound ACL must be extended as CBAC and must be able to permit traffic back in based on Layer 4 header information. These steps are:

1. **Choose the Interface** Determine whether to configure CBAC on an internal or external interface. Client sessions originate on the internal interface, and exit the router on the external interface. In the network shown in Figure 7.16, we will be inspecting traffic inbound to the Ethernet interface, and the return ACL will be applied inbound to the Serial interface.
2. **Configure ACLs** Create the ACLs for the CBAC configuration—oOne outbound for identifying all traffic to the Internet, and one inbound for permitting traffic regardless of CBAC inspection.
3. **Configuring Global Timeouts and Thresholds** You can use the default timeout and threshold values, or you can change to values more suitable to your security requirements. Set timeout and threshold values before you continue configuring CBAC. Table 7.12 lists available CBAC commands used to configure timeouts and thresholds.

4. **Inspection Rules** Specifies which application-layer protocols will be tested by CBAC at an interface. Must define at least one inspection rule. The inspection rule should specify each desired application-layer protocol, as well as TCP or UDP, if desired. The rule consists of statements, each listing a protocol and specifying the same inspection rule name.

Figure 7.16 Configuring CBAC

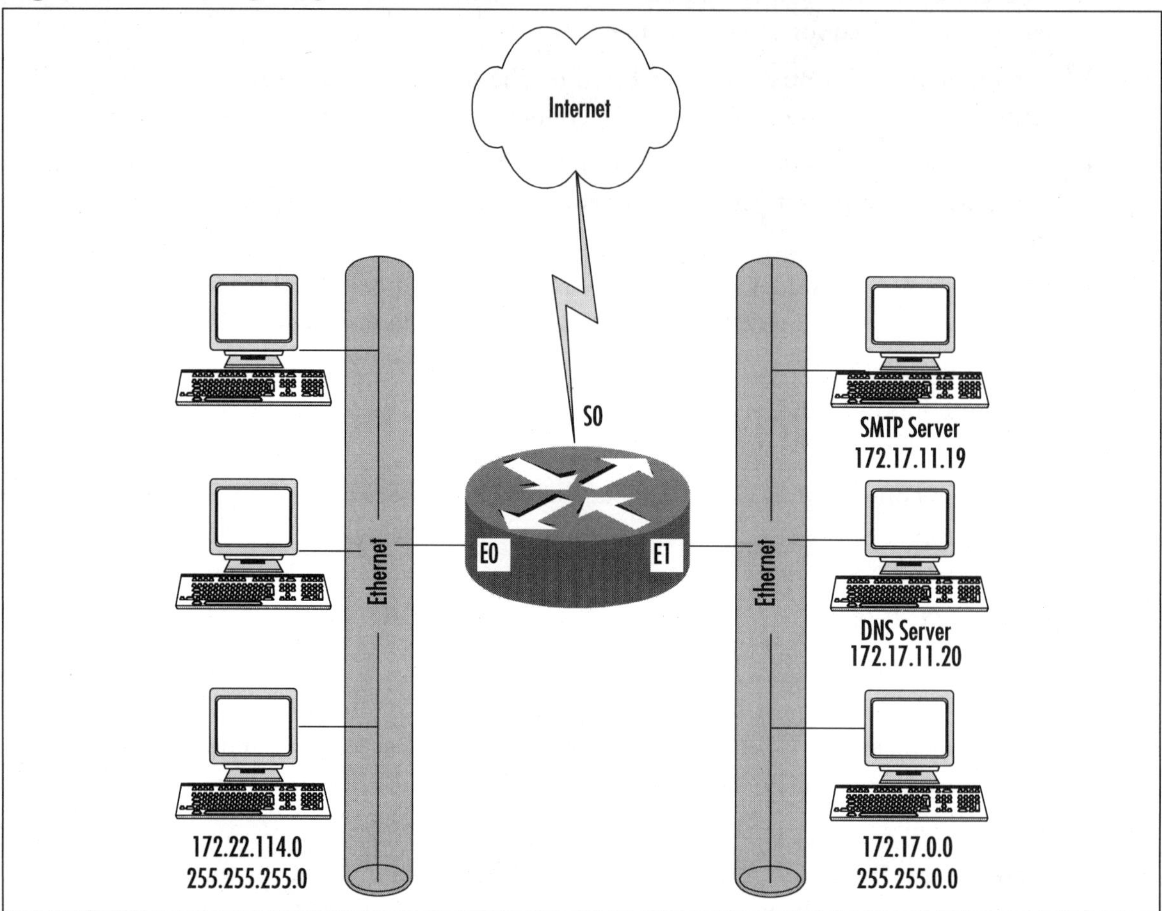

Table 7.12 Available Timeout Commands and Thresholds

Command	Description	Default values
ip inspect tcp synwait-time *seconds*	The length of time of wait for TCP session to be established	30 seconds
ip inspect tcp finwait time *seconds*	The length of time TCP is managed after FIN exchange	5 seconds
ip inspect tcp idle-time *seconds*	The TCP idle timeout	3600 seconds
ip inspect udp idle-time *seconds*	The UDP idle timeout	30 seconds
ip inspect dns-timeout *seconds*	The DNS lookup idle timer	5 seconds

Continued

Table 7.12 Available Timeout Commands and Thresholds

Command	Description	Default values
ip inspect max-incomplete high *number*	The maximum number of half-open connections before CBAC begins closing connections	500 sessions
ip inspect max-incomplete low *number*	The maximum number of half-open connections causing CBAC to stop closing connections	400 sessions
ip inspect one-minute high *number*	The rate of half-open sessions per minute before CBAC begins closing connections	500 sessions
ip inspect one-minute low *number*	The rate of half-open sessions per minute causing CBAC to stop deleting connections	400 sessions
ip inspect tcp max-incomplete host *number* block-time *seconds*	The number of existing half-open sessions with the same destination address before CBAC begins closing sessions	50 sessions

Inspection Rules

The following is the format for inspection rules:

```
ip inspect name inspection-name protocol [alert {on|off} [audit-trail{on|off}][timeout
seconds]
```

- **Alert** Allows CBAC to send messages to a SYSLOG server when an application violation occurs.
- **Audit Trail** Tracks connections used for a protected application. Here, the router logs information about each connection, including the ports used, the number of bytes transferred, and the source and destination IP address.

Applying the Inspection Rule

The final step is applying the rule to an interface using the same process as for any ACL. You must also specify inbound (for traffic entering the interface) or outbound (for traffic exiting the interface).

```
ip inspect inspection-name {in | out}
```

The following is an example of Java blocking. A list of permitted IP addresses must be created using a standard IP ACL. The following is an example:

```
access-list list-number {permit | deny} source-address [wildcard-mask] [log]
ip inspect name inspection-name http [java-list access-list] [alert {on | off}]
[audit-trail {on | off}] [timeout seconds}
```

By default, an undefined ACL in the java-list definition will deny all Java applets. CBAC can only block Java applets and not ActiveX.

There are several commands that are useful in gathering information about CBAC such as **show ip inspect config**.

```
Router# show ip inspect config
Session alert is enabled
One-minute (sampling period) thresholds are [400:500] connections
max-incomplete sessions thresholds are [400:500]
max- incomplete tcp connections per host is 50.
Block-time 0 minute.
tcp synwait-time is 30 sec - tcp finwait - time is 5 sec
tcp idle - time is 3600 sec - udp idle - time is 30 sec
dns - timeout is 5 seconds
```

The **show ip inspect interfaces** command shows the interfaces where CBAC inspection is configured.

```
Router# show ip inspect interfaces
Interface FastEthernet 3/0
Inbound inspection rule is Protector
tcp alert is on audit-trail is off timeout 3600
udp alert is on audit-trail is CBAC off timeout 30
fragment Maximum 50 In Use 0 alert is on audit-trail is off timeout 1
Inbound access list is 114
Outbound access list is not set
```

Configuring Port to Application Mapping

CBAC has certain limitations. For example, traffic going to a Web server on a port other than the standard HTTP port (80) cannot be inspected and protected using CBAC. A solution to CBAC and its limitations is Port to Application Mapping (PAM), which can customize TCP or UDP port numbers for network services. It builds a PAM table of ports associated with their default application; which includes all services supported by CBAC. The PAM table enables CBAC to handle non-standard ports. Otherwise, CBAC is limited to well-known ports and their applications.

Network services on non-standard ports require manual PAM table entries. You can create a separate entry in the PAM table for each port number in a range of ports. Entries are saved when the configuration is saved and are loaded at startup. Enter any non-standard ports for well-known services such as port 800 for Telnet instead of port 23.

Configuring PAM

When configuring PAM, the following format is used:

```
ip port-map application_name port port-number
```

The following is a mapping for well-known port 23 (Telnet) to port 8000:

```
ip port-map telnet port 8000
```

Now let's take this example a step farther and define a range of non-standard ports for use with Telnet. An example may look as follows:

```
ip port-map telnet port 8001
ip port-map telnet port 8002
ip port-map telnet port 8003
ip port-map telnet port 8004
```

We also have the option of mapping an application to a port for a specific host or subnet. Mapping an application to a host would look as follows:

```
access-list 1 permit host 172.16.144.1
ip port-map telnet port 8000 list 1
```

When mapping to a specific subnet, the list may look like this:

```
access-list 1 permit 172.16.144.0 0.0.0.255
ip port-map telnet port 8000 list 1
```

Protecting a Private Network

The solutions presented in the next sections demonstrate security techniques previously discussed. The first example shows a simple connection between two sites over a point-to-point circuit via Serial0. We are securing the connection between Company A and Company B. Figure 7.17 shows a basic architecture. The following is a summary of requirements that need to be properly secured:

1. All hosts belonging to Company A need to be able to access 10.150.200.5 on TCP port 1000.
2. Host 172.20.100.130 needs access to 10.150.150.56 on TCP port 1299.
3. Company B server 10.150.100.5 needs access to 172.20.100.155 on TCP ports 13000 through 13010.
4. Company B server 10.150.100.6 needs to have access to 172.20.100.156 on TCP port 12050.

Figure 7.17 Connection to a Private Network

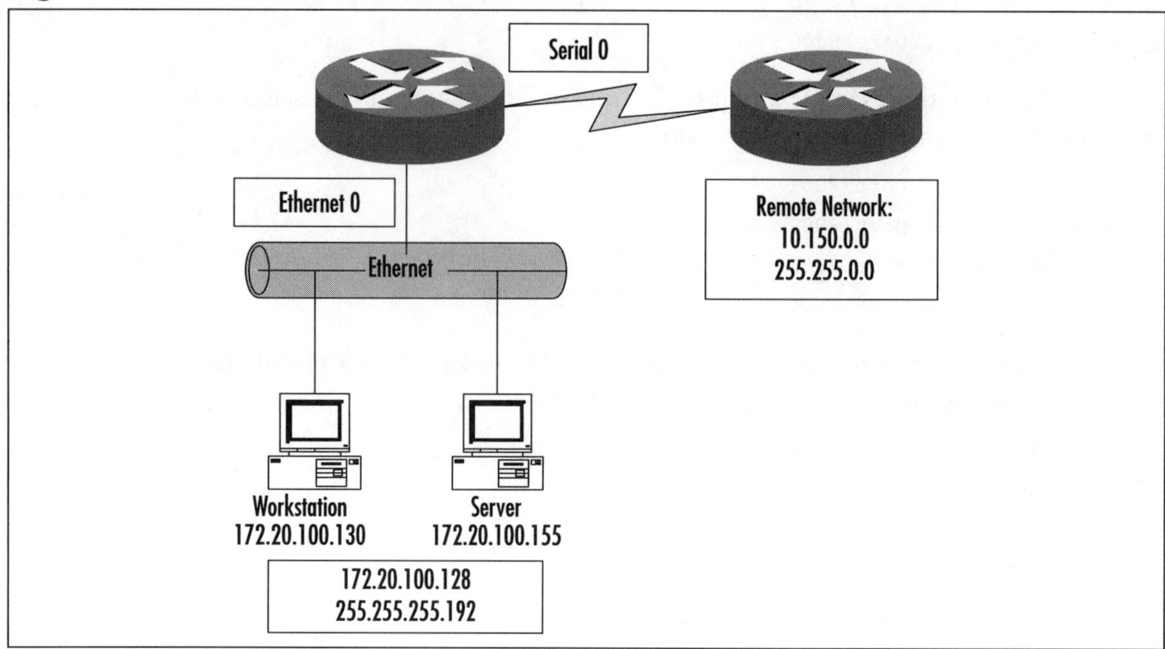

The following is the configuration we will need to create to protect our network.

```
interface Ethernet0
ip address 172.20.100.129 255.255.255.192
ip access-group ToCompanyB in

interface Serial0
ip address 172.16.0.1 255.255.255.252
ip access-group FromCompanyB in

ip access-list extended ToCompanyB
  evaluate EstSessionB
  permit tcp 172.20.100.128 0.0.0.63 host 10.150.200.5 eq 1000 reflect EstSession
  permit tcp host 172.20.100.130 host 10.150.150.56 eq 1299 reflect EstSession
  deny ip any any log

ip access-list extended FromCompanyB
  evaluate EstSessionA
  permit tcp host 10.150.100.5 host 172.20.100.155 range 13000 13010 reflect
EstSessionB
  permit tcp host 10.150.100.6 host 172.20.100.156 eq 12050 reflect EstSessionB
  deny ip any any log
```

Reflecting is bi-directional to protect both networks. We manually entered the **deny ip any any** statement so that we could use the **log** keyword with it. This will allow us to see any traffic that is denied by our ACL.

Protecting a Network Connected to the Internet

The next example configures basic protection for networks connected to the Internet. We would rather use CBAC to reduce problems with current network applications. For example, people may need to download files from an FTP server, or use RealAudio to stream a newscast. CBAC can handle FTP or RealAudio, while reflexive ACLs cannot.

The following is the configuration we will use to protect our network, which is shown in Figure 7.18:

```
ip inspect name CompanyA-FW tcp
ip inpsect name CompanyA-FW udp
ip inspect name CompanyA-FW ftp
ip inspect name CompanyA-FW http
ip inspect name CompanyA-FW realaudio

interface ethernet 0
 ip address 10.150.130.0 255.255.255.0
 ip access-group Outbound in
 ip inspect CompanyA-FW in

interface serial 0
 ip address 192.168.5.1 255.255.255.252
 ip access-group Inbound in

ip access-list extended Outbound
  permit ip 10.150.130.0 0.0.0.255 any
  deny ip any any log

ip access-list extended Inbound
  permit icmp any 10.150.130.0 0.0.0.255 echo-reply
  permit icmp any 10.150.130.0 0.0.0.255 traceroute
  permit icmp any 10.150.130.0 0.0.0.255 time-exceeded
  permit icmp any 10.150.130.0 0.0.0.255 unreachable
  deny ip any any log
```

Figure 7.18 A Network Attached to the Internet

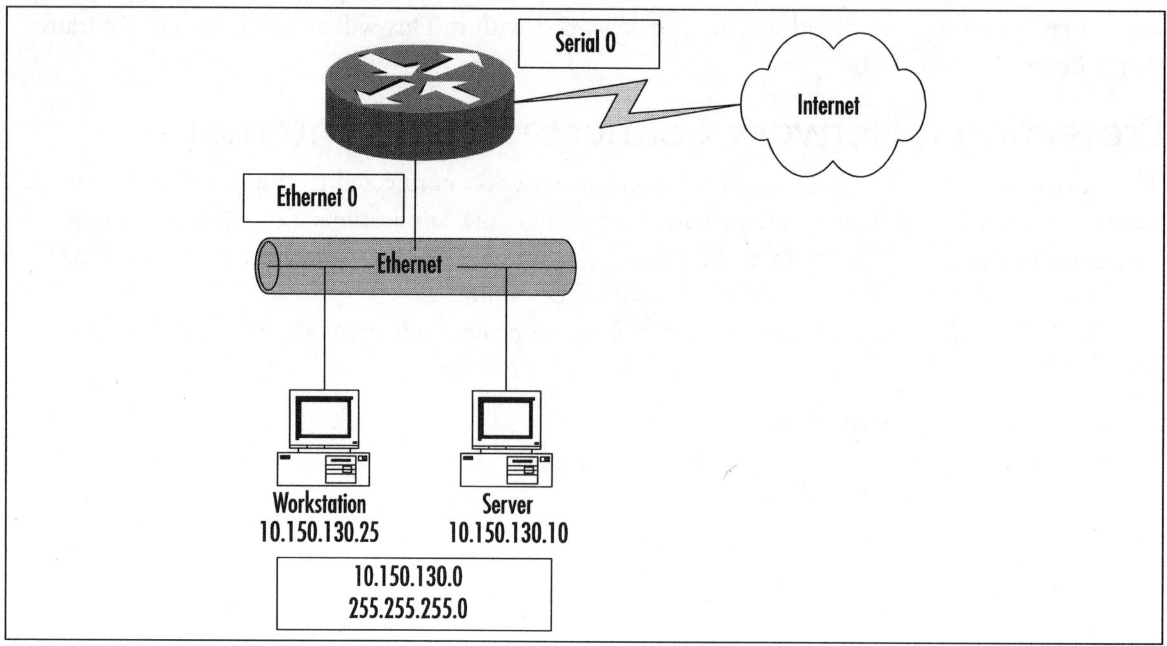

This configuration only allows traffic sourced from our subnet through the router. This blocks attacks performed with spoofed source addresses. The only address spoofing that could make it through the router is if a host spoofed their address to an address used by another host on our network. CBAC maintains a state table for Internet traffic and permits return responses. ICMP is permitted for troubleshooting purposes, but only if originated by us.

Protecting Server Access using Lock-and-Key

We will modify the previous configuration and network in Figure 7.18 to allow transient access to a particular server from outside our network. A permanent ACL would be counter to our security goals, so we will use a lock-and-key ACL. Specifically, "Bill" and "Susan" need to access the 10.150.130.10 server on port 110 (Post Office Protocol 3 [POP3]) from outside our network. The idle **timeout** specifies how long the dynamic lock-and-key entry remains in the ACL after a set period of inactivity; we are setting it to one minute. Our two users will be connecting from: 172.20.128.0 255.255.252.0, and 172.21.64.0 255.255.255.254.0.

After making the changes to our configuration, it should look like this:

```
username bill password needmyemail
username bill autocommand access-enable host timeout 1
username susan password letmein
username susan autocommand access-enable host timeout 1
username admin password supersecret

ip inspect name CompanyA-FW tcp
ip inpsect name CompanyA-FW udp
```

```
ip inspect name CompanyA-FW ftp
ip inspect name CompanyA-FW http
ip inspect name CompanyA-FW realaudio
!
interface Ethernet 0
 ip address 10.150.130.0 255.255.255.0
 ip access-group Outbound in
 ip inspect CompanyA-FW in
!
interface Serial 0
 ip address 192.168.5.1 255.255.255.252
 ip access-group Inbound in
!
ip access-list extended Outbound
  permit ip 10.150.130.0 0.0.0.255 any
  deny ip any any log
!
ip access-list extended Inbound
  permit icmp any 10.150.130.0 0.0.0.255 echo-reply
  permit icmp any 10.150.130.0 0.0.0.255 traceroute
  permit icmp any 10.150.130.0 0.0.0.255 time-exceeded
  permit icmp any 10.150.130.0 0.0.0.255 unreachable
  permit tcp 172.20.128.0 0.0.3.255 host 192.168.5.1 eq telnet
  permit tcp 172.21.64.0 0.0.1.255 host 192.168.5.1 eq telnet
  dynamic POPAccess permit tcp 172.20.128.0 0.0.3.255 host 10.150.130.1 eq 110
  dynamic POPAccess permit tcp 172.21.64.0 0.0.1.255 host 10.150.130.1  eq 110
  deny ip any any log
!
line vty 0 4
login local
exec-timeout 15 0
```

Protecting Public Servers Connected to the Internet

Our next example protects internal users accessing outside networks and servers that are also accessed by external users. The network will be divided into an internal network and a demilitarized zone (DMZ) network. Such DMZ networks contain servers and other devices that provide a limited set of services made accessible to outside users. DMZ networks are typically forbidden from initiating sessions to internal networks, thus reducing the chances that a hacked DMZ server can be used to launch an attack against internal networks. The DMZ serves as a way to isolate your public servers from your private ones.

Figure 7.19 has an internal network on Ethernet0, a DMZ network on Ethernet1, and an Internet connection on Serial0. CBAC will be used to protect this network. Inbound and outbound ACLs are on both Ethernet interfaces and an inbound list is on the serial interface. This controls what traffic is permitted to transit the interface. The configuration follows.

Figure 7.19 A Network with a DMZ and Internet Connection

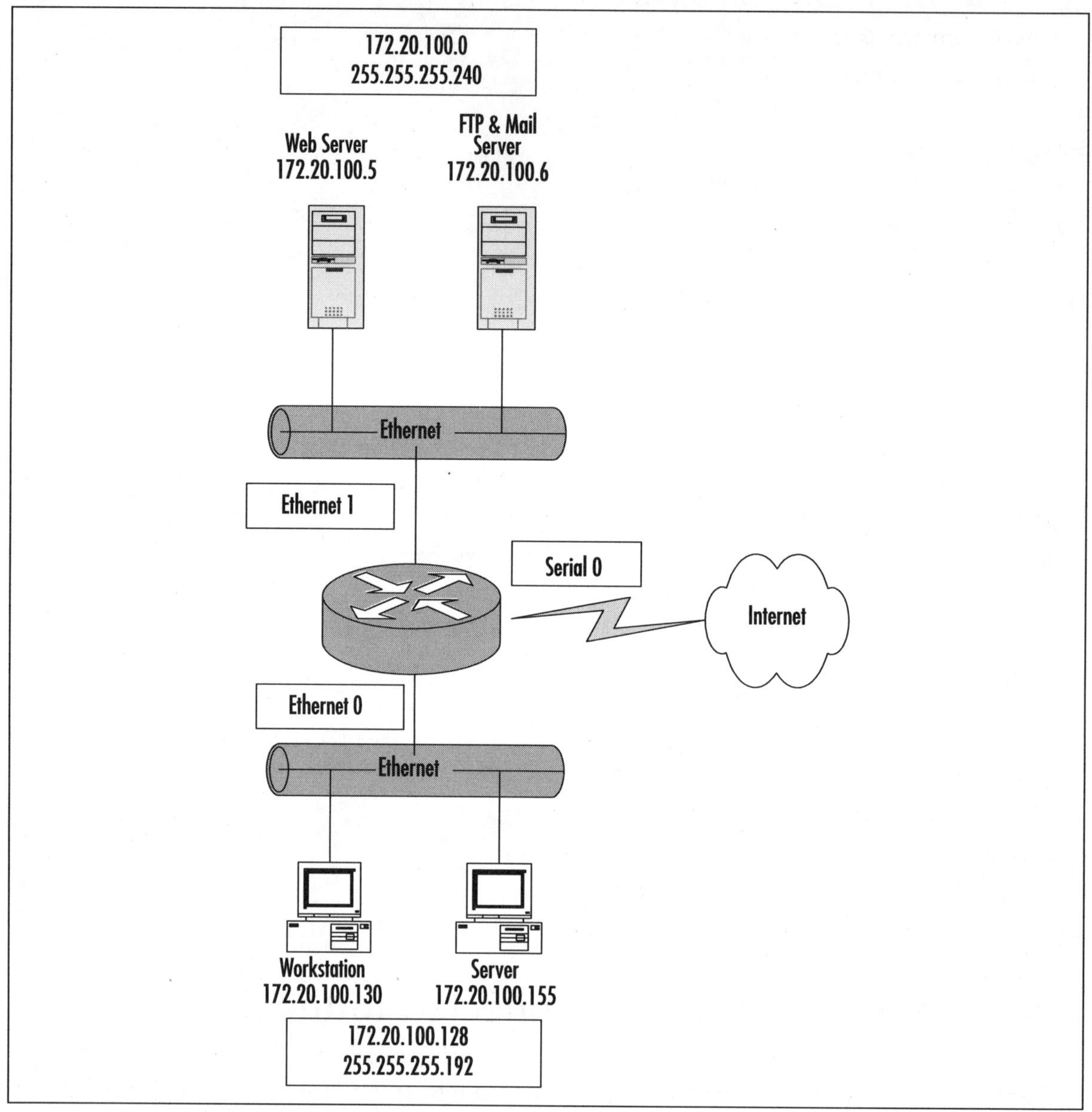


```
ip inspect name DMZ-FW tcp
ip inspect name DMZ-FW ftp
ip inspect name DMZ-FW http
ip inspect name DMZ-FW smtp
```

```
ip inspect name Internal-FW tcp
ip inpsect name Internal-FW udp
ip inspect name Internal-FW http
ip inspect name Internal-FW ftp
ip inspect name Internal-FW smtp
ip inspect name Internal-FW realaudio

interface ethernet 0
 ip address 172.20.100.129 255.255.255.192
 ip access-group Eth0-in in
 ip access-group Eth0-out out
 ip inspect Internal-FW in

interface ethernet 1
ip address 172.20.100.1 255.255.255.240
ip access-group Eth1-in in
ip access-group Eth1-out out
ip inspect DMZ-FW out

interface serial 0
 ip address 192.168.5.1 255.255.255.252
 ip access-group Serial-in in

ip access-list extended Eth0-in
  permit ip 172.20.100.128 0.0.0.63 any
  deny ip any any log-input

ip access-list extended Eth0-out
  permit icmp any 172.20.100.128 0.0.0.63 echo-reply
  permit icmp any 172.20.100.128 0.0.0.63 packet-too-big
  permit icmp any 172.20.100.128 0.0.0.63 time-exceeded
  permit icmp any 172.20.100.128 0.0.0.63 unreachable
  deny ip any any log-input

ip access-list extended Eth1-in
  permit icmp 172.20.100.0 0.0.0.15 any echo-reply
  deny ip any any log-input

ip access-list extneded Eth1-out
  permit tcp any host 172.20.100.5 eq www
```

```
  permit tcp any host 172.20.100.6 eq ftp
  permit tcp any host 172.20.100.6 eq smtp
  permit tcp 172.20.100.128 0.0.0.63 host 172.20.100.6 eq pop3
  permit icmp any 172.20.100.0 0.0.0.15 echo
  permit icmp any 172.20.100.0 0.0.0.15 echo-reply
  permit icmp any 172.20.100.0 0.0.0.15 packet-too-big
  permit icmp any 172.20.100.0 0.0.0.15 time-exceeded
  permit icmp any 172.20.100.0 0.0.0.15 unreachable
  deny ip any any log-input

ip access-list extended Serial-in
  deny ip 172.20.100.0 0.0.0.15 any log-input
  deny ip 172.20.100.128 0.0.0.63 any log-input
  permit ip any any
```

There are two **ip inspect** rules. One rule inspects and accepts HTTP, SMTP, and FTP for the DMZ network, and another handles UDP and possibly RealAudio for our internal network. Our users are permitted to go anywhere they want, but only responses are allowed into our network, as well as a few types of ICMP for troubleshooting. Placement is key. On our three-interface router in Figure 7.19, we have applied both the inbound and outbound ACLs to the Ethernet interfaces. Traffic received on Ethernet0 can either be routed to Ethernet1 or Serial0.

Since the servers on the DMZ network are publicly accessible and exposed to more risk than our internal network, strictly limit what traffic can originate from the DMZ. Only specific ports on the servers (HTTP, FTP, and so on) are accessible to outside networks, as well as responses to outside requests from the DMZ. If the DMZ network is compromised, no attacks can be launched from it. DMZ servers cannot initiate sessions to either the outside or inside network. The following describes what each ACL will do.

- **Eth0-in** Filters traffic from internal hosts entering Ethernet0. Permits all traffic with addresses from the internal network, and prevents spoofing attacks from being launched from this network. Packets allowed by this ACL are inspected by CBAC, which allows responses to transit Eth0-out interface.
- **Eth0-out** Filters traffic entering our internal network, and permits ICMP as CBAC cannot maintain state information on ICMP. All other traffic is denied as CBAC allows responses by adding temporary entries at the top of this list.
- **Eth1-in** Controls what traffic can be originated from DMZ hosts.
- **Eth1-out** Controls what traffic is allowed to the DMZ, which includes public access to HTTP, FTP, and SMTP services. POP3 is restricted to e-mail access from the internal network. ICMP is permitted on a limited scale for testing. Anything allowed through this list is inspected by CBAC and allowed to return back through the Eth1-in ACL.
- **Serial-in** Prevents spoofing attacks from outside our network. Packets with a source address of the internal network inbound to the serial interface are dropped.

Applying Perimeter Security in IPv6

At the time of this writing, the deployment of IPv6 is not widespread. As a result, we will limit our discussion to the ACLs that can help secure IPv6 networks. The two basic types of ACLs are **standard** and **extended**. Standard ACLs can filter based on only the source IP address within a packet. Extended ACLs can filter based on other packet parameters, including source and destination IP addresses, source and destination ports, and protocol. In addition, extended ACLs support logging.

Cisco supports only standard ACLs for IPv6 in IOS 12.2 and later, which represents Phase 1 of their roadmap to support IPv6. Extended ACLs will be supported in Phase 2 of their IPv6 roadmap. To configure standard ACLs of IPv6, you need to perform the following tasks:

1. Define the IPv6 standard ACL.
2. Apply the IPv6 standard ACL to an interface.
3. Verify the IPv6 standard ACL configuration.

The following list describes IPv6 ACL commands.

```
ipv6 access-list access-list-name {permit | deny} { source-ipv6-prefix/ prefix-length |
any} { destination-ipv6-prefix/ prefix-length | any} [priority value]
```

- ***access-list-name*** Specifies the name of the IPv6 ACL, which cannot contain a space or quotation mark.
- **deny** Specifies the deny conditions for the ACL.
- **permit** Specifies the permit conditions for the ACL.
- **source-ipv6-prefix/prefix-length and destination-ipv6-prefix/prefix-length** Mandatory. Prefix-length indicates the number of consecutive, most-significant bits used in the match. A slash (/) mark must precede the decimal value.
- **Any** Matches any prefix and is equivalent to the IPv6 prefix ::/0.
- **priority** This keyword specifies the order in which the statement is applied in the ACL. The acceptable range is from 1 to 4294967295.

```
interface interface-type interface-number
```

The **ipv6 traffic-filter** ***access-list-name*** **{in | out}** command applies the specified IPv6 ACL to the interface specified in the previous step.

- The **in** keyword filters incoming IPv6 traffic on the specified interface.
- The **out** keyword filters outgoing IPv6 traffic on the specified interface.

The **show ipv6 access-list** command verifies that the IPv6 standard ACLs are configured correctly.

The following example configures the ACL named **list2** and applies the ACL to outbound traffic on Ethernet interface 0. Specifically, the first ACL entry keeps all packets from the network fec0:0:0:2::/64 (packets that have the site-local prefix fec0:0:0:2 as the first 64 bits of their source IPv6 address) from exiting Ethernet interface 0. The second entry in the ACL permits all other traffic to exit Ethernet interface 0. The second entry is necessary because an implicit deny all condition is at the end of each IPv6 ACL.

```
ipv6 access-list list2 deny fec0:0:0:2::/64 any
ipv6 access-list list2 permit any any
interface ethernet 0
ipv6 traffic-filter dublin out
```

ACL Control Manager

ACLs are a line of defense against potential intruders and malicious hackers. Organizations often require additional security throughout the network to limit access to critical resources behind boundary defenses or to simply segment certain internal network traffic, which can be provided by ACLs. The maintenance of ACLs on multiple devices can become difficult due to complexity and quantity. A Cisco Works2000 component called ACL Manager (ACLM) can simplify the task of ACL management.

ACLM is included in the CiscoWorks2000 Routed WAN Management Solution set. ACLM develops and maintains ACLs on Cisco devices. The Web-based GUI controls IP and IPX ACLs and device access control from virtually anywhere on the network. VLAN and SNMP ACL management is also possible via ACLM. The interface eliminates the complexity and syntactical accuracy required to implement lengthy ACLs via the CLI.

ACLM version 1.4 supports most Cisco IOS routers, access servers, and switches with an IOS of 10.3 and later. ACLM can also manage Catalyst switches running Catalyst OS version 5.3 and later. ACLM includes full support for the following ACLs:

- Extended ACL for IP and IPX
- IPX SAP and Summary lists
- Rate Limit Lists (Precedence)
- Catalyst 6x00 VLAN ACL

The Basic Operation of ACLM

This section focuses on some of the basic operations of ACLM components. Since nearly all ACLM operations are configured via an easy-to-use GUI, we will simply provide an introductory overview.

Using Templates and Defining Classes

Templates ensure consistency across the network and reduce the time in deploying ACLs. Before using ACLM Template Manager, however, it is important to first configure networks, network classes, services, and service classes. To do so, administrators use the Class Manager to view, add, and change classes.

The services in the Class Manager include standard services and port numbers for well-known applications like FTP, HTTP, and Telnet. New, custom services can be added to the list of services as well. To add new services, simply select the type of IP service, UDP or TCP, enter a name to identify the new service, and enter the associated port number.

Using Diff Viewer

ACLs created and altered on the network via ACLM do not take effect immediately. Rather, changes are applied to specific routers and devices manually or at a scheduled, off-hours time with the ACL Downloader. When finished with ACL changes on the network, administrators can use the Diff Viewer to verify all current configurations, as well as the changes made to ACLs.

Using the Optimizer and the Hits Optimizer

The Optimizer and Hits Optimizer in ACLM help reduce processor cycles and increase packet-forwarding throughput through intelligent ACL regrouping and reordering. Large or inefficiently created ACLs can negatively impact the performance of network devices such as routers or switches. When a packet is received or forwarded out an interface, it must first be compared to all entries in the ACL until a match is found. Once a match for the specific traffic is located in the ACL, traffic is denied or permitted according to the ACE.

To prevent latency due to lengthy ACLs, the ACL Optimizer minimizes the number of ACEs used in ACLs. This is achieved by merging ACEs or removing redundant ACEs. In this manner, the Optimizer frees up processing resources and improves network performance. Table 7.13 exemplifies the positive effects of the Optimizer on some ACEs in an ACL.

Table 7.13 ACLM ACE Optimizer

Original ACEs	Optimized ACEs
permit ip any host 192.168.50.8	
permit ip any host 192.168.50.9	
permit ip any host 192.168.50.10	
permit ip any host 192.168.50.11	
permit ip any host 192.168.50.12	
permit ip any host 192.168.50.13	
permit ip any host 192.168.50.14	
permit ip any host 192.168.50.15	permit ip any 192.168.50.8 0.0.0.7

As can be seen, the Optimizer uses a process similar to that employed for route summarization on the network to improve network routing performance. Hits Optimizer is used to improve throughput performance related to ACLs on a device. Hits Optimizer rearranges ACLs by placing the most frequently matched ACEs at the top of the ACL and moving less frequently matched ACEs to the bottom. This is achieved based on the number of matches tracked by the device IOS.

Configuring the ACLM

Several pieces of information must be gathered prior to using ACLM. All Cisco devices to be managed must be configured to integrate with ACLM. Domain Name Service (DNS) entries must be configured for all devices on the network including forward and reverse resolution mapping. This information is used when adding devices to the Resource Manager Essentials inventory within CiscoWorks2000. The DNS entry should be a fully qualified domain name. When adding devices to the RME, the following information for each device on the network is required:

- Read Community String for SNMP
- Read/Write Community String for SNMP
- TACACS username and password, if used
- Local device username and password
- Telnet username and password
- Enable TACACS username and password, if used
- Enable password
- Enable secret password

Configuration Example: Creating ACLs with ACLM

The next example includes procedures for creating ACLs on a router. To do so, the following specific exercises are included:

- Adding a new router to the CiscoWorks2000 configuration
- Opening a new scenario to edit ACLs on the new router
- Adding an ACL and a specific ACE to the router

After successfully logging in to CiscoWorks2000, add the new router. Run ACLM and go through the following steps to create and apply your ACL.

A scenario must be created in association with the new ACL to be configured. Figure 7.20 shows the screen on which a scenario is configured. Enter a specific name for the new scenario and select the relevant information below. Click **Next** to select the devices to be used in the scenario.

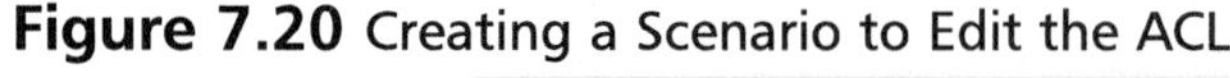

Figure 7.20 Creating a Scenario to Edit the ACL

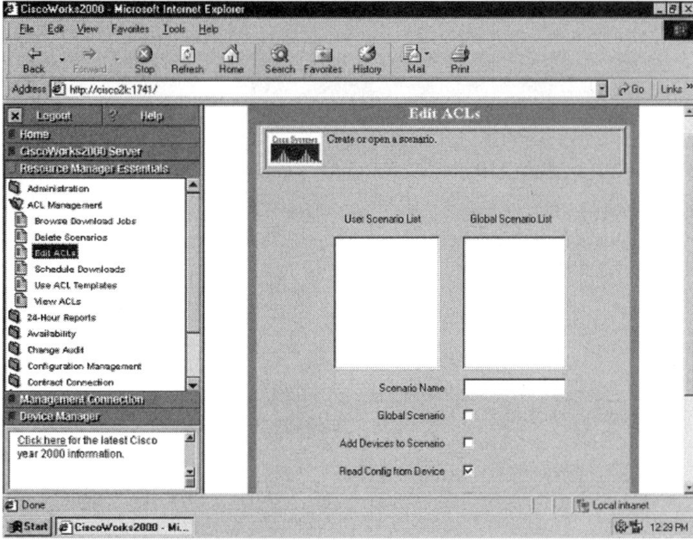

The next screen appears where the devices can be selected based on a custom view filter. Click **Add** to add the related device for the new scenario. Clicking **Next** opens a new Java applet window called "ACLM," which is used to configure the ACL. Apply it to the selected device. Figure 7.21 shows the ACLM applet window and sub-selections.

Figure 7.21 The ACLM Window

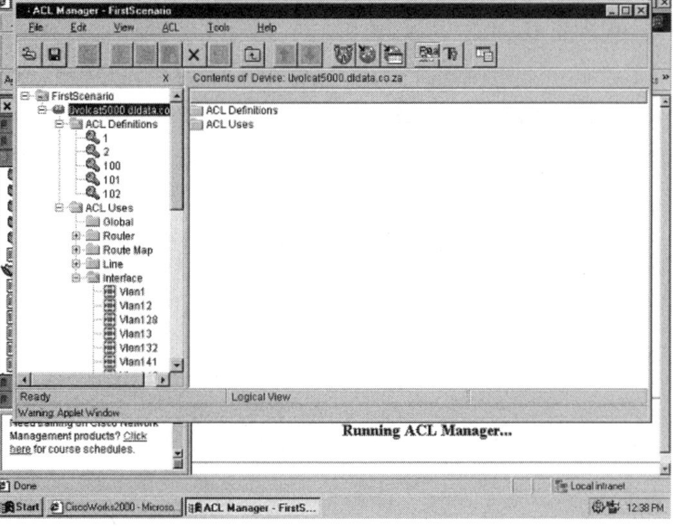

Next, add a specific ACL for the new ACE by right-clicking the **ACL Definitions** folder and selecting **New ACL**. Figure 7.22 shows the ACL Editor screen used to add an ACL to the selected router.

Figure 7.22 Adding an ACL to the Router

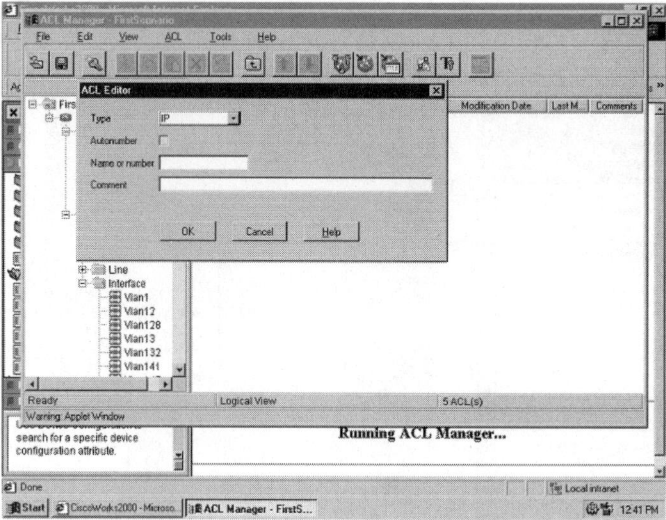

After clicking **OK**, notice the new ACL in the **ACL Definition** section. Right-click the new ACL to obtain a list of options available for it.

Finally, add the relevant ACEs for the specific security policy to the ACL. Figure 7.23 shows the first ACE for the new standard ACL that denies all traffic from 192.168.200.0. Click the **Expand…** button to see the list of IOS commands used to configure the selected router. To add another ACE to the ACL, click the **New** button.

Figure 7.23 Adding an ACE to the New ACL

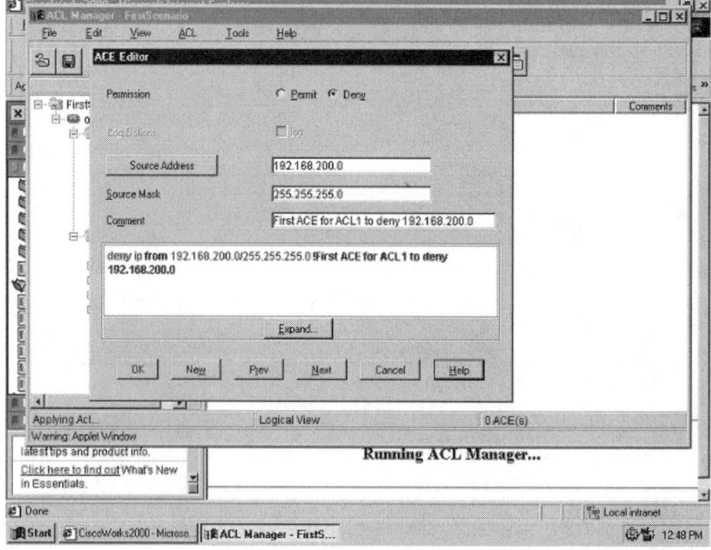

CSPM

CSPM is a Windows 2000 management tool for networks. It provides a complete management solution for Cisco VPN routers, IDS, and Cisco Secure PIX firewalls. Security administrators can effectively and securely manage the definition, enforcement and auditing of security policy from one intuitive administrative interface.

The significant features of CSPM are as follows:

- **Cisco PIX Firewall Management** Administrators can define and maintain PIX- and IOS-based security policies via the Cisco Secure Integrated Software feature set.
- **Cisco VPN Gateway Management** VPN Gateway Management enables IPsec VPN management on PIX firewalls and Cisco VPN devices running the IOS IPsec software.
- **Config Import** Firewall administrators can import topology and security polices from PIX and IOS security network devices.
- **Security Policy Management** Up to 500 Cisco security devices can be easily managed without extensive device knowledge and dependency on the command-line interface (CLI).
- **Notification and Reporting System** CSPM includes auditing tools to monitor, alert, and report Cisco security device and policy activity.

CSPM features and functions use are intuitive, and configuration is performed via a Web interface.

Overview of VPN Technologies

VPNs establish a secure network over insecure or public networks. VPNs can take many different forms and be implemented in various ways. VPNs achieve their security by encrypting the traffic that they transport, preventing eavesdropping or interception. In simplest terms, a VPN is fundamentally a secure tunnel established between two or more endpoints.

Tunneling VPNs

Tunnels can be created either between a source and destination router, router-to-router, or host-to host. Tunneling can be point-to-point or point-to-multipoint, but point-to-point tunneling is much more scaleable than point-to-multipoint.

A VPN could be constructed with or without the knowledge of the network provider, and could span multiple network providers.

Cisco's Generic Routing Encapsulation (GRE) is used for tunneling between source and destination router, router-to-router. GRE tunnels provide a specific pathway across a shared wide area network (WAN) and encapsulate traffic with new packet headers to ensure delivery to a specific destination. A GRE tunnel is configured between the source (**ingress**) router and the destination (**egress**) router. Packets are encapsulated with a GRE header, transported across the tunnel to the tunnel endpoint address, and stripped of their GRE header.

The IETF's L2TP and Microsoft's Point-to-Point Tunneling Protocol (PPTP) are used for host-to-host tunneling. PPTP should not be used without additional security features, such as those provided by IPsec, as it is known to have several security vulnerabilities. Some of these vulnerabilities have been addressed by the strengthening of PPTP's authentication mechanism, MS-CHAP, in the revised MS-CHAP version 2.

Host-to-host tunneling is considerably more secure than router-to-router tunneling due to the fact that with host-to-host tunneling the entire "conversation" can be encrypted. This is not the case in router-to-router tunneling, since only the tunnel can be encrypted while the host-to-router and router-to-host parts on both sides of the "conversation" remain in cleartext.

Virtual Private Dial Networks

Virtual Private Dial Networks (VPDNs) that utilize the Internet as a carrier for remote access (RAS) traffic are flexible and cost effective. L2TP and PPTP are fundamental to VPDN and provide the tunneling features through which the RAS traffic reaches the desired services.

Intranet VPNs

An Intranet VPN links enterprise customer headquarters, remote offices, and branch offices to an internal network over a shared infrastructure using dedicated connections. In Figure 7.24, we see a typical VPN dialup scenario.

Figure 7.24 VPN Client to Router VPN via Dialup

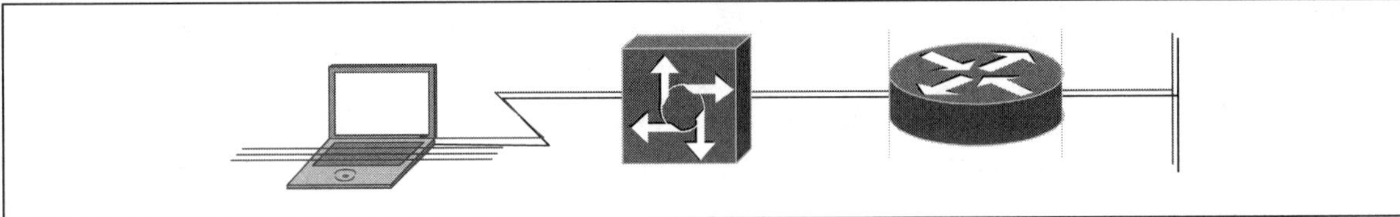

Extranet VPNs

An Extranet VPN links outside customers, suppliers, partners, or communities of interest to an enterprise customer's network over a shared infrastructure using dedicated connections (see Figure 7.25).

Figure 7.25 Router to Router VPN Gateway

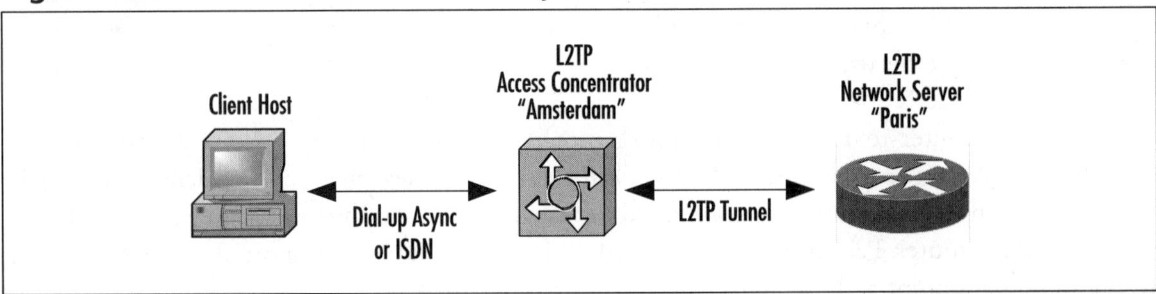

Access VPNs

An Access VPN provides RAS to an enterprise customer's intranet or extranet over a shared infrastructure (see Figure 7.26). Access VPNs use a variety of network types to connect mobile users, telecommuters, and branch offices.

Figure 7.26 Other Vendors to the Router VPN

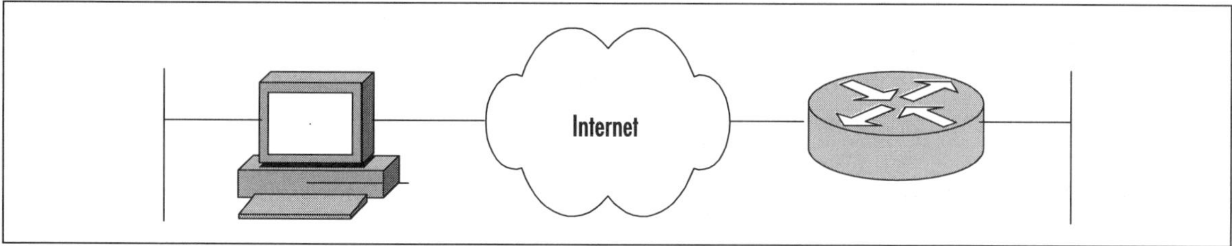

L2TP

L2TP is an Internet Engineering Task Force (IETF) standard that combines the best features of two existing tunnelling protocols: Cisco's L2F and Microsoft's PPTP. L2TP has actually replaced the L2F protocol.

L2TP can create a virtual tunnel to link customer's remote sites or remote users with corporate networks. L2TP allows organizations to provide connectivity to remote users by leveraging a service provider's existing infrastructure. L2TP is a not security protocol; instead it relies on IPsec for security.

The L2TP access controller (LAC) exchanges messages with remote users and communicates using L2TP requests and responses with the customer's L2TP network server (LNS) to set up tunnels (see Figure 7.27). L2TP passes packets through the virtual tunnel between endpoints of a point-to-point connection. Frames from remote users are accepted by the ISP's point of presence, stripped of any linked framing or transparency bytes, encapsulated in L2TP, and forwarded over the appropriate tunnel. The customer's home gateway accepts these L2TP frames, strips the L2TP encapsulation, and processes the incoming frames for the appropriate interface. L2TP is an extension of PPP and is vendor interoperable.

Figure 7.27 L2TP Architecture

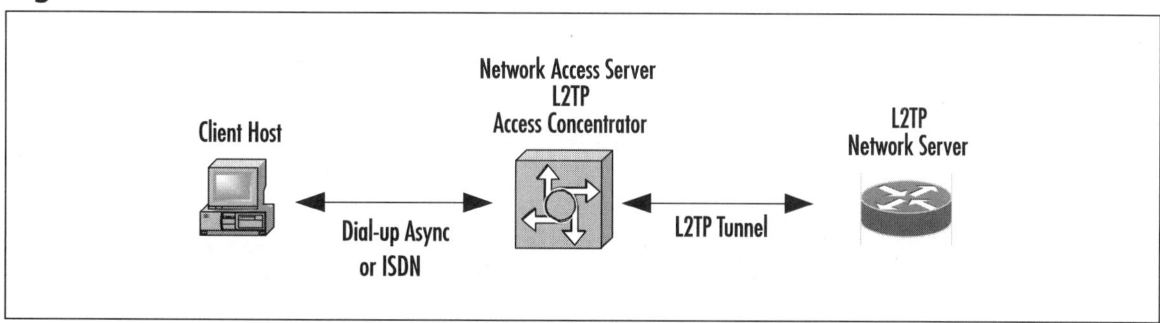

L2TP uses a *compulsory* tunnelling model, which means that the tunnel is created without any action from the user, and without giving the user a choice in the matter. In this scenario, a user dials into a NAS, authenticates either against a locally configured profile or against a policy server, and after successful authentication, a L2TP tunnel is dynamically established to a predetermined endpoint, where the user's PPP session is terminated.

Configuring Cisco L2TP

The following example illustrates how L2TP can be used to provide enterprise connectivity to remote users using a shared network such as a service provider. Figure 7.28 shows a typical L2TP scenario, displaying the LAC as well as the LNS.

Figure 7.28 L2TP Configuration

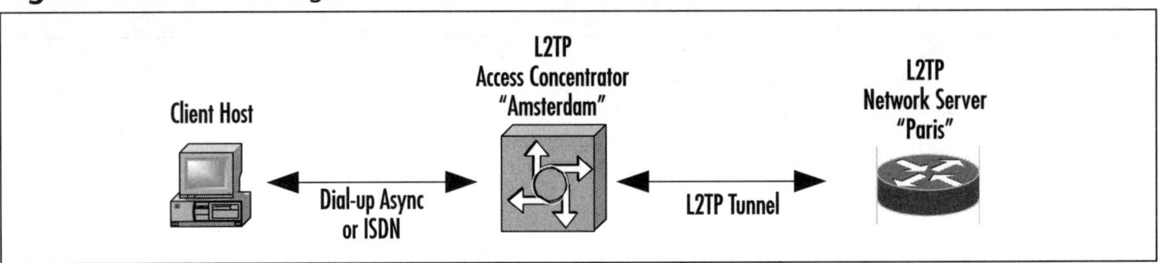

An LAC Configuration Example

The following is a basic LAC configuration for the scenario shown in Figure 7.28.

```
! Enable AAA.
aaa new-model
! Enable AAA authentication for PPP.
aaa authentication ppp default local
! Define the username as "Amsterdam."
username Amsterdam password 7 **********
! Enable VPDN.
vpdn enable
! Define VPDN group number 1.
vpdn-group 1
! Allow the LAC to respond to dial in requests using L2TP from the IP address
172.25.1.19 domain test.com.
request dialin l2tp ip 172.25.1.19 domain test.com
```

A LNS Configuration Example

The following is a basic LNS configuration for the scenario shown in Figure 7.28.

```
! Enable AAA.
aaa new-model
```

```
! Enable AAA authentication for PPP.
aaa authentication ppp default local
! Define the username as "Paris."
username Paris password 7 **********
! Create virtual-template 1 and assigns all values for virtual access interfaces.
interface Virtual-Template1
! Use the IP address from interface Ethernet 0.
ip unnumbered Ethernet0
! Disable multicast fast switching.
no ip mroute-cache
! Use CHAP to authenticate PPP.
ppp authentication chap
! Enable VPDN.
vpdn enable
! Create vpdn-group number 1.
vpdn-group 1
! Accept all dial-in l2tp tunnels from virtual-template from remote peer Amsterdam.
accept dialin l2tp virtual-template 1 remote Amsterdam
```

PPTP Overview

PPTP is much simpler than IPsec in its structure (see Figure 7.29). Each tunnel includes the following elements:

- The client
- A NAS (for example, an ISP's dialup server)
- The gateway or PPTP server

Figure 7.29 PPTP Functionality

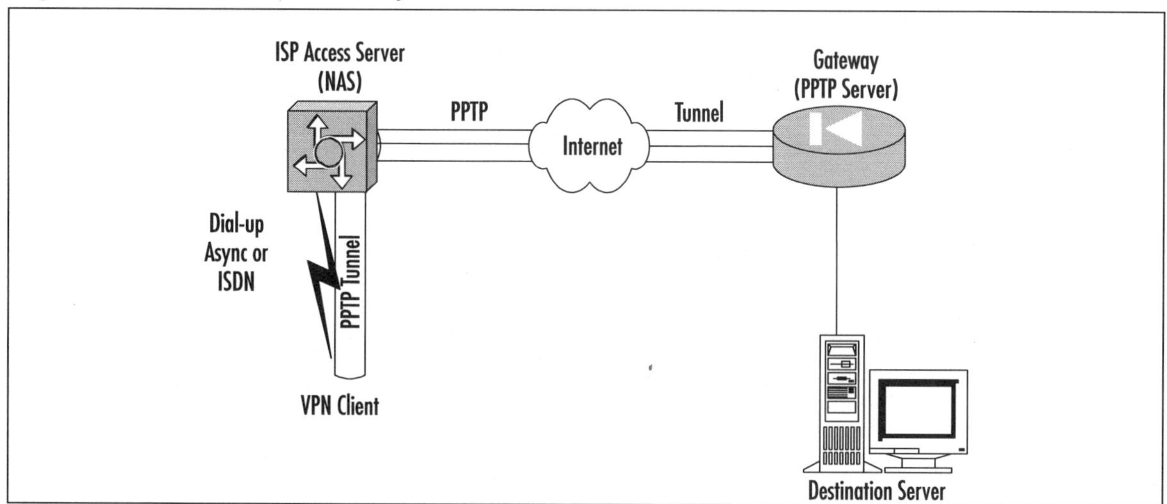

When a connection is being established, the following happens:

1. The client connects to the public network (via dialup, for example).
2. A PPTP control connection (from client to TCP port 1723 on the server) is established (PPTP tunnel).
3. A GRE tunnel is established over IP 47 (PPTP data tunnel).
4. Layer 3 protocols are encapsulated by the client into PPP packets and then transmitted through the GRE tunnel. This traffic is decapsulated twice (from GRE and from PPP) on the other side by the gateway and then forwarded to the private network.

As PPTP is PPP encapsulated into GRE, it uses all PPP authentication and encryption features. Authentication uses PAP, CHAP, or MS-CHAP. Authentication can be performed using a local database or external AAA servers (RADIUS or TACACS+).

Encryption can eliminate packet spoofing and insertion by third parties. Encryption is negotiated using PPP Compression Control Protocol (CCP). PPTP can use RC4 encryption with 40-bit or 128-bit keys—a part of Microsoft Point-to Point Encryption (MPPE) extensions. Longer keys are recommended, especially since RC4 is even weaker than DES. When MPPE is used, the external AAA server used for authentication must be RADIUS, and it should be able to return a MSCHAP_MPPE_KEY attribute.

The following configuration creates a basic PPTP configuration on an IOS router. Here, we have defined a single VPDN group and associated it with virtual interface 123.

```
username pptp password 0 cisco
ip subnet-zero
!
vpdn enable
!
vpdn-group 123
 accept-dialin
  protocol pptp
  virtual-template 123
 local name syngress

interface Ethernet0
 ip address 10.1.2.3 255.255.255.0
!
interface Virtual-Template123
 ip unnumbered Ethernet0
 ppp authentication ms-chap
```

Understanding Cryptography Concepts

The objective of cryptography is to hide information so that only the intended recipient(s) can "unhide" it; this is called *encryption*. The reverse process is *decryption*. A cipher is used to accomplish the encryption and decryption. The information being hidden is *plaintext*; and becomes *ciphertext* once it has been encrypted. Ciphertext is transported to the intended recipient(s), where it is decrypted back into plaintext.

Encryption Key Types

Cryptography uses two types of keys: *symmetric* and *asymmetric*. Symmetric keys utilize a single key for both encryption and decryption. Anyone in possession of the key can decrypt messages. Symmetric key algorithms used for encryption are well known, so only the key used remains a secret. Difficulties with symmetric keys include delivering and ensuring the send and receiver have the same key, key changes must be arranged and known to both sender and receiver, and theft of key threatens all data encrypted with that key.

Asymmetric cryptography (perhaps better known as *public key cryptography)* uses separate keys for encryption and decryption—a *public key* and a *private key*, respectively. The DH algorithm is used to securely exchange keys. The public key can be provided to any sender by the receiver in order to enable encryption of data to be transmitted to the receiver. Upon receipt, the receiver then uses their private key to decrypt the message.

Standard Cryptographic Algorithms

There are numerous algorithms available to provide different levels of security, speed, and ease of implementation. *Security* is the resistance to current and future attacks, *speed* measures processing power and time required to encrypt and decrypt a message, and *ease of implementation* is an algorithm's predisposition (if any) to hardware or software usage. Each algorithm has different strengths and drawbacks, and none of them is ideal in every way. The five most common algorithms that you will encounter are DES, Advanced Encryption Standard (AES) [Rijndael], International Data Encryption Algorithm (IDEA), DH, and RSA. All symmetric algorithms are also theoretically vulnerable to *brute force attacks*.

DES

DES algorithm is a complex symmetric algorithm encrypts data in 64 bit blocks. A 64-bit block of clear text goes into the algorithm along with a 56-bit key; the result is a 64-bit block of cipher text. Since the key size is fixed at 56-bits, the number of keys available (the key space) is 256 (about 72,000,000,000,000,000 keys).

DES uses a single 64-bit key—56 bits of data and 8 bits of parity—and operates on data in 64-bit chunks. This key is broken into 16 separate 48-bit subkeys, one for each round, which are called *Feistel cycles*. Figure 7.30 gives a schematic of how the DES encryption algorithm operates.

Figure 7.30 Diagram of the DES Encryption Algorithm

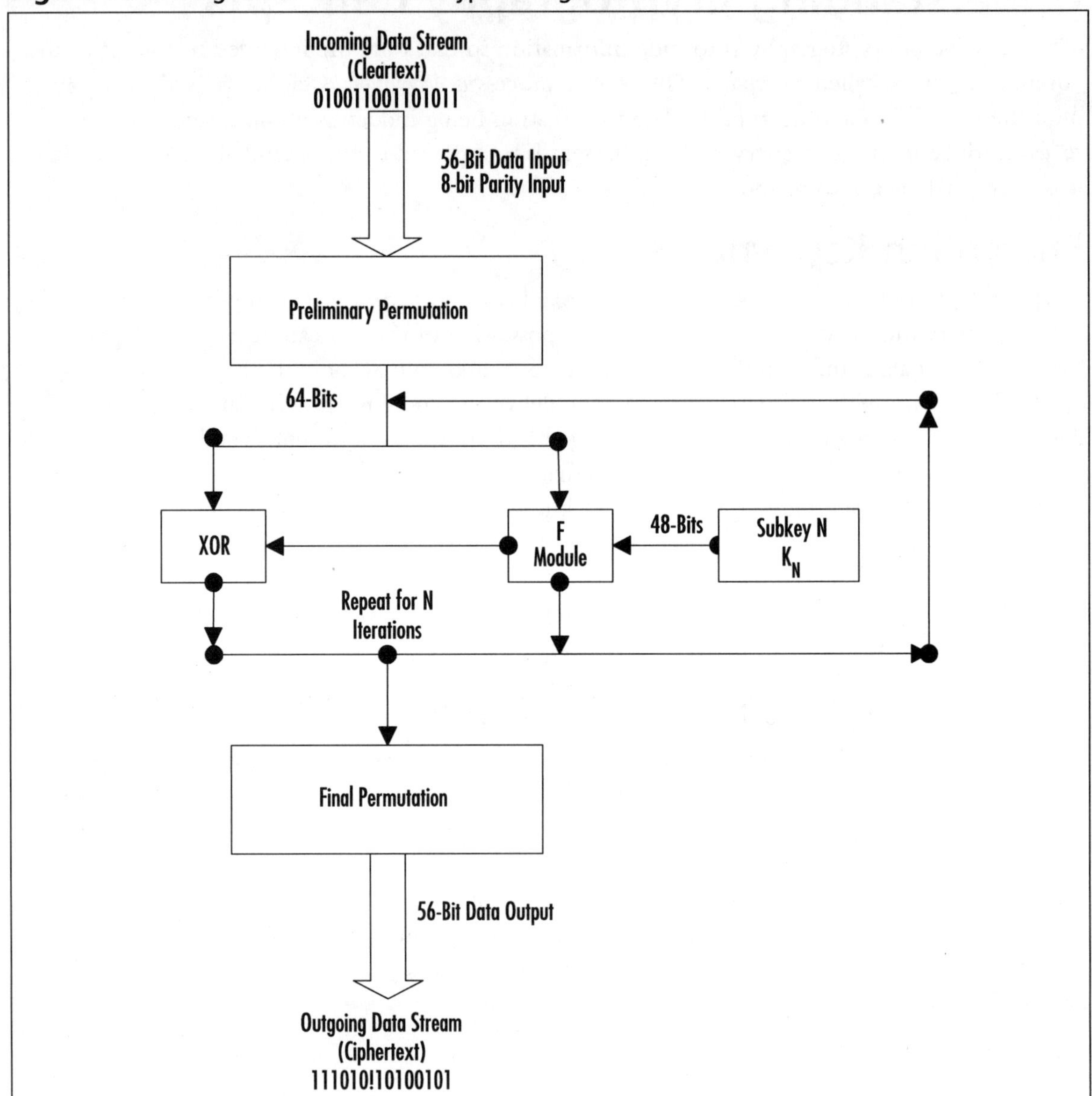

Each round consists of a substitution phase, wherein the data is substituted with pieces of the key, and a permutation phase, wherein the substituted data is scrambled (re-ordered). Substitution operations (AKA confusion operations) occur within S-boxes while permutation operations (AKA diffusion operations) occur in P-boxes. Both occur in the "F Module" shown in Figure 7.30. The non-linear nature of DES results in ciphertext that never resembles the original message. Permutation operations secure further by scrambling the already partially encrypted message.

The short 56-bit key length is a serious flaw in DES as shorter keys are more vulnerable to brute force attacks. DES was first publicly broken by a brute force attack in 1997. If you have a choice, opt for 3DES instead of DES.

3DES

Triple-pass DES (3DES) is a cryptographic system that uses multiple passes of the DES algorithm to increase the effective key space available to the system. The cleartext data is first encrypted with a 56-bit key. The resulting ciphertext is then decrypted with a different key, and that result is encrypted again with the first key. 3DES increases the effective key length from 56 bits to 112 bits. 3DES operates similarly to DES except that it encrypts three times with an effective key length of 168-bits. These "effective" 168 bits is achieved by using a different 56-bit key for each of the iterations of encryption.

3DES is a cryptographic system that uses multiple passes of the DES algorithm to increase the effective key space available. The same DES technique employed in 3DES is used, except that three different keys are used. This increases the effective key length to 168 bits for 3DES. The very strong encryption and security of the key make it the best solution when the highest security is needed. The drawback to 3DES is it requires more processing to compute such a complex algorithm.

IDEA

The European counterpart to DES is the IDEA algorithm. IDEA is considerably faster and more secure than DES. Its enhanced speed is due to the fact the each round consists of much simpler operations than the Feistel cycle in DES. These operations (XOR, addition, and multiplication) are much simpler to implement in software than the substitution and permutation operations of DES.

IDEA operates on 64-bit blocks with a 128-bit key, and the encryption/decryption process uses eight rounds with six 16-bit subkeys per round. The IDEA algorithm is patented both in the US and in Europe, but free non-commercial use is permitted.

AES (Rijndael)

AES is the successor to DES. AES (Rijndael) is a successor to 3DES that supports variable key lengths from 128-bit, 192-bit, and 256-bit. Like 3DES, it is a symmetric, cipher block algorithm. It can be used to replace 3DES or DES in an IPsec transform set. AES characteristics include:

- Private key symmetric block cipher (similar to DES).
- Stronger and faster then 3DES.
- Life expectancy of at least 20 to 30 years.
- Key sizes of 128-bits, 192-bits, and 256-bits.
- Royalty free, non-proprietary and unpatented.

AES was selected by NIST as the DES successor in October 2000 because of its high performance in both hardware and software implementations and its small memory requirement. The Rijndael algorithm is resistant to power- and timing-based attacks.

AES/Rijndael works by using iterative rounds like IDEA. Data is operated on in 128-bit chunks, which are grouped into four groups of 4 bytes each. The number of rounds is also dependent on the key size, such that 128-bit keys have 9 rounds, 192-bit keys have 11 rounds and 256-bit keys require 13 rounds. Each round consists of a substitution step of one S-box per data bit followed by a pseudo-permutation step in which bits are shuffled between groups. Then each group is multiplied out in a matrix fashion and the results are added to the subkey for that round.

Understanding Asymmetric Algorithms

Asymmetric algorithms require more than one key, usually a *public* key and a *private* key (systems with more than two keys are possible). Asymmetric algorithms rely on massively large integer mathematics problems. Many of these problems are simple to do in one direction but difficult to do in the opposite direction. For example, it is easy to multiply two numbers together, but it is more difficult to factor them back into the original numbers, especially if the integers you are using contain hundreds of digits. Security of asymmetric algorithms is dependent on the feasibility of performing difficult mathematical inverse operations and advances in mathematical theory that may propose new "shortcut" techniques.

DH

The DH algorithm is for key exchange and not intended for use as a general encryption scheme. It is concerned with transmitting a private key for DES (or some similar symmetric algorithm) across an insecure medium. DH, being 10 to 1000 times slower than DES, is not used for encrypting a complete message.

Key exchange using DH works as follows:

- The two parties agree on two numbers; one is a large prime number, the other is an integer smaller than the prime.
- Each of the two parties separately generates another number, which they keep secret. This number is equivalent to a private key. A calculation is made involving the private key and the previous two public numbers. The result is sent to the other party. This result is effectively a public key.
- The two parties exchange their public keys. They then privately perform a calculation involving their own private key and the other party's public key. The resulting number is the session key. Each party will arrive at the same number.
- The session key can be used as a secret key for another cipher, such as DES. No third party monitoring the exchange can arrive at the same session key without knowing one of the private keys.

The most difficult part of the DH key exchange to understand is that there are actually two separate and independent encryption cycles happening. Only a small message is being transferred between the sender and the recipient. It just so happens that this small message is the secret key needed to unlock the larger message. Knowledge of the public key does not compromise the message. Both the public and private keys are actually just very large integers. The algorithm is in wide use, most notably in the IPsec protocol.

RSA

RSA shares many similarities with the DH algorithm in that RSA is also based on multiplying and factoring large integers. However, RSA is significantly faster than DH, leading to a split in the asymmetric cryptography field that refers to DH and similar algorithms as Public Key Distribution Systems (PKDS) and RSA and similar algorithms as PKE. PKDS systems are used as session-key exchange mechanisms, while PKE systems are generally considered fast enough to encrypt reasonably small messages. However, PKE systems like RSA are not considered fast enough to encrypt large amounts of data such as entire file systems or high-speed communications lines.

RSA, DH, and other asymmetric algorithms use much larger keys than their symmetric counterparts. Common key sizes include 1024 bits and 2048 bits; the keys need to be this large because factoring, while still a difficult operation, is much easier to perform than the exhaustive key search approach used with symmetric algorithms.

The RSA algorithm has been in the public domain since RSA Security placed it there two weeks before the patent expired in September 2000. It is now freely available for use by anyone, for any purpose. It commonly used in applications such as PGP and SSH. In fact, you can download a freeware version of PGP from www.pgpi.org/products/pgp/versions/freeware if you want to experiment and learn more about PKE.

Skeme and Oakley Protocols

The Oakley protocol describes a series of key exchanges, called *modes,* and details the services provided by each (for example, perfect forward secrecy for keys, identity protection, and authentication). The Skeme protocol describes a versatile key exchange technique that provides anonymity, reputability, and quick key refreshment. Their relationship to Internet Security Association and Key Management Protocol (ISAKMP) is fairly straightforward: where Oakley defines modes of exchange, ISAKMP defines phases of when each is applied.

IPsec Concepts

The security architecture for IP (IPsec) is a suite of security services for traffic at the IP layer. It is an open standard, defined in RFC 2401 and several following RFCs. IPsec was developed by the IETF as part of IPv6 and can be implemented in IPv4. IPsec is a framework of open standards that operates at Layer 3 of the OSI model, which means that it can protect communications from the network layer (IP) and up.

IPsec protocols can supply access control, authentication, data integrity, and confidentiality for each IP packet between two participating network nodes. IPsec can be used between two hosts (including clients), a gateway and a host, or two gateways. IPsec establishes a secure tunnel between endpoints, and provides authentication and encryption services to protect transported data.

IPsec provides two security protocols used for transferring data: Encapsulating Security Payload (ESP) and Authentication Header (AH). AH provides connectionless integrity, data origin authentication, and anti-replay service for the IP packet. AH does not encrypt the data, but any modification of the data would be detected. ESP provides confidentiality through the encryption of the payload. Access control is provided through the use and management of keys to control participation in traffic flows.

The only required encryption algorithm in an IPsec implementation is DES, which is defined in RFC 1829. DES is considered inadequate protection and is being phased out in favor of stronger encryption such as 3DES, AES, and Blowfish. To provide authentication features, IPsec uses the two algorithms HMAC-SHA-1 and HMAC-MD5.

A security association (SA) is the agreement between two systems participating in an IPsec connection. A SA represents a simplex connection to provide a security service using a selected policy and keys, between two nodes. A Security Parameter Index (SPI), an IP destination address, and a protocol identifier are used to identify a particular SA.

The SPI is an arbitrary, 32-bit value selected by the destination system that uniquely identifies a particular SA among several associations that may exist on a specific node. The protocol identifier can indicate either AH or ESP, but not both. Separate SAs are created for each protocol, and for each direction between systems. If two systems were using AH and ESP in both directions, then they would form four SAs.

VPN Terminology

The follow technologies and mechanisms are integral to IPsec operations.

- **Transform-Set** Defines IPsec protocols to use for authentication and/or encryption.
- **Crypto Map** Binds transform set, the peer, and the data to be encrypted.
- **Dynamic Crypto Map** A crypto map before information is provided by the peer.
- **ISAKMP** The framework for policy negotiations and key management.
- **Internet Key Exchange (IKE)** Authenticates IPsec peers negotiates IKE and IPsec SAs. Also, it establishes keys for encryption algorithms used by IPsec.
- **MD5** The algorithm used to hash keys and pass the hash instead of passing the key or password. Hash algorithm used to authenticate packet data.
- **SHA-1** The algorithm used to hash keys and pass the hash instead of passing the key or password. The hash algorithm used to authenticate packet data.
- **AH** Data authentication and integrity for IP packets passed between two different systems, but not data confidentiality. Applies a keyed one-way hash function to the packet to create a message digest.
- **ESP** Data confidentiality, data origin authentication, integrity, and optional anti-replay. Encrypts the packet payload and/or authentication packets.
- **DES** Employs a 56-bit key to encrypt and decrypt packet data.
- **3DES** A variant of the 56-bit DES. Data is broken into 64-bit blocks and processed three times with three unique 56-bit keys.
- **DH** Public key cryptography protocol that allows two parties to establish a shared secret key used by encryption algorithms over some type of insecure channel.

- **RSA Signatures** Public key cryptographic system used for authentication.
- **Certificate Authorities (CA)** Digital identification card to each querying device.

IPsec

IPsec's main design goals are to provide the follow functionality:

- **Data Confidentiality** Encrypt packets before transmitting them across a network so only the communicating peers can read it.
- **Data Integrity** Authenticate packets sent by the IPsec sender to ensure the data has not been altered during transmission. Each peer can determine if a received packet was changed during transit.
- **Data Origin Authentication** Authenticate the source of the IPsec packets sent. The receiver can check the identity of a packet's sender.
- **Antireplay** The receiver can detect and reject replayed packets, protecting it from spoofing and MITM attacks.

IPsec Core Layer 3 Protocols: ESP and AH

ESP and AH are the main IPsec protocols used to protect data. Applying AH or ESP to an IP packet modifies its contents to varying degrees, from the header to the payload. An extra header is inserted between the IP header and the packet contents. See Figures 7.31 and 7.32 for illustrations of how these transformations are performed. AH provides no confidentiality because no encryption is used.

NOTE

AH is *always* broken by NAT.

Figure 7.31 AH Encapsulation

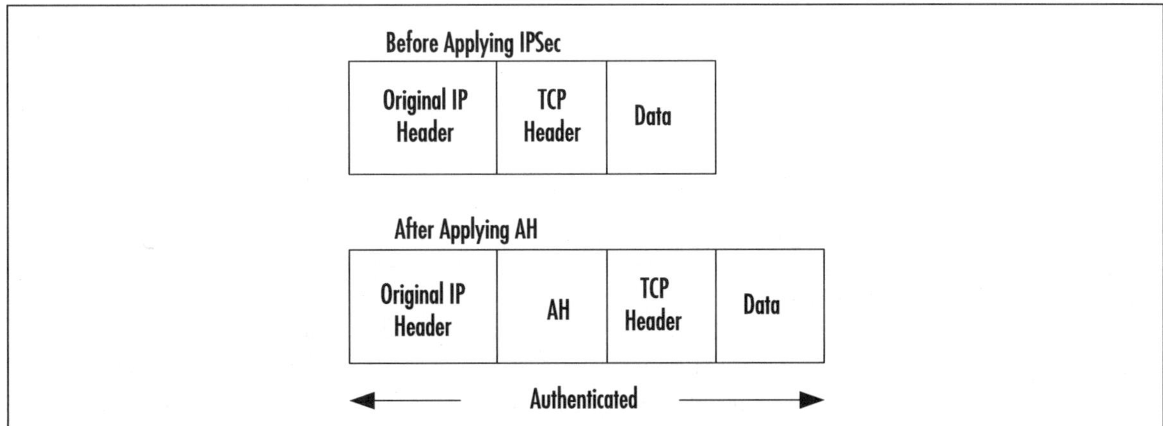

Figure 7.32 ESP Encapsulation

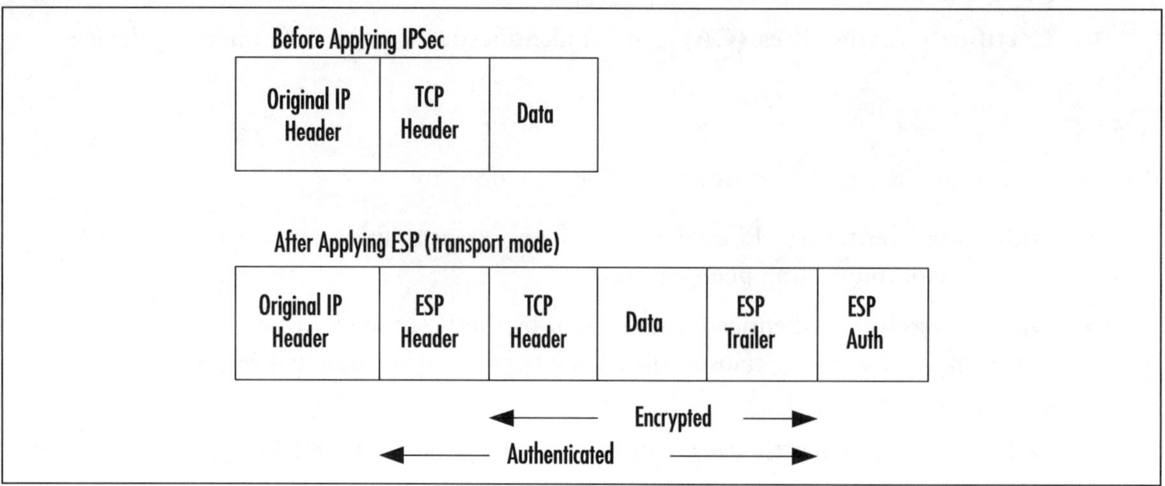

AH

The AH (RFC2402) provides packet authentication and anti-replay services. AH can be deployed in either **transport** or **tunnel** mode. In transport mode, the AH is inserted after the IP header and before an upper-layer protocol (such as TCP, UDP, and ICMP), or before any other previously inserted IPsec headers.

The AH (IP protocol 51) ensures:

- **Data Integrity** Calculates a hash of the entire IP packet, including the original IP header (not including variable fields such as the TTL), the data part of the packet, and the AH (excluding the field that will contain the calculated hash value) [either Message Authentication Code (MAC) or a digital signature]. MD5 or SHA-1 uses an extra value to calculate the hash (known only to the participating parties). The receiver performs calculations and compares to the sender's results: if they match, the packet is declared authentic.
- **Data Origin Authentication** The AH provides source IP authentication. Since the source IP is included in the data, its integrity is guaranteed.
- **Replay Protection** The AH uses an IPsec sequence number to protect against replay attacks.

In order to use Network Address Translation (NAT), you need to configure static NAT translations. This is due to AH being incompatible with NAT because NAT changes the source IP address. This, in turn, will break the AH header and cause the packets to be rejected by the IPsec peer or peers.

ESP

ESP (RFC2406) provides data encryption, data authentication, and optional anti-replay services. ESP can be used on its own or with AH packet authentication. ESP encapsulates the data and can be deployed in either transport or tunnel mode. In transport mode, ESP is placed after the IP header (and any options that it contains), and before the upper layer protocol. This makes ESP and AH compatible with non-IPsec-compliant routers.

Tunnel mode ESP may be employed in either hosts or security gateways. In tunnel mode, ESP protects the entire inner IP packet, including the entire inner IP header. The position of ESP in tunnel mode relative to the outer IP header is the same as for ESP in transport mode.

ESP (IP protocol 50) features:

- Pads a packet to prevent traffic analysis, and encrypts the result with ciphers such as DES, 3DES, AES, or Blowfish.
- Optional authentication using the same algorithms as the AH protocol. Header information is not included in the authenticated data, which allows ESP-protected packets to pass through NAT. Authentication data is calculated after encryption.
- Optional antireplay features.

ESP can perform most of AH's functions. ESP works on encapsulation principles: all data is encrypted and then placed between a header and a trailer. This differentiates it from AH, where only a header is created.

IPsec Communication Modes: Tunnel and Transport

IPsec has a transport mode and a tunnel mode. Transport mode only affects the data payload and does not modify the original IP header. In transport mode, the AH or ESP header is inserted after the IP header, but before any upper-layer protocol headers.

Tunnel mode encapsulates the entire original packet as the data portion of a new packet with its own IP header. (AH and/or ESP headers are created in both modes.) Transport mode is used when both the receiver and the sender are endpoints of the communication (for example, two hosts communicating directly to each other). Tunnel mode is more convenient for site-to site VPNs because it allows tunneling of traffic through the channel established between two gateways.

Transport Mode

Transport will place an AH or ESP header right after the original IP header and before upper-layer data (TCP header and application data). If ESP is applied to the packet, only this upper-layer data is encrypted. If optional ESP authentication is used, only upper-layer data, not the IP header, is authenticated. If AH is applied to the packet, both the original IP header and the upper-layer data are authenticated. Figure 7.33 shows what happens to the packet when IPsec is applied in transport mode.

Figure 7.33 Packet Structure in Transport Mode

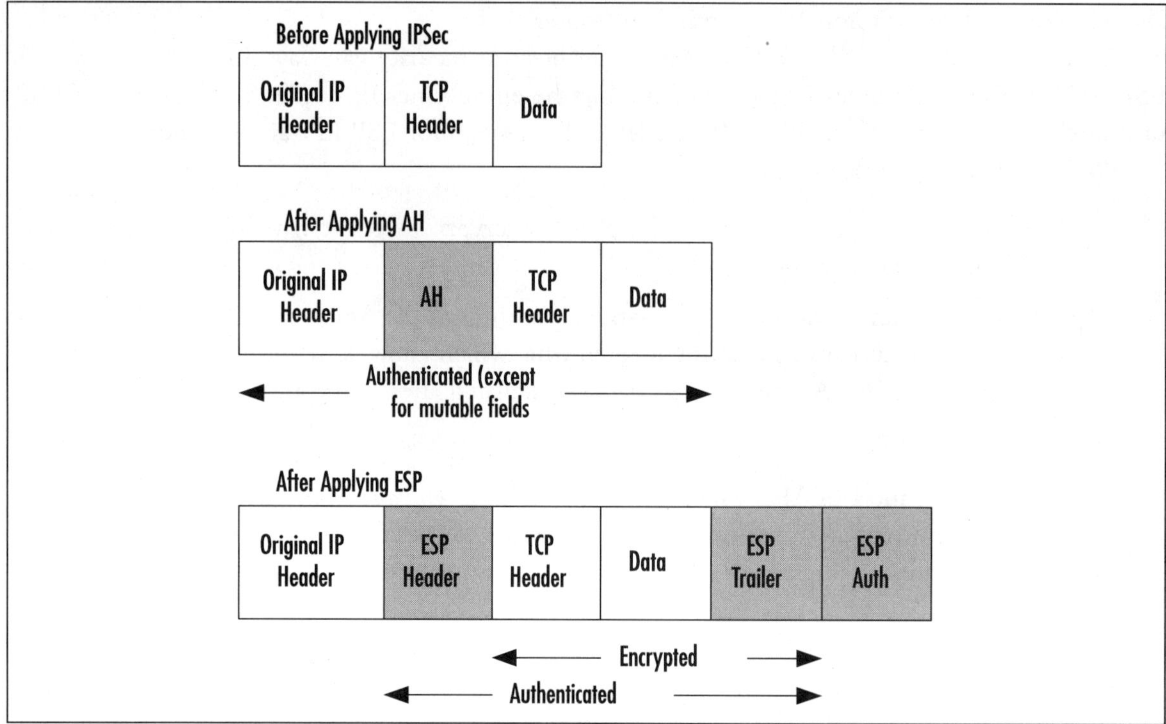

AH authenticates the original IP header, but does not protect the fields that are modified in the course of routing IP packets. ESP only protects what comes after the ESP header. If the security policy between two nodes requires a combination of security services, the AH header appears first after the IP header, followed by the ESP header. This combination of SAs is called an *SA bundle*.

Tunnel Mode

Tunnel mode, the most common mode of operation, allows the establishment of an encrypted and authenticated IP tunnel between two sites. The original packet is encrypted and/or authenticated and encapsulated as the data payload of a new IP packet. The new IP header is added to it with the destination address of the receiving gateway. The ESP and/or AH header is inserted between this new header and the data portion. The receiving gateway performs decryption and authentication of the packet, extracts the original IP packet (including the original source/destination IPs), and forwards it to the destination network. Figure 7.34 demonstrates the encapsulation performed in tunnel mode.

Figure 7.34 Packet Structure in Tunnel Mode

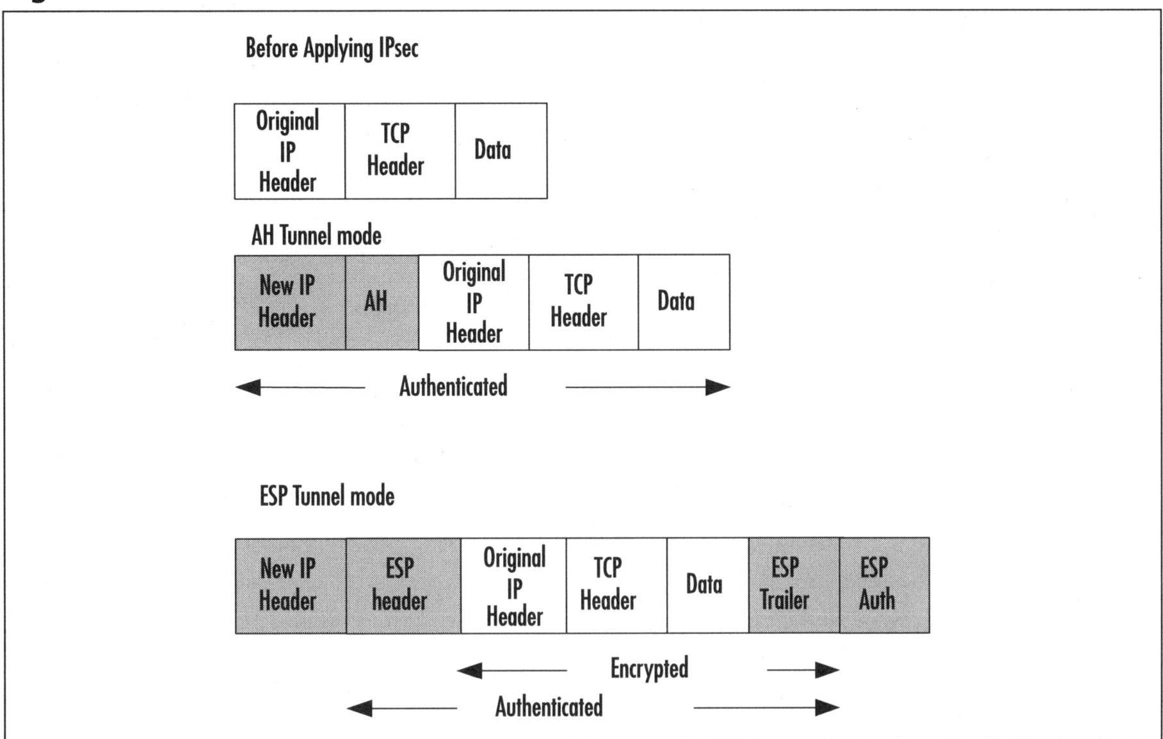

If the AH is used, both the original IP header and the new IP header are protected (authenticated), but if ESP is used, even with the authentication option, only the original IP address, not the sending gateway's IP address, is protected. This behavior makes it difficult to spoof an IPsec packet without knowing many technical parameters. The exclusion of the new IP header from authenticated data also allows tunnels to pass through devices that perform NAT. When the new header is created, most of the options from the original IP header are mapped onto the new one—for example, the ToS field.

In tunnel mode, the original IP header and payload are encapsulated by the IPsec protocols. A new IP header that specifies the IPsec tunnel destination is prepended to the packet. The original IP header and its payload are protected by the AH or ESP headers. In Figure 7.34, you can see that, as in transport mode, AH offers some protection for the entire packet, but does not protect the fields that are modified in the course of routing IP packets between the IPsec tunnel endpoints. It does, however, completely protect the original IP header.

IPsec Architecture

In simplified terms, IPsec provides three main functions:

- Authentication only, provided through the AH protocol
- Authentication and confidentiality (encryption), provided through the ESP protocol
- Key exchange, provided either manually or through the IKE protocol

IPsec provides secure communications between two endpoints (IPsec peers). These communications are essentially sets of SAs and define which protocols should be applied to sensitive packets, as well as the keying between the two peers. Multiple IPsec tunnels can exist between two peers, securing different data streams, with each communication having a separate set of SAs.

IKE

IKE is a key management protocol used in IPsec to create an authenticated, secure communication channel between two entities and then negotiate the SAs for IPsec. IKE offers several advantages over manually defined keys (manual keying):

- Eliminates manual configuration of keys
- Allows you to specify a lifetime for IPsec SA
- Allows encryption keys to change during IPsec sessions
- Supports the use of public key-based authentication and CAs
- Allows dynamic authentication of peers

ISAKMP and IKE

ISAKMP (RFC 2408) describes authenticated key exchange methods. This is a generic protocol and is not tied to IPsec or any other key-using protocol. It can be implemented directly over IP or any transport layer protocol. When partially combined with Oakley (RFC 2412) and Secure Key Exchange Mechanism (SKEME) key exchange protocols, the result is the IKE (RFC 2409). Although not strictly correct, the terms IKE and ISAKMP are often used interchangeably, even in Cisco where IKE is configured with the **isakmp** command.

IKE negotiates in two phases, both of which use UDP port 500.

1. **Phase 1** Peers negotiate and set up a secure, authenticated, bi-directional ISAKMP SA to handle Phase 2 negotiations. One such SA between a pair of peers can handle negotiations for multiple IPsec SAs. The peers agree on the encryption algorithm, hash algorithm, authentication method, and DH group to exchange keys and information.

   Peers mutually authenticate, agree on encryption and authentication algorithms to protect subsequent IKE traffic, exchange keys via DH, and lastly, establish an IKE SA (SA). IKE SAs are bi-directional; each IKE connection between peers has only one IKE SA associated with it.

2. **Phase 2** Peers negotiate IPsec (ESP and/or AH) as required. IPsec SAs are unidirectional (a different key is used in each direction) and are always negotiated in pairs to handle two-way traffic. There may be more than one pair defined between two peers. They agree on the IPsec protocol, hash algorithm, and encryption algorithm. Multiple SAs will result from Phase 2 negotiations. An SA is created for the inbound and outbound of each protocol used.

IKE Phase 2 negotiates one or more IPsec SAs to be used for the IPsec tunnel between these peers. It uses key material from IKE Phase 1 to derive IPsec keys. The initiating peer identifies what traffic it wants to protect and what encryption/authentication algorithms it supports. The receiving peer then agrees on a single protection set for this traffic and establishes keys needed for this protection set.

NOTE

Do not confuse IPsec SAs with IKE SAs. IKE SAs create the tunnel used by IPsec SAs. There is only one IKE SA between two devices, but there can be multiple IPsec SAs for the same IKE SA.

While having different phases adds some overhead in processing, there are advantages to this approach:

- Trust between peers is established in IKE Phase 1 and IKE Phase 2.
- Key material established in the first phase can be used in the second phase.
- Renegotiations of the first phase can be assisted by the second-phase data.

IKE Phase 1 has two modes: main mode and aggressive mode. Main mode uses three exchanges between peers; each exchange consists of two messages, a request, and a reply for a total of six packets exchanged.

- **First Exchange** Negotiates the parameters for protection of the IKE connection. Initiator sends a proposition that includes one encryption algorithm (DES, 3DES, and so on) and one authentication algorithms (pre-shared secret, RSA PKE with DH exchange group 1 and 2, or public key RSA signature (certificates). The receiver selects a pair that it can support; otherwise, no agreement means that the IKE tunnel cannot be established.

- **Second Exchange** DH key establishment between peers with exchange of **nonces** (hashes that only the other peer can interpret) , which confirm the message was sent by the same host of the previous exchange.
- **Third Exchange** Authentication of the peers using the agreed-on methods: public keys signatures, PKE, or a pre-shared secret. Protected by an encryption method selected in the first exchange.

At the end of the first phase, each host has an IKE SA, which specifies all parameters for this IKE tunnel: the authentication method, the encryption and hashing algorithm, the DH group used, the lifetime for this IKE SA, and the key values.

Aggressive mode exchanges only three packets. The first two packets in this exchange include almost everything in one message; each host sends a proposed protection set, DH values and authentication values. The third packet is for confirmation after the IKE SA is already established. Everything travels on the wire in cleartext and can be eavesdropped on or spoofed, though the only effective attack is an DOS to one of the peers.

Phase 2 quick mode is repeated several times using the same IKE SA established in Phase 1. Each exchange results in the establishment of two IPsec SAs by each peer. One is used for inbound protection, and the other for outbound protection. During the exchange, peers agree on the IPsec SA parameters and send each other a new nonce deriving DH keys from the ones established in Phase 1. When the IPsec SA lifetime expires, a new SA is negotiated in the same manner. Figure 7.35 summarizes the flow of the IKE protocol. Phase 2 Quick Mode can use Perfect Forward Secrecy (PFS) that uses encryption keys not derived from previous ones. PFS is achieved by performing a new DH key establishment in each quick mode.

Figure 7.35 IKE Phases and Modes

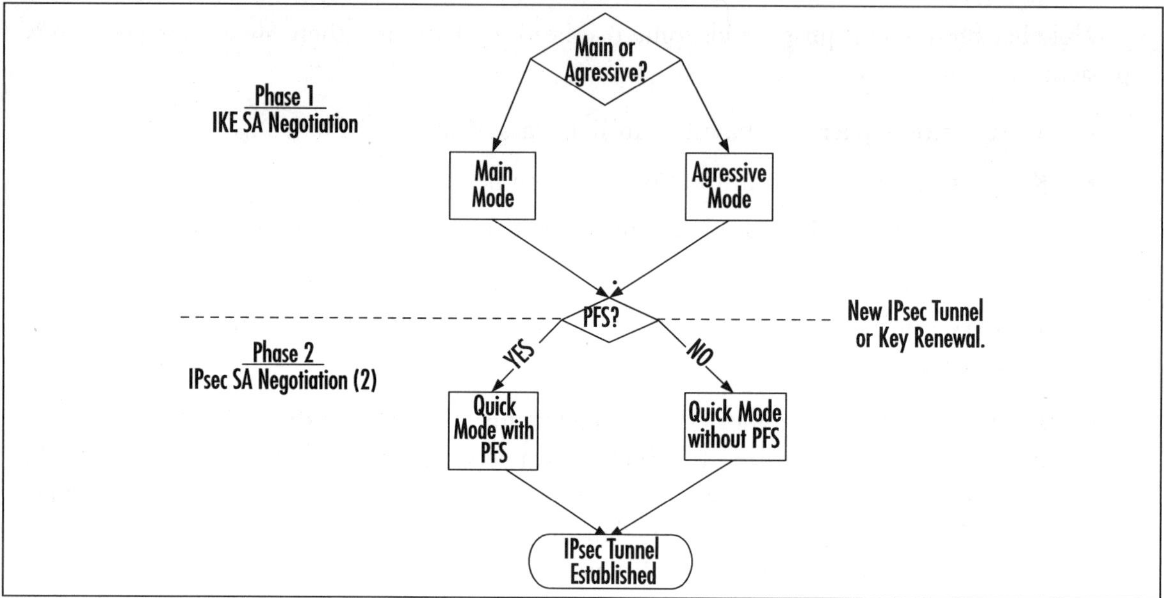

Another mode in Phase 2 is new group mode, which is not related to the setup of IPsec parameters and is used to change the parameters of the DH group used in IKE Phase 1.

SAs

IPsec SAs define how two or more IPsec peers will use security protocols (AH or ESP) to communicate securely on behalf of a particular flow. SAs contain the shared secret keys used to protect data in a particular flow, as well as their lifetimes. SAs are unidirectional connections and are unique per security protocol (AH or ESP). This means that if both AH and ESP services are required, two or more SAs have to be created. In a two-way communication, each party has at least two IPsec SAs: the sender and receiver each have one outgoing SA and one incoming SA, as shown in Figure 7.36.

Figure 7.36 IPsec SAs and Their use in Two-way Communication

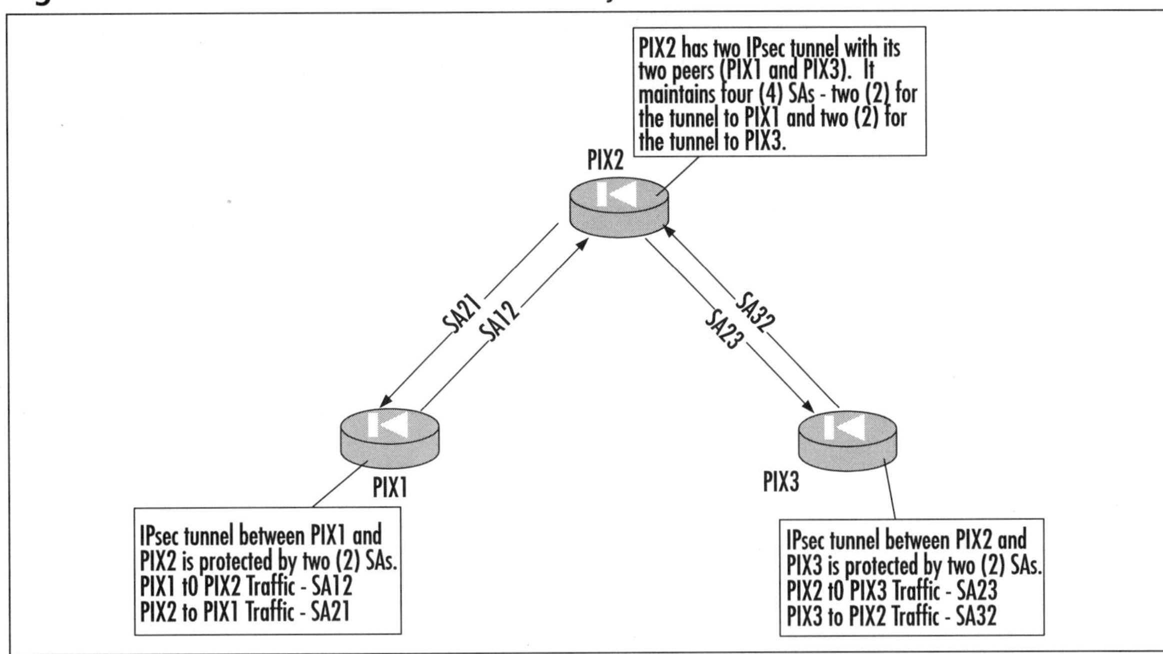

SAs can be created manually or with IKE. If created manually, the SAs are established as soon as they are created and do not expire. With IKE, SAs are established when needed and expire after a certain amount of time, or after a certain volume of traffic. The default lifetimes are 3600 seconds (one hour) and 4,608,000 kilobytes, and are periodically renegotiated.

Each SA can be uniquely identified by three parameters:

- **SPI** Pseudo-arbitrary 32-bit value assigned to a SA at creation. Both AH and ESP always contain a reference to an SPI. When SAs are manually created (IKE is not used), the SPI has to be manually specified for each SA.
- **IP Destination Address** The destination endpoint of the SA (host or network device).
- **Security Protocol Identifier** AH or ESP. SAs specify whether IPsec is used in transport or tunnel mode.
  - **Transport Mode SA:** Between two hosts.
  - **Tunnel Mode SA:** Between two gateways or between a gateway and a host.

Use the **show crypto IPsec security-association-lifetime** syntax to view the lifetimes of the SAs.

```
show crypto ipsec security-association-lifetime
Security association lifetime: 4608000 kilobytes/3600 seconds
```

Each peer maintains a Security Association Database (SAD) of active SAs for each direction (inbound and outbound) on each of its interfaces. SAs from these databases decide which encryption and authentication parameters are applied to packets. SAs may be fixed for the time of traffic flow (**manual IPsec**). When a key management protocol is used, they are renegotiated many times during the connection flow. For each SA, the SAD entry contains the following data:

- Destination address
- SPI
- IPsec transform (protocol and algorithm used—for example, AH, HMAC-MD5)
- Key used in the algorithm
- IPsec mode (tunnel or transport)
- SA lifetime (in kilobytes or in seconds); when this lifetime expires, the SA must be terminated, and a new SA established
- Anti-replay sequence counters
- Optional parameters such as Path MTU

The selection of encryption parameters and corresponding SAs is governed by another database, the Security Policy Database (SPD). An SPD is maintained for each interface and is used to decide:

- The selection of outgoing traffic to be protected
- Checking if incoming traffic was properly protected
- Tηε SAs to use for protecting this traffic
- What to do if the SA for this traffic does not exist

SPD specifies what security services are to be applied to IP packets and how, and distinguishes between protected and non-protected traffic. The SPD consists of a numbered list of policies, each associated with one or more selectors (ACLs). A **permit** statement means that IPsec should be applied to the matching traffic; a **deny** statement means that the packet should be forwarded and IPsec not applied. SPD policies are configured with the **crypto map** command. The resulting map and a crypto ACL are applied to the interface, creating an SPD for this interface.

For outgoing traffic, when the IPsec network stack layer receives data to be sent, it consults the SPD to determine if the traffic has to be protected. If it does, the SPD is used to recover a SA that corresponds to this traffic. If the SA exists, its characteristics are taken from the SAD and applied to the packet. If the SA does not exist yet, IKE is called upon to establish a new SA, and then the packet is protected with characteristics of this SA.

For incoming IPsec traffic, the SPI is recovered from the AH or ESP header, then used to find a corresponding SA in the SAD. If it does not exist, the packet is dropped. If an SA exists, the packet is checked/decrypted. The SPD is checked to ensure that this packet was correctly protected—for example, that it should have been encrypted using 3DES and authenticated with MD5 and nothing else. Figure 7.37 shows both sequences of events.

Figure 7.37 Processing of Outbound and Inbound Traffic by IPsec

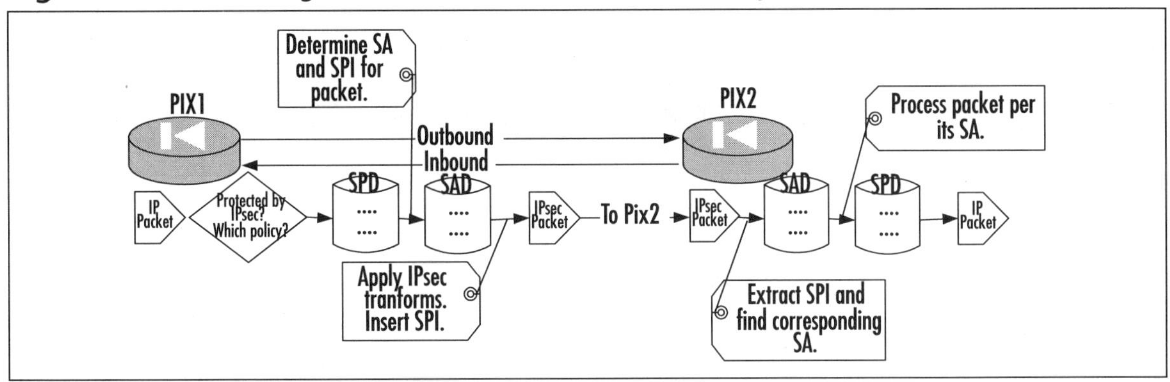

VPN Operation

There is often confusion over how IPsec, IKE, and ISAKMP work together to create a VPN. The flowchart in Figure 7.38 shows how they interoperate. Traffic entering the router is checked against an ACL associated with the crypto map applied to the ingress interface. A match triggers a check to determine if there is an IPsec SA with the peer for this traffic. If so, the traffic is encrypted and sent out the interface. If not, the router will check to see if it has an ISAKMP SA. If so, IKE will negotiate the IPsec keys and SAs necessary to encrypt and forward the traffic. If there is no ISAKMP SA, IKE will negotiate an IPsec SA, encrypt the data, and forward the traffic.

Figure 7.38 Interaction between IPsec, IKE, and ISAKMP

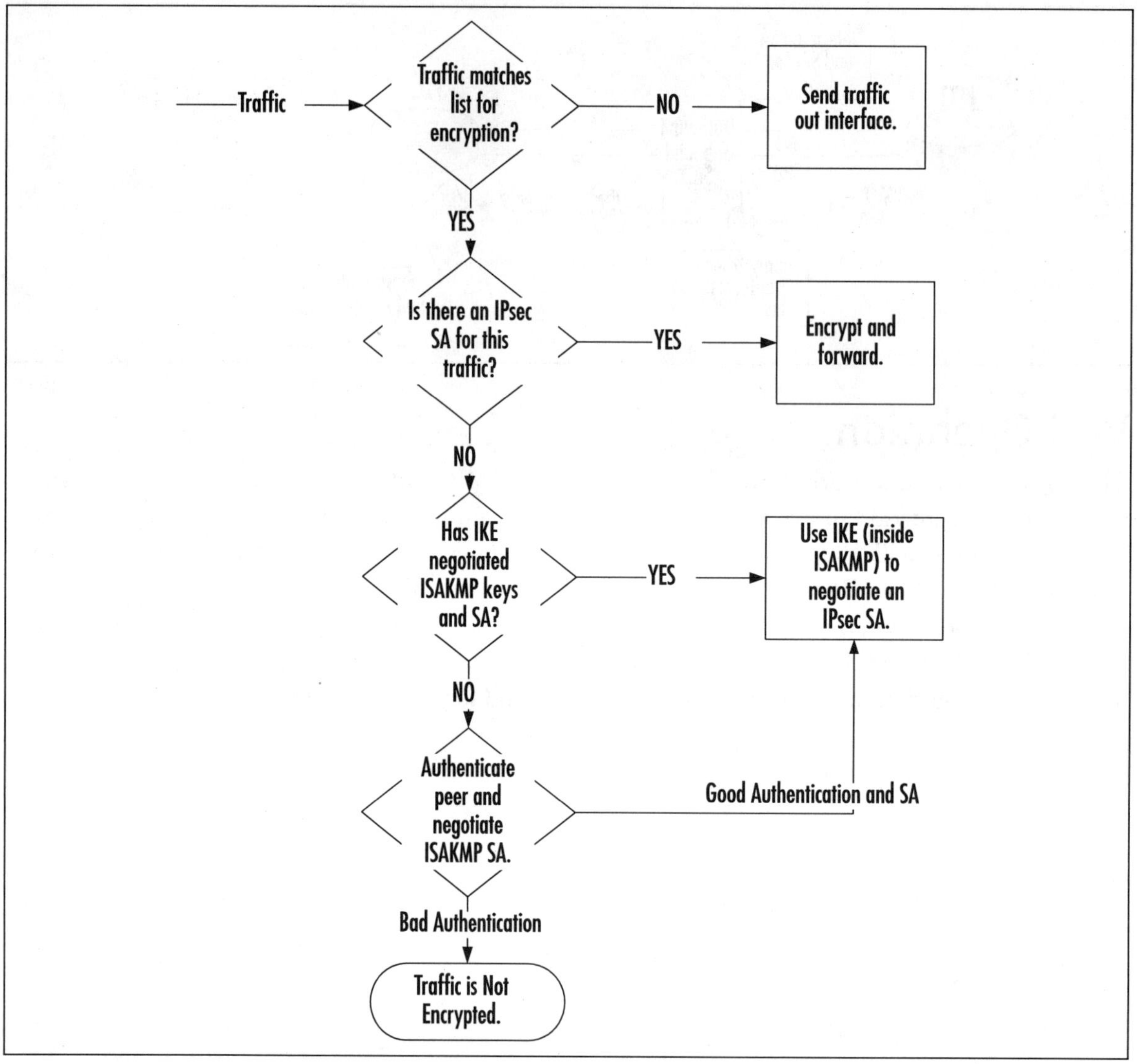

Traffic
Traffic matches list for encryption?
NO
Send traffic out interface.
YES
Is there an IPsec SA for this traffic?
YES
Encrypt and forward.
NO
Has IKE negotiated ISAKMP keys and SA?
YES
Use IKE (inside ISAKMP) to negotiate an IPsec SA.
NO
Authenticate peer and negotiate ISAKMP SA.
Good Authentication and SA
Bad Authentication
Traffic is Not Encrypted.

Authentication Methods

IPsec peers must negotiate and authenticate each other using a common authentication protocol. Multiple authentication methods are supported.

- **Preshared Keys** The same key is preconfigured on each peer. The peers authenticate each other by computing and sending a keyed hash of data that includes the preshared key. If the receiving side can independently re-create the same hash using its preshared key, it knows that both parties must share the same key.
- **PKE** Each party generates a pseudo-random number (nonce) and encrypts it in the other party's public key. The parties authenticate each other by computing a keyed hash

containing the other peer's nonce, decrypted with the local private key as well as other publicly and privately available information.

- **Digital Signatures** Each peer digitally signs a set of data and sends it to the other party. This method is similar to the public key cryptography one, except that it provides nonrepudiation (the ability for a third party to prove that a communication between the two parties took place).

Digital Certificates

When using digital certificates, each peer identifies itself by sending its name, its public certificate issued by a CA, and its RSA signature. A public key certificate contains a copy of the party's public key. The receiving party queries the same CA (of course, this CA should be trusted by the receiving party) to confirm that the certificate really belongs to the sender. If it does, the RSA signature is verified using the public key from the certificate, and the system's identity is verified. This scheme is easily scalable, especially in partial- or full-mesh environments. When a new peer is added to the IPsec network, the administrator only needs to enroll it with the CA and obtain a certificate from the CA.

To receive a certificate, a system must establish a trusted channel with the CA, generate a public/private key pair, and request a certificate. The CA then verifies the system's credentials somehow (usually using offline methods) and issues a certificate. A certificate can include the bearer's IP address, its name, the serial number of the certificate, the expiry date of the certificate, and a copy of the bearer's public key. The standard for the certificate format is X.509, of which Cisco supports version 3.

Cisco and VeriSign, Inc. co-developed a certificate management protocol called Certificate Enrollment Protocol (CEP), an early implementation of Certificate Request Syntax (CRS). CEP specifies how a device communicates with a CA, including how to retrieve the CA's public key, how to enroll a device with the CA, and how to retrieve a certificate revocation list (CRL). CEP uses RSA's public key cryptography standards (PKCS) 7 and 10 as key technologies. The IETF's Public Key Infrastructure (PKI) Working Group is working to standardize a protocol for these functions.

Figure 7.39 shows an example of multiple routers in a mesh topology where key management is not performed via a CA. Every time a new router is added, keys need to be created between each of the participating IPsec routers.

Figure 7.39 Management without Certificate Authority

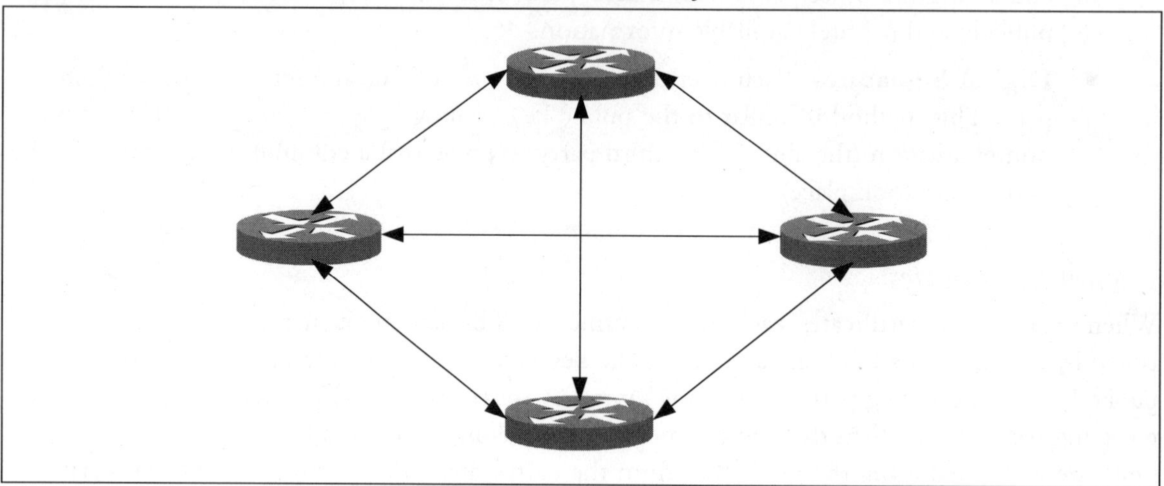

As an example, if you wanted to add an additional router to Figure 7.39, four additional two-part keys would be required to add just a single encryption router. The key's numbers grow exponentially as you add more routers and the configuration and management of these keys becomes problematic. A CA offers an ideal solution to such an environment. Figure 7.40 shows a typical scenario where key management is performed through a CA.

Figure 7.40 Key Management with CA

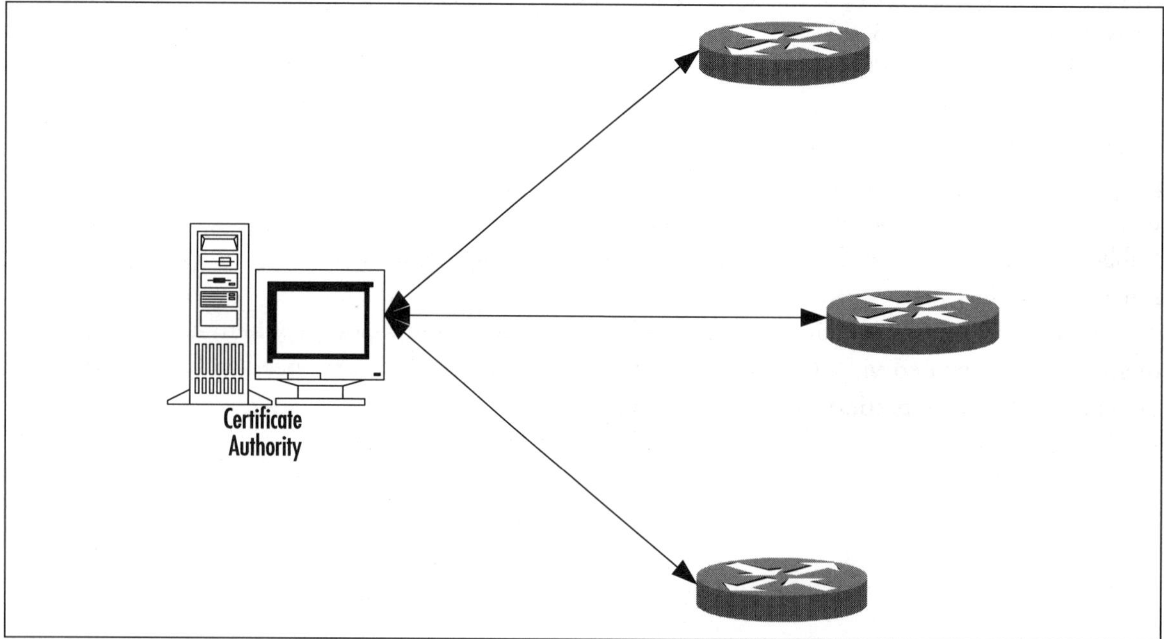

IPsec Limitations

One of the few limitations of IPsec is that it only supports unicast IP datagrams. No support for multicasts or broadcasts is currently provided. IPsec can have a significant impact on network performance. One of the drawbacks of network layer encryption is that it does complicate network troubleshooting and debugging. IDS sensors cannot analyze IPsec packets and determine if the packet contains any suspicious information.

Configuring ISAKMP/IKE

Unless you are doing manual IPsec, you should first configure ISAKMP policy to define the security parameters to be used in IKE negotiation. A peer must match one of the configured policies to begin negotiating the SA. No match, no SA, and therefore no VPN. Define and number an ISAKMP policy. Numbering enables you to have multiple policies and multiple peers. The lowest policy number takes precedence. In our example in Figure 7.41, we only need a single policy:

```
Central(config)# crypto isakmp policy 100
```

Determine the encryption protocol for data confidentiality (here we use DES):

```
Central(config-isakmp)# encryption des
```

Figure 7.41 Corporate to Branch Office VPN

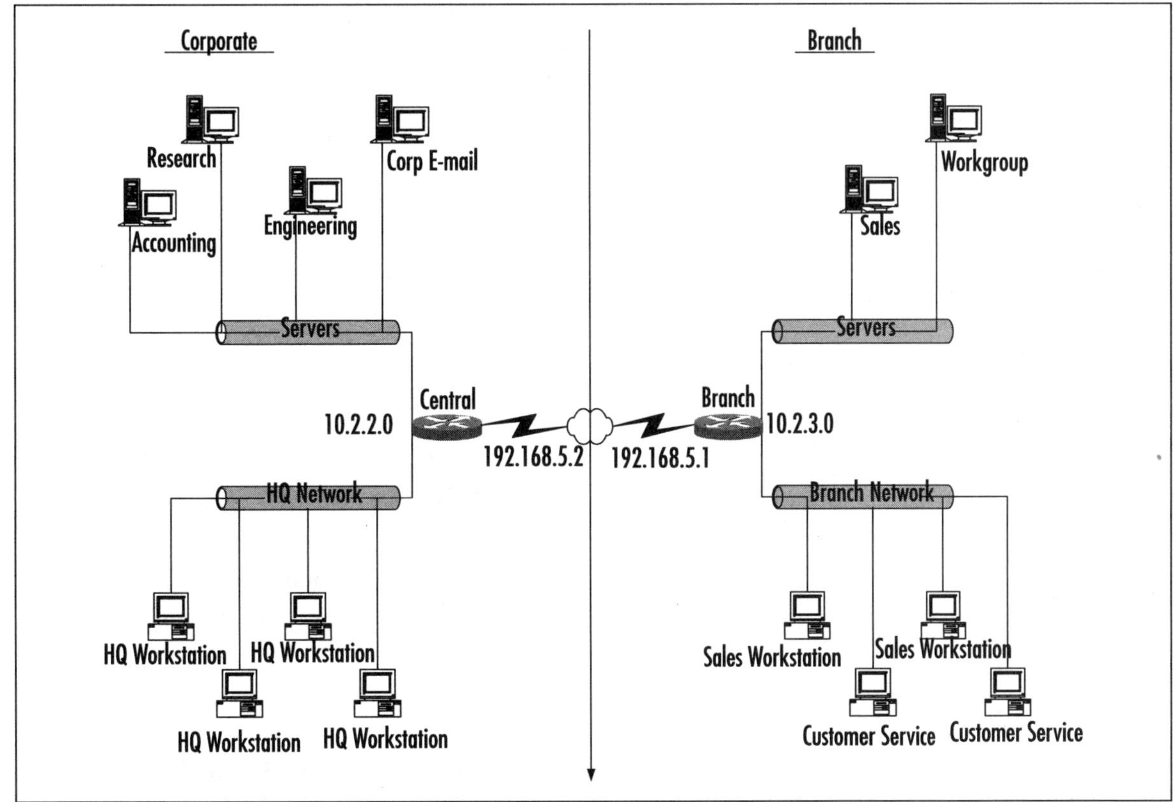

Define which hash algorithm to use. This could be MD5 or SHA.

```
Central(config-isakmp)# hash md5
```

Determine how the peers will authenticate each other. This can be done with pre-shared keys or digital certificates.

```
Central(config-isakmp)# authentication pre-share
```

Specify the DH 768-bit group identifier.

```
Central(config-isakmp)# group 1
```

Pre-shared keys require the identity of each peer: its hostname or IP address. The default is IP addresses for peer identity.

```
Central(config)# crypto isakmp identity address
```

Specify the pre-shared key and the identity (the IP address) of the encryption peer. The key will need to be the same on both ends.

```
Central(config-isakmp)# crypto isakmp key secretkey address 192.168.5.1
```

Verify the ISAKMP configuration.

```
Central router# show crypto isakmp policy
```

The **show crypto isakmp policy** displays the parameters of ISAKMP.

```
Protection suite of priority 100
encryption algorithm: DES - Data Encryption Standard (56 bit keys).
hash algorithm: Message Digest 5
Authentication method: Pre-Shared Key
Diffie-Hellman group: #1 (768 bit)
Lifetime: 86400 seconds, no volume limit
Default protection suite
encryption algorithm: DES - Data Encryption Standard (56 bit keys).
hash algorithm: Secure Hash Standard
authentication method: Rivest-Shamir-Adleman Signature
Diffie-Hellman group: #1 (768 bit)
lifetime: 86400 seconds, no volume limit
```

Next, configure the Branch router. The ISAKMP policy for the Branch router will be similar to the Central router. After we finish the ISAKMP parameters on both routers, we will move on to configuring IPsec.

Configuring IPsec

The first step in defining IPsec is to determine what traffic will be encrypted as specified in ACLs. These ACLs are used to define what traffic is encrypted/decrypted and what traffic is not. The crypto map references the ACL to IPsec and is applied to the interface.

Configure an ACL to define traffic that needs to be encrypted. You will configure a "mirror" ACL on the remote peer:

```
Central(config)# access-list 120 permit ip 10.2.2.0 0.0.0.255 10.2.3.0 0.0.0.255
```

Define a **transform set** that defines the authentication and encryption or data confidentiality you will use for IPsec. The first argument (**esp-md5-hmac**) defines the message hash for authentication; the second argument (**esp-des**) defines that the encryption will be 56-bit DES.

```
Central(config)# crypto ipsec transform-set MYSET esp-md5-hmac esp-des
```

Build the crypto map, which must contain compatible configurations between peers. Crypto map configurations are compatible if:

- Crypto map entries have "mirror" image ACLs, or in the case of a dynamic crypto map, the local crypto is permitted by the remote dynamic map.
- Crypto map entries properly identify the peer(s).
- Crypto map entries have at least one transform set in common between peers.

Name and number crypto maps identify the key negotiation and SA to be performed with ISAKMP:

```
Central(config)# crypto map MYMAP 2 ipsec-isakmp
```

Bind the previously defined ACL with the crypto map.

```
Central(config-crypto-map)# match address 120
```

Define the peer that we will be doing IPsec with:

```
Central(config-crypto-map)# set peer 192.168.5.1
```

Associate the transform set we want to use with the crypto map:

```
Central(config-crypto-map)# set transform-set MYSET
```

Apply it to the interface on the router.

```
Central(config)# interface serial0/1
Central(config-if)# crypto map MYMAP
```

Deploy a similar configuration on the Branch router.

To see your crypto map configuration on the Central router, issue the **show crypto map** command.

```
Central# show crypto map
Crypto Map "MYMAP" 2 ipsec-isakmp
Peer = 192.168.5.1
Extended IP access list 120
access-list 120 permit ip 10.2.2.0 0.0.0.255 10.2.3.0 0.0.0.255
Current peer: 192.168.5.1
Security association lifetime: 4608000 kilobytes/3600 seconds
PFS (Y/N): N
Transform sets={ MYSET, }
```

View the Branch router crypto map.

```
Central# show crypto map
Crypto Map "MYMAP" 2 ipsec-isakmp
Peer = 192.168.5.2
Extended IP access list 120
access-list 120 permit ip 10.2.3.0 0.0.0.255 10.2.2.0 0.0.0.255
Current peer: 192.168.5.2
Security association lifetime: 4608000 kilobytes/3600 seconds
PFS (Y/N): N
Transform sets={ MYSET, }
```

If you make changes to a crypto map, transform set, or any other item relating to your VPN, it may be necessary to issue the **clear crypto sa** command. This will clear the existing IPsec SAs so that renegotiation takes place and the changes are implemented immediately.

RAS VPN

Figure 7.42 shows a NAS providing access to the internal network using a dial-in connection. We do not want to pass information through the Public Switched Telephone Network (PSTN) unencrypted. The VPN tunnel will terminate on the asynchronous interface we use to dial in on. The VPN client is not limited to dial-up. It can be used across any type of network interface running TCP/IP. Let's begin our configuration on the NAS router.

Figure 7.42 Enterprise Dial-up VPN

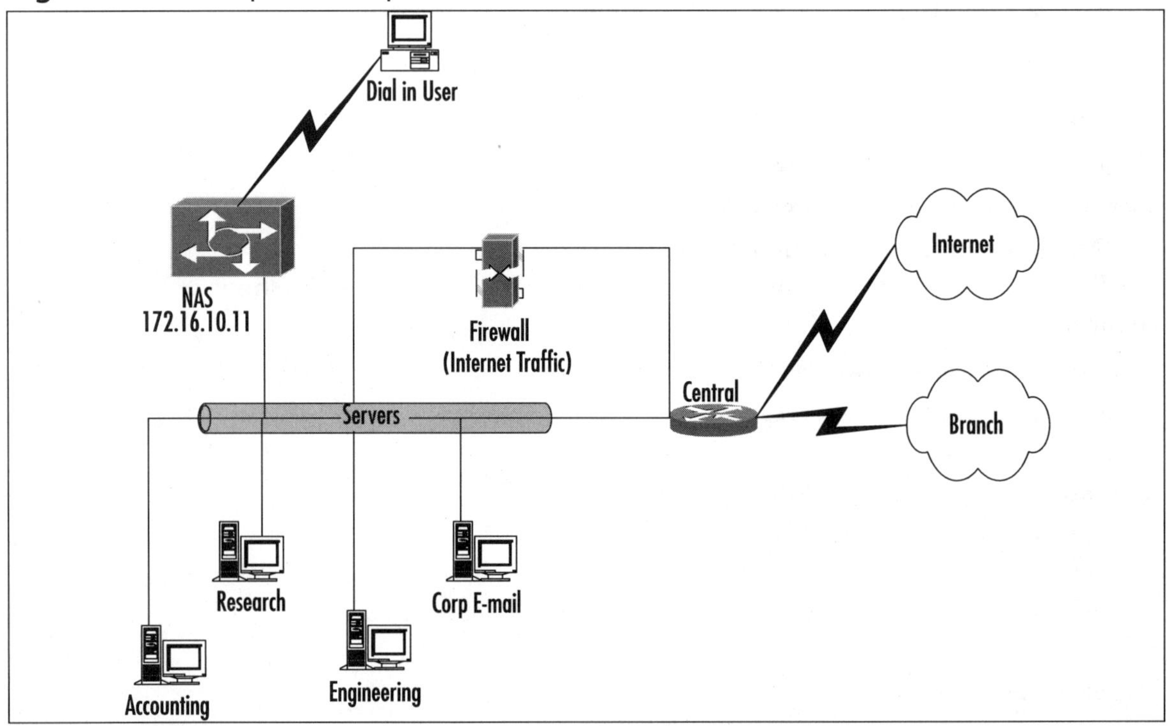

Configuring IPsec on the NAS

Create the IPsec transform set.

```
RouterNAS(config)# crypto ipsec transform-set vpnclient esp-des esp-shahmac
```

Create the ISAKMP policy.

```
RouterNAS(config)# crypto isakmp policy 100
RouterNAS(config-isakmp)# hash md5
RouterNAS(config-isakmp)# authentication pre-share
```

Configure a shared key and identify the peer.

```
RouterNAS(config)# crypto isakmp key dialclient address 10.1.1.1
```

Configure an ACL defining the traffic to be encrypted. This list will specify that any inside host with a destination of the VPN client (10.1.1.1) will get encrypted.

```
RouterNAS(config)# access-list 130 permit ip any host 10.1.1.1
```

Create a crypto map and associate the previous configurations.

```
RouterNAS(config)# crypto map dialclient 10 ipsec-isakmp
RouterNAS(config-crypto-map)# set peer 10.1.1.1
RouterNAS(config-crypto-map)# set transform-set vpnclient
RouterNAS(config-crypto-map)# match address 130
```

Apply the crypto map to the interface.

```
RouterNAS(config-if)# crypto map dialclient
```

Configure the VPN client as appropriate and establish your VPN to the NAS.

Configuring Cisco IPsec

The following examples show how IPsec can be used to encrypt and protect network traffic between two networks.

NOTE

When using ACLs or any form of filtering, remember that IKE uses UDP port 500 and IPsec ESP and AH use protocol numbers 50 and 51. These ports and protocols must not be blocked.

In very simplified terms IPsec is configured by:

1. Creating a SA (either manually or by using IKE)
2. Defining the SPD (ACLs that specify which traffic is to be secured)
3. Applying these ACLs to an interface by way of crypto map sets

IPsec Manual Keying Configuration

The following example (Figure 7.43) illustrates the use of IPsec Manual Keying to encrypt TCP/IP traffic between the 10.1.1.0/24 and 10.1.3.0/24 networks.

If a host on network 10.1.1.x wants to send a packet to a host on network 10.1.3.x, the packet from host 10.1.1.x is sent in cleartext to the Capetown router. The Capetown router uses the IPsec tunnel between the Capetown and London router to encrypt the packet and sends it to the London router that decrypts the packet and sends it to the host on network 10.1.3.*x* in cleartext.

NOTE

In IOS release 12.0, the crypto map statement **set security-association inbound**... has changed to **set session-key inbound**...

Figure 7.43 Network Diagram for IPsec Manual Keying

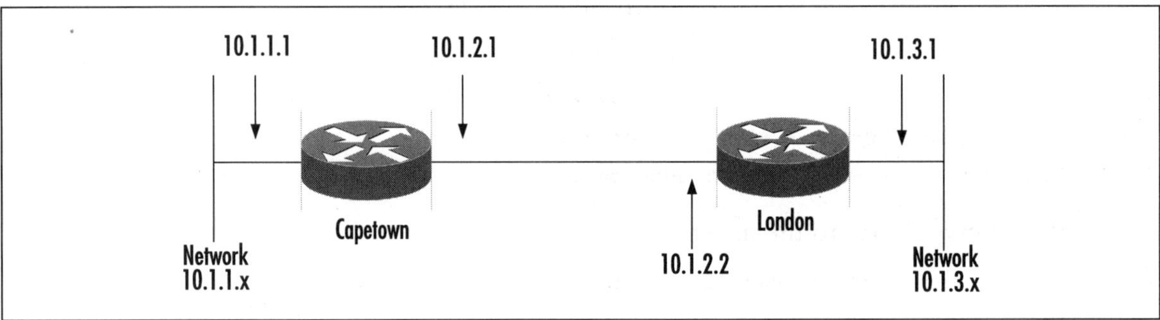


```
Capetown
no crypto isakmp enable
!
crypto ipsec transform-set encrypt-des esp-des
 !
 crypto map test 8 ipsec-manual
 set peer 10.1.2.2
 set security-association inbound esp 1000 cipher ****************
 authenticator 01
 set security-association outbound esp 1001 cipher ****************
 authenticator 01
 set transform-set encrypt-des
 match address 100
!
interface Serial0/0
 ip address 10.1.2.1 255.255.255.0
```

```
 no ip route-cache
 no ip mroute-cache
 crypto map test
!
interface Ethernet1/0
 ip address 10.1.1.1 255.255.255.0
!
access-list 100 permit ip 10.1.1.0 0.0.0.255 10.1.3.0 0.0.0.255
!

London
!
no crypto isakmp enable
!
crypto ipsec transform-set encrypt-des esp-des
!
 crypto map test 8 ipsec-manual
 set peer 10.1.2.1
 set security-association inbound esp 1001 cipher ****************  authenticator 01
 set security-association outbound esp 1000 cipher **************** authenticator 01
 set transform-set encrypt-des
 match address 100
!
interface Ethernet0/0
 ip address 10.1.3.1 255.255.255.0
!
interface Serial0/0
 ip address 10.1.2.2 255.255.255.0
 no ip route-cache
 no ip mroute-cache
 no fair-queue
 crypto map test
!
access-list 100 permit ip 10.1.3.0 0.0.0.255 10.1.1.0 0.0.0.255
```

To verify and debug the preceding example, use the **show crypto engine connections active** and **show crypto ipsec sa** commands.

```
capetown# show crypto engine connections active
ID  Interface   IP-Address   State   Algorithm    Encrypt  Decrypt
1   Serial0/0   10.1.2.1     set     DES_56_CBC   235      0
2   Serial0/0   10.1.2.1     set     DES_56_CBC   0        236
```

The **show crypto engine connections active** command shows active encryption connections for all crypto engines. Of particular interest are the encrypt counters that show encryption is working.

```
capetown# show crypto ipsec sa
interface: Serial0/0
    Crypto map tag: test, local addr. 10.1.2.1
   local  ident (addr/mask/prot/port): (10.1.1.0/255.255.255.0/0/0)
   remote ident (addr/mask/prot/port): (10.1.3.0/255.255.255.0/0/0)
   current_peer: 10.1.2.2
     PERMIT, flags={origin_is_acl,}
    #pkts encaps: 235, #pkts encrypt: 235, #pkts digest 0
    #pkts decaps: 236, #pkts decrypt: 236, #pkts verify 0
    #send errors 0, #recv errors 0
     local crypto endpt.: 10.1.2.1, remote crypto endpt.: 10.1.2.2
     path mtu 1500, media mtu 1500
     current outbound spi: 3E9
     inbound esp sas:
      spi: 0x3E8(1000)
        transform: esp-des ,
        in use settings ={Tunnel, }
        slot: 0, conn id: 2, crypto map: test
        no sa timing
        IV size: 8 bytes
        replay detection support: N
      inbound ah sas:
     outbound esp sas:
      spi: 0x3E9(1001)
        transform: esp-des ,
        in use settings ={Tunnel, }
        slot: 0, conn id: 1, crypto map: test
        no sa timing
        IV size: 8 bytes
        replay detection support: N
     outbound ah sas:
```

The **show crypto ipsec sa** command shows the settings used by current SAs. Of particular interest are local and remote crypto endpoints, the transform set used (encryption algorithm), and statistics of the packets encrypted and decrypted.

IPsec over GRE Tunnel Configuration

Figure 7.44 illustrates the use of IPsec over a GRE tunnel to encrypt non-IP-based traffic. In this example, Novell's Internetwork Packet Exchange (IPX) was used, but the same example holds true for other non-IP-based protocols such as AppleTalk. Please note that DES is no longer considered secure and wherever possible, a stronger cipher such as 3DES or AES should be used.

Figure 7.44 Network Diagram for IPsec over a GRE Tunnel

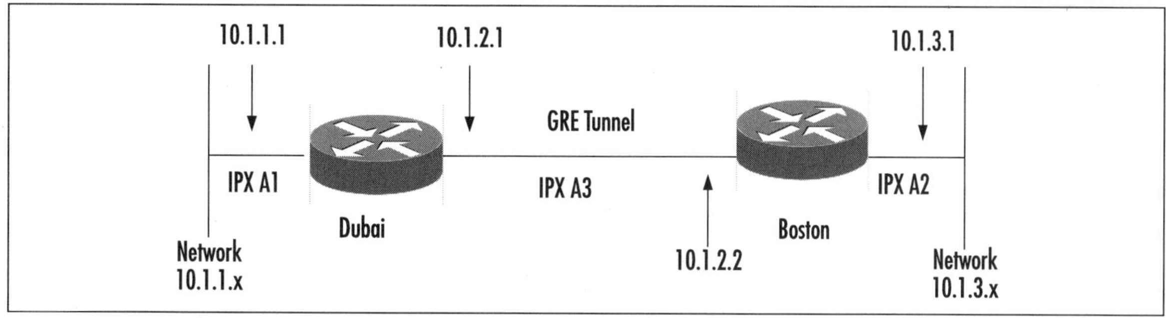


```
Dubai
crypto isakmp policy 10
 authentication pre-share
 group 2
 lifetime 3600
crypto isakmp key ****** address 10.1.5.1
!
crypto ipsec transform-set tunnelset esp-des esp-md5-hmac
!
 crypto map toBoston local-address Loopback0
 crypto map toBoston 10 ipsec-isakmp
 set peer 10.1.5.1
 set transform-set tunnelset
 match address 101
!
interface Loopback0
 ip address 10.1.4.1 255.255.255.0
!
interface Tunnel0
 no ip address
 no ip route-cache
 no ip mroute-cache
 ipx network A3
 tunnel source Serial0/0
 tunnel destination 10.1.2.2
```

```
 crypto map toBoston
!
interface Serial0/0
 ip address 10.1.2.1 255.255.255.0
 no ip route-cache
 no ip mroute-cache
 no fair-queue
 crypto map toBoston
!
interface Ethernet1/0
 ip address 10.1.1.1 255.255.255.0
 ipx network A1
!
access-list 101 permit gre host 10.1.2.1 host 10.1.2.2
!
Boston
!
crypto isakmp policy 10
 authentication pre-share
 group 2
 lifetime 3600
crypto isakmp key ****** address 10.1.4.1
!
crypto ipsec transform-set tunnelset esp-des esp-md5-hmac
!
 crypto map toDubai local-address Loopback0
 crypto map toDubai 10 ipsec-isakmp
 set peer 10.1.4.1
 set transform-set tunnelset
 match address 101
!
interface Loopback0
 ip address 10.1.5.1 255.255.255.0
!
interface Tunnel0
 no ip address
 no ip route-cache
 no ip mroute-cache
 ipx network A3
 tunnel source Serial0/0
```

```
 tunnel destination 10.1.2.1
 crypto map toDubai
!
interface Ethernet0/0
 ip address 10.1.3.1 255.255.255.0
 ipx network A2
!
interface Serial0/0
 ip address 10.1.2.2 255.255.255.0
 no ip route-cache
 no ip mroute-cache
 no fair-queue
 crypto map toDubai
!
access-list 101 permit gre host 10.1.2.2 host 10.1.2.1
!
```

To verify and debug the preceding example, use the **show crypto engine connections active** and **show crypto ipsec sa** commands.

```
dubai# show crypto engine connections active
ID    Interface    IP-Address    State   Algorithm           Encrypt  Decrypt
17    no idb       no address    set      DES_56_CBC          0        0
22    Tunnel0      unassigned    set     HMAC_MD5+DES_56_CB 0         20
23    Tunnel0      unassigned    set     HMAC_MD5+DES_56_CB 20        0
```

The **show crypto engine connections active** command displays all active encryption connections for all crypto engines. Of particular interest are the encrypt counters that show that the encryption is working.

Verifying and Debugging VPN Operation

You can verify and debug VPN operations using a combination of **debug** and **show** commands. The following commands will help you verify that the VPN is operating.

The **show crypto ipsec sa** command shows the SAs created for IPsec operation. It can be used to verify that the IPsec SA exists and that encryption is taking place.

```
show crypto ipsec sa
interface: Ethernet0
Crypto map tag: test1, local addr. 192.168.0.2
local ident (addr/mask/prot/port): (192.168.0.2/255.255.255.255/0/0)
remote ident (addr/mask/prot/port): (192.168.0.20/255.255.255.255/0/0)
```

You can see here that we have a peer and identify who the peer is.

```
current_peer: 192.168.0.20
```

```
PERMIT, flags={origin_is_acl,transport_parent,}
```

The following output shows us that we are encapsulating and encrypting outbound packets, as well as decapsulating and decrypting inbound packets. This verifies encryption operations and indicates that IPsec is operating between peers. This would be enough verification that a successful tunnel had been created.

```
#pkts encaps: 77, #pkts encrypt: 76, #pkts digest 76
#pkts decaps: 88, #pkts decrypt: 88, #pkts verify 88
#send errors 0, #recv errors 0
```

This shows us where your VPN tunnel is terminating locally, as well as the peer terminating point. You can also see the transform set in use and can tell that replay detection is on.

```
local crypto endpt.: 192.168.0.2, remote crypto endpt.: 192.168.0.20
path mtu 1500, media mtu 1500
current outbound spi: 1694080F
inbound esp sas:
spi: 0xF3F17E1(255793121)
transform: esp-des esp-sha-hmac ,
in use settings ={Transport, }
slot: 0, conn id: 2, crypto map: test1
sa timing: remaining key lifetime (k/sec): (4607998/57)
IV size: 8 bytes
replay detection support: Y
spi: 0x8CC2053(147595347)
[further output omitted....]
```

Another good indicator of successful VPN operations is the **show crypto engine connections** command. The following example shows both the command and the output it produces.

```
show crypto engine connections active
ID Interface IP-Address State Algorithm Encrypt Decrypt
46 Ethernet0 172.21.230.67 set HMAC_MD5+DES_56_CB 0 4
47 Ethernet0 172.21.230.67 set HMAC_MD5+DES_56_CB 4 0
```

Ethernet0 has an active crypto connection. It has encrypted and sent four packets and has decrypted four packets that it has received. In a single peer-to-peer VPN relationship, this would indicate that a good VPN operation is taking place. Using debug, we can see ISAKMP negotiates its own SA, then looks for and negotiates a matching IPsec transform set and does the IPsec SA.

```
debug crypto isakmp
20:26:58: ISAKMP (8): beginning Main Mode exchange
20:26:58: ISAKMP (8): processing SA payload. message ID = 0
```

ISAKMP starts trying to match ISAKMP policy. Once a policy match is made, the peers will begin the authentication phase, where they authenticate each other.

```
20:26:58: ISAKMP (8): Checking ISAKMP transform 1 against priority 10 policy
20:26:58: ISAKMP: encryption DES-CBC
20:26:58: ISAKMP: hash SHA
20:26:58: ISAKMP: default group 1
20:26:58: ISAKMP: auth pre-share
20:26:58: ISAKMP (8): atts are acceptable. Next payload is 0
```

IKE has found a compatible policy in the output above and will begin authenticating the peer in the output below.

```
20:26:58: ISAKMP (8): SA is doing pre-shared key authentication
20:26:59: ISAKMP (8): processing KE payload. message ID = 0
20:26:59: ISAKMP (8): processing NONCE payload. message ID = 0
20:26:59: ISAKMP (8): SKEYID state generated
20:26:59: ISAKMP (8): processing ID payload. message ID = 0
20:26:59: ISAKMP (8): processing HASH payload. message ID = 0
20:26:59: ISAKMP (8): SA has been authenticated
```

Now that the ISAKMP SA has been established, ISAKMP will begin negotiating IPsec transform sets and key exchange.

```
20:26:59: ISAKMP (8): beginning Quick Mode exchange, M-ID of 767162845
20:26:59: ISAKMP (8): processing SA payload. message ID = 767162845
20:26:59: ISAKMP (8): Checking IPsec proposal 1
20:26:59: ISAKMP: transform 1, ESP_DES
20:26:59: ISAKMP: attributes in transform:
20:26:59: ISAKMP: encaps is 1
20:26:59: ISAKMP: SA life type in seconds
20:26:59: ISAKMP: SA life duration (basic) of 600
20:26:59: ISAKMP: SA life type in kilobytes
20:26:59: ISAKMP: SA life duration (VPI) of 0x0 0x46 0x50 0x0
20:26:59: ISAKMP: authenticator is HMAC-MD5
20:26:59: ISAKMP (8): atts are acceptable.
```

ISAKMP has found a matching transform set and will begin negotiating the SA. A SA will be made in both directions: one for inbound IPsec traffic, and one for outbound traffic.

```
20:26:59: ISAKMP (8): processing NONCE payload. message ID = 767162845
20:26:59: ISAKMP (8): processing ID payload. message ID = 767162845
20:26:59: ISAKMP (8): processing ID payload. message ID = 767162845
20:26:59: ISAKMP (8): Creating IPsec SAs
20:26:59: inbound SA from 192.168.55.1 to 192.168.55.2 (proxy 192.168.55.1 to
192.168.55.2)
20:26:59: has spi 454886490 and conn_id 9 and flags 4
20:26:59: lifetime of 600 seconds
```

```
20:26:59: lifetime of 4608000 kilobytes
20:26:59: outbound SA from 192.168.55.2 to 192.168.55.1 (proxy 192.168.55.2 to
192.168.55.1)
20:26:59: has spi 75506225 and conn_id 10 and flags 4
20:26:59: lifetime of 600 seconds
20:26:59: lifetime of 4608000 kilobytes
```

Wireless Security

This section discusses the security options available to protect wireless communications. If you need a refresher on wireless technology, please read Chapter 3, which discusses wireless networking in great detail, as it enhances your understanding of wireless security.

Typically, wireless security is centered on the authentication of the wireless device, not on authenticating the user or station utilizing the wireless network. Public-key encryption is not used in the wireless encryption process. Although a few wireless vendors have dynamic keys that are changed with every connection, most wireless 802.11 vendors utilize shared-key authentication with static keys.

Shared key authentication is utilized by WEP functions with the following steps:

1. The station requests service by sending an authentication frame to its target AP.
2. The AP replies to the authentication frame with its own, which contains 128 octets of challenge text.
3. The station encrypts the challenge text with the shared encryption key and returns to the AP.
4. The AP decrypts the encrypted challenge with the shared key and compares it with the original challenge text. AP sends an acknowledgment to the station upon a match, otherwise, a negative acknowledgment is sent.

WEP does not authenticate the user or any resource the user might need to access. It is only a verification that the wireless client has the same shared secret key that the wireless AP has. Once authenticated, the client has full access to whatever devices and networks the AP is connected. You should use secure authentication methods to access these devices and prevent unauthorized access and use.

The IEEE 802.11 committee is working on 802.1x to provide a framework for 802-based networks authenticating from centralized servers. Cisco introduced Light Extensible Authentication Protocol (LEAP) authentication to their wireless products, which adds several enhancements to the 802.11 authentication system, including the following:

- Mutual authentication utilizing RADIUS.
- Securing the secret key with one-way hashes that make password reply attacks impossible.
- Force clients to re-authenticate more often, getting a new session key with each new session. This will help to prevent attacks where traffic is injected into the data stream.

- Changes to the initialization vector (IV) used in Wireless Encryption Protocol (WEP) encryption that make the current exploits of WEP ineffective.

Extensible Authentication Protocol

The Extensible Authentication Protocol (EAP) provides authentication within the PPP. EAP integrates third-party authentication packages that use PPP. EAP can support several authentication schemes, such as token cards, public keys, certificates, PINs, and on and on.

EAP will not select a specific authentication method at the Link Control Protocol (LCP) phase, but will wait until the Authentication phase. This allows the authenticator to request more information to decide the authentication method. This works with servers that can control authentication while the PPP authenticator passes through the authentication exchange.

APs do not need to understand each request type, because they will simply act as a conduit, or pass-through agent, for a server. The network device will only need to see if the packet has the success or failure code in order to terminate the authentication phase.

EAP defines one or more requests for peer-to-peer authentication. The request packet includes a type field, such as Generic Token, OTP, or an MD5 challenge. The MD5 challenge is very similar to the CHAP. EAP is able to provide a flexible, link-layer security framework (see Figure 7.45), by having the following features:

- EAP mechanisms are IETF standards–based and allow for the growth of new authentication types when your security needs change:
    1. Transport Layer Security (TLS)
    2. IKE
    3. GSS_API (Kerberos)
    4. Other authentication schemes (LEAP)
- No dependency on IP, because this is an encapsulation protocol.
- No windowing, as this is a simple ACK/NAK protocol.
- No support for fragmentation.
- Can run over any link layer (PPP, 802.3, 802.5, 802.11, and so on).
- Does not consider a physically secure link as an authentication method to provide security.
- Assumes that there is no reordering of packets.
- Retransmission of packets is the responsibility of the authenticator.

Figure 7.45 The EAP Architecture

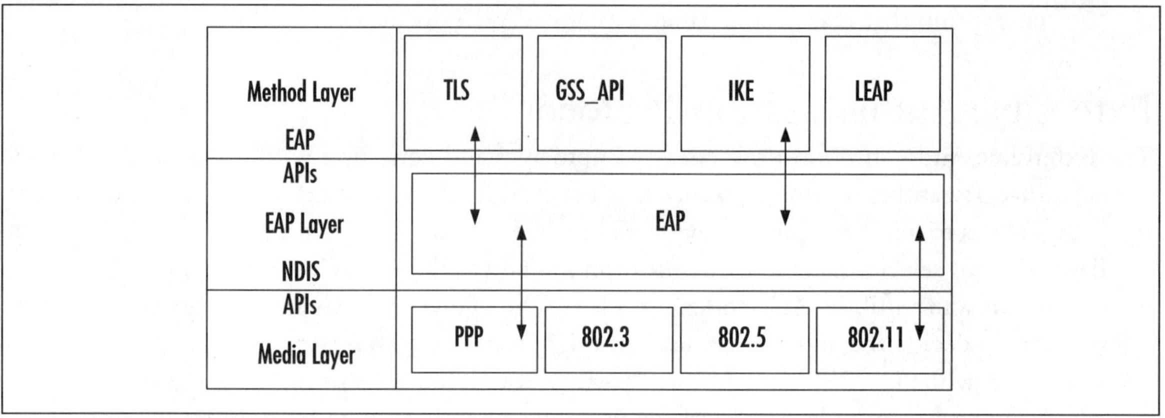

802.1x and EAP

By using the IEEE 802.1x standard, EAP, and Cisco LEAP as an end-to-end solution, you can provide enhanced functionality to your wireless network.

- EAP/LEAP allows all wireless clients to communicate with authentication servers such as RADIUS and TACACS+ servers.
- Implement the IEEE 802.1x standard for network access control that is port based for MAC filtering.

Wireless clients associated with APs will not be able to gain access to the network unless the user performs a network logon, after which the client and a RADIUS server will perform authentication, leading to the client being authenticated and access to the network and resources.

The RADIUS server and client device will receive a client-specific WEP key that is used by the client for that specific logon session. The user's password and session key will never be transmitted in the open.

Here is how authentication works and the WEP key is exchanged:

1. Wireless client will associate with an AP located on the wireless network.
2. AP will prevent all other attempts by that client to gain access until the client logs on to the network.
3. The client will supply a username and password for network logon.

Using the 802.1x standard and EAP/LEAP, the wireless client and a RADIUS server perform authentication through the AP. (If you are using LEAP, the RADIUS server will send an authentication challenge to the client.)

After authentication completes successfully, the following steps take place:

1. The RADIUS server and the client determine a WEP key that is unique for the client and that session.
2. The RADIUS server transmits this WEP key (session key) across the wired LAN to the AP.

3. The AP encrypts the broadcast key and the session key to send the new encrypted key to the client. The client will then use the session key to decrypt it.

The client and the AP activate the WEP. APs and clients will use the session and broadcast WEP keys for all communications that occur during the session. Session keys and broadcast keys are regularly changed at regular periods that are configured in the RADIUS server. This is graphically illustrated in Figure 7.46.

Figure 7.46 Cisco Security Solution using Session-based Encryption Keys

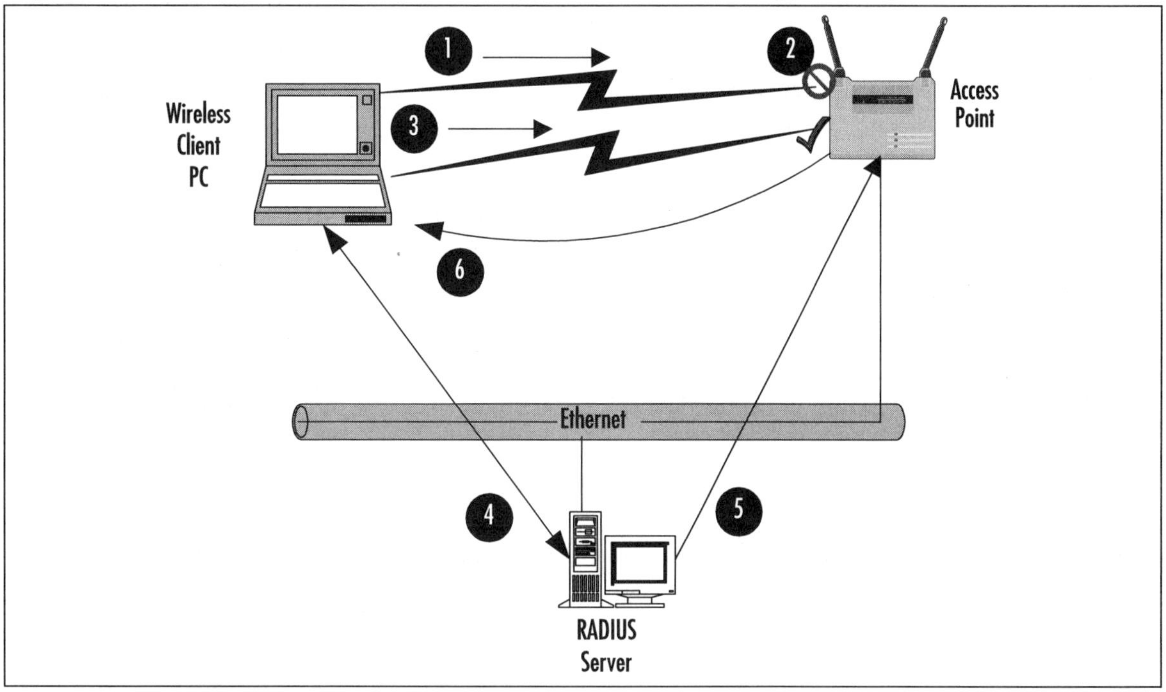

An Introduction to the 802.1x Standard

To understand 802.1x, you must understand the enhancements of current IEEE 802.11 security products and features. The current IEEE 802.11 standard is severely limited because it is available only for the current open and shared key authentication scheme, which is non-extensible.

Some of these requirements for the future security include the following:

- The creation of new 802.11 authentication methods.
- These authentication methods must be independent of the underlying 802.11 hardware.
- Authentication methods should be dynamic; otherwise, it is difficult to fix security holes.
- It must have the ability to support PKI and certificate schemes.

The Objectives of the 802.1x Standard

The IEEE 802.1x Working Group provides a security framework for port-based access control that resides in the upper layers such as new authentication and key management methods without changing current network devices.

The benefits that are the end result of this group are as follows:

- Significant decrease in hardware cost and complexity.
- More options, which allows you to pick and choose your security solution.
- Latest and greatest security technology will work with your existing infrastructure.
- Quick response to security issues as quickly as they arise.

802.1x in a Nutshell

When a client device connects to a port on an 802.1x switch and AP, the switch port can determine the authenticity of the devices. Only Extensible Authentication Protocol Over LAN (EAPOL) (see the following list) frames can be sent and received on that port until the authentication is complete. When the device is properly authenticated, the port switches traffic as though it were a regular port.

Following is some terminology for the 802.1x standard that you should familiarize yourself with:

- **Port** A port is a single point of connection to the network.
- **Port Access Entity (PAE)** Controls the algorithms and protocols associated with the authentication mechanisms for a port.
- **Authenticator PAE** Enforces authentication before it will allow access to resources on that port.
- **Supplicant PAE** Accesses the services that are allowed by the authenticator.
- **Authentication Server** Verifies the supplicant PAE, and decides if it is authorized to access the authenticator or not.
- **EAPOL** Encapsulates EAP messages so that they can be handled directly by a LAN MAC service. 802.1x tries to make authentication more encompassing, rather than enforcing specific mechanisms on the devices.
- **Extensible Authentication Protocol Over Wireless (EAPOW)** EAPOL messages are encapsulated over 802.11 wireless frames.

Making it Come Together - User Identification and Strong Authentication

The 802.1x standard identifies clients by username, not MAC addresses. This enhances security and streamlines the wireless AAA process. 802.1x supports extended forms of authentication, using password methods (such as one-time passwords, or GSS_API mechanisms like Kerberos) and nonpassword methods (such as biometrics, IKE, and smart cards).

Key Derivation can be Dynamic

802.1x allows per-user session keys, dispensing per-user, and/or per session-based WEP keys. These WEP keys are dynamically created at the client for every session. The Global key, like a broadcast WEP key, can be encrypted using a unicast session key and then sent from the AP to the client in a much more secure manner.

Mutual Authentication

The client and the authentication servers are mutually authenticating endpoints and will mitigate MITM attacks. To enable mutual authentication, you can use any of the following EAP methods:

- **TLS** The server supplies a certificate and establishes that it has possession of the private key.
- **IKE** The server shows possession of a pre-shared key or a private key (certificate authentication).
- **GSS_API (Kerberos)** The server demonstrates knowledge of the session key.

Per-Packet Authentication

EAP can support per-packet authentication and integrity protection, but this protection is not extended to all types of EAP messages. NAK (negative acknowledgment) and notification messages are not able to use this protection. Per-packet authentication and integrity protection works for the following (packet is encrypted unless otherwise noted):

- TLS and IKE derive session key
- TLS ciphersuite negotiations (not encrypted)
- IKE ciphersuite negotiations
- Kerberos tickets
- Success and failure messages that use derived session key (through WEP)

Possible Implementation of EAP on the WLAN

Two main authentication methods for EAP are EAP-MD5 and PKI with EAP-TLS. EAP-MD5 does not support mutual authentication between the access server and the wireless client. PKI is very computation-intensive on the client systems.

Cisco LEAP

LEAP is an enhancement to the EAP protocol. In LEAP, the client and RADIUS server have a shared secret (generally some permutation of a username and password). The server will then pass certain information to the AP so that the client and AP can derive encryption keys that are unique for this client/AP pair.

LEAP is worthy of consideration for authentication needs since it can offer mutual authentication, needs only minimal support from the client's CPU, can support embedded systems, and can support clients whose OS does not have the support for native EAP or allow for the use of the PKI authentication.

LEAP authentication works through three phases: the **start phase**, the **authenticate phase**, and the **finish phase**. The following sections show the process that the client and AP go through so that the client can also talk to the RADIUS server.

Start Phase for LEAP Authentication

In the start phase, information (in packet form) is transferred between the client and APs:

1. The EAPOW-Start (called EAPOL-Start in 802.1x for wired networks) starts the authentication process. This packet is sent from the client to the AP.
2. The EAP-Request/Identity is sent from the AP to the client with a request for the client's identity.
3. The EAP-Response/Identity is sent from the client to the AP with the required information.

Authentication Phase for LEAP Authentication

This phase depends on the mutual authentication method chosen for the client and the authentication server. For LEAP, the process is:

1. The client sends an EAP-Response/Identity message to the RADIUS server through the AP as a RADIUS-Access-Request with EAP extensions.
2. The RADIUS server then returns an access-request with a RADIUS-challenge, to which the client must respond.

Cisco LEAP authentication is a mutual authentication method, and the AP is only a pass-through. The AP in the authenticate phase forwards the contents of the packets from EAP to RADIUS and from RADIUS to EAP.

Finish Phase of LEAP Authentication

The steps for the finish phase are as follows:

1. If the client is considered invalid, the RADIUS server will send a RADIUS deny packet with an EAP fail packet embedded within it. If the client is considered to be valid, the server will send a RADIUS request packet with an EAP success attribute.
2. The RADIUS-Access-Accept packet contains the MS-MPPE-Send-Key attribute to the AP, where it obtains the session key that will be used by client.

The RADIUS server and client both create a session key from the user's password when using LEAP. The encryption for the IEEE 802.11 standard can be based on a 40/64-bit or 104/128-bit key. The key derivation process will create a key that is longer than is required. This is so that when the AP receives the key from the RADIUS server (using MS-MPPE-Send-Key attribute), it will send an EAPOL-KEY message to the client. This key will tell the client the key length and what key index that it should use.

The key value is not sent because the client has already created it on its own WEP key. The data packet is then encrypted using the full-length key. The AP will also send an EAPOL-KEY message that gives information about the length, key index, and value of the multicast key. This message is encrypted using the full-length session unicast key from the AP.

Configuration and Deployment of LEAP

This section discusses the installation and requirements for a LEAP solution consisting of a client, an AP, and a RADIUS server for key distribution in your network.

Client Support for LEAP

You can configure your client to use LEAP mode in one of two modes:

- **Network Logon Mode** Uses an integrated network logon for a single sign on for both the wireless network as well as the wired network. Authentication to the wireless network is transparent to the users.
- **Device Mode** The wireless LAN stores the username/password identification to enable non-interactive authentication into the wireless LAN. Used on wireless appliances where the devices that can authenticate themselves through these preconfigured credentials are enough security.

Access Point Support for LEAP

Access points provide 802.1x for 802.11 Authenticator support. Set 802.1x authenticator support:

- Configure the AP to use 40/64-bit or 104/128-bit WEP mode.
- Give the LEAP RADIUS server address and configure the shared secret key to enable the AP and RADIUS server to communicate securely.

Configuring your RADIUS server for LEAP

Configure the RADIUS server for authentication and key distribution users:

- Create the user databases.
- Configure the APs as NASs to enable users to use RADIUS.

Ensuring Authorization

Many of the early OSs and applications deployed had very small authorization groups. Generally, only user groups and operator groups were available for defining a user's access level. Cisco and others have implemented RADIUS authentication for their wireless devices. Now, utilizing stronger authentication methods, you can implement your authorization policies into your wireless deployments.

However, many wireless devices do not currently support external authorization validation. Plus, most deployments just ensure authorized access to the device, and do not control access to or from specific network segments. To fully restrict authorized users to the network devices they are authorized to utilize, you will still need to deploy an adaptive firewall between the AP and your network.

MAC Filtering

MAC forms the lower layer in the Data-Link layer of the OSI model. The purpose of the MAC sublayer is to present a uniform interface between the physical networking media (copper/fiber/radio frequency) and the Logical Link Control portion of the Data-Link layer. These two layers are found onboard a NIC, whether integrated into a device or used as an add-on (PCI card or PCMCIA card).

Where in the Authentication/Association Process does MAC Filtering Occur?

When a wireless device wants to connect to a WLAN, it goes though an authentication and authorization process. After both have been completed, the device is allowed access to the WLAN.

When a wireless device connects to a WLAN, it sends an authentication request to the AP (see Figure 7.47). This request will contain the SSID of the target network, or a null value if connecting to an open system. The AP will grant or deny authentication based on this string. Following a successful authentication, the requesting device will attempt to associate with the AP. It is at this point that MAC filtering is triggered. Depending on the AP make and model, MAC filtering either allows only the specified MAC addresses—blocking the rest, or it allows all MAC addresses—blocking specifically noted MACs. If the MAC address is allowed, the requesting device is allowed to associate with the AP.

Figure 7.47 MAC Filtering

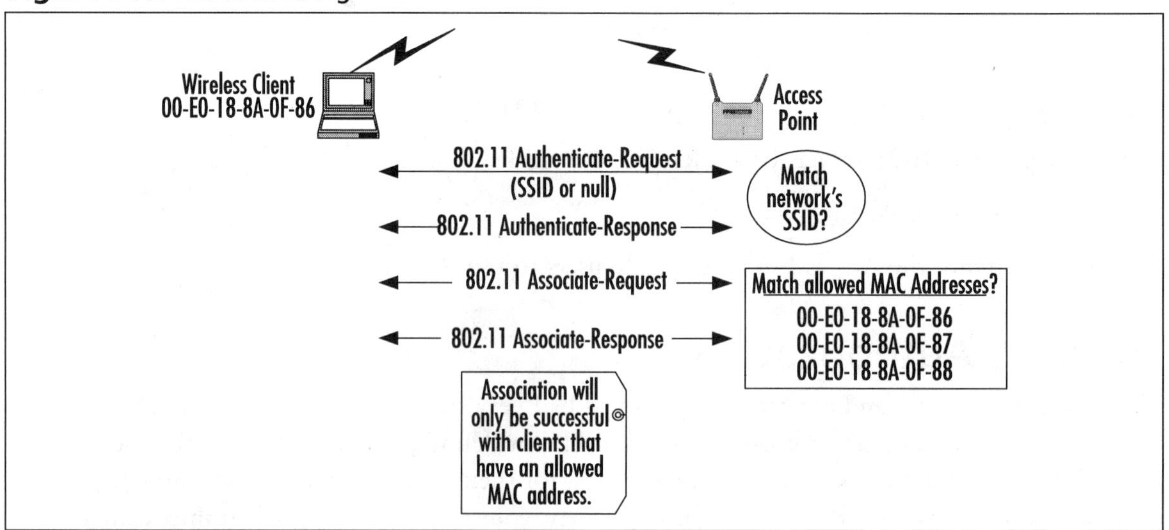

MAC Spoofing

MAC filtering can be circumvented by changing the MAC address (if allowed) to a MAC address permitted by the AP. Once you have modified the MAC address, you should be able to associate it with the AP. If the device bearing the MAC address you are spoofing is active on the network, you will not be able to use your device. Multiple duplicate MAC addresses will break ARP tables.

Accounting and Audit Trails

Auditing tracks and logs network and system activities, and binds them to specific user accounts or sources of activity. Most wireless APs do not offer any method of logging activity, but if your equipment provides the feature, you should enable it and then monitor it for inappropriate activity using tools such as **logcheck**. Wireless AP logging should, if available, log any new wireless device with its MAC address upon valid WEP authentication. It should also log any attempts to access or modify the AP itself. You can also segment the WLAN with a firewall, and use the firewall to log and track activity to and from that segment.

Implementing WEP

Despite its critics, WEP still offers a reasonable level of security, providing that all its features are used properly. This means greater care in key management, avoiding default options, and making sure adequate encryption is enabled at every opportunity. Most vendors advertise that they support WEP in at least 40-bit encryption, but often the 128-bit option is also supported. With data security enabled in a closed network, the settings on the client for the SSID and the encryption keys have to match the AP when attempting to associate with the network, or it will fail.

Defining WEP

The goal of WEP is to protect the privacy of the individual transmissions that in some way mirrors the privacy found on the wired LAN. WEP utilizes a cryptographic security countermeasure to ensure privacy, and provides authentication as well. This benefit is realized through a shared key authentication that allows the encryption and decryption of the wireless transmissions. Many keys can be defined on an AP or a client and rotated to add complexity for a higher security standard for your WLAN policy.

Creating Privacy with WEP

WEP comes in several implementations: no encryption and 40-bit and 104-bit encryption (usually advertised as 64- and 128-bit security respectively). Obviously, no encryption means no privacy. Transmissions are sent in cleartext, and can be viewed by any wireless sniffing application that has access to the RF propagated in the WLAN. In the case of the 40- and 128-bit varieties (just as with password length), the greater the number of characters (bits), the stronger the encryption. The initial configuration of the AP will include the setup of the shared key. This shared key can be in the form of either alphanumeric or hexadecimal strings, and is matched on the client.

WEP uses the RC4 encryption algorithm, a stream cipher. Both the sender and the receiver use the stream cipher to create identical pseudorandom strings from a known shared key. The process entails the sender to logically XOR the plaintext transmission with the stream cipher to produce the ciphertext. The receiver takes the shared key and identical stream and reverses the process to gain the plaintext transmission.

A 24-bit IV is used to create the identical cipher streams. The IV is produced by the sender, and is included in the transmission of each frame. A new IV is used for each frame to prevent the reuse of the key weakening the encryption. This means that for each string generated, a different value for the RC4 key will be used. Since the 24-bit space is small with respect to the potential set of IVs, in a short period of time, all keys are eventually reused. This weakness is the same for both the 40- and 104-bit encryption levels.

WEP incorporates a checksum in each frame to deter attacks that insert known text into the stream to attempt to reveal the key stream. Any frame not found to be valid through the checksum is discarded.

The WEP Authentication Process

WEP is a four-step process that begins when the AP receives a validated request for association. After the AP receives the request, a series of management frames are transmitted between the stations to produce the authentication. This includes the use of the cryptographic mechanisms employed by WEP as a validation.

The four steps break down in the following manner:

1. The requestor (the client) sends a request for association.
2. The authenticator (the AP) receives the request, and responds with a random challenge text and transmits it back to the requestor.
3. The requestor receives the transmission, ciphers the challenge with the shared key stream, and returns it.
4. The authenticator decrypts the challenge text and compares the values against the original. If they match, the requestor is authenticated.

WEP Benefits and Advantages

WEP provides some security and privacy in transmissions to prevent curious or casual browsers from viewing the contents of the transmissions held between the AP and the clients. WEP benefits include:

- All messages are encrypted using a checksum to prevent tampering.
- Privacy is maintained via the encryption. No key, no decryption.
- WEP is extremely easy to implement.
- WEP provides a very basic level of security for WLAN applications.
- WEP keys are user definable and unlimited. No predefined keys.

WEP Disadvantages

WEP has some inherent disadvantages.

- The RC4 stream cipher encryption algorithm uses a finite key and attempts to make an infinite pseudo-random key stream in order to generate the encryption.
- Changing the key requires informing all users as they must change their client configuration.
- Used on its own, WEP does not provide adequate WLAN security.
- WEP has to be implemented on every client as well as every AP to be effective.

Implementing WEP on the Cisco Aironet AP 3x0

Most Cisco APs are configured as shown in Figure 7.48. In this example, the Cisco AP340 supports 128-bit encryption, and is configured via HTTP connection or a serial connection. In Figure 7.48, you see the Web interface for an AP340. By using the drop-down menu, you can select **Full Encryption** and then **128 bit** for the key size. Finally, select the **WEP Key** radio button for the transmission key and type the string.

Figure 7.48 WEP Configuration on the Aironet

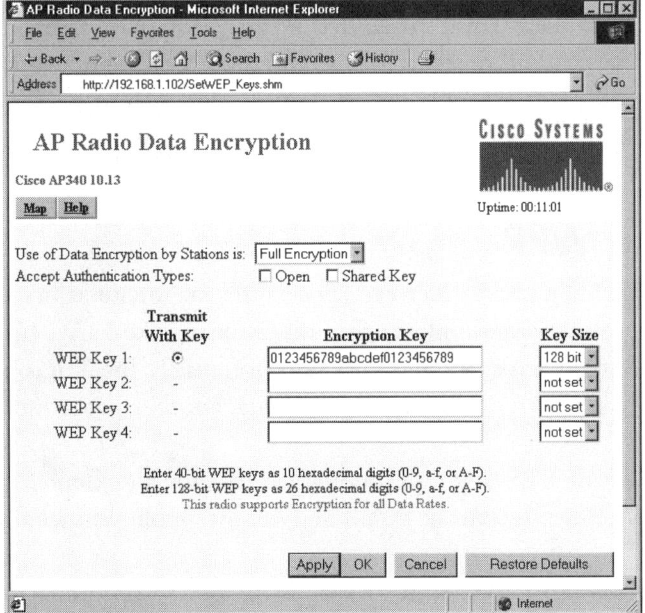

Exploiting WEP

There have been a number of well-publicized exploitations and defeats of WEP, from weaknesses in the encryption algorithm to weaknesses in key management. Although steps have been taken to overcome these weaknesses, attackers are not suffering from a lack of networks to exploit.

WEP reinitializes the encrypted data stream every time an Ethernet collision occurs. Even though the 802.11 protocol attempts to avoid them with CDMA/CA, collisions are a reality that will occur. If someone is listening in on the wireless conversation, they capture the IV information transmitted with each frame and in a matter of hours have all the data needed to recover the WEP key.

Security of 64-bit versus 128-bit Keys

It might seem obvious to a non-technical person that something protected with a 128-bit encryption scheme would be more secure than something protected with a 64-bit encryption scheme. This, however, is not the case with WEP. Because the same vulnerability exists with both encryption levels, they can be equally broken within similar time limits.

With 64-bit WEP, the network administrator specifies a 40-bit key—typically ten hexadecimal digits (0 through 9, a through f, or A through F). A 24-bit IV is appended to this 40-bit key, and the RC4 key scheme is built from these 64-bits of data. This same process is followed in the 128-bit scheme. The Administrator specifies a 104-bit key—this time 26 hexadecimal digits (0 through 9, a through f, or A through F). The 24-bit IV is added to the beginning of the key and the RC4 key schedule is built.

The vulnerability comes from capturing predictably weak IVs, so the size of the original key does not make a significant difference in the security of the encryption. This is due to the relatively small number of total IVs possible under the current WEP specification. Currently, there are a total of 2^{24} possible IV keys. You can see that if the WEP key was not changed within a strictly defined period of time, all possible IV combinations could be heard off of an 802.11b connection, captured, and made available for cracking within a short period of time. This is a flaw in the design of WEP, and bears no correlation to whether the wireless client is using 64-bit WEP or 128-bit WEP.

Strengthening WEP

Armed with a valid WEP key, an intruder can successfully negotiate association with an AP, and gain entry onto the target network. Unless other mechanisms like MAC filtering are in place, this intruder is now able to roam across the network and potentially break into servers or other machines on the network. If MAC filtering is occurring, another procedure must be attempted to get around this.

Keeping the same static WEP key in a production role for an extended period increases your vulnerability. If your WEP key is static, it could be become public knowledge to unscrupulous attackers.

One of the easiest ways to mitigate the risk of WEP key compromise is to regularly change the WEP key your APs and clients use. Although this may be an easy task for small WLANs, the task becomes extremely daunting when you have dozens of APs and hundreds of clients to manually re-key. Both Cisco and Funk Software have released ACSs that implement rapid WEP re-keying on both APs as well as the end-user client. Utilizing this form of software, even if a WEP key was to be discovered, you could rest assured that within a specified period of time, that particular key would no longer be valid.

Other options such as EAP and LEAP, and centralized authentication solutions such as RADIUS and TACACS+ also help strengthen wireless security.

Summary

This chapter focused on security for Cisco hardware and software, as well as solutions provided by the same. A big topic is IPsec, which has proven to be a useful and efficient method for securing networks. We did not have time to cover it in this chapter, but Cisco provides a wealth of security information at www.cisco.com/security. This Web site is a good supplement to the information provided in this chapter.

Your security is only as strong as your design. To that end, you should know your network before implementing any security measures. This will ensure that you have identified and secured all of your vulnerable points. All networks need to be secured, from wired to wireless. The 802.1x security is a holistic approach to security that overcomes inherent weaknesses in wireless networks. We leave you with this final thought on security: if it is in any way involved with the production, storage, or transport of your information, secure it!

Cha

Cisco PIX Firewall

Best Damn Topics in this Chapter:

- PIX Firewall Features
- Software Licensing and Upgrades
- Allowing Outbound Traffic
- Allowing Inbound Traffic
- TurboACLs
- Object Grouping
- Handling Advanced Protocols
- Filtering Web Traffic
- Configuring Intrusion Detection
- DHCP Functionality
- Fragmentation Guard
- AAA Floodguard
- SYN Floodguard
- Reverse-Path Forwarding
- Configuring Console Authentication
- Configuring Authentication for Traffic through the Firewall
- Configuring Accounting for Traffic Through the Firewall
- Failover Concepts
- Standard Failover Using a Failover Cable
- LAN-Based Failover
- Configuring Logging
- Configuring Remote Access
- Configuring Simple Network Management Protocol
- Configuring System Date and Time
- Configuring Virtual Private Networking
- Configuring Site-to-Site IPsec without IKE (Manual IPsec)
- Configuring Point-to-Point Tunneling Protocol
- Configuring Layer 2 Tunneling Protocol with IPsec
- Configuring Support for the Cisco Software VPN Client
- Troubleshooting PIX Firewall Hardware, Software, and Performance

Introduction

Cisco PIX firewalls offer world-class security and high levels of performance and reliability. They are a mature product, having been a part of enterprise and service provider networks since 1995. Cisco PIX firewalls can support small office/home office (SOHO) environments and large enterprises and service providers. This chapter introduces the Cisco PIX firewalls, and provides details on each model. This information is useful in determining which firewall is appropriate for your requirements.

The PIX provides a robust firewall that can protect your network from attacks, and can also restrict access to legitimate users and services. The PIX goes beyond its firewall nature by providing additional services such as encryption for data transported across insecure networks and basic intrusion detection.

Cisco PIX firewalls can be configured using a number of methods, including commands and web interfaces. Cisco also provides a graphical user interface (GUI [PIX Device Manager (PDM)]) for accomplishing most configurations.

Our goal in this chapter is to provide information that you can use to build a working PIX design, from initial planning to a robust configuration. We have gathered commands and built configurations that reflect common scenarios, to make this chapter particularly useful to you. The PIX has many practical features, and knowledge of these features will enable you to get the most out of your PIX.

PIX Firewall Features

The PIX 500 series firewalls provide robust performance and support scalable security architectures of all sizes. The PIX firewall provides stateful packet inspection, content filtering, virtual private network (VPN) termination, address translation, and security for multimedia applications.

Embedded Operating System

The PIX uses an embedded operating system (OS) where the OS is self-contained in the device and resident in read-only memory (ROM). The PIX is based on a hardened, specialized OS specific to security services. This OS allows for kernel simplification, which supports explicit certification and validation: The PIX OS has been tested for vendor certification such as ICSA Labs' firewall product certification criteria, as well as the very difficult-to-obtain International Organization for Standard(ISO) Common Criteria EAL4 certification. Kernel simplification has advantages in throughput as well; the PIX 535 supports up to 256,000 simultaneous connections, far exceeding the capabilities of a UNIX- or Windows-based OS on equivalent hardware. The PIX OS syntax is similar to the Cisco Internetwork Operating System (IOS), meaning a flatter learning curve for anyone familiar with Cisco software.

The Adaptive Security Algorithm

The Adaptive Security Algorithm (ASA) determines if packets should be allowed through the firewall in accordance with policy implemented on the firewall. The PIX evaluates packet information against existing state information and decides whether or not to pass the packet.

The information flow control policy is an expression of the information that is allowed to flow through the network. A sample policy might be, "If the datastream was initiated by someone on the inside, let it pass; if the datastream was initiated by someone from the outside, block it."

An access control list (ACL) table is a mechanism via which an administrator can try to implement this policy. It compares those distinguishing numbers against a database to see if the packet is consistent with policy. If it is not allowed by the database, the packet is dropped and perhaps logged.

A stateful packet filter allows for dynamic rule bases. For example, if the packet is coming from the outside toward the inside, the administrator should check to see if this packet was part of a previously opened datastream.

The biggest problem with fixed rules is that in order to allow certain traffic (for example, FTP), overly permissive ACLs need to be implemented. In File Transfer Protocol (FTP), two Transmission Control Protocol (TCP) data flows are developed: the command channel and the data channel. The firewall can monitor and maintain state information, and it can open only the necessary port for the inbound (return) data flow, and open it only while the transfer is active, dynamically changing the ACLs over time.

State

State is a history of the traffic that has passed, which is used to determine if new packets are part of an existing connection. If a packet is determined to be similar to those already passed, a full analysis against the firewall policy rules does not need to be followed. This allows the PIX to perform at line rate where static ACL might bog down.

A record of active connections is key to maintaining state information. This data is stored in the connections table (CONN). The PIX can translate addresses, which means that the translation and connection tables must be synchronized. Translations and connections are discussed later in this chapter.

Security Levels

The PIX allows the administrator to separate and classify networks at varying levels of security. The "inside" network has the highest security level, while the "outside" network has the lowest. Demilitarized (DMZ) networks fall somewhere between these two extremes. High security networks can access the resources of low security networks without an ACL, whereas an ACL is required to permit low to high communications.

How ASA Works

ASA allows traffic to flow from a higher security level to a lower security level, unless modified by **conduit** or **access-list** commands.

- No packets can traverse the PIX firewall without a connection and state.
- Outbound connections or states are allowed, except those specifically denied by ACLs. An outbound connection is one in which the originator or client is on a higher security interface than the receiver or server.

- Inbound connections or states, except those specifically allowed, are denied. An inbound connection or state is one in which the originator or client is on a lower security interface or network than the receiver or server. Multiple exceptions can be applied to a single **xlate** (translation) to permit access.
- All Internet Control Message Protocol (ICMP) packets are denied unless specifically permitted.
- All attempts to circumvent the previous rules are blocked and a message is logged.

Technical Details for ASA

The PIX is an Internet Protocol (IP) firewall that supports only IP. The PIX supports TCP by rewriting its checksums to compensate for address translation, or by maintaining state information using TCP port numbers. The PIX inspects TCP packets for several fields, notably source port, destination port, sequence and acknowledgment numbers, and TCP flags. Source and destination ports and information about the flags are listed in the CONN table.

User Datagram Protocol (UDP) is unreliable and unacknowledged, but still supported by the PIX. The PIX can recognize the first UDP packet in a datastream. When the first packet is permitted by the information flow control policy (either because it is traffic from a trusted net to a less trusted one or because of an explicit exception in the ACL), the same sort of process occurs, as shown in Figure 8.1. If permitted, an entry is made in the CONN table, and further packets with the same socket pairs are associated with that authorized datastream until an idle timeout occurs. (The idle timeout is set with the **timeout** command and defaults to two minutes.)

Figure 8.1 provides a diagram of how information flows through the PIX.

Figure 8.1 Basic ASA Operations

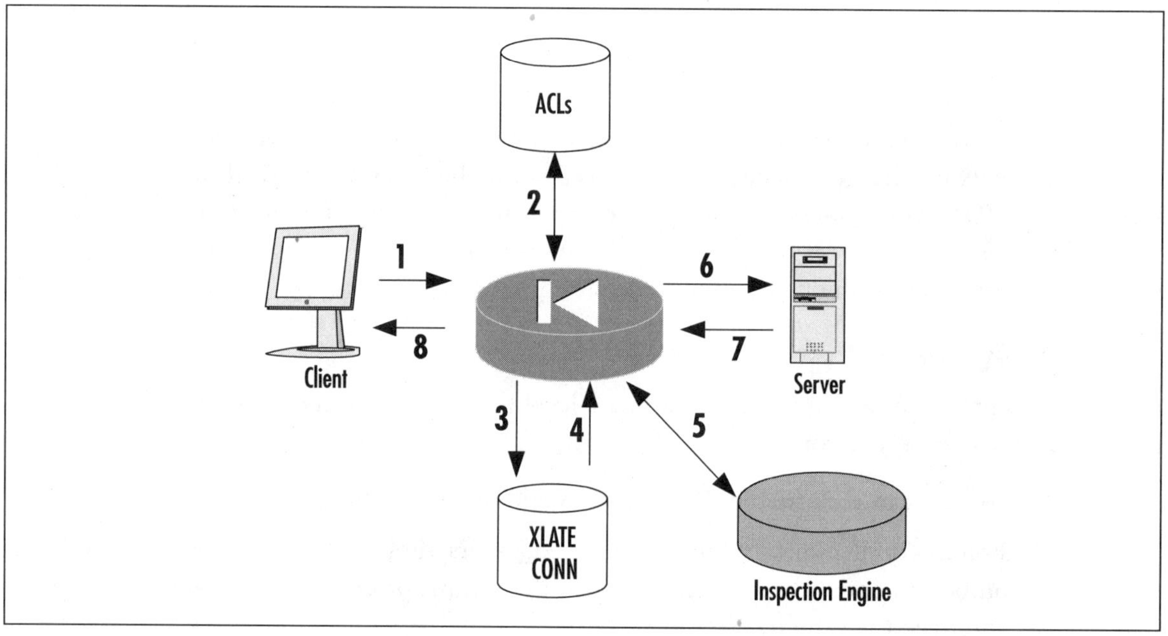

1. The client generates a SYN packet, headed toward the server, to establish a new connection.
2. The PIX investigates the ACL to determine if the information flow control policy should permit the new connection.
3. Assuming the connection is valid, the PIX updates the CONN table.
4. The XLATE table is updated as necessary.
5. If necessary, the stream is processed by the Application Inspection Engine, which may involve rewriting the packet.
6. The packet is sent on to the server.
7. On the reverse path, the server responds with its SYN/ACK.
8. However, since this is not an initialization request, inspection of the rule base is not required; it looks the packet up in the CONN table and then forwards it back to the client.

Advanced Protocol Handling

Providing support for complex protocols is a distinguishing characteristic of the PIX. The "fixup" proxies include FTP, Hypertext Transfer Protocol (HTTP), h323, Internet Locator Service (ILS), RSH, Real Time Streaming Protocol (RTSP), Simple Mail Transfer Protocol (SMTP), Serial Interface Protocol (SIP), SKINNY, and Structured Query Language (SQL). Some protocols, such as DNS Guard (which prevents multiple Domain Name System [DNS] responses from penetrating to the host), are supported in the native PIX services and do not need to be configured.

VPN Support

Packets flowing along a network are much like postcards sent through the mail; if you do not want the world reading your messages, you have to take additional care. The PIX provides confidentiality protection using VPNs. The PIX supports VPNs based on the Point-to-Point Tunneling Protocol (PPTP), Layer 2 Tunneling Protocol (L2TP), and Security Architecture for IP (IPsec).

URL Filtering

A uniform resource locator (URL), is how addresses are identified on the World Wide Web (WWW). The PIX firewall supports URL filtering by capturing a request and querying a database located on an N2H2 or Websense server. URL filtering provides a way to apply an acceptable use policy for Internet browsing and captures and analyzes how personnel are using the Internet. The servers themselves provide reporting capabilities so that the administrator can determine how well their policy is being followed.

NAT and PAT

Network Address Translation (NAT) re-maps IP addresses (or sockets) to provide address conservation or security. NAT allows "private" addresses to be used on inside networks, and translated to a public address when accessing external networks such as the Internet. NAT also provides a form of "security through obscurity." Since the private addresses are not advertised, an outside attacker does not necessarily know the true address of the source host. NAT can perform one-to-one translation, or one-to-many (better known as Port Address Translation [PAT]). NAT can be dynamic where translation occurs and is removed when it is static, where an administrator creates the necessary mappings.

High Availability

The term high availability usually refers to hardware fault tolerance. A firewall is a critical piece of equipment and is typically at the center of most networks. Its failure can be devastating. The PIX offers a failover feature where two firewalls operate in tandem, with one in stand-by mode ready to assume firewall duties should the primary fail.

PIX Hardware

Cisco offers different models of the PIX, each suitable for environments of differing sizes and needs, as summarized in Table 8.1. The Firewall Services Module (FWSM) 1.1 for the Catalyst 6500 series switches provides no physical interfaces. Instead, it provides support for up to 100 virtual local area network (VLAN) interfaces. For failover support, the FWSM has a dedicated logical interface.

Models

Five models are currently supported: the 501, the 506E, the 515E, the 525, and the 535. However, there are three models that may be deployed in enterprise environments: the 506, the 515, and the 520. Table 8.1 shows the vital characteristics of each of the models:

Table 8.1 PIX Model Characteristics

Model	End of Life?	Processor Type	Maximum Interfaces	Failover Support	Cleartext Throughput	VAC Available	3DES Throughput	RAM Memory
501	No	133 MHz AMD SC520	2	No	8 Mbps	No	3 Mbps	16 MB
506	Yes	200 MHz Intel Pentium MMX	2	No	8 Mbps	No	6 Mbps	32 MB
506E	No	300 MHz Intel Celeron	2	No	20 Mbps	No	16 Mbps	32 MB
515	Yes	200 MHz Intel Pentium MMX	6**	Yes	170 Mbps	No	10 Mbps	64 MB**
515E	No	443 MHz Intel Celeron	6**	Yes	188 Mbps	Yes	63 Mbps*	64 MB**
520	Yes	233 MHz Intel Pentium MMX	6	Yes	170 Mbps	Yes	60 Mbps*	128 MB
525	No	600 MHz Intel Pentium III	8	Yes	360 Mbps	Yes	70 Mbps*	128 MB
535	No	1 GHz Intel Pentium III	10	Yes	1 Gbps	Yes	100 Mbps*	1 GB**

***Mazimum 3DES throughput is achieved with the VAC; **maximum requires the unrestricted license.**

PIX 501

The PIX 501 is the basic entry fixed configuration model. It has a four-port 10/100 Mbps switch for inside connectivity and a single 10 Mbps interface for connecting to an Internet upstream device (such as a cable modem or DSL router). It provides 3 Mbps throughput on a 3DES IPsec connection, which should exceed a SOHO user's requirements. The base license is a 10-user license with DES IPsec; an optional license for a 50-user upgrade and/or 3DES VPN support is available. The PIX 501 is based on a 133 MHz AMD SC520 processor with 16MB of random-access memory (RAM) and 8MB of flash.

PIX 506

The PIX 506 is the basic remote fixed configuration office/branch office model. It provides two autonegotiate RJ45 10BaseT ports (inside and outside). The 506 supports 8 Mbps cleartext throughput, with 6 Mbps 3DES IPsec and can support hundreds of VPN users. The hardware is based on a 200 MHz Intel Pentium MMX, with 32MB of RAM and 8MB of flash.

PIX 506E

The PIX 506E replaced the PIX 506, and has the same chassis with a beefier central processing unit (CPU), a quieter fan, and a new power supply. The CPU is a 300 MHz Intel Celeron with 32MB RAM and 8MB flash. Cleartext throughput is 20 Mbps (wire speed) while 3DES throughput is 16 Mbps. Licensing on the 506E (and 506) is a single, unlimited-user license. The only extra license that might be needed is the 3DES license.

PIX 515

The PIX 515 supports small- to medium-sized businesses at wirespeed. It can handle up to 170 Mbps of cleartext throughput. The 1U rack-mount chassis is configurable with a slot for an additional single-port or four-port Fast Ethernet interface, allowing the inside, outside, and up to four additional DMZ networks. It has a 200 MHz Intel Pentium MMX with 32MB of RAM and 8MB of flash (the same as the 506E). The restricted license limits the number of interfaces to three and does not support high availability. The unrestricted license supports up to 64MB RAM, up to six interfaces, and failover.

PIX 515E

The PIX 515E replaced the 515 in May 2002, and has a 433 MHz Intel Celeron CPU. It can offload the arithmetic load of DES computation to a dedicated VPN accelerator card (VAC), which delivers up to 63 Mbps 3DES throughput and 2,000 IPsec tunnels. The restricted license is limited to three interfaces and no failover, whereas the unrestricted license supports up to 64MB memory, the VAC, failover, and up to six interfaces.

PIX 520

The PIX 520 has a PC-style rack-mount chassis that supports a wide mix of available media cards, including Token Ring and fiber. The 520 has a floppy drive and is on the 200 MHz Intel Pentium

MMX, and supports up to 128MB of RAM. The 520 license is based on the number of users. PIX-CONN-128 allows 128 simultaneous users, with upgrades for 1024 users or unlimited users.

PIX 525

The PIX 525 replaced the PIX 520 in June 2001. It is designed for large enterprise or small service provider environments. While it has no floppy drive, the 525 supports single- or four-port 10/100 Fast Ethernet, 4/16 Token Ring, and dual-attached multimode Fiber Distributed Data Interface (FDDI) cards, as well as Gigabit Ethernet. Based on the 600 MHz Intel Pentium III, the 525 boasts 360 Mbps cleartext throughput and, with the accelerator card, 70 Mbps of 3DES IPsec tunnel traffic. The restricted license limits the PIX 525 to 128MB of RAM and six interfaces. The unrestricted bumps RAM to 256MB, allows up to eight interfaces, and supports failover. As before, 3DES licensing is separate, if desired.

PIX 535

The PIX 535 is the current top-of-the-line model, suitable for service provider environments. It can provide up to 1 Gbps cleartext throughput, 500K simultaneous connections, and 7,000 connection initialization/teardowns a second. A VAC provides 100 Mbps 3DES throughput, with up to 2,000 simultaneous security associations (VPN tunnels). The PIX 535 is based on a 1 GHz Intel Pentium III, with up to 1GB of RAM. It has a 16MB flash and 256K cache running at 1 GHz, as well as a dual 64-bit 66 MHz Peripheral Component Interconnect (PCI) system bus. Cards available are the one- or four-port 10/100 Ethernet network interface cards (NICs) or 1GB Ethernet multimode "stick and click" fiber connectors.

Software Licensing and Upgrades

The PIX has customized licensing to enable or disable features to fit the administrator's needs. Features differ depending on the activation key. The activation key allows the administrator to enable features without acquiring new software. The activation key is computed by Cisco using the feature matrix and serial number. The serial number is based on the flash, so if the flash is replaced, the activation key must be replaced. The activation key enables feature-specific information such as interfaces, high availability, and type of encryption.

The **show version** command can be used to get information about the activation key. It shows the code version, hardware information, and activation key information. The **show activation-key** can also be used.

```
Serial Number: 480090153 (0x1c9d9829)


Running Activation Key: 0x75fe7c49 0xc08b4082 0x08979930 0xe4b4c4b0

Licensed Features:

Failover:             Enabled

VPN-DES:              Enabled

VPN-3DES:             Disabled

Maximum Interfaces: 6
```

```
Cut-through Proxy:  Enabled
Guards:              Enabled
URL-filtering:       Enabled
Inside Hosts:        Unlimited
Throughput:          Unlimited
IKE peers:           Unlimited
```

The **flash activation key** is the same as the running key. This machine is a PIX 515 and has an unrestricted license, with the maximum number of interfaces permitted, including failover.

Updating the activation key in version 6.2 of the PIX OS could not be simpler. The command **activation-key <activation-key-four-tuple>** sets the key to the new value. Note that activation of the four tuples are in hexadecimal, are case insensitive, and do not require the numbers to start with 0x. Thus, the previously mentioned machine could be set with:

```
PIX1(config)# activation-key 75fe7c49 c08b4082 08979930 e4b4c4b0
```

Updating the activation keys in prior versions is not much more complicated. Power-cycle the PIX, and send an Esc or Break to enter monitor mode. This presents you with a prompt:

```
monitor>
```

Type a **?** to see the options. Sample output is listed here:

```
Use ? for help.
monitor> ?
? this help message
address     [addr]    set IP address
file        [name]    set boot file name
gateway     [addr]    set IP gateway
help                  this help message
interface   [num]     select TFTP interface
ping        <addr>    send ICMP echo
reload                halt and reload system
server      [addr]    set server IP address
tftp        TFTP      download
timeout     TFTP      timeout
trace                 toggle packet tracing
```

Licensing

The three license categories are unrestricted, restricted, and failover. If you have a single PIX, you will want unrestricted or restricted licensing, depending on the number of interfaces you want to support. If you have two PIX appliances and want high availability (described previously), you will want one machine with an unrestricted license and another machine with a failover license.

Upgrading Software

The traditional way of managing images is via Trivial File Transfer Protocol (TFTP). you're the PIX OS us upgraded using TFTP. If using a very old version of the software (pre 5.1(*x*)), you must upgrade using monitor mode. You can follow the preceding notes or the following step-by-step procedure:

1. Enter monitor mode. Remember, this requires that you get a console session running, power-cycle the box, and press **Escape** within 10 seconds of the boot.
2. The PIX is currently unconfigured. Set up the download interface by doing the following:
   - Use **interface <*number*>** to set the TFTP interface. The default is 1, so you do not have to set it if the TFTP server is on the inside.
   - Use **address <*IP address*>** to set the IP address of the PIX.
   - If your TFTP server is not on the same network as the firewall, set a default gateway with **gateway <*IP address*>**.
3. Prepare the transfer information:
   - Use **server <*IP address*>** to set the IP address of your TFTP server.
   - Use **file <*filename*>** to set the name of the image to upload.
4. Execute the transfer. Use **tftp** to start the file.

This process installs the new image, which will become active upon rebooting.

Monitor mode is primarily used in the event of disaster. PIX firewalls with version 5.1 and later can bypass the monitor mode. Log into the PIX and enter enable mode. Ensure your TFTP server is reachable.

Get the version of the software onto your TFTP server, and copy the file to flash:

```
PIX1# copy tftp flash
Address or name of remote host [127.0.0.1]? 10.1.1.1
Source file name [cdisk]? pix621.bin
copying tftp://10.1.1.1/pix621.bin to flash
[yes|no|again]? yes
!!!!!!!!!!!!!!!!!!!!!!!!!!!!!!!!!!!!!!!!!!!!!!!!!!!!!!!
Received 1640448 bytes.
Erasing current image.
Writing 1640448 bytes of image.
!!!!!!!!!!!!!!!!!!!!!!!!!!!!!!!!!!!!!!!!!!!!!!!!!!!!!!!
Image installed.
```

Rebooting loads the new image.

Password Recovery

Passwords on the PIX are encrypted using Message Digest 5 (MD5) hash. The MD5 hash used on the PIX is significantly weaker than the Cisco type 5 hash used on Cisco routers. Cisco provides a technique for recovering passwords. Download a PIX OS specific version of this software from the locations specified in Table 8.2, and run it to reset the password to the default, **cisco**. This application is run in monitor mode. Select and download the image for your PIX OS version.

Table 8.2 PIX Password Recovery Binaries

Version	Filename	URL
4.3 and earlier releases	nppix.bin	www.cisco.com/warp/public/110/nppix.bin
4.4 release	np44.bin	www.cisco.com/warp/public/110/np44.bin
5.0 release	np50.bin	www.cisco.com/warp/public/110/np50.bin
5.1 release	np51.bin	www.cisco.com/warp/public/110/np51.bin
5.2 release	np52.bin	www.cisco.com/warp/public/110/np52.bin
5.3 release	np53.bin	www.cisco.com/warp/public/110/np53.bin
6.0 release	np60.bin	www.cisco.com/warp/public/110/np60.bin
6.1 release	np61.bin	www.cisco.com/warp/public/110/np61.bin
6.2 release	np62.bin	www.cisco.com/warp/public/110/np62.bin

1. Download the recovery image to your TFTP.
2. Reboot the PIX.
3. Within 10 seconds of the reboot, press **Esc** to enter monitor mode.
4. Use the **interface** command to identify the network where the TFTP server is connected.
5. Use the **address** command to address the interface.
6. Use the **server** command to specify the IP address of the TFTP server.
7. Use the **gateway** command to specify the default route if the TFTP server is on a remote network..
8. Use the **file** command to specify the filename of the recovery image chosen in Step 1.
9. Use the **ping** command to verify that you can connect to the TFTP server.
10. Use the **tftp** command to start the download.

At this point, you should be prompted to erase the passwords. The default password has now been set to **cisco**, with no enable password.

Factory Default Configurations

Like most Cisco hardware, the PIX provides a command line interface (CLI). The model of the PIX firewall determines what default configuration is shipped with it. The PIX 501 and PIX 506 ship with a basic default configuration that permits them to be integrated with a minimum of effort. The PIX 515, 525, and 535 models are more general-purpose firewalls, and require greater initial configuration to operate.

Access Modes

There are several access levels available on the PIX: user, enable, and monitor. User mode is unprivileged, with a very limited set of commands. Enable mode provides full administrative privileges to the firewall, including the ability to modify its configuration. Monitor mode bypasses the firewall configuration and security to enable the administrator to recover from errors while performing upgrades.

Logging on defaults to the unprivileged mode, as identified by the prompt that contains the hostname followed by a right-angle bracket (>). Only a few commands are available:

```
PIX1> ?
enable          Turn on privileged commands
help            Help list
login           Log in as a particular user
logout          Exit from current user profile, and to unprivileged mode
pager           Control page length for pagination
quit            Quit from the current mode, end configuration or logout
PIX1> show ?
checksum        View configuration information cryptochecksum
curpriv         Display current privilege level
history         Display the session command history
pager           Control page length for pagination
version         Display PIX system software version
PIX1> show version
```

Typing **enable** and entering the password places you in enable mode, providing access to more privileged commands. The prompt changes to a pound sign. Notice that the command set is much larger.

```
PIX1# ?
arp          Change or view the arp table, and set the arp timeout value
capture      Capture inbound and outbound packets on one or more interfaces
configure    Configure from terminal
copy         Copy image or PDM file from TFTP server into flash.
debug        Debug packets or ICMP tracings through the PIX Firewall.
disable      Exit from privileged mode
eeprom       Show or reprogram the 525 onboard i82559 devices
flashfs      Show, destroy, or preserve filesystem information
help         Help list
kill         Terminate a telnet session
```

```
logout      Exit from current user profile, and to unprivileged mode
logging     Clear syslog entries from the internal buffer
pager       Control page length for pagination
passwd      Change Telnet console access password
ping        Test connectivity from specified interface to <ip>
quit        Quit from the current mode, end configuration or logout
reload      Halt and reload system
session     Access an internal AccessPro router console
shun        Manages the filtering of packets from undesired hosts
terminal    Set terminal line parameters
who         Show active administration sessions on PIX
write       Write config to net, flash, floppy, or terminal, or erase flash
```

The **configure** command places you in the configuration mode, which allows you to make changes. This mode is indicated as shown.

```
PIX1(config)#
```

The previous commands executed can be listed with the **show history** command. Use the Up Arrow scroll through the past commands.

Basic Commands

The PIX firewall behaves similarly to a Cisco router as far as its command behavior and movement, as shown in Table 8.3.

Table 8.3 Basic Keystroke Shortcuts

Command	Result
Tab	Command line completion.
Ctrl + A	Moves the cursor to the start of a line.
Ctrl + B	Moves the cursor one character to the left (nondestructive).
Alt + B	Moves the cursor one word to the left.
Ctrl + D	Deletes the character under the cursor.
Ctrl + E	Moves the cursor to the end of the line.
Ctrl + F	Moves the cursor one character to the right.
Alt + F	Moves the cursor one word to the right.
Ctrl + H or Rubout	Erases the previous character.
Ctrl + R	Reprints a line.
Up Arrow or Ctrl + P	Displays the previous line.
Up Arrow or Ctrl + N	Displays the next line.
Help or ?	Displays help.

Hostname and Domain Name

The **hostname** command assigns a name to the PIX firewall, which also appears in the prompt. The **domain-name** assigns a DNS domain name to the firewall.

```
PIX1(config)# hostname PIX1
PIX1(config)# domain-name secret.com
```

Configuring Interfaces

Interface configuration is among one of the first tasks that you will perform. You will need to name the interface, establish its security level, and address it before it can be activated.

The nameif Command

The **nameif** command assigns the interface a logical name as well as a security level. The format of the **nameif** command is: **nameif <hardware_id> <interface> <security_level>**.

- **hardware_id** hardware associated with the interface, such as ethernet0.
- **Interface** descriptive name, such as dmz
- **security_level** Level of trust between 100 (trusted) and 0 (untrusted).

For example, to configure ethernet0 as the outside network with a security level of 0:

```
PIX1(config)# nameif ethernet0 outside security0
```

To configure ethernet1 as the inside network with a security level of 100:

```
PIX1(config)# nameif ethernet1 inside security100
```

The interface Command

The **interface** command **interface <hardware_id> <hardware_speed> [shutdown]** sets physical layer properties. **Hardware_id** corresponds to the value from the **nameif** command, and **hardware_speed** is chosen from Table 8.4.

The **shutdown** keyword disables the interface. An example of the **interface** command is:

```
PIX1(config)# interface ethernet0 100full
```

Table 8.4 Hardware Speed Types for the interface Command

Value	Description
10baset	10 Mbps Ethernet, half duplex
100basetx	Fast Ethernet, half duplex
100full	Fast Ethernet, full duplex
1000sxfull	Gigabit Ethernet, full duplex
1000basesx	Gigabit Ethernet, half duplex
1000auto	Gigabit Ethernet to autonegotiate full or half duplex

Continued

Table 8.4 Hardware Speed Types for the interface Command

Value	Description
aui	10 Mbps Ethernet, half duplex, for an AUI cable interface
bnc	10 Mbps Ethernet, half duplex, for a BNC cable interface
auto	Sets Ethernet speed automatically. Generally, it is better to hardcode the cable type, since autonegotiation has failed with some hardware devices.

The ip address Command

The **ip address** command **ip address <interface> <ip_address> <netmask>** sets the IP address and mask for an interface.

An example of this command is:

```
PIX1(config)# ip address dmz 192.168.0.1 255.255.255.0
```

Static Routes

The PIX does not have a wide selection of routing options. It is limited to static routes and Routing Information Protocol (RIP). Static routes are sufficient for most situations, and are entered with the following command.

```
route <if_name> <ip_address> <netmask> <gateway_ip> [metric]
```

To enter a default route, use the following (192.168.0.1 will be the gateway of last resort for this firewall; 0.0.0.0 and 0 mean the same thing; the 1 at the end is the metric of this route—the lower, the better):

```
PIX1(config)# route outside 0 0 192.168.0.1 1
PIX1(config)# route outside 0.0.0.0 0.0.0.0 192.168.0.1 1
```

Password Configuration

An administrator can set a virtual terminal (VTY) access password and an enable password on the PIX, using the commands shown. The PIX is limited to 16-byte case sensitive passwords. The passwd command sets the VTY password, while enable password is self-explanatory.

```
PIX1(config)# passwd cisco
PIX1(config)# enable password cisco
```

In the configuration, the password is stored in an encrypted fashion. The command then looks like this:

```
enable password 2KFQnbNIdI.2KYOU encrypted
passwd 2KFQnbNIdI.2KYOU encrypted
```

Managing Configurations

The PIX OS provides several commands and options for managing firewalls, including its configuration. When a change is made or firewall parameters are adjusted, the configuration must be saved or even copied to a external server as a backup. The following commands accomplish this and more.

- **write**
- **copy**
- **configure**
- **reload**

The write Command

The **write** command allows the administrator to save the configuration to various locations. Allowed variants are **write net**, **write memory**, **write standby**, **write terminal**, **write erase**, and **write floppy**.

The **write net [[server_ip] : [filename]]** command writes the configuration to a TFTP server and the **write memory [uncompressed]** command allows the administrator to store the configuration to flash (the PIX does not have or use Non-Volatile Random Access Memory (NVRAM) like Cisco routers). The **uncompressed** parameter specifies storing the configuration as an uncompressed string. Finally, to display the configuration use the **write terminal** command.

V6.2 added some standard IOS commands for configuration management: **show running-config** and **write erase**, both of which perform as they do on a Cisco router. The **write memory** will save the current running configuration to flash memory.

The copy Command

The **copy** command manages images; such as the **copy tftp** command which copies an image from a TFTP server to flash as shown.

```
copy tftp[:[[//location] [/tftp_pathname]]] flash[:[image | pdm]]
```

Images can also be downloaded from a Web server via conventional HTTP or over Secure Sockets Layer (SSL) as shown.

```
copy http[s]://[user:password@] location [:port ] / http_pathname flash
    [: [image | pdm] ]
```

If the Web server is running on a nonstandard port, it can be specified here by putting the port after a colon, similar to this:

```
copy http://fwadmin:cisco@10.10.10.1:99/pix_image flash
```

The configure Command

Configurations can be managed via the **configure** command, which performs similarly to the **write** command. The **configure terminal** command allows the administrator to change the configuration from the terminal.

These commands merge the configuration from the media with the existing configuration. The **clear configure** command is often used to wipe out the existing configuration. Another choice is to use the **configure [terminal|floppy|memory]** command.

Analogous to the **copy** command, the following command merges a configuration stored on a Web server with the running configuration:

```
configure http[s]://[<user>:<password>@]<location>[:<port>]/<pathname>

configure net [<location>]:[<pathname>]
configure factory-default [<inside_ip> [<mask>]]
```

Resetting the System

Generally, the PIX must be rebooted after installing a new image, or if you want to reboot back to a more stable configuration stored as the startup configuration.

The reload Command

The PIX can be restarted gracefully using the **reload** command.

```
PIX1# reload
Proceed with reload? [confirm]
```

To bypass pressing the second carriage return, use the **reload noconfirm** command.

Allowing Outbound Traffic

At a minimum, the PIX needs to be configured to allow outbound traffic (traffic from a higher security to a lower security interface) by configuring address translation or explicitly disabling it. Assuming that no ACLs or apply/outbound statements prohibit it, this will be sufficient to permit outbound sessions. When an outbound connection is initiated, traffic returning to that connection is allowed to traverse back from the lower security-level interface to the higher security-level interface.

Configuring Dynamic Address Translation

Address translation (or its deactivation) is sufficient to pass outbound traffic. Once NAT and/or PAT are configured, the ASA allows traffic to traverse from a higher security-level interface to a lower security-level interface on the PIX firewall (also known as *outbound connections*).

Configuration of NAT/PAT is a two-step process:

1. Use the **nat** command to identify the local addresses that will be translated.
2. Use the **global** command to define the global addresses to translate to.

Address translation records are known as *translation slots* (or *xlate*) and are stored in the *translation table*. To view the contents of this table, use the **show xlate** command. The xlate timer monitors the translation table and removes records that have been idle longer than the defined timeout. By default, this is three hours; current settings can be verified with the **show timeout** command. The syntax of the **nat** command is as follows:

```
nat [(<if_name>)] <id> <local_address> [<netmask> [outside] [dns] [norandomseq]
[timeout <hh:mm:ss>] [<connection_limit> [<embryonic_limit>]]
```

- **if_name** Applies the **nat** command to the interface where the traffic to be translated enters the PIX. If this parameter is not specified, the inside interface is assumed.
- **id** Integer between 0 and 2,000,000,000 used to map the local IP addresses (**local_address**) identified by the **nat** command to the global IP addresses specified by the **global** command. A 0 disables translations, and causes the local address to be treated as the global address.
- **outside** Allows external addresses to be translated.
- **dns** Configures the PIX to translate the IP address included in DNS responses using active entries in the translation table.
- **norandomseq** Stops randomization of TCP sequence numbers. This is necessary when performing address translation twice and does not require the sequence numbers to be randomized twice.
- **timeout** Defines how long to allow an entry in the translation table to stay idle.
- **connection_limit** Defines how many total concurrent active connections are allowed. The default is 0, which is unlimited.
- **embryonic_limit** Defines how many concurrent half-open connections are allowed. The default is 0, which is unlimited.

The syntax for the global command is **global [(<if_name>)] <id> { {<global_ip> [-<global_ip>] [netmask <global_mask>]} | interface}**. The parameters are as follows:

- **if_name** Defines the interface on which traffic will exit after being translated. The default is outside.
- **id** Binds one or more NAT statements to a global statement.
- **global_ip** Defines the global IP addresses to be used in translation. A single IP address specifies PAT, while a range specifies NAT. If the range for NAT is exhausted, the PAT is performed.
- **interface** Local addresses are translated to whatever address is assigned to the outgoing interface.

Figure 8.2 shows a simple address translation scenario. Three sets of local addresses are translated to corresponding global addresses.

Figure 8.2 A NAT Example

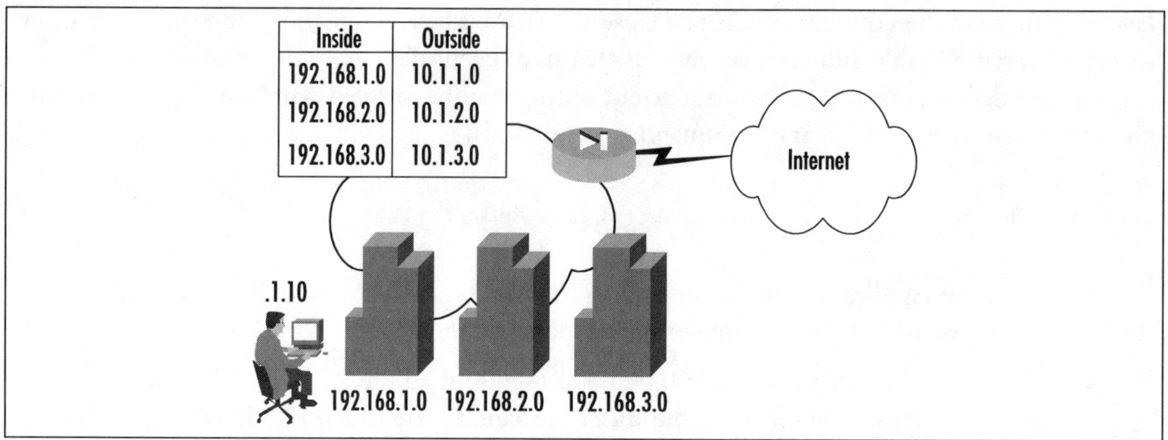

The configuration for Figure 8.2 is fairly straightforward. Traffic to be translated must be identified using the **nat** command and then mapped to a pool of global (outside) IP addresses defined by the **global** command.

```
PIX1(config)# nat (inside) 1 192.168.1.0 255.255.255.0
PIX1(config)# global 1 10.1.1.1-10.1.1.254 netmask 255.255.255.0
PIX1(config)# nat (inside) 2 192.168.2.0 255.255.255.0
PIX1(config)# global 2 10.1.2.1-10.1.2.254 netmask 255.255.255.0
PIX1(config)# nat (inside) 3 192.168.3.0 255.255.255.0
PIX1(config)# global 3 10.1.3.1-10.1.3.254 netmask 255.255.255.0
PIX1(config)# exit
PIX1# clear xlate
```

The **clear xlate** command is used to clear the translation table. It should be used after any translation configuration changes are made to remove stale xlate entries.

To make sure that everything was typed in correctly, use the **show nat** and **show global** commands:

```
PIX1# show nat
nat (inside) 1 192.168.1.0 255.255.255.0 0 0
nat (inside) 2 192.168.1.0 255.255.255.0 0 0
nat (inside) 3 192.168.1.0 255.255.255.0 0 0
PIX1# show global
global (outside) 1 10.1.1.1-10.1.1.254 netmask 255.255.255.0
global (outside) 2 10.1.2.1-10.1.2.254 netmask 255.255.255.0
global (outside) 3 10.1.3.1-10.1.3.254 netmask 255.255.255.0
```

In this configuration, the NAT was changed to PAT by setting the global pool to one address; all the addresses specified by the **nat 1** statements will be translated to this single address and distinguished by port numbers.

```
PIX1(config)# nat (inside) 1 192.168.1.0 255.255.255.0
PIX1(config)# nat (inside) 1 192.168.2.0 255.255.255.0
PIX1(config)# nat (inside) 1 192.168.3.0 255.255.255.0
PIX1(config)# global (outside) 1 10.1.1.1-10.1.1.1 netmask 255.255.255.255
PIX1(config)# exit
PIX1# clear xlate
```

NOTE

PAT works with DNS, FTP, HTTP, mail, Remote Procedure Call (RPC), Remote Shell (RSH), Telnet, URL filtering, and outbound traceroute. PAT does not work with H.323, caching name servers, and PPTP.

To enable NAT to work on multiple interfaces, separate **global** commands are needed for each interface. The key is using the same **id** on all **global** commands. Doing so allows one set of **nat** commands on the inside interface to translate a private IP address to one of many different global address ranges based on destination. For example, the following commands would configure the PIX to NAT the 192.168.1.0/24 network to either a 10.1.1.0/24 address or PAT to the DMZ interface IP address, depending on the outbound interface (outside or DMZ).

```
PIX1(config)# nat (inside) 1 192.168.1.0 255.255.255.0
PIX1(config)# global (outside) 1 10.1.1.1-10.1.1.254 netmask 255.255.255.0
PIX1(config)# global (dmz) 1 interface
PIX1(config)# exit
PIX1# clear xlate
```

Use the **no** keyword with the **nat** and **global** commands to remove them from the configuration.

Identity NAT and NAT Bypass

Private addresses are used in the examples as stand-ins for public addresses. In Figure 8.3, identity NAT (AKA NAT bypass) is used to disable the translation of local addresses to global addresses, as we want the local addresses to be the source addresses for outside communications. We are essentially turning off NAT, as seen in the configuration that follows.

Figure 8.3 An Identity NAT Example

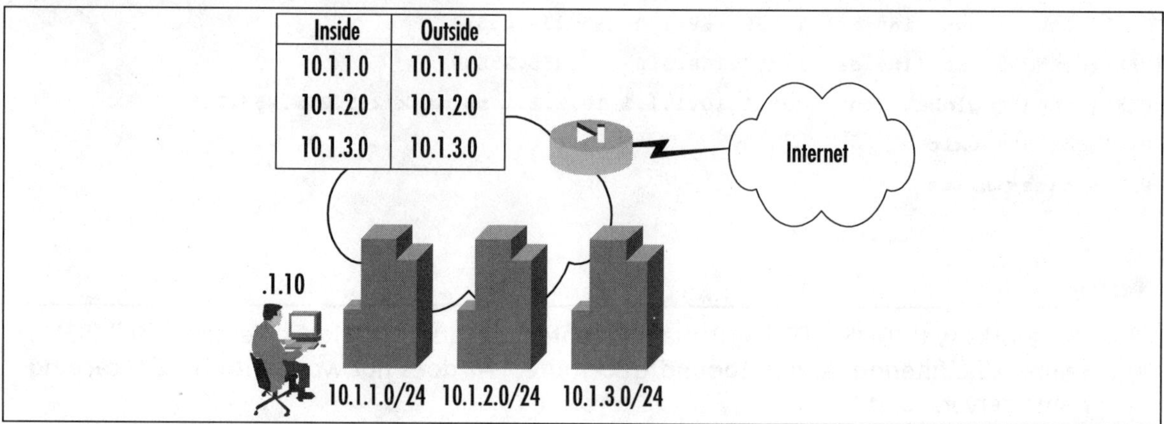

In identity NAT, instead of using an associated **global** command to define the global address, the internal address is mapped to itself when translating. To configure identity NAT, use the **nat** command with an **id** of 0, and do not define an associated **global** command. The commands to configure the PIX in Figure 8.3 are:

```
PIX1(config)# nat (inside) 0 10.1.1.0 255.255.255.0
nat 0 10.1.1.0 will be non-translated
PIX1(config)# nat (inside) 0 10.1.2.0 255.255.255.0
nat 0 10.1.2.0 will be non-translated
PIX1(config)# nat (inside) 0 10.1.3.0 255.255.255.0
nat 0 10.1.3.0 will be non-translated
PIX1(config)# exit
PIX1# clear xlate
```

To verify the configuration, use the **show nat** command to view the current NAT configuration:

```
PIX1# show nat
nat (inside) 0 10.1.1.0 255.255.255.0 0 0
nat (inside) 0 10.1.2.0 255.255.255.0 0 0
nat (inside) 0 10.1.3.0 255.255.255.0 0 0
```

As seen in Figure 8.3, the client opens a connection to a Web server on the Internet. Since the ASA defines that, by default, higher security-level interfaces can send traffic to lower security-level interfaces, the traffic should traverse the PIX and be listed in the xlate table. The **show xlate debug** command should show a mapping for this connection, and it should be flagged with an **I**, or identity flag.

```
PIX1# show xlate debug
1 in use, 1 most used
Flags: D - DNS, d - dump, I - identity, i - inside, n - no random,
    o - outside, r - portmap, s - static
```

```
NAT from inside:10.1.1.10 to outside:10.1.1.10 flags iI idle 0:01:27 timeout 3:00:00
```

NAT can also be bypassed using **nat 0** with an ACL. Define an ACL that identifies the traffic to be translated, and bind it to a **nat 0** statement. This can be a more granular approach allowing you to be more selective about what is and is not translated.

```
access-list <acl_name> permit ip <source_addr> <source_mask> <dest_addr> <dest_mask>
nat (<if_name>) 0 access-list <acl_name>
```

Using Figure 8.3 as an example, the commands to configure the PIX to bypass NAT using an ACL would be as follows:

```
PIX1(config)# access-list inside_public permit ip 10.1.1.0 255.255.255.0 any
PIX1(config)# access-list inside_public permit ip 10.1.2.0 255.255.255.0 any
PIX1(config)# access-list inside_public permit ip 10.1.3.0 255.255.255.0 any
PIX1(config)# nat (inside) 0 access-list inside_public
PIX1(config)# exit
PIX1# clear xlate
```

To verify the configuration, use the **show nat** and **show access-list** commands:

```
PIX1# show nat
nat (inside) 0 access-list inside_public
PIX1# show access-list
access-list inside_public; 3 elements
access-list inside_public permit ip 10.1.1.0 255.255.255.0 any (hitcnt=0)
access-list inside_public permit ip 10.1.2.0 255.255.255.0 any (hitcnt=0)
access-list inside_public permit ip 10.1.3.0 255.255.255.0 any (hitcnt=0)
```

Blocking Outbound Traffic

Controlling outbound traffic can be part of a well-designed security policy. This control can be accomplished using ACLs or outbound/apply statements. ACLs, introduced in PIX firewall software version 5.0, are the newer and recommended method for controlling outbound access on the PIX firewall. Use outbound/apply statements if necessary (for example, if using an older version of the PIX software).

ACLs

ACLs on the PIX firewall can be used to limit traffic based on several criteria, including source address, destination address, source TCP/UDP ports, and destination TCP/UDP ports. ACL configuration is a two-step process:

1. Define the ACL by grouping permit and deny statements using the **access-list** command.
2. Apply the ACL to the interface with the **access-group** command.

There are two protocol options for the **access-list** command: one for non-ICMP protocols, and one for ICMP.

```
access-list <acl_name> {deny | permit} <protocol> <src_addr> <src_mask>
[<dest_operator> <dest_port>] <dest_addr> <dest_mask> [<dest_operator> <dest_port>]

access-list <acl_name> {deny | permit} icmp <src_addr> <src_mask> <dest_addr>
<dest_mask> <icmp_type>
```

The **acl_name** parameter can be either a name or a number. The **protocol** parameter specifies the IP protocol or another protocol such as TCP or UDP. You can either enter the numerical value or specify a literal name, as shown in Table 8.5.

Table 8.5 Literal Protocol Names and Values

Literal	Value	Description
ah	51	Authentication header for IPv6, RFC 1826
eigrp	88	Enhanced Interior Gateway Routing Protocol
esp	50	Encapsulated Security Payload for IPv6, RFC 1827
gre	47	General Routing Encapsulation
icmp	1	ICMP, RFC 792
igmp	2	Internet Group Management Protocol, RFC 1112
igrp	9	Interior Gateway Routing Protocol
ip	0	IP
ipinip	4	IP-in-IP encapsulation
nos	94	Network OS (Novell's NetWare)
ospf	89	Open Shortest Path First (OSPF) routing protocol, RFC 1247
pcp	108	Payload Compression Protocol
snp	109	Sitara Networks Protocol
tcp	6	TCP, RFC 793
udp	17	UDP, RFC 768

To specify all networks or hosts, use the **any** keyword (equivalent to an address and mask combination of 0.0.0.0 0.0.0.0. Use the **host** keyword to specify a single host by IP address. PIX ACLs use standard wildcard masks, whereas on routers they use inverse wildcard masks. For example, when filtering a 24-bit subnet, you would use a mask of 255.255.255.0 on a PIX firewall and a mask of 0.0.0.255 on a Cisco router.

An operator comparison lets you specify a port or port range and is used in combination with the **tcp** or **udp** protocol keywords. To specify all ports, do not specify an operator and port. Operators include **eq** (single port), **gt** (greater than the specified port), and **neq** (all ports except the one specified). **Range** defines a specific range of ports. Ports can be specified using either a number or a literal name such as bgp or http instead of TCP port 179 or port 80, respectively.

The **icmp_type** parameter allows you to permit or deny access to ICMP message types such as type 0 (echo-reply) or type 11 (time-exceeded).

After configuring an ACL, apply it to an interface with the **access-group <acl_name> in interface <if_name>** command. The name associated with an ACL is specified as **acl_name**, whereas the name of the interface that the ACL will use to monitor inbound traffic is specified by **if_name**. An ACL, once applied to an interface using the **access-group** command, denies or permits traffic as it enters the PIX on the specified interface. ACLs on the PIX firewall can only be applied to traffic entering an interface, not traffic that is exiting an interface. This is unlike Cisco routers, on which ACLs can be applied in either direction.

ACLs on the PIX firewall have an implicit **deny all** attached to the end of the ACL. ACLs are processed sequentially from top to bottom. Only one ACL at a time can be applied to an interface.

Figure 8.4 shows a network with a PIX guarding a network addressed with 192.168.0.0/22, and with public addresses of 10.1.1.0/24.

Figure 8.4 The Secure Corporation ACL Example

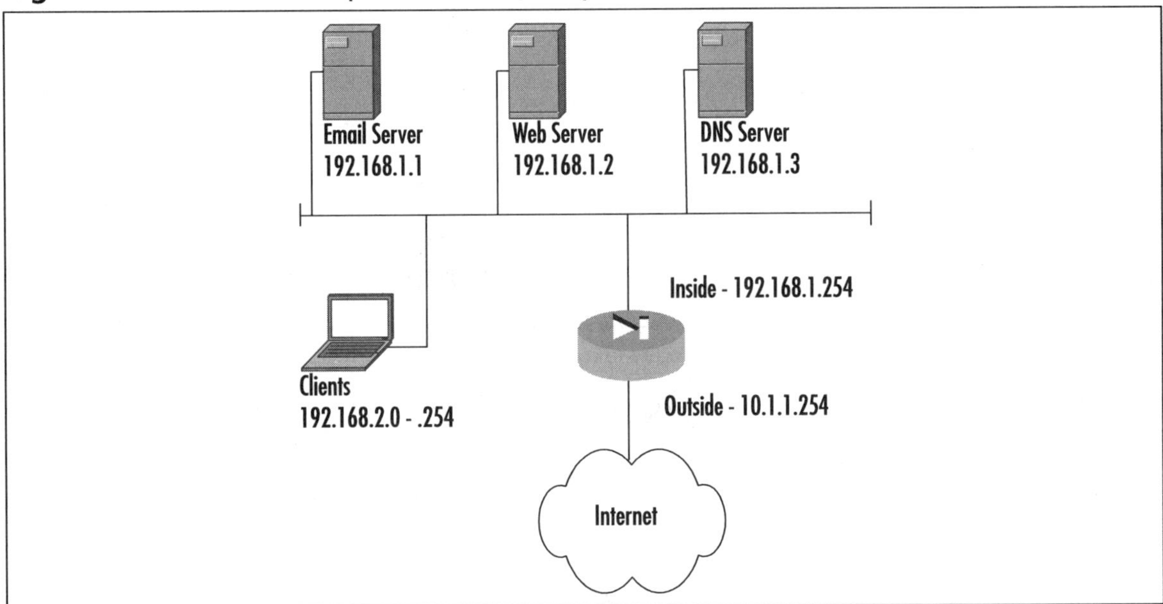

Workstations addressed with 192.168.2.0/24 need to be limited to outbound Web access only; the servers can initiate any IP sessions they want. All other traffic from the inside network is to be denied by default. The configuration to accomplish this is shown.

```
PIX1(config)# access-list inside_in permit tcp 192.168.2.0 255.255.255.0 any eq 80
PIX1(config)# access-list inside_in permit ip 192.168.1.1 255.255.255.255 any
PIX1(config)# access-list inside_in permit ip 192.168.1.2 255.255.255.255 any
PIX1(config)# access-list inside_in permit ip 192.168.1.3 255.255.255.255 any
PIX1(config)# access-group inside_in in interface inside
```

A good practice is to add an explicit **deny all** statement to the end of an ACL so you remember it is there when you do a **show access-list** command and to view its **hitcnt** counter:

```
PIX1(config)# access-list inside_in deny ip any any
PIX1(config)# exit
PIX1# show access-list
```

```
access-list inside_in; 4 elements
access-list inside_in permit tcp 192.168.2.0 255.255.255.0 any eq www
    (hitcnt=2)
access-list inside_in permit ip host 192.168.1.1 any (hitcnt=0)
access-list inside_in permit ip host 192.168.1.2 any (hitcnt=0)
access-list inside_in permit ip host 192.168.1.3 any (hitcnt=0)
access-list inside_in deny ip any any (hitcnt=40)
```

Publicly accessible servers should not be located on the inside network, but on a DMZ network created for that purpose. If a server on the DMZ network becomes compromised, it is possible to contain the compromise to the DMZ and away from a higher security level network such as the inside network. Figure 8.5 shows a revised network layout.

Figure 8.5 Secure Corporation Revised Network Layout

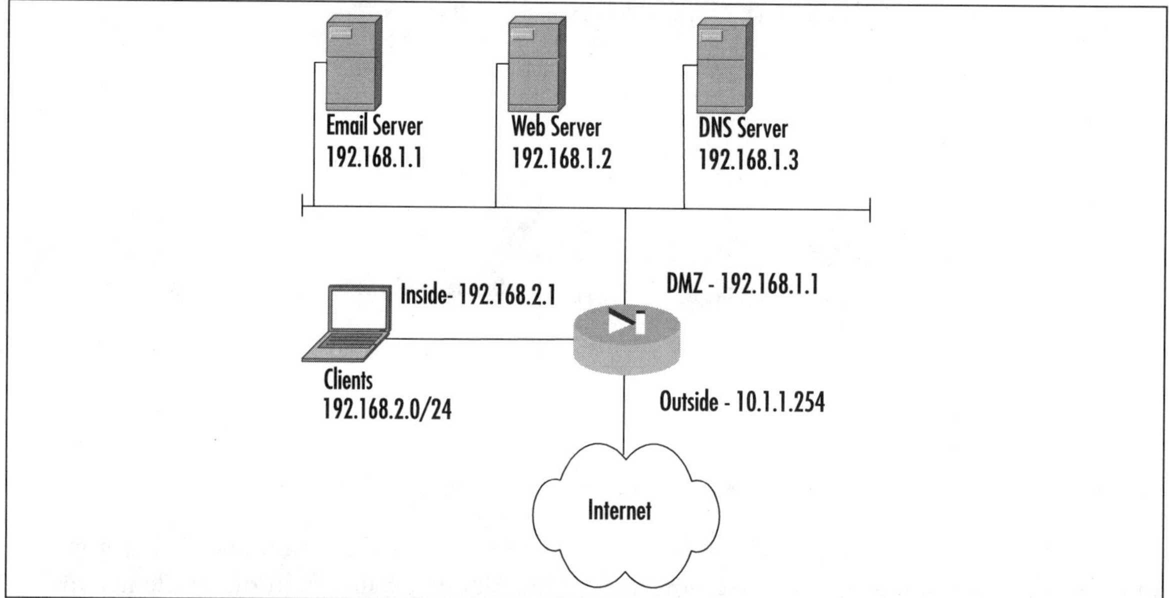

From the diagram, it is apparent that the network requirements have changed, because services the clients used to be able to get to without going through the firewall now need to be added to the ACLs. Unlike the ACL created before, the servers should not be allowed to access any IP address without restriction. A DMZ ACL should be created that locks down the services that the servers are able to use, because if these servers become compromised, you want to limit their ability to infect your network or even someone else's. The commands to create and apply these ACLs are:

```
access-list inside_in permit tcp 192.168.2.0 255.255.255.0 any eq www
access-list inside_in permit tcp 192.168.2.0 255.255.255.0 192.168.1.1 eq smtp
access-list inside_in permit tcp 192.168.2.0 255.255.255.0 192.168.1.1 eq pop3
access-list inside_in permit udp 192.168.2.0 255.255.255.0 192.168.1.3 eq domain
```

```
access-list inside_in permit tcp 192.168.2.0 255.255.255.0 192.168.1.3 eq domain
access-list inside_in deny ip any any

access-group inside_in in interface inside

access-list dmz_in permit tcp 192.168.1.1 255.255.255.255 any eq smtp
access-list dmz_in permit udp 192.168.1.3 255.255.255.255 any eq domain
access-list dmz_in permit tcp 192.168.1.3 255.255.255.255 any eq domain
access-list dmz_in deny ip any any

access-group dmz_in in interface dmz
```

One very useful feature in configuring the PIX is the **name** command, which allows you to define an alias for an IP address mapping to reference a host by name instead of IP address. Such descriptive names can help maintain and troubleshoot the PIX configuration. The syntax for the **name** command is **name <ip_address> <name>**. For example, the **name 10.1.1.10 mail** command maps the name mail to the IP address 10.1.1.10. The name mail can now be used in ACLs instead of an IP address.

Outbound/Apply

While no longer advocated by Cisco (which recommends using ACLs instead), the **outbound** and **apply** commands can control traffic. The **outbound** command only identifies traffic to be filtered. The **apply** command binds the outbound list to an interface, essentially activating it. The syntax for the **outbound** command is **outbound <list_id> permit | deny <ip_address> [<netmask> [<port>[-port>]] [<protocol>]**.

Once the **apply** command is bound to an interface, ingress traffic to that interface is filtered by the outbound list. The syntax for the **apply** command is **apply [(<if_name>)] <list_id> outgoing_src | outgoing_dest**.

An example outbound/apply configuration is provided:

```
outbound 20 permit 0.0.0.0 0.0.0.0 0
outbound 20 deny 0.0.0.0 0.0.0.0 echo
outbound 20 deny 0.0.0.0 0.0.0.0 discard
outbound 20 deny 0.0.0.0 0.0.0.0 chargen
apply (inside) 20 outgoing_src
```

The outbound **except** keyword reverse the filtering specified for the identified IP address. For example, if the normal behavior of a rule is to allow all source addresses to access all services, an **except** parameter would deny a specific destination. The **outbound 20 except 10.10.1.10 255.255.255.255 0** command applies the outbound statements to all hosts except 10.10.1.10. To verify a configuration, use the **show outbound [list_id]** command.

Allowing Inbound Traffic

The PIX ASA defines traffic originating from a lower security-level interface to a higher security-level interface as *inbound traffic*. Inbound traffic is denied by default, which protects higher security-level networks. Allowing inbound traffic to traverse the PIX is a two-step process. Static translations need to be defined, and an ACL or conduit needs to be created and applied. Similar to the **outbound** or **apply** commands, the **conduit** command has been replaced by ACLs.

Static Address Translation

Use the **static** command to create static translations to permit inbound access. This command creates a permanent translation in the PIX translation table for the global-to-local IP address mapping.

```
static [(<internal_if_name>, <external_if_name>)] {<global_ip> | interface} <local_ip>
[netmask <mask>] [<max_conns> [<em_limit>]] [norandomseq]
```

The **internal_if_name** interface is the interface name to which the address being translated is connected, while the **external_if_name** interface contains the incoming external network. The default value for both **max_conns** and **em_limit** is 0 (unlimited), and these parameters have the same meaning as they do in the **nat** command.

The following example maps the outside address (10.1.5.10) to the DMZ address 192.168.1.2.

```
PIX1(config)# static (dmz, outside) 10.1.5.10 192.168.1.2 netmask 255.255.255.255 0 0
```

The following example maps a range of outsides addresses (10.1.5.0/28) to a range of DMZ addresses 192.168.1.0/28.

```
PIX1(config)# static (dmz, outside) 10.1.5.0 192.168.1.0 netmask 255.255.255.240 0 0
```

The key thing is that **static** commands are required to enable lower to higher security communications. In the following example, the DMZ address 192.168.1.2 is *not* translated, and will access the inside network with its true source address. This is the static equivalent of **nat 0**.

```
PIX1(config)# static (inside, dmz) 192.168.1.2 192.168.1.2 netmask 255.255.255.255 0 0
```

Once the necessary static statements for inbound access are created, an inbound ACL or conduit must be defined and applied to actually permit traffic.

ACLs

The process of creating an inbound ACL is the same as for outbound ACLs, as discussed previously in this chapter. One key difference is that the inbound ACL is applied to the lower security-level interface where the incoming traffic originates.

Conduits

Conduit commands are no longer recommended by Cisco (which recommends ACLs instead), but can be used to permit inbound access. The **conduit** command syntax is provided; however, notice how awkward and counterintuitive is it.

```
conduit permit | deny <protocol> <global_ip> <global_mask> [<operator> <port>
[<port>]] <foreign_ip> <foreign_mask> [<operator> <port> [<port>]]
```

For example, if a Web server with an internal IP address of 172.16.1.10 resides on the DMZ network, the following commands would allow access to the Web server from any foreign IP address:

```
PIX1(config)# static (dmz, outside) 10.1.5.10 172.16.1.10 netmask 255.255.255.255 0
0
PIX1(config)# conduit permit tcp host 10.1.5.10 eq www any
```

The **show conduit** command displays all conduits currently configured.

```
PIX1# show conduit
conduit permit tcp host 10.1.5.10 eq www any (hitcnt=0)
conduit permit udp host 10.1.5.11 eq domain any (hitcnt=0)
conduit permit tcp host 10.1.5.11 eq domain any (hitcnt=0)
conduit permit tcp host 10.1.5.12 eq smtp any (hitcnt=0)
```

ICMP

Inbound ICMP traffic is controlled using the **icmp** command, which only filters ICMP traffic terminating on a PIX interface, as opposed to traversing the PIX. In other words, it filters ICMP traffic that enters any PIX interface.

```
icmp {permit|deny} <ip_address> <netmask> [<icmp_type>] <if_name>
```

For example, the following command permits the DMZ interface to respond to pings from the private network 172.16.0.0 255.255.240.0:

```
PIX1(config)# icmp permit 172.16.0.0 255.240.0.0 echo dmz
```

Port Redirection

Port redirection allows one public IP address to serve as the global IP address for more than one server located on inside or DMZ networks. Port redirection maps a session originating from an external network to a port on an inside or DMZ host. An inbound ACL is also required to permit incoming traffic. The **static** command, with a few modifications, is used to accomplish port redirection.

```
static [(<prenat_if_name>, <postnat_if_name>)] {tcp | udp} {<global_ip>| interface}
<global_port> <local_ip> <local_port> [netmask <mask>] [<max_conns> [<em_limit>]]
[norandomseq]
```

The parameters **global_port** and **local_port** are used to specify the TCP or UDP port used in the redirection. Instead of using a **global_ip**, the **interface** option should be used to specify the PIX interface to which local addresses will be translated. The example here configures port redirection for a Web server using the outside interface. Traffic to the IP address of the outside interface and port 80 will be redirected to 172.16.1.1 port 80 on the DMZ network. Figure 8.6 illustrates the port redirection process.

```
PIX1(config)# static (dmz, outside) tcp interface 80 172.16.1.1 80
```

In Figure 8.6, port redirection is also configured for Telnet, FTP, and another Web server as shown here. Since port 80 was used previously, 8080is used for the second Web server.

```
PIX1(config)# static (dmz, outside) tcp interface 23 172.16.1.2 23
PIX1(config)# static (dmz, outside) tcp interface 8080 172.16.1.3 80
PIX1(config)# static (dmz, outside) tcp interface 21 172.16.1.4 21
```

Figure 8.6 A Port Redirection Example

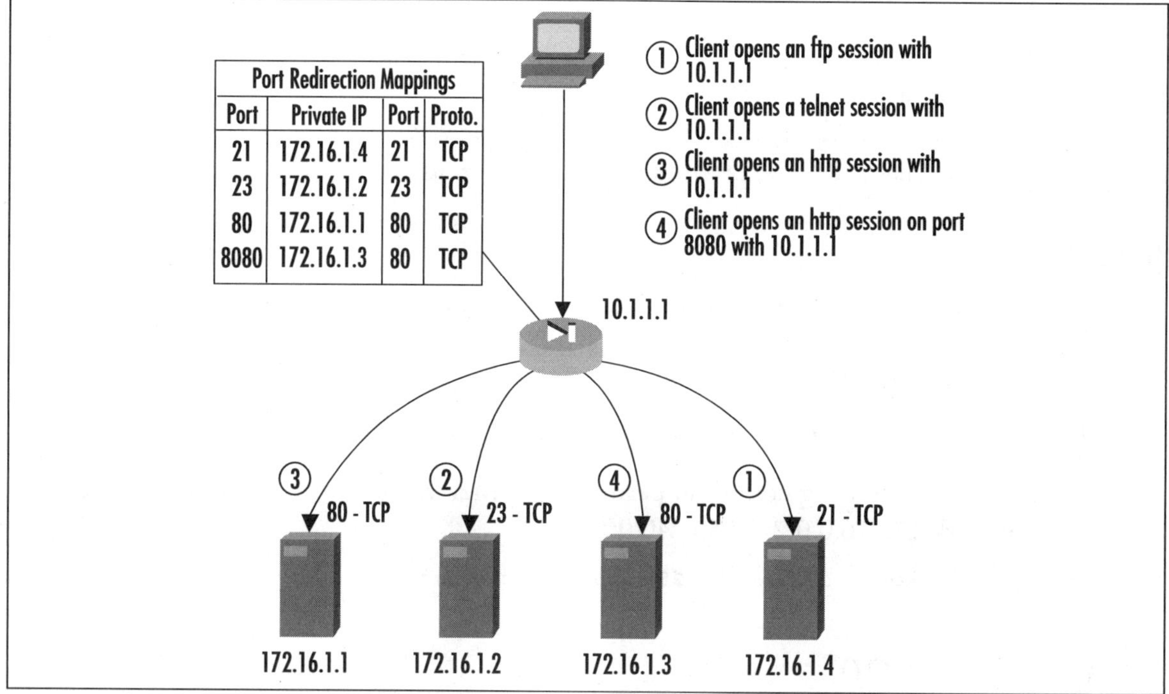

TurboACLs

TurboACLs are a new feature in PIX firewall software version 6.2 that compiles a long or complex ACL to enable faster processing of traffic through the ACL. TurboACLs do not speed up short ACLs; in fact, the PIX will not enable this feature on an ACL unless it is over 18 lines. TurboACL creates an index that enables the PIX to process the ACL faster.

The index created by a TurboACL requires a fair amount of resources, and should not be configured on anything lower than a 525 series firewall. To enable the TurboACL feature on all

ACLs of the PIX, use the **access-list compiled global** command, which compiles all ACLs over 18 lines long. To verify that the TurboACLs are indeed turned on, issue a **show access-list** command:

```
PIX1(config)# show access-list
access-list compiled
access-list inside_public turbo-configured; 3 elements
access-list inside_public permit ip 10.1.1.0 255.255.255.0 any (hitcnt=0)
access-list inside_public permit ip 10.1.2.0 255.255.255.0 any (hitcnt=0)
access-list inside_public permit ip 10.1.3.0 255.255.255.0 any (hitcnt=0)
```

TurboACLs can be turned on and off for individual ACLs with the **access-list <acl-name> compiled** command. This feature can be very useful if there are only a few ACLs that need to be optimized. An example of individual compiling is shown here.

```
PIX1(config)# no access-list compiled
PIX1(config)# access-list outside_in compiled
```

Object Grouping

Introduced in 6.2, *object grouping* makes very complex ACLs much simpler to maintain and support. Object groups define groups of network addresses, services, protocols, and ICMP types, thereby reducing the number of ACL entries needed.

For example, to deny inside users access to a number of external FTP servers requires an ACL be defined for each individual FTP server. With object groups, a network object group containing a list of IP addresses of the FTP servers can be defined and applied. The ACL can then deny this network object group, rather than individual entries for each FTP server. The ACL does not need to be modified if entries are added or removed from the object group.

Configuring and Using Object Groups

There are four types of object groups: *icmp-type, protocol, network,* and *service.* Each type corresponds to a field in the **access-list** or **conduit** command.

ICMP-type Object Groups

An *ICMP-type object group* is a group of ICMP-type numerical or literal values. ICMP-type object groups can replace the **icmp-type** parameter in an ACL or conduit (**object-group icmp-type <grp_id>**).

Once an object group has been defined, the subconfiguration mode enables the object group to be populated. An optional description can be specified using the **description** subcommand. To populate the ICMP-type object group, use the **icmp-object <icmp_type>** syntax.

For example, the following object group defines ICMP-type values that will be filtered with an ACL or conduit.

```
PIX1(config)# object-group icmp-type icmp-grp
```

```
PIX1(config-icmp-type)# description ICMP Type allowed into the PIX
PIX1(config-icmp-type)# icmp-object echo-reply
PIX1(config-icmp-type)# icmp-object unreachable
```

Network Object Groups

A *network object group* is a group of host IP addresses or networks that replace **src_addr** or **dst_addr** parameters in an **access-list** or **conduit** statement. To create a network object group, use the **object-group network <grp_id>** syntax.

Network object groups have two subcommands for defining the group of hosts and networks. For hosts, the subcommand is **network-object host <host_addr | host_name>**. The syntax for defining a network entry in the object group is **network-object <net_addr> <netmask>.**

For example, the following object group defines host and network values to be used later with an ACL or conduit:

```
PIX1(config)# object-group network net-grp
PIX1(config-network)# description List of Public HTTP Servers
PIX1(config-network)# network-object host 192.168.1.10
PIX1(config-network)# network-object host 172.16.10.1
PIX1(config-network)# network-object 172.16.2.0 255.255.255.0
PIX1(config-network)# exit
PIX1(config)# exit
```

Protocol Object Groups

A *protocol object group* is a group of protocol numbers or literal values that can replace the **protocol** parameter in an **access-list** or **conduit** command (**object-group protocol <grp_id>**).

Once an object group has been defined, the subconfiguration mode **protocol-object <protocol>** enables the object group to be populated. The **protocol** parameter is a protocol number or literal value. For example, the following object group defines a group of protocols that will be used later with an ACL or conduit to provide VPN access:

```
PIX1(config)# object-group protocol vpn-grp
PIX1(config-protocol)# description Protocols allowed for VPN Access
PIX1(config-protocol)# protocol-object ah
PIX1(config-protocol)# protocol-object esp
PIX1(config-protocol)# protocol-object gre
PIX1(config-protocol)# exit
PIX1(config)# exit
```

Service Object Groups

A *service object group* is a group of TCP and/or UDP port numbers or port number ranges that can replace the **port** parameter in an ACL or a conduit (**object-group service <grp_id> tcp | udp | tcp-udp**).

Since a service object group is a listing of ports and port ranges, the ports defined need to be configured as TCP, UDP, or both. The **tcp**, **udp**, and **tcp-udp** keywords define the common IP protocol for all ports listed in the object group (**port-object eq <port>**).

The sub-configuration command syntax to populate the service object group with a range of ports is: **port-object range <begin-port> <end-port>**.

For example, the following object group defines a group of ports that all Web servers within an organization need to have opened on the firewall:

```
PIX1(config)# object-group service websrv-grp tcp
PIX1(config-service)# description Ports needed on public web servers
PIX1(config-service)# port-object eq 80
PIX1(config-service)# port-object eq 8080
PIX1(config-service)# port-object range 9000 9010
```

To verify that an object group was created and populated with the correct information, the current object group configuration can be viewed using the **show object-group** command:

```
PIX1# show object-group
object-group icmp-type icmp-grp
  description: ICMP Type allowed into the PIX
  icmp-object echo-reply
  icmp-object unreachable
object-group network net-grp
  description: List of Public HTTP Servers
  network-object host 192.168.1.10
  network-object host 172.16.10.1
  network-object 172.16.2.0 255.255.255.0
object-group protocol vpn-grp
  description: Protocols allowed for VPN Access
  protocol-object ah
  protocol-object gre
  protocol-object esp
object-group service websrv-grp tcp
  description: Ports needed on public web servers
  port-object eq www
  port-object eq 8080
  port-object range 9000 9010
```

If one of the object groups does not look correct or is not needed, it can be removed using the **no object-group <grp_id>** command.

Object groups can be used in place of their respective values in ACLs or conduits, and must be preceded by the **object-group** keyword. For example, to allow the ICMP-type values defined in the **icmp-grp** object group to enter the PIX's outside interface, the **access-list** command is **access-list icmp_in permit icmp any any object-group icmp-grp**.

To allow access to the Web servers defined in the **net-grp** on the ports defined in **websrv-grp**, the command is **access-list outside_in permit tcp any object-group net-grp object-group websrv-grp**.

Object groups of the same type can be nested together. For example:

```
PIX1(config)# object-group network all-servers
PIX1(config-network)# group-object net-grp
PIX1(config-network)# network-object 172.16.3.0 255.255.255.0
```

Handling Advanced Protocols

One of the most important features of all firewalls is their ability to intelligently handle many different protocols and applications. Unfortunately, many applications, some of which were developed before the idea of a firewall emerged, act in a much more complicated manner than Telnet or HTTP. The general problem: these applications use more than one connection to operate and only one of these connections occurs on a well-known port, while the others use dynamically negotiated port numbers. Figure 8.7 shows an example of what happens when this situation occurs and no special measures are in place. (This is a simplified example of SQL*net session negotiation.)

Figure 8.7 Client Redirection without Application Inspection

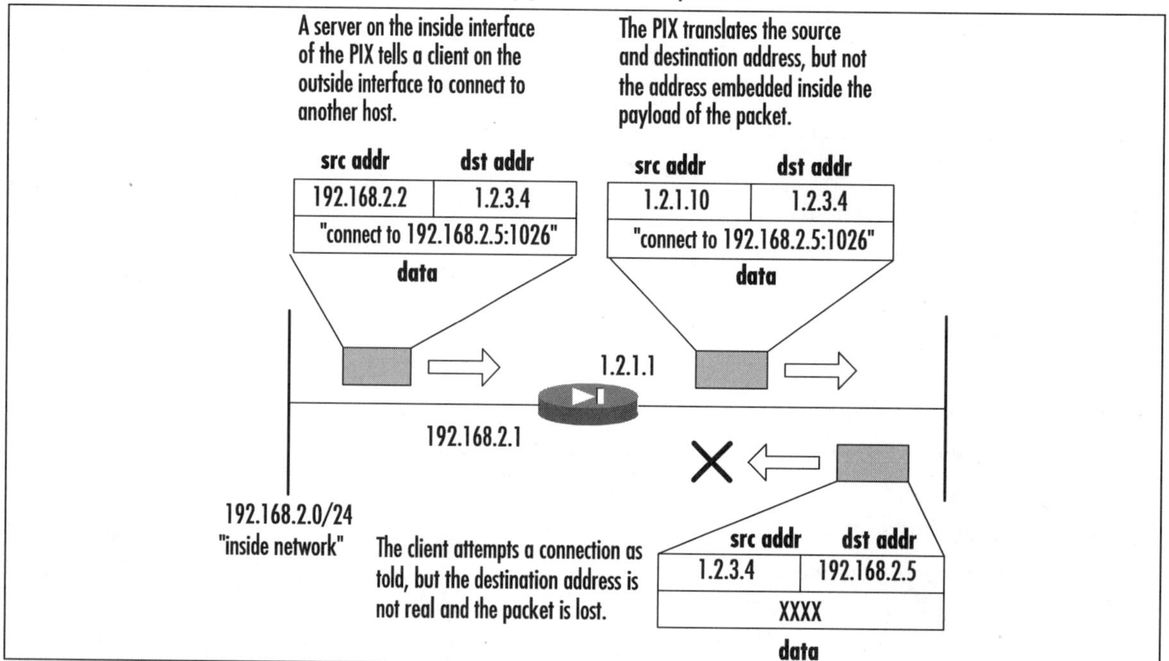

A firewall needs to monitor such applications, understand them, and adjust accordingly. This situation becomes even more complicated when NAT or PAT are involved; the firewall might need to change the data portion of a packet that carries embedded address information in order for the packet to be correctly processed by a client or server on the other side of PIX. There are many implementations of this feature for various firewalls (for example, the ASA of Cisco PIX devices).

The ASA uses several sources of information during its operation:

- ACLs that filter traffic based on hosts, networks, and the TCP or UDP ports involved.
- Embedded rules for application inspection, which allows automatic processing of most of the complicated cases mentioned. Although some of these rules are configurable, others are fixed.

The following steps are involved in processing a TCP packet by ASA, including application-level intelligence (not considering address translation):

1. If the packet is not the first one in a connection (with the SYN bit set), it is checked against internal tables to determine if it is a reply to an established connection. If not, it is denied.
2. If it is a SYN packet, check internal tables to determine if it is part of another established connection. If it is, the packet is permitted and tables are modified to allow return traffic for this connection.
3. If this SYN packet is not a part of any established communication, it is checked against ACLs.
4. If the SYN packet is permitted, create a new entry in internal tables (xlate and/or CONN table).
5. Determine whether the packet needs additional processing by application-level inspection algorithms. During this phase, the firewall can create additional entries in internal tables.
6. The inspected packet is forwarded to the destination.

The situation for UDP is similar, although simpler because there are no distinct initial packets in the UDP protocol, so the inspection simply goes through internal tables and ACLs and then through application inspection for each packet received. Figure 8.8 illustrates how the same example from Figure 8.7 would work with application inspection turned on.

Figure 8.8 Application Inspection in Action

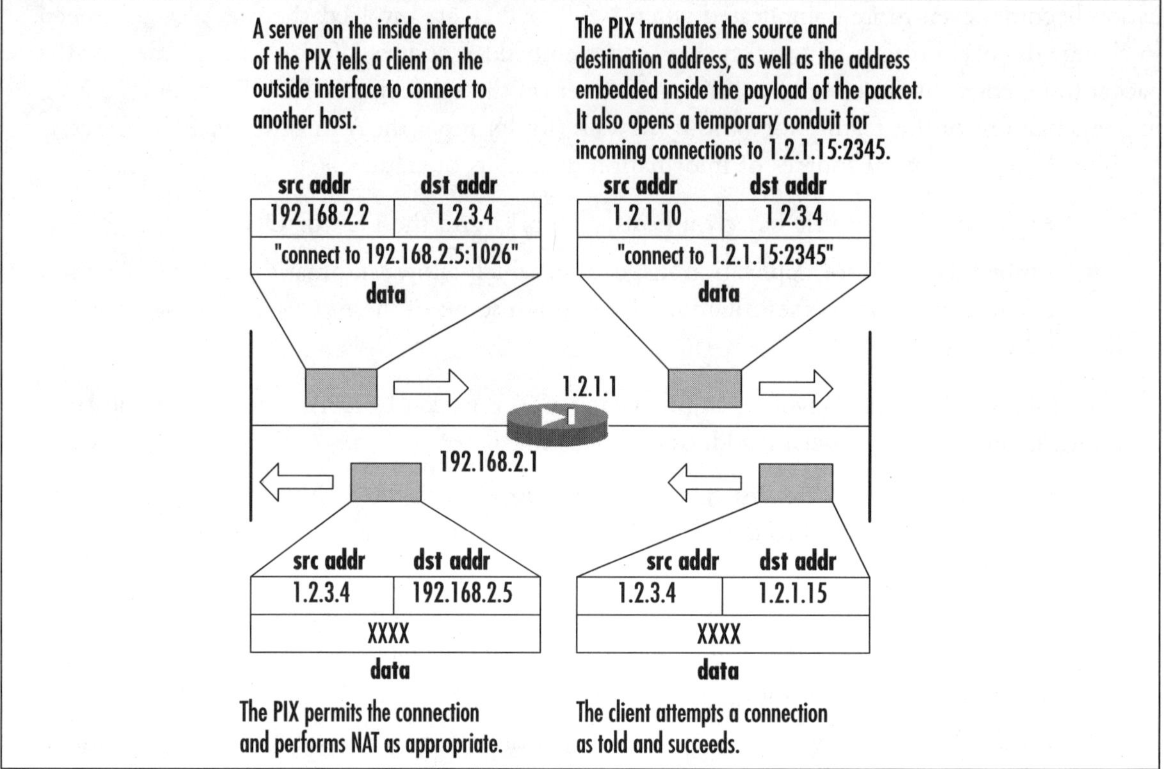

The PIX uses source/destination port numbers to decide if application inspection is needed for a particular packet. Some of these ports are configurable and others are not. Table 8.6 summarizes the application inspection functions provided by PIX firewall software version 6.2.

Table 8.6 Application Inspection Features of Cisco PIX Firewall Version 6.2

Application	PAT Support	NAT 1-1 Support	Configurable?	Default Port	Related Standards
H.323	Yes	Yes	Yes	TCP/1720 UDP/1718	H.323, H.245, H.225.0, Q.931, Q.932
H.323 RAS	Yes	Yes	Yes	UDP/1719	N/A
SIP	Yes	Yes	Yes No	TCP/5060 UDP/5060	RFC 2543
FTP	Yes	Yes	Yes	TCP/21	RFC 1123
LDAP (ILS)	Yes	No outside NAT	Yes	TCP/389	N/A
SMTP	Yes	Yes	Yes	TCP/25	RFC 821, 1123
SQL*Net v.1, v.2	Yes	Yes	Yes	TCP/1521 (v.1)	N/A
HTTP	Yes	Yes	Yes	TCP/80	RFC 2616
RSH	Yes	Yes	Yes	TCP/514	Berkeley UNIX
SCCP	No	Yes	Yes	TCP/2000	N/A
DNS	Yes	Yes	No	UDP/53	RFC 1123
NetBIOS over IP	See next two entries				
NBNS/UDP	No	No	No	UDP/137	N/A
NBDS/UDP	Yes	Yes	No	UDP/138	N/A
Sun RPC	No	No	No	UDP/111 TCP/111	N/A
XDCMP	No	No	No	UDP/117	N/A
RTSP	No	No	Yes	TCP/554	RFC 2326, 2327, 1889
CU-SeeMe	No	No	No	UDP/7648	N/A
ICMP	Yes	Yes	No	N/A	N/A
VDO Live	No	Yes	No	TCP/7000	N/A
Windows Media (NetShow)	No	Yes	No	TCP/1755	N/A

The main command used to configure the services stated as "configurable" in Table 8.6 (FTP, H.323, HTTP, ILS, RSH, RTSP, SIP, SSCP, SMTP, and SQL*Net) is the **fixup** command. Its basic syntax is **[no] fixup protocol [protocol] [port]**.

Filtering Web Traffic

PIX firewalls can enforce an acceptable use policy for Web access, as well as handle *active content* such as ActiveX or Java applets, which could be used to hide malicious codes.

Filtering URLs

It is possible to use ACLs to filter Web sites, but if the list of sites grows long, this solution will affect firewall performance. ACLs do not allow you to specify specific Web pages. One common approach is to offload these duties to a dedicated URL filtering server, which allows for fine-tuning of Web access controls. The sequence of events is as follows:

1. A client establishes a TCP connection to a Web server.
2. The client sends an HTTP request for a page on this server.
3. The PIX intercepts this request and hands it over to the filtering server.
4. The filtering server decides if the client should be allowed access to the requested page.
5. If the decision is positive, the PIX forwards the request to the server and the client receives the requested content.
6. If the decision is negative, the client's request is dropped.

Figure 8.9 demonstrates this process.

Figure 8.9 Interaction Among a Client, a Web Server, PIX, and a Filtering Server

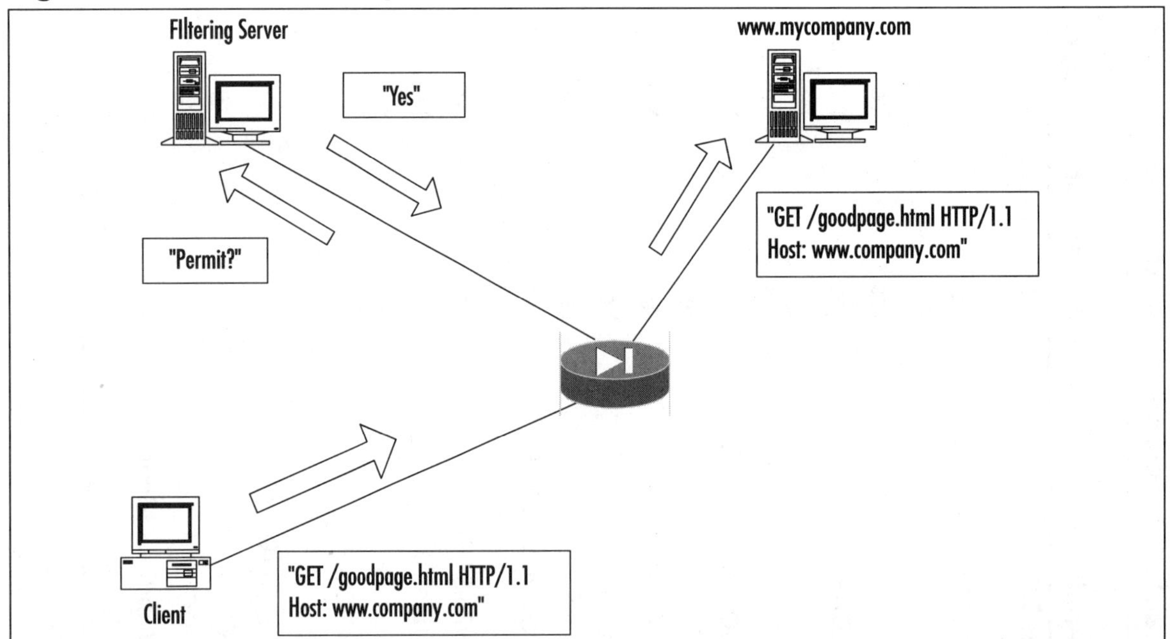

Websense and N2H2

The PIX can interact with two types of filtering servers: Websense (www.websense.com) and N2H2 (www.n2h2.com). Websense is supported in PIX version 5.3 and later, and N2H2 support was added in version 6.2. PIX URL filtering is applied only to HTTP requests. The PIX also does not inspect Hyper Text Transfer Protocol Secure (HTTPS) connections.

The command for specifying a filtering server for Websense is:

```
url-server (<if_name>) host <local_ip> [timeout <seconds>] [protocol <tcp> | <udp>
[version 1|4]]
```

For example, the following command specifies that the PIX should use a server with IP address 10.0.0.1, which is located on the interface "inside," and connects to it using TCP Websense protocol v4:

```
PIX1(config)# url-server (inside) host 10.0.0.1 protocol tcp version 4
```

The PIX uses **timeout** (default is five seconds) to specify how long it will wait for a reply before it tries the next configured server or takes a default action if there are no more servers available. It is possible to configure up to 16 servers, but they must all be of the same type; it is not possible to mix Websense and N2H2 filtering servers in the same configuration. Protocol type and version parameters specify the Websense protocol that should be used for communication with the server. It can be either TCP protocol version 1 (default) or 4 for UDP protocol version 4. If the application type is switched (that is, changed from a N2H2 server to a Websense or vice versa), all configuration of URL filtering is lost and must be re-entered.

The N2H2 server is specified by the command:

```
url-server (if_name) vendor n2h2 host <local_ip> [timeout <seconds>] [port
<port_number>] [protocol tcp | udp]
```

The next task is to configure the filtering policy itself. The relevant command is:

```
filter url <port>[-<port>] <local_ip> <local_mask> <foreign_ip> <foreign_mask> [allow]
[proxy-block]
```

This command specifies port numbers on which HTTP connections should be inspected (with the default of port 80). **local_ip** and **local_mask** specify which local clients are subject to monitoring (that is, the requests by the machines from this network will be checked with URL filtering server). The **foreign_ip** and **foreign_mask** parameters specify that only requests to a specific set of servers be checked. The **allow** parameter defines that the PIX should permit traffic through if it is unable to contact the primary URL filtering server. Finally, the **proxy-block** parameter specifies that all requests from any clients to proxy servers will be denied. For example, the following command defines that all HTTP requests to port 80 will be inspected:

```
PIX1(config)# filter url http 0 0 0 0
```

The following command inspects all HTTP requests to port 8080 from clients on network 10.100.1.0/24 to any server, and allows the request to pass through if a filtering server is unavailable:

```
PIX1(config)# filter url 8080 10.100.1.0 255.255.255.0 0 0 allow
```

Another variant of the **filter** command specifies certain traffic should be exempt from filtering:

```
filter url except <local_ip> <local_mask> <foreign_ip> <foreign_mask>
```

When entered after the **filter** command, this command excludes specified traffic from the policy. For example, the following sequence of commands means that all HTTP traffic to port 8080 will be inspected, excluding traffic from network 10.100.1.0/24:

```
PIX1(config)# filter url 8080 0 0 0 0
PIX1(config)# filter url except 10.100.1.0 255.255.255.0 0 0 allow
```

Fine-Tuning and Monitoring the Filtering Process

The **url-server** and **filter url** commands constitute a basic configuration for URL filtering, but some extra parameters might need to be configured. One of these is required to deal with the problem of long URLs, to store session and other information in the URL itself. A typical long URL could look like this:

```
http://www.somebettingcompany.com/?action=GoEv&class_id=1&type_id=2&ev_id=4288&class_na
me=%7CFootball%7C&type_name=%7CChampions+League%7C+%7CQualifying+Matches%7C&ev_name=%7C
Genk%7C+v+%7CSparta+Prague%7C
```

Until v6.2, the maximum supported URL length was 1159 bytes (for Websense only; N2H2 was not supported at all). In version 6.2, the maximum URL length for Websense filtering is 6KB and 1,159 bytes for N2H2. v6.2 introduced new options to the **filter** command to configure the firewall's behavior when the URL exceeds 1,159 bytes with a Websense server.

```
filter url [longurl-truncate | longurl-deny] [cgi-truncate]
```

The **longurl-truncate** parameter specifies that when the URL length exceeds the maximum, only the IP address or hostname from the request, instead of the full URL, is sent to the filtering server. The **longurl-deny** parameter specifies that all long URL requests should be dropped. The **cgi-truncate** parameter specifies that only the CGI script name and its location (the part of the URL before the **?** sign) should be passed as the URL to the Websense server. This skips the Common Gateway Interface (CGI) parameter list, which can be quite long. Without this option enabled, the entire URL, including the parameter list, is passed.

NOTE

Even in PIXv6.2, the default URL size passed to a Websense filtering server for processing is 2KB. To increase this size, use the command **url-block url-size <size_in_kb>**, where **size_in_kb** can be changed from 2 to 6.

There are also commands for fine-tuning performance. The most important is the **url-cache {dst | src_dst} size <kbytes>** command. This command tunes the process of caching replies from filtering servers. By default, the PIX sends requests to the URL filtering server for a decision and to the Web server for content at the same time, and if the Web server replies faster than the filtering server, the Web server's reply is dropped. The Web server is then contacted again if the filtering server permits the connection. To prevent these double requests, the filtering server replies can be stored locally instead of contacting the server every time. The **url-cache** command enables a cache of kilobytes for replies of filtering servers based either on destination (that is, Web server address) when the **dst** option is specified, or on both the source and destination when **src_dst** is specified. The first option is recommended when all users have the same access privileges (so there is no need to identify clients), and the second is recommended when different users have different access privileges. The statistics of the caching process, including the hit ratio, can be viewed by executing the **show url-cache stat** command.

For example, the **url-cache dst size 32**command enables a cache of 32KB for all outgoing HTTP requests. The following are cache statistics:

```
PIX1# show url-cache stat
URL Filter Cache Stats
------------------
Size : 32KB
Entries : 360
In Use : 200
Lookups : 2000
Hits : 1000
```

The **url-block block <block_buffer_limit>** command compensates for slow filtering server response by caching Web server replies and passing them to the client after the filtering server permits it. This command configures the size of the reply cache.

The **block_buffer_limit** defines how many blocks of memory will be used (1 to 128). Usage statistics for this memory pool can be viewed using the **show url-block block stat** command.

```
pix(config)# show url-block block stat

URL Pending Packet Buffer Stats with max block        1
-------------------------------------------------------
Cumulative number of packets held:                     0
Maximum number of packets held (per URL):              0
Current number of packets held (global):               0
Packets dropped due to exceeding url-block buffer limit:  0
Packet drop due to retransmission:                     0
```

The total amount of memory used for storing URLs and pending URLs (the ones for which no response from the filtering server has yet been received) is configured with the **url-block url-mempool <memory_pool_size>**command.

The size of the allocated memory pool is from 2KB to 10,240KB . Other commands for viewing the configuration of URL filtering are:

```
show filter
show url-server
show url-server stats
```

Here is some example output from these commands:

```
PIX1# show url-server
url-server (outside) vendor n2h2 host 192.168.2.17 port 4005 timeout 5
protocol TCP
url-server (outside) vendor n2h2 host 192.168.2.10 port 4005 timeout 5
protocol TCP
PIX1# show filter
filter url http 0.0.0.0 0.0.0.0 0.0.0.0 0.0.0.0
PIX1# show url-server stats
URL Server Statistics:
------------------------
Vendor n2h2
URLs total/allowed/denied 2556/2000/556
URL Server Status:
------------------------
192.168.2.17 UP
192.168.2.10 DOWN
```

The following monitoring commands can also be used for monitoring the performance of the URL filtering process:

```
show perfmon
show memory
show chunks
```

Active Code Filtering

Active content in Web pages could be considered undesirable from a security point of view. In HTML, active content is denoted by two types of tags. The first is:

```
<object>
...
</object>
```

These tags are more common for ActiveX content, but they also can be used by Java applets. There are also Java-only tags:

```
<applet>
...
```

```
</applet>
```

When configured to filter active content, the PIX simply comments out both of these tags inside a TCP packet and the content between them. This ensures the embedded code is not run. The only problem with this approach is when the first tag is in one packet and the closing tag is in another packet, the PIX cannot perform this operation and the Web page is passed as is.

Filtering Java Applets

To configure filtering of Java applets, use the filter java <**port**>[-<**port**>] <**local_ip**> <**mask**> <**foreign_ip**> <**mask**> command. Here is an example:

```
PIX1(config)# filter java 80 0 0 0 0
PIX1(config)# filter java 80 192.168.2.17 255.255.255.255 0 0
```

The first command configures the PIX to drop all Java applets from incoming Web pages; the second prohibits only one host, 192.168.2.17, from downloading Java applets. The **port** parameter specifies the TCP port on which to perform the inspection.

Filtering ActiveX Objects

Java has a more or less robust security model for its active code, but ActiveX objects have almost unrestricted access to the client's machine.

The command to configure filtering of ActiveX code (and all active content that is embedded in the **<object>** tags) is very similar to Java filtering:

```
filter activex <port>[-<port>] <local_ip> <mask> <foreign_ip> <mask>
```

Here is an example:

```
PIX1(config)# filter activex 80 0 0 0 0
```

This command configures the PIX to comment out all pairs of **<object>** tags from all incoming Web pages, disabling ActiveX and some Java applets.

Configuring Intrusion Detection

Cisco has a dedicated Intrusion Detection System (IDS) product called Cisco Secure IDS. A limited part of this IDS functionality is implemented in both Cisco IOS and Cisco PIX. Because the PIX is basically an OSI Layers 3 and 4 filtering device, it can detect only simple attacks that happen at these network communication layers and can be detected by inspecting a single packet in the data stream. PIX IDS signatures are a subset of the Cisco Secure IDS signature set. To upgrade signatures, the whole PIX firmware must be updated. Intrusion detection can be configured on each interface in inbound and outbound directions. When the PIX detects each signature, it generates an alert ("informational" or "attack," depending on the severity of the attack) and sends it via syslog to the configured destination.

Supported Signatures

Unfortunately, Cisco's own documentation is not clear about signatures supported in each specific version. The best way to check what your PIX can do in the area of intrusion detection is to browse a list of syslog messages produced by the specific version (*Cisco PIX Firewall System Log Messages* guide). For v6.2, syslog messages numbered from 400 000 to 400 050 are reserved for IDS messages. Their format is shown here:

```
%PIX-4-4000<nn>: : <sig_num> <sig_msg> from <IP_addr> to <IP_addr> on interface
<int_name>
```

This syslog message means that PIX has detected an attack with number (**sig_num**) and name (**sig_msg**). The two IP addresses show the origin and destination of this attack. For example:

```
%PIX-4-400013 IDS:2003 ICMP redirect from 1.2.3.4 to 10.2.3.1 on interface dmz
```

All signatures are divided into two classes: *informational* and *attack*. The division is rather deliberate and cannot be changed. For example, all Denial of Service (DoS) attacks are listed as attacks, and all informational requests only have informational status.

Configuring Auditing

Using the **ip audit** command, auditing can be turned on or off, different auditing policies can be created and applied to specific interfaces, and specific signatures can be turned on or off. The easiest configuration requires you to assign a name for the auditing policy, specify actions (one for informational signatures and one for attack signatures) to be taken, and apply the policy to an interface. The actions that can be taken are:

- **Alarm** Attacks are reported to all configured syslog servers.
- **Drop** PIX drops the offending packet.
- **Reset** PIX drops the packet and closes the connection if it was a part of an open connection.

The default action is alarm. Policy configuration usually takes no more than two commands:

```
ip audit name <audit_name> info action [drop | alarm | reset ]
ip audit name <audit_name> attack action [drop | alarm | reset ]
```

The following commands create a policy named **myaudit** specifiying that when an informational signature is matched, the PIX should send an alarm to syslog, and when an attack signature is matched, the PIX should drop the packet:

```
PIX1(config)# ip audit name myaudit info action alarm
PIX1(config)# ip audit name myaudit attack action drop
```

It is possible to omit the **action** parameter in the previous configuration. In this case, the default action is applied. If not changed, the default action is **alarm**. Default actions are configured via these commands:

```
ip audit info action [drop | alarm | reset ]
ip audit attack action [drop | alarm | reset ]
```

After creating a policy, it needs to be applied to an interface in order to activate IDS on the interface. This is done with the **ip audit interface outside myaudit** command. This means that all signatures and actions configured should be matched on the outside interface. The general form of this command is **ip audit interface <if_name> <audit_name>**.

- **if_name** An interface where the IDS has to check for packets.
- **audit_name** Name of the policy that describes which actions to take.

The **clear ip audit [name | signature| interface | audit | info | attack]** command allows easy clearing of all IDS configuration related to an interface, policy, or default action.

The following set of commands displays the corresponding configuration of IDS related to the interface, audit, or default action.

```
show ip audit interface <if_name>
show ip audit info
show ip audit attack
show ip audit name <audit_name>
```

Disabling Signatures

The amount of information logged can be reduced by using the **ip audit signature <sig_number> disable** command. For example, to disable the "ICMP echo reply" signature, use the **ip audit signature 2000 disable** command. After this command is entered, signature number 2000 ("ICMP echo reply") will no longer be detected by the PIX. Disabling a signature is global, and not just for a specific interface or audit.

It is possible to see the list of all disabled signatures with the command **show ip audit signature**.

You can enable a disabled signature with a **no** command in configuration mode. For example, **no ip audit signature <sig_number> disable**.

Configuring Shunning

Shunning is an IDS response that blocks traffic from a perceived attacking host. The basic syntax is **shun <src_ip> [<dst_ip> <sport> <dport> [<protocol>]]**.

This technique temporarily blocks all traffic from the specified source IP address. To block all traffic from source IP address 10.0.1.1, use the **shun 10.0.1.1**command.

The PIX deletes all matching connections from its internal connection table and drops all further packets that match the parameters. The action of this command takes precedence over ACLs and security levels on interfaces; all specified traffic is blocked, whether the offending host is on the inside or outside of the interface. In order to remove this blocking action, use the corresponding **no** command: **no shun 10.0.1.1**. This command is dynamic and is not displayed or stored in the configuration. To view active shuns, use the **show shun** command. The **clear shun** command deletes all shun entries.

Dynamic Host Control Protocol Functionality

The Cisco PIX firewall can be both a Dynamic Host Control Protocol (DHCP) server and a client. As a DHCP server, it is a gateway for its networks providing them with addresses and other IP information. As a client, it obtains the necessary IP information to connect its networks to other networks. DHCP functionality was specifically designed for PIX 501, 506, and 506E, although it is available on all PIX models. The DHCP server can only support a maximum of 256 clients (or even fewer, depending on the firewall model, version, and license). There is no Bootstrap Protocol (BOOTP) support and no failover support as the current state of DHCP server or client is not replicated.

DHCP Clients

When configured as a DHCP client, the PIX firewall can obtain the configuration of its outside interface from a designated DHCP server (for example, a server located at an Internet Service Provider [ISP]). This configuration includes the IP address, the subnet mask, and optionally, the default route. The DHCP client feature can only be configured on the "outside" interface of the PIX firewall.

For example, this address can be used as a PAT address for all outgoing communications. This is configured in the following way (assuming that the DHCP client is already configured):

```
nat (inside) 1 0 0
global (outside) 1 interface
```

This configuration PATs all outbound inside IP addresses to whatever IP address gets assigned to the outside interface.

To configure the DHCP client, the **ip address outside dhcp [setroute] [retry <retry_cnt>]** command should be used. The **setroute** keyword forces the PIX firewall to pick up not only the IP address and the subnet mask, but the default route as well. *Do not configure a static default route on the firewall if using the setroute option.* The **retry** option tells the PIX firewall to try to contact a DHCP server a specified number of times before giving up. If this keyword is not specified, no retries are attempted. The default number of retries is one without the retry keyword, and four with it. For example, **ip address outside dhcp setroute** configures a DHCP client on the outside interface to obtain an IP address, subnet mask, and default route from the DHCP server, and only one attempt is made.

The **ip address outside dhcp retry** command configures the DHCP client to obtain an IP address and subnet mask only, and tries at least four times before giving up if no DHCP servers are available.

There are no special commands for renewing and releasing a DHCP lease. Simply issue the same command again and the lease will be renewed.

The address obtained can be viewed using the **show ip address outside dhcp** command. This produces output similar to the following:

```
Temp IP Addr:123.1.2.3 for peer on interface:outside
Temp sub net mask:255.255.255.0
DHCP Lease server:123.1.2.31, state:3 Bound
DHCP Transaction id:0x4567
Lease:259200 secs, Renewal:129600 secs, Rebind:226800 secs
Temp default-gateway addr:123.1.2.1
Next timer fires after:100432 secs
Retry count:0, Client-ID:cisco-0000.0000.0000-outside
```

Troubleshoot any issues with the DHCP client using the following **debug** commands:

```
debug dhcpc packet
debug dhcpc detail
debug dhcpc error
```

DHCP Servers

The DHCP server can be configured only on the inside interface. There are a set number of active DHCP clients that can be supported, as shown in Table 8.7.

Table 8.7 Number of Clients Supported by the PIX DHCP Server

PIX Firewall Version	PIX Firewall Platform	Client Addresses (Active Hosts)
Version 5.2 and before	All platforms	10
Version 5.3 to version 6.0	PIX 506/506E	32
	All other platforms	256
Version 6.1 and after	PIX 501 with 10-user license	32
	PIX 501 with 50-user license	128
	All other platforms	256

A host is "active" if it has passed any traffic through the PIX, established a connection through the firewall, established a NAT or PAT translation entry, or authenticated itself to the firewall during the last 30 seconds.

A minimal configuration of the DHCP server requires only two commands: one for specifying a range of IP addresses that can be provided to clients and another one for actually turning the feature on.

```
PIX1(config)# dhcpd address 192.168.2.1-192.168.2.127 inside
PIX1(config)# dhcpd enable inside
```

It is possible to configure only one address pool. The domain name provided to a client is configured with the **dhcpd domain <domain_name>** command (for example, **dhcpd domain syngress.com**).

The DNS servers that a client should use are configured with the **dhcpd dns <dns1> [<dns2>]** command. Up to two DNS servers can be configured, using IP addresses (for example, **dhcpd dns 1.2.3.4 1.2.4.10**).

Windows Internet Name Service (WINS) servers are configured using the **dhcpd wins <wins1> [<wins2>]** command, with the same restrictions as DNS servers—up to two servers, configured using IP addresses.

To change the default lease time (the amount of time for which an IP address is provided to the client), the **dhcpd lease <lease_time>** command syntax isused. This command specifies the time in seconds. The default value is 3,600, and possible values are from 300 seconds to 2,147,483,647 seconds. The **dhcpd ping_timeout <ping_time>** command sets a maximum ping timeout in milliseconds (1/1000th of a second). The **ping_timeout** specifies how long the PIX will wait for a **ping** response to ensure that a host with the same IP address does not already exist on the network.

The **dhcpd auto_config outside** command allows the DHCP server to automatically obtain DNS, WINS, and domain parameters from a DHCP client configured on the outside interface.

Other commands show the current state of IP bindings (which client has been assigned which IP address) and general server statistics:

```
PIX1(config)# show dhcpd binding
IP Address Hardware Address Lease Expiration Type
192.168.2.210 0100.a0c9.777e 84985 seconds automatic
```

Here, a client with media access control (MAC) address 0100.a0c9.777e has obtained IP address 192.168.2.210, and this lease will expire in 84,985 seconds:

```
PIX1(config)# show dhcpd statistics
Address Pools 1
Automatic Bindings 1
Expired Bindings 1
Malformed messages 0
Message Received
BOOTREQUEST 0
DHCPDISCOVER 1
DHCPREQUEST 2
DHCPDECLINE 0
DHCPRELEASE 0
DHCPINFORM 0
Message Sent
BOOTREPLY 0
DHCPOFFER 1
DHCPACK 1
DHCPNAK 1
```

These statistics show the number of IP address pools configured, the number of active leases (bindings), expired bindings, messages received with errors, and a detailed breakdown on message type for correctly received and sent messages.

Fragmentation Guard

Fragmented packets are a challenge to firewalls. The firewall cannot decide what to do with the packet until it sees the entire TCP/IP header. Some firewalls simply pass the fragments without trying to reassemble the original packets, whereas others try to perform this reassembly. Reassembly can be a dangerous process. For example, it is very easy to send fragments that will cause the reassembled packet to be of illegal size, possibly crashing internal buffers of the IP stack implementation.

This feature is disabled by default and can be turned on or off on all interfaces simultaneously with the **sysopt security fragguard** command. The corresponding **no** command turns the feature off. The status of various settings, including FragGuard, can be checked with the **show sysopt** command.

FragGuard settings can be too restrictive at times. It is possible to manually tune the process of virtual reassembly with the **fragment** set of commands.

The following command sets the maximum number of blocks that can be used for fragment reassembly. This is a global setting; if no interface is specified, the setting is global. The default number of blocks is 200 and should never be greater than the total number of available blocks of 1,550 bytes' size. In general, a bigger database makes PIX more vulnerable to a DoS attack by flooding it with fragments and exhausting its memory (**fragment size <database-limit> [<interface>]**).

The **fragment chain <chain-limit> [<interface>]** command sets the maximum allowed number of fragments into which one IP packet is split. The default setting is 24 fragments and the maximum is 8,200. Further fragments will be discarded and the packet will not be reassembled.

The timeout setting specifies the time frame in which all fragments of one IP packet should be received. The command is **fragment timeout <seconds> [<interface>]**. The default timeout is 5 seconds and can be up to 30 seconds.

The last command, **clear fragment**, resets all three settings to their default values. The state of the fragments database can be displayed with the **show fragment** command:

```
pix(config)# show fragment outside
Interface:outside
Size:200, Chain:24, Timeout:5
Queue:150, Assemble:300, Fail:0, Overflow:0
```

This output shows that the database has default settings: 200 blocks in size, 24 fragments in a chain, 5-second timeout. There are 150 packets waiting to be reassembled, 300 were already successfully reassembled, and there were no failures or database overflows.

Authentication, Authorization, and Accounting Floodguard

Another flood-related problem is abuse of the PIX authentication, authorization, and accounting (AAA) authentication mechanism via a large number of login attempts without providing any login information, leaving the connections open. The PIX firewall then waits until a timeout expires. By making enough attempts, it is possible to exhaust AAA resources so that no further login attempts will be answered—a DoS on login resources.

```
floodguard enable
floodguard disable
show floodguard
```

SYN Floodguard

A well-known DoS attack is SYN flooding where an attacker sends large numbers of initial SYN packets to the host and neither closes nor confirms these half-open connections. This consumes a great deal of resources while waiting for confirmation, preventing new connections before the backlog of these half-open connections is cleared. The rate at which new connections are opened or the number of connections that are half-open is controlled by specifying a limit on the number of embryonic connections in the **static** and **nat** configuration commands. For example, **static (dmz, outside) 10.4.5.6 10.1.1.0 netmask 255.255.255.255 100 50** creates a static NAT entry for the DMZ server 10.1.1.0 with an external IP address of 10.4.5.6, with only 100 connections to this server from outside open at any given time. The number 50 is the number of half-open or embryonic connections to this server that can exist at any given time.

The **nat** command is similar: **nat (inside) 1 10.0.0.0 255.0.0.0 100 50**. The two numbers at the end specify the number of open and embryonic connections that can exist at any given time to each translated host. When any of these numbers is 0, the number of connections is not limited.

Reverse-Path Forwarding

The concept of reverse-path forwarding (RPF) checks the **source** address against a routing table. When a route to this source is found, it is assured that the packet has arrived on the same interface listed in the corresponding route entry (so the packet has arrived on the best path back to its origin). If the interface is correct, the packet has arrived from a verifiable source and is legitimate. If a reverse route is not found or the packet arrived on a wrong interface, it is presumed that the packet is spoofed, and it is discarded.

This feature is used for implementing ingress and egress filtering as specified in RFC 2267. It is turned off by default and can be enabled on a specific interface using the **ip verify reverse-path interface <interface_name>** configuration command:

Ingress filtering checks that outside hosts really have outside addresses, but because the PIX firewall cannot maintain the table of all possible routes on the Internet, most configurations check that packets arriving to the outside interface from the Internet do not have an "inside" source address. Egress filtering does exactly the opposite: It checks that the packets going to the Internet actually have internal source addresses. This filtering makes tracing any packet back to its origin much easier and prevents most spoofing attacks. Although this can all be accomplished using ACLs, the RPF feature provides a much easier solution.

Thus **ip verify reverse-path interface inside** provides egress filtering, whereas **ip verify reverse-path interface outside** provides ingress filtering.

RPF-related statistics can be viewed with the following command:

```
pix(config)# show ip verify statistics
interface outside: 5 unicast rpf drops
interface inside: 2 unicast rpf drops
```

The following commands delete **ip verify** commands from the configuration and clear packet counts, respectively:

```
clear ip verify reverse-path
clear ip verify statistics
```

Unicast Routing

Recall that routing involves collecting and storing information needed to forward traffic to its final destination. The PIX firewall was not meant to be a router, although it has a limited set of routing features, both static and dynamic.

Static and Connected Routes

To configure static routes on the PIX firewall, use the **route <interface> <ip_address> <netmask> <gateway_address> [<metric>]** command (for example, **route outside 0.0.0.0 0.0.0.0 1.2.3.4**). This command configures a static default route on the outside interface to gateway 1.2.3.4—a default gateway to be used for network traffic. If a **show route** command is issued, the output will include the following line:

```
route outside 0.0.0.0 0.0.0.0 1.2.3.4 1 OTHER static
```

OTHER simply means that this route is a manually entered static route.

It is possible to specify an IP address of an interface on the PIX instead of a gateway address. The PIX automatically creates routes of this type when an IP address is entered for an interface.

When a route is set to an interface, it is considered directly connected. The PIX sends an Address Resolution Protocol (ARP) request for the destination address itself instead of the gateway. The destination host does not have to be directly connected if it is connected via a router that has a proxy arp feature enabled. The router replies on behalf of the host, and the PIX forwards the packet to this router, which forwards it to the host. Cisco routers and PIX firewalls have proxy ARP turned on by default.

For example, if the inside interface has an IP address of 192.168.1.254/24 and two networks, 192.168.2.0/24 and 192.168.3.0/24, are connected to this interface via a router, the following two statements will configure correct routes to these networks. The router's address is not used, but the router has to be on the same network as the inside interface in this case.

```
PIX1(config)# route inside 192.168.2.0 255.255.255.0 192.168.1.254
PIX1(config)# route inside 192.168.3.0 255.255.255.0 192.168.1.254
```

The **show route** command displays the corresponding entries in the routing table as:

```
route inside 192.168.1.0 255.255.255.0 192.168.1.254 1 CONNECT static
route inside 192.168.2.0 255.255.255.0 192.168.1.254 1 OTHER static
route inside 192.168.3.0 255.255.255.0 192.168.1.254 1 OTHER static
```

The first entry here was created automatically by the PIX firewall when an IP address was configured on the inside interface. The other two are the result of the two static route entries. It is possible to turn the feature off on a specific interface with the **sysopt noproxyarp <interface>** command.

RIP

The PIX firewall supports RIPv1 and v2. RIP is a dynamic distance vector routing protocol that will broadcast (v1) or multicast (v2) its entire routing table to its neighbors.

Each PIX interface can be configured either to advertise itself as a default route for the network or to passively listen for routing updates from other routers. The simple syntax of the RIP configuration command is **rip <if_name> [default | passive] version [1 | 2]**. The **default** parameter specifies that a default route should be advertised, and **passive** means listening for updates from other routers, but not advertising. RIPv2 multicasts to 224.0.0.9 instead of broadcasts like RIPv1. RIPv2 supports authentication, while RIPv1 does not. RIPv2 is also a classless routing.

Here is an example of RIP v1 configuration:

```
PIX1(config)# show rip
rip outside passive
no rip outside default
rip inside passive
no rip inside default
PIX1(config)# rip inside default
PIX1(config)# show rip
rip outside passive
no rip outside default
rip inside passive
rip inside default
```

The first **show rip** command displays the default state of configuration—all interfaces listen passively. Then the inside interface is configured to broadcast itself as a default route. Note that the passive listening mode was not turned off by this mode. To do so, it would need to be disabled separately with **no rip inside passive**.

RIPv2 supports two types of authentication: cleartext passwords and MD5 hashes. Authentication is configured with the **rip <if_name> [default | passive] version 2 authentication [text | md5] <key_string> <key_id>** command.

The **rip inside default version 2 authentication text mysecretkey 1**command defines a cleartext password of **mysecretkey** while broadcasting the default gateway on the inside interface. Whereas the **rip outside passive version 2 authentication md5 anothersecretkey 2** command accepts only updates with a correct MD5 hash keyed by a key **anothersecretkey**. The **key_id** parameter is a key identification value and must be the same on all routers with which the PIX communicates.

The **clear rip** configuration mode command removes all RIP configuration statements from the PIX firewall.

Stub Multicast Routing

In multicasting, a host must join one or more *multicast groups*, represented by a specific IP address (these addresses are 224.0.0.0-239.255.255.255) and receive traffic destined for this group. The nature of broadcasting and multicasting implies that it can be used only for UDP transmission, because TCP always requires two endpoints.

Since multicast groups are not limited to one network by definition, messages need to be passed through routers and a means of informing routers if there are any hosts from a specific multicast group on a given physical network. This is done using Internet Group Management Protocol (IGMP).

IGMP is similar to ICMP in that it is also considered part of the IP layer (IPv2). Its basic functionality is as follows:

- When a host joins a multicast group, it informs the router by sending it an IGMP message.
- When a host leaves the group, it does not send any reports about this event (see the next two points).
- A multicast router regularly sends IGMP requests out each of its interfaces requesting connected hosts to report to the multicast groups to which they belong.
- A host responds to the request by sending one IGMP report for each group to which it belongs.

Figure 8.10 illustrates this IGMP exchange.

Figure 8.10 IGMP Used to Report Membership in a Multicast Group

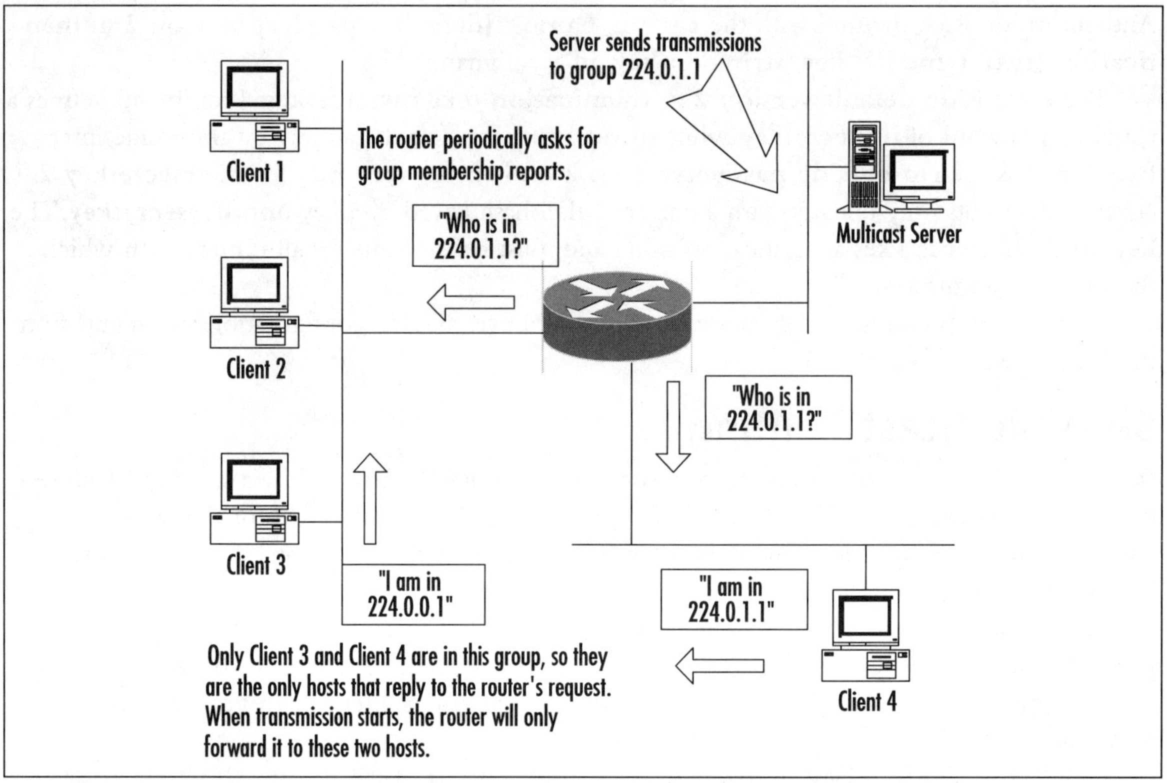

Since version 6.2, the PIX can process multicast and IGMP messages. It can act as a *stub router* or IGMP proxy agent, which means it forwards IGMP requests and replies between multicast routers and hosts. When the source and destination of multicast transmissions are divided by a PIX firewall, two obvious cases are possible: when the source of a transmission (or a multicast router) is on a lower security-level interface than the destination and when the source (router) is on a higher security-level interface than the destination.

SMR Configuration with Clients on a More Secure Interface

In this case, a multicast router and a server are on the outside interface of the PIX firewall, and clients are on the inside. The PIX needs to pass multicast traffic from the server and IGMP requests from the router to the inside hosts. It also needs to pass IGMP messages from the internal hosts to the outside router.

All SMR configurations start with the **multicast interface <interface> [max-groups <number>]** configuration mode command. The interface is placed into multicast promiscuous mode, and then it enters a submode of multicast configuration for a specific interface. (An optional **max-groups** parameter defines the number of multicast groups that can appear on the interface at any given time. The default setting is 500; the number can be up to 2,000. This mode has subcommands like **igmp <command>**.

In this case, the PIX needs to be able to receive multicast transmissions on its outside interface, which is done with the **multicast interface outside** configuration command. Once this is done, there is not much more to configure on the outside interface. An administrator can optionally configure counters and protocol options or access control. To configure multicast on the inside interface, the **multicast interface inside** configuration command is used.

While configuring the inside interface (**igmp forward interface outside**) the administrator needs to identify the interface to which the PIX should forward all IGMP messages from clients. This is the less secure interface where the router is located. If any clients on the inside network are not IGMP-capable, but still need to receive multicast traffic; their interface to join the multicast group statically should be configured with the **igmp join-group <multicast_address>** command. For example:

```
PIX1(config-multicast)# igmp join-group 224.1.1.1
```

With this interface configured, the PIX outside interface proxies for hosts interested in receiving transmissions for this group, and forwards the multicasts to them. Here is an example of the simplest multicast configuration:

```
PIX1(config)# multicast interface outside
PIX1(config-multicast)# exit
PIX1(config)# multicast interface inside
PIX1(config-multicast)# igmp forward interface outside
```

Here is a more complicated example with non-IGMP capable multicast clients who want to receive transmissions for group 224.10.0.9:

```
PIX1(config)# multicast interface outside
PIX1(config-multicast)# exit
PIX1(config)# multicast interface inside
PIX1(config-multicast)# igmp forward interface outside
PIX1(config-multicast)# igmp join-group 224.10.0.9
```

Here is an example of clients on two interfaces, **inside** and **dmz**:

```
PIX1(config)# multicast interface outside
PIX1(config-multicast)# exit
PIX1(config)# multicast interface inside
PIX1(config-multicast)# igmp forward interface outside
PIX1(config-multicast)# exit
PIX1(config)# multicast interface dmz
PIX1(config-multicast)# igmp forward interface outside
```

SMR Configuration with Clients on a Less Secure Interface

Enable multicast processing on both interfaces and create static multicast routes for passing traffic between the clients and the servers (and routers). Multicast processing is enabled with:

```
PIX1(config)# multicast interface outside
PIX1(config-multicast)# exit
PIX1(config)# multicast interface inside
```

Multicast routes are created using the **mroute <src> <srcmask> <in-if-name> <dst> <dstmask> <out-if-name>** command (which is not a subcommand of the multicast command). The **src** and **srcmask** parameters are the IP address and subnet mask of a multicast source host/router (just normal IP addresses, not multicast addresses.). The **in-if-name** parameter specifies the interface connected to the source. **dst** and **dstmask** are the multicast group address and subnet mask to which the server is sending its transmission. Finally, **out-if-name** is the interface connected to the multicast clients. For example:

```
PIX1(config)# mroute 192.168.2.25 255.255.255.255 inside 224.0.1.1 255.255.255.255
outside
```

Here is an example configuration in the case of two servers: 192.168.2.25 on the inside interface multicasting to group 224.1.1.1 and 10.2.3.4 on the dmz interface multicasting to the group 230.1.1.1 and no internal clients:

```
PIX1(config)# multicast interface outside
PIX1(config-multicast)# exit
PIX1(config)# multicast interface inside
PIX1(config-multicast)# exit
PIX1(config)# multicast interface dmz1
PIX1(config-multicast)# exit
PIX1(config)# mroute 192.168.2.25 255.255.255.255 inside 224.1.1.1 255.255.255.255
outside
PIX1(config)# mroute 10.2.3.4 255.255.255.255 dmz 230.1.1.1 255.255.255.255 outside
```

Access Control and Other Options

It is possible to restrict access to multicast transmissions using ACLs. The groups from which the internal hosts can receive transmissions could be restricted. For example, to allow only multicast transmissions to group address 224.1.1.1, an ACL similar to **access-list 10 permit igmp any 224.1.1.1 255.255.255.255** should be configured and then applied to the outside interface:

```
PIX1(config)# multicast interface outside
PIX1(config-multicast)# igmp access-group 10
```

Now only IGMP polls for group 224.1.1.1 will be able to pass through the PIX, and thus a multicast router will know only members of this group. This prevents the router from sending traffic destined for any other group address in this direction.

Other subcommands of the **multicast** command include: **igmp query-interval <seconds>**. This next command sets the interval at which IGMP messages will be sent out this interface. The default interval is 60 seconds. The maximum timeout for response (for IGMPv2 only) can be set using the **igmp query-max-response-time <seconds>** command. The default setting is 10 seconds.

Configured settings can be cleared using the corresponding **clear** commands. The **clear igmp group [<group-addr> | interface <interface-name>]** command clears the IGMP cache either for a specific group address or the whole cache on the specified interface:

The **clear mroute [<src-addr> | <group-addr> | interface <interface-name>]** command clears multicast routes for specified transmission source, for a group address, or all routes on the interface:

Another set of commands allows viewing of multicast configuration for the interface, multicast group, routes, and so on:

```
show igmp
show multicast [interface <interface-name>]
show igmp group [grou<p-addr> | interface <interface-name>]
show mroute [<src-addr> | <group-addr> | interface <interface-name>]
```

An example output of the **show igmp** command is:

```
pix(config)# show igmp
IGMP is enabled on interface inside
Current IGMP version is 2
IGMP query interval is 60 seconds
IGMP query timeout is 125 seconds
IGMP max query response time is 10 seconds
Last member query response interval is 1 seconds
Inbound IGMP access group is
IGMP activity: 0 joins, 0 leaves
IGMP querying router is 10.0.1.1 (this system)
IGMP Connected Group Membership
Group Address Interface Uptime Expires Last Reported
```

Two **debug** commands allow monitoring of multicast-related events. The **debug igmp** command monitors all IGMP messages passing through the PIX, while the **debug mfwd** command monitors all events related to multicast forwarding.

Point-to-Point Protocol over Ethernet

Point-to-Point Protocol over Ethernet (PPPoE), documented in RFC2516, is an encapsulation of Point-to-Point Protocol (PPP) for Ethernet. PPPoE is often used in SOHO environments because it allows ISPs to use their existing remote access infrastructure and supports authenticated IP address assignment. PPPoE links are established in two main phases:

- **Active Discovery Phase** PPPoE client attempts discovery of the PPPoE server (address concentrator [AC]). The PPPoE layer is established and a session ID is assigned.
- **PPP Session Phase** A PPP link is established (encapsulated in Ethernet) by the usual means: options and link layer protocols are negotiated and so forth. PPP authentication (Password Authentication Protocol [PAP], Challenge-Handshake Authentication Protocol (CHAP), or MS-CHAP) is performed.

After the session is established, data travels between endpoints encapsulated in PPPoE headers. v6.2 and later supports PPPoE. Most of the PPPoE configuration is performed using the **vpdn** command. PPPoE configuration starts with configuring the username and password to be used by the PIX in establishing a link to the server.

A VPDN group is created with the **vpdn group <group_name> request dialout pppoe** command. The **group_name** parameter can be anything;. it is used to group all PPPoE settings together. (for example, with the **vpdn group my-pppoe-group request dialout pppoe** configuration command).

The authentication type then needs to be selected (if required by an ISP) which can be accomplished with the **vpdn group <group_name ppp> authentication pap | chap | mschap** command. The ISP assigns the username and password to the system, and they are configured on PIX with the following commands:

```
vpdn group <group_name> localname <username>
vpdn username <username> password <pass>
```

The first command assigns the username to be used for a specific group and the second command associates a username with the password. For example:

```
PIX1(config)# vpdn group my-ppoe-group localname witt
PIX1(config)# vpdn username witt password cruelmail
```

These commands assign the username **witt** and password **cruelmail** to be used for the PPPoE dialout group **my-pppoe-group**. After configuring authentication, the next task is to enable the PPPoE client on the PIX. This is done in the configuration of the outside interface using **ip address outside pppoe [setroute]**. The current PPPoE session is terminated and a new one is established. The **setroute** parameter allows for automatically setting the default route for the outside interface. The Maximum Transmission Unit (MTU) on the outside interface is automatically set to 1492, which is the correct setting to provide PPPoE encapsulation. It is also possible to designate a fixed IP address for the outside interface. The PIX still has to provide the ISP with the correct username and password in order to establish the session:

```
PIX1(config)# ip address outside 1.2.3.4 255.255.255.0 pppoe
```

It is possible to use the **dhcp auto_config** command if you run the DHCP server on PIX contain DNS and WINS information from your provider via the PPPoE client:

```
PIX1(config)# dhcpd auto_config outside
```

To monitor and troubleshoot the PPPoE client, use the following commands:

```
show ip address outside pppoe
debug pppoe event | error | packet
show vpdn session pppoe [id <sess_id>|packets|state|window]
```

Examples of output are as follows:

```
PIX1(config)# show vpdn
Tunnel id 0, 1 active sessions
```

```
time since change 10240 secs
Remote Internet Address 10.0.1.1
Local Internet Address 192.168.2.254
1006 packets sent, 1236 received, 98761 bytes sent, 123765 received
Remote Internet Address is 10.0.1.1
Session state is SESSION_UP
Time since event change 10237 secs, interface outside
PPP interface id is 1
1006 packets sent, 1236 received, 98761 bytes sent, 123765 received
PIX1(config)# show vpdn tunnel
PPPoE Tunnel Information (Total tunnels=1 sessions=1)
Tunnel id 0, 1 active sessions
time since change 10240 secs
Remote Internet Address 10.0.1.1
Local Internet Address 192.168.2.254
1006 packets sent, 1236 received, 98761 bytes sent, 123765 received
PIX1(config)# show vpdn session
PPPoE Session Information (Total tunnels=1 sessions=1)
Remote Internet Address is 10.0.1.1
Session state is SESSION_UP
Time since event change 100238 secs, interface outside
PPP interface id is 1
1006 packets sent, 1236 received, 98761 bytes sent, 123765 received
```

Configuring Console Authentication

Authentication controls access *to* a network device or controls access to network resources *through* the network device. This section discusses PIX firewall AAA mechanisms to control access to the PIX firewall itself via the console port, Telnet, HTTP, or SSH. The general steps necessary to configure AAA authentication for firewall access are:

1. Configure the AAA authentication database that can be local on the firewall, or on a Remote Authentication Dial-In User Server (RADIUS) or Terminal Access Controller Access Control System (TACACS+) server.
2. Specify the methods of firewall access (serial port, Telnet, SSH, HTTP) and the AAA authentication database that should be used.

Configuring Local Console Authentication

If the PIX firewall is being configured to use a local database to authenticate users attempting to access the firewall itself, use the **username <username> {nopassword | password <password> [encrypted]} [privilege <level>]**command should be used to define users on the firewall. Use the **nopassword** keyword to create a local account with no password. Use the **password** keyword to assign a password to a local account, and specify the password. If the password being specified is already encrypted, use the **encrypted** keyword. To assign a privilege level to the user account, use the **privilege** keyword and specify the desired level between 0 and 15. Other options are:

- Delete a user with the **no username <username>**
- To view a list of configured usernames, use the **show username [<username>]** command.
- To remove the entire user database, use the **clear username** command in Configuration mode.

Once the local users are defined, you need to specify that the local database should be used for the various access methods by executing the **aaa authentication [serial | enable | telnet | ssh | http] console LOCAL** command. Use the **serial, enable, telnet, ssh,** or **http** keywords to specify the access method that requires authentication. For example, issue the following commands to establish a local user account and specify that the local database should be used when a user attempts to access the PIX firewall via Telnet, SSH, or HTTP (PIX Device Manager [PDM]):

```
PIX1(config)# username pixadm password pixpassword
PIX1(config)# aaa authentication telnet console LOCAL
PIX1(config)# aaa authentication ssh console LOCAL
PIX1(config)# aaa authentication http console LOCAL
```

The enable and SSH access methods allow three tries before denying authentication. Serial and Telnet continue to prompt the user until a successful login takes place.

Configuring RADIUS and TACACS+ Console Authentication

If configuring the PIX firewall to use RADIUS or TACACS+ to authenticate users attempting to access the firewall itself, first define a group for the AAA servers that the firewall will use with the **aaa-server <group_tag> protocol <auth_protocol>** command There is a maximum of 14. Then, specify a name for the server group (**group_tag**) and either tacacs+ or radius as the authentication protocol (**auth_protocol**).

By default, the PIX firewall communicates to RADIUS servers on port 1645 for authentication and port 1646 for accounting. Newer RADIUS servers may use port numbers 1812 and 1813. If a server uses ports other than 1645 and 1646, ports should be defined appropriately on the PIX firewall using the **aaa-server radius-authport** and **aaa-server radius-acctport** commands before defining the RADIUS servers with the **aaa-server** command.

The **aaa-server <group_tag> [(interface)] host <server_ip> [<key>] [timeout <seconds>]** command should then be used to define specific AAA servers that will be associated with the group:

- **group_tag** Specify the name of the group to which the server will belong.
- **interface** the interface on which the server will reside. Assumed to be the inside interface by default.
- **host** The IP address of the AAA server and secret key to be used between the AAA client and the server. If the key is not specified, unencrypted mode will be used.
- **timeout** Specifies the duration that the PIX firewall waits to retry (up to four times). The default value for the timeout is 5 seconds, and the maximum allowed is 30 seconds.

A maximum of 16 AAA servers can be specified in a group. To remove a server from the configuration, use the **no aaa-server** command.

Once AAA authentication servers have been designated using the **aaa-server** command, verify the configuration with the **show aaa-server** command.

Next, specify the AAA authentication database that should be used for the various access methods. Use the **aaa authentication [serial | enable | telnet | ssh | http] console <group_tag>** command to specify the authentication database. The syntax is very similar to using local authentication. The **group_tag** parameter identifies the AAA server group to use for authentication. For example, the following commands can be issued to create the AuthPIX server group, to assign a TACACS+ server to it, and to specify that the group should be used when a user attempts to access the PIX firewall via Telnet, SSH, and HTTP:

```
PIX1(config)# aaa-server AuthPIX protocol tacacs+
PIX1(config)# aaa-server AuthPIX (inside) host 10.5.1.20 TacacsKey
PIX1(config)# aaa authentication telnet console AuthPIX
PIX1(config)# aaa authentication ssh console AuthPIX
PIX1(config)# aaa authentication http console AuthPIX
```

Configuring Local Command Authorization

To implement command authorization using the PIX firewall local database, the various commands must first be assigned to the appropriate privilege levels using the **privilege [show | clear | configure] level <level> [mode {enable | configure}] command <command>** command. Select the appropriate command for which to set a privilege level (**show**, **clear**, or **configure**, or blank if it is not one of these). **level** specifies the privilege level assigned to the command, while **mode** specifies the mode (**enable** or **configure**).

Next, assign users to the appropriate privilege levels. If using the local database, use the **username** command with the **privilege** keyword.

Finally, enable AAA authorization on the PIX firewall using the **aaa authorization command LOCAL** command. Here is an example:

```
PIX1(config)# privilege show level 10 command access-list
PIX1(config)# privilege configure level 11 command access-list
PIX1(config)# privilege clear level 12 command access-list
PIX1(config)# username dora password wedidit privilege 12
```

```
PIX1(config)# username bootes password abre privilege 11
PIX1(config)# username swiper password noswiping privilege 10
PIX1(config)# aaa authorization command LOCAL
```

The **privilege** commands assign different command modifiers of the ACL command to different privilege levels. The **username** command defines users and assigns them privilege levels. Finally, the **aaa authorization command** command enables local user authorization services. The user **dora** is authorized to configure, clear, and show ACLs, the user **bootes** is authorized to configure and show ACLs, and the user **swiper** is authorized only to show ACLs.

To determine the privilege level to which a particular command is assigned, use the **show privilege command <command>** command. To determine the commands assigned to a particular level, use the **show privilege level <level>** command. To show all the commands and the levels to which they are assigned, use the **show privilege all** command.

Configuring Authentication for Traffic Through the Firewall

The PIX firewall can provide authentication and authorization of user access to services through the PIX firewall. Specifically, the PIX firewall allows you to implement authentication and authorization for inbound or outbound HTTP, FTP, Telnet; and other services with virtual Telnet. This functionality is provided through the cut-through proxy functionality.

Configuring Cut-through Proxy

Cut-through proxy controls services available through the firewall by user rather than by IP address. User connection requests can be authenticated or authorized against either a TACACS+ or a RADIUS server, but not against a local database. Using cut-through proxy functionality, the PIX transparently authenticates and authorizes the initial connection attempt at the application layer. Once authentication and/or authorization have been performed, the session is shifted and traffic flows directly between the two hosts while state information is maintained.

To implement AAA authentication to control user access to services through the PIX firewall:

1. Define the PIX firewall as an AAA client to the AAA server. Ensure that the appropriate authentication method (TACACS+ or RADIUS) is defined.
2. Define the users on the AAA server.
3. Define the AAA server group and AAA servers on the PIX firewall using the **aaa-server** command.
4. Enable and configure AAA authentication on the PIX firewall using the **aaa authentication** command syntax to control user access to services through the PIX firewall. The syntax of this command is as follows:

```
aaa authentication {include | exclude} <authen_service> {inbound | outbound |
<interface>} <local_ip> <local_mask> <foreign_ip> <foreign_mask> <group_tag>
```

- **include** Creates a new rule.
- **exclude** Creates an exception to a previous rule.
- **authen_service** **Any**, **ftp**, **http**, or **telnet**.
- **inbound** or **outbound** Specifies inbound or outbound services, respectively.
- **interface** Specifies the interface from which to authenticate connections.
- **local_ip** and **local_mask** Specifies the host or network that you want authenticated. Use 0 to specify all hosts.
- **foreign_ip** and **foreign_mask** Specifies the host or network that you want to access **local_ip**. To specify all hosts, use 0 for both.
- **group_tag** Specifies the AAA server group to use for authentication.

Here is an example of AAA authentication for Telnet services through the firewall:

```
PIX1(config)# aaa-server AuthOut protocol tacacs+
PIX1(config)# aaa-server AuthOut (inside) host 192.168.1.20 PIX1authkey
PIX1(config)# aaa authentication include telnet outbound 0 0 0 0 AuthOut
```

In this example, cut-through proxy is enabled for Telnet from any host to any host. After completing the configuration, any outbound Telnet session to a device through the PIX firewall results in an authentication challenge from the PIX firewall. The user is then connected to the device to which they initiated the session. For example, Figure 8.11 shows a successful Telnet connection through the PIX firewall to a Cisco router. The user authenticates against the PIX firewall, and then the Telnet session to the router is established.

Figure 8.11 Cut-Through Proxy Telnet Prompt

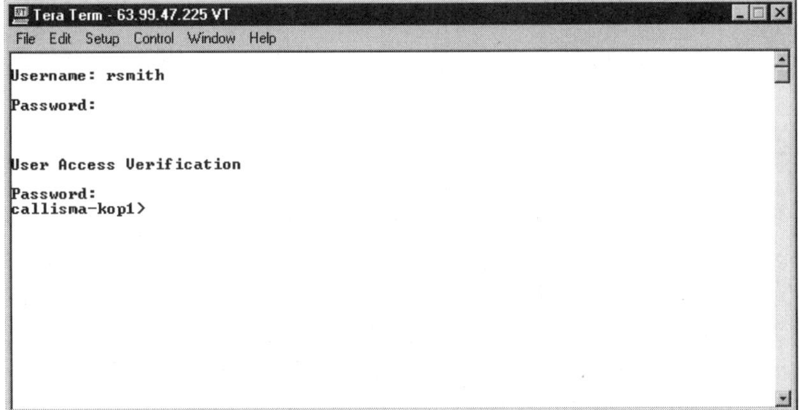

Here is an example of AAA authentication for FTP services through the firewall:

```
PIX1(config)# aaa-server AuthOut protocol tacacs+
PIX1(config)# aaa-server AuthOut (inside) host 192.168.1.20 PIX1authkey
PIX1(config)# aaa authentication include ftp outbound 0 0 0 0 AuthOut
```

In this example, any outbound FTP session to a host through the PIX firewall results first in an authentication challenge from the PIX firewall, then an authentication challenge from the device to which the user is connecting. For example, Figure 8.12 shows the cut-through proxy authentication prompt for an FTP connection request through the PIX firewall.

Figure 8.12 Cut-Through Proxy FTP Prompt

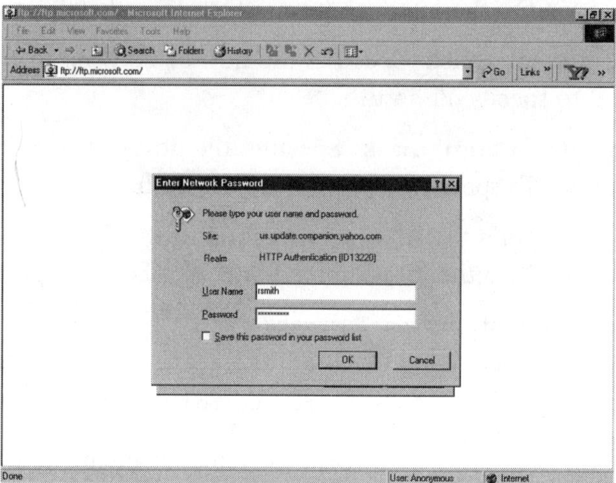

Here is an example of AAA authentication for HTTP services through the firewall:

```
PIX1(config)# aaa-server AuthOut protocol tacacs+
PIX1(config)# aaa-server AuthOut (inside) host 192.168.1.20 PIX1authkey
PIX1(config)# aaa authentication include http outbound 0 0 0 0 AuthOut
```

In this example, any outbound HTTP session to a host through the PIX firewall results first in an authentication challenge from the PIX firewall, then a session is established to the device to which the user is connecting. The HTTP host the user is connecting to may re-prompt for authentication

Virtual HTTP

With cut-through proxy authentication enabled for Web traffic (HTTP), users may experience some problems when connecting to Web sites based on Microsoft web servers using Basic Authentication or NT Challenge enabled. This is an issue when the Web server requires different login credentials from the PIX firewall's AAA server. When using HTTP authentication on a Microsoft web server with Basic Authentication or NT Challenge enabled, the browser appends the string "Authorization:Basic=Uuhjksdkfhk==" to the HTTP GET commands. Since this string contains the PIX authentication credentials and not the Microsoft authentication credentials, the user is denied access unless the user's AAA username and password match those defined on the Web server.

As a workaround, the PIX firewall provides a virtual HTTP feature. The Web browser's initial connection is redirected to the virtual HTTP IP address on the PIX firewall. The user is then authenticated, and the browser is redirected to the actual URL that the user requested. Virtual

HTTP is transparent to users. To define a virtual HTTP server, use the **virtual http <ip_address> [warn]** command. The **ip_address** parameter specifies an unused IP address that is routed to the PIX firewall. The **warn** keyword lets users know that their request was redirected and is only applicable for browsers that cannot redirect automatically.

For example, to enable virtual HTTP using the IP address 10.5.1.15, use the **virtual http 10.5.1.15** configuration command. Figure 8.13 illustrates the sequence of events that occur when virtual HTTP is enabled.

Figure 8.13 Virtual HTTP Operation

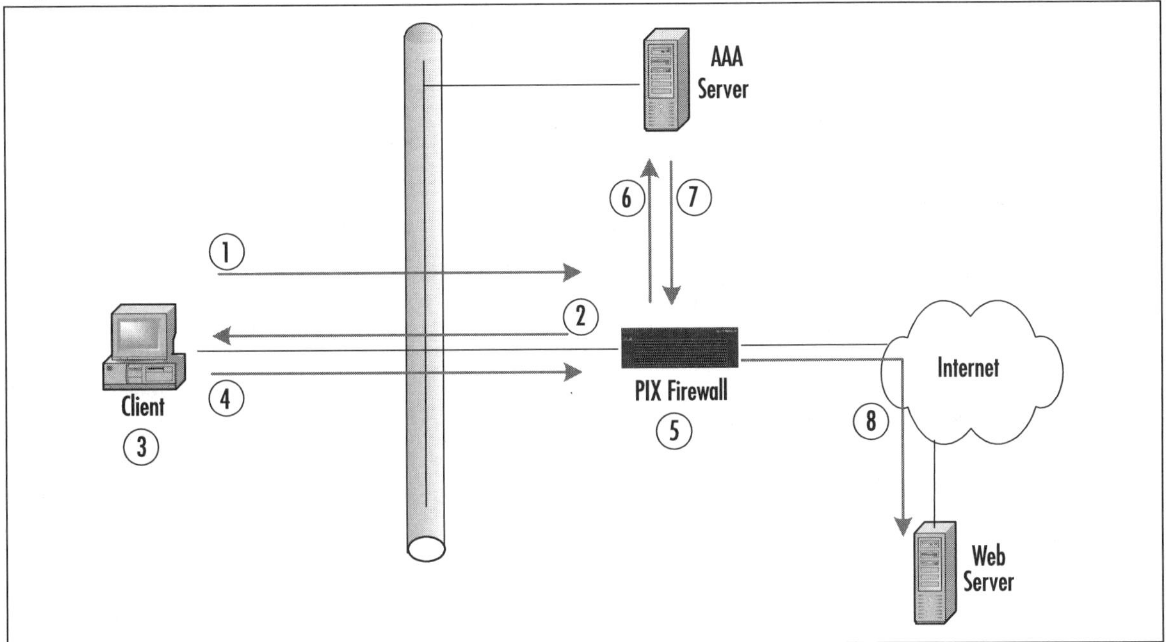

The steps identified in Figure 8.13 are described here:

1. The Web browser sends an HTTP request to the Web server.
2. The PIX firewall intercepts the connection attempt and replies with an HTTP 401 Authorization Required response.
3. The Web browser receives this reply, and displays a dialog box for the user to enter the username and password.
4. The Web browser resends the original HTTP request with the username and password embedded as a base64 encoding of "*username:password*." The actual field looks similar to the following:

```
Authorization: Basic ZnJlZDp0aGF0cyBtZQ==where ZnJlZDp0aGF0cyBtZQ== is the
base64 encoded "username:password" pair
```

5. The PIX firewall receives and splits the HTTP request into two requests: the AAA authentication request that contains the username and password and the original HTTP request without the username and password.

6. The PIX firewall sends the AAA authentication request to the AAA server.
7. The AAA server attempts to authenticate the user with the provided username and password and sends an ACCEPT or REJECT message.
8. If the authentication is successful, the PIX firewall then forwards the original HTTP request (without the username and password) to the Web server. If the Web server requires its own authentication, it sends its challenge back to the user.

With virtual HTTP enabled, once the user has authenticated, they will never have to authenticate again as long as there is a Web browser instance active. The **uauth** timer will not expire, because every subsequent Web request will include the encoded and embedded username and password.

Use the **show virtual http** command to show the configuration and the **no virtual http** command to disable the use of virtual HTTP.

Virtual Telnet

The **virtual telnet** command supports pre-authenticating users for services that do not support authentication (i.e., services other than HTTP, FTP, or Telnet). Virtual Telnet provides a way for users to authenticate themselves through Telnet before they use such services. For example, assume you enabled authentication for all protocols using the **any** keyword in the **aaa authentication include any outbound 0 0 0 0 AuthOut** command.

If a user's first outbound connection attempt is anything other than HTTP, FTP, or Telnet, the user will not be able to authenticate and gain access. However, a virtual Telnet server can be configured to pre-authenticate the user so they can gain access with the **virtual telnet <ip_address>** command. The **ip_address** parameter specifies an unused IP address that is routed to the PIX firewall. For example, to enable virtual Telnet on the PIX firewall using IP address 10.5.1.15 the configuration syntax would look like **virtual telnet 10.5.1.15**. The user can now Telnet to the virtual IP address and authenticate with their AAA username and password before using a service that does not support authentication. The PIX then authenticates them, closes the Telnet connection, and caches the authentication information for the duration of the **uauth** timer. Figure 8.14 shows an example of authentication using virtual Telnet.

Figure 8.14 A Virtual Telnet Session

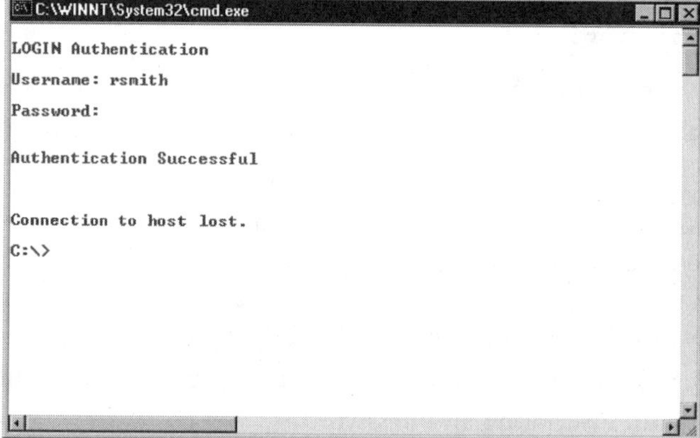

XVirtual Telnet can be used for logging in and for logging out. After successfully authenticating via virtual Telnet, you do not have to reauthenticate until the **uauth** timer expires. If you are finished with your tasks and want to prevent any further traffic from traversing the firewall using your authentication information, Telnet to the virtual IP address again to end the session and log out.

Use the **show virtual telnet** command to show the configuration and the **no virtual telnet** command to disable the use of virtual Telnet.

Configuring Authorization for Traffic Through the Firewall

Once authentication for traffic has been configured through the firewall using the cut-through proxy, the *authorization* for traffic can also be configured through the firewall. Authentication is a requirement for authorization. Authorization for traffic through the firewall requires a TACACS+ server. RADIUS servers and local databases are not supported for authorization of traffic.

After configuring the TACACS+ server for authorization, AAA authorization must be configured on the PIX firewall using the following command:

```
aaa authorization {include | exclude} <author_service> {inbound | outbound}
[<interface>] <local_ip> <local_mask> <foreign_ip> <foreign_mask> <group_tag>
```

Possible values for the **author_service** parameter are **any**, **ftp**, **http**, **telnet**, or **<protocol/port>**. The possible values for **protocol** are 6 (TCP), 17 (UDP), 1 (ICMP), and so on. The port value can range from 1 to 65535 and is only valid for the TCP and UDP protocols. Setting the port value to 0 indicates all ports.

For example, the following commands require authorization for all hosts for outbound Telnet, HTTP, and FTP service requests:

```
PIX1(config)# aaa authorization include telnet outbound 0 0 0 0 AuthOutbound
PIX1(config)# aaa authorization include http outbound 0 0 0 0 AuthOutbound
PIX1(config)# aaa authorization include ftp outbound 0 0 0 0 AuthOutbound
```

Configuring Accounting for Traffic Through the Firewall

Accounting for traffic through the firewall can only be configured with RADIUS and TACACS+:

```
aaa accounting {include | exclude} acct_service {inbound | outbound | <interface>}
<local_ip> <local_mask> <foreign_ip> <foreign_mask> <group_tag>
```

For example, the **aaa accounting include any outbound 0 0 0 0 AuthOutbound** configuration command generates accounting data for all hosts that generate any outbound service requests and sends the data to the AAA server in the **AuthOutbound** group.

Failover Concepts

The PIX failover feature deals with firewall failures by providing redundancy (not load balancing) between a pair of firewalls. With failover, a second PIX firewall automatically takes over in case the active firewall fails. Failover works with all interface types. The two firewalls must be identical in the following ways:

- They must have the same model of firewall (for example, a PIX 515 cannot be used with a PIX 515E)
- They must have the same amount of flash memory and RAM
- They must have the same software version (for example, software v6.1 cannot be used with software v6.2)
- They must have the same number and types of interfaces
- They must have the same activation key type (for example, DES or 3DES [discussed in Chapter 7] support)

In addition, there are some licensing restrictions for using failover:

- The primary firewall must be running an unrestricted license.
- The secondary firewall must be running either an unrestricted or a failover-only license.

Failover is only supported on the high-end models of the PIX firewall, such as the PIX 515, 515E, 520, 525, and 535. It is not supported on the PIX 501, 506, and 506E.

A firewall with a failover-only license may be used only as a secondary firewall for failover, not for standalone operation. If used in standalone mode, the firewall reboots once every 24 hours and displays the following message on the console. The reboots will continue until the firewall is reconfigured for operation as a failover unit.

```
=======================NOTICE =======================
    This machine is running in secondary mode without
     a connection to an active primary PIX. Please
      check your connection to the primary system.
                     REBOOTING....
=====================================================
```

In failover, one firewall is designated as **primary** and the other one is designated as **secondary**. In normal, error-free operations, the primary firewall is **active** and handles all the network traffic. The secondary firewall sits in **standby** state and is ready to take over the functions of the primary should it fail. If the standby firewall fails, the primary will not allow it to become active. Although the firewalls may switch the active and standby roles, the primary and secondary never change. This terminology of primary, secondary, active, and standby is extremely important to understand as they relate to other failover concepts.

Failure happens when any of the following conditions occurs:

- Block memory is exhausted for 15 consecutive seconds or longer on the active PIX firewall.
- The link status of any of the network interfaces on the active PIX goes down for more than twice the poll interval. This does not include interfaces that are administratively down.
- Hello packets are constantly exchanged between the primary and secondary PIX firewalls over all network interfaces. (They are sent out every 15 seconds by default, but this interval can be tuned.) If no hello messages are received for two poll intervals, the interface that did not respond is put into testing mode. If the interface does not pass testing, it and the firewall are considered failed.
- Hello packets are also exchanged between the primary and secondary PIX firewalls over the failover serial cable. If the standby firewall does not hear from the active firewall for two poll intervals and the failover cable status is declared okay, the standby PIX firewall becomes active itself. If the active unit does not hear from the standby firewall for two poll intervals, it considers the standby failed.
- If the standby firewall detects that the active firewall has been powered off or rebooted, the standby becomes active. If the failover cable is unplugged, no failover occurs.

There are two types of failover—standard failover and local area network (LAN)-based failover. The primary difference between them is the means used to exchange failover information between the primary and secondary firewalls. In standard failover, a special failover serial cable is used to connect the two firewalls. The failover cable is a Cisco proprietary modified RS-232 cable. LAN-based failover uses a dedicated Ethernet link to exchange failover information.

The failover information exchange includes:

- The MAC addresses of the firewalls
- Hello (keepalive) packets
- State information (active or standby)
- Network interface link status
- Configuration replication

Communication over the failover cable is performed using messages that must be acknowledged. If a message is not acknowledged by the other firewall within 3 seconds, it is retransmitted. After five retransmissions without an acknowledgment, the non-responsive firewall is declared failed.

Configuration Replication

Configuration replication is the process by which the configuration from the primary PIX firewall is replicated to the secondary firewall.

NOTE

The replication process occurs from memory-to-memory (running-config to running-config) only and is not saved in flash.

Therefore, after replication is complete, a **write memory** command should be issued on both the active and standby firewalls.

The replication process is automatically performed when:

- The standby PIX completes initial boot up. The primary firewall replicates its entire configuration to the secondary firewall.
- Commands are typed in on the active PIX firewall. As each command is entered on the active PIX firewall, it is sent to the standby across the failover connection.
- The **write standby** command is executed on the active PIX firewall. This forces the entire configuration to be replicated from the primary PIX firewall to the standby.

Any configuration changes made on the standby firewall are not replicated to the primary. If you try to enter commands on the standby firewall, the PIX warns you that you are trying to configure the wrong firewall.

IP and MAC Addresses Used for Failover

For each network interface on which you want failover configured, two IP addresses need to be reserved. One IP address is for the primary firewall, and one IP address is for failover. When functioning properly, the primary firewall uses its system IP and MAC addresses, and the secondary firewall uses the failover IP and MAC addresses. When failover occurs, the secondary firewall (now active) assumes the system IP and MAC addresses of the primary firewall. The primary firewall (now standby) assumes the failover IP and MAC addresses of the secondary firewall. Since the MAC addresses of the firewalls change in addition to the IP addresses, hosts connecting through the firewall do not have to re-ARP.

By default, the MAC addresses on the active firewall are the burned-in MAC addresses from the network interfaces of the primary firewall, and the MAC addresses on the standby firewall are the burned-in MAC addresses from the network interfaces on the secondary firewall. Instead of using these burned-in addresses, you have the option to use a virtual MAC address by using the **failover mac address <if_name> <active_mac> <standby_mac>**command. For example, the configuration command would look like **failover mac address inside 00c0.1715.3341 00c0.1715.3342**. To remove a virtual MAC address, use the **no** form of the command.

Failure Detection

The primary and secondary firewalls exchange hello packets with each other every 15 seconds by default over the failover cable and all network interfaces. To change the hello interval, use the **failover poll <seconds>** command. The minimum value for **seconds** is 3 seconds, and the maximum is 15 seconds. A shorter interval means faster failure detection, but also potentially unnecessary failover when the network is experiencing temporary congestion.

The PIX firewall monitors failover communication hello packets and the power status on the other firewall. If a failure not caused by a power loss or reboot of the secondary firewall is detected, the PIX firewall performs a series of tests to determine which firewall has failed:

- **Link Up/Down** The firewall tests the network link state to ensure it is up. If the interface passes, the PIX performs a network activity test. Otherwise, the interface and the corresponding firewall are considered failed.
- **Network Activity** The firewall listens for network activity for up to 5 seconds. If any packets are detected, the interface is considered operational and testing stops.
- **ARP** The PIX takes the 10 most recent entries in its ARP table and sends ARP requests for each one. The PIX then monitors all received traffic for up to five seconds. This continues until the list is exhausted or a response is received. If the list is exhausted and no traffic has been received, the PIX starts the broadcast ping test.
- **Broadcast Ping** The firewall sends out a broadcast ping on the interface and looks at all packets received for up to 5 seconds after the ping was sent. If any packets are received, the PIX firewall declares the interface operational and stops the test. If no packets are received, the firewall repeats the ARP test.

Stateful Failover

With stateful failover enabled, the primary firewall constantly replicates its TCP connection table to the secondary PIX firewall. If the primary firewall fails, the secondary firewall already has the connection table and therefore no connections are lost. Client applications continue to function without interruption.

When using stateful failover, the following information is replicated to the standby PIX firewall:

- xlate table with static and dynamic translations
- TCP connection table (including timeout information for each connection)
- System clock and uptime information

Most UDP connections are not replicated, with the exception of certain multi-channel protocols such as H.323. The following information is not replicated to the standby PIX firewall:

- Internet Security Association and Key Management Protocol (ISAKMP) and IPsec state information
- DHCP leases
- User authentication (**uauth**) table; when failover occurs, any authenticated users must re-authenticate
- Routing table; this means that all dynamically learned routes (through RIP) must be relearned
- The ARP table

By default, HTTP session information is not replicated. In PIXv6.2 and later, this feature can be enabled using the **failover replicate http** command.

The configuration of HTTP replication can be verified using the **show failover** command.

- Stateful failover requires a dedicated (failover-only traffic) Fast Ethernet or Gigabit Ethernet interface on each firewall (primary and secondary). (This as referred to as the *stateful failover interface.*)

Standard Failover Using a Failover Cable

The failover cable connects the primary and secondary PIX firewalls. One end of the failover cable is labeled primary, and the other end is labeled secondary. Do not connect the failover cable backward as this will replicate from the secondary firewall to the primary firewall and erase the entire configuration! This cable should be connected when the secondary firewall is turned off.

Configuring and Enabling Failover

Failover configuration is a straightforward affair, which is demonstrated using the network shown in Figure 8.15. In this example, PIX1 is the primary firewall and PIX2 is the secondary firewall. There are two interfaces in use: ethernet0 (outside) and ethernet1 (inside).

Figure 8.15 Standard Failover Example

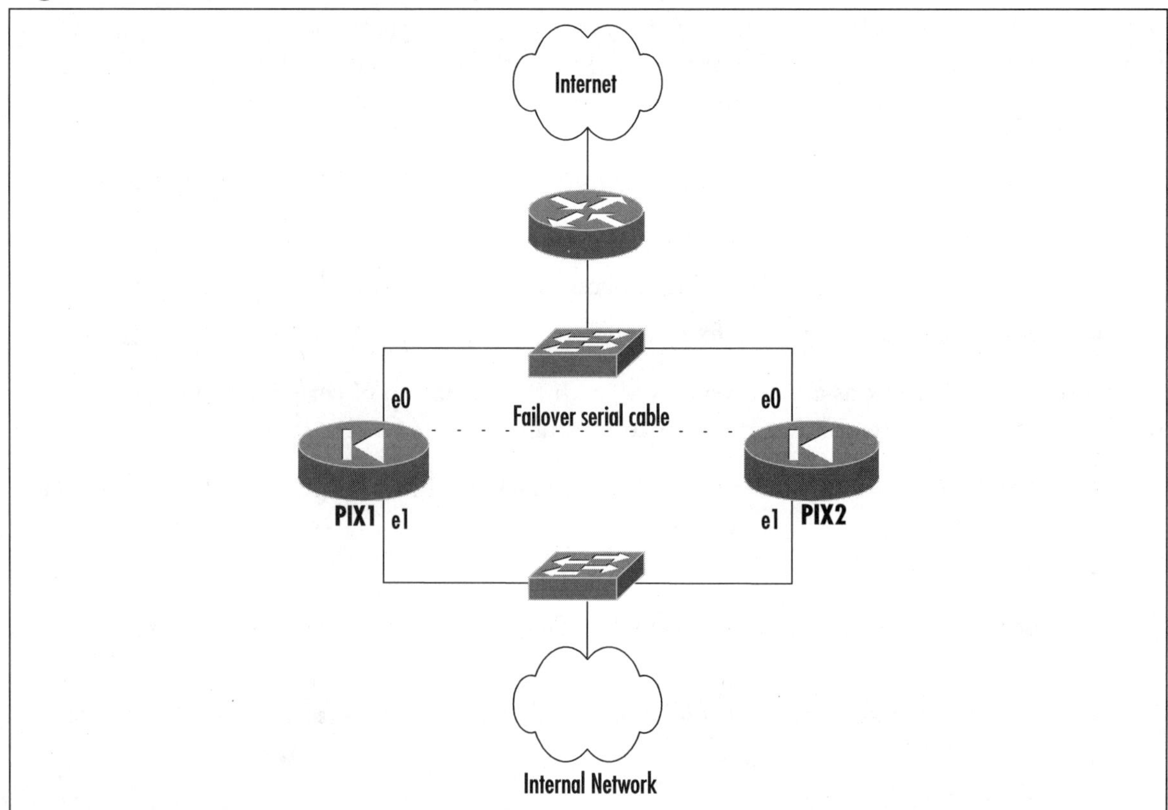

Connect the failover cable, but do not power on the secondary until the primary is fully configured.

The current IP addresses on the primary firewall should be the same as the system IP addresses. When failover occurs, the current IP addresses will change to the failover IP addresses.

To enable failover, the **failover** command is used on the primary firewall. Next, configure the failover IP addresses for each interface using the **failover ip address** command. In a normal state, these IP addresses will be assigned to their corresponding interfaces of the standby unit. Make sure that failover IP addresses are in the same subnet as the active IP addresses:

```
PIX1(config)# failover ip address inside 192.168.1.2
PIX1(config)# failover ip address outside 10.5.1.2
```

At this point, failover configuration is complete, and the secondary firewall can be turned on. After the secondary firewall boots up, the primary will detect it and start to synchronize the configurations. The **sync Started** message appears on the console. Once the synchronization is complete, the **sync Completed** message appears on the console.

To enable stateful failover, first set up a dedicated network link that will be used for exchanging state information. Figure 8.16 uses ethernet2 on each firewall for this function.

Figure 8.16 Standard Stateful Failover Example

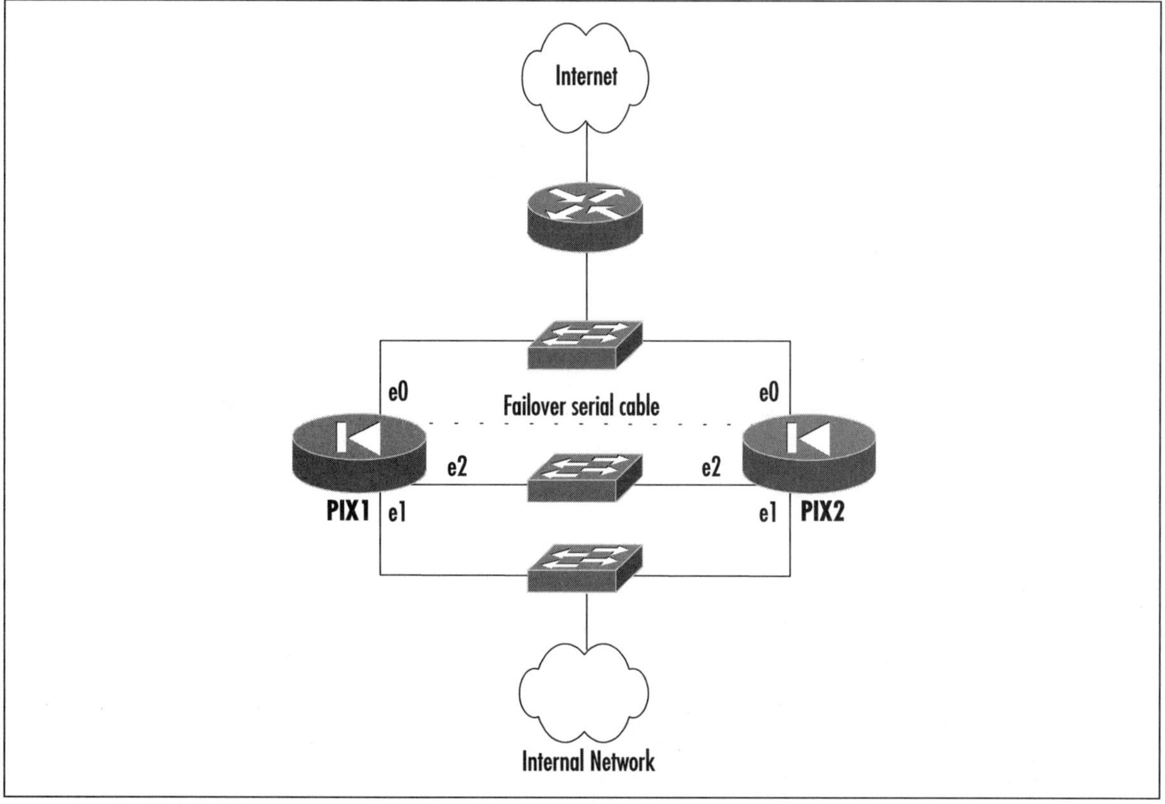

Configure **ethernet2** as follows.

```
PIX1(config)# nameif ethernet2 state security25
PIX1(config)# interface ethernet2 100full
PIX1(config)# ip address state 172.16.1.1 255.255.255.0
PIX1(config)# failover ip address state 172.16.1.2
PIX2(config)# nameif ethernet2 state security25
PIX2(config)# interface ethernet2 100full
```

Only a single command is required to make this the stateful failover interface:

```
PIX1(config)# failover link state
```

Monitoring Failover

The primary method of monitoring failover activity is the **show failover** command. This command relays everything you want to know about failover.

```
PIX1# show failover
Failover On
Cable status: Normal
Reconnect timeout 0:00:00
Poll frequency 3 seconds
        This host: Primary - Active
                Active time: 400 (sec)
                Interface state (172.16.1.1): Normal
                Interface outside (10.5.1.1): Normal
                Interface inside (192.168.1.1): Normal
        Other host: Secondary - Standby
                Active time: 0 (sec)
                Interface state (172.16.1.2): Normal
                Interface outside (10.5.1.2): Normal
                Interface inside (192.168.1.2): Normal

Stateful Failover Logical Update Statistics
        Link : intf3
        Stateful Obj    xmit        xerr        rcv         rerr
        General         3           0           3           0
        sys cmd         3           0           3           0
        up time         0           0           0           0
        xlate           0           0           0           0
        tcp conn        0           0           0           0
        udp conn        0           0           0           0
        ARP tbl         0           0           0           0
        RIP Tbl         0           0           0           0
```

```
Logical Update Queue Information
                    Cur      Max      Total
Recv Q:             0        1        3
Xmit Q:             0        1        3
```

Some of the output of this command merits further explanation. Status of the failover cable:

- **Normal** The primary and secondary firewalls are connected properly.
- **My Side Not Connected** The failover cable is not connected to the firewall on which the command was typed.
- **Other Side is not Connected** The failover cable is not connected to the other firewall.
- **Other Side Powered Off** The failover cable is connected, but the other firewall is powered off.

Interface status:

- **Normal** The interface is functioning properly.
- **Link Down** The line protocol on the interface is down.
- **Failed** The interface has failed.
- **Shut Down** The interface was administratively shut down.
- **Unknown** The interface was not configured with an IP address, and the status has not yet been determined.
- **Waiting** The monitoring of this interface on the other firewall has not yet started.

Stateful failover (logical unit status):

- **General** The sum of all objects.
- **sys cmd** Logical system update commands, such as login.
- **up time** Uptime information that is passed from the active to the standby unit.
- **xlate** The translation table.
- **tcp conn** TCP connection information.
- **udp conn** Dynamic UDP connection information.
- **ARP tbl** Dynamic ARP table information.
- **RIP Tbl** Dynamic routing table information.

For each of these stateful objects, the following statistics are available:

- **xmit** The number of packets transmitted to the other firewall.
- **Xerr** The number of errors that occurred while transmitting to the other firewall.
- **rcv** The number of received packets.

- **rerr** The number of errors that occurred while receiving packets from the other firewall.

The PIX firewall provides **debug** commands for monitoring failover operation (for example, **debug failover <option>**). Here, **option** can be any of the keywords listed in Table 8.8.

Table 8.8 Failover Debug Options

Keyword	Description
cable	Failover cable status.
fail	Failover internal exception.
fmsg	Failover message.
get	IP network packet received.
ifc	Network interface status trace.
open	Failover device open.
put	IP network packet transmitted.
rx	Failover cable receive.
rxdmp	Cable recv message dump (serial console only).
rxip	IP network failover packet received.
tx	Failover cable transmit.
txdmp	Cable xmit message dump (serial console only).
txip	IP network failover packet transmit.
verify	Failover message verify.
switch	Failover switching status.

LAN-Based Failover

PIX software v6.2 introduced support for LAN-based failover that uses an Ethernet link to monitor the failover status and exchange failover information. LAN-based failover overcomes the distance limitation (6 feet) of the serial failover cable. This Ethernet link must be a dedicated LAN interface. This link can also be used for stateful failover by configuring it to exchange state information. A hub or switch can be used, but not a crossover Ethernet cable. LAN-based failover does not detect power loss on the other firewall, a serious failing of this method.

Configuring and Enabling Failover

The example in Figure 8.17 is used to configure LAN-based failover. If a failover serial cable is connected to either of the two firewalls, it should be disconnected at this point. Connect all the network cables as shown in the diagram, beginning with the secondary firewall powered off.

Figure 8.17 A LAN-Based Failover Example

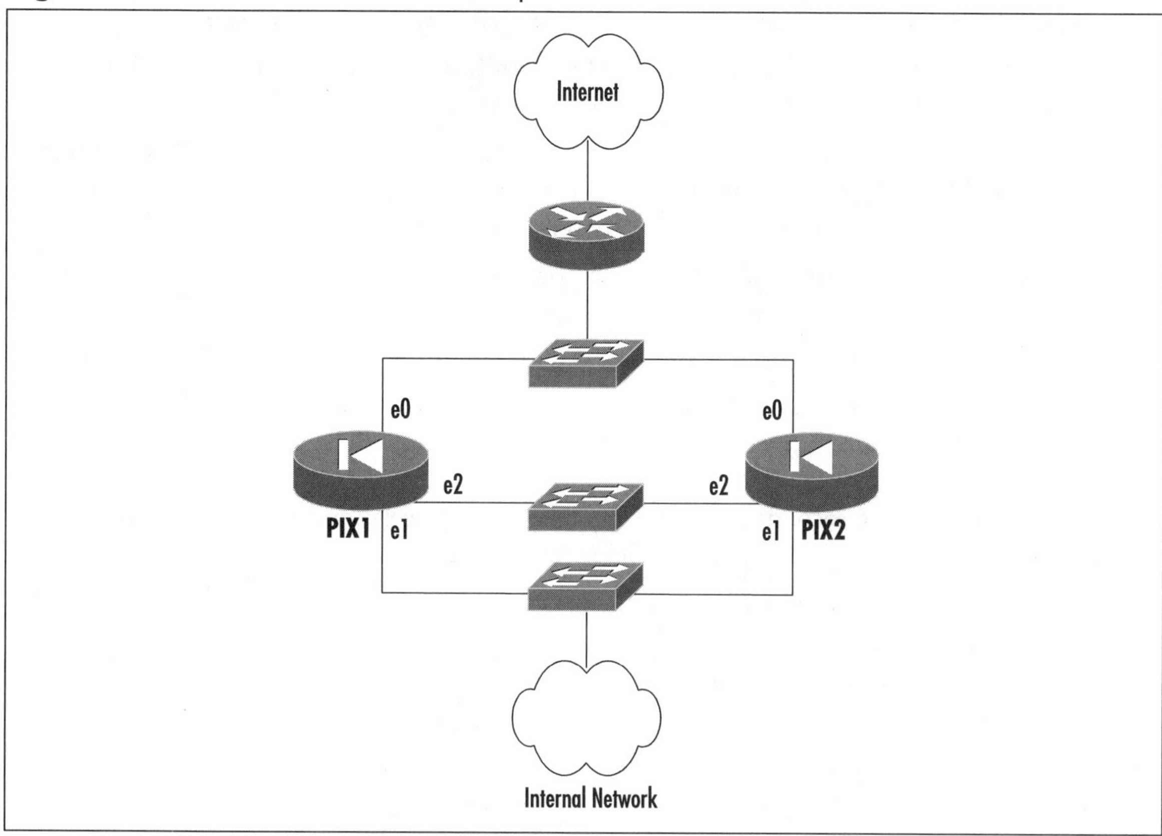

Here is what the configuration would look like in this example. **Ethernet2** is named **lanlink**.

```
PIX2(config)# nameif ethernet2 lanlink security25
PIX1(config)# interface ethernet0 100full
PIX1(config)# interface ethernet1 100full
PIX1(config)# interface ethernet2 100full
PIX1(config)# ip address inside 192.168.1.1 255.255.255.0
PIX1(config)# ip address outside 10.5.1.1 255.255.255.0
PIX1(config)# ip address lanlink 172.16.1.1 255.255.255.0
```

1. First, the failover we enabled on the primary unit with the **failover** configuration command.
2. Next, the failover IP addresses are configured using the **failover ip address** command:
   ```
   PIX1(config)# failover ip address inside 192.168.1.2
   PIX1(config)# failover ip address outside 10.5.1.2
   PIX1(config)# failover ip address lanlink 172.16.1.2
   ```
3. The primary firewall is designated for LAN-based failover with the **failover lan unit primary** configuration command.

4. The interface is specified on both the primary and secondary that will be used to as the failover interface with the command **failover lan interface <if_name>**.
5. In this example, the **failover lan interface lanlink** configuration command is entered on the primary firewall.
6. For better security (thought not required for failover), a manual pre-shared key should be used to encrypt and authenticate the contents of failover messages. This is accomplished with the **failover lan key <secret_key>** command.
7. In this case, the **failover lan key cisco** command is entered on the primary firewall and the key is set to **cisco**.
8. To enable LAN-based failover on the primary firewall, enter the following commands:

```
PIX1(config)# failover lan enable
PIX1(config)# failover
```

9. At this point, the secondary firewall can be powered on (after disconnecting the LAN-based failover interface). Enter the following commands:

```
PIX2(config)# interface ethernet2 100full
PIX2(config)# nameif ethernet2 lanlink security25
PIX2(config)# ip address lanlink 172.16.1.1 255.255.255.0
PIX2(config)# failover ip address lanlink 172.16.1.2
PIX2(config)# failover lan unit secondary
PIX2(config)# failover lan interface lanlink
PIX2(config)# failover lan key cisco
PIX2(config)# failover lan enable
PIX2(config)# failover
```

10. At this point, LAN-based failover is fully configured. Now the LAN-based failover interface can be reconnected. The following messages should appear on the secondary PIX firewall:

```
LAN-based Failover: trying to contact peer??
LAN-based Failover: Send hello msg and start failover monitoring
```

11. On the primary PIX firewall, the following messages should appear:

```
LAN-based Failover: Peer is UP
Sync Started
Sync Completed
```

12. If all connections are working and the configurations were typed in correctly, the **show failover** command will show that failover is operational.

```
PIX1# show failover
Failover On
Cable status: My side not connected
Reconnect timeout 0:00:00
Poll frequency 15 seconds
        This host: Primary - Active
                Active time: 400 (sec)
                Interface state (172.16.2.1): Normal
                Interface outside (10.5.1.1): Normal
                Interface inside (192.168.1.1): Normal
        Other host: Secondary - Standby
                Active time: 0 (sec)
                Interface state (172.16.2.2): Normal
                Interface outside (10.5.1.2): Normal
                Interface inside (192.168.1.2): Normal

LAN-based Failover is Active
  interface lanlink (172.16.1.1): Normal, peer (172.16.1.2): Normal
```

NOTE

The **failover MAC address** command is not available when using LAN-based failover.

The interface ethernet3 could be configured for exchanging state information (see Figure 8.18) and configured for stateful failover, though in the real world, this would "waste" an interface.

```
PIX1(config)# interface ethernet3 100full
PIX1(config)# nameif ethernet3 state security20
PIX1(config)# ip address state 172.16.2.1 255.255.255.0
PIX1(config)# failover ip address state 172.16.2.2
PIX1(config)# failover link state
PIX2(config)# interface ethernet3 100full
PIX2(config)# nameif ethernet3 state security20
```

Figure 8.18 A LAN-Based Stateful Failover Example

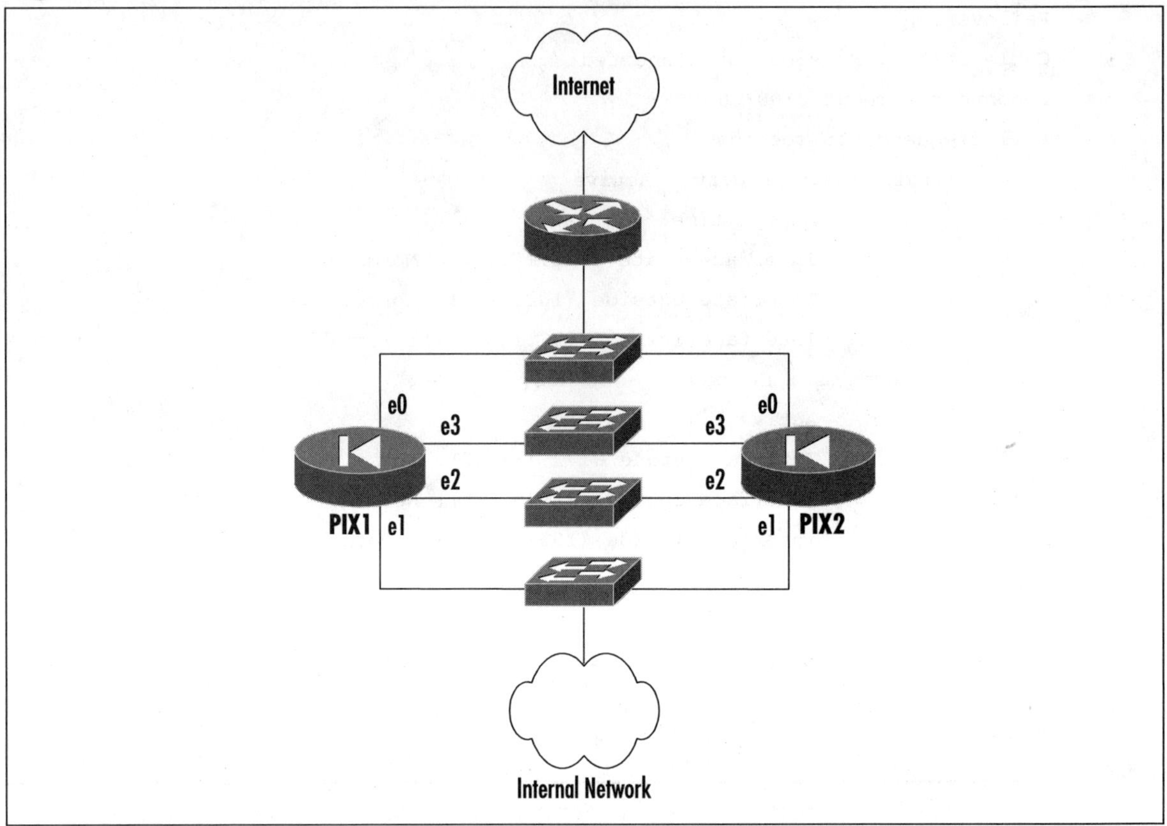

Monitoring Failover

The failover status can be viewed using the show failover command adjusted slightly to get a quick status of LAN-based failover:

```
PIX1# show failover lan
LAN-based Failover is Active
        interface fail (10.20.1.1): Normal, peer (10.20.1.2): Normal
```

To view LAN-based failover details, use the **show failover lan detail** command:

```
PIX1# show failover lan detail
LAN-based Failover is Active
This PIX is Primary
Command Interface is lanlink
My Command Interface IP is 172.16.2.1
Peer Command Interface IP is 172.16.2.2
My interface status is Normal
Peer interface status is Normal
Peer interface down time is 0x0
```

```
Total cmd msgs sent: 111, rcvd: 107, dropped: 0, retrans: 0, send_err: 0
Total secure msgs sent: 0, rcvd: 0
bad_signature: 2, bad_authen: 0, bad_hdr: 0, bad_osversion: 0,
    bad_length: 0
Total failed retx lck cnt: 0
Total/Cur/Max of 87:0:1 msgs on retransQ, 87 ack msgs
Cur/Max of 0:21 msgs on txq
Cur/Max of 0:1 msgs on rxq
Number of blk allocation failure: 0, cmd failure: 0, Flapping: 0
Current cmd window: 1, Slow cmd Ifc cnt: 0
Cmd Link down: 0, down and up: 0, Window Limit: 141
Number of fmsg allocation failure: 0, duplicate msgs: 0
Cmd Response Time History stat:
< 100ms:          84
100 - 250ms:      0
250 - 500ms:      0
500 - 750ms:      0
750 - 1000ms:     0
1000 - 2000ms:    0
2000 - 4000ms:    0
> 4000ms:         0
Cmd Response Retry History stat:
Retry 0 = 87, 1 = 0, 2 = 0, 3 = 0, 4 = 0
Failover enable state is 0x1
Failover state is 0x7d
Failover peer state is 0x58
Failover switching state is 0x0
Failover config syncing is not in progress
Failover poll cnt is 0
Failover Fmsg cnt is 0
Failover OS version is 6.2(2)
failover interface 0, tst_mystat = 0x0, tst_peerstat = 0x0
    zcnt = 0, hcnt = 1, my_rcnt = 10186, peer_rcnt = 23408
    myflag = 0x1, peer_flag=0x0, dchp = 0x80791f90
    act_ip: 10.5.1.171, stn_ip:10.5.1.2
    act_mac: 00d0.b7b2.97ee, stb_mac: 0090.273a.1240
failover interface 1, tst_mystat = 0x0, tst_peerstat = 0x0
    zcnt = 0, hcnt = 1, my_rcnt = 26191, peer_rcnt = 39296
    myflag = 0x1, peer_flag=0x0, dchp = 0x80791ff0
    act_ip: 192.168.1.1, stn_ip:192.168.1.2
```

```
    act_mac: 00d0.b783.9a79, stb_mac: 0090.273a.1288
failover interface 3, tst_mystat = 0x0, tst_peerstat = 0x2
    zcnt = 0, hcnt = 0, my_rcnt = 539, peer_rcnt = 404
    myflag = 0x0, peer_flag=0x0, dchp = 0x80791e10
    act_ip: 172.16.1.1, stn_ip:172.16.1.2
    act_mac: 00a0.c9ef.cfa0, stb_mac: 00a0.c9ef.cfa0
LAN-based Failover command link
```

Four **debug** commands are available (with the **debug failover <option>** command) when using LAN-based failover. See Table 8.9 for details.

Table 8.9 LAN-Based Failover Debug Options

Option	Description
lanrx	LAN-based failover receive.
lanretx	LAN-based failover retransmit.
lantx	LAN-based failover transmit.
lancmd	LAN-based failover main thread.

Failing Back

Once failover has occurred and the primary firewall is running in standby mode and the secondary firewall is running as the active, a failback does not automatically occur. When the primary firewall is restored and the failed condition has been fixed, it does not automatically become the active firewall (unless the secondary firewall fails). The primary firewall can be forced to become active by either:

- Using the **failover active** command on the primary firewall.
- Using the **no failover active** command on the secondary firewall.

After using one of these commands, the primary firewall becomes active. If stateful failover is enabled, no sessions will be dropped. Otherwise, connections will be dropped and applications will have to re-establish sessions through the firewall.

Disabling Failover

To disable failover, use the **no failover** command. To verify that failover has been disabled, use the **show failover** command:

```
PIX1# show failover
Failover Off
Cable Status: My side not connected
Reconnect timeout: 0:00:00
```

If disabling failover permanently, it is highly recommended that you clean up the configuration by removing the other **failover** commands. It would be best to erase the configuration completely from the secondary firewall.

Configuring Logging

System management is an important part of configuring and maintaining a firewall. Logging is invaluable for measuring system performance, identifying potential network bottlenecks, and detecting potential security violations.

There are two ways to log information: local and remote. Local logging is of limited value since it can only be used during a session on the PIX. Remote logging stores the messages and uses scripts to examine them in detail, manipulate the data, and generate detailed reports. Logging can be performed at several levels of detail. Level 3 (error) is the default for the PIX. Level 7 (debug) is the most verbose and is recommended only when troubleshooting the PIX. In normal network operations, Cisco recommends using Level 4 (warning) or Level 3 (error).

Normal logging (Level 3) records alerts (such as a failover link going down), error conditions (such as an ICMP being blocked), and informational messages (such as a memory allocation error). Higher levels can record connection setup and teardown, as well as the amount of traffic transferred in each session. This functionality can be useful if an administrator is trying to gather statistics on how much traffic is being exchanged per protocol or per session. It is possible to view logging messages in real time, either through a Telnet or SSH session or on the console port.

Local Logging

The three types of local logging are *buffered*, *console*, and *terminal*. Logging is disabled by default. To enable it and start logging to all output locations such as the buffer, console, terminal, or syslog server:

```
PIX1(config)# [no] logging on
```

To disable logging, use the **no** form of the command:

Buffered Logging

Buffered logging sends all messages to an internal buffer (up to 100 messages). To enable buffered logging, use **the logging buffered <level>** command.

The command, **show logging**, displays the logging configuration as well as buffered messages.

```
PIX1# show logging
Syslog logging: enabled
    Facility: 20
    Timestamp logging: disabled
    Standby logging: disabled
    Console logging: level debugging, 37 messages logged
    Monitor logging: disabled
    Buffer logging: level debugging, 9 messages logged
```

```
    Trap logging: disabled
    History logging: disabled
111008: User 'enable_15' executed the 'logging buffered 7' command.
111009: User 'enable_15' executed cmd: show logging
```

Use the **clear logging** command to clear out the buffer. To disable buffered logging, use the **no logging buffered** command in configuration mode.

Console Logging

Console logging sends log messages to the console of the PIX firewall. The configuration syntax is **logging console <level>**. Logging messages are displayed on the console. Console logging can enter with typing, as well as degrade firewall performance, so use sparingly. To disable console logging, use the **no logging console** command.

Terminal Logging

Terminal logging sends log messages to a Telnet or SSH session. To enable terminal logging, use the **logging monitor <level>** command. Logging must be enabled on a per-session basis with the **terminal monitor** command. Disable with the **terminal no monitor** command.

Syslog

To use syslog, configure the host (PIX firewall) that will send the messages and the server (syslog) that will receive them. The syslog server determines where to store and organize the log messages. It may write the messages to a file or send an alert by e-mail or pager.

As logging on the PIX is disabled by default, enable it with the **logging on** configuration command. To configure syslog on the PIX, identify the server to which to send the syslog messages with the **logging host [<interface>] <ip_address>** command.

The **interface** parameter specifies the outbound interface, and the **ip_address** parameter specifies the syslog server on that interface. If not specified, the interface is assumed to be the inside interface. No log messages will be sent to syslog until the logging level is configured using the **logging trap <level>** command.

The *level* parameter specifies the severity level.

Here is an example of configuring syslog on the PIX firewall:

```
PIX1(config)# logging host inside 192.168.50.8
PIX1(config)# logging trap debugging
PIX1(config)# logging on
PIX1(config)#
PIX1# show logging
Syslog logging: enabled
    Facility: 20
    Timestamp logging: disabled
    Standby logging: disabled
    Console logging: disabled
```

```
    Monitor logging: disabled
    Buffer logging: disabled
    Trap logging: level debugging, 38 messages logged
        Logging to inside 192.168.50.8
    History logging: disabled
```

In this example, logging is configured to send messages to the syslog server 192.168.50.8 on the inside interface with a severity level of debugging.

When configured to use syslog, the PIX firewall will send the log messages to the syslog server using UDP port 514 by default, which can be changed with the **logging host [<interface>] <ip address> [tcp|udp/<port_number>]** command. Either UDP or TCP can be configured for syslog, and the **port_number** parameter can be any value from 1025 to 65535. If the syslog server goes down when TCP is being used, the default behavior for the PIX firewall is that all network traffic through the PIX will be blocked. TCP also has more overhead and will be slower in sending syslog messages to the server.

In the following example, syslog is configured using TCP. The **port_number** parameter has been set to 1468, which is the default TCP port used by syslog servers that accept TCP syslog from PIX firewalls.

```
PIX1(config)# logging host inside 192.168.50.9 tcp/1468
PIX1(config)# logging trap debugging
PIX1(config)# logging on
```

If the syslog server is offline, the PIX will queue messages in memory and then overwrite older messages as necessary to make room for the newer messages. The size of the syslog message queue in memory is configured with the **logging queue <msg_count>** command. The default is 512 messages. If **msg_count** is set to 0, the queue size is unlimited and based on the available block memory.

To see the queue statistics and any discarded message statistics, use the following command:

```
PIX1# show logging queue
        Logging Queue length limit : 512 msg(s)
        Current 3 msg on queue, 5 msgs most on queue
```

Logging Levels

Although there are eight different severity levels used on the PIX (Levels 0 through 7), logging Level 0 (emergency) is not used. When a level is specified, the PIX firewall logs all events equal to the specified level as well as the levels below it. For example, the default severity level for the PIX is 3 (error), which also logs Level 2 (critical), Level 1 (alert), and Level 0 (emergency) events. A complete list of the keywords and equivalent levels is shown in Table 8.10.

Table 8.10 Logging Levels and Messages

Keyword	Level	Message
emergency	0	System unusable
alert	1	Immediate action needed
critical	2	Critical condition
error	3	Error condition
warning	4	Warning condition
notification	5	Normal but significant condition
informational	6	Informational message only
debugging	7	Only used during debugging

A system log message that the syslog server will receive is structured like **%PIX–Level-message_number: Message_text**. The syslog messages will be prefaced with a time and date stamp and the source IP address, followed by the level, which represents the logging level. When the PIX is configured to disable certain messages, the numeric code is used to identify which message to disable. Examples can be seen in Table 8.11.

Table 8.11 Sample Messages at the Various Logging Levels

Level 1	%PIX-1-101002: (Primary) Bad failover cable.
Level 2	%PIX-2-106016: Deny IP spoof from (IP_addr) to IP_addr on interface int_name.
Level 3	%PIX-3-201005: FTP data connection failed for IP_addr.
Level 4	%PIX-4-403110: PPP virtual interface int_name, user: user missing MPPE key from aaa server.
Level 5	%PIX-5-500001: ActiveX content modified src IP_addr dest IP_addr on interface int_name.
Level 6	%PIX-6-109005: Authentication succeeded for user 'user' from laddr/lport to faddr/fport on interface int_name.
Level 7	%PIX-7-702301: lifetime expiring.

The Cisco PIX firewall has the ability to log URL and FTP traffic. To enable URL logging, enable fixup for HTTP, set the logging level to 5 (notification), and look for the message type 304001. For example:

```
%PIX-5-304001: 192.168.0.10 Accessed URL 10.20.1.20:/index.html
```

To enable FTP logging, enable fixup for FTP, set the logging level to 6 (informational), and look for message type of 303002. For example:

```
%PIX-6-303002:  192.168.0.10 Retrieved 10.20.1.20:file1.bin
%PIX-6-303002:  192.168.0.10 Stored 10.20.1.20:file2.bin
```

Logging Facility

Each syslog message has a facility number that identifies where the message should be logged. There are 24 different facilities (RFC3164), with numerical codes ranging from 0 to 23. The eight facilities commonly used for syslog are local0 through local7. The syslog processes files or places the messages into the correct log file based on the facility or inbound pipe. On the PIX firewall, facility configuration is optional. If used, the facility must be specified using its numerical code with the **logging facility <facility_code>** command syntax. Table 8.12 shows the facility names associated with each of the numerical codes.

Table 8.12 Facility Numerical Codes and Names

Numerical Code	Name
16	local0
17	local1
18	local2
19	local3
20	local4
21	local5
22	local6
23	local7

The default setting for facility configuration on a Cisco PIX is local4 (20). By changing the facility number, the syslog messages can be directed from different Cisco PIX firewalls (or even different types and models of devices) to different files. For example, on a Linux/UNIX machine, the /etc/syslog.conf file is configured with the following command:

```
# PIX Firewall syslog messages
local7.*      /var/log/pix/pix1
```

The PIX firewall can be configured to send syslog messages to the local7 log file (/var/log/pix/pix1) using the **logging facility 23** configuration command. Now the PIX will send syslog messages to facility local7 on the Linux server. Any syslog message arriving at the Linux syslog process for facility local7 is stored in the /var/log/pix/pix1 log file, whereas any syslog message for local4 (20) will continue to go to the default message log file.

Disabling Specific Syslog Messages

At times, an administrator will want to disable certain syslog messages with the **no logging message <message_number>** command. The **message_number** parameter specifies the unique numeric message ID of each syslog message. For example, the configuration command would look similar to **no logging message 303002**.

To see which messages are disabled, use the **show logging disabled** command:

```
PIX1# show logging disabled
no logging message 303002
```

To clear the disabled message so that it will be logged again, use the **logging message <message_number>** command. The **message_number** parameter specifies the unique numeric ID of the disabled message. To re-enable all disabled messages, use the **clear logging disabled** command.

Configuring Remote Access

Telnet, SSH, Simplet Network Management Protocol (SNMP), and Cisco PDM can be used to access and manage the PIX firewall. Remote access is either command-line interface, or CLI or a GUI such as the PDM. The CLI provides a very fast and low-overhead method of management via SSH or Telnet while the user-friendly PDM requires more resources. The PIX firewall only supports SSH version 1, not SSH version 2.

Enabling SSH Access

In order for the PIX to accept SSH connections, the PIX firewall must be configured to support SSH.

1. To generate the RSA key, assign a hostname and a domain name to the PIX:

```
PIX1(config)# hostname PIX1
PIX1(config)# domain-name SecureCorp.com
```

2. Generate the RSA key pair (one public key and one private key) and save them to flash memory:

```
ca generate rsa key <modulus>
```

   Cisco recommends 1024 bits for the **modulus**. The larger the key, the longer it will take to generate the key and the longer it will take to crack it. An example:

```
PIX1(config)# ca generate rsa key 2048
```

   For **<key_modulus_size> >= 1024**, key generation could take up to several minutes.

3. View the new RSA public key:

```
PIX1(config)# show ca mypubkey rsa
% Key pair was generated at: 13:13:04 UTC Aug 1 2002
Key name: PIX1.SecureCorp.com
 Usage: General Purpose Key
 Key Data:
  30820122 300d0609 2a864886 f70d0101 01050003 82010f00 3082010a 02820101
  00b92dfe ac9a3fd1 f3c0bfd7 6920b498 b2722dbe d9aa8d4c f0bf0c0c a5bf1d3f
<<  output omitted  >>
% Key pair was generated at: 13:47:47 UTC Aug 10 2002
Key name: PIX1.SecureCorp.com.server
 Usage: Encryption Key
```

```
Key Data:
 307c300d 06092a86 4886f70d 01010105 00036b00 30680261 00c150ba b244378c
<<  output omitted  >>
```

NOTE

If an RSA key is already saved on the PIX, you will be asked to remove the existing key with the **ca zeroize rsa** command.

4. Save the RSA key pair to flash with the **ca save all** configuration command.
5. Identify hosts or subnets allowed to SSH to the PIX. The SSH inactivity timeout can also be set at this point. This is done with the **ssh <ip_address> [<netmask>] [<interface>]** command. If not specified, the netmask is assumed to be 255.255.255.255 and on the inside interface. For this example, the configuration command should follow the **ssh 192.168.50.0 255.255.255.0 inside** syntax.
6. By default, the PIX will disconnect an SSH session after 5 minutes of inactivity. The inactivity timeout can be set between 1 and 60 minutes. For our purposes set the inactivity timeout to 10 minutes with the configuration command **ssh timeout 10.**
7. Save the changes to flash with the **write memory** command.

To verify the SSH configuration, use the **show ssh** command in Enable mode. Now you can SSH to the firewall with the client of your choice. The default username for a Cisco PIX SSH connection that is not using AAA for authentication is pix. The passphrase is the password that is used for Telnet. Once the username and passphrase are authenticated, the SSH session will start. This authentication can take a few moments.

Troubleshooting SSH

At times an administrator will need to troubleshoot the reason that the SSH connection is failing. In this case, the **debug ssh** command should be used on the PIX. The debug output on PIX is relatively easy to understand and can be read easily without much trouble.

To see how many SSH sessions are on the PIX, use the **show ssh sessions [<ip_address>]** command. The optional **ip_address** parameter allows you to check for SSH sessions from a particular IP address.

```
PIX1# show ssh sessions
Session ID       Client IP        Version Encryption       State    Username
1                 192.168.50.8     1.5      DES               6         pix
```

To disconnect a specific SSH session, use the **ssh disconnect <session_id>** command. For example: **ssh disconnect 0**. The **session_id** parameter specifies the number associated with the SSH session that is shown by using the **show ssh sessions** command. To remove all SSH configuration statements from the Cisco PIX, use the **clear ssh** command.

Telnet

Telnet is the simplest and most insecure client that can be used to connect to the firewall. It is character-based and sends each character in cleartext across the network. SSH is recommend over Telnet, and is only covered briefly here.

NOTE

The Cisco PIX firewall can only be a Telnet server and not a Telnet client. This is unlike Cisco routers and switches, from which you can Telnet from one system to the next.

To configure Telnet on the PIX firewall, use the **telnet <ip_address> [<netmask>] [<interface>]** command (for example: **telnet 192.168.50.0 255.255.255.0 inside**). The idle timeout value can be set for the Telnet session. The timeout value is specified in minutes and must be a value from 1 to 60. The default timeout is 5 minutes.

The **show telnet** command shows the current list of IP addresses and their interfaces that are authorized to access the PIX via Telnet. For example:

```
PIX1# show telnet
192.168.50.0 255.255.255.0 inside
```

The **clear telnet** or **no telnet** commands remove the Telnet privilege from an authorized IP address.

```
clear telnet [<ip_address> [<netmask>] [<interface>]
PIX1(config)# clear telnet 192.168.50.0 255.255.255.0 inside
```

If no parameters are specified, the **clear telnet** command removes access for all hosts.

The **kill <telnet_id>** command terminates an active Telnet session. No warning is given the user when the session is dropped. The **telnet_id** parameter specifies the session number that is shown when you use the **who** command. For example: **kill 0**.

Configuring SNMP

SNMP is used to manage network devices, including collecting information from them. SNMP on the Cisco PIX is read only. Do not use a weak SNMP community string such as the default of public. The string chosen should not be a dictionary-based word (for example, **UcanN0tGuEe$$ME** rather than **SNMPString**). While there are currently three versions of SNMP, the PIX only supports version 1. Management software must be updated with the most current SNMP MIBs for the PIX.

SNMP uses queries and traps to get information from the PIX firewall. The host sends a query (polls) to the PIX and receives a response. Polling can retrieve information or values such as the software version, interface statistics, and CPU utilization that can be displayed by the SNMP management station. A *trap* is a message that the PIX sends based on an event that has occurred, such as a link going up or down or a syslog event.

Configuring System Identification

Basic SNMP identification is configured using the following commands.

```
snmp-server location <word>
snmp-server contact <word>
```

Both of these commands are optional for SNMP. The **word** parameter in both commands can be any string up to 127 characters. The location can describe a building, closet, rack location, or any other standard used on a network. The contact can be a contact person or company that is responsible for administering the PIX. The SNMP configuration can be verified using **show snmp**.

Configuring Polling

SNMP polling allows an SNMP management station to retrieve data using PIX SNMP Operation Ids (OIDs). To configure polling, establish a SNMP community by using the **snmp-server community <word>** command. This sets the SNMP "password" which is case sensitive and limited to 32 characters. The PIX firewall must be configured with the IP address of the polling station. This is done by using the **snmp-server host [<interface>] <ip_address> poll** command. If no interface is specified, the inside interface is assumed. The **poll** parameter specifies that the management station will query the PIX. Multiple polling station IP addresses can be specified by typing multiple **snmp-server host** commands.

Select OIDs are shown in Table 8.13. To find all the OIDs for the PIX firewall, go to ftp://ftp.cisco.com/pub/mibs/oid/ and download the appropriate MIB.

Table 8.13 Useful Cisco PIX OIDs

Description	OID
System description	1.3.6.1.2.1.1.1.0
System uptime	1.3.6.1.2.1.1.3.0
Memory used	1.3.6.1.4.1.9.9.48.1.1.1.5.1
Memory free	1.3.6.1.4.1.9.9.48.1.1.1.6.1
Failover status	1.3.6.1.4.1.9.9.147.1.2.1.1.1.4.7
Current connections in use	1.3.6.1.4.1.9.9.147.1.2.2.2.1.5.40.6
Most connections in use	1.3.6.1.4.1.9.9.147.1.2.2.2.1.5.40.7
CPU utilization (5 second)	1.3.6.1.4.1.9.9.109.1.1.1.1.3.1
CPU utilization (1 minute)	1.3.6.1.4.1.9.9.109.1.1.1.1.4.1
CPU utilization (5 minute)	1.3.6.1.4.1.9.9.109.1.1.1.1.5.1

Configuring Traps

SNMP traps are triggered by an event such as an interface going down. The SNMP traps are sent on UDP port 162 and are not encrypted. To configure and use SNMP traps, follow these steps:

1. Configure the SNMP community with the **snmp-server community Il0v3CiSCo** configuration command.
2. Configure the SNMP host that will receive the traps. The syntax is similar to configuring a host for polling, except the **trap** keyword is used instead of **poll**: **snmp-server host inside 192.168.50.8 tra**.

NOTE

If you configure an SNMP host without using the poll or **trap** keywords, the SNMP host will be used for both functions.

3. Enable SNMP traps by using the **snmp-server enable traps** command.
4. Set the logging level for SNMP traps using the **logging history** command (for example: **logging history errors**).
5. Start sending traps to the SNMP management station with the **logging on** command.
6. To stop SNMP traps, use the **no snmp-server enable traps** command.

Configuring System Date and Time

The clock and time zone allow the administrator to build an accurate timeline of what has happened in the log files. The Coordinated Universal Time (UTC) format can be used because the base time is always the same regardless of location. A number of hours is either added or subtracted from the UTC to get the local time. This log file timestamp consistency provides the one constant reference point across the network.

Setting and Verifying the Clock and Time Zone

The time zone can be adjusted and support can be configured for daylight savings time. These enhancements allow the administrator to view the clock information in a readily understandable time format without having to convert the internal UTC into their local time.

There are three approaches for configuring the PIX clocks across an enterprise network:

- Always display the "local" time zone for each device, based on where the device is located.
- Set all devices internally to the UTC format for a standard clock across multiple time zones.
- Set all devices to display the local "headquarters" time zone.

To check the time on a PIX firewall, use **show clock**. To set the local clock on the PIX use **clock set <hh:mm:ss month day year>**. The month should be the first three characters of the month, while days are numbered 1-31, and year from 1993 to 2035. PIX v6.2 supports daylight savings time (**summer-time**) and time zones:

```
clock summer-time <zone> date <week weekday month hh:mm week weekday month hh:mm
[offset]>
```

The **zone** parameter is the name of the time zone, such as PST. The other parameters are used to set the start and the end of summer time. If you want to make this a recurring event, change the command slightly:

```
clock summer-time <zone> recurring <week weekday month hh:mm week weekday month hh:mm
[offset]>
```

The parameter **recurring** will start and stop the **summer-time** adjustment each year at the same point. Here is an example:

```
PIX1# show clock
04:22:19.659 UTC Mon Oct 7 2002
PIX1# configure terminal
PIX1(config)# clock summer-time pst date 7 april 2002 00:00 27 october 2002 00:00
PIX1(config)#
PIX1# show clock
05:23:02.890 pst Mon Oct 7 2002
PIX1# show clock detail
05:23:05.751 pst Mon Oct 7 2002
Time source is user configuration
Summer time starts 00:00:00 UTC Sun Apr 7 2002
Summer time ends 00:00:00 pst Sun Oct 27 2002
```

To set the time zone for the display use only the **clock timezone <zone> <hours> [<minutes>]** command. **Clock timezone** only sets the displayed time; the internal time is still kept in UTC format. The **zone** parameter is the name of the time zone. The **hours** parameter is the time offset from UTC. To disable the time zone, use the **no clock timezone** command.

Use the **clear clock** command to clear the clock settings. The following example indicates that the command cleared the **summer-time** settings:

```
PIX1# show clock detail
17:01:43.480 pst Fri Sep 20 2002
Time source is user configuration
Summer time starts 00:00:00 UTC Sun Apr 7 2002
Summer time ends 00:00:00 pst Sun Oct 27 2002
PIX1# configure terminal
PIX1(config)# clear clock
PIX1# show clock detail
16:02:36.301 UTC Fri Sep 20 2002
Time source is user configuration
```

Configuring and Verifying the Network Time Protocol

Time keeping can be automated using the Network Time Protocol (NTP). NTP uses servers as the master reference point, and the NTP client (the PIX firewall) uses the NTP server to get accurate time. The NTP server gets its own time from a radio source or atomic clock. The NTP servers listen on UDP port 123 for requests. The Cisco PIX firewall queries an NTP server and updates its clock. Once NTP is configured on all of the PIX firewalls, all the log files will have consistent and accurate timestamps.

There are two strata, or classes, of NTP servers. Stratum 1 NTP servers are directly connected to the time source. Stratum 2 servers are the second level and consider Stratum 1 servers to be authoritative.

NOTE

Cisco supports only Stratum 2 servers.

You can get the time from public Stratum 2 servers on the Internet or configure your own NTP server on the LAN or WAN. To enable the Cisco PIX Firewall NTP client, use the **ntp server <ip_address> source <interface>** command. To remove an NTP server, use the **no ntp server <ip_address>** command.

The following example shows this command and how to check the configuration to ensure the PIX is talking with the timeserver correctly using the **show ntp status** and **show ntp association** commands:

```
PIX1(config)# ntp server 192.168.1.3 source inside
PIX1(config)# show ntp status

Clock is unsynchronized, stratum 16, no reference clock
nominal freq is 99.9967 Hz, actual freq is 99.9967 Hz, precision is 2**6
reference time is 00000000.00000000 (06:28:16.000 UTC Thu Feb 7 2036)
clock offset is -4.0684 msec, root delay is 0.00 msec
root dispersion is 0.00 msec, peer dispersion is 15875.02 msec
PIX1(config)# show ntp associations

address          ref clock     st   when   poll  reach   delay   offset      disp
~192.168.1.3     0.0.0.0       16     -     64     0      0.0     0.00       16000.
master (synced), # master (unsynced), + selected, - candidate, ~configured
```

The NTP configuration can be viewed using the **show ntp** command. To delete the NTP configuration, use the **clear ntp** command.

NTP Authentication

NTP authentication prevents unauthorized or manipulative clock resets by using trusted keys between the NTP server and the client. The 32-character authentication key must match on the PIX and the server.

1. NTP authentication is disabled by default on the PIX. It can be enabled by using the **ntp authenticate** command.
2. Define the authentication key with the **ntp authentication-key <number> md5 <value>** command. The only choice of encryption is MD5. The **number** parameter is a value from 1 to 4294967295 that uniquely identifies the key. The **value** parameter is an arbitrary string of 32 characters, including all printable characters and spaces.
3. Define the trusted key that will be sent in the NTP packets with the command **ntp trusted-key <key_number>.** The **key_number** parameter must be a number from 1 to 4294967295.
4. The last step is to configure the server association, which lets the Cisco PIX firewall synchronize to the other server. Use the command: **ntp server <ip_address> key <number> source <if_name> [prefer]**. **ip_address** specifies the IP address of the server to which you want the PIX to authenticate. The **key** is the number of the shared key used when you configured the trusted-key command. The **interface** is the interface that will send the NTP packets to the server. The optional **prefer** keyword will have the Cisco PIX go to this server first to set the time.

Here is an example of configuring NTP authentication:

```
PIX1(config)# ntp authenticate
PIX1(config)# ntp authentication-key 10 md5 ciscoisgreat
PIX1(config)# ntp trusted-key 10
PIX1(config)# ntp server 192.168.50.3 key 10 source inside
PIX1(config)# show ntp
ntp authentication-key 10 md5 ********
ntp authenticate
ntp trusted-key 10
ntp server 192.168.50.3 key 10 source inside
```

Configuring VPN

VPN technology provides confidential and authenticated secure communications between internal networks over a public network (such as the Internet). VPNs are commonly used to connect branch offices, mobile users, and business partners.

The PIX firewall supports both site-to-site and remote access VPNs using IPsec, L2TP, and PPTP. VPNs can be very complicated, and a single connection might be implemented using a combination of many protocols that work together to provide tunneling, encryption, authentication, access control, and auditing.

The following sections describe how to configure IPsec on the PIX firewall. Please note that the steps defining an ISAKMP pre-shared key and configuring certificate authority support are exclusive, and only one of them needs to be performed.

Allowing IPsec Traffic

The first task should be to confirm that the firewalls to be involved in IPsec can reach each other. IPsec will not work unless the underlying networking is functional.

The next task is to permit incoming IPsec traffic to reach the firewall. **sysopt connection permit-ipsec** can be used, which implicitly allows all IPsec-related traffic to reach the firewall. This is equivalent to adding the following lines to the ACL on the outside PIX interface:

```
PIX1(config)# access-list outside_access_in permit 50 any host 10.23.34.45
PIX1(config)# access-list outside_access_in permit 51 any host 10.23.34.45
PIX1(config)# access-list outside_access_in permit udp any host 10.23.34.45 eq 500
```

The first two lines allow any traffic with IP 50 (Encapsulated Security Payload [ESP]) and 51 (AH) to reach the outside interface, and the third allows Internet Key Exchange (IKE) traffic (UDP port 500). Instead of using the **sysopt** command, a more granular access control can be created for each firewall using ACLs or conduits, which are the second way to permit IPsec traffic. For example, the following ACL allows IPsec traffic only from 10.34.45.56 reach 10.23.34.45:

```
PIX1(config)# access-list outside_access_in permit 50 host 10.34.45.56 host
10.23.34.45
PIX1(config)# access-list outside_access_in permit 51 host 10.34.45.56 host
10.23.34.45
PIX1(config)# access-list outside_access_in permit udp host 10.34.45.56 host 10.23.34.45
eq 500
```

The **sysopt connection permit-ipsec** command is the preferred method for allowing IPsec traffic, because it is simpler and does not really open any holes in the firewall. Since IPsec packets are encrypted and authenticated, any packet that does not come from a correct peer will be discarded. With the **sysopt** command, all decapsulated IPsec traffic is allowed to pass through without additional conduits.

Enabling IKE

Configuration of IKE policies starts with enabling IKE on the outside interface of the firewall (or any other interface that is connected to the remote peer). This is completed with the **isakmp enable <interface_name>** command. In our example, this command needs to be on the outside interface of each firewall; therefore the command should be **isakmp enable outside.**

IKE is enabled on all interfaces by default. It can be turned off on a specific interface (to prevent DoS attacks on the interface) using the **no** form of the command (for example **no isakmp enable <interface_name>**).

By default, the PIX firewall uses its IP addresses to identify itself to its peers, although its hostname can also be used. The hostname should be used when peers are to be authenticated by

RSA signatures. (The remote peer must either be defined on the firewall using the **name** command, or it must be resolvable through DNS.) If the digital certificates include IP addresses, the IP address should be used for the identity method. To change the identity method, use the command **isakmp identity {address | hostname}**, but be sure to use the same method on both firewalls. If the identity method does not match, the peers will not be able to negotiate an IKE SA and thus no IPsec SA will be established.

Creating an ISAKMP Protection Suite

The PIX can have many IKE policies (*ISAKMP protection suites*), which are distinguished by their priority (an integer from 1 to 65,534). The smaller this number, the higher the priority. The IKE policy parameters between peers must match exactly. A policy with the smallest number is attempted first, and then, if it is not accepted by the remote peer, the next is attempted. This process continues until one of the policies is accepted by the other peer, or the policy list is exhausted and IKE establishment fails. To create a policy:

```
isakmp policy <priority> authentication {pre-share | rsa-sig}
isakmp policy <priority> encryption {des | 3des}
isakmp policy <priority> hash {md5 | sha}
isakmp policy <priority> group {1 | 2}
isakmp policy <priority> lifetime <lifetime>
```

These commands specify (in order) the encryption algorithm, the data authentication algorithm, the peer authentication method, the Diffie-Hellman group identifier, and the IKE SA lifetime in seconds. The lifetime can be any number of seconds between 2 and 3600.

According to our plan, the following will be configured on both firewalls using a priority of 10:

```
isakmp policy 10 encryption 3des
isakmp policy 10 hash md5
isakmp policy 10 group 2
isakmp policy 10 lifetime 2400
```

The default values for each of these parameters are **des** for encryption, **md5** for data authentication, **1** for DH group, and **3600** for IKE SA lifetime. The peer authentication method must also be specified. If using pre-shared keys, use the **isakmp policy 10 authentication pre-share** command.

If using digital certificates, use the f **isakmp policy 10 authentication rsa-sig** command (although it is the default and does not really need to be specified).

To verify the configuration of IKE policies, use the **show isakmp policy** command. If using pre-shared keys, the output should be as follows:

```
PIX1# show isakmp policy
Protection suite of priority 10
      encryption algorithm:   Three key triple DES
      hash algorithm:          Message Digest 5
      authentication method:  Pre-Shared Key
```

```
     Diffie-Hellman group:    #2 (1024 bit)
     lifetime:                2400 seconds, no volume limit
Default protection suite
     encryption algorithm:    DES - Data Encryption Standard (56 bit keys).
     hash algorithm:          Secure Hash Standard
     authentication method:   Rivest-Shamir-Adleman Signature
     Diffie-Hellman group:    #1 (768 bit)
     lifetime:                86400 seconds, no volume limit
```

There is also a default IKE policy with a priority of 65,535, although it is not shown here. If the configured ISAKMP policies do not match a proposal by the remote peer, the firewall tries this default policy. If the default policy also does not match, ISAKMP negotiation fails.

Defining an ISAKMP Pre-shared Key

The most common site-to-site VPN setup between two PIX firewalls is the configuration of an IPsec tunnel with IKE using a pre-shared key. If the firewall is used to establish a number of VPNs with different peers, it is highly recommended that the pre-shared key be unique for each pair of gateways. The key to be used for establishing an IKE tunnel with the particular peer is selected based on the peer's IP address. The key itself is a 128-character alphanumeric string that must be the same on both gateways: **isakmp key <keystring> address <peer-address> netmask [netmask]**.

We need to configure the key on both firewalls:

```
PIX1(config)# isakmp key mykey1 address 10.34.45.56 netmask 255.255.255.255
PIX2(config)# isakmp key mykey1 address 10.23.34.45 netmask 255.255.255.255
```

To use the same key for connecting to any peer, use 0.0.0.0 both as a peer address and as a netmask.

Configuring Certificate Authority Support

Certificate authorities (CAs) are useful for configuring a large network of interconnected peers, where peers can be added or removed at any time. CAs provide an easy method for configuring complicated or dynamic networks. Each peer is configured separately and independently from the others. Each peer has its own certificate that it presents to its peers during the IKE authentication phase. Peers confirm the authenticity and validity of received certificates by consulting a CA and, if legitimate, the IKE authentication is successful. The CA can either be a server on the network or a trusted external authority.

Enrollment is a complex process and includes the following steps:

1. The PIX generates its own RSA public/private key pair.
2. The PIX requests the CA's public key and certificate. This must either be done over a secure channel or be checked by some offline means (for example, by comparing certificate fingerprints).

3. The PIX submits a request for a new certificate. This request includes the public key generated at Step 1 and is encrypted with the CA's public key obtained in Step 2.
4. The CA's administrator verifies the requester's identity and sends out a new certificate. This certificate is signed by the CA, so its authenticity can be verified by anybody who has a copy of the CA's certificate.

The administrator must decide if they will be using certificate revocation lists (CRLs) maintained by the CA to identify revoked certificates. Enabling CRL support on the PIX means that each certificate is accepted after checking the CRL. If CRLs are not used, the administrator only needs connectivity with the CA during enrollment, and all authentication of certificates afterward is done using the CA's public certificate, which the firewall obtained from the CA during enrollment.

Configuring the Hostname and Domain Name

Enrollment starts by defining the firewall's hostname and domain name, which will be used in its certificate later.

```
hostname <hostname>
domain-name <domain-name>
```

In our example, we need to enter the following commands:

```
PIX1(config)# hostname PIX1
PIX1(config)# domain-name securecorp.com
PIX2(config)# hostname PIX2
PIX2(config)# domain-name securecorp.com
```

Generating an RSA Key Pair

A public/private RSA key pair is created with the **ca generate rsa key <key_modulus_size>** command. Key strength is specified using the **key_modulus_size** parameter. The default value is 768 bits, as well as 1,024 or 2,048 bits. Ensure that the host and domain names have been correctly configured for the PIX before generating the keys:

```
PIX1(config)# ca generate rsa key 1024
Key name:PIX1.securecorp.com
Usage:General Purpose Key
Key Data:
30819f30 0d06092a 864886f7 0d010101 05000381 8d003081 89028181 00c8ed4c
9f5e0b52 aea931df 04db2872 5c4c0afd 9bd0920b 5e30de82 63d834ac f2e1db1f
1047481a 17be5a01 851835f6 18af8e22 45304d53 12584b9c 2f48fad5 31e1be5a
bb2ddc46 2841b63b f92cb3f9 8de7cb01 d7ea4057 7bb44b4c a64a9cf0 efaacd42
e291e4ea 67efbf6c 90348b75 320d7fd3 c573037a ddb2dde8 00df782c 39020301
    0001
```

Generated keys are stored in flash memory. The public key can be viewed by issuing the **show ca mypubkey rsa key** command. The private key cannot be viewed.

Specifying a CA to Be Used

After the key pair is generated on the PIX firewall, specify the CA to use for certificate verification with the **ca identity <ca_nickname> <ca_ip_address>[:<script_location>] [<ldap_address>]** command. The **ca_nickname** parameter specifies an internal nickname that the PIX will use for this CA. The **script_location** parameter can be specified when the CA uses a nonstandard URL for the enrollment script, which by default should reside at /cgi-bin/pki-client.exe. For example, when using a Microsoft CA, specify **/CERTSRV/mscep/mscep.dll**. If the CA supports Lightweight Directory Access Protocol (LDAP) requests, the IP address of CA's LDAP server can be specified in the command as well.

The PIX supports only one CA at a time. To remove a CA, simply use the **no ca identity <ca_nickname>** command. For our example, we use the following configuration:

```
PIX1(config)# ca identity verisign 10.139.94.230
PIX2(config)# ca identity verisign 10.139.94.230
```

The CA identity settings can be verified using the **show ca identity** command.

Configuring CA Parameters

Configure CA parameters by using the **ca configure <ca_nickname> {ca|ra} <retry_period> <retry_count> [crloptional]** command. This command specifies whether **ca_nickname** is a CA or a registration authority (RA). An RA is a proxy for the CA but rarely used in small-to-medium-sized networks. The command also specifies the number of retries when contacting this authority and the timeout between requests (in minutes). The **crloptional** parameter tells the PIX to skip checking certificates against the CRL if the CRL is unavailable. If **crloptional** is not specified and the CRL is unavailable, the peer's certificate is rejected. Always use the **crloptional** parameter with both public and in-house versions of VeriSign CAs, because they do not provide a CRL.

We will use the following:

```
PIX1(config)# ca configure verisign ca 1 20 crloptional
PIX2(config)# ca configure verisign ca 1 20 crloptional
```

This means that the authority previously identified as **verisign** is a CA, it does not support CRLs, and the PIX should retry 20 times at 1-minute intervals. To view the CA configuration settings, use the **show ca configure** command.

Authenticating the CA

The next step is obtaining the CA's public key contained in its own digital certificate (signed by the CA). After obtaining this certificate, the PIX has to verify that it is using an offline method. This can be achieved by obtaining a special characteristic of the certificate, a "fingerprint," from the CA's administrator (or by other means). A fingerprint is a hash of the certificate's content, and if the calculated hash and received hash match, the certificate is original. The command used on

PIX for requesting the CA's certificate is **ca authenticate <ca_nickname> [<fingerprint>]**. If this command is used with only one parameter—the CA's nickname—the PIX simply requests the certificate from the CA and displays the results of this action:

```
PIX1(config)# ca authenticate verisign
Certificate has the following attributes:
Fingerprint: 1234 1234 5678 CDEF ABCD
```

The PIX also calculates a fingerprint of the received certificate (10 bytes in hexadecimal encoding) and displays it. The verification can be done automatically if the known fingerprint is entered as part of the command:

```
PIX1(config)# ca authenticate verisign 0123456789abcd012345
Certificate has the following attributes:
Fingerprint: 0123 4567 89AB CDEF 5432
%Error in verifying the received fingerprint. Type help or '?' for a list of available
commands.
```

In this case, the calculated fingerprint (0123 4567 89AB CDEF 5432) and the expected one (0123 4567 89ab cd01 2345) did not match, so the certificate is discarded. The **ca authenticate** command is not stored in the PIX configuration as there is no need to perform it more than once for each new CA. If the authority being used is an RA instead of a CA, it will return three certificates:

- The RA signing key
- The RA encryption key
- The CA general-purpose public key

The received certificate is stored in the memory area designated for storing the firewall's RSA keys (the whole record is called the *RSA public key chain*) and can be viewed with the **show ca certificate** command. It produces output similar to this:

```
RA Signature Certificate
Status: Available
Certificate Serial Number: 38231245
Key Usage: Signature

CA Certificate
Status: Available
Certificate Serial Number: 38231256
Key Usage: Not Set

RA KeyEncipher Certificate
Status: Available
Certificate Serial Number: 38231267
Key Usage: Encryption
```

CA certificates must be stored in flash memory using the **ca save all** command or they will be lost after a reboot. The **write memory** command does not save certificates.

Enrolling with the CA

The firewall requests a new certificate from the CA, to which the CA replies by signing the public key certificate it received from the firewall. It returns the signed results (a valid certificate) to the PIX. Certificate authenticity can be validated using the usual public key signature tools.

The enrollment is started by the **ca enroll <ca_nickname> <challenge_password> [serial] [ip_address]** command. The **ca_nickname** is a CA defined earlier using the **ca identity** and **ca authenticate** commands. The **challenge_password** parameter authenticates future requests for revoking a certificate. When the **ca authenticate** command is issued, the PIX requests one public key certificate for each of its RSA key pairs. If it has already been issued a certificate, the PIX will prompt you to delete existing certificates from its memory. Certificates can be removed using the **no ca identity <ca_nickname>** command. This command removes all certificates issued by the specified authority. The **ca enroll** command, including the challenge password, is not stored in the PIX configuration; only its results can be stored in flash memory by the **ca save all** command.

The **serial** and **ip_address** options allow inclusion of some extra information in the public key certificate. When the **serial** option is specified, the firewall's serial number is included in the certificate request and in the resulting certificate. This number is used by the CA administrator for additional authentication. By default, when the **ip_address** option is not specified in the **ca enroll** command, a certificate is bound only to the host and domain names of the PIX device (a fully qualified domain name [FQDN]), which have to be specified prior to any CA-related configurations. If the **ip_address** option is specified, an IP address of the firewall is also included in the certificate. As a result, this certificate can be used only by the device with this IP address. If the firewall is moved to a new address (even if its FQDN remains the same), you will need a new certificate.

In our example we use the previously defined CA **verisign** and host-based authentication, so the enrollment in this case is very simple: **ca enroll verisign midnightinmoscow**. Our configuration enrolls PIX1 to CA **verisign** and sets the challenge password to **midnightinmoscow**. The command **ca enroll verisign lunchtimeinLA** performs the same operation on PIX2 but sets a different challenge password:

Display obtained certificates on the firewall with the **show ca certificate** command. All CA-related information should be saved:

```
PIX1(config)# ca save all
PIX1(config)# write memory
```

Of all these **ca** commands, only **ca identity** and **ca configure** will be stored in the PIX configuration. The other commands just store their results, because there is no need to perform them when the firewall reboots.

Configuring Crypto ACLs

The first stage in the process of IPsec is specifying traffic to be protected by IPsec. This is accomplished by an ACL applied to an interface with a **crypto map** command. It is possible to apply multiple crypto ACLs to one interface to specify different parameters for different types of traffic. Actions can be **permit** or **deny**:

- **Permit** IPsec should be applied to the matching traffic
- **Deny** Packet should be forwarded and IPsec not applied

The following ACL entry on PIX1 will protect all IP traffic from 192.168.2.0/24 to 192.168.3.0/24 and responses between the two networks.

```
access-list crypto1 permit ip 192.168.2.0 255.255.255.0 192.168.3.0 255.255.255.0
```

A packet from 192.168.2.3 to 192.168.3.4 will be matched by ACL **crypto1** and submitted to the IPsec engine. A packet from 192.168.2.3 to www.cisco.com will not be matched and thus transmitted in the clear. If an IPsec packet arrives from 192.168.3.4 to 192.168.2.3, IPsec will check it. If the inbound packet originates from www.cisco.com, it will not be matched or checked by IPsec. Any cleartext packets from www.cisco.com will pass through and be permitted unmatched.

When the first **permit** entry in an ACL is matched, this entry defines the scope of SA that will be created for its protection. In our example, all traffic from network 192.168.2.0/24 to the network 192.168.3.0/24 will be protected by the same SA. Create an ACL on PIX1 using the following command set:

```
access-list crypto2 permit ip 192.168.2.0 255.255.255.128 192.168.3.0 255.255.255.0
access-list crypto2 permit ip 192.168.2.128 255.255.255.128 192.168.3.0 255.255.255.0
```

In this case, traffic originating from 192.168.2.0/25 and from 192.168.2.128/25 will be protected by two different IPsec SAs.

Let's now return to our earlier example and configure the firewalls with ACLs:

```
PIX1(config)# access-list crypto1 permit ip 192.168.2.0 255.255.255.0 192.168.3.0
255.255.255.0
PIX2(config)# access-list crypto2 permit ip 192.168.3.0 255.255.255.0 192.168.2.0
255.255.255.0
```

We are not applying these lists yet. This will be done later using a **crypto map** command.

NOTE

Source addresses in crypto ACLs should be the same as they appear on the firewall's outside interface. For example, if NAT translates the internal addresses, the global IP addresses must be stated as the ACL source, not the local IP addresses. For example, assume that the host 192.168.2.25 on the inside interface of PIX1 is translated to 10.23.34.55 on the outside by the **static (inside, outside) 10.23.34.55 192.168.2.25 netmask 255.255.255.255 0 0** command. In this case, an ACL entry for allowing IPsec for this host only should look like: **ACL crypto1 permit ip host 10.23.34.55 192.168.3.0 255.255.255.0**

Defining a Transform Set

A *transform set* is a set of parameters for a specific IPsec connection. It specifies the algorithms used for AH and ESP protocols and the mode (tunnel or transport) in which they are applied. There must be at least one set common to both peers for each crypto map entry. Transform sets are configured using the **crypto ipsec transform-set <transform-set-name> <transform1> [[<transform2>] [<transform3>]]** command. The default is tunnel mode. Transport mode is configured using the **crypto ipsec transform-set <transform-set-name> mode transport** command.

It is possible to configure up to three transforms in a single set: zero or one AH transforms; zero, one, or two ESP transforms. When two ESP transforms are configured, one of them must be an encrypted transform and the other an authentication transform. The available transforms are:

- **ah-md5-hmac** MD5-HMAC authentication algorithm for AH
- **ah-sha-hmac** SHA-1-HMAC authentication algorithm for AH
- **esp-des** DES encryption algorithm (56-bit key) for ESP encryption
- **esp-3des** Triple DES encryption algorithm (168-bit key) for ESP encryption
- **esp-md5-hmac** MD5-HMAC authentication algorithm for ESP
- **esp-sha-hmac** SHA-1-HMAC authentication algorithm for ESP

In our example, we use ESP encryption with DES and authentication with SHA-1-HMAC without AH:

```
PIX1(config)# crypto ipsec transform-set myset esp-des esp-sha-hmac
PIX2(config)# crypto ipsec transform-set myset esp-des esp-sha-hmac
```

Configured transform sets can be checked using the **show crypto ipsec transform-set** command:

```
PIX1(config)# show crypto ipsec transform-set
Transform set myset: { esp-des esp-sha-hmac }
will negotiate = { Tunnel, }
```

Bypassing NAT

Because we want to use IPsec on all traffic between the inside networks on each firewall, we must exclude it from NAT. To bypass NAT, use the **nat 0** command with the same ACL that defines our IPsec traffic:

```
PIX1(config)# nat 0 access-list crypto1
PIX1(config)# nat (inside) 1 0 0
```

```
PIX1(config)# global (outside) 1 10.23.34.46
PIX2(config)# nat 0 access-list crypto2
PIX2(config)# nat (inside) 1 0 0
PIX2(config)# global (outside) 1 10.34.45.57
```

Configuring a Crypto Map

A *crypto map* ties all IPsec parameters together and creates a serial presence detect (SPD) for a specific interface, through which IPsec traffic is tunneled. An interface can have only one crypto map assigned to it, although this map may have many different entries, identified by their sequence numbers. Entries are equivalent to the various policies in SPD. The first entry that matches the traffic will define methods of its protection. A crypto map entry for IPsec with IKE is created using the **crypto map <name> <seq-num> [ipsec-isakmp]** command. The keyword **ipsec-isakmp** is the default and can be omitted. In our example, we create the following entries:

```
PIX1(config)# crypto map pix1map 10 ipsec-isakmp
PIX2(config)# crypto map pix2map 10 ipsec-isakmp
```

Next, specify the traffic selectors for these entries using the **crypto map <map-name> <seq-num> match address <access-list-name>** command. In our case, these would look like:

```
PIX1(config)# crypto map pix1map 10 match address crypto1
PIX2(config)# crypto map pix2map 10 match address crypto2
```

Now we need to specify the IPsec peers with which the traffic protected by this entry can be exchanged. This is done with the **crypto map <map-name> <seq-num> set peer {<host-name> | <ip-address>}** command syntax. IPsec peers are identified either by their IP addresses or by their hostnames. It is possible to specify multiple peers by repeating this command for one crypto map entry. For our example, we use the following configuration:

```
PIX1(config)# crypto map pix1map 10 set peer 23.34.45.56
PIX2(config)# crypto map pix2map 10 set peer 12.23.34.45
```

Now we need to specify which transform sets can be negotiated for the traffic matching this entry. Multiple (up to six) previously defined transform sets can be specified here:

```
crypto map <map-name> <seq-num> set transform set <transform-set-name1> [<transform-set-name2> [<transform-set-name3> [<transform-set-name4> [<transform-set-name5> [<transform-set-name6>]]]]]
```

For two peers to establish an IPsec tunnel under this crypto map entry, at least one transform set in each firewall's corresponding crypto map entry must have the protocols and encryption/data authentication algorithms. For our example, we use one transform set on each firewall (**pix1map** on PIX1 and **pix2map** on PIX2):

```
PIX1(config)# crypto map pix1map 10 set transform-set myset
PIX2(config)# crypto map pix2map 10 set transform-set myset
```

In each case, **myset** is the transform set defined previously. It does not need to have the same name on each firewall, but the parameters must match.

The next two steps are optional: requesting that PFS should be used and selecting the SA lifetime. PFS is requested for a crypto map entry using the **crypto map <map-name> <seq-num> set pfs [group1 | group2]** command. The **group1** and **group2** keywords denote the DH group and are used for key exchange each time new keys are generated. In order to be effective, PFS has to be configured on both sides of the tunnel.

It is possible to configure a non-default IPsec SA lifetime for the specific crypto map entry using the following command:

```
crypto map <map-name> <seq-num> set security-association lifetime {seconds <seconds> |
kilobytes <kilobytes>}
```

This command limits the amount of time an IPsec SA can be used or the maximum amount of traffic that can be transferred by this SA. The renegotiations start 30 seconds before a timeout expires or when the volume of traffic is 256KB less than the specified volume lifetime. It is possible to change the default global IPsec SA lifetime using the following command, which has the same parameters:

```
crypto ipsec security-association lifetime {seconds <seconds> | kilobytes <kilobytes>}
```

If not specified, the defaults are 28,800 seconds and 4,608,000KB.

Apply the created crypto map to an interface with the **crypto map <map-name> interface <interface-name>** syntax. In our case, this will be:

```
PIX1(config)# crypto map pix1map interface outside
PIX2(config)# crypto map pix2map interface outside
```

You can check crypto map configuration using the following command:

```
PIX1(config)# show crypto map
Crypto Map: "pix1map" interface: "outside" local address: 12.23.34.45
Crypto Map "pix1map" 10 ipsec-isakmp
  Peer = 23.34.45.56
  access-list crypto1 permit ip 192.168.2.0 255.255.255.0 192.168.3.0 255
      .255.255.0 (hitcnt=0)
  Current peer: 23.34.45.56
  Security association lifetime: 4608000 kilobytes/28800 seconds
  PFS (Y/N): N
  Transform sets={ myset, }
```

The state of established IPsec SAs can be checked with the **show crypto ipsec sa** command:

```
PIX1(config)# show crypto ipsec sa
interface: outside
    Crypto map tag: pix1map, local addr. 12.23.34.45
```

```
local  ident (addr/mask/prot/port): (192.168.2.0/255.255.255.0/0/0)
   remote ident (addr/mask/prot/port): (192.168.3.0/255.255.255.0/0/0)
   current_peer: 23.34.45.56
     PERMIT, flags={origin_is_acl,}
    #pkts encaps: 10, #pkts encrypt: 10, #pkts digest 0
    #pkts decaps: 12, #pkts decrypt: 17, #pkts verify 0
    #pkts compressed: 0, #pkts decompressed: 0
    #pkts not compressed: 0, #pkts compr. failed: 0, #pkts decompress
        failed: 0
    #send errors 2, #recv errors 0
```

Configuring Site-to-site IPsec without IKE (Manual IPsec)

IPsec can work without IKE, meaning all IPsec SAs are established manually. This configuration is more difficult to scale and requires knowledge of the IP addresses or DNS names of all peers. The main configuration differences with pre-shared key IKE, for example, are:

- No IKE configuration is involved.
- When creating a crypto map entry, specify **ipsec-manual** instead of **ipsec-isakm***p.*
- The crypto map configuration must specify keys used for ESP and AH for each tunnel.

Let's briefly go through configuration for a manual IPsec tunnel between PIX1 and PIX2. The first few steps are the same as for IPsec that uses IKE (permitting IPsec traffic, defining crypto ACLs, creating transform sets, and enabling NAT bypass):

```
PIX1(config)# sysopt connection permit-ipsec
PIX1(config)# access-list crypto1 permit ip 192.168.2.0 255.255.255.0 192.168.3.0
255.255.255.0
PIX1(config)# crypto ipsec transform-set myset esp-des esp-sha-hmac
PIX1(config)# nat 0 access-list crypto1
PIX1(config)# nat (inside) 1 0.0.0.0 0.0.0.0
PIX1(config)# global (outside) 1 10.23.34.46
PIX2(config)# sysopt connection permit-ipsec
PIX2(config)# access-list crypto2 permit ip 192.168.3.0 255.255.255.0 192.168.2.0
255.255.255.0
PIX2(config)# crypto ipsec transform-set myset esp-des esp-sha-hmac
PIX2(config)# nat 0 access-list crypto2
PIX2(config)# nat (inside) 1 0.0.0.0 0.0.0.0
PIX2(config)# global (outside) 1 10.34.45.57
```

The next step is the creation of crypto maps. The following commands specify manually configured IPsec SAs.

```
PIX1(config)# crypto map pix1map 10 ipsec-manual
PIX2(config)# crypto map pix1map 10 ipsec-manual
```

The rest of the crypto map configuration is the same as with IKE:

```
PIX1(config)# crypto map pix1map 10 match address crypto1
PIX1(config)# crypto map pix1map 10 set peer 10.34.45.56
PIX1(config)# crypto map pix1map 10 set transform-set myset
PIX2(config)# crypto map pix2map 10 match address crypto2
PIX2(config)# crypto map pix2map 10 set peer 10.23.34.45
PIX2(config)# crypto map pix2map 10 set transform-set myset
```

Next, configure the SAs for each transform such as ESP with encryption and ESP with authentication in the transform set **myset**: we need to specify two outbound SAs and two inbound SAs. (Remember, each SA exists for one transform and in one direction.) We will use the following command:

```
crypto map <map-name> <seq-num> set session-key inbound | outbound esp <spi> cipher
<hex-key-string> [authenticator <hex-key-string>]
```

The **spi** parameter is a numerical value of the Security Parameter Index. This number is arbitrary, although a SPI number of an IPsec SA one peer has to match that of the second peer. This holds true with the keys (**hex-key-string**); the key for an outbound SA on one peer has to be the same as the key for the corresponding inbound SA on the second peer. The key value can be 16, 32, or 40 hexadecimal digits. There are some minimal requirements on key length:

- If a transform set for this map entry includes DES encryption, specify at least a 16-digit key.
- If this transform set includes the MD5 algorithm, specify at least 32 digits per key.
- If this transform set includes the SHA-1 algorithm, specify at least 40 digits per key.

If a longer key is specified, it is simply hashed (not truncated) to the required length. For PIX1, we will specify the following SPIs and keys:

```
PIX1(config)# crypto map pix1map 10 set session-key inbound esp 300 cipher
1234455667788909 authenticator 123445566778890acdefacd91234455667788909
PIX1(config)# crypto map pix1map 10 set session-key outbound esp 400 cipher
9887766554344556 authenticator acdefacd12238474646537485956745637485635
```

They include a 16-digit DES key and a 40-digit SHA-1 key.

On the second firewall we have to create a "mirror" configuration of keys and SPIs, applying the same commands but with **inbound** and **outbound** interchanged:

```
PIX2(config)# crypto map pix2map 10 set session-key outbound esp 300 cipher
1234455667788909 authenticator 123445566778890acdefacd91234455667788909
```

```
PIX2(config)# crypto map pix2map 10 set session-key inbound esp 400 cipher
9887766554344556 authenticator acdefacd12238474646537485956745637485635
```

If we were using AH for traffic authentication, we would add the command **crypto map <map-name> <seq-num> set session-key outbound ah <spi> <hex-key-data>**twice (one for the inbound and one for the outbound IPsec SA) to the configuration of each firewall. This uses the same agreements but requires only one key for each SPI. After applying the crypto map to the outside interfaces on both firewalls, the configuration is complete:

```
PIX1(config)# crypto map pix1map interface outside
PIX2(config)# crypto map pix2map interface outside
```

Configuring PPTP

PPTP (RFC 2637) establishes VPNs. PPTP works at Layer 2 and can support any Layer 3 traffic, including non-IP protocols. Although PPTP is usually associated with Microsoft, it was actually designed by the PPTP Forum.

Configuration

Most of the PPTP configuration tasks on the PIX are performed using VPDN (Virtual Private Dialup Networking) commands. VPDN is a common term for PPTP, L2TP, and PPPoE configurations. The first step is to permit incoming PPTP traffic with the **sysopt connection permit pptp** command. This command implicitly allows all traffic from authenticated PPTP clients to pass to its destination without additional conduits or ACLs. Without this command, the administrator would need to create and expand their ACLs.

The rest of the configuration consists of the following:

1. Creating an address pool for PPTP clients
2. Creating an AAA scheme if external AAA servers are used
3. Creating a dial-in group (VPDN group) and configuring authentication and encryption variables.
4. Creating ACLs to allow PPTP clients to access internal servers (only if you did not specify the **sysopt connection permit pptp** command)

An IP address pool is created using the **ip local pool <pool_name> <pool_start_address>[-<pool_end_address>]** command syntax. In this case the command will look like **ip local pool mypool 10.1.1.1-10.1.1.10.** This command allocates 10 IP addresses to the pool of available addresses. The state of this pool can be displayed using the **show ip local pool <pool_name>** command:

```
PIX1# show ip local pool mypool
Pool      Begin        End          Free      In use
mypool    10.0.1.1     10.0.0.10    10        0
Available Addresses:
```

```
10.0.1.1
...
10.0.1.10
```

When the pool is depleted, new allocation attempts fail and the PIX creates a syslog message of the type: %PIX-3-213004: PPP virtual interface number client ip allocation failed.

Assuming that we will not be using external AAA servers, we have to configure local usernames and passwords with the **vpdn username <name> password <pass>**command. For example:

```
PIX1(config)# vpdn username user1 password password1
PIX1(config)# vpdn username user2 password password2
```

These two commands create two users, **user1** with password **password1** and **user2** with password **password2.** The next step is to create a VPDN group. The minimal configuration without any authentication requires three commands:

```
vpdn group <group_name> accept dialin pptp
vpdn group <group_name> client configuration address local <address_pool_name>
vpdn enable <interface>
```

The first command enables processing of PPTP traffic by the group. The second specifies the IP address pool to be used for clients. The third command applies VPDN settings to the interface. If local authentication is used, the following commands are added:

```
vpdn group <group_name> ppp authentication {pap | chap| mschap}
vpdn group <group_name> client authentication local
```

The first command selects the authentication mode (PAP, CHAP, or MS-CHAP {version 1}). The same authentication protocol should be configured on PIX and on the client. If this command is not present in the PIX configuration, no authentication is performed and any client is allowed. The second line specifies that a local database will be used for authentication. When an external AAA server is used, this server is configured by usual AAA means.

```
PIX1(config)# aaa-server myserver (inside) host 192.168.2.99 key mysecretkey
PIX1(config)# aaa-server myserver protocol radius
```

This server is then specified in a VPDN group using the **vpdn group <group_name> client authentication aaa <aaa-server-group>** command syntax. In our case, this will be: **vpdn group mygroup client authentication aaa myserver.**

Encryption is specified by the **vpdn group <group_name ppp> encryption mppe 40 | 128 | auto [required]** command. Here, 40, 128, or "auto" specifies the length of the encryption key. The **auto** keyword means that the PIX will accept both 40- and 128-bit keys. The **required** keyword means that if the client refuses to support encryption with the key of specified length, the connection will be dropped.

It is possible to specify DNS and WINS server settings to be passed on to the client:

```
vpdn group <group_name> client configuration dns <dns_server1> [<dns_server2>]
```

```
vpdn group <group_name> client configuration wins <wins_server1> [<wins_server2>]
```

The following is a configuration with local MS-CHAP authentication and no encryption:

```
ip local pool mypool 192.168.3.1-192.168.3.10
vpdn username user1 password password1
vpdn username user2 password password2
vpdn group 1 accept dialin pptp
vpdn group 1 ppp authentication mschap
vpdn group 1 client authentication local
vpdn group 1 client configuration address local mypool
vpdn enable outside
sysopt connection permit pptp
```

If we need more granular access to internal servers, we can replace the **sysopt** command from the preceding listing with an ACL on the outside interface.

```
ip local pool mypool 192.168.3.1-192.168.3.10
vpdn username user1 password password1
vpdn username user2 password password2
vpdn group 1 accept dialin pptp
vpdn group 1 ppp authentication mschap
vpdn group 1 client authentication local
vpdn group 1 client configuration address local mypool
vpdn enable outside
static (inside, outside) 10.23.34.99 192.168.2.33
access-list acl_out permit tcp 192.168.3.0 255.255.255.240 host 10.23.34.99 eq telnet
access-group acl_out in interface outside
```

The status of PPTP tunnels can be displayed using several commands:

```
PIX1# show vpdn tunnel
% No active L2TP tunnels
% No active PPTP tunnels
```

If any tunnels were active, statistics on their number and traffic would have been displayed:

```
PIX1# show vpdn tunnel pptp packet
PPTP Tunnel Information (Total tunnels=1 sessions=1)
LocID    Pkts-In     Pkts-Out       Bytes-In       Bytes-Out
1         1234        23             200323          553
```

The preceding command shows only the traffic statistics for active PPTP data tunnels. Another command is used to monitor PPTP tunnels themselves:

```
PIX1# show vpdn tunnel pptp summary
PPTP Tunnel Information (Total tunnels=1 sessions=1)
```

```
LocID       RemID       State       Remote Address          Port Sessions
1             1          estabd      172.16.38.194           1723 1
```

The following commands display transport layer statistics and session information, respectively:

```
show vpdn tunnel pptp transport
show vpdn pptp session
```

Configuring L2TPwith IPsec

L2TP tunnels Layer 2 traffic over public network. L2TP is a hybrid of Cisco's Layer 2 Forwarding Protocol (L2F) and PPTP. L2TP by itself does not protect the traffic it tunnels; it requires IPsec to do that. L2TP/IPsec works by establishing an IPsec tunnel in **transport** mode, encapsulating traffic between the networks in PPP packets, and transmitting between UDP ports 1701 on the client and the server through the IPsec tunnel (see Figure 8.19). Thus, configuration consists of two parts: IPsec configuration and VPDN configuration (the latter is very similar to PPTP).

Figure 8.19 L2TP Packet Structure

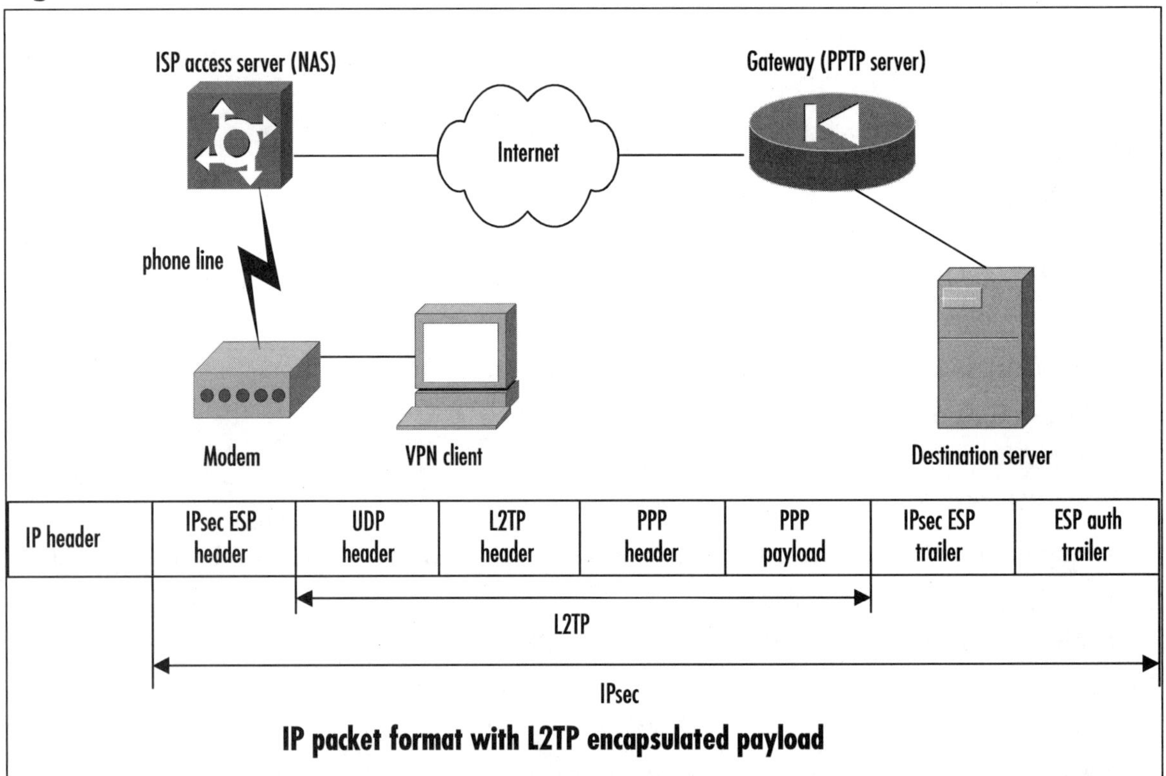

Many features of the PIX L2TP server are similar to the PPTP server implementation. L2TP can be configured only on one interface, and uses PPP authentication methods for client authentication. The PIX cannot serve as an L2TP client. Dynamic crypto maps are used with L2TP.

Dynamic Crypto Maps

A dynamic crypto map is a crypto map without all parameters configured. It is part of the crypto map and is used to establish IPsec connections with peers whose IP addresses are not known in advance. When using dynamic crypto maps, the client must first authenticate to the firewall by something (hostname, for example) during IKE exchange. Afterwards, their traffic is processed under the rules defined by the dynamic crypto map entry.

To configure a dynamic crypto map entry, specify only a transform set. All other parameters can be accepted from the other peer's proposals. Dynamic maps can be used only for incoming connections and must be the lowest priority. When the PIX uses a specific dynamic, it creates a temporary crypto map entry and installs it into its SPD. The entry is filled in with the results of IKE negotiations. Once established, this temporary entry is used as normal. When all IPsec SAs associated with this entry expire, the temporary entry is deleted.

Configuration commands for the dynamic crypto maps are similar to those for static crypto map entries:

```
crypto dynamic-map <dynamic-map-name> <dynamic-seq-num>
crypto dynamic-map <dynamic-map-name> <dynamic-seq-num> match address <acl_name>
crypto dynamic-map <dynamic-map-name> <dynamic-seq-num> set peer {<hostname> | <ip-address>}
crypto dynamic-map <dynamic-map-name> <dynamic-seq-num> set pfs [group1 | group2]
crypto dynamic-map <dynamic-map-name> <dynamic-seq-num> set security-association lifetime {seconds <seconds> | kilobytes <kilobytes>}
crypto dynamic-map <dynamic-map-name> <dynamic-seq-num> set transform-set transform-set-name1 [transform-set-name2 [transform-set-name3 … [transform-set-name9]]]
```

Only the transform set specification must be present in the configuration of a dynamic crypto map entry. It is also recommended that an ACL be specified in the **match address** command to increase security. A configured dynamic crypto map is then assigned as an entry in a regular crypto map. For example:

```
crypto ipsec transform-set myset1 esp-des esp-md5-hmac
crypto ipsec transform-set myset2 ah-sha-hmac
crypto dynamic-map dynmap 10
crypto dynamic-map dynmap set transform-set myset2
crypto dynamic-map dynmap match address 101
crypto dynamic-map dynmap 20
crypto dynamic-map dynmap set transform-set myset1
crypto dynamic-map dynmap match address 102
crypto map gorilla 10 ipsec-isakmp
crypto map gorilla 10 set peer 10.34.45.56
crypto map gorilla 10 set transform-set myset1 myset2
crypto map gorilla 10 match address 103
crypto map gorilla 20 ipsec-isakmp dynamic dynmap
```

```
access-list 103 permit ip 192.168.3.0 255.255.255.0 any
access-list 101 permit ip host 192.168.2.33 any
access-list 102 permit ip host 192.168.2.34 any
```

The crypto map, **gorilla**, has a dynamic map entry called **dynmap** with priority 20. This means that the PIX will first evaluate the static entry with priority 10 (the one with peer 10.34.45.65), and if this entry does not apply, it will try the dynamic map.

Configuration

Configuring L2TP on the PIX consists of three phases:

1. Configure IKE.
2. Configure IPsec in transport mode.
3. Configure VPDN dial-in settings for L2TP.

IKE is configured as before. In our example, clients will be allowed access to an internal host 192.168.2.33. IKE authentication will be done using VeriSign certificates, and user authentication will be handled by a RADIUS server. First, we need to make IPsec and L2TP traffic exempt from conduits:

```
PIX1(config)# sysopt connection permit ipsec
PIX1(config)# sysopt connection permit l2tp
```

CA support is configured the same as before:

```
PIX1(config)# hostname PIX1
PIX1(config)# domain-name securecorp.com
PIX1(config)# ca generate rsa key 1024
PIX1(config)# ca identity verisign 205.139.94.230
PIX1(config)# ca configure verisign ca 1 20 crloptional
PIX1(config)# ca authenticate verisign
PIX1(config)# ca enroll verisign midnightinmoscow
PIX1(config)# ca save all
PIX1(config)# write memory
```

IKE is configured the same as before:

```
PIX1(config)# isakmp policy 10 authentication rsa-sig
PIX1(config)# isakmp policy 10 encryption 3des
PIX1(config)# isakmp policy 10 hash md5
PIX1(config)# isakmp policy 10 group 2
PIX1(config)# isakmp policy 10 lifetime 2400
PIX1(config)# isakmp identity hostname
PIX1(config)# isakmp enable outside
```

Continue the IPsec configuration by defining the crypto ACL and configuring the NAT bypass:

```
PIX1(config)# access-list 99 permit ip 192.168.2.0 255.255.255.0 any
```

IPsec traffic has to be exempt from the NAT, as it was before:

```
PIX1(config)# nat (inside) 0 access-list 99
```

Configure the transform set and specify that the IPsec mode is **transport**:

```
PIX1(config)# crypto ipsec transform-set myset esp-des esp-md5-hmac
PIX1(config)# crypto ipsec transform-set myset mode transport
```

We create a simple dynamic crypto map to process mobile clients with unspecified IP addresses:

```
PIX1(config)# crypto dynamic-map mobileclients 10 set transform-set myset
PIX1(config)# crypto dynamic-map mobileclients 10 match address 99
```

We configure and apply the regular crypto map, which includes this dynamic map as an entry:

```
PIX1(config)# crypto map partners 20 ipsec-isakmp dynamic mobileclients
PIX1(config)# crypto map partners interface outside
```

IKE and IPsec configuration is now complete. Next we need to configure the VPDN settings. Almost all the commands are identical to PPTP:

```
vpdn group <group_name> accept dialin l2tp (enables L2TP)
vpdn group <group_name> l2tp tunnel hello <hello_timeout>
vpdn group <group_name> client configuration address local <address_pool_name>
vpdn group <group_name> client configuration dns <dns_ip1> [<dns_ip2>]
vpdn group <group_name> client configuration wins <wins_ip1> [<wins_ip2>]
vpdn group <group_name> client authentication aaa <aaa_server_group>
vpdn group <group_name> client authentication local
vpdn group <group_name> ppp authentication {pap | chap | mschap}
vpdn group <group_name> client accounting <aaa_server_group>
```

The resulting VPDN configuration is as follows:

```
PIX1(config)# ip local pool mypool 192.168.5.1-192.168.5.10
PIX1(config)# aaa-server myserver (inside) host 192.168.2.99 key mysecretkey
PIX1(config)# aaa-server myserver protocol radius
PIX1(config)# vpdn group 1 accept dialin l2tp
PIX1(config)# vpdn group 1 ppp authentication mschap
PIX1(config)# vpdn group 1 client authentication aaa myserver
PIX1(config)# vpdn group 1 client configuration address local mypool
PIX1(config)# vpdn group 1 client configuration dns 192.168.2.33
```

```
PIX1(config)# vpdn group 1 client configuration wins 192.168.2.34
PIX1(config)# vpdn enable outside
```

Configuring Support for the Cisco Software VPN Client

The Cisco software VPN client is used with Cisco VPN concentrators, PIX, and IOS-based devices. The VPN client is installed on a client computer and takes preference over the internal Windows IPsec client. Installation of the Cisco VPN client is straightforward, and it gathers pertinent details from you while installing.

Mode Configuration

IKE mode configuration allows you to assign an internal IP address to the VPN client during the IKE negotiation process. The client uses this address in its communications over the IPsec tunnel.

IKE mode configuration occurs between Phases 1 and 2 of IKE negotiation. During this process, it is possible to download an IP address and other IP-related settings such as DNS servers to the client. There are two types of IKE mode configuration negotiation:

- **Gateway Initiation** Server initiates the configuration mode with the client. After the client responds, IKE modifies the sender's identity, the message is processed, and the client receives a response.
- **Client Initiation** Client initiates the configuration mode with the gateway. The gateway responds with an IP address it has allocated for the client.

There are three steps for configuring IKE mode configuration on PIX firewall:

1. Define an IP address pool, as was done in the section about L2TP, with the **ip local pool pool_name pool_start_address[-pool_end_address]** command syntax.
2. Reference the IP address pool in the IKE configuration with the **isakmp client configuration address-pool local <pool-name> [<interface-name>]** command. This command states that IKE on interface ***interface-name*** should use the address pool named ***pool-name*** to assign local IP addresses to VPN clients.
3. Define the crypto map settings that should negotiate IKE mode configuration with the client and whether the client or gateway will be initiating this process. The relevant command is: **crypto map <map-name> client configuration address initiate | respond. Map-name** is the name of crypto map, **initiate** means that the gateway initiates IKE mode configuration, and **respond** means that client should start the process itself and the gateway responds. For example:

```
ip local pool modeconf 172.16.1.1-172.16.1.126
isakmp client configuration address-pool local modeconf outside
crypto map mymap client configuration address initiate
```

These settings (if all the rest of IKE and IPsec is configured) will initiate IKE mode configuration with each client who matches crypto map **mymap**. Clients will be assigned IP addresses from the 172.16.1.1 through 172.16.1.126 address range.

One slight complication arises if the same interface is used for terminating both VPN clients and peers with static IP addresses (site-to-site gateways). Such peers have to be excluded from the IKE mode configuration process. This is accomplished with the **isakmp key <keystring> address <ip-address> [<netmask>] no-config-mode** command.

To specify that a peer 10.34.45.56 uses the pre-shared key **mysecretkey** for IKE authentication and needs to be excluded from IKE mode configuration, use the command: **isakmp key mysecretkey address 10.34.45.56 255.255.255.255 no-config-mode.**

Extended Authentication

IKE Extended Authentication (**xauth**) is useful when configuring the Cisco software VPN client to access the PIX firewall because it allows authentication after IKE Phase 1 and before Phase 2. With **xauth,** IKE can support user authentication by allowing the server to request a username and password from the client. The user is verified against an external RADIUS or TACACS+ server. (Local authentication cannot be used.) If verification fails, the IKE SA for this connection is deleted and the IPsec SAs will not be established. **xauth** negotiation is performed before IKE mode configuration.

Before you enable **xauth**, define an AAA server group with AAA servers:

```
aaa-server <group_tag> protocol <auth_protocol>
aaa-server <group_tag> [(interface)] host <server_ip> [<key>] [timeout <seconds>]
```

For example:

```
PIX1(config)# aaa-server vpnauthgroup protocol radius
PIX1(config)# aaa-server vpnauthgroup (inside) host 192.168.2.33 secretkey timeout 60
```

xauth negotiation is enabled in the crypto map. This is done using the following command:

```
crypto map <map-name> client authentication <group_tag>
```

The **crypto map mymap client authentication vpnauthgroup** command configures IKE negotiations under map **mymap** to use **xauth** and authentication will be performed using the previously defined server 192.168.2.33.

Xauth faces the same problems as IKE mode configuration when the same interface is used for termination of both clients with dynamic addresses and site-to-site tunnels. Exclude the static devices from xauth: **isakmp key <keystring> address <ip-address> [<netmask>] no-xauth** (for example: **isakmp key mysecretkey address 23.34.45.56 255.255.255.255 no-xauth**).

VPN Groups

A Cisco VPN client logs into a VPN group in order to download its security parameters. A group is configured on PIX using the **vpngroup** set of commands:

```
vpngroup <group_name> address-pool <pool_name>
vpngroup <group_name> default-domain <domain_name>
vpngroup <group_name> dns-server <dns_ip_prim> [<dns_ip_sec>]
vpngroup <group_name> idle-time <idle_seconds>
vpngroup <group_name> max-time <max_seconds>
vpngroup <group_name> password <preshared_key>
vpngroup <group_name> pfs
vpngroup <group_name> split-tunnel <acl_name>
vpngroup <group_name> wins-server <wins_ip_prim> [<wins_ip_sec>]
```

The default idle timeout is 1800 seconds. The default connection time is unlimited. The **password** command specifies an IKE pre-shared key. In reality, when a VPN client connects to the PIX, it specifies its group name and the PIX tries to perform IKE negotiation using this password as a shared IKE key. The group name and password can be set in VPN Dialer when creating an entry. There is another option for assigning passwords (shared keys) for IKE authentication. It is possible to use a single pre-shared key for all possible peers using the **isakmp key <keystring> address 0.0.0.0 netmask 0.0.0.0** command. This is called a *wildcard* IKE key.

If an IKE Phase 1 negotiation is successful, IKE mode configuration is performed (it always has to be configured when a VPN client is used) and possibly xauth too (if configured, it is an optional feature). During IKE mode configuration, a client is assigned an internal IP address using either one common pool (must be in **initiate** mode) or the pool specific for this VPN group. If a group with the name **default** is configured, it will match any group name suggested by the VPN client. Group-specific pools are defined by **vpngroup <group_name> address-pool <pool_name>**.

After IKE negotiation succeeds, all parameters defined for this VPN group are downloaded to the client and an IPsec tunnel is established. By default, all traffic from the computer where the VPN client is installed is tunneled to the PIX. One of the problems arising due to this process is that the client's Internet access will be terminated, because all client traffic is sent to the PIX. Separate the traffic into two parts: one that should be tunneled and one that will be transmitted in the clear with the **vpngroup <group_name> split-tunnel <acl_name>** command syntax. This command specifies an ACL, which defines the traffic to be tunneled. Permit means that matched traffic should be tunneled from client to PIX. If the destination matches a deny statement or does not match anything in this ACL at all, the IP packet will be transmitted by the client in the clear. The following provides an example configuration using only pre-shared keys authentication and no xauth) of a VPN group on PIX1 with split tunneling and corresponding IPsec settings.

```
: only traffic between 192.168.2.0/24 and 192.168.10.0/24 will be tunneled
access-list 90 permit ip 192.168.2.0 255.255.255.0 192.168.10.0 255.255.255.0
: clients are assigned with ip addresses from 192.168.10.0/24
ip local pool vpnpool 192.168.10.1-192.168.10.254
: common dynamic map settings
crypto ipsec transform-set vpnset esp-des esp-sha-hmac
```

```
crypto dynamic-map dynmap 20 set transform-set vpnset
crypto map dialinmap 10 ipsec-isakmp dynamic dynmap
: pix will initiate ike mode configuration
crypto map dialinmap client configuration address initiate
crypto map dialinmap interface outside
: usual isakmp settings
isakmp enable outside
isakmp identity hostname
isakmp policy 5 authentication pre-share
isakmp policy 5 encryption 3des
isakmp policy 5 hash md5
isakmp policy 5 group 1
: vpn group "mygroup" is defined
: clients will be assigned ip addresses from "vpnpool"
vpngroup mygroup address-pool vpnpool
: dns, wins and domain are pushed to the client
vpngroup mygroup dns-server 192.168.2.33
vpngroup mygroup wins-server 192.168.2.34
vpngroup mygroup default-domain securecorp.com
: splitting according to access list 90 is defined
vpngroup mygroup split-tunnel 90
: timeouts are defined
vpngroup mygroup idle-time 1800
vpngroup mygroup max-time 86400
: ike shared key for this group is defined.
: it is actually shown as ****** in the PIX configuration
vpngroup mygroup password mypassword
```

Sample Configurations of PIX and VPN Clients

This section provides a configuration example of the PIX and a VPN client. Our example uses IKE with pre-shared keys, IKE mode configuration, and extended authentication (xauth) of the client against an internal RADIUS server. After that, we briefly discuss the changes needed in order to use digital certificates for IKE authentication. The network setup is shown in Figure 8.20.

Figure 8.20 Network Setup for Cisco VPN Client Configuration

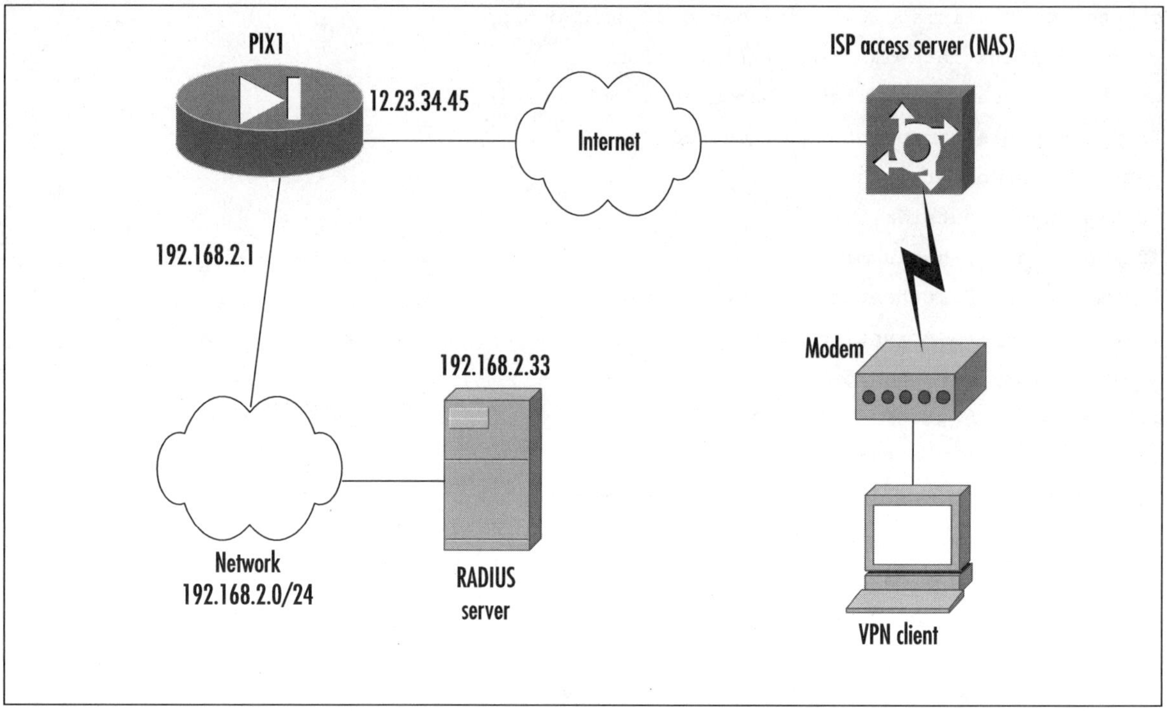

Clients will be assigned IP addresses from the pool 192.168.10.1 through 192.168.10.254, and IKE authentication will use a wildcard key. Only the default VPN group will be configured. Configuration (assuming that PIX IP addresses are already configured) starts with defining an authentication server:

```
PIX1(config)# aaa-server vpnauthgroup protocol radius
PIX1(config)# aaa-server vpnauthgroup (inside) host 192.168.2.33 abcdef timeout 5
```

Next an IKE policy is configured (3DES encryption and MD5 hashing):

```
PIX1(config)# isakmp enable outside
PIX1(config)# isakmp policy 10 encryption 3des
PIX1(config)# isakmp policy 10 hash md5
PIX1(config)# isakmp policy 10 authentication pre-share
```

Cisco VPN client 3.*x* requires use of Diffie-Hellman Group 2 (1024-bit keys), not the default Group 1 (768-bit keys):

```
PIX1(config)# isakmp policy 10 group 2
```

A wildcard pre-shared key is configured so that all clients will use the same key:

```
PIX1(config)# isakmp key mysecretkey address 0.0.0.0 netmask 0.0.0.0
```

An ACL for split tunneling is configured. Only traffic to or from network 192.168.2.0/24 will be protected:

```
PIX1(config)# access-list 80 permit ip 192.168.2.0 255.255.255.0 192.168.10.0
255.255.255.0
```

No-NAT is configured for IPsec traffic:

```
PIX1(config)# nat (inside) 0 access-list 80
```

transform sets and crypto maps are configured and applied. This is a simple crypto map with only a dynamic map as a subentry.

```
PIX1(config)# crypto ipsec transform-set strong esp-3des esp-sha-hmac
PIX1(config)# crypto dynamic-map cisco 10 set transform-set strong
PIX1(config)# crypto map partner-map 20 ipsec-isakmp dynamic cisco
PIX1(config)# crypto map partner-map interface outside
```

xauth is enabled for this map:

```
PIX1(config)# crypto map partner-map client authentication authserver
```

IKE mode configuration is enabled and an IP pool is created:

```
PIX1(config)# ip local pool dealer 192.168.10.1-192.168.10.254
PIX1(config)# isakmp client configuration address-pool local dealer outside
PIX1(config)# crypto crypto map partner-map client configuration address initiate
```

Initiate mode is optional for VPN client 3.*x* but must be used with version 2.*x*. The preceding two lines set global IKE mode configuration settings. They can be substituted by one command:

```
PIX1(config)# vpngroup default address-pool dealer
```

The default group and its setting will be applied for any group name supplied by the VPN client. If global IKE mode is configured, it will also be applied to site-to-site tunnel endpoints, so if there are any, they may need to be excluded. Other VPN group settings are configured:

```
PIX1(config)# vpngroup default dns-server 192.168.2.44
PIX1(config)# vpngroup default wins-server 192.168.2.45
PIX1(config)# vpngroup default default-domain securecorp.com
PIX1(config)# vpngroup default split-tunnel 80
PIX1(config)# vpngroup default idle-time 1800
```

IPsec connections are implicitly permitted:

```
PIX1(config)# sysopt connection permit-ipsec
```

The following shows the full configuration of PIX1.

```
nameif ethernet0 outside security0
nameif ethernet1 inside security100
nameif ethernet2 dmz security10
enable password 8Ry2YjIRX7RXXU24 encrypted
```

```
passwd 2KFQnbNIdIXZJH.YOU encrypted
hostname PIX1
domain-name securecorp.com
fixup protocol ftp 21
fixup protocol http 80
fixup protocol smtp 25
fixup protocol h323 1720
fixup protocol rsh 514
fixup protocol sqlnet 1521
names
pager lines 24
no logging on
interface ethernet0 auto
interface ethernet1 auto
interface ethernet2 auto
mtu outside 1500
mtu inside 1500
mtu dmz 1500
ip address outside 12.23.34.54 255.255.255.0
ip address inside 192.168.2.1 255.255.255.0
no failover
failover ip address outside 0.0.0.0
failover ip address inside 0.0.0.0
arp timeout 14400
nat (inside) 1 0.0.0.0 0.0.0.0 0 0
access-list 80 permit ip 192.168.2.0 255.255.255.0 192.168.10.0 255.255.255.0
nat (inside) 0 access-list 80
global (outside) 1 12.23.34.55
route outside 0.0.0.0 0.0.0.0 12.23.34.254 1
timeout xlate 3:00:00 conn 1:00:00 half-closed 0:10:00 udp 0:02:00
timeout rpc 0:10:00 h323 0:05:00
timeout uauth 0:05:00 absolute
ip local pool dealer 192.168.10.1-192.168.10.254
aaa-server TACACS+ protocol tacacs+
aaa-server RADIUS protocol radius
aaa-server authserver protocol radius
aaa-server authserver (inside) host 192.168.2.33 abcdef timeout 5
no snmp-server location
no snmp-server contact
snmp-server community public
```

```
no snmp-server enable traps
crypto map partner-map client configuration address initiate
crypto ipsec transform-set strong esp-3des esp-sha-hmac
crypto dynamic-map cisco 10 set transform-set strong-des
crypto map partner-map 20 ipsec-isakmp dynamic cisco
crypto map partner-map client authentication authserver
crypto map partner-map interface outside
isakmp key mysecretkey address 0.0.0.0 netmask 0.0.0.0
isakmp enable outside
isakmp policy 10 authentication pre-share
isakmp policy 10 encryption 3des
isakmp policy 10 hash md5
isakmp policy 10 group 2
vpngroup default address-pool dealer
vpngroup default dns-server 192.168.2.44
vpngroup default wins-server 192.168.2.45
vpngroup default default-domain securecorp.com
vpngroup default split-tunnel 80
vpngroup default idle-time 1800
sysopt connection permit-ipsec
telnet timeout 5
terminal width 80
```

Since the Cisco VPN client provides a simplified installation process as well as a wizard to guide you through the intricacies of VPN configuration, we will not discuss it. Instead, see www.cisco.com/en/US/partner/products/sw/secursw/ps2308/products_user_guide09186a00800bd983.html for more information.

To use digital certificates, the CA is configured (we will use VeriSign as before) and IKE is reconfigured correspondingly. The whole configuration changes just a few commands. The following is a listing of PIX configurations with new or changed commands in boldface.

```
nameif ethernet0 outside security0
nameif ethernet1 inside security100
nameif ethernet2 dmz security10
enable password 8Ry2YjIRX7RXXU24 encrypted
passwd 2KFQnbNIdIXZJH.YOU encrypted
hostname PIX1
domain-name securecorp.com
fixup protocol ftp 21
fixup protocol http 80
fixup protocol smtp 25
fixup protocol h323 1720
```

```
fixup protocol rsh 514
fixup protocol sqlnet 1521
names
pager lines 24
no logging on
interface ethernet0 auto
interface ethernet1 auto
interface ethernet2 auto
mtu outside 1500
mtu inside 1500
mtu dmz 1500
ip address outside 12.23.34.54 255.255.255.0
ip address inside 192.168.2.1 255.255.255.0
no failover
failover ip address outside 0.0.0.0
failover ip address inside 0.0.0.0
arp timeout 14400
nat (inside) 1 0.0.0.0 0.0.0.0 0 0
access-list 80 permit ip 192.168.2.0 255.255.255.0 192.168.10.0 255.255.255.0
nat (inside) 0 access-list 80
global (outside) 1 12.23.34.55
route outside 0.0.0.0 0.0.0.0 12.23.34.254 1
timeout xlate 3:00:00 conn 1:00:00 half-closed 0:10:00 udp 0:02:00
timeout rpc 0:10:00 h323 0:05:00
timeout uauth 0:05:00 absolute
ip local pool dealer 192.168.10.1-192.168.10.254
aaa-server TACACS+ protocol tacacs+
aaa-server RADIUS protocol radius
aaa-server authserver protocol radius
aaa-server authserver (inside) host 192.168.2.33 abcdef timeout 5
no snmp-server location
no snmp-server contact
snmp-server community public
no snmp-server enable traps
crypto map partner-map client configuration address initiate
crypto ipsec transform-set strong esp-3des esp-sha-hmac
crypto dynamic-map cisco 10 set transform-set strong-des
crypto map partner-map 20 ipsec-isakmp dynamic cisco
crypto map partner-map client authentication authserver
crypto map partner-map interface outside
```

```
isakmp enable outside
isakmp policy 10 authentication rsa-sig
isakmp policy 10 encryption 3des
isakmp policy 10 hash md5
isakmp policy 10 group 2
vpngroup mygroup address-pool dealer
vpngroup mygroup dns-server 192.168.2.44
vpngroup mygroup wins-server 192.168.2.45
vpngroup mygroup default-domain securecorp.com
vpngroup mygroup split-tunnel 80
vpngroup mygroup idle-time 1800
ca identity verisign 205.139.94.230
ca configure verisign ca 1 20 crloptional
sysopt connection permit-ipsec
telnet timeout 5
terminal width 80
```

The group name was changed from the default because in digital certificates the name of the group must match the Organizational Unit section of the Cisco VPN client certificate. This certificate must be obtained and installed before configuring the connection entry. The process of obtaining the certificate is described in VPN client documentation at www.cisco.com/univercd/cc/td/doc/product/vpn/index.htm. Client certificates are managed by Certificate Manager, which is installed together with the VPN client.

So far, our efforts have focused on getting the PIX configured to provide its services. Equally important is being able to troubleshoot and resolve problems that arise.

Troubleshooting PIX Firewall Hardware, Software, and Performance

Knowing the details of each PIX firewall model can validate a configuration and troubleshooting. It is important to know whether the PIX firewall being used is adequate for the demands planned for it. For example, if you have a network on which 100,000 simultaneous connections will be requested through the firewall and you are using a PIX 501, no amount of troubleshooting and configuration will enable the PIX 501 to support the load. The capacity of each firewall model determines the load that can be placed on that firewall.

Cisco ceased PIX firewall support for Token Ring and FDDI networks, starting with PIX software v5.3. Only models 515 up and support interfaces other than Ethernet.

The memory architecture of the PIX firewall is somewhat similar to that of Cisco routers with the exception that there is no NVRAM memory. The PIX uses flash memory to store the firewall OS (image) and the configuration file. The flash memory should be big enough to hold the software image and the configuration. Main memory is used to store data that is waiting to be processed or forwarded. Main memory can potentially have the most significant impact on performance since it is the working space of the firewall. You can never have too much, and you will definitely notice when you have too little, because packet loss will increase or IPsec traffic will become lossy or laggardly.

During the PIX boot sequence, the power-on self-test (POST) can provide a wealth of information to help determine from the onset whether the PIX firewall is healthy or ill. An example boot sequence is used to guide our discussion.

```
CISCO SYSTEMS PIX-501
Embedded BIOS Version 4.3.200 07/31/01 15:58:22.08
Compiled by morlee
16 MB RAM

PCI Device Table.
Bus Dev Func VendID DevID Class              Irq
 00  00  00   1022   3000  Host Bridge
 00  11  00   8086   1209  Ethernet            9
 00  12  00   8086   1209  Ethernet            10

Cisco Secure PIX Firewall BIOS (4.2) #6: Mon Aug 27 15:09:54 PDT 2001
Platform PIX-501
Flash=E28F640J3 @ 0x3000000

Use BREAK or ESC to interrupt flash boot.
Use SPACE to begin flash boot immediately.
Reading 1536512 bytes of image from flash.
#########################################################################
16MB RAM
Flash=E28F640J3 @ 0x3000000
BIOS Flash=E28F640J3 @ 0xD8000
mcwa i82559 Ethernet at irq  9  MAC: 0008.e317.ba6b
mcwa i82559 Ethernet at irq 10  MAC: 0008.e317.ba6c
-----------------------------------------------------------------------
                                 ||        ||
                                 ||        ||
                                ||||      ||||
                            ..:||||||:..:||||||:..
                           c i s c o S y s t e m s
                          Private Internet eXchange
  -----------------------------------------------------------------------
                          Cisco PIX Firewall
```

```
Cisco PIX Firewall Version 6.2(2)
Licensed Features:
Failover:            Disabled
VPN-DES:             Enabled
VPN-3DES:            Disabled
Maximum Interfaces: 2
Cut-through Proxy:  Enabled
Guards:              Enabled
URL-filtering:      Enabled
Inside Hosts:        10
Throughput:          Limited
IKE peers:           5
****************************** Warning ******************************
  Compliance with U.S. Export Laws and Regulations - Encryption.

<<  output omitted  >>
  ****************************** Warning ******************************


Copyright (c) 1996-2002 by Cisco Systems, Inc.


                Restricted Rights Legend


<<  output omitted  >>
Cryptochecksum(unchanged): 38a9d953 0ee64510 cb324148 b87bdd42

Warning: Start and End addresses overlap with broadcast address.
outside interface address added to PAT pool
Address range subnet is not the same as inside interface
```

The boot sequence identifies the version of the PIX OS loaded on firmware used to initially boot. In this example, it is 4.3.200. This is important to know because this is the OS that will be used if there is no software image in flash memory. Notice that the first line identifies the model of firewall—information that can be useful if you are checking the firewall remotely.

The boot display provides information about the PIX firewall hardware such as the amount of flash and main memory it has, and the number and type of network interfaces installed.

The exact version of the OS is identified—in this case v6.2(2). VPN-DES is supported, whereas VPN-3DES is not. This firewall supports cut-through proxy and URL filtering.

The last few lines of the boot screen can highlight errors that the OS encountered when it parsed the configuration file. These messages should be studied to determine if and how they must be fixed. In our example, we have several problems with the way we have allocated our IP addresses. We also know that the outside interface address is now part of the PAT pool, which is something that we might or might not want.

These are several commonly used commands to check the composition and health of your PIX firewall at Layer 1. The **show version** command provides a quick snapshot of the PIX firewall. Use this command when you need information about your firewall's software and hardware. Some of the output is similar to what you saw during the boot sequence.

```
PIX1# show version
Cisco PIX Firewall Version 6.2(2)
Cisco PIX Device Manager Version 2.1(1)
Compiled on Fri 07-Jun-02 17:49 by morlee

PIX1 up 23 secs

Hardware:   PIX-501, 16 MB RAM, CPU Am5x86 133 MHz
Flash E28F640J3 @ 0x3000000, 8MB
BIOS Flash E28F640J3 @ 0xfffd8000, 128KB
0: ethernet0: address is 0008.e317.ba6b, irq 9
1: ethernet1: address is 0008.e317.ba6c, irq 10

Licensed Features:
Failover:            Disabled
VPN-DES:             Enabled
VPN-3DES:            Disabled
Maximum Interfaces: 2
Cut-through Proxy:  Enabled
Guards:              Enabled
URL-filtering:      Enabled
Inside Hosts:        10
Throughput:          Limited
IKE peers:           5

Serial Number: 406053729 (0x1833e361)
Running Activation Key: 0xc598dce8 0xf775fc1c 0xbd76cee8 0x3f41e74b
Configuration last modified by  at 06:28:16.000 UTC Thu Feb 7 2036
```

When troubleshooting, the **show version** command should be one of the first (if not *the* first) commands executed to obtain an inventory of the PIX firewall. It is especially vital that you know which features are supported by the firewall before you begin troubleshooting; otherwise, you could squander valuable time trying to determine why an unsupported featured is not working.

The **show interface** command can provide information applicable to different layers of the troubleshooting process. It provides details on the network interfaces. As with Cisco routers, this command enables you to check the state of an interface and determine if it is operational. You can also see what each interface is named.

```
interface ethernet1 "inside" is up, line protocol is up
  Hardware is i82559 ethernet, address is 0008.e317.ba6c
  IP address 10.10.2.1, subnet mask 255.255.255.0
  MTU 1500 bytes, BW 10000 Kbit full duplex
  4 packets input, 282 bytes, 0 no buffer
  Received 0 broadcasts, 0 runts, 0 giants
  0 input errors, 0 CRC, 0 frame, 0 overrun, 0 ignored, 0 abort
  4 packets output, 282 bytes, 0 underruns
  0 output errors, 0 collisions, 0 interface resets
  0 babbles, 0 late collisions, 0 deferred
  0 lost carrier, 0 no carrier
  input queue (curr/max blocks): hardware (128/128) software (0/1)
  output queue (curr/max blocks): hardware (0/1) software (0/1)
```

Troubleshooting PIX Cabling

After ascertaining that the PIX hardware is functional, the next step in troubleshooting should be to corroborate cabling. The PIX firewall has a limited number of cable types that are important in the context of troubleshooting: Ethernet and failover cables.

Certain models of the PIX firewall support Token Ring and FDDI networks in older software versions (up to v5.3). Cisco has discontinued the sale of Token Ring and FDDI for PIX firewalls starting August 2001 and June 2001, respectively. Support is slated to cease in August 2006 and June 2006, respectively. Token Ring and FDDI cables are not discussed in this book.

Regardless of the cables you are troubleshooting, you should adopt a structured approach. Table 8.14 summarizes some steps you should first take to check your cabling. Ensure that you perform these steps to avoid missing a minor cabling glitch that could be causing a major problem.

Table 8.14 Cable Troubleshooting Checklist

Problem	Troubleshooting Step
Correct cable connected to the correct interface?	Check cable and verify slot and port number.
Correct end of cable connected to correct interface?	*Failover cable only:* Primary end to the primary firewall and secondary end to the secondary firewall.
Correct cable type connected to equipment?	Cross cables, rollover cables, and so on to the correct ports.
Cable pinouts correct?	Visually inspect and check with cable tester.

Continued

Table 8.14 Cable Troubleshooting Checklist

Problem	Troubleshooting Step
Cable verified as good?	Test with a cable tester or swap with known good equipment and test.

Troubleshooting Connectivity

Translation can be particularly critical since all addresses must be translated in order for internal and external networks to communicate with each other.

Get in the habit of executing **clear xlate** to clear any current translations whenever you make a change to NAT, global, static, ACLs, conduits, or anything that depends on or is part of translation. Since translation is mandatory on PIX firewalls, this covers just about any feature that can be configured.

Traffic from a higher security level to a lower security level is permitted by default but still requires translations. Traffic from a lower security level to a higher security level (such as outside-to-inside) requires an ACL or conduit, as well as corresponding translations.

Syslog provides an ongoing, real-time report of activities and errors—information that can be vital to troubleshooting success. For example, if a host on a lower security-level interface wants to communicate with a host on a higher security-level interface and translation is enabled for it, but no conduit or ACL is configured, the following message will be logged:

```
106001: Inbound TCP connection denied from x.x.x.x/x to x.x.x.x/x
```

This is your first clue that you need an ACL or conduit to permit this access. If the reverse is the case (ACL or conduit is present, but no translation is configured), the following message will be logged:

```
305005: No translation group found for...
```

For more information about syslog message numbers and descriptions, see www.cisco.com/univercd/cc/td/doc/product/iaabu/pix/pix_61/syslog/pixemsgs.htm.

Checking Addressing

As with any IP device, unless basic IP addressing and operation are configured correctly and working, none of the PIX firewall troubleshooting efforts regarding routing, ACLs, and translation will matter. Figure 8.21 shows PIX1 and PIX2 connected to each other.

Figure 8.21 IP Addressing Problem

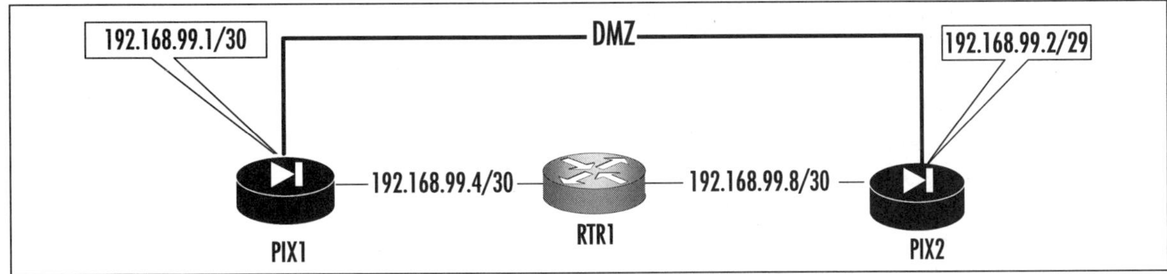

In the figure, there is an addressing problem on the LAN connecting the two firewalls (which is labeled DMZ in the configuration). For starters, PIX1 has a subnet mask of /30, while FW2 has a mask of /29 for the DMZ network (192.168.99.0), a common network between them. This is confirmed using the **show ip address** command on both firewalls. Notice the differences highlighted in the command output shown.

```
PIX1# show ip address
System IP Addresses:
        ip address outside 192.168.99.5 255.255.255.252
        ip address DMZ 192.168.99.1 255.255.255.252
Current IP Addresses:
        ip address outside 192.168.99.5 255.255.255.252
        ip address DMZ 192.168.99.1 255.255.255.252

PIX2# show ip address
System IP Addresses:
        ip address outside 192.168.99.9 255.255.255.252
        ip address DMZ 192.168.99.2 255.255.255.248
Current IP Addresses:
        ip address outside 192.168.99.9 255.255.255.252
        ip address DMZ 192.168.99.2 255.255.255.248
```

The fix here is simply to correct the mask on PIX2. As on Cisco routers, the **show interface** command can also be used to check addressing on a PIX firewall. Incorrect addressing will prevent advanced features of the PIX firewall from working, even if you configure them correctly.

Checking Routing

The inability to reach a destination is a prime indicator of routing problems. The PIX firewall uses both static and dynamic routing, as previously discussed. The tools of choice for troubleshooting routing issues are primarily **show route**, **show rip**, and **ping**. Determine if there is a reachability problem by attempting to ping the destination. If that fails, use **show route** to determine if there is a route (static or RIP) to reach the network. You can use the **show rip** command to confirm the dynamic routing configuration. The **ping** command should be a litmus test to verify that the destination cannot be reached. The syntax of the **ping** command is **ping [<if_name>] <ip_address>**. For example:

```
PIX1# ping 192.168.99.2
        192.168.99.2 response received -- 20ms
        192.168.99.2 response received -- 20ms
        192.168.99.2 response received -- 20ms
```

Does the PIX have a default route, a static route, or a dynamically learned route? Check your routing table with the **show route** command. For example:

```
PIX1# show route
      outside 192.168.99.0 255.255.255.252 192.168.99.1 1 CONNECT static
      inside 192.168.100.0 255.255.255.252 192.168.100.1 1 CONNECT static
      DMZ 192.168.1.0 255.255.255.0 192.168.1.1 1 CONNECT static
```

In our case, 192.168.99.2 is on our directly connected outside network. To perform a side-by-side comparison of RIP peers, use the **show rip** command. The **clear rip** command removes all existing RIP commands and parameters from the configuration.

Checking Translation

The PIX firewall performs address translation. In order for internal networks to communicate with external networks, and vice versa, addresses must be translated. Translation is not optional.

NOTE

To pass traffic through the PIX traffic, you must translate it, even if this means you will translate IP addresses to themselves.

When translation does not work, the administrator needs to know where to start and finish their troubleshooting. Cisco provides several commands that can be used to validate various aspects of translation. First, look at which private addresses are being translated to which public addresses. This information will determine if the translation parameters have been configured correctly. Two commands used to perform this task are **show nat** and **show global**:

```
PIX1# show nat
nat (dmz) 0 192.168.1.10 255.255.255.255 0 0
nat (inside) 1 0.0.0.0 0.0.0.0 0 0
nat (dmz) 99 0.0.0.0 0.0.0.0 0 0
PIX1# show global
global (outside) 99 192.168.99.4-192.168.99.254 netmask 255.255.255.0
global (outside) 1 192.168.99.3 netmask 255.255.255.0
```

Our NAT configuration specifies a nontranslation for the DMZ server at address 192.168.1.10 network (as evidenced by the **nat 0** command). The **nat 99** specifies that all remaining addresses in the DMZ should be translated. The global command defines two pools of addresses to be used for translation purposes. The numerical ID is referenced by the NAT command to perform the actual translation. The **global 99** command is used for NAT, whereas **global 1** with its single IP address is used for PAT. In actual practice, you would know at this point if you had configured the translation parameters correctly. Both of these commands provide enough data for making this determination. Once you have corrected any errors (the most common being typos or incorrect IP addresses), you can then check to see if connections are being made and translated.

Next, determine if connections have been made by using the **show conn detail** command:

```
PIX1# show conn detail
1 in use, 1 most used
Flags: A - awaiting inside ACK to SYN, a - awaiting outside ACK to SYN,
       B - initial SYN from outside, D - DNS, d - dump,
       E - outside back connection, f - inside FIN, F - outside FIN,
       G - group, H - H.323, I - inbound data, M - SMTP data,
       O - outbound data, P - inside back connection,
       q - SQL*Net data, R - outside acknowledged FIN,
       R - UDP RPC, r - inside acknowledged FIN, S - awaiting inside SYN,
       s - awaiting outside SYN, U - up
TCP outside:192.168.11.11/24 dmz:192.168.99.2/80 flags UIO
```

The workstation has established a connection to our HTTP server on the DMZ network (as confirmed by its destination port, 80). Notice that the workstation established the connection to the public address of this server rather than to its internal DMZ address (192.168.1.2), which it cannot reach. Now we have a valid connection attempt, but has the translation taken place as it should? To determine that, use the **show xlate detail** command:

```
PIX1# show xlate detail
1 in use, 1 most used
Flags: D - DNS, d - dump, I - identity, i - inside, n - no random,
       o - outside, r - portmap, s - static
TCP NAT from DMZ:192.168.1.2/80 to outside:192.168.99.2/80 flags ri
```

This command displays a current listing of active translation slots. The output of this command confirms that our host's attempt to access the Web server at 192.168.99.2 has resulted in the correct translation to 192.168.99.2. Such verification is particularly important if you are providing services that must be accessible by outside users.

There is one more command that can be used to gather information about the translation operations. The command that can provide the copious information is the **debug packet** command. The syntax of the command is as follows:

```
debug packet <if_name> [src <source_ip> [netmask <mask>]] [dst <dest_ip> [netmask
<mask>]] [[proto icmp] | [proto tcp [sport <src_port>] [dport <dest_port>]] | [[proto
udp [sport <src_port>] [dport <dest_port>]] [rx | tx | both]
```

In our case, the command we would actually enter to find out which addresses are attempting to use our Web server is:

```
PIX1(config)# debug packet outside src 0.0.0.0 netmask 0.0.0.0 dst 192.168.99.2 netmask
255.255.255.0 rx
```

This command captures packet data that comes into the outside interface destined for the Web server's public IP address. Since we do not know exactly which protocols (TCP, UDP, or ICMP) will be used, we have opted not to specify one. After we have captured our data, we can determine which translation parameters we need to enter.

Checking Access

The PIX firewall provides several mechanisms for controlling access through it. This section covers several of these mechanisms and discusses some ways to monitor and verify their functionality. The default state of the PIX firewall is to permit access to sessions originated from a higher security-level interface to a lower security-level interface, as long as a translation is configured. Traffic that originates from a low security-level interface to a high security-level interface has to be specifically permitted using conduits or ACLs (and of course, translations).

Problems with lack of access become apparent when machines are unreachable. Access problems can include typos, overly restrictive or loose ACLs or conduits, the wrong networks being denied or permitted access, or ACLs applied to the wrong interface.

The main command for verifying conduit configuration is **show conduit**. For example:

```
PIX1# show conduit
conduit permit tcp host 192.168.4.2 host 192.168.1.2 eq www (hitcnt=3)
```

This conduit permits 192.168.4.2 to access the Web server at 192.168.1.2. This is the only PIX command for checking conduits. If **clear conduit** is used in the Configuration mode, it removes all conduit statements from the PIX firewall configuration.

The **show access-list** command can be used to confirm which ACLs are configured on the PIX firewall and what they are permitting and denying:

```
PIX1# show access-list
access-list 99; 2 elements
access-list 99 deny ip host 192.168.1.2 any (hitcnt=1)
access-list 99 permit ip any any (hitcnt=0)
access-list 100 permit tcp host 192.168.4.2 host 192.168.1.2 eq www
    (hitcnt=5)
```

An ACL only affects incoming traffic to an interface. Verify that it has been applied to the correct interface with the **show access-group** command for this purpose.

```
PIX1# show access-group
access-group 99 in interface dmz
access-group 100 in interface outside
```

The **in** keyword is mandatory and serves as a reminder that the ACL is applied only to traffic coming into the interface. Cisco provides a **debug** command for troubleshooting ACL events as they occur. Be aware that when you use this command it debugs all ACLs. The **debug access-list** command can provide feedback on the ACL and whether it is permitting or denying the traffic that it should. The command syntax is: **debug access-list {all | standard | turbo}**.

The **fixup** feature does not seem to be access related, but since it curtails the operations of selected protocols, one can argue that access to certain features of the "protected" protocol have been negated. There is a standard set of protocols for which the **fixup** capability is enabled automatically, such as HTTP, SMTP, FTP, and so on. To determine for which protocols **fixup** is enabled, run the **show fixup** command. For example:

```
PIX1# show fixup
fixup protocol ftp 21
fixup protocol http 80
fixup protocol h323 h225 1720
fixup protocol h323 ras 1718-1719
fixup protocol ils 389
fixup protocol rsh 514
fixup protocol rtsp 554
fixup protocol smtp 25
fixup protocol sqlnet 1521
fixup protocol sip 5060
fixup protocol skinny 2000
```

Troubleshooting IPsec

We focus our efforts on using the tools Cisco provides to troubleshoot IPsec problems with the assumption that IKE (not manual IPsec) is used. Misconfigurations, mismatched parameters, keys, routing, IP addressing issues, and other problems can conspire to make IPsec fail. The administrator needs to be able to isolate and resolve these issues by first recognizing the symptoms and then using the correct tools to pinpoint the cause.

IKE

The chief mission of IKE is to negotiate parameters for IPsec by establishing a secure channel over which IPsec will establish its peering. The **show isakmp** command shows how IKE is configured on the PIX firewall. For example:

```
PIX1# show isakmp
isakmp enable outside
isakmp key ******** address 192.168.3.1 netmask 255.255.255.255
isakmp identity address
isakmp policy 99 authentication pre-share
isakmp policy 99 encryption des
```

```
isakmp policy 99 hash md5
isakmp policy 99 group 1
isakmp policy 99 lifetime 9999
```

The **show isakmp** or **show crypto isakmp** commands display the current IKE parameters configured on a PIX firewall. You should run this command on both peers and compare the resulting output to ensure that there will be agreement on at least one security policy. If you desire more detail or need more information about exactly what each parameter does, use the **show crypto isakmp policy** command.

```
PIX1# show crypto isakmp policy
Protection suite of priority 99
    encryption algorithm:   DES - Data Encryption Standard (56 bit keys).
    hash algorithm:          Message Digest 5
    authentication method:  Pre-Shared Key
    Diffie-Hellman group:   #1 (768 bit)
    lifetime:                9999 seconds, no volume limit
Default protection suite
    encryption algorithm:   DES - Data Encryption Standard (56 bit keys).
    hash algorithm:          Secure Hash Standard
    authentication method:  Rivest-Shamir-Adleman Signature
    Diffie-Hellman group:   #1 (768 bit)
    lifetime:                86400 seconds, no volume limit
```

Another useful aspect of the **show crypto isakmp policy** command is that it shows the default values that will be used if no values are specified. This information can be useful if you need to determine what a particular unspecified parameter would be if it is not configured specifically.

The most common problems that occur during the IKE phases are mismatched preshared keys and mismatched security policy parameters. The first step in troubleshooting IKE is to compare the configurations of each peer. This can be done with the commands discussed previously. After you have ascertained that you have an IKE policy that will work on each firewall, initiate the IKE process after executing the appropriate **debug** command. That way, you can monitor its progress or lack thereof.

If you do not define an IKE security policy common to both peers or if you neglect to define a security policy at all, IKE will try the defaults for the various values. This means using DES for encryption, SHA for calculating the hash values, RSA for authentication, and Diffie-Hellman Group 1 (768 bits) with a lifetime of 86,400 seconds. Policy mismatches will be apparent when the output of the **show crypto isakmp sa** command shows "no state," meaning that the peers did not and could not negotiate main mode successfully due to the mismatch. The "no state" error also appears if there is key (password) disagreement between the two peers. Hash calculations will also fail, which is something that can be watched with the **debug crypto isakmp** command.

Cisco provides a **clear crypto isakmp sa** command that can be used to delete existing security associations and force a re-initialization. This command can be useful not only to clear an invalid security association, but is also helpful in monitoring the IKE negotiation process with **debug**.

IPsec

After IKE successfully negotiates the parameters such as the method to be used for encryption, authentication, and the size key to use, IPsec is then ready to perform its mission of creating a VPN.

To check which transform sets have been configured, use the **show crypto ipsec transform-set** command. Notice that this command tells you if IPsec will negotiate AH, ESP, or a combination of both. Here is an example:

```
PIX1# show crypto ipsec transform-set


Transform set FW1: { ah-md5-hmac  }
   will negotiate = { Tunnel,  },
   { esp-des esp-md5-hmac  }
   will negotiate = { Tunnel,  },
```

It is important for IPsec peers to have in their transform sets common parameters on which they can agree. Crypto maps are used to specify the traffic to be encrypted. Execute the **show crypto map** command to confirm your maps. For example:

```
PIX2# show crypto map


Crypto Map: "pixola" interfaces: {outside }


Crypto Map "pixola" 1 ipsec-isakmp
        Peer = 192.168.2.1
        access-list 100 permit ip 192.168.2.0 255.255.255.0 any (hitcnt=1)
        Current peer: 192.168.2.1
        Security association lifetime: 4608000 kilobytes/28800 seconds
        PFS (Y/N): N
        Transform sets={ pix, }
```

This command also identifies the IPsec peer and the interface to which the map is applied. In this example, PIX2 has the crypto map **pixola** applied to its outside interface. It is peering with PIX1 (at IP address 192.168.2.1) and will encrypt traffic that matches ACL 100. It even tells you how many matches have been made against that ACL—a quick way to determine if anything is being checked for IPsec processing.

After verifying that there is agreement in the transform sets and the crypto maps are defined correctly, confirm that data is actually being protected. To verify, use the **show crypto ipsec sa** command as shown.

```
PIX1# show crypto ipsec sa
interface: outside
Crypto map tag: pixola, local addr. 192.168.2.1

local ident (addr/mask/prot/port): (192.168.2.1/255.255.255.0/0/0)
remote ident (addr/mask/prot/port): (192.168.3.1/255.255.255.0/0/0)
current_peer: 192.168.3.1
PERMIT, flags={origin_is_acl,}

#pkts encaps: 5, #pkts encrypt: 5, #pkts digest 5
#pkts decaps: 5, #pkts decrypt: 5, #pkts verify 5
#pkts compressed: 0, #pkts decompressed: 0
#pkts not compressed: 0, #pkts compr. failed: 0, #pkts decompress
    failed: 0
#send errors 0, #recv errors 0

local crypto endpt.: 192.168.2.1, remote crypto endpt.: 192.168.3.1
path mtu 1500, ipsec overhead 56, media mtu 1500
current outbound spi: 3a18fca2
inbound esp sas:
spi: 0x61af4121(2451330208)

transform: esp-des esp-md5-hmac
in use settings ={Tunnel, }
slot: 0, conn id: 1, crypto map: pixola
sa timing: remaining key lifetime (k/sec): (4000159/9460)
IV size: 8 bytes
replay detection support: Y

inbound ah sas:
inbound pcp sas:

outbound ESP sas:
spi: 0x61af4121(2451330208)
transform: esp-des esp-md5-hmac
in use settings ={Tunnel, }
slot: 0, conn id: 1, crypto map: pixola
sa timing: remaining key lifetime (k/sec): (4000159/9460)
IV size: 8 bytes
replay detection support: Y
```

```
outbound ah sas:
outbound PCP sas:
```

The output of this command can be very abundant. The **crypto map** tag identifies the crypto map being used, whereas **local** and **remote ident** show the IP addresses of the local and remote peers. The **pkts** counters track how many packets have been encrypted, decrypted, and compressed. So far, five packets have been sent and received encrypted. This is an earmark of successful IPsec operation.

The crypto **endpt** section identifies the IPsec peers. Notice that the path MTU as well as the media MTU are shown, which can be useful in determining if fragmentation will occur. The SPI is a unique identification for this tunnel. We can also view the transform set parameters being used and whether it is operating in tunnel or transport mode. The **lifetime** indicates the amount of time left before the SA will be renegotiated. The last section, **outbound sas,** verifies that both inbound and outbound SA have been established. It also indicates how many seconds and kilobits are left before the SA must be renegotiated.

Check the SA lifetime with the **show crypto ipsec security-association** command. For example:

```
PIX1# show crypto ipsec security-association lifetime
Security association lifetime: 4608000 kilobytes/28800 seconds
```

The IKE SA or IPsec SA establishment can be debugged using the **debug isakmp** and **debug ipsec** commands. These commands tend to produce a lot of output, but they are easy to understand if you know how IPsec works. For example, the following part of a log tells us that IKE negotiations were completed successfully:

```
ISAKMP (0): Checking ISAKMP transform 1 against priority 9 policy
ISAKMP:      encryption DES-CBC
ISAKMP:      hash SHA
ISAKMP:      default group 1
ISAKMP:      auth pre-share
ISAKMP:      life type in seconds
ISAKMP:      life duration (VPI) of  0x0 0x1 0x51 0x80
ISAKMP (0): atts are acceptable. Next payload is 0
ISAKMP (0): SA is doing pre-shared key authentication using id type ID_IPV4_ADDR
return status is IKMP_NO_ERROR
```

On the other hand, something similar to the following output will tell you that the IKE main mode exchange failed (IKMP_NO_ERROR_NO_TRANS) because a common proposal (transform set) was not found:

```
VPN Peer: ISAKMP: Added new peer: ip:PIX2 Total VPN Peers:3
VPN Peer: ISAKMP: Peer ip:PIX2 Ref cnt incremented to:1 Total VPN
Peers:3
ISAKMP (0): beginning Main Mode exchange
```

```
crypto_isakmp_process_block: src PIX2, dest PIX1
return status is IKMP_NO_ERR_NO_TRANS
ISAKMP (0): retransmitting phase 1...
```

At any time, an SA negotiation can be forced to occur with the **clear crypto ipsec sa** command. The **clear crypto ipsec sa** command deletes existing security associations (all of them) and forces the establishment of new associations if there is an active trigger such as a crypto map. You can get very specific with this command, such as specifying a particular peer with **clear crypto ipsec sa 192.168.2.***1*.

Capturing Traffic

Cisco has provided an excellent tool for capturing and analyzing network traffic in version 6.2. When the **capture** command is used, the PIX can act as a packet sniffer on the target interface. This command captures both inbound and outbound traffic.

The packet capture feature was introduced in PIX firewall version 6.2 and is only available for Ethernet interfaces. The syntax of the command is as follows.

```
capture <capture-name> [access-list <ID>] [buffer <bytes>] [ethernet-type <type>]
[interface <if_name>] [packet-length <bytes>]
```

- **capture-name** Defines a name for this particular capture. All other parameters are optional.
- **access-list** Specifies an ACL to limit the source and destination of the traffic captured. By default, all IP packets are matched.
- **buffer** Specifies the size of the buffer (in bytes) used to store captured packets. Default buffer size is 512K, and once the buffer fills up, the packet capture stops.
- **ethernet-type** Specifies the protocols to capture (**ip**, **arp**, **rarp**, **ip6**, or any protocol number between 1 and 65535). By default, all Ethernet types are captured. (Setting the Ethernet-type parameter to 0 specifies capturing all types.)
- **interface** Parameter specifies the interface on which to capture packets.
- **packet-length** Specifies how much of each packet to capture.

Usually for troubleshooting, only the first few bytes of a packet are necessary, and the PIX captures up to 68 bytes. For example:

```
PIX1# capture inside-traffic access-list 100 buffer 20000 interface inside packet-
length 200
```

In this example, we capture the first 200 bytes of traffic matching ACL 100 on the inside interface. We have allocated 20,000 bytes for buffer storage of these captured packets.

Multiple traffic captures can be run simultaneously. To view the list of captures, use the **show capture** command. For example, the following command shows two simultaneous captures, **cap1** and **cap2**, being performed:

```
PIX1# show capture
```

```
capture cap1 interface inside
capture cap2 interface outside
```

To clear a capture buffer without stopping the capture, use the **clear capture <capture-name>** command. For example:

```
PIX1# clear capture cap1
```

To stop a capture and clear the associated buffer, use the **no capture <capture-name>** command. For example:

```
PIX1# no capture cap2
```

To stop a capture and save the associated buffer, use the **no capture <capture-name> interface <if_name>** command. For example:

```
PIX1# no capture cap1 interface inside
```

Monitoring and Troubleshooting Performance

Three key components of the PIX firewall that affect performance are the CPU, memory, and network interfaces. An administrator needs to understand how to monitor these components and ensure that their load is not reaching the limits. The monitoring of these three components is discussed in the following sections. The ultimate question is, can your firewall handle the loads you will place on it?

CPU Performance Monitoring

Your CPU does it all: passes traffic, creates VPN tunnels, and performs encryption on demand. The rule of thumb is that during normal operational mode, the CPU load should stay below 30 percent, on average. During peak traffic hours and attacks, the CPU will surge up higher, but that is normal. However, if the CPU utilization consistently stays above 30 percent with normal network activity, consider upgrading to a more powerful model.

The show processes Command

If CPU utilization is high, you will often need much more detail than the **show cpu usage** command provides. This is where the **show processes** command comes in. This command identifies every process running on the PIX firewall, how much memory it is using, and CPU cycles. This information is collected from the time the PIX firewall was started. As shown in Figure 8.22, the output of this command is voluminous; in fact, this is an abbreviated listing of the actual output from a PIX 501 firewall, the lowest end of the PIX firewalls. Here we do not explain every row of this of the display, but we do discuss how to interpret what you see in the columns. A detailed analysis of this command is available on Cisco's Web site at www.cisco.com/warp/public/110/pix_shproc.html.

Figure 8.22 Output of the show processes Command

```
PIX1# show processes

    PC       SP       STATE        Runtime    SBASE     Stack     Process
Hsi 800b0e09 80759798 8052ddd8           0 80758810 3532/4096  arp_timer
Lsi 800b5271 8077c880 8052ddd8           0 8077b908 3912/4096  FragDBGC
Lwe 8020685d 808b8e20 80507300           0 808b6ed8 7644/8192  Logger
Hwe 8020a550 808bbee8 805075b0           0 808b9f70 8008/8192  tcp_fast
Lsi 80137edd 809400f0 8052ddd8           0 8093f168 3928/4096  xlate clean
Lsi 80256f4d 8096c430 8052ddd8           0 8096b4a8 3900/4096  route_process
Mwe 800d2671 809b19e0 8052ddd8           0 809afa68 6940/8192  IPsec timer
Lwe 8012ff5a 809daac8 80539908           0 809d9c50 3704/4096  pix/trace
Lwe 8013016a 809dbb58 80539fd0           0 809dace0 3704/4096  pix/tconsole
Hwe 800b2dd0 809ddbe8 80753b9c           0 809dbd70 7196/8192  pix/intf1
H*  80015207 7ffffe2c 8052ddc0         200 809e1ea0 12652/16384 ci/console
Csi 801299b3 809e6e88 8052ddd8          10 809e5f30 3440/4096  update_cpu_usag

 A     B        C        D           E        F         G         H
```

The first character of the first column refers to the priority of the process, which (ranked highest to lowest) can be: Critical, High, Medium, or Low. The next two characters refer to the current operating state of the process, which can be any of the values shown in Table 8.15.

Table 8.15 Process Operating States

Value	Description
*	The process is currently running.
E	The process is waiting for an event to occur.
S	The process is ready to run—gave up processor time slice (idle).
rd	The process is ready to run—conditions for activation have occurred.
we	The process is waiting for an event.
sa	The process is sleeping until an absolute time.
si	The process is sleeping for a given time interval.
sp	The process is sleeping for a given time interval (alternate).
st	The process is sleeping until a timer expires.
hg	The process is hung and will never run again.
xx	The process has terminated but has not been deleted.

The next column (PC) is the program counter, and the one after it (SP) is the stack pointer. Column D (STATE) identifies the thread queue used by the process. The thread queue may be shared with other processes. The fifth column (Runtime) is how much CPU time in milliseconds the process has consumed since it started. The Stack Base Address (SBASE) column shows the starting address space for the process, and the Stack column shows the ratio of used and total stack space in bytes allocated to the process. Bad processes will attempt to invade the space used by other processes. The last column (Process) identifies the process name.

The show perfmon Command

One extremely useful command for performance monitoring on the PIX firewall is the **show perfmon** command. This is the only command that can be used to view the "average" values for the number of translations and connections on the firewall. The parameters for the **show perfmon** command can be seen in Table 8.16.

```
PIX1# show perfmon
PERFMON STATS:    Current       Average
Xlates                0/s           0/s
Connections           0/s           0/s
TCP Conns             0/s           0/s
UDP Conns             0/s           0/s
URL Access            0/s           0/s
URL Server Req        0/s           0/s
TCP Fixup             0/s           0/s
TCPIntercept          0/s           0/s
HTTP Fixup            0/s           0/s
FTP Fixup             0/s           0/s
AAA Authen            0/s           0/s
AAA Author            0/s           0/s
AAA Account           0/s           0/s
```

Table 8.16 Values in the show perfmon Command

Parameter	Description
Xlates	Translations built up per second.
Connections	Connections established per second.
TCP Conns	TCP connections per second.
UDP Conns	UDP connections per second.
URL Access	URLs (Web sites) accessed per second.
URL Server Req	Requests sent to Websense/N2H2 per second (requires the filter command).
TCP Fixup	Number of TCP packets that the PIX forwarded per second.
TCP Intercept	Number of SYN packets per second that have exceeded the configured embryonic limit.
HTTP Fixup	Number of packets destined to port 80 per second (requires the fixup protocol http command).
FTP Fixup	FTP commands inspected per second.
AAA Authen	Authentication requests per second.
AAA Author	Authorization requests per second.
AAA Account	Accounting requests per second.

Memory Performance Monitoring

Memory utilization can be as important in determining performance as the CPU.

The show memory Command

The **show memory** command provides an easily comprehensible overview of how much memory is installed and how much is currently being used. This command simply shows the amount of total and free memory at the time that you run the command. Here is an example of the **show memory** command:

```
PIX1# show memory
16777216 bytes total, 4517888 bytes free
```

To optimize the usefulness of this command, run it on a PIX firewall that has a very basic configuration. That is, run it on a PIX firewall that is not running encryption or other functions and record that information. Then as you add features, execute the command and compare the output. Doing so enables you to record approximately how much memory is consumed by each process.

The show xlate Command

One process that consumes memory is address translation. Each translation requires approximately 56 bytes of memory. Knowing this, you can run the **show xlate** command. For example:

```
PIX1# show xlate
100 in use, 341 most used
```

Multiply the number of translations by 56 bytes to determine how much memory has been consumed for translations. In our example, we have 100 translations in use, which means we have 5,600 bytes of memory allocated for translation alone.

The show conn Command

Each connection made to the firewall also consumes memory. The amount of memory consumed depends on the type of connection. A UDP connection consumes 120 bytes; a TCP connection requires 200 bytes. This memory consumption is necessary to build the connection and maintain state information. Here is an example of the **show conn** command:

```
PIX1# show conn
2 in use, 2 most used
```

If 100 TCP connections are made through this PIX firewall, they will require 20K of main memory. Of course, this is a transitory number and will fluctuate depending on the times of the day.

The show block Command

The PIX firewall reserves certain amounts of memory to handle special traffic after the configuration is loaded and running and before any other memory allocation occurs. Certain amounts of memory are allocated into variable byte-sized blocks. Predefining such set-sized blocks relieves the firewall from having to carve memory on the fly. You can use the **show blocks** command to view the currently set block sizes. For example:

```
PIX1# show blocks
  SIZE     MAX    LOW    CNT
     4    1600   1563   1600
    80     400    386    400
   256     500    143    500
  1550    1700   1102   1315
 16384       8      8      8
```

We need to clarify the output of this command starting with the SIZE column, which is measured in bytes. The 4-byte blocks are reserved for certain traffic types such as DNS, IKE, and TFTP (traffic that is small and bursty). The 80-byte blocks are used to store failover hellos and TCP intercept acknowledgements. The 256-byte blocks store stateful failover messages. The 1550-byte blocks support Ethernet (10 and 100) packets as they pass through the firewall. The 16384-byte blocks will never be used unless you have Gigabit Ethernet interfaces, something you will only see on high-end firewalls.

The MAX column identifies the maximum number of each type of memory blocks available. The LOW column indicates the lowest number of blocks that have been available since the firewall booted. Subtract LOW from MAX to get the maximum number of blocks that were used at any particular time. The CNT column shows the available number of blocks. Use the **clear blocks** command to reset the LOW and CNT counters.

Network Performance Monitoring

Congested network interfaces can degrade overall performance. Administrators need to ensure that the interfaces on their PIX firewall can handle the demands placed on them. Cisco offers several commands to check the status of interfaces.

The show traffic Command

The **show traffic** command provides statistics on the number of packets and bytes passed through each interface. As seen in the following output, **show traffic** tells how long the interface has been in operation (either the firewall below has been in operation almost three hours or that much time has elapsed since the clearing of the statistics). The command output displays the amount of traffic transmitted and received in that amount of time.

```
PIX1# show traffic
outside:
        received (in 10035.150 secs):
                2 packets        678 bytes
                0 pkts/sec       0 bytes/sec
        transmitted (in 10035.150 secs):
                14 packets       1026 bytes
                0 pkts/sec       0 bytes/sec
inside:
        received (in 10035.150 secs):
```

```
                0 packets          0 bytes
                0 pkts/sec         0 bytes/sec
        transmitted (in 10035.150 secs):
                15 packets         900 bytes
                0 pkts/sec         0 bytes/sec
```

The traffic counters can be reset using the **clear traffic** command, which resets the counters to 0.

Summary

It was our goal in this chapter to present you with information about network security in general, and on the PIX firewall in particular. This chapter should serve as a handy reference for performing all manner of tasks with the PIX firewall.

Firewall architectures often include one or more DMZ networks, which enable services to be made available to the Internet while keeping them protected by the firewall and segmented from the internal LAN.

The PIX is a dedicated firewall appliance based on a special-purpose, hardened OS. The simplified kernel and reduced command structure (compared with firewalls based on general-purpose OSs) means that all other things being equal, the PIX will have higher throughput and more reduced maintenance costs than the general-purpose device. In addition, the similarity to IOS provides an edge to security administrators who are familiar with the Cisco environment.

The AS uses two databases—a table of translations and a table of known connections—to maintain the state of the traffic transiting the network and to dynamically allow packets through the filter. The ASA inspects packet header information (source/destination address, and TCP and UDP socket information), as well as packet contents for certain protocols, to make intelligent decisions on routing the packets. ASA has additional features: It will rewrite packets where necessary, as part of its inspection engine where the protocols are well known.

NAT allows an organization to use private, non-unique addresses on their internal networks. These addresses are translated to globally unique addresses for routing on the Internet. NAT also provides security by hiding internal network details from the outside.

VPNs are supported by most major firewalls today. They enable remote sites and users to gain authenticated, confidential access to the enterprise from the Internet.

Knowing the various models of PIX firewalls and their capabilities is extremely important to troubleshooting. Certain models of the PIX firewall, such as models 501 and 506, do not support failover. Knowing such details should prevent you from wasting your time attempting to solve problems with features not supported on a particular model. Other useful information to know about the PIX firewall includes the number of supported connections as well as the number and types of NICs supported (such as Token Ring and Ethernet).

Chapter 9

Cisco Voice over IP

Best Damn Topics in this Chapter:

- Telephone Calls–The "Traditional" Way
- Analog
- Basic Telephony
- Digital Transmission Techniques and Formats
- Call Control Signalling
- Inside the Private Branch eXchange
- PBX Terminology
- Non-IP Alternatives to Traditional Telephony
- Introduction to IP Telephony
- IP Telephony Components
- Cisco IP Telephony Applications
- Prepping the Network for Voice Service
- VoIP Protocols
- H.323 Call Stages
- Session Initiation Protocol
- Skinny Station Protocol
- Simplified Messaging Desk Interface
- Cisco VoIP Hardware and Software
- Installing VNMs and VICs
- Quality of Service
- Configuring Voice Ports
- Voice Port-Tuning Commands
- Configuring Dial Plans and Dial Peers
- Configuring Trunking
- Configuring ISDN for Voice
- Configuring Gateways and Gatekeepers
- Troubleshooting VoIP

Introduction

You have a choice, thanks to technological advancements in networking, and for those you reading this, especially for the feature rich hardware and software of Cisco. Your telephone calls can be made with little or no involvement of your telephone company. In years past, you had to purchase telephone service in the form of lines and numbers to enable your organization to communicate via voice and fax. If you were an organization of any meaningful size, the cost of these lines may have been quite prohibitive. All of this is possible by the convergence of voice and data over the same network.

Establishing telephone calls (voice, fax, or analog modem) over data networks using Internet Protocol (IP) now seems inevitable, given the benefits. VoXX implementations become even easier to justify if you have available capacity on your data networks to support voice traffic. One of the main driving factors for deploying voice over IP (VoIP) networks is the cost savings associated with doing so. Cisco has become quite a leader in forging ahead with robust VoIP solutions, from transport device to user- and network-friendly telephones. In this chapter you will also be introduced to VoIP and its configuration on a variety of Cisco products.

Throughout this chapter are several diagrams of network design concepts. We detail specific equipment and configuration issues. This chapter also highlights the opportunities in moving to a packetized voice architecture.

Most companies have spent exorbitant amounts of money to install and maintain their telephone equipment, an investment that can now be kept for other purposes. Packetizing voice allows for tremendous cost savings now and in the future. As more standards are ratified, the cost of deploying a VoIP network continues to drop. This is quite a different model from the traditional telephony cost trends of the last few decades.

As VoIP becomes more widespread and ubiquitous, we will begin to see new applications for packetized voice. Moving voice to an open standards-based architecture will revolutionize the phone industry and the world as much as the Internet has in terms of communication and the way business is transacted.

Telephone Calls—The "Traditional" Way

When you place a call, the circuit-switched network essentially dedicates a 64Kbps circuit for the duration of your call. This means that if you are calling from New York to Los Angeles, a dedicated circuit is set up from one end of the line to the other (see Figure 9.1). When you talk, 64Kbps of bandwidth is utilized, and when you are silent, you still consume 64Kbps. No matter what you do, you are tying up 64Kbps as long as you remain connected. If a switch goes down or someone cuts a fiber, your call ends.

Figure 9.1 A Simple, Traditional Circuit-Switched Call

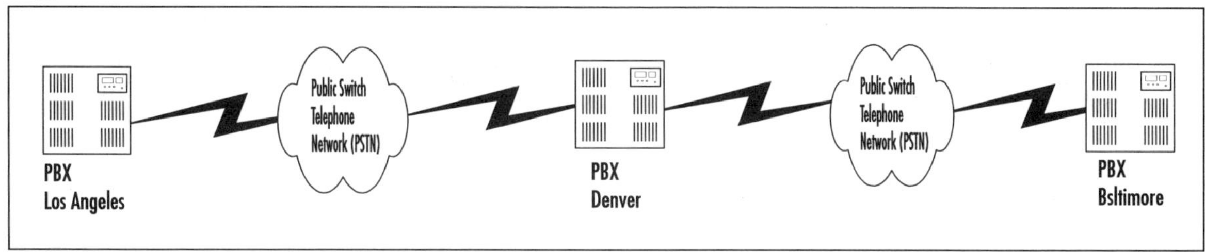

This is not very efficient or cost effective. A driving force behind VoIP networks is the desire to reduce or eliminate such bandwidth waste and expense for calls.

Toll Bypass

The public switched telephone network (PSTN) offers voice services with charges, or *tolls*. *Toll bypass* is the avoidance of PSTN charges by using data networks, such as the Internet, to carry voice conversations. Figure 9.2 shows a simple example of toll bypass using gateways that provide an interface between an IP network and a traditional Private Branch eXchange (PBX). Calls between the three locations are transported over the IP network, with little or no involvement of the telephone company.

Figure 9.2 Toll Bypass with Gateway Routers

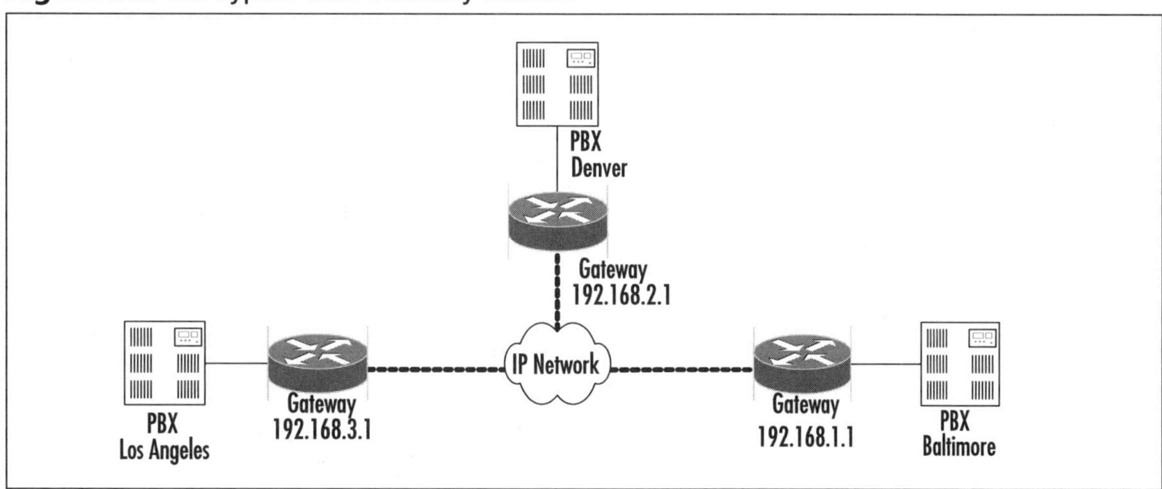

Before you can master VoIP, you need to have a good fundamental understanding of telephony concepts and terminology. We open this chapter with a review of these basics before we cover topics specific to Cisco. The most elemental thing about voice communications is that they are analog at their origin.

Analog

Analog is the transmission of electronic information by adding signals of varying frequency or amplitude to a carrier wave of a given frequency. Traditional broadcast media such as radio, television, and PSTN use analog technology, typically represented as a series of varying sine waves. The term *analog* can be traced to the similarity between the actual fluctuations of the human voice and the "analogous," or comparable, modulation of a carrier wave. The human voice occupies the 20Hz to 20KHz range, with most energy in the 300 to 3300Hz range. Viewed graphically, as in Figure 9.3, both the human voice and a modulated carrier wave display periods of little or no activity followed by periods of activity.

Figure 9.3 Analog Sine Wave

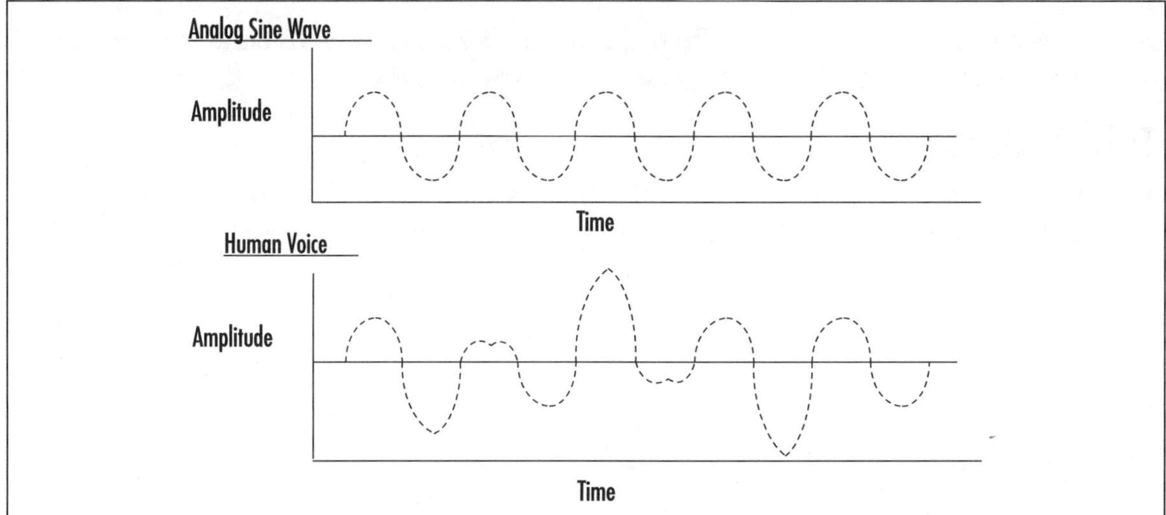

Analog signals are continuous waves that are capable of representing an unlimited number of values. These analog waves have a range of values that represent transmitted information. These signals are susceptible to many forms of interference, and appear as a continuous wave. There is no absolute value within the wave—it varies as the strength of the signal increases or decreases. This is a problem because static and amplification can alter the waveform.

Static and amplification will cause the waveform to achieve higher highs and lower lows. Spikes of noise will alter (and distort) the waveform. The receiver will perceive this as a change in pitch, volume, and tone, and, should this degradation continue through multiple amplifiers and noise-prone circuits, the original waveform may be so disrupted that communications are impossible.

There is a way to convert from analog to digital using a coder-decoder (CODEC). The CODEC samples the analog stream and creates a digital representation. It can also convert digital to analog. Foreign Exchange Office (FXO), Foreign Exchange Station (FXS), and earth & magnet (E&M) are all analog connection methods that we will discuss later.

Basic Telephony

Telephone systems convert *sound waves*, vibrations that move in the air, into electrical signals. Each telephone handset contains a transmitter covered by a diaphragm and a receiver composed of a coil attached to a speaker cone that vibrates, producing sound waves. When the telephone handset is lifted to make a call, the switchhook contacts are closed, energizing a relay, which initiates a search for an open line. A connection to the telephone central office (CO) is established and a dial tone is generated. The line finder then prepares the telephone company switching equipment to receive a telephone number.

Standard telephone cabling is a single pair of twisted-pair copper wiring. The telephone network termination point is an RJ-11 jack. The two-wire connection has two pins, designated *tip* and *ring*.

The process of making a call is as follows:

1. Both telephone sets are on hook with circuits open.
2. Lifting the handset (*off hook*) closes the switch and causes current to flow, which sends a signal to the CO, generating a dial tone.
3. Customer dials a destination telephone number, which are received *in band* by the CO switch.
4. Destination CO sends a ringing signal to the destination receiver and to the sender to indicate that the call request has been completed and the call is proceeding.
5. When the call is answered, another signal is sent to the CO to stop ringing and start the accounting process. The time it takes for the CO to complete the connection between the person calling and the person called is referred to as *call setup time*.
6. Hanging up the phone (*on hook*) opens the switch, which stops current and dial tone.

Dissecting an Analog Network

As shown in Figure 9.4, an analog telephone network consists of several components:

- Telephones
- Drop wires
- Local loops
- A CO containing an electronic switch system (ESS), analog and digital carrier system, DC voltage generation units, and billing, monitoring, and line maintenance computer systems
- Toll trunks

Figure 9.4 Telephone System Components

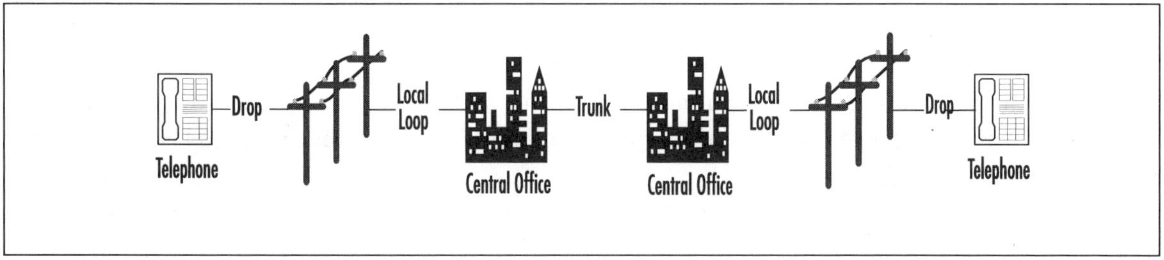

The CO is the building or buildings containing telephone switching equipment for a designated geographical area of responsibility within the greater telephone network. A typical telephone network consists of a multitude of cross-linked and redundantly switched COs, sometimes referred to as *nodes*. Depending on its location in the world, a telephone system node may contain one or more of the telephone switching systems shown in Table 9.1.

Table 9.1 Telephone System Switches

Switch	Description
Basic-NET3	Basic rate switches for the United Kingdom and Europe
Basic-5ESS	AT&T basic rate switches
Basic DMS100	NT DMS-100 basic rate switches
VN2	French VN2 ISDN switches
VN3	French VN3 ISDN switches
NTT	Japanese NTT ISDN switches
Basic-1TR6	German 1TR6 ISDN switches
Basic-NI1	National ISDN-1 switches
Basic-TS013	Australian TS013 switches (obsolete by Basic-NET3)
Primary-4ESS	Lucent 4ESS switch type for the United States
Primary-5ESS	Lucent 5ESS switch type for the United States
Primary-DMS100	Northern Telecom DMS-100 switch type for the United States
Primary-NET5	NET5 switch type for the United Kingdom, Europe, Asia, and Australia
Primary-NI	National ISDN Switch type for the United States
Primary-NTT	NTT switch type for Japan
Primary-QSIG	QSIG switch type
Primary-TS014	TS014 switch type for Australia (obsolete by Primary-NET5)

The local CO is a two-wire switch permitting conversations in both directions over the same pair of wires. When a signal has to be transmitted over long distances, the signal must be amplified and transmitted over a four-wire configuration. A hybrid transformer designed to permit full-duplex operation performs two- to four-wire conversion.

Four-wire circuits have two pairs of wires for simultaneous conversations in both directions. Physical separation of the transmitter and receiver are needed to process traffic and to permit amplifiers to increase signal levels. The CO must conduct loop-side testing, which requires access from the local loop to the CO switch to enable fault detection and permit corrective and preventative system maintenance.

Designed to support 10,000 telephones or more, a CO is typically identified by the first three numbers of a seven-digit telephone number in the United States. For example, 294-*xxxx* might indicate a CO in Paola, Kansas.

Should a call require switching between two COs, it would use a line called a *toll trunk line*. The CO is actually designed to handle only a portion of the calls it receives. A CO's design is typically based on the amount of projected or measured traffic received at peak hours, from 10:00

A.M. to 11:00 A.M. and from 2:00 P.M. to 3:00 P.M. Multiple COs are connected to provide redundancy and reliability.

When all of an individual COs facilities are in use, the CO is said to *blocking*. The grade of service provided by the CO is the proportion of blocked calls to attempted calls expressed as a percentage. Most telephone switching equipment is designed to handle individual telephone calls lasting approximately three minutes.

Each telephone CO in North America is described according to an office class and name. Table 9.2 describes a common telephone network hierarchy.

Table 9.2 Telephone Network Exchange Class Hierarchy

Class	Name
1	Regional center
2	Sectional center
3	Primary center
4C	Toll center
4P	Toll point
4X	Intermediate point
5	End office

Long distance switching is normally performed by Class 1, 2, 3, and 4 exchanges, with Class 1 holding the topmost position of the telephone switching tree. A mixture of Class 2, 3, 4, and 5 exchanges may occupy Layer 2 of the hierarchy, with Class 5 and Class 5 variations at the bottom of the tree.

Sites with multiple users typically use a specialized on-site switch called a *PBX*. A PBX connects telephone sets to each other and to a PSTN. Telephones connected to the PBX have a unique extension number enabling intra-switch calls. PBXs may also be connected to other PBXs over dedicated trunk lines.

Key systems are PBX alternatives; as small telephone switches, they allow multiple phone sets to share a number of external phone lines. Each line connected to a key system has its own unique number and can be dialed directly from an outside line.

Signaling is the communication process. Signaling between switches can occur in-band through the same talk channel or out-of-band through some communication path other than the talk channel.

Each CO manages all telephone calls within its area, either switching the call to the called party within the same exchange or switching the call to a trunk and into another COs area. The side of the CO connecting to another CO is called the *trunk-side interface*. The side of the CO closest to the local subscriber is called the *line-side interface* or *local loop*. Line-side interfaces provide:

- **Battery Feed** Typically 48 volts DC to the customer telephone, including telephone signaling, high alternating current (AC) impedance, and low DC resistance. Most U.S.-based telephone sets require from 10 to 23 milliamps for operation, with 400ohms of resistance. Resistance in non-U.S. telephones can range from 380 to 800ohms.

- **Over-Voltage Protection** Protects the telephone user and telephone from transient voltages due to short circuits, lightning surges, and electrical power lines.
- **Telephone Set Ringing** CO provides to the subscriber telephone inform of incoming calls. Typically 90 volts at 20Hz is provided after switching completes the connection.
- **Call Supervision** Monitoring the off-hook/on-hook state of a circuit, and reporting the status to the connected (and one would hope, communicating) equipment.
- **Signal Coding** Modification of carrier signal to transport information.
- **Hybrid Two-Four Wire Conversion** Point where two wire is converted to four-wire and vice versa.
- **Circuit Testing** Process of validating circuit's functionality and capability to transport calls.

Voice Encoding: Standards and Techniques

Coder-Decoders encode voices electrically for transmission over physical lines. There are three classes of speech CODECs (sometimes called *voice encoders* or *vocoders* if source CODECs are used):

- **Waveform** Older CODECs with high bit rates and very good speech reproduction.
- **Source** Very low bit rates but tend to produce speech that sounds artificial or tinny.
- **Hybrid** Use techniques from both source and waveform coding with intermediate bit rates, and provide good-quality speech.

CODECs model a segment of the speech waveform on the order of 20ms. Speech model parameters are then estimated, quantized (that is, the set of values is limited), coded, and transmitted over a communications channel. The receiver then decodes the transmitted values and reconstructs synthesized speech.

Waveform Encoding

Pulse code modulation (PCM) CODECs are the simplest waveform CODECs. They sample and quantize the input waveform. Narrowband speech is typically sampled 8000 times per second (8KHz), and each speech sample is quantized. If linear quantization is used, about 12 bits per sample are needed, giving a bit rate of about 96kbps. Nonlinear quantization samples 8 bits per sample which is sufficient for resulting speech quality nearly indistinguishable from the original signal, resulting in a bit rate of 64kbps. Two nonlinear PCM CODECs still widely used today were standardized in the 1960s: *u-law* in the United States and *a-law* in Europe.

PCM CODECs are simple, introduce very little delay, and reproduce high-quality speech. The only drawback to PCM CODECs is that they require a relatively high bit rate and are highly susceptible to channel or line errors.

Differential pulse code modulation (DPCM) predicts the value of the next sample from previous samples. This approach works as a result of repeated vocal patterns present in each speech sample. If predictions are correct, error signals between predicted and actual samples will have lower variance than the original speech samples and the error signal may be quantized with fewer bits than the original speech signal.

Improvements to the preceding CODEC technique can be made if the algorithm can adapt to match the characteristics of the coded speech. *Adaptive differential PCM (ADPCM)* CODECs use this approach, resulting in a 32kbps transmission rate and providing speech quality very near the 64kbps PCM CODECs. ADPCM CODECs operating at 16, 24 and 40kbps are also now in use.

Source Encoding

Sometimes called *vocoders*, source CODECs represent voice as a time-varying filter excited with white noise source for unvoiced speech segments, or a series of pulses separated by the pitch period for vocalized speech. Information sent to the decoder includes filter specification, a voiced/unvoiced flag, the necessary variance of the excitation signal, and the pitch period for voiced speech. This information is continually updated every 10ms to 20ms, following the non-stationary nature of speech.

Vocoders operate at 2.4kbps or less and produce acceptable but far from natural speech. Increasing the bit rate much beyond 2.4kbps is not possible due to limitations in the coder's performance and the simplified source signal model. Vocoders are typically found in military applications for which a very low bit rate is needed to support signal encryption.

Transcoders

Transcoders translate digitized voice from one CODEC to another. Since the various CODECs are not compatible with each other, transcoders are used to translate from one CODEC region to another. Transcoders are important in conference calling when the participants are not using the same CODEC.

DSP Provisioning

Digital Signaling Processor (DSP) provisioning is easily overlooked in the rush to deploy VoXX solutions. A DSP translates voice and fax signals into VoIP data streams. The number of conversions a DSP can perform is based on which CODEC complexity is being used. Cisco supports medium and high CODEC complexity.

- **Medium complexity** G.711 (a-law and µ-law), G.726, G.729a, G.729ab, and Fax-relay
- **High-complexity** G.728, G.723, G.729, G.729b, and Fax-relay

Cisco's voice-enabled routers currently support G.711, G.726, G.728, G.729, G.729a, and G.723.1 encoding schemes. These CODEC compression algorithms convert the voice signals into packets ranging in size from 64K to 5.3K. The level of complexity, which is affected by the algorithm used by the compression CODEC, determines the number of calls a DSP can process. By using medium complexity, each DSP can process four calls, whereas with high complexity, only two calls can be processed per DSP. Compression methods will affect the bit rate and quality of the call.

The quality of speech generated using analog-to-digital encoding is subjective. To help quantify the quality of a given technique, the mean opinion score (MOS) scale was developed. To compile the MOS numbers, listeners listen to various speech patterns sent through each compression technique. The test listeners then rate the quality of the sound on a scale of 1 to 5, with 5 being the best. The results are averaged to produce the MOS.

Table 9.3 includes the current International Telecommunications Union (ITU) encoding standard compression techniques and each technique's bit rate, MOS, coding delay, and the processing power required for compression.

Table 9.3 Voice Encoding and MOS Ratings

Encoding	ITU-T Standard	Bit Rate (Kbps)	MOS Score	MIPS	Frame Size (msec)	Coding Delay (msec)
PCM	G.711	64	4.1	.34	.125	.75
ACELP	G.723.1	5.3	3.65	16	30	30
MP-MLQ	G.723.1	6.3	3.9	16	30	30
ADPCM	G.726	32	3.85	14	.125	1
LD-CELP	G.728	16	3.61	33	.625	3-5
CS-ACELP	G.729	8	3.92	20	10	10
CS-ACELP	G.729a	8	3.7	10.5	10	10

Cisco voice DSP modules are 72-pin single inline memory modules (SIMMs), and are used on a variety of router and switch platforms. A DSP farm is a pool or group of DSP SIMMs located in Cisco switch and router modules. DSP provisioning is the process of allocating DSP resources for Cisco CallManager clusters to provide hardware conferencing and transcoding functions. CallManager also supports software-based conferencing and transcoding. To aid planning of DSP resources and provisioning, you must consider all the applications and users that will be communicating with G.711 applications, such as voice messaging and interactive voice response (IVR) packages and IP Wide Area Network (WAN) conferencing.

PCM uses the most bandwidth and least processing power, yet receives the best MOS rating. These factors have made PCM inexpensive to deploy and highly effective in transporting voice traffic over long distance. By contrast, CS-ACELP provides significant bandwidth savings at the expense of increased processing requirements, increased latency, and a lower MOS rating.

Analog Signaling

Signaling refers to the specific signals transmitted over telephone circuits to pass line control information, user data, and voice conversations. Dial pulse (DP) and dual-tone multifrequency (DTMF) are the address-signaling methods implemented from telephone to switch in the telephone network. Earth and magnet (E&M) signaling is the most commonly utilized method of analog trunking (described in more detail later in the chapter). Start dial supervision protocols define how the equipment seizes an E&M trunk and passes address signaling information. The main start dial signaling protocols used on an E&M circuit are loop and ground start signaling.

Analog signals are continuous varying electrical signals with amplitude, frequency, bandwidth, phase, and period characteristics. *Amplitude* measures the loudness of the signal in decibels, as known as the level of the signal. Signal level is usually expressed in terms of the power the signal delivers to the data load, as shown:

$Pload = es^{2/Z}$

where

Pload = Power in watts

es = Signal level in volts

Z = Independence in ohms

Each telephone in the United States uses a single pair of copper wires with an impedance of 400 ohms. *Impedance* in an AC circuit is similar to resistance in a direct current (DC) circuit. Signal level in telephone circuits is measured in terms of 1 milliwatt of power to the load. If *Pload* = 1 milliwatt (0.001 watt) and $Z = 400$ ohms, then:

$1\text{mW} = es^{2/400\ \text{ohms}}$

$400 \times 1 \times 10^{-3} = es^2$

$0.4 = es^2$

$0.633 = es$

A signal level of .633 volts applied across 400 ohms of resistance produces 1 milliwatt of power. Too much power on the line can cause *crosstalk*, where a single voice signal to interfere with other conversations traveling on the same wires in close proximity. *Attenuation* is the reverse of this problem—a dissipation of power on a line during a call as the signal travels.

Frequency is the number of vibrations per second, and is typically diagrammed as a sine wave; each complete wave is a *cycle*. The human ear can hear frequencies ranging from 20Hz to 15,000Hz. Speech has a frequency ranging from 300Hz to 15,000Hz. The PSTN supporting voice transmission operates in the 300Hz to 3300Hz frequency range.

Bandwidth is the difference between the upper-level and lower-level frequencies. All transmission media have limited frequency bandwidth. These limitations are due to the physical properties of the medium or artificial limitations placed on the medium to prevent crosstalk or interference from other signal sources. Telephone signal bandwidth may be calculated by subtracting the lower frequency range from the upper frequency range. The result will be typical telephone bandwidth.

For example, to calculate telephone bandwidth, we would use this equation:

3300Hz – 300Hz = 3000Hz

Claude Shannon developed a formula to calculate the maximum capacity of a transmission channel, limited by bandwidth and random noise:

$C = W \times \text{Log}_2[1 + (S/N)]$ bits per second

where

C = Capacity

S = Power of the signal in watts through the channel

N = Power of the noise in watts out of the channel

W = Bandwidth of the channel in Hertz

Using this formula, we can calculate the "theoretical" limit to binary transmission on a single channel. This is thought of as a theoretical limit due to the formula's inability to incorporate other significant real-world variables such as transmission medium characteristics, distance, and software and hardware enhancements. This formula should be used only as a rough estimate of the capacity of the designated channel due to the variables not taken into account by Shannon's formula. Let's take a look at an example. Given:

S = .0001 watts

W = 3000 Hertz

N = .0000004 watts

3000 x Log_2[1 + (.0001/.0000004) = 24,000 bits per second

The PSTN can use frequencies as high as 4000Hz but uses only up to 3000Hz to provide a buffer or guard band to eliminate interference from other signals. *Signal phase* is the relative position of the sine wave measured in degrees. A *phase shift* occurs when a sine wave breaks in the middle of its phase and starts its cycle again. Phase shifts are used more frequently in data-encoding algorithms for data transmission than for voice transmission. A *period* is the time a signal takes to complete one cycle. PSTN uses analog-switched lines to provide voice communications. Data communication over analog lines has limited transmission speed because of the narrow bandwidth of voice lines.

Noise on a line can degrade call quality. Noise originating from outside the system is inversely proportional to the frequency and directly proportional to the wavelength. In other words, at a low frequency such as 300KHz, atmospheric and electrical noise is much more severe than at a high frequency like 700MHz. Noise generated inside wireless receivers, known as *internal noise*, is less dependent on frequency. Engineers are more concerned about internal noise at high frequencies than at low frequencies because the less external noise there is, the more significant the internal noise becomes.

E&M Signaling

Ear and mouth or, more correctly, *earth and magnet* (E&M) signaling is the most prevalent method of providing analog trunking and inter-PBX tie line trunking. The *earth* portion represents electrical ground; the *magnet* portion represents the electromagnet used to generate tone in the telephone handset. E&M signaling provides signaling states indicating on-hook and off-hook conditions, decreasing the likelihood of *glare*, where a two-way trunk is seized simultaneously at both ends.

E&M signaling is used for two-way switch-to-switch or switch-to-network connections across long-haul inter-CO and short-haul toll trunks. E&M uses an extra pair of wires in the local and distant end trunk lines with one designated as the *E lead* and one designated as the *M lead*. The E lead receives signals and the M lead transmits signals.

E&M signaling defines a signaling side (PBX) and a trunking side (Telco, channel bank, or voice router) for each connection. The signaling side sends its on-hook/off-hook indicators over the M lead, and the trunking side sends its on-hook/off-hook indicators over the E lead.

There are five different types of E&M signaling, each providing a different method to indicate on-hook and off-hook conditions between the PBX and the CO switch. E&M signaling is supported in both two- and four-wire implementations. Cisco currently supports four of the five E&M signaling types in its VoIP products. All except Type IV are supported by Cisco.

- **Type I** Common in the United States. During inactivity, the E lead is open and M lead is connected to ground. A PBX indicates an off-hook condition by connecting the M lead to the battery. The router or CO side indicates an off-hook condition by connecting the E lead to ground. Type I is a two-wire signaling scheme. It uses a separate wire for the E and a separate wire for the M; signaling information comes in on the E and goes out on the M.
- **Type II** Used in the United States. During inactivity, both the E and M leads are open. A PBX indicates an off-hook condition by connecting the M lead to the signaling battery (SB) lead, which is connected to the battery at the CO side. The router or CO side indicates an off-hook condition by connecting the E lead to signal ground (SG), which is connected ground at the PBX side. Type II signaling is symmetrical and allows for signaling nodes to be connected back-to-back using a crossover cable. Type II is a four-wire signaling scheme. It has a wire for the E, a wire for the M, a wire for SG, and a wire for SB. There is no common ground for the signaling; it is created on an ad hoc basis by the E and M return paths riding on the SG and SB wires, respectively.
- **Type III** Type III is similar to Type II, except that it provides a common ground. Type III is not commonly used. During inactivity, the E lead is open and the M lead is grounded by connecting it to the SG lead from the CO. A PBX indicates an off-hook condition by disconnecting the M lead from the SG lead and connecting it to the SB lead from the CO. The router or CO side indicates an off-hook condition by connecting the E lead to ground.
- **Type IV** This signaling type is not currently supported by Cisco.
- **Type V** Used in the United States and common in Europe. During inactivity, both the E and M leads are open. A PBX indicates an off-hook condition by connecting the M lead to ground. The router or CO side indicates an off-hook condition by connecting the E lead to ground. Type V signaling is symmetrical and allows for back-to-back connections using a crossover cable. Type V is similar to Type I in that it is a two-wire signaling scheme. Type V has a common ground on its SG wire.

E&M uses six to eight pins on an RJ-48 jack, depending on the type of E&M signaling used. Off-hook and incoming calls are signaled using one of the five types of E&M signaling. E&M interfaces typically don't use a dial tone but instead use immediate-start, wink-start, or delay-start signaling to indicate an off-hook state or to indicate incoming calls.

Signaling rate is the number of times per second a signal on a circuit changes amplitude, frequency, or phase. *Tone signaling* uses single-frequency or multiple-frequency tones to indicate control and line status. To indicate a functioning line in the United States, the CO sends a continuous tone called a *dial tone* by combining a 350Hz tone with a 440Hz tone. To indicate a busy signal or off-hook condition, the CO sends a 480Hz tone combined with a 620Hz tone in intermittent half-second increments. If the receiver remains off-hook for more than a few minutes, the busy signal changes to a much louder 400Hz, 2060Hz, 2450Hz, and 2600Hz combination tone. Table 9.4 shows call progress tones.

Table 9.4 Call Progress Tones

Tone	Frequency	On Time	Off Time
Dial	350 + 440	Continuous	N/A
Busy	480 + 620	0.5 seconds	0.5 seconds
Normal ringback	440 + 480	2 seconds	4 seconds
PBX ringback	440 + 480	1 seconds	3 seconds
Toll congestion	480 + 620	0.2 seconds	0.3 seconds
Local call reorder	480 + 620	0.3 seconds	0.2 seconds
Receiver off-hook	1400 + 2060 + 2450 + 2600	0.1 seconds	0.1 seconds
Number doesn't exist	200 to 400	Continuous frequency modulated at 1Hz	N/A

COs commonly use either in-band or out-of-band tone signaling to indicate signal status. In-band signaling most commonly uses a 2600Hz tone; out-of-band signaling uses a 3700Hz tone. E&M signals use a single-frequency tone for transmission on carrier-based systems. A tone indicates on-hook; a lack of tone indicates off-hook. If multifrequency tone signaling is used, frequencies are used in pairs between toll facilities to indicate numbers 0 through 9 and additional control functions. Multifrequency tones include 700Hz, 900Hz, 1100Hz, 1300Hz, 1500Hz, and 1700Hz.

Analog Loop and Ground Start

There are two basic methods for detecting subscriber off-hook and initiating a series called *busy notification* or billing tasks: loop start lines and ground start lines. *Loop start lines* signal off-hook by completing a circuit at the telephone. When the subscriber lifts the handset, current flows from the loop-side battery through the closed switchhook contacts and energizes the line relay. A set of line relay contacts close, signaling that the subscriber desires service. A CO switch called a *line finder* provides dial tone and connects the subscriber into CO switching equipment and onto an available circuit.

Used on local loops to connect PBXs to the CO, *ground start lines* are, in effect, partially operational at all times. Current flows through one-half the line relay as a result of grounding the ringside path. When a PBX needs connectivity, the CO line finder provides dial tone and connectivity to CO switching equipment. When a dial tone is detected, the ground start contact is opened and the remainder of the line is instantly activated.

Dial-Pulse Signaling

Two basic methods of address signaling are used to place a telephone call: older and fast-fading dial pulseand the more popular DTMF. Since DP continues to be on its way out, we will not discuss its details.

Dual-Tone Multifrequency (AKA Touch Tone)

DTMF uses an audible two-tone signal to indicate a single number. Two audible tones are placed on the line to indicate the key pressed. For instance, if you dial the number 1, the higher-frequency tone placed on the line will be 1209MHz, whereas the lower-frequency tone associated with the number 1 will be 697MHz, as referenced in Table 9.5.

Table 9.5 DTMF Tones

		High	Frequency	Tones	
		1209MHz	**1336MHz**	**1477MHz**	**1633MHz**
Low	**697MHz**	1	2	3	A
Frequency	**770MHz**	4	5	6	B
Tones	**852MHz**	7	8	9	C
	941MHz	*	0	#	D

Telephone company switches decode the signals and make the desired connection, resulting in higher accuracy, with much quicker call setup and connection time. Using DTMF, a telephone system can recognize a single digit tone in 50 milliseconds or less with a typical between-digit wait time of another 50 milliseconds or less. The maximum time needed to process a single DTMF digit is 100 milliseconds, or approximately 1/10 of a second.

While analog telephony remains a force to be reckoned with, digital alternatives have made their inroads, especially at the CO level.

Digital Transmission Techniques and Formats

Digital signals are binary in nature, and are either on or off. These states are very precise, and the signal can be regenerated with accuracy regardless of noise and interference. Digital transmission breaks data down into a series of 0s and 1s; all data and voice traffic is expressed as 0s and 1s. While digital systems are not impervious to noise and static, they can detect and recover better than analog. This is made possible by the absolute values transmitted on the wire. Figure 9.5 illustrates a digital waveform.

Figure 9.5 The Digital Waveform

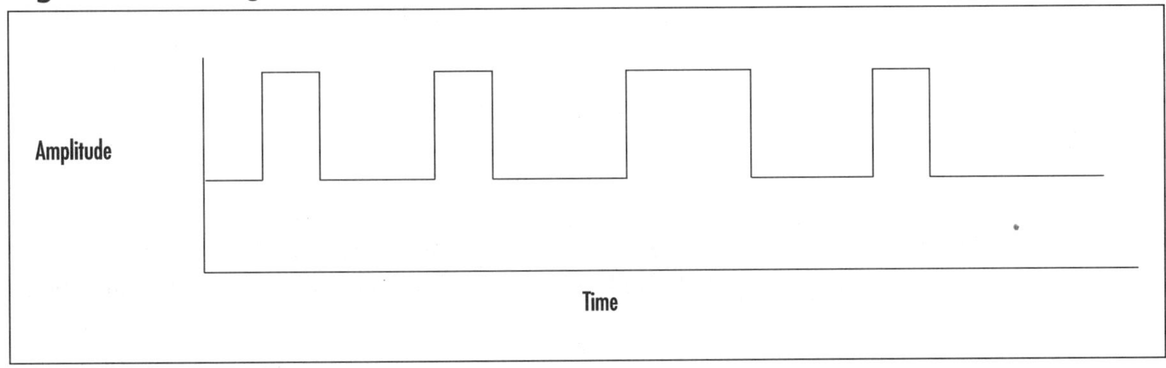

Digital transmission is more robust and of better quality than analog, though more bandwidth (but less expense) is required. Digital systems in telephony can take advantage of this binary state and augment communications with additional features that are not available in analog systems, including compression. This allows speech to be sent in fewer bits than in analog format. The data stream can actually be stopped when a party stops speaking. This can greatly increase the volume of connections that can concurrently occur in the network.

Time division multiplexing (TDM), a digital transmission technique, and integrated services digital network (ISDN) signaling are the most common elements of a digital communications network. The most widely used digital transmission formats are provided by the T-carrier system and the E-carrier system.

Time-Division Multiplexing

Time-division multiplexing is a digital transmission technique for carrying multiple voice, data, or video signals simultaneously over a single carrier line by interleaving bits of each signal in a time-synchronized string.

TDM converts all signals to a digital format, reducing any signal to a unique bit stream of 1s and 0s. With voice, for example, an analog signal in the range of 300Hz to 3,400Hz bandwidth is converted to a 64,000bps digital channel. Twenty-four such 64Kb channels are then multiplexed together in a T-1 at great speed, transmitting all voice and data in a "string." In effect, information from up to 24 different sources is placed on a single digital channel.

The "trunk" used to carry a digital transmission in North America is called T-1, with the electrical interface and framing defined in ANSI T-1.403. A T-1 line can carry 24 fixed voice and data channels, digitized at 64Kb, for an aggregate carrying capacity of 1.544Mb. Outside North America, the trunk used to carry a digital transmission is called an E-1, with the electrical interface and framing defined in ITU-T G.703 and G.704. An E-1 line can carry 30 fixed voice and data channels, digitized at 64Kb, for an aggregate carrying capacity of 2.048Mb.

The standard unit of bandwidth used for all digital transmission is 64Kb. It is derived from the fact that the voltage of an analog signal must be sampled in time to be accurately recreated digitally. Specifically, an analog signal is sampled at 256 different voltage levels, 8000 times a second. The resulting signal is then transmitted on a pair of twisted wires as a 64Kb digital bit stream. TDM establishes dedicated, point-to-point bandwidth between a sender and receiver to support multiple communications simultaneously across a WAN.

Integrated Services Digital Network Signaling

ISDN technology is standardized according to the ITU. These recommendations describe the protocols and architecture to implement a worldwide digital communications network. Generally, ISDN networks extend from the local telephone exchange to the remote user and include all the telecommunications and switching equipment in between. ISDN was developed to transport digital services across copper wiring originally intended to carry analog signals only.

The high throughput offered by ISDN, rapid call setup, and the high level of accuracy inherent to digital transmission are its main attractions. ISDN makes better use of carrier resources by doubling the bandwidth potential of existing wiring to subscribers' homes and businesses (the local loop) and reducing the maintenance costs that are associated with analog carrier equipment.

Voice and data are carried by bearer channels (known as *B channels*) occupying a bandwidth of 64Kb, though some switches limit this to 56Kb. A data channel (*D channel*) handles signaling at 16Kb or 64Kb, depending on the service type. There are two types of ISDN service: Basic Rate Interface (BRI) and Primary Rate Interface (PRI). BRI consists of two 64Kb B channels and one 16Kb D channel, for a total of 144Kb. In North America, a PRI consists of 23 64Kb B channels and one 64Kb D channel and gives total available bandwidth of 1.544Mb. In Europe and other parts of the world, an E-1 provides 31 64Kb B channels and one 64Kb D channel, providing a total aggregate bandwidth of 2.048Mb.

ISDN Reference Points

ISDN devices include terminals, terminal adapters (TAs), network-termination devices, line-termination equipment, and exchange-termination equipment.

- **Terminal equipment type 1 (TE-1)** Specialized ISDN terminals that.connect to the ISDN network through a four-wire, twisted-pair digital link.
- **Terminal equipment type 2 (TE2)** Non-ISDN terminals, such as DTEs that predate the ISDN standards that connect to the ISDN network through a TA.
- **Terminal Adapter (TA)** Either a standalone device or a board inside the TE2.
- **Network termination type 1 (NT-1)** Connects the four-wire subscriber wiring to the conventional two-wire local loop. North America: Customer premises equipment (CPE) device; elsewhere, provided by carrier.
- **Network termination type 2 (NT2)** Connects the four-wire subscriber wiring to the conventional two-wire local loop. Found in digital PBXs and that performs Layer 2 and 3 protocol functions and concentration services.

ISDN specifies a number of reference points that define logical interfaces between functional groups; such as TAs and NT-1s. ISDN reference points include the following and are illustrated in Figure 9.6.

- **R** between non-ISDN equipment and a TA.
- **S** between user terminals and the NT2.
- **T** between NT-1 and NT2 devices.
- **U** between NT-1 devices and line-termination equipment in the carrier network. Relevant only in North America, where the NT-1 function is not provided by the carrier network.

Figure 9.6 ISDN Reference Points

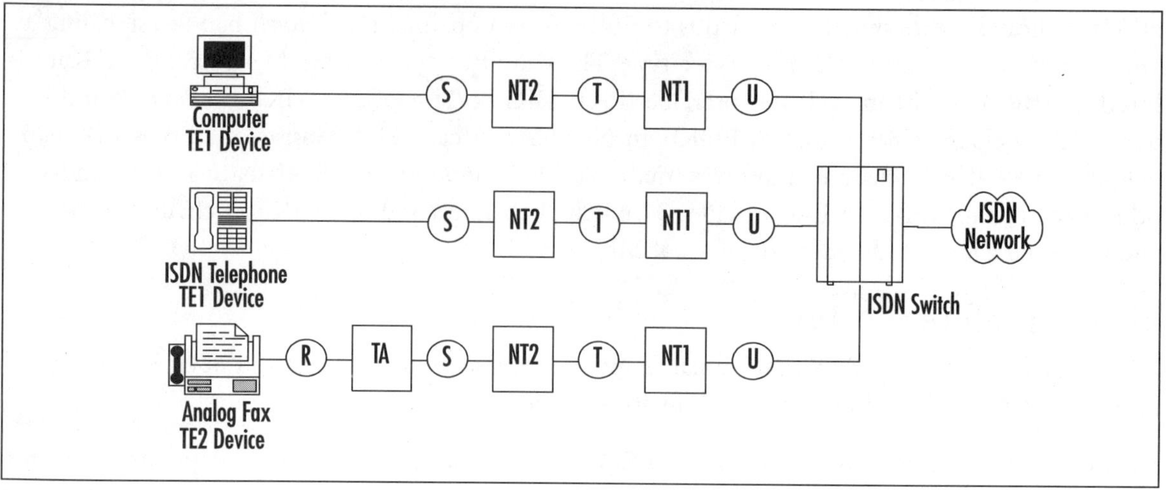

Call Control Signaling

Analog transmission signaling utilizes *Channel Associated Signaling (CAS)*. With the advent of digital transmission, Common Channel Signaling (CCS) was developed, and is the current favorite for call control signaling.

Channel Associated Signaling

CAS was the only form of automatic signaling until 1976, when CCS was introduced. Although CAS is still used mostly in developing countries, CCS is gradually replacing it. There are two main characteristics to CAS that differentiate it from CCS:

- CAS signaling is mainly analog.
- CAS signals travel on different paths on the same network that carries voice and data services, rather than on a separate network.

CAS is also referred to as *in-band signaling* because signaling information is placed within the actual circuit that is used to carry voice.

Common Channel Signaling

CCS was developed as an alternative form of call control signaling for trunks, where individual trunks do not carry signaling information. Instead, a signaling network, consisting of signaling data links (SDLs) and signal transfer points (STPs), transfers digital signaling messages between the exchanges. The channel used for CCS does not carry user information. CCS originally evolved from System No. 6 to System No. 7.

Signaling System 7

Signaling System 7 (SS7) protocols define how PSTN nodes exchange information over a digital signaling network for call setup, routing, and control. The ITU definition of SS7 allows for national variants such as the American National Standards Institute (ANSI) and Bell Communications Research (Telecordia Technologies) standards that are specific to North America and Europe.

SS7 defines the architecture, network elements, interfaces, protocols, and management procedures for transporting control information between switches, and between switches and databases. The North American version is sometimes called Common Channel Signaling 7 (CCS7).

Signaling across the PSTN is accomplished by two methods: *in-band signaling,* which sends information in the voice band or voice channel, and *out-of-band signaling*, which uses a separate 64Kb data channel. SS7 is an out-of-band signaling protocol that uses separate data links to support packet signaling between switches and databases (for network services such as the 800 service) and is the preferred signaling protocol of the past dozen years or so.

SS7 can deliver additional call-related information across the network, such as calling party identification (CPID). If CPID is delivered to the destination office, enhanced call features such as call forwarding, calling party name and number display, and three-way calling are possible. SS7 establishes and terminates calls faster than CAS, and utilizes the network more efficiently. Expensive long-haul trunks are no longer tied up during call setup.

Signaling Points

Each signaling point in the SS7 network is uniquely identified by a numeric point code. Point codes are carried in signaling messages between signaling points to identify the source and destination of each message. Each signaling point uses a routing table to select the appropriate path for each message.

There are three kinds of signaling points in the SS7 network:

- **Service switching point (SSP)** Switches equipped with SS7 hardware, software, and signaling links (DMS-100, 5ESS, GTD-5, AXE, or EWSD) that originate, terminate, or tandem calls. Sends signaling messages to other SSPs to set up, manage, and release voice circuits required to complete a call. An SSP may also send a query to a centralized database (SCP) to route a call.
- **Signal transfer point (STP)** High-speed, ultra-reliable, special-purpose packet switches for signaling messages in the SS7 network. Network traffic between signaling points may be routed via STPs. Network switches and SCPs connect directly to STPs for message routing. An STP routes each incoming message to an outgoing signaling link based on routing information contained in the SS7 message. There is no need for direct links between signaling points.
- **Service control point (SCP)** Highly reliable computer and database systems that run service logic programs (SLP) to provide customer services through SSPs. Centralized databases form the basis for *advanced intelligent networks (AINs).* SLPs instruct the SSP how to proceed with processing the call.

Signaling Links

All SS7 signaling points are interconnected via signaling data links. SS7 messages are exchanged between network elements over 56Kb or 64Kb bi-directional channels called *signaling links*. Signaling links are logically organized by link type (A through F) according to their use in the SS7 signaling network, as illustrated in Figure 9.7.

Figure 9.7 SS7 Signaling Links

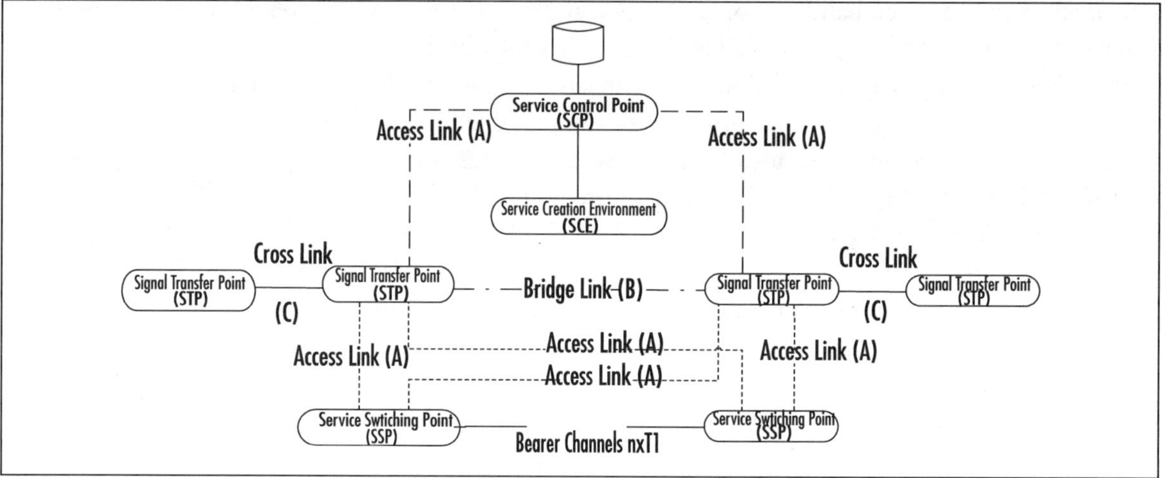

Types A through F, according to their use in the SS7 signaling network are described here:

- **Access (A) link** Between the SSP and the STP; and the SCP and STP to provide access to the network and to databases through the STP.
- **Bridge (B) link** Connect mated STPs to other mated STPs at the same hierarchical level. Bridge links are deployed in a quad fashion.
- **Cross (C) link** Connect an STP to its mate STP in pairs to maintain redundancy in the network. Normal SS7 traffic is not routed over these links except when congestion on the network exists.
- **Diagonal (D) links** Connect mated STP pairs at a primary hierarchical level to STP pair at a secondary hierarchical level. Not all networks use a hierarchical network architecture.
- **Extended (E) link.** Connect to remote STP pairs from an SSP. The SSP connects to its home STP pair. May be connected to a remote STP pair as well, using E links for diversity.
- **Fully associated (F) link** Used when a large amount of traffic exists between two SSPs or when an SSP cannot be connected directly to an STP. Allow SSPs to use the SS7 protocol and access SS7 databases when it's not economical to provide a direct connection to an STP pair.

SS7 Protocol Stack

The SS7 protocol stack consists of the Message Transfer Part (MTP), the Signaling Connection and Control Part (SCCP), and the Transaction Capabilities Application Part (TCAP). North American networks use the ISDN (ISUP), whereas European networks use the Telephony User Part (TUP). The SS7 protocol elements as dictated by the International Organization for Standardization (ISO) are depicted in Figure 9.8.

Figure 9.8 SS7 Protocol Stack

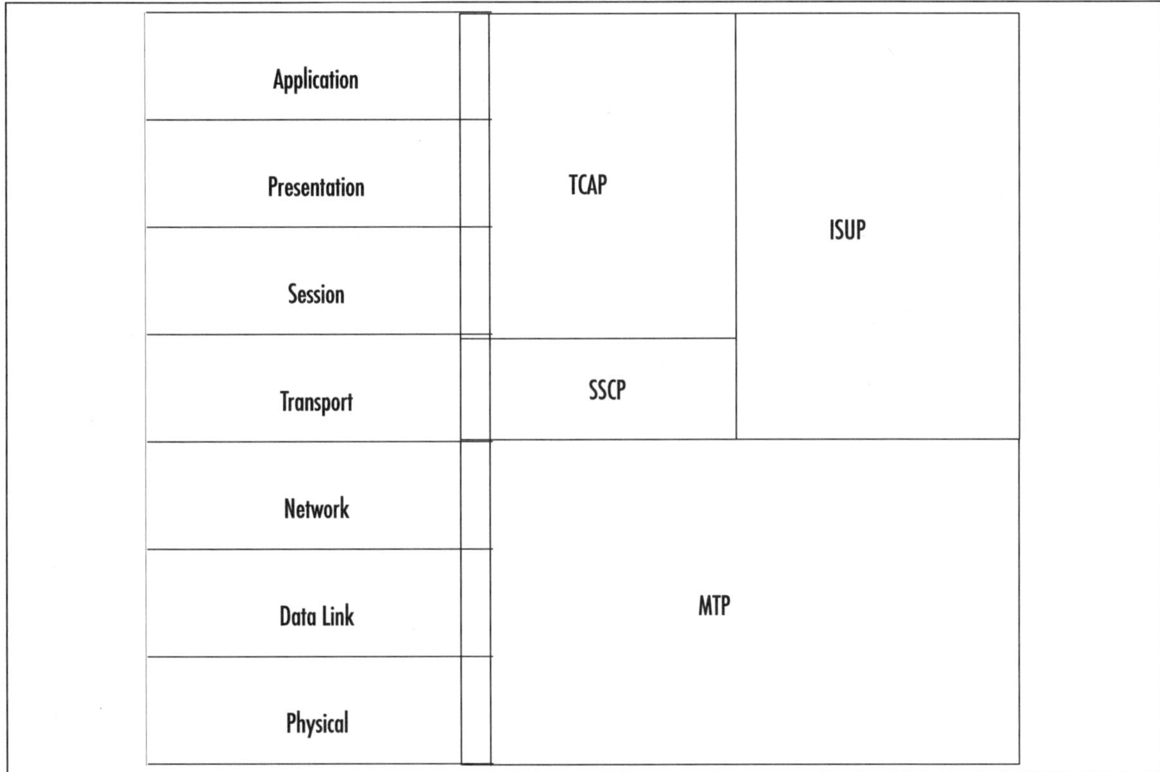

Each layer of the SS7 protocol (the right hand side of diagram shown in Figure 9.8) is described in the following section.

The Message Transfer Part

The MTP is divided into three levels.

- **MTP Level 1 (Physical Layer)** Defines the physical, electrical, and functional characteristics of the digital signaling link. Physical interfaces defined include E-1 (2048kbps; 32 64kbps channels), DS-1 (1544kbps; 24 64kbps channels), V.35 (64kbps), DS-0 (64kbps), and DS-0A (56kbps).
- **MTP Level 2 (Data Link)** Provides the network with sequenced delivery of all SS7 message packets. Concerned only with the transmission of data from one node to the next, not to its final destination in the network. Sequential numbering is used to deter-

mine if any messages have been lost during transmission. SS7 uses CRC-16 error checking.

- **MTP Level 3 (Network Layer)** Routes messages between signaling points and controls traffic when congestion occurs using its mechanisms for flow control and congestion control and procedures for changeover and changeback to enhance reliability.

The ISDN User Part

The ISUP establishes, manages, and releases trunk circuits that carry voice and data between terminating line exchanges (calling party and a called party). ISUP is used for both ISDN and non-ISDN calls. ISUP supports ISDN supplementary voice services and interoperates with Q.921 and Q.931. ISUP supports both basic bearer services and supplementary services for voice and non-voice applications, as well as circuit-switched telephone service and data services. ANSI adopted ISUP to replace the TUP, which does not support data transmission or digital circuits.

Broadband-ISUP (B-ISUP) supports Frame Relay and asynchronous transfer mode (ATM). The most significant difference between the ISUP and the B-ISUP protocols is in the circuit assignment and the type of circuits supported. ATM and broadband ISDN circuits are virtual circuits rather than physical circuits. The network must assign and maintain these virtual circuits. Because of the number of circuits available in broadband networks, a new circuit-numbering convention was adopted.

The Transaction Capabilities Application Part

The TCAP requests processing of an operation at a remote node, and defines the information flow to control the operation and the reporting of its result. Operations and their results are carried out within a *dialogue* or a *transaction*. The operations and their results are conveyed in information elements known as *components*. TCAP stores components for transmission received form the higher layers until a dialogue-handling information element is received, at which time all stored components are formatted into a single TCAP message and sent through SCCP to the peer TCAP. A network entity does not have to be a switch.

The Signaling Connection and Control Part

The SCCP supports applications that require enhanced transport capabilities. SCCP routes messages through the network using intermediate nodes as routers without knowing the individual addresses of the intermediate nodes.

The number of MTP users is limited to 16 (0 through 15). The MTP at any node is concerned only with passing the message to the next node so it only uses the SCPs of the adjacent nodes. SCCP provides for up to 255 users by employing subsystem numbers. This enhancement allows the SCCP to provide end-to-end routing as it makes use of all the SCPs for all locations in the network, whether linked to its local node or not.

SCCP provides users with four service classes.

- **Class 0** Basic connectionless service.
- **Class 1** Connectionless service with sequence control.

- **Class 2** Basic connection-oriented service.
- **Class 3** Connection-oriented service with flow control.

The Telephone User Part

The TUP is an analog protocol that performs basic telephone call connects and disconnects. It has been replaced by ISUP but is still used in some parts of the world, such as China. The TUP provides conventional PSTN telephony services across the SS7 network.

A workhorse of telephony that implements certain of the concepts that we have talked about is a private branch exchange. For most people, the PBX is "the" telephone network.

Inside the Private Branch eXchange

A PBX consists of hardware and software that emulates the PSTN within an organization, and provides paths into the PSTN. It is important to remember that voice services are based on TDM, the basis for most connections. A DS-0 is a single voice digital channel of traditional voice bandwidth—8Hz at 8 bits per sample. These systems can be categorized into four primary areas, with each area containing one or more functions:

- Extension termination
- Trunk termination
- System logic and call processing
- Switching

These functions are illustrated in Figure 9.9 and described in greater detail in the next section.

Figure 9.9 The Basic Functions of a PBX

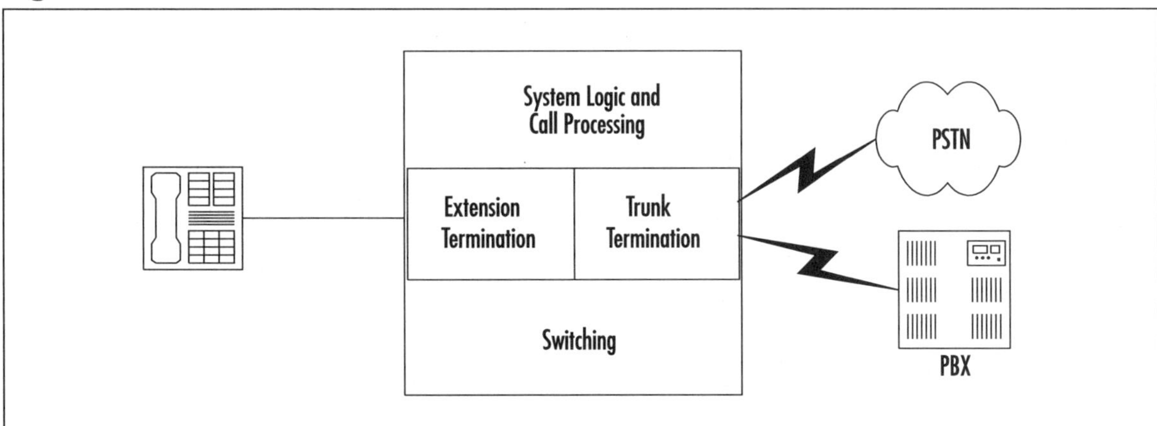

Extension Termination

Resources on the private side of the PBX are called *extensions*, and have a direct one-for-one connection to a port on the PBX. While typically digital, there are analog extensions. The PBX must also provide these extensions with dial tone generation, just as the PSTN switch provides for non-PBX attached phones. These interfaces also pass the DTMF tones to the call-processing engine.

Trunk Termination

Most PBX systems are connected by at least one T-1 circuit to either the PSTN or another PBX. A trunk is a T-1 or other circuit that can carry multiple channels, or TDM data stream. A T-1 can support up to 24 voice connections, while E-1 allows 30 user channels. *Tie lines* are trunks that connect PBXs to each other.

Call Processing and System Logic

Dial plans compare DTMF tones to route calls along paths configured on the PBX. These tones represent the numeric values of the buttons, in addition to the asterisk (*) and pound (#) keys. This addressing is used to route calls.

Switching

Switching maps a channel on one interface to a channel on another interface. This may involve linking a DS-0 to a DS-1 (T-1), or an FXS port to a T-1 trunk on another PBX. The logic that decides which path to be taken is part of the call processing function. Once established, however, the switching of these TDM packets is transparent to the processor until the call is torn down.

PBX Terminology

The following is a list of terms that you should be comfortable using when working with PBXs.

- **T-1** 24 voice channels (DS-0s), with total bandwidth of 1.544 Mbps.
- **ISDN PRI – T-1** Uses T-1 framing, but uses one DS-0 for upper layer signaling (23 voice channels).
- **E-1** European standard. 2.048 Mbps (32 voice channels).
- **ISDN PRI – E-1** Uses two channels for signaling and framing, (30 voice channels).
- **E&M** Analog signaling method. Used for trunk or tie lines between switches (network-to-network), and for connections to voice mail or legacy PBX systems.
- **Foreign Exchange Station** Link between the switch and an extension. Sometimes used to describe a connection that services an analog device attached to the PBX.
- **Foreign Exchange Office** Link between the PBX and the central office. It is a analog DS-0 tariffed at a flat-rate.
- **Loop start** Removing the receiver from the hook closes a circuit and creates a loop, allowing connections.
- **Ground start** Earth ground is needed to complete the loop and allow connectivity.
- **Central office** Local telephone company termination point for all numbers in a given area, and commonly connects to PBXs via T-1s.

- **Coordinated Dial Plans (CDP)** Defines numbers on your network and how callers will reach numbers outside your dial plan (for example, a coordinated dial plan may require a nine to be dialed to reach an external number).
- **Call routing** Physical act of routing a call through the network, and processing the call. This is static in PBX systems.
- **Tip-and-Ring** In single pair copper connections, identifies which end supplies the voltage on the wire.
- **Direct Inward Dial (DID)** Establishes a relationship between the extension and a public number. Assigns a block of numbers to a trunk line from the telephone provider to the PBX, and the PBX administrator can route those numbers to related extensions. Figure 9.10 illustrates the logical mapping of number 415-555-1706 to extension 51706. Please note that it is quite common to create five-digit extensions in North America that relate to the assigned DID numbers.

Figure 9.10 Direct Inward Dialing Illustrated

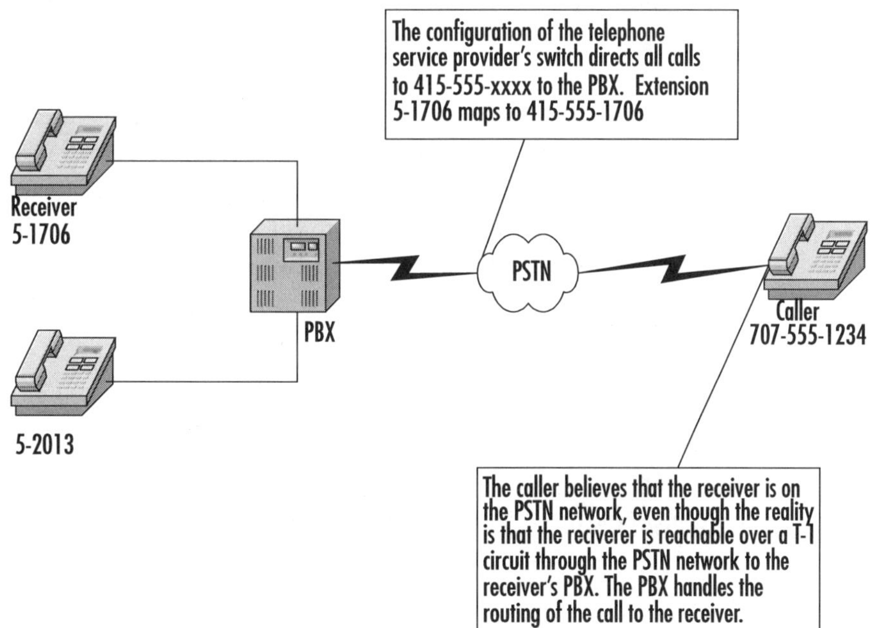

Our discussion so far has focused on traditional means of providing voice telephone service. The information provided thus far will help you to transition to accomplishing the same tasks using IP networks and techniques.

Non-IP Alternatives to Traditional Telephony

The focus of this chapter is the use of IP networks to transport calls of all kinds. However, we would be amiss if we did not briefly cover several viable alternatives that may serve your needs just as well, if not better than, VoIP. To that end, Frame Relay and ATM might be of interest to you for the transport of your voice traffic.

Voice over Frame Relay

Voice over Frame Relay (VoFR) uses Frame Relay networks to carry digitized voice packets. Building a private network to carry voice and data might not be financially feasible for many companies. VoFR does not use IP as voice traffic is actually addressed and encapsulated in Frame Relay frames. VoFR is typically used for site-to-site voice communications. As Frame Relay is a Layer 2 protocol, it is actually faster than VoIP as there is one less layer in the mix.

Frame Relay has been around for several years, and its standards are mature, with stable interoperability. VoFR allows voice to be compressed and transferred across a Frame Relay permanent virtual circuit (PVC).

A gateway router can connect directly to the frame circuit through either a multiflex trunk (MFT) interface or through a digital signal unit (DSU) attached to its serial interface. Using the compression algorithm G729A, you can squeeze voice calls down to about 8Kbps (total with overhead would be about 10.8Kbps). With a 768Kbps circuit and G729A encoding, you could theoretically support 70 concurrent calls.

Most installations require that voice traffic share a PVC with data traffic. Frame relay works on the principle of having a committed information rate that is guaranteed and a port speed that you can burst to, which differs by provider. Any frames that stray into the burst area are tagged and could be dropped.

What happens if the data traffic starts pushing the bandwidth into the burst area? Voice traffic will mix with data traffic, and it could be tagged for discard. Imagine how a conversation might sound if every other second was dropped. Quality of service (QoS) issues are critically important when it comes to packetizing voice. Implementing QoS on VoFR is easier than with other VoIP implementations. If configuration of QoS is not done correctly, you could end up with a very expensive project as everyone starts calling long distance just to have a coherent conversation.

Frame Relay Benefits

Frame Relay offers several benefits:

- Costs are relatively low compared with other types of circuits.
- Once a port is purchased, adding PVCs between two ports is simple and usually inexpensive.
- Can be oversubscribed which allows more bandwidth to be mapped to a port than the port would theoretically allow, though this could have a severe impact on voice traffic.
- It is available just about everywhere.
- It can support a wide range of bandwidth, from 16Kbps up.

When Does Frame Relay Make More Sense?

The single most useful aspect of VoFR lies in taking advantage of existing or low-cost circuits to provide tie-line functionality between PBXs. The header for frame relay takes up only a little more bandwidth. A call that has been compressed using G.729A uses about 8Kbps, and with frame relay overhead, that increases to 10.8Kbps.

With a typical tie-line replacement, this level of compression and bandwidth savings provide much more room for data to travel over the same circuit (Figure 9.11).

Figure 9.11 Bandwidth Savings with VoFR

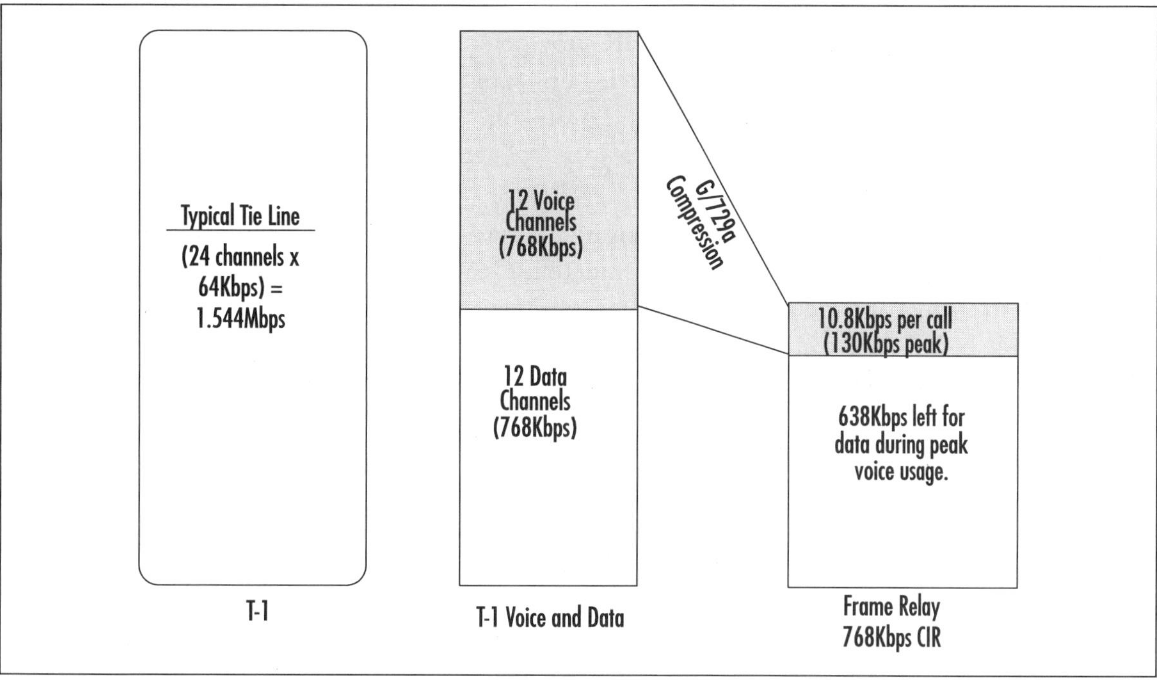

One of the most important things to avoid when packetizing voice is a multiple compressing and decompressing occurrence during a call. Every time the call goes through a CODEC, there is a delay as the call is encoded or decoded which degrades quality. It is important to note that the CODEC used at each end must match. Once the router has converted the bits into an analog waveform, it sends the call out of the appropriate phone port (Figure 9.12).

Figure 9.12 Encoding and Decoding a Voice Call

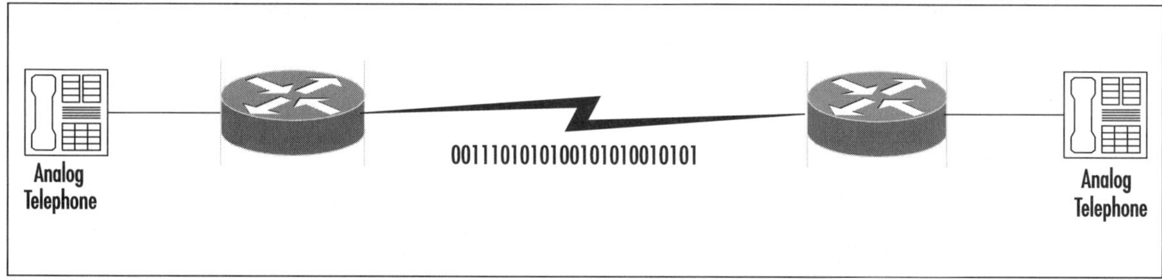

When end-to-end calls are needed across multiple locations, it becomes an opportunity for other Layer 2 solutions such as ATM or point-to-point circuits. VoFR has the edge from an ease-of-implementation and management standpoint as well as for long-term cost savings.

Voice over ATM

Voice over asynchronous transfer mode (VoATM) uses ATM to carry digitized voice packets in fixed, 53-byte cells (5-bytes of header plus 48-bytes of payload). ATM switches are extremely fast, a very high quality of service. ATM offers various classes of service (CoS) such as constant bit rate (CBR) specifically for transporting voice. CBR provides a better quality of service by minimizing time variations in the transmission of voice cells, a phenomenon known as *jitter*. As with VoFR, VoATM is faster than VoIP since it is a Layer 2 protocol.

Where to Use It

ATM will never match gigabit Ethernet when it comes to LAN interconnections, though it can provide true QoS for voice and video. These inherent QoS capabilities allow ATM to outperform IP solutions in many bandwidth-intensive, time-sensitive applications.

VoATM is best used if you already have ATM networks in place, or to interconnect remote offices. The network in Figure 9.13 shows ATM supporting end-to-end calls.

Figure 9.13 An ATM Network Providing End-to-End Calls

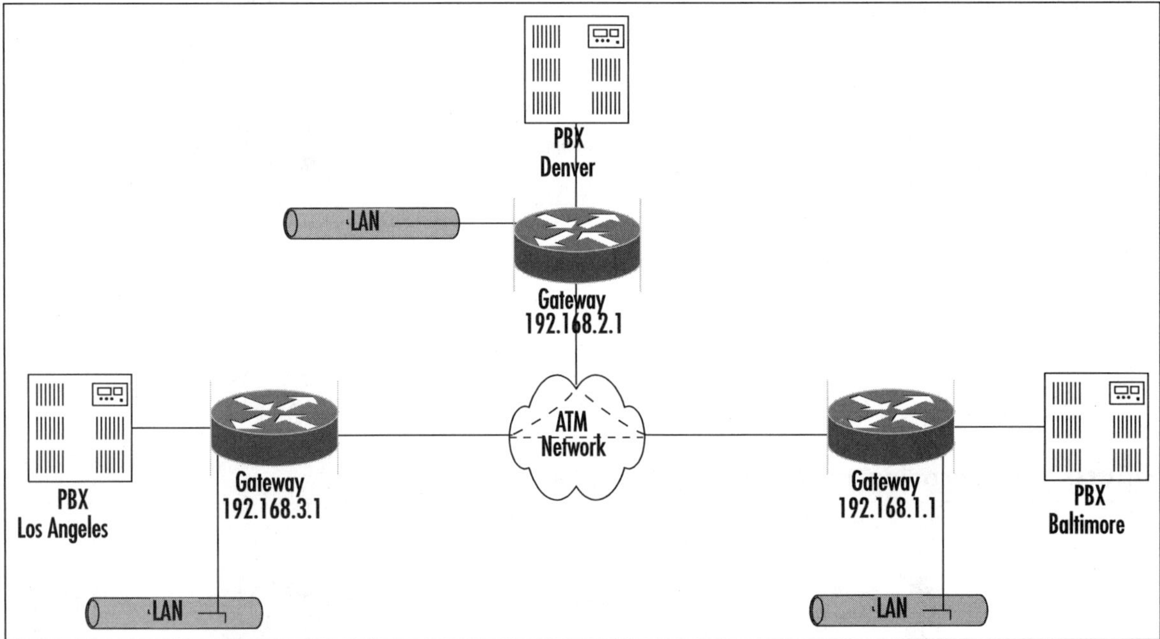

Calls can originate in Baltimore, pass through Denver, and end in Los Angeles without having to encode or decode the call multiple times. ATM QoS features ensure the timely arrival of calls without any degradation in quality. Data and voice are placed in queues that are treated differently throughout the ATM network.

Figure 9.14 illustrates how priority can be given to voice traffic over data traffic. In this example, a CBR is specified for voice traffic, which means that a fixed bit rate is assigned to minimize jitter. The data traffic is relegated to an available bit rate (ABR) queue. The data traffic on the ABR queue does not have a guaranteed bandwidth, but it can be allocated more bandwidth than the voice traffic when bandwidth is available. This type of queuing scheme can satisfy both voice and data traffic within the same network.

Figure 9.14 QoS Queuing with Voice and Data Traffic

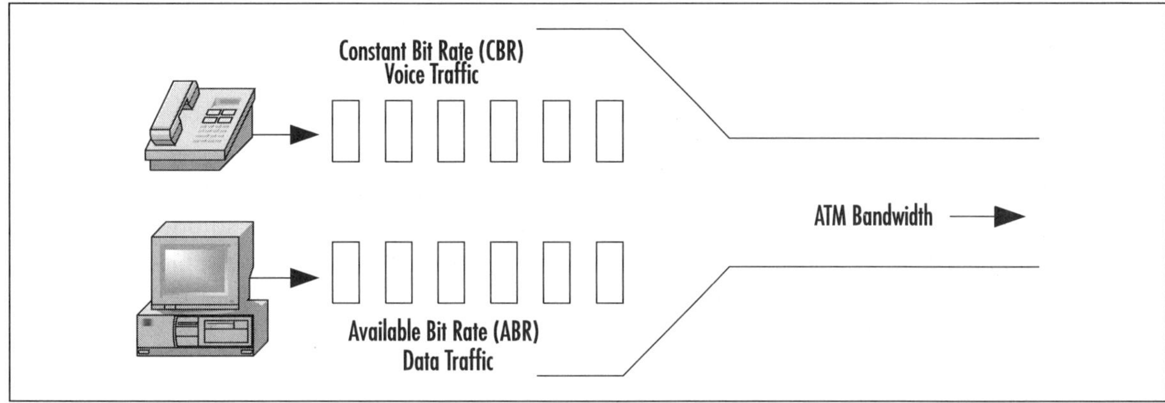

When ATM's QoS measures are used, the tagging information is carried for the life of the cell. As long as the voice call is carried through the ATM network, it can retain its higher QoS tag. ATM is a completely different method of handling data flow.

One characteristic of ATM is that it segments data into *fixed* 53-byte cells. In a frame-based network such as Ethernet, the frame size can vary. This variance causes the switches to have to either wait for the entire frame (also called *store and forward*) or start sending the frame out the destination port as soon as it is received. Because ATM cells are always 53 bytes, the ATM switches know when the end of the cell has been received without an end-of-frame identifier or delimiter. This knowledge allows ATM switches to switch cells very rapidly.

ATM places as much data as possible in a cell, and if there is any space left over, it pads the cell, which potentially wastes space. The same voice call that was discussed in the VoFR section using G.729 for compression now takes up 14.13Kbps of bandwidth. Using G.729 results in voice being segmented into 30-byte payloads. This results in 23 bytes of overhead, almost as much as the payload itself (Figure 9.15). This overhead can consume a lot of bandwidth on slower connections, so it is important to understand the ramifications of using ATM on anything under T-1 speeds.

Figure 9.15 ATM Cell and Potential Overhead

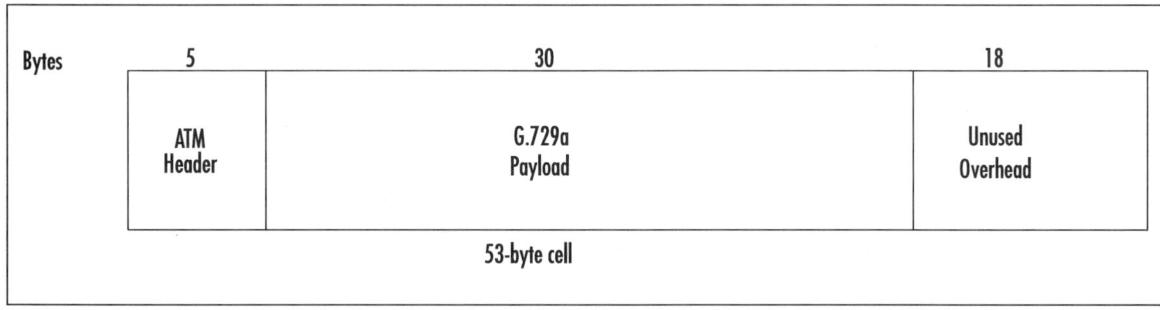

Continuous Bit Rate

ATM provides a CBR service to handle real-time information such as voice. Configuring an ATM link for CBR minimizes variations in time delay or jitter between successive voice cells, providing a high QoS to the end user.

CBR service provides a specific bit rate for voice traffic. There is an unavoidable delay between the transmission and delivery of a voice packet. Although important to minimize that delay, it is also important to minimize the variations in the time delay between successive voice packets. Ideally, each voice packet must arrive on cue, not late and not early.

Costs associated with ATM are still higher than Frame Relay. Equipment costs have come down quite a bit, and in a campus environment, ATM can be a very attractive solution. However, ATM service provider circuits are typically more expensive than Frame Relay circuits. This could make it difficult to justify ATM as opposed to Frame Relay. Keep in mind the following advantages that VoATM has over VoFR:

- Complete and detailed QoS measures
- End-to-end call routing without multiple encoding and decoding
- ATM popularity is still growing and services will be available everywhere in the near future
- ATM in the backbone as well as the WAN means a homogenous topology throughout

Voice over HDLC

If your particular network situation involves a point-to-point T-1 circuit, you might want to consider voice over High-level Data Link Control (VoHDLC). HDLC is a Layer 2 protocol typically used for point-to-point circuits. VoHDLC is similar to VoFR in that it allows multiple calls to be placed over the T-1 using compression. In the instance of tie-line replacement using T-1s and Cisco equipment, VoHDLC can be an attractive alternative. One of the major drawbacks to VoHDLC is that it has very limited scalability. It was originally designed for point-to-point connections between Cisco routers (Figure 9.16).

Figure 9.16 VoHDLC Configuration

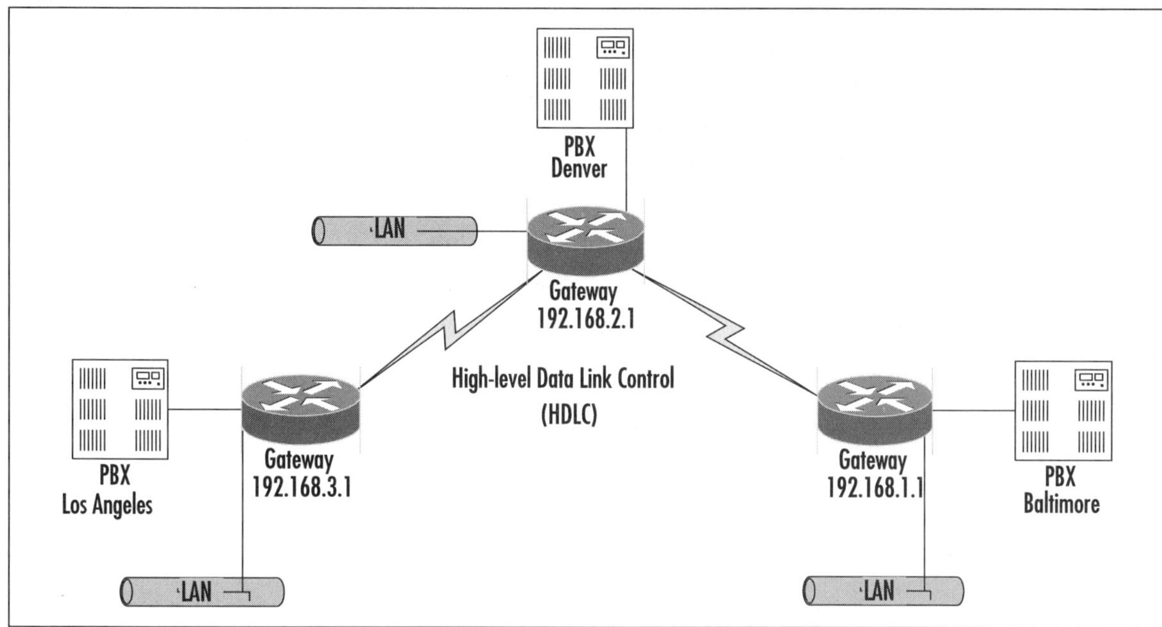

As you can see, you have a fair selection of technologies at your disposal for bypassing or supplementing your PSTN needs. No one technology is the "best"; instead, your requirements determine which you will need. VoIP best leverages the investment that you have likely made in your data network to handle your voice needs.

Introduction to IP Telephony

IP telephony describes products and solutions to transport voice traffic over IP. You can use IP to create a converged network to transport voice, video, and data communications. There are numerous benefits to this type of infrastructure, including simplified administration, cost savings on telecommunications fees, and unified messaging services.

Voice traffic and data traffic require two completely different solutions. Data traffic is relatively resilient and tolerant of slow WAN links, lost packets, and unsequenced packets. Voice traffic, on the other hand, is not. Voice requires packets to be received in the *same* order in which they were sent; if a packet is lost, it should remain lost, as retransmitting the packet would only confuse the person on the receiving end of the call.

There are several components that must be added to your infrastructure. These components include, but are not limited to, specialized router interfaces, specialized LAN switch modules and interfaces, IP telephone handsets, Cisco CallManager servers, and Cisco Unity Mail, as well as other unified messaging solutions.

Conferencing and Transcoding, and Other Services

Conferencing allows multiple participants to communicate in a single call. Cisco technologies support two types of conferencing: ad-hoc and meet-me. In ad-hoc conferencing, the originating caller controls the conference, and determines who will be on the call. The participants may even continue the call after the originating caller hangs up.

A meet-me conference allows participants to participate in a conference by calling an assigned number out of a pool of numbers. More participants can continue to join the conference call until the maximum number allowed is reached. DSP resources support both types of conferencing, and the Cisco CallManager uses DSP resources to provide conferencing services, as shown in Figure 9.17.

In this scenario, an IP phone caller joins another IP phone and an outside or PSTN initiated caller in a three-way conference call. This is an example of an ad-hoc conference. The Catalyst DSP resources are one way a Cisco CallManager is able to provide a conference bridge. A four-way G.711 conference call would utilize four DSP resources, one for each participant to stream into a single call.

Figure 9.17 Conferencing

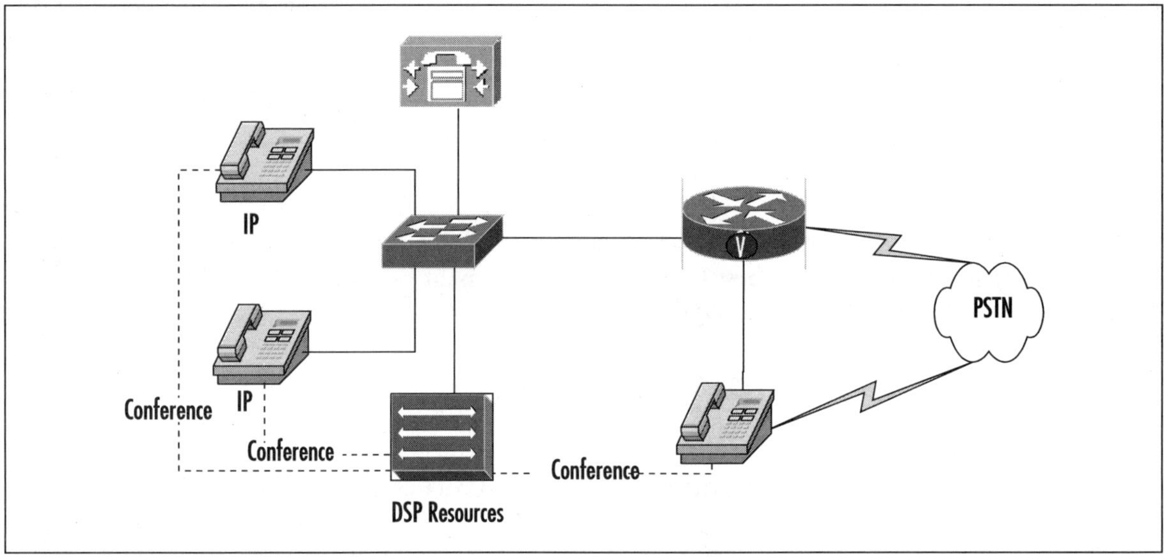

Software conferencing is based on G.711, whereas hardware-based solutions support G.711, G.729a, and G.723. The newer Cisco IP phones 7900 Series supports G.711 and G.729a, but the older style supports G.711 and G.723.

Transcoding is the process of converting IP packets of voice streams between a low bit-rate (LBR) CODEC to and from a G.711 CODEC. An LBR is a CODEC such as G.729a or G.723. An example of a need for transcoding is when a user across the IP WAN wants to access a voice mail system which only supports G.711 and CallManager is configured to initiate remote IP calls using a G.729a CODEC, as shown in Figure 9.18. In this scenario, transcoding must be performed to convert the G.729a voice stream to G.711 in order to communicate with the voice mail system.

Figure 9.18 Transcoding

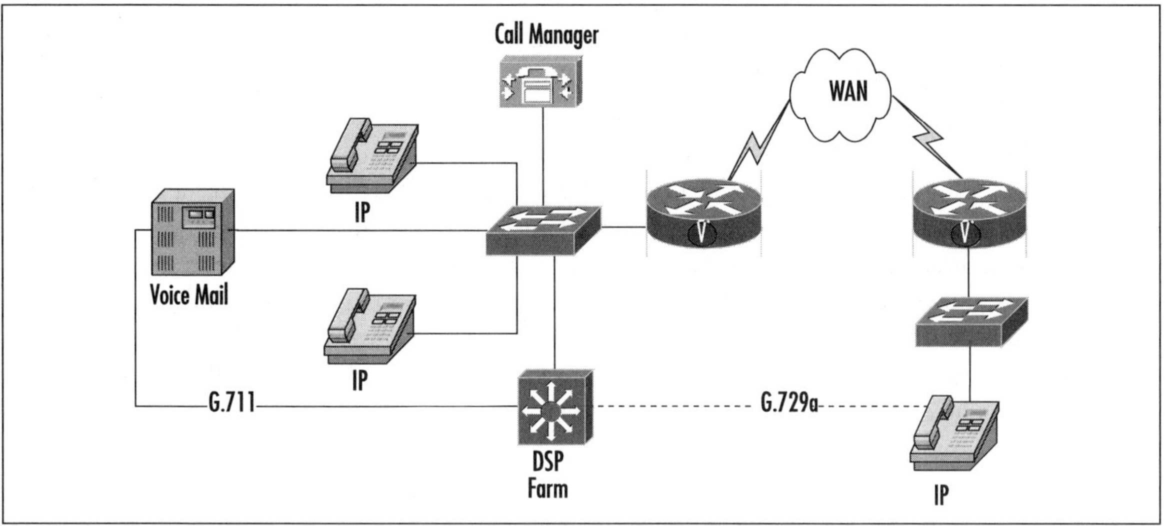

Figure 9.18 serves to illustrate that there are several components necessary to make your voice network a dream come true. Being familiar with these components is one of your first steps to achieving your voice goals. There are also several common telephone functions that any system should be able to provide, regardless of whether they are traditional PSTN or VoIP.

Call Transfer

Cisco IP phones support call transfer. By signaling back to the Call Manager (CM), a call can be transferred to the final destination.

Call Forward

Cisco IP telephony supports three types of call forwarding:

- **Call Forward All** Forwards all calls.
- **Call Forward Busy** Forwards calls only when the line is in use.
- **Call Forward No Answer** Forwards calls when the phone is not answered within a certain configurable number of seconds.

Call Park and Call Pickup

The Call Park feature allows a person to receive a call at another telephone for privacy. A Park soft key allows the receiver to place the caller on hold and dial a designated extension number. At another phone, the extension number can be dialed to pick up the call.

The Call Pickup feature is used to answer an incoming call that is ringing at an unattended telephone. Buttons or soft keys may be configured to activate this function.

Music on Hold

Music on Hold plays music when a caller is on hold, and the music stream may be a .WAV file or a fixed external device controlled by the CM.

Interactive Voice Response

IVRs are useful for routing calls to the appropriate person or department and are less expensive than having an individual do it. In most typical situations, there is an IVR on any public incoming line. Support on Cisco products for IVR is achieved with Tool Command Language (TCL) scripts and voice files, which are referenced in the configuration. When a call comes into the router and matches a set of criteria, the script is queried. The script runs and, depending on the digits it captures, plays an audio file. This audio file is stored in the router's flash and loaded into memory. The audio files use the standard .AU format. The scripts also have the capability to reroute calls.

IP Telephony Components

The components that must be added to your infrastructure in order to facilitate IP telephony blur the line between the traditional voice infrastructure and your data infrastructure. In this section, we will discuss some of these components and their features. The VoIP portion of the evolving Cisco Architecture for Voice, Video, and Integrated Data (AVVID) is Cisco IP Telephony, or CIPT shown in Figure 9.19.

Figure 9.19 Cisco IP Telephony

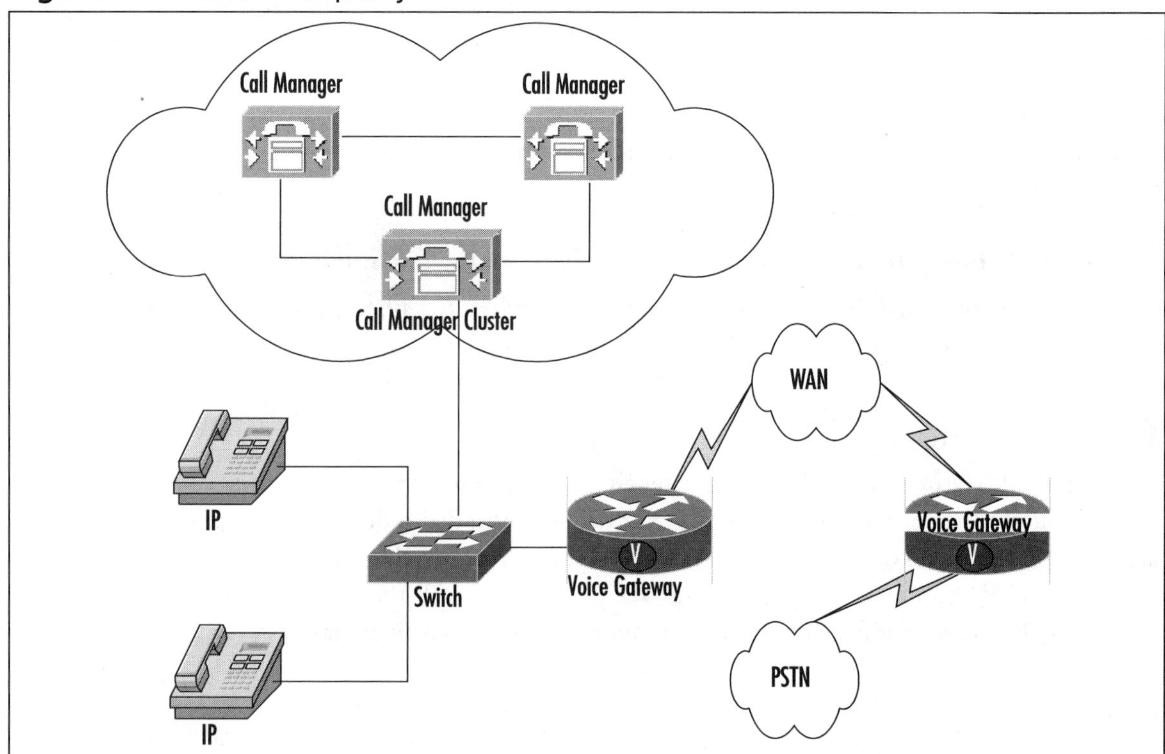

Cisco CallManager

Cisco CallManager provides a software-based call processing platform that runs on a Cisco Media Convergence Server (MCS). Cisco's CallManager offers a scalable, reliable, and manageable solution for an organization. While it may not be the ultimate choice for IP telephony, it has set a standard of performance for IP telephony call processing. The Cisco CallManager (CCM) takes the place of a PBX and performs several key functions:

- Registering IP telephony devices
- Call processing
- Administering dial plans and route plans
- Managing resources

The CCM provides a central point for call processing, connection services, signaling, and registration for IP telephone handsets, analog and digital gateways, and legacy telephony devices such as PBX systems. Communication with IP telephony devices is enabled by the use of several IP telephony protocols such as Skinny Station Protocol, H.323, Media Gateway Control Protocol (MGCP), and Simplified Message Desk Interface (SMDI). CallManager offers an open programming interface utilizing the Telephony Application Programming Interface (TAPI) and the Java Telephony Application Programming Interface (JTAPI).

Current releases of the CallManager platform allow a single CallManager server to support up to 30,000 IP telephones per cluster and up to 8 servers per cluster. CallManager is currently in release version 3.3 and offers increased reliability and scalability via *clustering*. Clustering allows multiple CallManager servers to be interconnected, in order to service more IP telephony devices and to provide redundancy. We will provide more detail on clusters later.

Clustering

Clustering, combines two or more CallManager servers into a logical unit known as a *group*. A group consists of the CallManager servers and their associated devices such as IP telephones, gateways, and logical devices such as the software-based Cisco IP Softphone. All the CallManager servers in the cluster share the same configuration database. Clustering provides enough servers so that if one fails, the other servers within the cluster assume its load without compromising service.

Cisco has outlined four primary roles a server can take on in the cluster:

- Primary CallManager server
- Backup CallManager server
- Database publisher server
- Trivial File Transfer Protocol (TFTP) server

The primary and backup CallManager servers are self-explanatory. The database publisher server maintains and distributes the master-configuration database. A second but equally important task is the storage of call detail records (CDRs), which is a record of the IP telephony call. The TFTP server provides the system image for devices such as IP telephones and gateways.

Call Detail Recording and Data Mining

Even with the lowered costs associated with using IP-based telephony systems, companies still want complete accounting records. This is true for the business user, as in the smaller company that wants to track where calls are being placed. This is a proactive strategy that emphasizes managed growth. Without understanding where calls are being placed, it is impossible to determine where bandwidth might need to be increased. Accounting records are also a major part of business for companies reselling phone services. A good accounting strategy involves CDR as well as bandwidth analysis obtained from the network. Without both, there is no way to determine if bottlenecks are being caused by voice calls or data traffic.

Call Detail Records

Many of the various pieces of the Cisco voice solution include the ability to capture call detail records. The CCM software can track a number of details and report them to a Radius or TACACS+ server. Those details include:

- Calling number
- Called number
- Call start time
- Call end time
- Bandwidth utilized

Cisco CM also supports output of its CDR to either a Microsoft Access database or an Open Database Connectivity (ODBC) database such as SQL. Once the data has been compiled to a database, a front-end interface can be designed to format the data in a useful way.

There are some limitations to consider before implementing a cluster. A cluster cannot cross a WAN link, so all cluster servers must exist on the same LAN. Servers must be interconnected at minimum by a 10 Mbps switched (not shared) connection. This is to ensure the proper QoS is maintained. A cluster is limited to 30,000 IP telephones. A maximum of 100 clusters can be interconnected, allowing support for up to 1,000,000 IP telephones within an organization. Figure 9.20 shows typical cluster architecture; notice that one of the backup servers has assumed the load of the failed primary server.

Figure 9.20 CallManager Clustering in Action

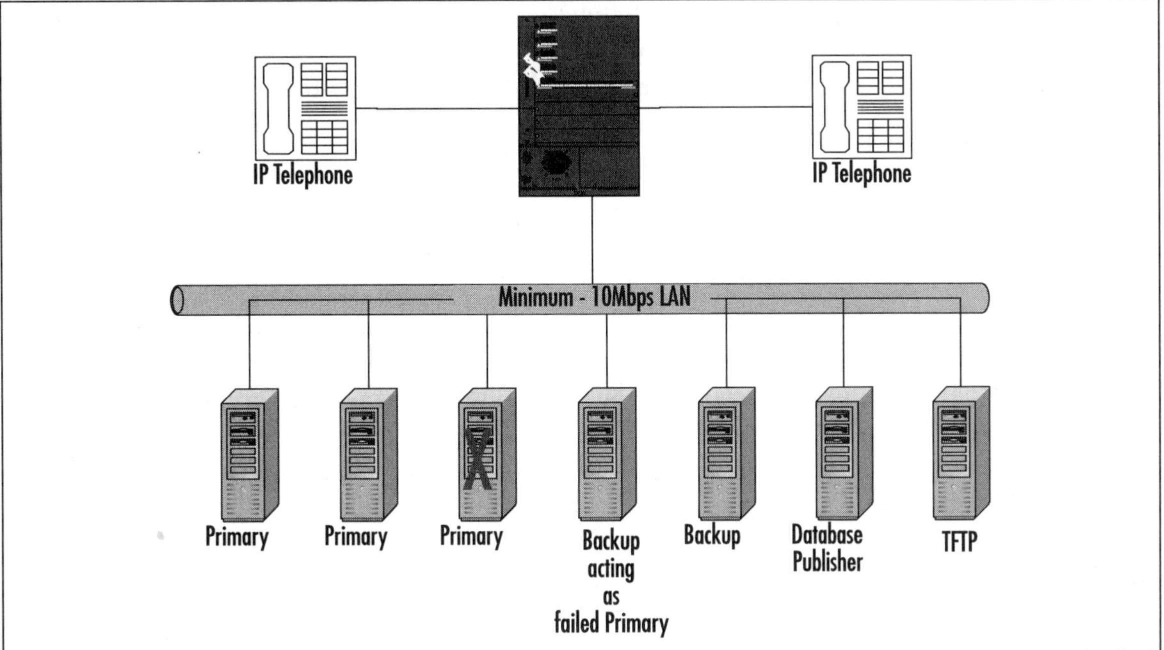

Cisco IP Phones

Cisco IP telephones provide the end-user with an interface to the IP telephony architecture. They contain digital signal processors to perform this function. There have been two generations of IP telephones produced by Cisco. Second-generation phones such as the 7940 and 7960 offer an LCD screen for a menu-based feature set, and utilize inline power via a specialized inline-power patch panel or modules for the Catalyst switch line.

There are currently several phones in Cisco's second-generation phone offering:

- **Cisco IP Conference Station 7935** Polycom conference technology full duplex conversations with inline power. Supports Dynamic Host Configuration Protocol (DHCP), coordinated dial plans, and auto-configuration of telephony features. Single RJ45 10/100BaseTX interface.
- **Cisco IP Phone 7905G (single user)** Basic IP Phone. Supports CDP, 801.1q, TFTP, and DHCP. Single RJ45 10BaseT interface. Inline power.
- **Cisco IP Phone 7910G and 7910G+SW (public/lobby area)** Basic IP Phone. Supports DHCP and CDP. Single RJ45 10BaseT interface 7910G. 7910G+SW model provides 2-port 10/100BaseT switch. External power.
- **Cisco IP Phone 7940G** Full-featured IP Phone with Lightweight Directory Access Protocol (LDAP) organizational directory support and advanced messaging features. Supports web information such as weather or stock reports. Supports DHCP, 802.1Q, TFTP, and CDP. Provides 2-port 10/100BaseT switch Inline power.

- **Cisco IP Phone 7960G** "Executive" full-featured IP Phone with LDAP organizational directory support and advanced messaging features. Supports web information such as weather or stock reports. Supports DHCP, 802.1Q, TFTP, and CDP. Provides 2-port 10/100BaseT switch. Interoperates with CallManager systems, H.323, and Session Initiation Protocol (SIP) Inline power.

Cisco Gateways

Gateways connect your IP telephony infrastructure to the PSTN or to legacy PBX systems. These devices allow calls between the VoIP locations and off-net or PSTN locations. Calls made from your office IP phone to a traditional analog phone and vice versa pass through a gateway. Cisco's product line currently includes over 20 different gateway products that support various types of gateway protocols. Currently there are three different types of gateways supported by the Cisco IP telephony solution: SIP, H.323, and MGCP.

Gateways also provide redundancy. When the VoIP network is congested or when the WAN carrying VoIP traffic is down, the gateway can redirect your outgoing call to the PSTN. The caller's gateway converts the digital voice packets into a traditional time-division multiplexed voice stream and transmits the call through the PSTN. The destination gateway converts the incoming TDM voice stream into digital packets for processing by the destination IP phone.

Switches

Cisco Catalyst switches support IP phones and can provide transmission speeds of up to 1Gbps on a LAN. Transmissions from one IP phone are not broadcast to other IP phones on the same switch. Many Cisco switches can supply inline power to the IP phones via the Ethernet cable. This eliminates the need to provide separate power to the IP phones.

Cisco IP SoftPhone

Cisco IP SoftPhone allows users to utilize IP telephony on any networked computer with a microphone and speaker to obtain a fully functional IP telephone. The IP telephony software digitizes the voice signals and sends the voice packets across the IP network. A graphical user interface (GUI) on the Windows computer provides a dial-pad and other functions of a standard IP telephone. IP SoftPhone consumes 20 device units on a CallManager server, as opposed to the one used by a standard IP telephone handset. It must be installed with Microsoft NetMeeting.

Cisco IP Telephony Applications

Cisco has developed software solutions to enhance their IP telephony solutions. IP telephony applications allow Cisco to augment their IP telephony hardware with features and services to provide an even more viable solution.

Cisco Web Attendant

Cisco WebAttendant is Windows Web-based TAPI software that allows the user to receive and dispatch calls from any IP telephone on the network. WebAttendant allows the IP phone to interface directly with the CallManager to direct calls and to monitor the status of lines, much like a traditional receptionist console. WebAttendant offers many of the same features of traditional PBX systems such as *hunt groups* and multiple attendant consoles.

WebAttendant is included in the basic CallManager package. It can scale to meet the size of almost any IP telephony infrastructure. A single WebAttendant console can monitor up to 26 calls at a time. A single CallManager cluster utilizing WebAttendant can support up 32 hunt groups with 16 members per hunt group. Also, a cluster can support up to 96 WebAttendant consoles, which means support for up to 512 (96 consoles x 26 calls) calls at one time.

Internet Communications Software

Internet Communications Software (ICS) is a suite of five tools for service and application providers to further gain the benefits of IP telephony.

- **Network Applications Manager (NAM)** A management console that enables utilization of Automatic Call Distribution (ACD), Intelligent Contact Mangement (ICM), CIS, and IP Contact Center (IPCC).
- **Automatic Call Distribution** Part of NAM, it reroute calls to different customers serviced via the same CO.
- **Cisco IP Contact Center** Allows call centers using IP telephony to receive regular POTS calls as well as IP telephony calls.
- **Intelligent Contact Management** Directs and relays customer contact information between resources such as Web, voice, and e-mail.
- **Customer Interaction Suite** Allows corporations and service providers to interact with their customers on the Internet or network in real-time. Four components: Cisco Media Manager, Cisco Media Blender, Cisco E-Mail Manager, and Cisco Collaboration Server:

Prepping the Network for Voice Service

To support voice traffic, several enhancements must be made to your existing infrastructure, such as specialized router interfaces and specialized switch cards. Your infrastructure must be voice *and* data friendly. We'll discuss the Layer 2 and Layer 3 devices that will help achieve this goal. Cisco has developed several routers that allow a network to make the change to a converged network. There are several types of voice interfaces that you can install on Cisco routers to support voice traffic.

Analog Voice Interfaces

Cisco routers utilize analog voice interfaces to interface directly with telephone handsets, or to connect to legacy PBXs or the PSTN. There are currently three types of analog interfaces supported by Cisco routers: Foreign Exchange Station, Foreign Exchange Office, and earth and magnet.

Foreign Exchange Station Interface

The FXS port connects the router to standard telephony devices and endpoint stations, such as basic telephone equipment, keysets, or fax machines. FXS ports can supply ring voltage, dial tone, and other basic signaling to an end station. The FXS port is configured with a standard RJ-11 connection port (see Figure 9.21). Do not connect to a PSTN.

Figure 9.21 Standard RJ11 Pinout

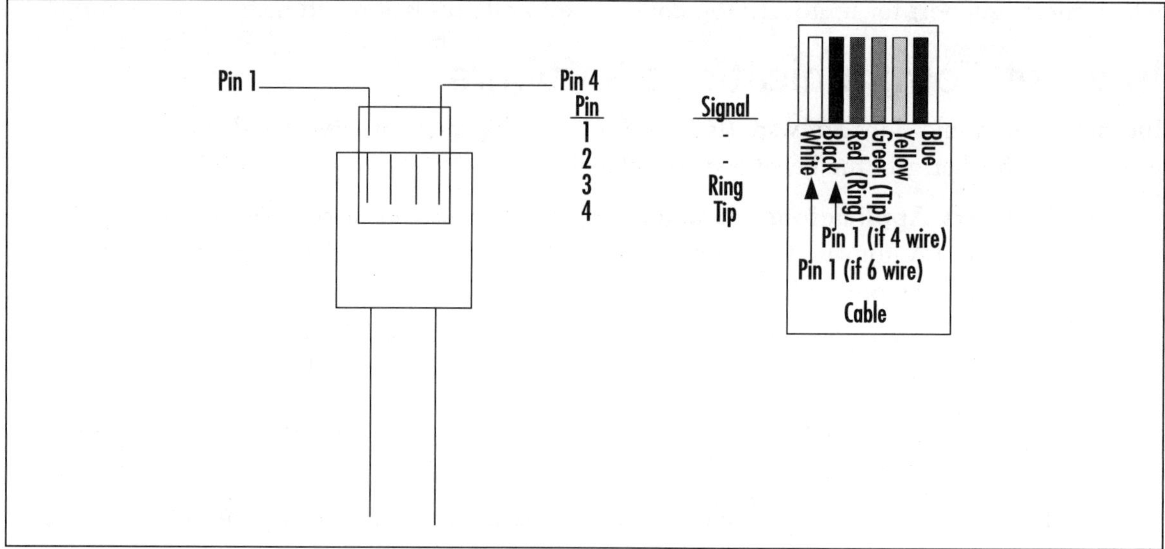

Foreign Exchange Office Interface

The FXO port is also configured with an RJ-11 connection port. FXO ports connect the IP network to off-premises equipment such as a PSTN CO or to a PBX tie-line interface. The FXO port connects to the line side of the switch, which allows the switch to think it is connected to a telephone. You can set several parameters that are compatible with tie-line features on a PBX. FXO ports are country specific, and are *not* interchangeable with FXS.

FXS/FXO signaling

FXS and FXO interfaces share the same signaling types, of which there are two. Loop-start and ground-start are used to "seize" a line in preparation for making a call. This line seizure is also called *starting*, since it completes the circuit, enabling voltage to flow and thus "starting" the line.

Both loop-start and ground-start have three states. In the *idle state,* the handset is on-hook and no ring voltage is being applied to indicate an incoming call. The *seizure state* occurs when you take the handset off-hook, thus completing the loop and allowing current to flow. In the *ring state*, voltage is passed to the ring generator to indicate an incoming call. The same wires that carry voice are used by loop-start and ground-start to supply signaling. This enables telephone companies to reduce the number of wires that they need to bring into a location.

Loop-Start

Loop-start signaling is used on local loops to initiate a call, as shown in Figure 9.22. When a call comes in, the CO or PBX supplies AC current to the ring line, causing the ring generator to activate, thus ringing the phone. When you pick up the handset, you complete the loop, and voltage ceases to flow to the ring generator.

Figure 9.22 Loop-Start Signaling

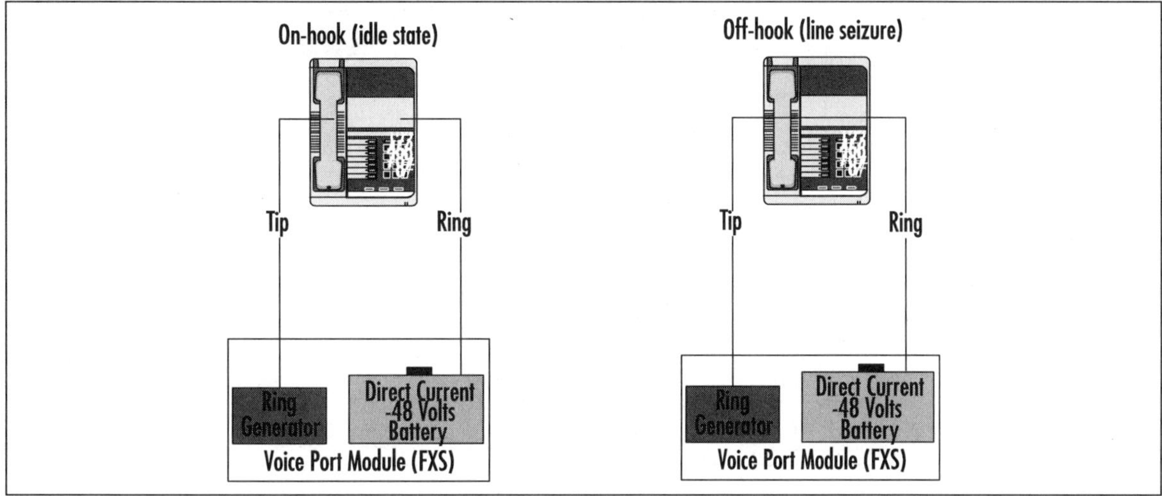

If you were initiate a call instead of responding to one, the mere act of lifting the handset would complete the loop, and the CO or PBX would generate your dial tone. When you dial your digits, the tones are sent back to the PBX or CO, and the call is completed.

Loop-start works well for simple, single-line locations such as residences. However, it is prone to *glare*, a condition that occurs when two parties call each other simultaneously, thus getting a busy signal and preventing the call from being completed. It is for this reason that ground-start signaling was developed.

Ground-Start

Ground-start signaling is similar to loop-start, but without the inherent glare weaknesses. Ground-start signaling can detect when loops have been seized at both ends. Figure 9.23 shows ground start in action.

Figure 9.23 Ground-Start Signaling

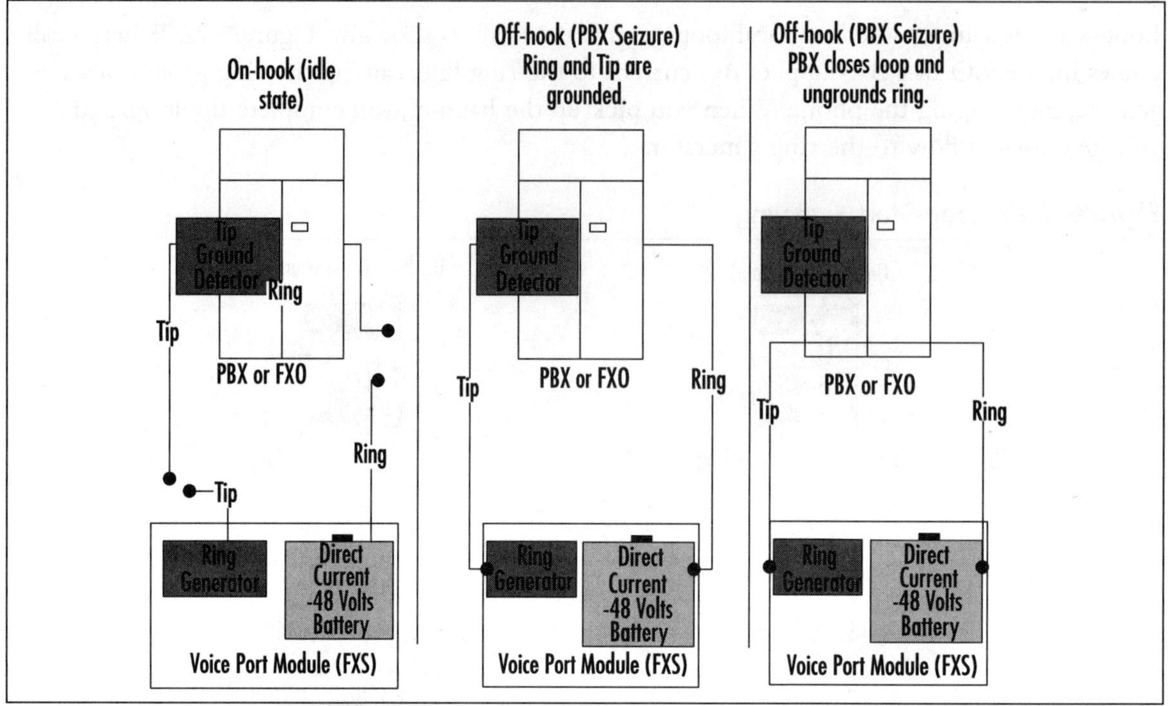

When the line is idle, no voltage is supplied, as shown in the left side of the figure. When the line goes off-hook in preparation for making a call, voltage is supplied to tip and ring, and digits can then be passed to initiate the call, shown by the middle section of Figure 9.23. As with loop start, should a call come in, AC voltage flows over the ring wire, causing the ring generator to produce ringing. Should you lift the handset to make a call, you will complete the loop and get a dial tone.

E&M Interface

The E&M interface is an RJ-48C type connector (see Figure 9.24) for connecting specifically to PBX trunk lines (*tie lines*) between PBXs. The E&M interface can be programmed with special attenuation, gain, and impedance settings that can conform to the specific attributes of different PBX systems. E&M is a signaling technique for two-wire and four-wire telephone and trunk lines. The connections and pinout specifications are listed in Table 9.6. Do not connect an E&M port to the PSTN, as this can cause disruptions and unpredictable results at the CO.

Figure 9.24 An RJ-48C Pinout

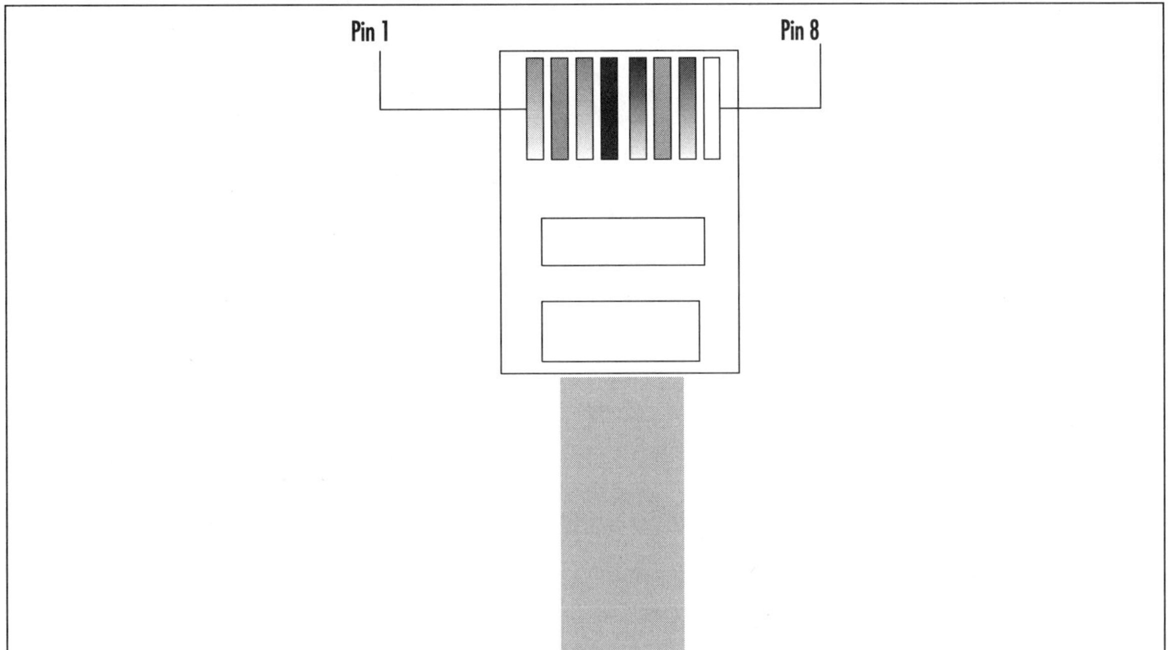

Table 9.6 E&M Pinouts

			Two-Wire Operation, Type				Four-Wire Operation, Type			
Pin	**Signal**	**Description**	**1**	**2**	**3**	**5**	**1**	**2**	**3**	**5**
1	SB	–48V signaling battery		SB	SB	–	–	SB	SB	–
2	M-lead	Signaling input	M	M	M	M	M	M	M	M
3	R	Ring, audio input	–	–	–	–	R	R	R	R
4	R or R1	Ring, audio input/output or output	R	R	R	R	R1	R1	R1	R1
5	T or T-1	Tip, audio input/output or output	T	T	T	T	T-1	T-1	T-1	T-1
6	T	Tip, audio input	–	–	–	–	T	T	T	T
7	E-lead	Signaling output	E	E	E	E	E	E	E	E
8	SG	Signaling ground return	–	SG	SG	–	–	SG	SG	–

Signaling is used for signaling from the PBX to the router, signaling between routers, and signaling from the router to the PBX. Without these procedures, calls would not be possible.

Signaling Between Routers and PBXs

When signaling from PBX to router, lifting the handset produces an off-hook condition. The connection appears as a trunk line to the PBX, which signals the router to seize the trunk. The PBX then forwards the dialed digits to the router in the same manner the digits would be forwarded to a telephone company switch or another PBX. The signaling interface may be any of the common signaling methods used to seize a trunk line, such as FXS, FXO, E&M, or T-1/E-1 signaling.

As you can see in Figure 9.25, the PBX seizes a trunk line to the router and forwards the dialed digits. Within the router, the dial plan maps the dialed digits to an IP address and initiates a Q.931 call establishment request to the remote peer router that is indicated by an IP address (Figure 9.26). This control channel is used to set up the Real-time Transport Protocol (RTP) audio streams, and the RSVP protocol may be used to request a guaranteed QoS.

When the remote router receives the Q.931 call request, it signals a line seizure to the PBX. After the PBX acknowledges this seizure, the router forwards the dialed digits to the PBX and signals a call acknowledgment to the originating router. Figure 9.27 shows this line seizure.

Figure 9.25 PBX-to-Router Signaling

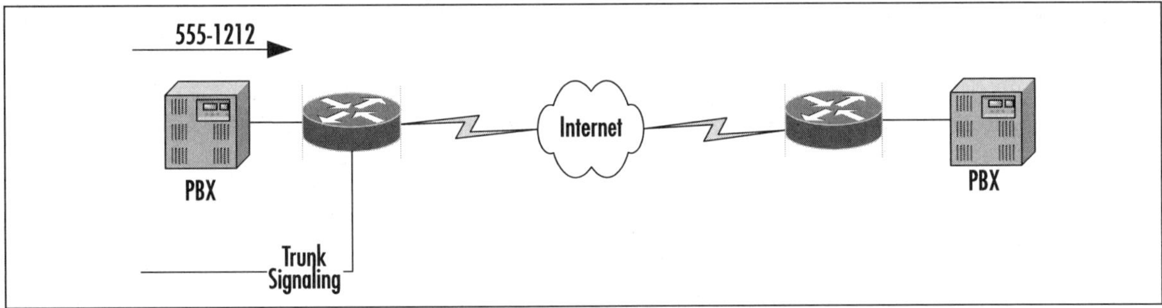

Figure 9.26 Router-to-Router Signaling

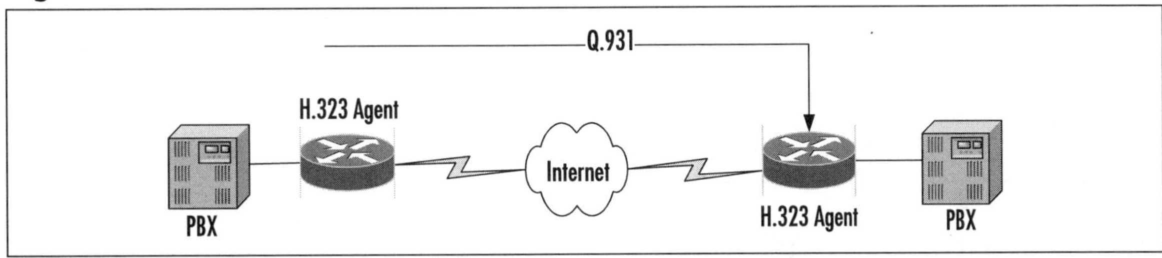

Figure 9.27 Router-to-PBX Signaling

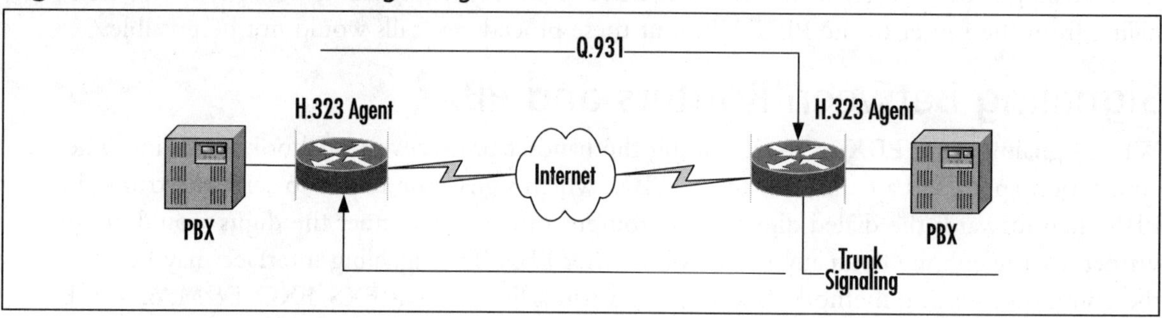

VoIP Protocols

With VoIP signaling, end stations perform signaling and session establishment. To successfully emulate voice services across an IP network, enhancements to the signaling stacks are required. For example, an H.323 agent is added to the router for standards-based support of the audio and signaling streams. The Q.931 protocol is used for call establishment and teardown between H.323 agents or end stations.

RTCP provides reliable information transfer once the audio stream has been established. A transport protocol such as TCP carries the signaling channels between end stations. RTP, which uses UDP, transports the real-time audio stream. RTP uses UDP since it has lower delay than TCP and voice traffic tolerates low levels of loss and cannot effectively exploit retransmission.

H.245 control signaling negotiates channel usage and capabilities. H.245 provides for capabilities' exchange between endpoints so that CODECs and other parameters related to the call are agreed upon by the endpoints. It is within H.245 that the audio channel is negotiated. Table 9.7 depicts the relationship between the ISO reference model and the protocols used in IP voice. We will discuss several of these protocols in detail in the next few sections.

Table 9.7 ISO Reference Model and H.323 Standards

ISO Protocol Layer	Standard
Presentation	G.711, G.729, G.729a, etc.
Session	H.323, H.245, H.225, RTCP
Transport	RTP,UDP
Network	IP, RSVP, WFQ
Link	RFC1717(PPP/ML), Frame, ATM, etc.

H.323 Standard and Protocol Stack

The H.320 series of standards was defined for ISDN videophones and videoconferencing systems. H.323 is an ITU-T set of standards that defines the components, protocols, and procedures necessary to provide multimedia (audio, video, and data) communications over *IP* networks. It is probably the most important standard for packetized voice technology. H.323 provides a method to enable other H.32x-compliant products to communicate. In addition to *control* and *call setup* standards, H.323 encompasses protocols for audio, video, and data as follows:

- **Audio** The compression algorithms H.323 supports for audio are all proven ITU standards (G.711, G.723, and G.729). All H.323 terminals must have at least one audio CODEC support specified by G.711.
- **Video** Optional. Any video-enabled H.323 terminal must support the ITU-T *H.261* encoding and decoding recommendation. (H.263 is optional.)
- **Data** H.323 references the T.120 specifications for data conferencing, which addresses point-to-point and multipoint data conferences. It provides interoperability at the application, network, and transport levels.

Figure 9.28 shows the roles and interoperability of the various H.323 protocols. H.323 is a suite of protocols that provide end-to-end call functionality in a converged network. The H.323 protocol relies heavily on the services provided by other protocols such as TCP, IP, and UDP as well as RTP. The protocols that make up the H.323 protocol are Registration, Admission, and Status (RAS), H.245, and H.225.

Figure 9.28 H.323 Protocol Interoperability

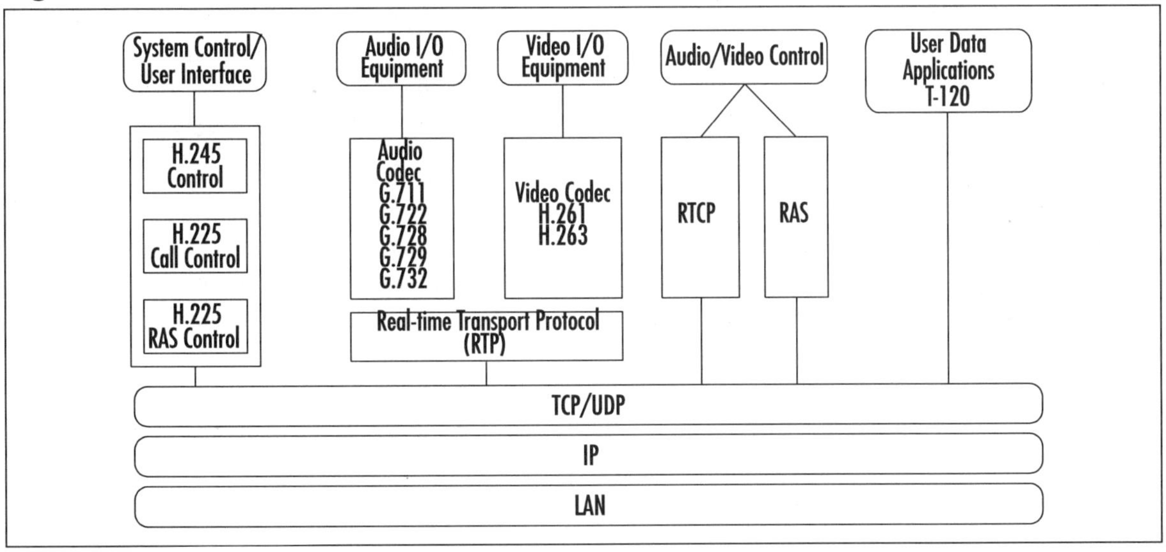

H.225

H.225 establishes and controls calls between two H.323 endpoints, functions that the ITU Q.931performs for ISDN. Q.931 uses 22 messages, and 29 in case of Q.932. H.225 adopted a subset of Q.931 messages and parameters such as alerting, call processing, connect, setup, release complete, status, status inquiry, and facility (Q.932).

H.245

H.245 control signaling negotiates channel usage and capabilities. H.245 exchanges end-to-end control messages managing the operation of the H.323 endpoint. Control messages carry information related to:

- Capabilities exchange
- Opening and closing logical channels used to carry media streams
- Flow control messages
- General commands

After call setup, all communications are over logical channels. H.245 defines procedures for mapping logical channels. Logical channel 0 is for H.245 control for the duration of the call while multiple logical channels of varying types, such as video, data, voice, are allowed for a single call.

Real-Time Transport Protocol

RTP provides end-to-end network transport functions suitable for applications transmitting real-time data such as audio, video, or simulation data, over multicast or unicast network services. It is used to transport data via UDP. *RTP does not address resource reservation and does not guarantee QoS for real-time services.* It is augmented by a control protocol (RTCP) to allow monitoring of the data delivery in a manner scalable to large multicast networks and to provide minimal control and identification functionality. RTP and RTCP are designed to be independent of the underlying transport and network layers. The protocol supports the use of RTP-level translators and mixers.

RTCP provides a control transport for RTP by providing feedback on the quality of data distribution and carries a transport-level identifier for an RTP source used by receivers to synchronize audio and video.

Registration, Administration, and Status

RAS is a protocol used between endpoints (terminals and gateways) and gatekeepers to perform registration, admission control, bandwidth changes, and status and to disengage endpoints from gatekeepers. RAS uses UDP port 1719.

A solid understanding of H.323 components, their functions, and their importance is paramount. All devices that fall within the H.323 protocol stack can be categorized as one of four types of devices. These device types are terminals, gateways, gatekeepers, and multipoint control units (MCUs).

H.323 Terminals (Endpoints)

H.323 terminals provide the user interface for real-time, two-way multimedia communications. All endpoints must support voice communications and, optionally, video or data communications. For voice, the H.323 terminal is generally an IP telephone. H.323 is deployed as software such as Microsoft NetMeeting . In order to qualify as an H.323 terminal, the device in question must have the following three items:

- A network interface
- Audio CODECs
- H.323 software

H.323 terminals must support audio (G.711 is mandatory, and G.723.1 and G.729 are recommended for networks of low bandwidth). Video and data support is optional; H.261 is mandatory when video is supported. H.245 and H.225 are required for control functions, and RTP is required for sequencing media packets.

H.323 Gateways

Gateways translate communications between H.323 and non-H.323 entities (for instance, between H.323 terminals and telephones on the circuit-switched network). They provide call control functions such as address translation and bandwidth management. H.323 gateways enable H.323 networks to communicate with other networks such as the PSTN or PBXs. Gateways provide translation and call control between dissimilar networks. Encoding, protocol translation, and call control mappings occur in gateways between two endpoints. Gateways provide many functions, including:

- **Translating protocols** Allows the PSTN and the H.323 network to set up and tear down calls.
- **Converting information formats** Enables different networks to freely exchange information such as speech and video.
- **Transferring information** Transfers information between dissimilar networks.

Gateway functionality is generally provided by a router, such as the 2600 or 3600 series, a Catalyst gateway module such as the 6000 T-1 gateway module, or dedicated gateway devices such as the VG200 and DT-24+.

H.323 Gatekeepers

Gatekeepers perform call control and policy administration for registered H.323 endpoints. *Gatekeepers in H.323 networks are optional.* If present, it is mandatory that endpoints use their services. The H.323 standards define several mandatory services that the gatekeeper *must* provide:

- **Address translation** Translate an alias address into a transport address, which is a PSTN-based phone calling a phone on an IP network (an E.164 number such as 555-555-2121 will be translated into an IP network address such as 192.168.12.78).
- **Admissions control** Defines RAS messages to authorize network access. Does not define the rules or policies used to authorize access to network resources. To do so, the gatekeeper can interface with an existing authorization mechanism.
- **Bandwidth control and management** Determines if there is no bandwidth available or no additional bandwidth available for calls requesting increases. Can instruct a call to reduce its bandwidth usage.
- **Zone management** An H.323 "zone" is the collection of all components—terminals, gateways, and MCUs—managed by a single gatekeeper. Gatekeeper must provide required functions (for example: address translation, admissions control, bandwidth control) to devices within its zone.

The gatekeeper can also perform *optional* functions such as:

- **Call authorization** Authorize or reject a given call; the provider of the H.323 service specifies the reasons for authorization and rejection.
- **Call control signaling** Process all call signaling associated with the endpoints registered with it (*gatekeeper routed call signaling*) or allow the call signaling messages to pass directly between the endpoints.
- **Call management** Provide intelligent call management. The call management may be based on address translation functions providing call screening, call forwarding/redirection, and call routing based on time of day, network congestion, or least-cost path.

As with gateways, routers are typically incorporated to provide gatekeeper functionality.

Multipoint Control Units

MCUs provide conference facilities for users who want to conference three or more endpoints together. MCUs do not provide a direct interconnection to the H.323 protocol stack. Rather, they provide a method for H.323 to interconnect voice and videoconferencing.

All terminals participating in the conference establish a connection with the MCU. It manages conference resources and negotiations between endpoints to determine which audio or video CODEC to use. The MCU might or might not handle the media stream. An MCU has two functional components:

- **Multipoint controller (MC)** Mandatory. Controls where media streams go. Has a reconciliation capability (common mode) and may be located in the terminal, gateway, or gatekeeper.
- **Multipoint processor (MP)** Optional. Mixes, switches, and processes media streams, including some or all of the streams in the conference call (video, data, or audio).

H.323 Call Stages

The process of establishing and maintaining an H.323 call is a very complex one. We will break this process down into a logical and hierarchical order to show what is occurring at each stage and the requirements and resources used for each stage.

H.323 Discovery and Registration

The five stages of an H.323 call and details of each of these connections are listed.

1. Discovery and registration
2. Call setup
3. Call-signaling flows
4. Media stream and media control flows
5. Call termination

A lot happens within each of these stages; from the time the call is requested to the time it is terminated.

Device Discovery and Registration

The gatekeeper initiates a "discovery" process to determine the gatekeeper with which the endpoint must communicate, as shown in Figure 9.29. This discovery can be either a statically configured address or through multicast traffic. Once this is determined, the endpoint or gateway registers with the discovered gatekeeper.

Registration is used by the endpoints to identify a zone with which they can be associated (a *zone* is a collection of H.323 components managed by a single gatekeeper). H.323 can then inform the gatekeeper of the zones' transport address and alias address.

Figure 9.29 H.323 Gatekeeper Call Control/Signaling: Discovery and Registration

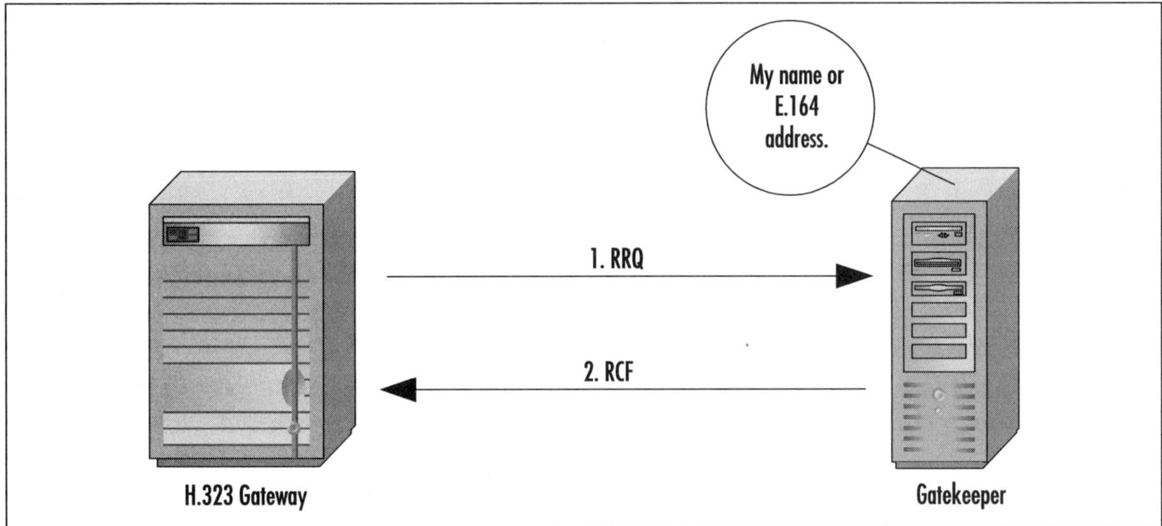

In Figure 9.29:

1. A H.323 gateway (or terminal) sends a request to register (RRQ) message using H.225 RAS on the RAS channel to the gatekeeper.
2. The gatekeeper confirms or denies the registration by sending a registration confirmation (RCF) or a "Reject registration" message back to the gateway.

Intra-zone Call Placement

Once the registration and discovery process is complete, we can place a call. Figure 9.30 shows Gateway X placing a intra-zone call to a terminal connected to Gateway Y, Gateway X sends an admission request (ARQ) message to the gatekeeper requesting permission to place a call to a phone number serviced by Gateway Y.

Figure 9.30 H.323 Gatekeeper Call Control/Signaling: Call Placement (Intra-zone)

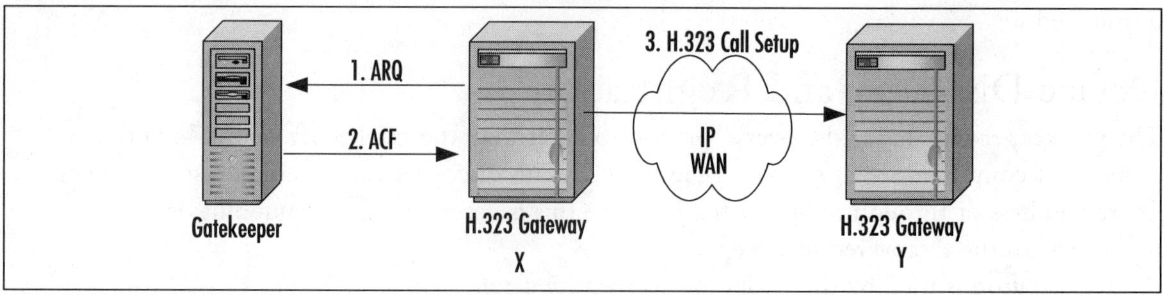

In Figure 9.30:

1. Gateway X sends an ARQ message using H.225 RAS to the gatekeeper.
2. Gatekeeper requests direct call signaling by sending an admission confirmation (ACF) to Gateway X.
3. H.323 call setup is initiated.

Inter-zone Call Placement

The process of placing an inter-zone call is somewhat more complicated and resource–intensive, as the network is larger and divided into multiple zones. In Figure 9.31, Gatekeeper A controls Zone A, and Gatekeeper B controls Zone B. Gateway X (or Terminal X) is registered with Gatekeeper A, and Gateway Y is registered with Gatekeeper B.

To place a call to Gateway Y terminal, Gateway X first sends an ARQ message to the gatekeeper requesting permission to make the call. Since Gateway Y is not registered with the gatekeeper in Zone A, we assume that the gateways (terminals) are already registered.

Figure 9.31 H.323 Gatekeeper Call Control/Signaling: Call Placement (Inter-zone)

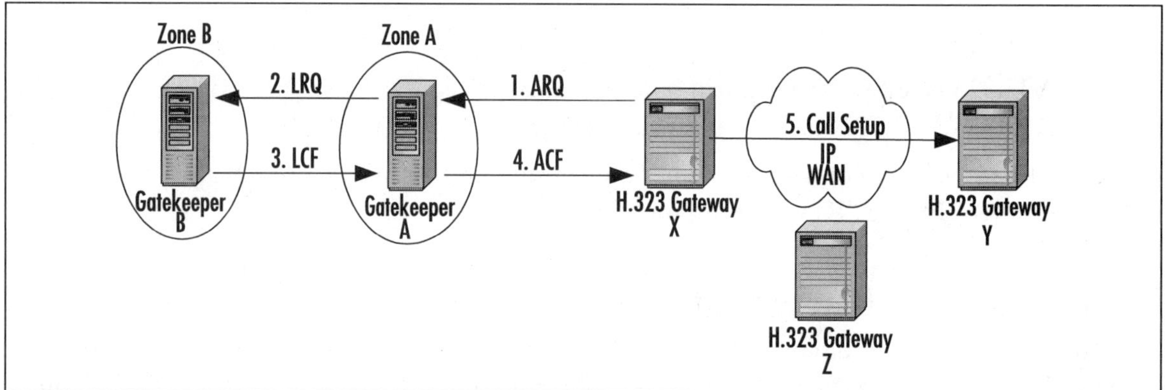

Figure 9.31 shows five distinct phases in an inter-zone call placement.

1. **ARQ** Gateway X requests a connection to Gateway Y from its local gatekeeper.
2. **Location request (LRQ)** Local gatekeeper for Gateway X does not know the IP address of Gateway Y and is requesting the address from Gateway Y's local gatekeeper.

3. **Location confirm (LCF)** Gateway Y's local gatekeeper responds to Gateway X's local gatekeeper with the IP address of Gateway Y.
4. **ACF** The local gatekeeper responds to Gateway X's request and provides the remote IP address of Gateway Y.
5. **Call established** The H.323 call is established between Gateway X and Gateway Y.

H.323 Call Setup

After discovery, registration, and call placement are complete, the H.323 call moves into the *call setup* stage. At this stage, the gateways are communicating directly to set up the connection. An alternative is *gatekeeper-routed call signaling,* where all call setup messages traverse the gatekeeper. Figure 9.32 helps us conceptualize this process.

Figure 9.32 H.323 Call Setup

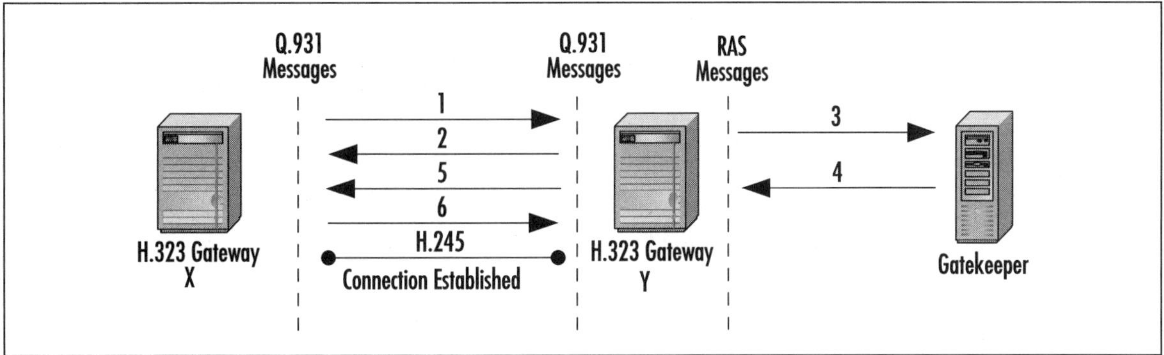

The call setup is based on the ITU-Q.931 (H.225 is a subset of Q.931), which provides a means to establish, maintain, and terminate network connections across an ISDN. This process comprises six distinct phases, as shown in Figure 9.32.

1. Gateway X sends an H.225 call-signaling setup message to Gateway Y to request a connection.
2. Gateway Y sends an H.225 message back to Gateway X, advising that it may proceed with the call.
3. Gateway Y sends an RAS message (ARQ) on the RAS channel to the gatekeeper to request permission to accept the call.
4. Gatekeeper confirms that the call can be accepted by sending a message (ACF) back to Gateway Y.
5. Gateway Y sends an H.225 message to Gateway X, alerting that the connection has been established.
6. Gateway Y sends an H.225 message to Gateway X, confirming call connection to establish the call.

Logical Channel Setup

After call setup, all communications travel over logical channels. The H.245 manages these logical channels. Multiple logical channels of varying types (video, audio, and data) are allowed for a single call.

The H.245 Logical Channel Signaling Entity (LCSE) opens a logical channel for each media stream. Channels may be unidirectional or bi-directional. Figure 9.33 helps us visualize how the H.323 utilizes virtual channels.

Figure 9.33 Media Channel Setup

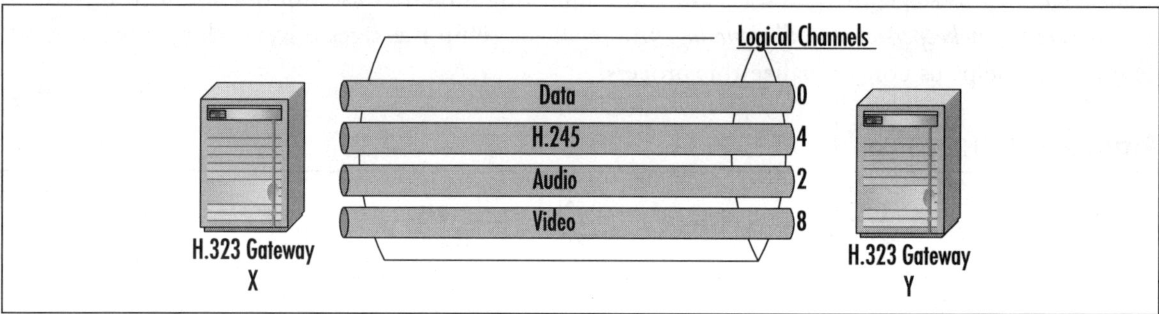

The H.245 control channel is established between Gateway X and Gateway Y. Gateway X uses H.245 to identify its capabilities via a Terminal Capability Set (TCS) message to Gateway Y. The media channel setup flow is as follows:

1. Gateway X exchanges its capabilities with Gateway Y by sending an H.245 TCS message.
2. Gateway Y acknowledges Gateway X's capabilities by sending an H.245 TCS Acknowledge message.
3. Gateway Y exchanges its capabilities with Gateway X by sending an H.245 TCS message.
4. Gateway X acknowledges Gateway Y's capabilities by sending an H.245 TCS Acknowledge message.
5. Gateway X opens a media channel with Gateway Y by sending an H.245 Open Logical Channel (OLC) message and includes the transport address of the RTCP channel.
6. Gateway Y acknowledges the establishment of the logical channel with Gateway X by sending an H.245 OLC Acknowledge message, including:
   - RTP transport addresses (used to send the RTP media stream) allocated by Gateway Y
   - RTCP address previously received from Gateway X
7. Gateway Y opens a media channel with Gateway X by sending an H.245 OLC message and includes the transport address of the RTCP channel.
8. Gateway X acknowledges the establishment of the logical channel with Gateway Y by sending an H.245 OLC Acknowledge message and includes:

- RTP transport addresses (used to send the RTP media stream) allocated by Gateway X
- RTCP address previously received from Gateway Y

Figure 9.34 highlights this process:

Figure 9.34 Media Channel Setup Call Flow

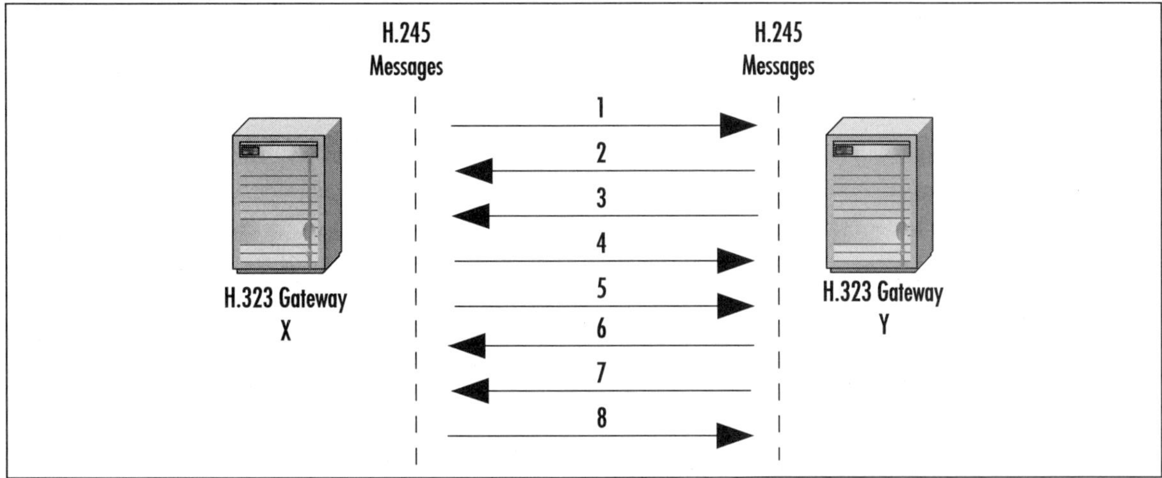

Media Stream and Media Control Flows

RTP media streams are transported over UDP ports 16384 through 16384 + 4*x* (where *x* is the number of voice ports on the gateways). For example, a Cisco 3620 router with four E&M ports would use UDP ports 16384–16400 for RTP flows.

RTCP manages media streams in the H.323 call flow by supporting QoS feedback from receivers. The source may use this information to adapt encoding or buffering schemes. RTCP uses a dedicated logical channel for each RTP media stream. Figure 9.35 illustrates the steps in this stage of the H.323 call flow.

Figure 9.35 Media Stream Communication

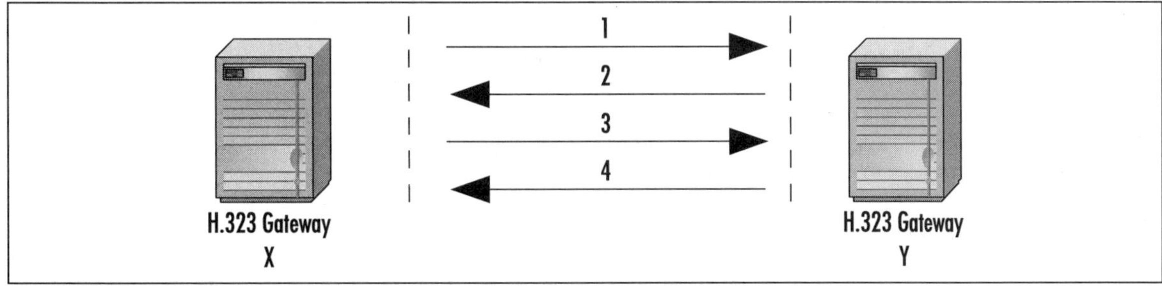

In the example shown in Figure 9.34, four actions are occurring:

1. Gateway X sends the RTP encapsulated media stream to Gateway Y.
2. Gateway Y sends the RTP encapsulated media stream back to Gateway X.

3. Gateway X sends the RTCP messages to Gateway Y.
4. Gateway Y sends the RTCP messages back to Gateway X.

Endpoints may seek changes in the amount of bandwidth initially requested and confirmed. The gatekeeper must be asked for bandwidth increases or decreases. Endpoints must comply with gatekeeper responses and requests. The bandwidth change flow is diagramed in Figure 9.36. This process consists of six stages:

1. The initiating gateway sends a bandwidth request (BRQ) to the gatekeeper to request the desired bandwidth.
2. The gatekeeper responds with a bandwidth confirmation (BCF) message for the requested bandwidth.
3. A logical channel is established between the two gateways with the specified bandwidth.
4. A BRQ is sent from the remote router to the gatekeeper to change the bandwidth of the connection.
5. The gatekeeper responds to the gateway with a BCF to confirm the new bandwidth.
6. The logical channel is re-established with the new bandwidth.

Figure 9.36 Bandwidth Change Request.

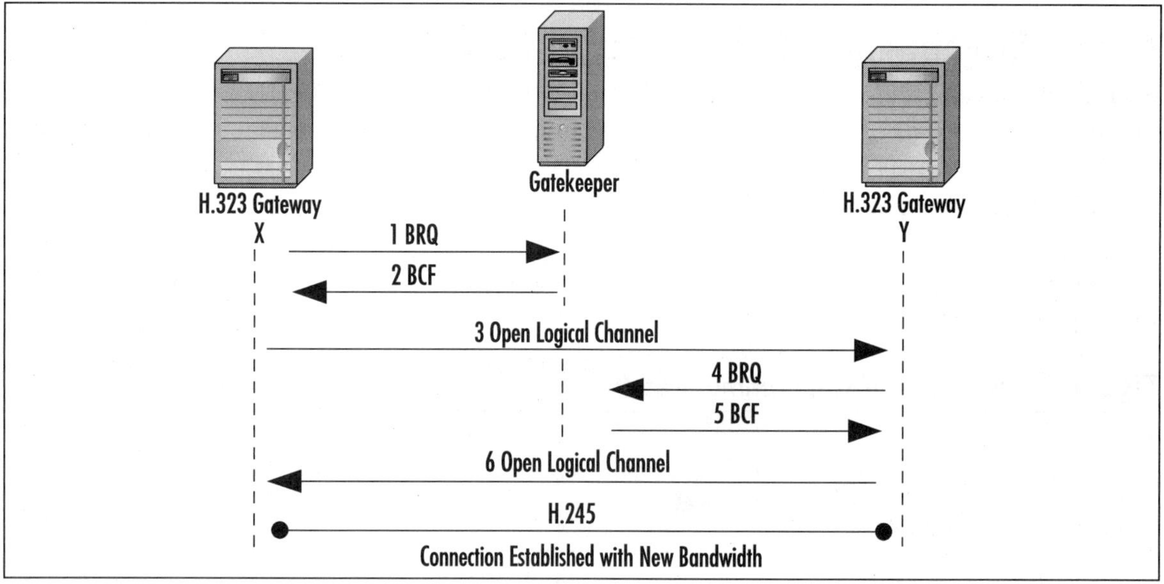

Call Termination

Call termination stops the media streams and closes the logical channels, and may be requested by any endpoint or gatekeeper. It ends the H.245 session, releases H.225/Q.931 connections, and provides disconnect confirmation to the gatekeeper via RAS. Figure 9.37 shows call termination flow and is described as follows:

1. Gateway Y initiates call termination by sending an H.245 End Session Command (ESC) message to Gateway X.
2. Gateway X releases the call endpoint and confirms with an H.245 ESC message to Gateway Y.
3. Gateway Y completes the call release by sending an H.245 Release Complete message to Gateway X.
4. Gateway X and Gateway Y disengage with the gatekeeper by sending a RAS DRQ message.
5. Gatekeeper disengages and confirms by sending DCF messages to both Gateway X and Gateway Y.

Figure 9.37 Call Termination (H.245/H.225/Q.931/RAS)

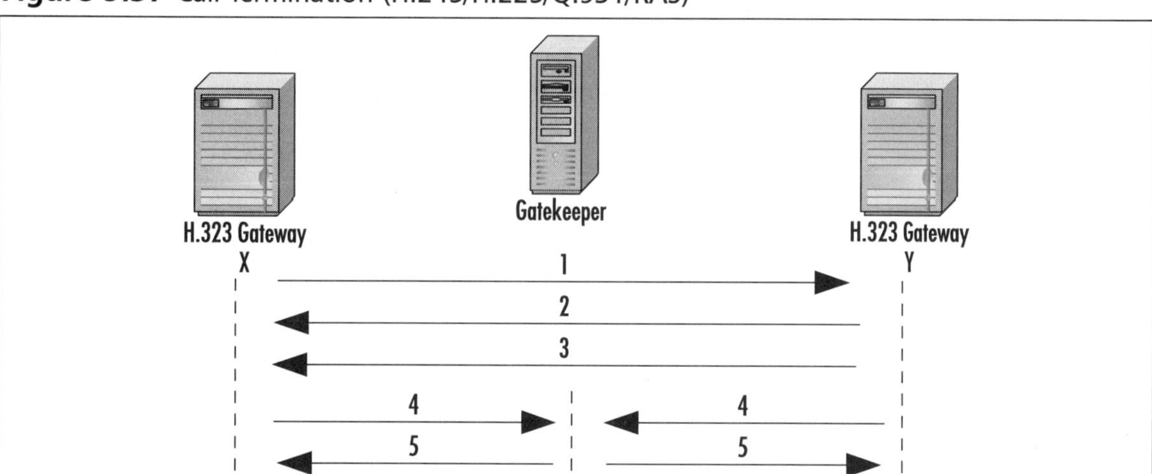

H.323 Endpoint-to-Endpoint Signaling

Assuming that endpoints (clients) know each other's IP addresses, the H.323 signaling is shown in Figure 9.38. This figure is based on the steps described in the previous section, "Call Termination."

Figure 9.38 H.323 Endpoint-to-Endpoint Signaling

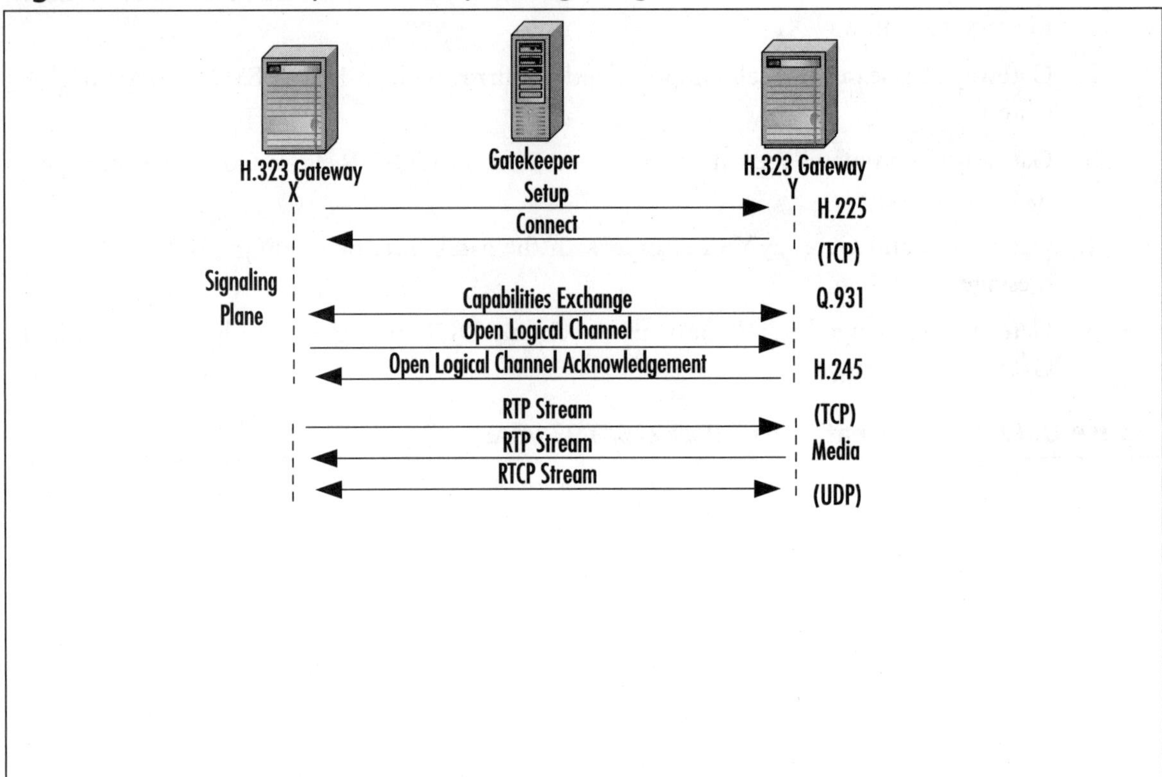

Session Initiation Protocol

SIP (RFC2543) is a simple signaling protocol for Internet conferencing and telephony. Based on Simple Mail Transfer Protocol (SMTP) and HyperText Transfer Protocol (HTTP), SIP was developed by the Internet Engineering Task Force's (IETF's) Multiparty Multimedia Session Control (MMUSIC) working group. SIP specifies procedures for telephony and multimedia conferencing over the Internet. SIP is an application-layer protocol independent of lower layer protocols (TCP, UDP, ATM, X.25).

SIP is based on a client/server architecture in which the client initiates the calls. By conforming to these existing text-based Internet standards (SMTP and HTTP), troubleshooting and network debugging are facilitated. The protocol can be read without decoding the binary ASN.1 payload required in non-text-based protocols, such as H.323. SIP is widely supported and is not dependent on a single vendor's equipment or implementation.

SIP is a newer protocol than H.323 and does not have maturity and industry support at this time. However, because of its simplicity, scalability, modularity, and ease with which it integrates with other applications, this protocol is attractive for use in packetized voice architectures. Some of the key features that SIP offers are:

- Address resolution, name mapping, and call redirection
- Dynamic discovery of endpoint media capabilities using the Session Description Protocol (SDP)

- Dynamic discovery of endpoint availability
- Session origination and management between host and endpoints

Session Initiation Protocol Components

The SIP system contains two components: user agents and network servers. A *user agent* (UA) is an endpoint, which makes and receives SIP calls.

- **User agent client (UAC)** Initiates SIP requests.
- **User agent server (UAS)** Receives the requests from the UAC and returns responses for the user.

SIP clients can include:

- IP telephones (UACs or UASs)
- Gateways to provide conferencing and translation

There are three kinds of SIP servers:

- **Proxy server** Determines the server to which the request should be forwarded. Request can actually transit many SIP servers to its destination. Responses return in reverse order.
- **Redirect server** Notifies the calling party of the actual location of destination.
- **Registrar server** Provides registration services for UACs at their current locations. Often deployed with proxy and redirect servers.

Figure 9.39 illustrates the interaction between SIP components.

Figure 9.39 SIP Components

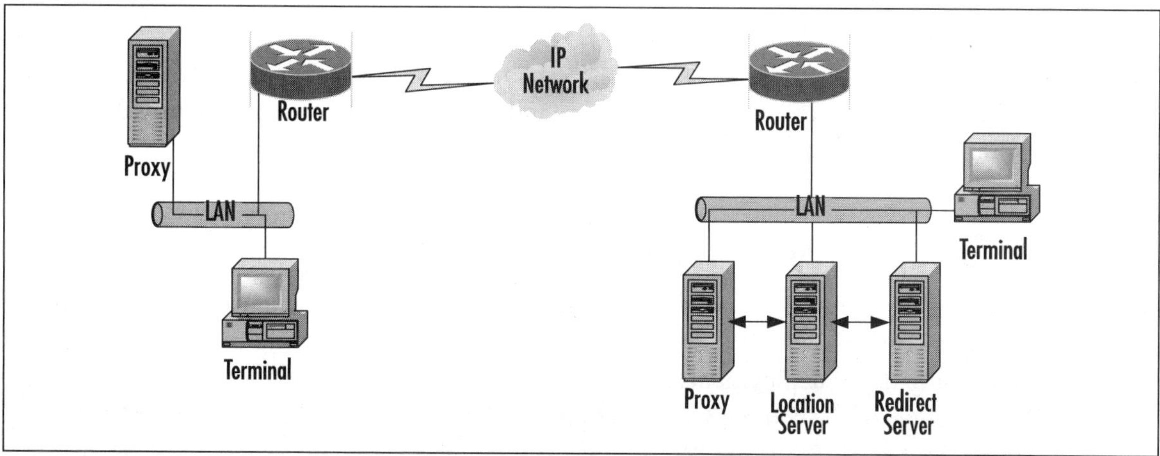

Session Initiation Protocol Messages

SIP works on a simple premise of client/server operation. Clients or endpoints are identified by unique addresses. These addresses come in a format very similar to that of an e-mail address: **user@domain.com**.

- SIP addresses are URLs: user@host
- User: name, telephone (E-164 address), number
- Host: domain, numeric network (IP) address

The users or clients register with SIP servers to provide location contact information.

SIP uses *messages* for call connection and control. There are two types of SIP messages: requests and responses. SIP messages are defined as follows:

- **Invite** Used to invite a user to a call. Header fields contain:
  - Addresses of the caller and the person being called
  - Subject of the call
  - Call priority
  - Call routing requests
  - Caller preferences for the user location
  - Desired features of the response
- **Bye** Used to terminate a connection between two users.
- **Register** Conveys location information to a SIP server, allowing a user to tell the server how to map an incoming address into an outgoing address that will reach the user.
- **ACK** Confirms reliable message exchanges.
- **Cancel** Cancels impending requests.
- **Options** Solicits information about the capabilities of the end being called, such as the difference between a plain old telephone handset and a fully-featured multimedia phone.

Media Gateway Control Protocol

MGCP (RFC 2705) is a relatively new protocol and as such, it is not as widely deployed as its H.323 and SIP predecessors. MGCP offers many key benefits and is growing in popularity, especially in Cisco CallManager deployments.

MGCP is a merger of the Simple Gateway Control Protocol (SGCP) and the Internet Protocol Device Control (IPDC). SGCP calls for a simplified design and a centralized intelligent call control. IPDC was designed to provide a medium to bridge VoIP networks and traditional telephony networks. MGCP is a media control protocol, suited for large-scale IP telephony deployment, and supports VoIP only.

MGCP incorporates *media gateway controllers (MGCs)* or *call agents* to perform all call connection and call control within an MGCP network. These MGCs signal to, and control, media gateways (MGs) to connect and control VoIP calls. All the information for making and completing a VoIP call is held in the MG.

MGs have very little intelligence and receive all their marching orders from the MGC; they cannot function without a controlling MGC. In a Cisco CallManager deployment, the MGC is often a CallManager server and the media gateway is a router used to connect to a dissimilar network. Examples of gateway applications are:

- **Trunking gateways** Interfaces between the telephone network and a VoIP network. Manage a large number of digital circuits.
- **Voice over ATM gateways** Interface to an ATM network.
- **Residential gateways** Provide a traditional analog (RJ11) interface to a VoIP network. Examples of residential gateways include cable modem/cable set-top boxes, and broadband wireless devices.
- **Access gateways** Provide a traditional analog (RJ11) or digital PBX interface to a VoIP network. Examples of access gateways include small-scale VoIP gateways.
- **Business gateways** Provide a traditional digital PBX interface or an integrated "soft PBX" interface to a VoIP network.
- **Network access servers** Can attach a modem to a telephone circuit and provide data access to the Internet. We expect that in the future, the same gateways will combine VoIP services and network access services.

When a gateway device detects that an end-user phone connection goes off-hook, it is directed by the MGC to provide a dial tone to the phone and receives the dialed digits and forwards them to the MGC for call processing.

MGCP Connections

In an MGCP connection, there are two basic types of logical devices: endpoints and connections. *Endpoints* are the physical, or logical interfaces that either initiate or terminate a VoIP connection. Endpoints are most often analog or digital ports in routers acting as gateway devices or digital interfaces into a PBX system.

Connections are temporary logical flows that are created to establish, maintain, and terminate a VoIP call. Once the call is complete, the connection is torn down and the resources that were allocated for that connection can be reused to support another connection. A *one-to-one connection* is really a point-to-point connection; a single endpoint signals to another single endpoint for the purposes of completing a single VoIP connection. *Multipoint calls* are used for conferencing and broadcast to multiple endpoints simultaneously.

MGCs manage connections in an MGCP network using the Session Description Protocol. SDP uses ASCII commands over IP/UDP to perform all call management functions. A series of eight connection messages is used by the MGC in order to control endpoints.

- CreateConnection
- ModifyConnection
- DeleteConnection
- NotificationRequest
- Notify
- AuditEndpoint
- AuditConnection
- RestartInProgress

Skinny Station Protocol

Skinny Station Protocol SSP is a Cisco proprietary communications protocol based on the industry standard Simple Gateway Control Protocol. Skinny Station Protocol enables communication between first generation IP telephone handsets/Gateways and CallManager servers. Products that support Skinny Station Protocol include the DT-24 and DE-30 gateways, the Catalyst 6000 8-Port T-1/E-1 voice service modules, as well as the Catalyst 6000 24 port FXS module. Skinny Station Protocol relies on the CallManager server to relay configuration and control information. It is built on TCP/IP and utilizes TCP ports 2000-2002.

Simplified Messaging Desk Interface

SMDI is a standard voice-mail protocol for integrating voice-mail systems with legacy PBX systems and/or other similar devices.

Cisco VoIP Hardware and Software

Up to this point, this chapter has been focused on the underlying technologies and concepts that are integral to VoIP. We will now turn our attention to Cisco-specific information. Cisco offers a variety of hardware and software solutions for implementing VoIP. Its routers and switches can be adapted to support voice communications, usually with the addition of voice modules and software in many cases.

Voice Modules and Cards

Routers and switches use voice modules to transform and transport voice traffic across the IP network. They use Voice Interface Cards (VICs) to provide connectivity to telephone equipment. Voice Network Modules (VNMs) and VICs are configured using Cisco IOS VoIP commands. Digital signal processors are used in various Cisco voice-enabled routers in order to convert analog voice signals to digital for transmission across an IP network and to convert back to analog once the packet has arrived at the destination router. DSPs can be found as modules inserted onto the motherboard, as on the 1700 series routers, or as slots built onto a VNM that is placed in the router. For more information on DSPs, refer back to the section entitled "DSP Provisioning".

Voice Network Modules

VNMs convert analog voice into a digital form for transmission over the IP network. At least one VNM is needed to enable the router to handle voice traffic. VNMs come in several different models for the 2600/3600 series routers. Figure 9.40 shows several models of VNMs available for the 26XX and 36XX routers.

Figure 9.40 Voice Network Modules

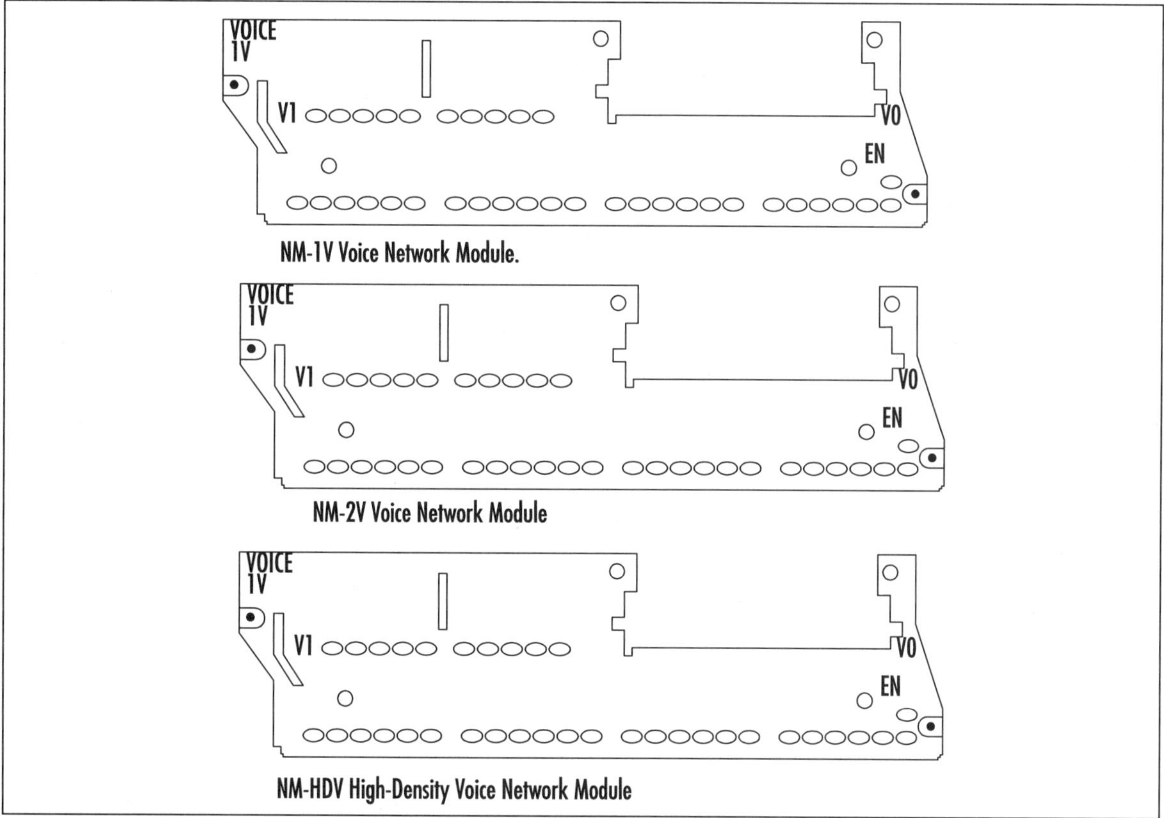

Only VICs are supported in the carriers with a *V* in the name. The NM-1V is a one-slot VNM. You can install one VIC in the NM-1V to gain up to two voice ports. The NM-1V/2V does not support WAN interface cards (WICs). The NM-2V is a two-slot version of the VNM. You can install up to two VICs in the NM-2V, providing up to four voice ports. The NM-HDV high-density VNM. This network module consists of five slots, one for the voice WIC (VWIC) and four for the packet voice DSP modules (PVDM). You can install one VWIC in the NM-HDV, providing up to two voice ports. The VNMs are the housings for the actual voice interface cards that provide the necessary functionality and connectivity to achieve voice communications.

Voice Interface Cards

Voice Interface Cards (VICs) are inserted in the VNM to provide the necessary interface and support for the desired type of voice configuration (FXS, FXO, or E&M). Figure 9.41 shows several VICs to give you an idea of what is available; this is not an exhaustive list, as Cisco continues to expand in this area.

Figure 9.41 Voice Interface Cards

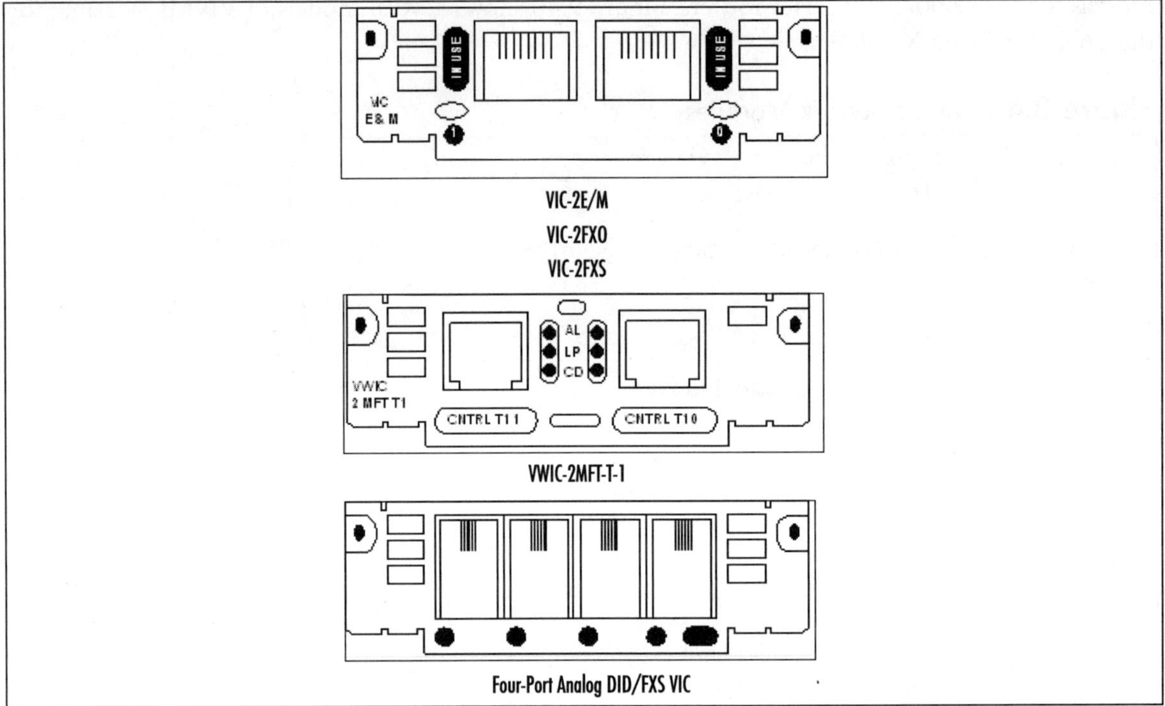

One thing we would caution you about is that physically and outwardly, there is no difference between the FXS and FXO connectors; it can be easy to plug a telephone into what you think is an FXS port, but is actually an FXO port. Ensure that you are using the proper port type by checking the color and labels before attempting to connect.

- **VIC-2E/M** The two-port E&M module VIC-2E/M connects an IP network directly to a PBX system. It can be configured for special settings associated with tie-line ports on most PBXs. E&M ports are color-coded brown.
- **VIC-2FXS** The two-port FXS module VIC-2FXS connects to endpoint equipment such as a telephone, keypad, or fax. These ports provide ringing voltage, dial tone, and other endpoint specific functionality. FXS ports are color-coded gray.
- **VIC-2FXO** The two-port FXO module VIC-2FXO connects to a PBX or PSTN. FXO ports are color-coded pink. Other types of FXO cards for use outside North America are capable of providing switching and signaling techniques used in other geographic regions such as VIC-2FXO-EU for use in Europe.
- **VWIC-2MFT-T-1** The two-port VWIC multiflex trunk interface card is a two-port card that can be used for voice, data, and integrated voice/data applications. The multiflex VWIC can support data-only applications as a WAN interface on the Cisco 1700, 2600, or 3600. It can also integrate voice and data with the Drop and Insert multiplexer

functionality and/or configured to support packetized voice (VoIP) when in the digital T-1/E-1 network module.

- **Two-Port ISDN BRI Card** Two two-port ISDN BRI VICs are available for the Cisco 1700, 2600, and Cisco 3600 series routers. These cards are available as ISDN BRI S/T or NT interfaces for terminating to an ISDN network.
- **Four-Port Analog DID/FXS VICs** Two direct inward dial interface cards are available. One card is a two-port RJ-11 that supports DID only. These cards are used for providing DID service to extensions on a PBX so that users may transparently dial directly to extensions.

Installing VNMs and VICs

The types of router chassis described in this section demonstrate how VNMs, VICs, and additional voice port adapters are installed on the various platforms. We chose a sampling of Cisco routers to structure our discussion, but the concepts and processes are similar for all Cisco routers, with a few minor adjustments.

E-1/T-1 Voice Connectivity

Digital E-1 and T-1 connectivity allows Cisco series routers and switches to provide E-1 or T-1 voice connectivity to PBXs or to a CO. T-1 voice connections are available for various routers and switches, including, but not limited to Cisco 1700, 2600, 3600, 3700, MC3810, 7200, 7500, AS5300, AS5800, and Catalyst 4000 and 6000 series equipment.

The 1700, 2600, 3600, 7200, and 7500 series routers are capable of VoFR and VoIP. The MC3810 (now end of sale) supports VoFR, VoATM, and VoIP. The AS5300 is able to perform VoIP, VoHDLC, or VoFR functions.

The 7200, 7500 series, and AS5300 series are primarily used as tandem switch points from T-1 tie lines to PBXs and the PSTN to the internal IP network. An example of the use of tandem switch points is receiving a voice call on one VoIP interface and switching it back out another VoIP interface to its final destination. The 1700, 2600, and 3600 routers series can perform this function because support for voice T-1/E-1 interfaces with up to two T-1/E-1 circuits per card has been added. The T-1/E-1 enhanced voice port adapter is used in the 7200 and 7500 series routers and can support up to two T-1s per card. The AS5300 series access switch uses the T-1 carrier card that can support up to four T-1s.

The 7200, 7500, and AS5850 can terminate T-1s for voice traffic into the WAN and forward the signals and transmissions to the 1700, 2600, 3600, and AS5300 series routers for complete processing. The 7200 Series offers a four- or six-slot configuration, with interfaces including ATM, Synchronous Optical Network Technologies (SONET), ISDN BRI, ISDN PRI, T-1, E-1, T3, and E3. Its multi-service interchange (MIX) allows the 7200 to support digital voice as well as gateway functionality through the use of two different trunk interfaces, the high-capacity and medium-capacity T-1/E-1 trunk interface cards. The primary difference between the two cards is that the high-capacity card includes an on-board DSP card for compression. The 7200 Series can support up to 120 voice calls, depending on the module configuration used. This router also supports analog voice applications through the use of voice interface cards (VICs).

1700 Series Router Configurations

The 1700 series modular access routers are designed for small- to medium-sized businesses. The 1700 family has several chassis for different applications, but the two that were designed specifically for voice applications are the 1751 and the 1760. These two modular chassis use the Cisco IOS along with various VICs to support analog and digital voice traffic over the IP network.

Cisco 1751 Modular Access Router

The Cisco 1751 is a standalone chassis that can support up to three voice interface slots. It comes in two models: a base model suited primarily for data, but with an easy upgrade path to voice, and a multiservice model (identified with a *V*) that includes all features for immediate integration of data and voice. Both models include three slots for data/voice interface cards as well as a 10/100 Ethernet port, a console port, and an auxiliary port. The 1700 series VICs are interchangeable with the Cisco 2600 and 3600 series routers.

The Cisco 1751 includes one PVDM-256K-4 (one DSP) that supports one analog VIC. If two analog VICs or one or more digital ISDN VICs are used, additional DSPs are required. The Cisco 1751 has two DSP slots to support additional voice channels. A PVDM is required to support VICs on the Cisco 1750 and 1760 routers. These two chassis require PVDMs to be placed on the motherboard, unlike the Cisco 2600, 3600, and 3700 routers, which have DSP support on the VNMs.

The Cisco 1760 Modular Access Router

The Cisco 1760 has four slots for VICs, and is available in two models. The base model is suited for data networking, but can be upgraded to support voice. The multi-service model (identified with a *V*) includes all features for immediate integration of data and voice. Both models include four slots for data/voice interface cards and a 10/100 Ethernet port.

The Cisco 1760 includes one PVDM-256K-4 (one DSP) that supports one analog VIC. If two analog VICs or one or more digital ISDN VICs are used, additional DSPs are required. The Cisco 1760 has two DSP slots to support additional voice channels.

3600 and 3700 Series Router Configurations

Cisco's 3600 and 3700 series routers come in a variety of base configurations that differ in the amount and/or type of standard network interfaces (RJ-45 ports, serial ports, and ISDN ports) that are available. The Cisco3600 and 3700 are designed primarily for traditional and power branch office solutions.

The 3600 series router comes in three varieties: the 3620, which has two network module slots; the 3640, which has four network module slots; and the 3660, which is equipped with six network module slots. The 3640 is end of sale as of this writing.

The 3700 series router comes in two varieties: the 3725, which has three integrated WIC slots and two network module slots, and the 3745, which has three integrated WIC slots and four network module slots. Currently, the built-in WICs do not support VICs.

Most Cisco 1700 VICs can be used for the 3600 and 3700 series except that a VNM is required in these higher-end routers. Installation of these VNMs is covered later in this chapter.

NOTE

For 3700 platforms, the minimum IOS release is IOS 12.2(8) T for all network modules and VICs.

7500 Series Router Configurations

The 7500 series high-end routers support voice, video, and data. The Cisco 7500 series includes the Cisco 7505, the Cisco 7507, and the Cisco 7513 with 5, 7, and 13 slots, respectively. Cisco 7500 adapters include the two-port T-1 and E-1 high-capacity enhanced digital voice port adapter, the two-port T-1 and E-1 moderate-capacity enhanced digital voice port adapter, and the one-port T-1 and E-1 enhanced digital voice port adapters.

AS5350 and 5850 Universal Gateway Configuration

The Cisco AS5350 and AS5850 universal gateways provide from 2 to 96 T-1s or E-1s to support data, voice, wireless, and fax services on any port. The AS5350 is only one rack unit high and supports 216 voice, dial, or universal ports. The AS5350 is mainly intended for ISPs and enterprises, whereas the Cisco AS5850 was designed for large service providers. The AS5850 is 14 rack units high and supports 2688 voice or universal ports. Both chassis support hot-swappable cards and fans to minimize service interruption. The AS5350 supports two-, four-, or eight-T-1/E-1 configurations; the AS5850 supports up to four 24-port T-1 cards for a total of 96 T-1s.

NOTE

The minimum IOS release for the Cisco AS5850 platform is IOS 12.2(1)XB for the 24-channel T-1 card.

Cisco Switches

Catalyst switches operate at Layer 2, but Layer 3 switching is also possible with a Route Switch Module (RSM). Certain Cisco switches were designed specifically to support IP telephony with features such as inline power and gateway functionality. We will discuss three lines that meet this challenge: the 3500, 4000, and 6000 Series.

The Catalyst 4000 series with the Access Gateway Module (WS-X4604-GWY) can support up to three VICs for T-1/E-1 voice connectivity. The Catalyst 6000 series utilizing the T-1 Service Module (WS-X6608-T-1) can support up to eight T-1s for voice connectivity.

Catalyst 3500 Series Switches

The 3500 series is a scalable, entry-level solution for small- to mid-sized networks. It is a wholly Cisco-developed switch, with a router-like IOS. The 3500 Series of switches are fixed configuration switches, and all offer 10/100 Ethernet ports and Gigabit Interface Converter (GBIC) ports. The 3550-24PWR is the only switch in the 3500 Series that supports inline power.

Catalyst 4x00 Series Switches

The Cisco Catalyst 4000 series switches are modular chassis available in several configurations. They are designed primarily for enterprise offices, branch offices, and multi-site campuses. Both chassis can provide inline power for end-user Cisco IP phones and thus can also centralize power management.

The 4x00 Series is a step up from the 3500, offering a modular configuration in several different switches: the 4003, 4006, 4503, 4506, and 4507R. The 4x00 Series also offers supervisor engine functionality, similar to that of the 5500 Series. Within the 4x00 Series, only the 4003 does not offer inline power. The 4x00 Series also offers voice-gateway functionality through the use of the Series 4x00 WS-X4604-GWY module, which provides support for both H.323 and SSP (in the future it will support MGCP).

Catalyst 4000 Modules

The Catalyst 4000 currently offers a mid-range hardware-based conferencing and transcoding solution. The Access Gateway Module (AGM) is equipped with slots for DSP modules, high-density analog, Gigabit Ethernet, and three slots for VICs. The AGM provides the following services: IP WAN routing, VoIP, and IP telephony. It supports VICs and WICs from the 1600/1700/2600/3600 Series routers. The AGM supports the following ports and slots:

- Two VIC/WIC slots (VWICs, VICs, and WICs)
- One dedicated VIC slot (VWICs and VICs)
- FlexSlot High Density Analog (8 port RJ-21 FXS module)
- Four DSP SIMM slots
- 64 or 128MB memory SIMM slot (Integrated Service Adapter)

VoIP gateway mode requires DSP resources to convert voice calls into data packets. The Cisco IOS IP/DSP Plus feature set is another requirement to allow VoIP gateway capabilities. The AGM supports the following interfaces as a VoIP gateway:

- T-1 and E-1 ISDN PRI
- T-1 Channel Associated Signaling
- Foreign Exchange Office
- Foreign Exchange Station
- E&M

The AGM can function as a DSP farm for Cisco CallManager, which can be configured to provide hardware-based conferencing. The Catalyst 4000 gateway module has four DSP SIMMs, with each SIMM having six DSPs for a total of 24 DSP resources. Table 9.8 summarizes the Catalyst 4000 AGM capabilities.

Table 9.8 Catalyst 4000 AGM DSP Resources.

Function	Capability
PSTN gateway	96 channels of G.711 voice
Conferencing	24 channels of G.711 conferencing (4 conferences x 6 through 8 x 3)
MTP transcoding	16 channels of LBR to G.711

Figure 9.42 depicts how the DSP resources are provisioning within the Catalyst 4000 after it is configured for gateway mode.

Figure 9.42 Catalyst 4000 Gateway Mode DSP Resources

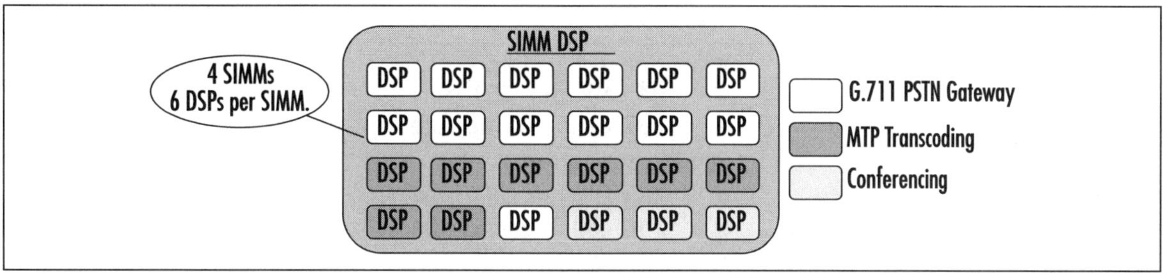

The Catalyst 4000 DSPs can only support G.711 conferencing sessions. This is not to say that there can be a conference session on a Catalyst 4000 with only G.711 participants, but that transcoding DSP resources must be involved to convert those participants to the G.711 CODEC for the conference. The Catalyst 4000 AGM module supports up to 16 transcoding sessions per module via hardware and would handle up to 104 channels in software.

Cisco Catalyst 4200

The Cisco Catalyst 4200 is a small branch office device that can provide voice gateway capabilities, IP routing, and Ethernet switching in a single chassis. It comes equipped with a 24-port 10/100 switch that can provide inline power to Cisco IP phones and a built-in eight-port FXS module for support of legacy analog telephony equipment. It is capable of using the same voice/WAN interface cards as the 1700, 2600, and 3600 families of routers.

Catalyst 6500 Series Switches

The 6500 Series has highly scalable, enterprise-class switches. The 6500 Series offers a completely modular design, utilizing supervisor modules, with the capability for redundant supervisor modules, if necessary. There are five switches in the 6500 Series family: the 6503, 6506, 6509, 6506, 6509, and 6513; the last two digits indicate the number of slots on each chassis. The 6500 Series provides inline power through its specialized 48-port switching modules. Gateway functionality is provided via the WS-X6658-x1 module, which supports SSP and MGCP. The 6500 Series also offers an eight-port voice T-1/E-1 and services module to provide connectivity to legacy PSTN or PBX systems, as well as a 24-port FXS module for analog telephone connectivity.

Catalyst 6000 Modules

The Cisco WS-6608-T-1/E-1 module for Catalyst 6000 offers similar functionality as the Catalyst 4000 AGM, only targeted at CO or headquarters environments. This module provides Digital T-1 or E-1 PSTN and PBX gateway services, transcoding, and conference bridging with eight T-1 or E-1 ports to support common channel signaling or ISDN PRI signaling. Each port can be configured as a PSTN/PBX gateway, MTP transcoder, or a conference bridge. Table 9.9 summarizes the DSP resource capabilities of the Catalyst 6000 Voice T-1/E-1 and Services module.

Table 9.9 Catalyst 6000 DSP Resources

Function	Capability
PSTN gateway	WS-6608-T-1 module: ■ 24 calls per DS1 port ■ 192 calls per module WS-6608-E-1: ■ 30 calls per DS1 port ■ 240 calls per module
Conferencing	G.711 or G.723: ■ 32 conferencing participants per physical port ■ Maximum conference size of six participants ■ 256 conference participants per module G.729: ■ 24 conferencing participants per physical port ■ Maximum conference size of six participants ■ 192 conference participants per module
MTP transcoding	G.723 to G.711: ■ 31 MTP transcoding sessions per physical port ■ 248 sessions per module G.729 to G.711 ■ 24 MTP transcoding sessions per physical port ■ 192 sessions per module

The 8-port T-1/E-1 Voice and Services module performs 24 transcoding sessions per port when translating from G.729 to G.711. It does 31 sessions per port for G.723 to G.711. The 8-port module can handle 192 or 248 sessions per module, depending on the LBR CODEC utilized. The Catalyst 6000 can perform a mix of transcoding and conferencing within the same DSP.

Each port on WS-6608-T-1/E-1 is configured with an IP address making it a PSTN gateway, conferencing, or transcoding resource in Cisco CallManager. A TFTP server must be configured to download the configuration.

Inline Power Options

Second-generation phones are superior to their first-generation counterparts because they offer support for *inline power*. First-generation telephones require an external power source. Inline power can be offered to second-generation telephones either via a powered patch panel or through inline power modules installed in the switch.

LAN Queuing for Video/Voice

Queuing has traditionally been a Layer 3 function for WAN connections, but when discussing a converged network, specifically that dealing with voice or video traffic, attention must also be given to the LAN. Layer 2 traffic can be classified by type of service using the 802.1Q protocol. You should separate voice and video traffic from data traffic into a high-priority queue. 802.1Q specifies seven classes of service, with 0 being the lowest priority and 7 being the highest priority. CoS 4-7 should be used for voice and video, and that 0-3 for data traffic. An important note to make regarding Layer 2 queuing is that once the packet encounters a router, the Layer 2 information is lost—in other words, 802.1Q is only a LAN solution. For traffic crossing WAN links, Layer 3 queuing must be incorporated.

Quality of Service

Voice traffic and data traffic have different characteristics. Unlike data traffic, voice traffic occurs in real time and is delay-sensitive. Voice packets tend to be smaller than data packets. When voice and data networks are merged, it is important to deliver an acceptable QoS for the voice traffic.

Voice traffic must be prioritized to minimize delay and jitter. *Delay* is the amount of time between the original transmission of the voice information and the final processing by the receiving station. *Jitter* is the variation in the delay between successive voice packets. Packet loss due to network errors or congestion will impact jitter. QoS depends on the ability to control these two factors that impact voice quality.

QoS tools can be divided into three categories:

- **Classification** Voice packets can be classified or marked with a specific priority to enhance QoS.
- **Queuing** Use separate queues for voice and date to ensure consistency and QoS for voice.
- **Provisioning** Circuits carrying voice traffic should be provisioned with enough bandwidth or capacity to minimize delay and jitter.

The increasing deployment of VoIP can be attributed to the improvements made in QoS. QoS is a set of ideas, procedures, practices, and numerous protocols that provide for reliable and efficient transportation across data networks.

What Is Quality of Service?

QoS is simply a set of tools to ensure that a minimum level of service will be provided to certain traffic. Many protocols and applications are not critically sensitive to network congestion. File Transfer Protocol (FTP), for example, has a rather large tolerance for network delay or bandwidth limitation.

Applications such as voice and video are particularly sensitive to network delay. If voice packets take too long to reach their destination, the resulting speech sounds choppy or distorted. QoS can be used to assure services to these applications. Critical business applications can also use QoS.

Applications for Quality of Service

When would a network engineer consider designing QoS into a network? Here are a few reasons to deploy QoS in a network topology:

- To prioritize certain mission-critical applications in the network.
- To maximize the use of the current network investment in infrastructure.
- To provide better performance for delay-sensitive applications such as voice and video.
- To respond to changes in network traffic flows.

When deploying QoS, analyze the traffic flowing through the bottleneck, determine the importance of each protocol and application, and determine a strategy to prioritize the access to the bandwidth. QoS allows control over bandwidth, latency, and jitter and minimizes packet loss within the network by prioritizing. Bandwidth is the measure of capacity on the network or a specific link. Latency is the delay of a packet traversing the network, and jitter is the change of latency over a given period of time.

Deploying certain types of QoS techniques can control these three parameters. QoS is not widely deployed within many networks. With the push for applications such as multicast, streaming multimedia, and VoIP, the need for QoS is more apparent, especially since these applications are susceptible to jitter and delay. Poor performance is immediately noticed by the end-user. However, QoS is not the magic solution to every congestion problem; it may very well be that upgrading the bandwidth of a congested link is the proper solution to the problem.

Levels of QoS

QoS can be divided into three different levels, also referred to as *service models*. These service models describe a set of end-to-end QoS capabilities. *End-to-end QoS* is the network's ability to provide a specific level of service to network traffic from one end of the network to the other. The three service levels are best-effort service, integrated service, and differentiated service.

Best-Effort Service

Best-effort service is when the network will make every possible attempt to deliver a packet to its destination. With best-effort service, there are no guarantees that the packet will ever reach its intended destination. An application can send data in any amount, whenever it needs to, without requesting permission or notifying the network.

Integrated Service

The integrated service model provides applications with a guaranteed level of service by negotiating network parameters end to end. Applications request the level of service necessary for them to operate properly and rely on the QoS mechanism to reserve the necessary network resources prior to the beginning of transmission. The application will not send traffic until it receives confirmation that the network can handle the load and provide the requested QoS end to end. To accomplish this task, the network uses a process called *admission control.*

Cisco IOS uses RSVP and intelligent queuing. RSVP is currently in the process of being standardized by the IETF in one of its working groups. Intelligent queuing includes technologies such as Weighted Fair Queuing and Weighted Random Early Detection (WRED).

RSVP works in conjunction with the routing protocols to determine the best path through the network that will provide the QoS required. RSVP routers create dynamic access lists to provide the QoS requested to ensure that packets are delivered at the prescribed minimum quality parameters.

Differentiated Service

Differentiated service includes a set of classification tools and queuing mechanisms to provide certain protocols or applications with a certain priority over other network traffic. Differentiated services rely on edge routers to perform the classification of the types of packets traversing a network. Network traffic can be classified by network address, protocols and ports, ingress interfaces, or whatever classification that can be accomplished through the use of a standard or extended access list.

Why QoS Is Essential in VOIP Networks

The challenge facing a converged infrastructure is to provide the efficiency of a packet-switched network with the reliability of a legacy network. This is the role that QoS fills.

QoS, through a variety of methods, gives reliability and availability to a converged infrastructure and still affords it the same benefits of efficient utilization of resources by providing the following:

- Managed response times
- Jitter (variation in delay) control
- Prioritization of delay-sensitive traffic
- Congestion management
- Congestion avoidance
- Support and enforcement of dedicated bandwidth requirements
- Management and recovery of packet loss

With QoS, converged infrastructures can provide end users with a convenient, low-cost, scalable, and above all, reliable solution for the majority of their communications. Without QoS, a converged infrastructure would be comparable to anarchy, with little to no reliability, convenience, or scalability—to a level where a single FTP session could shut down your entire VoIP infrastructure.

Configuring Voice Ports

We have now discussed the basic hardware installation for VNMs and VICs. The next step is to configure the cards on the Cisco router IOS. Voice card configuration is covered in the following sections. Some basic configuration parameters must be set in order for a voice port to operate. To configure a voice port, complete the following steps.

1. Enter Privileged Exec mode:

   ```
   router> enable
   ```

2. Check the DSP voice channel activity with the following command:

   ```
   router# show voice dsp
   ```

3. Enter Global Configuration mode:

   ```
   router# configure terminal
   ```

4. Enter Voice Card Configuration mode. On the router, the slot must be 0:

   ```
   router(config)# voice-card slot
   ```

5. Enter the CODEC type for the voice card:

   ```
   router(config-voicecard)# CODEC {med | high}
   ```

This series of steps sets the CODEC compression technique, which is either high or medium complexity. High complexity can handle fewer calls per DSP. This is due to the higher CPU utilization required for high CODEC complexity operation. High and medium complexity CODECs:

- **High complexity** Specifies two voice channels encoded in any of the following formats: G.711ulaw, G.711alaw, G.723.1 (r5.3), G.723.1 Annex A (r5.3), G.723.1 (r6.3), G.723.1 Annex A (r6.3), G.726 (r16), G.726 (r24), G.726 (r32), G.728, G.729, G.729 Annex B, and fax relay.
- **Medium (default) complexity** Specifies four voice channels encoded in any of the following formats: G.711ulaw, G.711alaw, G.726 (r16), G.726 (r24), G.726 (r32), G.729 Annex A, G.729 Annex B with Annex A, and fax relay.

Configuring FXO or FXS Voice Ports

All these parameters have default settings, and FXS and FXO port default configuration values are adequate for most situations. Therefore, user intervention is rarely needed. The following settings are mandatory to any FXS/FXO port configuration:

- Signal type
- Call progress tone
- Ring frequency
- Ring number
- Dial type (FXO only)
- PLAR connection mode
- Music threshold

- Description
- Voice activity detection (VAD)
- Comfort noise

Follow these steps to complete a basic setup for all FXS/FXO voice ports:

1. Enter Privileged Exec mode:

```
router> enable
```

2. Enter Global configuration mode:

```
router# configure terminal
```

3. Identify which port to configure on a 2600 and 3600 series router:

```
router(config)# voice-port nm-module/vic-module/port-number
router(config)# voice-port slot/port      (Cisco 175x/1760 and MC3810)
```

4. Select the appropriate signaling for the start of a call:

```
router(config-voiceport)# signal [loop-start|ground-start]
```

5. Select the appropriate country codes for call progression signaling. The default is *northamerica*:

```
router(config-voiceport)# cptone country-code
```

6. Configure the voice port connection mode type. If the connection will be to a PBX, use the **tie-line** option. If the connection will be for private line automatic ringdown (PLAR), use the **plar** option. If the connection will be for PLAR off-premises extension (OPX), use the **plar-opx** option.

```
router(config-voiceport)# connection {tie-line | plar | plar-opx} string
```

7. Assign the appropriate out-dialing dial type (FXO only):

```
router(config-voiceport# dial-type{dtmf | pulse}
```

8. Configure the frequency in Hertz of ringing for the system that is attached on a Cisco 1750, 2600, and 3600 series router (FXS only):

```
router(config-voiceport)# ring frequency [25| 50]
router(config-voiceport)# ring frequency [20| 30]
```

9. Configure the maximum number of rings allowed before answering a call (FXO only):

```
router(config-voiceport)# ring number number
```

10. Specify an existing pattern for ring tone or define a new one (FXS only). Each pattern specifies a ring-pulse time and a ring-interval time:

```
router(config-voiceport)# ring cadence {[pattern01 | pattern02 … pattern12]
[define pulse interval]}
```

11. Specify the termination impedance, which needs to match the specifications of the PBX it is attaching to:

```
router(config-voiceport)# impedance [600c|600r|900c|complex1|complex2]
```

12. Configure the threshold in decibels for hold music:

```
router(config-voiceport)# music-threshold number
```

13. (Optional) Configure a text string to the configuration that describes the connection for this voice port:

```
router(config-voiceport)# description string
```

14. Configure background noise generation for the comfort of a user when there is no noise:

```
router(config-voiceport)# comfort-noise
```

15. (Optional) Enable voice activity detection:

```
router(config-voiceport)# vad
```

Configuring E&M Ports

E&M default settings are usually *not* sufficient to enable voice transmissions over IP. This is because E&M ports are designed to connect directly to a PBX and therefore must match the particular PBX's specifications. The following settings are mandatory to implement an E&M port:

- Signal type
- Call progress tone
- Operation
- Type
- Impedance

The following commands complete a basic setup for all E&M voice ports:

1. Enter Privileged Exec mode:

```
router> enable
```

2. Enter Global Configuration mode:

```
router# configure terminal
```

3. Identify which port to configure on a 2600 and 3600 series router:

```
router(config)# voice-port nm-module/vic-module/port-number
router(config)# voice-port slot/port (Cisco 175x/1760 and MC3810)
```

4. Select the appropriate signaling for the interface:

```
router(config-voiceport)# signal [wink-start|immediate|delay-dial]
```

5. Select the appropriate country codes for call progression signaling. The default is *us*. The *northamerica* keyword is for the Cisco MC3810 multiservice concentrator for versions prior to Cisco IOS Release 12.0(4)T and for ISDN PRI:

```
router(config-voiceport)# cptone country code
```

6. Define cabling scheme operation:

```
router(config-voiceport)# operation [2-wire|4-wire]
```

7. Select the appropriate E&M interface type:

```
router(config-voiceport)# type [1|2|3|5]
```

8. Specify the termination impedance, which needs to match the specifications of the PBX the port is attaching to:

```
router(config-voiceport)# impedance [600c|600r|900c|complex1|complex2]
```

Some optional configurations for the E&M port are not required for operation. As with the FXS/FXO ports, the following configurations are used for optimization and usability:

- Connection mode
- Music threshold
- Description
- Comfort tone (VAD-activated only)

Use the following commands to adjust any of these optional configuration parameters for E&M ports:

1. Enter Privileged Exec mode:

```
router> enable
```

2. Enter Global Configuration mode:

```
router# configure terminal
```

3. Identify which port to configure on a 2600 and 3600 series router:

```
router(config)# voice-port nm-module/vic-module/port-number
router(config)# voice-port slot/port (Cisco 175x/1760 and MC3810)
```

4. Specify that the port configured for PLAR (which we discuss in more detail later in this chapter):

```
router(config-voiceport)# connection plar string
```

5. Define the threshold in decibels for hold music:

```
router(config-voiceport)# music-threshold number
```

6. Specify a description field for port:

```
router(config-voiceport)# description string
```

7. Set comfort noise to generate background noise for the user when there is no sound on the line:

```
router(config-voiceport)# comfort-noise
```

Voice Port-Tuning Commands

Voice port fine-tuning commands adjust timing, delay, impedance parameters, input gain, and output attenuation. Once these adjustments are made, you can fine-tune volume control, how the number pads are dialed, and how long a voice port will wait before hanging up a signal.

Concepts of Delay and Echo

The most challenging part of designing a VoIP network is the transmission of real-time traffic. Voice communication is sensitive to delays and echo. Speech patterns become awkward and indistinguishable if there is too much delay in the voice traffic. Minimize delay as much as you can to get the voice traffic as close to real time as possible. In today's voice trafficking, two different kinds of delay must be handled: fixed delay and variable delay. The various delay points are illustrated in Figure 9.43.

Echo is the reflection of voice traffic back to the source of that traffic. A certain amount of echo is acceptable and desirable because it assures the source that voice traffic has been generated and sent. Too much echo is disruptive because the speaker will not be able to discern between his voice and the echo.

Figure 9.43 Voice Packet Delay

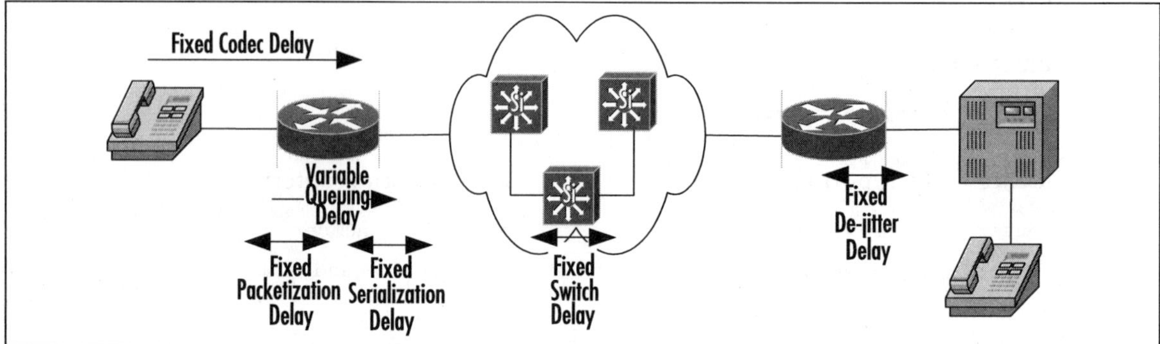

Fixed delay is the amount of time the signal needs to transverse the medium, such as copper, fiber, or microwave. This time is fixed because the laws of physics dictate how fast the data signals will go on particular media. Acceptable levels for most users are below 150ms one-way per ITU G.114. Fixed delays are composed of CODEC delays, packetization delays, and serialization.

- **CODEC induced delay** Compression/decompression of a voice packet from analog to digital format and vice versa. It ranges from 0.75ms to 30ms, depending on the CODEC used.
- **Packetization delay** Time it takes the equipment to actually produce a data packet. Should be under 30ms.
- **Serialization** Time it takes to clock a voice or data frame onto a network interface. Affected by the frame size and line speed.

Variable delays are synonymous with jitter and are caused by queuing variances during the transmission of a packet through the network. As the packets are transferred out of the queue, there can be a delay between voice packets that sounds like stuttering speech. QoS features can be used to alleviate the effects of jitter by prioritizing the voice traffic over other traffic. You can curb delay using several methods.

- **Queuing** Time it takes for a packet to exit the output queue of the device that is routing the data. Measured from the time the data is generated into the input queue to when it is released by the output queue.
- **Network switching** Delay across the public network such as a Frame Relay or ATM network.
- **De-jitter** Voice traffic works best if there is a constant flow of packets. Jitter must be minimized to improve the quality of the conversation. De-jitter buffers are utilized on the receiving end to adjust the variable delays into a fixed delay.

The command that adjusts the Cisco de-jitter buffering is **playout-delay.** The **playout-delay** command was configured under the voice-port configuration mode before IOS release 12.1(5)T. Release 12.1(5)T and later implement the command under the dial-peer configuration mode. The following steps are used to configure playout delay:

1. Enter Privileged Exec mode:

```
router> enable
```

2. Enter Global Configuration mode:

```
router# configure terminal
```

3. Identify the port to configure on a 2600 and 3600 series router:

```
router(config)# voice-port nm-module/vic-module/port-number
router(config)# voice-port slot/port (Cisco 175x/1760 and MC3810)
```

4. Determine the mode in which the jitter buffer will operate for calls on this voice port.
   - **Adaptive** Adjusts the jitter buffer size and amount of playout delay based on current network conditions. This is the default setting.
   - **Fixed** Defines the jitter buffer size as fixed so that the playout delay does not adjust. A constant playout delay is added.

   ```
   router(config-voiceport)# playout-delay mode {adaptive| fixed]
   ```

5. Tune the playout buffer to accommodate packet jitter caused by switches in the WAN:

   ```
   router(config-voiceport)# playout-delay {nominal value| maximum value
       | minimum {default | low | high}}
   ```

Fine-Tuning FXS/FXO Ports

Special parameters can be adjusted to fine-tune the ports, minimizing issues of delay and echo. In most cases, the default parameters for FXO/FXS ports will be sufficient, but special values can be set for the following parameters:

- Input gain
- Output attenuation
- Echo-cancel coverage
- Nonlinear processing
- Initial digit timeouts
- Interdigit timeouts
- Timing other than timeouts

To change any of these parameters, follow these steps:

1. Enter Privileged Exec mode:

   ```
   router> enable
   ```

2. Enter Global Configuration mode:

   ```
   router# configure terminal
   ```

3. Identify the port to configure:

   ```
   router# (config)voice-port nm-module/vic-module/port-number
   ```

4. Specify the amount of receiver gain on the interface in decibels. Value can be (–6) to 14:

   ```
   router(config-voiceport)# input gain value
   ```

5. Specify the amount of transmit attenuation on the interface in decibels. Value can be 0 to 14:

```
router(config-voiceport)# output attenuation value
```

6. Enable echo-cancellation for voice signals sent out of the interface and received back on the same interface. Excessive echo can cause disruption to normal conversation patterns.

```
router(config-voiceport)# echo-cancel enable
```

7. Adjust the size of the echo-cancel coverage time in milliseconds. Values are 16, 24, or 32:

```
router(config-voiceport)# echo-cancel coverage value
```

8. Enable "nonlinear" processing, which shuts off any signal if no speech is detected on the near end. This is used in conjunction with echo cancellation:

```
router(config-voiceport)# non-linear
```

9. Configure how long the system will wait for the first digit to be input by the user after an off-hook state is detected. This value can be anywhere between 0 and 120 seconds:

```
router(config-voiceport)# timeouts initial seconds
```

10. Configure how long the system will wait for subsequent digits after the initial digit is received. This value can be anywhere between 0 and 120 seconds:

```
router(config-voiceport)# timeouts interdigit seconds
```

11. Specify how long the digital signal lasts for DTMF digit signals. The range is from 50 to 100 milliseconds, with a default of 100 milliseconds:

```
router(config-voiceport)# timing digit milliseconds
```

12. Specify the delay between digit signals for DTMF digit signals. Range is from 50 to 100 milliseconds, the default being 100 milliseconds:

```
router(config-voiceport)# timing inter-digit milliseconds
```

13. Configure the length of pulse signal. This command is for FXO ports only using pulse signals. The range is 10 to 20 milliseconds and the default is 20 milliseconds:

```
router(config-voiceport)# timing pulse-digit milliseconds
```

14. Configure length of delay between digit signals. This command is for FXO ports only using pulse signals. The range is from 100 to 1000 milliseconds and the default is 500 milliseconds:

```
router(config-voiceport)# timing pulse-inter-digit milliseconds
```

Fine-Tuning E&M Ports

E&M ports may require fine-tuning. The following steps are used to fine-tune E&M ports:

1. Enter Privileged Exec mode:

```
router> enable
```

2. Enter Global Configuration mode:

```
router# configure terminal
```

3. Identify the port to configure:

```
router# (config)voice-port nm-module/vic-module/port-number
```

4. Specify the amount of receiver gain on the interface in decibels. Value can be (–6) to 14:

```
router# (config-voiceport)input gain value
```

5. Specify the amount of transmit attenuation on the interface in decibels. Value can be 0 to 14:

```
router# (config-voiceport)output attenuation value
```

6. Enable echo-cancellation for voice signals sent out of the interface and received back on the same interface.

```
router# (config-voiceport)echo-cancel enable
```

7. Adjust the size of the echo-cancel coverage in milliseconds. Values are 16, 24, or 32:

```
router# (config-voiceport)echo-cancel coverage value
```

8. Enable *nonlinear* processing, which shuts off any signal if no speech is detected on the near end. This is used in conjunction with echo cancellation:

```
router# (config-voiceport)non-linear
```

9. Configure how long the system will wait for the first digit to be input by the user after an off-hook state is detected. This value can be anywhere between 0 and 120 seconds:

```
router# (config-voiceport)timeouts initial seconds
```

10. Configure how long the system will wait for subsequent digits after the initial digit is received. This value can be anywhere between 0 and 120 seconds:

```
router# (config-voiceport)timeouts interdigit seconds
```

11. Specify how long the digit signal will last for DTMF digit signals. The range is from 50 to 100 milliseconds:

```
router# (config-voiceport)timing digit milliseconds
```

12. Specify the delay between digit signals for DTMF digit signals. The range is from 50 to 500 milliseconds:

```
router#(config-voiceport)timing inter-digit milliseconds
```

13. Specify the pulse-dialing rate. This is used for pulse dialing only. The range is from 10 to 20 pulses per second:

```
router# (config-voiceport)timing pulse pulse-per-second
```

14. Configure the delay between digit signals. This is used for pulse dialing only. The range is from 100 to 1000 milliseconds:

```
router# (config-voiceport)timing pulse-inter-digit milliseconds
```

15. Configure the delay signal time for delay dial signaling. The range is from 100 to 5000 milliseconds:

```
router#(config-voiceport)timing delay-duration milliseconds
```

16. Configure the minimum time for outgoing seizure to out-dial address. The range is from 20 to 2000 milliseconds:

```
router# (config-voiceport)timing delay-duration milliseconds
```

17. Specify the time between generations of "wink-like" pulses. The range is from 0 to 5000 milliseconds:

```
router# (config-voiceport)timing delay-pulse min-delay milliseconds
```

18. Specify the minimum amount of time between the off-hook signal and the call being completely cleared. The range is from 200 to 2000 milliseconds:

```
router# (config-voiceport)timing clear-wait milliseconds
```

19. Specify the delay signal time for delay dial signaling. The range is from 100 to 5000 milliseconds:

```
router(config-voiceport)timing delay-duration milliseconds
```

20. Configure the maximum wink-wait duration. The range is from 100 to 400 milliseconds:

```
router(config-voiceport)# timing wink-duration milliseconds
```

21. Configure the maximum wink-wait duration for wink-start signal. The range is from 100 to 5000 milliseconds:

```
router(config-voiceport)# timing wink-wait milliseconds
```

Some added features always need to be adjusted for the DID ports. Contrary to the default settings of the FXO/FXS ports, in most cases DID ports require fine-tuning adjustments. Follow these steps to fine-tune DID ports:

1. Enter Privileged Exec mode:

   ```
   router> enable
   ```

2. Enter Global Configuration mode:

   ```
   router# configure terminal
   ```

3. Identify the port to configure:

   ```
   router(config)# voice-port nm-module/vic-module/port-number
   ```

4. This command sets the maximum time to wait for wink signaling after an outgoing seizure is sent. This is optional for wink-start ports only:

   ```
   router(config-voiceport)# timing wait-wink milliseconds
   ```

5. This command sets the maximum time to wait before sending wink signals after an incoming seizure is detected. This is optional for wink-start ports only:

   ```
   router(config-voiceport)# timing wink-wait milliseconds
   ```

6. This command sets the duration of a wink-start signal. This is optional for wink-start ports only:

   ```
   router(config-voiceport)# timing wink-duration milliseconds
   ```

7. This command sets the duration of the delay signal. This is optional for delay dial ports only:

   ```
   router(config-voiceport)# timing delay-duration milliseconds
   ```

8. This command sets the delay interval after an incoming seizure is detected. This is optional for delay dial ports only:

   ```
   router(config-voiceport)# timing delay-start milliseconds
   ```

Configuring Dial Plans and Dial Peers

The *dial plan* is the architecture for the numbers and patterns that the user dials to reach the receiving party, or the routing plan for dial numbers. Dial plans are *manually* configured on Cisco routers. A collection of dial peers creates a dial plan. Devising the most optimal dial plan allows for growth and ease of manageability. If an existing plan is used, it should be reviewed for scalability and to meet VoIP's unique requirements. A number of extra items should be accounted for:

- Voice-mail extensions
- Call parking

- Reserved or preplanned voice conferencing
- Special outbound gateways
- Third-party TAPI applications that could require dialing numbers

These numbers might not be accounted for with an existing PBX system. If this system is being added to a new WAN that is covering many remote sites, you might need a new dial plan. The gateways and CM can forward calls based on wildcard digits. When call a remote location, the digits can be forwarded to the gateway once a wildcard for that site has been reached, as shown in our example in Figure 9.44. Using an initial four-digit plan is not too taxing on the users and will prevent many headaches down the road.

Figure 9.44 Simple Dial Plan

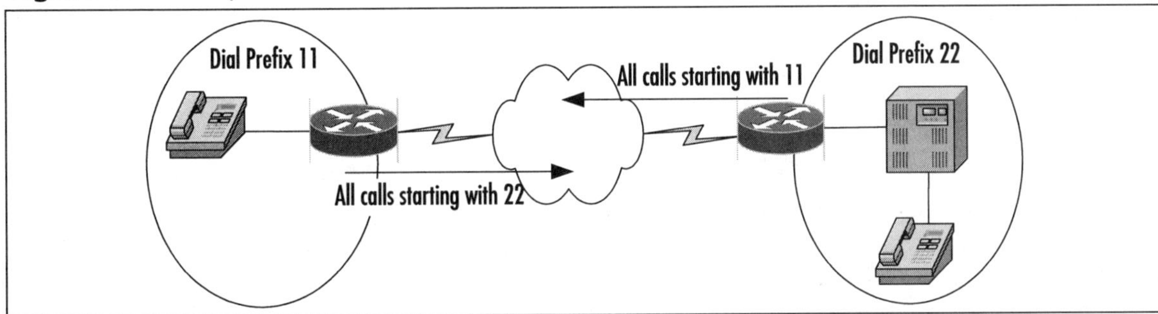

Call Legs: POTS vs. Voice Network Dial Peers

Call legs are individual segments between two voice termination points such as phone or PBX and a VoIP router. Another leg would be between two VoIP routers via a Frame Relay, IP, or ATM cloud. The call legs are configured via dial-peer statements. There are two types of dial peer: POTS and voice network. The voice network dial peers can be VoIP, VoFR, or VoATM.

The POTS dial peers are analog or digital connections to a telephone, fax, PBX, and PSTN. Figure 9.45 illustrates the call legs involved to complete a call. These steps equate to four dial-peer statements, with each router requiring two statements, since Call Leg 2 must be configured on both routers.

Figure 9.45 Dial-Peer Call Legs

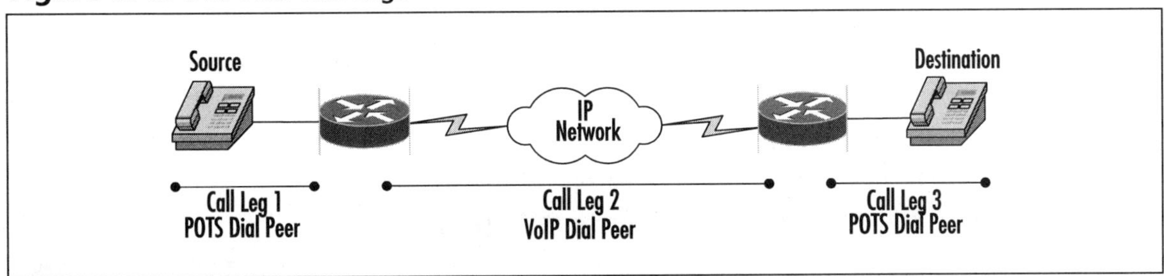

Call Legs 1 and 3 are considered inbound call legs, whereas Call Leg 2 is an outbound leg. An inbound leg is the POTS dial peer. An outbound leg in this example is the leg where the call transverses the voice network, which can be VoIP, VoATM, or VoFR. The concepts of inbound and outbound are from the router's perspective.

Creating and Implementing Dial Plans

We have a main/headquarter site and a branch/remote site, as shown in Figure 9.46. The scenario is simplified to help explain the items that need to be captured for the dial plan and then configured in the routers.

Figure 9.46 Basic Dial Plan Architecture

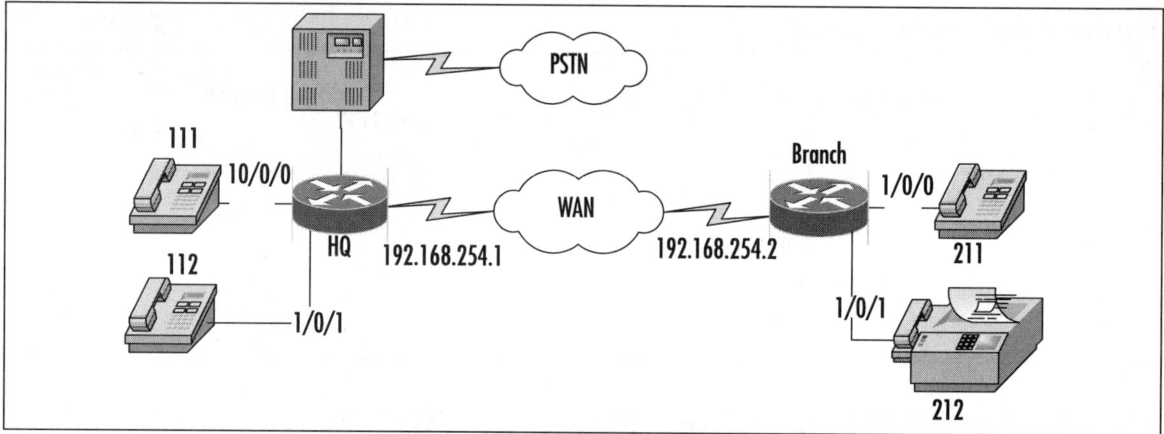

Let's complete the chart below based on the information in Table 9.10.

Table 9.10 Basic Dial Plan Information.

Router/Dial-Peer Tag Number	Number Expansion Extension	Destination Pattern	Type of Peer	Voice Port	Session Target	CODEC
HQ	1...	4046781...				
111		111	POTS	1/0/0		
112		112	POTS	1/0/1		
9		9T	POTS	1/1/0		
21		21.	VoIP		ipv4:192.168.254.2	G729r8
Branch	1...	4046781...				
211		211	POTS	1/0/0		
212		212	POTS	1/0/1		
9		9T	VoIP		ipv4:192.168.254.1	G729r8
11		11.			Ipv4:192.168.254.1	G729r8

One of the fields that requires further explanation is the destination pattern, which is the string of digits that will be dialed. Table 9.11 gives a description of all the possible symbols that can be used in the pattern.

Table 9.11 Destination Pattern

Symbol	Description
..	Indicates a single-digit placeholder. For example, 555.... matches any dialed string beginning with 555, plus at least four additional digits.
[ ]	Indicates a range of digits. A consecutive range is indicated with a hyphen (-); for example, [5-7]. A nonconsecutive range is indicated with a comma (,); for example, [5,8]. Hyphens and commas can be used in combination; for example, [5-7,9]. Please note that only single-digit ranges are supported. For example, [98-102] is invalid.
( )	Indicates a pattern; for example, 408(555). It is used in conjunction with the symbols ?, %, or +.
?	Indicates that the preceding digit occurred zero times or one time. Enter **Ctrl-v** before entering **?** from your keyboard.
%	Indicates that the preceding digit occurred zero or more times. This functions the same as the * used in regular expressions.
+	Indicates that the preceding digit occurred one or more times.
T	Indicates the inter-digit timeout. The router pauses to collect additional dialed digits.

With this information in hand, we can begin configuring dial peers on the routers. The basic LAN and WAN information should already be planned, designed, and configured prior to executing any commands.

Configuring Dial Peers

There are several commands to configure the POTS and voice network dial peers. The POTS dial peer requires the following variables for a basic setup:

- Tag number (we recommend using a tag number that relates to the destination pattern)
- Destination pattern
- Voice port

Only a few commands are necessary to set up a basic POTS dial-peer configuration. The steps are:

1. Enter Privileged Exec mode:

```
router>enable
```

2. Enter Global Configuration mode:

```
router# configure terminal
```

3. Enter dial-peer mode. Set the tag number to relate to the destination pattern. The dial-peer type is POTS:

   ```
   router(config)# dial-peer voice tag-number  pots
   ```

4. Define the destination pattern that is to be reached by this router:

   ```
   router(config-dial-peer)# destination-pattern string
   ```

5. Specify the voice port number that this call will be routed through:

   ```
   router(config-dial-peer)# port location
   ```

The following is an example of the dial-peer commands for the POTS connections from the HQ site, which are also summarized in Table 9.12:

```
dial-peer voice 111 pots
 port 1/0/0
 destination-pattern 111
!
dial-peer voice 112 pots
 port 1/0/1
 destination-pattern 112
```

Table 9.12 Optional Dial-Peer Commands for POTS

Optional Related Command	Description
answer-address *string*	Selects the inbound dial peer based on the calling number.
incoming called-number *string*	Selects the inbound dial peer based on the called number to identify voice and modem calls.
direct-inward-dial *string*	Enables the DID call treatment for the incoming called number.
forward-digits {*num-digit* | *all* | *extra*}	Configures the digit-forwarding method used by the dial peer. The valid range for the number of digits forwarded (num-digit) is 0 through 32.
max-conn *number*	Specifies the maximum number of allowed connections to and from the POTS dial peer. The valid range is 1 through 2147483647.
numbering-type {*abbreviated* | *international* | *national* | *network* | *reserved* | *subscriber* | *unknown*}	Specifies the numbering type to match, as defined by the ITU Q.931 specification.
preference *value*	Configures a preference for the POTS dial peer. The valid range is 0 through 10, where the lower the number, the higher the preference.

Continued

Table 9.12 Optional Dial-Peer Commands for POTS

Optional Related Command	Description
prefix *string*	Includes a prefix that the system adds automatically to the front of the dial string before passing it to the telephony interface. Valid entries for the string argument are 0 through 9 and a comma (,). Use a comma to include a one-second pause between digits to allow for a secondary dial tone.
translate-outgoing {*called* | *calling*} *name-tag*	Specifies the translation rule set to apply to the calling number or called number.

The voice network can be over IP, Frame Relay, or ATM. The focus of this chapter is VoIP. The VoIP dial-peer setup requires the following variable for a basic setup:

- Tag number (we recommend using a tag number that relates to the destination pattern)
- IP address for session target
- Destination telephone number pattern

The following are the basic dial-peer commands necessary for VoIP:

1. Enter the dial-peer mode for VoIP peer. *Tag-number* is a unique decimal number that identifies the peer. It is locally significant so the same number can be used on other routers for different peers.

   ```
   router(config)# dial-peer voice tag-number voip
   ```

2. Specify the IP address of the router connected to the remote telephony device:

   ```
   router(config-dial-peer)# session target {ipv4:destination-address
       | dns:[$s$. | $d$. | $e$.| $u$.] host-name}
   ```

3. Define the CODEC for the dial peer:

   ```
   Router(config-dialpeer)# CODEC {g711alaw | g711ulaw | g723ar53 |
       g723ar63 | g723r53 | g723r63 | g726r16 | g726r24 | g726r32 |
           g728 | g729br8 | g729r8
   [pre-ietf]} [bytes]
   ```

4. Define the destination pattern that is to be reached by this router. Example: 11, which is a group of phone numbers that can be reached across the connection. Table 9.13 lists all the options available for the string:

   ```
   router(config-dial-peer)# destination-pattern string
   ```

The following example shows the dial-peer commands for the VoIP connections from the HQ site:

```
dial-peer voice 11 voip
```

```
 CODEC g729r8
 ip precedence 5
 session target ipv4:192.168.1.1
 vad
 destination-pattern 11.
!
dial-peer voice 9 voip
 CODEC g729r8
 ip precedence 5
 session target ipv4:192.168.1.1
 vad
 destination-pattern 9T
```

Table 9.13 Optional Dial-Peer Commands for VoIP

Optional Command	Description
answer-address *string*	Selects the inbound dial peer based on the calling number.
incoming called-number *string*	Selects the inbound dial peer based on the called number to identify voice and modem calls.
dtmf-relay *[cisco-rtp] [h245-signal] [h245-alphanumeric]*	Configures the tone that sounds in response to a key-press on a touch-tone telephone. DTMF tones are compressed at one end of a call and decompressed at the other end.
fax rate {*2400* | *4800* |*7200* | *9600* | *12000* | *14400* | *disable* | *voice*}	Specifies the transmission speed of a fax to be sent to this dial peer. The disable keyword turns off fax transmission capability. The voice keyword, which is the default, specifies the highest possible transmission speed supported by the voice rate.
numbering-type {*abbreviated* | *international* | *national* | *network*| *reserved* | *subscriber* | *unknown*}	Specifies the numbering type to match, as defined by the ITU Q.931 specification.
playout-delay mode {*adaptive* | *fixed*}	Specifies the type of jitter buffer playout delay to use.
playout-delay {*maximum value* | *nominal value* | *minimum* {*default* | *low* |*high*}}	Specifies the amount of time that a packet is held in the jitter buffer before it is played out on the audio.
preference *value*	With multiple dial peers pointing to the same destination, the preference can be set for the preferred one.
tech-prefix *number*	Specifies that a particular technology prefix be prepended to the destination pattern of this dial peer.

Continued

Table 9.13 Optional Dial-Peer Commands for VoIP

Optional Command	Description
translate-outgoing {*called* | *calling*} name-tag	Specifies the translation rule set to apply to the calling number or called number.
vad	Enables voice activity detection, which suppress voice packets during periods of silence.

Number Expansion

It is not (and should not) always be necessary to dial the entire number to make a call; the last few digits (extension) should be more than sufficient To ease the process and usability, use the **num-exp** command on the dial-peer configuration as follows:

```
num-exp 66.. 55566..
```

Now, when someone dials the pattern 66**,** the router expands that number into 55566**....** For example, if the site has phone numbers 5556601 through 5556625, the router would only need the last four digits to identify where the call is to be routed. When working out your dial plan, try to keep all number expansions unique on the VoIP network.

Direct Inward Dialing

DID allows voice customers to have many private voice numbers without actually purchasing actual lines to service those numbers. Configuring analog DID ports allows connections to the PSTN in which calls are routed to phones as if they all had direct lines to the PSTN

DID can be used on digital and analog circuits. The key to using DID over VoIP is configuring the router to pass the DID information directly over to the DID-enabled PBX. The first scenario is where the router has a T-1/E-1 connection to the PSTN and you want DID capabilities on this circuit. Telcos use the Digital Number Identification Service (DNIS) to send the called number. The configuration on the router is done by enabling DID on the dial–peer, as shown in the following example:

```
router(config)# dial-peer voice number pots
router(config-dial-peer)# direct-inward-dial
router(config-voiceport)# signal did [wink-start|immediate|delay-dial]
```

In the situation with just an analog connection to the PSTN, the DID VIC can be configured to support DID. This capability was added in IOS releasE-12.1(5)XM and integrated later into 12.2(2)T. It is a simple configuration that uses the the following command:

```
voice-port 1/1/0
  signal did wink-start
```

Several of the wink-timing commands might need to be entered to make the appropriate adjustments with the PSTN connection. To verify that the command was successfully enabled, execute the **show voice port 1/1/0** command:

```
Router# show voice port 1/1/0
Foreign Exchange Station with Direct Inward Dialing (FXS-DID) 1/1/0 Slot
        is 1, Sub-unit is 1, Port is 0
  Type of VoicePort is DID-IN
  Operation State is DORMANT
  Administrative State is UP
  No Interface Down Failure
  Description is not set
  Noise Regeneration is enabled
  Non Linear Processing is enabled
  Music On Hold Threshold is Set to -38 dBm
  In Gain is Set to 0 dB
  Out Attenuation is Set to 0 dB
  Echo Cancellation is enabled
  Echo Cancel Coverage is set to 8 ms
  Playout-delay Mode is set to default
  Playout-delay Nominal is set to 60 ms
  Playout-delay Maximum is set to 200 ms
  Playout-delay Minimum mode is set to default, value 4 ms
  Playout-delay Fax is set to 300 ms
  Connection Mode is normal
  Connection Number is not set
  Initial Time Out is set to 10 s
  Interdigit Time Out is set to 10 s
  Call Disconnect Time Out is set to 3 s
  Ringing Time Out is set to 180 s
  Wait Release Time Out is set to 3 s
  Companding Type is u-law
  Region Tone is set for US

  Analog Info Follows:
  Currently processing none
  Maintenance Mode Set to None (not in mtc mode)
  Number of signaling protocol errors are 0
  Impedance is set to 600r Ohm
  Station name Richard Flanagan, Station number 4326534

  Voice card specific Info Follows:
  Signal Type is wink-start
  Dial Type is dtmf
```

```
In Seizure is inactive
Out Seizure is inactive
Digit Duration Timing is set to 100 ms
InterDigit Duration Timing is set to 100 ms
Pulse Rate Timing is set to 10 pulses/second
InterDigit Pulse Duration Timing is set to 750 ms
Clear Wait Duration Timing is set to 400 ms
Wink Wait Duration Timing is set to 200 ms
Wait Wink Duration Timing is set to 550 ms
Wink Duration Timing is set to 200 ms
Delay Start Timing is set to 300 ms
Delay Duration Timing is set to 2000 ms
Dial Pulse Min. Delay is set to 140 ms
Percent Break of Pulse is 60 percent
Auto Cut-through is disabled
Dialout Delay for immediate start is 300 ms
```

Configuring Trunking

A *trunk* is a line that carries multiple voice or data channels between two telephone systems. As far as VoIP is concerned, the trunk is a virtual connection between two PBXs. The virtual connection can be either permanent or switched. These virtual connections are implemented with the **connection** command.

The **connection** voice port configuration command allows special modes to be set for specific voice ports. If the **connection** command is not configured, the session application assumes that there is a "standard" connection being initiated and it will output a dial tone when the interface senses an off-hook state. The dial tone persists until enough digits are collected to match a dial peer and complete the call or until the timeout for digit entry is met. The syntax for the **connection** command is as follows:

```
connection [plar | tie-line | trunk | plar-opx] string
```

- **string** Represents the destination telephone number.
- **plar** Automatically dials a destination pattern as soon as the receiver is lifted and the port is activated. No digits have to be entered to establish the connection.
- **tie line** Specifies that the particular port is a tie-line connection to a PBX. It is used when a dial plan requires that additional digits are added in front of any digits dialed by the PBX and the combined set of digits is used to route the call via the dial-peer settings and into the network.
- **trunk** Specifies that the particular port is a straight tie-line connection to a PBX. The "connection trunk" mode can be used for E&M-E&M trunks, FX0-FXS trunks, and

FXS-FXS trunks. It should be noted that signaling would not be transported for FXS-FXS trunks since they do not support signaling parameters between them.

- **plar-opx** Specifies a private line automatic ringdown (PLAR) connection to an off-premises extension. Using this option, the local voice port provides a local response before the remote voice port receives an answer. This method ensures that the call is answered before the call flow is completed.

Trunks

Use the command **connection trunk** to provide a permanent connection between two PBXs, as shown in Figure 9.47. The connections between the router and the PBX must be T-1 CAS. T-1 CAS to E-1 CAS mapping does not work by default; bit-order manipulation must be performed. T-1 CCS is not supported. Voice port combinations that are supported are E&M-E&M, FXS-FXO, and FXS-FXS.

Figure 9.47 Connection Trunk Example

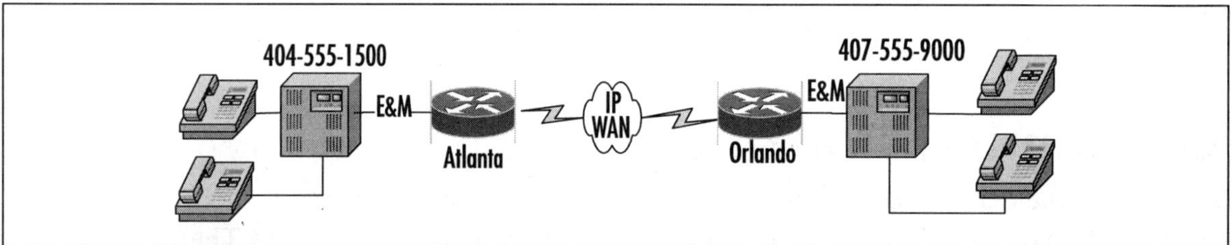

The partial configuration in the following list is from the Atlanta and Orlando routers, as illustrated in Figure 9.47. Here is the Atlanta configuration:

```
voice?card 1
!
controller T-1 1/0
framing esf
linecode b8zs
ds0?group 1 timeslots 1-24 type e&m
clock source line
!
voice?port 1/0:1
connection trunk
!
dial-peer voice 404 pots
destination-pattern 4045551500
port 1/0:1
!
dial-peer voice 407 voip
session-target ipv4:192.168.254.2
```

```
destination-pattern 4075559000
```

Here is the Orlando configuration:

```
voice?card 1
!
controller T-1 1/0
framing esf
linecode b8zs
ds0?group 1 timeslots 1-24 type e&m
clock source line
!
voice?port 1/0:1
connection trunk
!
dial-peer voice 407 pots
destination-pattern 4075559000
port 1/0:1
!
dial-peer voice 404 voip
session-target ipv4:192.168.254.1
destination-pattern 4045551500
```

Tie Lines

The **connection** command variable **tie-line** has a similar effect to the **trunk** variable, but the connection between the two PBXs emulates a temporary tie-line trunk. If you need to prepend additional digits to be sent to the PBX, use the **connection tie-line** command. The following is an example of the complete syntax:

```
voice-port 1/0/0
connection tie-line 4326534
```

Private Line Automatic Ringdown

PLAR automatically dials a remote phone when the local telephone is taken off-hook. PLAR works with any of the signaling types—E&M, FXO, or FXS. A voice port can be configured to accept either digits dialed or a PLAR connection. The configuration is enabled by simply adding the command **connection plar string** to the voice port, where **string** is the number to automatically be dialed. To verify that the command is enabled correctly on the voice port, type **show voice port *nm-module/vic-module/port-number*** at the Exec Privileged mode prompt. Note that the following output is from a 3600 router with **plar** configured to destination 1500 (part of the **show** command results):

```
branch# show voice port 1/0/0
```

```
Foreign Exchange Office
 Type of VoicePort is FXS
 Operation State is DORMANT
 Administrative State is UP
 The Last Interface Down Failure Cause is Administrative Shutdown
 Description is not set
 Noise Regeneration is enabled
 Non Linear Processing is enabled
 Music On Hold Threshold is Set to -38 dBm
 In Gain is Set to 0 dB
 Out Attenuation is Set to 0 dB
 Echo Cancellation is enabled
 Echo Cancel Coverage is set to 8 ms
 Connection Mode is plar
 Connection Number is 1500
```

plar-opx Commands

The **connection plar-opx** command allows connectivity between FXS and FXO interfaces to provide an acknowledgment prior to the remote FXS device answering the call. For example, if a call comes in and the remote end device does not answer the call, the PBX could roll the call to voicemail if voicemail is installed.

Direct Voice Trunking versus Dial-Digit Interpretation

Trunking allows for semi-transparent connections between two PBXs, a PBX and a local extension, or some other combination of telephony devices permanently linked. There is no need to analyze the digits for a destination pattern, since the connections are permanently trunked together and data will automatically pass between the two interfaces. Route analysis is unnecessary since the connection is up all the time.

The following are some advantages of using trunking technology:

- Less overhead on the routers passing the traffic.
- The destination patterns need not be interpreted or analyzed to determine the destination path.
- Packets are passed to the PBX for analysis and interpretation.

Some disadvantages of using trunking technology are:

- No control of incoming packets.
- The external PBX handles all the end-station routing.
- You cannot fine-tune the voice ports or special configurations in this mode.

- Special attention must be given to CODEC management; by passing information on trunk connections, all CODECs have to match along the entire path of transmission.
- Proper CODECs must be used for each FXO port connected to the tandem switch.

Standard Dialing Analysis: Digit Interpretation

If trunking is not being used, the router that receives an initiating call signal must access and analyze the incoming dialed digits (destination pattern). The router uses its dial-peer configurations to determine where to route the call over the IP network.

An advantage to using this method is that call routing is completely controlled by the routing architecture, which allows for greater control and fine-tuning of the VoIP system. Some disadvantages are:

- More overhead on the routers, since the processors must interpret the dial peers rather than just passing on the data in a trunking format.
- Increased latency in passing packets through the system, because the router must interpret all the calls.

supervisory Disconnect

supervisory disconnect is a command used when the router's FXO interface is connected to the PBX, PSTN, or a key system. The FXO interface closes the loop to specify that it is off-hook. Normally, the phone controls its interaction with the switch to tell the switch to end the call by hanging up. Unfortunately, the router cannot perform this action, so some of the other options are E&M, ground-start signaling, power denial, battery reversal, and supervisory disconnect tone.

Ground-start signaling is mainly used with FXO and PSTN, but it might not be available with the PBX. *Power denial* is the situation where the PBX or the PSTN CO has a 600ms interruption of power on the line. The router translates this interruption into a supervisor disconnect. *Battery reversal* changes the polarity on the line and router interprets this change as the supervisor disconnect. This is supported when the **battery-reversal** command is used. The *supervisory disconnect tone* is a detectable tone sent from the PSTN or PBX; the router senses this tone and disconnects the call. This method is supported only on analog FXO loop start configurations. The command to enable this functionality is **supervisory disconnect**. The steps to configure supervisory disconnect tone are:

1. Configure the voice class to specify the tones to be detected.
2. Assign the voice class to an FXO voice port.

The following are the steps to set up a supervisory disconnect voice class:

1. Create a voice class for defining one tone detection pattern:

```
router(config)# voice class dualtone tag
```

2. Specify the two frequencies, in Hz, for a tone to be detected (or one frequency if a non-dual tone is to be detected):

```
router(config-voice-class)# freq-pair tone-id frequency-1 frequency-2
```

3. Specify the maximum frequency deviation that will be detected, in Hz:

```
router(config-voice-class)# freq-max-deviation frequency
```

4. Specify the maximum tone power that will be detected, in dBmO:

```
router(config-voice-class)# freq-max-power dBm0
```

5. Specify the minimum tone power that will be detected, in dBmO:

```
router(config-voice-class)# freq-min-power dBm0
```

6. Specify the power difference allowed between the two frequencies, in dBmO:

```
router(config-voice-class)# freq-power-twist dBm0
```

7. Specify the timing difference allowed between the two frequencies, in 10ms increments:

```
router(config-voice-class)# freq-max-delay time
```

8. Specify the minimum tone on-time that will be detected, in 10ms increments:

```
router(config-voice-class)# cadence-min-on-time time
```

9. Specify the maximum tone off-time that will be detected, in 10ms increments:

```
router(config-voice-class)# cadence-max-off-time time
```

10. Specify a tone cadence pattern to be detected. Specify an on-time and off-time for each cycle of the cadence pattern. This is an optional configuration:

```
router(config-voice-class)# cadence-list cadence-id cycle-1-on-time
    cycle-1-off-time cycle-2-on-time cycle-2-off-time cycle-3-on-time
        cycle-3-off-time cycle-4-on-time cycle-4-off-time
```

11. Specify the maximum time that the tone onset can vary from the specified onset time and still be detected, in 10ms increments. This is an optional configuration:

```
router(config-voice-class)# cadence-variation time
```

12. Specify a tone cadence pattern to be detected. Specify an on-time and off-time for each. This is an optional configuration:

```
router(config-voice-class)# exit
```

Once the voice class has been created, apply it to the voice port interface. The following steps enable the voice class and supervisory disconnect commands on a Cisco 2600 router with FXO port 1/0/0 and voice class number 100:

```
router# config terminal
router(config)# voice-port 1/0/0
router(config-voiceport)# supervisory disconnect dualtone voice-class 100
router(config-voiceport)# exit
```

Trunk Seizure: Wink-Start Signaling versus Immediate-Start Signaling versus Delay-Start

To pass calls, E&M voice ports must seize the trunk using one of three techniques. We briefly cover them in this section. The figures in this section show PBX-to-PBX communications; the PBX icon in each figure can be an actual PBX or an E&M port performing PBX functions. Regardless, the signaling issues are applicable to both.

Wink-Start Signaling

Wink-start signaling derives its name from the fact that it technique has a certain wink appearance, as shown in Figure 9.48, from initiation to termination. In wink-start signaling, when the trunk goes off-hook, the remote PBX transmits an off-hook pulse at a set interval (measured in milliseconds). The originating switch waits a set interval (also in milliseconds) and then sends the telephone digits to the PBX. Wink-start signaling is very common.

Figure 9.48 Wink-Start Signaling

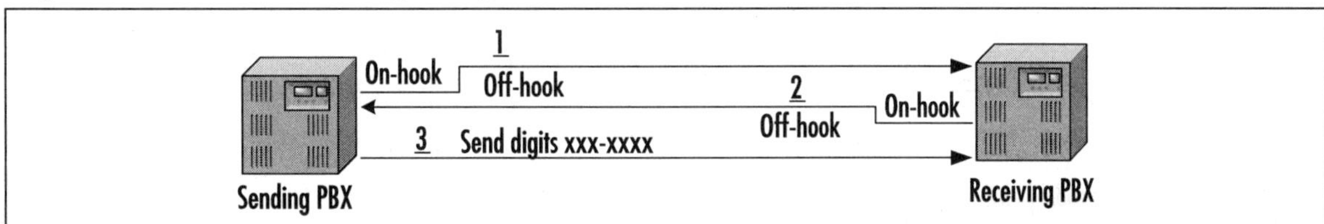

1. The sending PBX goes off-hook, which gets noted at the receiving PBX.
2. The receiving PBX responds by also going off-hook.
3. Upon receiving the "wink" (off-hook) condition from the receiving PBX, the send PBX then starts transmitting the digits.

Immediate-Start Signaling

With immediate-start signaling, the originating switch places the trunk in an off-hook condition, waits a set interval, and then starts the transmission of telephone digits to the PBX. Figure 9.49 shows a graphical representation of this behavior. This is different from wink-start signaling, in which the digit transmission does not start until the off-hook pulse is received from the remote switch. The originating switch goes off-hook for a certain amount of time, usually less than 200ms, and starts sending digits.

Figure 9.49 Immediate Start Signaling

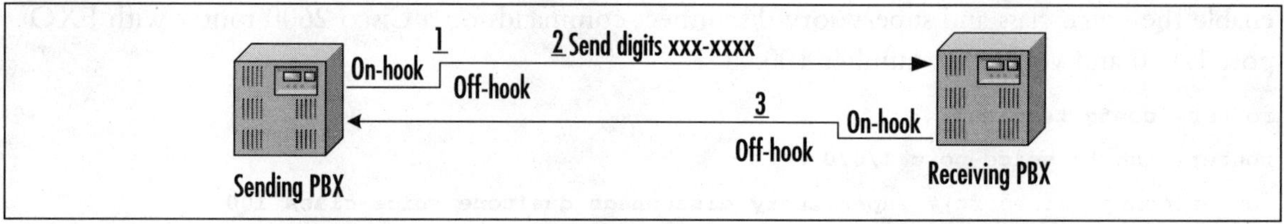

1. In immediate-start signaling, the sending PBX goes off-hook and waits approximately 200 milliseconds.
2. Once that interval has lapsed, the sending PBX starts transmitting the digits to the destination PBX.
3. The receiving PBX goes off-hook upon detecting the off-hook state of the sending PBX; this can be during the wait interval or upon receiving digits from the sending PBX.

Delay-Start Signaling

Delay-start signaling was developed to address a problem with wink-start signaling, wherein the remote switch might not be ready to receive the digits, even though it sent the off-hook pulse. In delay-start signaling, when the originating side goes off-hook at the start, so does the remote side. The remote side remains off-hook until it can receive the digits, at which point it goes back on-hook. When the digits arrive, the remote side goes off-hook, and the call proceeds as normal. This behavior is illustrated in Figure 9.50.

Figure 9.50 Delay-Start Signaling

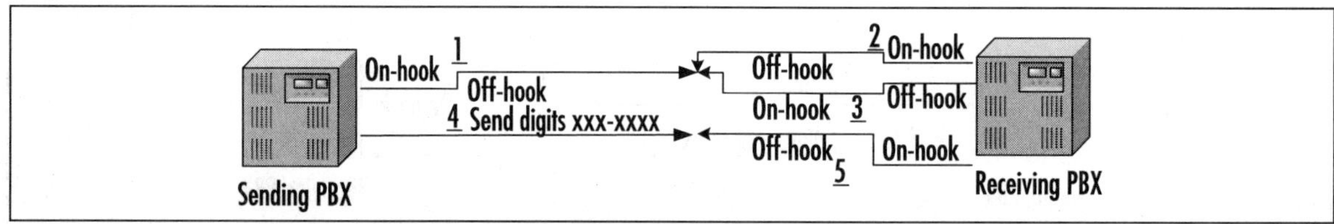

1. The sending PBX starts by going off-hook.
2. The receiving PBX responds by also going off-hook.
3. No digits are transmitted until the receiving PBX signals its readiness by going back on-hook.
4. When this on-hook state is detected by the sending PBX, it starts transmitting digits.
5. The receiving PBX responds to these incoming digits by going off-hook and completing the loop, thus completing the call.

The advantage of wink start versus immediate is that wink start offers an acknowledgment between the originating and terminating switches, which helps in situations where one side is too busy to answer or both are trying to seize the line at the same time.

The detailed wink-start commands are listed in the section, "Fine-Tuning E&M Ports," as Steps 20 and 21. An example of the configuration steps follows:

```
router# configure terminal
router(config)# voice-port 1/0/0
router(config-voiceport)# timing wink-duration 250
router(config-voiceport)# timing wink-wait 300
router(config-voiceport)# exit
```

To confirm that the commands are enabled on the voice port, enter the following **show** command:

```
router# show voice port 1/0/0
recEive And transMit 1/0/0 Slot is 1, Sub-unit is 0, Port is 0
 Type of VoicePort is E&M
 Operation State is DORMANT
 Administrative State is UP
  .
 Interdigit Time Out is set to 10 s
 Call-Disconnect Time Out is set to 60 s
 Region Tone is set for US

 Analog Info Follows:
 Currently processing none
 Maintenance Mode Set to None (not in mtc mode)
 Number of signaling protocol errors are 0
 Impedance is set to 600r Ohm

 Voice card specific Info Follows:
 Signal Type is wink-start
 Operation Type is 2-wire
 E&M Type is 2
 Dial Type is dtmf
 In Seizure is inactive
 Out Seizure is inactive
 Digit Duration Timing is set to 100 ms
 InterDigit Duration Timing is set to 100 ms
 Pulse Rate Timing is set to 10 pulses/second
 InterDigit Pulse Duration Timing is set to 500 ms
 Clear Wait Duration Timing is set to 400 ms
 Wink Wait Duration Timing is set to 300 ms
 Wink Duration Timing is set to 250 ms
```

```
Delay Start Timing is set to 300 ms
Delay Duration Timing is set to 2000 ms
Dial Pulse Min. Delay is set to 140 ms
```

Configuring ISDN for Voice

ISDN connectivity can play a major role in VoIP by providing circuits to connect to the PSTN and PBXs. Both ISDN PRI and BRI are supported on Cisco routers. Cisco supports Q.931 network and user-side, Q.SIG, and CCS ISDN configurations. Cisco plans to support BRI NT ISDN interfaces for the Cisco 2691 and 3700 series routers.

Configuring ISDN BRI Voice Ports

Cisco routers support several types of ISDN voice interface cards such as VIC-2BRI-S/T-TE and VIC-2BRI-NT/TE, which can provide connectivity to a PBX or PSTN. A benefit of using the ISDN BRI VIC rather than the analog VIC modules is the additional calling information that is passed.

Up to four calls are supported when the VIC-2BRI is installed in the NM-2V module. The BRI VIC needs to be installed in Slot 0 of the NM-2V for both ports to be active. If an additional VIC is installed in the second slot of the NM-2V, the second port on the first VIC will be disabled. This is based on the two ports of the BRI VIC requiring four DSPs. The VIC interface modules support both ISDN network and user-side configurations. The following are the steps necessary to configure ISDN BRI to a PBX:

1. Enter global configuration mode:

   router# **configure terminal**

2. Set the global ISDN switch type. The only NT supported type is basic-net or basic-qsig:

   router(config)# **isdn switch-type** *switch-type*

3. Set the ISDN BRI interface slot and port:

   router(config)# **interface bri** *slot/port*

4. Ensure that no IP address is configured for the ISDN interface (voice only):

   router(config-if)# **no ip address**

5. Specify incoming voice calls over ISDN:

   router(config-if)# **isdn incoming-voice voice**

6. Shut down the interface. Configure the physical layer type. Enable interface with no shutdown:

   - Enter **user** to configure the port as TE and to function as a clock slave. This is the default.

- Enter **network** to configure the port as NT and to function as a clock master.

```
router(config-if)# shutdown
router(config-if)# isdn layer1-emulate {user | network}
router(config-if)# no shutdown
```

7. Turn on or off the power supplied from an NT-configured port to a TE device:

```
router(config-if)# [no] line-power
```

8. Configure the Layer 2 and Layer 3 port protocol:

```
router(config-if)# isdn protocol-emulate {user | network}
```

9. Exit global configuration mode:

```
router(config)# end
```

Figure 9.51 illustrates a scenario with ISDN BRI connectivity to a PBX and PSTN. A partial configuration lists the commands pertaining to the PSTN and PBX interfaces.

Figure 9.51 ISDN BRI PBX and PBX Scenario

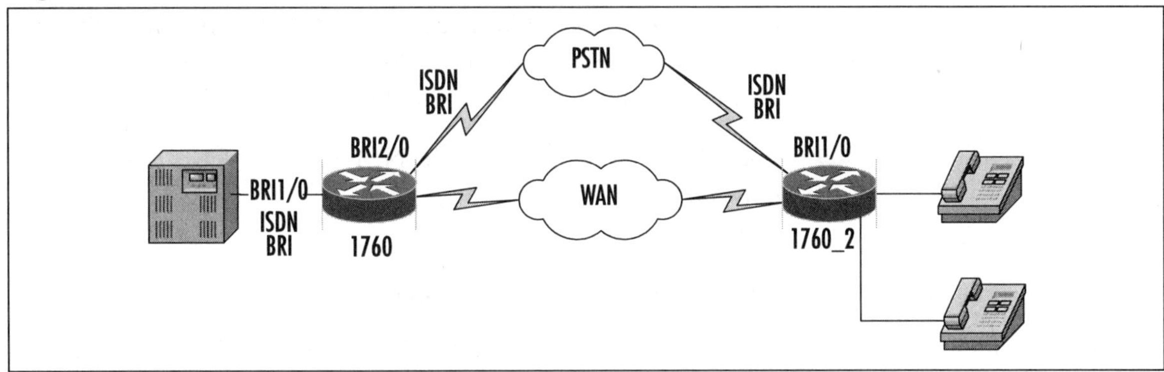


```
(Partial Cisco 1760 configuration)
!
hostname 1760
!
 isdn switch-type basic-net3
!
interface BRI 1/0
 no shutdown
 description connected to PBX
 no ip address
 isdn switch-type basic-net3
 isdn incoming-voice voice
 shutdown
```

```
 isdn layer1-emulate user
 no shutdown
 isdn protocol-emulate user
!
interface BRI 2/0
 no shutdown
 description connected to PSTN
 no ip address
 isdn switch-type basic-net3
 isdn incoming-voice voice
 isdn overlap-receiving
 shutdown
 isdn layer1-emulate network
 no shutdown
 isdn protocol-emulate network
```

Configuring ISDN PRI Voice Ports

Earlier in the chapter, we discussed the analog VICs modules such as the E&M, FXO, and FXS, but larger organizations that need higher-density interfaces to the PSTN or PBX typically use digital T-1/E-1 modules. The following is a list of digital voice interfaces and supported platforms:

- Digital T-1/E-1 Packet Voice Trunk Network Module, NM-HDV (VWIC-1MFT and VWIC-2MFT) Cisco 2600 and 3600 series.
- Digital voice interface card (DVM) Cisco MC3810.
- Octal or Quad T-1/E-1/PRI feature card Cisco AS5300 universal access server.
- Channelized trunk card and voice feature card Cisco AS5800 universal access server.
- T-1/E-1 high-capacity digital voice port adapter Cisco 7200 and 7500 series.

As with analog, the VICs are inserted into the VNMs to create the digital T-1 voice module for the Cisco 2600 and 3600 series routers. The Cisco 1760 router can use the individual VWIC-2MFT-T-1 card as an interface to a PBX or PSTN for digital connectivity. The card uses a RJ-48 crossover cable for connection to a PBX. The pinouts are listed below:

- **Pin 1** RX ring
- **Pin 2** RX tip
- **Pin 4** TX ring
- **Pin 5** TX tip

The items needed for configuration of the controller settings are the following:

- **Line interface** T-1 or E-1
- **Signaling interface** FXO, FXS, or E&M and ISDN PRI or BRI—Q.SIG or CCS

- **Line coding** AMI or B8ZS for T-1, and AMI or HDB3 for E-1
- **Framing format** SF (D4) or ESF for T-1, and CRC4 or no-CRC4 for E-1
- **Number of channels**

The controller configuration steps for an ISDN PRI connection to a PBX follow:

```
router# config terminal
router(config)# isdn switch-type basic-ni1
router(config)# controller T-1 1/0
router(config-controller)# framing esf
router(config-controller)# clock source internal
router(config-controller)# linecode b8zs
router(config-controller)# pri-group timeslots 1-24
```

This produces the following configuration:

```
(Partial Router configuration)
!
hostname router
!
memory-size iomem 15
voice-card 1
!
isdn switch-type ni1
!
controller T-1 1/0
framing esf
clock source line
linecode b8zs
pri-group timeslots 1-24
!
interface Serial1/0:23
no ip address
no logging event link-status
isdn switch-type primary-ni1
isdn incoming-voice voice
isdn T310 60000
no cdp enable
!
voice-port 1/0:23
!
```

Configuring Q.931 Support

Q.931 establishes and terminates ISDN circuits. This occurs at the network layer in the protocol stack. The basic steps to configure ISDN PRI with Q.931 are as follows:

1. Select the service provider ISDN PRI switch type:

   ```
   router(config)# isdn switch-type primary-net5
   ```

2. Configure the ISDN T-1/E-1 controller by setting the time slots, which are used for a T-1. The range is 1–23:

   ```
   router(config)# controller {T-1 | E-1} slot/port
   router(config-controller)# pri-group timeslots range
   ```

3. Exit from the T-1/E-1 controller configuration mode:

   ```
   router(config-controller)# exit
   ```

4. Configure the ISDN D channel interface:

   ```
   router(config)# interface serial0/0:n
   ```

5. Configure the ISDN protocol as primary slave or the primary master:

   ```
   router(config)# isdn protocol-emulate {network | user}
   ```

6. Enable or disable power supplied from an NT configured port:

   ```
   router(config-if)# [no] line-power
   ```

7. Allow incoming voice calls:

   ```
   router(config-if)# isdn incoming-voice voice
   ```

Configuring CAS

Figure 9.52 is a configuration for PBX to router with T-1 CAS signaling.

Figure 9.52 T-1 CAS Example

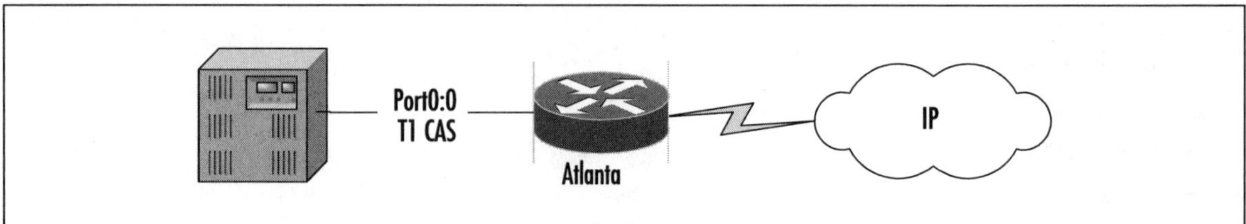

The configuration commands that pertain to the T-1 CAS example are:

```
controller T-1 0
  framing esf
```

```
clock source line primary
linecode b8zs
cas-group 0 timeslots 1-24 type e&m-fgb dtmf dnis
```

The remainder of the configuration is similar to the other scenarios. The command **cas-group 0 timeslots 1-24 type e&m-fgb dtmf dnis** sets the T-1 CAS group number and channels with the type of signaling. The other types of signaling are shown in Table 9.14.

Table 9.14 CAS Signaling Types

Signaling Type	Description
e&m-fgb	E&M Type II FGB
e&m-fgd	E&M Type II FGD
e&m-immediate-start	E&M immediate start
fxs-ground-start	FXS ground start
fxs-loop-start	FXS loop start
p7	P7 switch
r2-analog	R2 ITU Q411
r2-digital	R2 ITU Q421
r2-pulse	R2 ITU supplement 7
sas-ground-start	SAS ground start
sas-loop-start	SAS loop start

Configuring CCS

Figure 9.53 shows a basic example of PBX to router with ISDN PRI CCS signaling.

Figure 9.53 ISDN PRI CCS Example

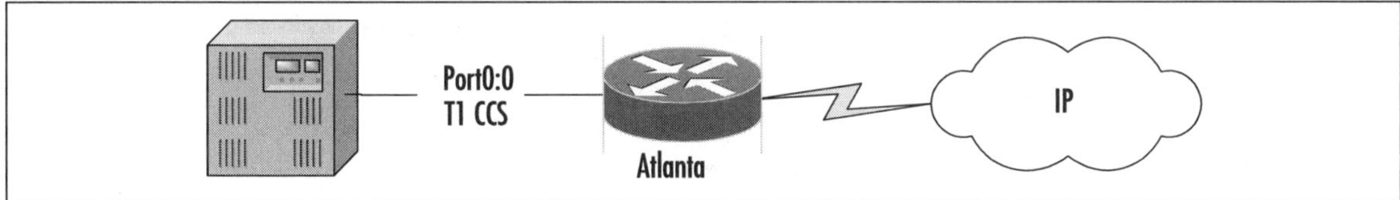

The partial configuration that follows lists the basic commands necessary for the Atlanta router with ISDN PRI connectivity to a PBX with CCS signaling.

```
isdn switch-type primary-dms100
!
controller T-1 0
 framing esf
 clock source line primary
 linecode b8zs
 pri-group timeslots 1-24
```

```
!
dial-peer voice 5000 pots
  destination-pattern 5...
  direct-inward-dial
  port 0:D
```

Configuring T-CCS

T-CCS uses a dedicated channel for signaling. There are three modes for configuring T-CCS: cross-connect, clear-channel CODEC, and frame forwarding.

T-CCS is supported with VoATM, VoFR, and VoIP. An example using T-CCS is illustrated in Figure 9.54, with two sites connected via IP and their respective telephone extensions per PBX.

Figure 9.54 T-CCS Example

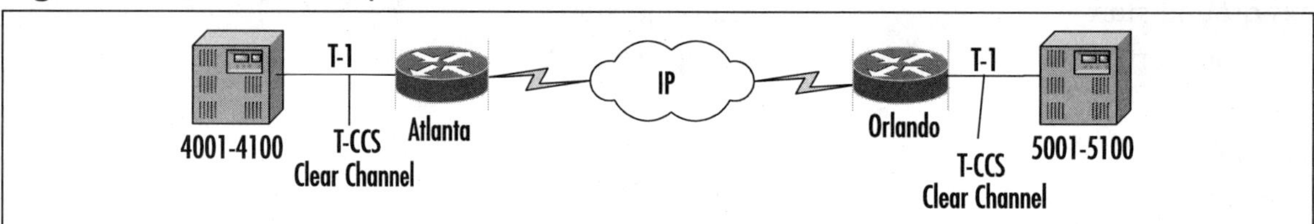

Based on the example in Figure 9.74, the following steps are needed to complete a basic T-CCS configuration to the router at the Atlanta location. The Orlando configuration would be very similar and have mirrored dial-peer statements:

1. Configure the T-1 controller:

   `router(config)# controller T-1 1/0`

2. Set the T-1 channels that are used and the signaling associated with each channel:

   `router(config-controller)# ds0-group 0 timeslots 1-24 type ext-sig`

3. Enable the T-1 controller:

   `router(config-controller)# no shutdown`

4. Exit from Controller Configuration mode:

   `router(config-controller)# exit`

5. Set up the local dial peer for the connection to the PBX:

   `router(config)# dial-peer voice 4000 pots`

6. Set up the local destination pattern for the connection to the PBX:

   `router(config-dialpeer)# destination-pattern 4...`

7. Associate the T-1 ds0-group to the dial peer:

```
router(config-dialpeer)# port 1/0:0
```

8. Exit dial-peer configuration mode:

```
router(config-dialpeer)# exit
```

9. Set up the dial peer for the connection to the remote PBX:

```
router(config)# dial-peer voice 5000 voip
```

10. Set the CODEC complexity to clear channel:

```
router(config-dialpeer)# CODEC clear-channel
```

11. Set up the destination-pattern for the connection the remote PBX:

```
router(config-dialpeer)# destination-pattern 5...
```

12. Configure the IP session target for the dial peer pointing to the remote router:

```
router(config-dialpeer)# session target ipv4:192.168.254.2
```

Configuring Gateways and Gatekeepers

The H.323 systems work primarily around two entities on the network: gateways and gatekeepers. Gateways perform the function of controlling access to resources on the network, and gatekeepers control the access to the gateways. In this section, we discuss the basic configuration steps for each entity.

Configuring H.323 Gateway

To configure a basic H.323 gateway, enable VoIP gateway functionality using the *gateway* command.

1. Enter Global Configuration mode:

```
router# configure terminal
```

2. Enable the VoIP gateway:

```
router(config)# gateway
```

3. Exit Gateway Configuration mode:

```
router(config-gateway)# exit
```

Next, configure the gateway interface parameters. Define which interface will be the gateway's H.323 interface to the VoIP network. *Only one interface is allowed to be the gateway interface.* You can select either the interface connected to the gatekeeper or a loopback interface.

After you define the gateway interface, you configure the gateway to discover the gatekeeper (multicasting or a specific host). Finally, configure the gateway's H.323 identification number and any technology prefixes that this gateway should register with the gatekeeper.

Use the next set of commands to define the Ethernet 1/0 interface to be used as the H.323 gateway interface and configure the H.323 gateway interface parameters, beginning in Global Configuration mode. For this example, assume that the gateway and gatekeeper's IP addresses are 192.168.1.1 and 192.168.1.254, respectively:

1. Enter Interface Configuration mode:

   ```
   router(config)# interface ethernet 1/0
   ```

2. Configure an IP address for this interface with subnet mask:

   ```
   router(config-if)# ip address 192.168.1.1 255.255.255.0
   ```

3. Designate this interface as being the H.323 gateway interface:

   ```
   router(config-if)# h323-gateway voip interface
   ```

4. Specify an H.323 name (ID) for the gateway associated with this interface. The gateway uses this ID when it communicates with the gatekeeper. Usually, the H.323 ID is the name given to the gateway, with the gatekeeper domain name appended to the end:

   ```
   router(config-if)# h323-gateway voip h323-id interface-id
   ```

5. Specify the name (ID) of the gatekeeper associated with this gateway and how the gateway finds it. The gatekeeper ID configured here must exactly match the gatekeeper ID in the gatekeeper configuration. The gateway determines the location of the gateway in one of three ways: by a defined IP address, through multicast, or via RAS.

   ```
   router(config-if)# h323-gateway voip id atl2600gk 192.168.1.254 1719
   ```

6. Define the H.323 name of the gateway, identifying this gateway to its associated gatekeeper:

   ```
   router(config-if)# h323-gateway voip h323-id atl2600gw1@cisco.com
   ```

7. Specify a technology prefix. A technology prefix is used to identify a type of service that this gateway is capable of providing. This is an optional configuration.

   ```
   router(config-if)# h323-gateway voip tech-prefix 9#
   ```

Configuring H.323 Gatekeeper

Setting up a Cisco router as a gatekeeper requires registering a zone of influence, stating other gatekeepers for other zones, and registering any zone prefixes, technology prefixes, and E.164 addresses with the gatekeeper.

H.323 ID Addresses

Interzone communications are handled via domain name registration (in DNS). H.323 interzone communications work very much like any DNS registration. Every gatekeeper is responsible for its own zone. The zone is registered as an H.323 domain, and each domain has a domain name. For example, to resolve an address *gateway1@zonE-1.com*, the end station's gatekeeper will find a gatekeeper that has the *zonE-1.com* domain registered. It will then send a request for an IP address resolution to that gatekeeper in the form of an LRQ request to resolve the *gateway1* entity.

Zone Prefixes

Zone prefixes perform the same functionality as domain names, but in a different numeric fashion. A good example of zone prefixes is an area code on the PSTN. When placing a local call, you do not have to include the area code with the telephone number if the destination is within the same area (zone). To get to a number outside your area code, you need to dial the destination area code first so that the telephone company can route the call properly. Zone prefixes are the internal functions that handle this problem.

Consider this example: The local gatekeeper knows that if it receives a telephone call with a zone prefix of 404*xxxxxxx* (the area code of 404 followed by seven arbitrary digits), the call is to be forwarded to the gatekeeper registered with that zone (atlgk in the following example). This command is issued on the local gatekeeper using the following syntax:

```
Atlanta(config-gk)# zone prefix atlgk 404. . . . . . .
```

In this case, the **zone remote** command will also be specified to indicate that the zone is not handled by the local gatekeeper. This helps the gateway to handle the transmission more efficiently by sending a LRQ to the remote gatekeeper for resolution. If this command is not used, the local gatekeeper is queried first. It will have to perform general broadcasts for resolution to other gatekeepers. With the **zone remote** command, this process is streamlined and performance is improved. In conjunction with the **zone remote** command, the **zone local** command identifies a zone as belonging to the local gatekeeper. The resolution process is again streamlined by pre-qualifying the zone as local.

The **zone remote** command sends the call from the Atlanta gatekeeper to the gatekeeper in Orlando. The call is received by the Orlando gatekeeper and is routed out to its final destination zone. If the E.164 address for the destination is registered with the gatekeeper, it will route the call to the H.323-enabled device. Usually, the device is not an H.323-enabled device and is not registered with the gatekeeper. The call is most likely going to a standard telephone that is not registered directly with the gatekeeper and needs to be forwarded to a gateway for processing. The gatekeeper looks at zone prefixes or technology prefixes to determine the proper gateway. Figure 9.55 illustrates the local and remote zone concepts.

Figure 9.55 Gatekeeper Zone Prefix

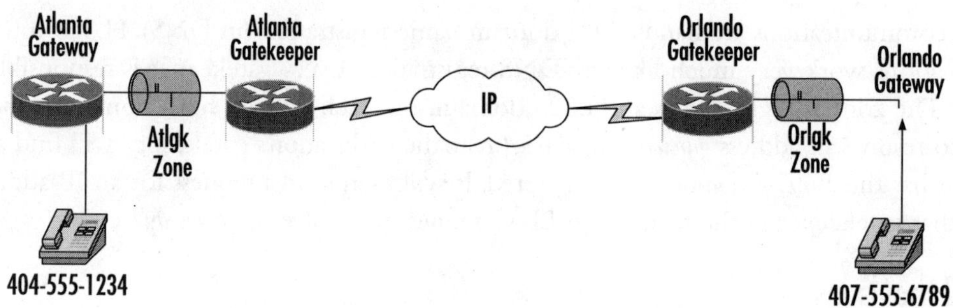

Let's discuss the steps to configure a gatekeeper based on the example scenario in Figure 9.55. The steps to take to configure a Cisco router to act as an H.323 gatekeeper are:

1. Enter Global Configuration mode:

   ```
   router# configure terminal
   ```

2. Activate the gatekeeper functionality on the router:

   ```
   router(config)# gatekeeper
   ```

3. Specify a zone controlled by a gatekeeper:

   ```
   router(config-gk)# zone local gatekeeper-name domain-name [ ras-IP-address]
   ```

4. Set a static entry for another zone's gatekeeper address so that information for that zone can be forwarded:

   ```
   router(config-gk)# zone remote other-gatekeeper-name other-domain-name other-gatekeeper-ipaddress [port number]
   ```

5. Configures the gatekeeper to acknowledge its own or remote prefixes:

   ```
   router(config-gk)# zone prefix gatekeeper-name e.164-prefix
   ```

6. Configure a technology prefix for the various types of service in the zone. The *hopoff* command tells to which gatekeeper to pass off the tech prefix, if appropriate. Configure the gatekeeper to acknowledge its own or remote prefixes:

   ```
   router(config-gk)# gw-type-prefix type-prefix [hopoff gkid] [default-technology] [[gw ipaddr ipaddr [port]]…]
   ```

The following is a partial configuration clip from the Atlanta gatekeeper router:

```
gatekeeper
  zone local Atlgk1 cisco.com
  zone remote Orlgk1 cisco.com 192.168.2.1 1719
  zone prefix Atlgk1 404.......
  gw?type?prefix 404#*
  no shutdown
```

Enter the following command to verify gateway and gatekeeper configuration from the Atlanta gateway:

```
Atlgw1# show gateway
Gateway Atlgw1@cisco.com is registered to Gatekeeper Atlgk1
Alias list (CLI configured)
  H323-ID Atlgw1@cisco.com
Alias list (last RCF)
  H323-ID Atlgw1@cisco.com
```

Troubleshooting VoIP

Troubleshooting VoIP can be challenging, especially if you do not structure your efforts. You will have more success if you have use a logical and methodological approach to testing, troubleshooting, and supporting VoIP. Before you can successfully troubleshoot, you need to have a thorough understanding of the steps and commands necessary to configure VoIP. The testing and troubleshooting information contained in this chapter is by no means exhaustive; rather, it provides a framework that you can expand to fit your own VoIP troubleshooting situations.

To make your troubleshooting logical and structure, use the Open System Interconnection (OSI) reference model. When you begin troubleshooting, start at Layer 1, the physical layer. Often you will find the cause of the problem here in the form of faulty hardware or mis-wired cable. Once you have ascertained that Layer 1 components are not at fault, move on to the next layer, Layer 2, and so on, until you have resolved the problem.

Layer 1 is the physical layer of the OSI model. It is concerned with the transmission and reception of bits on the physical media. By that definition, all hardware in and attached to a router operates at the physical layer. This means testing and verifying physical components such as the router, its modules, cards, interfaces, and cables. Your goal in troubleshooting this layer is to eliminate physical components as the chief suspects in causing the problem.

Troubleshooting Equipment, from Power On to Operating State

At Layer 1, the bare minimum is the router should be able to power up and enable you to inventory its hardware. When you power on your router, watch its power-on self-tests (POSTs) and note any errors. After a successful power on, log on to the router and execute the **show version** command to obtain a hardware and software. The output of this command is:

```
Cisco Internetwork Operating System Software
IOS (tm) 3600 Software (C3640-IS-M), Version 12.1(2)T,  RELEASE
    SOFTWARE (fc1)

Copyright (c) 1986-2000 by cisco Systems, Inc.
Compiled Tue 16-May-00 12:47 by ccai
Image text-base: 0x600088F0, data-base: 0x6101A000
```

```
ROM: System Bootstrap, Version 11.1(20)AA2, EARLY DEPLOYMENT RELEASE
     SOFTWARE (fc1)

usa3640 uptime is 26 minutes
System returned to ROM by reload
System image file is "flash:c3640-is-mz.121-2.t.bin"

cisco 3640 (R4700) processor (revision 0x00) with 60416K/5120K bytes
     of memory.
Processor board ID 19592029
R4700 CPU at 100Mhz, Implementation 33, Rev 1.0
Bridging software.
X.25 software, Version 3.0.0.
SuperLAT software (copyright 1990 by Meridian Technology Corp).
Primary Rate ISDN software, Version 1.1.
2 Ethernet/IEEE 802.3 interface(s)
2 Serial network interface(s)
2 Channelized T-1/PRI port(s)
2 Voice FXS interface(s)
2 Voice E & M interface(s)
DRAM configuration is 64 bits wide with parity disabled.
125K bytes of non-volatile configuration memory.
32768K bytes of processor board System flash (Read/Write)

Configuration register is 0x2102
```

For example, if you installed what you thought were FXO interfaces and this display shows only FXS interfaces, then either you need an IOS upgrade or your router hardware is faulty, *or* you actually installed FXS voice ports. Possible fixes include powering down the router and reseating modules, moving the module to a different slot, or considering the possibility that your version of IOS does not support the module.

As a rule of thumb, your IOS generally should be at least version 12.1 or later; this will vary by router platform and voice hardware. Some newer hardware requires at least version 12.2 or 12.3; you can, check the voice hardware compatibility matrix at www.cisco.com.

Several other commands that can give useful hardware information are **show controllers** (to list the various controllers installed in your router) and **show diagnostic** (to list information about your router's components).

Troubleshooting Cabling

Cables used in VoIP configurations are fairly straightforward and are probably one of the easiest components to troubleshoot, given the standard cables used and the wide variety of cable-testing equipment available to you. Cisco routers can support a large variety of cable types, ranging from simple RS232 and V.35 to ATM DS3 cables—far too many to cover in a single troubleshooting chapter. We have opted to provide you a structured checklist of cable troubleshooting steps, shown in Table 9.15.

Table 9.15 Checklist of Troubleshooting Steps

Possible Problem	Check
Right cable connected to right interface?	Check cable and verify slot and port number.
Right end of cable connected to right interface?	DCE vs. DTE: verify with **show controllers**.
Right cable type connected to communications equipment?	RS232, V.35, etc.
Cable pinouts correct?	Visually inspect and check with cable tester?
Cable verified as good?	Test with cable tester or swap equipment.

You'll use specific telephony cables to build your VoIP network. These are the registered jack (RJ) standards such as RJ11, RJ45, and RJ48. The most common problem with these types of cables occurs with their pinouts: they must be correct or they will not work, or, even worse, they will work intermittently. Figure 9.56 shows the wire diagram for the RJ11, RJ45, and RJ48 cables.

Figure 9.56 RJ11, RJ45, and RJ48 Wire Pinouts

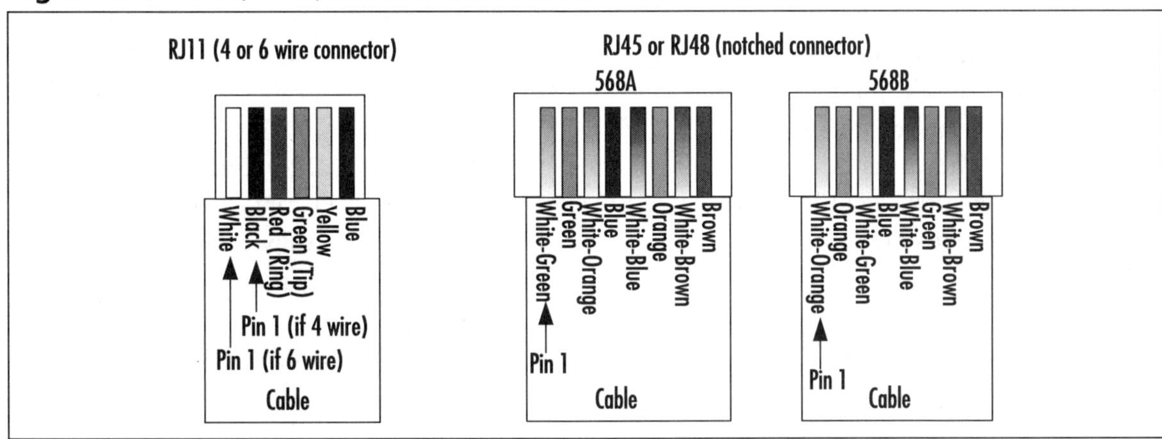

The RJ11 standard is typically used for most analog telephone communications. RJ11 connects FXS and FXO interfaces to various communications devices such as telephones and PBXs. As shown in Figure 9.56, the RJ11 standard uses two wires for analog telephone communications: one for receive (ring) and one for transmit (tip), corresponding in our figure to the red and green wires, respectively. The RJ11 connector can be either a four-pin or a six-pin connector, but only two wires are used for analog telephone communications.

VoIP networks use RJ45 and RJ48 connectors if E&M voice ports are involved. The RJ45 and the RJ48 standards are similar in that they both have eight wires (four pairs). The RJ45 standard was developed for high-speed LANs such as 100BaseT, whereas the RJ48 standard is geared more toward data communications such as T-1 circuits. Both standards can handle the same load requirements; they were merely designed for different purposes.

One difference between the RJ48 and RJ45 standards is that the RJ48 has a connector that is keyed to a slotted jack and the RJ45 does not. Interestingly enough, the RJ45 can be substituted for an RJ48 cable since its lack of a slot does not prevent it from fitting into a RJ48 jack. The converse is not true: A RJ48 connector cannot fit into a RJ45 jack, because the notch on the RJ48 prevents it from fitting into the RJ45 jack.

There are two wiring schemes for the RJ45 standard: TA568A and TA568B. It is important that your cable adhere to either one of these standards to prevent interference (crosstalk). If you were to dismantle an RJ45 cable, you would see that it has four pairs of wires. In each pair, the two wires are twisted around each other to minimize crosstalk. If you were to pick wires at random and crimp them into the RJ45 connector, chances are you would experience problems with your cables. TA568A/B cables are optimized to prevent such interference.

Troubleshooting cabling is relatively easy thanks to the numerous cable testers on the market, ranging from simple pin-checking devices (like the one you can find at www.copperandfiber-tools.com/testers.asp) to expensive full-featured testers such as those offered by Fluke (www.fluke.com).

Your first step in verifying RJxx cable is to visually inspect the cable for breaks. Check the wiring pinouts against Figure 9.56. If they match and appear to be in good physical shape, your next step is to test the cable using a cable tester. Most cable testers allow you to map the wiring to ensure that Pin 1 goes to Pin 1, Pin 2 to Pin 2, and so on; pin mismatches are a very common problem. If you still have problems with the cable after it passes the cable tester (it shouldn't, if you have a good tester), throw the cable away and get a new one. Chances are, you have a rare bad mix of plastic and metal composition that went into the making of that cable, and it is interfering with the cable's ability to transport electrons. If you do not have a cable tester and are not sure of the cable, replace it.

Figure 9.57 shows the "standard" deployment of these cables in a VoIP network. Remember that an RJ45 cable can stand in for an RJ48 cable. For example, an RJ11 cable can also fit into RJ45 and RJ48 ports. You could easily insert an RJ11 cable where you really need to use an RJ45 cable.

Figure 9.57 RJ11 and RJ45 Use

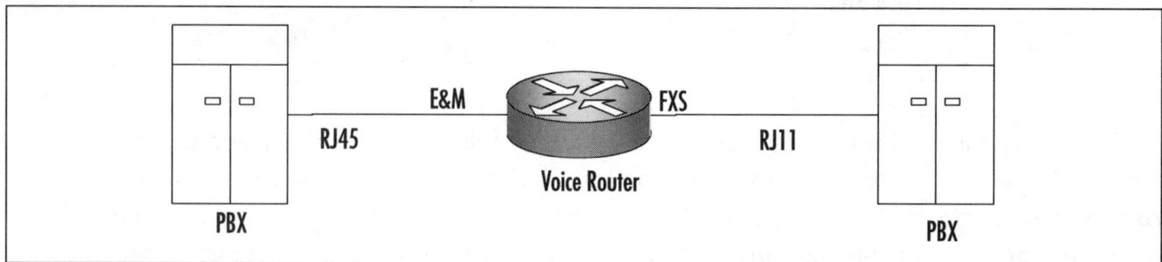

Troubleshooting Ports

Cisco routers (such as the 2600 or 3600 series) or the multifunction chassis (MC3810) have voice ports to provide telephony services. These voice ports can be classified as FXS, FXO, or E&M. What does this mean to troubleshooting efforts?

An FXS voice port is typically used to connect end-user telephony devices such as analog telephones, fax machines, and modems. FXS voice ports have standard RJ11 jacks. As with a "normal" telephone line, FXS voice ports supply the necessary dial tone, ring, and voltage to the end device, enabling the telephone to ring on incoming calls and dial tone to sound for outgoing calls. As far as the telephony device is concerned, it is plugged into the telephone network. Figure 9.58 shows some typical uses of FXS ports on Cisco routers.

Figure 9.58 FXS Port Uses

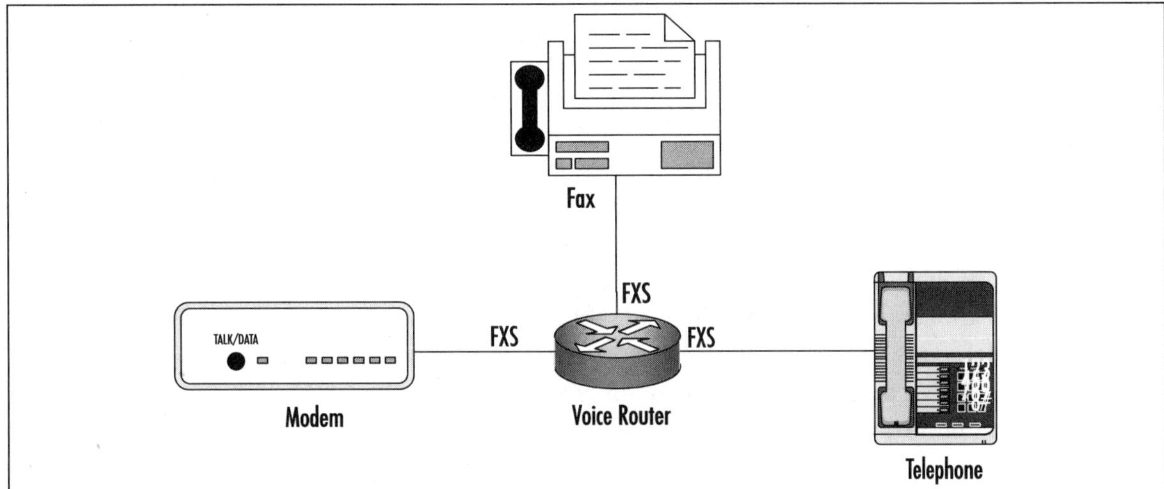

An FXO voice port is typically used for trunk support, such as connecting the VoIP network to a PSTN CO. FXO voice ports can be used in situations in which you want to connect a VoIP network to a PSTN. FXO ports do not provide dial tone, ring, or voltage, meaning that they cannot be used with the analog devices supported by the FXS interface. FXO interfaces use the same RJ11 connectors and jacks as any analog device. Figure 9.59 shows some typical uses of FXS ports on Cisco routers.

Figure 9.59 FXO Port Use

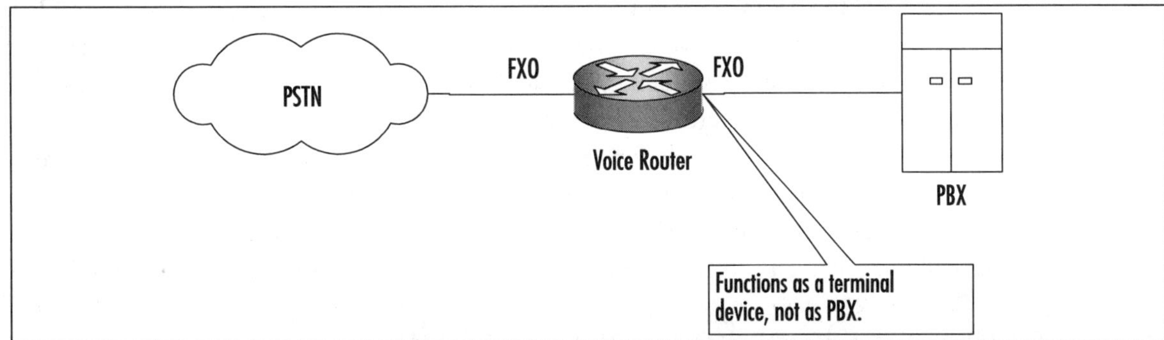

E&M ports provide an analog trunk to connect two or more PBXs over a network (IP, Frame Relay, or ATM). This can be useful in situations in which you have multiple remote locations with numerous telephone lines and a PBX at each location. A router with an E&M port can tie these PBXs together and route calls between them, as shown in Figure 9.60. Contrast this scenario with the alternative, which is purchasing a trunk from the telecommunications to each site. The cost savings can be significant if you use VoIP for tie-line replacement instead.

Figure 9.60 E&M Ports Connecting PBXs

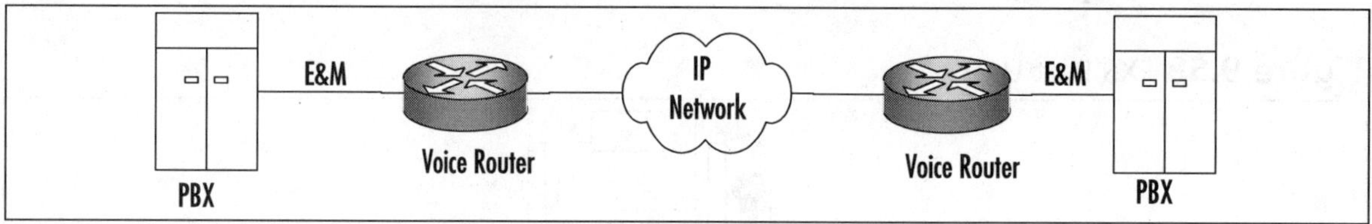

The E&M standard uses RJ48, which you will recall is more or less a keyed (notched) RJ45 connector and jack. The trunk line provided by E&M can be either two-wire or four-wire, although there might actually be six or eight physical wires.

At Layer 1, troubleshooting voice ports is relatively simple. A common problem is misidentifying the ports and attempting to use them for other than their designed purpose. For example, plugging an analog telephone into an FXO port is a common mistake. Another problem could involve connecting a crossover cable with RJ45 connectors into the E&M port (which is RJ48): The cable used must be straight-through cable.

Each port type (FXS, FXO, and E&M) must be used for its intended purpose, as described in the previous section. Avoid problems by plugging in the correct equipment with the correct cable. Once each port has been configured in the software, you can perform simple tests such as lifting the telephone handset and listening for dial tone (in case of FXS ports) or placing a call from one PBX to another connected over a WAN via E&M ports.

In case of E&M configuration, you can eliminate the local PBX as a source of problems by dialing another telephone connected to that PBX. If that is successful, the problem lies with the E&M port and/or the VoIP configuration.

Problems with E&M ports can occur due to the way E&M operates. E&M configuration can be relatively complex, so its Layer 1 troubleshooting must be logical and thorough. At Layer 1, the singular cause of problems for E&M ports is the physical cable. You need to ensure that the cable can support whatever E&M type you have configured. Each type of E&M has a different way of handling the E and M wires as well as signaling. The local device signals its off-hook condition via the E wire, whereas off-hook conditions on a remote device are indicated on the M wire.

E&M types I and V use only two wires for signaling, though there are six physical wires present. Types II, III, and IV use four wires for E, M, signal grounding, and signal battery and have eight physical wires. If the cable you are using lacks the necessary wires or a critical wire in the cable is bad, you will experience problems. Ensure that your cable is verified before you use it.

Troubleshooting Other Physical Layer Issues

Problems can occur in other Layer 1 aspects of voice communications. Components such as PBX, CO, and circuits can have a significant impact on your VoIP network. This is not an exhaustive list; you might have other unique components in your network. You should have a complete inventory of the devices that are used to support your VoIP network.

Troubleshooting Private Branch eXchange Problems

Unless you are a telephony specialist, you might not be familiar with PBXs and what they do. In simplest terms, a PBX is a hub for telephone lines. PBXs reduce the number of physical wires that a telephone company has to install to support a location that needs multiple telephone lines.

Generally speaking, the PBX is an install-and-forget device. You will not often have much to do with a PBX. However, if you want to connect the PBXs of different locations to each other or connect the PBX to a PSTN over a VoIP network, you need to know how to configure and troubleshoot the E&M ports on Cisco routers.

By developing your dial plan, dial peers, and so on, and then connecting each location PBX to an E&M port on the voice router, you can use your existing WAN links to transport your calls, as opposed to paying expensive trunk costs. In addition, you have much tighter control over your telephony network with this design.

Problems that occur with this arrangement will most likely be mismatch or misconfiguration issues between the PBX and the E&M port. In addition to configuring the Cisco E&M port, you also need to configure the PBX, using its native operating system commands.

The make of PBX determines whether the Cisco E&M port supports it. Currently, at this writing, Cisco supports Lucent, Nortel, and select NEC PBXs on its E&M ports. Check for an updated list at www.cisco.com/univercd/cc/td/doc/product/access/acs_mod/cis3600/sw_conf/pbx_int/index.htm. If this link does not work for you, do a search on www.cisco.com for *PBX interoperability*. Check this list before you attempt to connect a Cisco voice router to your PBX; if your device is not on this list, the device will not work.

Troubleshooting Central Office Problems

The CO is usually an unmanned building where trunk lines from the PBXs or telephone-line junction boxes terminate to connect to the PSTN. In context of VoIP networks, the trunk line from the PBX over which all the telephone lines ride connects to the CO, and from there, the CO is connected to the PSTN. Figure 9.61 shows a common CO arrangement.

Figure 9.61 Central Office Residential Line to PBX Line

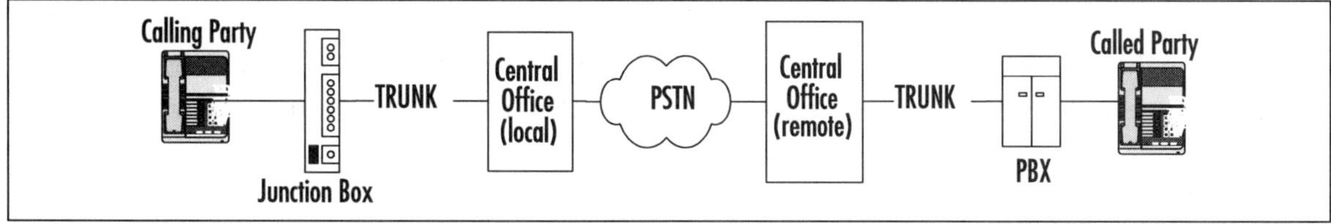

For most problems with a CO, there is little that you, as an end-user, can do to resolve them. What you can do is call your local telecommunications provider *after* you have performed in-house troubleshooting and have confidently proven that the problem does not lie with your network, your wiring, or your configuration. Last-mile providers are notorious for their skepticism regarding the part of the telephone network in which the problem lies.

To prove your hypothesis that there is a problem with the CO or with the connection to the CO, try a few simple tests. If you can call another number internal to the same PBX, you can generally be sure that your PBX is operating normally. If you have several PBXs connected to each other via an E&M port on your voice router and each location can call the other, your VoIP configuration is working. If you cannot reach non-organizational numbers (which normally traverse outside your PBX and VoIP network), the problem is definitely between your PBX and the CO, between the CO and its PSTN connection, or with your dial plan.

To test the connection between your PBX and the CO, try calling another number not on your PBX that terminates at the CO. If you can call successfully, the connection between your PBX and your CO is fine. However, this test requires that you know another number that terminates at the same CO. If that test is successful, try calling a number that terminates somewhere in the PSTN. If you are unable to make that call, the problem lies between that CO and the PSTN, in which case it becomes a problem for the provider to resolve.

Ensure that your dial plan is perfect and is functioning as intended. If your dial plan is faulty, there is a possibility your VoIP network is not routing the call as you think it is. Ensure that the number destination is configured correctly and that it does indeed pass through the provider's equipment and network before you call them.

If the problem occurred after you made changes to your PBX to accommodate your new PBX-to-voice-router E&M connection, chances are good that you made an error in the PBX configuration. Check your PBX configuration, and if possible, consult an expert who knows the PBX inside and out. If you do not know how to verify or configure your PBX, it is best that you consult a company or engineer.

After doing all this, you should call the telecommunications and inform your representative that there is a problem with the Telco network. Be prepared to provide details such as trunk information, any support agreements you have, contact information, location information, and so on. At this point, the value of a good service level agreement will become quite apparent.

Troubleshooting Underlying Circuit and Network Problems

At some point, your VoIP network is going to have its calls transported over various network media, whether point-to-point T-1 circuits, ATM DS3, Ethernet, ISDN, or the like. There are a large number of circuit types—too many to cover individually in this chapter. Instead, we present a simple methodology for troubleshooting suspect circuit problems.

At Layer 1, your concerns about any circuit or network are physical. Physical problems that can occur include problems with circuit equipment, cable problems, and interface failure. The following sections detail steps you can take to troubleshoot your suspected circuit and network problems.

Testing and Verifying Cable

We covered cable testing and verification in the Layer 1 troubleshooting section; here we revisit this topic with an eye toward circuits and networks. Cable verification can be either simple or an exercise in futility if you do not have cable testers or a known good cable to replace faulty cable. When you're verifying cable, start with a visual inspection. Check to ensure that no pins are bent, broken, or missing. With RJ45, RJ11, and RJ48 cables, ensure that their pinouts are what you expect (that is, not configured in some unique, nonstandard configuration). If the cables are in a nonstandard pinout, either rewire them to be standard or replace the cable. These cables should be in a straight-through configuration.

Cables that connect to a serial interface on Cisco routers can be a little trickier to troubleshoot. This is due to the fact Cisco cables typically have a proprietary high-density DB60 connector on the end that connects to the router serial interface, and they auto-configure to adapt to the other end. The other end is typically an industry-standard connector such as RS232, V.35, RS535, and so on. Most commercial cable testers cannot easily (if at all) test such cables. The easiest and most economical test is to swap your existing cable with a known good one.

The **show controllers** command confirms whether or not the router correctly sees your cable. A simple test you can do is to remove the cable, execute **show controllers** to verify you are connecting to the port you think you are, and the cable should disappear from the listing.

```
RR1# show controllers
insert show controllers output here.
  Interface 1 is Serial0, electrical interface is V.35 DCE
    10 total RX buffers, 11 buffer TX queue limit, buffer size 1520
    Transmitter delay is 0 microseconds
    High speed synchronous serial interface
```

Notice that **show controllers** tells us that there is a V.35 cable attached to our serial 0 interface and that it is DCE, not DTE. This is a useful bit of information for troubleshooting.

Testing and Verifying Communications Equipment

Your VoIP network might use many different types of communications equipment.

A channel service unit/data service unit (CSU/DSU) connects to digital lines. CSUs connect circuits with bandwidths ranging from 56k to T-1/E-1 speeds. Your make and model of CSU/DSU determines the features you have.

At a minimum, most CSUs support loopback testing, arguably one of the most important features of any CSU. Loopback testing is the capability to wrap a circuit so that test traffic is returned to the CSU of origin rather than the remote CSU. This function enables you to verify that a circuit is good, regardless of the state of the CSU at the distant end. Figure 9.62 shows local and remote loopbacks and their reach.

Figure 9.62 Local and Remote Loopbacks

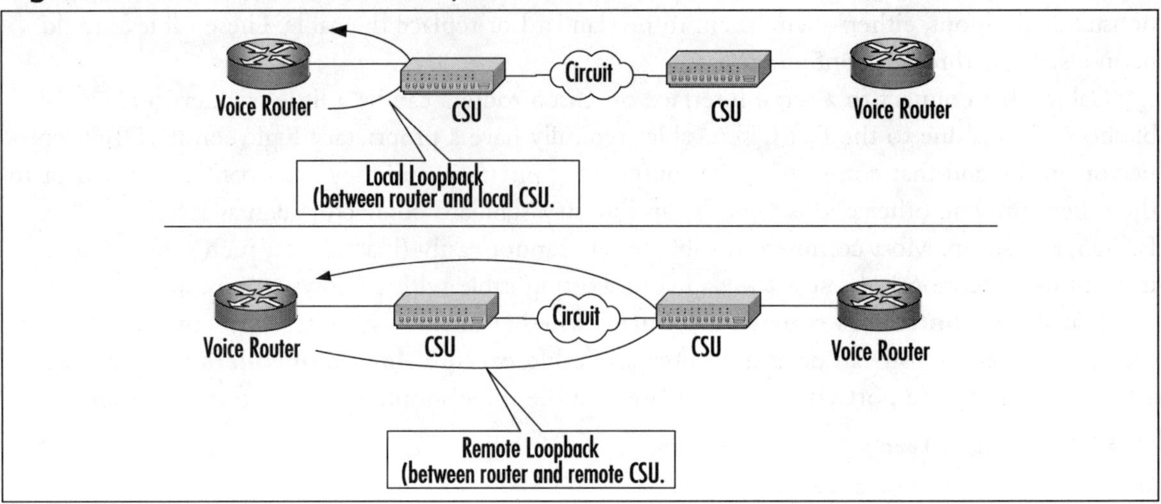

Your first loopback test should be local to verify good connectivity between the CSU and the router. Start by putting the CSU into a local loopback. Log onto the router, and execute a **show interface**; you should see a looped state as shown. Have the router ping its own interface. If the ping is successful, and you see the loop on the router, connectivity is good. When you use the **show interface serial x/x** command, if communications are good between your router and your CSU, your display should look like the following:

```
Serial x/x is up, line protocol is up (looped)
(output abbreviated)
```

This output confirms that communications between the router and the CSU is good, and it confirms that the CSU is operating correctly. Next, replace the local loopback with a remote loopback, and repeat the steps you performed with the local loopback. If the loop is visible, there is good connectivity all the way back to the distant-end Telco location, up to where the circuit connects to the distant end CSU. If you do not see the loop, there is a problem with the circuit between your CSU and the distant end. You will need to work with your Telco provider to have its staff troubleshoot the circuit.

LAN troubleshooting can start with viewing switch port lights. If the lights are green and transmitting keepalives regularly, you have a good LAN connection. This is true at least at the physical layer. Be aware that just because you have good connectivity between the router and the switch does not mean that the switch or its Virtual LANs (VLANs) are configured correctly.

Your next step in troubleshooting is to check the switch configuration. Ensure that the ports are enabled and are in the right VLAN. Some router interfaces have problems with full-duplex communication, so try turning it off. You can also manually set the speed to 10Mbps or 100Mbps, as opposed to using auto-negotiation, which is notorious for causing connectivity issues.

Testing and Verifying Cisco Router Interfaces

After we have ascertained that neither the cabling nor the circuit nor the communications equipment is the problem, we are ready to turn our attention to the Cisco router. Two of your best troubleshooting tools are **show** and **debug.** Both can provide useful Layer 1 information to aid your troubleshooting efforts. Here we highlight a few of those commands. The **show** command provides a quick snapshot of the current state of your hardware; **debug** affords a real-time display of events as they occur. The **debug** command can be quite resource-intensive and can generate copious amounts of data, so it should be used sparingly and very specifically.

Let's start with a discussion of several **show** commands that can be useful in troubleshooting your VoIP router. The commands we present here are by no means complete; rather, they form the basics of your **show** toolbox.

The **show version** command can give you a quick snapshot of the version of IOS you are running on your router, how much memory and flash it has, how it is booting (from ROM or flash), the interfaces and ports that are installed, and so on. Sample output from this command is as follows:

```
---------------- show version -----------------
Cisco Internetwork Operating System Software
IOS (tm) 3600 Software (C3640-IS-M), Version 12.1(2)T, RELEASE
    SOFTWARE (fc1)
Copyright (c) 1986-2000 by cisco Systems, Inc.
Compiled Tue 16-May-00 12:47 by ccai
Image text-base: 0x600088F0, data-base: 0x6101A000

ROM: System Bootstrap, Version 11.1(20)AA2, EARLY DEPLOYMENT RELEASE
     SOFTWARE (fc1)

usa3640 uptime is 26 minutes
System returned to ROM by reload
System image file is "flash:c3640-is-mz.121-2.t.bin"

cisco 3640 (R4700) processor (revision 0x00) with 60416K/5120K bytes
    of memory.
Processor board ID 19592029
R4700 CPU at 100Mhz, Implementation 33, Rev 1.0
Bridging software.
X.25 software, Version 3.0.0.
SuperLAT software (copyright 1990 by Meridian Technology Corp).
Primary Rate ISDN software, Version 1.1.
2 Ethernet/IEEE 802.3 interface(s)
2 Serial network interface(s)
```

```
2 Channelized T-1/PRI port(s)
2 Voice FXS interface(s)
2 Voice E & M interface(s)
DRAM configuration is 64 bits wide with parity disabled.
125K bytes of non-volatile configuration memory.
32768K bytes of processor
```

The **show diagnostic** command provides great detail on the cards and modules installed in your router. In the following display, we see that Slot 2 has a four-port voice module installed and that module has an E&M and an FXS voice port installed. Notice that you can also get the serial number of your hardware with this command:

```
Slot 2:
 4 PORT Voice PM for MARs Port adapter
 Port adapter is analyzed
 Port adapter insertion time unknown
 EEPROM contents at hardware discovery:
 Hardware revision 1.1           Board revision C0
 Serial number      10260117   Part number      800-02491-02
 Test history       0x0            RMA number      00-00-00
 EEPROM format version 1
 EEPROM contents (hex):
   0x20: 01 65 01 01 00 9C 8E 95 50 09 BB 02 00 00 00 00
   0x30: 60 00 00 00 98 10 08 17 FF FF FF FF FF FF FF FF

 WIC Slot 0:
 E&M Voice daughter card (2 port)
 Hardware revision 1.1           Board revision C0
 Serial number      10259431   Part number      800-02497-01
 Test history       0x0            RMA number      00-00-00
 Connector type     Wan Module
 EEPROM format version 1
 EEPROM contents (hex):
   0x20: 01 0F 01 01 00 9C 8B E7 50 09 C1 01 00 00 00 00
   0x30: 60 00 00 00 98 10 07 01 FF FF FF FF FF FF FF FF

 WIC Slot 1:
 FXS Voice daughter card (2 port)
 Hardware revision 1.1           Board revision C0
 Serial number      11242899   Part number      800-02493-01
 Test history       0x0            RMA number      00-00-00
 Connector type     Wan Module
```

```
 EEPROM format version 1
 EEPROM contents (hex):
   0x20: 01 0E 01 01 00 AB 8D 93 50 09 BD 01 00 00 00 0
```

The **show controllers** command details information about your interfaces, as shown here. In this case, we see that a V.35 DTE cable is connected to serial 0/0. You can also check your buffers to see if they are being overwhelmed, which could indicate that you need to control your traffic or upgrade to a high-speed connection:

```
Interface Serial0/0
Hardware is Quicc 68360
DTE V.35 TX and RX clocks detected.
Comment:  Is the correct type of cable connected to your router?

(output omited)

buffer size 1524
QUICC SCC specific errors:
0 input aborts on receiving flag sequence
0 throttles, 0 enables
0 overruns
0 transmitter underruns
0 transmitter CTS losts
0 aborted short frames

Comment:  Are you experiencing conditions here which indicate that
    your buffers are being overwhelmed?
```

The **show interface** command is one of Cisco's workhorse commands. It enables you to check the current status and configuration of your interfaces, as shown in the following output. Information you can verify includes the Layer 1 and Layer 2 state of your interface, IP addressing, buffers, and so on. We will return to this command later; at this point, you should know to use this command to verify your interface is operational and that is able to handle the load placed on it:

```
Serial0/0 is up, line protocol is up
  Hardware is QUICC Serial
  Internet address is 10.99.99.101/24
  MTU 1500 bytes, BW 2048 Kbit, DLY 20000 usec,
     reliability 255/255, txload 1/255, rxload 1/255
  Encapsulation FRAME-RELAY, loopback not set
  Keepalive set (10 sec)
  LMI enq sent  158, LMI stat recvd 158, LMI upd recvd 0, DTE LMI up
```

```
LMI enq recvd 0, LMI stat sent  0, LMI upd sent  0
LMI DLCI 1023  LMI type is CISCO  Frame Relay DTE
Broadcast queue 0/64, broadcasts sent/dropped 700/7, interface
    broadcasts 63
Last input 00:00:00, output 00:00:03, output hang never
Last clearing of "show interface" counters 00:26:23
Input queue: 0/75/0/0 (size/max/drops/flushes); Total output drops: 0
Queueing strategy: weighted fair
Output queue: 0/1000/64/0 (size/max total/threshold/drops)
   Conversations  0/2/256 (active/max active/max total)
   Reserved Conversations 0/0 (allocated/max allocated)
5 minute input rate 1000 bits/sec, 1 packets/sec
5 minute output rate 0 bits/sec, 0 packets/sec
   940 packets input, 196639 bytes, 0 no buffer
   Received 0 broadcasts, 0 runts, 0 giants, 0 throttles
   0 input errors, 0 CRC, 0 frame, 0 overrun, 0 ignored, 0 abort
   920 packets output, 182938 bytes, 0 underruns
   0 output errors, 0 collisions, 0 interface resets
   0 output buffer failures, 0 output buffers swapped out
   0 carrier transitions
   DCD=up  DSR=up  DTR=up  RTS=up  CTS=up
```

The **debug** commands can be useful in monitoring and capturing information as they occur. These commands enable you to track the consequences of a specific event at a specific point in time. Several **debug** commands can be useful, but use them with caution on a production system. Since they generate copious amounts of information, we do not provide examples of output. Instead, we call your attention to specific **debug** commands that can aid you in troubleshooting your interfaces.

Cisco also provides several beneficial commands for troubleshooting serial interfaces. The **debug serial interface** command captures serial interface events such as keepalive activity, outages, and buffer overflows. If you want information on packets as they flow through a serial interface, use **debug serial packet**. Be warned: This command tracks every single packet that flows through that interface. At the very least, it will enable you to confirm that your voice packets are being passed.

Layer 2 Troubleshooting

Once we have confirmed that Layer 1 has no problems, we are ready to start our Layer 2 (data link) troubleshooting. Layer 2 is not called the data link layer for nothing; it is the linkage between Layer 1 and Layer 3. Layer 2 packages data it receives from Layer 3 in a format that can be handed off to Layer 1. From there, Layer 1 puts the data on the wire as strings of 0s and 1s (binary data). It does the reverse upon receiving frames from Layer 1: It repackages them in the appropriate format for Layer 3 (IP packets, etc.).

You can accomplish several troubleshooting tasks at Layer 2. Many more troubleshooting options are available than we present here. Serial interfaces, Frame Relay, and ATM happen to be among the most common used to support VoIP networks.

Troubleshooting Serial Interfaces

When troubleshooting serial interfaces at Layer 2, you can look at several key items. Start with the **show interface serial x** command, where *x* is the interface number. Here is a sample display:

```
RR1# show interfaces serial 0/0
Serial0/0 is up, line protocol is up
Comment:  Is the interface operating at layer 2 (line protocol is up?)

  Hardware is QUICC Serial
  Internet address is 10.99.99.101/24
  MTU 1500 bytes, BW 2048 Kbit, DLY 20000 usec,
Comment:  Is this the correct MTU for this network?

     reliability 255/255, txload 1/255, rxload 1/255
  Encapsulation FRAME-RELAY, loopback not set
Comment:  Is the encapsulation correct?

  Keepalive set (10 sec)
  LMI enq sent  158, LMI stat recvd 158, LMI upd recvd 0, DTE LMI up
  LMI enq recvd 0, LMI stat sent  0, LMI upd sent  0
  LMI DLCI 1023  LMI type is CISCO  Frame Relay DTE
Comment:  In case of Frame Relay, are LMI messages being sent and
    received?  Is the LMI type correct?

  Broadcast queue 0/64, broadcasts sent/dropped 700/7, interface
      broadcasts 63
  Last input 00:00:00, output 00:00:03, output hang never
  Last clearing of "show interface" counters 00:26:23
  Input queue: 0/75/0/0 (size/max/drops/flushes); Total output drops: 0
  Queueing strategy: weighted fair
  Output queue: 0/1000/64/0 (size/max total/threshold/drops)
     Conversations  0/2/256 (active/max active/max total)
     Reserved Conversations 0/0 (allocated/max allocated)
  5 minute input rate 1000 bits/sec, 1 packets/sec
  5 minute output rate 0 bits/sec, 0 packets/sec
     940 packets input, 196639 bytes, 0 no buffer
```

```
Received 0 broadcasts, 0 runts, 0 giants, 0 throttles
0 input errors, 0 CRC, 0 frame, 0 overrun, 0 ignored, 0 abort
920 packets output, 182938 bytes, 0 underruns
0 output errors, 0 collisions, 0 interface resets
0 output buffer failures, 0 output buffers swapped out
0 carrier transitions
DCD=up  DSR=up  DTR=up  RTS=up  CTS=up
```

The first line, **[1] Serial 0/0 is up, line protocol is up**, is key to troubleshooting serial interface problems. It indicates whether the problem is at Layer 1, Layer 2, or both. Table 9.16 explains the possible states you can see with this command and their meanings.

Table 9.16 Interface States and Explanations

Serial Is	Line Protocol Is ...	Cause Is ...
Up	Up	Interface is up with no problems.
Up	Up (looped)	There is a loop on communications equipment.
Up	Down	High error rates (due to circuit or communications problems) causes disabled state.
Administratively Down	Down	Interface is shut down.
Down	Down	Nothing is connected to interface, or communications equipment is off.

You can also look at the input and output queues. Keepalive intervals should match at both sides, and traffic counters should increment to show them being sent. Interface resets are another indication of problems; if they increment, it means that the circuit, communications equipment, or interface has toggled between up and down that number of times. Excessive carrier transitions can indicate a problem with the circuit (cable or communications equipment) attached to this interface. Increasing input or output errors can indicate that the interface cannot handle the amount of traffic passing through it. If that's the case, you should investigate the traffic being passed and ways to curb it (perhaps allow only certain traffic). CRC errors indicate line noise or problems with clocking.

Troubleshooting Frame Relay

Frame Relay is a packet-switching network technology that uses data link circuit identifiers (DLCIs) to build permanent and switched virtual circuits. The same issues that impact serial interfaces also affect Frame Relay connections. In troubleshooting Frame Relay problems, ensure that you troubleshoot both sides of the connection.

DLCIs, which are Layer 2 addresses, identify a virtual circuit and are presented to the router by the Frame Relay switch. Ensure you have the correct DLCI information, because a common problem is using incorrect DLCIs.

DLCIs (Layer 2) are mapped to Layer 3 addresses (IP, for example) to enable connectivity via Frame Relay. The *local* DLCI of the PVC connected to your router is mapped to the *remote* IP address of the distant router. In Figure 9.63, RR2 maps its DLCI to RR1's IP address, and vice versa. Regardless of the topology you use, the DLCI-to-IP address mapping must be valid in order for the routers connected via Frame Relay to communicate with each other. The concept is fundamental for IP operation over Frame Relay.

Figure 9.63 Frame Relay DLCI and IP Address Mapping

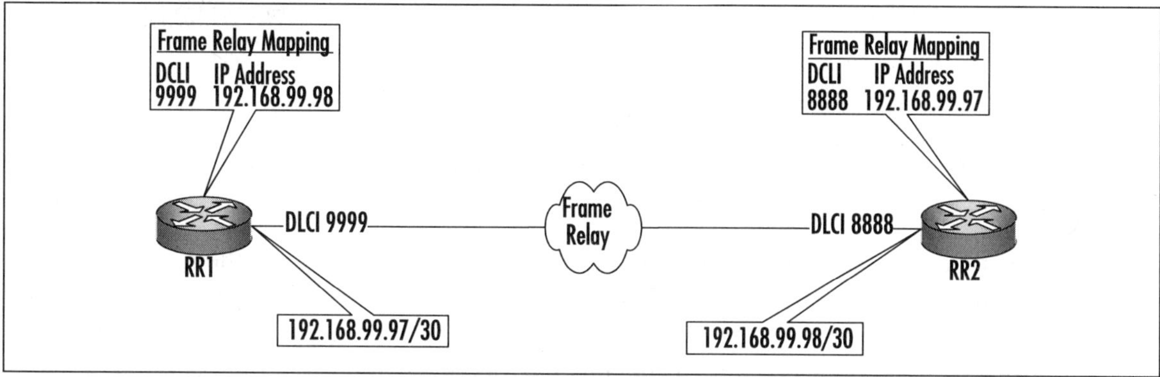

This mapping can be done automatically via inverse ARP or manual mappings that you engineer yourself. Unless you have a partial mesh topology or multiple DLCIs on a single circuit, it is best to let inverse ARP handle the mappings. Be aware that using map statements for IP on a particular DLCI automatically disables all inverse ARP for that DLCI for IP; in other words, you might need other map statements to all other IP addresses reachable via that DLCI.

If your PVC is on a physical interface on either a point-to-point or a full mesh network, let inverse Address Resolution Protocol (ARP) work out the mappings. You do not need to use the **frame-relay interface-dlci** command to lock the DLCI to this interface. However, if this physical interface has more than PVC associated with it (a multipoint interface), you need to manually map remote IP addresses to local DLCIs with **frame-relay map x.x.x.x yyyy.** This can become unmanageable as your Frame Relay network grows.

Sub-interfaces provide a workaround for this mapping requirement. Each sub-interface is a separate network segment, and therefore, mapping is automatic. If you break your physical interfaces into point-to-point sub-interfaces, you only need to execute the **frame-relay interface-dlci** command to ensure each point-to-point interface gets the right DLCI associated with it, and mapping is accomplished automatically by inverse ARP.

Point-to-multipoint interfaces are slightly trickier. Figure 9.64 shows a common spoke-and-hub configuration (a type of partial mesh topology). In this case, we would configure the hubs (RR2 and RR3) as point-to-point and the spoke (RR1) as point to multipoint.

Figure 9.64 Frame Relay Hub and Spoke

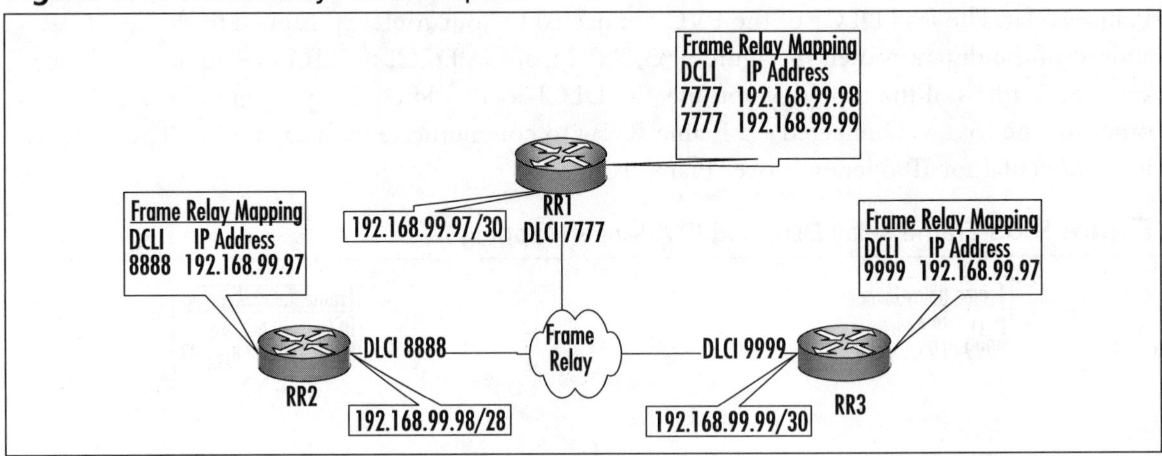

However, there is a problem: Although each hub can ping the spoke, and the spoke can ping each hub, neither hub can ping the other. This is due to the default nature of Frame Relay mapping on Cisco routers: Inverse ARP on RR1 creates mappings to RR2 and RR3, whereas RR2 and RR3 have their endpoints (RR1) mapped to RR1. Since neither RR2 nor RR3 is an endpoint to the other, no mapping occurs.

This is a problem if the VoIP peering has to be from RR2 to RR3. If they cannot reach each other at the network layer, they will not be able to pass calls to each other. There are several solutions to fix this problem. You can set up a separate PVC between the spokes, which will change your topology from a hub and spoke to a full mesh (this solution might not be possible if you are on a budget). Alternatively, you can configure a Frame Relay map and make the hub the next hop for each spoke. Or you can configure a Frame Relay map on each spoke to the other spoke. You can even execute static routes on each spoke to point to the hub as the next hop for the other spoke. Regardless of the solution you implement, the spokes must be able to reach each other in order to become VoIP peers.

Encapsulation issues are easier to troubleshoot. They either match or they don't. They are set with the **encapsulation frame-relay [ietf]** command. They must match on all routers on the same circuit. You can check the encapsulation type that is set on each router using either **show running or show interface**.

Cisco provides several commands that can be useful in troubleshooting Frame Relay.

The **show frame-relay pvc** command lists the PVCs that have been configured and whether they are operational or not. In the following example, DCLI 102 is configured and currently active, whereas the PVC attached to DCLI 103 is not used and is not active, indicating a problem with either the configuration or between this router and the Frame Relay network:

```
RR1# show frame-relay pvc

PVC Statistics for interface Serial0 (Frame Relay DTE)

              Active     Inactive      Deleted       Static
```

```
  Local          0          0          0          0
  Switched       0          0          0          0
  Unused         8          3          0          0

DLCI = 102, DLCI USAGE = UNUSED, PVC STATUS = ACTIVE, INTERFACE = Serial0

  input pkts 0              output pkts 1             in bytes 0
  out bytes 34              dropped pkts 0            in FECN pkts 0
  in BECN pkts 0            out FECN pkts 0           out BECN pkts 0
  in DE pkts 0              out DE pkts 0
  out bcast pkts 1          out bcast bytes 34            Num Pkts Switched 0
  pvc create time 00:00:08, last time pvc status changed 00:00:08

DLCI = 103, DLCI USAGE = UNUSED, PVC STATUS = INACTIVE, INTERFACE = Serial0

  input pkts 0              output pkts 0             in bytes 0
  out bytes 0               dropped pkts 0            in FECN pkts 0
  in BECN pkts 0            out FECN pkts 0           out BECN pkts 0
  in DE pkts 0              out DE pkts 0
  out bcast pkts 0           out bcast bytes 0             Num Pkts Switched 0
  pvc create time 00:00:11, last time pvc status changed 00:00:11
```

The **show frame-relay map** command displays the DLCI-to-IP address mappings. When troubleshooting, you should use this command to verify that the mappings are correct, regardless of whether they were dynamic or static.

The **debug frame-relay packet** command can be useful to catch DCLI-to-IP mapping errors. If there is no mapping to a particular IP address that you attempt to access while this command is running, you will get an error similar to the following:

```
debug frame packet
Serial0 : Encaps failed--no map entry link 7 (IP).
```

If you made changes and your INARP mappings are no longer valid, you can clear the mapping cache with the **clear frame-relay –inarp** command. The **debug frame-relay lmi** command is very important because it checks communications between the router and the Frame Relay switch. This command can determine whether they are communicating properly and whether you are using the correct DLCI (the command enables you to see what DLCI the switch is sending the router).

Troubleshooting Asynchronous Transfer Mode

ATM is similar to Frame Relay in that it shares some of its genetic composition. Its support for constant and time-sensitive traffic such as voice and video and its ability to guarantee a set quality of service make it a superior choice over Frame Relay—or pretty much any other network technology.

Another facet of ATM that makes it a superior transport for voice traffic is that it uses fixed-length 53-byte cells (a 5-byte header preceding a 48-byte payload). Like Frame Relay, it builds and transports these cells over permanent and switched virtual circuits. Its negotiation process is borrowed from Broadband ISDN (B-ISDN). ATM also supports a wide range of bandwidth, from 2Mbps up to OC-192, making it ideal for the support and expansion of your voice networks.

IP packets are segmented by the ATM module into cells and then transported to their destinations through the ATM network. At their destinations, these cells are reassembled into IP packets. The small and uniform size, as opposed to the large and differing sizes of other network technologies, enables ATM to easily and quickly transport the cells.

Two problems that can occur with an ATM PVC configuration involve cells being dropped in the ATM provider's network or PVCs not being established all the way through. You can determine if the ATM network is dropping cells by sending pings. Responses that are less than 100-percent successful could indicate that cells are being dropped. If possible, do the ping test from both sides of the PVC. Once you determine that cells are consistently dropped, you need to check several possible causes.

The **show controller** command can be used to check for physical errors in either the router or the ATM module. Two loopback test options are available with ATM. You can physically loop the RX port to the TX port of the ATM interface, thus creating a hard local loopback; this option verifies that your interface is good. Cisco also provides a command to accomplish the same thing: **loopback diagnostic**. If the interface has no hardware problems, it will achieve an "up/up" state that you can view with the **show interface** command. Either way, once the loop is up, you should be able to ping the local interface, which essentially confirms that it is operational from Layers 1 to 3.

You can check the status of your ATM interface with **the show interface atm (module/port)** command as shown. You can use the output from this command to determine if the amount of data being transferred is exceeding the bandwidth of the ATM circuit (which can result in dropped cells):

```
RR1# show interface atm 1/0
ATM1/0 is up, line protocol is up
  Hardware is ENHANCED ATM PA
  MTU 4470 bytes, sub MTU 4470, BW 149760 Kbit, DLY 80 usec,
     reliability 255/255, txload 1/255, rxload 1/255
  Encapsulation ATM, loopback not set
  Keepalive not supported
  Encapsulation(s): AAL5
  4096 maximum active VCs, 4 current VCCs
  VC idle disconnect time: 300 seconds  Signalling vc = 1, vpi = 0,
      vci = 5
  UNI Version = 4.0, Link Side = user
  0 carrier transitions
  Last input 00:05:16, output 00:08:23, output hang never
  Last clearing of "show interface" counters never
```

```
  Input queue: 0/75/0 (size/max/drops); Total output drops: 0
  Queueing strategy: Per VC Queueing
  5 minute input rate 0 bits/sec, 0 packets/sec
  5 minute output rate 0 bits/sec, 0 packets/sec
     345 packets input, 6544 bytes, 0 no buffer
     Received 0 broadcasts, 0 runts, 0 giants, 0 throttles
      2 input errors, 2 CRC, 0 frame, 0 overrun, 0 ignored, 0 abort
     345 packets output, 4278 bytes, 0 underruns
     0 output errors, 0 collisions, 1 interface resets
     0 output buffer failures, 0 output buffers swapped out
```

You can also check on the status of a PVC with the **show atm pvc module/port** command that follows. For voice traffic, it should be CBT (for *constant bit rate*). The peak rate is the highest-speed bandwidth available on this PVC; if it is below the level voice requires, your voice quality will suffer:

```
RR1# show atm pvc 1/23
ATM1/0.23: VCD: 7, VPI: 1, VCI: 23
VBR-NRT, PeakRate: 2000, Average Rate: 1000, Burst Cells: 32
AAL5-LLC/SNAP, etype:0x0, Flags: 0x20, VCmode: 0x0
OAM frequency: 0 second(s), OAM retry frequency: 1 second(s), OAM retry
     frequen)
OAM up retry count: 3, OAM down retry count: 5
OAM Loopback status: OAM Disabled
OAM VC state: Not Managed
ILMI VC state: Not Managed
InARP frequency: 15 minutes(s)
Transmit priority 2
InPkts: 57634, OutPkts: 589623, InBytes: 6778670, OutBytes: 6751812
InPRoc: 64351, OutPRoc: 62986, Broadcasts: 0
InFast: 0, OutFast: 0, InAS: 0, OutAS: 0
InPktDrops: 0, OutPktDrops: 0
CrcErrors: 0, SarTimeOuts: 0, OverSizedSDUs: 0
OAM cells received: 0
F5 InEndloop: 0, F5 InSegloop: 0, F5 InAIS: 0, F5 InRDI: 0
F4 InEndloop: 0, F4 InSegloop: 0, F4 InAIS: 0, F4 InRDI: 0
OAM cells sent: 0
F5 OutEndloop: 0, F5 OutSegloop: 0, F5 OutRDI: 0
F4 OutEndloop: 0, F4 OutSegloop: 0, F4 OutRDI: 0
OAM cell drops: 0
Status: UP
```

IP address-to-ATM address mappings can be either static (you create the map) or dynamic (inverse ARP [INVARP] creates the map). INVARP is enabled with the **pvc [name] vpi/vci** command, which is executed on a per-interface basis. Once that command is entered, ATM creates its mappings via the exchange of INVARP messages. You can create mappings statically using the **protocol ip x.x.x.x [[no] broadcast]** command; however, this command disables INVARP on whatever interface you execute it. The technique you use to obtain your mappings depends on your particular network situation. The **show atm map** command can be used to check your mapping, as shown in this example:

```
RR1# show atm map

Map list test : PERMANENT

ip 192.168.99.99 maps to VC 999
```

Layer 3 Troubleshooting

VoIP uses IP as its network protocol for transporting its calls. Problems with IP are problems for VoIP; VoIP cannot be separated from IP. Before you start troubleshooting your VoIP configuration, verify that your IP network is functioning correctly. You might also want to address additional Layer 3 issues such as QoS, queuing, and choosing the right bandwidth reservation schemes.

Troubleshooting IP

Common IP troubleshooting tasks include identifying and correcting addressing and routing problems. Issues with QoS, queuing, and other IP-based features will also crop up. Understanding these features used to support VoIP operation and troubleshooting them is important to VoIP. In this section, we discuss testing and verification measures you can take to ensure that your VoIP configuration is healthy.

IP Addressing and Routing

Entire books have been written on IP, covering every aspect of it from subnetting to extensive troubleshooting. There is almost no end to the list of things that can go wrong with IP. Here we provide you with the fundamental tools and commands you can use to perform the testing and verification necessary to make VoIP function.

One of the first things you should do is check to ensure that the IP address and mask on each router is correct and consistent with the addressing and routing plan you developed and implemented. Determine if the peers can reach each other via ping test. You can use several commands to troubleshoot various IP addressing and routing problems. The **show ip interface** command can provide detailed information about a router's interfaces. You can obtain a snapshot of the routing protocols that are configured on a router with **show ip protocols**. The **show ip route** command enables you to view the contents of your routing table to confirm that the correct routes are being advertised and learned.

Troubleshooting Voice Ports

Troubleshooting processes for FXS and FXO type ports are similar, whereas E&M ports have their own checklist of troubleshooting steps. We will cover some problems that you could encounter and provide tools with Cisco commands that you can use to isolate and resolve your problems.

Troubleshooting FXS and FXO Voice Ports

FXS ports connect end devices such as telephones, fax machines, analog modems, and so on. FXO ports are used to connect to telecommunications equipment such as PBXs. This is an important distinction to keep at the forefront of your mind as you configure VoIP on your equipment.

We will use the simple VoIP network in Figure 9.65 to guide our voice port troubleshooting discussion. R1 and R2 are dial peers to each other, servicing VOIP Users 1 and 2, respectively.

Figure 9.65 VoIP Network Port Troubleshooting

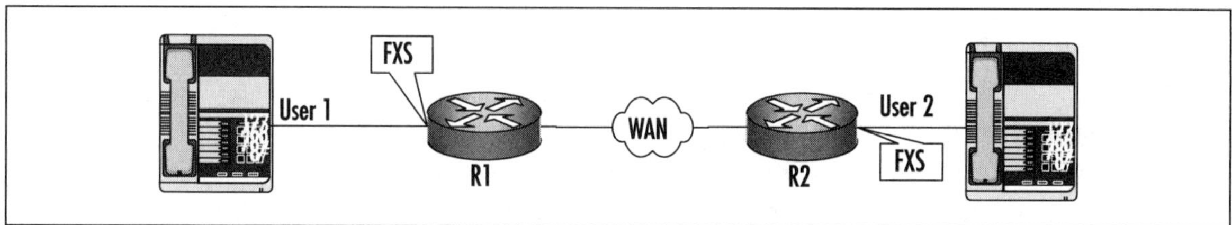

Start by ascertaining that everything is operational and healthy at Layer 1 by using **show version** to ensure that the router correctly recognizes the VoIP ports. You should get a display like the following:

```
R1# show version

Cisco Internetwork Operating System Software

(omitted content)

2 Voice FXS interface(s)
2 Voice E & M interface(s)
DRAM configuration is 64 bits wide with parity disabled.
125K bytes of non-volatile configuration memory.
32768K bytes of processor boar
```

Each router should recognize the ports as FXS voice ports, as shown in the preceding display. At this point, you can rest assured that your FXS card is installed and seated firmly, thus eliminating many physical Layer 1 problems.

If your telephones are plugged in, lift the handset. You should get a dial tone. If you do not get a dial tone, ensure that your telephone is plugged into an FXS port and not an FXO port (which does not generate dial tone). This is a common mistake on routers that have both voice port types, since they look very similar. If the telephone is plugged into the FXS port and you still don't have dial tone, use the **show voice-port** command:

```
Foreign Exchange Station 2/1/0 Slot is 2, Sub-unit is 1, Port is 0
 Type of VoicePort is FXS
 Operation State is DORMANT
 Administrative State is UP
 The Last Interface Down Failure Cause is Administrative Shutdown
 Description is Left Side Phone
 Noise Regeneration is enabled
 Non Linear Processing is enabled
 Music On Hold Threshold is Set to -38 dBm
 In Gain is Set to 0 dB
 Out Attenuation is Set to 0 dB
 Echo Cancellation is enabled
 Echo Cancel Coverage is set to 8 ms
 Connection Mode is normal
 Connection Number is not set
 Initial Time Out is set to 10 s
 Interdigit Time Out is set to 10 s
 Call-Disconnect Time Out is set to 60 s
 Ringing Time Out is set to 180 s
 Companding Type is u-law
 Region Tone is set for US

 Analog Info Follows:
 Currently processing none
 Maintenance Mode Set to None (not in mtc mode)
 Number of signaling protocol errors are 0
 Impedance is set to 600r Ohm
 Wait Release Time Out is 30 s

 Voice card specific Info Follows:
 Signal Type is loopStart
 Ring Frequency is 50 Hz
 Hook Status is On Hook
 Ring Active Status is inactive
 Ring Ground Status is inactive
 Tip Ground Status is inactive
 Digit Duration Timing is set to 100 ms
```

```
InterDigit Duration Timing is set to 100 ms
Ring Cadence is defined by Cadence Pattern03
Ring Cadence are [15 35] * 100 mse
```

Check to see if your voice port is administratively shut down. Enable it with the **no shutdown** command. Lift the handset again, and you should have a dial tone. Ensure that the telephone you use for this test is a known good telephone and that it is not a digital telephone, which can have its own special requirements. Lift the handset and dial a number, any number; dial tone should cease.

You can monitor voice port activity in real time with the **debug** commands. The **debug voice cp [slot/port]** command shows call activity on a particular interface. Here is an example:

1. Voice call processing state machine debugging is on:

   ```
   R1# debug voice cp 3/3
   ```

2. Handset is taken off-hook:

   ```
   3/3: CPD( ), idle gets event seize_ind
   3/3: CPD( ), idle gets event dsp_ready
   ```

3. Telephone number digit is entered:

   ```
   3/3: CPD(in), collect gets event digit
   3/3: CPD(in), collect gets event addr_done
   ```

4. Digits are completely entered and the call is initiated:

   ```
   3/3: CPD(in), collect ==> request
   3/3: CPD(in), request gets event call_proceeding
   ```

5. Waiting for response at called end (in this case, the telephone was answered):

   ```
   3/3: CPD(in), request ==> in_wait_answer
   3/3: CPD(in), in_wait_answer gets event call_accept
   3/3: CPD(in), in_wait_answer gets event call_answered
   ```

6. Call has been completed, and the two peers are connected to each other:

   ```
   3/3: CPD(in), in_wait_answer ==> connected
   3/3: CPD(in), connected gets event peer_onhook
   ```

7. Call is disconnected (hang up):

   ```
   3/3: CPD(in), connected ==> disconnect_wait
   3/3: CPD(in), disconnect_wait gets event idle_ind
   3/3: CPD(in), disconnect_wait ==> idle
   ```

Troubleshooting E&M Voice Ports

If a router has an E&M interface, it is performing PBX functions or communicating directly with a PBX as a PBX, complete with standard PBX functions and features.

Initial troubleshooting is similar to the troubleshooting of FXS and FXO ports. We will use Figure 9.66 to guide our E&M voice port troubleshooting discussion. Figure 9.66 shows a simple configuration in which two PBXs are tied together via VoIP routers (R1 and R3). Note that RR2 has no voice capabilities of any kind; it is merely routing traffic between RR1 and RR3. RR1 and RR3 have their E&M ports connected to their respective PBXs.

Figure 9.66 E&M Configuration

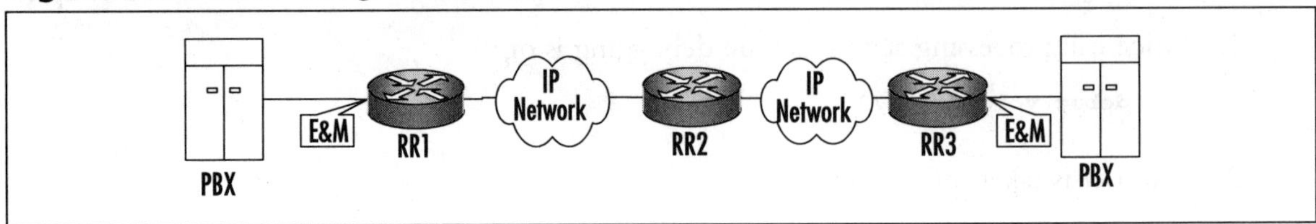

The initial troubleshooting process is similar to what you did for FXS and FXO ports, so you'll execute the same commands, such as **show version**, **show voice port**, and **ping** tests. Once successful, you can then focus specifically on E&M port issues.

If the router does not recognize the E&M interface at this point, power down the router and reinsert the voice modules. If the router still does not recognize the presence of the voice ports, you might need to upgrade your IOS to obtain VoIP support and to support the E&M cards. If, after doing all this, it the router does not recognize the cards, you might have faulty hardware, either with the router or with the E&M cards themselves.

If you have completed all the previous steps and detected no problems, you are ready to start troubleshooting the configuration of your E&M cards. PBXs have their own operating system and their own features that you need to configure the router to support. Currently, Cisco supports only a limited number of makes and models of PBX. Before you start extensive troubleshooting on your router, go to www.cisco.com and do a search for *PBX interoperability application notes* to obtain information on the PBXs Cisco supports. Any special configuration options you need to enable on either the router, the PBX, or both will be provided on this Web page.

Before configuring the router to interoperate with your PBX, you need to have in hand certain information about your PBX. What is the E&M signaling used by the PBX? Cisco supports I, II, III, and V, and only V (written as 5 in IOS configuration) is supported for U.S. configurations. Does the PBX use a two-wire or four-wire configuration for calls? How does the PBX signal call initiation—that is, the start of the dialing? PBXs can use wink-start, immediate, and delay-dial. You'll need to configure support for this function on your voice router. Is dial tone or dial pulse used? Nowadays, almost all new implementations are dial tone. Once you have this information in hand, you are ready to configure and troubleshoot your router configuration.

Check the configuration of the E&M interface by viewing the router's configuration file with the **show running** command. You can check the current status of the E&M voice port using the **show voice-port** command to obtain output, as shown in the following example.

Notice that the type is E&M, and the port is up but currently not in use (*dormant*). Numerous timer values are also displayed:

```
R1# show voice port
recEive And transMit 1/1/0 Slot is 2, Sub-unit is 1, Port is 0
 Type of VoicePort is E&M
 Operation State is DORMANT
 Administrative State is UP
 No Interface Down Failure
 Description is not set
 Noise Regeneration is enabled
 Non Linear Processing is enabled
 Music On Hold Threshold is Set to -38 dBm
 In Gain is Set to 0 dB
 Out Attenuation is Set to 0 dB
 Echo Cancellation is enabled
 Echo Cancel Coverage is set to 8 ms
 Connection Mode is normal
 Connection Number is not set
 Initial Time Out is set to 10 s
 Interdigit Time Out is set to 10 s
 Call-Disconnect Time Out is set to 60 s
 Ringing Time Out is set to 180 s
 Companding Type is u-law
 Region Tone is set for US
```

PBX communications can be monitored in real time with several **debug** commands. The **debug vtsp dsp** command enables you to confirm whether telephone digits are exchanged between the E&M port and the PBX. In the following example (shortened for brevity), the E&M interface has sent the digits 20 to the PBX:

```
Jun 9 05:35:19.100: vtsp_process_dsp_message: MSG_TX_DTMF_DIGIT_OFF:
    digit=2, duration=110
Jun 9 05:35:19.500:: vtsp_process_dsp_message: MSG_TX_DTMF_DIGIT_BEGIN:
    digit=0, rtp_timestamp
```

Troubleshooting Dial Peers

Cisco defines four types of dial peer. One is the POTS dial peer, which is the simple mapping of a dial string to a voice port. The remaining three dial peers are VoFR, VoATM, and VoIP. The voice peer configuration starts with the command shown in the following example. The thrust of this chapter is VoIP, so we focus on troubleshooting VoIP dial peers.

At a minimum, in order for a VoIP peer configuration to be valid, it must have a destination pattern and a session target. The destination pattern is the digits or digits and wildcards of your telephonic destination; this would be a telephone number. It is entered with the dial peer sub-command **destination-pattern.** The session target in the case of VoIP is an IP address of the remote VoIP peer. The session target is entered with **session target ipv4:*x.x.x.x***, where ***x.x.x.x*** is the IP address of the remote peer. The answer address parameters are not required for calling but can make it easier to identify any calls from this peer. If this is not used, then incoming voice port identification information is used. It is entered with **answer-address *xxx***, where ***xxx*** is the telephone number you want presented to the remote peer.

The following configuration shows the bare minimum configuration required to make a VoIP peer work:

```
dial-peer voice 11 voip

destination-pattern 9999.

session target ipv4:192.168.99.99

answer-address 3601
```

A large number of problems can occur with a VoIP configuration. Rather than attempting to address each scenario here, we discuss commands you have at your disposal to verify and support your configuration. We assume that you have already performed your troubleshooting at Layer 1 and 2 and that routing itself is not a problem. If you are at this point and have not done the troubleshooting as outlined previously in our methodology, go back and do so before diving into VoIP-specific troubleshooting commands.

Table 9.17describes the commands you have at your disposal to check your dial peer configuration.

Table 9.17 Troubleshooting Commands

Command	Description
show call active voice	Displays a list of active calls (calls in progress).
show call history voice	Displays a history of calls made.
show controllers voice	Displays hardware information about voice modules and ports.
show diag	Displays information about the router hardware.
show dial-peer voice	Displays dial peers configured on the router.
debug vpm all	Debugs the voice-processing module (VPM) on the router.
show dialplan number xxxx	Shows how the digits you enter will be expanded and switched (the designation they are switched to).
debug cpm dsp	Debugs communications between VPM and DSP.
debug vpm port	Caution! Much output! Captures real-time port activity as the call progresses.
debug vpm signal	Captures signaling information.

Table 9.18 summarizes common VoIP problems, how to detect them, and how to resolve them. This is not an all-inclusive list, but it does cover several issues that you are likely to encounter.

Table 9.18 Common VOIP Issues

VoIP Issue	Resolution
Poor quality of calls	cptone might not be configured correctly.
Excessive echo	Adjust output of originating voice port with **output attention** command or try enabling **echo-cancel enable**. Try adjusting the echo-cancel coverage command.
Telephone does not ring	Use the **show voice port** command and ensure that the ring tone is configured correctly.
Slow or dropped voice traffic	Voice tolerates a maximum of 150ms one-way trip time; use a ping test to determine if the network is the problem and check your network for congestion.
Unable to make or receive calls	Ensure that peer statements are correct (**show running**).

Summary

Modern telecommunications have evolved from the advent of the telephone, and many systems today are related in some way to the first calls. Analog signaling provided continuous waveforms on which data, including voice, could be transmitted. Digital signaling added compression, error correction and other services to the network.

IP telephony and IP-based video conferencing solutions present many opportunities to your organization, and at the same time introduce an entirely new set of challenges to overcome. IP telephony benefits your organization by providing simplified administration, toll bypass, and a unified messaging platform. All of these benefits have the potential to save your organization a great deal both administratively and monetarily when implemented correctly.

Cisco provides a myriad of hardware and software to enable the transport of voice traffic over non-telephony networks. Cisco makes several models of IP telephones, as well as providing a software-only solution for desktop calling. Many Cisco routers can be adapted to support voice with the addition of specialized modules and cards. Cisco switches can provide inline power to IP telephones.

The configuration of VoIP can be accomplished using the Cisco IOS commands. The process is similar as for any technology or feature configured on a Cisco product. A key to success is ensuring that you have a good plan and understanding prior to starting configuration.

Index

B

C

D

E

J

K

L

S

U

V

W

X

Y

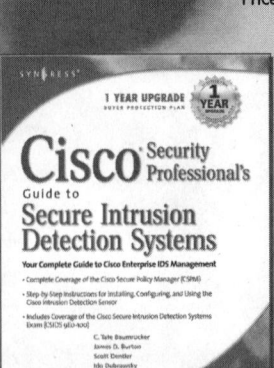